SOURCES AND ANALOGUES OF

Chaucer's
Canterbury Tales

SOURCES AND ANALOGUES OF

Chaucer's Canterbury Tales

CARLETON BROWN · GERMAINE DEMPSTER · G. H. GEROULD
W. M. HART · J. R. HULBERT · H. S. V. JONES · LAURA H. LOOMIS
EARL LYON · R. A. PRATT · R. K. ROOT · MARGARET SCHLAUCH
J. BURKE SEVERS · EDGAR F. SHANNON · J. W. SPARGO
J. S. P. TATLOCK · ARCHER TAYLOR · STITH THOMPSON
FREDERICK TUPPER · B. J. WHITING · J. A. WORK · KARL YOUNG

Edited by

W. F. BRYAN and GERMAINE DEMPSTER

General Editor   *Associate General Editor*

HUMANITIES PRESS
New York

First Published 1941
Copyright 1958 by
THE HUMANITIES PRESS, Inc.

Printed in U.S.A. by
NOBLE OFFSET PRINTERS, INC.
NEW YORK 3, N. Y.

PREFACE

THIS volume, *Sources and Analogues of Chaucer's "Canterbury Tales,"* is a collaborative undertaking by members of the Chaucer Group of the Modern Language Association of America. The purpose is to present in so far as possible the sources of the *Canterbury Tales* as Chaucer knew these sources or, where the direct sources are not now known, to present the closest known analogues in the form in which Chaucer presumably may have been acquainted with them. Since attention has thus been focused upon such material as may be significant in the study of Chaucer's use of his sources, remote analogues and late derivative versions have not been included. The content as well as the purpose of this work accordingly differs very materially from that of the Chaucer Society's *Originals and Analogues* (London, 1872–88). *Sources and Analogues* treats all twenty-four of the tales, with additional sections on the general framework and on two prologues to tales, whereas *Originals and Analogues* was concerned with only thirteen tales; the present work, moreover, reproduces only twenty-two of the one hundred and eleven versions and duplicates only about one-fourth of the material presented in the earlier work. Further, in only two of the thirteen tales treated in *Originals and Analogues* does *Sources and Analogues* fail to make significant additions to those analogues which it reproduces from the older work.

One of the most important direct sources—the *Teseida* of Boccaccio for the *Knight's Tale*—has been omitted. The inclusion of the *Teseida* would have so increased the bulk of the present work and added so greatly to the cost of production as to have made financing the publication very problematical. Fortunately, the recent issue of a new critical text of the *Teseida*,[1] which should be generally accessible, made inclusion of this work unnecessary. *Sources and Analogues*, however,

[1] Giovanni Boccaccio, *Teseida*, edizione critica per cura di Salvatore Battaglia ("Autori classici e documenti di lingua pubblicati dalle R. Accademia della Crusca" [Florence: G. C. Sansoni, 1938]).

vii

includes material designed to make this newly published text more readily serviceable to Chaucerians.

The primary intent has been not to present a series of studies on Chaucer's sources but to present texts and thus to make readily accessible the material for the study of sources and influences. Accordingly in most instances the individual contributors have reduced comment and discussion to the barest necessary minimum. Every care has been exercised in selecting texts and in presenting them accurately. Since, however, the texts are intended not for paleographical or linguistic but for literary study, except in special circumstances they are not diplomatic reproductions: obvious contractions have been silently expanded, and punctuation and capitalization have been modernized where this modernization was necessary for intelligibility. To make the texts readily intelligible the most unusual or puzzling words and phrases have been explained in footnotes. To add to the convenience of the reader, the texts have been provided with brief marginal summaries except in the few instances where such summaries appeared unnecessary. Although the general editors have felt perfectly free to offer suggestions and criticism, each individual contributor has, of course, had final responsibility for the selection and preparation of the texts in his section and for the presentation of his material in whatever way seemed most suitable to his considered judgment. With so many contributors and such varied material, any attempt to insist upon complete consistency would have been impossible.

As will be seen at a first glance, the order of the tales is not that of the edited Six-Text reprint adopted by Skeat, for example, but the order of the better manuscripts, followed by Manly in his monumental critical text of the *Canterbury Tales* and by Robinson in his indispensable edition of *Chaucer's Complete Works*. This arrangement is followed as a matter of convenience to the user and is not to be construed as implying any opinion upon the question of the order contemplated by Chaucer. To facilitate the use of this work in connection with editions of Chaucer which follow the Six-Text order, wherever reference is made to a passage in the *Canterbury Tales*, the reference is accompanied by the notation of the fragments as A, B, C, etc.

In a work of this character, the preparation of which has extended over a number of years, obligations for assistance have been so numerous that it is hardly possible to acknowledge all of them suitably. The first acknowledgment must be made to Dr. Beatrice Daw (Mrs. Carleton) Brown, who as secretary of the Chaucer Group initiated the work by proposing it as a collaborative undertaking for members of the Group and who aided effectively in the early stages of organization. In the actual preparation of the work, the services of Dr. Dempster, the associate general editor, have been invaluable; there are very few sections which do not show some reflection of her scholarship, energy, and resourcefulness. The members of the Advisory Board have been most generously helpful in the solution of many problems which have constantly arisen; their interest and knowledge have been a firm prop and support. Throughout the long and sometimes tedious process of preparation and revision the sympathetic co-operation of the editors of the individual sections has lightened and brightened the task of the general editors. Particular acknowledgment for assistance of various kinds is gratefully given to Professors Edward C. Armstrong, Alfred Foulet, George L. Hamilton, C. H. Beeson, William A. Nitze, Joseph Mansion, and John W. Spargo. Finally, acknowledgment is made to the University of Chicago Press for considerateness and painstaking care shown by many members of this organization.

A substantial grant from the Research Fund of the Graduate School of Northwestern University with a small grant from the Research Fund of the Modern Language Association enabled the general editor to cope with the very considerable expenses incident upon the preparation of this work. A very generous grant from the American Council of Learned Societies made publication possible.

Sources and Analogues has felt the loss of two distinguished contributors and helpers. Professor Edgar F. Shannon died very soon after he had completed the final revision of his section on the *Physician's Tale*, and Professor John M. Manly, a member of the Advisory Board, died shortly before actual publication got under way.   W. F. BRYAN

NORTHWESTERN UNIVERSITY
    December 1, 1940

TABLE OF CONTENTS

THE LITERARY FRAMEWORK OF THE CANTERBURY TALES

By ROBERT ARMSTRONG PRATT AND KARL YOUNG

INTRODUCTION

ANY survey of the literary antecedents of the framework
of the *Canterbury Tales* may well begin with the observation that, when Chaucer definitely approached the composing of this work in its present form, presumably about the
year 1387,[1] he needed no reminder of the usefulness of a framing
device and needed no literary model for the particular device
that he chose. He had recently experimented with the matter
tentatively in the *Legend of Good Women*,[2] he had already, perhaps, written the first version of the *Monk's Tale* according to a
design of a series of "falls,"[3] and he had produced the *House of
Fame*, which is sometimes interpreted as a prologue for a collection of unwritten stories.[4] Certainly Chaucer was familiar with

[1] See J. S. P. Tatlock, *The Development and Chronology of Chaucer's Works*
("Chaucer Society Publications, Second Series," No. 37 [London, 1907]), pp.
141–42; F. N. Robinson (ed.), *The Complete Works of Geoffrey Chaucer* (Boston,
etc., 1933), p. 1 ("The plan of the tales was probably adopted soon after 1386"),
and pp. 751–52.

[2] See Tatlock, pp. 131 and 141.

[3] See W. W. Skeat, *The Complete Works of Geoffrey Chaucer*, III (2d ed.; Oxford, 1900), 373, 427; G. L. Kittredge, *The Date of Chaucer's Troilus* ("Chaucer
Society Publications, Second Series," No. 42 [London, 1909]), pp. 41–52; Robinson, p. 852. Tatlock (p. 172), however, rejects the view that the series of stories
in the *Monk's Tale* was written before the *Canterbury Tales* were under way.
Boccaccio's *De casibus virorum illustrium* (issued in 1363–64) is a "framed" series
in that it represents a long procession of famous unfortunates, each of whom, in
general, appears before the author seated at his desk, and some of whom tell
their own "tragedies," after which Boccaccio comments. If Chaucer wrote a
version of the *Monk's Tale* before the period of the *Canterbury Tales*, he may have
used some such framing device. For a reference to the *De casibus* as "eine Art
Rahmenerzählung" see G. Koerting, *Boccaccio's Leben und Werke* (Leipzig, 1880),
p. 730.

[4] See J. M. Manly, in *Anniversary Papers by Colleagues and Pupils of George
Lyman Kittredge* (Boston, 1913), pp. 73–81. Objections to Manly's interpretation
have been expressed by W. O. Sypherd, in *MLN*, XXX (1915), 65–68, by F. C.
Riedel, in *JEGP*, XXVII (1928), 442, and by B. H. Bronson, in *University of Cali-*

the frame-story as an artistic resource. For his particular device of a group of persons on a pilgrimage to Canterbury on horseback he needed only to draw upon life about him. Although we have no authentic intimation that Chaucer himself ever participated in such a religious pilgrimage, we know very well that he observed, and heard of, others who did so.[1] If he lived for a considerable time at Greenwich, on the Canterbury road, groups of pilgrims must have passed near his residence.[2] Certainly he traveléd that road frequently on business journeys, and certainly he heard talk and taling from those who accompanied him and those whom he met. Thus the device of a pilgrimage as a narrative framework was repeatedly presented to him in actual life, and he was at liberty to adopt it for his literary purpose with whatever degree of realism he found convenient.[3] The fact that Chaucer could have conceived his design through his own observation, however, does not annul our interest in the similar literary devices of his predecessors and contemporaries. It is still important that we understand his place in the tradition of framed stories and weigh the possibility that other writers inspired him to activity of this sort or provided suggestions in

---

fornia Publications in English, III, No. 4 (1934), 175–76. Tatlock (p. 132, referring to A. W. Ward, *Chaucer* ["E.M.L. Series," New York, 1880], pp. 95–96) writes, "The germ of *C. T.* is in the house of Rumour in *H. F.* (lines 2121–36)," and mentions the "sketches of ancient heroines" in the *House of Fame* as the sort of writing from which a frame-story might "develop spontaneously."

[1] Tatlock (pp. 131–35) shows that there are no supporting facts for "the idea that the basis of the poem is an actual pilgrimage made by Chaucer."

[2] Tatlock (p. 141) writes: "It may be taken as a certainty, then, that from 1385 till well into the nineties (probably till 1399) Chaucer lived in Greenwich. . . . . Since Canterbury pilgrims went past Greenwich, Chaucer's daily familiarity with them probably dated from his residence there." For a less assured statement as to the possibility of Chaucer's having resided in Greenwich see J. M. Manly (ed.), *Canterbury Tales by Geoffrey Chaucer* (New York, 1928), p. 26.

[3] For facts concerning actual journeys between London and Canterbury see F. J. Furnivall, *A Temporary Preface to the Six-Text Edition of Chaucer's Canterbury Tales*, Part I ("Chaucer Society Publications, Second Series," No. 3 [London, 1868]), pp. 12–18, 26, 39–41, 119–32; H. Littlehales, *Some Notes on the Road from London to Canterbury in the Middle Ages* ("Chaucer Society Publications, Second Series," No. 30 [London, 1898]); R. E. G. Kirk and F. J. Furnivall, *Analogues of Chaucer's Canterbury Pilgrimage* ("Chaucer Society Publications, Second Series," No. 36 [London, 1903]); J. S. P. Tatlock, "The Duration of the Canterbury Pilgrimage," *PMLA*, XXI (1906), 478–85.

detail. Above all, a survey of the literary contrivances of others is essential for disclosing clearly, by contrast, those aspects of Chaucer's art which are unmistakably his own.[1]

I

Of these original aspects the one most directly apparent is the series of portraits of individual pilgrims in the *Prologue*. Behind these personal descriptions, to be sure, lies a long literary tradition.[2] The portrait, as a formal enumeration of physical characteristics for purposes of literary embellishment, arose in the late Latin poetry of the Roman Empire.[3] The development of such portraiture may have been encouraged by the presence of the formal *iconismos* in Latin historical prose[4] and by the rhetor-

[1] Perhaps the most comprehensive single study of framing devices in general is that of O. Löhmann, *Die Rahmenerzählung des Decameron: ihre Quellen und Nachwirkungen* ("Romantische Arbeiten," ed. K. Voretzsch, Vol. XXII [Halle, 1935]). Bibliography relevant to Chaucer is given by Eleanor P. Hammond, *Chaucer: A Bibliographical Manual* (New York, 1908), pp. 150–53, and J. E. Wells, *A Manual of the Writings in Middle English* (New Haven, 1916), p. 874 (with additions in the seven *Supplements*). The matter has been more or less comprehensively surveyed by Koerting, pp. 648–50; M. Landau, *Die Quellen des Dekameron* (Stuttgart, 1884), pp. 60–70, 314–16; J. C. Dunlop, *History of Prose Fiction*, II (London, 1888), 4–23; Skeat, III, 371–72; M. Landau, in *Beilage zur allgemeinen Zeitung*, No. 270 (1906), p. 351; H. B. Hinckley, *Notes on Chaucer* (Northampton, 1907), pp. 1–3; L. Morsbach, "Chaucers Plan der *Canterbury Tales* und Boccaccios *Decamerone*," *ES*, XLII (1910), 43–52; J. S. P. Tatlock, "Boccaccio and the Plan of Chaucer's *Canterbury Tales*," *Anglia*, XXXVII (1913), 69–117; K. Young, "The Plan of *The Canterbury Tales*," in *Anniversary Papers by Colleagues and Pupils of George Lyman Kittredge*, pp. 405–17; H. S. V. Jones, "The Plan of the *Canterbury Tales*," *MP*, XIII (1915), 45–48; W. F. Schirmer, in *GRM*, XII (1924), 290; Manly, *Canterbury Tales*, pp. 74–77; K. Voretzsch, *Introduction to the Study of Old French Literature* (New York, 1931), pp. 374–77; Robinson, pp. 1–2, 751; J. L. Lowes, *Geoffrey Chaucer* (Boston, 1934), pp. 192–97; H. B. Hinckley, "The Framing-Tale," *MLN*, XLIX (1934), 69–80; B. D. Brown, "A Thirteenth-Century Chaucerian Analogue," *MLN*, LII (1937), 28–31.

[2] This tradition, with particular reference to Old French and Middle English literature, is being investigated by Mr. L. A. Haselmayer, Jr., to whom we are gratefully indebted for the present section of our introductory essay. For references to earlier studies see Robinson, pp. 752, 885, 947.

[3] For examples see the *Epithalamium de Nuptiis Honorii Augusti* of C. Claudianus, in *Carmina*, ed. J. Koch (Leipzig, 1893), p. 100, ll. 264–75; *Anthologia Latina*, Part I, ed. A. Reise (Leipzig, 1894), No. 217, ll. 1–8; *The Elegies of Maximianus*, ed. R. Webster (Princeton, 1900), p. 28, No. 1, ll. 91–100.

[4] See E. C. Evans, "Roman Descriptions of Personal Appearance in History and Biography," *Harvard Studies in Classical Philology*, XLVI (1935), 43–84; S. Misener, "Iconistic Portraits," *CP*, XIX (1924), 97–123.

ical authorization of personal description found in the *Ad Herennium* of Cornificius.[1] The introduction of this literary device into medieval poetry resulted partly, no doubt, from direct imitation of classical practice, and partly from the instruction of medieval rhetoricians, who maintained the tradition of Cornificius and advocated the amplifying of poetical composition through the abundant use of formal personal description.[2]

After becoming established as an approved, and almost inescapable, form of literary embellishment, the portrait was widely used in medieval verse, appearing in a considerable variety of poetical genres in Latin, French, English, and other languages.[3] Such personal description was confined almost exclusively, however, to extolling the physical beauty of isolated individuals of the upper classes, and the conventionality and inflexibility of its phraseology precluded any substantial effect of reality or personal differentiation. The essence of the tradition is reflected in Chaucer's portraits of Blanche in the *Book of the Duchess*, of Venus in the *Knight's Tale*, and of Sir Thopas.[4]

The isolated and conventional description characteristic of the general medieval tradition obviously provides no adequate model for a sustained series of portraits such as that in Chaucer's *Prologue*. Here the personages are a considerable group, drawn from a variety of social positions, and all included within

[1] See the definition of *effictio* in *Cornifici Rhetoricorum ad C. Herennium Libri IIII*, ed. C. L. Kayser (Leipzig, 1854), p. 201.

[2] For the opinions and illustrations of medieval rhetoricians see Matthew of Vendome, *Ars versificatoria*, in E. Faral, *Les Arts poétiques du xiie et du xiiie siècle* (Paris, 1924), pp. 119, 129–30; Geoffrey of Vinsauf, *Poetria nova*, in Faral, pp. 214–15, ll. 563–97; John of Garland, *Poetria*, ed. G. Mari, in *Romanische Forschungen*, XIII (1902), 915.

[3] For examples in Latin verse see the *Dissuasio amoris Venerei* of Marbodus, in *Carmina varia*, ed. Migne, *Patrologia Latina*, Vol. CLXXI, col. 1655; and the *Descriptio cujusdam Puellae* of Giraldus Cambrensis, in *Opera*, ed. J. S. Brewer, I (London, 1861), 349–50. For Old French see Renaut de Beaujeu, *Le Bel inconnu*, ed. G. P. Williams (Paris, 1929), p. 5, ll. 135–46; and Guillaume de Machaut, *Le Jugement dou Roy de Behaigne*, in *Oeuvres*, ed. E. Hoepffner, I (Paris, 1908), p. 104, ll. 1234–55. For Middle English see the *Romance of Guy of Warwick* ("E.E.T.S.: Extra Series," No. 42), ed. J. Zupitza (London, 1883), Part I, pp. 5–7, ll. 59–94; and the *Confessio amantis* of John Gower, VI, 767–90, in *The Complete Works of John Gower*, ed. G. C. Macaulay, III (Oxford, 1901), 188.

[4] See *Book of the Duchess*, 816–1041; *Knight's Tale*, A 1955–66; *Sir Thopas*, B 1905–37.

a single fictitious narration. Perhaps the only comparable grouping of personal descriptions in earlier medieval literature is found in the several versions of the story of Troy, of which the most attractive is the *Roman de Troie* of Benoît de Sainte-Maure.[1] In his own treatment of the theme of Troy in *Troilus and Criseyde* Chaucer pays tribute to the group of portraits in the works of his predecessors by incorporating fragments of it into his poem.[2] One could hardly suggest, however, that the conventionalized descriptions of Greeks and Trojans depicted in the several forms of the Troy story served as a model for Chaucer's group-portraiture in the *Prologue* to the *Canterbury Tales*. For such service the portraits of Benoît de Sainte-Maure and his successors are much too limited in social variety and in realistic detail.[3] Neither in this group, therefore, nor in the whole range of earlier portraiture, do we find anything that could be exhibited in the present volume as a source or appropriate analogue for Chaucer's miscellaneous company of vivid and living personalities.[4]

[1] The earliest text of these portraits which concerns us here is found in the *De excidio Trojae historia* of Dares Phrygius, ed. F. Meister (Leipzig, 1873), pp. 14–17. Dares' brief prose descriptions are elaborated in French verse in the twelfth century in the *Roman de Troie* of Benoît de Sainte-Maure, ed. L. Constans, Vol. I (Paris, 1904), ll. 5119–76. In the thirteenth century Benoît's text was translated into Latin prose in the *Historia destructionis Troiae* of Guido de Columnis, ed. N. E. Griffin (Cambridge, Mass., 1936), pp. 83–87. During the latter half of the fourteenth century Guido's portraits were rendered in English alliterative verse in the *"Gest Hystoriale" of the Destruction of Troy*, ed. G. A. Panton and D. Donaldson ("E.E.T.S.: Original Series," Nos. 39 and 56 [London, 1869, 1874]), pp. 121–30, ll. 3741–4017. At the end of the twelfth century, Dares' portraits were elaborated in Latin hexameters in the so-called *De bello Trojano* of Joseph of Exeter, ed. S. Artopoeus (London, 1825), Lib. IV, 40–192.

[2] See the portraits of Diomedes, Criseyde, and Troilus in *Troilus and Criseyde*, V, 799–840. As Professor R. K. Root has shown (*MP*, XV [1917–18], 6–18), Chaucer borrows here chiefly from Benoît and Joseph of Exeter. See L. A. Haselmayer, "The Portraits in *Troilus and Criseyde*," *PQ*, XVII (1938), 220–23.

[3] The limitations of Benoît's portraits are stressed by Lowes, pp. 198–99.

[4] Concerning the realistic aspect of some of Chaucer's portraits see especially J. M. Manly, *Some New Light on Chaucer* (New York, 1926), *passim;* see also L. A. Haselmayer, "The Portraits in Chaucer's Fabliaux," *RES*, XIV (1938), 310–14. There was, of course, at least a faint strain of realism in portraiture throughout the Middle Ages. Descriptions of pagan kings, old hags, allegorical personages, and ugly men, for example, often attained a certain degree of distinctiveness. For illustrations see the *Geta* of Vitalis Blessensis, ed. G. Cohen, *La "Comédie" latine en France au xiie siècle*, I (Paris, 1931), 48, ll. 331–40; *Le*

II

When we pass from the portraits of the *Prologue* to the comprehensive narrative framework within which they are inclosed, we have before us a literary device of still greater antiquity, and one to which Chaucer's work has been thought to be related much more directly.

The oldest extant collection of framed stories is the fragmentary one preserved in the Westcar Papyrus, which antedates the Christian Era by some sixteen or eighteen centuries.[1] The tales are brought forward by the demand of King Khufu, or Cheops, that his sons narrate to him accounts of wonders wrought by magicians. Eventually, one of the sons informs his father that there lives a magician more remarkable than any of those whose performances have been recounted. Thereupon the magician referred to is summoned and required to exhibit his powers in the king's presence. The framing device in this ancient collection is obviously very simple and offers almost nothing in the way of characterization of the persons concerned.

Although this Egyptian collection antedates anything of the kind preserved elsewhere, the actual invention of the framing device is usually attributed to India. From that region, in any case, derive a number of venerable examples which have had wide currency in Western Europe. Of these the most remarkable is the *Panchatantra*, the lost original of which was probably composed in the third or fourth century of our era.[2] Among the

---

Couronnement de Louis, ed. E. Langlois (Paris, 1888), p. 25, ll. 504–10; Chrétien de Troyes, *Yvain*, in *Werke*, ed. W. Foerster, II (Halle, 1887), 12–13, ll. 288–307; *Le Roman de la Rose*, ed. E. Langlois, II (Paris, 1920), 8, ll. 139–51; *Oeuvres complètes de Eustache Deschamps*, ed. Queux de Saint-Hilaire, Vol. IV (Paris, 1884), No. 774, ll. 6–20; *Morte Arthure*, ed. G. G. Perry ("E.E.T.S.: Original Series," No. 8 [London, 1865]), pp. 32–33, ll. 1078–1101.

[1] See A. Erman (ed.), *Die Märchen des Papyrus Westcar* ("Königliche Museen zu Berlin: Mittheilungen aus den orientalischen Sammlungen," Vol. V [Berlin, 1890]), pp. 7 ff.; J. H. Breasted, *A History of Egypt* (London, 1906), pp. 122, 203; E. A. Wallis Budge, *The Literature of the Ancient Egyptians* (London, 1914), pp. 25–36; A. Erman, *The Literature of the Ancient Egyptians* (London, 1927), p. 36; Hinckley, in *MLN*, XLIX (1934), 69–70.

[2] Concerning the *Panchatantra* and its derivatives see I. G. N. Keith-Falconer, *Kalilah and Dimnah, or the Fables of Bidpai* (Cambridge, 1885), pp. xiii ff.; Dunlop, II, 4–8; J. Hertel, *Das Pancatantra: seine Geschichte und seine Verbreitung* (Leipzig and Berlin, 1914), reviewed by F. Edgerton, in *AJP*, XXXVI (1915),

translations and redactions of this is the eighth-century *Kalilah and Dimna*, or *Fables of Bidpai*, from which are descended the numerous European versions. In this collection it is represented that the stories are related at the request of a king of India by his philosopher, Bidpai, or Pilpay, by way of enforcing moral precepts. At the end of each narrative the king comments briefly and prescribes the nature of the next one. Though simple in itself, each of the tales commonly engenders one or more parenthetical stories or anecdotes, in such a manner that there is some confusion among the narratives ensphered one within another. In many of them the roles are taken by animals which conduct themselves like men and women. This collection became especially accessible to Western readers through the thirteenth-century Latin version of John of Capua, entitled *Directorium vitae humanae*.[1]

Another collection which arose in India, perhaps in the fifth century, is commonly called *The Seven Sages*. This was widely known in Western Europe through translations, the one in English, of the thirteenth century, presenting the frame and fifteen tales in 4,328 lines.[2] The framing story centers in the desperate jealousy of the Roman empress, Milisant, shown toward her stepson, Florentine, who is being educated in seclusion by seven wise men. The empress conspires with a witch to effect the murder of Florentine if he speaks during the first seven days after his coming to court. When the prince arrives, the wise men charge him to keep silence for a week, and each of the seven engages to speak on his behalf on one of the seven days. On the

---

44–69, 253–79; M. Winternitz, *Geschichte der indischen Litteratur*, III (Leipzig, 1920), 272–311; A. B. Keith, *A History of Sanskrit Literature* (Oxford, 1928), pp. 246–65; Löhmann, pp. 8–17. For a translation into English see A. W. Ryder, *The Panchatantra* (Chicago, 1925). The migration of tales from the Orient to the West is discussed by F. Max Müller, *Chips from a German Workshop*, IV (London, 1875), 145–89. For a study of the frame-story of the *Katha Sarit Sagara* see N. M. Penzer (ed.), *The Ocean of Story, Being C. H. Tawney's Translation of Somadeva's Kathā Sarit Sāgara*, IX (London, 1928), 94–121.

[1] Edited by J. Derenbourg, *Johannis de Capua Directorium vitae humanae* (2 fascs.; Paris, 1887, 1889).

[2] The English text is edited, with discussion of manuscripts and versions, by Killis Campbell, *The Seven Sages of Rome* (Boston, 1907). See also Löhmann, pp. 18–36.

first day the empress undertakes to seduce Florentine, and, after failing to prevail against the boy's silent resistance, accuses him to the emperor of having assaulted her. The emperor postpones the execution of the prince until the next day, and at night the empress recounts to her husband a story designed to persuade him to carry out the punishment without further delay. The next morning, one of the wise men stays the execution by telling a story counseling deliberation. On the following six nights the empress recounts to the emperor her persuasive tales, and on each succeeding morning one of the sages narrates a story successfully advising delay. On the eighth day the prince himself tells a story, and eventually exposes the empress's guilt, thus saving his own life and bringing about her death. After each story occurs a short narrative link, or *intermezzo*, presenting the mental conflict of the emperor and introducing the succeeding tale.

Probably of Indian origin also is the best known of all framed collections, the *Arabian Nights*, or *Thousand and One Nights*.[1] The story inclosing this Arabian compilation, derived perhaps through a Persian intermediary, is at least as old as the tenth century. The framework chiefly concerns a king who put to death each of his successive wives on the morning after the consummation of the marriage, until he married Scheherazade, who saved her life by telling her husband a succession of enchanting stories. The tales eventually gathered within this inclosing narrative, in the course of centuries, are of diverse oriental origin.

Famed during the latter Middle Ages was another collection derived largely from oriental sources, the Latin *Disciplina clericalis* composed in Spain by the converted Jew, Petrus Alphonsi, in the twelfth century. This work was translated into English and several other vernaculars and was freely drawn upon by compilers of *exempla*. The thirty stories are framed within a

---

[1] See P. Rajna, "Per le origini della novella proemiale delle *Mille e una notte*," *Giornale della Società asiatica italiana*, XII (1899), 171–96; V. Chauvin, *Les mille et une nuits*, I ("Bibliographie des ouvrages arabes," Vol. IV [Liège and Leipzig, 1900]), 1–8; R. A. Nicholson, *A Literary History of the Arabs* (New York, 1907), pp. 456–59; E. Cosquin, "Le Prologue-Cadre des Mille et une nuits, les légendes perses, et le Livre d'Esther," *Revue biblique* (1909), 7–49, 161–97; D. B. MacDonald, "The Earlier History of the *Arabian Nights*," *JRAS* (1924), pp. 353–97; and Löhmann, p. 45.

somewhat disordered dialogue between an Arabian philosopher and his son, whom the father is attempting to instruct in Christian morals.[1]

III

In a group apart from the conscious framing devices of these oriental, or orientalized, collections are one or two examples of the "boxing" of tales which have sometimes been cited from the literature of Greece and Rome. In the classical epics, for example, one finds short narrations or anecdotes which appear to be separable insertions, and which may be regarded, in a sense, as framed by the inclosing epic narrative. Probably the most striking of such insertions are the fabulous tales which Odysseus recites to Alcinous at the court of the Phaeacians.[2] It can hardly be said, however, that incidental stories in epics and romances are really and consciously framed, since in such works the comprehensive inclosing narrative exists for reasons of its own and is not composed specifically for introducing the episodic short tales.

A more precise approach to a framing-tale is found in the episode of the daughters of Minyas in Ovid's *Metamorphoses*.[3] The story is that, during a festival of Bacchus, the three maidens irreverently flout that deity by gathering to do their spinning and weaving. One of them proposes that they lighten their labors by reciting tales, she herself beginning with the story of Pyramus and Thisbe. A second daughter then narrates Vulcan's discovery of the intrigue of Mars and Venus. After a brief discussion of this tale and of what the next shall be, the third daughter tells of Salmacis and Hermaphroditus. Then the outraged Bacchus ends the storytelling by transforming the three girls into bats and their implements into vines. It has been sug-

---

[1] The Latin text of Migne, *Patrologia Latina*, Vol. CLVII, cols. 671–706, is superseded by that of A. Hilka and W. Söderhjelm, *Die Disciplina clericalis des Petrus Alfonsi* (Heidelberg, 1911). The Middle English translation has been edited, with a general discussion of other versions, by W. H. Hulme, *Peter Alphonse's Disciplina clericalis* ("Western Reserve University Bulletin," Vol. XXII, No. 3 [new ser.; Cleveland, 1919]). See also Löhmann, pp. 37–42.

[2] See *Odyssey*, Books vii–xii; Löhmann, pp. 47–48; Keith, pp. 244–45; Hinckley, in *MLN*, XLIX (1934), 73–74.

[3] See iv. 1–415; Löhmann, pp. 53–55.

gested that this Ovidian episode may have served Boccaccio in some fashion in his designing of the *Decameron*,[1] and there can be no doubt that Chaucer also was familiar with it, since he was a devoted reader of the *Metamorphoses* and actually borrowed from the story of Pyramus and Thisbe as found in the passage under discussion.[2] It is conceivable that Ovid was among those who reminded Boccaccio or Chaucer, or both, that stories could be framed and could be told for sheer entertainment. Beyond this germinal suggestion the episode in the *Metamorphoses* could offer little of significance.

Except in matters of external circumstance, one draws no nearer to Chaucer's conception through considering the *Confessio amantis* of his friend, John Gower. If, indeed, the first form of the *Confessio* was completed by 1390,[3] some knowledge of it might have reached Chaucer before he had formed the final plan of his own long poem. It is highly probable, however, that Chaucer had designed, and partly written, the *Canterbury Tales* before 1390.[4] In any case, there is virtually no specific resemblance between Chaucer's design and Gower's. In the *Confessio amantis* the author-lover is represented as dreaming that Venus sends him to her priest, Genius, to confess his short-

---

[1] See Landau, *Die Quellen des Dekameron*, pp. 314–15; Morsbach, p. 45; Tatlock, *Anglia*, XXXVII (1913), 76–77; V. Cian, "L'Organismo del Decameron," in *Studii su Giovanni Boccaccio*, ed. O. Bacci (Castelfiorentino, 1913), pp. 202–13, esp. p. 205; Löhmann, pp. 53–55; L. Morsbach, *Chaucers Canterbury Tales und das Decameron*, in *Nachrichten von der Gesellschaft der Wissenschaften zu Göttingen* ("Philologisch-historische Klasse" [N.F.], Fachgruppe IV, Band I, No. 4 [Göttingen, 1934]), pp. 49–70, esp. pp. 49–51.

[2] See Tatlock, in *Anglia*, XXXVII (1913), 76. Tatlock also notes here that the *Metamorphoses* exhibits other examples of tales within tales.

[3] See G. C. Macaulay (ed.), *The Complete Works of John Gower*, II (Oxford, 1901), xxi.

[4] See Tatlock, *Development*, pp. 142, 150; Robinson, p. 751. Manly (*Canterbury Tales*, pp. 76–77) summarizes the matter as follows: "Whether Gower's plan became known to Chaucer, and in turn set him to devising the plan of the *Canterbury Tales*, can probably never be determined. We have no certain knowledge when Chaucer first conceived his plan or even when he first began to execute it. And we do not know that Chaucer ever read the *Confessio Amantis* through, though we can be fairly certain that he had heard of it and knew something about its contents. . . . . In any event, only the barest impulse to make a large collection of stories could have come to Chaucer from Gower's example, for the *Confessio Amantis* is structurally not in the least like the *Canterbury Tales*."

comings. To the confessions and inquiries of the author, Genius replies with instruction illustrated by stories. These narratives are all recounted by Genius himself, and their purpose is to elucidate to the author the seven chief sins and all their branches and twigs. In comparison with Ovid's vivacious and pleasurable sketch, Gower's didactic and static undertaking, for all its fluency and comprehensiveness, seems even more remote from the form and temper of the *Canterbury Tales*.

IV

A far more significant approach to Chaucer's work is through the several examples of the framing of stories in the work of his foreign contemporary, Giovanni Boccaccio.[1] Important among these is the one found in the *Ameto*, written about 1341.[2] This pastoral romance recounts the adventures of the young, un-tutored Tuscan huntsman, Ameto, in the course of his amour with the nymph, Lia. The part of the narrative with which we are especially concerned is localized in a wooded meadow, where, on a festival of Venus, Lia and six other nymphs, along with Ameto, entertain themselves during a hot afternoon with storytelling.[3] Each of the seven nymphs agrees to narrate her experiences in love and, at the end of her recital, to sing in honor of the deity whom she particularly reveres. Ameto is appointed to preside and call upon the narrators in turn. There are, then, seven stories, six of them recounting autobiographically the love of a disillusioned wife for a youthful paramour. The seventh narrative, by Lia, is concerned chiefly with the history of Florence. The *intermezzo* after each recital presents Ameto's re-

---

[1] The most comprehensive study of Boccaccio's framing devices, in themselves and in relation to Chaucer, is that by Tatlock, "Boccaccio and the Plan of Chaucer's *Canterbury Tales*," *Anglia*, XXXVII (1913), 69–117, mentioned above. See also S. Battaglia, "Schemi lirici nell' arte del Boccaccio," *Archivum romanicum*, XIX (1935), 61–78. Boccaccio's fondness for frame-stories is noticed by Koerting, pp. 655 and 730.

[2] See H. Hauvette, *Boccace: étude biographique et littéraire* (Paris, 1914), pp. 106, 119; Tatlock, in *Anglia*, XXXVII (1913), 80–108; Cian, p. 206; L. di Francia, *Novellistica* ("Storia dei generi letterari italiani," I [Milan, 1924]), pp. 103–4; Battaglia, pp. 68–70; Löhmann, p. 75; Morsbach, *Chaucers Canterbury Tales und das Decameron*, pp. 51–52. The text used is *Opere volgari di Giovanni Boccaccio*, ed. Moutier, Vol. XV (Florence, 1834).

[3] See *Opere volgari*, XV, 23 ff.

flections and his wish that he might have been the paramour of the reciter.

Broad resemblances to Chaucer's plan appear in the following general features of the Boccaccian episode: the telling of the tales by the several members of an organized group of wanderers; the foregathering of these persons on a special religious occasion; the joining of the narratives by links; and the appointing of a person to preside over the storytelling. In addition to these general resemblances, one can point to certain verbal and thematic similarities between the *Ameto* and various parts of the *Canterbury Tales*.[1] The evidence, however, seems insufficient for demonstrating Chaucer's specific use of the framework of the Italian episode.[2]

A more extended experiment in the framing of stories is found in Boccaccio's *Filocolo*, a long prose romance composed during the period 1336–41 upon the well-known theme of Flore and Blancheflore.[3] The extended episode in this work that concerns us is placed in the midst of Florio's long wanderings in search of his beloved Biancofiore.[4] In the course of a sojourn at Naples, the young hero and five of his friends are invited to join a group of young people seeking diversion in a shady spot near the city. One of the company, Fiammetta, daughter of the king of Naples, persuades her companions to agree that one of their number shall preside as "king" and that each of the others shall submit to him some problem relating to love (*una questione d'amore*). The sovereignty is subsequently awarded to Fiammetta herself, who calls upon Florio for the first *questione*, ar-

[1] See Tatlock, in *Anglia*, XXXVII (1913), 93–108. For similarities between the *Ameto* and the *Merchant's Tale* see text quoted on pp. 339–40 in the present work.

[2] Tatlock (*Anglia*, XXXVII [1913], 109) does not claim a demonstration. Complete skepticism is expressed by H. M. Cummings, *The Indebtedness of Chaucer's Works to the Italian Works of Boccaccio* ("University of Cincinnati Studies," Vol. X, Part II [Cincinnati, 1916]), pp. 33–42.

[3] See Hauvette, pp. 60–73, 118–30. We are not concerned here with assigning separate parts of the *Filocolo* to separate years within the period 1336–41. The text used is S. Battaglia, *Giovanni Boccaccio: Il Filocolo* ("Scrittori d'Italia" [Bari, 1938]). See Cian, pp. 205–6; Tatlock, *Anglia*, XXXVII (1913), 70–80; Francia, I, 101–2; Löhmann, pp. 74–78; Morsbach, *Chaucers Canterbury Tales und das Decameron*, pp. 52–54; Battaglia, pp. 63–68.

[4] See *Giovanni Boccaccio: Il Filocolo*, pp. 293–366; Tatlock, in *Anglia*, XXXVII (1913), 70–80; Cian, pp. 205–6.

ranges that the others shall be summoned in the order in which they are sitting, opens the discussion which follows the discourse of each speaker, and passes judgment upon each problem formally presented. Of the thirteen *questioni* submitted, the greater part include a considerable amount of narrative, and at least four are genuine tales; hence we may regard the thirteen discourses as a series of stories within a framework.

Like the framing device used in the *Ameto*, the one before us resembles that of the *Canterbury Tales* in several general aspects: the stories (or *questioni*) are presented by the several members of an organized group; the stories are separated by *intermezzi;* and the ordering of the series is in the hands of a presiding person. In one respect the frame in the *Filocolo* is less like Chaucer's than the one in the *Ameto:* in the *Filocolo* the storytellers are not brought together by a special occasion. As a possible model for the framing of the *Canterbury Tales*, therefore, the *Filocolo* has even less claim to consideration than the *Ameto*.[1] Even though it is generally believed that Chaucer was well acquainted with the *Filocolo*, and used it both within the *Canterbury Tales* and elsewhere, we have no clear evidence that he was specifically influenced by it in designing the frame for his collection of stories.[2]

V

Though the *Filocolo* had no demonstrable influence upon Chaucer's plan, it had an important bearing upon the later work of Boccaccio himself, for the episode of the *questioni d'amore* in it has long been recognized as a preliminary form of the design executed with amplitude and richness in the *Decameron* (1348–53).[3] This later work, moreover, brings us for the first time into

[1] See Tatlock, p. 80.

[2] Opinions concerning Chaucer's general use of the *Filocolo* are sufficiently referred to by Robinson, pp. 826 and 923. See also Tatlock, in *Anglia*, XXXVII (1913), p. 70, and, for the probable source of the *Franklin's Tale*, pp. 377–83 in the present work. It is unnecessary to consider in detail the slight framework of Ser Giovanni's *Il Pecorone*, begun in 1378, for a discussion of which see Löhmann, pp. 122–24.

[3] See especially P. Rajna, "L'Episodio delle Questioni d'Amore nel *Filocolo* del Boccaccio, *Romania*, XXXI (1902), 28–81; R. Fornaciari, "Dal *Filocolo* al *Decameron*," in *Studii su Giovanni Boccaccio*, ed. Bacci, pp. 196–201; Löhmann, pp. 76–78; G. Lipparini, *La Vita e l'opera di Giovanni Boccaccio* (Florence, 1927), pp. 28–30, 71, 73; Francia, I, 100–102.

inescapable contact with the *Canterbury Tales*, for it has been persistently asserted, and denied, that the framework of the *Decameron* was Chaucer's model for the design of his longest narrative work.[1] We are, therefore, bound to examine the plan of the *Decameron* with some care.[2]

On a Tuesday morning during the plague of 1348, Boccaccio tells us, seven young women of Florence, dressed in deep mourning, met by chance at divine service in the church of Santa Maria Novella. They were all attached to one another either through blood or through close friendship, and their ages differed only through a range of ten years, from eighteen to twenty-eight. In order of seniority Boccaccio calls them Pampinea, Fiammetta, Filomena, Emilia, Lauretta, Neifile, and Elissa. After participating in the liturgy, they seated themselves in a circle in a corner of the church for conversation about the misfortunes of the times. Presently one of their number, Pampinea, proposed that, to avoid calamity to themselves, they leave town with their maids, and seek retirement and diversion in one or another of the numerous country estates in their possession (*nostri luoghi in contado*),[3] changing their residence from day to day, and enjoying the charms of the region. This proposal was applauded by the other six ladies, who promptly began discussing plans for their immediate departure from Flor-

---

[1] Opinions upon the question of Chaucer's knowledge and use of the *Decameron* are summarized sufficiently by P. Rajna, in *Romania*, XXXII (1903), 244–57; Tatlock, *Development*, pp. 131–32; Hammond, pp. 151–52; Morsbach, in *ES*, XLII (1910), 44–47; R. K. Root, in *ES*, XLIV (1912), 1–7; Tatlock, in *Anglia*, XXXVII (1913), 69–117; Cummings, pp. 176–80; W. E. Farnham, in *MLN*, XXXIII (1918), 193–203, and in *PMLA*, XXXIX (1924), 123–39; Hertha Korten, *Chaucers literarische Beziehungen zu Boccaccio* (Rostock, 1920); M. Praz, in *Monthly Criterion*, VI (1927), 140–49; Robinson, p. 751; Morsbach, *Chaucers Canterbury Tales und das Decameron*, pp. 55–70; Löhmann, pp. 226–27.

[2] The edition used is that of A. F. Massèra, *Giovanni Boccaccio: Il Decameron* ("Scrittori d'Italia" [2 vols.; Bari, 1927]). For special studies of the frame of the *Decameron*, in itself or in relation to the *Canterbury Tales*, see E. Fueter, "Die Rahmenerzählung bei Boccaccio und Chaucer," in *Beilage zur allgemeinen Zeitung*, No. 265 (1906), pp. 305–7; No. 266 (1906), pp. 315–16; Landau, *Beilage zur allgemeinen Zeitung*, No. 270 (1906), p. 351; E. Hutton, *Giovanni Boccaccio* (London, 1910), pp. 291–304; Hauvette, pp. 207–24; Cummings, pp. 176–80; Korten, pp. 12–42; W. F. Schirmer, in *GRM*, XII (1924), 290–93; Francia, I, 104–69; Lipparini, pp. 73–85; U. Bosco, *Il "Decameron": Saggio* (Rieti, 1929), pp. 11–64, 199; Löhmann, pp. 63–120, 226–27; Battaglia, pp. 70–78.

[3] See Massèra, I, 20.

ence. The discreet Filomena, however, advised against undue haste, pointing to the fact that women, being naturally fickle, obstinate, timid, and suspicious, were unlikely to fare well in such an undertaking without the steadying presence of men. Elissa took the same view of the matter but was perplexed when she remembered that the greater part of their male acquaintance had already died. At this opportune moment the ladies were joined by three young men, named Panfilo, Filostrato, and Dioneo, all beyond twenty-five years of age, and each of them in love with one of the ladies present. Pampinea explained to them the plan in hand and invited them to participate. After some jesting the young men accepted the invitation and joined in the preparations for departure next morning. On Wednesday at dawn, accordingly, the seven ladies, the three gentlemen, four maidservants, and three menservants—seventeen persons in all—set forth from the city and, after traveling two short miles (*né oltre a due piccole miglia*),[1] reached their first destination, a palace surrounded by gardens and meadows upon a slight eminence. After they had adjusted themselves to the comforts of the place, Pampinea proposed that they choose a separate person (*principale, maggiore*) to regulate the diversions of each day, and was herself elected for that Wednesday. Upon her head was placed a garland, which was to be handed on to the other persons presiding in turn on succeeding days. As the accepted "queen" (*reina*), Pampinea assigned duties to the servants and gave the ladies and gentlemen liberty until dinner time at nine in the morning. The interim was spent in strolling through the gardens, singing love songs, and weaving garlands of flowers. After dinner the company engaged in music and dancing and then retired for a siesta. Soon after three the queen summoned the ladies and gentlemen forth into a shaded meadow, arranged them in a circle, proposed that each of the ten tell a story, and appointed Panfilo as the first narrator. After some of the stories there was brief comment, but these *intermezzi* were short. By the end of the tenth story, told by Pampinea, the cool of the day had arrived, and the queen transferred her authority and garland to Filomena for the next day. Then followed supper, singing and dancing, and retirement for the night. This

---

[1] Massèra, I, 23.

order of diversions was the usual one for the days on which tales were told, with such variations as were brought about through the removal of the company to different localities. The company was absent from Florence for fourteen days, on ten of which ten stories were told.

Because of the analogy to the plan of the *Canterbury Tales* some emphasis should be given to the movement of Boccaccio's storytellers from place to place. The first stage in their journeying, as we have seen, was on a Wednesday morning, from the city to the first palace, a distance of two short miles. Here they sojourned four days, telling stories on Wednesday and Thursday but occupying themselves in more sober pursuits on Friday and Saturday. At sunrise on Sunday they journeyed a short distance (*senza essere andata oltre a dumilia passi*)[1] to a second palace, remaining there four days, and recounting stories each day. On the fourth of these days—the second Wednesday of their absence from Florence—in addition to the storytelling, the ladies and the gentlemen, in separate parties and at separate times, walked a mile or so (*né guari più d'un miglio*)[2] from the second palace to the Valley of Ladies (*Valle delle donne*) and back. This place was so agreeable, with its lake and umbrageous surroundings, that arrangements were made for the whole company to spend the next day there. On the following morning (Thursday), therefore, the party walked to the Valley of Ladies, spent the day there in telling stories and in other diversions, and returned at night to the second palace.[3] The next five days (Friday, Saturday, Sunday, Monday, and Tuesday) were passed at the second palace, only the last three, however, being

---

[1] Massèra, I, 183.   [2] Massèra, II, 34.

[3] We are not greatly concerned here with attempts to identify the two palaces and the Valley of Ladies with real places on the slopes south of Fiesole. For discussions of the matter see D. M. Manni, *Istoria del Decamerone di Giovanni Boccaccio* (Florence, 1742), pp. 140–41; [C. Giannini], *Il Ritrovo delle Novellatrici e dei Novellatori del Decameron di Giovanni Boccacci nelle Ville Gherardi e Palmieri* (Florence, 1893); N. Masellis, "I due Palagi di Rifugio e la Valle delle Donne nel Decamerone," *La Rassegna nazionale*, CXXXVII (1904), 92–115; W. J. Stillman, "The *Decameron* and Its Villas," *Nineteenth Century*, XLVI (1899), 289–301; Hutton, pp. 298–304; Hauvette, pp. 217–19; Lipparini, pp. 81–82; Bosco, pp. 58–63; Löhmann, pp. 112–14; L. Russo, "I Luoghi, i novellatori, l'architettura e la peste del *Decameron*," *Annali della R. Scuola normale superiore di Pisa* (*Lettere, storia e filosofia*), VI (2d ser.; 1937), 201–4.

devoted to storytelling. On the next day—the third Wednesday
of absence from the city—the whole company returned from the
second palace to Florence, the gentlemen taking leave of the
ladies at the church of Santa Maria Novella.[1] It is clear, therefore, that Boccaccio's Florentines did a considerable amount of
journeying, in short stages, and that his framing device cannot
be characterized as static.

The *intermezzi* after the first nine tales of each day are usually
brief, mentioning the laughter of the listeners, or the blushes of
the ladies, or some brief comment. The succeeding speaker
sometimes pretends to derive his tale from a suggestion in the
recital of his predecessor. The links following the final tales of
the days are considerably longer. At the close of the tenth novel
of each day the next "queen" or "king" is appointed, and the
appointee proposes a general subject or type for the tales of the
day to follow.[2] Then the members of the company are allowed
to divert themselves freely until supper, after which there are
singing and dancing until bedtime. One or two of these longer
links mention other matters. At the end of the second day, for
example, Neifile explains that there are to be no tales on Friday
and Saturday because those are the times for duties such as
laying in provisions, bathing, and religious observances.[3] She
also points to the desirability of their removing from the first
palace if they wish to avoid admitting to their circle certain
visitors who are likely to discover their retreat.[4] Particularly
lively are some of the occurrences recounted as occurring at the
end of the fifth day and at the beginning of the sixth.[5] The
queen suppresses the vivacious Dioneo when he undertakes to
sing ribald trash;[6] and, as she is about to introduce the first
narrator of the sixth day, she has to call upon him to settle a

---

[1] See Massèra, II, 321.

[2] For the first and ninth days no such general subject is prescribed.

[3] Such recognition of religious observance by Boccaccio's worldlings is an interesting commentary upon the absence of this element from the links of the *Canterbury Tales*.

[4] See Massèra, I, 177–78.

[5] In such instances the numbering refers to the days on which stories are told
and not to the whole succession of fourteen days of absence from Florence.

[6] See Massèra, I, 409–10.

noisy quarrel between the servants, Licisca and Tindaro. The realistic quality of this episode appears from the fact that the spicy language of Licisca "caused the ladies to laugh with such heartiness that you might have drawn all their teeth!"[1]

From the details in such an incident one might infer that the personages in the framing-story are characterized with considerable distinctness, but, in reality, only a few of the seventeen persons are clearly individualized at all, and none of them is described in a "portrait."[2] Of the seven servants, only Licisca is brought before us in any vividness.[3] Of the gentlefolk, only Dioneo is given a lively vitality. At the outset he is introduced to us as "the pleasantest youth of them all and full of words."[4] At the end of the first day's entertainment he asks that he be given exceptional liberty in the choice of his tales and be permitted, on each of the succeeding days, to speak last. This request the queen grants, knowing him to be "a merry and mirth-provoking fellow."[5] Of his subsequent vivacity an instance has been mentioned above. Of the other two gentlemen we can infer only that they are devoted and pensive lovers, Panfilo being somewhat the more cheerful in his outlook. Among the women Pampinea is the oldest, the most widely experienced, and the most inclined to reflection and discussion. Neifile is the young-

[1] See Massèra, II, 4: "facevan le donne sí gran risa, tutti i denti si sarebbero loro potuti trarre." The element of realism in the *Decameron*—as well as in the related parts of the *Filocolo* and the *Ameto*—is emphasized by Cian, pp. 205–13; Francia, I, 104–6, 141–42, 158–61.

[2] For attempts to differentiate these personalities see A. Albertazzi, *Parvenze e Sembianze* (Bologna, 1892), pp. 161–99 ("I Novellatori e le Novellatrici del Decamerone"); H. Hauvette, in *Journal des savants* (1905), pp. 489–91; Hauvette, *Boccace*, pp. 220–24; Francia, I, 112–17; Lipparini, pp. 76–80; Bosco, pp. 17–18, 20–53, 199–200; Löhmann, pp. 111–12; Russo, pp. 204–10. The lack of differentiation is stressed by Hutton, pp. 297–98. Historical identification was attempted by Manni, pp. 141–44.

[3] The names and duties of the seven servants are mentioned in the *Introduzione* (Massèra, I, 25). The three menservants are Parmeno, Sirisco, and Tindaro; the four maidservants are Misia, Licisca, Chimera, and Stratilia.

[4] See Massèra, I, 23: "Dioneo, il quale oltre ad ogni altro era piacevole giovane e pieno di motti."

[5] See Massèra, I, 68: "La reina, la quale lui e sollazzevole uomo e festevole conoscea, ed ottimamente s'avvisò, questo lui non chieder se non per dovere la brigata, se stanca fosse del ragionare, rallegrare con alcuna novella da ridere, col consentimento degli altri lietamente la grazia gli fece."

est and most sensitive, being given to blushes, timidity, and reverence. Filomena is tall, affable, and discreet. Emilia shows less tendency to reflection and prudence. Elissa is not free from harshness and disdain. Lauretta and Fiammetta are hardly individualized at all. What we know of the personality of each of the ten young gentlefolk must be inferred from an occasional adjective, from the attitudes of his companions toward him, and from his slight responses to the stories told. None of these persons, it must be repeated, appears before us in a descriptive and characterizing "portrait."

From this outline it appears that the frame of the *Decameron* resembles that of the *Canterbury Tales* in the following general aspects: the tales are told by the several members of an organized group; the storytellers are brought together by special external circumstances; between the tales there are narrative and conversational links; the conduct of the company and the succession of tales are controlled by a presiding person (or persons); it is agreed that each person shall tell more than one tale and that the storytelling shall continue during several days; and there is a certain amount of journeying from place to place.[1] Chaucer's plan differs from Boccaccio's in such general considerations as these: the storytellers represent not one, but many, social classes; the same person presides over the storytelling throughout; in the assigning of tales to individuals, conspicuous attention is given to the appropriateness of the stories to their personalities; the individual pilgrims are made known to us in detail through descriptive and characterizing "portraits"; and the essential element in the frame is a pilgrimage on horseback, in the course of which the stories are told, not at the resting-places, but as the pilgrims travel along the road.[2]

---

[1] Unpersuasive resemblances in detail are mentioned by Tatlock, in *Anglia*, XXXVII (1913), pp. 92–93; Korten, pp. 33–42; Morsbach, *Chaucers Canterbury Tales und das Decameron*, pp. 56–69.

[2] Critics have genially recorded certain slight violations of realism in Chaucer's plan—such as the fiction of making a tale audible to a cavalcade of thirty persons on horseback, to the accompaniment of clattering from one hundred and twenty hoofs. See M. Landau, *Beiträge zur Geschichte der italienischen Novelle* (Vienna, 1875), p. 47; A. P. Stanley, *Historical Memorials of Canterbury* (London, 1883), pp. 213–14; P. Rajna, in *Romania*, XXXII (1903), 251; Fueter, in *Beilage zur allgemeinen Zeitung*, No. 265 (1906), p. 307; Tatlock, *Development*, p. 138; Morsbach, in *ES*, XLII (1910), 48–49; A. Brusendorff, *The Chaucer Tradition* (London,

In view of these differences it is clear that the frame of the *Decameron* could not be regarded as Chaucer's "model" in any precise or thoroughgoing sense. In spite of its embryonic element of journeying, for example, its basic conception is that of a succession of aristocratic garden scenes rather than of a moving pilgrimage of diverse and discordant personalities. Nevertheless, no one acquainted with Chaucer's literary powers and practice would dare to deny that he could have transformed the polished orderliness and elegance of the *Decameron* into the varied realism and humanity of the *Canterbury Tales*, if he had known the Italian collection, and if he had chosen to undertake the transformation. The fundamental reason for doubting Chaucer's indebtedness to the *Decameron*, therefore, is not that it lacks suggestiveness but that we have no decisive evidence that Chaucer was acquainted with it. Although his thorough knowledge and use of certain other works of Boccaccio is well known, his acquaintance with the most famous of them all cannot be established. Chaucer does not mention the *Decameron*, he borrows no stories directly from it, and no copy or translation of it can be traced in England during the period of his life.[1] It is possible that he saw it, and probable that he heard of it, during his journeying in Italy or elsewhere; and he may have been influenced by what he saw or heard; but of this we cannot be certain.

VI

Whether Chaucer ever possessed any information about the *Decameron* or not, it is sufficiently clear that this work did not, in any adequate form, provide the conception of storytelling in

1925), pp. 123–25; Robinson, p. 2. A warning against too much attributing of "realistic finish" to Chaucer's poems is expressed by J. S. P. Tatlock, in *MLN*, L (1935), 292.

[1] In *MLN*, XXXIII (1918), 193–203, W. E. Farnham presents verbal resemblances between the *Clerk's Tale* and *Decameron*, X, 10, which in themselves might point to Chaucer's direct or indirect use of Boccaccio's story. The whole matter of the sources of the *Clerk's Tale* is treated by J. B. Severs elsewhere in this work. In *MLN*, LIII (1938), 257–58, T. H. McNeal presents a resemblance between the *Man of Law's Tale* and *Decameron*, V, 2, which might indicate that Chaucer used the *Decameron* or one of its sources. The restricted circulation of the *Decameron* during the period 1353–1500, in England and elsewhere, is discussed by Farnham, in *PMLA*, XXXIX (1924), 123–29; Praz, pp. 140–49. See above, p. 14, n. 1.

the course of a moving pilgrimage, which is fundamental in the design of the *Canterbury Tales*. For this device, accompanied by other similarities to Chaucer's work, we must turn to the large collection of *novelle* prepared by Giovanni Sercambi (1347–1424), an imitator of the *Decameron* and a contemporary of the English poet.[1] Sercambi was a citizen of Lucca.[2] Although he was of humble birth, he early took part in the military struggles of his city and, by 1369, had gained distinction as a soldier. In 1372 he was made a member of the *Consiglio generale* of Lucca and was elected one of the four *pennonieri* of his *contrada*. In 1382 he served successfully as an ambassador from Lucca to the adventurer, Alberigo da Barbiano, stationed threateningly at Arezzo. During his more mature years Sercambi allied himself to the powerful Guinigi family of Lucca, and from 1392 to 1400 held various public offices. In 1399 he was an ambassador from Lucca to Florence, and his prominence in public activities continued until the time of his death. The fact that throughout his life he exercised the profession of *speziale*, selling books as well as parchment, ink, and drugs, may account for Sercambi's interest in literary matters. His writings include the *Monito*, a book of advice to the Guinigi family; the *Croniche*, recording the history of Lucca for the period 1164–1423; a commentary on Dante's *Paradiso*, appropriated from Jacopo della Lana; and the collection of *novelle* with which we are chiefly concerned here.

[1] Perhaps the first to mention the possibility that Chaucer knew Sercambi's work is Landau, *Beiträge zur Geschichte der italienischen Novelle*, pp. 38–44, 47. P. Rajna, in *Romania*, XXXII (1903), 254–56, mentions Sercambi and Chaucer together but seems to assume that there is no literary relationship between them. The possibility of such a relationship is studied, with indecisive conclusions, by Hinckley, *Notes on Chaucer*, pp. 2–3, and by Young, pp. 405–17. The latter of these studies was the first to print substantial passages from the unpublished *intermezzi* of Sercambi's collection. These studies have often been mentioned by later Chaucerian critics, without fresh evidence or decisive conclusions.

[2] Concerning the life and works of Sercambi see R. Renier, *Novelle inedite di Giovanni Sercambi* (Turin, 1889), pp. x–lxiii; G. Volpi, *Il Trecento* (Milan, n.d.), pp. 135–36; A. Gaspary, *Storia della letteratura italiana*, trans. V. Rossi, II (Turin, 1891), pp. 62–63; C. Minutoli, *Alcune Novelle di Giovanni Sercambi* (Lucca, 1855), pp. v–xliv; S. Bongi (ed.), *Le Croniche di Giovanni Sercambi*, I (Rome, 1892), vii–xvi; Francia, I, 223–60 (Francia refers to the *Novelle* as the *Novelliero*); and, particularly for Sercambi's life, A. G. Dinucci, "Giovanni Sercambi e le sue Croniche," *Rassegna nazionale*, LVII (2d ser., 1927), 43–67, 93–103.

This collection of tales Sercambi composed in two different forms, at two different times. The earlier and shorter form, the *Novelliero*, containing one hundred stories, is said to have been written in 1374. The one recorded manuscript of this version has been lost.[1] The later form of the collection, the *Novelle*, is found in one manuscript, written in the fifteenth century.[2] This version could not have been composed, or at any rate completed, until after the death of Bernabò Visconti, on December 19, 1385.[3] Of these two forms of Sercambi's collection, either

[1] See Renier, pp. xlix-lii. One tale (No. 35) of the *Novelliero* has been preserved, and it corresponds to tale No. 34 of the *Novelle* (see Renier, pp. xlix–l, and p. l, n. 2). Both versions are printed by D'Ancona (*Novelle inedite di Giovanni Sercambi* ["Collezione di operette inedite o rare pubblicate dalla Libreria Dante in Firenze," No. 12 (Florence, 1886)], pp. 29–34, 59–65), and their only differences are in orthography or wording. D'Ancona (pp. 5–7; p. 59, n. 1) suspected the *Novelliero* to be a first version of the *Novelle*, and Renier (p. li) agreed with him. If the first tale of the Trivulzian manuscript has been lost (see below, p. 41, n. 2), then tale No. 34 of the *Novelle* was originally No. 35 and held the same position that it had in the *Novelliero*. The story conjecturally lost from the *Novelle* may have been that mentioned by Luigi Baroni (see p. 29 below; the *Novelle* contains no story corresponding to this one). To what extent the content of the *Novelle* followed that of the *Novelliero* we can only conjecture.

[2] MS 193 in the Biblioteca Trivulziana, Milan, written on paper in a crude cursive hand of the fifteenth century. A defective copy of this volume, made by Bartolomeo Gamba early in the nineteenth century, is preserved in MSS 194 and 195 in the same library. From Gamba's copy certain others were made. From MS 193 or from Gamba's copy, various editors have published various groups of the tales at different times, so that all 155 tales of the *Novelle* (except the most licentious or fragmentary) are now in print (see Renier, pp. xl-xlviii). The *Proemio* is printed by Renier, pp. 3–8. Hitherto the *intermezzi*, presenting (along with the *Proemio*) the framework of the *Novelle*, have been printed only in slender excerpts, chiefly by Young (see n. 1, p. 21, above). Further selections from the text of the *intermezzi* are now printed for the first time, together with the text of the *Proemio*. Mr. J. W. Alexander, at the University of Virginia, is working on the entire manuscript.

[3] Three of the tales (Nos. 5, 82, 91) begin, "Fu in Milano città di Lombardia al tempo di messer Bernabò," or with similar phraseology. See Renier, pp. 32, 190, 214, whose text is sufficiently accurate here. Concerning the death of Bernabò Visconti see G. Giulini, *Memorie spettanti alla storia, al governo ed alla descrizione della città e campagna di Milano*, V (Milan, 1856), 660. Bernabò's wife, Regina, similarly mentioned in tale No. 91 (Renier, p. 214), died in 1384 (Giulini, V, 643). The same conclusion regarding the date of the *Novelle* is reached by Francia (I, 226), who further proposes that tale No. 135 (Renier, pp. 341–45) was composed before the death of Giovanni dell'Agnello in 1387. Because of these dates, and because of information regarding the plague in Lucca (derived from Sercambi's *Croniche*), Löhmann (p. 125, n. 1) presents the theory that the journey described in the *Novelle* began in February, 1384, instead of 1374, the latter date being a scribal error. Löhmann failed to note, however, that the year 1374 (see below, p. 29) is mentioned also in association with the *Novelliero*.

one might conceivably have become known to Chaucer before
the period when he committed himself finally to the design of
the *Canterbury Tales* as we know it;[1] but, if it were possible, one
would give attention especially to the earlier *Novelliero*, for this
version antedated the *Canterbury Tales* by a longer period[2] and
was probably being produced during the period of Chaucer's
travels in Italy. Since the *Novelliero* is lost, however, we can
approach it only through the later and more highly developed
Novelle. Fortunately, as we shall see, the two versions did not
differ greatly in the aspect in which we are primarily interested:
namely, the general plan, or framework.

As we see from the *Proemio* and *intermezzi*, printed in large
portions below, the narrative framework of the *Novelle* takes the
following form:

During the ravages of a plague in Lucca in the year 1374, a
number of men and women of various stations and occupations
decide to leave town until the pestilence shall have subsided
and, in the interim, to travel about through Italy. One Sunday
in February, therefore, after attending Mass and performing
other prudent acts, these persons foregather in the church of
Santa Maria del Corso. At this meeting a certain prominent
citizen, named Aluisi, rises to address the company, suggesting
that they appoint some one person to whom they shall pay
reverence and obedience during their travels, and who shall
control their pleasures, arrange the itinerary, and conduct them
safely home. To this proposal they readily assent and for their
leader (*preposto* or *proposto*) choose Aluisi himself.

At the request of Aluisi the travelers promptly provide a
purse of three thousand florins for common expenses and promise more when this sum shall have been spent. The leader ap-
points a treasurer to take charge of the money, and stewards to
supervise expenditures, and arranges for the daily observance
of the offices of the Church. As amusements for so various a
company Aluisi provides that there shall be edifying conversation, fencing, erudite discussion, instrumental music, dancing,
and songs of love, of honor, and of worship. Finally he an-

---

[1] See below, pp. 31–32.

[2] Assuming that the *Novelle*—completed and probably largely prepared at some
time after December 19, 1385—antedated the *Canterbury Tales* at all.

nounces that there shall be an official storyteller for the journey, who shall respond whenever the *preposto* shall call upon him. Through an acrostic sonnet recited by Aluisi, Sercambi recognizes that he himself is the chosen narrator, and begins *Novella* I (*De Sapientia*), during the recital of which, one infers, the travelers set forth from Lucca somewhat speedily, for by the end of this tale of some three thousand words they have already left Pisa behind them.[1]

In the course of their journey the travelers visit the following places: Pisa, Volterra, San Miniato, Pistoia, Prato, Florence, Incisa, Siena, Civitella, Arezzo, Castiglione Aretino, Cortona, Città di Castello, Borgo San Sepolcro, Passignano, Massa di Maremma, Grosseto, Civitavecchia, Populonia, Maschona, Castro Povero, Bolsena, Orvieto, Assisi, Perugia, Todi, Narni, Terni, Montefiascone, Viterbo, Rome, Spoleto, Jesi, Aversa, Arpi, Aquila, Naples, Benevento, Salerno, Reggio di Calabria, Dierta, Squillace, Forati, Brindisi, Sant' Angelo, Scariotto, Ascoli, Fermo, Recanati, Ancona, Sinigaglia, Fano, Pesaro, Fossombrone, Gubbio, Urbino, Cagli, Cesena, Cervia, Bertinoro, Ravenna, Forlì, Faenza, Imola, Meldola, Bologna, Lagellino, Torre della Fossa, Ferrara, Francolino, Chioggia, Venice, Murano, Treviso, Feltre, Cividale, Vicenza, Padua, Verona, Brescia, Cremona, Mantua, Bergamo, Barzano, Monza, Milan, Como, Novara, Pavia, Vercelli, Alessandria, Tortona, Piacenza, Lodi, Parma, Reggio Emilia, Modena, Asti, Savona, Genoa, and Luni.[2] It appears, then, that, with some

---

[1] This appearance of unaccountable speed may result from the lacuna in the manuscript immediately before *Intermezzo* 1–2 (see below, p. 41, n. 2). The position of a particular *intermezzo* is indicated here by a dash between the numbers of the *novelle* which the *intermezzo* connects. In referring to the *novelle* we follow the numbering of the Trivulzian MS 193, as used by Renier in his list, pp. 429–33.

[2] For this list we cannot claim exhaustive accuracy, since, in some particulars, the text leaves the journey obscure. The route is largely imaginary and will not bear close scrutiny either in geography or in time-scheme. For the north of Italy, which was more or less familiar to Sercambi, the itinerary is fairly credible, but, as soon as the travelers leave Rome, their route becomes extravagant. For example, they visit Naples twice: *Int.* 58–59 mentions Partenopia, while *Int.* 68–69 finds the company at the same city, this time designated by its modern name. Moreover, they spend two days traveling from Naples to Benevento, 50 miles away, but two days suffice for their walking from Salerno to Reggio Calabria—a distance of about 250 miles (see *Int.* 78–79, 79–80, 80–81, 83–84, 84–85, 85–86). In such instances Sercambi is trusting to the list of places given in the third book of Fazio

tortuousness and retracing of steps, the travelers pass south-
ward from Lucca down the west coast of Italy, cross the penin-
sula at the southern end, pass northward along the east coast,
and, after touring in the north, end the journey—so far as the
defective manuscript carries us—at Luni, not many miles north-
west from Lucca. Sercambi's complete plan provided, no doubt,
for a return to Lucca itself. In general, the travelers spend only
a single night in a town; in a few of the larger and more interesting cities, however, they linger for a longer time—ten days, for
example, in Rome,[1] and five days in Naples.[2] The journey is
accomplished, for the most part, on foot. Between Bologna and
Treviso, in Venice and its neighborhood, the company travels
by boat.[3] On the road from Ferrara to Francolino they seem to
have used wagons.[4] We are given no indication of their traveling on horseback.

The tales are told sometimes on the road between towns and
sometimes in innyards or gardens in the towns themselves. In a
considerable number of instances there is an intentional relationship between the subject of the story and the region which
the company is, at the time, traversing.[5] During the ten days'
sojourn in Rome, for example, stories are drawn from Roman
history.[6] In the region about Venice the travelers listen to
stories on Venetian subjects.[7] On the road to Verona is told a
story of Veronese life.[8]

From this sketch of the framework of Sercambi's *Novelle* it is
obvious that in its fundamental conception his narrative plan
resembles Chaucer's more closely than does any of the others

---

degli Uberti's *Dittamondo*, the first fifteen chapters of which he included in his
Croniche (see Bongi, II, 83–117, 144–54.) Certain places along the route are best
explained by reference to the *Dittamondo*, their actual source; in so doing one
should use the version in the *Croniche*, for this seems to represent the text Sercambi knew, and is at times more accurate than even the best edition of the poem,
that published in Milan in 1826 (see *Croniche*, II, 448–49). A list of bibliographies
of editions and studies of the *Dittamondo* is given by N. Sapegno, *Il Trecento*
("Storia letteraria d'Italia" [Milan, 1938]), p. 138.

[1] See *Int.* 38–39.   [2] See *Int.* 67–68.

[3] See *Int.* 120–21, 121–22, 122–23, 123–24, 124–25, 125–26, 126–27.

[4] See *Int.* 121–22.

[5] See Renier, pp. lv–lvi.   [7] See *Novelle* CXXIV, CXXVI–CXXIX.

[6] See *Novelle* XL–XLIX.   [8] See *Novella* CXXXII.

adduced hitherto. The essential of the two narrative schemes is a journey made by a miscellaneous group of persons under a leader, in the course of which stories are told. In view of this basic resemblance we may appropriately examine certain likenesses and differences in detail.

1. *The group of travelers.*—Like the miscellaneous company that gathered in the Tabard Inn in Southwark, the travelers of Sercambi who assembled in the church of Santa Maria seem to have represented a great variety of conditions in life. Although the number of the Lucchese travelers is not mentioned, there are clear indications that the *brigata* was large. At the outset Aluisi addresses the company thus:

> Cari fratelli e a me maggiori et voi chare et venerabili donne che qui d'ongni condissione sete qui raunate....[1]

In the course of the journey, in singling out this or that group as his particular audience for a particular story, the narrator addresses bankers,[2] merchants,[3] young men,[4] nuns,[5] public officials,[6] ecclesiastics,[7] servants,[8] judges,[9] rulers,[10] and others in less definite categories.[11] The company includes also singers, dancers, and musicians, who frequently provide entertainment in the intervals between stories.[12] It is fair to say, however, that, of all these persons, none is really "portrayed" after Chaucer's manner and that, aside from the *preposto* Aluisi, and Sercambi himself, the only persons of whom the reader is generally aware are the *religiosi*, the *cantarelli*, and the *cantarelle*, who provide the company with entertainment. Most of the other travelers seem to have been invented as a mere part of the mechanism for joining the *intermezzi* to the tales. Only in a technical sense can

---

[1] See below, p. 38.

[2] See *Int.* 21–22.

[3] See *Int.* 21–22, 91–92.

[4] See *Int.* 94–95.

[5] See *Int.* 98–99.

[6] See *Int.* 103–4, 106–7, 137–38, 143–44.

[7] See *Int.* 109–10, 124–25.

[8] See *Int.* 118–19.

[9] See *Int.* 110–11.

[10] See *Int.* 134–35, 138–39.

[11] Among these are cheats (*Int.* 20–21, 145–46), widows (27–28), rich men (101–2), gluttons (107–8), and murderers (116–17).

[12] See, e.g., *Int.* 127–28, 128–29, 130–31, 134–35.

such mechanical figures be regarded as persons. They serve to sketch the narrative design but contribute no human reality.[1]

2. *The leader.*—In the manner of his appointment, as well as in some of his activities, the leader, or *preposto*, in the *Novelle* resembles the parallel personage in the *Canterbury Tales.* Just as Harry Bailey, after offering himself to the Canterbury pilgrims as guide and purveyor of amusement, is promptly acclaimed as such, so Aluisi, after suggesting that someone be appointed governor, is immediately chosen for this office.[2] In calling forth a tale, both guides sometimes mention the town which the band is passing or is soon to reach.[3] Like the English leader, Aluisi occasionally comments upon the tales recounted.[4] Although the Italian's observations seem lifeless in comparison with Harry Bailey's breezy outbursts, they show a similarity in the two narrative plans. One of the few really human touches in the *intermezzi* is the mention of Aluisi's falling asleep during the recital of the third tale[5]—an occurrence which reminds us of Harry Bailey's weariness at the end of Chaucer's *Sir Thopas,*[6] and his exhortation to the Clerk:

> Ne that thy tale make us nat to slepe.[7]

3. *The activities of the travelers on the journey.*—Although the *intermezzi* of Sercambi are conventional and monotonous, they do give us an impression of the behavior of the Italian travelers during the periods when they were not listening to stories. In the inns at night, we are told, there were dancing, instrumental music, songs by accomplished men and women singers, and moral pieces by the *religiosi.* We hear of sightseeing and religious observances and also of arrangements for meals and sleep-

[1] M. Praz (*Monthly Criterion*, VI [1927], 149–50) infers that even Chaucer's pilgrims, in the first instance, "sprung up from the stories themselves," through "an embodiment of the spirit of each work in a concrete person." For the reality and comprehensiveness of the series of portraits in Chaucer's *Prologue* there is no adequate literary precedent. See above, pp. 3–5.

[2] See *Canterbury Tales*, A 769–818; *Proemio*, below, p. 38.

[3] See *C.T.*, A 3905–8, B 3116–17; *Int.* 35–36, 36–37.

[4] See, e.g., *C.T.*, A 3114–17, B 3079–86; *Int.* 124–25, 144–45.

[5] See *Int.* 3–4.

[6] See *C.T.*, B 2109–11.   [7] See *C.T.*, E 14; see also B 3984–88.

ing.[1] Such activities are, of course, only a conventional and lifeless parallel to the clashes of personality and the sharp verbal encounters recorded in Chaucer's links, but they do show a resemblance in general situation.[2]

4. *The application of the tales to the travelers.*—Certainly, one of the most human and vivacious aspects of Chaucer's plan is found in the personal applications of the stories. The mutual lampooning of the Miller and the Reeve and the salacious exchange of the Friar and the Summoner are only ribald examples of the way in which the tales are applied to the persons present on the pilgrimage. To this aspect of the *Canterbury Tales* there are suggestive parallels in the *intermezzi* of Sercambi, for, as we have already observed, the Italian narrator rather frequently addresses his tales to professional or other groups of persons who are thus assumed to be among the listeners. More specific parallels might be drawn between Sercambi's address "A voi merchadanti" in introducing *Novella* XCII[3] and the Man of Law's prefatory challenge beginning, "O riche marchauntz,"[4] and between the warning "A voi iudici" prefixed to *Novella* CXI[5] and the Host's outburst at the end of the *Physician's Tale* against "a fals justise" and against "thise juges and hire advocatz."[6]

5. *The narrator.*—A striking difference between the Italian collection and the English arises from the fact that, whereas Sercambi's *novelle* all come from the lips of the author himself—a formally appointed reciter—Chaucer's tales are told by the individual pilgrims and, in many instances, are finely adjusted to the characters of the narrators. It should be observed, however, that, although the *preposto* elicits all the formal *novelle* from the author himself, he calls for other sorts of recitation from other members of the company. From the *religiosi* he re-

---

[1] For an account of the usual occupations of the evening see, e.g., *Int.* 122–23.

[2] The activities recounted in Sercambi's *intermezzi* often arouse one's regret that the *Canterbury Tales*, in their unfinished state, do not describe the evening amusements of the inn at Dartford, or Rochester, or Ospringe, and do not recognize explicitly the obvious probability that some of the English pilgrims must, now and then, have glanced at the offices of the Church.

[3] See *Int.* 91–92.

[4] See *C.T.*, B 122.

[5] See *Int.* 110–11.

[6] See *C.T.*, C 289, 291.

quests *qualche bello exenplo morale*,[1] *alcuna cosa .... che sia piace-vole*,[2] *qualche bella cosa*,[3] *qualche moralità*,[4] or *qualche cosa morale*,[5] and in at least two such instances the piece recited is called—perhaps in error—a *novella*.[6] Moreover, the burden of entertainment placed upon the *religiosi* is often shared by the *cantarelli* and *cantarelle*, whose *canzoni* are in frequent demand.[7] In spite of the fact, then, that in Sercambi's plan the regular *novelle* are all assigned to the author himself, the recitals by several of the other travelers provide at least a remote parallel to the brilliant arrangement developed by Chaucer.

From our examination of Sercambi's *Novelle*, completed at some time after 1385, we must now draw what conclusions we can concerning the nature of the earlier *Novelliero*, apparently of the year 1374, supporting our inferences by a few belated records. A former owner of the lost manuscript of the *Novelliero*, Bernardino Baroni (1694–1781), wrote concerning it the following note:

Oltre queste [i.e., Sercambi's *Croniche*] scrisse ancora ad imitazione del *Decameron* del Boccaccio cento novelle, raccontate da una brigata di uomini e di donne, quali per fuggire la pestilenza che era in Lucca, intraprendono un viaggio per la Toscana; e per sollevare il disagio del cammino, sono raccontati varii casi e accidenti con sentenze morali e poesie. Questo manoscritto codice, che forse unico e autografo si conserva presso di me, prego sia guardato e custodito come cosa pregevole.[8]

In a letter of July 17, 1793, another member of the Baroni family writes as follows:

Il ms. del Sercambi ha per titolo *Novelliero di ser Giovanni Sercambi, lucchese;* lo scriveva nel 1374, come apparisce da una novella di un giudice che comincia: *In questo dì 4 aprile 1374 avvenne in Lucca che uno Giudice Marchigiano, ecc.* Sono cento novelle, con rime alla fine di ogni diecina, e dette novelle sono avventure accadute a suo tempo, nominando la famiglia e le campagne del lucchese Stato dove accadute.[9]

[1] See *Int.* 122–23.   [2] See *Int.* 124–25.

[3] See *Int.* 126–27. Cf. 127–28, 128–29, 129–30, 131–32, 132–33.

[4] See *Int.* 141–42. Cf. 144–45, 150–51, 151–52.

[5] See *Int.* 136–37. Cf. 137–38, 140–41.   [6] See *Int.* 136–37, 142–43.

[7] See, e.g., *Int.* 122–23, 123–24, 126–27, 127–28, 130–31, 133–34, 134–35, 138–39, 139–40, 142–43, 143–44, 144–45, 147–48.

[8] Printed by Renier, p. xlix. Concerning the *Novelliero* see also above, pp. 22–23.

[9] This passage is printed by Renier, p. l. Concerning the *novella* mentioned in this passage see above, p. 22, n. 1.

These records indicate that the *Novelliero* contained one hundred tales, in direct imitation of Boccaccio's *Decameron:* that, unlike the *Decameron*, it had as its essential narrative framework the fiction of a journey;[1] that the tales were recounted "per sollevare il disagio del cammino"; that the tales were divided into ten sections, corresponding to the ten days of the journey; that *canzoni*—and presumably dancing and refreshments—were provided at the end of each day; and that the towns visited were named in the course of the journey. It is to be presumed that in the *Novelliero*, as in the *Decameron* and the *Novelle*, the participants were under the control of a leader (or of leaders) and that the stories aroused a certain amount of comment. It is entirely possible that the personages represented as present in the action of the *Novelliero* were as various in their social types as the participants in the *Novelle*. If so, the figures in the earlier work probably resembled those of the later in their lack of vitality. Whether the stories in the *Novelliero* were narrated by a single person or by the individual travelers we cannot tell. Since, however, the *Novelle* seems to follow the *Novelliero* closely in its general plan, it seems unlikely that, when Sercambi revised and expanded the *Novelliero*, he would have eliminated all trace of the individual storytelling if it had been present in the earlier work. In a summary way, then, one can infer that in the fundamental device of framing stories within the fiction of a journey the *Novelliero* resembled the *Canterbury Tales* as closely

---

[1] As a part of the frame, the journey in the *Decameron* is embryonic and incidental. In view of what Chaucer could have observed in real life—if not in the works of Boccaccio or Sercambi—we hardly need seek the source of his fiction of a pilgrimage in the journeyings recounted in general literature, outside the tradition of framed stories. The accumulating might well be endless. Praz (pp. 150–52) mentions the well-known journey in Dante's *Divina commedia*. In this connection one might urge that in his *Commedia* Dante has "framed" a number of stories, one of which—about Ugolino of Pisa—was used by Chaucer. Conceivably, the *Commedia* may again have been in Chaucer's mind when, as the Canterbury pilgrims neared their destination, the parson compared their "viage" to "thilke parfit glorious pilgrymage That highte Jerusalem celestial" (see *C.T.*, I 50–51). In regard to the motif of pilgrimage in *Piers Plowman* see Dorothy L. Owen, *Piers Plowman* (London, 1912), pp. 61–71, 134 ff. H. S. V. Jones (*MP*, XIII [1915], 46) draws attention to the *Roman de Carité* and the *Pèlerinage* of Deguilleville. Concerning attempts to find other motifs in the structural design of the *Canterbury Tales* (e.g., the service of Venus, or the seven deadly sins) see the studies referred to by Robinson, p. 751.

as the *Novelle* does. Concerning detailed resemblances between Sercambi's lost version and Chaucer's work we are left in considerable uncertainty.

Of Chaucer's actual acquaintance with Sercambi's collection of tales we have no proof. If we take the usually accepted view that Chaucer definitely approached the composing of the *Canterbury Tales* about 1387, and that he may have experimented with his plan for several years thereafter,[1] we find that there was ample time for previous acquaintance with the *Novelliero*, which is believed to have been composed in 1374, or slightly later.[2] The possibility of his knowing anything about the completed *Novelle* is distinctly less, since this latter work was not finished, and perhaps not begun, until an undetermined date after December 19, 1385.[3] Concerning the possibility of Chaucer's access to information about Sercambi's writings we have at least some suggestive facts. We know, for example, that in the late winter or early spring of 1373 Chaucer traveled from Genoa to Florence and back, thus undoubtedly passing twice through Lucca, the home of Sercambi.[4] How much time Chaucer may have spent in this small city we do not know. At that date the young Italian writer, some twenty-six years of age, may already have been engaged upon his *Novelliero*, and he, or his literary undertaking, may have become known to the young English poet. Since Sercambi had already taken part in the public affairs of his municipality, he was not an altogether obscure person.[5] Whatever Chaucer's experiences may have been when he visited Lucca in 1373, he had another opportunity for hearing about the Lucchese writer in the summer of 1378, when

[1] See Tatlock, *Development*, pp. 131–50, and the references given by Robinson, pp. 751–52.

[2] See Renier, pp. l, lviii; Löhmann, p. 124; and above, p. 22.

[3] See above, p. 22.

[4] In regard to this Italian journey of Chaucer see R. E. G. Kirk, *Life-Records of Chaucer*, Part IV ("Chaucer Society Publications, Second Series," No. 32 [London, 1900]), Nos. 68, 70, 72, 75, 78; F. J. Mather, in *MLN*, XI (1896), 419–25; XII (1897), 10–11, 18–21; Young, pp. 414–16; J. S. P. Tatlock, "The Duration of Chaucer's Visits to Italy," *JEGP*, XII (1913), 118–21; A. S. Cook, "Chaucerian Papers—I," in *Transactions of the Connecticut Academy of Arts and Sciences*, XXIII (1919), 39–44.

[5] See Dinucci, pp. 45–48; and above, p. 21.

he was a member of an English embassy to Milan, to treat with
Bernabò Visconti of that city and Sir John Hawkwood.[1] The
relations between Milan and Lucca were lively,[2] the rulers of
Milan were collectors of books and patrons of literature,[3] and
affairs in the vicinity of Lucca were well known to Sir John
Hawkwood.[4] Such opportunities, however, along with any
others that may have arisen, have left no convincing evidence
that Chaucer ever read any writings by Sercambi.[5] It is possible, of course, that Chaucer may have heard of the pilgrimage
framework of the *Novelliero* without having actually seen it.

[1] Concerning Chaucer's Italian journey of 1378 see *Life-Records*, Nos. 118, 120,
121, 122, 140, Addition No. 8; H. Braddy, in *MLN*, XLVIII (1933), 507–11;
J. M. Manly, in *MLN*, XLIX (1934), 209–16.

[2] See S. Bongi, *Paolo Guinigi e le sue ricchezze* (Lucca, 1871), *passim*.

[3] See F. Novati, "Il Petrarca ed i Visconti," in *F. Petrarca e la Lombardia*
(Milan, 1904), pp. 21–47; Giulini, pp. 513–18; G. d'Adda, *Indagini storiche,
artistiche, e bibliografiche sulla Libreria Visconteo-Sforzesca del Castello di Pavia,
Parte prima* (Milan, 1875), and the *Appendice alla Parte prima* (Milan, 1879); O. E.
Schmidt, "Die Visconti und ihre Bibliothek zu Pavia," *Zeitschrift für Geschichte
und Politik*, V (1888), 444–74; L. Delisle, *Le Cabinet des manuscrits de la Bibliothèque Impériale*, I (Paris, 1868), 125–38. For studies based on certain of these
materials see R. A. Pratt, "Chaucer and the Visconti Libraries," *ELH*, VI (1939),
191–99; D. M. Robathan in J. W. Thompson, *The Medieval Library* (Chicago,
1939), pp. 552 ff. Concerning the early years of the university founded by the
Visconti see M. Mariani, *Cenni storici intorno all'Università di Pavia* (Pavia, 1900),
pp. 1–7.

[4] G. Temple-Leader and G. Marcotti, *Giovanni Acuto* (Florence, 1889), pp.
109 ff.

[5] A comparison of the *novelle* of Sercambi with those stories by Chaucer which
are parallel to them fails to suggest borrowing for the *Legend of Thisbe* (*Novella
CXXX*), the *Legend of Lucrece* (*Novella XLII*), or the *Clerk's Tale* (*Novella
CLII*). A trick described in *Novella XXI* resembles one used in the *Canon's
Yeoman's Tale* (see the text quoted below in the present work, pp. 694–95).
A device described in *Novella LI* resembles, but is not likely to have been a source
of, the Pardoner's "gaude" (see the text quoted below in the present work,
pp. 413–14; see also B. J. Whiting, "More on Chaucer's Pardoner's Prologue
[VI (C), 377–390]," *MLN*, LI [1936], 324–25). This resemblance was pointed out
by C. P. Wagner in his paper, "Analogues to the Pardoner's Gaude," presented
to the Chaucer section of the Modern Language Association in Cincinnati, January 1, 1936. A comparison of *Novella XXXI*, however, with the *Shipman's Tale*
and *Decameron*, VIII, 1, reveals that Chaucer and Sercambi, but not Boccaccio,
agree in their time-schemes and also in certain minor details—a matter lying
beyond the scope of the present essay (see the text quoted below in the present
work, pp. 443–46; see also R. A. Pratt, "Chaucer's *Shipman's Tale* and Sercambi,"
MLN, LV (1940), 142–45.

Yet one must not forget that, about the time he planned the framework for his *Canterbury Tales*, Chaucer took up residence in Kent, perhaps near the road commonly followed by pilgrims to Canterbury.[1]

To the present writers this brief survey of some of the framing devices used by Chaucer's predecessors and contemporaries seems serviceable chiefly in pointing toward the English poet's own originality. He may have known one or more of the works reviewed, and, as has already been intimated, he may have derived from them both the impulse to compose a collection of stories and certain hints for details in his own literary design. An examination of the efforts of others, however, discloses the salient fact that what he could have borrowed from others is slight in comparison with what he certainly created himself. Whatever his obligations to those who preceded him, his chief dependence was upon his own observation of life, and his own genius for portraying it.

PROEMIO AND *INTERMEZZI* OF THE *NOVELLE* OF GIOVANNI SERCAMBI

EDITORIAL NOTE

Since virtually all the text that follows is now printed for the first time, the editors may well explain briefly the principles followed. The *Proemio*[2] and *intermezzi* of Sercambi's *Novelle* are here edited from their unique original source, MS 193 of the Trivulzian Library in the Archivio Storico Civico of Milan,[3] which is described in the following words by Renier:[4] "Il cod. n° 193 della biblioteca Trivulzio.... è un grosso cartaceo di cc. 277 e di dim. 290×200, scritto nel secolo XV col brutto corsivo del tempo. La scrittura veramente orribile, tanto che conviene assuefarvisi per capirla, è ora più serata, ora meno. In fine del codice l'inchiostro ha talora corroso la carta."

[1] See above, p. 2.

[2] Most of this was printed by Renier (pp. 3–8), though with numerous errors; the titles "Proemio," "intermezzo," and "Novelle" are not found in the manuscript, but have originated with various editors.

[3] For *Sources and Analogues* we have also edited from this manuscript texts of *Novella* XXI and of fragments of *Novelle* XXI and LI, in connection with the *Shipman's Tale*, the *Canon's Yeoman's Tale*, and the *Pardoner's Prologue*, respectively. See below, pp. 443–46, 694–95, and 413–14.

[4] Pp. xlii–xliii.

The editors have indicated the title of each *novella* in its place, together with a reference to its location in a printed text, and the titles or location of parallel stories by Boccaccio and Chaucer. We are following Renier's numbering of the *novelle*, using for this purpose capital Roman numerals.[1] We have indicated in pointed brackets the pages of the manuscript covered by the *Proemio*, each *intermezzo*, and each *novella*. Since the texts of the *novelle* are not printed here, however, and since an *intermezzo* often begins in the middle of a page, the folio number placed at the beginning of an *intermezzo* (or with the title of a *novella*) should not be misunderstood as indicating that the text begins at the very top of the page.

Except as stated below and in the footnotes, we have given the text as it is found in the manuscript. Inclosures in pointed brackets represent the editors' additions to the text, excepting the titles of the *novelle* and the accompanying Roman numerals.[2] Inclosures in square brackets represent restorations of illegible passages. For several of these restorations we have drawn upon other versions of poems referred to below and upon a copy of Gamba's transcription of MS 193 (MSS 194 and 195) referred to above (p. 22, n. 2). Some initial letters have not been illuminated; but they are usually found minutely written in the margin. Dots represent lacunae and passages for which no restoration is offered.

In expanding abbreviations we have used italics only when the scribe's intention could be doubted. Abbreviations of words for which the scribe elsewhere uses more than one spelling are expanded (without italics) to the predominant form: thus *t'po*[3] is expanded to *tenpo*, which appears more often than *tempo;* likewise, *senpre* occurs more frequently than *sempre*, and *exenplo* than *exemplo*. In all instances other than these three, the superscribed straight line is interpreted as *m* or *n* according to modern usage. Further, *v'tù* is expanded as *virtù*, which is more common than *vertù*. Such forms of the future and conditional of *essere* as *s'anno* are expanded to *seranno*, etc.; for, although the *ser-* and *sar-* forms occur with about equal frequency, *ser-* is more typically Lucchese.

Abbreviations for words for which the scribe elsewhere uses only one spelling are expanded (without italics) to that form: thus *de'ri* and *d'ri* become *denari; Luc'* becomes *Lucha; s'to* and *s'ti* become *santo* and *santi*, respectively; and the third person plural of the past absolute (e.g., *cenar'o*) is expanded to the scribe's usual form (*cenarono*) rather than to other forms that do not occur in our text (as *cenarno* or *cenaron*). The abbreviations *ess'r* and *ess'* are both expanded to *esser*, but *ess'e* becomes *essere*. Such abbreviations as *av'e*, *pet'e*, and *piac'e*, become *avere*, *petere*, and *piacere*, respectively. For

---

[1] If the abbreviation *Ex.°* always refers to the *novella* preceding, then Renier numbered the entire collection erroneously. The possibility that the folio missing between fols. 3 and 4 may have contained the first *novella* of the collection is mentioned above on p. 22, n. 1, and below on p. 41, n. 2.

[2] We have modernized the form of these Roman numerals.

[3] We use the apostrophe to indicate abbreviations that cannot be imitated in type.

the scribal forms *Cp'o*, *C'iano*, and *C'iani*, we print *Cristo*, *cristiano*, and *cristiani*, respectively (but *Christus*, etc., in the lines of Latin verse). The Tironian notes for the conjunction *e* is transcribed as *e* (and once as *è*), except in the Latin titles of *novelle* and in the lines of Latin verse, where the form *et* is used. Following A. Schiaffini (*Testi fiorentini del dugento e dei primi del trecento* [Florence, 1926], p. li), we have modernized *u* and *v* (thus avoiding such spellings as *auvto* [*avuto*]), and we have not reproduced the elongated *i* (*j*), except in the Latin titles of the *novelle;* on the other hand, we have preserved the *j* in its function of final letter of Roman numerals, even introducing it when lacking (except for the numbers assigned to the *novelle*).

We have preserved the scribe's spelling, and we have not attempted to improve the Latinity of the Latin headings of stories; but we have modernized the punctuation[1] and capitalization and have accented final oxytones (including the third person singular of the past definite when reflexive, as *voltòsi*). Where the scribe has written *de*, we have interpreted as follows: for *de* and *deve*, we print *de* (following Schiaffini, p. liv); for *diede*, *dè;* for *dei*, *de';* and for *deh*, *de!* Since the scribe is at times inconsistent or ambiguous in the division of words, the division indicated by the editors is often arbitrary and on occasion possibly wrong. Usually a preposition (but never the conjunction *e*) has been joined to a following definite article in compliance with the scribe's general practice, even though fifteenth-century practice varied on this point. The aim of the punctuation (in the guidance of which the scribe is not always helpful) has been clarity rather than consistency, and we have ventured to indicate pauses and stops with the realization that for many portions of the text there may be other interpretations than ours. When indirect discourse breaks into direct discourse, and vice versa, the attempt has not always been made to distinguish the direct discourse by inclosing it within quotation marks. Particularly among the verses are passages which yield little or no sense. In conveying these, the editors omit virtually all punctuation.

We have only sparingly commented upon medieval usage and have made no attempt to rectify passages which are ungrammatical according to modern standards. A score or two of the scribe's forms of words may raise difficulty; in certain instances we have explained the meanings of such words. No doubt, certain readers will feel that we have given too many of such meanings; others will feel that we have given too few. For example, we have not commented on the form *voltosi*, which we sometimes give as a past participle (*voltosi*), and sometimes interpret as meaning *voltossi* (*voltòsi*, i.e., *si voltò*). In general, the editors have assumed that the Lucchese dialect of the fifteenth century is sufficiently similar to modern Tuscan to enable the reader readily to recognize such forms as *altore*, *aultore*, *auctore* (*autore*); *auto* (*avuto*); *ò, oe* (*ho*); *à* (*ha*); *fare'* (*farebbe*); *furno* (*furono*); *gungere* (*giungere*); *u'* (*ubi*); and the others, whether the variations be morphological or simply orthographic.

Other, and usually better, versions of many of the poems—especially those

---

[1] Direct quotations we have punctuated according to English rather than Italian usage.

of the Florentine poet, Niccolò Soldanieri—are found in Sercambi's *Croniche;* in G. Carducci, *Cantilene e ballate, strambotti e madrigale, nei secoli xiii e xiv* (Pisa, 1871); in F. Trucchi, *Poesie italiane inedite di dugento autori,* Vol. II (Prato, 1846); and in MS Rediano 184 of the Laurentian Library in Florence (to whose folios we refer by their stamped rather than by their written numbers). In the footnotes reference has been made to these versions, which have occasionally yielded restorations for illegible passages.[1] Reference has also been made to Renier's edition of the *Novelle* (R).

Both in our study of the literary framework of the *Canterbury Tales* and in our editing of the text of the *Proemio* and *intermezzi* of Sercambi's *Novelle,* we have enjoyed the courteous help of scholars in Italy and America, and of these we cannot fail to mention a few. Dr. Luigi Foscolo Benedetto, of Florence, and Dr. Salvatore Battaglia, of Naples, have offered useful guidance in editorial principles. Professor Dino Bigongiari, of Columbia, and Professor Charles S. Singleton, of the Johns Hopkins University, have given generously of their time to aid us in a variety of ways. Professor Kenneth MacKenzie, of Princeton, has allowed us to consult him regarding problems of Italian paleography. Professor Angelo Lipari, of Yale, has given us liberal and invaluable assistance in the reading and interpretation of the entire text. Dr. Teresa Lodi, Director of the Laurentian Library in Florence, Dr. Caterina Santoro, Director of the Archivio Storico Civico in Milan, and Professor Walter Ll. Bullock, of Manchester, England, have forwarded our work by their active interest in our problems. We wish also to acknowledge the favors and unflagging interest shown by the former Director of the Trivulzian Library, Dr. Giuseppe Galli, Honorary Canon of the Cathedral of Milan. Above all, the editors desire to make use of this opportunity to express their debt of profound gratitude to His Excellency, the late Prince Luigi Alberico Trivulzio, for his hospitality in the library and his generosity in permitting photostats to be made of his manuscript of Sercambi's *Novelle.*[2] It should be understood, finally, that none of these benefactors is responsible for any errors that may appear below.

PROEMIO AND *INTERMEZZI*

⟨fol. 2ʳ⟩[3] Lo sommo e potente Dio, dal quale tutti i beni derivano, e lla natura humana creata e fatta da lui a sua somiglansa acciò che

[1] In referring to the poetry in the *Croniche* we have not made reference to the useful annotations found near the end of each volume.

[2] These photostats are to be found in the Library of Congress, Modern Language Association Deposit, No. 299, which was used by the editors. Since these photostats were made, the Biblioteca Trivulziana has become a part of the Archivio Storico Civico of Milan.

[3] The beginning of the manuscript is lost. Fols 1ʳ and 1ᵛ contain the end of a list of the titles of the *novelle.* Certain of these titles are marked with a point, and at the bottom of fol. 1ᵛ is written: "Tutte quelle che sono miniate di nero non sono da leggere in presensia di donne da ben. Nota lettore." See Renier, p. xliii.

tale humana natura la celestiale corte debbia possedere se di pechati
non è ripieno; e quando per follia d'essa dal cilestie paradizo è privata,
non se ne de dare la colpa se non ad essa humana natura; e simile se
eli dae diversitadi per li nostri pechati comisse. Però che moltissime
volte s'è veduto per li nostri pechati Idio avere conceduto alli spiriti
angelichi et malingni podestà sopra di molti; e a' corpi celesti, li quali
mediante la potensia di Dio ànno a guidare et condurre i corpi di
sotto, coè noi, e tutte le piante et bestie, con tutte le cose elementate;
e spesso per alcuni pechati commessi venuto fuocho e aque et sangue
da cielo per purgare et punire li malifattori; e molte ciptà e paezi som-
mersi et arsi; e di tutti i sengni quanti in nelle scritture antiche si
trovano scripto e di quelli che tutto dì si veghano, neuno ne vuole
prendere exemplo. E non che da' visii si voglano astenere, ma con
ongni solicitudine s'ingengnano con quanti modi sanno di far male. E
chi far nol può, insenga ad altri il modo di farlo. E per questo
modo quella creatura che Dio più fe' beata et che a sua similitudine
la creò, più vituperosamente da Dio si parte. E per tanto non è da
meraviglarsi, se alcuna volta la natura humana pate afflitioni di
guerre e pestelentie, fame, inciendi, rubare et storsioni, chè se da'
pechati s'astenesse, Idio ci dare' quel bene che ci promisse, coè in
questo mondo ongni grasia, e in el altro la sua gloria. Ma perchè la
natura humana al contrario del bene s'accosta et quello segue, à dis-
posto la potensia di Dio mandare di que' sengni che mandò a Faraone,
acciò che partendoci[1] da' visii ci amendiamo. E noi duri, et indurati i
nostri cuori come è quello di Faraone, spettando l'ultima sentensia in
nelle glorie[2] eterne ci farà collocare. E nonn è da meraviglarsi se hora
in Mccclxxiiij° la moria è venuta. E neuna medicina può riparare,
nè ricchessa, stato, nè altro argomento che prender si possa, sia soffi-
cente a schifar la morte; e altro ch'è solo il bene ch'è quello che da
tutte pestilensie schanpa. E quella è la medicina che salva l'anima e
'l corpo. E non prendendo la via di tal bene, necessaria cosa d'andare
in nella mala[3] via[4].... che acostandosi la persona col malato e sensa
febra la morte il giunge; quine non bizongna esser ghaglardo; quine
non vale stato che[5] parenti da tal colpo li possa difendere. Et essendo
alquanti homini e donne, frati et preti, et altre della ciptà di Lucha,
la moria e lla pestilensia in nel contado, diliberonno se piacere di
Dio fusse per alcun[6].... E prima acostarsi con Dio per bene adoperare

God sends afflictions to make us leave our sins.

Now in 1374 the plague is come.

Several men and women, brothers and priests, and others of the city Lucca, ...

---

[1] partendoci] *The* c *is not distinct (MS).*

[2] glorie] pene *(emend. R).*

[3] mala] *Inserted above the line (MS).*

[4] At this point a word is lost *(MS).*

[5] che] nè *(emend. R).*   [6] At this point most of a line is lost *(MS).*

et da tutti i visii[1] astenersi; e questo faccendo, la pestilensia et li altri mali, che hora et per l'avenire si spettano, Idio per sua pietà da noi cesserà. Veduto adunqua i sseri homini e donne, frati e preti, la ⟨fol. 2ᵛ⟩ pestilentia multiplicare, prima ben disposti verso Idio, pensonno con um bello exercisio passare tenpo tanto l'arie di Lucha fusse purifichata et di pestilensia netta. E raunati insieme, li ditti diliberonno di Lucha partirsi e per la Ytalia fare i⟨l⟩ loro camino con ordine bello et con honesti e santi modi. E del mese di febraio, un giorno di domenicha, fatto dire una messa et tutti comunichatosi et fatto loro testamento, si raunonno in nella chieza di Santa Maria del Corso, parlando cose di Dio. E levatosi in piè uno excellentissimo homo et gran riccho nomato Aluizi et disse: "Cari fratelli e a me maggiori et voi chare et venerabili donne che qui d'ongni condissione sete qui raunate per fuggire la morte del corpo et questa pestilensia, prima che ad altro io vengna, dirò che poi che diliberati siemo per canpare la vita et fuggire la peste, debiamo esiandio pensare di fuggire la morte dell'anima, la quale è più d'averne chura che lo corpo. E acciò che l'uno e l'altro pericholo si fugha, è di necessità preghare[2] la via di Dio e suoi comandamenti e con quelli savi modi che si denno guidare le nostre persone. E questo far non si può se prima tra noi non è persona a chui tutti portino reverensia, hobidendolo in tutte le cose honeste. Et lui come honestissimo non comandi se non cosa che sia piacere della brigata sensa pechato. Et fatto questo tale dispongna il no⟨stro⟩ camino la vita e 'l modo che tener si de, sì che sensa lesione o male e sensa verghongna salvi alla nostra ciptà e alle nostre case possiamo lieti e allegri tornare, avendo lui a tutte le terre dato buoni exempli." Ditto che Aluizo ebbe le ditte parole, subbito la brigata fra loro dissono: "Per certo in questa brigata miglor di lui non si potrebe trovare." Et subito a vive voci dissono tutti: "Noi voglamo che Aluizi sia il preposto di questa brigata e lui preghiamo che tale officio acepti, disposa noi tutti maschi e femmine a ubidire il suo comandamento però che in lui sentiamo tanta virtù che altro che d'oneste cose ci richiederà. Et per lo suo gran senno et lungho veder, sani col nome di Dio a Lucha ci condurrà."

Aluizo, che ode la brighata, non potendo altro, disse: "Charissimi fratelli e maggiori et voy honestissime donne, io cognoscho in questa brigata esser di quelli molto più savi e più intendenti e di magore veduta di me che tale officio farenno meglo in una ora che io in uno anno, e bene era che aveste altri eletto. Ma poi che a voi piace che io vostro preposto sia chiamato, sto per contento, preghando tutti

seeing the pestilence increase,

planned to pass the time journeying through Italy.

One Sunday in February they met in the church of Santa Maria del Corso.

Aluizi, an excellent rich man, suggested that the brigata select a leader.

The brigata elected Aliuzi to be preposto.

He asked that they obey his commands; they agreed to do so.

---

[1] visii] *The first* i *is inserted above* (*MS*).

[2] preghare] seguire (*emend. R*).

che quello che comanderà sia ubidito." Tutti disseno: "Chomandate, e serà fatto."

Lo preposto disse: "Prima che ad altro atto si vengna, bizongna che si faccia una borsa di denari, acciò che in nelle cose necessarie siamo per li nostri denari soccorsi." Subito misseno mani a denari et fatto um monte di fiorini 3,000[1] in mano del preposto dati, dicendo: ⟨fol. 3ʳ⟩ "Quando questi saranno spesi, metteremo dell'altri." Lo preposto, vedendo la quantità de' denari et la buona volontà di mettere de' nuovi, disse: "Omai stiamo allegri che la brigata chapiterà bene." *Aluizi had a purse made up for their expenses*

Avuto il preposto denari, parlò alto dicendo: "Omai che andar dobiamo per salvare le persone, vi comando a tutti omini e donne mentre che abiamo a ffare il viagio nessuna dizonesta cosa tra noi nè tra altri si faccia; et quale avesse pensieri d'altro fare, prima che in camino ci mettiamo si ritorni in Lucha; et se alcuno denaio pagato avesse, vengna che renduti li seranno." La brigata ciò udendo, rispuoseno tutti: "O preposto, siate certo che noi staremo con tanta honestà, mentre che il camino faremo, che la mogle col marito nè con altri uzerà; et così per contrario in questo nostro viagio non s'acosteranno per dizonesto modo." *and had the travelers declare their intention to conduct themselves with honestà.*

Lo preposto, essendo certo che disonestità non si de fare, ordinò uno chamarlingho leale, lo quale più tosto are' del suo messo a sostentamento della brigata, che di quel tezoro che il preposto li diede n'avesse uno denaio tolto o soccelato.[2] Et per questo modo la brigata spera d'esser dalle necessità ben servito. *He selected a treasurer,*

Ordinato il camarlingho,[3] dispuose il preposto che du' spenditori fusseno, l'uno al servigio delli homini, et l'altro al servigio delle donne. E perchè senpre tali offici si denno dare et atribuire a persone secondo quello che ànno a ministrare, dispuose il preposto che al servigio delli homini fusse uno govane spenditore savio e non d'avarisia pieno; et dal servigio delle donne fusse uno omo di matura età e discreto in nelo spendere, acciò che tutta la brighata di niente se potesse lamentare. *and stewards to supervise expenditures,*

Apresso ordinò che la mattina per alcuni de' preti della brigata fusse ditta la messa, alla quale volea che tutta la brigata vi fusse a udire. E lla sera, sensa che lla brigata vi fusse, dicesseno tutte l'ore e compieta, acciò che per loro alchuna negligensa si possa imputare. *and arranged for religious observances*

---

[1] 3,000] $\frac{m}{3}$ (*MS*).

[2] soccelato] The *dialectal* socelare *means* sottrare beni o denari al fisco (see *Croniche*, III, 472).

[3] camarlingho] samarling'o (?*MS*).

Fatto questo ordine, ordinò coloro che colli homini alla cena e al
desnare doveano con diletto, e canti di giostre e di moralità cantare, e
ragionare con alcuni stormenti, e talotta colle spade da schermire per
dare piacere a tutti; et alcuni tra loro che disputasero in nelle liberali
sciensie; et questi eletti solo per la brigata delli homini e prelati.[1]...
altri ordinò che di leuti e stormenti dilettevoli con voci piane[2] e basse
et con voci puerili cansonette d'amore e d'onestà dicesseno alle donne;
e perchè ve n'avea date alchune obligagone e ⟨a⟩ achasata e vedove,
ordinò alchuni pargoletti saccenti col salterio sonare un salmo et
una gloria; et quando s'udiva la messa et al levare del nostro Singnore
uno santus santus deus, et per questo modo volea che la m⟨fol. 3ᵛ⟩at-
tina, quando si dicesse la messa, fusse sonato; et al desnare e alla
cena diversamente secondo le condisioni delli homini fusse lo suono
et così delle donne. Apresso ordinò che tali stormenti e sonanti doppo
il desnare e lla cena contentassero la brigata di suoni di diletto sensa
vanagloria e tutto ordinatamente misse in effetto.

Dipoi rivoltosi lo preposto alla brigata parlando per figura disse:
"A colui il quale sem'[3] cagone à di molte ingurie sostenete, et a lui
sensa colpa sono state fatte, comando che in questo nostro viaggio
debbia esser autore e fattore di questo libro e di quello che ongni dì
li comanderò. E acciò che non si possa schuzare che a llui per me
non si sia stato per tutte le volte comandato, e ancho per levarlo se
alchuno pensiero di vendetta avesse, contrò uno sonetto in nel quale
lo suo proprio nome col sopranome vi troverà; et pertanto io comando
sens'altro dire che ongni volta che io dirò, 'Autore della tal cosa,'
lui sens'altra schuza la mia intensione."[4] E parlando alto disse:

Già trovo che si diè pace Ponpeo,
Immaginando il grave tradimento,
Omicidio crudele e violento,[5]
Volendo ciò Cezare e Tolomeo.
Am[6] Echuba quel reo
Nativo d'Antinore, il chui nome sia spento,
Naschose in sul altare; coè gran pasione
Il convertir ringrasiando Deo.

---

[1] At this point several words are lost (*MS*).

[2] piane] piani (*?MS*).

[3] sem'] *Meaning* senza.

[4] *After* intensione *a verb, such as* comprenderà, *seems to have been omitted. R
emends to* senz'altro segua.

[5] violento] violente (*MS*).

[6] Am] *Meaning* anco.

Sotto color di pace ancora Guida
El nostro salvator Cristo tradio,
Radendose di vita in morte cruda.
Considerando ciò, dommi pace io,
Avendo sempre l'anima mia cruda
Mossa a vendetta, chancello il pensier mio;
Ben dico che la lingua colla mente
Imsieme non disforma in leal gente.

E udendo ciaschuno della brigata lo sonetto piacevole, et neuno potendo intendere a chi il preposto parlava salvo colui il quale, comprendendo le parole et versi del sonetto, vi si trovò pronome et sopranome; sens'altro dire comprese che lui dovea esser autore di questo libro; et sens'altro parlare si stava come li altri cheto.[1]

Only Giovanni Sercambi understood who was intended.

Avendo il preposto dispensato parte de' suoi offici, et ordinato chi de condurre la brigata....[2]

⟨fol. 4ʳ⟩ Que' cui trovo alcuni che sia
Al mio piacere[3] bel come colui,
Lo coglio e bacio e parlomi con lui
E ciò che 'l cuor dizira
E com'io son, l'amico mio sia,
E colli altri il metto in ghirlanda bella
E co' miei crini biondi e legieri.

A love song.

E quel piacere ch'è di natura il fiore,
Alli occhi porgi e sì mi 'l vedea
Che s'io vedesse la propria dea
Che preso m'à del suo proprio amore.
Quel che mi faccia più el suo odore
Sprimer nol porrei colla favella,
Ma io so' spinta nè so testimon veri.

Lingua giamai non escim del mio petto
Dell'altre donne aspere nè grava
Ma si vegon di fuori cald' e soavi.

---

[1] The text from this point to the title, *De sapiensia*, is omitted by Renier.

[2] Thus, at the bottom of fol. 3ᵛ, the text breaks off. The next folio has been lost and replaced by an unnumbered leaf of paper blank on both sides. The lost text clearly included the following: (1) an account of the concluding activities at Lucca, of the departure from Lucca, and of the journey to a point beyond Pisa; (2) possibly a lost *novella* (see above, p. 24, n. 1); (3) Aluizi's actual request for one or more *novelle;* (4) possibly an earlier part of the poem written on the upper part of fol. 4ʳ.

[3] piacere] spiacere (? *MS*)

E al mio amore se ne vanno in cospetto,
Il qual, com'elli 'l sente a dar diletto,
Dise: "A me si muove cui come in quella
Ch'io son per dire, 'De! vien, ch'io non disperi.' "

Exenplo[1] j°.

Ditta la bella cansona, l'altore per ubidire il preposto, essendo fuora del prato, disse:

⟨Here appears:
Novella I,[2] *De sapiensia* (fols. 4^r–7^r), printed by Renier, pp. 9–16.[3]
Then follows *Intermezzo 1–2*.⟩

⟨fol. 7^r. U⟩dito il preposto la dilettevole novella de' tre iovani e del calì,[4] parendoli esser stata di grande sentensia ad avere sentimento delle cose non vedute, essendosi già partiti da Pisa et voltosi al'altore, dicendoli che segua qualche bella novella piacevole fine che gungeranno alla città di Volterra, l'altore presto a ubidire disse:

Having left Pisa already, the author tells a story on the way to Volterra.

⟨Here appear the following:
Novella II, *De sinplicitate* (fols. 7^r–7^v), printed by Renier, pp. 17–18.
Intermezzo 2–3 (fol. 8^r), recounting that, during the remainder of the day, on the way to the castle of San Miniato, the author tells a story.

[1] At the end of each *novella* is a concluding rubric beginning with the abbreviation *Ex*° (*Ex*° j, *Ex*° ij, etc.). We interpret this abbreviation to mean throughout *exenplo*, and so expand it here. It might be urged that *explicit* is the author's, or scribe's, intention. Elsewhere we have disregarded the abbreviation and have preserved only the number. See the note following.

[2] The numbers of the *novelle* appear in the manuscript immediately after the *novelle* and immediately before the *intermezzi*. Renier (perhaps erroneously; see above, p. 22, n. 1) interpreted these numbers as referring to the succeeding *novelle*. In following Renier, we have presented the number of each *novella* as if it accompanied the title given at the beginning of the *novella*. Thus in the manuscript the number of each *novella* actually precedes the *intermezzo* introducing that *novella*, and immediately follows the conclusion of the *preceding* novella. But the titles always immediately precede the *novelle* themselves.

[3] Ten publications, in addition to his own, in which one or more of the *novelle* may be found, are mentioned by Renier, pp. xl–xli, 429–33. All the *novelle* are printed (or summarized) in one or another of the following three volumes: R. Renier, *Novelle inedite di Giovanni Sercambi* (Turin, 1889)—(Renier); A. D'Ancona, *Novelle di Giovanni Sercambi* ("Scelta di curiosità letterarie inedite o rare dal secolo xiii al xvii, No. 119 [Bologna, 1871])—(D'Ancona, *Scelta*); A. D'Ancona, *Novelle inedite di Giovanni Sercambi* ("Collezione di operette inedite o rare pubblicate dalla Libreria Dante in Firenze, No. 12 [Florence, 1886])—(D'Ancona, *Libreria Dante*). In the present publication we refer only to Renier or another of these three volumes. Of certain fragmentary or salacious *novelle* Renier (pp. 411–27) has given only summaries. Of these, *Novella CLV* was printed by G. Sforza in 1922 (see below, p. 81).

[4] calì] *Meaning* califfo.

Novella III, *De malvagitate et Malizia* (fols. 8ʳ–9ʳ), printed by Renier, pp. 19–21.

Then follows *Intermezzo* 3–4.⟩

⟨fol. 9ʳ⟩ Essendo stato il preposto a dormire mentre che l'altore dicea la ditta novella, sveglandosi sentendo le donne et li homini ridere, dimandò qual era la cagone; fulli per alquante govanette baldansose ditta la novella del marcifaccio; et quella intesa come loro, incominciò a ridere, dicendo al'altore che ne dica una la quale lui sensa dormire ascolterà volentieri fine che alla ciptà di Pistoia perveranno; l'altore rispuose che sarà fatto e disse:

⟨Here appear the following:

Novella IV, *De mangna prudentia* (fols. 9ʳ–12ᵛ), printed by Renier, pp. 22–31.

Intermezzo 4–5 (fols. 12ᵛ–13ʳ), recounting that, on the way to the castle of Prato, the author tells a story.

Novella V, *De summa justisia* (fols. 13ʳ–13ᵛ), printed by Renier, pp. 32–33.

Intermezzo 5–6 (fol. 13ᵛ), recounting that the next day, on the way to Florence, the author tells a story.

Novella VI, *De justitia et crudelta* (fols. 13ᵛ–14ᵛ), printed by Renier, pp. 34–35.

Intermezzo 6–7 (fol. 14ᵛ), recounting that the company will use two days to reach Siena; and that the next morning, on the way to Incisa, the author tells a story.

Novella VII, *De transformasione nature* (fols. 14ᵛ–17ᵛ), summarized by Renier, pp. 411–13.

Intermezzo 7–8 (fols. 17ᵛ–18ʳ), recounting that they eat supper at Incisa; and that the next day, on the way to Siena, the author tells a story.

Novella VIII, *De sinplici juvano* (fols. 18ʳ–19ʳ), printed by Renier, pp. 36–38.

Intermezzo 8–9 (fol. 19ʳ), recounting that the next day, on the way to Civitella, the author tells a story.

Novella IX, *De latro e sinplici mercadante* (fols. 19ʳ–20ᵛ), printed by Renier, pp. 39–42. A similar story is narrated by Boccaccio, *Decameron*, II, 5.

Intermezzo 9–10 (fol. 20ᵛ), recounting that, on the way to Arezzo, the author tells a story.

Novella X, *De visio lusurie in prelati* (fols. 20ᵛ–23ʳ), summarized by Renier, pp. 413–15. A similar story is told in *Novella* XI.

Intermezzo 10–11 (fols. 23ʳ–23ᵛ), recounting that the next day, on the way to Castiglione Aretino, the author tells a story.

Novella XI, *De vituperio prelaty* (fols. 23ᵛ–24ᵛ), printed by Renier, pp. 43–45. A similar story is told in *Novella* X.

Intermezzo 11–12 (fol. 24ᵛ), recounting that the next day, on the way to Cortona,[1] the author tells a story.

[1] See *Int.* 107–8 below.

The leader, having fallen asleep during the story, asks for one that will keep him awake while they journey to Pistoia. The author begins.

Novella XII, *De Mulier volubili* (fols. 24ᵛ–25ᵛ), printed by D'Ancona, *Scelta*, pp. 138–43.

Intermezzo 12–13 (fol. 25ᵛ), recounting that the next day, on the way from Cortona to Città di Castello, the author tells a story.

Novella XIII, *De mulieri adultera* (fols. 25ᵛ–27ʳ), printed by Renier, pp. 46–49.

Intermezzo 13–14 (fol. 27ᵛ), recounting that the author tells a story on the way to Sansepolcro.

Novella XIV, *De bono fatto* (fols. 27ᵛ–31ʳ), printed by Renier, pp. 50–57.

Intermezzo 14–15 (fol. 31ʳ), recounting that two days will be used to reach Massa di Maremma; and that, on the way to Passignano di Perugia, the author tells a story.

Novella XV, *De ventura im matto* (fols. 31ʳ–33ᵛ), printed by D'Ancona, *Scelta*, pp. 172–85.

Intermezzo 15–16 (fol. 33ᵛ), recounting that the next day the author tells another story.

Novella XVI, *De tristitia et viltate* (fols. 33ᵛ–34ʳ), printed by D'Ancona, *Libreria Dante*, pp. 9–11.

Intermezzo 16–17 (fol. 34ʳ), recounting that the author tells a story to conduct the company from Massa to Grosseto.

Novella XVII, *De pericolo in amore* (fols. 34ʳ–35ᵛ), a fragmentary story, summarized by Renier, pp. 415–16.

Intermezzo 17–18 (fol. 35ᵛ), recounting that the author tells a story to conduct the company through the Maremma.

Novella XVIII, *De nuovo modo furandi* (fols. 35ᵛ–36ᵛ), printed by Renier, pp. 58–59.

Intermezzo 18–19 (fol. 36ᵛ), a fragment, implying that between Grosseto and Civitavecchia the author tells a story.

Novella XIX (fol. 37ʳ), a fragmentary story, with no title given in the manuscript, summarized by Renier, p. 416.

Intermezzo 19–20 (fols. 37ʳ–37ᵛ), recounting that the author tells a story to conduct the company toward Populonia.

Novella XX, *De furto extra natura* (fols. 37ᵛ–38ʳ), printed by Renier, pp. 60–61.

Intermezzo 20–21 (fols. 38ʳ–38v), recounting that the author tells a story to conduct the company toward Maschona.

Novella XXI, *De falsari* (fols. 38ᵛ–41ʳ), printed by D'Ancona, *Scelta*, pp. 155–68. Fragments of this *novella* are printed below in connection with the *Canon's Yeoman's Tale* (see pp. 694–95).

Intermezzo 21–22 (fol. 41ʳ), recounting that the author tells a story to conduct the company to Castro.

Novella XXII, *De inghanno e falsitate* (fols. 41ʳ–42ᵛ), printed by Renier, pp. 62–64. The same story is told in *Novella* XC.

Intermezzo 22–23 (fol. 42ᵛ), recounting that, the next day, the author tells a story to conduct the company to Bolsena.

Novella XXIII, *De somma avarisia* (fols. 42^v–44^r), printed by Renier, pp. 65–68.

Intermezzo 23–24 (fol. 44^r), recounting that the author tells a story to conduct the company from Bolsena to a meadow.

Novella XXIV, *De sinplicitate e stultia* (fols. 44^r–45^r), printed by D'Ancona, *Libreria Dante*, pp. 11–15.

Intermezzo 24–25 (fols. 45^r–45^v), recounting that the author tells a story in the meadow.

Novella XXV, *De placebili sentensia* (fols. 45^v–46^r), printed by Renier, pp. 69–70.

Intermezzo 25–26 (fol. 46^r), recounting that the author tells a story of *madonna* Banbacaia.

Novella XXVI, *De sentensia vera* (fols. 46^r–46^v), printed by D'Ancona, *Libreria Dante*, pp. 15–17.

Intermezzo 26–27 (fol. 46^v), recounting that the author tells another story.

Novella XXVII, *De pulcra rispontione* (fol. 46^v), printed by D'Ancona, *Libreria Dante*, pp. 17–18.

Intermezzo 27–28 (fols. 46^v–47^r), recounting that the maidens dance and that then the author tells a story on the way to Orvieto.

Novella XXVIII, *De astusia in juvano* (fols. 47^r–50^r), printed by Renier, pp. 71–77.

Intermezzo 28–29 (fol. 50^r), recounting that, after a fowling song, the author tells a story on the way to Assisi.

Novella XXIX, *De inghanno* (fols. 50^r–51^v), printed by Renier, pp. 78–80.

Intermezzo 29–30 (fols. 51^v–52^r), recounting that the author tells a story on the way to Perugia.

Novella XXX, *De libidine* (fols. 52^r–53^r), summarized by Renier, p. 417.

Intermezzo 30–31 (fols. 53^r–53^v), recounting that, after the *religiosi* present a *moralità*, the author tells a story on the way toward Todi.

Novella XXXI, *De avaritia et luzuria* (fols. 53^v–55^r), printed by Renier, pp. 81–84. The same story is narrated by Boccaccio, *Decameron*, VIII, 1, and by Chaucer, the *Shipman's Tale*, in connection with which this *novella* is printed below (see pp. 443–46).

Intermezzo 31–32 (fol. 55^r), recounting that, not yet halfway to Todi, the author presents a *moralità* and then a story.

Novella XXXII, *De prudentia et castitate* (fols. 55^r–56^v), printed by Renier, pp. 85–88.

Intermezzo 32–33 (fol. 56^v), recounting that, after spending the night at Todi, the author presents a *moralità* and a story on the way to Narni.

Novella XXXIII, *De vana luzuria* (fols. 56^v–59^v), printed by D'Ancona, *Libreria Dante*, pp. 18–29.

Intermezzo 33–34 (fol. 59^v), recounting that, the next day, the author tells a story on the way to Terni.

Novella XXXIV, *De novo inghanno* (fols. 59^v–60^v), printed by D'Ancona, *Libreria Dante*, pp. 29–34; on pp. 60–65 he prints the version of this story found in the *Novelliero*. See above, p. 22, n. 1.

Intermezzo 34–35 (fols. 60ᵛ–61ʳ), recounting that the author presents a story on the way to Montefiascone.

Novella XXXV, *De malitia et prudensia* (fols. 61ʳ–62ʳ), printed by Renier, pp. 89–91.

Then follows *Intermezzo* 35–36.⟩

Being more than halfway to Montefiascone, the author tells a story.

⟨fol. 62ʳ⟩ Ditta la dilettevole novella, lo preposto al'altore disse: "Noi non siamo ancora più che al messo il camino di Montefiaschoni gunti, e lla bella novella ditta à molto la brigata ralegrata; e acciò che 'l camino che ci resta sia d'una novelletta consolata";[1] a chui l'altore disse: "E io contenterò ognuno di una bella novellussa," parlando:

⟨Here appears:

Novella XXXVI, *De turpi tradimento* (fols. 62ʳ–63ʳ), printed by Renier, pp. 92–94.

Then follows *Intermezzo* 36–37.⟩

The author tells a story on the way to Viterbo.

⟨fol. 63ᵛ. L⟩a dilettevole novella ditta à molto consolato la brigata, e pertanto il preposto comandato al'altore che una bella novella dica fine che a Viterbo seranno andati, al quale l'altore disse: "Poi che io oe sentito nomare Viterbo, vi prego che lli spenditori e quelli che ordinare denno la cena, faccino di fuori apparchiare per buona cagone." Il preposto ciò udendo disse li piacea, e così coloro che servir doveano fenno; e voltosi l'altore alla brigata parlò dicendo:

⟨Here appear the following:

Novella XXXVII, *De malitia in guvano* (fols. 63ᵛ–65ʳ), printed by D'Ancona, *Scelta*, pp. 144–54.

Intermezzo 37–38 (fol. 65ʳ), recounting that, having spent the night near Viterbo, the leader plans to use two days to reach Rome, so that they may visit the church of San Paulo. The author presents a *moralità* and a story.

Novella XXXVIII, *De superbia et pauco bene* (fols. 65ʳ–66ᵛ), printed by Renier, pp. 95–97.

Then follows *Intermezzo* 38–39.⟩

Having reached the church of San Paulo, they plan to arrive at Rome the next day and to remain there ten days. The author presents a *moralità* and a story.

⟨fol. 66ᵛ. U⟩dito il preposto la bella novella e devota, gunti alla chieza di San Paulo, rivoltòsi al'autore dicendoli che per lo dì seguente debbia ordinare bella novella al camino da Roma; e simile comandò a quelli che aparechiar denno, notificando che in Roma dovea la brigata almeno x dì dimorare, li quali ciaschiduno s'aparechi a ubidire; "Ma ben vo' che l'altore dicha in presente qualche moralità"; lui presto disse:

Tanta de santa fiamma il cuor è acceso
Che parte ne do suso al cielo a Ddio,
E parte guso al prossimo mio.[2]

---

[1] Here Aluisi's actual request for a *novella* appears to have been omitted.

[2] See *Croniche*, II, 211.

E dapoi voltosi l'altore alla brigata parlò dicendo:

⟨Here appear the following:

Novella XXXIX, *De vera amicitia et charitate* (fols. 66ᵛ–70ʳ), printed by Renier, pp. 98–104.

Intermezzo 39–40 (fols. 70ʳ–70ᵛ), recounting that, after they reach Rome, the author presents a *moralità*. The company visits churches, and then the author tells a story.

Novella XL, *De fide bona* (fols. 70ᵛ–71ᵛ), printed by Renier, pp. 105–8.

Intermezzo 40–41 (fol. 71ᵛ), recounting that, the next day, they visit churches, and then the author tells a story.

Novella XLI, *De puritade* (fols. 71ᵛ–72ʳ), printed by D'Ancona, *Libreria Dante*, pp. 34–35.

Intermezzo 41–42 (fol. 72ʳ), recounting that, the next day, they visit points of historic interest, and after supper the author tells a story.

Novella XLII, *De castitade* (fols. 72ʳ–73ʳ), printed by Renier, pp. 109–10. The same story is narrated by Chaucer, the *Legend of Lucrece*.

Intermezzo 42–43 (fol. 73ʳ), recounting that, the next day, they visit churches and palaces, and after supper the author tells a story.

Novella XLIII, *De re publica* (fols. 73ʳ–73ᵛ), printed by Renier, p. 111.

Then follows *Intermezzo* 43–44.⟩

⟨fol. 73ᵛ. A⟩vendosi levato la mattina la brigata e 'l preposto andando ragonando per Roma l'antichissime cose romane, maravigliandosi di quella agulla[1] alta, d'um pesso, dove vidde di sopra una palla in che sta la cenere di Cezari, primo imperadore di Roma; e ritornati la sera a lloro abitagione narrando doppo la cena le meraviglose cose vedute dicendo: "Tutte le cose meraviglose che i Romani vedeano in alcuna parte del mondo, tutte le faceano a Roma venire." Et per non tenere molto la brigata a dizagio disse al'altore che una novella dica, avendo loro dato piacere quella che ditta avea; l'altore che presto era a ubidire disse:

The next day they visit an obelisk and other ancient things, and then the author tells a story.

⟨Here appear the following:

Novella XLIV, *De re publicha* (fols. 73ᵛ–74ʳ), printed by Renier, p. 112.

Intermezzo 44–45 (fol. 74ʳ), recounting that, the next day, after visiting the city and after supper, the leader discusses Roman gentility, and the author tells a story.

Novella XLV, *De leeltate* (fols. 74ʳ–74ᵛ), printed by D'Ancona, *Libreria Dante*, 52–53.

Intermezzo 45–46 (fol. 74ᵛ), recounting that, the next day, they discuss the laws of the Romans, and after supper the author tells a story. (Most of this *intermezzo* was printed by D'Ancona, *Libreria Dante*, pp. 53–54.)

Novella XLVI, *De falso pergurio* (fols. 74ᵛ–75ᵛ), printed by Renier, pp. 113–14.

---

[1] agulla] *For* aguglia, *meaning* obelisco.

Intermezzo 46–47 (fol. 75^v), recounting that, the next day, they see and discuss Roman books, and after supper the author tells a story.

Novella XLVII, *De amore et crudeltate* (fols. 75^v–76^r), printed by Renier, p. 115.

Intermezzo 47–48 (fol. 76^r), recounting that, the next day, they visit merchants, and after supper the author tells a story.

Novella XLVIII, *De cecho amore et giusta vendetta* (fols. 76^r–77^r), printed by Renier, pp. 116–17.

Intermezzo 48–49 (fol. 77^r), recounting that, the next day, they visit craftsmen, and after supper the author tells a story.

Novella XLIX, *De prudentia in consiliis* (fols. 77^r–79^r), printed by Renier, pp. 118–21.

Intermezzo 49–50 (fol. 79^r), recounting that, the next day, the leader advises all to get pardons, since they are to leave Rome on the morrow. They compare the ancient Roman religion with Christianity, and after supper the author tells a story.

Novella L, *De falsitate mulieris* (fols. 79^r–81^v), printed by Renier, pp. 122–27.

Intermezzo 50–51 (fols. 81^v–82^r), recounting that, the next day as they set out for Spoleto, the author tells a story.

Novella LI, *De ypocriti et fraudatores* (fols. 82^r–83^v), printed by Renier, pp. 128–31. Fragments of this *novella* are printed below in connection with the *Pardoner's Prologue* (see pp. 413–14).

Intermezzo 51–52 (fol. 83^v), recounting that, after dinner, the author presents a *moralità* and a story.

Novella LII, *De pigritia*[1] (fols. 83^v–84^r), printed by D'Ancona, *Scelta*, pp. 169–71. The same story is narrated by Boccaccio, *Decameron*, I, 9.

Intermezzo 52–53 (fol. 84^r), recounting that, having reached Spoleto, they enjoy singing and dancing and, after supper, more music. The next day, as they start for Jesi, the author tells a story.

Novella LIII, *De placibili loquela* (fols. 84^r–84^v), printed by D'Ancona, *Libreria Dante*, pp. 36–38.

Intermezzo 53–54 (fol. 84^v), recounting that, after supper at Jesi, the leader orders a story for the next day's journey along the road toward Naples to where Medea was buried. The author presents a *moralità* concerning Medea, and the next morning he tells a story.

Novella LIV, *De falsitate et tradimento* (fols. 84^v–86^v), printed by Renier, pp. 132–35.

Intermezzo 54–55 (fol. 87^r), recounting that, having gone halfway to where Medea was, they dine, enjoy music, and then rest in a meadow while the author tells a story.

Novella LV, *De sapientia et vero judicio* (fols. 87^r–88^r), printed by D'Ancona, *Libreria Dante*, pp. 54–58.

Intermezzo 55–56 (fol. 88^r), recounting that, after dancing and refresh-

---

[1] *pigritia*] *prigritia*, with the first *r* crossed out (*MS*).

ments, the author tells a story. (Most of this *intermezzo* was printed by D'Ancona, *Libreria Dante*, p. 59).

Novella LVI, *De natura femminili* (fols. 88ʳ–89ʳ), printed by Renier, pp. 136–37.

Intermezzo 56–57 (fol. 89ʳ), recounting that, after a performance by the singers, the company eats supper and enjoys dancing and music. The next day, while they go to the place where Medea was, the author tells a story.

Novella LVII, *De paulcra et magna sapientia* (fols. 89ʳ–91ᵛ), printed by D'Ancona, *Scelta*, pp. 83–96.

Then follows *Intermezzo* 57–58.⟩

⟨fol. 91ᵛ. I⟩l preposto e lla brigata inteso la savia casticasione fatta a' generi di ser Piero, con piacere gunti dovea Medea morta iace, cenarono al modo uzato; e quando fu tenpo d'andare a dormire si volse al'altore comandandoli che per lo dì seguente ordini bella novella per andare verso Napoli, pensando prima trovare ad Aversa. E fatto il comandamento, la brigata posta a dormire fine alla mattina, e levati, udita la messa, si missero in camino; l'altore disse:

The next day after Mass they proceed toward Naples. While they travel to Aversa the author tells a story.

⟨Here appear the following:

Novella LVIII, *De bona respontione* (fols. 91ᵛ–92ʳ), printed by D'Ancona, *Libreria Dante*, pp. 38–41. The same story is narrated by Boccaccio, *Decameron*, I, 10.[1]

Intermezzo 58–59 (fol. 92ᵛ), recounting that they have supper at Aversa and, the next day on the way to Partenopia,[2] the author tells a story.

Novella LIX, *De dizonesto adulterio et bono consilio* (fols. 92ᵛ–[94]ᵛ),[3] printed by Renier, pp. 138–44.

Intermezzo 59–60 (fol. [94]ᵛ), recounting that, after supper, the author presents a *moralità* and, the next day as they proceed to Arpi, he tells a story.

Novella LX, *De superbia contra rem sacrata*[4] (fols. [94]ᵛ–96ᵛ), printed by Renier, pp. 145–49.

Intermezzo 60–61 (fols. 96ᵛ–97ʳ), recounting that, after supper, the author presents a *moralità* and, the next day as they travel, he tells a story.

Novella LXI, *De conpetenti consilio de adultera* (fols. 97ʳ–98ʳ), printed by Renier, pp. 150–52.

Intermezzo 61–62) (fol. 98ᵛ), recounting that, after dinner, they dance, and then in a meadow the author tells a story.

Novella LXII, *De justa sentensia* (fols. 98ᵛ–99ᵛ), printed by Renier, pp. 153–55.

Intermezzo 62–63 (fol. 99ᵛ), recounting that, after dancing and refreshments, the author presents a *moralità* and a story.

[1] This parallel was pointed out to the editors by Mr. James W. Alexander.

[2] See above, p. 24, n. 2.

[3] Two consecutive folios are numbered "94," of which this is the second.

[4] *sacrata*] *facrata* (?*MS*).

Novella LXIII, *De meretricis et justo judicio*[1] (fols. 99ᵛ–100ᵛ), printed by Renier, pp. 156–57.

Intermezzo 63–64 (fols. 100ᵛ–101ʳ), recounting that the singers perform and, the next day on the way to Aquila the author tells a story.

Novella LXIV, *De dizonestitate viry* (fols. 101ʳ–102ᵛ), printed by Renier, pp. 158–61.

Intermezzo 64–65 (fols. 102ᵛ–103ʳ), recounting that, after supper at Aquila, the author presents a *moralità* and, the next day as they continue toward Naples, he tells a story.

Novella LXV, *De nova malisia in tiranno* (fols. 103ʳ–103ᵛ), printed by Renier, pp. 162–63.

Intermezzo 65–66 (fols. 103ᵛ–104ʳ), recounting that, at a village twenty-five miles from Naples, it being Saturday, they eat food suitable for a fast day and do not dance. The author presents a *moralità* and a story.

Novella LXVI, *De ebrietate et gulozitate in prelato* (fol. 104ʳ), printed by Renier, p. 164.

Intermezzo 66–67 (fol. 104ᵛ), recounting that the author tells another story.

Novella LXVII, *De smemoragine prelati* (fols. 104ᵛ–105ʳ), printed by Renier, pp. 165–66.

Intermezzo 67–68 (fol. 105ʳ), recounting that, on Sunday after Mass, the leader announces that in the evening they will reach Naples, where they will remain at least five days. As they proceed, the author presents a *moralità* and a story.

Novella LXVIII, *De doctrina data a puero* (fols. 105ʳ–106ʳ), printed by D'Ancona, *Scelta*, pp. 38–43.

Intermezzo 68–69 (fols. 106ʳ–106ᵛ), recounting that, at Naples before supper, they enjoy a song. The next day they see sights, and after dinner the author tells a story in the cloistered garden of the inn.

Novella LXIX, *De vidua libidinosa* (fols. 106ᵛ–107ᵛ), summarized by Renier, pp. 417–18.

Intermezzo 69–70 (fol. 107ᵛ), recounting that, after dancing and a love song, they eat supper. The next morning they visit Naples, and after dinner the author tells a story.

Novella LXX, *De bonis moribus* (fols. 107ᵛ–108ᵛ), printed by D'Ancona, *Scelta*, pp. 62–66.

Intermezzo 70–71 (fol. 108ᵛ), recounting that, after dancing, refreshments, and a song, the author tells a story.

Novella LXXI, *De justa responsione* (fols. 108ᵛ–110ʳ), printed by D'Ancona, *Scelta*, pp. 67–74.

Intermezzo 71–72 (fol. 110ʳ), recounting that, after the singers perform, the author tells a story.

Novella LXXII, *De presuntione stulti* (fols. 110ʳ–111ʳ), printed by Renier, pp. 167–68.

---

[1] *judicio*] The last four letters are blurred by scribal tracings (*MS*).

Intermezzo 72–73 (fol. 111ʳ), recounting that, after dancing, they have supper. The next morning they attend Mass, visit the sights of Naples, have dinner, and dance. The author presents a *moralità* and a story.

Novella LXXIII, *De amicisia provata* (fols. 111ʳ–112ʳ), printed by D'Ancona, *Scelta*, pp. 44–50.

Intermezzo 73–74 (fol. 112ᵛ), recounting that, after dancing and refreshments, the author presents some verses and a story.

Novella LXXIV, *De conpetenti mizura* (fols. 112ᵛ–113ᵛ), printed by Renier, pp. 169–71.

Intermezzo 74–75 (fol. 113ᵛ), recounting that, after a love song, they eat supper. The next morning they see sights, and after dinner the author tells a story.

Novella LXXV, *De vituperio mulieris* (fols. 113ᵛ–115ᵛ), printed by Renier, pp. 172–75. A similar story is told in *Novella* LXXXVI.

Intermezzo 75–76 (fol. 115ᵛ), recounting that, after refreshments, the singers perform and the author tells a story.

Novella LXXVI, *De vituperio fatto per i stipendiari* (fols. 115ᵛ–116ᵛ), printed by Renier, pp. 176–77.

Intermezzo 76–77 (fol. 116ᵛ), recounting that the next morning they see sights, and after dinner the author presents some verses and a story.

Novella LXXVII, *De sinplicitate viri et uxoris* (fols. 116ᵛ–117ᵛ), printed by D'Ancona, *Scelta*, pp. 16–22.

Intermezzo 77–78 (fols. 117ᵛ–118ʳ), recounting that after refreshments there is a love song, and the author tells a story.

Novella LXXVIII, *De mulier adultera e tristitia viri* (fols. 118ʳ–118ᵛ), summarized by Renier, pp. 418–19.

Then follows *Intermezzo* 78–79.⟩

⟨fol. 118ᵛ. L⟩evati la mattina, essendo ditto la messa e bel tenpo, il preposto disse alla brigata che stessero atenti d'andare stretti e ordinate perchè il paese che ànno a ffare molti gorni è paese di malandrini e di mafattori, amonendoli di fare buone gornate per uscire tosto del paese. E l'altore comandò che di bella novella consoli la brigata acciò che 'l camino non rincrescha; et essendo tutti amaestrati, disse al'altore che comincasse qualche moralità, e poi una novella dicha fine a tanto che lla brigata ⟨fol. 119ʳ⟩ sarà iunta a Benevento; e se 'l camino fusse magore, che per uno die se ne faccia du', come è stato fatto fine a qui; l'altore e li altri, al servigio presti, disseno di ubidire, e voltòsi l'altore e disse:

The next morning after Mass they set forth toward Benevento through a country full of rascals and malefactors. The author presents a moralità and a story.

> Guarda che Negligensa non s'anidi
>   In casa tua, che non ne va per gridi.
> La Negligensa albergo mai non pigla
>   Che non vi meni Povertà, sua figla.

Non ti rechar, figluolo, al punto stremo
Chè molti n'a ingannati "Già faremo."
Madonna Negligensia fu la madre
Di "Già faremo," e da l'Indugio il padre.[1]

E di poi disse:

⟨Here appears:
Novella LXXIX, *De bona providentia contra homicida* (fols. 119ʳ–119ᵛ), printed by Renier, pp. 178–80.
Then follows *Intermezzo* 79–80.⟩

After dinner, instead of dancing or singing, the company hears the author tell a story.

⟨fol. 120ʳ⟩ Lo preposto, udito lo subito rimedio che l'altore prese di quel malandrino traditore, parlando alla brigata che prendeano exenplo dalla dilettevole novella; e trovando le vivande[2] apparechiate per desnare, posto che fusse passato nona, nondimeno diliberò che in quel bello albergo per lo dì si restasse per non avere a caminare di notte; comandò che si desni sensa suoni o canti, ma che l'altore per ristoro de' balli e canti una novella ordini fine alla sera che quine[3] denno dormire; l'altore, desnato che ongni persona ebbe, disse:

⟨Here appears:
Novella LXXX, *De dizonesta juvinaa et equali corretione* (fols. 120ʳ–122ʳ), printed by Renier, pp. 181–85.
Then follows *Intermezzo* 80–81.⟩

The next morning as they travel to Benevento the author tells a story.

⟨fol. 122ʳ⟩ Venuta l'ora della cena colla dilettevole novella, cenarono e a posare n'andarono fine alla mattina; e mossi come è d'uzansa, lo preposto allo autore disse che una novella dica fine che a Benevento saranno iunti; l'autore rivoltosi alla brigata disse:

⟨Here appear the following:
Novella LXXXI, *De devotione in santo Juliano* (fols. 122ʳ–123ᵛ), printed by Renier, pp. 186–89. The same story is narrated by Boccaccio, *Decameron*, II, 2.
Intermezzo 81–82 (fol. 123ᵛ), recounting that, after supper, the singers perform *sotto voce*. The next morning after Mass the author presents a *moralità*. As they proceed toward Salerno he tells a story.
Novella LXXXII, *De Crudelta massima* (fols. 123ᵛ–124ᵛ), printed by Renier, pp. 190–91.
Intermezzo 82–83 (fol. 124ᵛ), recounting that, after dinner, they continue toward Salerno, the author presenting a *moralità* and a story.
Novella LXXXIII, *De bona providensa* (fols. 124ᵛ–126ᵛ), printed by Renier, pp. 192–94.
Then follows *Intermezzo* 83–84.⟩

---

[1] These verses were printed by Renier, p. liv.

[2] vivande] *Reading uncertain (MS).*

[3] quine] *The MS appears to read* quime. *Apparently, however, the scribe has retouched the final strokes of the word, leaving his intention slightly in doubt.*

⟨fol. 126ᵛ. G⟩unti a Salerno colla dilettevole novella e quine cenarono; e perchè la brigata era stanca, sens'altro dire se n'andarono a
dormire fine al dì seguente che levati funno; e dato l'ordine di chami-
nare, il preposto comandò al'altore che alla brigata dicha una novella
perchè lo camino di verso Reggio di Chalabria era un pogo lunghetto;
a tal camino per lo gorno ordini di bella novelle actte secondo il luogo[1]
dove sono; ma prima che si muovano, dicha qualche cansona morale;
l'altore disse che fatto serà, e voltosi alla brigata disse:[2]

⟨Here follows a moral song[3] ("Canson, chi vuol ben iudicar, il fine")
printed in *Croniche*, II, 258.⟩

E seguendo disse:

⟨Here appears:
Novella LXXXIV, *De bona fortuna in aversitate* (fols. 126ᵛ–127ᵛ), printed
by Renier, pp. 195–96.
Then follows *Intermezzo* 84–85.⟩

⟨fol. 127ᵛ. L⟩a prudensia di Santo condusse con piacere la brigata
all'ora del desnare in una villa bene de borghi piena, e in uno la brigata
trovò aparechiato; lo preposto sentendo il camino dubievole dispuose
che la sera s'aparachiasse in quel luogo, dove comandò che l'altore
contentasse la brigata di bella novella fine alla cena sensa che stormenti s'udisseno, ma prima dicesse qualche moralità; lui presto disse:

> Io sono francha Magnaminitade
> Di sì alto e magnifico inteletto;
> Doppo 'l[4] pensiero fornisco il diletto.[5]

E poi l'altore, fatta la brigata condurre in um bellissimo chiostro,
rivoltòsi a essa dicendo:

⟨Here appears:
Novella LXXXV, *De magnaminitate mulieris et bona ventura juvani* (fols.
127ᵛ–130ʳ), printed by Renier, pp. 197–202. The same story is narrated by
Boccaccio, *Decameron*, II, 3.
Then follows *Intermezzo* 85–86.⟩

⟨fol. 130ʳ. C⟩olla dilettevole novella la brigata fu condutta dove
aparechiato da cena honorevilmente era; e cenato, a dormire n'andono
fine ala mattina, che levati furno lo preposto parlò dicendo al'altore

Side notes:

After supper they sleep at Salerno, and the next morning as they travel the author presents a *moralità* and a story.

After dinner the author presents a *moralità*, and then in a cloister he tells a story.

The next day on their way to Reggio Calabria the author tells a story.

---

[1] luogo] viag'o (*MS*).

[2] At this point, rather than below, appears the title of the next *novella*.

[3] Here, and below, have been omitted all but the first line of each of a number
of poems. As we have noted, other versions of many of these have been printed
elsewhere. We have throughout referred to the poems as "songs," whether sung
or spoken, and whether appearing in printed versions alone or as portions of longer
poems.

[4] 'l] *Followed by a stroke, the intention of which is uncertain* (*MS*).

[5] See *Croniche*, II, 212.

che una novella dica fine che a Reggio la brigata fi' condutta, e voltòsi l'altore dicendo:

⟨Here appear the following:

Novella LXXXVI, *De pericolo in ytinere* (fols. 130ʳ–131ʳ), printed by D'Ancona, *Scelta*, pp. 75–82. A similar story is told in *Novella* LXXV.

Intermezzo 86–87 (fols. 131ʳ–131ᵛ), recounting that, the next day as they
proceed from Reggio Calabria toward Dierta, the author presents a song
and a story.

Novella LXXXVII, *De rasionabili dominie et bona iustitia* (fols. 131ᵛ–
132ᵛ), printed by Renier, pp. 203–5.

Intermezzo 87–88 (fol. 132ᵛ), recounting that, after dinner, they proceed
to Dierta with a story.

Novella LXXXVIII, *De latrones et bona justitia* (fols. 132ᵛ–133ᵛ), printed
by Renier, pp. 206–7.

Intermezzo 88–89 (fol. 133ᵛ), recounting that, the next day after Mass,
they go to Squillace, the author telling a story.

Novella LXXXIX, *De malitia hospitatoris* (fols. 133ᵛ–135ʳ), printed by
Renier, pp. 208–10.

Intermezzo 89–90 (fol. 135ʳ), recounting that the next day a story is told
as they travel to Forati.

Novella XC, *De falsatores et bona justitia* (fols. 135ʳ–136ʳ), printed by
Renier, pp. 211–13. The same story is told in *Novella* XXII.

Intermezzo 90–91 (fol. 136ʳ), recounting that, the next day as they go to
Brindisi, the author tells a story.

Novella XCI, *De massimo furto* (fols. 136ʳ–137ᵛ), printed by Renier, pp.
214–17.

Then follows *Intermezzo* 91–92.⟩

The next day, instead of going to Bari, where the plague has started, they travel to Sant' Angelo, the author telling a story.

⟨fol. 137ᵛ. L⟩o preposto e lla brigata gunsero a Brandisio, e quine
ebbeno sentimento come a Bari e in quelle parti la moria era comincata e pertanto dispuose che il loro camino fusse verso Santangelo;
e la mattina quando da Brandisio si vennero a partire, comandò
al'altore che una novella dicha; l'altore presto comincò a dire: "A
voi merchadanti non intendenti, li quali disiderando di guadagnar
tosto a quanti pericoli venite, e a voi che la fortuna v'à ristorati che
di ciò dovete esser grati, dirò ad exenplo una novella fine che gungeremo a Santangelo in questa forma coè:"

⟨Here appear the following:

Novella XCII, *De restauro fatto per fortuna* (fols. 137ᵛ–139ʳ), printed by
D'Ancona, *Scelta*, pp. 119–26. The same story is narrated by Boccaccio,
Decameron, II, 4.

Intermezzo 92–93 (fol. 139ʳ), recounting that at Sant'Angelo they enjoy music and dancing; and the next day the author tells a story as they proceed
toward Scariotto, where Judas was found.

Novella XCIII, *De malvagitate ypocriti* (fols. 139ʳ–141ʳ), printed by Renier, pp. 218–21.

Intermezzo 93–94 (fol. 141ʳ), recounting that halfway to Scariotto they rest, and then the author tells a story during the remainder of the journey.

Novella XCIV, *De malitia in inganno* (fols. 141ʳ–142ʳ), printed by Renier, pp. 222–24.

Intermezzo 94–95 (fol. 142ʳ), recounting that after supper they dance and, the next day while they travel to Ascoli, the author presents a love song and a story.

Novella XCV, *De cecho amore* (fols. 142ʳ–143ᵛ), printed by Renier, pp. 225–27.

Intermezzo 95–96 (fols. 143ᵛ–144ʳ), recounting that, the next morning on their way toward Fermo, the author tells a story.

Novella XCVI, *De cattivitate stipendiari* (fols. 144ʳ–145ᵛ), printed by Renier, pp. 228–31.

Intermezzo 96–97 (fol. 145ᵛ), recounting that before dinner the singers present a love song, and on the way to Fermo the author tells a story.

Novella XCVII, *De viltate* (fols. 145ᵛ–147ʳ), printed by Renier, pp. 232–34.

Intermezzo 97–98 (fol. 147ʳ), recounting that, after supper at Fermo, there is a love song, and the next day on the way to Recanati[1] the author tells a story.

Novella XCVIII, *De falsitate mulieris* (fols. 147ʳ–149ʳ), printed by Renier, pp. 235–38. A similar story is narrated by Boccaccio, *Decameron*, II, 5.

Intermezzo 98–99 (fols. 149ʳ–149ᵛ), recounting that, after supper at Recanati, there is music and, the next day on the way to Ancona, the author tells a story.

Novella XCIX, *De malitia hominis* (fols. 149ᵛ–151ʳ), printed by Renier, pp. 239–42. The same story is narrated by Boccaccio, *Decameron*, III, 1.

Intermezzo 99–100 (fol. 151ᵛ), recounting that, the next day on the way to Senigallia, the author tells a story.

Novella C, *De subita malitia in muliere* (fols. 151ᵛ–152ᵛ), printed by Renier, pp. 243–45.

Intermezzo 100–101 (fols. 152ᵛ–153ʳ), recounting that, at Senigallia that evening, there is music; and the next day, on the way to Fano, the author presents a moral song and a story.

Novella CI, *De mala corretione* (fols. 153ʳ–154ᵛ), printed by Renier, pp. 246–48.

Then follows *Intermezzo* 101–2.⟩

⟨fol. 154ᵛ. L⟩o preposto e lla brigata gunseno a Fano sensa alcuno dizagio là u' la sera stenno con piacere fine al'altra mattina, che 'l preposto al'altore comandò che una novella dicha fine che gunti seranno a Pesale, ora prima dicha cansone; il quale ubidendo disse:

The next day on the way to Pesaro the author presents a moral song and a story.

---

[1] See *Int.* 106–7 below.

⟨Here (fols. 154ᵛ–155ʳ) follows a moral song ("Le dilitie quagiù, a voi mondani") printed in *Croniche*, II, 237.⟩

E ditta, disse: "A voi homini ricchi che l'avaritia vi tiene stretti intanto che quello che di necessità tener dovete per tal vizio fugite per la spesa non tenere, ad exenplo dirò una novella in questo modo, coè":

⟨Here appear the following:

Novella CII, *De avaritia mangna* (fols. 155ʳ–156ᵛ), printed by Renier, pp. 249–52.

Intermezzo 102–3 (fol. 156ᵛ), recounting that, the next day on the way to Fossombrone, the author presents a love song and a story.

Novella CIII, *De inganno in amore* (fols. 156ᵛ–158ʳ), printed by Renier, pp. 253–55. The same story is narrated by Boccaccio, *Decameron*, III, 2.

Intermezzo 103–4 (fol. 158ʳ), recounting that, the next day on the way to Gubbio, the author presents a *moralità* and a story.

Novella CIV, *De invidia* (fols. 158ʳ–159ᵛ), printed by Renier, pp. 256–58.

Intermezzo 104–5 (fol. 159ᵛ), recounting that, the next day on the way to Urbino, the author tells a story.

Novella CV, *De lungo inganno* (fols. 159ᵛ–162ʳ), printed by Renier, pp. 259–63.

Intermezzo 105–6 (fol. 162ʳ), recounting that, before supper at Urbino, there is a love song and, the next day on the way to Cagli, the author tells a story.

Novella CVI, *De malitia mulieris adultera* (fols. 162ʳ–164ᵛ), printed by Renier, pp. 264–68. The same story is narrated by Boccaccio, *Decameron*, III, 3.

Intermezzo 106–7 (fol. 164ᵛ), recounting that, the next day on the way to Recanati,[1] the author presents a short song (?) and a story.

Novella, CVII, *De presuntuosi* (fols. 164ᵛ–165ᵛ), printed by Renier, pp. 269–71.

Intermezzo 107–8 (fol. 166ʳ), recounting that, the next day on the way to Cortona,[2] the author presents a *moralità* and a story.

Novella CVIII, *De somma golozitate* (fols. 166ʳ–167ʳ), printed by Renier, pp. 272–73.

Intermezzo 108–9 (fol. 167ʳ), recounting that, having reached Cesena, the company enjoys singing and dancing before supper. The next day on the way to Cervia, the author presents a *moralità* and a story.

Novella CIX, *De mangna golozitate* (fols. 167ʳ–168ʳ), printed by Renier, pp. 274–76.

Intermezzo 109–10 (fols. 168ʳ–168ᵛ), recounting that, the next day on the way to Bertinoro, the author presents a *moralità* and a story.

Novella CX, *De prelato adultero* (fols. 168ᵛ–170ᵛ), printed by Renier, pp. 277–80. The same story is narrated in *Novella* CXVI and by Boccaccio, *Decameron*, III, 4.

Then follows *Intermezzo* 110–11.⟩

[1] See *Int*. 97–98 above.   [2] See *Int*. 11–12 above.

⟨fol. 170ᵛ. L⟩a dilettevole novella sensa dizagio condusse la brigata a Bertinoro, dove il preposto comandò che alquanto si dansasse e dapoi una piacevole cansone si dicesse in questo modo:

⟨Here follows a love song ("Tra tuo fugir e 'l mio seguir sarà") by Soldanieri, printed by Carducci, *Cantilene*, p. 267.⟩

E, ditta, andasero a cenare e dapoi a posar si vada, fine alla mattina che levati furono, dove il propòsto comandò al'altore che una novella dica fine che gunti seranno a Ravenna; il quale per ubidire disse: "A voi iudici che avete a dare sententie, quando iustamente iudicate sete molto commendati, e faccendo il contrario sete biasmati, ad exemplo dirò una novella in questo modo":

⟨Here appear the following:

Novella CXI, *De justo juditio* (fols. 170ᵛ–173ᵛ), printed by D'Ancona, *Scelta*, pp. 23–37.

Intermezzo 111–12 (fol 173ᵛ), recounting that, after supper at Ravenna, there is a song and, the next day on the way to Forlì, the author tells a story.

Novella CXII, *De avaro* (fols. 173ᵛ–175ʳ), printed by Renier, pp. 281–83.

Intermezzo 112–13 (fol. 175ʳ), recounting that, after supper at Forlì, there is a song and, the next day on the way to Faenza, the author tells a story.

Novella CXIII, *De ponpa bestiale* (fols. 175ʳ–176ʳ), printed by ˏD'Ancona, *Scelta*, pp. 11–15.

Intermezzo 113–14 (fol. 176ʳ), recounting that, after supper at Faenza, the leader speaks and, the next day on the way to Imola, the author tells a story.

Novella CXIV, *De mala custodia* (fols. 176ʳ–177ᵛ), printed by Renier, pp. 284–85.

Intermezzo 114–15 (fol. 177ᵛ), recounting that, at Imola before supper, there is a love song and, the next day on the way to the castle of Meldola, the author tells several stories.

Novella CXV, *De pigritia* (fols. 177ᵛ–181ʳ), consisting of several stories, and printed by Renier, pp. 286–91.

Intermezzo 115–16 (fol. 181ʳ), recounting that, at Meldola before supper, there is dancing and, the next day on the way to Bologna, the author tells a story.

Novella CXVI, *De pessima malitia in prelato* (fols. 181ʳ–182ʳ), summarized by Renier, pp. 419–20. The same story is narrated in *Novella* CX and by Boccaccio, *Decameron*, III, 4.

Intermezzo 116–17 (fol. 182ʳ), recounting that at Bologna there is singing before supper, and afterward dancing; the next morning in Bologna, the author tells a story.

Novella CXVII, *De nemico reconciliato ne confidetur* (fols. 182ʳ–183ʳ), printed by Renier, pp. 292–93.

Then follows *Intermezzo* 117–18.⟩

At Bertinoro occur dancing and singing, and the next day on the way to Ravenna the author tells a story.

⟨fol. 183ʳ⟩ Odito quanto de l'uomo guardarsi di fidare la sua persona al suo nimico, per la qual cosa il proposto lodò molto l'altore che
di tale cosa avea amaestrato la brigata; e perchè era assai buonora
prima che fusse l'ora del desnare, il proposto comandò a' cantatori che
una cansona dicesseno fine che l'ora serà d'andare a desnare. E
presto uno cantatore con una damigella cominċono una cansona in
questo modo:

⟨Here follows a love song ("Io prego che ongni donna cruda invechi") by
Soldanieri, printed by Carducci, *Cantilene*, pp. 291–92.⟩

Ditta la cansone, le vivande aparechiate, lavate le mani, a seder si
puoseno; e desnato, preso le danse, in uno giardino se n'andarono dove
lo proposto comandò al'altore che una novella dicha fine che l'ora
serà d'andarsi a posare per lo gorno che caldo era; l'altore atto a
ubidire si voltò alla brigata parlando: "A voi homini che v'afrigete
trovando le vostre donne in fallo, non pensando che natura l'à con-
dutte a tale atto, e però ad exenpro dirò una novella, non però che
le donne debiano di ciò prendere sigurtà, chè radi si troverenno pasi-
enti, come in nella precedente novella sentirete in questo modo":

⟨Here appear the following:
Novella CXVIII, *De ingenio mulieris adultera* (fols. 183ʳ–188ʳ), printed
by Renier, pp. 294–99.
Intermezzo 118–19 (fol. 188ʳ), recounting that the company enjoys dancing,
a siesta, more dancing, and then a story by the author.
Novella CXIX, *De dizonesto famulo* (fols. 188ʳ–189ᵛ), printed by Renier,
pp. 300–302.
Intermezzo 119–20 (fols. 189ᵛ–190ʳ), recounting that, after singing and
dancing, supper is served; and the next morning they embark in boats for
Lagellino, and the author tells a story.
Novella CXX, *De pulcra responsione* (fols. 190ʳ–190ᵛ), printed by D'An-
cona, *Libreria Dante*, pp. 41–43. The same story is narrated by Boccaccio,
Decameron, VI, 1.
Then follows *Intermezzo* 120–21.⟩

⟨fol. 190ᵛ. L⟩a dilettovole novella ditta condusse sensa dizagio a
Lugellino dove quine sensa uscire di barch[a] dienno ordine di cenare;
e sensa altro fare doppo cena si dienno a dormire, avendo il proposto
prima comandato al'altore che domattina quando serà tenpo di
caminare dicha una bella novella fine alla Torre della Fossa, sperando
quine esser a desnare. E così la notte passò, et venuto il gorno li
marinai, le vele alsate e co' remi in punto, si mossero. L'altore per
ubidire il comandamento del proposto disse: "Io vorei prima dire
qualche moralità." Lo proposto lieto, lui disse:

Io, Tenperansa, tenpero mia vita,
E tutti i miei nimici tengno a freno,
Di quanti voglio far nè più nè meno.[1]

Dicendo: "Poi che noi siamo sopra l'aque e di necessità di racontare alchuna novella actta secondo i⟨l⟩ luogo, e pertanto dicho, a voi donne che avete tanta volontà di bere aqua non guardando s'ella è netta o no, dirò ad exemplo una novella in questo modo coè":

⟨Here appears:
Novella CXXI, *De apetito chanino et non tenperato* (fols. 190v–192v), printed by Renier, pp. 303–6.
Then follows *Intermezzo* 121–22.⟩

⟨fol. 192v. G⟩unta la brigata, alquanto passato nona, colla dilettevole novella alla Torre della Fossa dove trovarono aparechiato da desnare, e usciti delle barche, a taula si puoseno e con piacere desnarono; e desnato, lo proposto fatto ogni persona mettere in sulle barche de' Ferraresi per caminare a Ferrara dove la sera volea che la brigata dormisse; e come in barca funoro,[2] ⟨fol. 193r⟩ il proposto chomandò a' cantarelli che una cansona dichano, e gunti poi a Ferrara, sens'altro fare s'intenda a cenare; li cantatori presti cominconno a cantare dicendo:

⟨Here follows a love song ("Chi d'altra donna sia, certa sia tu") by Soldanieri, printed by Carducci, *Cantilene*, p. 287.⟩

After dinner on shore at Torre della Fossa, they listen to a love song while traveling in boats to Ferrara.

Ditta la cansone e gunti a Ferrara dove si ridusseno al'abergo e quine trovato aparechiato da cena cenarono e poi a dormire s'andarono fine alla mattina che levati furono; il proposto disse al'altore che ordini dire una novella quando montati seranno in sulle carrette per andare a Francolino, là dove vuole che la sera si stia; l'altore presto a ubidire spettò che tutti montati furono, e voltòsi alla brigata dicendo: "A voi homini parsiali, li quali non per rispetto di Dio charità faite, ma per l'animo della parte quello faite, dirò una novella ad exemplo in questo modo coè":

After supper and a night at Ferrara, they go to Francolino in wagons, while the author tells a story.

⟨Here appears:
Novella CXXII, *De inganno placibili* (fols. 193r–194v), printed by D'Ancona, *Scelta*, pp. 1–10.
Then follows *Intermezzo* 122–23.⟩

⟨fol. 194v. L⟩a dilettevile novella di frate Tomazino à molto la brigata condutta sensa dizagio a Francolino prima che fusse l'ora della

At Francolino dancing and singing take place both before and after supper;

[1] See *Croniche*, II, 211.

[2] funoro] *Meaning* funoro; *above the word appears a superfluous line indicating abbreviation* (MS).

cena perchè agiati assai erano iti; e come gunti furono, il proposto missosi a ssedere in una camera d'uno albergo dove tutta la brigata dintorno si puose, il quale proposto comandò a' dansatori che una dansa facesseno; e fatta, li cantatori una cansonetta cantasero; e ditta, la brigata a cenare andasero. E fatto il comandamento, le danse prese, li stormenti sonando tanto che le danse restarono; e restate, i cantarelli e cantarelle ⟨ fol. 195ʳ⟩ con voci puerili cantarono in questo modo una cansona:

⟨Here follows a love song ("Io vo' ben a chi vuol bene a me") by Soldanieri, printed by Carducci, *Cantilene*, p. 290, and Trucchi, p. 197.⟩

Compiuta la novella,[1] la morale cansona, le taule poste, le vivande aparechiate, dato l'aqua alle mani e posti a mensa, cenarono di buona vogla; e cenato, per poter alquanto smaltire il cibo cominconno i dansatori sensa sensa comandamento a dansare, li stormenti a sonare, facciendo dolci melodie, parendo esser come in villa, più volte mutando danse e suoni; e per non dar molta faticha a' dansatori, essendo assai buonora, fatto restare li suoni, con honesto parlare lo proposto disse: "A voi religiosi, li quali, ora che siemo fuora della cittade, consolate la brigata di qualche bello exenplo morale morale." Intanto le religiosi per ubidire disseno:

⟨Here follows a moral song ("Errar non può colui, che si rimete") printed in *Croniche*, II, 257–58, and III, 90–91.⟩

the company then sleeps until midnight, when they board boats; as soon as they start out for Chioggia, the author tells a story. Udito il proposto il savio dire, piacendoli, fatto fare collatione al modo uzato, comandò che tutti a posar n'andasero acciò che a messanotte in su lengno montar possano per caminare alla città di Chioggia, dove comandò che quine sia aparechiato per la cena; "E a te, altore, che levati e entrati in barcha, dichi una bella novella fine alle Bebe; e dapoi i cantatori ⟨fol. 195ᵛ⟩ una cansonetta cantino; e perchè molto m'è piaciuto il dire de' religiosi, dico che doppo le cansone qualche cosa dichano, e così con piacer giungeremo alla città di Chioggia." Ognuno inteso che à 'l proposto, a dormire si puoseno, e la notte chiamati da' padroni in barcha se ne vanno, e dato de' remi in aqua e fatto silensio, l'altore parlò dicendo: "A voi conti e signori che vi disperate per adenpiere il vostro dizio, dirò ad exemplo una novella la quale in questo modo si conta":

⟨Here appears:
Novella CXXIII, *De disperato dominio* (fols. 195ᵛ–197ʳ), printed by Renier, pp. 307–9.
Then follows *Intermezzo* 123–24.⟩

Ashore at the Bebe the singers present a love song, ⟨fol. 197ʳ⟩ Li cantatori che atento stavano, gunti che alle Bebe funno, e sposati di barcha per dovere quine la sera dormire, asettati

---

[1] la novella] *Possibly crossed out* (*MS*).

in uno albergo sotto un bello fraschato, cominconno a cantare in questo modo una cansonetta dicendo:

"Donna, se inganni me, chi poi ti crede?"
"Sai chi? Un altro te,
 Che crede avere per dar stra me se me."[1]
"Non è in altrui far beffe in donna bello."
"Io beffo te per non esser beffata."
"Lasso! tu 'l fai per volgermi mantello."
"Come ch'io sia, i' son dizamorata."
"Non m'ami tu, sendo da me amata?"
"Sì, se non fusse fè:
 Ma huomo donna ama a diletto di sè."
"Come se' di dolce stata ria?"
"Sai come se' tu fatto reo?"
"I' son ben reo amando te, iudea."
"Iudea ⟨fol. 197ᵛ⟩ non sono, ma tu se' ben iudeo."
"S'io t'ò messo nel messo del cor mio,
 Metti me in quel di te."
"Io non ti metterei al suol del pè."[2]

Ditta la dilettevole cansona, per non fare contro [alla] volontà del proposto, li religiosi cominconno a dire con quelle melo[die] in cant[iche] si richiede in questo modo: *and the religiosi recite a moralità accompanied by music.*

⟨Here follows a moral song ("Tu, ingnorante, segui le richesse") by Soldanieri, printed in *Croniche*, II, 373.⟩

Lo proposto udite le dolce melodie, essendo l'ora della cena e aparechiato, comandò che a cena si andasse e poi a posare per far buona levata per esser a Chioggia al desnare; e al'altore comandò che d'una bella novella in nel camino la brigata contentasse: l'altore presto disse che fatto serae; e dormiti fine [a quel] punto che da' padroni delle barche funno desti, e intrati in barcha, l'altore disse: "A voi homini che colle donne altrui dizonestamente e con pechato uzate e poi vi fidate di chi à ricevuto la vergogna, ad exemplo dirò una novella in questo modo": *After supper they sleep, and the next day, as they proceed in boats toward Chioggia, the author tells a story.*

⟨Here appears:
Novella CXXIV, *De mala fiducia di nimicy* (fols. 197ᵛ–198ᵛ), printed by Renier, pp. 310–11.
Then follows *Intermezzo* 124–25.⟩

[1] We cannot make sense out of this line; here and elsewhere this version of Soldanieri's dialogue between a lover and his lady appears to be corrupt.

[2] By Soldanieri; the first ten lines are given by Carducci on pp. 281–82 of the *Cantilene,* and the last seven lines on pp. 270–71.

⟨fol. 198ᵛ⟩ Lo proposto come savio, avendo a....io, udito la morte di Lancilotto, disse: "O per certo a lui e ali altri che di simile pechato involti fusseno diverre, quando di tali si fidass[ero], e pertan-[to] se male nelli colse, non n'è da meraviglarsi, e pertanto il belista l'à aparechiato e se savio non fu n'à portato la pena e con quella si rimangna. E noi intendiamo ora che presso siamo a Chioggia a darci piacere et pertanto dico a voi religiosi che alcuna cosa dichiate che sia piacevole [fine] che questo pogo di camino infine a Chioga saremo." Loro presti dissero:

⟨Here (fols. 198ᵛ–199ʳ) follows a moral song ("Ricognoscha ciascum quel ch'à ond'ebbie") printed in *Croniche*, II, 257.⟩

Livro[1] il bel dire de' religiosi, i navigli gunti al porto di Chioga, lo proposto e li altri sciesi a terra, e in nell'abergo dov'era aparechiato per lo desnare se n'andarono, dove di vantagio funno ben serviti; e desnato, lo proposto comandò che alquanto si mettesseno a cercare la terra, e le barche si mettesseno in punt[o acciò] che la sera in Vinegia sia la loro stansa; e così fenno che, cerchato la terra e montati in barcha, comandato al'altore che una novella dicha fine a Vinegia, l'altore presto a ubidire disse: "A voi homini grossi di pasta, che v'è mostrato con dan[no e ver]ghongna la luna per lo sole, [e a] voi frati, che dovreste d'exenpli buoni amaestrare i vostri subditi, e voi con vituperio il contrario fate, ad [exe]np[lo] dirò una novella in questo modo coè":

⟨Here appears:

Novella CXXV, *De tradimento fatto per monacum* (fols. 199ʳ–201ʳ), printed by Renier, pp. 312–15. The same story is narrated by Boccaccio, *Decameron*, III, 8.

Then follows *Intermezzo* 125–26.⟩

⟨fol. 201ᵛ⟩ Gunta a Vinegia colla dilettevole ⟨novella⟩ uno sabato sera, una vigilia di festa, dove, andati al'abergo, trovarono di vantagio aparechiato; et per la cena, e perch'era tardi, e ancho perchè sentia Vinegia alquanto [la] peste per l'aire cattiva, deliberò il proposto che ognuno a dormire doppo cena n'andasse, acciò che di buonora si possa caminar verso Murano; al'altor comandò che una novella ordini per lo dì seguente.... e una cansonetta dicano li cantarelli; allora loro presti disseno: "Da che più serveno a una donna e io bene."[2] E questo messo in effetto, [cenarono] e sensa che di quine si partisseno a dormire n'andarono; e la mattina, udita la messa, e entrati in barcha, e l'altore per adenpiere la volontà del [proposto] disse: "A voi donne che uzando con altri e di loro ingravidare e parturendo pensate che i

---

[1] Livro] *Syncopated form of* liverato, *meaning* terminato.

[2] "Da.... bene."] *Apparently this is the first line of a song.*

vostri mariti siano sì sciochi che non debbiano cognoscere quello che fatto avete, ad exenplo dirò una novella in questo modo coè":

⟨Here appears:

Novella CXXVI, *De malitia mulieris adultera et simile maltia viri* (fols. 201ᵛ–203ʳ), printed by Renier, pp. 316–18.

Then follows *Intermezzo* 126–27.⟩

⟨fol. 203ʳ⟩ Colla dilettevole novella la brigata giunse a Murano in sul deznare dove trovonno bene aparachiato; e desnato che la brigata ebbe, il proposto disse a' cantatori che alquanto cantassero; e ditta una cansona, si prendesse una dansa; e questo fatto, si cerchi alquanto Murano, e poi tornati prenderemo pensieri ad altro. Li cantatori per ubidire comincorono a cantare in questo modo:

After dinner at Murano there are singing and dancing; they see sights, hear a song by the religiosi, and have supper.

⟨Here follows a moral song ("Chi 'l dover fa, mal dire non churi altrui") by Soldanieri, printed by Carducci, *Cantilene*, p. 290, and in *Croniche*, III, 182.⟩

Ditta la piacevole cansona, li sonatori sonando, le danse prese e una dansa ⟨fol. 203ᵛ⟩ facciendo fine che a proposto parve di dovere andar vedendo Murano; e fatto restare le danse e suoni, si mosse per vizitare l'inocenti in nella chieza magore, e, quelli veduti, si dienno a vedere le belle botteghe de' bichieri e opra di vetro, et così ongni particularità ricercando, piacendo a ongni persona il sito di tale città; e come tutto ebeno proveduto, ritornando verso l'abergo, dove [la cena era ap]arechiata, e posti a sedere in um bel chiostro, il preposto disse: "A voi religiosi, vi pregho che la brigata si consoli di qualche bella cosa." Loro presti con canto disseno:

⟨Here follows a moral song ("Per poter da superbia star rimoto") by Soldanieri, printed in *Croniche*, II, 311.⟩

Udito il proposto e li altri sì bella cosa, li stormenti sonando, dato l'aqua alle mani e posti a cena, cenarono di buona vogla; e cenato, il proposto disse che ungnuno riposar andasse e di buonora s'intrasse in barcha acciò che sensa faticha possiamo domane esser a Trivigi; e l'altore comandò che di bella novella consoli la brigata. E questo ditto, ciaschuno a posar andò; e levati e entrati in barcha, l'altore disse: "A voi donne, che vi lassate vituperare sotto spesie di moneta, e come matte per tal difetto ij inganni ricevete, ad exenplo dirò una novella in questo modo":

The next day as they proceed by boat to Treviso the author tells a story.

⟨Here appears:

Novella CXXVII[1] (fols. 203ᵛ–204ᵛ), printed by D'Ancona, *Libreria Dante*, pp. 43–46. The same story is narrated in *Novella* CXLV and by Boccaccio, *Decameron*, VI, 3.

Then follows *Intermezzo* 127–28.⟩

[1] No title given in manuscript.

⟨fol. 204ᵛ⟩ La bella novella condusse la brigata a Trivigi di buonora, e prima che a cenar s'andasse, essendo riposati alquanto [in uno] albergo dov'erano belli giardini, in [uno de' quali] lo proposto comandò che aparechiato fusse, e quine a' religiosi disse che una bella cosa dicesseno in canto, li qu[ali] per ubidire disseno così:

⟨Here follows a moral song ("Tu che se' su, perch'el mundo t'onora").⟩

Piaciuto il bel dire de' religiosi, per prender altro diporto il proposto comandò alle cantarelle che una cansonetta dicesseno; e ditta, le danse si prendeano fine che a cena serà l'ora d'andare; e tutte preste a ubidire comecionn[o] dicendo:

⟨Here follows a love song ("Se tu pensassi al torto che mi fai") by Soldanieri, printed by Carducci, *Cantilene*, pp. 282–83, and Trucchi, pp. 190–91. And then, on fol. 205ʳ, the *intermezzo* continues.⟩

Ditta la piacevole cansone, li stormenti comincati a sonare, le danse prese fine che l'ora della cena fu venuta, e dato l'aqua alle mani e posti a mensa, là u' funno di vantagio ben serviti, e levati da taula, il proposto in nel gardino postosi a sedere, per non stare osioso, disse a ad alquanti cantarelli che una piacevole cansonetta dicano, e ditta, ognuno a posar vada; coloro presti a ubidire disseno:

⟨Here follows a love song ("Donna, i' so ben che servon più d'uno due") by Soldanieri, printed by Carducci, *Cantilene*, p. 280, and Trucchi, pp. 194–95.⟩

E ditta, a posar n'andarono e fine alla [mattina] con p[oco] dormire, e levati e udita la messa, si misseno in via, avendo il proposto fatto comandamento al'altore che una novella dicha fine che gunti saranno alla ciptà di Feltre; l'altore presto disse: "A voi donne, che per disidireo[1] di contentare vostra vogla ongni vituperio de' vostri mariti faite, e vedendo che scoperte de' falli sete, con nuovo schuzare alcuna volta schanpate la vita, ad exenplo dirò una novella in questo modo coè":

⟨Here appears:
Novella CXXVIII, *De pauco sentimento in juvano* (fols. 205ʳ–206ᵛ), printed by Renier, pp. 319–22.
Then follows *Intermezzo* 128–29.⟩

⟨fol. 206ᵛ⟩ La smemoragine del nostro ciptadino à fatto alquanto la brigata meraviglare, e con tale meravigla gunse a Feltri, dove per quelli che deputati erano a servire fu aparechiato per la cena assai in abundansia, et ⟨fol. 207ʳ⟩ perch'erano alquanto caldi per lo caminare, lo proposto, postosi a sedere, essendoli piacuto il ditto de' religi-

---

[1] disidireo] *Reading uncertain* (*MS*).

osi, disse loro che con uno bello canto dicesseno qualche bella cosa; loro volentieri rispuoseno che tutto faranno, e fatto fare silentio comincorono a dire:

⟨Here follows a moral song ("Color che per santier dirieto vanno") by Soldanieri, printed in *Croniche*, II, 394–95.⟩

Molto piacuto il bel ditto al preposto, perchè l'ora non era ancora della cena, per trapassar tenpo disse a' cantarelli che una cansonetta dicessero; e loro presti a ubidire, fatto reverensa, comincarono in questo modo:

⟨Here follows a love song ("O govin donne che 'l tenpo perdete") by Soldanieri, printed by Carducci, *Cantilene*, p. 285.⟩

Udito la dolce melodia de' cantatori, venute le vivande, dato l'aqua alle mani e posto a mensa, cenarono di vantagio; e levati da cena, i dansatori con li stormenti fatto alcune danse tanto che l'ora fu d'andare a dormire; e dormiti fine alla mattina che, ditta la messa e mossi, il proposto disse al'altore fine che gunti seranno a Civitale d'una novella contenti la brigata; l'altore presto disse: "A voi gelozi che sensa ragione o[1] cagione contra le vostre donne fate stranesse e, non facciendo noi il dovere, se di tal fallo puniti sete, non n'è da prenderne amirasione; ad exenplo dirò una novella in questo modo": *(margin: The next day after Mass they proceed to Civitale while the author tells a story.)*

⟨Here appears:
Novella CXXIX, *De mangna gelozia* (fols. 207ʳ–208ᵛ), printed by Renier, pp. 323–25.
Then follows *Intermezzo* 129–30.⟩

⟨fol. 208ᵛ. L⟩o proposto gunto a Civitale colla dilettevole novella assai innanti cena, e in uno albergo allogiati, e rinfreschati di buoni vini e d'alquanti ⟨fol. 209ʳ⟩ frutti, si puoseno a ssedere; e parlando il proposto che i religiosi d'una bella cosa contentino la brigata e poi si ceni, loro presti a ubidire disseno: *(margin: At Civitale there are refreshments, a recitation by the religiosi, supper, and dancing.)*

⟨Here follows a moral song ("Gente ci à assai che non guochano a zara") by Soldanieri, printed in *Croniche*, II, 374.⟩

Piaciuto il savio ditto al preposto, e l'ora della cena venuta, l'aqua alle mani, e posti a mensa, le vivande preste, con diletto cenarono; e levati da mensa, per dar piacere alla brigata, li stormenti sonando, le danse prese, fine al'ora del dormíre si dansò, e dapoi iti a dormire fine alla mattina là u' il proposto disse al'altore che una bella novella dicha fine che gunti saranno a Vicensa; l'altore presto disse: "A voi amanti che disponete a morire per tale amore, e a voi neganti le cose giuste che far non si debiano, dirò ad exenplo una novella; *(margin: The next day as they go to Vicenza the author tells a story.)*

---

[1] o] a (*MS*).

posto che più volte la dobiate avere intesa, non dimeno per ricordarla di nuovo la conterò in questo modo coè":

⟨Here appears:

Novella CXXX, *De juvano futtili in amore* (fols. 209ʳ–210ᵛ), printed by Renier, pp. 326–28. The same story is narrated by Chaucer, the *Legend of Thisbe.*

Then follows *Intermezzo* 130–31.⟩

At Vicenza before supper the *religiosi* recite a *moralità* to music, ⟨fol. 210ᵛ. A⟩ Vicensa gunse il proposto colla brigata alquanto presso a cena, dove volse che i religiosi dicessero con canto suave alcuna cosa e lo⟨ro⟩ presti disero:

⟨Here follows a moral song ("Prova non fa d'amicho a proferirsi") by Soldanieri, printed in *Croniche*, II, 388.⟩

and afterward there is a love song and refreshments. Udito la dilettevole cosa, e dato l'aqua alle mani, e posti a mensa, cenarono di vamtaggio; e dapoi, ridutti in un pratello, il proposto volendo prendere piacere disse: "Su, cantarelli, e una cansonetta si canti e poi a dormire ognuno si vada." Coloro presti comincarono a cantare in questo modo:

Ama chi t'ama sempre a buona fè;
Serve qualuncha e non guardar perchè.
Così facciendo pur tenpo verrà
(La fama è cosa che va qua e chulì)
Che um solo per tutti ti meriterà,
E per un certo farò quel che a ti.[1]
⟨fol. 211ʳ⟩ Cosa non è che amor più tiri a si
Come a servire sensa sperar mercè.
Un grande error è fra noi gente mo,
Di servir solo a cui pur serve a mi.
Quest'è contra natura quanto pò,
S'al principio di noi guardemo sì
Che alcuno del'altro non fu dato più,
Nè mai virtù serrà dov'esser de.[2]

Ditta la cansone, e dato de' confetti e alquanto bere, il proposto licensiò che ognuno s'andasse a dormire; e così oservato, fine alla mattina si posarono; e levati da dormire, il proposto, udita la messa, disse The next day after Mass they proceed to Padua while the author tells a story. al'altore che una novella dicha fine che gunti saranno a Padova; l'altore presto disse: "A voi malvagi, li quali dimostrate esser amici, e altri fidandosi come da amico, e voi come traditori inghannate chi[3] di voi si fida, ad exenplo dirò una novella in questo modo":

---

[1] This line particularly does not yield much sense.

[2] By Soldanieri; see *Croniche*, II, 242, where, in general, a better version of the song is presented.

[3] chi] di chi, *with* di *crossed out* (MS).

⟨Here appears:

Novella CXXXI, *De prava amicitia* (fols. 211ʳ–214ᵛ), printed by Renier, pp. 329–34.

Then follows *Intermezzo* 131–32.⟩

⟨fol. 214ᵛ⟩ La iusta vendetta udita per lo proposto e per la brigata piaque molto, e con tal novella iunseno a Padova, dove era aparechiato per la cena; ma perchè il camino era stato alquanto lungho volse che prima che si cenasse in uno gardino si riposasse alquanto la brigata; e così riposati, lo proposto disse a' religiosi che qualche bella cosa dicesseno. Loro presti dissero: *At Padua the religiosi recite a moralità before supper.*

> Chi gola segue al[tri arrà] il comendare:
>> Perchè natura è vagho,
>> Il suo diletto ragion ne periscie;
>> Perdendo del veder la chiara luce,
>> Come porcho in bancho[1]
>> S'involge; involge se in le ipeticie.
>> Chi fa stinensa ciò non concupiscie,
>> Ansi sea casto quanto vuol misura;
>> E pur se lla natura
>> Vel chiama, allora honesto vi s'inchina.
>> Col matrimonio sol questo li piace;
>> Ongn'altro uzar li spiace,
>> Perchè ci el vieta ongni ragon divina,
>> Che vuole che qui l'un dell'altro naschi,
>> Ne uzi così come bestia viva o pascha.[2]

Piacuto il bel detto di religiosi, essendo l'ora della cena, e dato l'aqua alle mani, cenarono; e dapoi, perchè il gorno non aveano posato, andarono a dormire, e levati, il proposto disse al'altore che una novella dicha fine che iunti saranno a Verona; lui presto a ubidire disse: "A voi che con altrui a star vi ponete, e vituperando la famigla di casa, pensando sempre poter godere, se male ve ne aviene non è da maraviglarsi, e però ad exenplo dirò una novella in questo modo coè": *and the next day while they proceed to Verona the author tells a story.*

⟨Here appears:

Novella CXXXII, *De malvagio famulo* (fols. 214ᵛ–216ʳ), printed by Renier, pp. 335–37.

Then follows *Intermezzo* 132–33.⟩

⟨fol. 216ʳ. G⟩unti a Verona colla dilettevole novella del suo Veronese quasi presso a cena, ma, per potere avallare la faticha del caminare, volse il proposto che prima che si cenasse per li cantarelli si dicesse *At Verona the singers present a love song*

---

[1] in bancho] *Possibly for* in fangho.

[2] By Soldanieri; see Florence, Bibl. Laur., MS Redi. 184, fols. 107ᵛ–108ʳ; neither of these versions yields complete sense.

alcuna cansonetta, e poi secondo il tempo si seguirà; e comandato, rispuoseno che fatto serà incomincando:

> Non temo, donna, di pianger giamai
>> Poi che 'l ben ch'io perdei *p*renduto m'ài.
>> ⟨fol. 216ᵛ⟩ O che dogla o che martirio avere porrei
>> Per lo qual mai mi si tingesse il volto?
>> I' fui in gloria e poi a terra dei,
>> E or tenpo felice m'à ricolto.
>> Eli è sì dolce in riquistar il tolto
>> Che trar non può più, chè 'l prova guai.[1]

and the *religiosi* a *moralità* before supper,

Udendo il proposto non esser tenpo ancora da cena, per non perder tempo disse: "O religiosi, piaciavi di bella cosa contentar la brigata?" Lor presti disseno:

> Io fui ieri uno, e un altro son oggi,
>> E non so se dimane
>> Sarò quel c'ora, nè a chui vicino.
>> Passare ò aque, selve e aspri poggi
>> Con opere urbi e vane,
>> Venendo per lo mal mortal camino.
>> Non dicha ch'io sia Piero si fui Martino
>> Quel uomo che delle fonti mi trassi,
>> Ma per diversi passi
>> Meno la vita mia al dì sessaio,
>> Torcendo certe vie ond'io già venni;
>> Chè vegio a viza, e senti
>> Men da fallir, ben che si mettan vaio,
>> E cercho honesto nel voler volare.
>> Lasso a chi n'à il dispensar podere.[2]

Ditto la moral cansonetta, l'ora venuta del cenare, e dato l'aqua alle mani, e posti a mensa, cenarono; e sens'altro dire ciaschuno a posar si diede fine alla mattina che levati funno, dove il proposto disse al'altore che una novella dicha fine che gunti serano a Brescia; l'altore prestc disse: "A voi fideli e leali conpangni, li quali non come avari seguite vostra compagnia, ma come fideli sempre state, ad exenplo dirò una novella in questo modo coè":

and the next day on the way to Brescia the author tells a story.

⟨Here appears:

Novella CXXXIII, *De perfetta sosietate* (fols. 216ᵛ–218ᵛ), printed by D'Ancona, *Scelta*, pp. 127–37.

Then follows *Intermezzo* 133–34.⟩

[1] By Soldanieri; see Carducci, *Cantilene*, p. 273.

[2] By Soldanieri; see Florence, Bibl. Laur., MS Redi. 184, fol. 105ᵛ, which indicates that many of our readings are corrupt.

⟨fol. 218ᵛ⟩ La leale compagnia piaque molto alla brigata e con gran At Brescia before supper there is a love song, and the *religiosi* present a *moralità;*
piacere gunsero a Brescia in sul vespro, dove aparechiato era di van-
tagio per la cena; ma perchè era assai buonora, il proposto, volendo
alquanto piacere prima che si cenasse, comandò a' cantatori che una
cansonetta dicessero, li quali presti presti a ubidire dessero che fatto
serà, comincando:

⟨Here follows a love song ("Donna, non spero che 'l morir mi gravi") by
Soldanieri, printed by Carducci, *Cantilene*, p. 273.⟩

Quanto honestamente i cantatori ànno ditto, e non parendo al proposto ancora d'esser a cena disse: "O religiosi, li quali sempre d'ones-
tissime cose e di buone sustanse avete contentato la brigata, ora vi
pregho che d'una ne contentiate fine che a cena n'andremo." Loro
presti dissero:

⟨Here follows a moral song ("L'animo tuo non menimi nè prescha") by
Soldanieri, printed in *Croniche*, II, 311–12.⟩

Ditto la bella moralità, dato l'aqua alle mani, e posti a mensa, cenarono, et per poter la mattina per tenpo levarsi, il proposto licensiò
ognuno che a dormire andasse a così si fe'; e la mattina levati, il the next day on the way to Cremona the author tells a story.
proposto al'altore comandò che una novella dicha fine che gunti
seremo alla città di Cremona; l'altore presto disse: "A voi donne di
pogo sentimento, che sotto spesie di darvi a credere che i vostri
mariti di falli non s'avegano, e a voi matti che simile credensa avete,
se male ve n'aviene l'avete ben comperato, ad exenplo dirò una
novella in questo modo coè":

⟨Here appears:

Novella CXXXIV, *De prava amicisia vel sosietate* (fols. 218ᵛ–220ʳ), printed
by Renier, pp. 338–40. The same story is narrated by Boccaccio, *Decameron*,
IV, 9.

Then follows *Intermezzo* 134–35.⟩

⟨fol. 220ʳ. G⟩unta la brigata a Cremona assai di buonora, piacendo At Cremona before supper the *religiosi* perform,
la terra e 'l sito, il proposto diliberò che prima che si cenasse i religiosi
decessero qualche buona cosa; e pregati, rispuoseno esser presti, e
con dolce melodie disseno:

> Così del mondo e stato alcun ti sida¹
> Come di fogla al vento
> Che lla non volga a um gran soffio lato.
> Fermo del suo, non da me, fermo sfida,
> ⟨fol. 220ᵛ⟩ Se da' a chui il à spanto
> Delle richesse suor in questo stato.
> I' vegho far d'un gran singnor soldato,

¹ sida] *Probably for* fida.

> Così d'un merchadante altrui scrivano,
> Morir subito un sano,
> E spesse volte un povoro arrichire;
> E veggio se un conpra, un altro vende;
> Talor salì che scende,
> E tale scese vegho risalire.
> Tale è forte il batteo c'oggi il trastulla;
> Tal 'eri fe' grande c'oggi non è nulla.[1]

Lo proposto disse: "Per certo a' savi s'apartiene le cose di gran sustansa, et però il bel dire m'è piacuto; ma per dare a' grossi alchuno *and the singers likewise;* piacere comando che i cantatori dicano qualche chansonetta." Loro presti dissero:

> Ciaschun faccia per sè,
> Ch'i' non son più [d'a]ltrui, che altri di me.
> Chara mi gosta [la mia] libertà,
> E la gran fè ch'i' ò portato altrui,
> Però che molto è fuor sì di bontà
> Che 'l tradimento si chiama virtù,
> E io tradito fu'
> Mostrando con amor libera fe'.[2]
> Disposto sono pure a far per me,
> Poi che per ben servire ò rotto il chò;[3]
> E per tradir colui che me trade
> Col'arco teso in man senpre starò,
> E così viverò;
> Volpe con volpe e non con lupo be'.

Intesa la notabile cansonetta de' cantatori non meno piaciuta che quella de' religiosi, essendo l'ora della cena, e dato l'aqua alle mani, e posto a mensa, il proposto colla brigata cenato, licensiò ognuno che *the next day on the* a posare andasse; levati la mattina, comandò al'altore che una novella *way to Mantua the* dicha fine che iunti seranno alla città di Mantova; lui presto a ubidire *author tells a story.* disse: "A voi, li quali da altri fatti sete grandi, e singnori con proferte grandi avete promesse, e poi trovandovi in singnoria ogni proferte ronpete, e per ingratitudine pensate tali del mondo for partire, ad exenplo dirò una novella incomincando in questo modo coè"[4]:

---

[1] By Soldanieri; see *Croniche*, II, 372–73.

[2] At least to this point the poem may be attributed to Soldanieri; see Trucchi, pp. 192–93.

[3] chò] *Meaning* capo.   [4] coè] ite (*? MS*).

⟨Here appear the following:

Novella CXXXV, *De tiranno ingrato* (fols. 220ᵛ–223ʳ), printed by Renier, pp. 341–45.

Intermezzo 135–36 (fols. 223ᵛ–224ʳ), recounting that, at Mantua before supper, the company discusses the conditions in Lucca during its servitude to Pisa, and the *religiosi* present a hunting song. The next day on the way to Bergamo the author tells a story.

Novella CXXXVI, *De summa ingratitudine* (fols. 224ʳ–225ᵛ), printed by Renier, pp. 346–48.

Then follows *Intermezzo* 136–37.⟩

⟨fol. 225ᵛ⟩ Montata[1] la cost[a] e gunta la brigata a Bergamo, aven- do [in]teso la schognoscensa di messer Saulo e sentito la sua[2] fine, il proposto disse: "Di vero altro [non me]ritava." E intrati in l'abergo dove aparechiato era per la cena, essen[do an]cora grande ora del die, parendo al proposto di dovere da' religiosi udire qualche cosa morale, disse loro che la brigata contentasero; loro presti disero: — At Bergamo before supper the *religiosi* recite;

⟨Here follows a moral song ("Più solo un'ora val che tutto quello") by Soldanieri, printed in *Croniche*, II, 373–74.⟩

La bella novella de' religiosi fe' molto lieta la brigata, e venuta l'ora della ⟨fol. 226ʳ⟩ cena, dato l'aqua alle mani, cenaro, e sensa altro dire a dormire si puoseno, e fine alla mattina che, levati si funno e mossi per caminare, il proposto comandò al'altore che una novella dicha fine che gunti saranno a Basciano. L'altore presto disse: "A voi donne malisiose che con uno bello modo vituperando voi e i vostri mariti date a credere loro la luna esser il sole, non pensando che mai tali mariti del fallo acorgere si possano, e però ad exenplo dirò una bella novella incomincando in questo modo coè": — the next day on the way to Barzano the author tells a story.

⟨Here appears:

Novella CXXXVII, *De malitia mulieris adultera* (fols. 226ʳ–227ᵛ), printed by Renier, pp. 349–52. The same story is narrated by Boccaccio, *Decameron*, VII, 2.

Then follows *Intermezzo* 137–38.⟩

⟨fol. 227ᵛ. G⟩unti a Basciamo, avendo come uzati erano desnato a messo il camino, e con piacere in sul vespro si trovonno in uno albergo dove trovonno di molto pescio aparechiato, perch'era vernadì; e perchè non[3] era l'ora della cena, di stormenti volse che li religiosi dices- seno sensa canto qualche cosa morale e di piacere; li quali prestamente disero in questo modo coè: — At Barzano the *religiosi* present a *moralità*, half in Latin, and, it being Friday, the company sups on fish.

---

[1] Montata] Nontata (*MS*); *but a marginal* m *gives the correct reading.*

[2] sua] sia (*MS*).   [3] non] era non, *with* era *crossed out* (*MS*).

Quosienscunque e audieat iustitia
Per l'universo pondo della terra
Indica furore molestia e guerra
E latrocinium surgit cum negligensia.
Duo sunt in celo solistitia,
Ch'ongni creato in vegitar non erra,
E 'l frutto al tenpo dal seme diserra
E sie disposuit creato con letisia.
Così ciaschun singnor che se governa
Severitas in supliciis bene competet,
⟨fol. 228ʳ⟩ Sensa furia misuri e dicerna[1]
Quia si precepta dei male optinet
Aspetti in sè la ruina superna:
Qua nunquam iudicare retto penitet
Yesus Christus iudex mangnus in Iuzafach
Iudicherà ciascun qual avrà fat.

O quanto p[iacque] al proposto e ali altri il bel dire de' religiosi! E sens'altro dire, dato l'aqua alle mani e posti a mensa, cenarono. E dapoi, stato alquanto, n'and[a]rono a dormire; e levati la mattina,[2] il proposto comandò al'altore che una novella dica fine che gunti seremo a Moncia. L'altore presto disse: "A voi homini che in nelle città prendete parti, e colli amici vostri sete fatti magiori, e poi sensa richiesta di quelli che con voi sono stati a cacciare i vostri nimici, tali nimici rimettete e più che ali ofici tali richiederete, e se male alcuna volta ve ne aviene l'avete bene comprato; e pertanto ad exenplo dirò una novella in questo modo coè":

The next day on the way to Monza the author tells a story.

⟨Here appears:
Novella CXXXVIII, De summa et justa venditta de ingrato (fols. 228ʳ–229ᵛ), printed by Renier, pp. 353–56.
Then follows Intermezzo 138–39.⟩

⟨fol. 229ᵛ. L⟩o savio partito di messer Pipino di punire lo 'ngrato consolò molto la brigata, e con quella iunseno a Monca lo sabato, dove volse il proposto che li religiosi dicesseno in canto, o per che modo loro fusse di piacere, qualche bella cosa. Loro presti dissero:

⟨Here follows a moral song ("Leggi se vuoi saper, se non se odi") printed in Croniche, II, 235–36.⟩

L'una cosa doppo l'altra piacuto al proposto e alla brigata, non essendo ancora l'ora della cena, il proposto comandò ai cantarelli che una cansonetta dicesseno; loro presti a ubidire disseno:

At Monza before supper the *religiosi* and the singers perform;

---

[1] dicerna] *Between the* n *and the* a *is a vertical line slightly resembling an* i (*MS*).

[2] *Here the words* l'altore presto disse *were written and crossed out* (*MS*).

Perchè se', donna, in farmi grasia lenta?
Che di vedermi tuo pa[r] si contenta.
Chi à tenpo e tenpo aspetta e' tenpo perde;
E tal perduta mai non si raquista.
Donna, chi non fioriscie in tenpo verde,
Di frutto fare al tenpo perde vista.
Non frutto, ripresension chi 'n ciò l'aquista,
Nel tenpo no li patirà perchè si penta.[1]

⟨fol. 230r⟩ Ditta la piacevole cansonetta, data l'aqua alle mani e cenato, lo proposto disse che ognuno a dormire vada per poter la gornata seguente fare di buonora, e così si fe'. E levati, il proposto disse al'altore che una novella dicha che sia grande acciò che con essa possiamo andare alla ciptà di Milano dove quine faremo uno gorno almeno riposo. L'altore presto disse: "A voi re e singnori che non vastandovi quello che voi avete, con inganno e tradimento l'altrui rubare volete, e se Dio di tal cosa ne mostra il vero non ve ne dovete turbare, ad exenplo dirò una bella novella la quale, posto che sia alquanto lungha, per comandamento del nostro proposto me la conviene dire, la quale in questo modo cominca":

⟨Here appears:
Novella CXXXIX, *De bona et justa fortuna* (fols. 230r–239r), printed by Renier, pp. 357–73.
Then follows *Intermezzo* 139–40.⟩

⟨fol. 239r⟩ Colla lunga e dilettevole novella gunse la brigata a Milano, dove[2] trovarono aparechiato di vantagio; ma perchè non era l'ora della cena, il proposto, volendo alquanto da' cantarelli piacere, comandò loro che una chansonetta dicessero con bello tinore.[3] Loro presti a ubidire dissero:

⟨Here follows a love song ("I' servo e non mi pento, ben che a 'ngrato") by Soldanieri, printed by Carducci, *Cantilene*, pp. 283–84.⟩

Lo proposto piaciutoli la bella cansonetta rivoltòsi a' religiosi dicendo loro: ⟨fol. 239v⟩ "Poi che s'apressima l'ora della cena, vi pregherei che una bella cosetta dicesce, et, ditta, si vada a cena." Loro presti dissero che volentieri lo contenterenno dicendo in questo modo:

⟨Here follows a moral song ("Colui che 'l tutto fe' a ordinato") by Soldanieri; see Florence, Bibl. Laur., MS Redi. 184, fol. 107v.⟩

the next day on the way to Milan the author tells a story.

At Milan the singers and then the religiosi perform, and after supper there is dancing.

[1] By Soldanieri; see Carducci, *Cantilene*, pp. 272–73.

[2] Here dove *was written a second time and then crossed out* (MS).

[3] tinore] *The usual spelling is, of course,* tenore, *and the usual meaning that of the English word* tenor; *here the meaning may be that of* armonia.

Lo chuocho avendo cotte le vivande, se ne venne a proposto dicendo che a taula si ponessero; e' servidori presti, dato l'aqua ale mani, e posti a mensa, cenarono; e dapoi fatto fare una dansa con suoni se n'andarono a dormire. Et la mattina, levati, il proposto disse: "Oggi staremo in Milano, e però ciaschuno vada vedendo la terra e a buonora si torni a desnare." Et cosa s'oservò, e venuto l'ora del dormire desnarono di vantagio, e dapoi andati in uno giardino dove si dansò con istormenti più ore, e poi il proposto comandò al'altore che una novella dicha fine che l'ora della cena serà venuta. L'altore presto disse: "A voi homini che vi sete dati a servire Idio solo per aquistare la gloria di paradizo, e voi mattamente il contrario fate, e a voi donne sinplici e scioche che per ogni picholo pensieri che in nel'animo vi viene sotto inganno sete vituperate, ad exenplo dirò una novella in questo modo":

⟨Here appears:

Novella CXL, De romito adultero et inganno[1] (fols. 239ᵛ–240ᵛ), summarized by Renier, pp. 420–21. The same story is narrated by Boccaccio, *Decameron*, III, 10.

Then follows *Intermezzo* 140–41.⟩

⟨fol. 240ᵛ⟩ Lo proposto, udito lo modo che quel romito trovò ad inganare sè pensando ingannare la iovana, molto li dispiaque, ma ben piaque la sinplicità della iovana che sotto sinplicità sasiò il suo apetito. E fatto sonare li stormenti, e preso alcuna dansa, cenarono, e doppo cena comandò a' cantatori che una cansonetta discessero. Loro presti dissero:

⟨Here follows a love song ("Amor, verso costei l'archo disera") by Soldanieri, printed by Carducci, *Cantilene*, p. 271.⟩

Udito il proposto e la brigata la bella cansonetta, rivoltatosi a' religiosi, dicendo ⟨fol. 241ʳ⟩ che qualche cosa morale dicano fine che l'ora sia d'andare a dormire, loro ubidenti disseno in questo modo:

⟨Here follows a moral song ("Puon Salamone amicho un gran tezoro") by Soldanieri, printed in *Croniche*, II, 388.⟩

Ditta la bella moralità, e l'ora venuta del dormire, ongnuno a posare andò, e fine alla mattina dormiro; e levati, il proposto comandò al'altore che una novella dicha fine che iunti seranno a Como. Lui presto a ubidire disse: "A voi che desiderate udire novità, io raconterò una novella che vi parà più tosto meravigla che altro, e nondimeno ad exenplo di quelle iovane che prima che si maritino si provano con molti, dirò una novella in questo modo coè":

The next day they see Milan, and before supper there is dancing, and the author tells a story.

There is more dancing, and then after supper there is a love song, and the *religiosi* present a *moralità*.

The next day on the way to Como the author tells a story.

---

[1] *inganno*] The last three letters, hidden by a repair to the *MS*, we supply from the list of titles found on fol. 1ᵛ.

⟨Here appears:

Novella CXLI, *De bona ventura* (fols. 241ʳ–245ʳ) printed by Renier, pp. 374–82.

Then follows *Intermezzo* 141–42.⟩

⟨fol. 245ʳ⟩ La dilettevole e bella novella ditta condusse la brigata allegra a Como, dove era da vantagio aparechiato da cena, però che in nel camino aveano deznato; e non parendo al proposto ancora della cena comandò a' cantatori che una cansonetta dicessero; loro per ubidire, fatto reverensa, dissero:

At Como before supper the singers and the religiosi perform, and afterward there is dancing.

⟨Here follows a love song ("De! quando mi farai, donna, contento") by Soldanieri, printed by Carducci, *Cantilene*, p. 274, and Trucchi, p. 196.⟩

Piaciuto il bel dire de' cantarelli, non essendo ancora l'ora della cena, voltatosi a' religiosi dicendo che qualche moralità dicano, loro presti cominconno a dire in questo modo:

⟨Here (fols. 245ʳ–245ᵛ) follows a moral song ("Chi tiene stato al mondo senpre teme") by Soldanieri, printed in *Croniche*, II, 394.⟩

Colla bella moralità fu venuta l'ora della cena, e data l'aqua alle mani, cenarono; e dapoi, dato alquante danse con suoni, se n'andaronno a dormire, dove fine alla mattina si posarono. E levati, il proposto comandò al'altore che una novella dicha fine che a Novara saranno iunti. L'altore, presto a ubidire, disse: "A voi homini gelozi, li quali pensando, stando gelozi, guardare la donna, e loro come malvage ne fanno di peggo, posto che poi del fallo punite siano, ad exenplo dirò una novella in questo modo coè":

The next day on the way to Novara the author tells a story.

⟨Here appears:

Novella CXLII, *De gelozo et mulier malisiosa* (fols. 245ᵛ–246ᵛ), printed by D'Ancona, *Scelta*, pp. 55–61. The same story is narrated by Boccaccio, *Decameron*, VII, 4.

Then follows *Intermezzo* 142–43.⟩

⟨fol. 246ᵛ⟩ Lo casticamento fatto della mala mogle condusse la brigata con piacere a Noara quazi in sul vespro, e perchè le vivande non erano ancora ben cotte il proposto comandò a' cantarelli che una cansonetta si dicha. Loro presti disseno:

At Novara there are presented a love song before supper and a moralità afterward,

⟨Here follows a love song ("Se ali occhi li ochi pietà di costei") by Soldanieri, printed by Carducci, *Cantilene*, p. 291.⟩

Ditta la bella cansona, le vivande preste, e dato l'aqua alle mani, cenarono; e dapoi sensa ballare nè suoni comandò il proposto che a' religiosi pia⟨c⟩esse dire una bella novella. Loro presti disseno:

⟨Here (fols. 246ᵛ–247ʳ) follows a moral song ("Il ciel colle virtù di noi aspetta").⟩

Con quanta la bella moralità è piacuta al proposto, e con questo ciascuno s'andò a posare fine alla mattina che levati furo, dove il proposto
comandò al'altore che una novella dicha fine che iunti seranno alla
ciptà di Pavia. Lui presto a ubidire disse: "A voi singnori e homini
di grande stato, i quali per vostra follia prendete gelozia di vostre
donne, non guardando quanto a tali singnori sea male esser gelozo,
e se alcuna volta di tal gelozia sete ingannati non è da meraviglarsi, e
però ad exenplo dirò una novella fine che iunti saremo a Pavia, città
bellissima, dicendo":

⟨Here appears:
Novella CXLIII, *De placibili furto unius mulieris* (fols. 247ʳ–251ᵛ), printed
by D'Ancona, *Scelta*, pp. 97–118.
Then follows *Intermezzo* 143–44.⟩

⟨fol. 251ᵛ. D⟩el[1] ganno piacevole del tollere la donna al soldano
di Babilonia gelozo ralegrò molto le damigelle della brigata, e con
tale alegressa lo proposto gunse colla brigata salvi a Pavia, dove
trovarono per la cena bene aparechiato; e perchè era assai buonora
lo proposto, postosi a sedere in una dilettevole loggia dell'albergo,
disse a' religiosi che una moralità discesseno, acciò che lo spettare non
faccia rincrescimento alla brigata. Loro presti a ubidire con canti
suoni dessero:

⟨Here follows a moral song ("Colui pover non è che di' ch'à pogo") by
Soldanieri, printed in *Croniche*, II, 374.⟩

Lo proposto sentito il bel dire, voltatosi a' cantarelli dicendo che una
cansonetta cantando dicesero, e ditta si ceni, loro presti con voci
consonanti e alte disseno:

⟨Here follows a love song ("Questa colmor di pietra margarita") by Soldanieri, printed by Carducci, *Cantilene*, pp. 274–75.⟩

Fatto fine al canto e l'aqua data ale mani, le vivande venute e loro a
mensa posti, cenarono; e doppo la cena, alquanto dansato fine al
dormire, che fine alla mᵃttina ognuno posò; e levati e preso pensieri al
caminare, lo proposto disse al'altore che una novella dicha fine gunti
seranno a Vercelli. L'altore presto disse: "A voi homini di bassa
mano, li quali avendo provato l'essere fuora di casa vostra per le
parti e poi col braccio delli amici rimessi e fatti singnori, e voi ingrati
contra di chi è stato cagione di tal dominio, se male di tale ingratitudine v'interviene l'avete meritato; ad exenplo dirò una novella in
questo modo coè":

[1] ⟨D⟩el] *The D has not been illuminated, but is given in the margin. The reading*
El *would have been preferable.*

and the next day on
the way to Pavia
the author tells a
story.

At Pavia before
supper there are
presented a *moralità*
and a love song,

and the next day on
the way to Vercelli
the author tells a
story.

⟨Here appears:

Novella CXLIV, *De massima ingratitudine* (fols. 251ᵛ–254ʳ), printed by Renier, pp. 383–86.

Then follows *Intermezzo* 144–45.⟩

⟨fol. 254ʳ⟩ Lo proposto e li altri, avendo udito sì bella novella, non meraviglandosi dissero: "Per certo la morte di tali singnori è certa, e a ciascuno iustamente diverre."[1] E parlando il proposto a tutti disse: "A noi non è debito di dire per tale anima neuno paternosso, ma intendere a darci piacere. E però dico a voi religiosi, poi che colla ditta novella siamo gunti a Vercelli e ancora non è l'ora della cena, a contentamento di noi voi religiosi dite qualche moralità in canto soave." Loro presti dissero:

At Vercelli before supper there are presented a moralità and a love song,

⟨Here follows a moral song ("Roma fu già del secol la colonna") printed in *Croniche*, II, 208–9.⟩

Chantato la dolce moralità per li sacerdoti, il proposto, volendo più altre udire, rivoltosi a' cantarelli, disse che una cansonetta dicessero, e ditta ognuno si riducha verso la cena; loro per vogla di mangare, fatto reverensa, con canti alti disero:

⟨Here follows a love song ("Sol d'un piccol sospiro l'anima mia") by Soldanieri, printed by Carducci, *Cantilene*, p. 289.⟩

Ditta la cansonetta, e poi cenato, e fine alla mattina di buona vogla dormito, e levati il proposto comandò all'altore che una novella dicha fine che iunti seranno a Allexandria della pagla. L'altore presto disse: "A voi homini e donne che mottegando altrui di disonesta cosa, se ricevete motti dizonesti non vi dovete corucciare, ma cognoscere prima se sol motto che dir vuole li può a lui vergongna tornare, e però ad exenplo dirò una novella in questo modo coè, posto che d'altra parte quazi una simile ne sia contata dicendo":

and the next day on the way to Alessandria the author tells a story.

⟨Here appear the following:

Novella CXLV, *De mocto placibili* (fols. 254ʳ–255ʳ), printed by D'Ancona, *Scelta*, pp. 51–54. The same story is narrated in *Novella* CXXVII and by Boccaccio, *Decameron*, VI, 3.

Intermezzo 145–46 (fols. 255ʳ–255ᵛ), recounting that, at Alessandria before supper, there are refreshments, a *moralità*, dancing, and a love song. The next day, on the way to Tortona, the author tells a story.

Novella CXLVI, *De falsatores* (fols. 255ᵛ–256ᵛ), printed by Renier, pp. 387–88.

Intermezzo 146–47 (fols. 256ᵛ–257ʳ), recounting that, at Tortona before supper, the singers present a *moralità* and the *religiosi* recite and, the next day on the way to Piacenza, the author tells a story.

---

[1] diverre] *Probably for* diverse *or* diversa.

Novella CXLVII, *De justo matrimonio* (fols. 257ʳ–259ʳ), printed by Renier, pp. 389–92. The same story is narrated by Boccaccio, *Decameron*, V, 4. Then follows *Intermezzo* 147–48.⟩

At Piacenza before supper the *religiosi* present a *moralità* and the singers present a love song, ⟨fol. 259ʳ⟩ La piacevole novella della malisia di Iovanna fe' contenta la brigata, e con tale novella si gunse di buonora a Piagensa lo sabato innanti cena. Et posati in una loggia dell'albergo, il proposto disse a' religiosi che una bella cosa dicessero per contentamento della brigata. Loro presti dissero:

Àmi fortuna tanto misso al fondo
    Che per questa cagone
    Non posso [a quest]'andata far riparo;
    Chè chi vuol vivere con ragone al mondo
    De seguitar ragone,
    Che quanto buon più e giuso più è charo.
    Io non vo' in questa andata come avaro,
    Ma perchè più honore mi segue andare
    Che qui com'io sto stare.
    Disprego mia per meglo finir vita
    Chè chi non à e non se ne progaccia
    Non à virtù nè faccia;
    Ond'io per questo fo da lei partita,
    Non curando che[1] morte qui mi privi
    Po' ch'io non seguo lo stil de' gattivi.[2]

Piacuto al proposto il bel dire, per più consolatione della brigata comandò a' cantarelli che una cansonetta dicessero. Loro ubidenti dissero:[3]

⟨fol. 259ᵛ⟩ Amor, tu sai ch'i' fui per te ferito
    Da una donna, e non piansi tanto
    C'un pogho di pietà li desse vanto.
    Ond'io veggendo lei non voler patti
    Di me schanpar, fuggir le forse suoi:
    E or di nuovo un'altra con suoi atti
    Mi vuol far suo com'io di questa fui.
    Dich'io per questo inganno[4] sto tradire
    Che di colei costei abbia apetito:
    Temo e non ne so piglar partito.[5]

---

[1] che] *Inserted above the line (MS).*

[2] By Soldanieri; see Florence, Bibl. Laur., MS Redi. 184, fol. 105ʳ.

[3] At the bottom of fol. 259ʳ are written (and then crossed out) lines 4, 5, and 3 of the song that follows at the top of fol. 259ᵛ.

[4] inganno] ingann'o (*MS*).

[5] By Soldanieri; see Carducci, *Cantilene*, p. 283.

Livro la cansonetta, l'ora della cena venuta, l'aqua dato alle mani e posti a mensa, cenarono; e sens'altro dire se n'andarono a dormir, e fine alla mattina che levati furono si posarono. Il proposto volta- *and the next day on the way to Lodi the author tells a story.* tosi al'altore disse che d'una bella novella contentasse la brigata fine che gunti seranno alla città di Lodi. L'altore presto a ubidire rivoltatosi alla brigata disse: "A voi homini da pogo e pogo intendenti, li quali del vituperio fatto delle donne vostre in nella vostra presensa, multiplicando vergongna, disponete le vostre menti, ad exenplo dirò una novella incomincando in questo modo coè":

⟨Here appear the following:

Novella CXLVIII, *De subito amore acceso in muliere* (fols. 259ᵛ–261ᵛ), printed by Renier, pp. 393–96.

Intermezzo 148–49 (fol. 262ʳ), recounting that, at Lodi, the *religiosi* and the singers perform before supper, and afterwards there is dancing. The next day on the way to Parma the author tells a story.

Novella CXLIX, *De novo ludo* (fols. 262ʳ–264ʳ), summarized by Renier, pp. 421–22.

Intermezzo 149–50 (fols. 264ʳ–264ᵛ), recounting that, at Parma, there are a *moralità* and a love song before supper, and afterward dancing. The next day on the way to Reggio the author tells a story.

Novella CL, *De inganno in amore* (fols. 264ᵛ–266ʳ), printed by Renier, pp. 397–400. The same story is narrated by Boccaccio, *Decameron*, VII, 3.

Intermezzo 150–51 (fols. 266ʳ–266ᵛ), recounting that, at Reggio, there are a *moralità* and a song before supper, and afterward dancing. The next day on the way to Modena the author tells a story.

Novella CLI, *De muliere voluntarosa in libidine* (fols. 266ᵛ–269ʳ), summarized by Renier, pp. 423–24.

Then follows *Intermezzo* 151–52.⟩

⟨fol. 269ʳ. C⟩olla novella di madonna Vessosa gunse la brigata a *At Modena the religiosi present a bisticcio,* Modona assai di buonora; e riduttasi in uno gardino il proposto comandò a' religiosi che qualche cosa di piacere dicessero con bella moralità. Loro presti dissero:

Dapoi ch'io sento sanctus e terribile
   Tra salmi del salterio si saltare,
   I Roma remo non poria voghare,
   La nuova nave ch'è cotanto oribile
   Iocundus homo che ama cum possibile
   Non par che vogla quel voglio quel fare
   Che fuora i ferri che faria trottare,
   In sul trottiero el trattar ch'è 'nvizibile:
   O Nerone, nè rana nè ranochio
   Fu mai in fosso nè in fesso nè in bucho
   Che tu nibbio n'abbi men festucho.

Dapoi che ài aperto la porta dell'ochio
A providensa, provedi anti tratto
Con richo rocho darà schacho matto.
Benchè mon roccho con monarcha si tengna
Non par che vogla quel veglio che vengna.

⟨fol. 269ᵛ⟩ Le cantarelle, udendo il bel bisticcio ditto per li religiosi, chinate le ginochia il proposto, disseno che se lli era[1] in piacere, loro direnno per risposta del ditto alcuna cosa. Lo proposto che vede la volontà delle cantarelle disse ch'era contento; e loro dissero canson ive che stia per cameriera:

and then the singers do likewise; after supper there is dancing.

Se 'l serpente sur ponta ferocibile
  Con prava prova per forsa fersa trare,
  Colli centurion centoriare,
  Che venom cum Venere[2] sì curutibile,
  Paladio paladina transibile
  Che nimbratta cum Nembrot per non fare
  La torre alla terra elli ta ramentare
  Per forsa d'arme si fit fortibile,
  Quel malbrich ne becha de nosochio
  Ma sfalsa e sfelsa e sfilsa col firrucho
  Che più che lonza lenza lanza el verucho
  Se 'l turchio sel torchia col suo fero[chio]
  Vincere, che[3] crede che croda e per mesfatto,
  E perdere per dar vincer misfatto
  Se di sirocho saracho s'inprengna
  Di morte cruda darà dura insegna.

La brigata e 'l proposto udita la dilettevola risposta, lodarono molto tali cantarelle, e venuta l'ora della cena, dato l'aqua alle mani e posti a mensa, cenarono. E dapoi prese alcune danse fine al dormire dansarono, e dapoi levati la mattina da dormire, il proposto voltatosi al'altore che una novella assai lungha dicha fine che gunti seranno ad Asti che un pogo di lungi è al nostro camino; l'altore presto disse: "A voi donne honestissime, le quali per accidente che a voi avengna dal bene ad operare non vi partite, ma ferme al ben fare l'animo vostro sea, io dirò una novella ad exenplo di voi e dell'altre che qui non sono in questo modo coè":

The next day on the way to Asti the author tells a story.

⟨Here appears:
Novella CLII, *De muliere costante* (fols. 269ᵛ–273ᵛ), printed by Renier,

---

[1] era] erano (*MS*), *from which the last two letters have been crossed out.*

[2] Venere] *Possibly* Vinere (*MS*).   [3] che] *Inserted above the line* (*MS*).

pp. 401–8. The same story is narrated by Boccaccio, *Decameron*, X, 10, and by Chaucer, the *Clerk's Tale*.

Then follows *Intermezzo* 152–53.⟩

⟨fol. 273ᵛ⟩ La piacevole novella detta consolò la brigata, non os-
tante che 'l camino fusse assai lungo; non di meno li condusse tal
novella sani ad Asti, dove trovarono ben da cena; e perchè il caldo
avea un pogo le brigate riscaldate, per non mangare sì tosto, volse
che li religiosi dicesseno una melodia; li quali presti disseno:

At Asti before sup-
per the *religiosi* pre-
sent a *moralità;*

⟨Here follows a moral song ("Il senno e lle virtù che sono in noi") printed
in *Croniche*, II, 256.⟩

Ditta la piacevole moralità, per non perder tenpo si dè l'aqua alle mani,
e posti a mensa cenarono; e dapoi sens'altro fare andaro a posare che
bizogno n'aveano; fine ala mattina dormirono; e levati, il proposto
disse al'altore che una novella dicha fine che alla città di Saona seranno
iunti. L'altore presto disse: "A voi donne male honeste, e con vergogna vituperate voi e vostri mariti, e non guardandovi per un bel
modo lo vostro vituperio s'apalesa, ad exenplo dirò una novella in
questo modo coè":

and the next day on
the way to Savona
the author tells a
story.

⟨Here appear the following:

Novella CLIII, *De pauca sapiensia viri contra muliere* (fols. 273ᵛ–275ᵛ),
summarized by Renier, pp. 424–26.

Intermezzo 153–54 (fol. 275ᵛ), recounting that, at Savona, the *religiosi* perform before supper, and afterward there is dancing. The next day on the way
to Genoa the author tells a story.

Novella CLIV, *De falsitate juvini* (fol. 275ᵛ), a fragment, summarized by
Renier, p. 426.

Intermezzo 154–55 (fol. 277ʳ),[1] in a fragmentary form, recounting that, on
the way to Luni, the author tells a story.

Novella CLV, *De pauco sentimento domini* (fols. 277ʳ–277ᵛ), a fragment,
summarized by Renier, pp. 426–27, but printed by G. Sforza, "La Distruzione
di Luni nella leggenda e nella storia," in *Miscellanea di storia italiana*, Terza
Serie, XIX (L of the collection), (1922), 14–15.⟩

[1] After fol. 275ᵛ a folio has been lost and replaced by an unnumbered sheet of
blank paper. The lost folio contained all but the first line of *Novella* CLIV and
the beginning of the present *intermezzo*.

The preparation of this chapter was greatly furthered by a grant to Robert
A. Pratt from the American Council of Learned Societies. This assistance is
gratefully acknowledged by Dr. Pratt and by the general editor.

THE KNIGHT'S TALE

By ROBERT ARMSTRONG PRATT

I

IT HAS, of course, been long established that Chaucer based his *Knight's Tale* primarily on *Il Teseida* of Giovanni Boccaccio.[1] The Italian poet wrote the *Teseida* in 1339–40 toward the close of his long sojourn in Naples and when his liaison with Maria d'Aquino—the Fiammetta to whom he dedicated the poem—seemed to have reached an almost hopeless conclusion. The amatory and psychological content of the *Teseida* was largely autobiographical.[2] The poem was modeled largely on Statius' *Thebaid,* and partly on Virgil's *Aeneid* and, possibly, the *Roman de Thèbes.*[3] Because he knew the *Thebaid* in an annotated manuscript, Boccaccio prepared for the *Teseida* a commentary in the form of explanatory and interpretative notes. These notes are included in Professor Salvatore Battaglia's critical edition of the poem, which is based on the newly discovered autograph collated with other manuscripts. The availability of Battaglia's excellent edition and the expense of reprinting have made it seem inadvisable to reproduce the text in the *Sources and Analogues,* and students are consequently referred to this critical text,[4] the use of which may be facilitated by the summary of the *Teseida* on pages 93–105 below.[5] It may

[1] Source materials of secondary importance are mentioned below on p. 88. A translation of the *Teseida* is in preparation by Professor Margaret Rooke.

[2] Regarding the *Teseida,* see N. Sapegno, *Il Trecento* ("Storia letteraria d'Italia" [rev. ed.; Milan, 1938]), pp. 312–19, 396, n. 30. For a bibliographical introduction to Boccaccio see Sapegno, p. 391; V. Branca, *Linee di una storia della critica al "Decameron" con bibliografia boccaccesca completamente aggiornata* ("Biblioteca della Rassegna," Vol. XXIII [Rome, 1939]), pp. 79–186.

[3] For references to the literary sources of the *Teseida* see F. N. Robinson (ed.), *The Complete Works of Geoffrey Chaucer* (Boston, etc., 1933), p. 771; Sapegno, p. 396, n. 30.

[4] S. Battaglia (ed.), *Giovanni Boccaccio: Teseida* ("Autori classici e documenti di lingua pubblicati dalla R. Accademia della Crusca" [Florence, 1938]).

[5] Among other summaries should be mentioned those of G. Koerting (*Boccaccio's Leben und Werke* [Leipzig, 1880], pp. 593–616) and T. Tyrwhitt (reprinted

be serviceable also to summarize the manuscript problem as presented by Battaglia in his introduction so that the variant readings may be interpreted without excessive reference to that introduction itself.

Until the publication in 1938 of Battaglia's critical edition of the *Teseida*, scholars for over a century relied for a text chiefly on Moutier.[1] By collating and classifying editions and manuscripts of the poem,[2] Battaglia had already completed a critical reconstruction of the text when, in 1928, the Italian government acquired at a sale a manuscript of the *Teseida* which proved to be an autograph and is now in the Laurentian Library at Florence.[3] Aside from the autograph (Aut. Laur.), the texts fall into two distinct families, designated by Battaglia as a and β. Aut. Laur. represents yet a third reading, which at times appears to belong to a, and at others to β.[4] To the relationship of Aut. Laur. to the two families a and β, Battaglia has de-

---

from Tyrwhitt's "Introductory Discourse" by W. W. Skeat, *The Complete Works of Geoffrey Chaucer*, III [2d ed.; Oxford, 1900], 392–94, and by R. D. French, *A Chaucer Handbook* [New York, 1927], pp. 211–14), and that based on Koerting by R. K. Root (*The Poetry of Chaucer* [Boston, etc., 1934], pp. 164–66).

[1] G. Boccaccio, *La Teseide* (*Opere volgari di Giovanni Boccaccio*, ed. I. Moutier, Vol. IX [Florence, 1831]). Battaglia discusses Moutier's edition and lists a number of its variants (pp. xl–xli, lxxiv–lxxviii); although a few of the variants here listed (about 10 out of about 380) occur where Chaucer followed the *Teseida* rather closely, they are slight verbal substitutions which do not alter the sense, and Moutier's text appears to be fairly satisfactory for the study of Chaucer's use of the *Teseida*. Furthermore, this edition is based on two conservative manuscripts of group z (less zz) of family a, the very section to which Chaucer's manuscript appears to have belonged (see below, pp. 85–87).

[2] Battaglia makes use of significant editions and twenty-eight manuscripts, and he lists five other manuscripts; Levi lists six additional manuscripts which Battaglia does not seem to mention. See Battaglia, pp. xi–xlv; C. S. Singleton, reviewing Battaglia, in *Speculum*, XIV (1939), 373–76 (esp. p. 376); E. Levi, "Adriano de' Rossi," *Giornale storico della letteratura italiana*, LV (1910), 201–65 (esp. pp. 239–40). Yet another manuscript of the *Teseida* is in the University of Chicago Library, PQ 4270, f.T4.1430.

[3] The autograph is numbered Doni e Acquisti 325 (see Battaglia, p. xi). A reproduction of this manuscript is in the Library of Congress, Modern Language Association Deposit, No. 311. Regarding the autograph, see Battaglia, pp. xi–xv; G. B. Vandelli, "Un Autografo della *Teseide*," *Studi di filologia italiana*, II (1929), 5–76; here Vandelli showed that the title of the poem is (Il) *Teseida*.

[4] Battaglia, pp. xlvii–lv.

voted careful study, the course and results of which can here be but briefly indicated.[1]

At first, writes Battaglia, one might be inclined to attribute to scribal carelessness or ingenuity those readings of a which disagree with the combined authority of Aut. Laur. and β. But examination of Aut. Laur. reveals that in at least seven such cases the reading of Aut. Laur. and β is, in Aut. Laur., a correction written over an erasure of the reading found in a, all in Boccaccio's own hand.[2] Aut. Laur., then, presents the process of certain slight revisions by Boccaccio and thus tends to give to the readings of a the value of early, original readings, even when they disagree with the combined authority of Aut. Laur. and β.

The relationships of the manuscripts suggest to Battaglia that the three following hypotheses are the most probable.

a) The readiest hypothesis, writes Battaglia, is that both families derive from Aut. Laur., a at an early period, and β later. But this disregards the variants of a, a family with readings which appear authentic even when differing from the combined authority of Aut. Laur. and β; furthermore, the text offered by a (especially in certain manuscripts) shows itself to be extremely conservative and presents readings which have every indication of being genuine.[3]

b) One may suppose that there was an earlier autograph, designated Aut$_1$ by Battaglia (the manuscript destined for Fiammetta, or its twin), from which were descended, first, a;

---

[1] Battaglia, pp. lxxix–cx. The remainder of the present section is intended to serve merely as a bare summary of a detailed analysis which is at once delicate, involved, and controversial. For Battaglia's evidence and reasoning the reader must perforce turn to the introduction itself. The validity of his conclusions is questioned by Germaine Dempster in a review article in *Modern Philology*, Vol. XXXVIII (November, 1940).

[2] E.g., in *Teseida*, VIII, 6, 1, *Pachin* appears in a, and *Appennin* in β, while in Aut. Laur. *Pachin* was first written, and then erased, and replaced by *Appennin*, all in Boccaccio's hand. The reading *Pachin* was a geographical error on the part of Boccaccio, Battaglia writes; but, were it not for the evidence of Aut. Laur., the presence of this error would have been attributed to a copyist, and family a would seem of slight or no authority. For this and further examples see Battaglia, pp. lxxix–lxxxv.

[3] Battaglia, pp. lxxxv–lxxxvii.

and, second, Aut. Laur., from which, after revision and the addition of the commentary, came β.[1]

c) In preparing Aut. Laur., Boccaccio produced at least twenty-three *varianti d'autore*[2] at points where all the manuscripts of α and β are in complete accord with one another and against the authority of Aut. Laur. In other words, it may be that none of the known manuscripts descends from Aut. Laur.; and Aut. Laur. may represent a transcription parallel and probably posterior to those from which descended α and β. In any case, the readings of Aut. Laur. must here and there be corrected.[3]

After offering these various hypotheses, Battaglia then presents his own conclusions. The reading of α, he states, is certainly prior to those of β and Aut. Laur.; and many of the variants of α are authentic. The text of Aut. Laur. appears to be a rapid transcription of the hypothetical and anterior Aut_1, with light and spontaneous verbal modifications. To this text (Aut. Laur.) Boccaccio added the notes, of which no example is found in α; and Aut. Laur. thus came to constitute the redaction which was then reflected in the manuscripts of β. Battaglia has therefore based his critical text on Aut. Laur., making note of the manuscript tradition whenever the autograph appears in error, and presenting the variants of α.[4] The textual variants are presented in footnotes at the bottom of the page, while Boccaccio's notes are printed immediately beneath the text.

II

Chaucer's extensive paraphrasing of the *Teseida* and close translation of portions of it—in the *Knight's Tale* and elsewhere—suggest that it was among his "sixty bokes olde and newe";[5] his use of it, moreover, is sufficient to provide indica-

---

[1] Battaglia, pp. lxxxvii–lxxxviii, where it is pointed out that the notes appear in Aut. Laur. and in some manuscripts of β, but never in those of α.

[2] Regarding these *varianti* see the illuminating review of Battaglia by G. Contini, in *Giornale storico della letteratura italiana*, CXII (1938), 86–96, where it is suggested that most of these represent involuntary scribal distractions rather than true *varianti d'autore*.

[3] Battaglia, pp. lxxxviii–xcix.

[4] Battaglia, pp. c–cxi. [5] See *Legend of Good Women*, G 273.

tions of the nature of his manuscript of the Italian poem and to enable the fitting of his manuscript into the classification determined by Battaglia. Thus the phrase *with water of a welle*[1] suggests that Chaucer's manuscript read *di fontano liquore*[2] rather than *di sovrano liquore* and was therefore unlike MS P_2 of family β.[3] The lines

> Was whilom wyf to kyng Cappaneus
> That starf at Thebes

and

> We losten alle oure housbondes at that toun,
> Whil that the seege theraboute lay[4]

indicate that the couplet

> davanti a Tebe, dove trista sorte
> ciascuno alto baron tolto ha con morte[5]

was not missing from Chaucer's manuscript, as it is from those of group *x*, which constitutes the rest of family β.[6] Thus two slight indications appear to eliminate Chaucer's manuscript from family β.

Family *a* is made up of the two groups *k* and *z*. Three manuscripts of *k* (S, L_2, and R_4) err at a crucial line: the other manuscripts have *e 'l forte arcione li premette 'l petto*,[7] while these three read *e 'l forte Arcita ....*;[8] Chaucer follows the regular tradition.[9] These same three manuscripts lack stanzas which were present in Chaucer's text.[10] Group *k* as a whole is distinguished by the reading *questo gli altri tutti alluminava*, where the rest of the manuscripts have *altari*,[11] and Chaucer: *maden every auter for to brenne*.[12] Group *k* is thus eliminated. Finally, subgroup *zz*

---

[1] *Canterbury Tales*, A 2283.

[2] *Teseida*, VII, 72, 5. [6] Battaglia, p. liii.

[3] Battaglia, p. lii. [7] *Teseida*, IX, 8, 2.

[4] *Canterbury Tales*, A 932–33, 936–37. [8] Battaglia, p. lx.

[5] *Teseida*, II, 29, 7–8. [9] *Canterbury Tales*, A 2691.

[10] These are *Teseida*, V, 93 (see *Canterbury Tales*, A 1821–26) and *Teseida*, VIII, 5 (*see Canterbury Tales*, A 2600); MSS L_2 and R_4 lack *Teseida*, VII, 32–33 (see *Canterbury Tales*, A 1982–98); see Battaglia, p. lxi.

[11] *Teseida*, VII, 59, 4; Battaglia, p. lvii.

[12] *Parliament of Fowls*, 249.

of group *z* lacks five stanzas which seem to have been present in Chaucer's manuscript.[1]

In each of these cases the evidence is extremely slight, for Chaucer's close translation of the *Teseida* is so limited that, when fifty variants distinguish two groups of manuscripts, perhaps only one of these readings can serve to indicate the classification of his manuscript. A slightly different type of testimony is afforded by study of Boccaccio's notes, for there are passages which Chaucer almost certainly would have written differently had the notes been within his reach.[2] This evidence falls in with the conclusion that his manuscript belonged to family *a*, no representative of which has the commentary. Thus we have a series of delicate manifestations which, in their collective entirety, suggest that Chaucer's manuscript was more closely related to group *z* (less *zz*) of family *a* than to any other group or manuscript.[3] This is the most conservative and the largest section and contains ten manuscripts.[4]

III

Chaucer shows indebtedness to the *Teseida* chiefly in four poems, and there are slight verbal echoes elsewhere.[5] Seven stanzas are the source of portions of *Anelida and Arcite;*[6] at least sixteen more were closely imitated in the *Parliament of Fowls;*[7]

---

[1] *Teseida*, VIII, 123–27 (see *Canterbury Tales*, A 2652, 2680–83); Battaglia, p. lxiv; the fragmentary MS M₇ of this subgroup contains none of Book VIII (see Battaglia, p. xxvi).

[2] The evidence that Chaucer did not have Boccaccio's notes is too lengthy for inclusion here; I plan to present it in the near future.

[3] The only variant even tending to present evidence to the contrary is in *Teseida*, VII, 47, 4, where family *β* and Aut. Laur. read *di possedere il disio del mio amore*, and family *a* has *core* instead of *amore* (Battaglia, p. xlix); in *Canterbury Tales*, A 2249–50, Chaucer wrote:

> Youre vertu is so greet in hevene above
> That if yow list, I shal wel have my love.

In my opinion this paraphrase throws no light on the problem.

[4] Battaglia, pp. lxiii–lxvi.

[5] See, e.g., Robinson, pp. 826–30 (*Franklin's Tale*), 955–56, 965–66 (*Legend of Good Women*).

[6] Robinson, pp. 898–99.

[7] Robinson, pp. 902–4. These sixteen stanzas (*Teseida*, VII, 51–66) were translated into English by W. M. Rossetti; see F. J. Furnival, *Trial-Forewords to My*

at least five went into *Troilus and Criseyde*;[1] and the poem as a whole forms the basic material of the *Knight's Tale*, originally entitled *Palamon and Arcite*.[2]

Next in importance to the *Teseida* in the preparation of the *Knight's Tale* was Boccaccio's model and chief literary source, the *Thebaid* of Statius.[3] Chaucer perhaps used also the *Roman de Thèbes*.[4] In addition, he drew upon his knowledge of such other writings as the poetry of Ovid,[5] the *De consolatione philosophiae* of Boethius,[6] the *Speculum majus* of Vincent de Beauvais,[7] the *Roman de la rose* of Guillaume de Lorris and Jean de Meun,[8] and English romances.[9]

Chaucer's treatment of the *Teseida* in the *Knight's Tale* has been the subject of numerous studies, of which only a few need be mentioned here.[10] The problem was simplified in 1907, when Tatlock disposed of the once widely accepted theory of

---

"Parallel-Text Edition of Chaucer's Minor Poems" ("Chaucer Society Publications, Second Series," No. 6 [London, 1871]), pp. 60–66; reprinted by W. W. Skeat, *The Complete Works of Geoffrey Chaucer*, I (2d ed.; Oxford, 1899), 68–73.

[1] Robinson, pp. 923, 928–31, 936, 939, 941, 945–47, 949–51.

[2] See *Legend of Good Women*, F 420 (G 408).

[3] See B. A. Wise, *The Influence of Statius upon Chaucer* (Baltimore, 1911), pp. 46–54, 78–115.

[4] Wise, pp. 127–37.

[5] See E. F. Shannon, *Chaucer and the Roman Poets* (Cambridge, 1929), pp. 302–7.

[6] See B. L. Jefferson, *Chaucer and the Consolation of Philosophy of Boethius* (Princeton, 1917), pp. 130–32, 142–43.

[7] See P. Aiken, "Arcite's Illness and Vincent of Beauvais," *PMLA*, LI (1936), 361–69.

[8] See D. S. Fansler, *Chaucer and the Roman de la rose* (New York, 1914), *passim* (see p. 257 for an index of the references to the *Knight's Tale*).

[9] See R. M. Smith, "Three Notes on the *Knight's Tale*," *MLN*, LI (1936), 320–22; see also S. Robertson, "Old English Verse in Chaucer," *MLN*, XLIII (1928), 234–36.

[10] For further references see E. P. Hammond, *Chaucer: A Bibliographical Manual* (New York, 1908), pp. 270–74; D. D. Griffith, *A Bibliography of Chaucer: 1908–1924* (Seattle, 1926), pp. 75–80; W. E. Martin, Jr., *A Chaucer Bibliography: 1925–1933* (Durham, 1935), pp. 52–53; J. E. Wells, *A Manual of the Writings in Middle English* (New Haven, 1916), pp. 692–94, 877, and the seven *Supplements*; in these bibliographies reference is made to reviews and criticisms of the books and articles mentioned below.

a stanzaic *Palamon and Arcite*,[1] so that this poem and the *Knight's Tale* may now be considered as essentially the same.[2] Tatlock finds reason to believe that Chaucer treated his material in a light and satirical tone. Both Tatlock and Fairchild point out that in the *Teseida* Palemone and Arcita are hardly distinguished and show how Chaucer differentiates between them.[3] Fairchild's conclusion that Arcite is supposed to represent a type of the active and Palamon of the contemplative life is not so easy to accept as his analysis of the two characters. On the other hand, Hulbert feels that Palamon and Arcite are without individuality and that Chaucer's aim was to present a question of love regarding two equal rivals.[4] Robertson points out that, whereas the actual translations from the *Teseida* consist chiefly of such things as descriptions, speeches, and prayers, most of Chaucer's important changes are in the direction of realism.[5] Cummings discusses many of Chaucer's additions, omissions, and changes and points out that in the process of condensation Chaucer disregarded many elements of pseudo-classicism in Boccaccio's epic and inserted many concrete elements of feudal realism, thus giving the tale a new and English atmosphere.[6] Curry shows how, in paraphrasing the *Teseida*, Chaucer discarded ancient mythological machinery and substituted as motivating forces Boethian destiny and the planetary influences of medieval astrology.[7] Other useful discussions

[1] See J. S. P. Tatlock, *The Development and Chronology of Chaucer's Works* ("Chaucer Society Publications, Second Series," No. 37 [London, 1907]), pp. 45–66, where sufficient references are given for the stanzaic theory.

[2] Tatlock, pp. 66–70; W. J. Wager, "The So-called Prologue to the *Knight's Tale*," *MLN*, L (1935), 296–307.

[3] See Tatlock, pp. 231–33; another comment on Chaucer's treatment of the *Teseida* is on p. 67, n. 2; H. N. Fairchild, "Active Arcite, Contemplative Palamon," *JEGP*, XXVI (1927), 285–93.

[4] See J. R. Hulbert, "What Was Chaucer's Aim in the *Knight's Tale?*," *SP*, XXVI (1929), 375–85.

[5] See S. Robertson, "Elements of Realism in the *Knight's Tale*," *JEGP*, XIV (1915), 226–55.

[6] See H. M. Cummings, *The Indebtedness of Chaucer's Works to the Italian Works of Boccaccio* ("University of Cincinnati Studies," Vol. X, Part II [Cincinnati, 1916]), pp. 123–46.

[7] See W. C. Curry, *Chaucer and the Mediaeval Sciences* (New York, 1926), pp. 119–63.

of the two poems are presented by Kissner,[1] Clerke (with verse translations of twenty-seven significant stanzas of the *Teseida*),[2] Mather (with parallel summaries),[3] Patch (who finds Chaucer's treatment humorous rather than romantic),[4] Torraca (who finds Chaucer has not done very well),[5] and Looten.[6]

Several scholars have prepared tables of correspondences between the *Knight's Tale* and the *Teseida*. H. L. Ward presented marginal references to the *Knight's Tale*, indicating 272 lines translated from the *Teseida*, 379 showing a general likeness, and 131 showing a slight likeness to passages in the Italian poem.[7] Skeat prepared a brief table of general correspondences,[8] and Mather printed parallel summaries of the two poems.[9] Tatlock prepared a table of parallels, adding a few lines to those indicated by Ward.[10] Cummings listed the further borrowing of episodes and has shown that Chaucer used the materials of the *Teseida* in from seven hundred to

---

[1] See A. Kissner, *Chaucer in seinen Beziehungen zur italienischen Litteratur* (Marburg, 1867), pp. 58–66.

[2] See E. M. Clerke, "Chaucer and Boccaccio," *National Review*, VIII (1886), 379–91.

[3] See J. M. Mather (ed.), *The Prologue, the Knight's Tale, and the Nun's Priest's Tale from Chaucer's Canterbury Tales* (Boston, etc., 1899), pp. lxi–lxxiii.

[4] See H. R. Patch, "Chaucer and Mediaeval Romance," in *Essays in Memory of Barrett Wendell* (Cambridge, 1926), pp. 95–108; this essay is reprinted with slight changes and additions in H. R. Patch, *On Rereading Chaucer* (Cambridge, 1939), pp. 195–212.

[5] See either F. Torraca, "The *Knightes Tale* e la *Teseide*," *Atti della reale Accademia di Archeologia, Lettere e Belle arti*, X (new ser.; 1928), 199–217; or F. Torraca, *Scritti vari* (Milan, etc., 1928), pp. 89–107.

[6] See [C.] Looten, *Chaucer, ses modèles, ses sources, sa religion* ("Mémoires et travaux publiés par des professeurs des facultés catholiques de Lille," *Fasc.* XXXVIII [Lille, 1931]), pp. 55–72, 148–51.

[7] See either F. J. Furnival (ed.), *The Cambridge MS of Chaucer's Canterbury Tales*, Part I ("Chaucer Society Publications, First Series," No. 4 [London, 1868]), pp. 25–88; or F. J. Furnival (ed.), *The Lansdowne MS of Chaucer's Canterbury Tales*, Part I ("Chaucer Society Publications, First Series," No. 7 [London, 1868]), pp. 25–88.

[8] See W. W. Skeat (ed.), *The Complete Works of Geoffrey Chaucer*, V (2d ed.; Oxford, 1900), 60; this table was reprinted, with a slight addition, by Robinson, p. 771.

[9] See Mather, pp. lxii–lxix.   [10] See Tatlock, pp. 226–30.

eight hundred more lines than those previously noted.[1] Skeat's
table as modified by Robinson is reprinted below and is followed by a new table of the chief verbal correspondences between Chaucer's works and the *Teseida*, with the closest resemblances indicated by italics. These tables, together with the
summary in English, which appears immediately after them,
should facilitate a general comprehension of Chaucer's treatment
of the *Teseida* and serve as an introduction to the critical text
provided by Battaglia.

A TABLE OF GENERAL CORRESPONDENCES BETWEEN THE *KNIGHT'S TALE* AND THE *TESEIDA*[2]

Knight's Tale	Teseida
865– 883	I and II
893–1027	II, 2–5, 25–95
1030–1274	III, 1–11, 14–20, 47, 51–54, 75
1361–1448	IV, 26–29, 59
1451–1479	V, 1–3, 24–27, 33
1545–1565	IV, 13, 14, 31, 85, 84, 17, 82
1638–1641	VII, 106, 119
1668–1739	V, 77–91
1812–1860	V, 92–98
1887–2022	VII, 108–10, 50–64, 29–37
2102–2206	VI, 71, 14–22, 65–70, 8
2222–2593	VII, 43–49, 68–93, 23–41, 67, 95–99, 7–13, 131, 132, 14, 100–102, 113–18, 19
2275–2360	VII, 71–92
2600–2683	VIII, 2–131
2684–2734	IX, 4–61
2735–2739	XII, 80, 83
2743–2808	X, 12–112
2809–2962	XI, 1–67
2967–3102	XII, 3–19, 69–83

[1] See Cummings, pp. 131–34.   [2] From Robinson, p. 771.

A TABLE OF THE CHIEF VERBAL CORRESPONDENCES BETWEEN CHAUCER'S WORKS AND THE *TESEIDA*[1]

Teseida		Chaucer's Works	Teseida		Chaucer's Works
I	1–3	AA 1–21	VII	74–77	2290–99
				79–81	2297–2313
II	1	TC v 8–11		84–85	2317–25
	10–12	AA 50–66		88–93	2331–65
	22	AA 36–40		94	*TC v 274–78*
	25–31	898–947		96–100	2506–31
	50	965–67		99	2202–5
	85–89	1005–24		106	1638–46
	95–98	1027–32		108–10	1887–94
III	5	TC ii 50–56		113	2571–75
	8–11	1040–76		114	2581–83
	12	F 1016–17		119	1641–42
IV	37–38	1391–92; 1402–7	VIII	124–26	2680–83
	43	F 1031–37	IX	1	TC v 1
	60–63	F 925–43		7–8	2686–91
	82	1563–68		48–49	2694–97
	84–85	1553–58	X	55	2765–66
V	13	1624–26; F 764–66		102, 104	2771–76
	77	1668–78		112–13	*2799–2808*
	83	1708–11	XI	1–3	*TC v 1808–27*
	95–98	1829–60		6	*2809*
VI	21–22, 36	2130–42		7–11	2827–52
	65	2182–83; 2190–94		13–16	*2853–80*
	69–70	2195–2203		18–19	2913–16
VII	12	2543–47; 2559		20–29	2915–38
	14	2560–64		30–31	*2881–86*
	19	2587–93		35	2889–96
	23–28	2371–2417		37	2907–8
	29–37	1971–2022		38	2899–2900
	39–41	2423–35		40	2905–6; 2910–12
	43	*2219–24*		51, 53–55	2949–55
	45–49	*2227–58*		90	TC v 311–12
	50	1936–37	XII	3	2967–69
	51–60	*PF 183–259*		4–5	*2975–86*
	55–57	*1925–29*		6	*2843–46*
	61–62	*PF 281–89*		7–12	3017–56
	63–66	*PF 260–76*		19	3068–70
	67	*2438–41*; 2445–46		80	2735–36
	71–72	2275–83		83	2739; 3101–2

[1] The letters "AA" indicate lines in *Anelida and Arcite;* "F," *Canterbury Tales,* V(F), or the *Franklin's Tale;* "PF," *Parliament of Fowls;* and "TC," *Troilus and Criseyde.* Numbers without letters indicate lines in *Canterbury Tales,* A, or the *Knight's Tale.* The closest resemblances are indicated by italics.

A SUMMARY IN ENGLISH OF THE *TESEIDA*

TO FIAMMETTA

O cruel lady, your unjust disdain cannot extinguish the flame your beauty has kindled in my soul. Nor do I tire of faithful service. Therefore, I have reduced an ancient story to *latino volgare* and rhyme. In it you will discern things done by you and me, and stories, fables, and hidden meanings. The argument. Discerning my affection, you can turn my misery back into happiness. I pray Love that he rekindle in you the spent flame and restore you to me.

SONNET

The general argument of the whole book.

BOOK I

Argument.

(1) O Castalian sisters that in the mount Helicon dwell content, about the sacred Gorgonian fount, under the shade of the fronds loved by Phoebus, hear my prayers. (2) I wish to write in rhyme an ancient story, so hidden in time that no Latin author tells it; make my labor pleasing. (3) Be present, O rubicund Mars, severe and ferocious in thine arms, and thou, mother of Love. (4) And you, who I hope will see this, be attentive.

(6) When Egeo was king of Athens, there were women in Scythia who would not be subjugated by their men. (7) They killed their males (8) and elected Ipolita queen. (10) Men who came there and would not leave were killed. (13) Teseo proposed to purge such a sin. (18) With a band of men (20) he sailed. (21) Ipolita (22) addressed her council: (26) "Teseo comes; (28) oppose him (33) boldly." (37) She armed her country. (41) Teseo arrived (44) and attempted to treat with her, (45) but in vain. (49) Teseo and his men (51) were prevented from landing. (57) Teseo cried: (58) "O cruel Mars, O despitous god, I shall win without thee!" (61) Then to his men: "Do women make you flee? (64) May he who is worthy take up arms." (66) He landed, (67) the Greeks behind him. (73) After long fighting, (76) Teseo won the shore (80) and encamped. (85) Ipolita prepared. (91) Teseo besieged her (94) many months, (95) and finally undermined the wall.

(96) Ipolita sent Teseo a letter: (102) "I know not why thou besiegest me; (107) cease, or I will drive thee away!" (108) Teseo replied: (110) "We avenge villainy; (111) surrender, or die!" (113) To the messengers he said, "I should be sorry to treat your queen roughly." (115) Ipolita, having heard, said: (118) "We must choose; (121)

I think it better to surrender." (124) A pact was made that she be Teseo's bride. (125) Ipolita was beautiful and young. (128) Teseo was met by Ipolita and her dear little sister, Emilia. (134) Teseo wedded Ipolita. (136) He noticed the beauty of Emilia (137) and planned to wed her to his kinsman Acate.

BOOK II

Argument.

(1) Two years after the Greeks had left Athens, (2) in a vision (3) Teseo (4) was addressed by Peritoo: "Why dost thou dally in Scythia?" (9) With Ipolita and Emilia he set sail for Athens.

(10) Mars had aroused the Greeks against the Thebans, (11) and had caused great slaughter at Thebes, (12) which was soon seized by Creonte. (13) He, hating the Greeks, prohibited the burning or burial of any of their bodies; (14) whence the Greek women proposed to pray Teseo to avenge such injury. (15) At Athens (17) they waited in the temple of Clemency.

(18) Teseo returned toward Athens. (19) The Athenians had prepared festivities, (21) a rich triumphal car, and a crown of laurel. (22) Teseo mounted the car with Ipolita and Emilia, (23) entered the city, (25) and came to the throng of weeping women. (26) "Who are these?" (28) Evannes said, "Each of us was a king's wife or mother or sister or daughter. (29) Each great noble died before Thebes. (30) We must bury them. (31) Creonte denies burial to the Greek bodies; they are eaten by animals. (33) Be pitiful." (36) Teseo, touched, (39) swore to defeat Creonte. (42) [Ipolita] and Emilia dismounted from the car, (43) and Teseo addressed his men: (47) "Let us humble Creonte."

(49) He left Athens. (50) The ensigns were raised, and the knights followed the disconsolate women to Thebes. (51) He challenged Creonte (53) and the armies came together in a field. (54) They fought. (58) Teseo encountered Creonte, (60) unhorsed him, (61) and said: "Now thou shalt be punished." (64) Creonte defied him (66) and died. (70) The enemy fled to the mountains. (72) Teseo entered Thebes (73) and gave his people license to pillage. (74) Teseo performed exequies for Creonte (76) and told the Greek women to do likewise for their kings. (79) With many plaints they collected the bodies, (81) burned them, (82) thanked Teseo, (83) and took home the ashes.

(85) While the Greeks ransacked the field, they found two wounded youths; (86) they lay not far apart; their shining arms and haughty mien showed them to be royal. (87) The Greeks carried them in their arms to Teseo, (88) who learned they were of the blood of Cad-

mo (89) and had them cured and imprisoned. (90) Teseo returned to Athens with his men (91) and entered in a triumphal car, (92) before which went Arcita and Palemone. (93) Ipolita and Emilia greeted him. (94) In the temple of Mars (95) he offered the leaves of Peneis from his brow, (96) and then returned to the palace. (97) After several days he summoned Palemone and Arcita (98) and condemned them to eternal imprisonment. (99) They were held in a room in the palace, and served according to their pleasure, so as to make them comfortable because they were of royal blood.

BOOK III

Argument.

(1) Cupid invoked.

(3) The two imprisoned Thebans (4) were given by Venus a new occasion for further sighing. (5) [Between mid-April and mid-May], (7) the season of love, (8) Emilia at dawn, in a garden near her chamber, sang love songs. (10) One morning (11) Arcita opened a little window, (12) saw her, (13) and exclaimed, "Palemone, come to see Venus!" (14) Palemone, seeing her, said, "Surely this is Cytheraea!" (16) "In her eyes I see [Cupid], (17) and he has wounded me." "And me also!" (18) Hearing Palemone, Emilia looked at the window and then retired. (20) The two lovers complained, (26) wondered whether she were goddess or woman, (27) and sighed violently. (28) Whenever Emilia was in the garden, she furtively watched the window, (29) and sang delightfully if she saw them, (30) not for love but for vanity of her beauty. (31) Every morning they watched and fell more in love. (34) They slept and ate but little, (35) wept, (36) forgot everything except Emilia, (38) wrote songs, (40) and finally learned her identity. (43) [In the autumn] (44) Emilia no longer came into the garden, (45) and the two lovers were desperate.

(47) Teseo mentioned the prisoners to his noble visitor, Peritoo, (48) who thereupon asked to see them. (49) Palemone was strong-limbed, somewhat dark, clever in speech, subtle, solemn in movement, and bold. (50) Arcita was rather slender, blond, open in speech, active, and agile. (51) Peritoo knew Arcita (52) and said to Teseo, "Please release him." (53) "Certainly, but he must never return to my kingdom, (54) on pain of losing his head." (55) Arcita, released, thanked Peritoo (56) and Teseo. (58) Arcita received gifts from Teseo (59) and sadly left the palace. (60) Palemone was miserable. (61–68) Peritoo vainly tried to comfort Arcita, who longed to remain in Athens. (69–72) Arcita tried to find comfort for himself in his release from prison, (73) and then took leave of Peritoo. (74) Arcita

found Palemone and said, (75–76) "You will see her in the spring, but I cannot hope to." (77) "I shall be sad without you, (78) but you can travel about and alleviate your pain." (80) They wept together (81) and embraced, and Arcita departed. (82) He mounted his horse and prayed for a glimpse of Emilia. (83) She appeared on a balcony. (84) He saw her (85) and sadly rode from Athens.

BOOK IV

Argument.

(1) [In October] (2) Arcita left Athens for Boetia (3) with his retinue, calling himself Penteo. (5) He lamented his unhappy condition, (12) and finally came to Thebes, (13) whose destruction he lamented. (18) He went to Corinth, and then to Messenia, where he served Menelao. (19) His hardships had disguised his features. (20)· After about a year he went to Aegina, (21) where he hoped to hear news of Emilia. (22) He served [Pelleo] as a low servant (23) and often lamented, (26) sighed, and wept in his unhappiness. (27) His appearance (29) and voice became horribly changed. (31) He felt that his end was near. (33) A small vessel arrived from Athens, and he was invited to go there in it. (34) Penteo inquired of Emilia. (35) "No goddess is more lovely; recently, alas, her fiancé, Acate, died." (36) His ardent desire determined Penteo (37) to return to Athens. (38) "I am so changed that I can serve Teseo without being recognized. (39) Even if I were, death were kinder than this everlasting languishment." (40) He came to Athens as a poor servant; (42) in the temple of Apollo he prayed (47) that he might not be recognized; (48) he knew by a sign that his prayer was granted. (49) He was received into the service of Teseo, (50) and became stronger. (51) Teseo gave a feast, at which Emilia was the most beautiful. (52) Penteo rejoiced: "Nothing can harm me now, (53) for I see her who is my delight!" (56) Emilia had not yet felt love; she alone recognized Arcita, (57) and she said to herself, "What is he doing here?" (58) She pretended that she had never seen him before. (59) Penteo served Teseo so well that [Teseo] loved him more than any other servant. (60) Although he loved fervently, Penteo ever kept his desire hidden. (61) At times he looked intently at Emilia, and she pretended not to know she was loved.

(63) To hide his desire, he used to go alone to sleep in a grove (64) about three miles from the city. (66) There he would complain to Love; (72) and in the midst of his torments he would fall asleep. (74) In the morning (75) he would pray Phoebus and Venus to encourage Emilia to love him. (78) Such prayers he would sing and then

return to Athens. (79) One morning he thus lamented: (80) "O wretched Fortune! (82) Teseo imprisoned me; then love entered my heart, (83) and then Peritoo caused me to be driven from prison. (84) In lowly disguise, Penteo being transformed from Arcita, (85) I have madly returned as a servant, for Emilia's beauty has routed my fear of Teseo." (89) While Penteo thus blasphemed his fortune one morning, Panfilo, one of Palemone's servants, chanced to pass that way and hear him. (90) He marveled greatly and returned to tell Palemone. (91) But Penteo, ignorant of this, returned joyfully to Athens.

BOOK V

Argument.

(1) Palemone remained in prison, (2) fearing that Arcita might be out of prison through Emilia's solicitation. (5) Panfilo informed Palemone that Penteo was Arcita. (6) "I don't believe it." "He is in the grove, and greatly changed." (14) "I would leave prison and conquer Emilia by arms." (20) "There came here recently Alimeto, the Theban physician, wise and trustworthy. (21) You will feign sickness, and I shall bring him to you; he will put on my garments, you his. (22) You will leave me in your place and say I am resting. You will find Arcita in the grove." (23) The preparations were made, (24) and Panfilo intoxicated the guards with wine. (25) They changed clothing, and Palemone left prison with Alimeto, (26) telling the guards to leave the prisoner alone all night.

(27) Palemone slept at the inn, and in the morning armed himself, (28) went toward the grove where Arcita slept, (33) and found him. (35) "This is certainly he, nor can his beard conceal him. (36) O praiseworthy friend, we shall soon end our rivalry." (37) The birds began to sing, and Penteo, awaking, turned to Palemone. "Knight, what are you seeking in this wood, all armed?" (38) "Thee." Penteo recognized him. (39) Palemone said, "I love Emilia (40) and so dost thou, but we cannot both have her; consent that she be mine." (42) "Concede her to Arcita, thy kinsman." (43) "We shall settle our difference with swords." (45) Penteo tried to suggest other possible courses, (54) but Palemone was insistent: "Prepare, for I believe I shall win." (55) "Alas, I feel the wrath of the gods. (56) We shall have an inglorious end like our predecessors: (59) it remains for us, the last of Theban blood, to kill each other." (61) Quickly Penteo armed himself. (65) They charged fiercely; (66) Arcita struck Palemone, (67) who lay as dead. (69) He removed Palemone's helmet, bathed his face, (70) and wept: "My valorous companion is dead; I never desired the battle. Why did I ever love?" (72) At this,

Palemone arose, having been only stunned: (73) "I am not yet vanquished; expect no pardon because of thy pity." (75) With prayers to Mars, Venus, and Emilia, they charged like dragons (76) and fought long, neither having the advantage.

(77) Teseo and Emilia entered the grove with a company; (78) they went here and there, hunting, and Emilia came to where the battle was. (80) Recognizing her, they fought more fiercely. (81) She summoned Teseo, (82) who watched the fighters, and then rode up to them: (83) "Tell me who you are and why you fight so." (84) They drew apart, and Penteo replied, "We are knights who try our valor for love." (85) Teseo said: "Tell who you are." "If you promise us your peace." "You have it, for you are so valorous." (86) "I am Penteo." (87) "I am your Palemone." (88) "Tell me how you both fell in love, (89) and with whom." Palemone told how things had happened. (92) "I often committed folly for love; my great pity pardons you (93) on condition that you promise to do as I say." They promised faithfully. (94) "I intended to give the maiden you love as bride to our cousin Acate, but he died. (95) I could not give her better than to one of you, but both of you cannot have her. (97) You shall settle the question by arms, each with one hundred chosen companions, in our theater. (98) He who drives out the other party shall be her husband; the other shall obey her judgment. The term shall be an entire year." Thus it was confirmed. (105) Teseo took them to the palace.

BOOK VI

Argument.

(1) The effects on the two Thebans of Fortune, (5) whose mutations are not to be foreseen. (6) They lived in friendship, (7) spent freely, and were popular. (8) They entertained lavishly, and had goshawks, falcons, and hounds. (9) They were full of largess, held jousts, and tried to please Emilia. (10) Each intended to win or die. (11) Each invited friends (12) and made preparations.

(13) The day approached, and each asked his men to come. (14) Ligurgo came to aid Arcita. (15) Pelleo came, (16) dressed in gold cloth, with many stones; (17) his saddle was of gold, (18) and he was greatly admired. (19) Many nobles accompanied him so as to win honor. (20) Niso came. (21) On a car drawn by four great bulls came Agamenone, with a black beard, and large and strong-limbed. (22) He did not wear gold or stones, but the skin of a bear. (23) Behind him came Menelao; (25) Castore and Polluce followed him. (27) Cromis came, wearing the skin of a lion, (29) and Ippodomo, (30) and Nestore, son of Neleo, (32) richly armed. (35) Evandro came (36)

with the skin of a bear whose nails were covered with shining gold, (38) and with an elaborate shield. (41) Peritoo came, crowned with leaves of laurel, (44) [Ulisse] came, and Diomede, (45) Pigmaleone, and Sicceo; (46) [Minos], (47) Radamante, and Sarpedone; (51) Anchelado, (52) and Ida; (55) and Ameto—all with much company. (58) Many others came also (64) to acquire fame and honor through valor; (65) all were received with the highest and most joyful honors. (67) Nor were Arcita and Palemone considered foolish for striving for such a treasure. (70) There was feasting. (71) Never had such great nobility been gathered there.

BOOK VII

Argument.

(1) The appointed day approached, and Teseo took the nobles (2) and the people to the theater and addressed them: (3) "Everyone knows of the question between the Thebans and of my arrangement. (4) I planned only a palestral game; (5) I did not expect all Greece to come out for so little a thing. (8) This battle ought to savor of love, not hate. (11) A hundred are to be named for each side. (12) The winner will have the lady and the glory." (15) To Arcita (16) came various men, (17) and others to Palemone. (18) The men of each chose their best followers so as to be a hundred. (20) Teseo led them back through the city.

(22) The day before the battle Palemone and Arcita prayed to the gods. (23) Arcita prayed in the temples of Mars: (24) "O strong god, (26) without thee I am little powerful. (27) If I win, I shall have the delight and thou the honor. (28) Thy temples shall be adorned." (29) The Orison of Arcita saw the house of Mars, (30) in the cold Thracian fields, (32) all of polished steel. (33) And she saw Ire, Fear, (34) Treasons, (35) and Death. (36) The temple was all ornamented with histories of plunder and the like. (38) Mars heard the Orison, (39) the temples heard their god, (40) and signs were given to Arcita that his Orison was heard.

(42) Palemone prayed to Cytheraea: (43) "O beautiful goddess, (45) only thou canst turn my suffering into delight. (46) I do not ask thee for victory; I seek only Emilia. (48) Thy temples shall always be honored by me." (50) The Orison of Palemone went to the temple of Cytheraea on Mount Cithaeron (51) and saw a pleasant garden (54) wherein were Cupid, Pleasure, (55) and many others. (59) She entered the temple, (62) decorated with the histories of lovers, (63) and was told that Venus was in the most secret part, (64) where she saw her lying nude on a bed. (66) The prayer was

granted. (67) A new strife arose in heaven between Venus and Mars; but they found a way to content both prayers. (68) Palemone remained in prayer.

(70) Emilia prayed to Diana, (72) in whose temple (75) she kindled two fires. (79) "O chaste goddess, (81) I am a virgin of thy troops, more apt to hunt in the woods than to please a husband with love. (82) Quench the desire of the lovers; (85) but if I must have one, let it be he who desires me more. (86) Tell me which by these flames." (88) The company of Diana appeared and said: (89) "It is decided among the gods, but hidden a little from you." (90) The arrows of Diana's quiver sounded, and Emilia understood that her prayers were worthy. (91) One fire went out and then relighted itself; (92) the other looked like blood and went out.

(94) Morning came; (96) in the palace were many people; (100) Teseo magnificently appeared; (101) and the two Thebans, greeted by shouts. (102) Teseo took them to the temple of Mars for sacrifices. (104) Each took his men to the theater. (108) The circular theater, a mile around, with a marble wall, had two entrances with well-wrought gates; (110) more than five hundred stone tiers arose, where people sat to watch without hindering one another. (111) Egeo and Teseo came first, (112) and the Greeks, all disarmed, and the Thebans; (113) last came Ipolita and Emilia. (114) Arcita, with his men, entered from the east; (118) Palemone entered from the other direction. (122) Arcita saw Emilia and said to himself: (125) "Disdain not my love." (128) Palemone said almost the same thing. The first call of the battle sounded; (130) Teseo arose (131) and said: "Those of you who are taken will leave their arms. (132) He who is victorious shall have the lady." (133) Teseo made the second call, Arcita encouraged his men, (145) and Palemone did likewise.

BOOK VIII

Argument.

(1) The third call sounded. (6) The two bands came together, swifter than floods, (8) and were repelled by equal blows. (11) Palemone and Arcita charged. (18) The various nobles fought (20) and wounded one another. (21) Arcita encountered Almeone; Palemone met Polluce (22) and was rescued by Ulisse, who was taken. (26) Diomede (27) fought fiercely (30) but was taken. (31) After furious fighting (37) Minos was taken. (38) Evandro and Sicceo fought (40) and were so bruised (45) that their men carried them off. (46) Pelleo was stunned (47) and carried from the theater. (51) Ameto (52) wounded many; (53) Arcita attacked him; (54) together with their men they

had a fierce battle. (58) Ida attempted to take Arcita, (62) but after a struggle (65) Arcita's men captured Ida. (66) Seeing this, Ameto attacked Arcita's standard bearer, (67) whom Ligurgo guarded; (72) many were wounded. (78) Arcita rested a little; (79) a glimpse of Emilia restored him; (81) he terrified all. (85) He did marvels; Palemone did likewise. (87) The field was wet with blood. (89) Teseo watched (90) the actions of the combatants; (92) the captured fighters were with him.

(93) Ipolita watched and wished to fight. (94) Emilia watched (96) and said to herself: (99) "The souls of the dead combatants will haunt me. (101) What a hard lot love brings to me, who never burned with desire! (104) Of all women only I am sought by the energy of many. (105) Each is so beautiful and noble that I do not know which I would choose. (108) Oh, that Teseo had let them fight alone in the grove! (109) Thus, Love, hast thou done."

(111) The combatants were perplexed and tired. (112) Mars, (113) in the form of Teseo, said to Arcita: "What cowardice stops you?" (114) Arcita, inflamed, (115) fought courageously; (116) the battle became fiercer than ever. (120) The stallion of Cromis bit Palemone's arm so that he fell; (122) he was disarmed by Arcita. (123) Whether Palemone was then full of grief, each may decide. (124) Emilia's heart turned to Arcita, and no longer cared for Palemone. (125) Each man beware of falling: he who was loved before is now abandoned. (126) Now Emilia admires Arcita, whereas before they had appeared equal to her. (127) Already she considers herself wed to Arcita. (129) Palemone, taken, vainly cried: "Hold the field!" (130) Arcita, aroused, circled the field (131) with his men in joy.

BOOK IX

Argument.

(2) As they watched, Venus said to Mars: "Thy part is finished." (3) "Do as thou wilt." (4) She directed Erinis, (7) who, horrible, went right in front of Arcita's running steed, which reared and fell backward. (8) Arcita fell beneath, and the saddlebow crushed his chest so that all his body seemed a wound. (10) Emilia became deathly pale, (11) saying to herself: "How brief was my happiness!" (13) He was disarmed and his face bathed, but he could not speak. (18) Emilia cursed the love that had brought him to this; (20) his men were so sad that they did not seem to have won. (21) Palemone grieved for both Arcita's and his misfortunes.

(22) Teseo emptied the theater (23) and had doctors care for Arcita, (24) who was told that he had won the field and Emilia.

(25) "Let me hear her voice and die in her hands." (26) Teseo said to her: "Content him." (27) "I can hardly bear your hurt, my sweet husband." (30) Teseo summoned a triumphal car (32) in which Arcita sat with Emilia, (33) who comforted him. (34) The others arranged themselves (35) as was customary in triumphs. (38) They issued from the theater, and Arcita had the arms offered to Mars.

(48) They reached the palace, (49) where Arcita was placed on a great bed and comforted. (50) Palemone and his men stood downcast; (51) Teseo said to them: (53) "Man cannot resist the fates, (58) and you ought to approve the pleasure of the gods; (60) you are all free except Palemone, who is Emilia's prisoner." (63) Palemone kneeled to Emilia: "I am your prisoner." (66) "I should have loved thee; (67) but I may have only one. (68) The Greek cities are full of beauties. (70) I give thee liberty and this ring." (78) "I shall love only you." (81) Arcita said to Teseo: "May I have Emilia?" (82) "I wish you married." (83) They were wed.

BOOK X

Argument.

(1) At night the Greeks (2) told their men (3) to burn the slain. (4) All was prepared at the theater, (7) the bodies burned, (8) and the ashes taken to the temple of Mars. (10) All the wounded Greeks recovered (11) except Arcita, who was so torn within. The great Itmone examined him (12) and said to Teseo: "Arcita is dead; (13) Esculapio could not cure him. (14) Make him go content where Dis holds every light extinguished."

(16) Arcita became worse (17) and called to Teseo: (18) "I go, leaving my love unconsummated. (27) I am honored by the victory. (28) May Palemone receive the lady." (32) "Thou wilt be cured. (34) Emilia is thine; take comfort." (37) Arcita called Palemone: (40) "Hardly married, I must die; (41) pray perform my rites, (42) and accept Emilia." (49) "Thou and thy children will outlive me." (52) Ipolita and Emilia came, (54) and Arcita said: (57) "May Emilia take me in her hands when I die." (59) Emilia said: "If thou diest, what shall I do?" (61) "My kinsman Palemone is more worthy to be wed than I; (63) I should like thee to be his rather than another's. (64) I feel about my heart the coldness that accompanies death. (65) I commend my soul to thee. (66) Kiss me."

(68) "O husband dearer to me than life, the gods are not wrathful at thee but at me; (69) Cytheraea took Acate, my betrothed, (70) and now takes thee. (71) Alas, that I was born! (73) Now I understand Diana's signs to me. (75) I shall die in grief. (80) If I outlive thee, I

shall follow Diana, a virgin; (81) if Palemone wishes to marry, he will find another. (82) After kissing thee I shall kiss no more." (84) She fell on him and kissed him. (86) Everyone wept.

(89) After nine days Arcita said: (90) "Tomorrow I wish to sacrifice to Mercury." (93) The sacrifice was made and Arcita prayed: (94) "O god, carry my soul away gently." (100) Then he said to the others: (101) "Now Arcita's life will fail; (102) death is cruel to me; (103) where, Arcita, has thy strength fled? (104) O beautiful Emilia, desire of my heart! (106) I shall always be full of grief without thee. (108) Where am I leaving you all? (110) I must lose so much!" (111) He looked at Emilia as death (112) came from his feet up toward his breast. (113) He murmured: "To God, Emilia!" and said no more.

BOOK XI

Argument.

(1) Arcita's soul went toward the concavity of the eighth heaven. (2) Hence he turned down to regard the earth and the place where he had left his body, (3) and to himself he laughed at the doleful laments of the Greek throng; and hence he departed to the place that Mercury dealt out to him. (4) All listened to Arcita and wept at his death; Emilia said: (5) "Where art thou? I would come to thee." (6) But when she saw that his spirit had changed house, they, with Palemone weeping, closed his eyes, nose, and mouth. (8) All wept. (9) No one could console Teseo or Egeo. (11) [Egeo] said that deaths and mutations, and grief and song, one after the other every man often sees.

(13) Teseo decided he would have the pyre made in the grove. (14) He commanded that a forest near the grove be cut. (15) He had a bier brought and furnished with a most beautiful cloth of gold, and had Arcita similarly clad (16) and carried into the palace. (17) In Athens one heard only weeping. (18) The forest was cut to prepare a great pyre. (21) The animals and birds fled. (22) Many kinds of trees were cut. (27) The pyre was built, (29) and the summit covered with a cloth of Tyrian purple tinged with gold. (30) Everyone wept. (38) The greatest of the Greeks carried the bier from Athens to the pyre. (40) There came Palemone, Egeo, and Teseo; then Emilia, carrying in her hand the funeral fire. (41) Emilia wept: "O sweet Arcita, I did not think to enter thy chambers in this guise; (42) O pitiless gods, where is your love? It is gone with the empty winds. (43) Receive these flames." (44) She put the flames to the pyre and swooned. (47) Palemone had cut his beard and hair; (48) he cast them on the pyre, together with arms and jewels. (49) The fire increased. (51) The cups of foaming wines, and of dark blood, and the white milk

felt the fire. (52) Greek knights, each wearing some outer vestment of [Arcita], (53) three times rode about the pyre to the left hand, and there resounded lances struck on lances. (54) Those arms gave a horrible noise four times; the ladies wept; then all turned to the right. (55) Their covering and the horses' they cast into the fire during the fourth circling. (56) Some also cast lance, spear, helmet, or quiver; some, bows; and some, swords; some, chariots; some, horses. (57) Toward night the things were in ashes. (58) The next day Egeo collected the ashes in a golden urn, which he put in the temple of Mars. (59) Games were ordered: running, (62) oily wrestling, (64) the cestus, (66) and the discus.

(69) Palemone had a temple to Juno built where the pyre was, for Arcita's ashes. (70) In it were represented all the adventures of Arcita: (71) Teseo's return from Scythia, (73) his battle with Creonte, (75) the capture of Palemone and Arcita, (77) the maiden in the garden, (78) Arcita's wanderings (79) and return as Penteo, (81) the escape of Palemone, (82) the battle in the grove, (85) the battle in the theater, (86) the marriage, the mourning for Arcita, (87) and the pyre. (88) Only his fall from the horse was omitted. (90) In the midst was a column of marble on which was placed an urn of gold, inscribed: (91) "I preserve the ashes of Arcita."

BOOK XII

Argument.

(1) Emilia wept (2) and became pale and thin. (3) After several days, it was generally agreed that the sad lamentations cease and Emilia be married to Palemone. (4) Palemone was called by Teseo to Emilia. (5) Teseo said: (6) "All die; (9) if one is happy, the manner and place do not matter. (11) To make virtue of necessity, when needful, is wisdom; this applies to us. (12) The valorous life leaves fruit of fame after the flower. (14) Arcita has been bewept enough; (17) let us rejoice. (18) He requested that Emilia be given to Palemone; (19) before any depart we shall celebrate the wedding of these two." (20) Palemone replied: (21) "You say true; (22) but regarding Arcita's wish, (23) my duty conquers my desire. (25) My love for Arcita was the greatest ever, (27) and would be denied if I took Emilia. (28) Arcita was courteous; I would not be villainous." (29) Teseo said: (30) "It would not be infamy; (32) follow my will." (33) Palemone was silent and then prayed: (34) "O Jove, (35) Diana, and Cytheraea, (36) and thou, O soul of Arcita, pardon me if I obey Teseo." (38) Teseo said to Emilia: "Fulfil my wish." (39) "Hear me, and if thou wishest, I will do what thou hast commanded. (40) I

was vowed to Diana, (41) who has already taken vengeance on Acate and Arcita; (42) unless you hate Palemone, it would be better for me to serve Diana." (43) "If Diana were angry, her wrath would have come on thee, not those." (44) All changed their vestments; (45) Athens rejoiced.

(48) The marriage day came. (49) Teseo, Palemone, and the kings went to the temple of Venus; (51) also Ipolita, and Emilia, (54) whose golden hair was crowned, (58) whose cheeks were like lilies and roses, (65) and who was richly dressed in green. (69) Palemone wedded her. (70) All feasted at the palace. (75) Emilia entered a chamber with Palemone (76) for the night. (77) The next day (79) the feasting recommenced (80) and lasted fifteen days, with great gifts. (82) Each king took leave, (83) and Palemone remained in joy and solace with his lady.

(84) O Book, thou singest of Mars in *latino volgare;* (85) thou cleavest unplowed waves; (86) here we lower sail and await rewards.

SONNET

O Muses, carry these crumbs from your table, to my lady, and with her give them a name.

REPLY OF THE MUSES

We have carried your verses. Your lady would have them named the Theseid of the wedding of Emilia.

THE MILLER'S TALE

By STITH THOMPSON

THOUGH no direct literary source has ever been discovered for the *Miller's Tale*, and though such future discovery seems unlikely, the presence of the tale in oral tradition of the poet's day is well established. Through the work of R. Köhler,[1] of H. Varnhagen,[2] and of A. J. Barnouw,[3] the relation of the extant literary and oral versions has been made sufficiently clear.

The argument for a lost French fabliau as Chaucer's immediate source is strengthened by the presence of a fourteenth-century fabliau in Flemish. This may be an adaptation of a contemporary French poem. Chaucer's version differs from it in many particulars. He places the seducer in the household, provides enough tubs to rescue all three members, and forgets that the duped lover should appropriately be a smith. A second French fabliau intermediate between the first and Chaucer has been proposed to account for the differences. And it may even be that Chaucer heard the tale narrated orally.

In the *Miller's Tale* (Aarne-Thompson, *Types of the Folk-Tale* [1928], No. 1361) and its analogues three principal motifs are to be found.

I. *The flood.*[4]—(1) (*a*) A carpenter or (*b*) rich merchant hears a prediction that at a certain time the world is to be destroyed by flood. (2) The prediction is made (*a*) by a disinterested priest at church or (*b*) by a priest who wants to have access to the dupe's wife. (3) The husband makes provision against the flood by making (*a*) a tub for himself or (*b*) tubs for himself, his wife, and her lover.

---

[1] "Zu Chaucer's The Milleres Tale," *Anglia*, I (1878), 38 ff.

[2] "Zu Chaucer's Erzählung des Müllers," *Anglia*, VII (1884), Anzeiger, 81–84.

[3] "Chaucer's 'Milleres Tale,' " *MLR*, VII (1912), 145–48, and *Zesde Nederlandsche Philologencongress* (Leiden, 1910), pp. 125–39.

[4] K 1522 in S. Thompson's, *Motif-Index of Folk-Literature* (Helsinki and Bloomington, 1932–37).

II. *Misdirected kiss.*[1]—(1) The faithless wife has (a) three lovers or (b) two lovers. (2) When the second of the three lovers arrives, the first hides (a) in a window projection or (b) in a hanging tub. (3) While the favorite lover (usually the priest) is present an unwelcome lover, (a) a smith or (b) a parish clerk, arrives and will not leave until promised a kiss. (4) He is tricked into kissing through the window the posterior of (a) the wife or of (b) the successful lover.

III. *The branding.*[2]—(1) The ill-treated lover returns and asks a second kiss and brands with a hot iron the successful lover's rump. (2) At the cry of "Water!" the (a) husband or (b) first lover in the tub, thinking the flood has come, cuts the ropes and falls.

ANALOGUES

We list all the close analogues known, quoting the texts of only those that give us valuable suggestions touching the lost source of the *Miller's Tale*.

(1) German, fifteenth century: Hanz Folz, *Fastnachtspiel* (H. A. Keller, *Fastnachtspiele aus dem 15. Jahrhundert* [Stuttgart, 1853], I, 330). *Kiss* only.

(2) English ballad, early sixteenth century (E. Flügel, "Liedersammlungen des XVI. Jahrhunderts," *Anglia*, XXVI [1903], 273). *Kiss* only.

(3) Italian, 1520: Morlini, forty-sixth *novella*. (See E. Kölbing, "Zu Chaucer's Erzählung des Müllers," *Zeitschrift für vergleichende Litteraturgeschichte*, XII [1898], 449 for Latin text). *Flood.* Priest prophesies flood so as to frighten husband from home and enjoy woman.

(4) Italian, 1476: *Il Novellino di Masuccio Salernitano, restituto alla sua antica lezione da L. Settembrini* (3a ed.; Napoli, 1891), Novella XXIX, pp. 314–21.[3] *Kiss and branding.* Three visitors to woman at appointed hours. First hides in window when second lover, priest, comes. Priest's rump kissed. He is branded by third lover, a smith.

[1] *Ibid.*, K 1225.

[2] *Ibid.*, K 1577.

[3] For later versions based on Masuccio see J. Bolte, *Stuttgart Lit. Verein,* CXCVII (1893), 385.

NARRAZIONE

Viola, the carpenter's lusty young wife, promises each of her three lovers that she will satisfy him when her husband goes away for the night.

Il prossimo passato Jennaro fè un anno che in Napoli fu un bon omo lignaiuolo, il mestiero del quale a niuna altra cosa si estendea che in fare zoccoli, il quale tenea casa a fitto di costa a la Sellaria a un larghetto posto dietro la Zecca vecchia, e avendo una vaga e bellissima moglie, la quale ancora che come a giovane non fosse punto schifa nè sdegnosa dei vagheggiamenti dei suoi quasi infiniti amatori, pure tra la molta brigata tre ne erano da costei, che Viola aveva nome, più che altri amati e favoriti: l'uno era fabro suo vicino, l'altro un mercante genoese, e il terzo un frate, del nome e abito del quale come che non me ne ricordo pure so che era un esperto e famoso corsalo: a li quali tutti tre senza l'uno de l'altro avea promesso come il marito pernot-

The husband soon leaves on business, each of the lovers hearing of it during the day.

tava fuori di casa satisfarli di loro desiderio. Ove accadde che non passaro molti di che il marito andò a Ponte a Selece per condurre un somaro carico di zoccoli smarriti, per poscia polirli in Napoli come era già solito fare, per lo cui bisogno dovendovi insino al seguente dì dimorare, fu da tutti tre gli aspettanti tale partire e pernottare saputo. E come che ciascuno di loro da per sè si ponesse in ordine,

The first to claim his right is a Genoese.

pure el primo che si representò alle battaglie a l'uscio de la nostra Viola, e forse per essere più fervente amante, fu il genoese, e caramente la pregò che la notte lo aspettasse a cena e ad albergo, facendole

Viola arranges that he is to come as soon as it is dark.

le più larghe promesse come in simili contratti fare si sogliono, de modo che Viola per non tenerlo in tempo gli disse contentarsi ma che venisse tanto di notte che non fosse dalle brigate della contrada veduto. Il genoese lietissimo rispose, Sia col nome de Dio; e da lei partito se n'andò spacciatamente a la Loggia o tal volta al Pendino,

He sends a supper to her house.

e comparò due avantaggiati caponi grossi bianchi e lunghi, e con pane fresco, e de più maniere d' ottimi vini, occultamente li mandò in

The second lover, a friar, comes straight from divine offices.

casa de la giovene. Il frate celebrati li divini uffucii, desideroso che la fatta promessa gli fosse osservata, postasi la via tra'piedi, traversando di molte strate, come famelico lupo s' abattesse in alcuna smarrita pecora de la greggia, pervenne ove era la Viola, e chiamatala le disse che lui intendea per ogni modo venire a stare la notte con lei. Viola che per cosa alcuna il Genoese averia ingannato; e per conoscere il frate temerario e fastidioso molto, · non gli averia di contentarlo possuto negare, così confusa non sapea che deliberare; pur come a prudente di subito le occorse con acconcia maniera a tutto provvedere, e al frate con piacevolezza rispose, essere al suo volere presta,

He is told to come during the night, on the pretext that a cousin of Viola's will stay with her and will not be asleep until then.

ma che non venesse prima de le cinque ore, per cagione che un piccolo suo cognato venea a stare con lei, il quale insino a tale ora non saria addormito; e satisfatto che avesse il suo desiderio se n'andasse

subito con Dio. Il frate vedendo che pur era ricevuto, non curando
del resto, disse di farlo, e andò via. Il fabro che in Doana era stato The last to demand
her favors is Mauro,
a smith, who lives
close by. He is the
favored one.
insino al tardo occupato al traere de certo ferro, retornandosene
verso casa trovò Viola a la fenestra, e le disse: Pur questa notte che
tuo marito non vi è mi potrai ricevere in grazia, e ben per te se il
fai, altrimenti tieni per fermo ogni tuo disegno da me ti sarà turbato.
Viola che molto lo amava, e non poco lo temeva, pensando pur che
tempo le avanzava de la lunga notte di tutti e tre li avventori poter
liberare, come a li due aveva trovata maniera, così propose al terzo,
ancora che ultimo fosse, dare recapito, e gli disse: Mauro mio, tu Viola bids him wait
until dawn on the
pretext that the
neighbors will keep
watch on her dur-
ing the night.
sai come ne sono io male tollerata in questa contrada, e quanto tutte
con giusta cagione cercheriano di cacciarmene; e sono di quelle che
me fanno la guardia sino a mezza notte, e imperò a tale che loro in-
sidie non me abbiano a offendere, dimora a venire per sino all'alba,
a quell'ora che solito se'levarti, e faraimi segno, che io te aprirò,
e staremo un pezzo insieme per questa prima volta, che col tempo
provvederemo per migliore cammino. Il fabro canoscendo che lei
con colorate ragioni si movea, e che lui pur averia sua intentione,
senza altro replicare restò a tale ordine contento. Lo Genoese come While Viola and the
Genoese are waiting
for the capons to
cook for supper,
notte fu occultamente se n' entrò in casa di Viola, il quale ancora che
da lei fosse lietamente raccolto, e più volte baciatisi, nondimeno da
la sua infreddata natura non gli essendo concesso senza caldo di letto
o di altri argomenti li concupiscibili appetiti svegliare, si pose a
cavallo e cominciò a fare sua salatuccia fin che i caponi si penavano
ad arrostire per mal foco o che altro ne fosse stata cagione, ancora
che la giovene tutta si andasse struggendo, dubitando non le soprav-
venesse la seconda vivanda avanti che avesse la prima assaggiata:
pure erano già sonate tre ore, e la loro cena non era incominciata.
E in questi termini sentero piccare l'uscio: il genoese molto impaurito the importunate
friar arrives much
too early.
disse: Ei mi pare che l'uscio nostro sia tocco. La giovene rispose:
Tu di'vero, e certo io dubito che sia mio fratello; ma non temere che io
provvederò che non te vederà: e però esci per questa fenestra, e poniti Viola hides the fear-
ful Genoese on the
window-box, al-
though it is raining
and cold, and locks
the window.
a sedere a questo arvarello de erbicciole che è qui, che io vederò chi è, e
quello che vole dire, e ne lo manderò presto. Il genoese più timido che
caldo d'amore, come che una minuta pioggia facesse da freddissimo
vento menata che molti per neve l'avrebbeno giudicata, pure fe' quanto
per Viola gli fu ordinato; la quale serratogli dietro, e, per estimare chi She hides the supper and admits the
friar.
era colui che aveva picchiato, occultata la cena, se ne venne all'uscio;
e certificata che era l'importuno frate, alquanto turbata gli disse:
Tu sei molto presto venuto, e non hai servato l'ordine te donai:
trista me che per non aspettare un poco de tempo vorrai che io sia
morta. E con queste ed altre simili parole pur gli aperse; il quale

entrato, senza cerimonie di baci come il genoese fatto avea, rattissi-
mamente a non serrar l'uscio le donò per una volta plenaria remissione,
non per autorità che il generale gli avesse donata ma da sua poderosa
natura concessagli: e credendo Viola che quello gli bastasse a farnelo
contento ritornare, il vide che montava in casa: di che lei serrato
l'uscio seguendolo per le scale, gli dicea: Vattene per l'amore di Dio,

che mio cognato non è anco addormito, e del certo ti sentirà. Il frate
non curando del suo dire, salito su, e trovato ancora il foco calente,
scalfatosi un poco, appicciata un' altra volta la Viola cominciò a
sonare un novo ballo, con più piacevole melodia che quella che il
poveretto Genoese col battere dei denti pel soverchio freddo facea;

il quale per le fessure della finestra ogni cosa vedendo, quanto da
tale dolore, dal timore d'essere sentito e dal gran freddo che senteva
fosse afflitto, ciascuno a sè pensando ne potrà fare giudicio. E più
volte del saltare lui avria il partito preso, se non che la oscurità era
si grande che non gli facea l'altezza scorgere, e anco che pur dimorava
in speranza che il frate per essere più del dovere satisfatto, e da la

giovane de continuo al partirsi sollicitato, se n'andasse. Ma il frate
dal piacere della bella giovene riscaldato, senza togliersi la Viola
di braccia avendo di più e diversi tratti de' moderni balli non che a
lei ma al Genoese che con poco piacere li mirava insegnati, avea
deliberato di mai partirsi di là fin che dalla chiarezza del giorno non

ne fosse cacciato. E così stando insino alle dieci ore, sentì il fabro
che col preso segno inquietava l'uscio di Viola: el che lui alla giovene
rivolto disse: chi tocca il tuo uscio? Lei rispose: Egli è il continuo
stimolo di questo fabro mio vicino, il quale nè con bona nè con rea
risposta me l'ho possuto togliere dinanzi. Il frate che facetissimo

era subito gli occorse fare una nova piacevolezza, e rattissimo se
ne venne giù a l'uscio, e con sommessa voce, come Viola fosse, disse:
Chi se' tu? Lui rispose: Sono io, non mi conosci tu? aprimi, ti prego,
che tutto mi bagno. Esso disse: Dolente me, che io non posso per
questo uscio che aprendolo fa tanto rumore che ne seguiria scandalo.
Lui non avendo dove fuggir l'acqua sollicitava che gli aprisse, che
tutto si struggea per amore suo. Il frate che con gran piacere lo

tenea in tempo per farlo ben bagnare gli disse: Anima mia, baciami
un tratto per questa fessura che è ben larga, per sino a che vederò
di piano aprire questa maledetta porta. Il fabro sel crese, e molto
lieto a baciare s'acconciò: il frate che fra quello mezzo s'avea cavate
le brache gli porse la bocca per la quale si rigetta il soverchio de la
sentina: il fabro credendosi appicciare i dolci labbri di Viola, de
continente cognobbe e per tatto e per odore ciò che di vero già era,
ed estimò quello essere altro cacciatore il quale più sollecito di lui
gli aveva tolto il piacere e dipoi in tale maniera il beffeggiasse.

Di che subito propose tale ricevuto scorno non passare irremunerato; *Mauro, determined on revenge, pretends to be duped. He says he must go for a rain cloak,*
e facendo vista di mordere e leccare, gli disse: Viola mia, fra questo
mezzo che tu vederai di aprirme io anderò per un mantello, che non
posso più durare l'acqua. Il frate rispose: Va col nome di Dio e
torna presto, ridendo con la giovene in maniera che non si posseano
in piedi tenere. Il fabro entrato in bottega fe' spacciatamente una *but instead, has a red-hot spit prepared in his smithy.*
verga di ferro a modo di spido e ben focante lasciò stare, e disse al
garzone: Sta attento, e quando io sputo e tu leggiero te ne vieni
a me con questa verga. E ciò detto si ritornò a tenere in trame *Returning, he interrupts the friar and Viola in their laughter by calling for another kiss. The friar hastens down to repeat his act; the smith signals his apprentice for the spit and thrusts it into the friar. At his roars the neighbors assemble.*
dell'entrare, e da una parola a un' altra il fabro disse, Baciatemi
un' altra volta. Il frate che era più presto a tale volgimento che una
scimia, subito gli porgè la solita voragine: Mauro dato il segno, al
suo garzone, prestissimo gli presentò il focante ferro, il quale recatosi
in mano, e preso tempo, gli donò una stoccata presso vallescura che
ve lo pose quasi un palmo dentro. Il frate sentendo la fiera percossa
fu costretto a buttare un grido che toccò il cielo, e mugliando di
continuo come un toro ferito. Tutti i vicini destatisi con lumi in mano
si faceano per le finestre, e ognuno dimandava di tale novità la
cagione. Il dolente genoese che era in maniera assiderato che poco *The Genoese, fearing discovery,*
più gli bisognava stare che convertito in giazzo ivi si averiano i
suoi giorni terminati, udendo tale rumore, e vedendo tanti lumi per
la contrada, e già appressare l'alba, per non essere quivi trovato
a modo di ladro posto in vergogna, preso per ultimo partito di but- *at last summons courage to jump from the window. He breaks his leg and adds his cries to those of the friar.*
tarsi giù; e pigliato core, e raccomandandosi a Dio così fece. E gli
fu la fortuna così favorevole che al percotere in terra trovò una pietra
sopra la quale dato il piede e voltatosi in maniera che si fraccò una
gamba in più pezzi; il quale dal fiero dolore oppresso non meno che
il frate fu costretto al gridare fortissimo i suoi oimai. Il fabro correndo al rumore, e trovato e cognosciuto il Genoese, e vista la cagione
del suo gridare, alquanto pietoso divenuto, con aiuto del suo garzone
con difficoltà non piccola il menorono in bottega, e saputo da lui *Mauro finds him and hears the whole story. He then quiets the neighbors with an explanation of the noise and confusion.*
tutto il fatto come era andato, e chi era il frate, si cavò fuori e pose
silenzio al molto abbaiare dei vicini, dicendo che erano stati due suoi
garzoni che si avevano feriti. Ed essendo ognuno quieto, come il
frate volse, la Viola chiamò piano il fabro, il quale in casa intratogli
e trovato il frate mezzo morto, dopo molti e diversi debatti, col suo
fante sel posero in spalla e insino al suo convento nel condussero; e *He has the Genoese and the friar carried away, and he himself enjoys Viola and the capons.*
ritornato ne fece il Genoese sopra un somaro portare a la sua stanza.
E lui in casa di Viola rientrato essendo omai dì, mangiatisi insieme i
caponi, e oltre a ciò satisfatto intieramente al suo desiderio, lietissimo
se ne tornò a battere il martello. E così il maestro come ad ultimo
corretore fe'restare i compagni con beffe e danno e con dolore.

(5) English, 1631: Thomas Brewer, *The Merry Devil of Edmonton*. (See L. Proescholdt, "Eine prosaische Nachbildung der 'Erzählung des Müllers' aus Chaucer's Canterbury Tales," *Anglia*, VII [1884], 117–19). *Kiss and branding*. First lover a barber. Second (a smith?) is unwelcome. Kisses first lover's rump. Branding.

(6) Flemish, second half of fourteenth century,[1] unpublished verse fabliau: MS II, 1171. Bibliothèque royale de Belgique (Thorpe MS), Brussels, 330ʳ–331ᵛ. (See A. J. Barnouw, "Chaucer's 'Milleres Tale,'" *MLR*, VII [1912], 145–48.) Garbled *flood* episode, *kiss, branding*. Three visitors. When second (priest, favorite) arrives, she hides first in a tub hanging from rafters. Priest tells woman of approaching flood and frightens first lover. Third lover, smith, appears. Kisses priest's rump. Branding. "Water!" First lover falls. Moral ending.

Dits van Heilen van Beersele	Of Heile of Bersele
Die de .iii. jaghede te spele	Who brought trouble on three men.

1 Ghi hebt gehoert te menegher ure — You have often heard
Vertrecken scone avonture — fine adventures told
Van messeliken dinghen — about wonderful things,
Beide vedelen ende singhen — both by fiddling and singing
5 Ende somtijt spelen metter herpen; — and sometimes by playing on the harp.
Maer alsoe vremde alse t'Antwerpen — But I think not everyone has heard one so strange as that
Hier voermaels ene ghesciede — which happened once here in
Sone hebben alle die liede — Antwerp
Niet gehoert, wanic wale,
10 Alsoe ic u in dietscher tale — and which I shall tell you in
Vertellen sal dore ene bede — Flemish at the request of a good friend
Die .i. goet geselle ane mi dede, — friend
Dies mi niet enwoude verlaten. — who would not release me from the promise.

T'Antwerpen in der coperstraten — In Antwerp in the Market Street
15 Woende, alse ic mi versinne, — lived, as I understand,

[1] The appearance of the manuscript indicates a date about 1400, more probably before than after.

Ene harde goede ghesellinne
Ende hiet van Bersele Heile,
Die hare dicke[1] maecte veile[2]

Goeden gesellen dien sijs onste

20 Ende dien si toende hare conste.
    Eens gevielt, hoerdic vertellen,
Dat ane hare quamen .iij. gesellen
Op enen dach, alsic versta,
Deen vore, ende dander na,
25 Ende die hare alle om vrienscap
    baden
Dat si hen wilde ghestaden
Te comene daer si ware.
Si wilden spreken iegen hare
Hiemeleke ende anders niet.
30   Alse Heile van Bersele siet
Dat hare soe scone gevel,

Peinset si in hare herte wel,
Si souds hen allen saden gerume
Hare en faelgierde hare dume.[3]
35   Dat ierste was des geloeft
Een moeldre hiet Willem Hoeft.
Dien hiet si comen ter selver stont
Rechts in den avont.
Dander was .i. pape; dien hiet si
    comen
40 Alse hi die slaepclocke hadde ver-
    nomen.
Terde was hare gebuer .i. smet;

Dien hiet si comen al ongelet

Alse die diefclocke geluut ware.
    Dus saeden si alle .iij. van hare

45 Van goeden troeste ende blide,
Ende elke wachte wel sijn getide.

a very good companion,
who was called Heile of Bersele,
who very often offered herself for
sale

to good fellows to whom she
granted her favor
and to whom she showed her skill.
    Once it happened, as I heard tell
that to her came three fellows
in one day, as I understand,
one after the other,
and all of them begged her, as a
favor,
that she would let them come
where she was.
Each wanted to speak to her
in secret and not otherwise.
    As Heile of Bersele saw
that things were falling out so
well for her,
she thought in her heart
that she would satisfy them all
fully.
    The first who was promised it
was a miller named William Hoeft.
Him she bade come exactly in the
evening.
The second was a priest. Him she
bade come
as soon as he heard the sleep-bell
ring.
The third was her neighbor, a
smith.
Him she told to come without
waiting
as soon as the thief-bell was rung.
    Thus, they were all three well
satisfied with her,
full of hope and joy
and each watched well his time.

[1] Often.   [2] Venal.   [3] An obscure line.

Alst quam tuschen dach ende
    nacht,
Quam Willem diet hadde gewacht.

Heile ontfing kene blidelike
50 Ende was met hem heimelike;
Oec speelden si der minnen spel
Want si conste dat ambacht wel.
Dus laghen si in hare jolijt
Tote dat was slaepcloc tijt.
55 Doe quam die pape met fieren
    sinne
Ende seide, "Heile, laet mi inne.
Ic ben hier, ghi wet wel wie."
    "Ay, Heile, dat u lieue ghes-
    cie,"
Sprac Willem, "wie es daer?"
60   "Willem, in weets niet, maer
Het dunct mi die pape wesen;
Hi soude mi over thoeeft lesen

Ende beteren mi dat mi deert."

    "Ay, lieve Heile, werweert[1]

65 Maghic haestelike dan vlien
Dat mi die pape niue mach sien?"

    Heile seide, "Daer boven hangt
    .i. bac
Dies ic hier voermaels ghemac
Hadde te menegen stonden.

70 Ane die haenbalke es hi gebonden
Met enen vasten zele wel.
Daer sidi bat dan ighering el."

    Doe hiet Willem den pape in
    doen
Ende es in den bac gevloen.
75   Heile dede den pape te ghemake,

When it was between daytime
and night,
William, who had been awaiting
the hour, came.
Heile received him gladly
and was with him secretly.
Also they played the game of love,
for she knew that office well.
Thus lay they in their joy
until it was time for the sleep-bell.
Then came the priest with eager
spirit
and said, "Heile, let me in.
I am here. You know who I am."
    "Ah, Heile, heaven help you,"
said William, "who is there?"
    "I don't know, William, but
I think it is the priest;
he should give me much instruction
and correct what is wrong with
me."
    "Ah, dear Heile, where shall I
run then
so that the priest cannot see me
anywhere?"
    Heile said, "Up there hangs a
trough
which I have previously found
convenient in many circumstances.
It is well bound to the rafters
by a strong rope.
There you will be better than
anywhere else."
    Then William told her to let the
priest in
and escaped into the trough.
    Heile satisfied the priest,

[1] Whereto.

Ende alsi die wiekewake
Driewerf hadden gheslaghen
Ghinc die pape liggen ghewaghen[1]
Uter ewangelien menech woert;
80 Oec soe seidi dit bat voert
Dat die tijt noch soude comen
Dat God die werelt soude doemen

Beide met water ende met viere,
Ende dat soude wesen sciere,

85 Dat al die werelt verdrinken
        soude,
Grote ende clene, ionge ende
        oude.
     Dit hoerde Willem daer hi sat

Bouen hoge in ghenen bac,
Ende peinsde het mochte wel
        waer wesen,
90 Sidermeer dat papen lesen
Ende dewangelie gheeft getughe.
     Hieren binnen soe quam Hughe
Van Bersele die smet,
Die te langhe waende hebben ge-
        let
95 Ende gemert bouen sinen wille.

Vore die tore clopte hi stille.
Heile sprac, "Wie es daer?"
     "Ay, Heile, dat benic vore
        waer!"
     Doe sprac Heile, "Ghine moget
        niet inne."
00   "Ay, Heile, wel lieve minne,
Seldi v gelof dan breken?

Ic moet u emmer endelike sprek-
        en."
     "Ghine selt," sprac Heile, "teser
        stont
Want in ben niet wel ghesont

and when they had three times
done the "wiekewake,"
the priest . . . . quoted words from
the scriptures.
Also he proceeded saying this,
that the time should come
when God would punish the
world
both with water and with fire
and that it would happen forthwith and
that all the world should be
drowned,
the great and the small, young
and old.
     All this heard William where
he sat
high above in that trough
and thought that this might well
be,
since the priests explained it
and the gospels gave evidence.
     In the meantime now came
Hugh of Bersele, the smith
who thought that he had been
patient too long
and had waited longer than he
wished.
He knocked softly at the door.
Heile said, "Who is there?"
     "Ah, Heile, it is I, for sure!"

Then said Heile, "You may not
come in."
     "Ah, Heile, my dear love,
shall you then break your promise?
I really must speak to you."

     "You shall not this time," said
Heile,
"for I am not well.

[1] An obscure line.

105 Ghine moget niet in comen nu."
    "Ay, lieve Heile, soe biddic u,
Ochtic mach teser stont,
Dat ghi mi cussen laet uwen
    mont."
    Doe seide Heile toten pape,
110 "Ay, here, laet cussen desen knape
U achterste inde hi sal wanen wel
Dat ict ben ende niemen el."
    "Sone," saeghdi, "boerde nie
    goet."[1]
    Die pape stont op metter spoet
115 Ende sette die cauele sijn
Tehans vore een vensterkijn,
Ende Huge waende dat Heile ware

Ende custe spapen ers al dare
Met soe heten sinne
120 Dat sine nese vloech daerinne
Soe dat die smet sonder waen
Harde wel waende sijn gevaen
Gelijc der mese in der clouen.
    Van torne wart hi al verscouen,
125 Want hine was niet soe verdoert,
Hine heeft gevoelt ende gegoert
Dat hi gecust heeft .i. ers,
Want die mont dochte hem staen
    dwers
En die cauele op ende neder.
130   "Wetkerst,"[2] peinst hi, "hier
    comic weder."
    Hi liep thuus alse die was erre.

Hi woende van daer niet verre.
Een groet ijser nam hi gereet

Ende staect int vier ende maket
    heet

You may not come in now."
    "Ah, dear Heile, I beg you if I
may this time that I may kiss
your mouth."

    Then said Heile to the priest,
"Now, sir, let this fool kiss your
behind, and he shall think that it
is I and no one else."
    "There never was so good a
joke," he said.
    The priest got up in a hurry
and forthwith put his tail out a
little window,
and Hugh thought that it was
Heile
and kissed the priest's arse with
such fury and zeal that his nose
went inside
so that the smith had no doubt
that he was caught like a mouse
in a trap.
    He was consumed with anger,
for he was not so stupid
as not to feel and smell that he
had kissed an arse,
for the mouth seemed to him to
be athwart and the cheeks above
and below.
    "Upon my word," thought he,
"I shall come back."
    He ran home as if he were a
madman.
He did not live far from there.
He took a great iron without
hesitation,
stuck it in the fire, made it hot

---

[1] A difficult line. *Boerde* may be a verb: "Such a woman, he said, never invented a joke so well."

[2] MHG "wizze Krist."

135 Soe dat gloyde wel ter cure

Ende lieper mede vore Heilen
    dure
Ende riep, "Heile, lieve minne,
Ic moet nu endelike inne,
Ochtic moet cussen u mondekijn;

140 Deen vanden tween moet emmer
    sijn,
Ochtic sta hier al den nacht.
Hier toe dwingt mi uwer minnen
    Kracht."
    Die pape die sijns niet vergat

Hine sette weder sijn achterste gat
145 Daer hijt te voren hadde gheset
Ende die smet stac onghelet
Tgheloyende ijser in den ers.
Doe sanc hi lude dit vers,
"Water! water! ic ben doet!"
150 Dit riep hi met anxte groet

Ene harde lange stont;
Dat woerd verstarf hem in den
    mont.
    Doe wert Willem in groten
    sorghen
Die daer bouen lach geborghen.
155 Hi peinsde, "Nu eest waerheide
Van dat die pape te nachte seide:
Dwater es comen sekerlike,
Nu sal verdrinken al erterike.
Maer eest dat ic henen drive
160 Die bac houd mi wel te liue."

Sijn mes hi gegrepe
Ende sneet ontwee den repe
Daer die bac mede hing.
    Doe seide Willem dese ding,
165 "Nu wouds God ende goed geval

so that it glowed wonderfully
well,
and ran with it to Heile's door

and called out, "Heile, my love,
I must come in now at last,
or else I must kiss your little
mouth.
One of the two things surely
must be,
or I shall stand here all night.
The power of your love forces me
to this."
    The priest, who did not forget
himself,
again set his behind
where he had set it before,
and the smith without waiting
stuck the glowing iron in his arse.
Then loudly he sang this verse,
"Water! Water! I am dead!"
This he cried out with great
anguish
for a long time.
The word died in his mouth.

    Then was William, who lay
hidden there above, in great concern.
He thought, "Now is the truth
of what the priest said tonight.
The water has surely come.
Now all the earth shall drown.
But if I float away from here
this trough will let me keep
alive."
He grasped his knife
and cut in two the rope
that the trough hung by.
    Then William said this thing,
"Now may God and good fortune

Ochte Willem Hoeft iet zeilen sal." / be propitious if William Hoeft is to have a sailing!"[1]

Aldus quam Willem met allen / Thus came William falling with

Ter erden neder ghevallen / everything to the ground,

Dat hem dede harde wee, / and suffered great pain,

170 Want hi doe brac ontwee / for he broke in two

Sinen arm ende sinen dic scinkel. / his arm and his thigh.

Die pape scoet in een winkel / The priest ran into a corner

Ende waende dat die duvel ware. / and thought that it was the devil.

In enen vulen putte viel hi dare. / There he fell into a foul pit

175 Alsoe als men mit doet weten, / According to what people tell me,

Quam hi thuus al besceten / he came home all befouled

Ende sinen ers al verbrant / and his arse all burned,

Te sceerne gedreven ende ghescant. / and was put to scorn and shamed.

Hi hadde bat gebleven thuus / He would better have stayed at home

180 Ende ghesongen sinen benedicant. / and sung his benediction.

Aldus voeren Heilen gaste. / Thus fared the guests of Heile.

Die smet hadde eet onraste, / The smith had something of a hard time,

Maer hi verdroeght vele te bat / but he stood it very much the better

Dies die pape cloyde sijn gat; / for the fact that the priest had his behind burned.

185 Daer met hadde hi hem wel gewroken. / He had revenged himself well.

Met orloue es dit gesproken, / With your leave be it spoken,

Wie met hoeren omme gheet, / if anyone goes around with whores,

Toren, scade, scande ende leet / anger, damage, shame, and pain

Es hem nakende sonder spel. / are surely coming his way.

190 Dat scene Heilen gasten wel. / This was shown to the guests of Heile.

(7) German, 1559: Valentin Schumann, *Nachtbüchlein*, No. 2 (ed. J. Bolte, *Stuttgart Lit. Verein*, CXCVII [Tübingen, 1893], 12–14).[2] *Flood, kiss, branding.* Flood prediction from disinterested priest. Husband (rich merchant) prepares one tub. Favored lover a priest. Second lover, a smith, kisses priest's rump. Branding. "Water!" Husband falls. Moral ending.

[1] Or "Now, if God and good fortune grant it, William Hoeft will have a sailing."

[2] For later adaptations of Schumann's version see Bolte, p. 384.

EIN ANDERE HYSTORIA, VON EINEM KAUFFMANN, DER FORCHTE SICH VOR DEM JÜNGSTEN TAGE

Ein reicher kauffmann ist vor zeyten zu Nördlingen gesessen, des namen ist mir unbekandt, aber es solt doch war sein. Der kame auff ein zeyt in ein kirchen, da höret er, das der predicant saget, wie es zur zeyt des jüngsten tags wurde zugehen, das es da wurde feür regnen und verbrennen alles, was auff erden were, unnd was das feür wurde uberlassen, das wurde das wasser erseüffen. Der kauffmann gedachte: "Wie möchte ich doch disem wasser entrinnen?" *(A rich merchant of Nördlingen hears the preacher at church predict the destruction of the world by a flood.)* unnd gieng heim, liess ihm ein schiff machen, dasselb liess er mit eysenem blech wol beschlagen und mit bech auff das allerbeste vergiessen. Als es nun fertig was, da liess er im ein gross starck sayl machen und des nachtes allerley speiss sampt wein unnd bier, auch was zur leibs narung gehört, in das schiff tragen und liess das schiff auffziehen und also hangen für und für. Wann es dann nacht war, so stige er auff einem brett inn das schiff und lag also alle nacht in dem schiff. *(He has a boat made, hangs it by a rope to the roof, and sleeps in it at night.)*

Nun hett der kauffmann ein auss der massen schön weib, der thet wehe, das der mann alle nacht in dem schiff lag, und hette vil leiber gesehen, er were bey ihr und dem beth gelegen; dann sie hett wol bedürfft und lag ir vil an dem nachthunger, das man ir den gebüsst hette. *(His lustful wife, in his absence from bed, receives occasionally two lovers, a priest and a smith.)* Dardurch die gůt fraw in liebe entzündet ward gegen einem jungen pfaffen und auch gegen einem schmidt, damit, wann der mann des nachts in das schiff stige, dz sie ir dieweil den nachthunger büssten. Dessen die frau gar wol zukam und zufriden was, auch der mann nichts wusste von solchen sachen, vermeinet, er hett ein frommes weib. Nun trůg sich zu, das auff ein zeyt der pfaff bey der frawen war, mit ir schertzt; nach dem zusamen sassen, truncken und assen unnd waren frölich. *(Once when the priest is with her, the smith knocks on the window, but she orders him away.)* In dem so kompt der schmid auch, wolt zu der frawen, klopfet an dem fenster an; da fragt die fraw: "Wer ist da?" Der schmid antwort: "Fraw, thůnd auff!" Die fraw fragt den pfaffen: "Herr, soll ich auffthun?" Der pfaff sprach nein. Da sprach die kauffmännin zum schmid: "Ich kan euch jetzt warlich nicht herein lassen." Da sprach der schmid: "Liebe fraw, so lasst mich euch doch nur einmal kussen zu gůter nacht!" Das hört der pfaff und sprach: *(The smith begs for a kiss. The priest goes to the window, and the smith kisses his arse.)* "Halt, fraw, ich will ihm recht thůn!" und zoch das gesesslin ab und wuscht mit blossem arss zum fenster zu. Der gůt schmid mainet, es were die fraw, unnd kusst den pfaffen auff den arss; der sprang von dem banck und schlug das fenster zu.

Der schmid gieng haimwertz, und fiel im auff dem weg ein, der pfaff wurd da sein unnd wurd ihm ein schalckheit haben gethan, gieng heim und namm ein gross eysen, macht das glüet heiss, gieng wider *(The smith goes for a hot iron, again asks for a kiss, and the priest goes to the window.)*

an das fenster, klopfet an. Die fraw fragt wider, wer da sey. Der schmid sprach: "Liebe fraw, thůnd auff!" Die fraw fragt den pfaffen widerum, ob sie solt aufthůn. Der pfaff sprach nein, sie antwort wie vor. Da bat sie der schmid, sie solt in nur noch einmal kussen lassen. Da sprach der pfaff wider: "Halt, fraw!" und wider das gesesslein
The smith burns his arse with the hot iron. The priest cries: "Water!" herab zoch und mit dem arss zum fenster nauss. Das merckt der schmid und nam das heyss glüend eysen, stiess das dem pfaffen in den arss hinnein, so tieff als er kundt, darvon der pfaff ward springen und in der stuben anfieng zu schreyen: "Wasser, wasser, wasser!" und mit dem geschrey zum hauss hinauss lieff, schrey immer fort.
Hearing "Water," the merchant above thinks the last day has come, cuts the rope, and falls. Das hört der kauffmann oben in seinem schiff, das der pfaff so laut schrye: "Wasser, wasser, wasser!" vermeinet, as käme der jüngste tag, wuschte von stund an auff unnd schnit das seyl ab, vermeinet, er wolt also dahin faren. Da fiel er darnider, dass das schiff zu stucken und zu drümmer fiel, auch der kauffman halber tod auss dem schiff in sein hauss wurd tragen.
Each of those three men gets what he deserves. Also der kaufmann durch sein verstandt und weltliche weisshait kam umb sein gůt und bracht sein weib umb ir ehr, auch sich umb leib und leben, auch der pfaff umb sein grobe schalckhait umb seine gesundthait. Ich wolte, das es allen also gienge, die den frommen männern ire weyber nicht wolten mit friden lassen, sondern tag und nacht mit bitt unnd geschenck nachlauffen, wie der schmid, und ihn die frawen liessen in hindern kussen; so behielt mancher mann ein frommes weib.

(8) German popular tale, 1845: Bowdlerized version. (K. Müllenhoff, *Sagen, Märchen und Lieder aus Schleswig, Holstein, und Lauenburg* [1st ed.; Kiel, 1845], p. 481, No. 619.) *Flood, kiss, branding.* Farmer hears of flood at church. One tub. Uncorrupted wife allows smith only to kiss her hand. Disappointed smith burns her hand with hot iron. "Water!" Husband cuts down tub.

(9) German, 1580: Latin poem. Caspar Cropacius, *Poemata* (Noribergae, 1581), page 291, "Fabula de sacerdote et simplice rustico." (Reprinted in *Stuttgart Lit. Verein*, CXCVII [1893], 291). *Flood, kiss, branding.* Flood a deliberate lie by priest (otherwise like Schumann).

(10) German, 1537: Hans Sachs, *Der schmit im pachdrog* (*Neudrücke deutscher Litteraturwerke des 16. und 17. Jahrhunderts*, Nos. 164–69, p. 163 [No. 69][1]). *Flood, kiss, branding.*

[1] Reference to this version by Barnouw in *MLR*, VII (1912), 145, is incorrectly given.

Prediction in church by priest to get rid of the husband, a smith. One tub. Favored lover priest; second the husband's servant boy. Kisses priest's rump. Branding. "Water!"

DER SCHMIT IM PACHDROG

1

1   Zw Dettelpach ein schmid sas, ein einfeltig man,
    Der het ein schönes weib, das puelet der caplon.
    Nün war der schmit dag unde nacht im hawse,
    Das der pfaff künt den seinen aufrit haben nicht;
5   Darümb er ein selczame abentewer dicht.
    Um süntag frwe, als die predig war aufe,
      Sprach er: "Ir lieben kint, habt acht!
    Es wirt ein grose wasser gües vür rinnen,
    Wen sich heint[1] schaidet tag und nacht.
10   Fliecht auf den perg und wie er müegt entrinnen."
    Des schmides haus stünd an dem pach;
    Wie pald wart er im einen sin erdencken
    Und wart hinaüf unter das tach
    Sein pachtrog an vier starcke wiede hencken[2]
15   Und leget sich haimlich darein,
    So palt das wasser keme,
    Das er sich den abschnit allein
    Und sitlich fein
    Herab fiel in dem pachdrog sein
20   Und aüf dem wasser schweme.[3]

2

    Zw nacht meint die schmidin, es war der schmit darfon,
    Und schicket heimelich(e) ir maid nach dem caplon,
    Der kam in ir kamer heimlich geschlichen.
      Auch het die schmidin vor gepült mit dem schmid-
        knecht,
25   Der selbig mainet aüch, er wer allein der recht,
    Gedacht, der schmid wer aus dem haüs entwichen.
      Pald sich die schmidin niderlegt,
      Kam der knecht an ir kamertüer zw klopfen

Marginal notes:

A simple smith in Dettelbach remains at home too much for the priest, who loves his wife.

At church the priest predicts the flood.

The smith prepares a baking-trough as boat, ropes it to the roof, and sleeps there.

The wife thinks him absent and summons the priest.

The smith's servant boy, thinking that his master is absent and that he is the only lover, comes while the priest is with her.

[1] Tonight.

[2] Ll. 12–14, "Soon he began (*wart*) to devise for himself a thought, and began to hang his trough up under the roof with four strong ropes."

[3] Ll. 16–20, "As soon as the water would come he would loosen (*abschnit*) it (the trough) for himself, and neatly would come down in the trough and swim on the water." *Allein* and *sein* seem used only for the sake of the rhyme.

Und mit vil pitten sie auf wegt.

She orders him
away but consents
to give him a kiss.

30 Sie sprach: "Ge nür von mir weg, allers dropfen,
Wan es müs heint gestorben sein."
Er sprach: "Küest mich doch vor, e den wir sterben."
Die kamer het ein fensterlein,

The priest goes to
the window, and
the smith kisses his
rump.

Der pfaff für aüf, hielt im darfuer sein kerben;
35 Der schmidknecht küest [in] aüf das loch,
Das leichnam ubel stancke.
Der schmidknecht sich des kümert hoch,
Gedacht idoch,
Es kem her von dem pfaffen noch,
40 Erdacht er im ein rancke.

3

He heats an iron
and goes for
another kiss.

Er ging hin vür die ess und macht ein eysen hais,
Ging darmit zw dem fensterlein und es aüfrais,
Sprach: "Kuest mich zw lecz, kert eüch an kein
    hasser!"

He burns the
priest's arse.
"Water!"

Der pfaff recht naüs sein ars und den schmid-
    knecht anplies,
45 Das glüent eysen er im ein die kerben sties;
Der pfaff schray: "Wassrio, wasser, o wasser!"

The husband above
cuts the rope and
falls.

Das gschray erhört der güete schmid,
Unter dem dach lag in dem pachdrog münder,
Aufüer er ünd die wied abschnid
50 Und vil herab, als schlueg ins haüs der dünder.
Der pfaff schmiczt nackat hinden naüs,
Vermaint, er höret einen doner knallen.
Der schmid lag unden in dem haüs
Und het schir all sein rib im leib zerfallen.

The foolish smith is
injured and the
priest put to shame.

55 Der schmid war zw einfeltig gar,
Müest den öllgoczen dragen;[1]
Der pfaff was gar zw listig zwar,
Den zalt man par,[2]
Wie er gemessen het vurwar,
60 Und dorft es neimant klagen.

[1] "He had to carry the oil idols (the painted images of saints), *that is*, he had to be made the dupe."

[2] "He was repaid in kind."

Other versions of all or part of the *Miller's Tale* are listed, as above noted, in J. Bolte's edition of Schumann's *Nachtbüchlein* (*Stuttgart Lit. Verein*, CXCVII, 384); in Bolte's edition of Frey's *Gartengesellschaft* (*Stuttgart Lit. Verein*, XLVIII [1897], 251, 269, 277); and in A. Andrae, "Zu Longfellow's und Chaucer's Tales," *Anglia Beiblatt*, XXVII (1916), 61. They give ample witness to the popularity of the tale in oral tradition since the Renaissance.

THE REEVE'S TALE

By W. M. HART

AFRENCH fabliau resembling the *Reeve's Tale* of Chaucer—the *Miller and the Two Clerks*[1]—is extant in two manuscripts:

A. Bibliothèque de Berne, MS 354, folio 164. Printed by T. Wright, *Anecdota litteraria* (1844), pages 15–23; by the Chaucer Society, *Originals and Analogues* (London, 1872), pages 93–100; and by Montaiglon-Raynaud, *Recueil général et complet des fabliaux* (Paris, 1883), V, 83–94.

B. Berlin, Hamilton MS. Printed by H. Varnhagen, *Englische Studien*, IX (1886), 241–46.

Varnhagen regarded B as an unintentional transformation of A. Mrs. Dempster, however, has shown that B, though an inferior text, is not derived from A, since it contains matter not included in A.[2]

Matter peculiar to A or to B is found also in the *Reeve's Tale;* both are therefore printed in the present volume, Text A on the even-numbered pages, Text B on the odd, corresponding passages facing each other as far as possible.

The superiority of A is manifest: in it the story is more nearly complete; it is free from bungling repetitions; lines occur in their proper order; there is due regard to the requirements of rhyme. Matter peculiar to A includes hints of character and details of action which give a greater liveliness to the narrative.

B has the air of being a reproduction of an excellent text badly remembered: essential details are omitted; forgotten passages are supplied by the repetition of earlier lines; changes

---

[1] The fabliau *De Gombert et des deux clers* was printed in the Chaucer Society's *Originals and Analogues* of 1872. It contains no reference to a miller, or to grain to be ground, and has nothing in common with the *Reeve's Tale* that is not found also in the *Miller and the Two Clerks*. It is, therefore, not reprinted in the present volume.

[2] Germaine Dempster, "On the Source of the *Reeve's Tale*," *JEGP*, XXIX (1930), 473–88.

in the order of the lines distort the narrative; rhyming is defective or wholly neglected.

Where there are verbal differences, it is sometimes A, sometimes B, that provides the better word.

Resemblances of the *Reeve's Tale* to A, or to B, or to both,[1] slight enough in some cases, are sufficient, in the aggregate, to suggest a connection. They will be indicated by references to the *Reeve's Tale* appended to the marginal summaries of the fabliau or to the texts. Most of the marginal summary of text A applies to B; marginal notes to B are confined to important features absent in A.

[1] *Resemblances to both A and B: CT* A 4002: A 1, 6–9, 14, 16; B 6–11, 14, 16; *CT* A 4111, 4183: A 108–9; B 92–93, 169, 183; CT A 4169: A 190; B 180; *CT* A 4233: A 257; B 244; *CT* A 4273: A 288; B 268. *Resemblances to A only: CT* A 3922: A 55; *CT* A 3971: A 160; *CT* A 4014: A 2; *CT* A 4226: A 251; *CT* A 4251: A 261; *CT* A 4288, 4291: A 294; *CT* A 4210: A 273. *Resemblances to B only: CT* A 4100: B 113; *CT* A 4117: B 114; *CT* A 4163, 4165–68: B 177; *CT* A 4236: B 247; *CT* A 4221: B 248.

TEXT A[1]

LE MEUNIER ET LES .II. CLERS

Two poor Clerks[2]

1　Dui povre clerc furent jadis
　　Né d'une vile et d'un païs;[3]
　　Conpeignon et diacre estoient

lived in a forest;

　　En un boschage, o il menoient,
5　O il orent esté norri,

a dearth came,

　　Tant c'uns chiers tans lor i sailli,
　　Con il fait mout tost et sovant:
　　C'est domage à la povre gent.

　　　. . . . .

　　　. . . . .

　　Li clerc virent la mesestance;
10　Si en orent au cuer pesance,
　　Ne il ne sevent conseillier,

they couldn't earn
anything,

　　Car il ne sevent rien gaaignier
　　N'en lor pais, n'en autre terre;
　　Honte avroient de lor pain querre,
15　Tant por lor hordre, et tant por el.[4]

and they had noth-
ing to live on.

　　Il n'avoient point de chatel
　　Don se poïssent sostenir,
　　Ne il ne sevent où ganchir.

　　　. . . . .

　　　. . . . .

　　.I. diemanche, après mangier,
20　Sont alé devant lo mostier;
　　Illuec se sont entretrové.
　　Puis s'an sont de la vile alé,
　　Por dire .I. po de lor secroi.

One asks the other
what they are to do.

　　Li uns dist à l'autre: "Antan moi;

[1] The text is given as printed by A. de Montaiglon and G. Raynaud, *Recueil général et complet des fabliaux*, V, 83–94. Mrs. Dempster believes that "A is very likely to be derived from a fabliau written in the North of France."

For substantial aid in the interpretation of both texts thanks are due to Professor P. B. Fay of the University of California.

[2] Cf. *CT* A 4002. The idea of the Clerks' poverty is present both in A (1, 6–9, 14, 16) and in B (6–11, 14, 16). In the *Reeve's Tale*, however, the event proves, as Varnhagen points out, that they are not poor. In several *CT* manuscripts the word *povre* does not occur.

[3] Cf. *CT* A 4014.　　　　　　　　　[4] Other reasons.

TEXT B[1]

LE MEUNIER ET LES .II. CLERS

1   De .II. clers qui furent jadis
      Nez d'une terre et d'un païs.
      Conpainon diacres estoient
      En .I. boscage, ou il manoient,
5   Ou il orent esté norri,
      Tant c'un chier tens les asailli,
      Comme ci fet c'est mout sovent;
      C'est grant domage a povre gent.
      La fein la povre gent greva,
10   Le païs mout en enpira.
      Les clers virent leur mesestance,
      Si en orent au cuer pesance,

      .   .   .   .

      .   .   .   .

      Qu'en leur païs ne en lor terre
      N'osent por honte lor pein qerre,
15   Tant por lor ordre et tant por el,
      Ne il n'orent point de chatel,

      .   .   .   .

      .   .   .   .

      Ne ne savoient nul mestier,
      Ou il peüsent gaagnier.[2]
      .I. diëmenche aprés menger
20   S'en vienent devant le mouster,

      .   .   .   .

      .   .   .   .

      Por dire .I. poi de lor segroi.
      "Conpains," fet l'un, "entent a moi;

---

[1] The text is reprinted, with minor corrections, from H. Varnhagen, *Englische Studien*, IX (1886), 241–46. He thinks that the manuscript dates from the second half of the thirteenth century. Mrs. Dempster shows that this version is derived from one first written in Artois, "in the region through which English travelers, including Chaucer himself, used to pass, as well as French travelers on their way to or from the English town of Calais" (p. 486).

[2] Cf. A 12.

25 Nos ne nos savon conseillier,
Car ne savon rien gaaignier,
Et voiz là fain qui nos destraint,
C'est une chose qui tot vaint;
Nus ne se puet de li deffandre,
30 Ne nos n'avon rien nule o prandre.[1]
As tu nule rien porveü
Par quoi nos soions maintenu?"

L'autre respont: "Par saint Denise,
Je ne te sai faire devise,
35 Mais que jo ai un mien ami,
Je lo que nos aillon vers li,
Por prandre .I. setier[2] de fromant,
A la vante que l'an lo vant;
Et il m'an querra[3] les deniers
40 Mout longuemant et volantiers
Jusq'à la feste saint Johan,
Por nos giter de cest mal an."

Li autres a lors respondu:
"Il nos est très bien avenu;
45 Car j'ai un mien frere ensemant,
Qui a une grasse jumant;
Je la prandrai, pran lo setier,
Et si devandron bolangier.
L'an doit toute honte endosser
50 Por soi de cest mal an giter."
Ensi lo font, plus n'i atant:

.   .   .   .

Au molin portent lor fromant.

.   .   .   .

Li molins si loin lor estoit,
Plus de .II. liues i avoit.
55 C'estoit lo molin à choisel,[4]
Si seoit juste un bocheel:[5]
Il n'ot ilueques[6] environ
Borde, ne vile, ne maison,
Fors sol la maison au munier,
60 Qui trop savoit de son mestier.
Li clerc ont tost l'uis desfermé,

*The Second says,
"Let's borrow a
sack of wheat from
a friend of mine."*

*"And I'll take my
brother's mare, and
we'll turn bakers."*

*They take their
wheat to the mill,*

*which stands quite
alone.*

---

[1] To draw upon.   [2] Two hundred and forty pounds.
[3] querra: *B 31 reads* crerra (*from* croire), "he will give me credit for."
[4] With a mill-race. Cf. *CT* A 3922–23.
[5] Small wood, grove.   [6] Thereabouts.

. . . .
. . . .
. . . .
. . . .
. . . .
. . . .

T'ies tu ore rien porveü
De quoi nos soion soustenu?"

25   Il li respont: "Par seint Denise
Je ne t'en sai fere devise,
Ne mes que j'ai .I. mien ami,
Qui tut oan m'a asailli
De prendre .I. seter de froment,

30   A la vente que hom le vent;
Et il m'en crerra les deniers
Mout bonement[1] et volenters
Si qu'a la feste seint Jehan,
Por nos geter de cest mal en."

35   Enroment l'autre a respondu,
"Mout nos est or bien avenu;
Car j'ai .I. mien frere ensement,
Qui a une bonne[2] jument;
Je la prendrai, pren le seter,

40   Si devendron mes boulenger."

. . . .

. . . .

Einsi le font, plus n'i atendent:
La jument et le seter prenent;
Au molin en vienent errant,
(En un sac[3] portent lor froment.)

45   Le molin loing d'iluec estoit:
.II. bones leues i avoit;

. . . .

. . . .

Et d'une fort leue environ
N'avoit ne borde ne meson,
Ne mes sans plus cele au mouner,

50   Qui mout savoit[4] de son mestier.

. . . .

---

[1] bonement: longuement (A 40) better fits the context.

[2] bonne: grasse (A 46) is more specific.

[3] sac: Varnhagen supplies this line from A 52, where, however, the word *sac* does not occur.

[4] mout savoit: trop savoit (A 60) is more suggestive of the Miller's character.

They throw their sack inside the door and turn their mare into a meadow.

Si ont lo sac dedanz gité:
Après ont mis en un prael
La jumant, joste lo choisel.

One Clerk stays at the mill, the Second goes to fetch the Miller

65 Li uns remest por tot garder,
L'autre ala lo munier haster,[1]
Que il les venist avancier.
Mais il s'an fu alé mucier;
Bien ot les clers veü venir,
70 Je cuit à aus voldra partir.

. . . .

. . . .

. . . .

. . . .

Chiés lo munier en vient corant,
La dame a trovée filant:
  "Dame," fait il, "por saint Martin,
O est li sires do molin?

75 Bien fust que il nos avançast."

from the wood.

  —"Sire clers, point ne m'an pesast:
En ce bois lo porroiz trover,
Se il vos i plaist à aler,
Qui ci est joste ce molin."
80 Et ii clers se mest au chemin,
Querre lo vait mout vistemant.

The First Clerk gets tired of waiting

A son conpeignon qui l'atant
Poise mout qu'il demore tant;
En la maison en vient corant:

. . . .

. . . .

85 "Dame," fait il, "por amor Dé,

and goes after the Second.

O est mon conpeignon alé?"
  —"Sire, si aie je hanor,
Il en vait querre mon seignor
Qui orandroit issi là hors."
90 Ele ot bien ce mestier amors:

. . . .

. . . .

L'un des clers après l'autre envoie,
Et li muniers aquiaut sa voie;
Si vient au molin auramant,[2]

[1] On ll. 63–66 cf. B 54–57.

[2] auramant: *for* erraumant *or* erranmant, "quickly."

.   .   .   .

.   .   .   .

.   .   .   .

.   .   .   .

.   .   .   .

.   .   .   .

Quant le mouner les vit venir,
Bien sot qu'a eus voudra partir;
Lors s'est en la chambre mucié.
L'un mena la jument en pré,
55   (Et lors remest por tot garder.)
L'autre ala le mouner haster;
Ques le mouner en vint errant,[1]

.   .   .   .

Si trueve sa fame filant;
"Dame," fet il, "por seint Martin,
60   Ou est li sire du molin?"

.   .   .   .

"Sire," fet el, "par seint Omer,
En cel bois le poëz trover,

.   .   .   .

Tres par dejouste cel molin."
Or est li clerc mis au chemin.

.   .   .   .

65   A son conpaignon qui l'atent,
Sachiez, anuie mout forment;

.   .   .   .

Ques le mouner revint errant
Et trueve sa fame filant:
"Dame," fet il, "por seint Omé,
70   Ou est mon conpaignon alé?"
"Sire," fet ele, "par m'aneur,
Il ala qerre mon seigneur

.   .   .   .

.   .   .   .

En cel bois jouste cel molin."
Or s'est li clers mis au chemin.
75   L'un clerc aprés l'autre en envoie;
Le mouner raprise sa voie,

.   .   .   .

[1] On ll. 54–57 cf. A 63–66.

Lo sac lieve sor la jumant

. . . .

The Miller and his
wife hide the sack in
their house;

95   O sa fame qui li aida,
En sa maison tot enporta.

he goes to his mill.

Tant a en sa maison[1] mucié,
Puis est au molin repairiez;

The Clerks come

Et li clerc ont tant cheminé
100 Que il sont au molin torné.

and ask him to get
on with their corn.

"Munier," font il, "Deus soit o vos!
Por amor Deu, avanciez nos."

"With what?"

—"Seignor," fait il, "et je de quoi?"

"Our corn here!"

—"De nostre blé qu'est ci, par foi."

But they cannot
find corn or mare.

105 Qant durent prandre lo fromant,

. . . .

Ne trovent ne sac ne jumant.
L'uns d'aus a l'autre regardé:
"Qu'est ice? somes nos robé"[2]

They cry out that
they've been
robbed.[3]

—"Oïl," fait ce l'uns, "ce m'est vis!
110 Pechiez nos a à essil mis."
Chascuns escrie: "Halas! halas!
Secorez nos, saint Nicolas!"

"What's the mat-
ter?" asks the
Miller.

Fait li muniers: "Qu'est ce c'avez?
Por quoi si durement criez?"

. . . .

"We've lost our all.

115 —"Munier, ja avon tot perdu:
Malemant nos est avenu,
Car n'avons ne jumant ne el:
Tot i estoit notre chatel."
—"Seignor," fait il, "n'en sai noiant."

Where can we go to
find it?"

120 —"Sire," font il, "ne vos apant.

. . . .

Fors tant que de nos asener
Quel part nos poïssiens aler
Querre et tracier nostre domage."
—"Seignor," fait il, "en cest bochage:
125 Ne vos sai je pas conseillier,

---

[1] maison: granche (A 315; B 81), "grange, barn."

[2] *Robé* is manifestly more specific than *gabé*, B 92. However, in the passages that follow, B (169, 184–85) places more emphasis than A upon the robbery as a motive.

[3] Cf. *CT* A 4111, 4133.

Le sac lieve sus la jument
Et le trouse delivrement,
Et sa fame li a edié;
80   En sa granche tot a lancié.
Tot a en sa granche mucié,
Puis est ariere reperié.
Les clers ont le mouner trové.
Meintenant l'ont aresoné:
85   "Sire," dist l'un, "por seint Thommas,
Bien fust que l'en nos avanchast!"
"Avanchast, diex? Et je de quoi?"
"Ja le verres!" "Et je l'otroi."

. . . .

Au molin en vienent errant,
90   Ne truevent ne sac ne jument.
L'un clerc a l'autre regardé:
"Qu'est ce, diex? Sommes nos gabé?"
"Oïl," dist l'autre, "ce m'est vis!
Maupechié nos a ici mis."
95   Il s'escrïent: "Elas! Elas!
Que feron nos, seint Nicolas?"
Dist le mouner: "Et que avés?"

. . . .

"Certes, nos sommes mal menés.
Sire, nos avon tot perdu,
100   Maupechié nos est avenu:
Ne trovon ne sac ne jument."

. . . .

Dist le mouner: "N'en vi noient."
"Sire, de riens a vos n'apent,
Ce vos di bien veroiement,
105   Fors que nos voilliez enseigner
Ou peüson aler cercher
Nostre perte et nostre damage."
Dist le mouner: "Tot est boscage,
Par quoi ne vos sai enseignier;

"In the wood near
the mill."

> Mais en cel bois alez cerchier,
> Qui ci est joste cest molin."

The Clerks start.

> Li clerc se mestent au chemin.
> Maintenant sont el bois entré,
130 Et li muniers s'an est alé.

. . . .

One says, "It's no
use seeking; goods
come and go like
straw.

> Li uns clers à l'autre parla:
> "Certes," font il, "voir dit i a,
> Fous est qui en vain se travaille;
> Avoir vient et va comme paille,

. . . .

Let's go and lodge
at the Miller's."

135 Alons nos huimais herbergier."
> —"Nos? en quel leu?"—"Chiés lo munier,
> O no alon en cel molin,
> Deus nos doint l'ostel saint Martin!"

They go there

> Errant vindrent chiés lo munier.
140 Lor venir n'avoit il point chier,
> Ainz lor demande aneslopas:[1]
> "Que vos a fait saint Nicolas?"

and ask the Miller
to take them in.

> —"Munier," font il, "ne .I. ne el."

. . . .

> —"Or gaaignez autre chatel,

. . . .

145 Car de cest estes vos trop loing;
> Ne l'avroiz pas à cest besoing."
> —"Munier," font il, "ce puet bien estre:
> Herbergiez nos, por saint Servestre,
> Ne savon maishui o aler."
150 Et li muniers prant à panser,

. . . .

> Or seroit il pire que chiens,
> S'il ne lor faisoit aucun bien
> Del lor, car il lo puet bien faire.

---

[1] aneslopas: *enelepas, isnel le pas, in ipsum illum passum,* "immediately."

110 Mes cel bos vos lo a cercher
  Tres par dejouste cel molin."
  Or sunt li clers mis au chemin.

  . . . .

  . . . .
  Tant ont et haut et bas alé,[1]
  Que le soleil fu escoussé[2]
115 Et que li .I. l'autre apela:
  "Conpaing," fet il, "voir dit i a,
  Fous est qui en vein se travaille,
  Avoir vient et va comme paille.
  Nos porriön fere tel chose
120 De quoi nos nos dondriön pose:
  Je lo, nos aillon herbegier
  Jusqu'a demein ches le mouner,
  Ou nos entron en cel molin;
  Diex nos doint l'ostel seint Martin!"
125 Quant le mouner les vit venir,
  Sachiez que il n'osa guenchir,
  Einz s'escria inelepas:
  "Que vos a fet seint Nicolas?"
  "Ne nos a fet ne ce ne el."
130 "Je le croi bien, par seint Omel!
  Or gaagniez autre chatel,
  Que bien vos siet ou let ou bel;
  Car icestui vos est mout loing,
  Pas ne l'arez a cest besoing."
135 "Je le croi bien, par seint Omel!
  Porriön nos avoir l'ostel?"

  . . . .
  Lors se porpense le mouner:
  "Nos n'avon ore del mestier!"[3]
  Mes trop seroit pire d'un chien,
140 Se ne lor fesoit aucun bien
  Du leur, quant il le puet bien fere.

---

[1] Cf. *CT* A 4100.   [2] Cf. *CT* A 4117.
[3] del mestier: *for* d'el mestier?—"We have no need of anything else."

He says they must, sleep in the one room,

and they agree.

He has a wife, a little child,³ and a pretty daughter,

whom he puts at night in a bin, locks it outside,

and gives her the key through a hole.

They all sup;

one Clerk with the daughter,

the other with the Miller.

In an andiron is a movable ring.

The Clerk with the daughter hides the ring

"Seignor," fait il, "nient fors l'aire[1]

155 Ice[2] avroiz, se plus n'en avez."

  —"Munier," font il, "ce est assez."

Li vilains n'ot pas grant cointie:

Il n'ot que soi, cart de maisnie,

Sa fille q'an doit metre avant,

160 Sa fame, et un petit enfant.

  . . . .

La fille estoit et bele et cointe,

Et li muniers, qu'el ne fust pointe,

En une huche[4] la metoit

Chascune nuit, o el gisoit,

165 Et l'anfermoit par de desus,

Et li bailloit par un pertuis

La clef, et puis s'aloit cochier.

A noz clers devons repairier.

La nuit, qant ce vint au soper,

170 Li muniers lor fait aporter

  . . . .

Pain et lait, et eues, et fromage,

C'est la viande del bochage;

Aus .II. clers assez en dona.

L'un o la pucele manja,

  . . . .

175 L'autre o la dame et lo munier.

En l'aitre[5] ot un petit andier,

O il avoit un anelet,

Que l'an oste sovant et met.

Cil q'o la pucele manja

180 De l'andier l'anelet osta,

  . . . .

Bien l'a et repost et mucié.

---

[1] aire: "the floore of a house or barne" (Cotgrave); "lieu, place, salle" (Godefroy); "Tenne, Hofraum" (Tobler). "Room" is the better meaning: l. 238, the Clerk is said to have fallen (*chaüz*=*cheüt* from *choir*) from his bed; l. 227, it is said that the Miller's wife

> "Par de devant lo lit trescort
> Au clerc, qui en l'aire gisoit."

If his bed were on the floor, she could hardly mistake it for her own.

[2] Ice: l'ostel (B 143) is clearer.   [3] Cf. *CT* A 3971–72.

[4] huche: "A Hutch or Binne; a kneading Trough, or Tub; also a Mill-hopper" (Cotgrave).

[5] Fireplace.

Dist le mouner: "N'i a fors l'ere;
L'ostel arez, se plus n'avez."
"Sire, cest a mout grant plentez !"
145   Le mouner n'ot pas grant mesnille,

. . . .

. . . .

. . . .

Lui et sa fame et une fille,[1]
Qui tant estoit et belle et cointe;
Por ce qu'ele ne fust trop cointe,
En une huche la couchoit

. . . .

. . . .

150   Et par deseure li bailloit
Le clef, et puis s'aloit coucher.

. . . .

Quant ce vint au soir au menger,
Asez lor fist apareiller
Tot quant qu'i lor estoit mestier,
155   Pein et oes et let et formage,
C'est la viande du boscage.

. . . .

L' .I. o la pucele menja
Et tot dis du pié la bouta,
Et l'autre o li e sa moiller.
160   En l'aitre si ot .I. lander;
El lander ot .I. anelet,
Que l'en oste sovent et met.
Cil qu'o la pucele menja
Du lander l'anelet osta,
165   Qui les le feu iert aprochié;
Si l'a bien repus et muchié.

[1] B fails to mention child or cradle until the moment when the clerk displaces them (l. 230).

and at night watch-
es how the Miller
locks her in her bin

La nuit qant il furent cochié,
Li clers de li grant garde prist:
Bien vit que li muniers li fist;

. . . .

. . . .

. . . .

185   Con en la huche la bouta,
        Et par de desus l'anferma;

. . . .

. . . .

and gives her the
key through the
hole.

Con il li a la clef bailliée,
Par un pertuis li a lanciée.

When all are set-
tled,

Qant il furent aseüré,[1]

. . . .

. . . .

this Clerk pokes the
other.[2] "I will go
to the girl."

190   Il a son conpaignon bouté:
        "Conpainz," fait il, "je voil aler
        A la fille au munier parler,
        Qui est en la huche enfermée."

. . . .

. . . .

"Are you crazy?"

—"Viaus tu," fait cil "faire mellée,
195   Et estormir ceste maison?
        Verité est, tu ies bricon,
        Tost nos en porroit mal venir."
        —"Je ne voldroie por morir,
        Que ne m'en aille à li savoir
200   S'el me porroit de rien valoir."

. . . .

He goes, scratches
on the bin,

A la huche vient erraumant,

. . . .

.I. petit grate, et el l'antant:

. . . .

"Q'est ce," fait ele, "là defors?"

and tells the daugh-
ter he's dying for
her

—"C'est celui qui por vostre cors
205   Est si destroiz et mal bailli,
        Se vos n'avez de lui merci,

[1] Settled down.   [2] Cf. *CT* A 4169.

Tant com se dut aler coucher,

. . . .

. . . .

Car il estoit aprés menger,
Son sac vit apert et son blé,
170 Que le mouner lor ot emblé.
Aprés vit le mouner qui muche
Sa fille dedenz une huche;
Iluec la muce et sovent tremble,
Grant paour a c'on ne li emble.
175 Et la pucele tot soëf
Par le pertus reçoit la clef.

He sees his stolen corn.

. . . .

Adont se couche et ronfle fort
Icel mouner et tost s'endort.
.I. des clers qui ce escouta
180 De sa mein l'autre clerc bouta:
"Conpaing," fet il, "je veil aler
A la fille au mouner parler."

The Miller snores loudly.[1]

The Clerk listens to the snoring.[2]

. . . .

"Qu'est ce, deäble? Es tu desvé?
Ne t'est or gueres de nos blé
185 Que le mouner nos a enblé?
Nos veus tu ci fere honir
Et estormir ceste meson?
Veritez est, tu es gloton."[4]

"Don't you remember our corn stolen by the Miller?"[3]

. . . .

"Or nel leroie por avoir
190 Qu'orendroit[5] ne voise savoir."

. . . .

De son lit saut inellement,
A la huche vient enroment;
A la huche s'est acosté,
Si a .I. petitet graté,
195 Et el l'avoit mout bien oï:
"Qui est ce, diex? Qui est la hors?"
"C'est celi qui por vostre cors
Est si destruit et maubailli,
Se vos n'avez de li merci,

[1] Cf. *CT* A 4163.   [2] Cf. *CT* A 4168.   [3] Cf. *CT* A 4183.
[4] gloton: "knave, rascall, filthie fellow" (Cotgrave).
[5] "I would not refrain for a fortune from going to find out."

Jamais nul jor joie n'avra,
C'est celui qui o vos manja,

and has brought her
a ring of gold

Qui vos aporte un enel d'or,
210   Onques n'aüstes tel tresor;

of which the stone
will restore virgin-
ity.

Bien est esprové et saü
Que la pierre en a tel vertu
Que ja fame, tant soit legiere,
Ne tant par ait esté corsiere,[1]
215   Qui chaste et pucele ne soit,
S'au matin en son doi l'avoit.
Tenez, gel vos en faz presant."

She gives him the
key; he opens the
bin;

Errant cele la clef li tant,
Et il desferme errant la huche,
220   Dedanz se met, ele s'acluche.[2]

they take their
pleasure.

Or puent faire lor deduit,
Car ne trovent qui lor anuit.

The Miller's wife
gets up and goes
naked into the
court.

La fame o munier, ainz lo jor,
Se leva d'enprès son seignor;
225   Tote nue vait en la cort.
Par de devant lo lit trescort
Au clerc, qui en l'aire gisoit.

. . . .

The Second Clerk
sees her,

Li clerc au trespasser la voit;
Qant il la vit, si l'esgarda,

thinks on his mate's
enjoyments,

230   De son conpaignon li manbra,
Qui en la huche fait ses buens;
Mout convoite faire les suens.
Pansa que il la decevroit
Au revenir, se il pooit:
235   Puis repansoit no feroit mie,
Tost en porroit sordre folie.
.I. autre angin li est creüz:
S'anprès est de son lit chaüz,

goes to the Miller's
bed,

A l'autre lit s'an va tot droit,
240   Là o li muniers se gisoit;

and pulls the cradle
to his own.
When the wife
comes back,

L'anfant à tot lo briez[3] aporte,
Et qant la dame entre en la porte,

. . . .

---

[1] Gadabout.

[2] ele s'acluche: "crouches"? (Ital. *accoccolarsi*). This is the only known occurrence of the word.

[3] Cradle.

200   James nul jor joie n'avra.—
       Le cler qui avec vos menja,
       Qui vos aporte .I. anel d'or;
       Diex ne fist si riche tresor.
       La pierre en est de tel vertu,
205   Bien l'ai esprové et seü,
       Qu'il n'est souz ciel fame legerre,
       Qui par terre eit esté corsiere,
       Se l'anelet a en son deit,
       Que toz jorz pucele ne soit.
210   Tenez, je vos en faz present!''
       Cil li baille, la clef li tent;
       Or a la huche desfermée,
       Avec la pucele est entrée.
       Or en puet fere son delit,
215   Car or ne trueve qui li nuit.
       La fame au mouner ainz le jor
       Se lieve d'ovec son seignor,
       Tote nue vet en la court;

       . . . .

       . . . .

       Et le clerc si fremist trestot.
220   Le clers autres passer la vit,

       . . . .

       De son conpaignon li sovint,
       Qui en la huche fet ses bons;
       Et il a si petit des soens,
       Qu'il jure deu et seint Thommas,
225   C'au revenir la retendra.
       Il repense nen fera mie,
       Tost l'en porroit venir folie.
       .I. autre engin li est creü:
       De son lit se lieve tot nu,

       . . . .

       . . . .

230   Le berz a tot l'enfant enporte.
       Et la dame a reclos la porte,
       Au lit est venue tot droit,

the Clerk makes her
child cry,

. . . .
Li clers tire à l'anfant l'oroille,
Et l'anfes crie, si s'esvoille.
245 Cele ala à son lit tot droit,[1]
Qant ele oït o cil estoit;

she goes to the
cradle,

Puis est erraument retornée,
Au cri de l'anfant est alée:
Lo briez trove, don s'aseüre,
250 Puis solieve la coverture,

and lies down in the
Clerk's bed.[2]
He amuses himself.

Dejoste lo clerc s'est cochiée
Et cil l'a estroit enbraciée.
Vers soi l'atrait, formant l'acole,
A son deduit tote l'afole;
255 Si sofre tot, si se mervoille.

The First Clerk, at
cock crow,[3] gets out
of the bin and comes
to his bed;

 Et l'autres clers si s'aparoille,
Qant il oït le coc chanter,
Car il cuidoit trop demorer.
De la huche s'an est issuz,

. . . .
260 Puis est droit à son lit venuz:

. . . .

but finds the cradle
by it[4]

Lo briez trove, si s'esbaïst;
N'est pas mervoille s'il lo fist.
Il ot peor, et neporqant
.I. petit est alez avant;

. . . .

and two heads in it.

265 Et qant .II. testes a trovées,
Erraumant les a refusées.

So he goes to the
other bed,

A l'autre lit o se gisoit
Li muniers, s'an va cil tot droit.
Dejoste li s'estoit cochiez,
270 Ne s'est pas encore esveilliez,
Ne ne s'est mie aparceüz,

and says to the
Miller, "Mate,

"Compainz," fait li clers, "que fais tu?
. . . .
Qui toz jorz se tait rien ne valt,[5]

---

[1] "She goes toward her own bed, but when she hears where the child is, she goes in that direction and finds the cradle."

[2] Cf. *CT* A 4226. [3] Cf. *CT* A 4233. [4] Cf. *CT* A 4251–53.

[5] Cf. *CT* A 4210, where the clerk quotes the proverb before lying with the maid.

La ou son mari se gesoit.
S' a tiré a l'enfant l'oreille,
235   Il bret et ele s'esmerveille.

. . . .

. . . .
Si est ariere retornée,
Au bret de l'enfant est alée,
Le bers trueve, si s'aseüre,
Li souzlieve la coverture,
240   Et el s'estoit dedenz mucée,
Et il l'a estroit enbracée.
Or en puet fere son delit,
Car il ne trueve qui li nuit.

. . . .
Celui oï le coc chanter
245   Qui en la huche se gesoit.

. . . .
De la huche ist inellement,
A la pucele congié prent,[1]
Au lit s'en est venu tot droit,
La ou son conpaignon gesoit.

. . . .

. . . .

. . . .
250   (Si a tot belement tasté)[2]
Les .II. testes i a trovées,
Enroment les a refusées.
A l'autre lit revint tot droit,
La ou le mouner se jesoit:

. . . .

. . . .

. . . .
255   "Beau conpaing," fet il, "que fes tu?
Comment t'est anuit avenu?

. . . .

---

[1] Chaucer expands this hint to a speech of four lines (cf. *CT* A 4236–39). This leads to Malyne's confession of the theft. In both A and B the confession is made at the end of the tale, dramatically and naturally enough, by the wife, enraged by her husband's reproaches (though those dropped out of B). Chaucer, then, might find in either A or B a suggestion for confession by a member of the family. It is curious that he fails to show that Symkin was aware of his wife's misadventure.

[2] Cf. *CT* A 4222. In Chaucer the subject is, of course, the Miller's wife.

Or sai je bien, se Deus me salt,

I've had a good
night,

275   Que j'ai aü boene nuitiée:
Mout est la pucele envoisiée,
La fille à cest nostre munier;
Mout par si fait mal anvoisier[1]

. . . .

. . . .

Et si fait trop bon foutre en huche.

280   Conpeignon, car va, si t'i muce,
Et si pran do bacon ta part;
Assez en a jusq'à la hart;[2]

and swived the Miller's daughter seven
times,

Par .VII. foiz l'ai anuit corbée,
Dès or sera boene l'asnée,[3]

all for an andiron
ring."

285   El n'a fors l'anel de l'andier;
Si ai je bien fait mon mestier."

The Miller seizes
him by the throat,[4]

Qant li muniers entant la boíe,
Tantost prant lo clerc par la gole
Et li clers lui, qui s'aparçoit.

but the Clerk soon
nearly kills the
Miller.

290   Tantost lo met en si mal ploit
A po li fait lo cuer crever;[5]
Et la dame aquialt à boter
L'autre cler, qui o lui gisoit:

His wife says the
Clerks will strangle
one another.[6]

"Sire," fait ele, "ce que doit?"

295   Se viaus, car nos levon tost sus,
Ja s'estranglent cil cler laissus."

Her bedfellow says,
"Let 'em."

   —"Ne te chaut,"[7] fait il, "lai ester,
Lai les musarz entretuer."
Il savoit bien, si n'ot pas tort,

300   Que ses conpainz ere plus fors.
   Qant li muniers pot escháper,

As soon as the Miller escapes, he goes
to light the fire;

. . . .

Tantost cort lo feu alumer;
Et qant il sa fame aparçoit,

sees his wife with
the other Clerk

Qui avoc lo clerc se gisoit:

and calls her a
proved whore.

305   "Or sus," fait il, "pute provée,
Qui vos a ici amenée?

[1] "Amusing one's self is very wicked indeed, and yet there is good swiving in the bin." B 260 is clearer.

[2] Cord by which bacon was hung.

[3] The load of an ass, good measure.   [4] Cf CT A 4273.

[5] cuer crever: l'a estranglé (B 271) is more appropriate.

[6] Cf. CT A 4288, 4291.   [7] It does not heat, does not concern, you.

. . . .

Mout ai eü bone nuitiée,
Mout est la pucele envoisiée,
La fille a cest nostre mouner;
260   Mout fet bon avec li coucher.
Et VI. foiz l'ai anuit eüe
Entre mes braz trestote nue:
Mout par fet bon coucher en huche.
Conpains, car va et si t'i muche,
265   Et si pren du bacon ta part;
Mout en i a jusqu'a la hart."

. . . .

. . . .

. . . .

. . . .

Quant le mouner entent la boule,
S'avoit le clerc pris a la goule;
Et quant le clerc dont s'aperchoit,
270   Si l'avoit mis en si mal ploit,
Qu'a poi que ne l'a estranglé,

. . . .

. . . .

. . . .

. . . .

. . . .

. . . .

. . . .

. . . .

Mes le mouner est eschapé.
Quant vit que il pot eschaper,
Errant vint le feu alumer;
275   Au lit s'en est venu tot droit,
La ou sa fame se gesoit,

. . . .

. . . .

Certes, il est de vos tot fait."

. . . .
. . . .
. . . .

. . . .

She says she's one through guile,

    —"Sire," fait ele, "autrement vait,
Car se je sui pute provée,
310 Par engin i fui atornée;

whereas he's a proved thief, as he's stolen the Clerk's corn and mare.

Mais vos estes larron prové,
Qui en cez clers avez emblé
Lor sac de blé et lor jumant,
Dont vos seroiz levez au vant:[1]
315 Tot est en vostre granche mis."

. . . .

The Clerks then thrash the Miller

Li dui clerc ont lo vilain pris;
Tant l'ont folé et debatu
Par po qu'il ne l'ont tot molu,

. . . .

and have their corn ground at another mill.

Puis vont modre à autre molin.
320 Il orent l'ostel saint Martin,
Et ont tant lor mestier mené
Q'il se sont do mal an gité.

Explicit

[1] Hanged.

.   .   .   .

Estes vos sa fame desvée,
Et entre en grande pensée.
"Par deu, il est de vos tot fet,
280   Vos avez commencé mauplet;[1]

.   .   .   .

Que se je sui fame desvée,
Par enging i fui amenée.
Mes vos estes lerre prové,
Qui avez au .II. clers enblé
285   Leur sac de blé et leur jument;
S' en devez estre mis au vent."

.   .   .   .

Quant les clers entendent la boule,
S' ont le mouner pris a la goule,
Tant l'ont foulé, tant l'ont batu,

.   .   .   .

290   Que tot lor blé lor a rendu.   The Miller returns
.   .   .   .   the corn.

.   .   .   .

Puis ont lor mester tant mené;
Qu'il se sunt du mal en geté;
A deu et a seint Nicolas
Entendent grasces haut et bas.

Explicit

[1] "You have started an evil quarrel."

THE COOK'S TALE

By EARL D. LYON

I F WE should care to assume that Chaucer was, as usual, following an at least partly ready-made story when he began the *Cook's Tale*, we have enough of the fragment to justify a search—which will, however, prove fruitless—for its source (or a close analogue) with some hope of recognizing it should we find it. From the personality of the Cook, from the kind of story that moved him to tell his own, from his announcement that he would tell of "a litel jape that fil in oure citee" (A 4343), and from the tone of the fragment itself we may be sure that the Cook was going to cap the fabliau of the Reeve with another not unlike it. In the fragment itself we have an elaborately introduced character who is to be expected, from the openings of the other fabliaux in the *Canterbury Tales*, to play an important part in the "jape." This character has been dismissed by an angry master, a victualer, and he has a confederate who is married to a prostitute. We infer that he and the confederate are to live a life of riot, debt, and theft (A 4415–17). We may look, therefore, for a humorous tale involving certainly the "Revelour" and probably the others and dealing with a way of life implied in the last lines of the fragment. So much is obvious. We have, besides, in the trick of association by which the "litel jape" is drawn into the Cook's mind, a bare clue as to the theme for which to look. The theme of the *Reeve's Tale*, which so amuses the Cook, is tit for tat:

Hym thar nat wene wel that yvele dooth [A 4320].

The miller stole the clerks' flour; the clerks enjoyed the miller's women. Only a condition of the clerks' revenge is the miller's "herbergage." Yet Roger seizes upon this condition as if it were the point of the story, worries it into a brief homily, and offers to cap the tale (A 4327–43). Though it is true that the "herberwynge" causes most of the humor in the *Reeve's Tale*, the Cook's lighting upon it alone for insistent comment suggests that something on his mind enforces such an emphasis.

148

At the moment the thing uppermost in Roger's mind is the "litel jape." Is it the point of his own tale that Roger sees in the miller's "perilous herberwynge," and is Roger's little sermon a modulation, as it were, on a common theme?[1] Though far from conclusive, such evidence may contribute its bit.

Parallels to the story elements here listed, taken singly, are as abundant as one might expect, especially in the humorous stories of Renaissance England and of fifteenth-century Germany, of which latter the *Schwänke* of Hans Sachs are the most elaborate. The reveler was, or came to be, traditional stuff;[2] sometimes he was a burgher or the servant or apprentice of a burgher.[3] There are stories in which man and master or rogue and burgher are opposed: a shoemaker dismisses an apprentice;[4]

[1] At least twice in the *Canterbury Tales* Chaucer uses equally subtle psychological transitions from tale to tale. The Friar, pregnant with his "game" of a summoner, clears the way for it by complimenting the Wife of Bath on her learning and then suggesting that "game" were more appropriate conversation "heere as we ryde by the weye." The Merchant is reminded by the Clerk's story, and perhaps by the Host's comments on it, of the woes of those "that wedded been." There surges into his mind the sorrow caused him by his own wife, so unlike Griselda. He complains briefly, stints, then tells his tale in the same tone of sad disillusionment. Cf. the whole "Marriage Group."

[2] E.g.:

> "Und genczlich und gar war ergeben
> Aim wolüestig und frechen leben,
> Und ob keinr sach wolgfallen het,
> Den was dem leib sanft und wol thet,
> Als essen, trinckn und schlemerey,
> Spillen und faülkeit mancherley,
> Hoffart, danczen und hoffiren,
> Büelen, feyren und spaciren
> Mit ander meins geleichen gselen,
> Die weder nach güet noch eren stelen."

(Hans Sachs, *Sämtliche Fabeln und Schwänke*, ed. Edmund Goetze and Carl Drescher ["Neudrucke deutscher Litteraturwerke" (6 vols.; Halle, 1893–1913)], II, No. 375, p. 609). Cf. *ibid.*, I, No. 45, p. 141; No. 68, p. 215; No. 24, p. 77; No. 48, p. 147; III, No. 108, p. 232; *The Meeting of Gallants at an Ordinarie*, ed. J. O. Halliwell ("Percy Society" [London, 1841]), pp. 21–25; *Shakespeare's Jest Book. A Hundred Mery Talys*, ed. Hermann Oesterley (London, 1866), No. XCI, pp. 145–50 (a dicer and unthrift, passing as a "prentice," steals from a country maltman by a series of city-slicker tricks).

[3] Sachs, II, No. 294, p. 321; No. 293, p. 316; V, No. 812, p. 340; No. 694, p. 142. *Shakespeare Jest-books*, ed. W. C. Hazlitt (London, 1864), III, 14.

[4] Sachs, II, No. 311, p. 378.

servants overcome bad masters;[1] servants cheat their masters, and rogues cheat tradesmen;[2] servants play pranks on tradesmen and craftsmen;[3] and one craftsman plays such a trick on his servant as must have avenged his whole class.[4] Rogues work together in pairs,[5] and rogue cheats rogue.[6] Man and wife collaborate in roguery.[7] And in three stories two men and a woman so collaborate. A fabliau by Hugues Piaucele tells how a man and his wife dispose of the bodies of three murdered priests with the aid of a natural, their friend.[8] But the characters in no way suggest Chaucer's. W. C. Hazlitt[9] ascribes to the youthful Sir Thomas More "A Mery Jest how a Serjeant wolde lerne to be a Frere," wherein a merchant's son who through dissipation and bad investments loses his patrimony and goes into debt finally takes refuge in the home of a married friend. At the instigation of the creditors a sergeant disguises

[1] Sachs, I, No. 126, p. 342; II, No. 365, p. 586; IV, No. 459, p. 332; V, No. 632, p. 50.

[2] Samuel Rowlands, *Greenes Ghost Haunting Connie-catchers* (*Complete Works* [Glasgow, 1880]), p. 17 (a cutpurse steals a cheesemonger's purse while the latter loads the cheese into the hood of his cape), pp. 18, 20; *The Knave of Clubbes* (*ibid.*), pp. 18 ff.; Boccaccio, *Il Decameron*, VI, 4; IX, 4; Sachs, III, No. 142, p. 291; II, No. 246, p. 162.

[3] Eulenspiegel is the type. For examples of his crudities see the convenient *The Marvellous Adventures . . . . of Master Tyll Owlglass*, ed. and tr. Kenneth R. H. Mackenzie (London, 1890), Nos. 8, 20, 29, 44–45, etc.

[4] Sachs, VI, No. 990, p. 234.

[5] Robert Greene, *The Second Part of Conny-catching* (*The Life and Complete Works in Prose and Verse . . . .* [London and Aylesbury, 1881–86]), pp. 110 ff. (rogues feign quarrel; one throws meal on the other. While meal-merchant dusts him off, he cuts the meal-merchant's purse); Rowlands' *Greenes Ghost Haunting Connie-catchers*, pp. 44 ff. (two hungry rogues get lodging and money by setting up as a seer and his assistant); *The Knave of Clubbes*, pp. 10 ff.; *The Knave of Harts*, pp. 42–43; *Shakespeare Jest-books*, I, 110; Masuccio, *Il Novellino*, ed. Luigi Settembrini (Napoli, 1874), No. XVII; *Gesta Romanorum*, ed. Hermann Oesterley (Berlin, 1872), Cap. 108, p. 440; *Recueil général et complet des fabliaux . . .* , ed. Anatole de Montaiglon and Gaston Raynaud (Paris, 1872–90), Vol. III, No. LXII; Sachs, IV. No. 565, p. 477.

[6] Montaiglon-Raynaud, Vol. V, No. CXVI; Sachs, IV, No. 437, p. 300; *The Meeting of Gallants at an Ordinarie*, pp. 19–21.

[7] Greene, *Thirde and Last Parte of Conny-catching*, pp. 156, 172; *A Disputation between a Hee Conny-catcher, and a Shee Conny-catcher*, pp. 203 ff.; *A Notable Discovery of Coosnage*, pp. 39 ff.

[8] Montaiglon-Raynaud, Vol. I, No. XIX, pp. 198 ff.

[9] *Remains of the Early Popular Poetry of England* (London, 1864–66), III, 98–100, 119 ff.

himself as a friar, gets admittance to the house, and seizes the debtor. The housewife and the maid come to the guest's assistance; they pull the "friar's" hood down over his eyes and throw him thus blinded out of the house. The characters of the *Cook's Tale* could have performed this "jape." But there is no reason to suppose Chaucer had it in mind. This wife is no prostitute, and the story does not appear, to my knowledge, before More's time. A tale more appropriate to the Cook's three rogues is told by Robert Greene in *The Blacke Bookes Messenger*.[1] Two rogues and a prostitute "cross-bite" a citizen: the prostitute entertains the victim; the one rogue surprises them, accuses the citizen of dishonoring his wife, and calls in a "constable," who is the second rogue. But though this is the kind of thing one would expect Perkyn and his friends to go in for, there is nothing to tie it to the *Cook's Tale*, no apprentice, and, in the Cook's sense, no "perilous herberwynge." And it appears in literature late.

The *Cook's Tale*, therefore, falls into the group of Chaucer's stories for which we lack sources and complete analogues— stories in most of which he probably attempted a fresh combination of traditional elements. Of these, the *Canon's Yeoman's Tale* is merely a simple narrative of an alchemist's tricks, some parallels to which have been found. The others— the *Anelida and Arcite, Sir Thopas*, the *Squire's Tale*, and the *Cook's Tale*—are fragments.[2] From the fact that the tales for which we lack sources are, with the one exception, the fragments, we infer that the creation of original "plots" was not, for Chaucer, a satisfactory procedure and that, when he attempted it, he was likely to bog down. Probably, then, if Chaucer was following literary sources in the *Cook's Tale*, he was attempting a fresh combination of story elements.[3]

---

[1] Pp. 12 ff.   [2] Cf. also the *House of Fame*.

[3] The state in which Chaucer left the tale allows, to a degree reinforces, this inference. There is an apparent inconsistency between the *Cook's Prologue* and that of the Manciple, wherein the Host calls on the Cook as if for the first time; an inconsistency aggravated by the fact that we do not know which prologue Chaucer wrote first. If, as is possible, he went back after writing the latter to add the *Cook's Prologue and Tale* to Fragment A, it is probable either (1) that he intended to write only a fragment and have it broken off, through the interruption of the Host, perhaps, who is anxious to have the tales go "thriftily," or through that of one of the "gentils," as later in the pilgrimage; (2) that he began a story and found that he could not finish it to his satisfaction; or (3) that he never got

There is reason to believe, however, that in this, his tale of London life, Chaucer was not drawing on literary sources. As is evident in the representative selection of references above, almost all the parallels to elements of the *Cook's Tale* appear after Chaucer's death. Rogues, doubtless, there have always been in literature. But tales of rogues in a bourgeois setting became common only with the development and formulation of a bourgeois morality.[1] The probability is that Chaucer was taking the stuff for the *Cook's Tale* not from literature but, as the prologue says (A 4343), from London life, whence, in all probability, he took the Cook;[2] for the London records of Chaucer's time, and before, afford as many parallels to the elements of the *Cook's Tale* as do the storybooks of the centuries immediately following.[3] Offending apprentices were common[4]

---

around to finishing it. It is probable, however, that the *Cook's Prologue and Tale* is the earlier work. (The *Reeve's Tale* was fresh in Chaucer's mind when he wrote the *Cook's Prologue*, for he alludes in the latter to a sentence in the former: "argument of herbergage" [A 4329]; "by argumentes make a place" [A 4123]; cf. Robinson's statement of probabilities [*Chaucer's Complete Works*, p. 791].) If it is the earlier, we may believe that Chaucer did not intend to have the *Cook's Tale* interrupted by one of the pilgrims. Had he so intended, he would probably not have left the discrepancy in the *Manciple's Prologue*. Likewise we may set aside the possibility that he never got around to finishing the Cook's fragment, for what he wrote in the *Manciple's Prologue* seems to indicate that he intended not to finish but to cancel it, together with its prologue. It is possible (1) that he decided, on writing the last lines of the fragment, to cancel it because he had too many vulgar stories in a row; or (2) that, when he began the *Cook's Tale*, he intended to compose a complete story and that he left it unfinished because he was unable, for some reason, to sustain the creative impulse. The inference in the text above offers the most probable reason for the failure of the impulse.

[1] For which cf. Werner Sombart, *The Quintessence of Capitalism* (New York, 1915), pp. 103 ff.; Louis B. Wright, *Middle-Class Culture in Elizabethan England* (Chapel Hill, 1935), pp. 165–66, 196, 637 n., *et passim*.

[2] Argued in my note, "Roger de Ware, Cook," *MLN*, LII (1937), 491–94.

[3] The matter of the *Liber vagatorum* "was drawn in part from manuscript accounts of criminal trials at Basel (1475), which may also have furnished lore for the 'Narrenschiff' " (Frank W. Chandler, *The Literature of Roguery* [Boston and New York, 1907], I, 27). Cf. Taylor's "Wit and Mirth. Chargeably Collected Out of Taverns, Ordinaries, Innes, Bowling-Greens and Allyes, Ale-houses, Tobacco Shops, Highwayes, and Water-passages" (*Shakespeare Jestbooks*). Poggio drew his material from observation and conversation (see *The Facetiae* [Paris, 1879], *passim*).

[4] Gambling: *Calendar of Plea and Memoranda Rolls . . . . of the City of London . . . .*, 1323–1364, ed. A. H. Thomas (Cambridge, 1926), p. 113; *ibid., 1364–*

and were commonly given "acquitance."[1] Rogues, alone and in company, perpetrated "wikked japes."[2] Two brothers, for example, were enticed by a decoy into playing at tables and "quek" (a game played on a checker-board) with a certain tailor. "Wondering at their continued losing," they examined the board and found that on three quarters of it the black squares were depressed and on the fourth quarter, the white. When they refused to play further, one of them was stripped of his cloak. The tailor and his accomplice were haled into court, forced to make restitution, and, on the prosecution of Ralph Strode, "common Serjeant," sentenced to stand in the pillory, their checker-board being burned beneath them and the reason for their punishment being proclaimed by the sheriff.[3] This, one of many such cases, is cited here because it shows how public the punishment commonly was and because the prosecutor was probably Chaucer's friend, the philosophical Strode. There were many ruses more elaborate,[4] the most daring of which occurred in 1387: One William Frenkysshe, claiming to be the son of the Earl of Ormond, in hiding, imposed mightily on the hospitality and generosity of John Tylneye, inducing John to sell part of his estate for expenses incurred, and sleeping with John's seven-year-old daughter.[5] Even the wife who

> heeld for contenance
> A shoppe, and swyved for hir sustenance

was of a kind known in London. One Elizabeth Moring took in young women as apprentices, "under colour of the craft of

---

81 (Cambridge, 1929), p. 130; theft: *Calendar of Select Pleas and Memoranda of the City of London* .... , *1381–1412* (Cambridge, 1932), pp. 89–90, 102–3, 126; William Bullen, "Boxyng and Neckeweede" ("E.E.T.S.": *The Babees Book* [London, 1868]), p. 241; imprisonment for various breaches of contract: *Plea and Memoranda Rolls, 1323–64*, p. 276; ibid., *1364–81*, pp. 107, 128, 129; *Select Pleas and Memoranda*, p. 170.

[1] *Plea and Memoranda Rolls, 1364–81*, p. xlvi.

[2] *Ibid., 1323–64*, p. 113; ibid., *1364–81*, pp. 47, 52, 89, 115, 116, 130, 211; *Calendar of Letter-Books* .... *of the City of London*, ed. Reginald R. Sharpe (London, 1899–1912), H, 174–75.

[3] *Memorials of London and London Life*, ed. and tr. Henry Thomas Riley (London, 1868), pp. 395–96.

[4] *Letter-Book*, H, pp. 18–19, 295; *Memorials*, pp. 404, 412, 419, 430; Charles Pendrill, *London Life in the Fourteenth Century* (New York, 1925), p. 197.

[5] Told at length in *Memorials*, pp. 496–98.

broidery," really to hire them out to "friars, chaplains, and other such men as desired to have their company." She was caught pawning the stolen breviary of a chaplain loath to pay, and sentenced by Mayor Brembre, Chaucer's associate, to the pillory for women.[1]

It is clear, then, that the London underworld was rich in story stuff. The criminals were prosecuted by Chaucer's probable and certain associates and were dramatically punished in the streets of London. Their crimes were proclaimed. Though the published records contain no evident source or analogue of the *Cook's Tale*, parallels to elements of it were published, day by day during Chaucer's life, at the pillory on Cornhill. Most probably, therefore, Chaucer was fictionalizing contemporary people and events.[2]

[1] 1385. This case is not unique; "through such women and the like deeds many scandals had befallen the city" (*Memorials*, pp. 484–86).

[2] I am grateful to Professor J. S. P. Tatlock for guidance and criticism in the preparation of this study.

THE MAN OF LAW'S TALE

By MARGARET SCHLAUCH

INTRODUCTION

IN COMPOSING his *Man of Law's Tale*, Chaucer used as direct source a lengthy passage in the Anglo-Norman *Chronicle* of Nicholas Trivet, who wrote early in the fourteenth century. This fact was first pointed out in 1845 by the Swedish scholar Bäckström.[1] Trivet's story, in its turn, is but one of a large number of medieval romances in many languages which recount the sorrows and adventures of a beautiful, innocent heroine who is falsely accused or otherwise persecuted, either by her stepmother, her mother-in-law, her father, her envious sister, or a rejected lover; who endures such trials as exile, imprisonment, loss of her children, or servitude; and who is finally restored to her husband and family with her reputation completely cleared and her persecutions ended by the defeat and punishment of her enemies.[2] The *Man of Law's Tale*, Trivet's story, and Gower's *Confessio amantis*, II, 587 ff., constitute a group of three closely connected tales within the general cycle. Both identity of plot and close verbal similarities prove that Chaucer and Gower used Trivet; but the relation of Chaucer to Gower is not so readily determined. E. Lücke has argued[3] from a detailed study that Chaucer used not only Trivet but also Gower, yet verbal similarities alone are not enough to prove this; they might as readily have resulted from a use of Chaucer by Gower. The indications within the poems themselves (our only evidence) indicate an earlier date for Gower. In the first place, his rather mediocre narrative shows no sign of demonstrable influence by Chaucer's more original

---

[1] In the notes to the Swedish folk book, *Helena Antonia af Constantinopel,* ed. in *Svenska Folkböcker,* I (Stockholm, 1845), 221 ff.

[2] For a survey of the cycle see M. Schlauch, *Chaucer's Constance and Accused Queens* (New York, 1927).

[3] "Das Leben der Constanze bei Trivet, Gower und Chaucer," *Anglia,* XIV (1892), 77–112 and 149–85.

and moving tale; in the second place, certain lines in Chaucer's tale and the introduction to it have been construed as references to another version (in English) already in circulation long enough to be known by a literary audience. When in the head link to the *Tale* the Man of Law expresses his disapproval of such "unkinde abhominaciouns" as the stories of Canace and Apollonius of Tyre, both of which involve incest, it is supposed that he is referring to the *Confessio amantis*, which contains them together with the more acceptable Constance story; when Chaucer disagrees explicitly (B 1086 ff.) with the version of a minor episode as reported by "som men" (otherwise unspecified), this too is supposed to refer to Gower as well as to Trivet. These indications are slight, but they point to Gower's priority.[1]

The *Chronique* into which Trivet introduced the story of Constance was written for Princess Marie, daughter of Edward I, after she had become a nun at Almesbury convent. The long and romantic digression, like the extended Arthurian passages, may have been inserted to interest the royal patroness, or because of a request on her part. The tale of Constance is attached to the name of the Emperor Tiberius Constantius, who acceded to the throne of the East in A.D. 578. As authority or source Trivet vaguely refers to "chronicles of the Saxons," otherwise unspecified. No such story is contained in any Anglo-Saxon source known to us; only the name Alla (for Ælle) could be thence derived. There are two versions of the general cycle of persecuted queens, however, which stand close to Trivet's in several respects. One of these is the *Vitae duorum Offarum*, attributed to Matthew of Paris, and the other the French romance *La belle Hélène de Constantinople* of the latter thirteenth or early

---

[1] For a summary of the arguments see Schlauch, pp. 132–34. G. C. Macaulay (*Complete Works of John Gower*, II [Oxford, 1900], 483) also recapitulates Lücke's arguments but arrives at an opposite conclusion. He thinks Chaucer wrote first and Gower copied him. The significance of this head link and prologue to the *MLT*, both for the chronology of the *Canterbury Tales* and for Chaucer's literary relations with Gower, has been presented recently at some length by Carleton Brown, "The Man of Law's Head-Link and the Prologue of the *Canterbury Tales*," *SP*, XXXIV (1937), 8–35, as part of an argument that Group B originally stood at the head of the *CT*. For a possible connection with Boccaccio see Thomas H. McNeal, "Chaucer and *The Decameron*," *MLN*, LIII (1938), 257 f.

fourteenth century.[1] In both of these the heroine flees from her father to avoid an incestuous marriage with him, takes refuge in England, marries a prince of that country (as does Constance), and is falsely accused by means of exchanged letters. The *Vitae*, probably written in the early twelfth century, makes the heroine a daughter of a King of York and uses a war of Offa against the Scots, in behalf of the King of Northumbria, as an occasion for the accusation by means of exchanged letters. This version was no doubt easily accessible to Nicholas Trivet, and from it he may have taken the northern English locality (Knaresburgh) and the war against the Scots by King Alla. *La belle Hélène* also places this part of the story in England, but in the south, near Dover. The feature of *La belle Hélène* which would appeal to Trivet is its preoccupation—at least to a certain extent—with hagiography. The very name of the romance suggests Helena the mother of Constantine.[2] The name of Constance, on the other hand, suggests Constantia, daughter of Constantine. The Hélène of the romance is made the mother of both St. Martin of Tours and St. Bricius (Brice in the romance). It is the pleasure of the romancer to make them twin brothers; in reality we know from Gregory of Tours that Bricius was the successor of Martin, but there is no indication that he was in any way related to him. It is appropriate, however, that he should appear in the tale of an innocent calumniated queen since it is reported that he too was the subject of a false accusation involving adultery, was cleared by a miracle, but only restored to his city after years of exile.[3] It is to be noticed that Trivet has the pious Elda, King Alla's constable, die at Tours and receive burial at St. Martin's.

Trivet uses hagiographical and pseudo-hagiographical ma-

---

[1] *Vitae duorum Offarum*, ed. Wil. Wats (London, 1684), in *Mathaei Paris Historia major*; also in Chaucer Society, *Originals and Analogues* (London, 1872). *La belle Hélène* is not yet printed (see Laura Hibbard Loomis, *Mediaeval Romance in England* [New York, 1924], p. 27 and n.). A summary (taken from the prose redaction) is given by Florian Frocheur, *Messager des sciences historiques* (Ghent, 1846), pp. 169–209.

[2] The relation of these characters to St. Helena and Constantine was first pointed out by Edith Rickert, *Emare* ("E.E.T.S.: Extra Series" [London, 1908]), Introd.

[3] W. Arndt and Br. Krusch, *Gregorii Turonensis Opera, Mon. Germ. Hist., Script. Rerum Merov.* (1884), Book ii, chap. 1 (p. 59).

terial to a still greater extent than *La belle Hélène*. His Constance, like St. Ursula and the heroine of the contemporary *King of Tars*, is persuaded to marry a heathen prince in order to help the Christian cause. His Tiberius Constantius, Roman emperor and father of the heroine, is a historical personage who reigned at Constantinople (not Rome), A.D. 578–82. (He corresponds to the Emperor Antonius of Constantinople in *La belle Hélène*.) Tiberius selected Maurice of Cappadocia to succeed him and gave him his daughter in marriage. "It was during the reign of Maurice that the mission went from Rome for the conversion of the English, and this may have had something to do with the story that Maurice was partly of English origin."[1] (Trivet makes him a grandson of the Emperor.) In similar fashion Geoffrey of Monmouth had created the legend that Helena, Constantine's mother, was English. Trivet uses the name of St. Helena but transfers it from the heroine to her cousin, the wife of Senator Arsenius. Pope Pelagius, referred to several times in the Constance story, was pontiff in A.D. 555–60. Pope John, mentioned at the beginning, is the second of that name (533–35), the predecessor of Pelagius.

In general, Trivet seems to have been guided even in his choice of names for fictitious characters by historical persons who flourished in the latter fifth and sixth centuries. For instance, the name of Hermengild, prince of Spain, martyred by his Arian father (a Visigoth) in 585, is transferred to the wife of the constable of Northumbria. St. Hermengild had been converted to Catholic Christianity by his wife, just as Alla had been converted by Constance. It is significant that Trivet refers expressly to the martyrdom of St. Hermengild immediately before recounting the legend of Constance.[2] King Alla corresponds to Ælle of Northumbria (d. 560). There is a curious inconsistency in the account of the kindly senator who harbors Constance in Rome during her exile. At first, Trivet calls him Tarquinius, but later he abandons this name, presumably be-

---

[1] Macaulay, *Complete Works of John Gower*, II, 484. On the conversion theme see Lillian H. Hornstein, "Trivet's Constance and the *King of Tars*," *MLN*, LV (1940), 355–57.

[2] For St. Hermengildus see Gregory the Great *Dialogues* iii. 31; *Acta sanctorum*, April, II, 136 f. Bede, *De temporum ratione*, gives the date of Hermengild's death as 529, but cf. *Bibliotheca Hag. Lat.* ("Bollandist Society" [Brussels, 1898]), I, 574.

cause of its unpleasant associations, in favor of Arsenius. This was the name of a hermit saint of Lybia who flourished in the fifth century. His *vita* indicates no connection with our story, however.

The miracles associated with Constance—namely, the restoration of a blind man's sight by Hermengild and the direct chastisement of Constance's accuser by divine intervention—are rather commonplace, and it is therefore difficult to surmise what saint's life inspired them; but a few parallels to the former incident, taken from the period in which Trivet places his action, will indicate the type of material he drew on. Bede tells us that in 510 Pope John I, during a visit to Constantinople, restored the sight of a blind man whom he met near the Golden Gate to the city.[1] A youth named Tholosanus is said to have been cured of blindness by visiting the tomb of St. Martin Abbot (d. *ca.* 590–600); his name suggests that of the villain Thelous, also written Tholous, in the story of Constance.[2] Most likely, however, is Trivet's indebtedness to the *Vita* of St. David of Wales, mentioned by him in the Arthurian section of his *Chronicle*, especially since a certain "Lucius, Bishop of Bangor in Wales," plays a fairly important part in the Constance story. It is told of David that in the very act of being baptized he caused a blind man's sight to be restored, and later he cured his teacher Paulinus of blindness, although his excessive modesty had kept him from ever gazing on the face of his master. David, like Hermengild, was at first too timid to make the attempt; but he obeyed his master's words: "Leua tantum manum, tangens oculos, nec tamen cernens, et sanabor." This is done by making the sign of the cross over the eyes of Paulinus, as Hermengild is bidden to do by the blind Briton.[3] A certain Paulinus was also cured of incipient blindness by St. Martin of Tours; the incident is recounted by Ælfric and is important here because of the connection between this particular saint and *La belle Hélène*.

[1] *De temporum ratione*, ed. Th. Mommsen, *Mon. Germ. Hist.*, *Auctores Antiquissimi*, XIII, 247 ff.

[2] *Acta sanctorum*, October, X, 811.

[3] "Factumque est, vt congregatis in vnum discipulis, ex Magistri rogatu, singuli oculos Magistri Crucis impressione tangentes benedicerent, vt eorum oratione & benedictione sanaretur" (*Acta sanctorum*, March, I, 42).

The cumulative effect of these parallels of name and incident is to indicate the hagiographical interest in Trivet's *Constance*. Considering the pious and edifying tone thus imparted to the tale, it is no wonder that Trivet chose to deviate from the numerous stories of persecuted queens—like *La belle Hélène*—in which the heroine begins her adventures by flight from an incestuous father. To avoid this shocking episode, Trivet could do no better than to duplicate the motive of persecution by a mother-in-law, so that Constance is first exiled by the Sultan's mother, and later by King Alla's. The repetition is awkward, but at least the offending episode is thus suppressed.

The ultimate origin of the cycle of persecuted heroines has been discussed more than once, and the various episodes have been compared with motives in folk tales and romance.[1] In a very important study Josef Schick has suggested that the legend of Constance and other related groups are derived from the third-century Greek romance with hagiographical and theological flavoring known as the *Clementine Recognitions*. Professor Schick cites a story in the *Kaiserkronik* (A.D. 1147) as an intermediate stage between the *Recognitions* and the so-called *Crescentia* version of the cycle. Since *Crescentia* and *Constance* are in turn clearly related, the chain of connections is thus complete. All the romances of the cycle use the literary device of bringing together the scattered members of a family at the end of the story for a general reunion; such a "recognition scene," as it is technically called, is notoriously common in Greek romance. Not only the names of some of the characters but also the plot in which they appear would, therefore, come ultimately from Byzantium.[2]

The origin of the Constance legend in the area of Byzantine influence has been reaffirmed by A. H. Krappe, who uses the geographical diffusion of folk tales as evidence. He distinguishes three types of folk tale and relates the romances of the Constance cycle to one or another of these types. Recapitulat-

[1] A. B. Gough, *On the Constance-Saga* (*Palaestra*, Vol. XXXIII [1902]); M. Schlauch, *Chaucer's Constance*; Arthur Dickson, *Valentine and Orson* (New York, 1929), esp. pp. 38 ff.

[2] J. Schick, "Die Urquelle der Offa-Konstanze Sage," *Britannica* ("Festschrift Max Förster" [Leipzig, 1929]), pp. 31–56.

ing the list of historical names in the Constance version, he argues that these were not original with Trivet but were first introduced into a lost source which "presumably was a compilation like those of Wace and Jeffrey Gaimar, professing to satisfy the curiosity of the Normans about the past history of the British Isles." It is possible, to be sure, that Trivet was following "an older model written in Latin or Norman French"; but it would have been very easy for Trivet himself to make the innovations. The Greek connections had already been suggested in *La belle Hélène;* so had the hagiographical elements; all that remained to be done was to suppress the incident of the incestuous father, add to the hagiographical material, and look up the names of some sixth-century saints and rulers in a handbook like Bede's *De ratione temporum.* Since Trivet was writing for a royal nun, it would seem as likely that he did this himself as that he depended upon a "lost original" for the change.[1]

Besides hagiography, pseudo-history, and moral instruction, our story also contains motives drawn from the general body of migratory plots, superstitions, and popular beliefs commonly known as folklore. Their presence has been recognized by all students since Gough made the first extended investigation of the cycle. The use of wicked mothers-in-law as persecutors, of an accusation of monstrous birth and consequent exile of the accused heroine, imparts something of the terror and unreality of a *märchen* world to our romantic and edifying theme. It remained for Chaucer, however, to add the greatest quality of all: to infuse into the quaint, traditional plot the pathos of sentient and suffering human beings; to elevate what was dead and conventional into the realm of art. It is worth while to read the simpler versions of Trivet and Gower, if only to realize afresh from the contrast how far Chaucer stands above them.[2]

---

[1] A. H. Krappe, "The Offa-Constance Legend," *Anglia,* LXI (1937), 361–69.

[2] The following stories in the cycle of accused and persecuted queens may be added to those discussed by me in *Chaucer's Constance:* the *vita* of St. Dympna, *Acta sanctorum,* May, III, 478 ff. (*init.*); *Van den Keyserinne van Rome,* discussion by C. G. N. de Vooys, *Middelnederlandse Legenden en Exempelen* (The Hague, 1926), pp. 123–25 (see Paul Zaunert, *Marienlegenden* [Jena, 1925], pp. 3 ff.); *Mírmans saga,* ed. Eugen Kölbing in *Riddarasögur* (Strassburg, 1872); Johannes Junior, *Scala Coeli* (Ulm, 1486), fols. 27ᵇ f. (see A. Wesselski, *Märchen des Mittelalters* [Berlin, 1925], pp. 29–31 and notes on p. 200).

MANUSCRIPTS

The French *Chronique* of Trivet is preserved in the following manuscripts:

Ar   Arundel 56, British Museum, fourteenth century, used by E. Brock in his edition for the Chaucer Society. Brock was aware of the existence of only two manuscripts:—Ar and S. Ar is mentioned in the *DNB*, under the life of Trivet, by its old number, Gresham College C 56. The old notation is repeated by J. Vising, *Anglo-Norman Language and Literature* (Oxford, 1923), Index, p. 91.

F   Fairfax 10 [3890], Bodleian Library, Oxford, fourteenth century.[1]

M   Magdalen College 45, fourteenth century, earlier than Ar. (See Thomas Duffus Hardy, *Descriptive Catalogue*, III, 349.)

S   Stockholm, Kungl. Biblioteket D 1311*a* (formerly No. 3), collated by Brock (whose variants have been used in the present edition). Omitted by Vising and Hardy.

R   Rawlinson B 178 [11,545], Bodleian Library, Oxford, fourteenth century.

Fr   Fonds français 9687, Paris, Bibliothèque Nationale; a decorated manuscript of the fourteenth century. (See Henri Omont, *Ancien suppl. fr.*, Vols. I–III: *Nos. 6171–15,369 du Fonds fr.* [Paris, 1893], p. 22.) This manuscript was unknown to Brock, Hardy, and Vising.

G   Gale O.4.32 [1262] in Trinity College, Cambridge, fourteenth century.

D   Douce 119 [21,693], Bodleian Library, Oxford, fifteenth century. The folios covering the years 33–583 are missing, so that the Constance story is incomplete; the remainder goes as far as the reign of Richard I.

The manuscripts containing our story fall into three groups: Ar, M, and S; R, Fr, and D; and F and G. In the second group, D may be eliminated since the lacuna covers most of the Constance story. G represents a distinct aberration from all the manuscripts of the other groups: it shows about twice as many hyperforms and pseudo-learned forms as they; it introduces many minor inversions of word order, and in many detailed readings it has obvious corruptions (*Moris* for *monstre; aloinez* for *alliez; fossez* for *estoffe*, etc.). F, which resembles it closely, must be eliminated for similar reasons. Of the two

---

[1] Information concerning the existence of this manuscript reached me from Miss Ruth Dean of Mount Holyoke College while the present volume was going through the press. It was unknown to Vising and Hardy, but discovered by Mr. Denholm-Young while he was preparing publication of the *Summary Catalogue*. Unfortunately, I have not been able to include variants from the text of F, although Miss Dean's generous communication has enabled me to list it and to include remarks concerning its relation to other manuscripts.

remaining groups, it must now be decided which probably stands closer to Trivet's original text of the Constance story.

Ar, M, and S may be called Group A, and R, Fr, and D, Group B. From the variants recorded by Brock, it appears that S in Group A may be eliminated from it as later than and inferior to Ar. Group A has readings which improve on B, but B also improves on A almost as often. B frequently shows more ample readings, but upon examination most of these appear to be due to the insertion of unnecessary synonyms, or to the repetition of proper nouns, rather than to the preservation of words elsewhere lost from the original. Moreover, there are two rather important omissions on the opening pages of the Constance story, where A gives the complete text. (This argument would not, of course, constitute a determining factor in the choice of a basic manuscript for the whole text of the *Chronique*. It is decisively important, however, in editing the Constance story alone.)

A study of the dialect gives some further indication that Group A may be closer to the original. In the fourteenth century any cultured Anglo-Norman was likely to know Ile-de-France French, especially if (like Trivet) he had studied in Paris. Hence arguments based on comparison with an ideally "pure" dialect have little validity. Nevertheless, the preservation of Anglo-Norman characteristics such as *ei* for French *oi*, *u* before liquid or nasal, simplified diphthongs, and inflectional archaisms will offer some guidance. On the whole, Group A shows the greater number of these characteristics,[1] being near a hypothetical Anglo-Norman text of the early fourteenth century, if this showed linguistic characteristics of the "pure" dialect. Within Group A the choice falls on M for several reasons: first, it is older than Ar and S; second, it is most clearly Norman; and, finally, it has fewest instances of glaring grammatical mistakes (such as feminine adjectives with masculine nouns, archaic nominative endings added to oblique cases,

[1] The precise counting of such forms is extremely difficult because of the ambiguous orthography. Moreover, spelling no doubt lagged behind actual changes in pronunciation. Tables of forms do offer an approximate guide to manuscript relations, however. They have been omitted here to save space. In her forthcoming edition of the entire Trivet text, Miss Dean uses R as basic manuscript.

etc.). For these reasons, M has been chosen as the basic manuscript.

In printing the text, abbreviations have been expanded, and the capitalization, punctuation, and division into sentences have been modernized. Variant readings from other manuscripts are recorded only when they improve on M. The very few variations from Brock's reading of M have been noted. The variants in S are taken from the notes to Brock's edition.

The text of Gower's version of the story has already been critically edited in G. C. Macaulay's *Complete Works of John Gower*, Volume II; *Confessio amantis*, II, 587–1612. A description of the several families of manuscripts is given by Macaulay in his introduction (II, cxvii ff.). It appears that there are no less than three recensions of the *Confessio*, among which the manuscripts are divided as follows: twenty-five belong to the first recension (in subdivisions of seven, eight, and ten manuscripts, respectively); seven belong to the second (in subdivisions of two and five, respectively); and nine belong to the third. The basic text of Macaulay's edition is, naturally, the best of the last or third recension—Fairfax 3 in the Bodleian Library, Oxford. So far as the story of Constance is concerned, there is no significant difference between one recension and another. Macaulay's reading of Fairfax 3 has been checked with the original, and a few slight deviations are recorded. In addition, the other chief manuscripts of the third recension have been consulted:

H_2 Harleian 3869, British Museum
H_3 Harleian 7184, British Museum
M   Magdalen 213, Oxford
N   New College 226, Oxford

and besides

H_4 Harleian 7333 (selections, including the *Constance*).

K and P^3 (in private possession), W (late and full of mistakes), Hn (from Caxton's edition) were not consulted. A few additional variants have been recorded, but those already given in Macaulay's excellent edition are not repeated. The capitalization of the text has been modernized.

TRIVET'S LIFE OF CONSTANCE[1]

⟨fol. 51*a*⟩ En le tenps cist Thiberie Constantin, emperour, com dient les vns cronikes, estoit vn tresuailaunt cheualer del pais de Capadoce, apele Moris. Cist Moriz fu eslu par le auant dist Thiberie destre emperour ⟨fol. 51*b*⟩ oue lui; e lui dona femme Constaunce sa fille, e la[2] clama son heir. Mes come dient les aunciene cronikes de Sessouns, cist Moris nestoit mes de dissept antz quant il fu ordine par Tyberie al empire, trop gracious juuencel, merueilousement vigerous de son age, e de sen sages e agu. Cist, solom lestoire de Sessouns auant dites, estoit le fitz Constaunce, la fille Tyberie, de vn rei de Sessouns, Alle, auant nome, que estoit le secund rei de Northombre; e fu dist de Capadoce, quar dozze anz estoit norri en la court le senatour Tarquinius de Rome, questoit de Capadoce. Dount fait assauoir que cist Tyberie Constantin, taunt com il gouerna la court e lez prouinces del empire souz lemperor Justin, com auant est dist al comencement del quarauntime sisme estoire, engendra de sa femme Ytalie vne fille Constaunce. E pur ceo que nul autre enfaunt auoyt, pur ceo a grant diligence la fist enseigner la fey Cristien, e endoctriner par mestres sachaunz en lez sept sciences, que sount logicience, naturel, morale, astronomie, geometrie, musique, perspectiue, que sount philosophies seculeres apelez, e la fist endoctriner en diuerses langages. Puis, quant ele estoit entree le trezime aan de soun age, vindrent a la court son pere Tiberie, marchauntz paens hors de la grande Sarazine, portaunts divers e riches marchaundies, a queus descendi Constaunce pur auiser lour richesses; si lour demaunda de lour terre e de lour creaunce. E quant ele entendi qil estoient paens, lour prescha la fey Cristienn. E puis qil auoient assentu a la fey, les fist baptizer e enseiner parfitement en la fei Iesu Crist.

Constance preaches Christianity to Saracen merchants.

Puis retournerent a lour terre. Et quant reconustrent la foi deuant lour veisines e parens Sarazins, estoient accuses al haut soudan de lour fey. E apres qil estoient amenes deuaunt lui, furent repris par les sages de lour ley qil deueyent crere en vn homme crucefie e mortel. Mes puis qil aueyent suffisauntment defendu la ley Iesu Crist encountre les paens qi ne sauoient plus countredire, comenserent de preiser la pucele Constaunce qui les auoyt conuertu, de trop haute e noble sen e sapience e de graunde[3] merueilouse biaute e gentirise e noblesce de saunc; par quelez paroles lui soudan, trop suppris del amour de la pucele (com il estoit homme de joeuene age), maunda de nouel mesmes ceux Cristiens qil[4] conuerti a la fei, e ouesqes eus vn

They praise her to their Sultan; he is enamored of her and proposes marriage.

---

[1] Taken from Nicholas Trivet, *Les Chroniques ecrites pour Marie d'Angleterre, fille d'Edward I.* (Text from MS Magdalen 45, Oxford.)

[2] lui *G.*   [3] et *added F, R.*   [4] ia *S, F, R, G.*

admiral paen oue graunt aparail et richesses e presentz a Tyberie
e a sa fille, en demaundaunt la pucele en mariage oue grant promesce
de pees e daliance countre[1] lez parties de Cristiens e Sarazins. E
puis que Tyberie auoit counseile sur ceste demaunde le pape Johan[2]
(de qi est auaunt dist en le quarauntisme sisme estoire) e les autrez
grantz de seint eglise, e lez Romeyns del senat, respoundy al admiral e
as messagers, qe si luy soudan se voleit assenter de reneer sez maumetz
e sa mescreaunce, e resceiuere bapteme e la lei Iesu Crist, a cest couenaunt Tyberius sassentireit a laliaunce, mes ne pas en autre fourme.
E sur ceo maunda sez lettres a lui soudan, e grantment honura les
messagers. E cist,[3] a lour retourner, sur toute riens preiserent la
pucele a lui soudan, e la nobleye, e la court, e la genti ⟨fol. 52a⟩
seignurie Thiberie. Et lui admiral deuaunt le soudan e deuant tot
soun[4] counseil se vowa a la fey Cristien si le soudan sassentisit.

The Sultan is will-
ing to be baptised
in order to win Con-
stance as wife.
Puis apres poy de iours le soudan maunda mesmes cesti admiral e
solempnes messagers dez plus grantz de sa terre e en lour conduyt
duzze enfauntz Sarazins fitz a grauntz Sarazins, hostages a Thiberie,
en fourme de seurte pur sa fille. E a ceo maunda son assent, haut e
baas, de lordinaunce des Cristiens, e a ceo enuoya sez lettres asseles
[de bone][5] e entere pees entre tous Cristiens e tous Sarazins, e fraunche
passage de aler fraunchement e marchaunder, e pur visiter lez seintz
luz del sepulcre, e del mount de Caluarie, e de Bethleem e de Nazareth
e del val de Josaphat e tous autres[6] seyns deins les marches de son
power. Et la cite de Ierusalem abaundona a la seignurie des Cristiens
pur enhabiter, e ffraunchises as euesques Cristiens e a lour clergie de
precher, e enseigner les gentz de sa terre la dreite foy, e de baptizer
e deglises fere, e les temples de maumetz destrure. E a ceo enuoya
ses lettres a lapostoile e a la clergie, e a Tyberie e a la pucele Constaunce, e a tut le senat, oue riche douns e tresours par[7] persones. E
pur lour conunes[8] sur cest maundement tous se acorderent e en tenps
maunderent la pucele hors de la mesoun son piere e hors de sa conisaunce, entre estraunges barbaryns a grant doel e lermes e crie e
noise e pleinte de toute la citee de Rome. En cele veiage estoit enueye
vn euesqe cardinal e[9] vn prestre cardinal[9] oue grant noumbre de
clergie e vn senatour de Rome oue noble cheualerie e grant e riche

---

[1] entre S, F, R, G.

[2] le tiers added F, R.

[3] ils S; ceux G.

[4] Thus Ar; Brock reads sun.

[5] Om. M, Ar.

[6] lieux added S.

[7] grantz added S.

[8] Sic; comunes Ar, F, R; conues S; comies G; for the meaning ("in behalf of
their communes or towns") see Godefroy, commune (1).

[9] e ... cardinal om. G.

aparail e oue grant noumbre dez Cristiens qe i alerent, les vns pur
pelerinage, les autres pur la seysine de Jerusalem.

Avynt que la mere le soudan, que vnquore viuoit (allas! si ne fut
la volunte dieu), veaunte que sa ley estoit ia en poynt destre destrute
par Cristiens qi furent[1] en Saraisines, senpensa de mal e de tresoun.
Dount puis qele auoit priue aliaunce de couenaunt ouesqe sept
[cenz][2] Sarazyns qe sabaundonerent de viuere e morir en la querele,
mist[3] a soun fitz quant ele oy la venue de la pucele e de Cristiens bien
pres de la terre a poy des iourneis e comensca mout mercier e loer
dieu qel auoit le purpos de la ley Cristien, e lui iura qe par grant tenps
auoit ele este en mesme la volunte priuement; dount finaument pria
soun fitz le soudan qe lui grauntast la prime feste auant les esposailes,
e il en merciaunt ly octrei. Puis fu la pucele e les Cristiens resceu
del souldan e de sa mere a grant honur e a grant nobleye. E le primer
iour de lour venue fu la feste purweue en le paleys le soudane, e estoit
la mangerie ordeyne issint qe[4] les hales li soudan mangasent tous
madles, Cristiens e Sarazins, e qe en les hales e en la feste le soudane
fusent soules femmes sauntz les sept centz Sarazins lowes[5] qe furent
ordeines pur seruice del vne feste e del autre. E ces sept centz lowis,
quant la fest fust plus lee, vyndrent armes oue vne autre graunde
multitude de lour reteinaunce sur lez mangeauntz. E solom lordinaunce de la soudane, tuerent tous les Cristiens, madles e femeles,
fors soule la pucele; e occirent le soudan et ladmiral e lez autres
conuertiez a la fei. E par tote la court quantqil trouerent del
comun peouple des Cristiens, mistrent a la mort. ⟨fol. 52b⟩ Mes treis
vallez Cristiens eschaperent, quant primerement oierent lefray, e
vindrent a Rome e counterent al emperor la mescheaunce e le traisoun
e la mort sa fille Constaunce, come il entendirent. A ceste nouele
estoit lemperour e tote la clergie e senat affraietz; a grant doel fu
demene par mi Rome.

A ceste manere demorra Constaunce soule, degarre, toute en lez
meins ses enemis. Puis, apres que ele ne voleit pur nule bele promesse
de richesse ne de honur, ne pur nul manace de peyne ne de mort,
reneier sa fei, le membre au diable, la soudane, senpensa de lui[6] nouel
turment, que tut li uensit de cruele volunte,—nepurquant la purueaunce dieu ni faili poynt, qi en tribulacioun ia ne faut a ceaus qi
ount en lui esperaunce. Dount ele fist estorer vne neefs de vitaile,

[margin] Constance is received by the Sultan's mother, who plans to ambush and murder the Christian guests.

[margin] The massacre. Three youths escape and bring the news to Rome.

[margin] Constance is set afloat in a ship without rudder or sail by order of the Sultan's mother.

[1] qestoient G; suruenauntz added S.

[2] Om. M, Ar; sept C dez S, G; sept cenz F, R.

[3] vient F, R.   [5] I.e., "mercenaries."

[4] qen F, R, G.   [6] dune S; de vne F; de vn R; dun G.

de payn quest apele bisquit, e de peis e de feues, de sucre et[1] de meel e de vyn pur sustenaunce de la vie de la pucele pur treis aunz. E en cele neef fist mettre tote la richesse e le tresour que lempire Tyberie aueit maunde oue la pucele Constaunce, sa fille; e en cele neef fist la soudane mettre la pucele saunz sigle e sauntz neuiroun e sauntz chescune manere de eide de homme. E issint la first mener par autres neefs tanqe a la haute meer, e[2] ou nule terre lour apparut; e issint les mariners la lesserent soule e la comaunderent a quatre ventz. Mes dieu estoit soun mariner, quar par treis aunz entiers fu ele mesme en la graunde occean; en tut le tenps vnqes homme ne neef ne vist ne encountra. Mes dieux soul lauoit conforte e conseile de sa parlaunce.

Puis le oytime moys del quart aan, dieux, qi gouerna la neef le seint home Noe en le graunde diluuie, maunda vn vent couenable e enchasca la neef en Engletere, de south[3] vn chastel en la reaume de Northombre, pres Humbre; e ariua la neef la veile de la natiuite Jesu Crist. E quant les mariners que estoient pres de la riuail en lour neefs virent ceste meruaile, ceo est assauoir vne pucele de bele e genti afeiture, mes descoloure, en estraunge atir e estoffe de graunt tresour, alerent al gardeyn del chastel que adounque estoit vn Sessoun quy auoit a noun Elda[4] (quar les Bretounz[5] auoient ia perdu la seingnurie del isle, come auant est countee en la fin del quarantisme quint estoire), e lui counterent la meruaile. Et Elda descendi a la pucele en sa neef e lui demaunda de son estre. E ele lui respoundi en Sessoneys, qe fu la langage Elda, come cele questoit aprise en diuerses laungages, com auant est dist, e lui disoit qe quant a sa creaunce ele estoit de Cristiene fey; quant a linage, qele estoit de riches e nobles gentz estret; e qe par soun linage estoit ele done en mariage a vn grant prince; mes pur ceo qe ele desplut as grantz de la terre, pur ceo fu ele en tiele manere exilee. E entre sez dys riens ne voleit reconustre de Tyberie lemperor, soun piere, ne del soudan; quar laauenture del mourdre del soudan e de les Cristient estoit ia conue par totes terres. E puis qe Elda lauoit oy si renablement parler sa launge, e troua oue lui si grant tresour, esperoit qe ele estoit fille de ascun rey de Sessoneys outre meer, com de Alemayne ou de Sessoyne, ou de Swete, ou de Denemarch. E a graunt ioye, curteisement e honurablement la resceut en le chastel; e le tresour qil auoyt oue lui troue, ferma eyns vne huche souz double serure, de quele il baila[6] la pucele le vne clef, e deuer sei retint lautre. E comaunda sa compayne quele resceut la pucele honurablement en sa chaumbre.

---

[1] se *in MS.*

[2] *Om.* S, F, R, G.

[3] de souz S, F, R, G.

[4] Olda S, F, R, G (*so throughout*).

[5] brutons F, R (*et passim*).

[6] a *added* G.

Puis apres vn poy de tenps, qele estoit bien auigoure de bones viaundes e counforte de bayns e dautre esemenz, ele reprist sa beaute e sa bele colour. E tut fust ele bele a merueile de corps, nepurquant ele passa en biaute dez vertues com cele que dieux auoit predestine a grace e vertue e temptacioun e joye. Dount ⟨fol. 53a⟩ quant Hermyngild, la femme Elda, aparceut sa noble vie e vertuouse, taunt fu de samour supprise, qe riens ne lui poeit avenir qe ele ne freit a sa volunte.

Lors, quaunt plusours foitz lui auoit ceste parole afferme, vn jour com Hermingyld lui rehersa autre foitz la parole, la seinte pucele lui respoundi: "Et puis que riens ne est," dist ele, "qe vous ne freez a ma volunte, dount vous serrez mesme tiel come ioe suy." Et Hermyngild lui respoundi: "A ceo," dist ele, "ja ne purray ioe ateyndre, quar vous etez en terre sauntz peer en vertue." E Custaunce lui respount: "A ceo poez vous venir, si crere voudrez en celi dieu quest seignur de toute vertue." (¹Hermingyld e Elda e lez autres Sessouns qe auoient dounque la seignurie de la terre estoient vnquore paens.) E Hermin- gild homblement e deuoutement escota la doctrine de la fei par la bouche Constaunce, que lui aprist la puissaunce dieu en la fesaunce de tut le mound, e sa vengeaunce quyl prist² par la grant deluuie, e apres par les grantz cites qil enfoundri en enfern pur pesche, e³ hommes, e bestes, e quantque leins estoit. Puis li moustra le grant amour dieu en sa nesaunce, sa boneirte e vertue en sa mort e en sa passioun, e la vertue de la deite⁴ Iesu Crist en sa resurrexioun e en sa ascensioun, e tote la nature de vn soul dieu e treis persones⁵ en la venue del seint espirit. E quant par plusours iours lauoit de la fei apris, e lez sacre- mentz, e de les⁶ comaundementz,⁷ lui aprist amour e desir e la joye de ciel, e les peines denfern douter. Dont Hermigyld, apres ceste aprise, devotement pria destre baptize solom la fourme de seint eglise; mes pur ceo qe soun baroun estoit paen, ele ne poeit vnquore purseure soun purpos.

E avint qe ausint com Helda e Hermingild e Constaunce alerent vn iour de veer la marine e les pessoners peschauntz en la meer, (e) voient encountraunt vn pouere Cristien Britoun enveugles. Cist, questoit de tous estraunge, mes apris del seint espirit, comensca de crier deuant touz: "Hermyngild, la femme Elda e la deciple Coun- staunce, te⁸ pri en le noun Jesu en qui tu crois, que tu me facis le signe de la crois sur mes eus enweugles." A ceste parole, Hermigild, trop affraie, estoit abaie; mes Constaunce, entendaunte la vertue

---

¹ qar added S, F, R, G.

² de pecche added S, F, R, G.

³ oue S, F, R, G.

⁴ I.e., "deity, godhead."

⁵ en trinite et added S.

⁶ .x. added S.

⁷ puis added S.

⁸ le in MS.

dieu en la parole lenueugle, conforta Hermigild[1] e lui dist: "Ne mucez pas, dame, la vertue qe dieu te ad done." E Hermigild, deuaunt Elda e sa mene qe lui suy, de bone fei e ferme fist sur lez eus de lui ennueugles la seinte crois e lui dist en sa laungge Sessone: "Bisene man, in Iesu name in rode ysclawe, haue thi[2] sith."[3] E si meintenaunt fu allumine, e regardoit bien e clerement. Quant Elda auoit ceo veu, mout senmerueila ou sa femme auoit aprise si bele mestrie. Et apres qil auoit demaunde, ele lui respoundi qe si il escotat soun conseil, tiele merueile freyt e plus graunde. Puis Hermigild e Constaunce ne cesserent [de precher][4] a Elda e a tote sa menee la fei Iesu Crist. E cil pouere Britoun receuerent e sustindrent pur lamour Iesu Crist. Lors Elda trop ioiusement resceut la doctrine de la fey; e par comun assent maunderent priueement le dist Britoun en Gales, ou estoient le plus de Britouns fuitz, come auant est dist en la fyn del quarauntisme quint estoire, pur amener de illoeqes vn euesqe Britoun qi poeit Elda e sa femme e lour meine baptizer. E en le mene tenps, Elda fist debruser[5] lour Mahouneth, qil auoient aoure, e les comaunda gettre en longgaynes.

Puis cist pouere Britoun, returnaunt de Gales, amena ouesqe lui Lucius, vn dez euesques de Gales,[6] de Bangor. Cist Lucius, apres ceo qil auoit assae e esproue que Elda oue sa femme e sa menee estoient solom dreite fourme de la lei e fei enfourmes, loa dieux deuoutement e les baptiza al noumbre de quatre vinz e vnze. ⟨fol. 53b⟩ Puis Elda par grant auisement e priue counsil de lui mesmes ala a son seygnur le rey de Northombre, Alle, auant nome, e en priue counseil lui counta de la pucele Counstaunce com cely que par graunt affiaunce de leaute e seen auoit sa souereyne garde del reaume apres lui roys. E quant le rei auoit tous sez dis priue en counseil entre eus dois escote, mout fu desirous de la pucele veer et parler. E a cest desir promist a Elda qil priuement la vendreit visiter.

Elda and Hermengild are baptized by Bishop Lucius of Bangor in Wales.

En cel mesme tenps, vn cheualer Sessoun de la meyne Elda, entre lez autres ia baptize, a quy Elda auoit baile la garde del chastel taunque a sa venue del roys, estoit par priue temptacioun suppris en lamur la pucele Constaunce. Et[7] par maueise aprise e temptacioun del diable ala surquere la pucele Constaunce de assent de pesche char-

---

[1] *Thus Ar; Brock reads* hermigilde.

[2] ʒi *in MS.*

[3] sight *Ar, G;* siht *F, R.*

[4] *Om. MS and Ar.*

[5] debrusier *Ar; Brock reads* debruisier.

[6] qestoit *added F, R.*

[7] pur ceo qen labsence Olda tote la garde lui estoit demoree *added F, R;* pur ceo qen labsence tout la garde estoit a luy demure *S;* qen labsence de Olda toute la garde de lui estoit demorez *G.*

nel. E puis quele auoit[1] respris vne foitz e autre, la tierce foiz oue
grant qoer luy reuili en disaunt qil estoit com cheen, que apres si seinte
sacrement de son baptesme voleit retourner a son merde. Puis cist,
dotaunt qil fust acuse de sa mesprise a soun seignur Elda, a soun
retourner, de mal se purueint. Qar en la iournante de la nuyt a quele
Elda deuoit entrer le chastel en le returnaunt del rey, puis que Hermyngild e Constaunce estoient forment endormies apres longes veiletz
e oreisouns, cist, que tut estoit pris en la mayn al diable, trencha la
goule Hermingild, sa dame, e coste[2] Constaunce, qe fu forment en-
dormie en mesme le lyt. E quant il auoit parfait la felonie, musca le
coteil senglaunt en[3] Constaunt lorier[3] la pucele.

A ceo apres poy de tenps entra Elda le chastel, e en haste vint a
la chaumbre sa compaine pur counter nouele de la venue le rey.
Constaunce, qe oue la noyse estoit aueile, quidaunte la dame dor-
maunte, lui moueyt la mayn pur la veiler. E quant ele senti que le
corps lui estoit tut moil de saunc, a grant affray dist en criaunt:
"Ma dame est morte!" A quele parole Elda e qui estoient en present,
trop abais de la parole, come ceus que riens nentendirent de la felonie,
accriauns "Lumere! Lumere!" trouerent la goule Hermingild hidouse-
ment trenche e le corps tut envolupe en saunc. E quant tous acrierent
la crueute, en demaundaunt de Constaunce la verite, cist tretres,
qi auoyt fet la felonie, hugement surmist la mort sur la pucele, e
par countenaunce que la mort lui estoit plus pres a quoer qe as autres,
saili a toute pars com homme arage, taunqe il eust troue le coteil la
ou il lauoit mesmes musce; e deuant touz moustraunt le instrument
de la felonie, a huge crie apela la pucele de tresoun. Mes Elda, qi ne
poeit cele crueute penser de la pucele, bonement la defendi. E cil
maueys en haste prist entre mains le liure lesuesqe Lucius, auant nome,
questoit liure dez Ewangeiles, qe lez seintes femmes, Hermyngild e
Constaunce, chescune nuyt par deuocioun auyoent en coste eles; e sur
cel liure iura en criaunt, si dieu lui eydast e le Ewangeile e son baptesme, que ia nouelement auoit resceu, qe Custance fu la felonesse,
mordrere la dame. A peine auoit parfini la parole, qe vne mayn close
com poyn de homme apparut deuant Elda e quant questoient en
presence, e ferri tiel coup en le haterel[4] le feloun, qe ambedeus lez
eus luy enuolerent de la teste, e lez deentz hors de la bouche; e le
feloun chai abatu a la terre. E a ceo dist vne voiz en le oye de touz:

A wicked knight, having been re-buffed by Con-stance, kills Her-mengild and hides the dagger under the pillow of Con-stance.

Constance is ac-cused of murder by the wicked knight.

A hand from heav-en strikes the false accuser to earth; Constance vindi-cated.

---

[1] lauoit *F, R, G;* auoit lui *S.*

[2] *Sic;* en coste *F, R;* a coste *S;* a cost *G;* E ceste *Ar.*

[3] aderer loriler Constaunce *S;* de souz le oriler Constaunce *F;* de sour le oeiler
Constaunce *R;* et Constaunce lorir *G.*

[4] I.e., "neck; head."

"Aduersus filiam matris ecclesie ponebas scandalum; hec[1] fecisti et[2] tacui." Et pur ceo que la venue le rey fu pres, pur ceo ne voleit Elda iugement doner sur la tresoun iesqes a sa venue; e mist le feloun en prisoun. Puis deyns poy dez iours, par le rey fu le iugement done de sa mort. Puis le rey—pur ⟨fol. 54a⟩ le grant amour qil auoit a la pucele, e pur lez miracles par dieux moustrez—le rey Alle se fist baptizer del euesqe Lucius, auant nome; et esposa la pucele, qe conseut del rey [vn][3] enfaunt madle.

Puis, a vn demi aan passe, vint nouele al rey que les gentz de Albanye, qe sount les Escotz, furent passes lour boundes e guerrirent les terres le roy. Dount par comun conseil le rei assembla son ost de rebouter ses enemis. Et auant son departir veers Escoce, baila la reine Constaunce sa femme en la garde Elda le conestable du chastel e a Lucius, leuesque de Bangoor; si lour charga que quant ele fu deliueres denfaunt, qi[4] lui feisent hastifment sauoir la nouele. E sur toute riens lour charga que la reine fut a totez sez eises.

Vnquore a cel tenps estoit la mere le reis Alle en vie, bele dame e fere de corage, e que trop morteument hey Constaunce la reyne. Qar grant[5] engayn auoyt que le reis Alle auoit pur lamour vne femme estraunge, e qi lynage lui nestoit pas conu, sa primere ley gwerpi, quele touz ses auncestres auoient leaulment e enterement gardes. Dautre part graunt enuye lui auoit le quer naufre, que Constaunce estoit de toutes gentz, riches e pouueres, saunz comparisoun[6] de lui ou de nule[7] de la terre, plus grauntment preise de bounte e de seintete e de merueilouse beaute. E lui fu auis sa loaunge e sa glorie fu ia anentie pur le graunt pris de Constaunce. E mout lui encrut sa ire lez chaunssounz que lez puceles de la terre fesoient e chauntoyent de lui. La mare[8] auoit a noun Deumylde. Puis quant dieu e nature voleient, Constaunce fu deliuerez de vn enfaunt madle, bel enfaunt e graunt, ben engendre, bien norre nee,[9] e al baptisme fu nome Moris. Puis Elda e Lucius hastifuement maunderent noueles graciousez al rey de la reigne, que fu seigne e heite, e de son enfaunt dount ele estoyt deliueres. A cel tenps estoit Doumilde, le mere le rey, a Knaresbourth[10] entre Engleterre e Escoce, auxi come en la mene.[11] Avint que le

[1] hoc F, R, G.
[2] non added S, F, R, G.
[3] Om. M, Ar.
[4] qil F, R; quils G.
[5] auant in M, S.
[6] comparison Ar; Brock reads comparaison.
[7] autre added S.
[8] Miere Ar, G; mere F, R.
[9] bien nee Ar, F, R, G.
[10] knaresbourgh Ar, R; Knaresborugh F; knaresburgh G.
[11] en lieu men Ar, S, F, R; en lieu moien G.

messager maunda[1] par Elda e Lucius, ala par Knaresbourch pur porter e nuncier a la mere le rey bone nouele, com il quidoyt par resoun. E[2] ele, oye la nouele, feynt trop grant ioye en agard[3] de gentz, e al messager dona trop grauntz dounz e riches en moustraunce de ioie. Mes plus pensa que ne dist, qar cele nuyt enyueri taunt le messauger de vn maliciouse beyuere que luy purprist la cerueile, e si fort le lia les sens, qil iueut com sauntz sens e come homme mort. Puis, par lassent e le conseil le soun clerc, ouery la boiste le messager e ouery les lettres maundes al rey par le counte Elda e leuesque Lucius, e les fausa desouz mesmes lez seals, e escritz en lez nouns les dit seignurs altres lettres, tiele sentence portauntz: qe la reyne Constaunce, bailee en lour garde puis le departir le rei, fu en manere e en condicioun chaungee, come en vne autre creature; qar ele fu maueise espirit en fourme de femme; dount les merueiles que ele fist, que sembleient miracles, furent fesaunces del mauueys espirit en soun corps: "a qey temoine lenfaunt[4] de luy nee, que ne recemble pas a fourme de homme, mes a vne maladite fourme hidouse e dolorouse. E pur ceo, sire rei, qe a ta persone ne vensist a hountage e a toun real honur, feimes en moustraunce vn autre enfaunt baptizer e le nomamez Morys; e lautre fourme demoniac auoms priueement ferme en vne cage de feer taunque il plese a ta seignurie remaunder que nous estoit fere a toun honur de Constaunce e de sa hidouse engendrure. Cestes merueiles escriuoms a ta seignurie oue dolour e lermes soloms[5] qe nous sumes charges par toun seignurel comaundement a toy toute ⟨fol. 54b⟩ verite maunder de ta femme e de sa deliueraunce; a al portour de cetes la chose est desconue, qi autre quide sauoir qil ne seet."

Puis a matin se leua le messager, tut malade e deheite pur la malice del boire, que lui auoyt la cerule envenime; a apres fautz enbracemens e fauces promesses de Dounylde, sen ala son chemyn charge de retourner, a son departir del rey, mesme le chemyn. Et quant [il estoit][6] al rey venuz, de bouche lui counta veritable nouele et joyeuses. Mes [la][7] lettre ly fist retourner a dolour, e ly fist noun creable; quar ly roys, quant auoit lez lettres regarde, hastiuement suppris de grant dolour e parfond pensee, defendi al messager, a grantz manaces de peine, que riens de sa femme ne del enfaunt parlat. E meintenaunt rescrit a Elda e Lucius en responaunt a les lettres qil entendi auer

gives him a drugged beverage, and secretly changes the letters so that they report the birth of a monstrous and inhuman child. Constance is accused of being an evil spirit in human guise.

The King receives the exchanged letter while he is at war in Scotland. He replies with a command to have his wife and her offspring carefully guarded until his return.

---

[1] maunde *Ar, F, R;* mande *G.*

[2] come *added S.*

[3] I.e., "in the sight of."

[4] *Thus Ar; Brock reads* lenfant.

[5] I.e., "accordingly as."

[6] *Om. M, F, R;* il *om. S.*

[7] *Om. M, F, R, G;* la *S;* lez lettres *Ar.*

resceu de lour maundement e comaundement, que tout le fusent lez
noueles merueylouses e, sauue la grace de si bele[1] genz escriuant, a
poy noun creables, comaunda qe sauntz nul countredist feisent sa
femme sauuement garder, e le moustre de luy, taunque a son retourner.

Puis oue cestes lettres retourna le fol messager a mal houre par
Domylde, e quant estoit la venuz, durement se pleinout de la chere
le rey e de son lourd semblaunce. Mes la tretresce mout le conforta de[2] son[2] fauz semblaunt, e cele nuyt lenyueri com autre foiz.
E puis qe ele auoit lez lettres le rey ouert e regarde, aparceut qe cel

Domilde changes
the King's letter
into a sentence of
exile for Constance
and her son
Maurice.

maundement ne lui fut de riens fauorable; dount desouz mesme le
seal au rei escrit a Elda e Lucius en la persone le rey, en tiele sentence,
com par respouns fere a les primeres lettres par eus maundees: que
pur ceo que en estraunge pays puet homme souent noueles oyer plus
qe a mesoun en veisenage, pur ceo, par la resoun qil auoit nouele oy
de Constance, sa femme, qe si ele en la terre demorat, ceo auendreit
a guere e destruccioun de toute la terre par estraunge naciouns, e[3]
pur ceo comaunda a Elda, en forfeture de vie e de sez terres e quant
qil auoyt, e desheritement de tout son lynage, qe deins quatre iours
apres lez lettres luez feit apparailer vne neef e vitaile pur cync aunz
de manger e boire pur Constaunce, e en la neef mettre mesme le
tresor que fu en sa primere neef troue, e qe en mesme la manere en
cele neef, sauntz sigle e sauntz enviroun,[4] ou saunz nul autre engyn,
fut oue son enfaunt Moris de la terre exile, come ele en la terre entra.
E mesme la chose comaunda a Lucius, euesqe de Bangor, sur peyne
de perpetuel enprisonement.

Puis, quant lez dist seignurs auoient cestes lettrez resceu, graunt
duel e grant dolour demeneient. E pur ceo qe la beneite dame aparceut
lour semblaunt trop chaunge e mournes, e que a luy nul maundement
nestoit del rois venuz, soucha[5] la mort soun seignur; e a grant priere
lour requist qe nule verite luy fut celee. Lors ly dist luy messager qe
ly rois ly fist si dur encountrer qil ne voleit de la dame ne del enfaunt
nule parole oyer. Puis les seignurs ly ount les lettres le rois moustre
oue grant dolour e lermes. Mes Constaunce, pleine deu e prest a toutes
sez voluntez e a sez[6] ordinaunces, lour dist: "Ja ne veigne ceo iour
qe pur moy la terre feust destrute e que pur moy mes chers amiz
eusez[7] mort ou moleste. Mes puis que a dieu plest e a mon seignur,

---

[1] lele *Ar;* leles *F;* loilx *G.*

[2] dessouz *S.*

[3] *Om. S, F, R, G.*

[4] nauiroun *S;* viroun *F, R;* mariner *G.*

[5] I.e., "feared; was concerned for."

[6] *Thus Ar; Brock reads* ses.

[7] eussent *F, R, G;* sount (?) mys en *S.*

le rois, moun exil, a bon gree le doys prendre, en esperaunce qe dur
comencement amenera dieux a bon fyn, e qil me porra en la meer
sauuer qi en meer e en terre est de toute pusaunce."

Lors le quart iour fu ele exile oue Moriz son douz fitz, qi joeuenes
aprist marinage. E taunt de dolour e crie e plour fu en cite e ville,
de riches e pouerez, veuz e joeuenes, quant oyrent de la dolorouse
nouele, qe nul qoer ne le puet comprendre; ⟨fol. 55a⟩ qar toute[1] gentz
la weymenteient.[2] E tut ne vst il coupe, al rei Alle touz mauudisoient.
E pus qe sa neef par autre nauie estoit ia amene en la haute mere, ou
ia Engleterre ne autre terre lour apparut, lez mariners a grantz dolours
la comaunderent a dieu, en priaunt qe vnquore peust ele a joie a la
terre retourner.

Lors dieux gya sa neef tanqe en la mer despayne enveers la terre
del orient, desouz vn chastel de vn admiral de paens. Cist admiral
auoit le seon seneschal vn renee de la fei Cristiene, Thelous[3] nome.
Cist, quant il vist la dame de sa neef amene, oue son fitz, deuaunt
ladmiral, graunt pite en auoit, e par luy fu mout graciousement res-
ceue. E apres que ele estoit bien refete de manger e de boire, asseir
ne voleyt par ailours mes en sa neef herberger; qar il estoient paens,
e ele mout[4] auoit sa esperaunce en la gaste mer sour le gouernement
dieu floter, que entre lez enemis dieu herberger. Lors dieu, qi a sez
amis ia ne fause en tribulacioun, lui dona grace deuaunt ladmiral; qar
il comaunda a lui auant dist Thelous, son seneschal, qe il en eust
cure, que mal ne moleste par nuly avensist a la dame. Et Thelous,
de la garde trop lee e ioyous, en la nuyt parfounde descendi soul,
portaunt graunt tresour dor e dargent e peres preciousez. Et quant
auoit reconu a la dame soun errour, que cil qy auoit este Cristien fu
tretres reneez envers dieu pour pour de mort e pur coueitise de terrien
honur, lui pria qil se peut oue lui mettre en la meyn dieu pur retourner
acun lu[5] a sa fey par la grace [dieu][6] entre Cristiens. Puis, par eide de
sez priueez aloinez de la terre, vindrent al haute mer. E lenemy, qi
par tut senforce de mal fere, moueit le cheualer renee a greuose
temptacioun de ticer la dame a consent de pesche. Mes dieux, a qi
ele auoit done son qoer denfaunce, ne la voleit suffrir assentir a tiel
mal. Dount quant cist Theolous par dures manaces la voleit aforcer,
ele refreynt sa folye par resoun, qar lenfaunt Moris, que ia estoit de
doys anz enters puis qil estoit exiles dengleterre, poieit auoir entende-

---

[1] toutent *in MS.*

[2] I.e., "lamented."

[3] Tholous *G fol. 59b;* Theolous *Ar, S.*

[4] meus *S;* meuth *F, R;* auoit mieulz *G.*

[5] lieu *Ar, G;* liu *F, R.*

[6] *Om. M, F, R.*

ment e memoire de chose faite en sa presence (adonqe dount ceste fu
sa colour pur sei defendre de pesche), e pria a Thelous qil auisat de
tote parz si puet nule terre veer, e quant a la terre puissent attendre,
en lu couenable, parfreyt soun talent. Et cil, sur ceste promesse mout
corious, esteaunt en le vaunt partie de la nef, de toute pars auisa si
nule terre puet veir. Et taunt com fu plus curious, Constaunce, pur
sa chastete sawer, priueement luy vient rere au dos e le tresbucha en
la mer.

King Alla, returned
from the war, dis-
covers the treach-
ery and executes his
mother.
Deyns ceste tenps le rois Alle, ja espleite de la victorie en Escoce
de lez Pycteis, sez enemis, a grant desir e dolour se hasta en Engletere;
qar counte ly estoit par entrealauntz que sa beneyte femme, Constaunce, ia estoit par soun comaundement de sa terre oue son fitz
Moris exilez. Et com ly rois erra soun chemyn par cites e viles, de iour,
en Engletere, luy vindrent encountrauns hommes e femmes, enfauntz
e veilars, e le reuilerent de crie e ledengge, gettauntz sur lui et les
seuns tay e ordure e grosses peres, e femmes e enfauntz deuestuz par
despyt luy moustrerent lour derere; et tant dure fu la persecucioun
que lui couenoit e son ost desormes de nuyt prendre lour iourneis. Puis,
quant il estoit al auant dist chastel venuz, a grant poeur de sa vie,
fist apeler Elda e Lucius a grant felonie, demaundaunt ou fu sa femme
Constaunce qe yl apelerent maueys espirist en fourme de femme, e
ou fut deuenuz le demoniac moustre, soun enfaunt. E cil, abays de
la parole, se diseient riens sauoir de tiele chose, mes que sa femme
estoyt bone e seincte, e sa engendrure bele e graciouse. E cil, com
homme arage, lour demaunda qele resoun lour moueit si tresoneles
lettres a lui maunder, com apertement lour poeit moustrer. Puis,
veuuez lez lettres de vne part e de autre, ia le rey les lettres riens ne
conusoit qil vist de soun seal asselez, ne ceaus del autre part ausint.
Dount dautre part ne sauoient soucher la tresoun mes ver le messager.
E cist finaument dit qe de nul ⟨fol. 55b⟩ tresoun se senti coupable,
nepurquant bien lour reconust de sa yueresce en la court Dom-
mylde, la mere le rey; e si tresoun feust, la fu la source. Et le rey,
ia tut enflaume de ire, comensca de nuyz errer taunque il vynt ou
sa mere estoit. Et quant estoit entre sur sa mere ia endormis, ou
hidouse voiz la escria tretresce, e luy comaunda hastiuement moustrer les lettres qe ele auoit tretrousement fause. Et ele, sudeine-
ment supprise de pour, e veaunte le rey com homme hors de sens,
tenaunt lespeie nue, outre luy e bien sachaunte sey coupable de si
grant tresoun, sauntz plus de relees, en priaunte mercy, recunisoit
toute sa felonie. Et le rey a grant fierte ly dist que nul merci ne en
auereyt mes come sa tresoun demaunda. "Qar de moy, ne de ma
femme, ne de moun enfaunt vous ne nauiez pite, ne ioe de vous ia

pite naueray." E a ceo ly coupa la teste e le corps tut a pecees,
com ele iut[1] nue en soun lit. Lors Alle solempnement fit soun vou
deuaunt Lucius, leuesque de Bangor, qe iammes femme ne esposereit,
taunqe la misericorde dieu ly enueiat noueles de Constaunce.

Puis ceste Constaunce, le tierz aan apres qe ele auoit neey Theelous
en la mer, qe fu le quinte an de ceste exil, come ele fu flotaunte sur
la mer, regardoit de loins luy apparer com vn boys. E com soun
tresboun e courteys gyour, dieux, gya sa neef plus pres e plus, a
la fyn aparceut que ceo estoient mastode[2] vne graunde nauie qe reposa
en le port de vn cite sur la mer. Et quant les mariners virent vne
neef si merueilousement sur la mer flotaunte, sucherent qe ceo vst
este vne neef par tempeste veude de sez mariners. Mes quant estoient
venuz ades, trouerent vne femme e vn enfaunt de cynk aunz, richement estoffetz de tresor, mes trop poures de vitaile. E apres que lez
mariners auoient la dame aresones, amenerent luy e son enfaunt en
la cite a vn paleis, ou vn senatour de Rome, ne pas de la pucele des-
conu, estoit resette.[3] Cist estoit apele Arcemius[4] de Capadoce,
tresages cheualer e pruz, e mout excellent en lettrure, et del emperour
Tyberie Constantin, le pere Constaunce, mout ame e secre. Cist,
quant vist Constaunce, de riens la conisoyt, qe la dame prist a graunt
ioye. E cele assez luy conisoit, qar assetz lauoit veu en la meson
lemperour soun pere. Cist Arcemius estoit dustre de toute cele nauie.
E puis qil auoit demaunde le dame plusours demaundes de soun estre
e de sa fortune, e ele luy auoit sagement respoundu, sauntz riens des-
couerir de son lynage ou del emperour, e pur ceo qe sa fortune ne luy
estoit solom le secle tote graciouse, tut ly plust ele solom dieu, e
pur ceo qele estoit marie a vn riche seignur qi auoit engendre lenfaunt,
a qi par sa fortune ele nestoit pas plesaunte en touz poyns, e[5] pur
ceo suffri ele tiele penaunce. E puis qil auoit son noun demaunde,
[et][6] ele luy auoit respondu qe ele estoit Couste nome (qar issint la-
pelerent lez Sessoneys), puis luy demaunda la dame quey amounta
cele graunde nauie qil amena. E il ly respoundi qe ceo estoit la nauie
lemperour ⟨fol. 56a⟩ Tyberie, enveye par luy en la terre seynte encountre les Sarazins, qe auoyent tresterousement mourdre sa fille
Constaunce, e grant nombre des Cristiens, e le soudan e sez aliez
questoient amys a Cristiens; e luy disoyt que de toute parz dieu lour
auoyt done eurous espleyt de lour enemys, qar la soudane fu arse,
e de Sarazins estoyent plus de vnze mil tuez, mes vnques vn Cristien

---

[1] tut in MS; iut Ar; ieut F, R; geust G.

[2] mastes dune S, G; mastes de vn F, R.

[3] I.e., "had an abode."

[4] Arcenius S, F, R, G.

[5] Om. F, R.

[6] Om. M, Ar, S.

ne estoit perdue ne naufre en soun ost; e que touz lez corps de Cristiens auoyent yl e son ost trouez, que par Sarazins estoient mourdretz,
fors soulement le corps Constaunce, que solom le dist de Sarazins
estoit nee en la mer. Puis li pria la pucele qe ele peut en son conduyt
passer tanque a Rome. E Arsemius a graunt joye luy graunta, e la
prist en sa garde, e son fitz e tut son tresour. E puis qil estoyent a

Arcenius is married
to Helaine, cousin
of Constance; but
neither recognises
her.

Rome venuz, recomaunda Custe a sa femme Romeyne, Heleyne, la
fille Salustius, le frere lemperour Tyberie e le vncle Constaunce.
Ceste Heleyne, la nece Constaunce, taunt tendrement ama sa nece e
Moris son cosyn, que autre si graunt ioye en sa vie nauoyt. E pust
estre que sa joie ly eust escrue si Constaunce ly [eust][1] toute verite
countee. Puis Constaunce[2] oue son fitz Moris demora en la compaynie
Arsemye e Heleyne douzze auntz entiers, dame de toute seynteite e
verite. E Arsemius e Heleyne, que nul engendrure ne auoient, Moris
en amur e noriture, come lour fitz luy clamerent[3] lour eyr.

King Alla visits
Rome to seek ab-
solution for his
mother's death.

En cele mesme tenps Alle le rey dengletere, par le conceil Lucius,
euesqe de Bangor, e Elda, son seneschal e conestable, ala oue gentz
pur fere soun pelerinage a Rome e dauer absolucioun del pape de la
occisoun sa mere. En mesme le tenps baila la garde de soun reaume
a Edwyn son fitz, questeoyt le tierz roy apres luy. E quant Alle
estoit a sept journeis de Rome, maunda Elda deuaunt, pur honurable
purueaunce fere.[4] E quant Elda estoit a Rome venuz e auoit conquis
ou le rey dengleterre e sez gentz pussent honurablement herberger,
luy fu respoundu, qe Arsemius, le senatour de la cite, estoit noblement
dowe de plusours chasteaus e bieus paleys. Puis a ceste nouele Elda
ala a Arsemius de ceo prier; e il bonement ly fist moustrer sez chasteus
e maners questoient ia veudez sanz nul demoraunt. E puis que Elda
auoit pur le rey honurablement choysi, Arsemius sen est retourne a
son paleys. E puis qe il estoit en la chambre sa femme entre, ou
estoit Constance, lour demaunda si eles voleyent noueles oyer;[5] et
lour counta qe Alle, roys dengletere, deyns lez dis iours vendreit
en vile e serreit herberge en[6] sez chasteus, e a ceo auoyt maunde vn
grant counte e chasteleyn, soun mareschal. Et quant Constaunce oy
la nouele, de priuee e celee ioye chey en paunesoun.[7] Et puys qe
sez espiritz luy estoient reuenuz, a lour demaunde qe ele deuot,[8] se
acundut[9] par feblesse de sa seruele qe luy aynt en la mer. Puis

---

[1] *Om. M, Ar.*   [2] *MS Douce begins here.*   [3] et *added Ar.*

[4] encontre lui *added S;* contre lui *F;* countre lui *R, D.*

[5] noueles oyer nouueles *in MS.*

[6] e *in MS.*

[7] *Or* paimesoun (*thus Brock reads Ar*); paumeson *other MSS.*

[8] deuoit *Ar, F, R, D, G.*   [9] I.e., "excused."

eyns lez dist dys iours, quant le rois Alle fu en uenaunt pres a la cite
de Rome, Arsemius le senatour, qy le deuoit reseiuere deins sez
chasteus, ly ala encountraunt honurablement oue toute la cheualerye
de Rome e oue lez riches citeseynz Romeins, e le resceut curteyse-
ment. E come la femme le senatour, Heleyne, e Custaunce, esturent
sur vn bretage[1] ordine de gre, qe elez pusent veer le reys dengletere
e auiser la cheualerie, vn cheualer qe auoyt veu ⟨fol. 56b⟩ le reis auaunt
sa venue a la cite par chemyn, e qe estoit assigne pur les dames
moustrer la persone le rey, lour moustra la[2] persone com il cheuacha
desouz le bretage, e dist: "Vees si, dames, lui rois Alle." Et ly roys,
oyaunt son noun nomer, reguarda vers mount. E quant Constaunce
vist soun visage, chey enpres Heleyne paume, qi ne quidoit autre
mez feblesse.

A ceo tenps de la venue le rois a Rome, comensca Moris son diseoy-
time aan. Cist estoit apris priueement de sa mere Constaunce, qe
quant il irreit a la feste oue son seignur le senatur, que, toutez autrez
choses lesses, se meit deuant le rey dengletere, quant il fust assis
a manger, pur luy seruir; e que de nule part se remuat hors del regard
al rey, e qe il se aforsat bien e curteisement ly seruir; qar il durement
resembla sa mere. Puis, quant ly rois regarda lenfaunt, esteaunt
deuaunt luy, trop fu suppris de la resemblaunce, e ly demaunda
qi fitz estoit; e ly respoundi qil estoit fitz a Arsemie, le senatour, qy
luy seoit a destre. E a sa demaunde ly senatour lui dist qe son fitz
luy tint il, pur ceo qil lauoyt fest son heir. E sa mere sauoit il bien,
mes noun pas son piere; qar vnques sa mere ceo ne lui voleit reconustre, en le tenps de dozze aunz. E le juuencel ne sauoit, qar la
mere e luy estoient mis en exil, quant ne estoit forqe de dis semaynes.
A ceo le roy demanda del juuencel soun noun. E il respoundi qe son
noun fu Moris. Dount le rey deuynt en grant pensee, e del noun e de
la resemblaunce de visage, e pur le dis le senatour; e demaunda del
senatour si ly plust fere moustraunce de la dame, la mere le juuencel.
E il lui respoundi qe ele estoit en sa mesoun. Sur ceo le rey, trop conforte, fist hastier le manger. E quant yl estoit descendu al paleys le
senatour, parust sa femme, qe ly venoit encountre oue la femme le
senatour. E ly rois, apres qil auoyt la dame del paleys salue, par
certeyne conisaunce ala sa femme enbracer e beser. E taunt apert
moustraunces damour ly fesoit, que le senatur e la dame e quantqe i
esteint, ne esteient pas poi merueilez. E le rey a ceo, tut en haut
escrie: "Jeo ay troue ma femme!" Puis Elda e Lucius ount salue la
dame e a grant ioye ount dieux mercye, que iames ne faut a ceus qen
ly ount affiaunce. Lendemayn le rois ala prendre son absolucioun de

---

[1] I.e., "crenelated balcony or parapet."   [2] sa S, F, R, D, G.

la mort sa mere. E puis qil auoyt counte al pape Pelagie, auant nome, tote lez auentures, le pape rendi gracez a dieux.

Puis, apres quaraunte jours qe luy rois auoit demore a Rome, vne nuyt ly pria Custaunce qil demaundast al emperere, que demora de Rome a dozze lues, qil vousist luy fere lonur qe luy plust oue luy manger a Rome. E puz qe la priere plust au rey, Constaunce charga son fitz Morice del message; e luy dist, si lemperour ne luy grantast poynt sa priere, que dount ly request pur lamour qil auoit al alme sa fille Constaunce; qar dount sauoit ele bien qe lemperour ne luy deneieroit pas sa demaunde, com a nuly ne fist qe pur lalme sa fille riens ly priast. E puis, quant Morice estoit deuaunt lemperour venuz oue compaignie honurable, e auoyt son message fest[1] de part le rey son per, lemperour, trop suppris de lamur del juuencel, dist a sez cheualers en ploraunt: "Dieux! Com cel juuencel merueilousement resemble ma fille Constaunce! E puis qil auoit a Morice done grauunz douns, mes ne luy voleit otreyer sa priere, pur ceo que pur le doel qe il auoit pris pur sa fille, quil quida morte, vnqes apres ne voleit a feste de ioye manger ⟨fol. 57a⟩ ne menestraucie oyer. Dount luy pria Morice solom la fourme auaunt dist, e lemperor luy graunta.

Avynt la veile seynt Johan le Baptistre, la feste de sa natiuite, quant la feste se deueyt fere le jour ensuant, Constance dist al rey que a sa courteysie qil cheuachast honurablement encountre lemperour, pur ly resceyuere en la cite; e ensi fu fest.[1] E quant la noble cheualerye de Rome oue lez citeyseintz vyndrent en la compaynie le roys honurablement, Constance prya son seignur descendre de soun destrer e[2] encountre lemperor, qi ele ia veist venir de preez. E Constaunce, deuaunt toute la compaymye,[3] prist son seignur le rey en la mayn destre e Morys son fitz en la senestre, e vynt son pere saluer en ceste paroles: "Moun seignur e beau pere Tyberie, joe, Constaunce, vostre fille, mercie dieux qe vnqore a coe jour mad grante la vie, qe ioe vous vey en saunte." E puis qe lemperour out sa fille oy e bien conu,[4] ia de si sudeyne ioye auoit le qoer suppris que a poy estoit de son destrer tresbuche, mes le rois Alle e son fitz Moris le supporterent. Dount a bon dreit grant joye demenerent. E Custaunce counta a soun pere totes sez auentures, e coment ele auoit ia dozze auntz demore en la mesoun al senatour Arsemie e Heleyne, que ore primerement reconuseyt sa nece, la fille son vncle. Puz apres autre qaraunte jours passetz, quant le rey Alle sen returna en soun pais, lemperere Tyberie, par assent le pape Pelagie e de tout le senat de Rome, pur sa veilesse, prist Morice compeynoun de empire, e luy

---

[1] fait *F, R, D, G.*

[2] *Om. S, F, R, D, G.*

[3] compaignie *other MSS.*

[4] com *in MS.*

clama son eyr. E estoit Moris de Capadoce nome pour Arsemie,
questoit de Capadoce, com auant est dist al comencement de ceste
estoire. Cist Moris fu apele de Romeyns en Latin "Mauricius Cris-
tianissimus imperator," ceo est a dire, "Morice le Cristien emperor."

Puis Alle, le rei dengletere, le neofuime moys apres qil estoit venuz
en Engletere, rendi lalme a dieu seintement. E apoy apres vn demi
aan, Constaunce, que en grant honur e amur estoit a tute la terre,
returna a Rome pur la nouele qe ele oy de la maladie son piere;[1] le
tressime jour apres sa venue, morust Tyberie seintement deyns lez
bras sa fille, e rendi lalme a dieu. E ele, apres vn an, trespassa a
dieu, lan del incarnacion cync centz oitaunte quarte, le jor seint
Clement, e fu enterre a Rome pre de son pere en leglise de seint
Pere. Et Elda, qe auoit Constaunce remene a Rome, en retournaunt
vers Engletere, morust deuoutement a Tours, e par Lucius, euesqe
de Bangor, auaunt dist, fu enterre en leglise seint Martyn. Puz
Lucius retourna a sa eglise de Bangor. Le corps Alle fu enterre al
eglise seint Amphibel a Wyncestre, ou yl morust.

Deaths of Alla, Constance, and Elda.

GOWER'S TALE OF CONSTANCE[2]

⟨fol. 30*b*⟩   A worthi kniht in Cristes lawe
                     Of grete Rome, as is the sawe,
                     The sceptre hadde forto rihte;
590   Tiberie Constantin he hihte,
                     Whos wif was cleped Ytalie:
                     Bot thei togedre of progenie
                     No children hadde bot a maide;
                     And sche the God so wel apaide,
                     That al the wide worldes fame
                     Spak worschipe of hire gode name.
                     Constance, as the cronique seith,
                     Sche hihte, and was so ful of feith,
                     That the greteste of Barbarie,
600   Of hem which vsen marchandie,
                     Sche hath conuerted, as thei come
                     To hire vpon a time in Rome,
                     To schewen such thing as thei broghte;
                     Which worthili of hem sche boghte,
                     And over that in such a wise
                     Sche hath hem with hire wordes wise

Constance, daughter of the Roman Emperor, converts heathen merchants to Christianity.

---

[1] et *added* S, F, R, D, G.

[2] Taken from John Gower's *Confessio amantis*, II, 587 ff. (Text from MS
Fairfax 3, Bodleian, Oxford.)

Of Cristes feith so full enformed,
That thei therto ben al conformed,
So that baptesme thei receiuen
610 And alle here false goddes weyuen.
Whan thei ben of the feith certein
Thei gon to Barbarie ayein,
⟨fol. 31a⟩ And ther the Souldan for hem sente
And axeth hem to what entente
Thei haue here ferste feith forsake.
And thei, whiche hadden vndertake
The rihte feith to kepe and holde,
The matiere of here tale tolde
With al the hole circumstance.

Their Sultan, in
order to marry
Constance, agrees
to accept the faith.

620 And whan the Souldan of Constance
Vpon the point that thei ansuerde
The beaute and the grace herde,
As he which thanne was to wedde,
In alle haste his cause spedde
To sende for the mariage.
And furthermor with good corage
He seith, be so he mai hire haue,
That Crist, which cam this world to saue
He woll belieue: and this recorded
630 Thei ben on either side acorded.
And therevpon to make an ende,
The Souldan hise hostages sende
To Rome, of princes sones tuelue:
Whereof the fader in himselue
Was glad, and with the Pope auised
Tuo cardinals he hath assissed
With othre lordes many mo,
That with his doghter scholden go,
To se the Souldan be conuerted.

His jealous mother
pretends to approve
of his plans

640   Bot that which neuere was wel herted,
Envie, tho began trauaile
In destourbance of this spousaile
So priuely that non was war.
The moder which this Souldan bar
Was thanne alyue, and thoghte this
Vnto hirself: "If it so is
Mi sone him wedde in this manere,

Than haue I lost my ioies hiere,
For myn astat schal so be lassed."
650 Thenkende thus sche hath compassed
Be sleihte how that sche may beguile
Hire sone; and fell withinne a while,
Betwen hem two whan that thei were,
Sche feigneth wordes in his ere,
And in this wise gan to seie:
"Mi sone, I am be double weie
With al myn herte glad and blithe,
For that miself haue ofte sithe
Desired thou wolt, as men seith,
660 Receiue and take a newe feith,
Which schal be forthringe of thi lif:
And ek so worschipful a wif,
The doughter of an emperour,
To wedde it schal be gret honour.
Forthi, mi sone, I you beseche
That I such grace mihte areche,
Whan that my doughter come schal,
That I mai thanne in special
So as me thenkth it is honeste,
670 Be thilke which the ferste feste
Schal make vnto hire welcominge."
The Souldan granteth hire axinge,
And sche therof was glad ynowh: but prepares
treachery.
For vnder that anon she drowh
With false wordes that sche spak
Covine of deth behinde his bak.
And thervpon hire ordinance
She made so, that whan Constance
Was come forth with the Romeins,
680 Of clerkes and of citezeins   At a feast
A riche feste sche hem made:
And most whan that thei weren glade,
With fals covine which sche hadde
Hire clos envie tho sche spradde,
And alle tho that hadden be   all those who had
advised this mar-
riage are murdered,
Or in apert or in priue
Of conseil to the mariage,
Sche slowh hem in a sodein rage
Endlong the bord as thei be set,

690 So that it myhte noght be let;
Hire oghne sone was noght quit,
Bot deide vpon the same plit.

Bot what the hihe God vol spare
It mai for no peril misfare:
This vorthi maiden which was there
Stod thanne, as who seith, ded for feere,
To se the feste how that it stod,
Which al was torned into blod:
The dissh forthwith the coppe and al
700 Bebled thei weren oueral;
Sche sih hem deie on euery side;
No wonder thogh sche wepte and cride
Makende many a woful mone.
Whan al was slain but sche al one,
⟨fol. 31b⟩ This olde fend, this Sarazine,
Let take anon this Constantine
With al the good sche thider broghte,
And hath ordeined, as sche thoghte,

A nakid schip withoute stiere
710 In which the good and hire[1] in fiere
Vitailed full for yeres fyue,
Wher that the wynd it wolde dryue,
Sche putte vpon the wawes wilde.

After three years
her ship arrives in
Northumberland,
near a castle of
King Allee.

Bot he which alle thing mai schilde,
Thre yer, til that sche cam to londe,
Hire schip to stiere hath take in honde,
And in Northumberlond aryueth;
And happeth thanne that sche dryueth[2]
Vnder a castel with the flod,
720 Which vpon Humber banke stod
And was the kynges oghne also,
The which Allee was cleped tho,
A Saxon and a worthi knyht,
Bot he belieueth noght ariht.
Of this castell was chastellein

Elda the kinges chamberlein,
A knyhtly man after his lawe;
And whan he sih vpon the wawe
The schip driuende al one so,

[1] hiere F.　　　　　　　　　　[2] *Macaulay reads* dryveth.

730   He bad anon men scholden go
        To se what it betokne mai.
        This was vpon a somer dai;
        The schip was loked and sche founde;
        Elda withinne a litel stounde
        It wiste, and with his wif anon
        Toward this yonge ladi gon,
        Wher that thei founden gret richesse;
        Bot sche hire wolde noght confesse
        Whan thei hire axen what sche was.
740   And natheles vpon the cas
        Out of the schip with gret worschipe
        Thei toke hire into felaschipe,
        As thei that weren of hir glade:
        Bot sche no maner ioie made,
        Bot sorweth sore of that sche fond
        No Cristendom in thilke lond;
        Bot elles sche hath al hire wille,
        And thus with hem sche duelleth stille.

        Dame Hermyngheld, which was the wife
750   Of Elda, lich her oghne lif
        Constance loueth; and fell so
        Spekende alday betwen hem two,
        Thurgh grace of Goddes pourveance
        This maiden tawhte the creance
        Vnto this wif so parfitly,
        Vpon a dai that faste by
        In presence of hire housebonde,
        Wher thei go walkende on the stronde,
        A blind[1] man, which cam there lad,
760   Vnto this wif criende he bad,
        With bothe hise hondes vp and preide
        To hire, and in this wise he seide:
        "O Hermyngeld, which Cristes feith,
        Enformed as Constance seith,
        Receiued hast, yif me my sihte."

        Vpon his word hire herte afflihte
        Thenkende what was best to done,
        Bot natheles sche herde his bone

Hermengild, Elda's
wife, converted by
Constance,

miraculously gives
sight to a blind
man,

[1] blinde M, H₂, H₄.

And seide, "In trust of Cristes lawe

770 Which don was on the crois and slawe,

Thou bysne man,[1] behold and se."

With that to God vpon his kne

Thonkende he tok his sihte anon,

Whereof thei merueile e
euerychon,

whereupon Elda
also accepts the
faith.Bot Elda wondreth most of alle:

This open thing which is befalle

Concludeth him be such a weie

That he the feith mot nede obeie.

Elda goes to the
King and tells him
of Constance. Now lest what fell vpon this thing.

780 This Elda forth vnto the king

A morwe tok his weie and rod,

And Hermyngeld at home abod

Forth with Constance wel at ese.

Elda, which thoghte his king to plese,

As he that thanne vnwedded was,

Of Constance al the pleine cas

Als goodliche as he cowthe tolde.

The king was glad and seide he wolde

Come thider vpon such a wise.

790 That he him mihte of hire auise,

The time apointed forth withal.

During his absence
a false knight,
whose lust for Con-
stance had turned
into hate,This Elda triste in special

Vpon a knyht, whom fro childhode

He hadde vpdrawe into manhode:

To him he tolde al that he thoghte,

Whereof that after him forthoghte;

⟨fol 32a⟩ And natheles at thilke tide

Vnto his wif he bad him ride

To make redi alle thing

800 Ayein the cominge of the king,

And seith that he himself tofore

Thenkth forto come, and bad therfore

That he him kepe, and told him whanne,

This knyht rod forth his weie thanne;

And soth was that of time passed

He hadde in al his wit compassed

How he Constance myhte winne;

Bot he sih tho no sped therinne,

---

[1] I.e., "thou blind man."

Wherof his lust began tabate,
810   And that was loue is thanne hate;
Of hire honour he hadde envie
So that vpon his tricherie
A lesinge in his herte he caste.
Til he cam home he hieth faste,
And doth his ladi tunderstonde
The message of hire housebonde:
And thervpon the longe dai
Thei setten thinges in arrai,
That al was as it scholde be
820   Of euery thing in his degree;
And whan it cam into the nyht,
This wyf hire hath to bedde dyht
Wher that this maiden with hire lay.
This false knyht vpon delay
Hath taried til thei were aslepe,
As he that wolde his time kepe
His dedly werkes to fulfille;
And to the bed he stalketh stille,   *kills Hermengild*
Wher that he wiste was the wif;
830   And in his hond a rasour knif
He bar, with which hire throte he cutte
And priuely the knif he putte   *and puts his bloody*
Vnder that other beddes side,   *knife under the*
                                      pillow of Constance.
Wher that Constance lai beside.
Elda cam home the same nyht,   *When Elda returns*
And stille, with a priue lyht   *home that night*
As he that wolde noght awake   *and finds his wife*
His wif, he hath his weie take   *dead,*
Into the chambre, and ther liggende
840   He fond his dede wif bledende,
Wher that Constance faste by
Was falle aslepe; and sodeinly
He cride alowd, and sche awok
And forth withal sche cast[1] a lok
And sih this ladi blede there,
Whereof swounende ded for fere
Sche was, and stille as eny ston
She lay, and Elda therevpon
Into the castell clepeth oute,

[1] *Macaulay reads* caste.

850   And vp sterte euery man aboute,
       Into the chambre and forth thei wente.
       Bot he, which alle vntrouthe mente,

the false knight shows the bloody knife

       This false knyht, among hem alle
       Vpon this thing which is befalle
       Seith that Constance hath don this dede;
       And to the bed with that he yede
       After the falshed of his speche
       And made him there forto seche,
       And fond the knif, wher he it leide
860   And thanne he cride and thanne he seide,
       "Lo, seth the knif al blody hiere!

and accuses Constance of the murder.

       What nedeth more in this matiere
       To axe?" And thus hire innocence
       He sclaundreth there in audience
       With false wordes whiche he feigneth.
       Bot yit for al that euere he pleigneth,
       Elda no full credence tok:

He swears to her guilt

       And happeth that ther lay a bok
       Vpon the which, whan he it sih,
870   This knyht hath swore and seid on hih,
       That alle men it mihte wite,
       "Now be this bok, which hier is write,
       Constance is gultif, wel I wot."

but is struck down by the hand of heaven,

       With that the hond of heuene him smot
       In tokne of that he was forswore,
       That he hath bothe hise yhen lore;
       Out of his hed the same stounde
       Thei sterte, and so thei weren founde.
       A vois was herd, whan that they felle,
880   Which seide, "O dampned man to helle
       Lo, thus hath God the sclaundre wroke
       That thou ayein Constance hast spoke:
       Beknow the sothe er that thou dye."

confesses, and dies.

       And he told out his felonie
       And starf forth with his tale anon.
       Into the ground, wher alle gon,
       This dede lady was begraue:
       Elda, which thoghte his honour saue
⟨fol. 32b⟩   Al that he mai restreigneth sorwe.

890   For the seconde dai a morwe

The King comes to
the castle.

     The king cam, as thei were acorded;
     And whan it was to him recorded
     What God hath wroght vpon this chaunce,
     He tok it into remembrance
     And thoghte more than he seide.
     For al his hole herte he leide

For the love of
Constance he em-
braces the faith;

     Vpon Constance, and seide he scholde
     For loue of hire, if that sche wolde,
     Baptesme take and Cristes feith

900   Belieue, and ouer that he seith
     He wol hire wedde, and vpon this
     Asseured ech til other is.
     And forto make schorte tales,
     Ther cam a bisschop out of Wales
     Fro Bangor, and Lucie he hihte,
     Which thurgh the grace of God almihte
     The king with many an other mo
     Hath cristned, and betwen hem tuo
     He hath fulfild the mariage.

he marries her.

910   But for no lust ne for no rage
     Sche tolde hem neuere what sche was;
     And natheles vpon the cas
     The king was glad, how so it stod,
     For wel he wiste and vnderstod
     Sche was a noble creature.
     The hihe makere of nature
     Hire hath visited in a throwe
     That it was openliche knowe
     Sche was with childe be the king,

920   Whereof aboue al other thing
     He thonketh God and was riht glad.
     And fell that time he was bestad

While the King is
away fighting the
Scots,

     Vpon a werre and moste ride;
     And whil he scholde there abide,
     He lefte at hom to kepe his wife
     Suche as he knew of holi lif,
     Elda forth with the bisschop eke;
     And he with pouer goth to seke
     Ayein the Scottes for to fonde

930   The werre which he tok on honde.

The time set of kinde is come,
This lady hath hire chambre nome,
And of a sone bore full,
Wherof that sche was ioiefull,
Sche was deliuered sauf and sone.
The bisshop, as it was to done,
Yaf him baptesme and Moris calleth;
And thervpon, as it befalleth,
With lettres writen of record
940   Thei sende vnto here liege lord,
That kepers weren of the qweene:
And he that scholde go betwene,
The messager, to Knaresburgh,
Which toun he scholde passe thrugh,
Ridende cam the ferste day.
The kinges moder there lay,
Whos rihte name was Domilde,
Which after al the cause spilde:
For he, which thonk[1] deserue[2] wolde,
950   Vnto this ladi goth and tolde
Of his message al how it ferde.
And sche with feigned ioie it herde
And yaf him yiftes largely.
Bot in the nyht al priuely
Sche tok the lettres whiche he hadde,
Fro point to point and ouerradde,
As sche that was thurghout vntrewe,
And let do wryten othre newe
In stede of hem, and thus thei spieke:
960   "Oure liege lord, we thee beseke
That thou with ous ne be noght wroth,
Though we such thing as is thee loth
Vpon oure trowthe certefie.
Thi wif, which is of faierie,
Of such a child deliuered is
Fro kinde which stant al amis:
Bot for it scholde noght be seie,
We haue it kept out of the weie
For drede of pure worldes schame,
970   A pouere child and in the name
Of thilke which is so misbore

Constance bears a son, Maurice.

A messenger is sent to the King,

but his mother exchanges the letter;

she states that the child is a monster

and that, to avoid disgrace, they have put a poor child in its place.

---

[1] thong F (*also H₂*).   [2] *Macaulay reads* deserve.

We toke, and therto we be swore,
That non bot only thou and we
Schal knowen of this priuete:
Moris it hatte, and thus men wene
That it was boren of the qweene
And of thin oghne bodi gete.
Bot this thing mai noght be foryete,
That thou ne sende ous word anon
980   What is thi wille thervpon.''
⟨fol 33a⟩   This lettre, as thou hast herd deuise,
Was contrefet in such a wise
That noman scholde it aperceiue:
And sche, which thoghte to deceiue,
It leith wher sche that other tok.
This messager, whan he awok,
And wiste nothing how it was,
Aros and rod the grete pas
And tok this lettre to the king.
990   And whan he sih this wonder thing,
He makth the messager no chiere,
Bot natheles in wys manere
He wrot ayein, and yaf hem charge
That thei ne soffre noght at large
His wif to go, bot kepe hire stille,
Til thei haue herd mor of his wille.
This messager was yifteles,
Bot with this lettre natheles,
Or be him lief or be him loth,
1000   In alle haste ayein he goth
Be Knaresburgh, and as he wente,
Vnto the moder his entente
Of that he fond toward the king
He tolde; and sche vpon this thing
Seith that he scholde abide al nyht
And made him feste and chiere ariht,
Feignende as thogh sche cowthe him thonk.
Bot he with strong wyn which he dronk
Forth with the trauail[1] of the day
1010   Was drunke, aslepe and while he lay
Sche hath hise lettres ouerseie
And formed in an other weie.

The King writes
that his wife should
be kept under guard
until he gives fur-
ther orders.

The King's mother
again changes the
message

[1] *Macaulay reads* travail.

Ther was a newe lettre write,
Which seith, "I do you forto wite,
That thurgh the conseil of you tuo
I stonde in point to ben vndo,
As he which is a king deposed.
For euery man it hath supposed,
How that my wif Constance is faie;
1020   And if that I, thei sein, delaie
To put hire out of compaignie,
The worschipe of my regalie
Is lore; and ouer this thei telle,
Hire child schal noght among hem duelle,
To cleymen eny heritage.
So can I se non auantage
Bot al is lost, if sche abide:
Forthi to loke on euery side
Toward the meschief as it is,

and writes that
within four days
mother and child
must be left on the
sea in the ship in
which Constance
had come.

1030   I charge you and bidde this
That ye the same schip vitaile,
In which that sche tok ariuaile,
Therinne and putteth bothe tuo,
Hireself forthwith hire child also,
And so forth broght vnto the depe
Betaketh hire the see to kepe.
Of foure daies time I sette,
That ye this thing no lenger lette,
So that your lif be noght forsfet."[1]
1040   And thus this lettre contrefet
The messager, which was vnwar,
Vpon the kinges halue bar
And where he scholde it hath betake.
Bot whan that thei haue hiede take,
And rad that writen is withinne,
So gret a sorwe thei beginne,
As thei here oghne moder sihen
Brent in a fyr before here yhen:
Ther was wepinge and ther was wo,
1050   Bot finaly the thing is do.

Adrift, the dis-
tressed Constance
is chiefly concerned
with her child.

Vpon the see thei haue hire broght,
Bot sche the cause wiste noght.

[1] forsfet *for* forfet.

And thus vpon the flod thei wone,
This ladi with hire yonge sone:
And thanne hire handes to the heuene
Sche strawhte, and with a milde steuene
Knelende vpon hire bare kne
Sche seide, "O hihe mageste,
Which sest the point of euery trowthe,
1060   Tak of thi wofull womman rowthe
And of this child that I schal kepe."
And with that word sche gan to wepe,
Swounende as ded, and ther sche lay;
Bot he which alle thinges may
Conforteth hire, and ate laste
Sche loketh and hire yhen caste
Vpon hire child and seide this:
"Of me no maner charge it is
What sorwe I soffre, bot of thee
1070   Me thenkth it is a gret pite,
For if I sterue thou schalt deie:
So mot I nedes be that weie
⟨fol. 33b⟩   For moderhed and for tendresse
With al myn hole besinesse
Ordeigne me for thilke office
As sche which schal be thi norrice."
Thus was sche strengthed forto stonde;
And tho sche tok hire child in honde
And yaf it sowke, and euere among
1080   Sche wepte, and otherwhile song
To rocke with hire child aslepe:
And thus hire oghne child to kepe
Sche hath vnder the Goddes cure.

And so fell vpon auenture,
Whan thilke yer hath mad his ende,
Hire schip, so as it moste wende
Thurgh strengthe of wynd which God hath yiue,
Estward was into Spaigne driue
Riht faste vnder a castell wall
1090   Wher that an hethen amirall
Was lord, and he a stieward hadde,
Oon Thelous, which al was badde,
A fals knyht and a renegat.

The ship is driven
under a castle wall
in Spain.

Thelous, the stew-
ard of the castle,
attempts to do her
violence,

He goth to loke in what astat
The schip was come, and there he fond
Forth with a child vpon hire hond
This lady, wher sche was al one.
He tok good hiede of the persone
And sih sche was a worthi wiht,
1100   And thoghte he wolde vpon the nyht
Demene hire at his oghne wille,
And let hire be therinne stille,[1]
That mo men[2] sih sche noght that dai.
At Goddes wille and thus sche lai,
Vnknowe what hire schal betide;
And fell so that be nyhtes tide
This knyht, withoute felaschipe,
Hath take a bot and came to schipe,
And thoghte of hire his lust to take
1110   And swor, if sche him daunger make,
That certeinly sche scholde deie.
Sche sih ther was non other weie,
And seide he scholde hire wel conforte,
That he ferst loke out ate porte,
That noman were nyh the stede,
Which myhte knowe what thei dede,
And thanne he mai do what he wolde.
He was riht glad that sche so tolde,
And to the porte anon he ferde:

but her prayer is
heard, and Thelous
is drowned.

1120   Sche preide God, and he hire herde,
And sodeinliche he was out throwe
And dreynt, and tho began to blowe
A wynd menable fro the lond,
And thus the myhti Goddes hond
Hire hath conveied and defended.

After three more
years on the sea,
the ship drifts amid
a large fleet.

And whan thre yer be full despended,
Hire schip was driue vpon a dai
Wher that a gret nauye lay
Of schipes, al the world at ones:
1130   And as God wolde for the nones
Hire schip goth in among hem alle,
And stinte noght, er it be falle

[1] And in the ship he kept hir still M.
[2] That no men M, H₃, H₄ (also MSS of other recensions).

And hath the vessell vndergete,
Which maister was of al the flete,
Bot there it resteth and abod.
This grete schip on anker rod;
The lord cam forth, and whan he sih
That other ligge abord so nyh,
He wondreth what it myhte be,
1140   And bad men to gon in and se.
This ladi tho was crope aside,
As sche that wolde hireseluen hide,
For sche ne wiste what thei were:
Thei soghte aboute and founde hir there
And broghten vp hire child and hire;
And thervpon this lord to spire   *Questioned by the admiral,*
Began, fro whenne that sche cam,
And what sche was. Quod sche, "I am   *Constance tells part of her story,*
A womman wofully bestad.
1150   I hadde a lord, and thus he bad,
That I forth with my litel sone
Vpon the wawes scholden wone,
Bot why the cause was, I not:
Bot he which alle thinges wot
Yit hath, I thonke him, of his miht
Mi child and me so kept vpriht,
That we be saue bothe tuo."
This lord hire axeth ouermo
How sche belieueth, and sche seith,
1160   "I lieue and triste in Cristes feith
Which deide vpon the rode tree."
"What is thi name?" tho quod he.
"Mi name is Couste," sche him seide:
Bot forthermor for noght he preide   *but not her origin.*
⟨fol. 34a⟩   Of hire astat to knowe plein,
Sche wolde him nothing elles sein
Bot of hir name, which sche feigneth;
Alle othre thinges sche restreigneth,
That a word more sche ne[1] tolde.
1170   This lord thanne axeth if sche wolde   *She is willing to be taken to Rome.*
With him abide in compaignie,
And seide he cam fro Barbarie
To Romeward, and hom he wente.

[1] no *F, N, H₂*.

Tho sche supposeth what it mente,
And seith sche wolde with him wende
And duelle vnto hire lyues ende,
Be so it be to his plesance.
And thus vpon here aqueintance
He tolde hire pleinly as it stod
1180 Of Rome how that the gentil blod
In Barbarie was betraied,
And thervpon he hath assaied
Be werre, and taken such vengance,
That non of al thilke alliance,
Be whom the tresoun was compassed,
Is from the swerd alyue[1] passed;
Bot of Constance hov[2] it was,
That cowthe he knowe be no cas,
Wher sche becam, so as he seide.

1190   Hire ere vnto his word sche leide
Bot forther made sche no chiere.
And natheles in this matiere
It happeth thilke time so:
This lord, with whom sche scholde go,
Of Rome was the senatour,
And of hir fader themperour
His brother doughter hath to wyue,
Which hath hir fader ek alyue,
And was Salustes cleped tho;
1200 This wif Heleine hihte also,
To whom Constance was cousine.
Thus to the sike a medicine
Hath God ordeined of his grace,
That forthwith in the same place
This senatour his trowthe plihte,
For euere, whil he liue mihte,
To kepe in worschipe and in welthe,
Be so that God wol yiue hire helthe,
This ladi, which fortune him sende.
1210 And thus the schipe forth sailende
Hire and hir child to Rome he broghte,
And to his wif tho he besoghte
To take hire into compaignie:

This admiral is a senator, and husband of Helaine, a cousin of Constance,

[1] *Macaulay reads* alyve.   [2] *Macaulay reads* how.

And sche, which cowthe of courtesie
Al that a good wif scholde konne,
Was inly glad that sche hath wonne
The felaschip of so good on.
Til tuelue yeres were agon,
This emperoures dowhter Custe
1220   Forth with the dowhter of Saluste
Was kept, bot noman redily
Knew what sche was, and noght forthi
Thei thoghten wel sche hadde be
In hire astat of hih degre,
And euery lif hire loueth wel.

Now herke how thilke vnstable whel,
Which euere torneth, wente aboute.
The king Allee, whil he was oute,
As thou tofore hast herd this cas,
1230   Deceiued thurgh his moder was;
Bot whan that he cam hom ayein
He axeth of his chamberlein
And of the bisschop ek also,
Wher thei the qweene hadden do.
And thei answerde, there he bad,
And haue him thilke lettre rad
Which he hem sende for warant,
And tolde him pleinli as it stant,
And sein, it thoghte hem gret pite
1240   To se so worthi on as sche
With such a child as ther was bore,
So sodeinly to be forlore.
He axeth hem what child that were;
And thei him seiden, that naghere,
In al the world thogh men it soghte,
Was neuere womman that forth broghte
A fairer child than it was on.
And thanne he axede hem anon
Whi thei ne hadden write so:
1250   Thei tolden, so thei hadden do.
He seide "Nay"; thei seiden "Yis."
The lettre schewed, rad it is,
Which thei forsoken eueridel.
Tho was it vnderstonde wel

who welcomes her;

*she lives twelve
years with them,*

*her origin still a
secret.*

*King Allee of
Northumberland
has returned home*

*and discovered the
treason of his
mother.*

⟨fol. 34b⟩

That ther is tresoun in the thing:
The messager tofore the king
Was broght and sodeinliche opposed;
And he, which nothing hath supposed
Bot alle wel, began to seie
1260   That he nagher¹ vpon the weie
Abod, bot only in a stede;
And cause why that he so dede
Was, as he wente to and fro,
At Knaresburgh be nyhtes tuo
The kinges moder made him duelle.
And whan the king it herde telle,
Withinne his herte he wiste als faste
The treson which his moder caste;
And thoghte he wolde noght abide,
1270   Bot forth riht in the same tide
He tok his hors and rod anon.
With him ther riden mani on
To Knaresburgh and forth thei wente,
And lich the fyr which tunder hente,
In such a rage, as seith the bok,
His moder sodeinliche he tok

He makes her confess

And seide vnto hir in this wise:
"O beste of helle, in what iuise²
Hast thou deserved forto deie,
1280   That hast so falsly put aweie
With tresoun of thi bacbitinge
The treweste at my knowlechinge
Of wyues and the most honeste?
Bot I wol make this beheste,
I schal be venged er I go."

and has her burned to death.

And let a fyr do make tho,
And bad men forto caste hire inne;
Bot ferst sche told out al the sinne,
And dede hem alle forto wite
1290   How sche the lettres hadde write,
Fro point to point as it was wroght.
And tho sche was to dethe broght
And brent tofore hire sones yhe:
Wherof these othre, whiche it sihe
And herden how the cause stod,

¹ nowher H₄.   ² guise M; a wyse H₄.

Sein that the iuggement is good,
Of that hir sone hire hath so serued;
For sche it hadde wel deserued
Thurgh tresoun of hire false tunge
1300   Which thurgh the lond was after sunge,
Constance and euery wiht compleigneth.
Bot he, whom alle wo distreigneth,
This sorghfull king, was so bestad,
That he schal neuermor be glad,
He seith, eftsone forto wedde,
Til that he wiste how that sche spedde,
Which hadde ben his ferste wif:
And thus his yonge vnlusti lif
He dryueth forth so as he mai.

1310   Til it befell vpon a dai
Whan he his werres hadde achieued,
And thoghte he wolde be relieued   He goes to Rome to
Of soule hele vpon the feith   receive absolution
                                           from the Pope.
Which he hath take, thanne he seith
That he to Rome in pelrinage
Wol go, wher pope was Pelage,
To take his absolucioun.
And vpon this condicioun
He made Edwyn his lieutenant,
1320   Which heir to him was apparant,
That he the lond in his absence
Schal reule: and thus be prouidence
Of alle thinges wel begon
He tok his leue and forth is gon.
Elda, which tho was with him there,   Elda, sent ahead to
Er thei fulliche at Rome were,   make arrangements,
Was sent tofore to pourueie;
And he his guide vpon the weie,
In help to ben his herbergour,
1330   Hath axed who was senatour
That he his name myhte kenne.
Of Capadoce, he seide, Arcenne
He hihte, and was a worthi kniht.
To him goth Elda tho forth riht   speaks to the sena-
And told him of his lord tidinge,   tor (whose name is
                                           Arcenne),
And preide that for his comynge

He wolde assigne him herbergage;
And he so dede of good corage.

Whan al is do that was to done,
1340   The king himself cam after sone.

who tells his wife
and Constance of
the coming of King
Allee.
This senatour, whan that he com,
To Couste and to his wif at hom
Hath told how such a king Allee
Of gret array to the citee

Constance swoons
for joy.
Was come, and Couste vpon his tale
With herte clos and colour pale
Aswoune fell, and he merueileth
So sodeinly what thing hire eyleth,
⟨fol. 35a⟩   And cawhte hire vp, and whan sche wok,
1350   Sche syketh with a pitous lok
And feigneth seknesse of the see;
Bot it was for the king Allee,
For ioie wich[1] fell in hire thoght
That God him hath to tovne broght.

Allee has received
the absolution of
the Pope.
This king hath spoke with the pope
And told al that he cowthe agrope,
What grieueth in his conscience;

He plans a feast and
invites the senator.
And thanne he thoghte in reuerence
Of his astat, er that he wente,
1360   To make a feste, and thus he sente
Vnto the senatour to come
Vpon the morwe, and other some,
To sitte with him at the mete.
This tale hath Couste noght foryete,

At the feast,
Maurice, instructed
by his mother,
attracts the atten-
tion of Allee,
Bot to Moris hire sone tolde
That he vpon the morwe scholde
In all that euere he cowthe and mihte
Be present in the kinges sihte,
So that the king him ofte sihe.
1370   Moris tofore the kinges yhe
Vpon the morwe, where he sat
Ful ofte stod, and vpon that
The king his chiere vpon him caste,

who is reminded of
Constance,
And in his face him thoghte als faste
He sih his oghne wif Constance;
For nature as in resemblance

---

[1] *Macaulay reads* which.

Of face hem liketh so to clothe,
That thei were of a suite bothe.
The king was moeued in this thoght
1380 Of that he seth, and knoweth it noght;
This child he loueth kindely,
And yit he wot no cause why.
Bot wel he sih and vnderstod
That he toward Arcenne stod,
And axeth him anon riht there,   questions Arcenne,
If that this child his sone were.
He seide, "Yee, so I him calle,
And wolde it were so befalle,
Bot it is al in other wise."

1390   And tho began he to deuise   and is told how
How he the childes moder fond   Maurice and his
                                       mother Couste
Vpon the see from euery lond   came in a rudderless
Withinne a schip was stiereles,   ship.
And how this ladi helpeles
Forth with hir child he hath forthdrawe.
The king hath vnderstonde his sawe,
The childes name and axeth tho,
And what the moder hihte also
That he him wolde telle he preide.
1400 "Moris this child is hote," he seide,
"His moder hatte Couste, and this
I not what maner name it is."
But Allee wiste wel ynowh,   Allee hopes tnat
Wherof somdiel smylende le lowh;   this Couste is Con-
                                       stance;
For Couste in Saxoun is to sein
Constance vpon the word Romein.
Bot who that cowthe specefie
What tho fell in his fantasie,
And how his wit aboute renneth
1410 Vpon the loue in which he brenneth
It were a wonder forto hiere:
For he was novther[1] ther ne hiere,
Bot clene out of himself aweie,
That he not what to thenke or seie,
So fain he wolde it were sche.
Wherof his hertes priuete

[1] *Macaulay reads* nouther.

Began the werre of yee and nay,
The which in such balance lay
That contenance for a throwe
1420   He loste, til he mihte knowe
The sothe: bot in his memoire
The man which lith in purgatoire
Desireth noght the heuene more
That he ne longeth al so sore
To wite what him schal betide.
And whan the bordes were aside
And euery man was rise aboute,
The king hath weyued al the route,

he asks to be taken
to see her.

And with the senatour al one
1430   He spak and preide of him a bone,
To se this Couste, wher sche duelleth
At hom with him, so as he telleth.
The senatour was wel appaied,
This thing no lengere is delaied,
To se this Couste goth the king;
And sche was warned of the thing,
And with Heleine forth sche cam
Ayein the king, and he tho nam

They are happily
reunited.

God hiede, and whan he sih his wif,
1440   Anon with all his hertes lif
⟨fol. 35b⟩   He cawhte hire in his arm and kiste.[1]
Was neuere wiht that sih ne wiste
A man that more ioie made,
Wherof thei weren alle glade
Whiche herde tellen of this chance.

    This king tho with his wif Constance,
Which hadde a gret part of his wille,
In Rome for a time stille
Abod and made him wel at ese:

She still refuses to
tell her origin

1450   Bot so yit cowthe he neuere plese
His wif, that sche him wolde sein
Of hire astat the trowthe plein,
Of what contre that sche was bore,
Ne what sche was, and yit therfore
With al his wit he hath don sieke.
Thus as thei lihe abedde and spieke,

---

[1] keste F (also NH₂, H₃).

Sche preide him and conseileth bothe,
That for the worshipe of hem bothe
So as hire thoghte it were honeste

but suggests that
Allee invite the
Emperor.

1460   He wolde an honourable feste
Make, er he wente, in the cite,
Wher themperour himself schal be:
He graunteth al that sche him preide.
Bot as men in that time seide,
This emperour fro thilke day
That ferst his dowhter wente away
He was thanne after neuere glad;
Bot what that eny man him bad
Of grace for his dowhter sake
1470   That grace wolde he noght forsake;
And thus ful gret almesse he dede,
Wherof sche hadde many a bede.

This emperour out of the toun
Withinne a ten mile enviroun
Where as it thoghte him for the beste,
Hath sondry places forto reste;
And as fortune wolde tho,
He was duellende at on of tho.
The king Allee forth with thassent

1480   Of Couste his wif hath thider sent

Maurice is sent to
the Emperor,

Moris his sone, as he was taght,
To themperour, and he goth straght,
And in his fader half besoghte,
As he which his lordschipe soghte,
That of his hihe worthinesse
He wolde do so gret meknesse,
His oghne toun to come and se,
And yiue a time in the cite,
So that his fader mihte him gete
1490   That he wolde ones with him ete.
This lord hath granted his requeste;

who agrees.

And whan the dai was of the feste,
In worschipe of here emperour
The king and ek the senatour

Allee, Constance,
and others ride to
meet him.

Forth with here wyues bothe tuo
With many a lord and lady mo,
On horse riden him ayein;

Til it befell, vpon a plein
Thei sihen wher he was comende.

Constance rides
ahead

1500 With that Constance anon preiende
Spak to hir lord that he abyde,
So that sche mai tofore ryde,
To ben vpon his bienvenue
The ferste which schal him salue;
And thus after hire lordes graunt
Vpon a mule whyt amblaunt
Forth with a fewe rod this qweene.
Thei wondren what sche wolde mene,
And riden after, softe pas;
1510 Bot whan this ladi come was
To themperour, in his presence

and greets the
Emperor as her
father.

Sche seide alowd in audience,
"Mi lord, mi fader, wel you be!
And of this time that I se
Youre honour and your goode hele
Which is the helpe of my querele,
I thonke vnto the Goddes myht."
For ioie his herte was affliht
Of that sche tolde in remembrance;
1520 And whanne he wiste it was Constance,
Was neuere fader half so blithe.

He weeps for joy.

Wepende he keste hire ofte sithe,
So was his herte al ouercome;
For thogh his moder were come
Fro deth to lyue out of the graue,
He mihte nomor wonder haue
Than he hath whan that he hire sih.
With that hire oghne lord cam nyh
And is to themperour obeied;

All are deeply
moved.

1530 Bot whan the fortune is bewreied,
How that Constance is come aboute,
So hard an herte was non oute,
⟨fol. 36a⟩ That he for pite tho ne wepte.

Arcennus, which hire fond and kepte,
Was thanne glad of that is falle.
So that with ioie among hem alle
Thei riden in at Rome gate.
This emperour thoghte al to late

Til that the[1] pope were come,   The Pope joins
them,
1540   And of the lordes sende some
To preie him that he wolde haste:
And he cam forth in alle haste,
And whan that he the tale herde,
How wonderly this chance ferde,
He thonketh God of his miracle,   and thanks God for
this miracle.
To whos miht mai be non obstacle:
The king a noble feste hem made,
And thus thei weren alle glade.
A parlement, er that thei wente,
1550   Thei setten vnto this entente   Maurice is declared
heir apparent.
To puten Rome in full espeir
That Moris was apparant heir
And scholde abide with hem stille
For such was al the londes wille.

Whan euery thing was fulli spoke,
Of sorwe and queint was al the smoke,
Tho tok his leue Allee the king,   Allee and Con-
stance return to
Northumberland.
And with full many a riche thing,
Which themperour him hadde yiue
1560   He goth a glad lif forto liue;
For he Constance hath in his hond,
Which was the confort of his lond.
For whan that he cam hom ayein,
Ther is no tunge it mihte sein
What ioie was that ilke stounde
Of that he hath his qwene founde,
Which ferst was sent of Goddes sonde,
Whan sche was driue vpon the strounde,
Be whom the misbelieue of sinne
1570   Was left, and Cristes feith cam inne
To hem that whilom were blinde.

Bot he which hindreth euery kinde   After Allee's death,
And for no gold mai be forboght,
The deth comende er he be soght,
Tok with this king such aqueintance,
That he with al his retenance
Ne mihte noght defende his lif;

[1] *Om. F.*

And thus he parteth from his wif,
Which thanne made sorwe ynowh.

Constance returns
to Rome.

1580 　And thervpon hir herte drowh
To leuen Engelond for euere
And go wher that sche hadde leuere,
To Rome, whenne that sche cam:
And thus of al the lond sche nam
Hir leue, and goth to Rome ayein.

Her father soon
dies,

And after that the bokes sein,
Sche was noght there bot a throwe,
Whan deth of kinde hath ouerthrowe
Hir worthi fader, which men seide

1590 That he betwen hire armes deide.

and she the follow-
ing year.

And afterward the yer suiende
The God hath mad of hire an ende,
And fro this worldes faierie
Hath take hire into compaignie.

Maurice reigns.

Moris hir sone was corouned,
Which so ferforth was abandouned
To Cristes feith, that men him calle
Moris the Cristeneste of alle.

Thus love tri-
umphed,

And thus the wel meninge[1] of loue

1600 Was ate laste set aboue;

and the backbiters
were punished.

And so as thou hast herd tofore,
The false tunges weren lore,
Whiche vpon loue wolden lie.
Forthi touchende of this enuie
Which longeth vnto bacbitinge,
Be war thou make no lesinge
In hindringe of another wiht:
And if thou wolt be tawht ariht
What meschief bakbitinge doth

1610 Be other weie, a tale soth
Now miht thou hiere next suiende
Which to this vice is acordende.

[1] whiel moeuing H_3.

THE WIFE OF BATH'S PROLOGUE

By BARTLETT J. WHITING

THE Wife of Bath is perhaps Chaucer's richest, and certainly his ripest, character. Her *Prologue*, enlarging on the masterly sketch in the *General Prologue*, gives us a full-length portrait of an oxymoron in the flesh, this overpowering, shrewish mistress of the art of love. But her *Prologue* contains more, and in its eight hundred and fifty-six lines we get a compact and learned survey, adorned with precepts, *exempla*, and authorities of that medieval antifeminism which, rising in the Dark Ages with classical antecedents and ecclesiastical fostering, was to run its course well into the seventeenth century. A complete collection of parallels, whether analogues or originals, is manifestly impossible. To determine just where Chaucer found many of his unchivalrous commonplaces in disparagement of the sex would be to ask which tooth of the buzz saw cut off the finger. We can, however, assemble a number of illustrative passages, some of them certainly direct sources, and some, indeed overlapping, from works which Chaucer surely knew. I have brought together more or less representative groups of quotations, and have arranged them, in accordance with the editor's general ruling, in the order in which they occur in the works from which they are taken. Marginal notes give line references to the *Prologue* itself, and cross-references will lead the reader to quotations which, as notably in the case of Jerome and Deschamps, might have served as alternate sources. The quotations, most or all of which have been noted before, are taken from four works: Jerome's *Epistola adversus Jovinianum* (including the long quotation from Theophrastus),[1] Walter Map's "Dissuasio Valerii

---

[1] For Chaucer and St. Jerome see W. W. Woollcombe, "The Sources of the Wife of Bath's Prologue," *Essays on Chaucer*, Part III ("Chaucer Society" [1876]), pp. 297–304; E. Koeppel, "Chaucer und Innocenz der Drittens Traktat *De Contemptu mundi*," *Archiv für das Studium der Neueren Sprachen und Litteraturen*, LXXXIV (1890), 413–16; "Chauceriana," *Anglia*, XIII (1890), 177–81; T. R. Lounsbury, *Studies in Chaucer* (New York, 1892), II, 292; W. E. Mead, "The Prologue of the Wife of Bath's Tale," *PMLA*, XVI (1901), 399–402.

ad Ruffinum ne uxorem ducat,"[1] the *Roman de la rose*,[2] and Eustache Deschamps' *Miroir de mariage*.[3] It is, perhaps, worth while to comment on the way in which Chaucer worked in the material from his various sources. Ten of the fifteen quotations from Jerome are paralleled in the first one hundred and fifty lines of the *Wife's Prologue*, and the passage from Theophrastus is utilized mainly in the hundred lines after line 198. With the exception of one short passage, all the quotations from the *Miroir* find their counterparts in the two hundred lines of the *Wife's Prologue* after line 198, and at least three-quarters of these fall in the area influenced by Theophrastus and are, indeed, often themselves ultimately from Theophrastus. The "Dissuasio Valerii" is used mainly toward the end of the *Wife's Prologue*, and the influence of the *Roman de la rose* appears throughout.

I

(From Jerome's *Epistola adversus Jovinianum* [Migne, *Patrologia Latina*, Vol. XXIII (Paris, 1845), cols. 211 ff.]).

Jovinian has claimed support from Scripture:

Abraham and Jacob had more than one wife (D 55–58), and Abraham was blessed.

Currit ad Abraham, Isaac, et Jacob, e quibus prior trigamus, secundus monogamus, tertius quatuor uxorum est: Liæ, Rachel, Balæ, et Zelphæ; et asserit Abraham ob fidei meritum benedictionem in generatione filii accepisse [i. 5. col. 216; cf. i. 19. col. 237].

That one should eat barley (D 143–46) in preference to cow dung is not an argument against the goodness of wheat.

Velut si quis definiat: Bonum est triticeo pane vesci, et edere purissimam similam. Tamen ne quis compulsus fame comedat stercus bubulum, concedo ei, ut vescatur et hordeo. Num idcirco frumentum non habebit puritatem suam, si fimo hordeum præferatur? [i. 7. col. 219].

Jovinian is pleased that the Apostle does not claim authority to command virginity (D 59–68).

Hic adversarius tota exsultatione bacchatur: hoc velut fortissimo ariete, virginitatis murum quatiens: "Ecce, inquit, Apostolus profitetur de virginibus, Domini se non habere præceptum: et qui cum auc-

---

[1] See P. T[oynbee], "The Author of Chaucer's *Book Cleped Valerie*," *Academy*, XL (1891), 588–89; Koeppel, "Chauceriana," pp. 181–83; Lounsbury, 368–71.

[2] See W. E. Mead, "The Prologue of the Wife of Bath's Tale," *PMLA*, XVI (1901), 388–404; Dean S. Fansler, *Chaucer and the Roman de la rose* (New York, 1914), pp. 166–74 and 259.

[3] See J. L. Lowes, "Chaucer and the *Miroir de mariage*," *MP*, VIII (1911), 305–21; Lowes, "Illustrations of Chaucer," *Romanic Review*, II (1911), 120–21; C. Brown, "The Evolution of the Canterbury 'Marriage Group,'" *PMLA*, XLVIII (1933), 1049–50.

toritate de maritis et uxoribus jusserat, non audet imperare quod Dominus non præcepit. Et recte. Quod enim præcipitur, imperatur: quod imperatur, necesse est fieri, quod necesse est fieri, nisi fiat, pœnam habet. Frustra enim jubetur, quod in arbitrio ejus ponitur, cui jussum est." Si virginitatem Dominus imperasset, videbatur nuptias condemnare, et hominum auferre seminarium, unde et ipsa virginitas nascitur. Si præcidisset radicem, quomodo fruges quæreret? Nisi ante fundamenta jecisset, qua ratione ædificium exstrueret, et operturum cunneta desuper culmen imponeret? Multo labore fossorum subvertuntur montes: terrarum pene inferna penetrantur, ut inveniatur aurum. Cumque de granis minutissimis prius conflatione fornacis, deinde callida artificis manu fuerit monile compactum; non ille beatus vocatur, qui de luto excrevit aurum, sed qui auri utitur pulchritudine. Noli igitur admirari, si inter titillationes carnis, et incentiva vitiorum, Angelorum vitam non exigimur, sed docemur. Quia ubi consilium datur, offerentis arbitrium est: ubi præceptum, necessitas est servientis [i. 12. col. 227; cf. i. 36. col. 259].

Virginity could hardly be commanded without forbidding marriage (D 69–70), and without marriage whence could virgins come (D 71–72)? After all, gold adorns not the miner but the wearer.

In propatulo est cur Apostolus dixerit, De virginibus autem præceptum Domini non habeo; profecto quia præmiserat Dominus: Non omnes capiunt verbum, sed quibus datum est. Et, qui potest capere, capiat. Proponit ἀγωνοθέτης præmium, invitat ad cursum, tenet in manu virginitatis bravium: ostendit purissimam fontem, et clamitat: Qui sitit, veniat, et bibat. Qui potest capere, capiat (*Joan.* vii. 37) [i. 12. col. 228].

In this wicked world the angelic life is urged but n demanded (D 66 67, 80–82).

Quomodo enim virginibus ob fornicationis periculum concedit nuptias, et excusabile facit, quod per se non appetitur, ita ob eamdem fornicationem vitandam, concedit viduis secunda matrimonia. Melius est enim licet alterum et tertium, unum virum nosse, quam plurimos: id est, tolerabilius est uni homini prostitutam esse, quam multis. Siquidem et illa in Evangelio Joannis Samaritana, sextum se maritum habere dicens, arguitur a Domino, quod non sit vir ejus (*Joan.* iv, 17). Ubi enim numerus maritorum est, ibi vir, qui proprie unus est, esse desiit. Una costa a principio in unam uxorem versa est. Et erunt, inquit, duo in carne una (*Genes.* ii. 24): non tres, neque quatuor, alioquin jam non duo, si plures. Primus Lamech sanguinarius et homicida, unam carnem in duas divisit uxores: fratricidium et digamiam, eadem cataclysmi pœna delevit. [i. 14. col. 233].

Though all are not able, let him who can receive the word receive it. The great Starter calls for contestants, holds out the price of chastity (D 75–76), and points to the fount of purity.

Virgins may marry to avoid sin and widows similarly may remarry. One man, though he be second or third husband, is better than many.

The Samaritan woman (D 9–25) had too many, it would seem, and thus the original idea of marriage was destroyed.

Lamech (D 53–54), the bloody murderer, was the first bigamist.

Non damno digamos, immo nec trigamos, et, si dici potest, octogamos: plus aliquid inferam, etiam scortatorem recipio pœnitentem. Quidquid æqualiter licet, æquali lance pensandum est [i. 15. col. 234].

Not even octogamy (D 32–33) is damned.

Increase and multiply (D 26–29), said the Lord, for without planting there is no wood; but marriage fills the earth and virginity fills Heaven.

Quod autem ait: Crescite et multiplicamini, et replete terram (*Gen.* i, 28), necesse fuit prius plantare silvam et crescere, ut esset quod postea posset excidi. Simulque consideranda vis verbi, replete terram. Nuptiæ terram replent, virginitas paradisum [i. 16. col. 235].

When Solomon compared the love of women to hell, dry earth, and fire (D 371–75), he was thinking not alone of the wanton or the adulteress, but of women in general.

Sanguisuga diabolus est, diaboli filiæ sunt dilectione dilectæ, quæ satiari interfectorum cruore non possunt: Infernus, et amor mulieris, et terra arens, et ignis exæstuans (*Pr.* xxx, 16). Non hic de meretrice, non de adultera dicitur, sed amor mulieris generaliter accusatur, qui semper insatiabilis est, qui exstinctus accenditur, et post copiam rursum inops est, animumque virilem effeminat, et excepta passione quam sustinet, aliud non sinit cogitare. Simile quid et in sequenti

Three things shake the earth (D 362–70), and four would overwhelm it

parabola legimus: Per tria movetur terra, quartum autem non potest ferre: si servus regnet, et stultus si saturetur panibus, et odiosa uxor si habeat bonum virum: et ancilla si ejiciat dominam suam (*Prov.* xxx,

—and a wife is one of these evils.

21 seqq.). Ecce, et hic inter malorum magnitudinem uxor ponitur [i. 28. col. 250].

Jerome prepares to answer an unpleasantly anatomical question (D 115–34).

Et cur, inquies, creata sunt genitalia, et sic a conditore sapientissimo fabricati sumus, ut mutuum nostri patiamur ardorem, et gestiamus in naturalem copulam? Periclitamur responsionis verecundia, et quasi inter duos scopulos, et quasdam necessitatis et pudicitiæ συμπληγάδας hinc atque inde, vel pudoris, vel causæ naufragium sustinemus. Si ad proposita respondeamus, pudore suffundimur [i. 36. col. 260].

Frustra hæc omnia virorum habes, si complexu non uteris feminarum. Compellor aliquid loqui et insipiens fieri; sed vos me, ut loqui

He finds his answer (D 135–41) in the body and example of Our Lord.

audeam, coegistis. Dominus noster atque Salvator, qui cum in forma Dei esset, formam servi dignatus est assumere, factus obediens Patri usque ad mortem, mortem autem crucis, quid necesse erat, ut in his membris nasceretur, quibus usurus non erat? Qui certe ut sexum ostenderet, etiam circumcisus est. Cur Joannem apostolum et Baptistam sua dilectione castravit, quos viros nasci fecerat? Qui ergo in Christum credimus, Christi sectemur exempla [i. 36. cols. 260 f.].

The church does not damn matrimony, but rather uses it, as dishes of wood and clay are used in a great household (D 99–101).

Ecclesia enim matrimonia non damnat, sed subjicit: nec abjicit, sed dispensat: sciens, ut supra diximus, in domo magna non solum esse vasa aurea et argentea, sed et lignea et fictilia: et alia esse in honorem, alia in contumeliam: et quicumque se mundaverit, eum futurum esse vas honorabile, et necessarium in omne opus bonum præparatum [i. 40. col. 270].

Jerome has already said enough,

Sentio in catalogo feminarum multo me plura dixisse, quam exemplorum patitur consuetudo, et a lectore erudito juste posse reprehendi.

but the conduct of women forces him on,

Sed quid faciam, cum mihi mulieres nostri temporis, Apostoli ingerant auctoritatem; et necdum elato funere prioris viri, memoriter digamiæ præcepta decantent? Ut quæ Christianæ pudicitiæ despiciunt fidem, discant saltem ab Ethnicis castitatem. Fertur Aureolus Theophrasti liber de Nuptiis, in quo quærit, an vir sapiens ducat uxorem. Et eum definisset, si pulchra esset, si bene morata, si honestis parentibus, si ipse sanus ac dives, sic sapientem aliquando inire matrimonium, statim intulit: "Haec autem in nuptiis raro universa concordant. Non est ergo uxor ducenda sapienti. Primum enim impediri studia Philosophiæ; nec posse quemquam libris et uxori pariter inservire. Multa esse quæ matronarum usibus necessaria sint, pretiosæ vestes, aurum, gemmæ, sumptus, ancillæ, supellex varia, lecticæ et esseda deaurata. Deinde per noctes totas garrulæ conquestiones: Illa ornatior procedit in publicum: hæc honoratur ab omnibus, ego in conventu feminarum misella despicior. Cur aspiciebas vicinam? quid cum ancillula loquebaris? de foro veniens quid attulisti? Non amicum habere possumus [Al. possum], non sodalem. Alterius amorem, suum odium suspicatur. Si doctissimus præceptor in qualibet urbium fuerit, nec uxorem relinquere, nec cum sarcina ire possumus [Al. potest]. Pauperem alere, difficile est; divitem ferre, tormentum. Adde, quod nulla est uxoris electio, sed qualiscumque obvenerit, habenda. Si iracunda, si fatua, si deformis, si superba, si fetida, quodcumque vitii est, post nuptias discimus. Equus, asinus, bos, canis, et vilissima mancipia, vestes quoque, et lebetes, sedile ligneum, calix, et urceolus fictilis probantur prius, et sic emuntur: sola uxor non ostenditur, ne ante displiceat, quam ducatur. Attendenda semper ejus est facies, et pulchritudo laudanda: ne si alteram aspexeris, se existimet displicere. Vocanda domina, celebrandus natalis ejus, jurandum per salutem illius, ut sit superstes optandum; honoranda nutrix ejus, et gerula, servus patrinus, et alumnus, et formosus assecla, et procurator calamistratus, et in longam securamque libidinem exsectus spado: sub quibus nominibus adulteri [Al. adulteria] delitescunt. Quoscumque illa dilexerit, ingratis amandi. Si totam domum regendam ei commiseris, serviendum est. Si aliquid tuo arbitrio reservaveris, fidem sibi haberi non putabit; sed in odium vertetur ac jurgia, et nisi cito consulueris, parabit venena. Anus, et aruspices, et hariolos et institores gemmarum sericarumque vestium si intromiseris, periculum pudicitiæ est; si prohibueris, suspicionis injuria. Verum quid prodest etiam diligens custodia, cum uxor servari impudica non possit, pudica non debeat? Infida enim custos est castitatis necessitas; et illa vere pudica dicenda est, cui licuit peccare si voluit. Pulchra cito adamatur, fœda facile concupiscit. Difficile custoditur, quod plures amant. Molestum est possidere, quod nemo habere dignetur. Minore tamen miseria deformis habetur, quam formosa servatur. Nihil tutum

(margin notes)

and he will try to teach them chastity even from the pagans. Theophrastus declares that all the good qualities of a wife are seldom found in one woman.

No wise man needs to marry (D 274). A wife interferes with study (D 711 ff.), she has many wants,

complains all night,

and makes false accusations (D 235–378; cf. *Miroir*, ll. 1584–1611).

Poor she is bad, rich worse (D 248–52; cf. *Roman*, ll. 8579–86; *Miroir*, ll. 1755–59).
Her faults are concealed until after marriage—she is the only purchase a man makes without testing (D 282–92; cf. *Miroir*, ll. 1538–75).
She must be gazed on, praised, fêted;

even her family and hangers-on must be honored (D 293–302; cf. *Miroir*, ll. 1760–77).

However you treat her, you'll be sorry.

No custody will preserve chastity (D 357–61), nor does a chaste wife need to be guarded.

A fair wife is sought after, an ugly one lustful.
The sought-after is hard to guard—the uncoveted painful to hold (D 265–72).

Wooers have various charms, and what is often attacked is usually captured (D 253–64; cf. *Roman*, ll. 8579–8600; *Miroir*, ll. 1625–55). One marries for assistance and companionship, but a faithful and grateful servant is better in every way than a self-willed wife. Even in sickness friends and servants are more comforting than a weeping wife.[1]

est, in quod totius populi vota suspirant. Alius forma, alius ingenio, alius facetiis, alius liberalitate sollicitat. Aliquo modo, vel aliquando expugnatur, quod undique incessitur. Quod si propter dispensationem domus et languoris solatia, et fugam solitudinis, ducuntur uxores: multo melius servus fidelis dispensat, obediens auctoritati domini, et dispositioni ejus obtemperans, quam uxor, quæ in eo se existimat dominam, si adversum viri faciat voluntatem, id est, quod placet, non quod jubetur. Assidere autem ægrotanti magis possunt amici, et vernulæ beneficiis obligati, quam illa quæ nobis imputat [Al. imputet] lacrymas suas, et hæreditatis spe vendit [Al. vendas] illuviem, et sollicitudinem jactans, languentis animum desperatione conturbat [i. 47. cols. 276 f.].

Socrates had two wives who fought over him, beat him,

Socrates Xantippen et Myron neptem Aristidis, duas habebat uxores. Quæ cum crebro inter se jurgarentur, et ille eas irridere esset solitus, quod propter se fœdissimum hominem, simis naribus, recalva fronte, pilosis humeris, et repandis cruribus, disceptarent: novissime verterunt in eum impetum, et male mulctatum fugientemque diu persecutæ sunt. Quodam autem tempore cum infinita convicia ex

and one of whom poured water on his head (D 727–32).

superiori loco ingenerti Xantippæ restitisset, aqua perfusus immunda, nihil amplius respondit, quam capite deterso: Sciebam, inquit, futurum, ut ista tonitrua imber sequeretur [i. 48. cols. 278 f.].

Only the wearer knows where the shoe pinches (D 491–92; cf. *De nugis*, dist. iv, cap. iii).

Legimus quemdam apud Romanos nobilem, cum eum amici arguerent quare uxorem formosam et castam et divitem repudiasset, protendisse pedem, et dixisse eis: "Et hic soccus quem cernitis, videtur vobis novus et elegans: sed nemo scit præter me ubi me premat." Scribit Herodotus, quod mulier cum veste deponat et vere-

Herodotus identifies clothing and chastity (D 782–83).

cundiam. Et noster Comicus fortunatum putat, qui uxorem numquam duxerit [i. 48. cols. 279 f.].

Three wicked and lustful women (D 733–46).

Quid referam Pasiphaen, Clytemnestram, et Eriphylam: quarum prima deliciis diffluens, quippe regis uxor, tauri dicitur espetisse concubitus: altera occidisse virum ob amorem adulteri: tertia prodisse Amphiaraum, et saluti viri monile aureum prætulisse [i. 48. col. 280].

II

(From Walter Map's "Dissuasio Valerii ad Ruffinum philosophum ne uxorem ducat" [*De Nugis curialium*, ed. M. R. James ["Anecdota Oxoniensia; Mediaeval and Modern Series," XIV [Oxford, 1914]), 143 ff.].)

Pacuvius wept because his three wives had hung themselves on a single tree. Arrius, however, congratulated him on his unappreci-

Pacuuius flens ait Arro vicino suo "Amice, arborem habeo in orto meo infelicem, de qua se prima uxor mea suspendit, et postmodum secunda, et iam nunc tercia." Cui Arrius "Miror te in tantis successi-

---

[1] Chaucer used this passage in the *Merchant's Tale*, E 1295–1304.

bus lacrimas inuenisse," et iterum "Dii boni, quot dispendia tibi arbor illa suspendit!" et tercio "Amice, dede michi de arbore illa surculos quos seram." Amice, et ego tibi dico, metuo ne et te oporteat arboris illius surculos mendicare cum inueniri non poterunt [Dist. iv, cap. iii, pp. 151 f.]. ated good fortune, and begged for a shoot of the tree (D 757–64).

Sensit Sulpicius ubi ipsum calceus suus premebat, qui ab uxore nobili et casta diuertit. Amice, caue ne te premat calceus que auelli non potest [Dist. iv, cap. iii, p. 152]. Sulpicius, who left a noble and chaste wife, felt where his shoe pinched (D 491–92; cf. Jerome i. 48. cols. 274 f.).

Liuia uirum suum interfecit quem nimis odit; Lucilia suum quem nimis amauit. Illa sponte miscuit aconiton, hec decepta furorem propinauit pro amoris poculo. Amice, contrariis contendunt uotis iste; neutra tamen defraudata est fine fraudis feminee, proprio id est malo. Variis et diuersis incedunt semitis femine; quibuscunque anfractibus errent, quantiscunque deuient inuiis, unicus est exitus, unica omnium uiarum suarum meta, unicum caput et conuentus omnium diuersitatum suarum, malicia. Exemplum harum experimentum cape, quod audax est ad omnia quecunque amat vel odit femina, et artificiosa nocere cum vult, quod est semper; et frequenter cum iuuare parat obest, unde fit ut noceat et nolens. In fornace positus es; si aurum es, exibis aurum [Dist. iv, cap. iii, pp. 153 f.]. Livia killed a hateful husband, Lucilia a beloved one; the first willingly gave the poison, the second by mistake (D 747–56). Women move by various paths, but the end is ever the same—evil. They will do all for hate or love, injure when they wish and even when they do not.

III

(From Guillaume de Lorris and Jean de Meun, *Le Roman de la rose*, ed. E. Langlois ["Société des Anciens Textes Français" (5 vols.; Paris, 1914–24)].)

E qui veaut povre fame prendre, A poor wife requires expense,
8580 A nourrir la l'esteut entendre,
E a vestir e a chaucier.
E s'il tant se cuide essaucier a rich wife is proud and masterful,
Qu'il la preigne riche forment,
8584 A sofrir la ra grant torment,
Tant la treuve orguilleuse e fiere
E seurcuidiee e bobanciere.
S'el rest bele, tuit i acueurent, a pretty wife is pursued by many
8588 Tuit la poursivent, tuit l'eneurent,
Tuit i hurtent, tuit i travaillent,
Tuit i luitent, tuit i bataillent,
Tuit a li servir s'estudient,
8592 Tuit li vont entour, tuit la prient,
Tuit i musent, tuit la couveitent,
Si l'ont en la fin, tant espleitent, —a beleaguered tower which may fall—
Car tour de toutes parz assise

and a plain wife is
too anxious to
please (D 248–55;
cf. Jerome i. 47. col.
276, and *Miroir*, ll.
1625–55, 1734–59).

8596   Enviz eschape d'estre prise.
  S'el rest laide, el veaut a touz plaire;
 E coment pourrait nus ce faire
 Qu'il gart chose que tuit guerreient,
8600   Ou qui veaut touz ceus qui la veient? ...[1]

Hercules overcame
twelve monsters

 Cist Herculès ot mout d'encontres:
9192   Il vainqui doze orribles montres,
 E quant ot vaincu le dozieme,
 Onc ne pot chevir dou trezieme,
 Ce fu de Deïanira

but could not es-
cape Deïaneira's
poisoned shirt (D
724–26).

9196   S'amie, qui li descira
 Sa char de venin toute esprise
 Par la venimeuse chemise.
 Si ravait il pour Yolé
9200   Son cueur ja d'amour afolé.
 Ainsinc fu par fame dontez
 Herculès, qui tant ot bontez.

Samson was fearless
while he had his hair
but Delilah tricked
him (D 721–23).

 Ausinc Sanson, qui pas dis omes
9204   Ne redoutast ne que dis pomes
 S'il eüst ses cheveus eüz,
 Fu par Dalida deceüz ...[2]

La Vieille did not
learn of love in
school

12801   Bele iere e jenne e nice e fole,
 N'onc ne fui d'Amours a escole
 Ou l'en leüst la theorique,

but from years of
practical experience
(D 1 f.).

12804   Mais je sai tout par la pratique:
 Esperiment m'en ont fait sage,
 Que j'ai hantez tout mon aage;
 Or en sai jusqu'a la bataille,

It is but right that
she should share
her knowledge with
the young (cf. D
187).

12808   Si n'est pas dreiz que je vous faille
 Des biens aprendre que je sai,
 Puis que tant esprouvez les ai.
 Bien fait qui jennes genz conseille ...

Regrets are vain for
what is gone,

12924   Mais riens n'i vaut le regreter:
 Qui est alé ne peut venir.
 Jamais n'en pourrai nul tenir,
 Car tant ai ridee la face

and with wrinkles a
woman's power
fails,

12928   Qu'il n'ont garde de ma menace.
 Pieç'a que bien le me disaient
 Li ribaut qui me despisaient.
 Si me pris a plourer des lores.
 Par Deu! si me plaist il encores

but she can still get
pleasure in recalling
her good days.

 Quant je m'i sui bien pourpensee;

[1] Vol. III, p. 87, ll. 8578–8600. [2] Vol. III, pp. 111 f., ll. 9191–9206.

Mout me delite en ma pensee
E me resbaudissent li membre
12936 Quant de mon bon tens me remembre
E de la joliete vie
Don mes cueurs a si grant envie;
Tout me rejovenist le cors

It rejuvenates her to think at least she has had her joys (D 469–79).

12940 Quant j'i pens e quant jou recors;
Touz les biens dou monde me fait
Quant me souvient de tout le fait,
Qu'au meins ai je ma joie eüe,
12944 Combien qu'il m'aient deceüe.
Jenne dame n'est pas oiseuse

No girl wastes her time whose happy life pays her expenses.

Quant el meine vie joieuse,
Meïsmement cele qui pense
12948 D'aquerre a faire sa despense ...[1]
13452 E puis que fame est enivree,

A drunken woman is without defense,

Il n'a point en li de defense,
E jangle tout quanqu'ele pense,

babbles what she thinks,
and is at the mercy of everybody (D 467–68).

E est a touz abandonee
Quant a tel meschief s'est donee ...[2]
13517   E gart que trop ne seit enclose

No woman should stay indoors too much, for then her beauty will be little seen and sought,

Car, quant plus a l'ostel repose,
Meins est de toutes genz veüe
13520 E sa beauté meins queneüe,
Meins couveitiee e meins requise.
Souvent aille a la maistre iglise

but rather must she go to public events of every kind,

E face visitacions,
13524 A noces, a processions,
A jeus, a festes, a queroles,
Car en teus leus tient ses escoles

for there the rites of Love are found (D 555–58)

E chante a ses deciples messe
13528 Li deus d'Amours e la deesse.[3]

IV

From Eustache Deschamps' *Le Miroir de mariage* [*Œuvres complètes*, ed. the Marquis de Queux de Saint-Hilaire and G. Raynaud ("Société des Anciens Textes Français," Vol. IX [Paris, 1904])].

Répertoire de Science writes to Franc Vouloir of the married man's care and tells him that a wife, ever desirous of new clothes, will complain in this way:[4]

[1] Vol. III, pp. 262 f., ll. 12924–48.

[2] Vol. IV, p. 21, ll. 13452–56.   [3] Vol. IV, p. 24, ll. 13517–28.

[4] In connection with the *Merchant's Tale* a more detailed summary of the *Miroir* is given in the present work, pp. 333–39.

"My headdress is old and out of date, and I know a less worthy woman who has a far better one" (D 236–38).

1256 "Et si vous di bien que ma huve[1]
      Est vieille et de pouvre fasson:
      Je sçay tel femme de masson,
      Qui n'est pas a moy comparable,
1260 Qui meilleur l'a et plus coustable
      .Iiii. fois que le mienne n'est ..."
      A mon propos vueil revenir.
      Qui prandra femme, cilz l'ara

He who takes a wife must take her as he finds her,

1540 Toute tele qu'il la prandra,
      Soit juene, vieille, salle ou nette,
      Sotte, boiteuse ou contrefette,
      Humble, courtoise ou gracieuse,
      Belle ou borgne ou malicieuse,
1545 Car par devant se couverra;
      Mais ses meurs après ouverra,

but she will soon reveal what she concealed before.

      Et de près les fera sentir
      A tel qui en sera martir;
      Lors fera apparoir ses vices.

He is a foolish man who buys without testing.

1550 Si me semble que cilz est nices
      Qui, sanz cerchier ce qu'il veult prandre,
      L'achate et ne le puet reprandre.
      Se tu veulz achater bestail
      Pour garder ou vendre a detail,

No one purchases an animal without looking for defects,

1555 Soit buefs, vaiches, brebiz ou pors,
      Tu le verras au long du corps,
      Ou ventre, en la queue, en la teste
      Et es dens, s'il est juene beste,
      Et les metteras a l'essay;
1560 Et des chevaulx encore sçay,
      Quant ilz vendront en ton encontre,
      Ilz troteront dessus la monstre,[2]
      Tu les verras et chaux et frois,
      Et soubz la selle, c'est bien drois,
      Qu'ilz ne soient rouz[3] ou cassez;
      Et qu'ilz ne soient mespassez,[4]
      Leur tasteras parmi les jointes;
      Sus monteras, et donrras pointes
      Es costez de tes esperons.

[1] Headdress.

[2] Often "examination," "inspection"; here the place where horses for sale were made to show their gait.

[3] Broken (Sainte-Palaye).   [4] Jaded, overdriven.

1570 Mais autrement va des barons
  Et des aultres qui prannent femmes,
  Car sanz vir queuvrent leur diffames,
  Et les prannent sanz ce sçavoir
  Qu'elles font depuis apparoir,
1575 Comme plus a plain sera dit.
  Quant le povre deduit du lit
  Est passé par aucunes nuis,
  Lors te saudront les grans ennuis,
  Car tu ne pourras achever
1580 Son delit sanz ton corps grever,
  Qui adonc reposer vouldras;
  Mais Dieux scet que tu ne pourras
  Rendre le deu qu'elle demande
  Quant au delit. Or yert engrande
1585 D'avoir fremillez et affiches
  Et tu ne seras pas si riches
  Que tu puisses continuer
  Son estat et renouveler;
  Et elle verra ses voisines,
1590 Ses parentes et ses cousines,
  Qui nouvelles robes aront:
  Adonc plains et plours te saudront
  Et complaintes de par ta fame,
  Qui te dira: "Par Nostre Dame,
1595 Celle est en publique honourée,
  Bien vestue et bien acesmée,
  Et entre toutes suy despite
  Et povre, maleureuse ditte!
  Mais je voy bien a quoy il tient:
1600 Vous regardez, quant elle vient,
  No voisine, bien m'en perçoy,
  Car vous n'avez cure de moy;
  Vous jouez a no chamberiere:
  Quant du marchié venis arriere,
1605 L'autre jour, que li apportas?
  Las! de dure heure m'espousas!
  Je n'ay mari ne compaignon.
  Certes se vous me fuissiez bon,
  Et vous n'amissiez autre part,
1610 Vous ne venissiez pas si tart
  Comme vous faictes a l'ostel!" ...

Marginal glosses:

but it is far otherwise with men when preparing to marry (D 282–92; cf. Jerome i. 47, col. 276).

Marriage brings debts, grievous enough to pay (D 198 ff., 213 ff.),

and costs which shake the married man's estate.

A wife sees new gowns on every hand

and complains that others have fine attire, while she goes poorly clad (cf. *Miroir*, ll. 1256–61).

Her husband eyes the neighbor,

flirts with the maid;

if he loved her, he'd not come home so late.

A handsome wife
brings little peace,
for all will covet
her,

1625   Se tu la prens, qu'elle soit belle,
    Tu n'aras jamais paix a elle,
    Car chascuns la couvoitera,
    Et dure chose a toy sera
    De garder ce que un chascun voite
1630   Et qu'il poursuit et qu'il couvoite,
    Car tu as contre toy cent œulx,
    Et li desirs luxurieux
    Est toutes fois contre beauté,
    Qui est contraire a chasteté.
1635   A paine pourroit belle fame
    Sanz grant bonté eschuer blame,
    Com chascuns y tend et y rue,

and woo in various
ways,

    Soit en moustier soit en my rue,
    En son hostel ou aultre part.

with gifts and po-
ems and flattery,

1640   Ly uns des chapeaulx ly depart,
    L'autre robes, l'autre joyaulx,
    L'un fait joustes, festes, cembeaulx[1]
    Pour son amour, pour son gent corps:
    L'autre lui envoie dehors
1645   Chançons, lettres et rondelez,
    Fermaulx, frontaulx et annelez,
    Et dit que de sens n'a pareille,
    S'est de beauté la nompareille:
    Il art pour li, il muert, il pert;

dressing themselves
in green, or blue,
white, red or black
for her (D 253–56,
263–64; cf. Jerome
i. 47. col. 276).

1650   Li uns se vest pour li de vert,
    L'autre de bleu, l'autre de blanc,
    L'autre s'en vest vermeil com sanc,
    Et cilz qui plus la veult avoir
    Pour son grant dueil s'en vest de noir,
1655   Et dist qu'il vit a grant martire ...

A homely wife, by
contrast, is not
sought,

1734   Or regardons une autre chose,
    Que nulz homs ne veult ne souhaide:
    S'il est qui preingne femme laide,
    Nulz homs n'ara sur elle envie;

and who wants that
which no other man
desires (D 265–72)?

    Et ou sera plus mortel vie
    Qu'a celui qui possidera
1740   Ce que nulz avoir ne vourra,
    Que il possidera touz seulx?

This shames the
wretched man and
rouses strife.

    En tous temps le verrez honteux,
    Plain de courroux et d'atayne

---

[1] Tourneys, battles.

Et contre sa femme en hayne,
1745 En laidenges et en reprouches,
Qui ysteront de leurs deux bouches;
Et la clamera vile et orde.
Et ainsis seront en discorde,
Tousjours sanz paix et sanz amour,
1750 Et fera par tout sa clamour
Da sa femme laide qu'il a,
Ne jamais jour ne l'aimera.
Belle femme est envix domptée,
Et la laide est trop ahontée.

No wife is good, be she fair, ugly, rich or poor (D 248 ff.; cf. Jerome i. 47. col. 276; Roman, ll. 8579-8600).

1755 Se tu prans femme qui soit riche,
C'est le denier Dieu[1] et la briche[2]
D'avoir des reprouches souvent;
S'elle est povre, ce n'est que vent
Et tourment d'elle soustenir.

1760 S'en paix veulz ta vie finir,
Quelque chiere que femme face,
Il te fault encliner[3] sa face.
Soit belle, laide ou difformée,
Fain[4] qu'elle soit de toy amée:

To live in peace

1765 Il couvient sa beauté louer,
Et te tien d'autre regarder;
Il fault qu'apelée soit dame,
Et que tu jures Nostre Dame
Qu'elle passe tout en bonté.

a man must praise his wife's beauty

1770 Le jour de sa nativité
Te doit estre concelebrable,
Et le sa nourice amiable,
Son aieul, son frere et son oncle
Et son pere doiz tu a l'ongle

and her goodness,

remember her birth-day, and that of her nurse and honor all her kin (D 293-302; cf. Jerome i. 47. col. 276).

1775 Honourer, amer, conjouir,
Leurs mesgnies et gens jouir
Et livrer tout ce qu'il lui fault ...
1877 Tousjours veulent estre maistresses,
Et se tu consens que leurs tresses
A fil d'or soient galonnées

A man who lets his wife go gay with gold and silk imperils her chastity (D 337-47).

1880 Et qu'elles soient ordonnées
De soye et de fins autres draps,
Que feras tu? Tu nourriras

---

[1] Earnest-penny; see *NED, s.v.* "God's penny."   [3] Praise.

[2] Noose, snare; fig. (compulsory) way or means.   [4] Desirous.

Le vice d'impudicité,
Qui destruira leur chasteté.

After her husband's death a wife is sadly callous.

She takes whatever she can get,

1966   Elle emporte plus que le tiers,
Et s'a a part tout desrobé,
Sa proye prins comme un hobé[1]
Pour un autre qui la prandra.

thinks a short mass enough (D 496–500),

1970   Et sçavez vous qu'il advendra?
Du service, obseque et les lays
Oir vouldra parler jamais,
Excepté d'une courte messe;
Et regardera, en la presse

and searches the funeral crowd in hope to find herself another spouse (D 593–99, 627–29).

1975   A porter le deffunct en terre,
Quel mari elle pourra querre
Et avoir après cesti cy.

A wife's mother can be trusted to take her part and talk to the husband as follows:

"A wife who stays at home and hugs the fire brings little credit,

3208   "Se ta femme crout en maison
Et garde le feu et les cendres,

3210   Elle en vault pis, tes noms est mendres;
D'oneur ne sçara tant ne quant,

but is like a wandering goat,

S'iert comme une chievre vacant
Qui ne scet que brouter et paistre,

or cat whose fur is singed" (D 348–54).

Ou comme un chat qui est en l'aistre,

3215   Qui brulle son poil et qui l'art."

If the husband listens to his mother-in-law and lets his wife away from home, he suffers for it.

The wife whose husband long has waited for her must trick him by making the first complaint (D 387–92).

3600   Il fault que son mari deçoive
Au revenir, qui longuement
L'a attendue; et Dieux! comment
Il se cource de la demeure!
Et elle se commence en l'eure

3605   A plourer et a esmouvoir:
"Lasse! j'en doy bien tant avoir,
Qui ne finay huy a journée

"My marketing has taken the whole day,

D'aler! De maleure fuy née!
J'ay achaté ce qu'il me fault

3610   Et dont j'avoye grant default;

---

[1] *Falco subbuteo*: see *NED*, *s.v.* "Hobby," sb.[2]

Je ne bu huy ne ne mangay,
Et si m'ose vanter que j'ay
De lin, de chanvre et de semence,
Et de filé dont on me tance,
3615 D'aguilles, cannoulle et fuseaux,
De desvoudoirs, de bureteaux[1]
Plus pour .xx. soulz de parisis,
Que n'aroit femme de Paris
Ne d'ailleurs pour .xl. solz.
3620 Je croy que vous devenez fols
Qui ainsis m'alez riotant:
Or en alez querir autant!
Et je croy que vous y faurrez
Pour le pris: vous estes fourrez
3625 Et vestus comme un droiz prelas!
Il ne me faulroit pas un las
Ne ceans un morsiau de pain
Que je n'achate soir et main!
Mesler ne vous voulez de rien.
3630 Mais puis que femme fera bien,
Son mari la tourmentera
Ne jamès bien ne lui fera;
Bien l'apperçoy a vostre chiere.
Demandez a vo chamberiere
3635 Se j'ay en mauvais lieu esté:
J'ay tout ce mesnaige acheté
A grant paine: je m'en repent."
Puis le desvelope et l'espent
Par l'ostel devant son mary,
3640 Qui est a la moité guari,
Quant il oit ainsy sa deffense,
Et bien en son cuer se pourpense
Que mal fait quant ainsi la blame.
    Lors pour elle jetter de blame,
3645 Fuit en sa chambre d'un escueil
Et se couche la larme a l'ueil,
Pour plus son mary assoter.
Et adonc la va convoier
Sa chamberiere, et s'en retourne:
3650 Dolente est et fait chiere mourne;
Et ly maris la tient de plait,

Marginal notes:

and no woman ever found better bargains.

I have to buy everything,

you won't help at all. But then, a wife who does well is always tortured by her husband.

Ask the maid if I have been in any evil place" (D 233–34).

The poor husband is taken aback and begins to repent his injustice (D 390–91).

She goes to her room to cry;

her perplexed spouse questions the maid

[1] Sieves, bolters.

Demendans que sa femme fait.

and learns that she
sides with his wife
(D 231–34).

Et la chamberiere engigneuse

Respond: "Ma dame est maleureuse,

3655   Quant onques tel homme espousa."

If the husband remonstrates, he is repaid in kind:

"You woo the maid
and frequent com-
mon women (D
239–42, 393–99).

3920 "Vous avez nostre chamberiere

Requis d'amour .ii. foiz ou trois;

Vous estes alez pluseurs fois

Veoir Helot et Eudeline,

Ysabel, Margot, Kateline

3925   Et couché aux femmes communes.

It is that which
makes you suspect
me, for the evil can
think no good.

De la me viennent les rancunes,

Car lerres le larron mescroit,

Ne ly mauvès le bon ne croit,

Ains cuide que chascuns soit lerres:

3930   On ne verroit en nulles terres

Plus mescreant de vous sanz failles;

Tousjours avons plaiz et batailles.

J'ay long temps souffert vo pechié:

Comment m'avez vous reprouchié

3935   Que j'estoie trop villotiere?

I am better than
you are,

Meilleur vous suy et plus entiere

Que vous ne m'estes, par ma foy!

Lasse! vous doubtez vous de moy?

Je ne suy pas du lieu venue

and my family, at
least, is above re-
proach."

3940   Que pour fole soye tenue;

En mon linaige n'a putain:

Prenez les vostres par la main

Et celles de vostre linaige."

Et lors fait semblant qu'elle enrraige,

She cries and weeps
as though she were
mad

3945   Et crie si horriblement,

Et ploure si parfondement

Qu'il samble qu'elle soit dervée:

and complains that
she is even forbid-
den to go to church.

"Hé lasse!" fait elle, "il me vée

Neis que je voise au moustier!

Nor can she have
any friend (D 243–
45).

3950   Si n'ay je Robin ou Gautier

Ne homme, dont je soie acointe!"

Thus she lies and
deceives as many
women do.

Ainsis ly ment, ainsis l'apointe,

Ainsis le deçoit et confont,

Ainsis pluseurs femmes le font.

THE WIFE OF BATH'S TALE

By BARTLETT J. WHITING

THERE can be little doubt that Chaucer originally intended what is now the *Shipman's Tale* for the Wife of Bath. At a later time, however, he decided to substitute for it a story which would be more in keeping with the substance and tenor of the *Wife's Prologue*. With this in mind he turned to a tale so well calculated to illustrate the chief tenet of her faith that, as in the case of the tales of the Pardoner and the Canon's Yeoman, it may be described not as a tale following after the prologue but rather as an *exemplum* which clinches, by an appeal to authority, an argument which in the prologue was largely derived from experience. In the Wife's new tale two motifs are joined, that of the Loathly Lady, or hag transformed through love,[1] and that of the man whose life depends on the correct answering of a question.[2] The motifs are often found separately, and they are found combined in the three poems offered here as analogues to the *Wife's Tale:* Gower's *Tale of Florent*, the (fragmentary) *Marriage of Sir Gawaine*, and the *Weddynge of Sir Gawen and Dame Ragnell.*

There have been many discussions of the *Wife's Tale* and its analogues and parallels, of which the most important are G. H. Maynadier's *The Wife of Bath's Tale*,[3] Joseph W. Beach's "The Loathly Lady: A Study in the Popular Elements of the *Wife of Bath's Tale*,"[4] and a brief survey of the problem in the Introduction to Laura Sumner's edition of the *Weddynge of Sir Gawen and Dame Ragnell.*[5] Further bibliographical information will be found in the works cited and in J. E. Wells's *Manual*

[1] See Stith Thompson, *Motif-Index of Folk-Literature*, D 732.

[2] Thompson, H 530 ff. (where the question is often in the form of a riddle) and H 1388. 1.

[3] "Grimm Library," Vol. XIII (London, 1901).

[4] Unpublished Harvard doctoral dissertation, submitted in 1907, now on file in the Harvard College Library.

[5] "Smith College Studies in Modern Languages," Vol. V, No. 4 (Northampton, Mass., 1924).

of the Writings in Middle English (New Haven, 1916) and its various supplements.

Clearly enough the English poems have a common ancestor, but their relation to that ancestor is by no means clear nor, for that matter, is their relation to one another. Chaucer's version and Gower's agree in certain marked points as against the other two, but they differ too much in other respects to make it possible to speak of a common source. The ballad *Marriage of Sir Gawaine* has been held to be based on the romance *Weddynge of Sir Gawen and Dame Ragnell*, and, conversely, critics have found the ballad more primitive than the romance. Theories, fortunately, do not concern us here, and the poems must speak for themselves. One thing is certain: despite the varying merits of the other documents, no better proof of Chaucer's overwhelming literary power and artistry is to be found than in a comparison of the *Wife's Tale* with its analogues.

I. THE TALE OF FLORENT

(From John Gower's *Confessio amantis*, I, vss. 1396–1861, *The Complete Works of John Gower*, ed. G. C. Macaulay, II [Oxford, 1901], 74–86.)

Obedience in love often avails where strength would fail.

1396   Mi Sone, and I thee rede this,
        What so befalle of other weie,
        That thou to loves heste obeie
        Als ferr as thou it myht suffise:
1400   For ofte sithe in such a wise
        Obedience in love availeth,
        Wher al a mannes strengthe faileth;
        Whereof, if that the list to wite
        In a Cronique as it is write,
        A gret ensample thou myht fynde,
        Which now is come to my mynde.

Florent, a worthy knight, nephew of the Emperor,

        Ther was whilom be daies olde
        A worthi knyht, and as men tolde
        He was Nevoeu to themperour
1410   And of his Court a Courteour:
        Wifles he was, Florent he hihte,
        He was a man that mochel myhte,
        Of armes he was desirous,
        Chivalerous and amorous,
        And for the fame of worldes speche,

Strange aventures forte seche,
He rod the Marches al aboute.
And fell a time, as he was oute,

is taken by force to the castle of the parents of Branchus, whom he had killed.

Fortune, which may every thred
1420   Tobreke and knette of mannes sped,
Schop, as this knyht rod in a pas,
That he be strengthe take was,
And to a Castell thei him ladde,
Wher that he fewe frendes hadde:
For so it fell that ilke stounde
That he hath with a dedly wounde
Feihtende his oghne hondes slain[1]
Branchus, which to the Capitain
Was Sone and Heir, whereof ben wrothe
1430   The fader and the moder bothe.
That knyht Branchus was of his hond
The worthieste of al his lond,
And fain thei wolden do vengance

They would wreak vengeance on him, but fear the Emperor.

Upon Florent, bot remembrance
That thei toke of his worthinesse
Of knyhthod and of gentilesse,
And how he stod of cousinage
To themperour, made hem assuage,
And dorsten noght slen him for fere:
1440   In gret desputeisoun thei were
Among hemself, what was the beste.
Ther was a lady, the slyheste

The grandmother of Branchus finds a way to bring about the death of Florent without blame to anyone.

Of alle that men knewe tho,
So old sche myhte unethes go,
And was grantdame unto the dede:
And sche with that began to rede,
And seide how sche wol bringe him inne,
That sche schal him to dethe winne
Al only of his oghne grant,
1450   Thurgh strengthe of verray covenant
Withoute blame of eny wiht.
Anon sche sende for this kniht,
And of hire Sone sche alleide
The deth, and thus to him sche seide:
"Florent, how so thou be to wyte
Of Branchus deth, men schal respite

---

[1] Fighting, slain with his own hands.

As now to take vengement,

Unless he can answer a certain question, he must die.

Be so thou stonde in juggement
Upon certein condicioun,

1460 That thou unto a questioun
Which I schal axe schalt ansuere;
And over this thou schalt ek swere,
That if thou of the sothe faile,
Ther schal non other thing availe,
That thou ne schal thi deth receive.

He will be free to go and inquire,

And for men schal thee noght deceive,
That thou therof myht ben avised,
Thou schalt have day and tyme assised
And leve saufly forto wende,

but must come back to the castle at an appointed time.

1470 Be so that at thi daies ende
Thou come ayein with thin avys.''
This knyht, which worthi was and wys,
This lady preith that he may wite,
And have it under Seales write,
What questioun it scholde be
For which he schal in that degree
Stonde of his lif in jeupartie.
With that sche feigneth compaignie,[1]
And seith: "Florent, on love it hongeth

1480 Al that to myn axinge longeth:

The question is: What do women most desire?

What alle wommen most desire
This wole I axe, and in thempire
Wher as thou hast most knowlechinge
Tak conseil upon this axinge.''
Florent this thing hath undertake,
The day was set, the time take,

The agreement is made and sealed.

Under his seal he wrot his oth,
In such a wise and forth he goth

Florent first goes to the Emperor's court,

Home to his Emes court ayein;

1490 To whom his aventure plein
He tolde, of that him is befalle.
And upon that thei weren alle
The wiseste of the lond asent,

where he receives contradictory answers.

Bot natheles of on assent
Thei myhte noght acorde plat,
On seide this, on othre that.
After the disposicioun

[1] Fellowship, i.e., friendship.

Of naturel complexioun
To som womman it is plesance,
1500   That to an other is grevance;
Bot such a thing in special,
Which to hem alle in general
Is most plesant, and most desired
Above alle othre and most conspired,
Such o thing conne thei noght finde
Be Constellacion ne kinde:
And thus Florent withoute cure
Mot stonde upon his aventure,
And is al schape unto the lere,[1]
1510   As in defalte of his answere.
This knyht hath levere forto dye
Than breke his trowthe and forto lye
In place ther as he was swore,
And schapth him gon ayein therfore.
Whan time cam he tok his leve,
That lengere wolde he noght beleve,
And preith his Em he be noght wroth,
For that is a point of his oth,
He seith, that noman schal him wreke,
1520   Thogh afterward men hiere speke
That he par aventure deie.
And thus he wente forth his weie
Alone as knyht aventurous,
And in his thoght was curious
To wite what was best to do:
And as he rod al one so,
And cam nyh ther as he wolde be,
In a forest under a tre
He syh wher sat a creature,
1530   A lothly wommannysch figure,
That forto speke of fleisch and bon
So foul yit syh he nevere non.
This knyht behield hir redely,
And as he wolde have passed by,
Sche cleped him and bad abide;
And he his horse heved aside
Tho torneth, and to hire he rod,
And there he hoveth and abod,

Yet he must keep his word, and return on the appointed day.

Approaching the castle,

he sees a most loathly woman.

She calls him;

he stops.

---

[1] "Prepared for the loss" (Macaulay).

To wite what sche wolde mene.

1540   And sche began him to bemene,

She knows his
plight;
And seide: "Florent be thi name,
Thou hast on honde such a game,
That bot thou be the betre avised,
Thi deth is schapen and devised,
That al the world ne mai the save,
Bot if that thou my conseil have."
Florent, whan he this tale herde,
Unto this olde wyht answerde

he asks for advice.
And of hir conseil he hir preide.

1550   And sche ayein to him thus seide:

If she saves him,
"Florent, if I for the so schape,
That thou thurgh me thi deth ascape
And take worschipe of thi dede,
What schal I have to my mede?"
"What thing," quod he, "that thou wolt axe."
"I bidde nevere a betre taxe,"
Quod sche, "bot ferst, er thou be sped,
Thou schalt me leve such a wedd,
That I wol have thi trowthe in honde

he must marry her.
1560   That thou schalt be myn housebonde."
"Nay," seith Florent, "that may noght be."
"Ryd thanne forth thi wey," quod sche,
"And if thou go withoute red,
Thou schalt be sekerliche ded."

He offers other re-
wards, but she re-
fuses them.
Florent behihte hire good ynowh
Of lond, of rente, of park, of plowh,
Bot al that compteth sche at noght.

After much hesita-
tion
Tho fell this knyht in mochel thoght,
Now goth he forth, now comth ayein,

1570   He wot noght what is best to sein,
And thoghte, as he rod to and fro,
That chese he mot on of the tuo,
Or forto take hire to his wif
Or elles forto lese his lif.
And thanne he caste his avantage,
That sche was of so gret an age,
That sche mai live bot a while,
And thoghte put hire in an Ile,
Wher that noman hire scholde knowe,

1580   Til sche with deth were overthrowe.

And thus this yonge lusti knyht
Unto this olde lothly wiht
Tho seide: "If that non other chance
Mai make my deliverance,
Bot only thilke same speche
Which, as thou seist, thou schalt me teche,
Have hier myn hond, I schal thee wedde."
And thus his trowthe he leith to wedde.
With that sche frounceth up the browe:

1590   "This covenant I wol allowe,"
Sche seith: "if eny other thing
Bot that thou hast of my techyng
Fro deth thi body mai respite,
I woll thee of thi trowthe acquite,
And elles be non other weie.
Now herkne me what I schal seie.
Whan thou art come into the place,
Wher now thei maken gret manace
And upon thi comynge abyde,

1600   Thei wole anon the same tide
Oppose thee of thin answere.
I wot thou wolt nothing forbere
Of that thou wenest be thi beste,
And if thou myht so finde reste,
Wel is, for thanne is ther nomore.
And elles this schal be my lore,
That thou schalt seie, upon this Molde
That alle wommen lievest wolde
Be soverein of mannes love:

1610   For what womman is so above,
Sche hath, as who seith, al hire wille;
And elles may sche noght fulfille
What thing hir were lievest have.
With this answere thou schalt save
Thiself, and other wise noght.
And whan thou hast thin ende wroght,
Com hier ayein, thou schalt me finde,
And let nothing out of thi minde."

He goth him forth with hevy chiere,
1620   As he that not in what manere
He mai this worldes joie atteigne:
For if he deie, he hath a peine,

he agrees to her terms.

If some other answer can save him, well and good;

otherwise, let him answer that what women most desire is sovereignty over man's love.

Then he must come back to her.

And if he live, he mot him binde
To such on which of alle kinde
Of wommen is thunsemlieste:
Thus wot he noght what is the beste:
Bot be him lief or be him loth,

In the castle

Unto the Castell forth he goth
His full answere forto yive,

1630   Or forto deie or forto live.

the council is gath-
ered.

Forth with his conseil cam the lord,
The thinges stoden of record,
He sende up for the lady sone,
And forth sche cam, that olde Mone.[1]
In presence of the remenant
The strengthe of al the covenant
Tho was reherced openly,
And to Florent sche bad forthi
That he schal tellen his avis,

1640   As he that woot what is the pris.

All other answers
having failed,

Florent seith al that evere he couthe,
Bot such word cam ther non to mowthe,
That he for yifte or for beheste
Mihte eny wise his deth areste.
And thus he tarieth longe and late,
Til that this lady bad algate
That he schal for the dom final
Yive his answere in special
Of that sche hadde him ferst opposed:

Florent offers that
of the loathly lady,

1650   And thanne he hath trewly supposed
That he him may of nothing yelpe,
Bot if so be tho wordes helpe,
Whiche as the womman hath him tawht;
Wherof he hath an hope cawht
That he schal ben excused so,
And tolde out plein his wille tho.

which is accepted.

And whan that this Matrone herde
The manere how this knyht ansuerde,
Sche seide: "Ha treson, wo thee be,

1660   That hast thus told the privite,
Which alle wommen most desire!
I wolde that thou were afire."
Bot natheles in such a plit

[1] Crone (?). *NED*, *mone*, sb[2], quotes only this passage.

Florent of his answere is quit:
And tho began his sorwe newe,
For he mot gon, or ben untrewe,
To hire which his trowthe hadde.
Bot he, which alle schame dradde,
Goth forth in stede of his penance,
1670 And takth the fortune of his chance,
As he that was with trowthe affaited.
 This olde wyht him hath awaited
In place wher as he hire lefte:
Florent his wofull heved uplefte
And syh this vecke[1] wher sche sat,
Which was the lothlieste what
That evere man caste on his yhe:
Hire Nose bass, hire browes hyhe,
Hire yhen smale and depe set,
1680 Hire chekes ben with teres wet,
And rivelen as an emty skyn
Hangende doun unto the chin,
Hire Lippes schrunken ben for age,
Ther was no grace in the visage,
Hir front was nargh, hir lockes hore,
Sche loketh forth as doth a More,
Hire Necke is schort, hir schuldres courbe,
That myhte a mannes lust destourbe,
Hire body gret and nothing smal,
1690 And schortly to discrive hire al,
Sche hath no lith withoute a lak;
Bot lich unto the wollesak
Sche proferth hire unto this knyht,
And bad him, as he hath behyht,
So as sche hath ben his warant,
That he hire holde covenant,
And be the bridel sche him seseth.
Bot godd wot how that sche him pleseth
Of suche wordes as sche spekth:
1700 Him thenkth welnyh his herte brekth
For sorwe that he may noght fle,
Bot if he wolde untrewe be.
 Loke, how a sek man for his hele
Takth baldemoine with Canele,[2]

In sorrow he goes back to the loathly lady

—the ugliest thing on earth—

who bids him fulfil his promise.

In despair,

[1] Old woman. [2] Gentian with cinnamon.

And with the Mirre takth the Sucre,
Ryht upon such a maner lucre
Stant Florent as in this diete:
He drinkth the bitre with the swete,
He medleth sorwe with likynge,
1710   And liveth, as who seith, deyinge;
His youthe schal be cast aweie
Upon such on which as the weie

but resigned to his fate,

Is old and lothly overal.
Bot nede he mot that nede schal:
He wolde algate his trowthe holde,
As every knyht therto is holde,
What happ so evere him is befalle:
Thogh sche be the fouleste of alle,
Yet to thonour of wommanhiede
1720   Him thoghte he scholde taken hiede;
So that for pure gentilesse,
As he hire couthe best adresce,
In ragges, as sche was totore,

he takes her on his horse

He set hire on his hors tofore
And forth he takth his weie softe;
No wonder thogh he siketh ofte.
Bot as an oule fleth be nyhte
Out of alle othre briddes syhte,
Riht so this knyht on daies brode
1730   In clos him hield, and schop his rode
On nyhtes time, til the tyde
That he cam there he wolde abide;

and rides to his castle,

And prively withoute noise
He bringth this foule grete Coise[1]
To his Castell in such a wise
That noman myhte hire schappe avise,
Til sche into the chambre cam:

where he tells his friends that he must marry her.

Wher he his prive conseil nam
Of suche men as he most troste,
1740   And tolde hem that he nedes moste
This beste wedde to his wif,
For elles hadde he lost his lif.

Women clean and dress her,

    The prive wommen were asent,
That scholden ben of his assent:

---

[1] The *New English Dictionary* declares the etymology and meaning of "coise" to be uncertain. The sense, however, is undoubtedly derogatory.

Hire ragges thei anon of drawe,
And, as it was that time lawe,
She hadde bath, sche hadde reste,
And was arraied to the beste.
Bot with no craft of combes brode
1750 Thei myhte hire hore lockes schode,
And sche ne wolde noght be schore
For no conseil, and thei therfore,
With such atyr as tho was used,
Ordeinen that it was excused,
And hid so crafteliche aboute,
That noman myhte sen hem oute.
Bot when sche was fulliche arraied
And hire atyr was al assaied,
Tho was sche foulere on to se:
1760 Bot yit may non other be,
Thei were wedded in the nyht;
So wo begon was nevere knyht
As he was thanne of mariage.
And sche began to pleie and rage,
As who seith, I am wel ynowh;
Bot he therof nothing ne lowh,
For sche tok thanne chiere on honde
And clepeth him hire housebonde,
And seith, "My lord, go we to bedde,
1770 For I to that entente wedde,
That thou schalt be my worldes blisse":
And profreth him with that to kisse,
As sche a lusti Lady were.
His body myhte wel be there,
Bot as of thoght and of memoire
His herte was in purgatoire.
Bot yit for strengthe of matrimoine
He myhte make non essoine,
That he ne mot algates plie
1780 To gon to bedde of compaignie:
And whan thei were abedde naked,
Withoute slep he was awaked;
He torneth on that other side,
For that he wolde hise yhen hyde
Fro lokynge on that foule wyht.
The chambre was al full of lyht,

but she looks still worse.

The knight is married to her.

They go to bed,

but he turns away from her,

The courtins were of cendal thinne,
This newe bryd which lay withinne,
Thogh it be noght with his acord,

1790   In armes sche beclipte hire lord,

until, on her insist-
ent request,

And preide, as he was torned fro,
He wolde him torne ayeinward tho;
"For now," sche seith, "we ben bothe on."
And he lay stille as eny ston,
Bot evere in on sche spak and preide,
And bad him thenke on that he seide,
Whan that he tok hire be the hond.
    He herde and understod the bond,
How he was set to his penance,

1800   And as it were a man in trance

he turns over and
sees a most beauti-
ful eighteen-year-
old woman.

He torneth him al sodeinly,
And syh a lady lay him by
Of eyhtetiene wynter age,
Which was the faireste of visage
That evere in al this world he syh:
And as he wolde have take hire nyh,
Sche put hire hand and be his leve
Besoghte him that he wolde leve,
And seith that forto wynne or lese

He is to choose
whether to have her
fair by day or at
night.

1810   He mot on of tuo thinges chese,
Wher he wol have hire such on nyht,
Or elles upon daies lyht,
For he schal noght have bothe tuo.

After painful hesi-
tation

And he began to sorwe tho,
In many a wise and caste his thoght,
Bot for al that yit cowthe he noght
Devise himself which was the beste.
And sche, that wolde his hertes reste,
Preith that he scholde chese algate,

1820   Til ate laste longe and late

he leaves the choice
to her wisdom.

He seide: "O ye, my lyves hele,
Sey what you list in my querele,
I not what ansuere I schal yive:
Bot evere whil that I may live,
I wol that ye be my maistresse,
For I can noght miselve gesse
Which is the best unto my chois.
Thus grante I yow myn hole vois,

Ches for ous bothen, I you preie;
1830   And what as evere that ye seie,
Riht as ye wole so wol I."
    "Mi lord," sche seide, "grant merci,
For of this word that ye now sein,
That ye have mad me soverein,
Mi destine is overpassed,
That nevere hierafter schal be lassed
Mi beaute, which that I now have,
Til I be take into my grave;
Bot nyht and day as I am now
1840   I schal alwey be such to yow.
The kinges dowhter of Cizile
I am, and fell bot siththe awhile,
As I was with my fader late,
That my Stepmoder for an hate,
Which toward me sche hath begonne,
Forschop me, til I hadde wonne
The love and sovereinete
Of what knyht that in his degre
Alle othre passeth of good name:
1850   And, as men sein, ye ben the same,
The dede proeveth it is so;
Thus am I youres evermo."
Tho was plesance and joye ynowh,
Echon with other pleide and lowh;
Thei live longe and wel thei ferde,
And clerkes that this chance herde
Thei writen it in evidence,
To teche how that obedience
Mai wel fortune a man to love
1860   And sette him in his lust above,
As it befell unto this knyht.

Marginal glosses:

"Since you have given me sovereignty,

I will be fair all my life both day and night.

I am the daughter of the king of Sicily. By my stepmother I was transformed into an ugly woman

until a perfect knight would give me his love and sovereignty over him."

They lived very happily.

This shows the good effects of obedience in love.

II. THE MARRIAGE OF SIR GAWAINE

(From *Bishop Percy's Folio Manuscript*, ed. J. W. Hales and F. J. Furnivall, I [London, 1867], 103–18. The date of the manuscript is mid-seventeenth century.)

Kinge Arthur liues in merry Carleile,
    & seemely is to see,
& there he hath with him Qqueene Genever,
    that bride soe bright of blee.

Marginal gloss: King Arthur holds his court at Carlisle

And there he hath with Queene Genever,
    that bride soe bright in bower,
& all his barons about him stoode
    that were both stiffe and stowre.

celebrating Christ-
mas.

The King kept a royall Christmasse
    of mirth & great honor,
& when
    [*half a page missing, in which Arthur, to avoid
    fighting a Baron at Tearne Wadling, asks what
    his ransom will be. The Baron answers:*]

"You must tell me
what women most
desire."

"And bring me word what thing it is
    that a woman most desire.
this shalbe thy ransome, Arthur," he sayes,
    "for Ile haue noe other hier."

King Arthur then held vp his hand
    according thene as was the law;
he tooke his leaue of the baron there,
    & homeward can he draw.

Back at Carlisle
Arthur tells Gawain
of his encounter
with the bold bar-
on,

And when he came to Merry Carlile,
    to his chamber he is gone,
& ther came to him his Cozen Sir Gawaine
    as he did make his mone.

And there came to him his cozen Sir Gawaine
    that was a curteous knight,
"why sigh you soe sore, vnckle Arthur," he said,
    "or who hath done thee vnright?"

"O peace, O peace, thou gentle Gawaine,
    that faire may thee beffall,
for if thou knew my sighing soe deepe,
    thou wold not meruaile att all;

"ffor when I came to tearne wadling,
    a bold barron there I fand,
with a great club vpon his backe,
    standing stiffe and strong;

"And he asked me wether I wold fight,
    or from him I shold begone,
o[r] else I must him a ransome pay
    & soe depart him from.

"To fight with him I saw noe cause,
   methought it was not meet,
for he was stiffe & strong with-all,
   his strokes were nothing sweete;

"Therefor this is my ransome, Gawaine,
   I ought to him to pay,
I must come againe, as I am sworne,
   vpon the New yeers day.

and of the covenant.

He has sworn to be back on New Year's Day.

"And I must bring him word what thing it is"
   [half a page missing.]

Then king Arthur drest him for to ryde
   in one soe rich array
toward the fore-said Tearne wadling,
   that he might keepe his day.

Riding toward Tearne Wadling

And as he rode over a more,
   hee see a lady where shee sate
betwixt an oke & a greene hollen:
   She was cladd in red scarlett.

he sees a very ugly lady clad in scarlet.

Then there as shold haue stood her mouth,
   then there was sett her eye,
the other was in her forhead fast
   the way that she might see.

Her nose was crooked & turnd outward,
   her mouth stood foule a-wry;
a worse formed lady than shee was,
   neuer man saw with his eye.

To halch vpon him, King Arthur,
   This lady was full faine,
but King Arthur had forgott his lesson,
   what he shold say againe.

"What knight art thou," the lady sayd,
   "that will not speak to me?
Of me be thou nothing dismayd
   tho I be vgly to see;

"for I haue halched you curteouslye,
   & you will not me againe,
yett I may happen Sir Knight," shee said,
   "to ease thee of thy paine."

She tells him that she can help him.

"If you do, you
shall be married to
Gawain."

"Giue thou ease me, lady," he said,
    "or helpe me any thing,
thou shalt haue gentle Gawaine, my cozen,
    & marry him with a ring."

"Why, if I help thee not, thou noble King Arthur,
    Of thy owne hearts desiringe,
of gentle Gawaine" [*half a page missing.*]

At Tearne Wad-
ling the baron takes
Arthur's letters;

And when he came to the tearne wadling
    the baron there cold he finde,
with a great weapon on his backe,
    standing stiffe and stronge.

And then he took king Arthurs letters in his hands
    & away he cold them fling,
& then he puld out a good browne sword,
    & cryd himselfe a King.

he claims Arthur
and his kingdom.

And he sayd, "I have thee & thy land, Arthur,
    to doe as it pleaseth me,
for this is not thy ransome sure,
    therfore yeeld thee to me."

And then bespoke him Noble Arthur,
    & bad him hold his hand,
"& giue me leaue to speake my mind
    in defence of all my land."

Arthur then tells
him of the lady in
scarlet

He said "as I came over a More,
    I see a lady where shee sate
betweene an oke & a green hollen;
    shee was clad in red scarlett;

and her answer,
that women's chief
desire is to have
their will.

"And she says 'a woman will haue her will,
    & this is all her cheef desire':
doe me right, as thou art a baron of sckill,
    this is thy ransome & all thy hyer."

The knight curses
the lady (who is his
sister)

He sayes "an early vengeance light on her!
    she walkes on yonder more;
it was my sister that told thee this;
    & she is a misshapen hore!

and swears to take
his revenge on her.

"But heer Ile make mine avow to god
    to doe her an euill turne,
for an euer I may thate fowle theefe get[t],
    in a fyer I will her burne."
        [*about nine stanzas missing.*]

THE 2^d PART

Sir: Lancelott & Sir Steven bold
 they rode with them that day,
and the formost of the company
 there rode the steward Kay.

Soe did Sir Banier & Sir Bore,
 Sir Garrett with them soe gay,
soe did Sir Tristeram that gentle knight,
 to the forrest fresh & gay.

And when he came to the greene forrest,
 vnderneath a greene holly tree
their sate that lady in red scarlet
 that vnseemly was to see.

Sir Kay beheld this Ladys face,
 & looked vppon her smire,
"whosoeuer kisses this lady," he sayes,
 "of his kisse he stands in feare."

Sir Kay beheld the lady againe,
 & looked vpon her snout,
"whosoeuer kisses this lady," he saies,
 "of his kisse he stands in doubt."

"Peace cozen Kay," then said Sir Gawaine,
 "amend thee of thy life;
for there is a knight amongst vs all
 that must marry her to his wife."

"What! wedd her to wiffe!" then said Sir Kay,
 "in the diuells name anon,
gett me a wiffe where-ere I may,
 for I had rather be shaine!"[1]

Then some tooke vp their hawkes in hast,
 & some tooke vp their hounds,
& some sware they wold not marry her
 for Citty nor for towne.

And then be-spake him Noble king Arthur,
 & sware there by this day,
"for a litle foule sight & misliking"
 [*half a page missing.*]

With his knights

Arthur rides to the lady in scarlet.

Sir Kay comments on the kisses of such a creature,

but Gawain tells him that one of them must marry her.

Sir Kay and others swear that they would not do it.

[1] "Perhaps for slaine."

She tells Gawain
(her husband) that
he must choose
whether to have her
fair by day or at
night.

Then shee said "choose thee, gentle Gawaine,
 truth as I doe say,
wether thou wilt haue me in this liknesse
 in the night or else in the day."

And then bespake him Gentle Gawaine,
 with one soe mild of Moode,
sayes, "well I know what I wold say,
 god grant it may be good!

"Better be beauti-
ful at night."

"To haue thee fowle in the night
 when I with thee shold play;
yet I had rather, if I might,
 haue thee fowle in the day."

"Alas, I shall then
have to hide from
your companions."

"What! when Lords goe with ther seires," shee said,
 "both to the Ale & wine;
alas! then I must hyde my selfe,
 I must not goe withinne."

"Do as you wish."

And then bespake him gentle Gawaine,
 said, "Lady, thats but a skill;
And because thou art my owne lady,
 thou shalt haue all thy will."

"Bless you, I shall
be fair at all times.

Then she said, "blesed be thou gentle Gawain[e],
 this day that I thee see,
for as thou see me att this time,
 from hencforth I wilbe:

I was bewitched by
my stepmother."

"My father was an old knight,
 & yett it chanced soe
that he marryed a yonge lady
 that brought me to this woe.

"Shee witched me, being a faire young Lady,
 to the greene forrest to dwell,
& there I must walke in womans liknesse,
 Most like a feend of hell.

"She witched my brother to a Carlist B . . . .'
 [half a page missing.]

"that looked soe foule, & that was wont
 on the wild more to goe."

"Come kisse her, Brother Kay," then said Sir Gawaine, On Gawain's request
   "& amend thé of thy liffe;
I sweare this is the same lady
   that I marryed to my wiffe."

Sir Kay kissed that lady bright, Kay kisses the lady.
   standing vpon his ffeete;
he swore, as he was trew knight,
   the spice was neuer soe sweete.

"Well, Cozen Gawaine," sayes Sir Kay,
   "thy chance is fallen arright,
for thou hast gotten one of the fairest maids
   I euer saw with my sight."

"It is my fortune," said Sir Gawaine; All rejoice over the good fortune of Gawain.
   "for my vnckle Arthurs sake
I am glad as grasse wold be of raine,
   great Ioy that I may take."

Sir Gawaine tooke the lady by the one arme,
   Sir Kay tooke her by the tother,
they led her straight to King Arthur
   as they were brother & brother.

King Arthur welcomed them there all,
   & soe did lady Geneuer his queene,
with all the knights of the round table
   most seemly to be seene.

King Arthur beheld that lady faire
   that was soe faire and bright
he thanked christ in trinity
   for Sir Gawaine that gentle knight;

Soe did the knights, both more and lesse,
   reioyced all that day
for the good chance that hapened was
   to Sir Gawaine & his lady gay. *ffins.*

III. THE WEDDYNGE OF SIR GAWEN
AND DAME RAGNELL

(From *The Weddynge of Sir Gawen and Dame Ragnell*, a mid-fifteenth-century poem found in a manuscript [Rawlinson C 86] written at the beginning of the next century. The present text is that of Laura Sumner's edition ["Smith College Studies in Modern Languages," Vol. V, No. 4 (1924)] and is used here with the gracious permission of the editor and of the manager of the series. Through the courtesy of the Smith College Library I have been able to compare the printed text with a rotographic copy of the manuscript and thus to catch a few trifling misprints. "M" in the footnotes refers to Sir Frederick Madden's text in *Syr Gawayne* [London: Bannatyne Club, 1839], pp. 298–298*y*).

⟨fol. 128*b*⟩

Lythe and listenythe the lif of a lord riche,
The while that he lyvid was none hym liche,
Nether in bowre ne in halle;
In the tyme of Arthoure thys adventure betyd,
5   And of the greatt adventure that he hym-self dyd,
That kyng curteys and royalle.
Of alle kynges Arture berythe the flowyr,
And of alle knyghtod he bare away the honour,
Where-so-euere he wentt.
10   In his contrey was nothyng butt chyvalry,
And knyghtes were belovid[1] [by] that doughty,
For cowardes were eueremore shent.
Nowe wylle ye lyst a whyle to my talkyng,
I shalle you telle of Arthowre the kyng,

15   Howe ones hym befelle.
On huntyng he was in Ingleswod,
Withe alle his bold knyghtes good,
Nowe herken to my spelle.
The kyng was sett att his trestylle-tree,
20   Withe hys bowe to sle the wylde venere,
And hys lordes were sett hym besyde;
As the kyng stode, then was he ware,
Where a greatt hartt was and a fayre,
And forthe fast dyd he glyde.

25   The hartt was in a braken ferne,
And hard the g[r]oundes,[2] and stode fulle derne,
Alle that sawe the kyng.
"Hold you stylle, euery man,
And I wolle goo my-self, yf I can
30   Withe crafte of stalkyng."

---

[1] MS, *by* is inserted after *belovid*.   [2] M., *houndes*.

⟨fol. 129⟩

The kyng in hys hand toke a bowe,

And wodmanly he stowpyd lowe,

To stalk vnto that dere;

When that he cam the dere fulle nere,

35   The dere lept forthe into a brere,

And euere the kyng went nere and nere,

So kyng Arthure went a whyle,

After the dere, I trowe, half a myle,

And no man withe hym went;

40   And att the last to the dere he lett flye,

And smote hym sore and sewerly,—

Suche grace God hym sent.

Doun the dere tumblyd so deron,

And felle into a greatt brake of fferon;

45   The kyng folowyd fulle fast.

Anon the kyng bothe ferce and felle,

Was withe the dere and dyd hym serve welle.[1]

And after the grasse he taste.

As the kyng was withe the dere alone,

50   Streyghte ther cam to hym a quaynt grome,

Armyd welle and sure;

A knyghte fulle strong and of greatt myghte,

And grymly wordes to the kyng he sayd:

"Welle i-mett, kyng Arthour!

55   Thou hast me done wrong many a yere,

And wofully I shalle quytte the here;

I hold thy lyfe days nyghe done;

Thou hast gevyn my landes in certayn,

Withe greatt wrong vnto Sir Gawen.

60   Whate sayest thou, kyng alone?"

"Syr knyghte, whate is thy name withe honour?"

"Syr kyng," he sayd, "Gromer Somer Joure,

I telle the nowe withe ryghte."

"A, Sir Gromer Somer, bethynk the welle,

65   To sle me here honour getyst thou no delle,

⟨fol. 129b⟩

Be-thynk the thou artt a knyghte,

Yf thou sle me nowe in thys case,

Alle knyghtes wolle refuse the in euery place,

That shame shalle neuere the froo;

Marginal notes:

Alone, he stalked the hart for some distance,

and finally slew it.

A knight, strong and well armed, appears

determined to kill Arthur,

who had deprived him of his land.

"Killing me would only bring shame on you;

---

[1] M., *serve well* suggested in the notes; $vell, MS.

I shall amend what
is amiss."

70   Lett be thy wylle and folowe wytt,
     And that is amys I shalle amend itt,
     And thou wolt, or that I goo."

The knight (Sir
Gromer Somer)
swears that he shall
take Arthur's life.

     "Nay," sayd Sir Gromer Somer, "by hevyn kyng!
     So shalt thou nott skape withoute lesyng,
75   I haue the nowe att avaylle;
     Yf I shold lett the thus goo withe mokery,
     Anoder tyme thou wolt me defye;
     Of that I shalle nott faylle."

"Ask for anything
else, and I shall
grant it. You are
armed and I am
not."

     Now sayd the kyng, "So God me saue,
80   Save my lyfe, and whate thou wolt crave,
     I shalle now graunt itt the;
     Shame thou shalt haue to sle me in venere,
     Thou armyd and I clothyd butt in grene, perde."
     "Alle thys shalle nott help the, sekyrly,
85   Ffor I wolle nother lond ne gold truly;
     Butt yf thou graunt me att a certayn day,
     Suche as I shalle sett, and in thys same araye."
     "Yes," sayd the kyng, "lo, here my hand."
     "Ye, butt abyde, kyng, and here me a stound;

"Swear that in ex-
actly one year you
shall come back
alone, in the same
array, and tell me
what women love
best.

90   Ffyrst thow shalt swere vpon my sword broun,
     To shewe me att thy comyng whate wemen love
       best in feld and town;
     And thou shalt mete me here witheouten send,
     Evyn att this day xij. monethes end;
     And thou shalt swere vpon my swerd good,
95   That of thy knyghtes shalle none com with the,
       by the rood,
     Nowther frende[1] ne freynd.

If you cannot an-
swer that question,
you must die."

     And yf thou bryng nott answere withe-oute faylle;
     Thyne hed thou shalt lose for thy travaylle,—

⟨fol. 129*⟩

     Thys shalle nowe be thyne othe.
100   Whate sayst thou, kyng, lett se, haue done."

They agree;

     "Syr, I graunt to thys, now lett me gone;
     Thoughe itt be to me fulle lothe,
     I ensure the, as I am true kyng,
     To com agayn att thys xij. monethes end,
105   And bryng the thyne answere."
     "Now go thy way, kyng Arthure,

[1] M., *fremde*(?) suggested in notes.

Thy lyfe is in my hand, I am fulle sure,
Of thy sorowe thow artt nott ware.
Abyde, kyng Arthure, a lytelle whyle,
110 Loke nott to-day thou me begyle,
And kepe alle thyng in close;
Ffor and I wyst, by Mary mylde,
Thou woldyst betray me in the feld,
Thy lyf fyrst sholdyst thou lose."

115 "Nay," sayd kyng Arthure, "that may nott be,   Arthur pledges his
faith.
Vntrewe knyghte shalt thou neuere fynde me;
To dye yett were me lever.
Ffarwelle, Sir knyghte and evylle mett,
I wolle com, and I be on lyve att the day sett,
120 Thoughe I shold scape neuere."
The kyng his bugle gan blowe,   He gathers his com-
panions
That hard euery knyghte and itt gan knowe,
Vnto hym can they rake;
Ther they fond the kyng and the dere,
125 Withe sembland sad and hevy chere,
That had no lust to layk.
"Go we home nowe to Carlylle,   to ride home.
Thys hyntyng lykys me nott welle,"—
So sayd kyng Arthure.
130 Alle the lordes knewe by his countenaunce   The knights note
his distress.

⟨fol. 129*b⟩

That the kyng had mett withe sume dysturbaunce.
Vnto Carlylle then the kyng cam,
Butt of his hevynesse knewe no man,
Hys hartt was wonder hevy;
135 In this hevynesse he dyd a-byde,
That many of his knyghtes mervelyd that tyde,
Tylle att the last Sir Gawen   Gawain questions
him;
To the kyng he sayd than,
"Syr, me marvaylythe ryghte sore,
140 Whate thyng that thou sorowyst fore."
Then answeryd the kyng as tyghte,
"I shalle the telle, gentylle Gawen knyghte.   Arthur answers that
he had an encoun-
ter with a knight,
but is pledged not
to say any more.
In the fforest as I was this daye,
Ther I mett withe a knyghte in his araye,
145 And serteyn wordes to me he gan sayn,
And chargyd me I shold hym nott bewrayne;

Hys councelle must I kepe therfore,
Or els I am forswore."

Gawain would keep
the secret.

"Nay, drede you nott, lord, by Mary flower,
150 I am nott that man that wold you dishonour,
Nother by euyn ne by moron."

Arthur tells him the
story.

"Forsothe I was on huntyng in Ingleswod,
Thowe knowest welle I slewe an hartt by the rode,
Alle my-sylf alon;
155 Ther mett I withe a knyghte armyd sure,
His name he told me was Sir Gromer Somer Joure,
Therfor I make my mone.
Ther that knyghte fast dyd me threte,
And wold haue slayn me withe greatt heatt,
160 But I spak fayre agayn;
Wepyns withe me ther had I none,
Alas! my worshypp therfor is nowe gone."
"What therof?" sayd Gawen,
"Whatt nedys more I shalle nott lye,
165 He wold haue slayn me ther withe-oute mercy,

⟨fol. 130⟩

And that me was fulle lothe;
He made me to swere that att the xij. monethes end,
That I shold mete hym ther in the same kynde,
To that I plyghte my trowithe.
170 And also I shold telle hym att the same day,
Whate wemen desyren moste in good faye,
My lyf els shold I lese.[1]
This othe I made vnto that knyghte,
And that I shold neuere telle itt to no wighte,
175 Of thys I myghte nott chese.
And also I shold com in none oder araye,
Butt euyn as I was the same daye;
And yf I faylyd of myne answere,
I wott I shal be slayn ryghte there.
180 Blame me nott thoughe I be a wofulle man,
Alle thys is my drede and fere."

Gawain suggests
that Arthur ride in-
to distant regions,

"Ye, Sir, make good chere;
Lett make your hors redy,
To ryde into straunge contrey;

---

[1] M., *lese; leve,* MS.

185   And euere wher-as ye mete owther man or woman,
      in faye

inquiring for answers to the question;

    Ask of theym whate thay therto saye.
    And I shalle also ryde a-noder waye,
    And enquere of euery man and woman, and gett
      whatt I may

he shall do the same, and write the answers in a book.

    Of euery man and womans answere,
190   And in a boke I shalle theym wryte."
    "I graunt," sayd the kyng as tyte,

Arthur agrees.

    "Ytt is welle advysed, Gawen the good,
    Evyn by the holy rood."
    Sone were they[1] bothe redy,
195   Gawen and the kyng, wytterly.
    The kyng rode on way, and Gawen a-noder,

Each of them gathers many answers.

    And euere enquyred of man, woman, and other,
    Whate wemen desyred moste dere.
    Somme sayd they lovyd to be welle arayd,
200   Somme sayd they lovyd to be fayre prayed;

⟨fol. 130*b*⟩

    Somme sayd they lovyd a lusty man,
    That in theyr armys can clypp them and kysse
      them than;
    Somme sayd one; somme sayd other;
    And so had Gawen getyn many an answere.
205   By that Gawen had geten whate he maye,
    And come agayn by a certeyn daye,
    Syr Gawen had goten answerys so many,
    That had made a boke greatt, wytterly;
    To the courte he cam agayn.
210   By that was the kyng comyn withe hys boke,
    And eyther on others pamplett dyd loke.

They look at each other's books; Gawain thinks Arthur safe,

    "Thys may nott ffaylle,"[2] sayd Gawen.
    "By God," sayd the kyng, "I drede me sore,
    I cast me to seke a lytelle more

but Arthur will go to the forest of Ingleswood and keep inquiring.

215   In Yngleswod Fforest;
    I haue butt a monethe to my day sett,
    I may hapen on somme good tydynges to hytt,—
    Thys thynkythe me nowe best."
    "Do as ye lyst," then Gawen sayd,
220   "Whate-so-euere ye do I hold me payd,

---

[1] M., *they; the*, MS.   [2] M., *faylle* suggested in the notes; *ffayd*, MS.

Hytt is good to be spyrryng;
Doute you nott, lord, ye shalle welle spede;
Sume of your sawes shalle help att nede,
Els itt were ylle lykyng."

225   Kyng Arthoure rode forthe on the other day,
In-to Yngleswod as hys gate laye,

There he meets a
very ugly lady

And ther he mett withe a lady;
She was as vngoodly a creature,
As euere man sawe witheoute mesure.

230   Kyng Arthure mervaylyd securly.
Her face was red, her nose snotyd withalle,
Her mowithe wyde, her tethe yalowe ouere alle,
Withe bleryd eyen gretter then a balle,
Her mowithe was nott to lak;

⟨fol. 131⟩

235   Her tethe hyng ouere her¹ lyppes;
Her chekys syde as wemens hyppes;
A lute she bare vpon her bak.
Her nek long and therto greatt,
Her here cloteryd on an hepe,

240   In the sholders she was a yard brode,
Hangyng pappys to be an hors lode;
And lyke a barelle she was made;
And to reherse the fowlnesse of that lady,
Ther is no tung may telle, securly,

245   Of lothynesse inowghe she had.

seated on a gay pal-
frey.

She satt on a palfray was gay begon,
Withe gold besett and many a precious stone,
Ther was an vnsemely syghte;
So fowlle a creature withe-oute mesure,

250   To ryde so gayly, I you ensure,
Ytt was no reason ne ryghte.
She rode to Arthoure, and thus she sayd:

She tells him that
his life is in her
hands.

"God spede, Sir kyng, I am welle payd,
That I haue withe the mett;

255   Speke withe me, I rede, or thou goo,
Ffor thy lyfe is in my hand, I warn the soo,
That shalt thou fynde, and I itt nott lett."
"Why, whatt wold ye, lady, nowe withe me?"
"Syr, I wold fayn nowe speke withe the,

¹ M., *her*; *he*, MS.

260 And telle the tydynges good;
 Ffor alle the answerys that thou canst yelpe,
 None of theym alle shalle the helpe,
 That shalt thou knowe, by the rood,
 Thou wenyst I knowe nott thy councelle,
265 Butt I warn the I knowe itt euery dealle;
 Yf¹ I help the nott, thou art butt dead.
 Graunt me, Sir kyng, butt one thyng,

⟨fol. 131*b*⟩

 And for thy lyfe, I make warrauntyng,
 Or elles thou shalt lose thy hed."
270 "Whate mean you, lady, telle me tyghte,
 For of thy wordes I haue great dispyte,
 To you I haue no nede.
 Whate is your desyre, fayre lady,
 Lett me wete shortly;
275 Whate is your meanyng,
 And why my lyfe is in your hand,
 Telle me, and I shalle you warraunt,
 Alle your oun askyng."
 "Ffor-sothe," sayd the lady, "I am no qued,
280 Thou must graunt me a knyghte to wed,
 His name is Sir Gawen;
 And suche covenaunt I wolle make the,
 Butt thorowe myne answere thy lyf sauyd be,
 Elles lett my desyre be in vayne.
285 And yf myne answere saue thy lyf,
 Graunt me to be Gawens wyf,
 Advyse the nowe, Sir kyng;
 Ffor itt must be so, or thou artt butt dead,
 Chose nowe, for thou mayste sone lose thyne hed.
290 Telle me nowe in hying."
 "Mary," sayd the kyng, "I maye nott graunt the,
 To make warraunt Sir Gawen to wed the;
 Alle lyethe in hym alon.
 Butt and itt be so, I wolle do my labour,
295 In savyng of my lyfe to make itt secour,
 To Gawen wolle I make my mone."
 "Welle," sayd she, "nowe go home agayn,

Marginal glosses:
- None of his answers will help;
- she knows all about his plight;
- let him grant her one thing, and he will be safe.
- "What do you mean?"
- "Grant that I shall marry Gawain,
- and my answer will save your life;
- no other hope for you."
- "I cannot bind Gawain to this."
- "Go and tell him."

¹ In the MS *Butt I warn the* is repeated at the beginning of l. 266. Madden omits it.

And fayre wordes speke to Sir Gawen,
Ffor thy lyf I may saue;
300   Thoughe I be foulle, yett am I gaye,
Thourghe me thy lyfe saue he maye,
Or sewer thy dethe to haue."

"I am sorry for
him."
"Alas!" he sayd, "nowe woo is me,
That I shold cause Gawen to wed the,

⟨fol. 132⟩

305   For he wol be lothe to saye naye.
So foulle a lady as ye ar nowe one
Sawe I neuere in my lyfe on ground gone,
I nott whate I do may."

"Never mind my
ugliness;
"No force, Sir kyng, thoughe I be foulle,
310   Choyse for a make hathe an owlle,
Thou getest of me no more;

come back and
meet me here."
When thou comyst agayn to thyne answere,
Ryghte in this place I shalle mete the here,
Or elles I wott thou artt lore."[1]
315   "Now farewelle," sayd the kyng, "lady."
"Ye, Sir," she sayd, "ther is a byrd men calle an
    owlle,
And yett a lady I am."
"Whate is your name, I pray you telle me?"
"Syr kyng, I highte Dame Ragnelle, truly,
320   That neuere yett begylyd man."

Arthur parts from
the lady (called
Dame Ragnell).
"Dame Ragnelle, now haue good daye."
"Syr kyng, God spede the on thy way,
Ryghte here I shalle the mete."
Thus they departyd fayre and welle,

Back at Carlisle
325   The kyng fulle sone com to Carlylle,
And his hartt hevy and greatt.
The fyrst man he mett was Sir Gawen,
That vnto the kyng thus gan sayn,
"Syr, howe haue ye sped?"

he tells Gawain that
he is lost.
330   "Fforsothe," sayd the kyng, "neuere so ylle.
Alas! I am in poynt my-self to spylle,
For nedely I most be ded."

Gawain says he
would rather die
himself.
"Nay," sayd Gawen, "that may nott be,
I had lever my-self be dead, so mott I the,
335   Thys is ille tydand."

[1] In the folio there is the word *fowll*, which Madden omits.

"Gawen, I mett to-day withe the fowlyst lady,
That euere I sawe sertenly;
She sayd to me my lyfe she wold saue,
Butt fyrst she wold the to husbond haue,
340   Wherfor I am wo begon,
That in my hartt I make my mone."

⟨fol. 132b⟩

"Ys this alle?" then sayd Gawen,
"I shalle wed her and wed her agayn,
Thowghe she were a fend,
345   Thowghe she were as foulle as Belsabub,
Her shalle I wed, by the rood;
Or elles were nott I your frende,
For ye ar my kyng withe honour,
And haue worshypt me in many a stowre,
350   Therfor shalle I nott lett;
To saue your lyfe, lorde, itt were my parte,
Or were I false and a greatt coward,
And my worshypp is the bett."
"I-wys, Gawen, I mett her in Inglyswod,
355   She told me her name, by the rode,
That itt was Dame Ragnelle;
She told me butt I had of her answere,
Elles alle my laboure is neuere the nere,
Thus she gan me telle.
360   And butt yf her answere help me welle,
Elles lett her haue her desyre no dele,
This was her covenaunt;
And yf her answere help me, and none other,
Then wold she haue you, here is alle to-geder,
365   That made she warraunt."
"As for this," sayd Gawen, "[it]¹ shalle nott lett,
I wolle wed her att whate tyme ye wolle sett,
I pray you make no care;
For and she were the moste fowlyst wyghte,
370   That euere men myghte se withe syghte,
For your love I wolle nott spare."
"Garamercy, Gawen," then sayd kyng Arthor,
"Of alle knyghtes thou berest the flowre,
That euere yett I fond;

¹ M., *it* inserted.

Arthur tells him of the request of the foul lady.

"Is that all? For your sake I would wed the fiend."

Arthur tells of the covenant.

If he cannot be saved except by her answer, she is to have Gawain.

Gawain is ready for anything;

Arthur thanks and praises him.

375   My worshypp and my lyf thou savyst for-euere,
        Therfore my loue shalle nott frome the dyssevyr,

〈fol. 133〉

        As I am kyng in lond."
        Then within v. or vj. days,
        The kyng must nedys goo his ways,
380   To bere his answere.

They ride out to-
gether,

        The kyng and Sir Gawen rode oute of toun,
        No man withe them, butt they alone,
        Neder ferre ne nere.
        When the kyng was withe-in the Fforest,
385   "Syr Gawen, farewell, I must go west,
        Thou shalt no furder goo."

then part,

        "My lord, God spede you on your jorney,
        I wold I shold nowe ryde your way,
        Ffor to departe I am ryghte wo."
390   The kyng had rydden butt a while,
        Lytelle more then the space of a myle,

and Arthur soon
meets Ragnell,

        Or he mett Dame Ragnelle.
        "A, Sir kyng, ye arre nowe welcum here,

who tells him that
his answers won't
do.

        I wott ye ryde to bere your answere,
395   That wolle avaylle you no dele."

"Tell me yours;

        "Nowe," sayd the kyng, "sithe itt wolle none other be,
        Telle me your answere nowe, and my lyfe saue me,

Gawain has prom-
ised that he would
wed you."

        Gawen shalle you wed;
        So he hathe promysed me my lyf to saue,
400   And your desyre nowe shalle ye haue,
        Bothe in bowre and in bed.
        Therfor telle me nowe alle in hast,
        Whate wolle help now att last,—
        Haue done, I may nott tary."
405   "Syr," quod Dame Ragnelle, "nowe shalt thou
              knowe
        Whate wemen desyren moste of highe and lowe,
        Ffrom this I wolle nott varaye.

"Whatever others
may say,

        Summe men sayn we desyre to be fayre,
        Also we desyre to haue repayre,
410   Of diuerse straunge men;
        Also we loue to haue lust in bed,

⟨fol. 133b⟩

And often we desyre to wed,
Thus ye men nott ken.
Yett we desyre a-noder maner thyng,
415 To be holden nott old, butt fresshe and yong,
Withe flatryng and glosyng and quaynt gyn,
So ye men may vs wemen euere wyn,
Of whate ye wolle crave.
Ye goo fulle nyse, I wolle nott lye,
420 Butt there is one thyng is alle oure fantasye,
And that nowe shalle ye knowe:
We desyren of men aboue alle maner thyng,   what women most desire is sovereignty over men.
To haue the souereynte, withoute lesyng,
Of alle, bothe hyghe and lowe.
425 For where we haue souereynte alle is ourys,
Thoughe a knyghte be neuere so ferys,
And euere the mastry wynne;
Of the moste manlyest is oure desyre,
To haue the souereynte of suche a syre,
430 Suche is oure crafte and gynne.
Therfore wend, Sir kyng, on thy way,
And telle that knyghte, as I the saye,
That itt is as we desyren moste;
He wol be wrothe and vnsoughte,   The knight will curse her who told you."
435 And curse her fast that itt the taughte,
Ffor his laboure is lost.
Go forthe, Sir kyng, and hold promyse
Ffor thy lyfe is sure nowe in alle wyse,
That dare I well[1] vndertake."
440 The kyng rode forthe a greatt shake,
As fast as he myghte gate,
Thorowe myre, more, and fenne,
Where-as the place was sygnyd and sett then,   At the appointed place Arthur finds Gromer.

⟨fol. 134⟩

Evyn there withe Sir Gromer he mett.
445 And stern wordes to the kyng he spak withe that,
"Com of, Sir kyng, nowe lett se,
Of thyne answere whate itt shal be,
Ffor I am redy grathyd."

[1] M., well; wele, MS.

The kyng pullyd oute bokes twayne;
450 "Syr, ther is myne answer, I dare sayn
Ffor somme wolle help att nede."
but the correct an-
swer is not there;
he must die.
Syr Gromer lokyd on theym euerychon;
"Nay, nay, Sir kyng, thou artt butt a dead man,
Therfor nowe shalt thou blede."
455 "Abyde, Sir Gromer," sayd kyng Arthoure,
"I haue one answere shalle make al[l]e¹ sure."
"Lett se," then sayd Sir Gromer,
"Or els so God me help as I the say,
Thy dethe thou shalt haue with large paye,
460 I telle the nowe ensure."
"Now," sayd the kyng, "I se as I gesse,
In the is butt a lytelle gentilnesse,
By God that ay is helpand.
Here is oure answere and that is alle,
465 That wemen desyren moste specialle,
Bothe of fre and bond.
I saye no more, butt aboue al thyng,
Wemen desyre souereynte, for that is theyr lykyng,
And that is ther moste desyre;
470 To haue the rewlle of the manlyest men,
And then ar they welle, thus they me dyd ken,
To rule the, Gromer syre."
"May I see her burn
who told you! It is
my sister Ragnell.
"And she that told the nowe, Sir Arthoure,
I pray to God, I maye se her bren on a fyre,
475 Ffor that was my suster, Dame Ragnelle;

⟨fol. 134b⟩

That old scott, God geve her² shame,
Elles had I made the fulle tame;
Nowe haue I lost moche travaylle.
Go where thou wolt, kyng Arthoure,
480 For of me thou maiste be euere sure;
Alas! that I euere se this day;
Nowe, welle I wott, myne enime thou wolt be,
and shall never
again find you un-
armed."
And att suche a pryk shalle I neuere gett the,
My song may be welle-awaye!"
485 "No," sayd the kyng, "that make I warraunt,
Some harnys I wolle haue to make me defendaunt,
That make I God avowe,

¹ M., all; ale, MS.   ² M., her; he, MS.

In suche a plyghte shalt thou neuere me fynde,
And yf thou do, lett me bete and bynde,
490   As is for thy best prouf."
"Nowe haue good day," sayd Sir Gromer,

They part.

"Ffarewell,"[1] sayd Sir Arthoure, "so mott I the,
I am glad, I haue so sped."
Kyng Arthoure turnyd hys hors into the playn,
495   And sone he mett withe Dame Ragnelle agayn,

Arthur soon meets Ragnell;

In the same place and stede.
"Syr kyng, I am glad ye haue sped welle,
I told howe itt wold be euery delle;
Nowe hold that ye haue hyghte.
500   Syn I haue sauyd your lyf, and none other,
Gawen must me wed, Sir Arthoure,
That is a fulle gentille knyghte."
"No lady, that I you hyghte I shalle nott faylle,
So ye wol be rulyd by my councelle,
505   Your wille then shalle ye haue."
"Nay, Sir kyng, nowe wolle I nott soo,

she insists on riding with him openly

Openly I wol be weddyd, or I parte the froo,
Elles shame wolle y haue.
Ryde before, and I wolle com after,
510   Vnto thy courte, Syr kyng Arthoure;
Of no man I wolle shame;
Be-thynk you howe I haue sauyd your lyf.
Therfor withe me nowe shalle ye nott stryfe,
Ffor and ye do, ye be to blame."
515   The kyng of her had greatt shame;
Butt forthe she rood, thoughe he were grevyd,
Tylle they cam to Karlyle forthe they mevyd.

to Carlisle and into the court,

In-to the courte she rode hym by,
Ffor no man wold she spare, securly,—
520   Itt likyd the kyng fulle ylle.
Alle the contraye had wonder greatt,

to the amazement of all.

Ffro whens she com, that foule vnswete,
They sawe neuere of so fowlle a thyng;
In-to the halle she went, in certen:
525   "Arthoure, kyng, lett fetche me Sir Gaweyn,

"Call the knights and have Gawain pledge his troth in their presence."

Before the knyghtes, alle in hying,
That I may nowe be made sekyr,

---

[1] M., *Farewell; Farewele*, MS.

In welle and wo trowithe plyghte vs togeder,
Before alle thy chyvalry.
530   This is your graunt, lett se, haue done;
Sett forthe Sir Gawen, my love, anon,
Ffor lenger tarying kepe nott I."
Then cam forthe Sir Gawen the knyghte,

Gawain is ready to
keep his promise.

"Syr, I am redy of that I you hyghte,
535   Alle forwardes to fulfylle";
"Godhauemercy," sayd Dame Ragnelle then,
"Ffor thy sake I wold I were a fayre woman,

⟨fol. 135b⟩

Ffor thou art of so good wylle."
Ther Sir Gawen to her his trowthe plyghte,
540   In welle and in woo, as he was a true knyghte,
Then was Dame Ragnelle fayn.

All are sorry for
him;

"Alas!" then sayd Dame Gaynour;
So sayd alle the ladyes in her bower,
And wept for Sir Gawen.
545   "Alas!" then sayd bothe kyng and knyghte,
That euere he shold wed suche a wyghte,

his bride is so ugly.

She was so fowlle and horyble.
She had two tethe on euery syde,
As borys tuskes, I wolle nott hyde,
550   Of lengthe a large handfulle;
The one tusk went vp, and the other doun;
A mowthe fulle wyde, and fowlle igrown.
With grey herys many on;
Her lyppes laye lumpryd on her chyn;
555   Nek forsothe on her was none i-seen,—
She was a lothly on!

She insists that a
large company be
gathered for the
wedding,

She wold nott be weddyd in no maner,
Butt there were made a krye in all the shyre,
Bothe in town and in borowe.
560   Alle the ladyes nowe of the lond,
She lett kry to com to hand,
To kepe that brydalle thorowe.
So itt befylle after on a daye,
That maryed shold be that fowlle [lady],[1]
565   Vnto Sir Gawen.
The daye was comyn the daye shold be,

[1] M., *lady* inserted after *fowlle*.

Therof the ladyes had greatt pitey;
"Alas!" then gan they sayn.
The queen prayd Dame Ragnelle sekerly.

⟨fol. 136⟩

570 To be maryed in the mornyng erly,
"As pryvaly as we may."
"Nay," she sayd, "by hevyn kyng,
That wolle I neuere for no-thyng,
Ffor oughte that ye can saye;
575 I wol be weddyd alle openly,   to be done openly,
Ffor withe the kyng suche covenaunt made I;
I putt you oute of dowte,
I wolle nott to churche tylle highe masse tyme,   with High Mass,
And in the open halle I wolle dyne,
580 In myddys of alle the rowte."
"I am greed," sayd Dame Gaynour,
"Butt me wold thynk more honour,   in spite of the
And your worshypp moste."   queen's advice.
"Ye, as for that, lady, God you saue,
585 This daye my worshypp wolle I haue,
I telle you withoute boste."
She made her redy to churche to fare,
And alle the states that there ware,
Syrs, withoute lesyng.
590 She was arayd in the richest maner,   Richly arrayed,
More fressher than Dame Gaynour,
Her arayment was worthe iij. mlle. mark,
Of good red nobles styff and stark,
So rychely she was begon.
595 Ffor alle her rayment she bare the belle
Of fowlnesse that euere I hard telle,   but most ugly,
So fowlle a sowe sawe neuere man,
Ffor to make a shortt conclusion.

⟨fol. 136b⟩

When she was weddyd, they hyed theym home,   Ragnell is wedded.
600 To mete alle they went.
This fowlle lady bygan the highe dese,
She was fulle foulle and nott curteys,
So sayd they all verament.
When the seruyce cam her before,   At the feast she eats
605 She ete as moche as vj. that ther wore,   like six, in unseemly
                                                manner.

That mervaylyd many a man;
Her nayles were long ynchys iij⁰.,
Therwithe she breke her mete vngoodly,
Therfore she ete alone.
610   She ette iij⁰. capons and also curlues iij⁰.,
And greatt bake metes she ete vp, perde,
All men therof had mervaylle;
Ther was no mete cam her before,
Butt she ete itt vp lesse and more,
615   That praty fowlle dameselle.
Alle men then that euere her sawe,
Bad the deuille her bonys gnawe,
Bothe knyghte and squyre;
So she ete tylle mete was done,
620   Tylle they drewe clothes and had wasshen,
As is the gyse and maner.
Meny men wold speke of diuerse seruice,
I trowe ye may wete inowghe ther was,
Bothe of tame and wylde;
625   In king Arthours courte ther was no wontt,
That myghte be gotten withe mannys hond,
Noder in fforest ne in feld.
Ther were mynstralles of diuerse contrey.

[A leaf is here lacking.]

⟨fol. 137⟩

In bed she begs Ga-
wain to give her at
least a kiss.
"A, Sir Gawen, syn I haue you wed,
630   Shewe me your cortesy in bed,
Withe ryghte itt may nott be denyed.
I-wyse, Sir Gawen," that lady sayd,
"And I were fayre ye wold do a-noder brayd,
Butt of wedlok ye take no hed;
635   Yett for Arthours sake kysse me att the leste,
I pray you do this att my request,
Lett se howe ye can spede."
Sir Gawen sayd, "I wolle do more
Then for to kysse, and God before!"

He turns to her and
sees the fairest crea-
ture.
640   He turnyd hym her vntille;
He sawe her the fayrest creature,
That euere he sawe withoute mesure.
She sayd, "Whatt is your wylle?"
"A, Ihesu!" he[1] sayd, "whate ar ye?"

[1] M., *he; she,* MS.

645 "Sir, I am your wyf, securly;
    Why ar ye so vnkynde?"
    "A, lady, I am to blame;
    I cry you mercy, my fayre madame,—   *He is amased and*
    Itt was nott in my mynde.   *delighted.*
650 A lady ye are fayre in my syghte,
    And to-day ye were the foulyst wyghte,
    That euere I sawe withe myne ie.[1]
    Wele is me, my lady, I haue you thus";
    And brasyd her in his armys, and gan her kysse,
655 And made greatt joye, sycurly.
    "Syr," she sayd, "thus shalle ye me haue,   *"You must choose*
    Chese of the one, so God me saue,   *to have me fair*
    My beawty wolle nott hold;   *either by day or at*
    Wheder ye wolle haue me fayre on nyghtes,[2]   *right."*
660 And as foulle on days to alle men sightes,

⟨fol. 137b⟩

    Or els to haue me fayre on days,
    And on nyghtes on the fowlyst wyfe,
    The one ye must nedes haue;
    Chese the one or the oder,
665 Chese on, Sir knyghte, whiche you is leuere,
    Your worshypp for to saue."
    "Alas!" sayd Gawen, "the choyse is hard;   *"The choice is hard;*
    To chese the best itt is froward;
    Wheder choyse that I chese,
670 To haue you fayre on nyghtes and no more,
    That wold greve my hartt ryghte sore,
    And my worshypp shold I lese.[3]
    And yf I desyre on days to haue you fayre,
    Then on nyghtes I shold haue a symple repayre.
675 Now fayn wold I chose the best,
    I ne wott in this world whatt I shalle saye,
    Butt do as ye lyst nowe, my lady gaye,   *I leave it to you."*
    The choyse I putt in your fyst.
    Euyn as ye wolle I putt itt in your hand,
680 Lose me when ye lyst, for I am bond;
    I putt the choyse in you;
    Bothe body and goodes, hartt, and euery dele,

[1] M., *ie; ien*, MS.

[2] M., *nyghtes; nyght*, MS.   [3] M., *lese; lose*, MS.

Ys alle your oun, for to by and selle,—
That make I God avowe!"

685 "Garamercy, corteys knyghte," sayd the lady,
"Of alle erthly knyghtes blyssyd mott thou be,
Ffor now am I worshyppyd;

Thou shalle haue me fayre bothe day and nyghte,
And euere whyle I lyve as fayre and bryghte;

690 Therfore be nott greuyd.

Ffor I was shapen by nygramancy,
Withe my stepdame, God haue on her mercy,
And by enchauntement,

And shold haue bene oderwyse vnderstond,

695 Euyn tylle the best of Englond

⟨fol. 138⟩

Had wedyd me verament.

And also he shold geve me the souereynte
Of alle his body and goodes, sycurly,
Thus was I disformyd;

700 And thou, Sir knyghte, curteys Gawen,
Has gevyn me the souereynte serteyn,
That wolle nott wrothe the erly ne late.
Kysse me, Sir knyghte, euyn now here,
I pray the, be glad, and make good chere,

705 Ffor welle is me begon."

Ther they made joye oute of mynde,
So was itt reason and cours of kynde,
They two theym-self alone.
She thankyd God and Mary mylde,

710 She was recouered of that that she was defoylyd,
So dyd Sir Gawen;
He made myrthe alle in her boure,
And thankyd of alle oure Sauyoure,
I telle you, in certeyn.

715 Withe joye and myrthe they wakyd tylle daye,
And than wold ryse that fayre maye.[1]
"Ye shalle nott," Sir Gawen sayd,

"We wolle lye and slepe tylle pryme,
And then lett the kyng calle vs to dyne."

720 "I am greed," then sayd the mayd.
Thus itt passyd forth tylle mid-daye.

[1] M., *maye; mayd*, MS.

"Syrs,"[1] quod the kyng, "lett vs go and asaye,

Yf Sir Gawen be on lyve;

I am fulle ferd of Sir Gawen,

725   Nowe lest the fende haue hym slayn,

Nowe wold I fayn preve.

Go we nowe," sayd Arthoure the kyng.

"We wolle go se theyr vprysyng,

⟨fol. 138*b*⟩

Howe welle that he hathe sped."

730   They cam to the chambre, alle in certeyn.

"Aryse," sayd the kyng to Sir Gawen,

"Why slepyst thou so long in bed?"

"Mary," quod Gawen, "Sir kyng, sicurly,

I wold be glad, and ye wold lett me be,

735   Ffor I am fulle welle att eas;

Abyde, ye shalle se the dore vndone,

I trowe that ye wolle say I am welle goon,

I am fulle lothe to ryse."

Syr Gawen rose, and in his hand he toke

740   His fayr lady, and to the dore he shoke,

And opynyd the dore fulle fayre;

She stod in her smok alle by that fyre,

Her her[2] was to her knees as red as gold wyre,

"Lo! this is my repayre,

745   Lo!" sayd Gawen Arthoure vntille,

"Syr, this is my wyfe, Dame Ragnelle,

That sauyd onys your lyfe."

He told the kyng and the queen hem beforn,

Howe sodenly from her shap she dyd torne,

750   "My lord, nowe be your leve."

And whate was the cause she forshapen was,

Syr Gawen told the kyng both more and lesse.

"I thank God," sayd the queen,

"I wenyd, Sir Gawen, she wold the haue myscaryed;

755   Therfore in my hartt I was sore agrevyd;

Butt the contrary is here seen."

Ther was game, revelle, and playe,

And euery man to other gan saye:

"She is a fayre wyghte."

---

[1] M., *Syrs; Syr*, MS.   [2] M., *her; hed*, MS.

Marginal notes:

Wondering how Gawain is faring,

Arthur and his companions come to the chamber:

"Why sleep so late?"

"You will see."

He opens the door.

"This is Ragnell my wife."

He tells them how she had been transformed.

All rejoice.

Arthur tells them
how she saved his
life;

760   Than the kyng them alle gan telle,
       How did held hym att nede Dame Ragnelle,
   "Or my dethe had bene dyghte."
       Ther the kyng told the queen, by the rood,
       Howe he was bestad in Ingleswod,

⟨fol. 139⟩

765   Withe Sir Gromer Somer Joure;
       And whate othe the knyghte made hym swere,
   "Or elles he had slayn me ryghte there,
       Withoute mercy or mesure.
       This same lady, Dame Ragnelle,
770   Ffrom my dethe she dyd help me ryghte welle,
       Alle for the love of Gawen."

Gawain explains
more;

       Then Gawen told the kyng alle togeder,
       Howe forshapen she was withe her stepmoder,
       Tylle a knyghte had holpen her agayn;
775   Ther she told the kyng fayre and welle,
       Howe Gawen gave her the souereynte euery delle,
       And whate choyse she gave to hym;

Ragnell thanks
him for his cour-
tesy;

   "God thank hym of his curtesye,
       He savid me from chaunce and vilony,
780   That was fulle foulle and grym.
       Therfore, curteys knyghte and hend Gawen,
       Shalle I neuere wrathe the serteyn,
       That promyse nowe here I make,—

she will always
obey him.

       Whilles that I lyve I shal be obaysaunt,
785   To God aboue I shalle itt warraunt,
       And neuere withe you to debate."

Gawain is very
happy;

   "Garamercy, lady," then sayd Gawen,
   "With you I hold me fulle welle content,
       And that I trust to fynde."

he loves Ragnell.

790   He sayd, "My loue shalle she haue,
       Therafter nede she neuere more craue,
       For she hathe bene to me so kynde."
       The queen sayd, and the ladyes alle,
   "She is the fayrest nowe in this halle,
795   I swere by Seynt John!
       My loue, lady, ye shalle haue euere,
       For that ye savid my lord Arthoure,

As I am a gentilwoman."
Syr Gawen gatt on her Gyngolyn,

⟨fol. 139*b*⟩

800 That was a good knyghte of strengthe and kynn,
And of the Table Round.
Att euery greatt fest that lady shold be,
Of fayrnesse she bare away the bewtye,
Wher she yed on the ground.

805 Gawen louyd that lady Dame Ragnelle,
In alle his lyfe he louyd none so welle,
I telle you withoute lesyng;
As a coward he lay by her bothe day and nyghte,
Neuere wold he haunt justyng aryghte,
810 Ther-att mervayled[1] Arthoure the kyng.[2]
She prayd the kyng for his gentilnes,
"To be good lord to Sir Gromer, i-wysse,
Of that to you he hathe offendyd;"
"Yes, lady, that shalle I nowe for your sake,

815 Ffor I wott welle he may nott amendes make,
He dyd to me fulle vnhend."
Nowe for to make you a short conclusyon,
I cast me for to make an end fulle sone,
Of this gentylle lady.
820 She lyvyd with Sir Gawen butt yerys v.,
That grevyd Gawen alle his lyfe,
I telle you, securly.
In her lyfe she grevyd hym neuere,
Therfor was neuere woman to hym lever,

825 Thus leves my talkyng;
She was the ffayrest lady of al[l]e[3] Englond,
When she was on lyve, I vnderstand,
So sayd Arthoure the kyng.
Thus endythe the aduenture of kyng Arthoure,
830 That oft in his days was grevyd sore,
And of the weddyng of Gawen.
Gawen was weddyd oft in his days,
Butt so welle he neuere lovyd woman always,

[1] MS., *movaylyd.*

[2] M., *Arthoure the kyng; kyng Arthoure,* MS.   [3] M., *all; ale,* MS.

⟨fol. 140⟩

As I haue hard men sayn.
835   This aduenture befelle in Ingleswod,
As good kyng[1] Arthoure on huntyng yod,
Thus haue I hard men telle.
Nowe God as thou were in Bethleme born,
Suffer neuere her soules be forlorne,
840   In the brynnyng fyre of helle!
And, Ihesu, as thou were borne of a virgyn,
Help hym oute of sorowe that this tale dyd devyne,
And that nowe in alle hast,
Ffor he is be-sett withe gaylours many,
845   That kepen hym fulle sewerly,
Withe wyles wrong and wraste.
Nowe God as thou art veray kyng royalle,[2]
help hym oute of daunger that made this tale,
Ffor therin he hathe bene long;
850   And of greatt pety help thy seruaunt,
Ffor body and soulle I yeld into thyne hand,
Ffor paynes he hathe strong.

Here endythe the weddyng of
Syr Gawen and Dame Ragnelle
Ffor helpyng of kyng Arthoure.

IV. SUBSIDIARY MATERIAL

The Wife's characteristic account of Midas is cheerfully accredited to one of Ovid's "thynges smale."[3] The account of "gentilesse"[4] which served to prolong, if not to enliven, the Loathly Lady's bolster lecture has definite parallels in addition

[1] M., *kynge*.

[2] *Ryoall*, MS.

[3] See E. F. Shannon, *Chaucer and the Roman Poets* ("Harvard Studies in Comparative Literature," Vol. VII [Cambridge, Mass., 1929]), pp. 318 ff. It is perhaps worth noting that no striking divergence from Ovid is to be found in this part of the *Ovide moralisé* (ed. C. de Boer ["Verhandelingen der Koninklijke Akademie van Wetenschappen te Amsterdam," Afdeeling Letterkunde, N.R. XXXVII], IV, 133 ff.), xi. 651-770.

[4] On the general theme see G. M. Vogt, "Gleanings for the History of a Sentiment: Generositas Virtus, non Sanguis," *JEGP*, XXIV (1925), 102-24, and, though less directly related, S. Resnikow, "The Cultural History of a Democratic Proverb," *JEGP*, XXXVI (1937), 391-405.

to her acknowledged quotation from Dante's *Purgatorio*. Beyond a doubt the *canzone* which opens the fourth tractate of the *Convivio* was in her mind, and memories also of the *Roman de la rose*.

(From Ovid *Metamorphoses* xi. 180–93.)

Midas, won by Pan's music, earned Apollo's ire, and Phoebus, angered, gave him ass's ears.

Ille quidem celare cupit, turpique pudore
Tempora purpureis temptat velare tiaris.
Sed solitus longos ferro resecare capillos
Viderat hoc famulus, qui cum nec prodere visum
Dedecus auderet, cupiens efferre sub auras,
Nec posset reticere tamen, secedit humumque
Effodit et, domini quales aspexerit aures;
Voce refert parva terraeque inmurmurat haustae
Indiciumque suae vocis tellure regesta
Obruit et scrobibus tacitus discedit opertis.
Creber harundinibus tremulis ibi surgere lucus
Coepit et, ut primum pleno maturuit anno,
Prodidit agricolam: leni nam motus ab austro
Obruta verba refert dominique coarguit aures.

These same he hid

and yet the slave who shaved beheld and, all too human, told truth in a hole.

The reeds next year reported the fact.

Rade volte risurge per li rami
    L'umana probitate: e questo vuole
    Quei che la dà, perchè da lui si chiami,
              —*Purgatorio*, VII, 121–24

(From the *Convivio*, con prefazione e note di Giorgio Rossi [Bologna, 1925], pp. 156–58, Trattato Quarto, Canzone Terza.)[1]

21   Tale imperò[2] che gentilezza volse,
        secondo 'l suo parere,
        che fosse antica possession d'avere
        con reggimenti belli;
25   e altri fu di più lieve savere,
        che tal detto rivolse,
        e l'ultima particula ne tolse,
        che non l'avea fors'elli!
        Di retro da costui van tutti quelli

An emperor once held nobility to come from wealth inherited and one's own worth;

another said from wealth alone,

an opinion shared by many.

[1] See also Dante's commentary on this *canzone*, esp. chaps. iii, vii, and x–xx of Trattato Quarto.

[2] The emperor Frederic II, as explained by Dante in chap. iii of Trattato Quarto.

30   che fan gentile per ischiatta[1] altrui
      che lungiamente in gran ricchezza è stata;
      ed è tanto durata
      la cosi falsa oppinion tra nui,
      che l'uom chiama colui

35   omo gentil che può dicere: "Io fui
      nepote, o figlio, di cotal valente,"
      benchè sia da niente.

No man is more low than a degenerate descendant of a noble line.

      Ma vilissimo sembra, a chi 'l ver guata,
      cui è scorto 'l cammino e poscia l'erra,

40   e tocca a tal, ch'è morto e va per terra!

These same contend no man of humble birth or his descendants can win nobility,

61   Nè voglion che vil uom gentil divegna,
      nè di vil padre scenda
      nazion[2] che per gentil già mai s'intenda;
      questo è da lor confesso:

though they claim that nobility depends on time.

65   onde lor ragion par che sè offenda
      in tanto quanto assegna
      che tempo a gentilezza si convegna,
      diffinendo con esso.[3]

We are all of the same condition;

      Ancor, segue di ciò che innanzi ho messo,

70   che siam tutti gentili o ver villani,
      o che non fosse ad uom cominciamento;[4]
      ma ciò io non consento,
      ned ellino altressì, se son cristiani!

I hold their opinions false,

      Per che a 'ntelletti sani

75   è manifesto i lor diri esser vani,
      e io così per falsi li riprovo,
      e da lor mi rimovo;

and here declare in what gentility lies.

      e dicer voglio omai, sì com'io sento,
      che cosa è gentilezza, e da che vene,

80   e dirò i segni che 'l gentile uom tene.

[1] *Schiatta* (race, family).

[2] Lineage, family.

[3] Ll. 65–68: "Hence it appears that their reasoning confutes itself, in that it states that time is necessary to nobility, defining nobility in terms of time."

[4] "Unless there should not be to all men the same beginning."

(From *Le Roman de la rose*, publ. par E. Langlois [Paris, 1922], IV, 236–37, 239, and 241–42.)[1]

18607   E se nus contredire m'ose,
      Qui de gentillece s'alose,
      E die que li gentill ome,
18610   Si con li peuples les renome,
      Sont de meilleur condicion
      Par noblece de nacion
      Que cil que les terres coutivent
      Ou qui de leur labeur se vivent,

If one should claim that the nobles are by birth superior to the poor who work,

18615   Je respons que nus n'est gentis
      S'il n'est a vertuz ententis,
      Ne n'est vilains fors pour ses vices,
      Don il pert outrageus e nices.

then I reply that only virtue makes man gentle,

      Noblece vient de bon courage,
18620   Car gentillece de lignage
      N'est pas gentillece qui vaille
      Pour quei bonté de cueur i faille;
      Par quei deit estre en li paranz,
      La proëce de ses parenz,

and that nobility comes from a noble nature. He who shows not the virtue which his forebears showed has not their worth.

18625   Qui la gentillece conquistrent
      Par les travauz que granz i mistrent.
      E quant dou siecle trespasserent,
      Toutes leur vertuz emporterent,
      E laissierent aus eirs l'aveir,

They, being gone, leave but their wealth.

18630   Qui plus ne porent d'aus aveir.
      L'aveir ont, riens plus n'i a leur,
      Ne gentillece ne valeur,
      S'il ne font tant que gentill seient
      Par sens ou par vertuz qu'il aient.

Their heirs have no gentility unless they themselves gain it.

18677   E pour gentillece conquerre,
      Qui mout est enourable en terre,
      Tuit cil qui la veulent aveir
18680   Cete regle deivent saveir:

Those who would earn gentility must master one rule thoroughly:

      Quiconques tent a gentillece
      D'orgueil se gart e de parece,

Shun pride and idleness,

      Aille aus armes ou a l'estuide,
      E de vilenie se vuide.

instead seek arms or study;

18685   Humble cueur ait, courteis e gent,

humble be and kind to every man.

[1] Only short extracts will be quoted. The discussion of "gentillesse" in the *Roman de la rose* spreads over 330 lines (ll. 18561–18896, IV, 234–47).

En trestouz leus, vers toute gent,
Fors senz plus vers ses anemis,
Quant acorz n'i peut estre mis.

Honor the sex, but
trust them not too
far, lest evil come.

Dames eneurt e dameiseles,
18690 Mais ne se fie trop en eles,
Qu'il l'en pourrait bien meschoeir,
Car nus trop bien n'est bons a voeir.

Thus one gains
praise and gentle is,
otherwise not.

Teus on deit aveir los e pris,
Senz estre blasmez ne repris,
18695 E de gentillece le non
Deit receveir, li autre non.

A nobleman with-
out merit of his own
stands lower than
the son of a vaga-
bond.

18755 E cil qui d'autrui gentillece,
Senz sa valeur, senz sa proece,
Veaut emporter los e renom
Est il gentis? Je di que non;
Ainz deit estre vilains clamez,
18760 E vis tenuz, e meins amez
Que s'il estait filz d'un truant.

THE FRIAR'S TALE

By ARCHER TAYLOR

THREE recensions of a story similar to Chaucer's *Friar's Tale* occur in medieval and Renaissance literature.[1] Although these recensions show many agreements in detail and are evidently closely akin to Chaucer's tale, we cannot derive Chaucer's tale directly from any of them. Parallels to an incident which is characteristic of Chaucer's tale and which is not found in the other medieval or Renaissance texts are found in modern oral tradition.

The only version known to us which may have been available to Chaucer is illustrated by the following *exemplum:*

Quodam tempore quidam Rusticus surgens diluculo intendebat ire ad forum proxime ville. Cui demon in forma alterius rustici expectabat ante hostium suum, et cum rusticus exiret de doma sua demon salutavit eum et quesiuit quorsum tenderet. Et ille respondit se velle ire ad forum proxime ville. Demon dixit, "Et ego uolo illuc ire; simus ergo socii in via." Dixit Rusticus, "Placet michi." Et cum venissent ad uiam quesiuit Rusticus quis esset. Qui respondit, "Ego sum demon." Et ille, "O maledicte, quid tu vis facere in foro?" Ad quod demon, "Non propter aliud modo ibi vado, nisi quia uolo recipere quicquit michi spontanee offertur." Tunc Rusticus, "Sic bene pacior te ire mecum, quia spero quod michi nichil facias." Dixit demon, "Ne timeas." Procedentes igitur in uia et confabulantes in leticia; ecce venit quidam qui pascebat gregem suum, et cum vna ouis nimium discurreret ab aliis iratus super eam pastor maledixit ei et verbis tradidit dyabolo. Tunc Rusticus audiens dixit demoni, "Ecce ouis illa data est tibi; tolle eam." Cui demon, "O karissime, ista maledictio et donacio non procedit ex corde et ideo non possum eam tollere." Demum venerunt ad uillam, et ecce intra portam in prima domo sedebat quedam mulier in foribus domus sue habens in

Marginal glosses:

> A farmer on his way to the next village met the Devil in the guise of a farmer.

> The Devil said, "I am going to the next market place too; let us go together." To the farmer's question he said, "I am the Devil and seek that which is freely offered to me."

> The farmer points out a sheep which a driver curses.

> "That curse and gift does not come from the heart."

> A mother curses her child.

---

[1] See Archer Taylor, "The Devil and the Advocate," *PMLA*, XXXVI (1921), 35–59, and "Der Rihter und der Teufel," *Studies in Honor of Hermann Collitz* (Baltimore, 1930), pp. 248–51; R. T. Christiansen, "Fanden, Futen, Asbjørnsen og Ragna Nielsen," *Festskrift til bibliotekar Hj. Pettersen* (Oslo, 1926), pp. 253–63. An additional version of the *exemplum* (which I have not seen) is found in H. Ammann, *Praestantiorum aliquot codicum mss., qui Friburgi servantur, ad jurisprudentiam spectantium notitia* (Freiburg i.Br., 1836), pp. 4 ff.

sinu paruulum lactantem et nimium vagientem. Qua de re mulier nimium rapta furore cepit puero maledicere et cum verbis dyabolo

tradere. Quod audiens Rusticus demoni dixit iterum, "Ecce puer ille datus est tibi; tolle eum." Cui demon chaninando [? cachinando] respondit, "O nec ista maledictio procedit ex corde." Et sic pertransi-

erunt. Venientes autem super forum, subito apparuit quedam femina pauper, et videns Rusticum dixit, "O quod dyabolus vos accipiat cum corpore et anima quamdiu uultis affligere animam meam

cum mercede mea quam apud vos merui et michi non datis." Statim demon tenens Rusticum per collerium suum dixit. "Modo volo accipere quod datum est michi, quia hoc processit ex corde." Et ita deduxit eum permittente dei iudicio. Ne igitur nobis simile contingat, saltem in anima multum cauere debemus ne frauderimus mercennarios nostros mercede uel uictu suo, quia dicit Apostolus I ad Timo-[theum] V, "Qui suorum et maxime domesticorum curam non habet fidem negauit et est infideli deterior." Sed potius debemus studere esse liberales erga ipsos et alios pauperes. Tunc deus multiplicabit nobis bona etc.[1]

With minor variations—a sheep or a calf is substituted for the pig or the like—this story appears now and again in collections of *exempla*. It is probably derived ultimately from Cæsarius of Heisterbach's fragmentary *Libri octo miraculorum*,[2] with which text it agrees almost verbatim. In later books of *exempla* the compilers have usually removed the few and insignificant traces of localization belonging to the original version: "Retulit mihi [i.e., Cæsarius] quidam abbas ordinis Cisterciensis ante annos paucos in diocesi Bremensi. . . . ."

The form in which this story is told in some standard collections of *exempla* such as the *Promptuarium exemplorum*, a compilation by Johannes Herolt, a Dominican friar at Basel, resembles Chaucer's *Friar's Tale* in its mention of a lawyer as the Devil's victim. Herolt's compilation was made in the early years of the fifteenth century.

[1] British Museum Add. MS 15833, fol. 156ᵇ; cf. J. A. Herbert, *Catalogue of Romances*, III, 592, No. 108. First printed in *PMLA*, XXXVI (1921), 38–39. This manuscript was written in the fourteenth century. It once belonged to the Augustinian monastery of Waldhausen in Upper Austria.

[2] A. Meister, "Die Fragmente der Libri VIII Miraculorum des Cæsarius von Heisterbach," *Römische Quartalschrift für christliche Alterthumskunde und für Kirchengeschichte*, Supplementheft 13 (Rome, 1901), p. 90, Book ii, chap. xvii: "De advocato, quem diabolus vivum rapuit, dum iret facere exactionem."

Homo quidam erat diversarum villarum advocatus, immisericors, *A grasping lawyer, out to gather prey,*
avarus, faciens graves exactiones in sibi subditos. Die quadam, cum
propter exactionem faciendam ad villam unam properaret, diabolus in *met the Devil in the form of a man,*
specie hominis se illi in itinere sociavit, quem tam ex horrore quam ex
mutua collocutione diabolum esse intellexit. Ire cum eo satis timuit; *and could not get rid of him.*
nullo tamen modo, neque orando neque cruce signando, ab eo separari
potuit. Cumque simul pergerent, occurrit eis homo quidam pauper *A poor man, angry with his perverse pig, said, "Devil take you!"*
porcum in laqueo ducens. Cumque porcus huc illucque diverteretur,
iratus homo clamavit, "Diabolus te habeat!" Quo verbo audito,
advocatus sperans se tali occasione a diabolo liberari, ait illi, "Audi, *But, as he did not say it from his heart, the Devil could not take the pig.*
amice: porcus ille est tibi datus; vade tolle illum." Respondit dia-
bolus, "Nequaquam mihi illum ex corde donavit, et ideo illum tollere
non possum." Deinde transeuntes per aliam villam, cum infans *Nor could he take a child to which its mother said, "Devil take you!"*
fleret, mater in foribus domus stans, turbida voce dicebat, "Diabolus
te habeat! quid me fletibus tuis inquietas?" Tunc advocatus dixit,
"Ecce bene lucratus es animam unam! tolle infantem, quia tuus est."
Cui diabolus, ut prius, "Non mihi illum dedit ex corde: sed talis est
consuetudo hominibus loquendi, cum irascuntur." Incipientibus *When, however, some townsmen saw the lawyer coming,*
autem appropinquare loco ad quem tendebant, homines a villa longe
videntes, et causam ejus adventus non ignorantes, omnes una voce *they all cried out, "May the Devil take you!"*
simul clamabant, dicentes, "Diabolus te habeat, ac diabolo venias."
Quo audito, diabolus, caput movens et cachinnans, ait advocato, *As they did it from the bottom of their hearts, the Devil carried off the lawyer.*
"Ecce, isti dederunt te mihi ex intimo corde, et ideo meus es." Ac
rapuit eum in ipsa hora diabolus, et quid de eo fecerit ignoratur.
Verba mutuae confabulationis ac facta istius, per famulam advocati, *This the lawyer's servant, who was with him, has told.*
qui secum fuit in itinere, declarata sunt.[1]

The fifteenth-century *exemplum* in British Museum Cleo-
patra D VIII which was discovered by Thomas Wright is interesting for its stylistic peculiarities. In its rapid dialogue and in
its choice of details, the introductory episode shows a certain
degree of similarity to Chaucer's manner, but we need not think
of a connection. The text is as follows:

NARRATIO DE QUODAM SENESCALLO SCELEROSO

Erat vir quidam Senescallus & placitator, pauperum calumpniator. *A harsh seneschal*
& bonorum huiusmodi spoliator. Qui die quadam forum iudiciale
causa contencionis faciende lucrandi adiuit. ¶ Cui quidam obuiauit *is met by another man who asks him his business.*
in itinere dicens ei. "Quo vadis? Et quid habes officij?" Respondit
primus "vado lucrari." Et ait secundus. "Ego tui similis sum.

[1] Reprinted from *Originals and Analogues* ("Chaucer Society" [1872–78]), p. 106.

Eamus simul." Primo consciente, dixit secundus ei. "Quid est lucrum

tuum?" Et ille "emolumentum pauperum quamdiu aliquid habent. vt per lites contenciones & vexaciones siue iuste siue iniuste. Modo dixi tibi lucrum meum vnde est. Dic mihi queso. vnde est & tuum?"

Respondit secundus dicens. "quicquid sub maledictione traditur diabolo. computo mihi pro lucro." Risit primus. & derisit secundum. non intelligens quod esset diabolus. ¶ Paulo post cum

transirent per ciuitatem audierunt quemdam pauperem maledicere cuidam vitulo quem duxit ad vendendum quia indirecte ibat. Item audierunt consimilem de muliere fustigante puerum suum. Tunc ait primus ad secundum. "Ecce potes lucrari si vis. Tolle puerum & vi-

tulum." Respondit secundus "non possum. quia non maledicunt ex corde." ¶ Cum vero paululum processissent, pauperes euntes versus iudicium. videntes illum Senescallum. ceperunt omnes vnanimiter maledictiones in ipsum ingenere. Et dixit secundus ad primum, "audis quid isti dicunt." "audio" inquit. "Set nichil ad me." Et dixit secun-

dus. "Isti maledicunt ex corde & te traducunt diabolo. Et ideo meus eris." Que statim ipsum arripiens. cum eo disparuit.[1]

Since the *exemplum* contains a natural climactic sequence of events—a pig is cursed and then a child and then the lawyer— we may reasonably suppose it to represent the original form of the story. Minor variations appear in the Middle Ages and later. In the first half of the thirteenth century, for example, Der Stricker, an Austrian poet, versifies a form of the story in which a pig, one of a herd of cattle, and then a child are cursed, and finally a widow curses the lawyer. The casual enlargements of the story need not delay us, but the last incident may serve as a parallel to the curse which the old woman calls down on the summoner:

175 Da begunden si stille sten.
Do begunde ein witwe zuo gen.
Diu was beide siech und alt,
Ir armuot diu was manikvalt,
Des was vil groz ir ungehabe,
180 Si gie vil kume an einem stabe.

Do sie den rihter ane sach,
Si begunde weinen, unde sprach:

[1] I have printed the text from the *Originals and Analogues*, p. 105, but have not retained the italicization of expanded abbreviations. I have slightly simplified the punctuation.

"O we dir, rihtaere!   Alas, you are so
    Daʒ du so riche wære,   powerful and I so
185 Und ich so arme bin gewesen,   weak
    Und du trutest niht genesen,   and you thought
    Dun[en] habest mir, ane schulde   you had to take
    Und wider Gotes hulde,
    Min eineʒ kuelin genomen,   my only cow.
190 Da daʒ alleʒ von solde komen,
    Des ich vil arme solde leben.
    Mirn' ist diu kraft niht gegeben,   I do not have
    Daʒ mir der lip so vil tuge,   strength
    Daʒ ich dar nach gen muge,   to go where one
195 Da man mir eʒ gebe durch Got.   would give it to me
    Desn' hastu niht wan dinen spot.   for God's sake.
    Nu bit' ich Got durch sinen tot   I pray God by his
    Und durch die grimmeliche[n] not,   sufferings
    Die er an siner menscheit
200 Durch uns arme alle leit,
    Daʒ er gewer mich armeʒ wip,   to grant me that the
    Daʒ dine sele und dinen lip   Devil may carry off
    Der tiuvel mueʒe vueren hin!"   your body and
    Do sprach der tiuvel wider in: soul."
205 "Sich, daʒ ist ernest, nu nim war!"   The Devil seized
    Er greif in vaste in daʒ har   him by the hair
    Und begunde ze berge gahen,   and carried him up
    Daʒ eʒ alle die an sahen,   so that all in the
    Die an dem market waren.[1]   market place saw.

At the time of the Reformation, Johannes Pauli, an Alsatian
Franciscan, included the story in his *Schimpf und Ernst*, published in 1522. His version is marked by the reversal of the
order of the first two incidents: a child and then a pig is cursed.
Various jestbooks repeat this version of the story. About the
middle of the sixteenth century, Hans Sachs tells a version in
which only a child is cursed before the Devil bears off the un-
righteous man. These German versions seem to be corruptions
or contractions of the original story and bear witness to the
popularity of the story in oral tradition.

The differences in the three versions of the medieval *exemplum* which I have printed here suggest the existence of

[1] Printed from F. H. von der Hagen, *Gesammtabenteuer*, III (Stuttgart, 1850),
391–92 (No. LXIX, vss. 175–209). I have made a few changes in the punctuation.

other, unrecorded variations which may have been known to Chaucer and which may have agreed more closely in details with his story than do any of the versions in our hands. In particular, the animal which is cursed before the Devil bears off his victim is a different one in all the texts above. The first one has a sheep,[1] the second a pig,[2] the third a calf.[3] Such variations can easily have given rise to an incident in which a draft animal is cursed, as in Chaucer's tale, but we do not find an actual parallel to this incident older than three apparently independent stories written down in the nineteenth century. These three stories are a sophisticated *Novella* by A. F. E. Langbein, a story which makes literary use of Thuringian dialect, and a modern French folktale. Although the influence of Chaucer on Langbein has been suspected, we may infer that the incident was ultimately invented by tradition. The following passage from the French popular tale illustrates how this incident appears in tradition:

The Devil and the bailiff saw a man and woman plowing. She could not guide the young oxen,

Quand ils [le diable et l'huissier] eurent fait un bon petit bout de chemin, ils virent un homme et puis une femme qui étaient à la charrue. Cela était malaisé comme le cent diable, et puis la femme ne pouvait pas mener les bœufs comme il faut, c'était deux jouven-

and the man cursed her, "The Devil take you!"

ceaux. Ah, ma foi, l'homme jurait; il jurait qu'on n'ose pas le dire. Et puis voilà que tout d'un coup il lui dit: "Que le diable t'emporte, garce, va!"

Quand l'huissier entendit cela, il s'arrêta, et puis il regarda le diable.

"Didn't you hear?"

—"Eh bien? qu'il lui dit, est-ce que vous n'avez pas entendu? Ah, voilà bien votre affaire, mâtin, ce n'est pas la peine que vous alliez plus loin; fuyez vite la prendre, mâtin, fuyez vite!"

"There's nothing here for me."

—"Ah! c'est pour rire, tout cela, il ne le dit pas pour tout de bon; il n'y a rien à faire ici, il faut que j'aille plus loin."

The bailiff had to walk along with the Devil.

Cela ne faisait pas l'affaire de l'huissier du tout, il aurait bien voulu que le diable l'emportât, lui, le diable. Mais, ma foi, il fut encore obligé de marcher d'avec lui.[4]

[1] Above, p. 269. [2] Above, p. 271. [3] Above, p. 273.
[4] C. Roussey, *Contes populaires recueillis à Bournois* (Paris, 1894), pp. 120–26, No. 13. The passage quoted is found on pp. 121–22.

THE SUMMONER'S TALE

By WALTER MORRIS HART

On ne sait rien de précis sur l'existence de Jacques de Baisieux. Je conjecture, un peu aventureusement, qu'il fut le contemporain de Watriquet et de Jean de Condé, et comme eux ménestrel attitré de quelque seigneur. Ses poèmes allégoriques du dit *de l'Epée* et des *Fiefs d'amour*, ses rimes batelées et equivoquées sur *les cinq Lettres de Maria* ressemblent exactement aux pièces de ces trouvères.[1]

THIS conjecture places Jacques de Baisieux in the group of men of letters who, between 1300 and 1325, displaced the wandering jongleurs of the thirteenth century. These men took themselves seriously; they regarded themselves as preachers and teachers; they haughtily defended their calling against the Jacobins and the Friars Minor—the Dominicans and Franciscans—who still dared to attack them.

Their compositions were for the most part heavy, solemn, pretentious: the surprising thing is not that they should have been the last composers of fabliaux; the surprising thing is that they should have written fabliaux at all. Yet their few comic tales are not lacking in the gaiety characteristic of the type. Survivals of the preceding age, these stories had continued to live in oral tradition. They were now presented in competition with the fabliaux of the last wandering minstrels to satisfy the tastes of great lords who still found pleasure in amusing though scabrous tales.

Li Dis de le vescie à prestre was doubtless based upon a story current in oral tradition, in which jests at the expense of begging friars were not uncommon. Testaments, in which good things were bequeathed to friends, ill things to enemies, were not uncommon in folk literature. These were easily parodied[2] and readily became an instrument of satire. An anecdote, similar to *Le Vescie*, is recorded of a bequest of Jean de Meun to the Jacobin friars.

[1] Joseph Bédier, *Les Fabliaux* (1895), p. 419, n. 6.
[2] Cf. F. J. Child, *English and Scottish Popular Ballads*, I, 144.

275

In *Le Vescie* the story is well told, though in this respect it is neither better nor worse than many a thirteenth-century fabliau. The important matter of the Priest's wealth is emphasized in the beginning. He has already bequeathed it all; and it is the Friar's suggestion that he revoke some of his bequests that arouses his anger and leads him to plan revenge. The nature of his revenge is not revealed; the resulting suspense is maintained through one hundred and fifty lines—about one-half the fabliau. The author makes effective use of the opportunity, thus provided, for irony, conscious in the speeches of the Priest, unconscious in those of the Friars; present also in the whole situation and emphasized by the presence of Mayor and Aldermen at the close. Readers or hearers, enlightened by the title of the piece, will enjoy this irony to the full; yet, in so far as they are aware of the Friars' point of view, they will not forego the pleasure of suspense.

In the creation of his protagonist, however, Jacques de Baisieux goes beyond his predecessors; a character so complex and so highly idealized is scarcely to be found in the thirteenth-century fabliaux. The Priest has been eminently wise in the conduct of his affairs, generous, and hospitable. He greatly desires to make a good ending. He is thoughtful in his bequests: poor relations, poor of the town, people of small estate, orphans, nuns, Franciscans—none are forgotten; he names each individual beneficiary. He wishes to right any wrong that he may have done those among whom he has lived his life. He is genuinely troubled, at first, by his inability to leave something also to the Jacobins; it is only when the Friars urge him to revoke some of his bequests that his righteous indignation is aroused. He reveals then his skill in dissimulation. The situation which he himself creates and prolongs permits him to use his powers as a master of irony. He announces his gift at last with the comment: "It will last longer than leather; you can put your pepper in it."

These very excellences of *Li Dis de le vescie à prestre* might well lead one to think that Chaucer had never seen it: had he encountered the character of the Priest, had his attention been called to the possibilities for irony in speech and situation, he would surely have developed them in the *Summoner's Tale*, as he had developed similar matters in the *Friar's Tale*. But he had other fish to fry: the Summoner must tell a tale at the expense of a Friar; the character of the Friar must then be the important matter, not the plot, not the character of the sick man; and not irony, which, in any case, had just been exploited in the *Friar's Tale*.

E.-G. Sandras, who first called attention to this analogue of the *Summoner's Tale*, declared that "plusieurs passages sont imités fidèlement."[1] This is, manifestly, an overstatement. Yet there are resemblances or similarities, in thought if not in phrasing,[2] which suggest that Chaucer may well have known, perhaps in oral tradition, a tale very similar to *Li Dis de le vescie à prestre*.

LI DIS DE LE VESCIE
A PRESTRE

(Reprinted with minor corrections from A. de Montaiglon and G. Raynaud, *Recueil général ... des fabliaux*, III [1878], 106–17.)[3]

	En lieu de fable vos dirai	Instead of a fable. I'll tell you a true tale of a Priest ne: Antwerp,
	Un voir, ensi k'oï dire ai,	
	D'un prestre ki astoit manans	
	Deleis Anwiers; li remanans	
5	Estoit mut biaus de son avoir,	
	Car plains estoit de grant savoir.	a wise man
	Si n'avoit pas tot despendut,	
	A amasser avoit tendut,	
	S'estoit riches hons et moblés;	and a rich.
10	Buez et vaches, brebis et bleiz	
	Avoit tant c'on n'en savoit conte,	
	Mais li Mors, qui roi, duc ne conte	Being about to die
	N'espargne, l'ot par son message	
	Somont al naturel passage:	

[1] *Etude sur Chaucer considéré comme imitateur des Trouvères* (1859), pp. 237 ff.

[2] Cf. D 1765–68, 1772–73 with V, 45–51; D 1784–86 with V, 122–23; D 1873–75, 1906–8, 1936 with V, 128–29; D 1950–53 with V, 80–83; D 1955, 1958 with V, 112, 266; D 1974–77 with V, 130–31; D 2107–8 with V, 65; D 2121–25 with V, 132–39, 300; D 2126 with V, 247; D 2129 with V, 276; D 2153–54 with V, 292–95; D 2158–60 with V, 308–10. Those parallels will be recalled by references to the *Summoner's Tale* in the marginal summary or in the text of the fabliau.

[3] For substantial aid in interpretation thanks are due to Professor P. B. Fay of the University of California.

15   Eutropikes[1] ert devenus;
De nul home n'estoit tenus
Ki li promesist longe vie.
Li prestes, qui out grant envie
De bien morir et justement,

he sends for his Dean and his friends, and gives them all his property,

20   Manda tost et isnelement
Son doiien et toz ses amis,
Son avoir entre lor main mis
Por donner et por departir
Cant ilh verront que departir

to divide, when he's dead,

25   De son cors estovera l'ame:
Jouuel, cossin, pot ne escame,
Cuete,[2] tuelle, neiz une nape,
Brebis, moutons, buef, ne sa chape
Ne li remaint que tot ne donne,

among the people he names.

30   Et nome chascune persone
A qui ilh vuet c'on doinst ses chozes.

And open letters are written and authenticated in witness thereof.

Descovertes, et non pas clozes,
Lettres saeler et escrire
En fist. Que ne le vos puis dire

35   Plus briément, quant que il avoit
Ilh dona tot quant qu'il savoit,[3]
Con chil qui n'avoit esperance
D'avoir de son mal aligance,
Car sa maladie ert amere.

Two Jacobin Friars

40   Atant se sont d'Anwier dui Frere
De Saint Jake[4] issu por prechier,
Qui mut se vuelent estachier
Cant aucun desviiet ravoient.[5]
Cele part tot droit en lor voie

come to the Priest, expecting a good meal,[6]

45   Si sont chés le prestre venus.
I estre quidarent retenus
Al mangier, à joie et à feste

. . . .

Si c'autrefois esté i furent

---

[1] Dropsical.   [2] Mattress.

[3] Ll. 32–36: "He has open letters drawn up about it, and authenticated (*saeler*). In less time than I can tell you, he disposes of every earthly possession so far as his knowledge goes."

[4] Saint Jake: "Jacobin: A Jacobin or white Friar" (Cotgrave).

[5] "By bringing back to the true path anyone who has gone astray."

[6] Cf. D 1765–68, 1772–73, 1838–43.

50   Mais ne mengierent ne ne burent,
     Car malade ont trové le prestre.
     Non porquant li ont de son estre   ask how he is,
     Demandé et de son afaire.
     Ses mains manient, son viaire,   handle him,
55   Ses piés, ses jambes regarderent
     Et tot son cors mut bien tansterent;
     Si lor sembla bien par droiture   and think he must
     C'awoir ne poist de son mal cure   die.
     Ke ne l'en coviengne morir:
60   Trop lonc tans l'a laisié norrir,[1]
     Si n'est pas legiers à curer.
        "Mais des or nos covient curer,"   Friar Lewis says,
     Dist l'uns à l'autre,—"c'est passé[2]—   "We can't cure him,
                                               but he ought to give
     Ke de l'avoir k'a amassé   our house £20
65   Doinst à nostre maison .xx. livres   to mend our
     A lé,[4] por refaire nos livres;   books."[3]
     Se nos le poons ensi faire,
     A no Prius devera plaire
     Et si en seront liet no Frere."
70   —"Vos dites voir, par Dieu no pere,   "True," says Friar
     Frere Louuiz; or i para   Simon.[5]
     Liqueis miez à lui parlera
     Et mostrera nostre besongne."
        Al prestre, ki out grant esoingne   So they tell the sick
75   De maladie, ont dit sans faille: Priest that he must
                                               think of his soul,
     "Sire, chis maus mut vos travaille,   and give money for
     Vos nos sambleis mut agreveis,
     De vostre ame penser deveis;   God's use.
     Doneis por Dieu de vostre avoir."
80   Dist li prestes: "Ne puis savoir   The Priest says he's
     K'aie caché sortout ne cote   given everything for
                                               God.[6]
     Neis les linchuès[7] à coi me frote,
     Ke tout n'aie por Dieu doné."
        —"Comment aveis vos ordené,"   "Ah, but whom
85   Dient li Frere, "vo besongne?   have you given it
                                               to?
     Li Escriture nos temongne   Scripture says you
     C'on doit garder à cui on done,   must be careful."

---

[1] Develop.

[2] It is settled.   [5] Friar Simon is named in l. 249, below.

[3] Cf. D 2107–8.   [6] Cf. D 1950–53.

[4] As a bequest.   [7] Sheets.

S'emploiiet est à la persone[1]
A cui on vuet aumone faire."

The Priest says he's given his cattle to his poor relations,

90 Li prestes respont, sans contraire:
"J'ai à mes povres parentiaus
Doné brebis, vaces et viaus,

and £10 worth of corn to his poor townsmen,

Et à povres de cele vilhe
Ai doné ausi, par saint Gilhe,

95 De bleis qui vaut plus de .x. livres:
Por ce ke je soie delivres
De ce ke j'ai vers iaus mespris,
Car entor iaus mon vivre ai pris:
Si ai doné as orfenines,

besides legacies to the orphans and nuns,

100 A orfenins et à beguines
Et à gens de povre puissance,[2]
Et si ai laisiet, por pitance,
.C. souz as Freres de Cordeles."[3]

and 100 sous to the Franciscan Friars.

—"Ces amuenes si sont mut beles;

"But have you given nothing to us Jacobins?"

105 Et as Freres de no maison,
Aveis vos fait nule raison?"[4]
Ce dient li doi Frere al prestre.
"Naie, voir."—"Ce comment peut estre?

No. "What! When we're your neighbors,

En maison a tant de preudomes,

110 Et à vos prochain voisien somes,
Et si vivons mut sobrement,

and so good!

Vos ne moreis pas justement

You'll not die well if you give us nothing."[5]

Se del vostre ne nos laiiés."

The Priest says he's nothing left to give.

Li prestes trestous esmaiiés

115 Respont: "Par les oelz de ma teste,
A doner n'ai ne bleif ne beste,
Or ne argent, hanap ne cope."
Chascuns des Freres li rencope
Et li mostre par exemplaire

"Well, but you might revoke one of your other gifts, and give it us.

120 K'ilh puet un de ses dons retraire
Et rapeler por iaus doner:

We'll help your soul.[6]

"Nos nos vorimes mut pener
Ke vostre ame fust adrechie,
Car chaiens[7] a esté drechie

---

[1] Whether it is properly employed.　　　　[2] Of small estate.

[3] Freres de Cordeles: "Cordelier: A Grey Frier (of the Order of S. Francis), a Cordelier" (Cotgrave).

[4] Given no consideration.　　　　[6] Cf. D 1784–86.

[5] Cf. D 1955–58.　　　　[7] Here.

125 Soventes fois bien nostre escuele,[1]
    Et li amuene si est biele
    Ki est à nostre maison mise.
    Nos ne vestons nule chemise
    Et si vivomes en pitance.
130 Ce sache Dieus, por la valhance
    De vostre argent nel disons mie.''[3]
    Li prestes l'ot, si s'en gramie
    Et pense qu'il s'en vengera,
    S'ilh puet, et k'ilh les trufera,
135 Mar le vont or si près tenant.[5]
    As Freres respont maintenant:
        ''Appenseis sui, doner vos voelh
    .I. jouuel ke mut amer suel
    Et aime encore. Par saint Piere,
140 Je n'ai chose gaires plus chiere;
    Milh mars d'argent n'en prenderoie,
    Et, se je bien haitiés estoie,
    Je n'en voroie mie avoir
    .Ii\u2091. marchies[6] d'autre avoir;
145 Diez vos a chaiiens asseneis.
    Vostre Prieus me ramineis;
    Si vos en ferai conissanche
    Ains que de vie aie faillance.''
    Li Frere, sans duel et sans ire,
150 Ont respondut: ''Dieus le vos mire!
    Cant voleis vos que revenons,
    Et nostre Prieuz ramenrons?''
        —''Demain, je sui ou Dieu plaisir,
    Vo promesse deveis saisir
155 Ains que je trop agreveis soie.''
        Atant ont acueilli lor voie
    Li Frere; à Anwier sont venu,

(marginal glosses:)

And alms to us is so well bestowed; we never wear shirts,

and we fare hardly.''[2]

The Priest thinks he'll be revenged and trick them.[4]

So he says he'll give them a jewel

that he wouldn't take 1,000 silver marks for:

let them fetch their Prior, and he'll then tell them where the jewel is,

tomorrow.

The Friars go back to Antwerp, and tell their Chapter.

---

[1] Escuele *for* escole (*cf.* amuene *for* almosne, l. 126): ''It has been our will to take great pains that your soul should be kept in right paths, for right here (in your house) we have ofttimes conducted our schooling.'' Or, taking *escuele* to mean bowl: ''for right here in your house our bowl has had a place (on your table at mealtime).'' Either interpretation leaves the passage dubious, for the rhyme with *biele* is faulty.

[2] Cf. D 1873–75, 1906–8, 1936.   [3] Cf. D 1974–77.   [4] Cf. D 2121–23.

[5] ''To their misfortune they are pressing him so closely.''

[6] Two hundred marks; we should expect a larger figure than the *milh mars* of l. 141. The amount is reported as .Ii\u2091. *livres* in l. 163 below.

Si ont lor chapitre tenu.[1]
Chascuns s'aventure raconte,
160 Mais chil n'ont cure de lonc conte,
Ains ont dit haut en audience:
"Faites venir bone pitance.
.Ii^c. livres gaangniet avons
A .i. prestre ke nos savons
165 Malade chi à une vilhe."
Frere Nichole et Frere Gilhe,
Frere Guilhiame et Frere Ansiaus
Vinrent oïr ces nos nouviauz,
Ki mut forment lor abelissent.
170 De ces grans poisons mander fisent,
Viez vin, novel, flons[2] et pasteis.
Chil grans mangier fu mut hasteis;
Chascuns de lui bien aisier pense;
Ne burent pas vin de despense,
175 De boire et de mangier bien s'aisent,
Por le prestre le hanap baisent
Ki le jouuel lor ot promis.
Cant en lor testes orent mis
De ce bon vin, grant feste fisent;
180 Lor cloches sovent en bondissent
Ansi con ilh auuist cors saint;
N'i a voisin qui ne se saint,
Et se merveillent qui la[3] voient,
Qui miez miés[4] as preschors s'avoient
185 Por la grant merveilhe esgarder.
Nus d'iauz ne savoit garder
De mener vie deshoneste,
Car chascuns a serré la teste[5]
De bon vin et de lor pitance.
190 A lor diverse contenance
Et al maintieng et à lor estre
Semblerent bien hors de sens estre.
Chascuns ki les voit s'en merveilhe,
Et Frere Louuis s'aparailhe

Marginal notes:

A grand feast is ordered on the strength of the jewel:

big fish, old wine, flawns, and pasties.

They drink,

toast the dying Priest,

rejoice, and ring their bells as for a saint's corpse.

The neighbors wonder.

Friar Lewis asks how they can best get the Priest's promise out of him.

[1] Assembled; called a chapter meeting.

[2] flons: "Flans: Flawnes, Custards, Egge-pies" (Cotgrave).

[3] La: *the* grant feste *of l. 179.*

[4] In rivalry they come to the preachers.

[5] Pressed the head, stupefied himself.

195　De demander con faitement
　　　Il poroient plus sagement
　　　Al prestre querre lor promesse.
　　　　"Demain, auchois[1] c'on chante messe,　　*They settle that next day the Friars shall set off,*
　　　Se fera bon metre à la voie,"
200　Dist chascuns, "se Jhesus m'avoie,
　　　Anchois ke li Mors le sorprengne,
　　　Si comment ke la choze prengne,
　　　De no don aions conissance;
　　　Nos i arons mainte pitance:
205　Si s'en doit on mut bien pener.
　　　Frere Louuis, lesqueis miner　　　　　*Friar Lewis and*
　　　I voreis vos? Or le nos dites.
　　　　—"Frere Guilhiames, li ermites,　　*Friars William, Nicholas, and*
　　　En venra et Frere Nichole,
210　Bien saront dire la parole,
　　　Et si venra Frere Robiers;　　　　　*Robert (with their breviary),*
　　　Caiens[2] n'a si sage Convers,[3]
　　　Si portera no breviaire;
　　　De no Prieus n'avons ke faire."[4]　　*but not their Prior.*
215　Ensi ont le plait otriiet.
　　　　L'endemain se sont avoiiet　　　　*So in the morning the Friars go off*
　　　Tot droit vers la maison le prestre,
　　　Ja n'i cuidierent à tans estre;
　　　Mais, ains ke li jors fu passeis,　　*(though before night they wish they'd stopped at home),*
220　Amassent ilh mieus estre asseis
　　　A Anwiers dedens lor maison.
　　　Atant ont le prestre à raison
　　　Mis, et de Deu l'ont salué;　　　　*salute the Priest, and ask if he's better.*
　　　Puis demandent s'il a mué
225　Son mal en nul aligement.
　　　Li prestes mut trés sagement　　　　*The Priest welcomes them, and says he hasn't forgotten the gift for them.*
　　　Lor dit: "Bien soiiés vos venu,
　　　Je n'ai mie desconneü
　　　Le don ke promis vos avoie,
230　Encore en sui je bien en voie;

[1] auchois: *for* anchois, "before," *as in l. 201.*

[2] Here.

[3] Lay-brother, domestic servant of the convent.

[4] "With our Prior we have nothing to do; we do not require our Prior." "The priest asked the friars to bring him, but they do not. Thus there are only 4 friars, not 5, as l. 285 says" (Henry Nicol).

but they must fetch
the Aldermen and
Mayor,

Faites les eschevins[1] venir

Et le maieur, si k'awenir

Ne vos puist nule grevance;

Devant iaus la reconissance

235 Mut volentiers vos en ferai

and then he'll tell
them what and
where the jewel is.

Et la choze vos nomerai.

Et vos dirai u ele ert prise."

Entrues que li prestes devise,

Freres Robers a tant pené

Friar Robert fetch-
es the Aldermen
and Mayor.

240 K'ilh a le maieur aminé

Et toz les eschevins ensemble.

Li .IIII. Frere, ce me samble,

Les ont hautement benvigniés.

The Priest says,

Li prestes ki fu ensigniés,

245 Si a parlé premierement

Et lor a dit si faitement:

"My Friends,[2] yes-
terday Friars Lewis
and Simon came to
preach to me,

"Sangnor, vos estes mi ami,

Por Dieu, or entendeis à mi;

Frere Louuis, Frere Symons

250 Vinrent ier chi faire sermons,

K'ilh me cuidoient en santé,

Mais Dieus par sa grasce a planté

En moi maladie si grieve

C'aparant est ke mais n'en lieve.

255 Il me virent et esgarderent,

and asked if I'd
thought of my soul,

Et après si me demanderent

Se j'avoie pensé de m'ame,

Et je lor dis, par Nostre Dame,

Ke j'avoie trestot donet.

and if I'd given
their house any-
thing.

260 Ilh demanderent s'ordiné

A lor maison riens née avoie,

I said No;

Et je dis non; se Dieus m'avoie,

Il ne m'en estoit sovenu,

Or estoient trop tart venu;

265 Je n'avoie mais que doner.

and they told me I
should die in danger

" 'Non,' dissent ilh, 'trop malmener[3]

Vos voi, mavaisement moreis[4]

if I didn't give them
something.[5]

S'en cestui propoz demoreis,

Se vos ne nos doneis del vostre.'

[1] Aldermen, city fathers.

[2] Cf. D 2126.

[3] Going too far astray.

[4] You will make a bad ending, die in sin.

[5] Cf. D 1955–58.

270 Et je, par sainte patenostre,
    Ne vuelh pas morir malement.
    Si ai pensé si longement   So I've thought of a
                                                thing
    K'apenseis me sui d'une coze
    Ke j'ai en mon porpris encloze,
275 Ke j'aime mut et tieng mut chiere,   that I value very
                                                much, but that I
    Mais je lor doin en tel maniere   can't give away
    K'ilh ne l'aront tant con vivrai,   while I live,[1]
    Car onkes ne le delivrai
    En autrui garde k'en la moie.
280 Sachiés ke durement l'amoie   so much do I love it.
    Et amerai tote ma vie:
    Sans convoitise et sans envie   But I'll bestow it in
    Lor done chi en vo presence.   your presence."
        —Et ke nus n'i amene tenche,"
285 Dient al prestre li .v. Frere,[2]   The five Friars say,
                                                "Tell us what it is."
    "Dites quel choze c'est, biaz pere."
        —"Volentiers voir, c'est me vesie.   "Well, it's my
                                                Bladder.
    Se la voiiés bien netoiie,   If you'll have it
    Mieus ke de corduan varra[3]   cleaned, you can
                                                keep your pepper in
290 Et plus longement vos dura: it!"
    Se poreis ens metre vo poivre."
        —"Nos aveis vos ci por dechoivre   "False Priest!
                                                You've had us here
    Mandeis, foz prestes entesteis?   to shame us!"[4]
    Avoir nos cuidiés ahonteis,
295 Mais n'en aveis, par saint Obert,
    Bien nos teneis or por bobert."
        —"Mais vos, por beste me teneis,   "Quite true. You
                                                treated me like a
    Cant les dons que je ai doneis   brute; you asked me
    Me voleis faire recolhir.   to revoke my gifts,
                                                when I told you
300 Bien me faites le sanc bolir[5]   I'd nothing for
    Ki voleis ke je le rapiele;   you."
    Bien vos dis ke pot ne paele
    Ne riens née à doner n'avoie;
    Or me voleis metre en tel voie
305 K'en vos soit mieus l'amouene asise[6]

[1] C. D 2129–30.

[2] li .v. Frere: only four are mentioned in ll. 206–11; cf. note on l. 214.

Mieus ... varra: "It will be worth more."

[4] Cf. D 2153–54.

[5] Cf. D 2121–22.

[6] "That the alms should be better bestowed upon you."

K'en lieu u je l'euuise mise,[1]
Por ce ke de tos melhor estes."[2]

The Jacobins go
home with sorry
face;[3]

Li Jacobin baisent les testes,
Si se sunt retorné arriere

310 Vers lor maison à triste chiere,
Et tot chil ki là demorerent

and the neighbors
all laugh at them
about the cheat of
the Bladder,

De ris en aise[4] se pamerent
Por la trufe de la vesie,
Ke li prestes ot tant prisie[5]

that they feasted
over.

315 As Jacobins, ki bien en burent
Et mangierent et en rechurent[6]
De vin et de poissons pitance.

Jakes de Baisiu
translated this joke
because he

JAKES DE BAISIU, sans dotance,
L'a de Tieus[7] en Romanc rimée

enjoyed it.

320 Por la trufe qu'il a amée.

THE THREE *EXEMPLA* IN THE SUMMONER'S TALE[8]

The Friar is holding forth to Thomas concerning the sin of
anger, most dangerous when a wrathful man is set in high place.
To prove his point he recites three *exempla*. He names Seneca
as the author of the first but mentions no source for the others.
All three are to be found in the *De ira*.

(From Seneca, *Moral Essays*, ed. John W. Basore ["Loeb Classical Library"
(1928)].)

Gnaeus Piso con-
demned a soldier to
death because his
companion was
missing.

Cn. Piso fuit memoria nostra vir a multis vitiis integer, sed pravus
et cui placebat pro constantia rigor. Is cum iratus duci iussisset
eum, qui ex commeatu sine commilitone redierat, quasi interfecisset
quem non exhibebat, roganti tempus aliquod ad conquirendum non

The execution was
about to take place
when the com-
panion appeared.
The centurion led
both men to Piso,

dedit. Damnatus extra vallum productus est et iam cervicem porrige-
bat, cum subito apparuit ille commilito qui occisus videbatur. Tunc
centurio supplicio praepositus condere gladium speculatorem iubet,

[1] "Than in any place in which I might have bestowed it."

[2] "Because you are the best of all."

[3] Cf. D 2158–60. [5] Vaunted, extolled.

[4] Almost. [6] Received for it.

[7] Tieus, tiois: *MS* niex. "La présence dans ce fabliau de la ville d'Anvers nous
prouve bien que le *tiois* auquel il est emprunté est simplement du néerlandais"
(Montaiglon-Raynaud, III, 357 f.).

[8] D 2017–42, 2043–73, and 2079–84.

damnatum ad Pisonem reducit redditurus Pisoni innocentiam; nam militi fortuna reddiderat. Ingenti concursu deducuntur complexi alter alterum cum magno gaudio castrorum commilitones. Conscendit tribunal furens Piso ac iubet duci utrumque, et eum militem qui non occiderat et eum qui non perierat. Quid hoc indignius? Quia unus innocens apparuerat, duo peribant. Piso adiecit et tertium. Nam ipsum centurionem, qui damnatum reduxerat, duci iussit. Constituti sunt in eodem illo loco perituri tres ob unius innocentiam. O quam sollers est iracundia ad fingendas causas furoris! "Te," inquit, "duci iubeo, quia damnatus es; te, quia causa damnationis commilitoni fuisti; te, quia iussus occidere imperatori non paruisti." Excogitavit quemadmodum tria crimina faceret, quia nullum invenerat [I. xviii. 3–6].

who ordered three executions, that of the first soldier because previously condemned, the second as cause of this condemnation, the centurion for not having obeyed.

Cambysen regem nimis deditum vino Praexaspes unus ex carissimis monebat, ut parcius biberet, turpem esse dicens ebrietatem in rege, quem omnium oculi auresque sequerentur. Ad haec ille: "Ut scias," inquit, "quemadmodum numquam excidam mihi, adprobabo iam et oculos post vinum in officio esse et manus." Bibit deinde liberalius quam alias capacioribus scyphis et iam gravis ac vinolentus obiurgatoris sui filium procedere ultra limen iubet adlevataque super caput sinistra manu stare. Tunc intendit arcum et ipsum cor adulescentis, id enim petere se dixerat, figit rescissoque pectore haerens in ipso corde spiculum ostendit ac respiciens patrem interrogavit, satisne certam haberet manum.[1] .... Accessit itaque ad numerum eorum, qui magnis cladibus ostenderunt, quanti constarent regum amicis bona consilia [iii. xiv. 1–6].

King Cambyses, urged by his friend Praexaspes to drink less, said he could show that his eyes and hands could always perform their duty. He drank more, ordered the son of his critic to stand before him, and shot him through the heart. Advising kings is perilous.

Hic iratus fuit genti et ignotae et immeritae, sensurae tamen; Cyrus flumini. Nam cum Babylona oppugnaturus festinaret ad bellum, cuius maxima momenta in occasionibus sunt, Gynden late fusum amnem vado transire temptavit, quod vix tutum est, etiam cum sensit aestatem et ad minimum deductus est. Ibi unus ex iis equis, qui trahere regium currum albi solebant, abreptus vehementer commovit regem; iuravit itaque se amnem illum regis comitatus auferentem eo redacturum, ut transiri calcarique etiam a feminis posset. Hoc deinde omnem transtulit belli apparatum et tam diu adsedit operi, donec centum et octoginta cuniculis divisum alveum in trecentos et sexaginta rivos dispergeret, siccum relinqueret in diversum fluentibus aquis [iii. xxi. 1–3].

Cambyses raged against a people, Cyrus against a river. As he was fording the Gyndes, one of the horses of his chariot was swept away. He swore that he would reduce the river to almost nothing, had runways cut, and left the channel dry.

[1] The rest of the story shows that anger may be restrained by the stronger influence of fear; with that thesis Chaucer, manifestly, is not concerned.

THE CLERK'S TALE

By J. BURKE SEVERS

INTRODUCTION[1]

O F FOLK-TALE origin, the story of Griselda assumed literary form in the middle of the fourteenth century. Boccaccio first told the narrative in his native Italian and put it at the conclusion of his famous century of tales, the *Decameron* (1353). Thence Petrarch took it, twenty years later (1373–74), retelling the story in Latin and elaborating upon the almost bare outline which he had from Boccaccio. Almost simultaneously with Petrarch's redaction, Giovanni Sercambi, likewise relying upon Boccaccio, retold the story of the patient marchioness (*ca.* 1374), retaining the Italian language and condensing rather than expanding the *novella*. After these versions, all emanating from Italy in the third quarter of the fourteenth century and all based upon the original Italian version of Boccaccio, the scene shifts to France, the time changes to the last quarter of the century, and the model becomes Petrarch's Latin rather than Boccaccio's Italian. There appeared two prose French translations of Petrarch's version: one by Philippe de Mézières (1384–89)—the version which, with some changes, found its way into *Le Ménagier de Paris* (*ca.* 1393)—and, more important for our purposes, an anonymous prose translation, less verbose and more literal than De Mézières', of indefinite date, but certainly written before Chaucer created the *Clerkes Tale.* Before the close of the century Walter and his bride were also presented in a French play, *L'Estoire de la Marquise de Saluce miz par personnages et rigmé* (1395), based upon De Mézières' translation from Petrarch. One other telling of the story which originated in France may also have been in existence before Chaucer died: it is in Latin verse, based upon Petrarch, and, according to the unique manuscript in the Biblio-

[1] Proof of all generalizations made in this introduction will be found in the editor's study, "The Literary Relationships of Chaucer's *Clerkes Tale*" (see bibliography at end of this introduction).

thèque de Poitiers (MS 93, fol. 96ᵛ), "metrificata per P. de Hailles."

All these versions were antecedent to or contemporary with Chaucer's *Clerkes Tale;* but, of them all, the English poet used only two in composing his poem: Petrarch's Latin letter and the anonymous French prose translation of it. Claims have been brought forward also for Chaucer's dependence upon the *Decameron* and *Le Ménagier;* but the parallels between them and the *Clerkes Tale* are neither numerous enough nor important enough to be convincing. Of his two sources, Chaucer consulted both regularly throughout the composing process, from first stanza to last. He leaned more heavily, however, upon the French. Echoes of the French text are much more frequent than echoes of the Latin. Based upon the number of lines in the *Clerkes Tale* giving some hint as to their derivation, the ratio is almost five to three in favor of the French. Moreover, the intervals between such echoes from the French are much shorter than from the Latin; that is, there occur in the text of Chaucer's poem rather frequent patches of considerable length in which no definite echo of the Latin text appears, but such lengthy stretches between lines reflecting the French text are much less common.

Although Chaucer relied chiefly upon his French source, there is reason for believing that he started out—both in the poem as a whole and at the beginning of each part—with the intention of relying about equally upon Latin and French; his purpose, however, did not hold for long, and he soon yielded to the natural temptation of leaning more heavily upon the French redaction, which, because of its greater simplicity and smoother flow, lent itself more easily to conversion into English verse. Apparently, his method of procedure was to read a passage in Petrarch's Latin, then to read the corresponding passage in the French translation, and finally, under the immediate influence of this double recital, to set down his own version, stanza by stanza. Since his French source was a rather close translation of his Latin, Chaucer found the sequence of events in them identical; and he made no changes in this sequence. Indeed, discounting his frequent expansions and infrequent omissions, his tale is virtually a sentence-for-sentence paraphrase; and in not many more than half-a-dozen passages is there displacement of one of the sentences. Of course, instances of double translation, and especially of alternation of emphasis, now upon one source, now upon the other, are not uncommon.

Despite this close reliance upon his sources, Chaucer made significant changes in characterization, in narrative technique, and in the whole tone and spirit which informs the tale. Walter, for instance, emerges in Chaucer's version as more obstinately wilful, more heartlessly cruel than he had been in either the Latin or the French; and Chaucer cannot refrain from adding outspoken and vehement condemnation of the marquis and of the people who condoned the repudiation of Griselda. In this respect, Chaucer more nearly approaches the attitude of Boccaccio than of Petrarch, assuming a point of view intermediate between the two. Chaucer also sympathizes with Griselda more deeply than either Petrarch or the anonymous French translator. By adding half-a-dozen passages, ranging in length from a few lines to a stanza or more, he heightens throughout the gentle submissiveness and meek obedience of Griselda. Yet he saves her from utter colorlessness and the complete submersion of her will in that of her lord by portraying her as feeling more poignantly than the heroine of the sources her husband's cruelty and inconstancy; by bestowing upon her the courage to give utterance to her feelings; and by allowing her even to pass judgment upon her husband's actions in a speech which has more than a hint of implied reproach in it—all emphases which are original with Chaucer and not to be found in either Latin or French source. Other alterations in character he likewise effects: Janicola he makes more realistically emotional, the sergeant who takes away the children more darkly sinister, Walter's subjects more expressive of fealty and obedience. In the details of plot, Chaucer introduces numerous, though generally not very extensive, changes and additions, the nature of which can be indicated only by selected examples, such as Griselda's plea to the sergeant that she be allowed to say goodbye to her baby girl before it be borne away to its fate, and her stanza-long farewell to the infant; her going to the gate in her mean habiliments among the crowd of folk who stream forth to greet the new marquise; and her double swoon and long speech in the reconciliation scene—this last by all odds constituting Chaucer's longest single expansion in the whole poem.

In preparing the texts of the two sources which are presented in the following pages, the editor has in both instances selected as base that manuscript which in itself came closest to duplicating the readings of the text from which Chaucer worked when he wrote the *Clerkes Tale*. Selection of the base, therefore, involved a thorough, detailed study of the variants in all the manuscripts. This study revealed that the manuscripts of the Latin source fall into two groups: those giving an earlier version of the tale as Petrarch first wrote it in 1373 and those giving a final version containing a few revisory touches added by Petrarch when, just about a month before he died, in 1374, he inserted the story in the *Epistolae seniles*. Since Chaucer carried over into his poem clear echoes of Petrarch's final slight additions, we know that the Latin manuscript which lay before Chaucer as he composed his tale contained the final, somewhat fuller version of 1374,[1] and it is this text, of course, which is here presented.

The text of each source, Latin and French, has been accurately transcribed from the base manuscript, except that the manuscript symbols for *u-v* in both texts, and for *i-j* in the French, have been silently regularized, *u* and *i* being printed for vowels, *v* and *j* for consonants. Every other departure from the base, however slight, is recorded in the first set of variants, immediately below the last line of text on each page. Minor emendations are made with no indication of the manuscripts which have afforded the correct reading; but, in recording all emendations of any importance, I have added in parentheses the manuscripts from which the emendations have been drawn. Obviously erroneous readings in the base manuscript have been emended, but errors which there is reason to believe were also present in the text which Chaucer used are allowed to stand

---

[1] This bears upon the question whether Chaucer met Petrarch on his visit to Italy in 1373 and received personally from the great humanist's hands his manuscript of the Griseldis letter. Since the English poet left London on December 1, 1372, and returned May 23, 1373 (see F. J. Mather, "An Inedited Document concerning Chaucer's First Italian Journey," *MLN*, XI [1896], 419–25), he could hardly have been presented with a manuscript which was not finished until June 8, 1374! ("Inter colles Euganeos, vi Idus Iunias, MCCCLXXIIII," Lac, fol. 155ʳ).

unaltered. Emendations have also been made to rescue the Latin text from the peculiar, individual spelling of its scribe, and from his annoying habit of altering the word order. Since, however, every deviation from the base manuscript is scrupulously recorded in the first set of variants, the text and variants together afford an absolutely literal transcription of the base manuscript.

In the second set of variants, headed "Var.," have been recorded all manuscript readings which come closer to the content or phraseology of Chaucer's poem than do the corresponding readings in the base. If these variants are comparatively few, and if the correspondence between them and Chaucer's text frequently is weak or even apparently fortuitous, the editor would observe that precisely this condition is to be expected if the task of selecting the base manuscript has been carefully performed; for the closer the base manuscript to the text of the source that Chaucer actually employed, the fewer and weaker will be the correspondences between other manuscripts and Chaucer's poem. We may, therefore, feel confident that Chaucer's source manuscripts differed but little from the texts presented in the following pages.

The editor is responsible for the division of the Latin text into parts corresponding to the parts of Chaucer's tale; but the divisions in the French text, which do not always coincide with Chaucer's, are present in the manuscript itself. Punctuation and capitalization throughout have been brought into conformity with modern usage. The numbers in the margin to the left of the texts refer to the corresponding lines in the *Clerkes Tale*.

LIST OF MANUSCRIPTS

I. Latin[1]

Bay₅   Bayerische Staatsbibliothek, Munich. MS 5311. Fifteenth century. Fols. 245ʳ–253ʳ. Family *a*.

Bay₇   Bayerische Staatsbibliothek, Munich. MS 78. Fifteenth century (1451). Fols. 90ᵛ–95ʳ. Family *d*.

---

[1] The Latin manuscripts fall into four families: family *d* gives the original text composed by Petrarch in 1373; families *a*, *b*, and *c* give the text (in differing degrees of accuracy) as it was slightly revised by Petrarch in 1374 about a month before his death. The text which Chaucer used derived from family *a* of the 1374 version.

Bod Bodleian Library, Oxford. MS Lat. Misc. d.34. Late fifteenth century. Fols. 46^r–53^v. Family c.

CC$_2$ Corpus Christi College, Cambridge. MS 275. Fifteenth century. Fols. 163^r–168^v. Family b.

CC$_4$ Corpus Christi College, Cambridge. MS 458. Fifteenth century (1467). Fols. 108^r–121^v. Family d.

Chig Biblioteca Apostolica Vaticana, Rome. MS Chigiano L, VII, 262. Fifteenth century. Fols. 69^v–74^r. Family d, contaminated with family a and/or family b.

Cs Print. *Originals and Analogues of Some of Chaucer's Canterbury Tales*, Part II, pp. 151–70. London, 1875. This gives the text of "Petrarchae Opera, Basileae, 1581, p. 541" (p. 151); "Mr. Hales has .... kindly revised the Latin text" (p. 150). Family a, contaminated with family d.

Har$_2$ British Museum, London. MS Harley 2492. Fifteenth century. Fols. 288^v–293^v. Family d.

Har$_3$ British Museum, London. MS Harley 3081. Fifteenth century. Fols 223^r–228^v. Family a.

Lac Biblioteca Medicea Laurenziana, Florence. MS Acquisti e Doni 266. Fifteenth (?) century. Fols. 151^v–154^v. Family a.

Laur$_2$ Biblioteca Medicea Laurenziana, Florence. MS 78.2. Fifteenth century. Fols. 112^r–118^v. Family a.

Laur$_3$ Biblioteca Medicea Laurenziana, Florence. MS 78.3. Fifteenth century. Fols. 221^v–227^v. Family a.

Mgd Magdalen College, Oxford. MS Lat. 39. Fifteenth century. Fols. 24^v–34^r. Family c.

Mlb Biblioteca nazionale centrale, Florence. MS Magliabechiano II, IV, 109. Fifteenth century. Fols. 21^r–25^r. Family b.

P$_1$ Bibliothèque nationale, Paris. MS Lat. 11291. Fifteenth century. Fols. 11^v–18^r. Family d.

P$_6$ Bibliothèque nationale, Paris. MS Lat. 16232. Fifteenth century (beginning). Fols. 99^r–103^r. Family d.

P$_7$ Bibliothèque nationale, Paris. MS Lat. 17165. Fifteenth century (beginning). Fols. 191^r–193^r. Family d.

Pal Biblioteca Apostolica Vaticana, Rome. MS Pal. Lat. 1625. Fifteenth century (1479). Fols. 248^r–256^v. Family d.

Ra Print. *Francisci Petrarchae Florentini .... Opera quae extant omnia.* Basle, 1581. Four volumes in one. "Basiliae, per Sebastianvm Henric Petri, anno a virgineo partv MDXXCI mense martio" (at end of Vol. IV). Vol. I, pp. 540–46. (Yale, Hc 52.05.) Family a.

Rb Print. *Librorum Francisci Petrarche Impressorum Annotatio.* Venice, 1503. "Impressum Venetiis per Simonem Papiensem dictum Biuilaquam. Anno domini 1503 die uero 15 Iulii" (p. 493^r). Pp. 201^r–203^r. (Yale, z103.o126.) Family a.

Rc Print. *Epistola .... de Historia Griseldis. ....* Cologne, 1470? Edition of Ulrich Zell. Eleven unnumbered leaves. (British Museum, I.A. 2833.) Family *d.*

Ricc   Biblioteca Riccardiana, Florence. MS 805. Fifteenth century. Fols. 13^v–19^r. Family *b.*

Vat$_3$ Biblioteca Apostolica Vaticana, Rome. MS Vat. Lat. 3355. Fifteenth century. Fols. 129^v–136^r. Family *b.*

Vat$_6$ Biblioteca Apostolica Vaticana, Rome. MS Vat. Lat. 1666. Fourteenth century. Fols. 17^r–21^v. Family *a.* (This manuscript is the base for the present edition.)

II. FRENCH

BB   Stadtbibliothek, Bern. MS 209. Fourteenth or fifteenth century. Fols. 1^r–4^v.

PA   Bibliothèque de l'arsenal, Paris. MS 2076. Fifteenth century. Fols. 225^r–238^r.

PN$_1$ Bibliothèque nationale, Paris. MS fr. 1505. Late fifteenth century. Fols. 126^r–134^v.

PN$_2$ Bibliothèque nationale, Paris. MS fr. 1165. Early fifteenth century. Fols. 85^r–93^v.

PN$_3$ Bibliothèque nationale, Paris. MS fr. 12459. Fifteenth century. Fols. 135^r–142^v. (This manuscript is the base for the present edition.)

PN$_4$ Bibliothèque nationale, Paris. MS fr. 20042. Fifteenth century (1436). Fols. 50^v–59^v.

PN$_7$ Bibliothèque nationale, Paris. MS n.a. fr. 4511. Fifteenth century. Fols. 7^r–23^v.

SELECTED BIBLIOGRAPHY

AVENA, A. "Per la cronologia delle Epistole di Francesco Petrarca," *Atti e Memorie dell'Accademia d'Agricoltura, Scienze, Lettere, Arti, e Commercio di Verona,* Ser. IV, Vol. V, Fasc. 1 (Vol. LXXX of the whole collection). Verona, 1904–5. Pp. 21–27.

CATE, W. A. "The Problem of the Origin of the Griselda Story," *Studies in Philology,* XXIX (1932), 389–405.

COOK, A. S. "Chaucer's *Clerk's Tale* and a French Version of His Original," *Romanic Review,* VIII (1917), 210–22.

FARNHAM, W. E. "Chaucer's *Clerk's Tale,*" *Modern Language Notes,* XXXIII (1918), 193–203.

FRENCH, R. D. *A Chaucer Handbook.* New York, 1929. (Contains a translation of Petrarch's Latin prose tale, pp. 291–311.)

GOLENISTCHEFF-KOUTOUZOFF, E. *L'Histoire de Griseldis en France au XIVe et au XVe siècle.* Paris, 1933.

GRIFFITH, D. D. *The Origin of the Griselda Story.* "University of Washington Publications in Language and Literature," Vol. VIII. Seattle, 1931.

HENDRICKSON, G. L. "Chaucer and Petrarch: Two Notes on the 'Clerk's Tale,'" *Modern Philology,* IV (1906–7), 179–92.

JUSSERAND, J. J. "Did Chaucer Meet Petrarch?" *Nineteenth Century*, XXXIX (January–June, 1896), 993–1005.

MATHER, F. J. "On the Asserted Meeting of Chaucer and Petrarch," *Modern Language Notes*, Vol. XII (1897), cols. 1–18.

Originals and Analogues of Some of Chaucer's Canterbury Tales. "Chaucer Society Publications." London, 1872–87. Pp. 149–76, 525–40, 549–50.

PICHON, J. (ed.). *Le Ménagier de Paris.* Paris, 1846. I, 99–124.

SEVERS, J. B. "Chaucer's Source MSS. for the *Clerkes Tale*," *Publications of the Modern Language Association*, XLVII (1932), 431–52.

———. "The Job Passage in the *Clerkes Tale*," *Modern Language Notes*, XLIX (1934), 461–62.

———. "The Literary Relationships of Chaucer's *Clerkes Tale*." (Yale doctoral dissertation, 1935.)

[*EPISTOLAE SENILES*
BOOK XVII, LETTER III]

⟨fol. 17ʳ⟩ Francisci Petrarce, Poete Laureati, de Insigni
Obedientia et Fide Uxoris, ad Johannem
Bocacium de Certaldo . . . .[1]

[Pars I]

E 57, 45   ⟨fol. 17ᵛ⟩ Est ad Ytalie latus occiduum Vesullus ex Apenini   At the foot of the mountains
       iugis mons unus altissimus, qui, vertice nubila superans,   2   on one side of Italy lies the land of Saluzzo.
       liquido sese ingerit etheri, mons suapte nobilis natura, Padi

E 50   ortu nobilissimus, qui eius e latere fonte lapsus exiguo, orien-   4
       tem contra solem fertur, mirisque mox tumidus incrementis
       brevi spacio decurso, non tantum maximorum unus amnium   6
       sed fluviorum a Virgilio rex dictus, Liguriam gurgite violentus

E 51   intersecat; dehinc Emiliam atque Flaminiam Veneciamque   8
       disterminans multis ad ultimum et ingentibus hostijs in Adria-
       cum mare descendit. Ceterum pars illa terrarum de qua   10
       primum dixi, que et grata planicie et interiectis collibus ac
       montibus circumflexis, aprica pariter ac iocunda est, atque ab   12
       eorum quibus subiacet pede montium nomen tenet, et civi-

E 58   tates aliquot et opida habet egregia. Inter cetera, ad radicem   14
       Vesulli, terra Saluciarum vicis et castellis satis frequens,
       marchionum arbitrio nobilium quorundam regitur virorum,   16   Its first and greatest ruler,

E 64   quorum unus primusque omnium et maximus fuisse traditur   Walter, was young, hand- some, and noble.
       Valterius quidam, ad quem familie ac terrarum omnium   18
       regimen pertineret; et hic quidem forma virens atque etate,

E 71   nec minus moribus quam sanguine nobilis, et ad summam   20

(**Vat₆.**) Title: Laureati] leureati.
2   nubila] nubilla.
3   nobilis] nobillis.
4   nobilissimus] nobillissimus.
5   solem] sollem.
7   gurgite violentus] violentus gurgite.
14   egregia] eggregia.
16   nobilium] nobillium.
18   ad quem] atque *within the line is corrected to* ad quem *in the margin.*
20   nobilis] nobillis—summam] sumam.

(**Var.**) 15   vicis] aliis villis micis *P₆*.
18   quidam] nomine *CC₂*.

---

[1] The introductory "Librum tuum . . . . Hec prefatus, incipio" is
omitted.

LE LIVRE GRISELDIS

[Preface]

⟨fol. 135ʳ⟩ Au commandement et soubz la correccion de mon
maistre, et a l'exemplaire des femmes mariees et toutes autres,   2
j'ay mis, selon mon petit engin et entendement, de latin en françois
l'ystoire de Griseldis qui cy aprés s'ensuit de la constance et pacience   4
merveilleuse d'une femme. Laquelle hystoire translata de lombart en
latin un tres vaillant et moult solennel poete, appellez François Pe-   6
trach, dont Dieux ait l'ame. Amen.

Et commence le premier chappitre.   8

[I]

E 57   Au pié des mons en un costé d'Ytalie est la terre de Saluces, qui
jadis estoit moult peuplee de bonnes villes et chastiaulx, en laquelle   2
E 64 avoit plusieurs grans seigneurs et gentilz hommes, desquelz le premier
et le plus grant on treuve avoir esté un marquis appellez en son propre   4
nom Wautier, auquel principaument appartenoit le gouvernement
E 71 et dominacion d'icelle terre. Bel et jeune seigneur estoit, moult noble   6

E 78 omni ex parte vir insignis, nisi quod presenti sua sorte
contentus, incuriosissimus futurorum erat. Itaque venatui 22
aucupioque deditus, sic illis incubuerat ut alia pene cuncta
E 85 negligeret; quodque in primis egre populi ferebant, ab ipsis 24
quoque coniugij conscilijs abhorreret. Id aliquamdiu taciti
cum tulissent, tandem catervatim illum adeunt quorum unus 26
cui vel auctoritas maior erat vel facundia maiorque cum suo
E 92 duce familiaritas, "Tua," inquit, "humanitas, optime mar- 28
chio, hanc nobis prestat audaciam, ut et tecum singuli quociens
res exposcit devota fiducia colloquamur, et nunc omnium 30
E 99 tacitas voluntates mea vox tuis auribus invehat, non quod
singulare aliquid habeam ad hanc rem, nisi quod tu me inter 32
E 106 alios carum tibi multis indicijs comprobasti. Cum merito
igitur tua nobis omnia placeant, semperque placuerint, ut 34
felices nos tali domino iudicemus. Unum est, quod si a te
impetrari sinis teque nobis exorabilem prebes, plane felicissimi 36
finitimorum omnium futuri simus: ut coniugio scilicet animum
E 113 applices, collumque non liberum modo sed imperiosum legip- 38
timo subicias iugo, idque quam primum facias. Volant enim
E 120 dies rapidi, et quamquam florida sis etate, continue tamen 40
hunc florem tacita senectus insequitur, morsque ipsa omni
proxima est etati. Nulli muneris huius immunitas datur, 42
eque omnibus moriendum est; utque id certum, sic illud am-
E 127 biguum quando eveniat. Suscipe igitur, oramus, eorum preces 44
qui nullum tuum imperium recusarent. Querende autem
coniugis studium nobis linque, talem enim tibi procurabimus 46
que te merito digna sit, et tam claris orta parentibus ut de ea
E 134 spes optima sit habenda. Libera tuos omnes molesta solici- 48

(sidenotes:)

Occupied with the pleasures of the present, he was careless of the future—especially of marriage and offspring

One day his subjects came to him, and their spokesman said: "Noble marquis, we rejoice in such a kind and noble lord.

One boon, however, would make us the happiest of men: namely, that you marry as soon as possible for old age and death come quickly.

We shall select for you a worthy, noble wife. Free us we pray, of fear lest you die issueless, leaving us without a lord."

(Vat₆.) 22 Itaque] Itemque (Itaque *Cs, P₁, P₆, P₇, Ra, Rb, Rc, Lac, Laur₃, Chig, Vat₃, CC₄, CC₂, Mgd, Ricc, Mlb, Pal, Bay₇, Har₂, Har₃, Bod, Laur₂*).

    23 alia] allia.
    25 abhorreret] aboreret.
    25–26 taciti cum tulissent] cum tulissent taciti.
    30 exposcit] expossit—colloquamur] coloquamur.
    33 alios] allios.
    35 tali] talli.
    36 exorabilem] exorabillem.
    37 finitimorum] finittimorum.
    37–38 scilicet animum applices] animum scilicet aplices.
    38 collumque] columque.
    46 talem] tallem.

(Var.) 38 imperiosum] imperio *P₆*, imperio sub *Bay₅*, imperio cum *with* cum *corrected to* sum(?) *in the margin Bay₇.*

de lignaige et plus assez en bonnes meurs, et en somme noble en
78 toutes manieres, fors tant qu'il ne vouloit que soy jouer et esbatre   8
et passer temps ne ne consideroit point au temps ne es choses a venir.
Et ainsy tant seulement a chacier et a voler prenoit son desduit et   10
plaisir, car de toutes autres choses peu lui chaloit. Et mesmement
85 ne se vouloit point marier, dont sur toutes les autres choses le peuple   12
estoit courroucié, en tant que une fois ⟨fol. 135ᵛ⟩ tous ensemble alerent
a lui, desquelz un de plus grant auctorité, beau parleur et bien privez   14
92 dudit seigneur, lui va dire: "Ton humanité, sire marquis, nous donne
hardiesse que, toutesfois que besoing nous fait, parlions a toy feauble-   16
ment et hardiement; et veez cy que je te veul dire de par tous tes
99 hommes et subgez. Non pas que j'aye aucune singularité a ceste chose,   18
fors que entre les autres tu m'as chier de ta grace, comme en maintes
06 manieres je l'ay approuvé. Et comme, doncques, et a bonne cause,   20
tous tes fais nous plaisent et tousjours nous aient pleu, si que nous nous
tenons pour moult eureux que t'avons a seigneur. Mais une chose est,   22
laquelle se tu nous veulz accorder et ottroier, nous serons, ce nous
13 semble, les plus aises de tous noz voisins: c'est assavoir que tu te   24
20 vueilles marier sans plus attendre, car le temps passe et s'en va. Et
ja soit ce que soyes jeune et en fleur de jeunesce, toutesfois ceste fleur   26
viellesce, sans dire mot, la suist et chasse, et est la mort prochaine a
tout aage, ne aucun ne lui eschappe. Et ainsy fault il mourir l'um   28
comme l'autre; et ne scet homme ou, ne quant, ne comment. Or,
27 doncques, reçoys et accepte, nous te supplions, les prieres et requestes   30
de ceulx qui nulz tiens commandemens ne refuseroient. Et nous
vueilles chargier de toy querir femme; et nous la te procurerons telle   32
que sera digne de toy avoir, et de si bon et si grant lieu que, par raison,
34 devras esperer tout bien d'elle. Delivres nous doncques, nous t'en   34

(PN₃.) 14   un] *om.* (un *PN₂*, *PN₇*, *BB*, *PN₄*).

27   viellesce, sans dire mot, la suist et chasse] enveillist sans dire mot et la suit et chasse villesce (viellesce sans dire mot la suist et chasse *PN₂*, *BB*, *PA*).

(Var.) 7 plus] plain *PN₁*.
10   prenoit] prenoit tout *PA*.
14   de plus grant auctorité] des plus sages *PN₁*.
16   fait] est nous *PN₇*, *BB*, *PN₁*, *PA*.
31   nulz tiens commandemens ne refuseroient] nul tien commandement ne refuseroient *PN₂*, *PN₇*, *BB*, *PN₄*, nulle foiz refuieront(?) ton commandement *PN₁*.

tudine, quesumus, ne si quid humanitus tibi forsan accideret, tu sine tuo successore abeas, ipsi sine votivo rectore remane- 50
E 141 ant." Moverunt pie preces animum viri, et "Cogitis," in- quit, "me, amici, ad id quod michi in animum nunquam 52 venit; ⟨fol. 18ʳ⟩ delectabar omnimoda libertate, que in coni-
E 148 ugio rara est. Ceterum subiectorum michi voluntatibus me 54 sponte subicio, et prudencie vestre fisus et fidei. Illam vobis quam offertis querende curam coniugis remicto, eamque 56 humeris meis ipse subeo. Quid unius enim claritas confert
E 155 alteri? Sepe filij dissimillimi sunt parentum. Quicquid in 58 homine boni est, non ab alio quam a Deo est. Illi ego et status et matrimonij mei sortes, sperans de sua solita pietate, com- 60 miserim; ipse michi inveniet quod quieti mee sit expediens ac saluti. Itaque quando vobis ita placitum est, uxorem ducam: 62 id vobis bona fide polliteor, vestrumque desiderium nec
E 162 frustrabor equidem nec morabor. Unum vos michi versa vice 64 promictite ac servate: ut quamcunque coniugem ipse delegero,
E 169 eam vos summo honore ac veneratione prosequamini, nec sit 66 ullus inter vos qui de meo unquam iudicio aut litiget aut queratur. Vestrum fuerit me omnium quos novissem liber- 68 rimum iugo subiecisse coniugij; mea sit iugi ipsius electio; que- cumque uxor mea erit, illa, ceu Romani principis filia, domina 70
E 176 vestra sit." Promictunt unanimiter ac lete nichil defuturum, ut quibus vix possibile videretur optatum diem cernere nup- 72
E 183 tiarum, de quibus in diem certum magnificentissime ap-

Walter answered: "I never thought to marry, for I have rejoiced in my liberty. Yet I submit to your wish.

My wife, however, I shall choose myself. You, on your part, must promise that whomever I choose you will honor as your mistress."

They promised, and the marquis gave orders to pre- pare for the nuptials and fixed the wedding day.

(Vat₆.) 49 quesumus] quesimus (quesumus Cs, P₁, P₆, P₇, Ra, Rb, Lac, Laur₃, Chig, Vat₃, CC₄, Mgd, Ricc, Bay₇, Har₂, Har₃, Bod, Laur₂).
50 abeas] habeas *with* h *erased, and above is written* id est recedas.
58 filij dissimillimi] fillij disimilimi.
60 et matrimonij] matrimonij (et matrimonij Cs, P₁, P₆, P₇, Ra, Rb, Rc, Lac, Chig, Vat₃, CC₄, CC₂, Mgd, Ricc, Mlb, Pal, Bay₇, Bay₅, Bod, Laur₂).
60–61 commiserim] comiserim.
61 sit] scit (sit Cs, P₁, P₆, P₇, Ra, Rb, Rc, Lac, Laur₃, CC₄, CC₂, Mgd, Pal, Bay₇, Bay₅, Har₂, Bod)—ac] an (ac Cs, P₁, P₆, P₇, Ra, Rb, Lac, Laur₃, Chig, Vat₃, CC₄, CC₂, Mgd, Ricc, Mlb, Bay₇, Har₂, Har₃, Bod, Laur₂).
62 placitum est] placitum (placitum est Cs, P₆, P₇, Ra, Rb, Laur₃, CC₂, Mgd, Bod.)
66 summo] sumo.
69 iugi] iugij (iugi Cs, P₆, Ra, Rb, Lac, Laur₃, Bay₇, Bay₅, Har₃, Bod.)
70 filia] fillia.
72 possibile] posibille.

(Var.) 53 delectabar omnimoda libertate] delectabar enim mea lib- ertate CC₂.
59 ego] ergo P₁, P₆, Cs, Ra, Rb, Rc, CC₂, Pal, Bay₇, Laur₂.

prions, de grant cusençon affin que se tu mouroies nous ne demouris-
sions sans seigneur et gouverneur." 36

141   Lors esmeurent les doulces parolles de ses subgetz ledit seigneur, et
respondi: "Vous me contraignez, mes amis," dist il, "a ce que je n'euz 38
oncques en pensee. Je me delittoye en franchise, qui peu souvent
148 est en mariage, mais je me vueil soubmettre maintenant aux bonnes 40
voulentez et conseil de vous mes subgez, moy confiant de vostre foy,
loyauté, et prudence. Et vous laisse la cure et cusençon, comme vous 42
vous y offrez, de moy querir femme. Et puis qu'il vous plaist, je me
marieray, et je le vous promés en bonne foy, ne pas n'atendray longue- 44
162 ment. Une chose toutesfois vous me promettrez et garderez: que
quelconque que je esliray et prandray a femme, vous l'onnourerez 46
169 souverainement, ne ja aucun de vous ne mesparlera de mon jugement, plaindra ne murmurera ⟨fol. 136ʳ⟩ aucunement. Et vueil qu'il 48
soit en mon chois et voulenté de prendre telle femme comme il me
plaira. Et quelconque qu'elle soit, vous l'aurez en honnour et rever- 50
ence et pour dame la tendrez, comme se elle estoit fille d'emperiere
ou de roy." 52

176   Et lors tous lui promistrent et d'un consentement moult voulentiers, comme ceulx a qui il ne sembloit pas que ja peussent veoir le 54
183 jour des nopces. Et fut pris et ordonné un jour, dedens lequel le

(**PN₃.**) 53   d'un] du (d'un *PN₂, PN₇, BB, PN₄, PN₁, PA*).

(**Var.**) 37   parolles] prieres *PN₂, PN₇, BB*, parolles et prieres *PN₁, PN₄, PA*—
ledit seigneur] ledit marquiz *PN₇*.
    43   vous y offrez] m'offrés *PA*.

parandis domini iubentis edictum alacres suscepere. Ita e 74
E 190 colloquio discessum est, et ipse nichilominus eam ipsam nuptiarum curam domesticis suis imposuit, edixitque diem.   76

[Pars II]

E 197 Fuit haud procul a palacio villula paucorum atque in-
E 204 opum incolarum, quorum uni omnium pauperrimo Ianicole 2
nomen erat; sed ut pauperum quoque tuguria non numquam
gratia celestis invisit, unica illi nata contigerat Griseldis 4
E 211 nomine, forma corporis satis egregia, sed pulcritudine morum
atque animi adeo speciosa ut nichil supra. Hec parco victu, 6
in summa semper inopia educata, omnis inscia voluptatis, nil
E 218 molle nil tenerum cogitare didicerat, sed virilis senilisque 8
animus virgineo latebat in pectore. Patris senium inextimabili
refovens caritate, et pauculas eius oves pascebat, et colo inter- 10
E 225 im digitos atterebat; vicissimque domum rediens, oluscula et
dapes fortune congruas preparabat, durumque cubiculum 12
sternebat, et ad summam angusto in spacio totum filialis obedi-
E 232 encie ac pietatis officium explicabat. In hanc virgunculam 14
Valterius, sepe illac transiens, quandoque oculos non iuvenili
E 239 lascivia sed senili gravitate defixerat, et virtutem eximiam 16
supra sexum supraque etatem, quam vulgi oculis conditionis
obscuritas abscondebat, acri penetrarat intuitu. Unde effec- 18
tum ut et uxorem habere, quod nunquam ante voluerat, et
E 246 simul hanc unam nullamque aliam habere disponeret. Insta- 20
bat nuptiarum dies; unde autem ventura sponsa esset, nemo
E 253 noverat, nemo non mirabatur. Ipse interim et anullos aureos 22
et coronas et baltheos conquirebat, vestes autem preciosas et

Not far from the palace, in a poor village, dwelt Janicola, the neediest inhabitant of all, who had a daughter Griseldis, beautiful both in body and in spirit.

She cared for her aged father with love and faith, fully performed her home tasks.

Walter had often seen her and had noted her virtue. Her he decided to take as wife.

Everyone wondered who the bride was to be, but no one knew. Walter, meanwhile, made ready jewels and clothing.

(Vat₆.) 2 pauperrimo] pauperimo.
  8 senilisque] senillisque.
  9 in] im—inextimabili] in extimabilli.
  11 atterebat] atteirbat.
  12 cubiculum] cubicullum.
  13 summam] sumam.
  14 virgunculam] virguncullam.
  15 oculos] ocullos—iuvenili] iuvenilli.
  16 senili] senilli.
  18 penetrarat] penetraverat (penetrarat Cs, P₁, P₇, Ra, Rb, Lac, Laur₃, Vat₃, CC₂, Mgd, Ricc, Mlb, Bay₇, Har₃, Bod).
  20 aliam] alliam.

(Var.) 4 invisit] immisit CC₂, Mgd, Bay₇.

---

74 *suscepere.* Although *expectaverunt* would seem to make better sense here, as Professor French has noted (*Chaucer Handbook*, n. 75 on p. 274), yet all the manuscripts give *suscepere* in one form or another.

marquis dist et promist qu'il espouseroit; et ainsy leur parlement   56
190 fina et se departirent. Et commist et encharga ce dit seigneur a
aucuns siens privez et familliers l'appareil des nopces.   58

[II]

COMMENT le marquis voult avoir en mariage la pucelle Griseldis,
fille de Janicole, et comment et la maniere des nopces.   2

197   Pres de la cité et du palais ou demouroit ledit marquis, avoit une
204 villette ou habitoient et demouroient peu de gens et povres, entres   4
lesquelz estoit un et le plus povre, appellez Janicolle. Mais comme
aucune foiz la grace de Dieu descent en un petit hostel et mainnaige,   6
ledit bon homs avoit une fille, appellee Griseldis, de beauté de corps
211 et de membres assez belle, mais de bonté et de meurs et vertus tant   8
reamplie estoit que plus ne povoit. Ceste pucelle avoit esté nourrie
en grant povreté et ne savoit que c'estoit d'aise, riens mol ne riens   10
218 tendre n'avoit apris; et toutesfoiz courage meur et ancien estoit
muciez et enclos en sa virginité, et en tres grant chierté et reverence   12
nourrissoit son povre pere en sa viellesce. Et ne sçay quans brebis
avoient, qu'elle menoit en pasture, et en menant faisoit tousjours   14
225 aucune chose comme filler ou tillier chanve, et au retour apportoit
des chouz ou autre maniere d'erbettes pour eulx vivre. Et ainsy gou-   16
vernoit ce povre homme, son pere, moult charitablement et doulcement.
Briefment, toute obeïssance de bien, de pitié, qui en fille puet estre,   18
estoit en elle.

232   En ceste virginité ledit ⟨fol. 136ᵛ⟩ marquis, la aucune foiz passant   20
pour aler chacier ou vouler, maintes foiz gettoit ses yeux, non pas
par jeune mignotise ou delectacion mauvaise, mais par grant sapience   22
239 sa grant vertu, plus que en femme de tel aage ne seult avoir, que le
peuple n'avisoit pas, souvent consideroit ledit marquis et nottoit,   24
dont fut fait que il a femme avoir, ce que oncques n'avoit voulu par
avant, et celle seule et nulle autre se disposa et determina a prendre.   26
246 Le jour des nopces devant dit s'approuchoit desja fort, et nul encores
ne savoit ne oioit dire quelle femme ledit marquis prandroit, dont   28
253 chascun se merveilloit. Et il, ce temps pendant, faisoit faire aneaulx,
couronnes, robes, et joyaulx a la mesure d'une autre pucelle, qui estoit   30

(PN₈.) 10   riens mol] om. (riens mol PN₂, PN₇, BB).
22   sapience] pacience (sapience PN₂, PN₇, BB, PN₁, PA).
23   tel] te.
26   et celle] celle (et celle PN₄, PN₁, PN₂, PN₇)—se] om. (se PN₂, PN₇, BB, PN₄, PN₁, PA).

(Var.) 5   et le plus povre, appellez Janicolle] appellé Janicole lequel estoit le plus povre PA, povre homme qui estoit bon homme et le plus pouvre de celle villete lequel on appelloit Jehan nicholle PN₁.
13   ne sçay quans] quatre ou cinq PN₇.

calceos et eius generis necessaria omnia ad mensuram puelle 24
alterius, que stature sue persimilis erat, preparari faciebat.
E 260 Venerat expectatus dies, ⟨fol. 18ᵛ⟩ et cum nullus sponse rumor 26
audiretur, admiratio omnium vehementer excreverat. Hora
iam prandij aderat, iamque apparatu ingenti domus tota 28
E 267 fervebat. Tum Valterius, adventanti velut sponse obviam
profecturus, domo egreditur, prosequente virorum et ma- 30
E 274 tronarum nobilium caterva. Griseldis, omnium que erga se pa-
rarentur ignara, peractis que agenda domi erant, aquam e 32
E 281 longinquo fonte convectans, paternum limen intrabat, ut,
expedita curis alijs, ad visendam domini sui sponsam cum 34
E 288 puellis comitibus properaret. Tum Valterius, cogitabundus
incedens eamque compellans nomine, ubinam pater eius esset 36
interrogavit; que cum illum domi esse reverenter atque
humiliter respondisset, "Iube," inquit, "ad me veniat." 38
E 302 Venientem seniculum, manu prehensum, parumper ab-
E 309 straxit ac submissa voce, "Scio," ait, "me, Ianicola, carum 40
tibi, teque hominem fidum novi, et quecumque michi placeant
velle te arbitror. Unum tamen nominatim nosse velim: an me, 42
quem dominum habes, data michi hac tua in uxorem filia,
E 316 generum velis?" Inopino negotio stupefactus, senex obriguit, 44
et vix tandem paucis hiscens, "Nichil," inquid, "aut velle
debeo aut nolle, nisi quod placitum tibi sit, qui dominus meus 46
E 323 es." "Ingrediamur soli ergo," inquit, "ut ipsam de quibusdam
E 330 interrogem, te presente." Ingressi igitur, expectante populo 48
E 337 ac mirante; puellam circa patris obsequium satagentem. et
insolito tanti hospitis adventu stupidam invenere, quam hijs 50
E 344 verbis Valterius agreditur: "Et patri tuo placet," inquit, "et

On the appointed wedding day, Walter, followed by his train, issued from the castle as if to meet his bride.

As Griseldis, carrying water, was crossing her threshold, Walter, drawing near, asked for her father.

When the old man came, Walter requested his daughter in marriage.

Stupefied, stammering, Janicola assented. They entered the house, and Walter addressed Griseldis:

(Vat₆.) 25   persimilis] persimillis—stature] statura (stature P₆, P₇, Rc,
Laur₃, Chig, Vat₃, CC₂, Mgd, Ricc, Mlb, Pal, Bay₇, Har₂, Har₃, Bod).
   31   que] the abbreviation -que in the text is corrected to que in the margin.
   35   comitibus] comittibus—Tum] Dum (Tum Cs, Rc, Pal).
   37   interrogavit] interogavit—atque] ac.
   38   respondisset] respondidisset.
   39   seniculum] senicullum.
   42   velim] vellim.
   44   velis] vellis.
   46   nisi] ni (nisi Cs, P₁, P₆, P₇, Ra, Rb, Rc, Lac, Laur₃, Chig, Vat₃,
CC₄, CC₂, Mgd, Ricc, Mlb, Pal, Bay₇, Har₃, Bod, Laur₂).
   48   interrogem] interogem.

(Var.) 25   que stature sue persimilis erat] stature sueque persimilis
Bod.
   26   dies] dies nuptiarum Har₂, nuptarium dies Har₃.

E 260 de la grandeur et fourme d'icelle que prandre vouloit a femme. Vint
le jour des nopces, et l'eure du disner se approuchoit fort, et avoit 32
on fait grant appareil ou palais de paremens, viandes, et autrement,
E 267 comme au fait appartenoit. Et veez cy le marquis, ainsi comme s'il 34
alast au devant de sa femme, ist hors de sa maison acompaignié de
E 274 plusieurs nobles bonnes dames. Ne Griseldis de tout ce que pour elle 36
se faisoit riens ne savoit, mais bien avoit oÿ dire que son seigneur
E 281 se devoit marier; et pour ce s'estoit hastee et avancee de faire ce 38
qu'elle avoit a faire en leur maisonnette, et venoit desja de querir en
E 288 une croche de l'eaue de bien loing. Et tout ainsy qu'elle vouloit 40
E 295 entrer en leur maison, le marquis, tout pensis, vient au devant d'elle,
en lui demandant ou estoit son pere; laquelle lui respondi humblement 42
et en tres grant reverence: "Monseigneur," dist elle, "en nostre
hostel." 44
      "Ou lui dis," fait il, "qu'il viengne parler a moy."
E 302   Et quant ce bon homs fut venus, il le prist par la main et le tira a 46
E 309 part et en basse voix lui dist: "Je sçay," dist il, "Janicole, que tu
m'ainmes et as bien chier, et es mon homme feable, et que quelconques 48
choses me plaisent, tu les veulz et te plaisent. Une chose toutesfoiz
especiaulment vueil savoir: se il te plaist bien que j'aye ceste tienne 50
E 316 fille a femme et me vueille avoir ton gendre." Dont li bon homs, qui
riens ne savoit de ce fait, fut moult esmerveilliez; et tout rougis et 52
esbaÿs, en tremblant, a paine pot dire: "Riens," dist il, "sire, vouloir
ne doy que ce qui te plaist, qui es mon droiturier seigneur." 54
E 323   "Entrons doncques," dist le marquis, "seulz en ta chambre, car je
veil faire ⟨fol. 137ʳ⟩ a ta fille certaines demandes, toy present." 56
E 330 Lors y entrerent, le peuple attendant et soy merveillant des services
que la pucelle faisoit a son pere de l'ordonner en sa petitesce et povreté 58
E 337 a la venue de si grant seigneur. Laquelle ledit marquis arrengna en
E 344 ceste maniere: "Griseldis," dist il, "il plaist a ton pere et a moy aussi 60

(**PN₃.**) 46 fut venus] *om.* (fut venus PN₂, PN₇, BB, PN₄, PN₁, PA).
53 il] *om.*
60 il plaist] y plaist (il plaist PN₂, PN₇, BB, PN₄, PN₁, PA).

(**Var.**) 36 nobles bonnes dames] nobles hommes et bons gens PN₁, nobles et
bonnes dames et damoezelles PN₇.
41 leur] sa PN₁.
42 ou estoit son pere; laquelle] Dy moy ou est ton pere et elle PN₁.
43 Monseigneur] Seigneur BB, PN₄, PN₂, Sire PA—en] il est en PN₇, PA,
il est a PN₁.
48 quelconques] toutes les PA.
53 en tremblant] et tout en tremblant et tellement qu' PA—dire] mot dire
PN₇, dire mot PN₁, PA.

michi ut uxor mea sis. Credo id ipsum tibi placeat, sed habeo   52

E 351   ex te querere, ubi hoc peractum fuerit quod mox erit, an
volenti animo parata sis ut de omnibus tecum michi conveniat,   54
ita ut in nulla unquam re a mea voluntate dissencias et, quicquid tecum agere voluero, sine ulla frontis aut verbi repug-   56

E 358   nancia te ex animo volente michi liceat." Ad hec illa miraculo
rei tremens, "Ego, mi-domine," inquid, "tanto honore me in-   58
dignam scio; at si voluntas tua, sique sors mea est, nichil ego
unquam sciens, nedum faciam, sed etiam cogitabo, quod   60
contra animum tuum sit; nec tu aliquid facies, etsi me mori

E 365   iusseris, quod moleste feram." "Satis est," inquit ille; sic in   62
publicum eductam populo ostendens, "Hec," ait, "uxor mea,
hec domina vestra est; hanc colite, hanc amate, et si me carum   64

E 372   habetis, hanc carissimam habetote." Hinc ne quid reliquiarum
fortune veteris novam inferret in domum, nudari eam iussit,   66
et a calce ad verticem novis vestibus indui, quod a matronis
circumstantibus ac certatim sinu illam gremioque foventibus   68

E 379   verecunde ac celeriter adimpletum est. Sic horridulam virginem, indutam, laceramque comam recollectam manibus   70
comptamque pro tempore, insignitam gemmis et corona

E 386   velut subito transformatam, vix populus recognovit; quam   72
Valterius anullo precioso, quem ad hunc usum detulerat,
solempniter desponsavit, niveoque equo impositam, ad   74
palacium deduci fecit, comitante populo et gaudente. Ad
hunc modum nuptie celebrate, diesque ille letissimus actus   76

Right margin glosses:

52 "Your father and I desire that you shall be my wife. But first I have one thing

54 to ask: Will you agree never to dispute my wish and always allow me to do whatsoever I desire with you?"

Trembling, Griseldis replied: "I will never even

58 think anything contrary to your will; nor will anything you do ever vex me."

62 Satisfied, Walter led her before the people and proclaimed her his bride. He commanded that she be clad

64 with new garments, so that she was suddenly transformed.

72 Then Walter married her and led her to the palace.

(Vat₆.) 54   tecum michi] michi tecum.

55   dissencias] disencias.

57   miraculo] miracullo.

59   nichil] nil.

65   Hinc] Hic (Hinc *Lac, Laur₃, Har₃, Laur₂*).

66   inferret] inferet.

71   gemmis] gemis.

73   Valterius] Valterius animo *with* animo *cancelled*—anullo precioso] precioso anullo.

75   comitante] comittante.

(Var.) 71   pro tempore] coopertam cunctamque prope CC_2.

76   ille] totus *Laur₂*.

---

65 *Hinc.* Petrarch wrote *Dehinc*, since families *b, c, d,* Chig, and the Cs, Ra, Rb subgroup of family *a* unanimously give this reading. *Hinc* (or *Hic*) is found only in the Laur₃ subgroup of family *a;* but, since Chaucer's source manuscript probably came from this subgroup, the reading is allowed to stand.

que tu soies ma femme. Je croy que ce te plaist aussy, mais je t'ay
a demander et veil savoir de toy, se puis que ce sera fait qui sera   62
E 351   tantost, se de bon cuer et plain vouloir tu es preste et le veulx, et que
tout me loise, et puisse faire avec toy si que jamais en quelconque   64
maniere tu ne contrediras a ma voulenté et que tu vueilles et te plaise
quanqu'il me plaira."   66
E 358   A ces choses, de ce fait merveilleux toute tremblant, respondi:
"Je," dist elle, "monseigneur, sçay certainement que je ne suis pas   68
digne ne souffisant de si grant honneur. Et se ceste chose toutesfois
est ta voulenté et mon eur, jamais riens ne feray ne penseray quelque   70
chose a mon povoir qui soit contre ta voulenté ou plaisir, ne tu ne
feras ja chose, et me feisse mourir, que je ne seuffre pacienment."   72
E 365   "C'est assez," dist il; et ainsy la fist amener devant tous en publique
et dist au peuple: "Ceste," fait il, "ma femme et vostre dame est.   74
Honnourez la, amez la. Et se vous m'avez chier, je vous prie, aiez
E 372   la tres chiere." Et incontinent la commanda a devestir toute nue et   76
du pié jusques au chief la fist revestir de neuves robes tres richement par les bonnes dames qui la estoient. Laquelle chose firent moult   78
honteusement pour le regart des vilz et povres vestemens qu'elles lui
E 379   desvestoient aux precieuses que on lui vestoit. Et ainsi ordonnee et   80
paree de couronne et de pierrerie tres grandement, comme soudaine-
E 386   ment transmuee et changié, a paine la recongnust le peuple. Laquelle   82
le marquis solennelment espousa de l'anel precieux que a cest usaige
et pour ce especiaument il avoit fait faire. Et la fist mettre sur un   84
beau palefroy et mener au palays, le peuple la acompaignant et faisant
grant feste et liesce, et furent faites les nopces et passa le jour moult   86
joyeusement et liément.

(PN₃.) 63   vouloir] vouloie (vouloir PN₂, PN₇, BB, PN₄, PN₁, PA).
66   quanqu'il] quanqui (quanqu'il PN₂, PA).

---

82   *changié.* A feminine ending, not a masculine, is required. The scribe elsewhere errs in grammatical agreement: *presté* (V. 41), *vil* (V. 44), *eu* (V. 65),
recouvré (VI. 15), *recité* (VI. 32), etc. It is possible, however, that we may here
be dealing with a Picardism (*changie* instead of *changiee*). The text contains other
similar possible Picardisms, which therefore possibly ought to be printed without
the accent: *liément* (II. 87), *mucié* (II. 101), *changié* (III. 62), *lignié* (III. 72), *commancié* (IV. 27), *abaissié* (V. 95), *courroucié* (VI. 6), and *embrassié* (VI. 20). If these
are Picardisms, they are probably due to the scribe, for the remaining manuscripts
usually give the correct readings.

E 393 est. ⟨fol. 19ʳ⟩ Brevi dehinc inopi sponse tantum divini favoris
affulserat, ut non in casa illa pastoria sed in aula imperatoria   78
E 400 educata atque edocta videretur; atque apud omnes supra fidem
cara et venerabilis facta esset, vixque his ipsis qui illam ab   80
origine noverant persuaderi posset Ianicole natam esse,
E 407 tantus erat vite, tantus morum decor, ea verborum gravitas   82
ac dulcedo, quibus omnium animos nexu sibi magni amoris
E 414 astrinxerat. Iamque non solum intra patrios fines sed per   84
finitimas quasque provincias suum nomen celebri preconio
fama vulgabat, ita ut multi ad illam visendam viri ac matrone   86
E 421 studio fervente concurrerent. Sic Valterius, humili quidem
sed insigni ac prospero matrimonio honestatis, summa domi   88
in pace, extra vero summa cum gratia hominum, vivebat;
quodque eximiam virtutem tanta sub inopia latitantem tam   90
perspicaciter deprehendisset, vulgo prudentissimus habebatur.
E 428 Neque vero solers sponsa muliebria tantum ac domestica, sed   92
E 435 ubi res posceret, publica etiam obibat officia, viro absente,
lites patrie nobiliumque discordias dirimens atque compo-   94

Griseldis seemed to all to have been reared not in a shepherd's hut but in a king's court. So gracious were her manners, so sweet her speech, that all the people loved her.

Her fame spread, and Walter was held wise for having discovered such hidden virtue.

She attended not only to domestic but even to state affairs.

(Vat₆.)   80   venerabilis] venerabillis.
87   concurrerent] concurerent—humili] humilli.

(Var.)   78   imperatoria] imperatoris Har₃.
88–89   domi in pace] dei in pace CC₂, domini pace Har₂.
92   domestica] modestia Har₃.

---

88 *honestatis*. Professor Hendrickson has pointed out the corrupt-
ness of this reading, which is found also in the Latin glosses in MSS El, Hg,
Dd of the *Clerkes Tale;* at the same time he suggested emending to
honestatus (*MP*, IV, 188–92). Petrarch undoubtedly wrote *honestatus*.
It is found in fourteen of the twenty-four manuscripts, and these fourteen
represent all four families (P₁, P₆, P₇, Lac, Laur₃, Chig, Vat₃, CC₂, Mgd,
Mlb, Har₂, Har₃, Bod, Laur₂); whereas the rival reading *honestatis* appears only in certain manuscripts of family *a* (Vat₆, Bay₅, Cs, Ra, Rb).
Most probably the scribal error crept in through confusion from the use of
the symbol 9 (which usually denotes *-us*, sometimes *-is*). In four of the manuscripts used for this edition the ambiguous symbol concludes the word
(Rc, CC₄, Ricc, Pal). Chaucer's manuscript bore one of the corrupt readings, for his noun "honestetee" (*Clerkes Tale*, l. 422) clearly derives
from the noun *honestatis*, not from the participle *honestatus*. Hence,
honestatis is allowed to stand in the text.

88–89 *domi in*. The reading *domini* in Har₂ is obviously due to a
scribal misreading, since *in* and *ni*, requiring the same number of strokes,
are virtually indistinguishable in the manuscripts. The reading *dei*,
found in CC₂, seems to be an error for *domi* alone, since CC₂ retains the *in*.
Dei occurs also in the Latin glosses in MSS El, Hg, Dd of the *Canterbury
Tales;* either it, or *domini*, probably suggested Chaucer's "Goddes" in l. 423
(see Hendrickson, pp. 188–92, and cf. Cook, *Romanic Review*, VIII, 213–14).

E 393   Or crut Dieu et envoia tant grace en celle femme que non pas en   88
povre maison de villaige mais en hostel royal sembloit estre nourrie
E 400   et avoir esté nee. Et l'ost chascun tant chiere et en si grant honneur   90
et amour que ceulx qui savoient qui elle estoit et qui la congnoissoient
de nativité a paine povoient croire qu'elle ⟨fol. 137ᵛ⟩ feust fille a   92
E 407   Janicole, tant avoit en elle de honnesteté, belle vie, bonne maniere,
E 414   sagesse, et doulceur de parler que chascun se delittoit a la ouÿr. Et ja   94
non pas tant seulement en son pays, mais es pays et regions voisines
son bon nom et la grant louenge et la bonne renommee d'elle se pub-   96
lioit et croissoit, tellement que mains hommes et femmes pour le
E 421   grant bien d'elle l'aloient veoir. Et ainsi le marquis, humblement   98
mais virtueusement mariez, vivoit en bonne paix en sa maison et en
grant grace dehors; lequel, comme si tres grant et excellant vertus, en   100˙
E 428   si grant povreté mucié, eust prins, chascun l'en tenoit a saige; car
non pas tant seulement euvres et mesnages appartenans a femme   102
ladicte bonne creature faisoit, mais, ou le cas le requeroit, la chose
E 435   publique adresçoit et pourveoit; son seigneur absent et dehors, les   104
descors du pays et contencions si s'esmouvoient entre nobles ou

(PN)₃. 95   pays et] pays (pays et *PN₂*, *PN₇*, *BB*, *PN₄*, *PA*).
98   humblement] humble (humblement *PN₂*, *PN₇*, *BB*, *PN₄*, *PN₁*, *PA*).
100–101   en si grant povreté mucié, eust prins] et en si grant amitié l'eust pris
(en si grant povreté mucié eust prins *PN₂*).
102   et mesnages] en mariage (et mesnages *PN₂*, *BB*, *PN₄*, *PA*).

(Var.) 97–98   le grant bien] la grant bonté *BB*.
100–101   lequel, comme … tenoit a saige] Et le tenoit le peuple a moult sage
d'avoir pris telle femme ainsi plaine de grant vertu *PA*, Et l'en tenoit le peuple a
sage d'avoir pris tele femme ainsi plaine de grant vertu *BB*.

nens tam gravibus responsis tantaque maturitate et iudicij
equitate, ut omnes ad salutem publicam demissam celo 96
E 442 feminam predicarent. Nec multum tempus effluxerat, dum
gravida effecta, primum subditos anxia expectatione suspendit; 98
dehinc, filiam enixa pulcerrimam, quamvis filium maluissent,
tamen votiva fecunditate non virum modo sed totam patriam 100
letam fecit.

[Pars III]

E 449   Cepit, ut fit, interim Valterium, cum iam ablactata esset
infantula, mirabilis quedam quam laudabilis (doctiores 2
E 456 iudicent) cupiditas, sat expertam care fidem coniugis experi-
E 463 endi altius et iterum atque iterum retentandi. Solam igitur in 4
thalamum sevocatam, turbida fronte sic alloquitur: "Nosti,
E 470 O Griseldis,—neque enim presenti fortuna te preteriti tui 6
E 477 status oblitam credo,—nosti, inquam, qualiter in hanc domum
veneris. Michi quidem cara satis ac dilecta es; at meis nobili- 8
E 484 bus non ita, presertim ex quo parere incepisti, qui plebeie
domine subesse animis ferunt iniquissimis. Michi ergo, qui 10
cum eis pacem cupio, necesse est de filia tua non meo sed alieno
E 491 iudicio obsequi, et id facere quo nil michi posset esse molestius. 12
Id enim vero te ignara nunquam fecerim; volo autem tuum
michi animum accomodes, pacienciamque illam prestes quam 14

(Vat₆.) 99 filiam] filliam—pulcerrimam] pulcerimam—filium] fil-
lium.
   2   infantula] infantulla.
   5   alloquitur] aloquitur.
  14   michi animum accomodes] animum michi acomodes.

(Var.) 97   tempus] post CC_2.
   2–3   mirabilis quedam quam laudabilis (doctiores iudicent) cupiditas]
mirabilis quedam quam laudabilem doctores iudicent cupiditas P_6, mirabilis quedam quam laudabilem doctiores iudicent cupiditas Mgd.
   5   turbida] seva atque turbida $Laur_2$.

2–3 *mirabilis quedam quam laudabilis (doctiores iudicent) cupiditas.*
This is undoubtedly what Petrarch wrote. All but two (Har₃, Laur₂) of the
manuscripts in the best family (family a) have this reading; and three of
the manuscripts of family d (the early version) have it (Rc, CC₄, Pal). One
other reading finds support in two families, but only one manuscript in
each family contains it: P₆ and Mgd (families d and c) have *mirabilis
quedam, quam laudabilem doctiores [doctores in P₆] iudicent, cupiditas.* The
passage is awkward, as Professor French points out (*Chaucer Handbook,*
n. 77 on p. 299). Perhaps it should be corrected to read as the manuscripts in family b: *mirabilis quedam magis quam laudabilis (doctiores iudicent) cupiditas* (Vat₃, Ricc, Mlb).

autres gens, abaissoit et appaissoit tres saigement. Tans beaux et 106
saiges parlers et reponses, tant grant discrecion et hault jugement avoit
en elle, que plusieurs la tenoient et disoient estre envoiee des cielz au 108
E 442 salut du bien commun publique. Et ne demoura gueres qu'elle fut
grosse et enfanta une belle fille, combien que on eust mieulx amé un 110
filz. Toutesfoiz le marquis et tout le pays s'en esjoÿrent grandement.   112

[III]

COMMENT ledit marquis voult essaier et approuver Griseldis sa
femme par diverses manieres et veoir sa grant constance.   2
E 449 Et veez cy que je ne sçay quelle ymaginacion merveilleuse print
ledit marquis, laquelle aucuns saiges veulent louer, c'est assavoir de   4
E 456 experimenter et essaier sa femme plus avant, laquelle il avoit desja
assez essayee et approuvee, et de la tenter encores par diverses ma-   6
E 463 nieres. Vint une fois a elle de nuit en sa chambre, aussy comme tout
E 470 courrouciez et troublez, et lui va dire: ⟨fol. 138ʳ⟩ "Tu sces bien,   8
Griseldis,—et je croy que la dignité ou je t'ay mis ne te fait oublier
E 477 l'estat ou je te pris,—tu scez assez comment tu vins en ceste maison. 10
Tu m'es certainement bien chiere et si t'aime bien, comme tu scez;
E 484 mais ce ne font pas mes nobles, mesmement quant tu as commencié a   12
enfanter une fille, lesquelz se dient estre moult villenez qui soient subgés a telle femme de peuple comme tu es. Or, doncques, je qui desire   14
estre de tout mon cuer appaisié et vivre en paix avec eulx, maintenant
neccessité m'est a ordonner et faire de ta fille non pas a ma voulenté et 16
E 491 plaisir, mais au conseil et jugement d'autruy. Toutesfoiz, je n'en
veil riens faire sans ton sceu; je veil, doncques, que tu me prestes ton 18
consentement et accort, et aies celle pacience que tu me promis des
l'encommencement de nostre mariage."   20

(**PN₃.**) 12–13   a enfanter une fille] une fille (a enffenter une fille *PN₇*).
14   de peuple] *om.* (de peuple *PN₂, PN₇, BB, PN₄, PA*)—qui desire] cuidoie
(qui desire *PN₂, PN₇, BB, PN₄, PN₁, PA*).

(**Var.**) 110   amé] amé qu'elle eust enffanté *PN₇*.
3   Et veez cy que je] Et assez tost aprés l'enffantement *PN₇*, Et aprés ce ung
petit de temps je *PN₁*.
8   dire] dire en ceste maniere *PA*.

12–13   *a enfanter une fille.*   The evidence indicates that the translator wrote
merely *a enfanter*, since PN₂, BB, PN₄, and PA agree in this reading. PN₃
reads only *une fille* (without *a enfanter*); the reading adopted in the text appears in
PN₇. The editor retains *une fille* since Chaucer's source manuscript seems to have
had it: "And namely sith thy doghter was ybore" (*Clerkes Tale*, l. 484).

E 498 ab inicio nostri coniugij promisisti." Hijs auditis, nec verbo

mota, nec vultu, "Tu," inquit, "noster es dominus, et ego et 16

hec parva filia tue sumus; de rebus tuis igitur fac ut libet,

E 505 nichil placere enim tibi potest quod michi displiceat. Nichil 18

penitus vel habere cupio vel amittere metuo, nisi te; hoc ipsa

michi in medio cordis affixi, nunquam inde vel lapsu temporis 20

vel morte vellendum. Omnia prius fieri possunt quam hic

E 512 animus mutari." Letus ille responso, sed dissimulans visu 22

E 519 mestus abscessit, et post paululum unum suorum satellitum

fidissimum sibi, cuius opera gravioribus in negocijs uti con- 24

sueverat, quid agi vellet edoctum, ad uxorem misit, qui ad

E 526 eam noctu veniens, "Parce," inquid, "O domina, neque michi 26

imputes quod coactus facio. Scis, sapientissima, quid est esse

sub dominis, neque tali ingenio predite ⟨fol. 19ᵛ⟩ quamvis in- 28

E 533 experte dura parendi necessitas est ignota. Iussus sum hanc

infantulam accipere, atque eam—" Hic sermone abrupto, 30

quasi crudele ministerium silencio exprimens, subticuit.

E 540 Suspecta viri fama, suspecta facies, suspecta hora, suspecta 32

erat oratio, quibus etsi clare occisum iri dulcem filiam intelli-

geret, nec lacrimulam tamen ullam nec suspirium dedit, in 34

E [561], nutrice quidem, nedum in matre, durissimum. Sed tranquilla
E 547

fronte puellulam accipiens, aliquantulum respexit, et simul 36

exosculans, benedixit ac signum sancte crucis impressit,

E 568 porrexitque satelliti et "Vade," ait, "quodque tibi dominus 38

noster iniunxit exequere. Unum queso: cura ne corpusculum

hoc fere lacerent aut volucres, ita tamen nisi tibi contrarium 40

Griseldis replied: "We are yours; do as you will."

Soon after, Walter sent to her a follower, who said: "Blame me not for what I do unwillingly. I am ordered to take this infant."

Griseldis guessed her daughter was to be killed, yet showed no emotion. She kissed the child and gave it to the man, saying, "Do our lord's bidding; yet take care lest beasts or birds mutilate her body."

(**Vat₆.**) 17   tuis igitur] tuis (tuis igitur *Cs, P₁, P₆, P₇, Ra, Rb, Rc, Lac, Laur₃, Chig, Vat₃, Mgd, Ricc, Mlb, Pal, Bay₇, Bay₆, Bod*).

21   vellendum] velendum.

22–23   visu mestus] mestus (visu mestus *Cs, P₁, P₆, P₇, Ra, Rb, Lac, Laur₃, Chig, Vat₃, CC₄, CC₂, Mgd, Ricc, Mlb, Bay₇, Har₃, Laur₂*).

23   satellitum] satelitum.

28   neque] neque tibi (tibi *appears in the margin with a symbol indicating that it should follow* neque).

29   necessitas] necesitas.

30   infantulam] infantullam.

31   crudele] crudelle.

33–34   intelligeret] inteligeret.

36   puellulam] puelulam—aliquantulum] aliquantullum.

38   porrexitque] porexitque.

(**Var.**) 39   cura] a te *CC₄*.

E 498   Laquelle chose oyee, de visaige ne de parler ne s'esmeut, mais
meurement respondi a lui et saigement: "Tu es," dist elle, "mon   22
seigneur, et je et ceste petite fillette sommes tiennes; doncques fais
E 505 de ta chose comme il te plaist. Certainement riens ne te puet plaire   24
qui me desplaise, ne riens ne couvoite a avoir ne a perdre ne ne doubte
que toy. Et cecy ay je mis parfaitement en mon cuer, ne jamais ne   26
par laps de temps ne par mort ne s'en partira. Et toutes autres choses
se puent avant faire que ce courage a moy muer."   28
E 512   Le marquis de ceste response fut moult liez en cuer, mais il dissimula
et faingny qu'il feust courroucié et triste et se party d'elle. Et un peu   30
E 519 après envoia a elle un sien serviteur et sergent a lui feable, qu'il avoit
esprouvé en plus grans choses, et l'enforma bien comment il feroit,   32
E 526 lequel vint de nuit a elle. "Pardonne moy," dist il, "ma dame, ne
point ne me metz sus ne ne me saches mauvais gre de ce que je fay   34
contraint. Tu scez que c'est d'estre soubz grans seigneurs, et com-
E 533 ment il fault a eulx obeïr. Commandé m'est de prandre cest enffant."   36
Et en ce disant, ainsi qu'il voulsist faire crueuse et mauvaise chose,
comme le monstroit par signes, prist l'enfant par rude et lourde   38
E 540 maniere. Ce sergent estoit tenuz pour crueux homme, et estoit de
laide figure, et a heure souspessonneuse estoit venuz, et parloit comme   40
homme plain de mauvaise voulenté. Et aussi cuidoit la bonne dame
et simple qu'il alast faire mauvais fait de sa fillette que ⟨fol. 138ᵛ⟩   42
[561] tant amoit; toutesfoiz ne plours ne sospirs ne fist, qui dobt estre
E 547 tenue a tres dure chose en une nourrice. Et de plain front prist son   44
enffant et le regarda un pou et le baisa et beneist, et fist le signe de la
E 568 croix, et le bailla audit sergent. "Va," dist elle, "fay et excecute ce   46
que monseigneur t'a enchargié. Je te prie, toutesfoiz," dist elle, "que
tu gardes a ton povoir que les bestes sauvaiges ne devourent ou   48
menguent le corps de cest enffant, se le contraire ne t'est enjoint."

(PN₃.) 24 ta] om. (ta PN₂, PN₇, BB, PN₄, PN₁, PA).
37 faire] om. (faire PN₂, PN₇, BB, PN₄, PN₁, PA)—chose] om. (chose
PN₂, PN₇, BB, PN₄, PN₁, PA).
45 le baisa] la baisa (le baisa PN₂, BB, PN₄, PA).

Var.) 26 mis] om. BB.
32 esprouvé] par avant plusieurs fois essaié PN₇, autresfoiz esprouvé PA.

E 575   sit preceptum." Reversus ad dominum, cum quid dictum
quidve responsum esset exposuisset et ei filiam obtulisset,   42
vehementer paterna animum pietas movit; susceptum tamen

E 582   rigorem propositi non inflexit, iussitque satelliti obvolutam   44
pannis, ciste iniectam, ac iumento impositam, quieto omni

E 589   quanta posset diligencia Bononiam deferret ad sororem suam,   46
que illic comiti de Panico nupta erat, eamque sibi traderet
alendam materno studio, et caris moribus instruendam, tanta   48
preterea occultandam cura, ut cuius esset filia a nemine posset

E 596   agnosci. Ivit ille illico, et solicite quod impositum ei erat im-   50
plevit. Valterius interea, sepe vultum coniugis ac verba con-
siderans, nullum unquam mutati animi perpendit indicium: 52

E 603   par alacritas atque sedulitas, solitum obsequium, idem amor,
nulla tristicia, nulla filie mencio, nunquam sive ex proposito   54
sive incidenter nomen eius ex ore matris auditum.

The servant bore the little
girl to Walter, who was
moved with pity, yet
ordered her taken to Bologna
to his sister, wife of the
Count of Panago, where she
was to be cared for and
hidden from all.

Meanwhile Griseldis be-
trayed to Walter no altered
emotions or change of attitude, nor ever mentioned
her daughter.

[Pars IV]

E 610   Transiverant hoc in statu anni quatuor, dum ecce, gravida
iterum, filium elegantissimum peperit, leticiam patris in-   2

E 617   gentem atque omnium amicorum, quo nutricis ab ubere post
biennium subducto, ad curiositatem solitam reversus pater,   4

E 624   uxorem rursus affatur: "Et olim," ait, "audisti populum
meum egre nostrum ferre connubium, presertim ex quo te fe-   6
cundam cognovere, nunquam tamen egrius quam ex quo
marem peperisti. Dicunt enim—et sepe ad aures meas mur-   8

E 631   mur hoc pervenit—'Obeunte igitur Valterio, Ianicule nepos
nostri dominabitur, et tam nobilis patria tali domino subiace-   10
bit.' Multa quotidie in hanc sentenciam iactantur in populis;

Four years later, Griseldis
bore a son. When the child
was two years old, Walter
came to his wife and said:

"My people resent that
Janicola's grandson is heir
to their lord. I must, therefore, do with this child as I
did with the other."

(Vat₆.)   46   diligencia] dilligencia—deferret] defferet.
47   comiti] comitti.
49   occultandam] ocultandam.
50–51   implevit] adimplevit *with* ad *canceled.*
53   solitum] solitumque (soḷitum *Cs, P₁, P₆, P₇, Ra, Rb, Lac, Laur₃,
Chig, Vat₃, CC₄, CC₂, Mgd, Ricc, Mlb, Bay₇, Bay₅, Har₂, Har₃, Bod, Laur₂*).
55   ore] hore◂—auditum] auditui (auditum *Cs, P₁, P₆, P₇, Ra, Rb, Rc,
Lac, Laur₃, Chig, Vat₃, CC₄, CC₂, Mgd, Ricc, Mlb, Pal, Bay₅, Bay₇, Bod,
Har₂, Har₃, Laur₂*).
4   biennium] bienium.
6   connubium] conubium.

(Var.)   41   dominum] dominum servus *Har₃*—cum] eumque *Bay₇.*
45   iniectam] vectam *Rc, Chig, Pal.*
2   patris] patrie *Laur₂.*
4   pater] marchio *CC₂.*

E 575   Lequel sergent quant il fut retournez a son seigneur et lui raconta   50
la response de sa femme et lui presenta sa fille, il fut meu de grant
E 582   pitié. Neantmoins toutesfoiz ne desista il point de son propos, et   52
commanda audit sergent qu'il envelopast ladicte fillette bien et
E 589   seurement et qu'il la portast secretement a Bouloingne la grasse a une   54
sienne suer, qui estoit la mariee au conte de Paniquo, et a lui la
baillast a nourrir de par lui et a enseignier de science et de meurs,   56
comme sa fille, et si celeement la gardast que nul ne sceust ne ne peust
E 596   congnoistre ou apparcevoir qui elle feust. Et il y ala tantost et soing-   58
neusement accomplist ce que commis lui estoit. Et le marquis aprés
ce souvent avisoit et consideroit la chiere, les parolles, le semblant, et   60
le maintien de sa femme se point lui feroit semblant de sa fille, mais
E 603   en quelconque maniere ne la vit ou apparçut changié ou muee. Telle   62
liesce, telle obeïssance, tel service et amour, comme tousjours faisoit
par avant, lui rendoit, ne nulle tristesce, ne nulle mencion de sa fille   64
de propos ou par accident ne faisoit.
E 610   En cest estat se passerent iiii ans, tant qu'elle fut grosse et enfanta   66
un tres beau filz, dont le pere et tous les amis furent moult joyeux.
E 617   Lequel enfant puis qu'il ot deux ans et qu'il fut sevré de la nourrice, le   68
E 624   marquis de rechief vint a sa femme et lui dist: "Femme, tu as ouÿ
autrefoiz comment mon peuple est mal content et murmure de nostre   70
mariage, et maintenant especiaument, puis qu'ilz voient que tu portes
et es disposee et encline a avoir lignié, et mesmement que tu as masle.   72
E 631   Et dient souvent: 'Nostre marquis mort, le nepveu de Janicole sera
nostre seigneur, et sy noble pays sera subjet a tel seigneur'; et maintes   74

(PN₃.) 51   il fut] dont il fut (il fut PN₂, PN₇, BB, PN₄).

(Var.) 53   ladicte fillette] ledit enffant PN₇, l'enffent PN₁.
58   Et il y] Et ledit sergent ly PN₇, Et le serviteur PN₁.
66   tant] avant PA.
68   puis qu'il] quant il BB.
74   et sy noble ... tel seigneur] om. PA.

E 638 quibus ego, et quietis avidus et—ut verum fatear—michi 12
metuens, permoveor ut de hoc infante disponam quod de
sorore disposui. Id tibi prenuncio ne te inopinus et subitus 14
E 645 dolor turbet." Ad hec illa "Et dixi," ait, "et repeto, nichil
possum seu velle seu nolle nisi quod tu, neque vero in hijs 16
E 652 filijs quicquam habeo preter laborem. Tu mei et ipsorum
dominus; tuis in rebus iure tuo utere. Nec consensum meum 18
queras, in ipso enim tue domus introitu ut pannos sic et
voluntates affectusque meos exui; tuos indui; quacunque 20
E 659 ergo de re quicquid tu vis, ego etiam volo. Nempeque si
future tue voluntatis ⟨fol. 20ʳ⟩ essem prescia, ante etiam quic- 22
quid id esset et velle et cupere inciperem, quam tu velles; nunc
animum tuum, quem prevenire non possum, libens sequor. 24
Fac senciam tibi placere quod moriar, volens moriar, nec res
E 666 ulla denique nec mors ipsa nostro fuerit par amori." Ad- 26
mirans femine constanciam, turbato vultu abijt, confestimque
E 673 satellitem olim missum ad eam remisit, qui multum excusata 28
necessitate parendi, multumque petita venia siquid ei molestum aut fecisset aut faceret, quasi immane scelus acturus 30
poposcit infantem. Illa eodem quo semper vultu, qualicunque
animo, filium forma corporis atque indole non matri tantum 32
sed cunctis amabilem in manus cepit, signansque eum signo
crucis et benedicens ut filiam fecerat, et diuticule oculis in- 34
herens, atque deosculans, nullo penitus signo doloris edito,
E 680 petenti obtulit. "Et tene," inquid, "fac quod iussus es. 36
Unum nunc etiam precor: ut, si fieri potest, hos artus teneros
infantis egregij protegas a vexatione volucrum ac ferarum." 38
E 687 Cum his mandatis reversus ad dominum, animum eius magis ac
magis in stuporem egit, ut nisi eam noscet amantissimam filio- 40
rum, paulo minus suspicari posset hoc femineum robur quadam
E 694 ab animi feritate procedere, sed cum suorum omnium valde, 42
nullius erat amancior quam viri. Iussus inde Bononiam profi-
cisci, eo illum tulit quo sororem tulerat. Poterant rigidissimo 44

Griseldis replied: "My wish is your wish. If you desired even my death, I would gladly die."

Again Walter sent his follower, who demanded the child. Griseldis blessed and kissed her son, then gave him, too, over to the servant.

Walter, marveling at her constancy,

sent the boy where he had sent the girl.

(Vat₆.) 15   et repeto] repeto et.
19   pannos] panos.
21   volo] vollo.
29   necessitate] necesitate.
33   amabilem] amabillem.

(Var.) 32   animo] animo mestissima P_1, P_6, P_7, Rc, Vat_3, CC_4, $Ricc$, Mlb, Pal, Bay_7, Har_2.

42–43 *sed cum suorum omnium valde, nullius erat amancior quam viri.*
Despite the fact that this passage is decidedly elliptical (French, *Chaucer*

[*Continued on p. 318*]

E 638 telles parolles dist souvent le peuple. Lesquelles choses et parolles
je, qui veil vivre en paix et en doubtant aussi de ma personne, me   76
font vivre pensif et merancolieux. ⟨fol. 139ʳ⟩ Sy suy meu que de
cest enfant face comme j'ay fait de l'autre. Et ce je te fay premiere-   78
ment assavoir, affin que la douleur soudaine ne te troublast trop ou
nuisist."   80

E 645   A ce, "Je t'ay fait," elle dist, "et je le te recorde que je ne puis
riens vouloir, fors ce que tu veulx, ou non vouloir. Ne je n'ay riens   82
E 652 en ces enffans que l'enffantement. Tu es seigneur d'eulx et de moy:
use de tes choses a ton droit, ne en ce ne demande ou requier mon   84
consentement. Quant j'entray, il n'est riens plus vray, ou seul de ta
maison, je devesty mes robes et aussy mes voulentez et vesti les   86
tiennes. Quanque tu veulx, doncques, comment que ce soit, je veil.
E 659 Et pour certain, se je povoie avant savoir ta voulenté que toy meismes,   88
je la vouldroye et feroye avant que toy meismes; doncques maintenant
ta voulenté, que je ne puys devant savoir que la me dies, j'ensuivray   90
et feray voulentiers. Et s'il te plaist que je muire, je vueil morir tres
E 666 voulentiers, ne la mort ne se pourroit comparer a nostre amour."   92

[IV]

COMMENT ledit marquis envoia secondement son sergent a sa femme
Griseldis pour lui oster son filz, comme il avoit fait sa fille, et comment   2
benignement, sans faire nul semblant de courrous, elle lui bailla.

Quant le marquis apparçut ainsi et congnut la grant constance de   4
sa femme, se esmerveilla moult et, tout troublé, se parti d'elle, et
E 673 tantost envoia ce sergent que autresfoiz avoit envoié a elle. Lequel   6
sergent, en soy excusant comment il lui convenoit obeïr, ainsi comme
se il voulsist faire une grande inhumanité, demanda l'enfant comme   8
il avoit fait l'autre, et elle respondy de bonne chiere, ja fust ce que
bien estoit courroucee en cuer. Son filz moult bel et doulcet prist entre   10
ses bras et le beneist et seigna, comme elle avoit fait la fille, et un
petit longuement le regarda et le baisa, sans monstrer signe de douleur,   12
E 680 et au messaige le bailla. "Tien," dist elle, "fay ce a quoy tu es envoié.
Une chose, toutesfoiz, te requier chierement tant que je puis: ⟨fol.   14
139ᵛ⟩ que, se tu pues faire, tu vueilles garder et deffendre le corps
et membres de ce noble enffant, que bestes mauvaises ne le devourent   16
ou menguent." Lequel, enportant ledit enfant, retourna au marquis
E 687 et lui raconta ce qu'il avoit trouvé en sa femme, dont de plus en plus   18

(**PN₃**.) 87   que ce] qu ce.
12   monstrer] monstre (monstrer *PN₂, PN₇, BB, PN₄, PA*).
18   en plus] en plus en plus (en plus *PN₂, PN₇, PN₄, PN₁, PA*).

(**Var.**) 81   recorde que] recorderay *PN₇*.
5   se esmerveilla] il s'en merveille *BB*.

coniugi hec benivolencie et fidei coniugalis experimenta
E 701 sufficere; sed sunt qui, ubi semel inceperint, non desinant; ymo   46
E 708 incumbant hereantque proposito. Defixis ergo in uxorem ocu-
lis, an ulla eius mutatio erga se fieret contemplabatur assidue,   48

As before, Griseldis remained unchanged.

nec ullam penitus invenire poterat, nisi quod fidelior illi indies
E 715 atque obsequencior fiebat, sic ut duorum non nisi unus animus   50
videretur, isque non communis amborum sed viri dum taxat
unius, uxor enim per se nichil velle, ut dictum est, nichil nolle   52
E 722 firmaverat. Ceperat sensim de Valterio decolor fama crebres-
cere: quod videlicet effera et inhumana duricie, humilis peni-   54
tencia ac pudore coniugij, filios iussisset interfici, nam neque
pueri comparebant, neque ubinam gencium essent ullus audi-   56
E 729 erat; quo se ille vir alioquin clarus et suis carus multis infamem
odiosumque reddiderat. Neque ideo trux animus flectebatur,   58
sed in suscepta severitate experiendique sua dura illa libi-
E 736 dine procedebat. Itaque cum iam ab ortu filie duodecimus   60
E 743 annus elapsus esset, nuncios Romam misit, qui simulatas
inde literas apostolicas referrent, quibus in populo vulgaretur   62
datam sibi licenciam a Romano pontifice, ut pro sua et suarum
gencium quiete, primo matrimonio reiecto, aliam ducere   64
E 750 posset uxorem; nec operosum sane fuit alpestribus rudibusque
animis quidlibet persuadere. Que fama cum ad Griseldis   66
noticiam pervenisset, tristis, ut puto, sed ut que semel de se
E 757 suisque de sortibus statuisset, inconcussa constitit, ex- ⟨fol. 20ᵛ⟩   68
pectans quid de se ille decerneret cui se et sua cuncta sub-

The rumor spread that Walter had murdered his children, and his reputation grew black.

But, persisting in his severity, twelve years after the birth of his daughter he had papal bulls forged, leading the people to believe that the Pope had annulled his marriage and given him leave to take another wife.

Griseldis, hearing the news, awaited Walter's will.

(Vat₆.) 46   sufficere] suficere.
    48   assidue] asidue.
    54   et inhumana] inhumana (et inhumana Cs, P₁, P₆, P₇, Ra, Rb, Rc,
Lac, Laur₃, Chig, Vat₃, CC₄, CC₂, Mgd, Pal, Bay₇, Har₂, Har₃, Bod, Laur₂)—
humilis] humillis.
    56   gencium essent] gencium (gencium essent Cs, P₁, P₆, P₇, Ra, Rb,
Rc, Lac, Laur₃, Chig, Vat₃, CC₄, CC₂, Mgd, Ricc, Mlb, Pal, Bay₇, Har₂,
Har₃, Bod, Laur₂).
    57   alioquin] alioquim—infamem] infamen.
    62   referrent] refferent.
    66–67   Griseldis noticiam] noticiam Griseldis.

Handbook, n. 81 on p. 303), the manuscript evidence indicates that Petrarch intended it to read as it is printed in the text. All manuscripts (except those of families c and d, which omit cum suorum omnium valde) give
the reading essentially as it appears in the text. No manuscript gives an
expanded form of the passage. Professor French's emendation from
nullus of the Basle and Venice prints to nullius is borne out by a majority
of manuscripts in each of the families a, b, and d, and by half the manuscripts in family c (in all, by sixteen out of the twenty-four).

se merveilla, et tellement que, s'il n'eust sceu qu'elle amast parfaitement ses enffans, il l'eust tenue pour suspecte et mauvaise femme,   20
et eust creu celle fermeté et constance venir de couraige d'aucune
E 694 crueuse voulenté; mais seur estoit qu'elle riens plus n'amoit aprés   22
lui. Il envoia ce filz a Bouloingne a nourrir et a garder secretement,
comme il avoit fait sa fille.   24

Povoient, je vous prie, a ce seigneur ces experimens d'obeïssance
E 701 et de foy de mariage bien souffrire? Mais y sont aucuns que quant il   26
ont aucune chose commancié ou en propos qui continuent tousjours
E 708 plus. Or avisa plus que devant ledit marquis se sa dicte femme se   28
mueroit envers lui ou feroit semblant en aucune maniere de ses
enffans; mais en riens ne se changa qu'elle ne fust plus continuelment   30
E 722 a lui feable, plus obeïssante et serviciable que par avant. Si commen-
çoit du marquis une mauvaise renommee a courir: qu'il n'eust ce de   32
mauvais esperit meu, et pour honte de ce qu'il c'estoit si petitement
mariez, fait faire et fait perir et occirre ses enffans, car on n'en veoit   34
E 729 aucun ne on ne savoit ne oyoit dire ou ilz estoient; dont il, qui estoit
si noble et estoit si amez de ses subgés, en autre maniere se faisoit   36
haynneux et notter de son peuple. Et toutesfoiz ja pour ce son dur
couraige ne mua, mais en sa merancolie et dure ymaginacion de ap-   38
E 736 prouver sa femme proceda et continua encores plus avant; si que comme depuis la nativité de sa fille eust xii ans, il envoia a Romme ses   40
E 743 messages qui lui apporterent lettres faintes, par lesquelles il donnoit
a entendre au peuple que le pape pour la paix de lui et de ses gens lui   42
avoit donné congié et dispensacion de soy departir de sa femme et
E 750 prandre une autre. Et ne fut pas fort de le donner a entendre a ses   44
gens simples et rudes ce qu'il lui pleut. Laquelle chose quant elle vint
a la congnoissance Griseldis, elle ne s'en esbaÿst ne mua en aucune   46
E 757 maniere ne ne changa soy, attendant que cil, a qui elle avoit soubmis
tous ses fais, en ordonnast a sa voulenté. ⟨fol. 140ʳ⟩ Il avoit desja   48

(Var.) 29   lui] li son courage PA.
47   ne ne changa soy, attendant que cil] Ains attendoit touzjours moult
humblement que cellui PA.

E 764 iecerat. Miserat iam ille Bononiam, cognatumque rogaverat   70
E 771 ut ad se filios suos adduceret, fama undique diffusa virginem
illam sibi in coniugium adduci. Quod ille fideliter executurus,   72
E 778 puellam iam nubilem, excellentem forma preclaroque con-
spicuam ornatu, germanumque simul suum annum iam septi-   74
mum agentem ducens, cum eximia nobilium comitiva, statuto
die iter arripuit.   76

Walter sent to Bologna for his offspring, and let every-one believe that a maiden from there was to be his new bride. His relative the count set out with the two children.

[Pars V]

E 785   Hec inter Valterius, solito ut uxorem retemptaret ingenio,
doloris ac pudoris ad cumulum, in publicum adducte coram   2
E 792 multis, "Satis," inquit, "tuo coniugio delectabar, mores tuos
non originem respiciens; nunc quoniam, ut video, magna   4
E 799 omnis fortuna servitus magna est, non michi licet quod cuilibet
liceret agricole. Cogunt mei, et papa consentit, uxorem me   6
alteram habere, iamque uxor in via est statimque aderit.
E 806 Esto igitur forti animo, dansque locum alteri, et dotem tuam   8
referens, in antiquam domum equa mente revertere. Nulla
E 813 homini perpetua sors est." Contra illa, "Ego," inquit, "mi   10
domine, semper scivi inter magnitudinem tuam et humilitatem
meam nullam esse proporcionem; meque nunquam tuo, non   12
E 820 dicam coniugio, sed servicio dignam duxi, inque hac domo,
in qua tu me dominam fecisti, Deum testor, animo semper   14
E 827 ancilla permansi. De hoc igitur tempore quo tecum multo
cum honore longe supra omne meritum meum fui, Deo et tibi   16
gratias ago; de reliquo, parata sum bono pacatoque animo
E 834 paternam domum repetere, atque ubi puericiam egi senec-   18
tutem agere et mori, felix semper atque honorabilis vidua, que

Meanwhile Walter, still test-ing his wife, said to her: "Although I have delighted in our marriage, my people compel me to take another wife, who is even now on the way here. Take back your dowry, therefore, and re-turn to your old home."

She answered: "I have ever realized my unworthiness, and I give thanks for these years I have dwelt with you.

Willingly I return to my father's house, willingly yield to your new bride.

(Vat₆.) 71   filios] fillios.
73   nubilem] nubillem.
74   simul suum] suum simul.
75   nobilium] nobillium.
76   arripuit] aripuit.
2   cumulum, in publicum adducte] cumullum impublicum adductam (adducte Cs, P₁, Ra, Rb, Lac, Laur₃, Chig, Vat₃, CC₄, Mgd, Ricc, Mlb, Bay₇, Har₂, Har₃, Bod, Laur₂).
15   ancilla] ancila.
17   de reliquo] derelico (with co canceled and quo written above).

(Var.) 3   inquit] inquit Grisildis CC₂.
7   uxor] uxor mea Rc, Pal, Bay₇.
9   Nulla] Nulli Mgd, Bod.
11   humilitatem] parvitatem Mgd, paucitatem Bod.
12   nullam] nullam prorsus P₁, P₆, Rc, Chig, Vat₃, CC₄, Ricc, Mlb, Pal, Bay₇, Har₂, nullius prorsus P₇ —proporcionem] comparationem P₇.

764 envoié a Bouloingne et avoit escript au mari de sa suer que il lui
771 amenast ses enfans. La renommee courroit ja partout que le marquis   50
devoit prendre a femme une grant dame. Et ycellui conte de Paniquo,
qui estoit moult amis dudit marquis, en grant appareil et ordonnance,   52
et moult bien acompaignié de nobles, estoit desja au chemin, et
778 amenoit ycelle fille du marquis, moult belle et en point de marier, et   54
le frere d'icelle fille, qui avoit environ sept ans.

[V]

COMMENT ledit marquis dist a sa femme Griseldis qu'il failloit qu'il
preist autre femme qu'elle, et comment il la renvoia chiez son pere   2
toute nue, excepté tant seulement une povre chemise, et comment
Janicole, son pere, lui vint au devant, qui lui bailla ses povres veste-   4
mens qu'il avoit gardé.

785 Et ce temps pendant le marquis, vueillant sa femme plus que de-   6
792 vant essaier et tenter, vint a elle et lui dist: "Griseldis, je ne te veul
riens celer, et vueil que tu saches que j'avoye grant plaisir de toy   8
avoir a femme pour les biens et vertus que je savoye estre en toy, et
non pas pour ton lignaige, comme tu le dois savoir; mais je congnois   10
maintenant que toute grande fortune et seigneurie est grant servitute,
799 car il ne me loise ce qu'il loise et puet faire un povre homme. Mes   12
gens me contraingnent, et le pape consent, que je preigne une autre
806 femme, qui est ja en voie et sera tantost cy. Aies doncques bon   14
couraige et fort; fay lieu a l'autre, et pren le douaire que tu apportas
avecques moy et t'en retourne en la maison de ton pere. Ainsi est des   16
choses: nul n'est seur en son estat."
813 A ce dist elle: "J'ai tousjours sceu et tenu que entre ta grant magni-   18
ficence et mon humilité et povreté n'avoit nulle comparoison, ne moy
oncques je ne dis mie seulement d'estre ta femme, mais d'estre ta   20
820 chamberiere ne me reputay digne. Et j'en appelle Dieu en tesmoing,
qui scet tout, en ceste tienne maison ou ⟨fol. 140ᵛ⟩ tu m'as fait dame,   22
ay tousjours en cuer et me suy tenue pour ta chamberiere et servente.
827 De ce temps, doncques, que sans mes merites et trop plus que je ne   24
vail certainement moy honnourant j'ay esté avec toy, j'en rens
graces a Dieu et a toy. Quant au remenant, je suy preste de bon et   26
834 prompt courage de retourner chiez mon pere, ou j'ay esté nourrie en
m'enfance; et d'y estre en ma villesce, et la morir bien me plaist,   28
bieneureuse et honnourable vesve de si grant seigneur comme tu es.

(**Var.**) 12   il ne me loise] je n'ose mie faire *PA*.
15   fay] et fais *BB*, et fay *PA*.
18   elle] elle monseigneur *PN₂, PN₇, BB, PN₄, PA*.
28   estre] demourer *PA*.

E 841 viri talis uxor fuerim. Nove coniugi volens cedo, que tibi utinam 20
felix adveniat, atque hinc ubi iocundissime degebam quando ita

E 848 tibi placitum, non invita discedo. At quod iubes dotem meam 22

E 862 mecum ut auferam, quale sit video, neque enim excidit ut
paterne olim domus in limine spoliata meis, tuis induta 24
vestibus ad te veni, neque omnino alia michi dos fuit quam
fides et nuditas. Ecce igitur ut hanc vestem exuo, anulumque 26

E 869 restituo quo me subarrasti; reliqui anuli et vestes et ornamenta
quibus te donante ad invidiam aucta eram, in thalamo tuo 28
sunt. Nuda e domo patris egressa, nuda itidem revertar,

E 876 nisi quod indignum reor ut hic uterus in quo filij fuerunt quos 30

E 883 tu genuisti, populo nudus appareat. Quamobrem si tibi
placet, et non aliter, oro atque obsecro ut in precium virgini- 32
tatis quam huc attuli quamque non refero, unicam michi
camisiam linqui iubeas earum quibus tecum uti soleo, qua 34

E 890 ventrem tue quondam uxoris operiam." Abundabant viro
lacrime, ut contineri amplius iam non possent, itaque faciem 36
avertens, "Et camisiam tibi unicam habeto," verbis tre-
mentibus vix expressit, et sic abijt illacrimans. Illa, coram 38
cunctis sese exuens, solam sibi retinuit camisiam, qua con-

E 897 tecta, nudo capite pedibusque nudis, egreditur; atque ita prose- 40
quentibus multis ac flentibus fortunamque culpantibus, siccis
una oculis et honesto veneranda silencio, ⟨fol. 21ʳ⟩ ad paternam 42

E 904 domum remeavit. Senex, qui has filie nuptias semper sus-
pectas habuerat neque unquam tantam spem mente concepe- 44
rat semperque hoc eventurum cogitaverat, ut, sacietate sponse
tam humilis exorta, domo illam quandoque vir tantus et more 46
nobilium superbus abiceret, tunicam eius hispidam et attritam

E 911 senio, abdita parve domus in parte servaverat. Audito ergo 48
non tam filie tacite redeuntis quam comitum strepitu, occurrit

E 918 in limine et seminudam antiqua veste cohoperuit. Mansit illa 50

Marginal glosses (right column):

My dowry, I know, was but nakedness and faithfulness—

naked I came, naked will I go. Yet, for propriety's sake, allow me one shift to cover the belly in which I carried your children."

"Keep one shift," he said, with wet eyes and trembling voice.

Stripping to her shift, she went forth in that alone, dry-eyed and silent among many who followed her weeping and bewailing her fate.

Her old father, always suspicious of the marriage, had kept her coarse gown;

at his threshold he covered her with it. In kindness and humility she remained with him for some days.

(Vat₆.) 26 anulumque] anullumque.
31 populo] popullo.
33 refero] reffero.
46 humilis] humilli (humilis Cs, P₁, P₆, P₇, Ra, Rb, Lac, Chig, Laur₃, Vat₃, CC₄, Ricc, Mlb, Har₂, Har₃, Laur₂).
48 in parte] imparte.
49 redeuntis] reddeuntis.

(Var.) 22 discedo] discedam Cs, Ra, Rb.
23 excidit] animo excidit P₆, excidit *after which is inserted above, in almost illegible writing*, a mea memoria P₇.
30 filij] filij tui Bod.
47 et attritam] antiquam atritam P₆.

841 Et voulentiers feray lieu a ta nouvelle femme, laquelle soit en ton   30
boneur et aventure, comme de tout mon cuer le desire. Et de cy, ou
j'estoie et demouroie en grant plaisir, puis qu'il te plaist, voulentiers   32
848 me partiray. A quoy, toutesfoiz, me commande tu que je reporte
avec moy mon douaire, quel il l'est je le voy, ne je n'ay pas oublié   34
862 comment, quant pieça tu me voulz prendre a femme, je fus desvestue
sur le seul de mon pere des povres robes que j'avoye vestues, et fus   36
vestue des tiennes grandes precieuses, ne en tout n'aportay avec toy autre douaire que foy et loyauté. Veez cy, doncques, puis qu'il te plaist,   38
je te desvests ceste tienne robe et rens l'aneau de quoy tu m'espousas.
869 Les autres aneaux, vestures, couronnes, et autres ornemens, que   40
fortune m'avoit presté une espasse de temps avec toy et, en faisant
et paiant son deu, les me toust et reprent, sont en tes escrins. Nue   42
vins de chiez mon pere, et nue la retourneray, se tu ne repute et tien
876 chose vil et malgracieuse, comme je croy que tu feroyes, que ce   44
ventre cy, qui a porté les enffans que tu as engendrez, soit veu nus ne
883 descouvert au peuple. Pour laquelle chose, s'il te plaist et non autre-   46
ment, je te supplie que, ou pris et pour la virginité que je apportay
avec toy, laquelle je n'en reporte mie, laisse moy une des chemises que   48
j'avoie quant j'estoie appellee ta femme."
890   Lors ploura forment de pitié le marquis si que a paine contenir se   50
povoit; et ainsi, en tournant son visaige, en parler tout troublé,
a paine peust dire, "Doncques te demeure celle que tu as vestue."   52
Et ainsi se party celle sans plourer; et devant chascun se devesti,
et seulement retint la chemise que vestue avoit, et la teste toute des-   54
897 couverte et deschausse s'en va. Et en cest estat la suivent plusieurs,
plourans et maudisans fortune, et elle seule ne ⟨fol. 141ʳ⟩ plouroit   56
mie ne ne disoit mot. Et ainsy s'en retourna en l'ostel de son pere.
904 Et le bon homs son pere, qui adés avoit eu le mariage suspet ne oncques   58
n'en avoit esté seur, ains doubtoit tousjours que ainsy n'en avenist,
911 vint a l'encontre des gens a cheval sur son seul; et de la povre robette,   60
que tousjours lui avoit gardee, la couvry a grant mesaise, car la femme
estoit devenue grande et embarnie et la povre robe enrudiee et em-   62
918 piree. Et demoura avec son pere par aucuns jours en merveilleuse-

(**Var.**) 33   A quoy, toutesfoiz] Mais quant ad ce que tu *PA*.
34   quel il l'est je le voy] tel qu'il est. Tu scez bien *PA*.
52   dire] dire mot *PN₂, PN₇*—Doncques te demeure] doncques te demeure
dist il *PN₂, BB, PN₄*, doncques dit il te demeure *PN₇*, Je vueil bien dist il
adoncques que *PA*.
55   plusieurs] plusieurs gens *PN₂*.
60   vint] vient *PN₂, BB, PA*—des gens a cheval] d'elle et des gens qui la
suyvoient *PN₇*.
63   demoura] ainsi demoura *PA*.

cum patre paucos dies equanimitate et humilitate mirabili,
ita ut nullum in ea signum animi tristioris, nullum vestigium   52
E 925 fortune prosperioris extaret, quippe cum in medijs opibus inops
semper spiritu vixisset atque humilis.   54

[Pars VI]

E 939   Iam Panici comes propinquabat, et de novis nupcijs fama
undique frequens erat; premissoque uno e suis, diem quo Salu-   2
E 946 tias perventurus esset acceperat. Pridie igitur Valterius, ad
E 953 se Griseldim evocans, devotissime venienti, "Cupio," ait, "ut   4
puella cras huc ad prandium ventura magnifice excipiatur,
virique et matrone qui secum sunt, simulque et nostri qui con-   6
iugio intererunt, ita ut locorum verborumque honor integer
E 960 singulis pro dignitate servetur. Domi tamen feminas ad hoc   8
opus ydoneas non habeo; proinde tu, quamvis veste inopi,
hanc tibi, que mores meos nosti optime, suscipiendorum locan-   10
E 967 dorumque hospitum curam sumes." "Non libenter modo,"
inquit illa, "sed cupide et hoc et quecunque tibi placita sensero   12
faciam semper, neque in hoc unquam fatigabor aut lentescam
E 974 dum spiritus huius reliquie ulle supererunt." Et cum dicto,   14

A little before the Count of Panago was to arrive, Walter sent for Griseldis. "I desire," he said, "that the maiden and guests coming here tomorrow be fittingly received. Since I have no one able to do this, do you, despite your poor clothing, perform the task."

"Gladly," she replied, and took up the household implements and set to work.

(Vat₆.) 53   in] im.

1–2   fama undique] fama (fama undique *Cs, P₁, P₆, P₇, Ra, Rb, Rc, Lac, Laur₃, Chig, Vat₃, CC₄, CC₂, Mgd, Ricc, Mlb, Pal, Bay₇, Har₂, Har₃, Bod, Laur₂*).

4   venienti] vehenienti (*with* he *canceled*).

7   honor integer] honor (honor integer *Cs, P₁, Ra, Rb, Rc, Chig, Vat₃, CC₄, Mgd, Ricc, Mlb, Pal, Bay₅, Bod*).

9   opus ydoneas] ydoneas opus.

10   mores meos] meos mores.

10–11   suscipiendorum locandorumque] suscipiendorumque locandorum.

12   placita sensero] sensero placita.

(**Var.**) 53   extaret] exstaret verbumque beati Job compacientibus sibi respondit, "Dominus dedit, Dominus abstulit; sicut Domino placuit, ita factum est" *CC₄*.

6–7   *coniugio.* The true Petrarchan reading is *convivio*, which is found in twenty-two of the twenty-four manuscripts, Vat₆ and Har₂ alone giving *coniugio*. *Coniugio* is allowed to stand in the text because it is very slightly closer to Chaucer. In the twenty-two manuscripts Walter, when commanding Griseldis to come receive his guests, makes no mention of the marriage which is to occur on the morrow; in Vat₆ and Har₂, however, he mentions it in the word *coniugio*. Chaucer's Walter also alludes to the marriage:

"Grisilde," quod he, "my wyl is outrely
This mayden *that shal wedded been to me*," etc. (953–54).

ment grant humilité et pacience, si que nul signe de tristesce, nulz   64
remors de la prosperité qu'elle avoit eu ne faisoit ne monstroit en
925 aucune maniere; et ce n'estoit pas merveille, comme en ses grans   66
richesses tousjours en pensee humble eust vescu et fust maintenue.

939 Et ja le conte de Paniquo venoit de Bouloingne et approchoit fort,   68
et des nouvelles nopces se continuoit et publioit la renommee par tout
le pays; sy envoia ledit conte au marquis dire le jour qu'il seroit a lui.   70
946 Et un peu devant qu'il venist, le marquis manda Griseldis, qui venist
pour obeïr a ses commandemens moult voulentiers, et lui dist: 72
953 "Griseldis, je desire moult que celle pucelle, qui doit demain estre cy
pour estre ma femme, et ceulx qui vendront avec elle, et aussy tous   74
ceux qui seront au disner, soient receus bien et grandement, et que
chascun soit festoyé et ordonné selon sa personne et estat. Toutes-   76
960 foiz, ceans n'ay a present qui proprement sceut ce faire; pourquoy,
doncques, ja soit ce que tu soies mal vestue et povrement, pren la   78
cusançon de cecy, qui congnois mes meurs et les estres de l'ostel."

967 "Maintenant," dist elle, "non pas voulentiers tant seulement   80
mais de tres lié cuer, et ce et quelconque chose que je sentiroie qui
te pleust feray tousjours. Ne ja de ce ne me laisseray ne m'ennueray   82
974 tant que vive." Et en ce disant, commence a besoingnier, comme de

(**PN₃.**) 77   n'ay] n'a (n'ay PN_2, BB, PN_4, PA).

(**Var.**) 66   maniere] maniere semblant PN_2—comme] Car PA.
67   en pensee humble eust vescu et fust maintenue] vescu en grant humilité PA.
68   Et ja le] ja ce PN_2, PN_7, PN_4.
77   ceans] seans PN_2.
77–78   pourquoy, doncques, ja soit ce] aucune belle ordranance je vueil combien PA.
80   dist elle] dist elle monseigneur PN_7.

servilia mox instrumenta corripiens, domum verrere, mensas
instruere, lectos sternere, ortarique alias ceperat, ancille in 16

E 981 morem fidelissime. Proxime lucis hora tercia, comes super-
venerat; certatimque omnes et puelle et germani infantis 18
mores ac pulcritudinem mirabantur. Erantque qui dicerent

E 988 prudenter Valterium ac feliciter permutasse, quod et sponsa 20
hec tenerior esset et nobilior, et cognatus tam speciosus

E 1009 accederet. Sic fervente convivij apparatu, ubique presens 22
omniumque solicita Griseldis, nec tanto casu deiecta animo
nec obsolete vestis pudore confusa, sed sereno vultu intranti 24
obvia puelle, "Bene venerit domina mea," inquit. Dehinc

E 1016 ceteros dum convivas leta facie et verborum mira suavitate 26
susciperet, et immensam domum multa arte disponeret, ita
ut omnes et presertim advene unde ea maiestas morum at- 28
que ea prudencia sub tali habitu vehementissime mirarentur,

E 1023 atque ipsa imprimis puelle pariter atque infantis laudibus 30
saciari nullo modo posset, sed vicissim modo virgineam, modo
infantilem eleganciam predicaret. Valterius, eo ipso in tem- 32
pore quo assidendum mensis erat in eam versus, clara voce

E 1030 coram omnibus, quasi illudens, "Quid tibi videtur," inquid, 34
"de hac mea sponsa? Satis pulcra atque honesta est?"
"Plane," ⟨fol. 21ᵛ⟩ ait illa, "nec pulcrior ulla nec honestior 36
inveniri potest. Aut cum nulla unquam, aut cum hac tran-
quillam agere poteris ac felicem vitam; utque ita sit cupio et 38

E 1037 spero. Unum bona fide te precor ac moneo: ne hanc illis

The count arrived, and all commended the maiden and her brother.

Griseldis, unashamed in her old garments, greeted the maiden and the other guests, and managed all things so well that everyone wondered at her. She praised both the maiden and the boy.

As they were about to sit at table, Walter mockingly cried, "Griseldis, what think you of my bride?" "None prettier or finer could be found," she replied; "I wish you joy. But, I beg, do not treat her so harshly as you have another, for her delicateness could not bear it."

(Vat₆.) 15 verrere] verere.
16 ancille] ancile.
21 hec] habere is expunged and hec written above it.
32 infantilem] infantillem—ipso] ipso quo with quo expunged.
35 Satis] satin (Satis Cs, P₆, P₇, Ra, Rb, Rc, Chig, Vat₃, CC₄, Ricc, Mlb, Pal, Bay₇, Bay₆, Har₂).

(Var.) 16 alias] alicis Har₂.
20 permutasse] coniugium permutasse CC₄.
34 inquid] inquit Griseldis Cs, Ra, Rb.

25 *puelle.* After this word in the prints (Cs, Ra, Rb) occurs a passage (*flexo poplite servilem in modum vultuque demisso reverenter atque humiliter*) found in none other of the seventy-two manuscripts and early prints which I examined. Since the evidence is thus overwhelmingly against its authenticity, and since the passage finds no echo in Chaucer's poem, I have not included it in the text. Yet the addition must date from the fourteenth century, for both Philippe de Mézières' French translation, executed before 1389, and the version in *Le Ménagier*, composed about 1393, reflect the passage (cf. *Le Ménagier*, I, 122: "Vint de loing a l'encontre de la pucelle *et de loing humblement la salua a genoulx*, disant: 'Bien soiez venue, madame' ").

baloier la maison, mettre tables, faire liz, et ordonner tout et prier aux   84
autres chamberieres que chascune en droit soy feist au mieulx qu'elle
pourroit.   86

E 981   Il estoit ja environ tierce du jour que le conte, qui avoit amené et la
fille et le filz, estoit venuz, et chascun regardoit tres fort et voulentiers   88
la beauté de ses deux enfans, et se merveilloient tous. Et estoient ja
aucuns qui disoient que le marquis faisoit que saige de laissier la pre-   90
E 988   miere femme et de prendre celle belle jeusne femme, mesmement
qu'elle estoit tant noble et son frere tant bel. Et ainsy s'avançoit   92
C 1009 fort l'appareil du disner; et par tout aloit ⟨fol. 141ᵛ⟩ et couroit celle
Griseldis, sans avoir honte de ce qu'elle estoit si mal vestue, ne de ce   94
qu'elle estoit ainsy abaissié de son hault mariage, mais de bonne chiere
et liee vint a l'encontre de celle pucelle et dist, "Bien soiez venue, ma   96
C 1016 dame." Et en ceste maniere les seigneurs, dames, et damoiselles qui
la devoient disner de liee chiere tres doulcement et benignement elle   98
recevoit et ordonnoit du tout ce palays et mettoit a point tellement
que chascun, et especiaument les estrangiers, se merveilloient dont   100
telles meurs, tant grant sens soubz tel abit venoient, et s'en donnoient
grant esbaÿssement, et sur toutes choses ne se povoient souler de la   102
C 1023 regarder. Ne aussy ne se povoit souler Griseldis de parler des louenges
de ses deux enffans: maintenant de la vierge, maintenant du filz la   104
beauté et maintien recommandoit. Et le marquis, tout ainsy que on
devoit aler a table, en haulte voix dist a Griseldis devant tous, ainsi   106
C 1030 comme en soy jouant: "Dy, Griseldis, que te semble il de ma femme?
Est elle belle?"   108

"Plainement," dist elle, "ouy; ne je ne croy mie que plus belle ne
plus gente tu puisses trouver. Tu vivras en paix et euresement   110
avec elle, comme je prie a Dieu que ainsy le faces, et ay esperance
E 1037 que ce feras tu, ou jamais avec autre. Une chose toutesfoiz te vueil   112

(**PN₃.**) 90–91   premiere femme] premiere (premiere femme *PN₇, BB, PN₄, PA*).
100   se merveilloient] *om.* (se merveilloient *PN₂, PN₄*).

(**Var.**) 92   bel] belle que grant merveilles estoit de les veoir *PA*.
102–3   de la regarder. Ne aussy ne se povoit souler] *om. PN₂, PN₇, BB,
PN₄, PA*.

aculeis agites quibus alteram agitasti, nam quod et iunior et 40
delicatius enutrita est, pati quantum ego auguror non valeret."

E 1044 Talia dicentis alacritatem intuens, atque constanciam tociens 42
tamque acriter offense mulieris examinans, et indignam sortem

E 1051 non sic merite miseratus, ac ferre diucius non valens, "Satis," 44
inquit, "mea Griseldis, cognita et spectata michi fides est tua,
nec sub celo aliquem esse puto qui tanta coniugalis amoris 46
experimenta perceperit." Simul hec dicens, caram coniugem

E 1058 leto stupore perfusam et velut e somno turbido experrectam, 48
cupidis ulnis amplectitur et "Tu," ait, "tu sola uxor mea es;

E 1065 aliam nec habui, nec habebo. Ista autem quam tu sponsam 50
meam reris, filia tua est; hic qui cognatus meus credebatur,
tuus est filius: que divisim perdita videbantur, simul omnia 52

E 1072 recepisti. Sciant qui contrarium crediderunt me curiosum
atque experientem esse, non impium; probasse coniugem, non 54

E 1079 dampnasse; occultasse filios, non mactasse." Hec illa audiens,
pene gaudio exanimis et pietate amens iocundissimisque cum 56
lacrimis, suorum pignorum in amplexus ruit, fatigatque osculis,

E 1114 pioque gemitu madefacit. Raptimque matrone alacres ac 58
faventes circumfuse, vilibus exutam suis, solitis vestibus in-
duunt exornantque; plaususque letissimus et fausta omnium 60

E 1121 verba circumsonant, multoque cum gaudio et fletu ille dies
celeberrimus fuit, celebrior quoque quam dies fuerat nupti- 62

E 1128 arum. Multosque post per annos ingenti pace concordiaque
vixere; et Valterius inopem socerum, quem hactenus neglexisse 64
visus erat, ne quando concepte animo obstaret experiencie,
suam in domum translatum in honore habuit, filiam suam 66

E 1135 magnificis atque honestis nupcijs collocavit, filiumque sui
dominij successorem liquit, et coniugio letus et sobole. 68

Marginal glosses:

"Enough, Griseldis!" Walter exclaimed. "Your faithfulness to me has been proved."

Embracing her, he continued: "You are my only wife, and ever shall be. This maiden is your daughter; that youth, your son. Know all that I am not so evil as has been thought."

At these words Griseldis was overcome with joy.

Then the ladies clothed and adorned her very grandly. Everyone was happy; and that day was even more honored than had been her marriage day.

For many years they lived happily. Walter moved old Janicola into the castle and held him in esteem. For his daughter he arranged an honorable marriage; and his son succeeded him as his heir.

(**Vat₆.**) 42 alacritatem intuens] intuens alacritatem.

45 spectata] specta (spectata *Cs, P₁, P₆, P₇, Ra, Rb, Rc, Lac, Laur₃, CC₄, Mgd, Pal, Bay₇, Har₂, Bod*).

46 aliquem esse puto] puto aliquem esse.

48 experrectam] experectam.

55 occultasse] ocultasse.

59 solitis vestibus] vestibus solitis.

62 celeberrimus] celeberimus.

65 visus] iussus (visus *Cs, P₁, P₆, P₇, Ra, Rb, Rc, Lac, Laur₃, Chig, Vat₃, CC₄, CC₂, Mgd, Ricc, Mlb, Pal, Bay₇, Har₂, Har₃, Bod, Laur₂*).

67 collocavit] colocavit.

(**Var.**) 42 alacritatem] vultum alacriter *CC₂*.

50 habebo] habeo *P₁, Vat₃, CC₂, Bod*.

68 sobole] sobole. Et sic ex serie et stemate huius narrationis egregie patet quod pacientissima Grysildis post se talem non reliquit superstitem. *Explicit Bod.*

prier et requerir: que tu ne la poingnes des aguillons que tu as pointe
l'autre, car et plus jeune est et plus delicieusement nourrie; souffrir,   114
comme je croy, ne le pourroit."

[VI]

COMMENT le marquis rappella sa femme Griseldis et la remist en son
estat avec lui, et comment il lui monstra ses deux enfans qu'elle   2
cudoit qu'il eust fait morir et occirre.

1044   Et quant le marquis regarda la bonne et entiere voulenté de celle   4
femme, la constance et grant pacience, que tant de fois et tant durement courroucié avoit, et qui ainsy respondoit, dist a haulte voix: 6
1051 "C'est assez, Griseldis, j'ay a plain veu et congneu ta bonne foy et
vraye humilité, ne je ne croy mie que soubz le ciel soit aucun qui tant   8
ait veu ne approuvé de vraie amour et obeïssance de mariage que ⟨fol.
142ʳ⟩ j'ay en toy." Et en ce faisant et disant l'embraissa tres doulce-   10
1058 ment, et elle s'esbahyt tout ainsy que s'elle s'esveillast d'un songe.
1065 "Tu es," dist il, "seule ma femme; autre n'ay eu, ne ja n'auray. Ceste   12
cy, voy tu, que tu cuidoies estre ma femme est ta fille, et l'enfant ton
filz. Yceulx enffans que tu cudoies avoir perdu a deux foiz, tu les as   14
1072 maintenant recouvré tout ensemble. Saichent tous qui le contraire
ont cudié, moy avoir fait ce que j'ay fait pour toy approuver et essaier   16
tant seulement, et non pas avoir voulu faire tuer mes enffans, dont
Dieu me gart, ne oncques ne fu, puis que t'espousay, que pour ma   18
1079 femme ne te tenisse et reputasse." Et quant Griseldis oÿ ces nouvelles, toute pasmee et avenoiee, ainsi que le marquis l'avoit embrassié,   20
1114 se laissa cheoir.   Et lors tantost les bonnes dames qui la estoient la
devestirent de ses povres robes qu'elle avoit vestue, et la revestirent   22
1121 de ses bonnes et parerent tres grandement. Et adoncques chascun
commença a faire bonne chiere et joyeuse, car le seigneur le vouloit et   24
en prioit chascun. Et fist on plus grant solennité que on n'avoit fait
1128 aux nopces premieres. Et depuis grant temps et long furent ensemble   26
en grant paix et bonne amour ledit marquis et Griseldis. Et depuis,

(**PN₃.**) 10–11   tres doulcement] *om.* (tres doulcement *PA, PN₂, PN₇, BB,
PN₄*).
18   t'espousay] t'espousa (t'espousay *PN₂, PN₇, BB, PN₄, PN₁, PA*).
(**Var.**) 12   eu] *om. PN₇, PN₁*.
15   Saichent] Et les a nourriz ma suer et introduis abier et a tout honneur
faire comme tu le pues appercevoir. Et sachent *BB*.
16   moy avoir fait ce que j'ay fait] que j'ay ce cy fait tant seullement *PA*.
19   Et quant] quant *PA*.
21   laissa] laisse *PN₂*—estoient la] estoïent la prindrent gracieusement et
PN₇, estoient aprés ce qu'elle fut revenue de paulmoisons la *PA*.
23   de ses bonnes et parerent tres grandement] tres honnorablement et en
grant reverance de ses bonnes robes et parerent tres grandement et richement
PN₇, et reparerent grandement de robes riches et honnorables *PN₁*.
25   solennité] sollempnité et plus grant feste et plus joyeuse *PN₇*.

E 1142   Hanc historiam stilo nunc alio retexere visum fuit, non tam
ideo, ut matronas nostri temporis ad imitandam huius uxoris   70
pacienciam, que michi vix imitabilis videtur, quam ut legentes
E 1149   ad imitandam saltem femine constanciam excitarem, ut quod   72
hec viro suo prestitit, hoc prestare Deo nostro audeant, qui
licet (ut Jacobus ait Apostolus) intentator sit malorum, et   74
E 1156   ipse neminem temptet. Probat tamen et sepe nos multis ac
gravibus flagellis exerceri sinit, non ut animum nostrum sciat,   76
quem scivit ante quam crearemur, sed ut nobis nostra fragilitas notis ac domesticis indicijs innotescat. Abunde ego   78
constantibus viris ascripserim, quisquis is fuerit, qui pro Deo
suo sine murmure paciatur quod pro suo mortali coniuge rusti-   80
cana hec muliercula passa est.

I have told this story not to
arouse the ladies to imitate
Griseldis but rather to urge
all men to be steadfast to
God, when he tries us, as
this poor woman was to her
temporal lord.

(Vat₆.)   70   matronas nostri temporis] matronas (matronas nostri temporis Cs, P₁, P₆, Ra, Rb, Rc, Lac, Laur₃, Chig, Vat₃, CC₄, CC₂, Mgd, Ricc,
Mlb, Pal, Bay₇, Bay₅, Har₂, Har₃, Bod, Laur₂).
   71   imitabilis] imitabillis.
   72   imitandam] imittandum (imitandam Cs, P₁, P₆, P₇, Ra, Rb, Rc,
Lac, Laur₃, Chig, Vat₃, CC₂, Mgd, Ricc, Mlb, Pal, Bay₇, Bay₅, Har₃; Bod,
Laur₂).
   73   viro suo] suo viro.
   74   malorum] mallorum.
   75   et sepe nos] nos et sepe.
   76   exerceri sinit] sinit exerceri.
   77   nobis] nobis ut *with* ut *canceled.*
   77–78   fragilitas] fragilitas sit *with* sit *canceled.*
   78   innotescat] inotescat.
   81   est] est. Deo gracias amen. Explicit.

(Var.)   69   alio] alto CC₂.
   71   quam] sed CC₄, Mgd, Har₂.

69   *alio.* Of the seventy-two manuscripts and early prints which I
examined, all but five have *alio.* In CC₂ alone occurs *alto;* though in the
1473 print by Johannes Zeiner the word might be either *alco* or *alio.* It
looks as if the letter between *l* and *o* had not printed well, and had been
put in by hand; but it is exactly the same in both copies which I examined
(Bodleian, Douce 204; and British Museum, C.6.b.6). The letter is like
neither the *i* nor the *t* of the type, but if it should appear in a manuscript, I would take it for a *t* (*c*). Professor Hendrickson has pointed out
that Chaucer's "heigh style" (*Clerkes Tale*, ll. 18, 41, 1148) probably
came from a corruption or misreading of Petrarch's "stilo . . . . alio"
(Hendrickson, *MP,* IV, 188–92).

ce marquis son povre serorge, duquel n'avoit tenu compte jusques   28
alors pour mieulx faire son experiment de sa femme, fist venir en sa
maison, et le tint en grant honneur. Et maria sa fille tres haultement;   30
135 et succeda en grande et bonne prosperité son filz comme son heritier.
142   Ceste hystoire est recité de la pacience de celle femme, non pas   32
tant seulement que les femmes qui sont aujourd'uy je esmeuve a
ensuir ycelle pacience et constance, que a paine me semble ensuivable   34
et possible, mais aussy les lisans et oyans a ensuiir et considerer au
149 mains la constance d'icelle femme, afin que ce qu'elle souffrist pour   36
son mortel mary, facent et rendent a Dieu. Lequel, comme dist Saint
156 Jaque l'Apostre, ne tempte nul, mais bien appreuve et nous sueffre   38
maintes foiz tres griefment pugnir. Non pas qu'il ne congnoisse
nostre couraige et entencion devant que soyons nez, mais pour que   40
par jugemens clers et evidens recongnoissions et veons nostre fragile
humanité. Et en especial est ce escript aux constans hommes, se il   42
est aucun qui pour nostre createur et redempteur Jhesu Crist seuffre
et endure pacienment ce que pour son mary mortel endura ceste   44
⟨fol. 142ᵛ⟩ povre femmelette.

Explicit.

(**PN₃.**) 44 mortel] *om.* (mortel *PN₂, PN₇, BB, PN₄, PA*).

(**Var.**) 28   serorge] serourge dit Janicolle pere de sa femme *PN₇*.
30–31   tres haultement; et succeda] haultement et grandement et tres honnorablement selon son estat et aprés ledit marquis succeda son filz *PN₇*.
32   femme] femme grizelidiz *PN₇*.
36–37   ce qu'elle ... a Dieu] tout ainsi comme elle souffri les adversitez pacienment pour son mortel mary Nous vueillons aussi pacienment porter et souffrir
les adversitez et tribulacions de ce *plus an illegible word plus* en rendant graces
a dieu de tout ce qu'il nous envoye *PA*.
41–42   fragile humanité] fragillité humaine *PN₂, PN₇, BB, PN₄, PA*.

THE MERCHANT'S TALE

By GERMAINE DEMPSTER

OUR material will be presented under three main headings in accordance with a rough division of the tale into three somewhat overlapping portions. For the first of these, which leads up to January's marriage, and for a few features elsewhere in the tale, Section I will give the most significant passages of Deschamps' *Miroir de mariage;* as parallel to the portion on the relations of an old husband and a young wife, part of a story from Boccaccio's *Ameto* will be reprinted in Section II; in Section III we shall gather the closest analogues to Chaucer's last act, the story of the blind husband and the fruit tree.

I. DESCHAMPS' *MIROIR DE MARIAGE*

The situation all through Deschamps' long poem (12,000 lines) is that of the opening parts of the *Merchant's Tale*, both January and Franc Vouloir receiving contradictory advice on the question of taking a wife. As analogies in details almost prove Chaucer's use of the *Miroir* in that part of his tale, it seems possible and even likely that the whole episode was suggested by the French poem. Besides, the *Miroir* offers parallels to some passages in Chaucer's story of the blind husband and the fruit tree. Finally, that particular deception tale may quite possibly have been brought back to Chaucer's memory by passages in the *Miroir*.[1]

(From G. Raynaud, *Œuvres complètes d'Eustache Deschamps*, Vol. IX ["SATF" (Paris, 1894)].)

33 Le vray amy, se tu faiz mal,	If you err, a true friend will warn you,
Lui saichant, par especial	
Le te dira pour toy garder. ...	

---

[1] On Chaucer's debt to the *Miroir* see J. L. Lowes, "Chaucer and the *Miroir de mariage*," *MP*, VIII (1910–11), 165–86 and 305–34; G. Dempster, *Dramatic Irony in Chaucer* (Stanford, 1932), pp. 46–51; pp. 1045–50 in Carleton Brown, "The Evolution of the Canterbury 'Marriage Group,'" *PMLA*, XLVIII (1933); and B. J. Whiting on the *Wife of Bath's Prologue*, pp. 207 ff. in the present work. On the possibility that the *Miroir* called to Chaucer's mind the story of the blind husband see Lowes, pp. 180–81, and Dempster, p. 50, n. 91.

whereas a false
friend will acquiesce
in your folly.

42 Mais le faulx ami, par ma teste,
    Blandist, flatte et va decepvent,
    Et se tourne avecques le vent
    Et consentira ta folie
    Pour toy plaire. ...

Désir, Folie, Servitude, and Faintise, the false friends of
Franc Vouloir, have been urging him to marry:

Better marry than
burn.

106   ... Cilz vit folement
    Et contre la Saincte Escripture,
    Quant il art ou feu de luxure,
    Dont mieulx vault marier qu'ardoir.

St. Paul approves
of marriage for
procreation.

110 Car saint Pol le nous fait sçavoir
    Es epistres qu'il nous envoye,
    Mariage est moult bonne voye
    Qui la prant en entencion
    De faire generacion:

Many sins are thus
avoided.

115 On en laist maint autre pechié
    De quoy on puet estre entechié. ...

It is a most pleasant
union,
a lawful joining of
two bodies in one
flesh.

217 C'est tresdoulce conjunction,
    Ce sont deux corps en union,
    En une char par la loy joins,

220 Qui s'entraiment et près et loins.
    Homs doit par dehors ordonner,
    Femme doit dedenz gouverner.

Man's business is
outside;
woman's, at home.
Her gentle ways
soothe her
husband's temper.

    Elle est si doulce en sa parole,
    Son mari sert, baise et acole,

225 Et fait, quant il est a martire
    Qu'elle le puisse getter d'ire.

If he is ill, she
nurses him.

    S'il a griefté, celle le garde,
    Et piteusement le resgarde. ...

She takes care of
home and cattle,

231 Elle gouverne son hostel
    Et son bestail d'autre costel;

thriftily preventing
waste;

    Elle est guettant,[1] saige et apperte,[2]
    Et voit que rien ne voist a perte; ...

she saves and
spends opportunely,

    Espargnier scet et avoir soing

240 Pour le despendre a un besoing:
    Ce ne fait pas mesgnie estrange,

while strangers
would rob and loaf.

    Qui vuide l'escrin[3] et la grange
    Et ne pense fors de rober,
    De po faire et de temps passer.[4]

---

[1] Vigilant, heedful.   [2] Skilful.   [3] Coffer.

[4] In E 1296–1306 the Merchant gives us Theophrastus' very different view of
these matters. The source of this passage is quoted by B. J. Whiting in connection
with the *Wife of Bath's Prologue*, pp. 211–12 of the present work.

Examples mostly from the Old Testament are called upon to
strengthen the argument of the false friends:

252 Thobie perdit sa lueur,

Mais sa femme lui fut aidable,

Treshumble, doulce et charitable,

Tobit became blind, but his wife gently tended him,

255 Et a lui garder entendi

Tant que Dieux clarté lui rendi;[1] ...

until God restored his sight.

275 Celle Saire que nous disons

Fut si loyal qu'es benissons

Est nommée et es espousailles. ...

Faithful Sarah is mentioned in blessings.

280   Il fut uns roys

Qui diverses femmes ama

Et son propos en ce ferma

Que il n'aroit jamais espouse; ...

A king would not marry;

290 Maint bastart se vouldrent faire hoir

Qui le royaume destruisirent;

Et quant aucuns voisins ce virent,

Les destruisirent et regnerent,

Entr'eulx le regne diviserent ...

lack of legitimate heirs led to warfare and division of kingdom.

369 Si fait bon avoir droicte ligne

Et espouser femme benigne

D'onnestes parens et de bons

Tant qu'a merdailles n'a garsons

Par deffault d'oirs ne soit donnée

Terre d'autruy n'abandonnée. ...

Such examples show that it is advantageous to have lawful heirs by a kind wife born of respectable parents, so one's lands do not fall to knaves.

418 Or garde donc par quel maniere

Ta clarté n'estaingne ne faille,

Et que par mariage saille

De toy lumiere pardurable,

Belle au monde, a Dieu agreable,

See to it that your line be continued

Et que ta femme en tes vieulx jours

Soit a ta vieillesse secours,

and that your wife sustain your old age,

425 Ainsi comme fut la vieille Anne

as Anna did Tobit's.

Au grant Thobie. Et ne te dampne

Avoid carnal sins,

De suir en ce temps obscur

Pechié de char, car ou futur

En seroit ta vie abregiée,

430 Et en la fin t'ame dampnée; ...

which would shorten your life and damn your soul.

Franc Vouloir refuses to make a hasty decision:

493 S'ay bien mestier d'avoir advis.

Et si me samble que je vis,

I remember this saying of Solomon:

---

[1] Cf. E 1288–92 and the story of January recovering his eyesight. The example
of Anne and Thobie is brought in again in ll. 425–26 quoted below.

Comme je fu enfant d'escole,
De Salemon une parole,
Qui disoit assez plainement :

Act with
discernment,
ever regarding the
end,

"Se tu faiz rien, fay saigement,
Et resgarde en tous temps la fin."
500 Et ailleurs disoit en latin,
De quoi le françois veult retraire,

and do nothing
without advice,
which secures
success.

Qu'om ne doit nulle chose faire
Sanz conseil, car qui de lui euvre,
A bonne fin vient de son euvre; ...

He passes from fears (ll. 523–721) to great hopes:

I want my wife to
be kind,
meek, unaffected,
not talkative,
hard working, not
proud,
young and chaste,
sensible and grace-
ful, at least fifteen
to twenty years old,

722   Mais avoir vueil femme benigne,
Humble, simple, po enparlée,
Bien besongnant, pou eslevée,
725   Juene et chaste de bouche et mains,
Saige et gente, et qui ait du mains
De xv, xvi ou a vint ans,

rich and of good
family,
beautiful,

Qui soit riche et de bons parans,
Qui ait bon corps et qui soit belle,

gentle,

730   Et doulce comme columbelle,

obedient,

Obeissant a moy en tout, ...
746   Et se je des enfans lui fais,

loving her children,

Qu'elle les aimt, garde et nourrice,
Comme mere et douce nourrice,

and saving for their
future.

Et espargne pour les nourrir
750   Et pour eulx a estat venir.[1]
Se j'en puis trover une tele,
Plus l'ameray que riens mortele,

With such a wife I
shall end my life in
joy and peace,

En joie fineray mon temps,
Je n'aray noise ne contemps,
755   Je seray gaiz et envoisés,
Je seray tousjours bien aisés

free from the dan-
gers of light women,

Et hors de ces aultres perils
De foles femmes qui sont vils;
Nulz n'avra tel joie com moy :

and live within the
law.
She will be the
refuge of my youth
and staff of my age.

760   Je viveray selon la loy.
S'iert le retret de ma jonesse,
S'iert le baston de ma vieillesse,
Soustenent ma fragilité;

And when I shall
die,

Et quant je seray exité

[1] Situation, position.

765 A paier le treu[1] de nature,
    Celle ara de m'ame la cure
    Et prira pour l'ame de my: she will pray for my
                                                  soul;
    Ce ne feront pas mi amy;
    Et mes enfens qui demourront   and my children
                                                  shall remember me.
770 Moy leur pere ramenbreront:
    Ainsi demourra ma lumiere
    Glorieuse ça en arriere,
    Et croy que ce sera le mieulx. ...   This is the best
                                                  solution.

But he still hesitates and appeals to his faithful friend Répertoire de Science, whose answer is a long disquisition against the woes of married life and the vices of women.[2] A buyer of cattle examines them carefully, but men take wives without knowing what they will later reveal.[3] They are most exacting.[4]

1617 Et encor soit ly maris saiges, ...   Conflict is
                                                  inevitable.
1622 Ne puet il eschuer la guerre
    De sa femme, puis qu'il l'a prise,
    Ne la sarcine[5] de l'emprise.
1625   Se tu la prens, qu'elle soit belle,   If she is beautiful,
                                                  she will be hard to
    Tu n'aras jamais paix a elle,   keep for yourself.
    Car chascuns la couvoitera,
    Et dure chose a toy sera
    De garder ce que un chascun voite
1630 Et qu'il poursuit et qu'il couvoite. ...
2922   Juvenaulx les mariez tance   Juvenal maintains
                                                 that no woman
    Et content qu'il n'est femme chaste,   remains chaste if
                                                 pursued;
    S'on la poursuit et s'on la haste;
2925 Que la nature est enclinable   her nature tends to
                                                pity;
    D'estre a tout homme secourable,

[1] Debt.

[2] In this section Deschamps borrows freely from the speech of *Ami* in the *Roman de la rose* (ed. Langlois, ll. 8455–9492); cf., e.g., the passages quoted below and *Roman* 8587–96 (quoted in chapter on *Wife of Bath's Prologue*, pp. 213–14), and 9142–48 (note *Miroir* 2927–28 copied verbatim from *Roman* 9145–46). Though Chaucer must inevitably have been reminded of the *Roman*, there is no doubt that the parallel passages in *Mch. T.* are due primarily to his use of the *Miroir*.

[3] Cf. Justinus' words on the dangers of a hasty choice, E 1523–43. The passage in *Miroir* (ll. 1538–75; cf. *Roman de la rose*, 8667–77) is quoted on pp. 216–17 in connection with the *Wife of Bath's Prologue*, D 282–92.

[4] Cf. E 1547–48, 1561–64. The passage in *Miroir* (ll. 1576–98) is quoted on p. 217.

[5] Load, burden.

yielding to men is
the least of her sins.

Et que c'est ly mendres pechiez

Dont cuer de femme est entechiez

Que de livrer bersault aux hommes. ...

Herodotus says that
a woman is not
ashamed to lift her
dress anywhere;

Erodotes encor raconte

Que la femme n'a point de honte,

2945   Pour son grant delit achever,

De sa robe prandre et lever

En quelque lieu, en quelque place,

Tant que aucuns sa volunté face;

discovered, she has
ready excuses.

Et s'elle y estoit prinse apperte,

2950   Mais qu'elle soit tost recouverte,

Tant se scet de sa langue aidier

Qu'elle ara droit par son plaidier

Encontre cellui qui l'accuse.

The false friends repeat their former arguments and add more
examples.

Christian women
have shown in
martyrdom much
greater constancy
than men.

9063   Et encores, pour le voir dire,

Trueve femmes en leur martire

Avoir esté cent mille tans

Plus devotes et plus constans

Assez que les hommes ne furent, ...

For one bad woman
I can find a
thousand good ones.

9097   Car j'oseray gaigier et mettre

Que pour une qu'om treuve en lettre

Qui a mal fait, j'en trouveray

Mille bonnes. ...

Judith saved her
people.

9107   Que fist Judith pour sa cité[1]

Dont elle a le sang respité,

Quant elle a petit de harnès[2]

Couppa le chief Holofernès? ...

So did Esther.

9124   Ne rest digne de grant desserte

Hester pour son humilité? ...

9135   ... tant fist par son orison

Qu'elle impetra la garison

De son peuple qui estoit mort.

Amam en ot au derrain tort, ...

9143   Mardocheus pour lui regna,

Qui saigement se gouverna. ...

[1] The *Miroir* may have suggested to Chaucer this use of Scripture heroines,
but the direct source of E 1362–74 is unquestionably in Albertanus de Brescia
(cf. *Mel.* B 2290–95), where the four heroines are given in the same order as in
Mch. T., and the verbal similarity is striking.

[2] With little armament, with small equipment.

9150   N'est ce pas donques belle vie
      Que d'avoir belle et bonne dame
      Et de trover une tel femme?

How wonderful to have such wives!

In the course of this discussion between Franc Vouloir and his false friends, the poem abruptly breaks off.

II. BOCCACCIO'S *AMETO*

Seven nymphs in turn narrate their love affairs to pilgrims gathered for the festival of Venus. If Chaucer knew this frame-story, as he probably did, the resemblances between young Agapes' picture of her old husband and the description of January are not likely to be accidental.[1]

(Reprinted, with changes in punctuation, from *Opere volgari di Giovanni Boccaccio*, ed. Moutier, XV [Firenze, 1833], 123–26.)

I longed for a young and beautiful husband,

. . . . ma il mio pensiero era a una cosa, ma i cieli ne disposero un' altra. Perocchè a possedere la bellezza da me lungo tempo studiata fu dato un vecchio, avvegnachè copioso, ond' io mi dolsi, ma non osò passare a' detti[2] il mio dolore. Egli, da' patrocinanti le quistioni civili sopra nominate,[3] avente forse veduti più secoli che il rinnovante cervio, dagli anni in poca forma era tirato, e la testa con pochi capelli e bianchi ne davano certissimo indizio; e le sue guance per crespezza ruvide, e la fronte rugosa, e la barba grossa e prolissa, nè più nè meno pugnente che le penne d'un istrice, più certa me ne rendeano assai.

but was given to an old and rich man. I grieved in silence.

An old stag, he was withered with years. His sparse white hair, his deeply wrinkled cheeks and forehead, and his thick prickly beard revealed his great age.

His eyes, lips, and teeth are equally repulsive.[4]

E il sottile collo nè ossa nè vena nasconde, anzi tremante, spesso con tutto il capo muove le vizze parti; e così le braccia deboli, e il secco petto, e le callose mani, e il già voto corpo, con quanto poi seguita

His thin neck moves trembling and flabby; every part of his body bears the signs of age.

---

[1] See pp. 80–108 of J. S. P. Tatlock, "Boccaccio and the Plan of Chaucer's *Canterbury Tales*," *Anglia*, XXXVII (1913); Robert A. Pratt and Karl Young, pp. 11–12 of the present work. H. M. Cummings opposes Tatlock, without giving the question adequate treatment (*The Indebtedness of Chaucer's Works to the Italian Works of Boccaccio* ["University of Cincinnati Studies" (Cincinnati, 1916)], pp. 35–36 and 42).

[2] a' detti: into words. "But my grief did not dare express itself in words."

[3] A difficult passage which seems to mean: "as one dealing lawyer-wise with civil questions."

[4] The passages which we omit as not important in a comparison with *Mch. T.* add up to less than one-third of the section considered; most of them are mere expansions.

He walks stooped, looking at the earth, which I think will soon receive him, as it should have done, when it deprived him of his reason long ago. Happy, he took me into his house, where even the shortest nights seem long to me. In bed he takes me in his arms and weighs unpleasantly upon my neck, kisses me, moves his trembling hand to every part of my body.

alle parti predette risponde con proporzione più dannabile. Nel suo andare continovamente curvo la terra mira, la quale credo contempli lui tosto dover ricevere; ed ora l'avesse ella già ricevuto, perocchè di sua ragione gli ha di molti anni levato. A costui mi concessero i fati, il quale lieto mi raccolse nelle sue case, dove io ancora dimorante alcuna volta con lui nella tacita notte, delle quali mai niuna con esso, quanto che Febo si lontani alla terra, vi sento corta; stanti[1] nel morbido letto, mi raccoglie nelle sue braccia, e di non piacevole peso preme il candido collo. E poichè egli ha molte volte con la fetida bocca, non baciata, ma scombavata la mia, con la tremante mano tasta li vaghi pomi, e quindi le muove a ciascuna parte del mio male arrivato corpo, e con mormorii ne' miei orecchi sonevoli male mi porge lusinghe, e

Cold himself, he murmurs flatteries to kindle my passion.

freddissimo si crede me di sè accendere con cotali atti, là dove io piuttosto di lui accendo l'animo che 'l misero corpo. O ninfe, abbiate ora compassione alle mie noie! E poichè egli ha gran parte della notte

He exhausts himself in vain.

tirata con queste ciance, gli orti di Venere in vano si fatica di coltivare; .... vinto, alquanto si posa; e quindi alla seconda fatica, ...

Thus he makes me spend the whole night sleepless.

E per questo modo tutta la notte da spiacevoli ruzzamenti, e da sconvenevoli atti, senza sonno accidiosa mi fa trapassare. Elli col capo voto d'umidità, di poco sonno contento, con nuovi ragionamenti, senza dormire, invita mi tiene; elli mi racconta i tempi della sua gio-

He tells me of his youth and early love and how he could have satisfied many women; and when I think he will sleep, "You are the sole ruler of my house and myself; no other love could take me from you. I give you all you wish. Life is pleasant only when you are in my embrace.

vanezza, e come elli a molte femmine solo saria bastato, e dice i suoi amori, e le cose fatte per quelli. .... Quando io credo ch'egli voglia dormire, ricomincia, e dice: "O giovane donna, tra l'altre molto felice, ... tu sola se' della mia casa e di me donna; di me non puoi dubitare che amore d'altra donna mi ti tolga; da me vestiri, e tutte quelle cose che a grado ti sono, a te sono concedute; tu se' sola bene e riposo di me; niuna volta m'è graziosa la vita, se non mentre che tu nelle mie braccia dimori, e la tua bocca s'accosta alla mia. Se tu fossi pervenuta nelle mani di più giovane, poche di queste cose ti sarieno

A younger husband would have had other loves." If, near dawn, I succeed in making him sleep, his snoring keeps me awake.

concedute. I giovani hanno gli animi divisi in mille amori." ....
E appena al giorno vicini, posso fare che da me diviso si dorma alquanto; la qual cosa se avviene pur che faccia, russando forte il mio sonno impedisce. .... Questi atti, avvegnachè ancora il mio vecchio

In despair I decided to serve Venus

li servi, essendo io senza alcuna consolazione, quasi a disperazione m'aveano arrecata; ma per utile consiglio a me dato, proposi di servire Venere, ed alla sua deità più ch'altra pietosa, pensai di dolermi de'

and seek a remedy for my woes; I succeeded.

miei affanni, e di cercare ad essi alcuno rimedio per lo quale con meno fatica li sostenessi; e come fu l'avviso, così seguitai con l'effetto.

Agapes has found compensation in the love of a handsome young man.

---

[1] stanti: plural, refers to *il quale* and *io*.

III. THE BLIND HUSBAND AND
THE FRUIT TREE[1]

Our analogues fall into two classes: in A, as in the *Merchant's Tale*, the blind man's cure is the consequence of the interest spontaneously taken in him by two spectators (supernatural powers in all but one case); in B, it is granted in answer to his direct appeal to a deity.[2]

The only versions which Chaucer may have known in exactly their present forms are the Italian prose version in the *Novellino* (Class A) and the Latin fable of Adolphus (Class B). Nothing suggests that he read Adolphus. If he knew the *Novellino* version, he very probably combined it with one or more others lost to us.

CLASS A

1. THE *Novellino* VERSION

The *Novellino* tales were collected at the end of the thirteenth or the beginning of the fourteenth century.[3]

(Reprinted, with minor changes in punctuation, from G. Biagi, *Le Novelle antiche dei codici Panciatichiano-Palatino 138 e Laurenziano-Gaddiano 193* [Firenze, 1880], pp. 199–201.)[4]

[1] Generally referred to as the pear-tree story, a phrase responsible for endless and ever recurring confusion between our blind-husband story, of which no oriental version is known, and the distantly related pear-tree episode in the *Comoedia Lydiae* and in *Decameron*, VII, 9. Here, and in the very numerous—mostly oriental—close analogues, the husband sees perfectly well all through the tale but is made to believe in an optical illusion caused by an enchanted tree (sometimes a pear tree), or a window, or anything else. On the versions of that story see H. Varnhagen, "Zu Chaucers Erzählung des Kaufmanns," *Anglia*, VII *Anz.* (1884), 155–65; *Originals and Analogues*, pp. 183–88, 341–64, 544; Joseph Bédier, *Les Fabliaux* (Paris, 1895), pp. 469–70; V. Chauvin, *Bibliographie des ouvrages arabes* (Liège, 1892–1922), VI, 175 and VIII, 97–98; A. C. Lee, *The Decameron: Its Sources and Analogues* (London, 1909), pp. 236–44; R. Basset, "Contes et légendes arabes," *Revue des traditions populaires*, XVII (1902), 148–59, esp. 156–58, and *Mille et un contes, récits et légendes arabes* (Paris, 1924–27), II, 150–52.

[2] On the relations of the different versions to Chaucer's see Reinhold Koehler, "Due Novelle Antichissime," *Göttingische Gelehrte Anzeigen*, I (1869), 773–74, and *Kleinere Schriften* (Weimar, 1900), II, 568–69; H. Varnhagen; pp. 14 ff. of A. Schade, "Über das Verhältnis von Popes *January and May* und *The Wife of Bath*," *ES*, XXV (1898); M. Schlauch, "Chaucer's *Merchant's Tale* and a Russian Legend of King Solomon," *MLN*, XLIX (1934), 229–32; G. Dempster, "On the Source of the Deception Story in the *Merchant's Tale*," *MP*, XXXIV (1936), 133–54.

[3] See Letterio di Francia's introduction to *Le cento Novelle antiche, o libro di novelle e di bel parlar gentile, detto anche Novellino* (Torino, 1930), esp. pp. vii–xvi.

[4] Like many other stories found only in the *Panciatichiano* manuscript, ours is left out in most editions of the *Novellino*. It is found in Pietro Ferrato, *Due*

A uno tempo era uno riccho homo, ed avea una molto bella donna per molglie; et questo homo le volea tutto il suo bene, ed erane molto geloso. Or avenne, chome piacque a Dio, che questo homo li venne uno male nelgli occhi, donde aciechò, sicchè non vedea lume. Ora avenía che questo homo no' si partía da la molglie; tuttavía la tenea sì che no' la lasciava partire da ssè, per tema ch'ella no lli facesse fallo. Ora avenne che uno homo della contrada invaghío di questa donna, et non vedea chome le potesse favelare, però che 'l marito era tuttavía cho' lei; et questo homo moría di lei per senbianti ch'elli faciea a la donna; et la donna, vedendolo chosìe inamorato di lei, sìe ne le '(n)crebe,[1] et disse per senbianti, "Tue vedi chome io posso, chè questi non si parte mai da me!" Sì che il buono homo non sapea che si fare nè che si dire, et parea che volesse morire per senbianti; altro modo no' sapea trovare chome s'avenisse cholla donna; et la donna, vedendo i modi di questo gentile homo chome faciea, sì ne le '(n)crebe, et pensò di volere servire chostui. Ora fecie fare uno chanone di canna lungho, et puoselo a l'orecchie di questo gentile homo, et favelolli in questo modo, però che non volea che 'l marito l'odisse, et disse a questo gentile homo, "Di te m'increscre, e però oe pensato di servirti. Vattine nel giardino nostro, et sali in su 'n uno pero che v'àe molto belle pere, et aspettami là suso, ed io veròe là sùe a te." Il buono homo inchontanente n'andò nel giardino, et salíe in sul pero, ed aspettava la donna. Ora venne il tenpo che la donna era nel giardino, e volea andare a servire il buono homo, et il marito era tuttavía co' lei, et la donna disse, "E' m'è venuto volglia di quelle pere che sono in sùe quello pero, che sono cosíe belle." E' marito disse, "Chiama chi ti ne cholgha." Et la donna disse, "Io me ne cholglierò pure io, ch'altrimenti no' mi ne gioverebe." Alotta si mosse la donna per andare in sul pero, et il marito si mosse e venne co' lei infino a piè del pero, et la donna andoe in sùe il pero; et il marito abraccia il pedale del pero perchè non v' andasse persona dietro le'. Or avenne che la donna fue sùe pero cho' l'amico che lla aspettava, e istavano in grande solazzo, e il pero si menava tutto, sì che le pere chadevano in terra a dosso al marito. Onde disse il marito, "Che fai tue, donna, che no 'ne vieni? Tue fai cadere tante pere." Et la donna li rispuose, "Io volea delle pere d'uno ramo; non ne potea avere altrimenti." Ora volglio che sapiate che Domenedio et San Piero vedendo questo fatto, disse San Piero a Domenedio, "No' vedi tue la beffa che quella donna fae al marito? Dè! fae che 'l marito vegha lume, sicchè elli

novelle antichissime inedite (Venezia, 1868), p. 11; Papanti, Catalogo dei novellieri italiani (Livorno, 1871), Appendix to Vol. I, pp. xliii–xliv; E. Holthausen, "Die Quellen von Chaucers Merchant's Tale," ES, XLIII (1910), 168–69.

[1] Increscere: to be annoyed at, to be sorry for, to feel pity.

vegha cioe che la molglie fae." Et Domenedio disse, "Io ti dicho, San Piero, che sì tosto chome elli vedrà lume, la donna averà trovata la chagione, cioè là schusa, e però volglio che vega lume, et vedrai quello ch' ella dirae." Ora vidde lume et guatò in sùe, et vidde quello che la donna faciea. Alora disse a la donna, "Che fate voi co' cotesto homo? Non è onore ned a voi ed a me, et non è lealtà di donna." Et la donna rispuose incontanente di subito, et disse, "S' io non avessi fatto chosíe con chostui, tue non n'averesti mai veduto lume." Alotta udendo il marito chosíe dire, istette contento. Et chosíe vedete come le donne et le femine sono leali, et chome trovano tosto la schusa.

"St. Peter, as soon as he sees she will find an excuse. You will hear it."

The husband sees light and looks up. "What are you doing?"

Immediately she answers, "If I had not done this you would never have seen."

The husband is well pleased.

Such are women.

2. Von einem Plinten

This text can be placed between 1425, or very little before, and 1476, the date of the manuscript.[1]

(From A. von Keller, *Erzählungen aus Altdeutschen Handschriften*, ["Stut. Lit. Ver.," Vol. XXXV (Stuttgart, 1855)], pp. 298–305, with minor alterations mainly from Holthausen's reprint, *ES*, XLIII [1910], 170–75.)

A very jealous blind man knows that his beautiful young wife likes a student; he takes all possible precautions.

p. 299   Der schuler ging do er den plinten fant,
          Der furt oben an seiner hant
          Sein mynnigliches frewelein. . . . .

The student finds the blind man leading his lovely wife by the hand.

          Er neyget sich zu ir und sprach,
          "Mir ist leyt faßt dein ungemach."

He bends close to the woman and says he is sorry for her.

          Ein brieffllein gabe er ir in dy hant,
          Domit thet er ir gar bekannt
          Seinen syn und auch seinen mut.

He hands her a letter, which tells his desire.

          Das bedaucht dy schonen frawen gar gut.
          Do sie gelaß das kleyne briefflein,
          Sie sprach, "Ach, lieber meister mein,
          Ich sich dort einen pawm stan;
          Wir sullen werlich darunter gan,
          Ob uns des obbs mochte werden.

She thinks the matter over. After reading the letter, she says, "Dear husband, let us go to that tree for fruit.

          Mich gelustte noch nye hie auff erden
          Keyns dings nye also wol."

I never desired anything so much."

The suspicious blind man accompanies his wife; she goes to the tree.

p. 300   Des nam der schuler eben war,
          Wan er an das briefflein
          Hette geschriben den syn sein.

The student understands her move, for he had given instructions in his letter.

[1] The editor owes this information to Professor J. A. Walz.

He climbs a linden carrying a sack of fine apples.

The woman says, "How shall I go about getting fruit from that high tree?"

Sie sprach zu irem plinten,
"Nun wie sol ich es heben an,[1]
Das ich des obbs muge gehan,[2]
Wan der pawm ist so hoch?"

The blind man pulls out his stick and strikes among the branches until the student drops an apple.

Der plint palde seinen stecken zcoch
Und slug auf hin[3] an die este,
Das ein apfel vil hernider veste,
Den der schuler warffe herab.

The blind man and his wife divide the apple.

"Unless I have more, it will go ill with me."

"ich muß ir haben mere
Oder mir geschicht wirser dann wee."

Her husband strikes the branches again, but she cares nothing for the fruit thus gathered.

"You must let me climb into the tree

and fill my sack as full as I can."

"I am afraid another man might come to you."

"Clasp the trunk, so you will know whether another man could come to me.

He would get little anyway,

except perhaps hard blows."
The blind man thinks she is right, and helps her up the tree,

then grasps the trunk, and listens steadily.

p. 301 "Darumb saltu mich steygen lan
Auff den pawm oben hinan,
Das ich fulle vol meinen sack.
Ich gewynn ir so meynßt ich mag."[4]
Er sprach, "Frawe, so forcht ich mir
Das ein ander kum zu dir."
Die frawe sprach, "Des saltu kein sorge han;
Du salt here zu dem pawm gan
Und mit den henden yn greyffen an;
So weistu ob ein ander man
Zu mir auf den pawm mochte klimmen.
Der solte auch wol gewynnen
Lutzel und wenig an der fertt,[5]
Er gewinn dann doran streich hertt."[6]
Der plint gedacht, "Ia, du hast war."
Und halff ir auff den pawmen dar.
Do sie auff den pawmen kam,
Do umbfing der plint den stam
Und loßet da vil eben.

---

[1] Mod. Ger. *anheben*, to begin, originate.

[2] gehan: infinitive.   [3] auf hin: Mod. *hinauf*.

[4] "I will get of them (ir) as many (so meynßt) as I can (ich mag)."

[5] Dative of *fart*; Mod. *Fahrt*, journey, trip.

[6] dann: unless. "Unless he gets hard blows through it," i.e., in consequence of his climbing.

Der schuler begund mit der frawn zu streben.

Mit irem schonen stoltzen leybe

Wolte er nach luste kurtzweyl treybe.

The student has his pleasure of the woman.

Der plint ruffen do began,

"Schut den pawmen flucks oben an,[1]

Das etzwas falle herab!"

The blind man calls to her to shake down some fruit.

Der schuler was ein rechter knab,

Er begund sich mit der frawen rutteln

Und die opffell auß der kappen schutteln.

Er sprach, das were recht.

The student throws apples from his sack.

Unser Herr und auch sein knecht.

Sandt Peter gingen bede da fur.

Our Lord and St. Peter were passing by.

Das erhoret der plint geheur;[2]

Er sprach, "Wer geht da pey?

Wart, das er auch ein fremde sey."[3]

The blind man hears them. "Who goes by there?"

Sand Peter sprach, "Herre Meister, lug!

Sichstu nit das grosse ungefug,[4]

Die dem plinten thut das weip?

Ich wolte gern das sein leip

St. Peter says, "Lord, I wish he could see the great wrong she is doing him."

p. 302 Sehen solte den grossen mort."

Unser Herr Got sprach, "Sie funde wol ein antwort

Dannoch, ob es der man sehe an."[5]

"She would find an answer even then."

"Herre, wie wer das aber gethan?"

Sandt Peter sprach, "das höret ich gern."

"How could this be done? I would fain hear it."

Unser Herr sprach, "Wiltu sein nit enpern,[6]

So wil ich dich lassen sehen

Wie die frawe wirt jehen."[7]

"Very well, if you insist."

Den plinten er sehen ließ.

Der warde gar ein starcker ryeß.[8]

Our Lord gives the blind man his sight.

[1] Schut . . . . flucks oben an: "Shake it quickly up at the top."

[2] MHG *gehoere* as subs. ("the hearing") cannot fit in the line; as adj. it makes poor sense: "The obedient, or the gentle blind man heard it."

[3] A puzzling line. Replacing *das* by *ob* we might translate: "Watch out (i.e., pay attention, see) whether it is not a stranger."

[4] *Ungefug, ungevuoc* (misconduct, mischief) should be masculine as below and in Mod. Ger. *der Unfug.*

[5] This can be taken as direct or as indirect discourse.

[6] enpern: Mod. Ger. *entbehren.* "If you cannot do without it."

[7] Talk.

[8] MHG *riez*, a loud noise, makes acceptable sense ("Then, there arose a big noise"), but leaves *der* and *warde* unsatisfactory. *Ries*, giant, makes neither sense nor possible MHG rhyme with *liess.*

He looks up.

Do er nun do uber sich sach,

Gern möchte ir horen wie er do sprach:

"You harlot, what wrong are you doing me?

"Secht ir, frawe hur, was habt ir

Hewt gerochen[1] hie an mir?

You shall both die!"

Des müßt ir ewer beyder leben

Hie umb die lieb geben."

St. Peter says, "Lord, prevent this crime

Sand Peter sprach, "Herr Meister, lug,

Und went disen ungefug,

Das diser mort nit geschee,

and make this man blind again."
The woman answers,

Und heyß disen plinten nit gesehen!"[2]

Die frawe antwortten began

Auff dem pawm oben an.

"My dear husband,

Sie sprach, "Lieber man mein,

this love is what gives you your eyesight forever.

Diese lieb muß dir ein puß[3] sein,

Das du nymmer werdest plint.

Des half mir heut das himelische kint

Und auch dartzu der schuler.

The student taught me this.

Der lernet mich dise mere,[4]

Das du wider hast dein augen.

Des saltu dir also taugen,[5]

You should fall on your knees and thank us both,

Das du nyderfallest auf dein knye,

Und sag uns beyden gnade hye,

Dem guten schuler und auch mir,

and pray God you keep your eyesight.

Und pit Gote das dein augen dir

Pleiben, die du ytzunt hast.

O, how slow you are!"
He kneels down.

Ach, du thor, wie lanng du staßt!"

Er vil nyder auff seine knye

"Wife, I must reward you for this great service now and later.

p. 303   Und sprach, "Frawe, du lißt[6] mich nye.

Du hast mir gutlichen getan;

Des sol ich dich genyßen lan

Hewt und zu allen stunden,

---

[1] *Rechen:* Mod. Ger. *rächen,* nearly always has the more definite sense of punishing, avenging. "What are you avenging on me?" "What have I done to bring this on me?"

[2] gesehen: infinitive. "And order this blind man not to see."

[3] *Buoz, buss* means either a penance, or a remedy. "This love must be to you (you should accept this love as) a penance, a compensation, a ransom, owing to which you will never be blind again," or "This love is the remedy, etc. . . . ."

[4] MHG *maere, mere,* information, news, tidings.

[5] A difficult line. MHG *tugen, tügen* (Mod. Ger. *taugen*), to be fitting, proper, advantageous. Reading *sal* instead of *saltu* we could translate: "Therefore this (to fall on your knees) will be the fitting thing for you to do."

[6] An unexplained word, possibly some misspelled form of *lassen* or of *lügen.*

Das du so eben hast funden
Ein puß, das ich mein augen han.
Darumb saltu herab gan
Und auch dartzu der schuler."

Come down with
the student."

The blind man falls at the feet of the lovers; the student
receives ten pounds as recompense.

3. A Low German Version

This text is found in a manuscript of the last quarter, or at
least the second half, of the fifteenth century.[1]

(From a photostat of fol. 94ᵛ of MS 29 of the Royal Library of Stockholm.[2]
Abbreviations [only *m*'s and *n*'s] have been expanded; otherwise the spelling is
reproduced exactly.)

1 . . . . was eyn blynder man

A blind man

. . . . r nomen han
. . . . schone junc. Dat wyf
. . . . lef also syn lyf.

dearly loves his
beautiful young
wife.

5 . . . . gan to spele edder to der kerken
. . . . r hande se solde werken
. . . . ok jo by er syn.
. . . . vnwro de vrouwe fyn
. . . . se bẏ den klederen dat

She cannot take a
step away from
him.

10 . . . . em nychc enen trede en trat.
. . . . ener stunden
. . . . . . kede se eneme junghen

She bids a young
man make love to
her.

. . . . . se hauen wolde,
. . . . at en dat he se truten scolde.[3]

[1] Thus dated, in agreement with W. Seelmann (*Valentin und Namelos* [Norden,
1884], p. x), by Dr. Hans Reutercrona, of Stockholm, who kindly examined the
manuscript. For many of the explanations of difficult words in this text I am
indebted to the late Professor Joseph Mansion of the University of Liège.

[2] Previously published by G. W. Dasent, *Theophilus in Icelandic, Low-German
and Other Tongues* (London, 1845), pp. xxvi–xxviii, and (incompletely) by H.
Oesterley, *Niederdeutsche Dichtung im Mittelalter* (Dresden, 1871), pp. 38–39.

[3] The dots indicate the varying length of the passages lost. Trying to fill in the
gaps, one might translate ll. 1–14 as follows: "There was a blind man who had a
beautiful young wife. That woman was as dear to him as his own life. Whether she
was taking recreation or going to church or working with her hands, he was always
near her. She was annoyed. He held her by her clothing so she could not take a
step away from him. It happened at a certain time that she let a young man know
that she desired his love and that he should embrace her."

"I will do it gladly if you can find a chance."

She bids him go to an orchard, where she will embrace him;

he is to climb a tree and wait for her.

Eating at a table and speaking of apples with her husband,

she suggests going to the orchard.

He is ready to follow her.

In the garden

she asks, "How shall we get apples from this tree?

Bend over."

He makes no objection; she steps on his back and climbs up.

He grasps the tree

so no one can climb up. She finds the man she wants and bids him embrace her.

He looks hither and thither and notices three branches upon which he places her.

15 . . . sprak, "Vrouwe, yk dat gherne do,
Kone gy vynden stede dar to."
Se heyt en an enen bomgharden ghan,
Dar so wolde se ene al vmme van;[1]
(Eynen bomgha(r)den al vmme)[2]
20 Vp eynen bom dat he klŭmme,
Dar scholde he erer warden;
Se wolde komen in den gharden.
In ereme huse dat[3] se sat,
Met ereme manne dat se at,
25 Ouer tafelen dat se seten,
Van appelen dat se spreken,
Se sprak, "Wolde gy an den bomgharden ghan,
Dar de schonen appele stan?"
He sprak, "Vrouwe, ghat my vore;
30 Ik volghe jw al vpme[4] spore."
Do se in den gharden quemen,
Vnn nyne appele dar ynne vŏrnemen,[5]
Se sprak, "Wo schole wy des beghynnen,
Dat wy appele van desseme bome wynnen?"
35 Se sprak, "Bucket yw dar nedder."
De blynde sprak dar nycht wedder;
Se stech em up dat lyf;[6]
Vp den bom clam dat sulue wyf.
De blynde grep den bom al vmme
40 Vp dat dar nemant up en clŭmme.
Se want den se hebben wolde,
Vnn bat en dat he se truten solde.
De junghe sach hyr vnn dar.
Dryer telghen wart he vnwar[7]
45 Dar he se up legede.

[1] Dar: there, in that place. The adverb *so* reinforces *dar; ene*, him; *vmme van*, Ger. *umfangen*.

[2] "An orchard in the neighborhood." This seems to be a parenthesis brought in for the rhyme.

[3] dat: as.

[4] vpme: a contraction of *up* and the dative form of the definite article. "Go in front of me, I follow you *on the* footsteps."

[5] "And perceived no apple in it" (probably meaning on the ground or within easy reach). MDu. *negeen, neen, nin*, no, none.

[6] Body, trunk.

[7] MDu. *vnwar, onwar*, aware; *telghen*, Mod. Du. *telg*, twig.

Do beghunde de bom to roghende,[1]
De loue beghunden ruschen,[2]
De appele beghunden duschen.[3]
Des wart Sunte Peter vnwar.[4]

50 He sprak, "Here Scheppar,
Ghyf deme blynden manne syne øghen[5]—
Ik mach des nycht lengher døghen[6]—
Dat dyt de blynde man seghe,
Wo schemelyken dat syn vrouwe leghe."

55 Vnse He de sprak to hant,[7]
"Peter, nŭ sy des ghenant:[8]
De vrouwe de ys so wrot,[9]
Se vntlecht dat em[10] myt der spot."[11]
"Ach, Here Meyster, dorch dyne ghute,

60 Ghyf em dat he sen mote!"
To hant dar eyn teken schach
Dat de blynde man sach.
He sprak, "Wat do ghy nu?"
Se sprak, "Leve man, segý nu?

65 Deygher[12] bŏte hebbe yk wol[13] lxxii ghemaket
Er yk er eyn han gheraket
Dat gy, leue man, konne sen.
Des mote Gode lof schen.

The tree begins to move, the leaves to rustle, the apples to clatter down.

Noticing this, St. Peter says, "Lord Creator, I cannot stand it any more; let the blind man see this shame."

"Peter, be assured of this: the woman is so clever, she will argue him down in no time."

"O Lord, please, make him see!"

At once a miracle happens, and the blind man sees.

"What are you doing?" "Dear husband, do you see now? I have tried seventy-two treatments before I found one that made you see.

God be praised!

---

[1] MLG rogen, regen, MHG rugeln, to move.

[2] Mod. Du. ruisschen, to rustle.

[3] duschen: translated rauschen by A. Lasch and C. Borchling (Mittelniederdeutsches Handwörterbuch [Hamburg, 1928——], who note only this occurrence. I know of no related word and suspect a scribe's mistake for a form *druschen, corresponding to Mod. Ger. draüschen, "to fall thickly and noisily."

[4] See l. 44.

[5] The sign on the o cannot here mean an umlaut; the ø is found in this text in øghen and døghen only.

[6] MDu. doghen, A.S. dogian, Mod. Du. gedoogen, suffer, tolerate, allow.

[7] MHG zehant, immediately.

[8] ghenant: past part. of genenden or nenden, MHG and MDu., to dare, be bold, become bold; here, to feel sure about.

[9] MDu. vrot, vroet, Mod. Du. vroed, wise, prudent.

[10] MDu. enen iet ontleggen, persuade someone he is wrong about something.

[11] MLG spôt, MDu. spot, spoet, Mod. Du. spoed, speed, diligence. MDu. met der spoet very commonly means at once; sometimes, with success.

[12] MLG deger, MDu. deygher, deger, completely, counting them all.

[13] wol: as many as.

Des synt gý my nu to vluggh;[1]

Help in shaking the apples."
"Come down both of you.

70   Schudde gý de appele myt . . . ."
"Styghet af vnn latet allen
Wo desse dynk syn ge vallen[2]

Let us give thanks (?) for my restored sight."

. . . . nk syn gheschen
Dat yk blynde man kan sen."

4. A GREAT RUSSIAN VERSION

The date of this verse and prose ballad is uncertain.[3]

(From the English translation of Margaret Schlauch, "Chaucer's *Merchant's Tale* and a Russian Legend of King Solomon," *MLN*, XLIX [1934], 229–32.)[4]

A blind merchant and his wife are walking in their beautiful garden in Jerusalem. The woman gives her husband an apple; he eats it and asks her where she got it.

"There are still more of these apples,
But 'tis high up that they hang.
Do thou hold on to the tree with thy hands,
And I shall mount into that high tree
And pluck thee some apples."
On that tree she had a cradle,
And in the cradle was her lover,
Beside him she laid herself in the cradle.
    Now at that very same time
Tsar David perchance stood on his balcony
Together with his very fair Tsaritsa;
They saw the blind man holding the tree,
And Tsar David spoke with the Tsaritsa:
"If at this time God gave sight to the blind man,
What then would he do with his wife?"
The very fair Tsaritsa replies:

---

[1] "In consequence (i.e., because you can see) you are now too quick for me (i.e., nimbler than I)" or "About this you are now too hasty (in your judgment) toward me." The first interpretation agrees better with the usual meaning of *vlug* in LG and MDu. and makes better sense with the next line.

[2] "How this miracle occurred"?

[3] M. Schlauch thinks that our version, taken down in the nineteenth century, is corrupt or ill remembered but may go back to a medieval original (see *MLN*, XLIX, 231).

[4] The Russian text is printed by A. Veselovskii, *Slavyanskiya Skazaniya o Solomone i Kitrovase i Zapadnyya Legendy o Morol'fe i Merline* [St. Petersburg, 1872], pp. 102 f.

"My sister would find a way out!"
But the son in her womb [i.e., Solomon] cried:
    "Woman here judges in woman's manner!"
The mother spoke: "Poison will I drink,
And thee in my womb I will ruin."
And the son replied, "I will break through
        thy flank,
I will break thy rib, and thus come out!"

Then God gave the blind man his sight, so that he saw his wife with her lover in the cradle, and he cried out: "O thou wife, thou fool! How canst thou commit adultery over my very head?" His wife said, "Only suffer me to come to thee, for I am entirely thine. Do thou beat me, do thou break me, but only hearken to what I tell thee: at night I slept and I dreamed in my sleep that if I should commit adultery over thy head, God would give thee thy sight." Then the husband took his wife by the right hand and kissed her, and they went home.

The story closes with a short comment of the Tsar.

5. A LITTLE RUSSIAN VERSION

This prose version was taken down from oral tradition in the last century.

(From the French translation in *Kruptadia*, I [Heilbronn, 1883], 65.)

The couple are lovers already when the blind husband, a nobleman, becomes suspicious and watchful. There is no mention of either fruit or climbing, though the apple tree is kept as part of the scenery. A neighbor and his wife watch the scene from their window:

"Regarde donc, ma chère amie, ce qu'on fait sous le pommier. Qu'arriverait-il si Dieu ouvrait maintenant les yeux à l'aveugle et qu'il vît cette scène?"—"Sans doute il la tuerait."— "Oh, ma chère amie! Dieu inspirerait une excuse à notre soeur."—"Quelle excuse?" —"Tu le saurais alors."

The blind man recovers his sight. The woman explains that her purpose was to cure him according to instructions received in her sleep.

6. AN ITALIAN *Facezia*

This is one of the *facezie* of Lodovico Domenichi, collected probably about 1478.[1]

(From Albert Wesselski, *Die Schwänke und Schnurren des Pfarrers Arlotto* [Berlin, 1919], II, 333.)

La moglie del Nero monta sul pero e si trastulla con lo amante; il Nero geloso tiene abbracciato il pedale. Passa Christo a cauallo col diauolo in groppa, che andauano a una anima che era in quistione. Alluminano il cieco, il quale gli domanda quello che la su faccia. Rispose la moglie: "Facciamo acqua da occhi."

7. A PORTUGUESE ANALOGUE

This very short version was taken down for J. L. de Vasconcellos, who published it in *Giornale di filologia romanza*, IV (1883), 192–93. The husband and wife are replaced here by an old father and his unmarried daughter, who sends her lover to climb a cherry tree along the road. She takes her father to the spot and asks his permission to climb for cherries. The blind man cautiously keeps the trunk of the tree embraced. Christ and St. Peter pass by. Upon St. Peter's remarking on the situation, God restores the sight of the old man. He looks up, but the girl at once breaks in with her explanation. The lovers are married.

CLASS B

1. THE FABLE OF ADOLPHUS

(Reprinted, with alterations in spelling and punctuation, from Polycarp Leyser, *Historia poetarum et poematum* [Halae Magdeb., 1721], pp. 2008–9.)[2]

Adolphus gives 1315 as date of composition of his ten fables.[3] The verse and quantities are sometimes incorrect and the sense doubtful.

A blind man is jealous of his beautiful wife.

Caecus erat quidam, cui pulcra virago; reservans
20   Hanc puro pure[4] ne luat haec alias.

[1] See Wesselski, *Die Schwänke und Schnurren des Pfarrers Arlotto*, II, 308–43.

[2] Reprinted from Leyser in Thomas Wright, *A Selection of Latin Stories* (London, 1842), pp. 174–75; *Originals and Analogues*, p. 179; and H. Varnhagen, pp. 160–61.

[3] Leyser, p. 2036. On Adolphus see Gröber's *Grundriss*, II, Abt. 1, 414.

[4] This may mean "keeping her in a pure state for him who was pure too."

In curtis viridi resident hi cespite quodam
    Luce; petit mulier robur adire pyri.

In a garden, one day, she wishes to climb a pear tree.

Vir favet, amplectens mox robur ubique lacertis.
    Arbor adunca fuit, qua latuit juvenis.

He agrees and embraces the trunk. A lover is hidden in the forked tree. They fulfil their desire.

25   Amplexatur eam, dans basia dulcia; terram
    Incepit colere vomere cum proprio.

Audit vir strepitum; nam crebro carentia sensus
    Unius, in reliquo, nosco, vigere solet.[1]

The husband hears noise.

"Heu miser!" clamat, "te lædit adulter ibidem.
30   Conqueror hoc illi, qui dedit esse mihi."

"An adulterer is with you. I complain to Him who made me."

Tunc Deus omnipotens, qui condidit omnia verbo,
    Qui sua membra probat vascula velut figulus,[2]

Omnipotent God restores his sight.

Restituens aciem misero, tonat illico, "Fallax
    Femina! cur tanta fraude nocere cupis?

"False woman!

35   Heu mihi, quam fraude mulier mala varia sordet![3]
    Integra jura thori non tenet illa viro.

Alterius segetes semper putat uberiores.
    Yo,[4] confinis ubera magna tenet.

She always prefers another's bed to her husband's."

Alterius thalamo mala credit inesse sapinum,[5]
40   Quamvis sit spado, nil valeatque thoro."

Percipit illa virum; vultu respondet alacri,
    "Magna dedi medicis, non tibi cura fuit.

She answers promptly, "I wasted a lot on doctors.

Ast, ubi lustra sua satis uda petebat Apollo,
    Candida splendescens Cynthia luce mera,[6]

One evening,

45   Tunc sopor irrepsit mea languida corpora, quædam
    Astitit, insonuit auribus illa meis:

after I fell asleep, someone said in my ears,

'Ludere cum juvene studeas in roboris alto,
    Prisca viro dabitur lux cito, crede mihi.'

'Play with a youth high in a tree, and sight will be given to your husband.' I succeeded; you should thank me."

Quod feci. Dominus ideo tibi munera lucis
50   Contulit; idcirco munera redde mihi."

Addidit ille fidem mulieri, de prece cujus
    Se sanum credit, mittit et omne nefas.

He believes her, and forgives the sin.

Esse solet nullum pejus muliere venenum;
    Excolit hanc, adamat vir, alter eam.[7]

No poison is worse than woman.

---

[1] "For through the lack of one sense one generally grows strong in other respects." *Carentia* must be taken as ablative in spite of the meter.

[2] "Who tests his members as the potter the vessels."

[3] Perhaps "Alas, how defiled is a bad woman through various frauds!"

[4] Yo: probably an interjection. "Alas, the neighbor possesses great fruitfulness."

[5] *Sapinus:* a fir tree, or the unbranched part of the trunk of a fir tree (*Martinii lexicum filologicum*).

[6] "But as Apollo was seeking his watery resort, and fair Cynthia shone in the clear sky."

[7] "Her husband praises and loves her." The rest of the line lacks its verb.

2. Latin Prose from Steinhöwel's *Aesop*

Steinhöwel first published his collection of fables and stories about 1476 or 1477.[1]

(Reprinted, with minor alterations, from *Steinhöwels Aesop*, hrsg. von Hermann Oesterley ["*Stut. Lit. Ver.*," Vol. CXVII (Tübingen, 1873)], pp. 326–27.)[2]

DE CECO ET EIUS UXORE AC RIVALI

A blind man is jealous of his pretty wife.

She wishes to climb a pear tree to gather pears.

Lest someone should join her, he embraces the trunk. Hidden in the tree a youth was waiting.

They make love.

The blind man hears the noise. "O wicked woman! I hear you are with a lover! I complain to Jove who can give light to the blind."

His eyesight is restored. "O false woman!"

First frightened, she promptly invents a lie, and replies, "I thank all gods who granted my prayers. After wasting much on physicians I besought the gods to cure your blindness. Mercury appeared in my sleep and said,

Cecus erat quidam habens uxorem perpulcram, qui cum cruciatu mentis uxoris castitatem observabat, zelotipus namque fuerat. Accidit autem quodam die, ut in orto sederent ameno prope arborem pirum, uxori vero arborem cupienti ascendere ut pira legeret cecus assensit, ne tamen quis alter vir ipsam accederet, brachiis suis stipitem amplectitur. Erat autem arbor ramosa, in qua, priusquam uxor ceci ascenderet, iuvenis quidam se absconderat, mulieris expectans adventum. Conveniunt leti, amplexantur se, figunt basia, ac Veneris vomere terra colitur hirsuta umbrosumque nemus. Cumque iuvenis in opere fortis ageret ut potuit, mulier vero vim inferenti vices referret, audit cecus strepitus amborum, et dolens exclamat, "O mulier iniquissima, licet visu caream, auditus tamen et discursus[3] in me sunt intensiores, ut sentiam tibi astare adulterum. Conqueror hoc summo deo Iovi, qui gaudio tristium corda potest afficere et lumen cecis restituere." Simul his dictis ceco reddita lux est. Ille vero suspiciens in arborem adulteros vidit concubentes exclamatque subito, "O mulier fallacissima, cur has mihi cudis fraudes, cum te bonam castamque crediderim? Ve mihi! cum letum diem amplius tecum nunquam pervixero!" Mulier vero audiens maritum ipsam increpantem, licet primo parum territa, alacri tamen vultu, cito fraude inventa, respondit marito exclamans, "Gratias ago diis deabusque omnibus, qui preces meas exaudiverint et visum restituerint marito meo carissimo! Nam, coniux dilecte, te videre scias opera et precibus meis. Cum enim usque huc multa multa in vanum expenderem phisicis, orationibus institi deorum ut salvum te facerent ac visum restituerent. Tandem deus Mercurius, Iovis supremi iussu, mihi in sompno apparuit et ait,

[1] *Gesamtkatalog der Wiegendrucke*, Vol. I (Leipzig, 1925), No. 351.

[2] Previously published, probably from a later edition of Steinhöwel's *Aesop*, by Wright, pp. 78–79, and, from Wright, in *Originals and Analogues*, p. 180. Reprinted from Oesterley by Varnhagen, pp. 160–61. Our story is No. 12 in Alphonsus' *Disciplina clericalis;* on its appearance there see A. Schade, pp. 15–16. Steinhöwel's German version (Oesterley, pp. 327–28) is his translation of the Latin prose.

[3] Reason.

'Si ascendas in arborem pirum et Veneris ludum cum iuvene perficias, marito tuo lux pristina restituetur.' Quod ego perfici ut te sanarem. Munera ergo mihi debes ob meritum, cum tibi visum restituerim." Cecus uxoris dolo et fraudibus fidem dedit, ac nephas omne remisit, ac muneribus ipsam reconciliat quasi correptam inique.

'Climb in a pear tree and engage in the sport of Venus with a youth.' I deserve a recompense." The blind man believes her tale, and pacifies her with gifts, as if she had been unjustly criticized.

3. French Version from Julien Macho's *Esope*

The first known edition of the *Esope* of Julien Macho or Julien des Augustins is dated 1480. The work is largely a translation of Steihöwel's Latin *Aesop*.

(From *Les Subtilles Fables de Esope translatéez de latin en françois par Reverend Docteur en Theologie Frere Julien des Augustins de Lyon, auecques les Fables d'Avien, et Alfonse, etc.* [Lyon, 1480].)[1]

D'UNG AUEUGLE ET DE SA FEMME

Le temps passé estoit vng aueugle lequel auoyt vne belle femme de laquelle il estoit fort ialleux, laquelle il gardoyt qu'elle ne pouoyt aller en nul lieu, car tousiours il la tenoyt par la main. Et apres qu'elle fust enamourée de aulcun gentil compaignons ilz ne scauoient trouuer façon ne maniere ne lieu propice pour faire leur vouloir.

A jealous blind man keeps his beautiful wife constantly by his side, holding her by the hand. She falls in love with a fine fellow, but they find no chance to work their will.

Toutesfoys la femme qui estoyt fort ingenieuse conseilla a son amy qu'il vint en sa maison et qu'il entrast au iardin et qu'il montast sur vng poyrier qui la estoyt, lequel le fist. Et quant ilz eurent fait leur entreprinse la femme reuint en sa maison et dist a son mary: "Mon amy, ie vous prie que nous aillons esbatre en nostre iardin;" de laquelle priere l'aueugle fust bien content et dist a sa femme: "Bien, ma mye,[2] ie le vueil bien, allons." Et ainsi qu'ilz furent dessoubz le poyrier elle dist a son mary: "Mon amy, ie te prie que ie monte[3] sur ce poyrier et nous mengerons des belles poyres." "Et bien, ma mye," ce dit l'aueugle, "ie le vueil bien." Et ainsi que elle fust montée sur le poyrier le ienne filz commença a secoure le poyrier d'ung costé et la femme de l'autre. Et ainsi que l'aueugle ouyst secoure le poyrier

She tells him to climb a pear tree in the garden. He does so.

She comes back to the house. "My dear, let us go and disport ourselves in our garden." He gladly assents. When they reach the pear tree, "Allow me to climb this tree for the beautiful pears." "I am willing." She is up. The lovers shake the tree.

et le bruyt qu'ilz menoyent, il leur dist: "Ha, mauluaise femme, combien que ie n'y voye goute toutesfoys ie y entens bien, mais ie prie aux dieux qu'ilz me vueillent retourner la veue." Et incontinent qu'il

The blind man hears the noise. "Ah, wicked woman! I do not see but I can hear. May the Gods restore my sight!" Jupiter grants his

---

[1] It must be from this 1480 edition, of which only one copy is known (Tours, Bibliothèque municipale), that Caxton translated his *Aesop*. His *Fable of a Blynd Man and of His Wyf*, which follows Macho's version almost word for word, is printed in *Originals and Analogues*, pp. 181–82.

[2] Or *m'amye*.

[3] The 1480 edition has *que tu montes;* the later editions correct this error.

eut fait sa priere, Jupiter luy rendyst sa clere veue. Et quant il veit le personnaige sur le poyrier il dist a sa femme: "Ha, maleureuse, iamays n'auray bien auecques toy." Et pource que la femme estoyt prompte et malicieuse elle respondist a son mary: "Mon amy, tu es bien obligé a moy, car pour l'amour de moy les dieux t'on donné clereté, car ie rends grace[1] aux dieux et aux deesses qu'ilz ont exaulcé ma priere, car desirant que tu me peusses veoyr n'ay cessé de prier ne iour ne nuyct qu'il leur pleust de toy donner clereté. Et Venus s'est apparut a moy et m'a dist que se ie faisoit plasir a ces ienne filz que elle te donneroyt clereté, et ainsi pour moy tu as recepu lumiere et veu." Et adoncques le bon homme luy dist: "Ma mye, ie vous remercye car vous aues bon droyt et i'ay grant tort."

[1] The 1480 edition has *ie rendis*.

THE SQUIRE'S TALE

By H. S. V. JONES

THE best critical opinion favors the theory that Chaucer derived the material for his *Squire's Tale* from many quarters and worked inventively with a free hand.[1] Though we do not possess any unquestioned source of any portion of the tale or of any motif in it, we do find striking parallels to many of its features in various stories of oriental origin. These will be presented here under three headings: I, Prester John; II, the Cléomadès cycle; and III, analogues to the Canacee and Falcon episode.

I. PRESTER JOHN

The first known mention of Prester John,[2] the fabulous Christian monarch of Asia, is in the Latin chronicle of Otto of Freising, written shortly after 1145.[3] He is best known from

---

[1] Alfred W. Pollard, *Chaucer* ("Literature Primers" [London, 1895]), p. 118; H. S. V. Jones, "Some Observations upon the *Squire's Tale*," *PMLA*, XX (1905), 346–59; and Robert K. Root, *The Poetry of Chaucer* (1922), p. 270, who writes: "But no single narrative which Chaucer might have used has yet been discovered. Whether any such narrative existed, or whether Chaucer merely allowed his imagination to play freely with the familiar themes of Arabian magic, filling in his background with such scraps of knowledge about Tartary and the Far East as he had picked up in reading or conversation we cannot say. The general character of the tale, and in particular its unfinished state, would favor the latter theory." Cf. J. M. Manly, *Canterbury Tales* (1928), p. 597; and F. N. Robinson, *Chaucer's Complete Works* (1933), p. 821.

[2] For a brief account of the history of the legend see H. Yule's article in *Encyclopaedia Britannica* under "Prester John." For a full discussion of the subject and for the texts see Friedrich Zarncke, *Der Priester Johannes* (*Abhandlungen der Philologisch-historischen Classe der Königlich-sächsischen Gesellschaft der Wissenschaften*, VII [1879], 827–1030, and VIII [1883], 1–186 [referred to hereafter as Zarncke I and Zarncke II]); *Neue . . . . lateinische Redaction des Briefes der Priester Johannes* (*Berichte der Königlich-sächsischen Gesellschaft der Wissenschaften, Philologisch-historische Classe*, XXIX [1876], 111–56 [referred to as *Berichte*]); *Über zwei neue lateinische Redactionen des Presbyterbriefes* (*Berichte . . . .*, XXX [1878], 41–46). See also Gustav Oppert, *Der Presbyter Johannes in Saga und Geschichte* (Berlin, 1870). For a discussion of the analogies with the *Squire's Tale* see J. L. Lowes, "The Squire's Tale and the Land of Prester John," *Washington University Studies*, I, Part II (1913), 1–18.

[3] Zarncke I, pp. 847–48.

the *Epistola Presbyteri Johannis ad Emmanuelem regem Graeco-rum*,[1] which is mostly an account, supposedly by Prester John, of his prodigious power and wealth and the marvels of his kingdom. This document appeared about 1165.[2] It had an immense success,[3] and there are definite indications that it was known in England in Chaucer's time.[4] We shall quote (*a*) passages from the Latin *Epistola* which parallel features of the setting of the *Squire's Tale* and (*b*) selections from a German poem, where we find, woven into the material of the *Epistola*, an analogue to Chaucer's three gifts' episode.

A. The Latin *Epistola*

Our first quotation is from the text published by Zarncke as representing the earliest form of the *Epistola* (Zarncke I, pp. 919–24). The others are from enlarged versions.

On top of the highest column is a mirror which shows any plot against us.[5]

Armed men guard it.[6]

We are served by kings, dukes, and counts.

In summitate vero supremae columpnae est speculum, tali arte consecratum, quod omnes machinationes et omnia, quae pro nobis et contra nos in adiacentibus et subiectis nobis provinciis fiunt, a contuentibus liquidissime videri possunt et cognosci. Custoditur autem a XII milibus armatorum tam in die quam in nocte, ne forte aliquo casu frangi possit aut deici. Singulis mensibus serviunt nobis reges VII, unusquisque illorum in ordine suo, duces LXII, comites CCCLXV in mensa nostra, exceptis illis, qui diversis officiis deputati sunt in curia nostra [Zarncke I, p. 920, §§ 71–73].

There is a most wonderful chapel, which on our birth-

Juxta hoc palacium habemus capellam vitream non manu factam, mirabiliorem omnibus mirabilibus, quae cum nichil ibi esset, in prima

---

[1] The superscription varies in different manuscripts; instead of *presbyteri Johannis* it is often *Johannis regis*.

[2] See *Encycl. Brit.*, and cf. Zarncke I, p. 878.

[3] It is preserved in approximately one hundred manuscripts, was several times translated into German (Zarncke I, pp. 947–1028), and was used by Albrecht von Scharfenberg in *Der jungere Titurel* (Zarncke I, pp. 968–72).

[4] See Lowes, p. 14.

[5] For more analogues to this and other magic features of Chaucer's tale, see *On the Magical Elements in Chaucer's Squire's Tale*, by W. A. Clouston, pp. 263–476, of *John Lane's Continuation of Chaucer's Squire's Tale* ("Chaucer Society Publications: Second Series" [London, 1888]), No. 23.

[6] According to the Cambridge text (*Berichte*, p. 151, § 72), the guard by day consists of twenty armed soldiers, the night guard of thirty. Johannes Witte de Hese (Zarncke II, p. 167, § 35) says: "Ad quod speculum sunt electi tres valentissimi doctores, qui inspiciendo speculum vident omnia, quae fiunt in mundo, ut ibidem dicitur."

die nativitatis nostrae apparuit, ubi nunc est, ad gloriam et decorem *day[1] appeared where it stands now.*
nominis nostri [Zarncke I, p. 922 (D) aa[2]].

Cum ex parte vestra nobis revelatum sit, quod vos multum de- *You wish to know of our religion. We believe in the Triune God.[3]*
siderastis scire et noscere nos et regiones et terras nostras et qualem
deum colimus et adoramus, per tenorem praesencium pro certo
sciatis, quod nos credimus in verum deum, patrem et filium et spiritum
sanctum, trinum in personis et unum in essencia et in substancia . . . .
[Zarncke, *Berichte*, p. 119].[4]

Habemus alias gentes, quae solummodo vescuntur carnibus tam *Others of our subjects eat only flesh and consider it a most holy thing to eat human flesh.*
hominum quam brutorum animalium et abortivorum, quae nunquam
timent mori. Et cum ex his aliquis moritur, tam parentes eius quam
extranei avidissime comedunt eum, dicentes: "Sacratissimum est
humanam carnem manducare" [Zarncke I, p. 911, § 15].[5]

Sunt et in eisdem provinciis cati silvestres volantes; formicas in- *India produces large ants, eaten as a delicacy.*
super rubeas magnitudine parvuli cancri India producit, quas illi
populi pro summis deliciis comedunt [Zarncke II, p. 178, § 28].[6]

Some Christians, having escaped from the Saracens, arrive in
India, and are generously received by Prester John.

Tandem rogaverunt eum, ut arborem siccam, de qua multum saepe *They ask about the dry tree but are told it is the tree of Seth.[7]*
loqui audierant, liceret videre. Quibus dicebat: "Non est appellata

---

[1] Cf. Heidelberg MS (Zarncke I, pp. 1015–28), ll. 680–85. The king's birthday
is mentioned in a different connection in the early version of the *Epistola*
(Zarncke I, p. 922, § 96): "In die nativitatis nostrae et cotiens coronamur,
intramus palatium istud et tamdiu sumus intus, donec potuissemus ibi comedisse,
et inde eximus saturi, ac si omni genere ciborum essemus repleti"; and in the
Heidelberg version, ll. 605–18.

[2] This quotation is from Interpolation D of the *Epistola*, which Zarncke thinks
should be assigned to the middle of the fifteenth century (see Zarncke I, p. 897).

[3] Cf. Otto of Freising's account of the report of the bishop of Jibal, Syria:
"Narrabat etiam, quod ante non multos annos Johannes quidam, qui . . . . rex et
sacerdos cum gente sua christianus esset, sed Nestorianus, Persarum et Medorum
reges fratres . . . . bello petierit. . . . . Fertur enim iste de antiqua progenie illorum, quorum in evangelio mentio fit, esse magorum, eisdemque, quibus et isti,
gentibus imperans . . . ." (Zarncke I, p. 848).

[4] Hildesheim version, known in a fourteenth-century manuscript. On this
text and the French, Italian, and English versions based on it see *Berichte*, p. 111 ff.
We do not reproduce the italics and brackets by which Zarncke indicates different
interpolations.

[5] Interpolation C, which Zarncke thinks was known before 1221 (Zarncke I,
p. 892).

[6] *Tractatus pulcherrimus*, written in the second half of the fifteenth century
and incorporated in some editions of the *Epistola*. In many details this tractatus
agrees with Interpolation D of the *Epistola* (see Zarncke II, pp. 171–79).

[7] Cf. Heidelberg MS, ll. 1346–47, where it is stated that Frederick might come
back, conquer the Holy Land, and hang his shield "an den dorren ast." See,
further, Zarncke I, pp. 1010–11.

arbor sicca recto nomine, sed arbor Seth, quoniam Seth, filius Adae, primi patris nostri, eam plantavit." Et ad arborem Seth fecit eos ducere, prohibens eos, ne arborem transmearent, sed [si?] ad patriam suam redire desiderarent. Et cum appropinquassent, de pulcritudine arboris mirati sunt; erat enim magnae immensitatis et miri decoris. Omnium enim colorum varietas inerat arbori, condensitas foliorum et fructuum diversorum; diversitas avium omnium, quae sub coelo sunt. Folia vero invicem se repercutientia dulcissimae melodiae modulamine resonabant, et aves amoenos cantus ultra quam credi potest promebant; et odor suavissimus profudit eos, ita quod paradisi amoenitate fuisse[t] [Zarncke II, p. 128].[1]

They find it beautiful, very large,

full of fruits and birds,

melodious,

and exhaling an odor so sweet that it seems like Paradise.

B. Oswald's Poem (The Heidelberg Version)

This narrative, of which the letter of Prester John is only a part, is the work of Osswalt der Schribar, not otherwise known.[2] It was written probably about the middle of the fourteenth century.[3] Its version of the letter seems derived from an English form of the *Epistola*.[4]

The beginning of the poem is lost; the preserved fragment opens in the text of Prester John's letter, apparently about the middle of it. This letter is here addressed to the emperor Frederick.[5]

On top of a great and beautiful tower

is a mirror with wonderful properties.

405 Vor vnsers sales tewr,[6]
Als man gen wil herfur,
In dem hof an einer weyt[7]
Ein grosser vnd ein schoner turn lit:[8]
Daruf zu aller obrist
410 Ein spiegel clar gemeistert ist
Mit listeclicher meisterschaft,

[1] Version in a Cambridge University MS (Oo.7.48) of about 1300 (Lowes, p. 14, n. 1; cf. Zarncke I, p. 890, and *Berichte*, p. 134).

[2] The text is published by Zarncke I, pp. 1015–28; for commentary see pp. 1004–14. The manuscript is dated 1478; it is hastily written and full of mistakes and omissions.

[3] Jacob Grimm assigned it approximately to the year 1400; Zarncke, on the basis of the rhyme words, places it in the middle of the fourteenth century.

[4] Represented in MS Oo.7.48 of Cambridge University. See Lowes, p. 14.

[5] Such is the case in some other versions probably derived from the same Cambridge manuscript. On Emperor Frederick (Barbarossa or Frederick II) see Zarncke I, pp. 1009–10.

[6] Door.   [7] Willow tree.   [8] Lies; is situated.

Mit wunderlicher dugent kraft.

. . . .

Der spiegel, der ist ein cristal clar

An alle mal licht gevar;[1]

It is clear crystal without blemish.

450 Von kunstricher meisterschaft

Hat der spiegel solh kraft,

Das man alles darin siecht,

Das in vnserm land geschicht:

One sees reflected in it whatever happens in our land.

Wes vnser fursten vnd hern

455 Beginnent nahent oder verrn,[2]

Nacht vnd tag, spat vnd fru,

Was yr ygklicher[3] tu,

Das siecht allmenlich

In dem spiegel schimberlich.[4]

460 Ob yemant bossen willen hat

Gen vns oder vntrewn verrat,

Anyone who has schemes against us is at once stopped and punished

Das er sich wieder vns woll seczen,

Den lassen wir allezuhant[5] leczen[6]

An lib an ere vnd an gut,

465 Das er es nymer mer getut.

Zu aller zijt tusent man

Gewapent vmb den spiegel stan,

Armed men stand around the mirror to guard it.

Ye[7] darnach er siecht [?] fur war

Koment ander tusent dar:

470 Also yr dru tusent ist,

Di sin huttent[8] zu aller vrist,[9]

Das yn ye man an rur,

Noch zeprech noch zefur.[10]

Wir ghen all morgen dar

We go there every morning

475 Mit sampt vnserm rat fur war;

Wenn wir miss gehoret han,

So gen wir fur den spiegel stan

to detect possible evils and correct them.

Vnd beschauwen do by,

Ob icht in vnserm land sy

480 Vngerechts an keinen enden,

Das wir das zu hant wenden.

[1] Without any blemish; light colored.

[2] Near or far.

[3] Each of them.

[4] Clearly.

[5] At once.

[6] Hinder, bereave, harm.

[7] Ever.

[8] Guard.

[9] Time.

[10] Lest anyone touch it, or break or injure it.

Prester John describes a wonderful room of his palace:

Only on our birthday does our court accompany us there.[1]

605   Nûr zu eim mal yn dem jar,
      An dem selben tag vorwar,
      Daran wir geporn sin,
      So get mit sampt darin
      Alles vnser hofgesind,
610   Die by der stat dwil[2] sind.

There is also a beautiful chapel which miraculously appeared the day Prester John was born (ll. 675–86).[3] He is sending to Frederick three precious gifts: a garment of salamander skin which cannot burn, a bottle of water from the Fountain of Youth, and a ring.

This ring gives the wearer victory

      Das drit ist ein fingerlin
      Des rechten golds von Arabin:
      Das selb gold hat die kraft,
1050   Wer is by yme dreit,[4] der ist syghaft

and the strength of three men.

      Vnd alle die wil[5] gar
      Dryer man sterck fûr war.

Three precious stones are set in it.

      In dem selben gold sin
      Dry edel stein verwirckt in,

Holding the red stone in one's mouth one will not drown.

1055   Der ein rot vnd hat die art,
      Kein wasser nie so tief ward,
      Wer in hat in sinem mûnd,
      Der lege ein jar an dem grûnd,
      Das er nyemer stûrb
1060   Noch von des wassers not[6] verdûrb.
      Der ander der ist hiemelvar,

Whoever wears the blue one in his hand cannot be wounded.

     . . . .
      Wer in an der hend treit,
      Das den kein waeffen verschnit.[7]

The gold-colored makes invisible the man who holds it in his hand.

      Der drit der ist goldvar
1065   Vnd vbergilt[8] die andern gar:
      Der hat tûgent vnd die art,
      Wenn er verporgen vnd verspart[9]
      Wirt in einer, menschen hant,
      Der ist vnsichtig alle zû hant,[10]

---

[1] Cf. passage of the *Epistola* quoted above, p. 359, n. 1, from Zarncke I, p. 922, § 96.

[2] At that time.

[3] Cf. passage from Interpolation D, quoted on pp. 358–59.

[4] Wears.

[5] Time.

[6] Pressure.

[7] Wound.

[8] Is worth more than.

[9] Inclosed.

[10] Immediately.

1070 Das mans nicht siecht alle die vrist
     Vnd der stain verporgen ist.
     Dise kleinad senden wir   We send you these
     Zů minn vnd ze lieb dir: gifts as tokens of love.
     Die soltu versuchen lan   Test their virtue,
1075 Zů hant, ob sie die tůgent han,
     Die wir dir haben geschriben hie.
     Ob du dan erfindest die,
     So macht du wol an geůar   and then you will
     Das ander alles glauben gar.   believe everything else in this letter.

    . . . .   Here the letter ends.

     Der keiser selber den briff las,   The Emperor read the letter and wondered about the great power of Prester John.
     Want er wol geleret was;
     Ygclichs lase er besůnder:
     Yne nam des vil wůnder,
1155 Wie nůr vf der erden
     Solh herschaft mocht werden.
     Die cleinat er alle glich[1]   He tested the jewels,
     Selb versůcht tawgenlich.[2]
     Do er an yne allen sampt
1160 Die ganczen warheit erfant,
     Da glaupt er dester pas[3]   and believed all the more what was written in the letter.
     Das an dem bůch geschriben was.

He called a large gathering of princes and kings and had some of the gifts tested in their presence.

     Den rock von salamander tewr   The salamander garment, thrown in the fire, did not burn.
     Warff er vor yne yn ein fewr:
1215 Der mǎcht mit nicht verprinnen,
     Er ward nůr new vnd licht darinnen.
     Er gab den fůrsten alle sampt   The princes drank the water.
     Des pruns zu trincken alle zu hant;
     Yedoch der keiser das vermaid,
1220 Das er sin tugent nicht gar said.
     Do sie die warheit sahen,   They agreed that the riches of Prester John were unequaled.
     Gemeiniglich des jahen,[4]
     Das an richeit sin gelich
     Nyndert lebt von ertrich.[5]

One day, while hunting, Frederick took the magic ring in his hand, disappeared, and was never heard of again.

[1] Similarly.   [3] Better.

[2] In secret.   [4] Affirmed.   [5] Earth.

II. THE CLÉOMADÈS CYCLE

Stories of this cycle, besides presenting parallels to episodes
fully developed in the *Squire's Tale*, suggest the kind of plot
which Chaucer may have had in mind for the part of his story
that was never written.[1] We shall quote (a) a short Arabic
version and (b) portions of *Li Roumans de Cléomadès* by Adenès
li Rois.

A. The Arabic Story

On a feast day a king of Persia, who was a great lover of philosophy
and geometry, is visited by an Indian, a Greek, and a Persian. The
Indian presents the king with an image of a man with a golden trumpet. Should a spy enter the city, the man will immediately blow his
trumpet and the spy will fall dead. The Greek's gift is a silver basin
in the middle of which sits a golden peacock surrounded by twenty-
four young ones; at the passing of each hour, the mother-bird marks
the time of day by pecking one of its young and at the end of each
month it shows a moon in its mouth. The Persian, in turn, offers an
ebony horse adorned with gold and precious stones and furnished with
splendid harness; in a day by flying through the air it will carry its
rider a year's journey. The king tests the virtues of the presents and
is so pleased with them that he promises to grant any request that his
visitors might make. Taking him at his word, they ask for his three
daughters in marriage.

The youngest of the three daughters of the king is deeply distressed
because the Persian, to whom she has been promised, is as ugly as she
is beautiful. Her brother, siding with her, remonstrates with his
father and insists that the gift of the ugly suitor be tested. He will
mount the horse himself. The ugly suitor, resenting this opposition
to his marriage, acquaints the Persian prince only with the pin that
causes the horse to ascend, purposely omitting to teach him how to
come down. When, after a long flight, the Persian prince succeeds in
mastering the horse, he descends on the roof of the palace of a foreign

---

[1] This holds particularly for the story of Algarsif, who, during his courtship,
was saved from grave peril by the steed of brass. See H. S. V. Jones, "The
Cléomadès and Related Folk-Tales," *PMLA*, XXIII (1908), 557–98; "Some
Observations upon the *Squire's Tale*," ibid., XX (1905), 346–59; "The *Cléomadès*,
the *Méliacin*, and the Arabian Tale of the 'Enchanted Horse,' " *JEGP*, VI (1907),
221–43. For the *Cléomadès*, the *Arabian Nights* story, and other analogues see,
further, W. A. Clouston's "Notes on the Magical Elements in Chaucer's *Squire's
Tale* and Analogues" in F. J. Furnivall's edition of *John Lane's Continuation of
Chaucer's "Squire's Tale"* ("Chaucer Society: Second Series" [1888–90]), Nos.
24, 26.

king whose daughter, a princess of marvelous beauty, he finds sleeping in a room close by. She mistakes him at first for the suitor to whom she had been promised, but is soon disabused when the king her father, rushing into her room, demands angrily what the stranger is doing there. The prince of Persia rejoins that he will confront on his horse the whole army of the king, but once mounted he loses no time in making away, to the great consternation of the assembled host. At home again, he cannot control his longing to revisit his princess, and on this trip she is glad to return with him that he might make her his bride. Unfortunately, he leaves his beloved unprotected outside the city in order to have proper arrangements made for her reception by his father. In his absence the ugly suitor, representing himself as the prince's messenger, persuades her to mount the horse with him and takes her off to China. The king of that country rescues her but promptly takes over the role of the importunate and unwelcome suitor. She now feigns madness for her self-protection and when her lover, after a long journey, has discovered her whereabouts, he is admitted to her presence disguised as a physician. While pretending to exorcise a demon from the magic horse in order to make permanent the cure of the princess, he once more transports her to his native land, where he makes her his bride and lives with her happily ever after.[1]

B. *Li Roumans de Cléomadès*

Adenès li Rois wrote his long romance (18,688 lines)[2] at the request of Blanche, daughter of St. Louis and widow of the Spanish infanta.[3] Probably the common source of the *Cléomadès* and the very similar *Méliacin* by Girard d'Amiens[4] was a

---

[1] I have in this summary greatly condensed Gustav Weil's German translation (*Tausend und eine Nacht, zum erstenmale aus dem Urtext . . . . übersetzt*, v. Dr. Gustav Weil [Stuttgart 1889], I, 341–55) of the Breslau Arabic text of the *Arabian Nights* as edited by Habicht and Fleischer. This is not only the best and fullest version of our story (Richard F. Burton, *The Book of the Thousand Nights and a Night* [1885], V, 1, n. 1) but the one which comes nearest to the version of the French romances. However, it should not be overlooked that the version in Galland's diary communicated to him by a Maronite Christian from Aleppo in 1709 more nearly resembles in its introduction the beginning of the *Squire's Tale*. The Indian who presents the magic horse is not there, as in Bulak and the Breslau text, merely one of three artisans who bring gifts; he is given special prominence by appearing after the king had received presents from an indefinite number of ingenious artisans and the assembly was about to break up.

[2] *Li Roumans de Cléomadès par Adenès li Rois*, publié par André van Hasselt (Bruxelles, 1865).

[3] Van Hasselt, I, xx–xxi.   [4] The *Méliacin* has not been edited.

Spanish version[1] of the oriental story of the wooden horse.[2] It seems almost certain that Chaucer knew the romance of Adenès.[3]

Marcadigas, king of Sartaigne,[4] has a very accomplished son, Cléomadès, and three beautiful daughters. Three kings come as suitors, each of them bringing a marvelous gift; the first, a golden hen with three chickens that could walk and sing as though alive (ll. 1585–93); the second, a golden man with a trumpet that he would sound at any threat of treason (ll. 1594–1608); and the third, a wonderful horse.

Crompars made a wonderful wooden horse

Or vous dirai dou roi Crompart.
1610 Cil refist grandement sa part;
Car il fist un cheval de fust.
Je ne croi k'ainc puis nus tex fust.[5]
Si faitement[6] le sot ouvrer
Li rois Crompars, et arréer,[7]

on which he could in little time go wherever he wanted and come back.

[1] For arguments in favor of a Spanish source see van Hasselt, pp. xxi–xxiii, and H. S. V. Jones, "The *Cléomadès*, the *Méliacin* and the Arabian Tale of the Enchanted Horse," *JEGP*, VI (1906–7), 239–46.

[2] The closeness of a large portion of the *Cléomadès* to the Arabian story of the wooden horse is much greater than appears from our very short summaries of both.

For magic horse and other means of aerial locomotion used in stories more or less related to the *Squire's Tale* see Clouston, *Magic Elements in the "Squire's Tale"* ("Chaucer Society" [1889]), and H. S. V. Jones, "The *Cléomadès* and Related Folk-Tales," *PMLA* (1908), 557–98. On analogy with a dream reported by Froissart see H. Braddy, "Cambyuskan's Flying Horse and Charles VI's 'Cerf volant,'" *MLR*, XXXIII (1938), 41–44.

[3] The *Cléomadès* is mentioned in Froissart's *L'Espinette amoureuse*, a poem with which Chaucer was certainly familiar. At ll. 700 ff. the lady of the poem reads to her knight a portion of the romance. Possibly a suggestion for the mirror as one of Chaucer's gifts may have come from the passage beginning at l. 2382; there the lady gives her knight a mirror in which later he seems to see her reflection. One should note further the magic mirror in the story of Papirus and Idoree of which Froissart makes use at ll. 2667 ff. of *L'Espinette* and his allusion at ll. 2382 ff. to the mirror of Rome, mentioned by Chaucer, F. 231. See H. S. V. Jones, "Observations upon the *Squire's Tale*," *PMLA* (1905), 346–59.

[4] The geography of Adenès is hazy. Sartaigne may mean either Sardinia or Cerdagne, a region in the East Pyrenees (see van Hasselt, pp. xxii–iii). However, it is clear that Adenès nowhere thinks of the kingdom as an island, since he makes no mention of a voyage by water; note, e.g., ll. 425–28 and 1280 ff. Furthermore, Marcadigas is repeatedly called *roi d'Espagne*, and his subjects, *les Espagnols*. Seville appears to be his capital.

[5] I do not think that ever afterward any such existed.

[6] Skilfully.   [7] Areer: put together.

Que, quant il vouloit, il estoit
Assez tost où estre vouloit,
Et tout aussi tost retournés
Ert arriere quant c'ert ses grés.
    Li chevaus ert tous de benus,[1]

1620 Fors tant que desouz et desus
Avoit chevilletes d'acier.
Par ces chevilles adrecier
Povoit on faire le cheval,
S'on vouloit, amont ou aval,
Ou par en coste, ou de travers.
Par foi cil cheval fu divers;
Car, quant on l'avoit esmeü,
Jamais ne l'eüssent veü
Nule gent, ce sachiez de voir,

1630 S'il ne fussent à l'esmouvoir.
Nes cil qui au mouvoir estoient
En petit d'eure le perdoient;
Car trop plus tost ert esloigniés
Que karrel qui est descochiés.

. . . .

Gent de petit entendement

1640 Demandent à la fois comment
Tels choses pueënt estre faites
Que je vous ai ici retraites.
Aucun en sont tout esbahi.
Et savez vous que je leur di?
Je leur di que nigromancie
Est moult merveilleuse clergie;
Car mainte merveille en a on
Faite pieça,[2] bien le set on.
    Bien savez que Virgiles fist

1650 Grant merveille quant il assist
Il chastiaus seur II oes en mer;

. . . .

    A Naples fist il de metal
Seur I piler un tel cheval
Qui chascun cheval garissoit

1680 D'aucun mehaing, se il l'avoit,
Mais con le loiast au piler.

. . . .

Je croi qui à Naples iroit

Margin notes:

It was of ebony, with steel pegs to control it.

After it moved no one could see it except those who had seen it start,

but they too quickly lost sight of it.

People of slight understanding wonder how such things can be made,

but necromancy is a wonderful science.

Virgil placed two castles upon two eggs in the sea.

At Naples he made a metal horse,

which cured of any sickness any horse bound to the pillar.

[1] Ebony.   [2] Long since.

1690   K'encor le cheval trouveroit.

In Rome he made a
mirror,

A Ronme[sic] fist, c'est verités,
Virgiles plus grant chose assez;
Car il i fist I mireöir

in which one could
see anything plot-
ted against Rome.

Par quoi on povoit bien savoir,
Par ymage qu'il y avoit,
Se nus vers Romme pourchaçoit[1]
Ne fausseté ne trayson
De ceaus de leur subjection.

After description of other marvels wrought by Virgil, the poet returns to his story.

Crompars thinks
his two companions
and he should ar-
rive on the birthday
of King Marca-
digas,

Lors dist Crompars qu'il loëroit
Se chascun d'aus s'i acordoit,
Que il meüssent si à point[2]

1850   Qu'il venissent là à ce point[3]
Que rois Marcadigas fu nés.

an occasion for a
very great feast
with the Spaniards.

Ce seroit li mieudre d'assés;[4]
Car trop grant geste celui jour
Font Espaignol pour leur seignour.

The three kings arrive with their gifts.

Melocandis says:

1933   Melocandis premiers parla

. . . .

"We have brought
you three rich
jewels."

1942   Si li dist:—"Biau sire, aporté
Vous avommes de no pays
Trois joiaus riches et soutis."
    Lors li devise mot à mot

He describes them.

Quel force chascuns joiaus ot.
Et li rois les en mercia;

The king values
them greatly.

Car les joiaus forment prisa,
Car moult furent bien à prisier.

In gratitude for his presents, the king offers to give the suitors whatever they might ask in return. Crompars says they wish his daughters in marriage. Though he does not like to marry his three daughters on one day, the king will keep his covenant. The ugly and misshapen Crompars asks in marriage Marine, the most beautiful of the daughters. Her brother Cléomadès is greatly displeased. The king is advised to test the gifts. The

[1] Seek to bring about.   [3] Just at the time.
[2] In such a way.   [4] By far the best.

daughters observe from a window the suitors and the testing
of their gifts. Marine is distressed at the thought of marrying
the ugly Crompars. Her brother pleads with their father on
her behalf:

—"Sire," ce dit Cléomadès,
2370 "Ne savons se cil chevalès
    Est tex qu'il nous fait entendant,
    A tout le mains,[1] sachiez avant
    Se ce est veritez ou non
    Qu'il parait[2] de ma suer le don."
     Et li rois dist bien li plaisoit,
    Et k'à l'esprouver s'assentoit.
      Lors fu rois Crompars apelez
    Qui estoit boçus et pelez.

"Sire, we do not know if this horse is such as he would have us understand."

The king is willing to have the horse tested,

and Crompars is called.

Crompars, resenting the opposition to his marriage with
Marine, decides to be avenged.

      Cléomadès dist que savoir
    Veut dou cheval se tel povoir
    A en lui comme dit leur a.
    Dist Crompars:—"Vous le saurez jà.
    Et, se vous voulez esprouver
2390 Le chevalet et sus monter,
    Assez tost saurez vraiement
    Se je di voir ou se je ment;
    Et, se trouvez sui en mençongne,
    J'otro c'on me face vergongne,
    Car je l'arai bien desservi."
    Dist Cléomadès:—"Je l'otri;
    Sus monterai, comment qu'il aille,
    Ce vous ai je en couvent, sans faille.
    Tout maintenant essaierai
2400 Le cheval, plus n'arresterai."
    De ce mot fu Crompars moult liez,
    Car bien pensoit c'or iert vengiez
    De Cléomadès se il puet;
    Car de cuer la venjance vuet,
    Car moult crueus et fel estoit,
    Sa façon par droit le devoit.[3]

Asked to show the power of the horse

Crompars suggests that Cléomadès mount him.

Cléomadès assents.

Crompars is glad of this chance to avenge himself.

[1] At the very best.   [2] Is equal to, corresponds in value.
[3] His makeup, i.e., his being a hunchback, necessarily brought it about.

At the threat of treason the golden man sounds his trumpet but no one pays attention to him.

<table>
<tr><td>They lead the horse into the court.</td><td></td><td>Le cheval mainent en la court,
Et chascun i va et acourt
Pour savoir se ainsi iroit
Cis chevaus que Crompars disoit.</td></tr>
</table>

They lead the horse into the court.

Le cheval mainent en la court,
Et chascun i va et acourt
Pour savoir se ainsi iroit
Cis chevaus que Crompars disoit.

He had a good saddle of ebony,

Sele y ot bonne et bien séant
2430   De benus, forte et bien tenant,

stirrups that adjusted themselves to a tall or a short man,

Et estriers tels et si faitis
Que s'uns grans hom ou s'uns petis
I montast, trestout à droiture
Fussent à point et à mesure.

and a suitable bit.

Fraint y ot tel qu'il convenoit
Et k'à tel cheval aferoit.

Marcadigas advises caution,

Marcadigas dist à son fill
Qu'il sache s'il y a perill
Ainçois que il soit sus montés.

but Crompars says that the horse never turns over but always goes straight.

2440   Dist Crompars:—"Sire, n'en doutés
Que jamais ne se verseroit
Cis chevaus, ains va tous jors droit;
Tex est li chevaus, sans mentir."
Cléomadès ne volt souffrir
Que nus sur le cheval montast
Ne la grant merveille essaiast

Cléomadès mounts the horse. Crompars goes in front,

Fors il. Et il [y] est montez,
Et Crompars est avant passez.
Au front dou cheval vint tout droit.

turns a peg,

2450   Une chevillete y avoit;
Un petitelet la tourna,

and the horse is soon out of sight.

Et li chevalès s'en ala
Si très tost, que cil qui le virent
Mouvoir, assez tost le perdirent,
Ne sorent qu'il fu devenus.
S'en fu chascuns tout irascus.

Everybody is angry. Marcadigas bids Crompars call the horse back.

Dist Marcadigas à Crompart:
—"Faites retourner ceste part
Le cheval, trop est esloigniez;
2460   Il me samble assez essaiez;
Je ne quier que on plus l'essait."

Crompars says he cannot,

—"Sire," dist Crompars entresait,
"Je n'ai povoir dou retorner;

Car j'oubliai à deviser
A Cléomadès, au partir,
Comment il porroit revenir.
Ne m'en souvint s'en fu alés."

and forgot to teach Cléomadès how.

Crompars is thrown into prison and the weddings are postponed.

A tant me tairai or de lui;
Quant tans en iert g'i revenrai.

2650 De Cléomadès parlerai.
Qui seur le chevalet s'en va.
En petit de tans le porta
Si loing qu'il ne sot où il fu.
Lors vit il bien que deceü
L'avoit Crompars et engingnié;
Mais n'ot pas le cuer esmaié,
Ains l'ot si ferm en seürté
Com cil où ains n'ot lascheté.

Cléomadès is taken very far.

He knows he has been tricked

but is too brave to be frightened.

. . . .

Lors se commence à aviser
C'une cheville vit torner
Crompart, droit ou front dou cheval.

2670 Lors tasta amont et aval
Pour savoir que ce povoit estre.
A une chevillete à destre
Assena, et il l'a tournée;
Et li chevaus, sans demorée,
S'est tantost à destre tournés.
Lors tasta au senestre lés;
Pluseurs chevilles i trouva;
L'une après l'autre ressaia,
Tant qu'il vit bien qu'il torneroit

2680 Le cheval quel part qu'il vorroit.
Moult durement li abeli
Que la chose trouva ainsi.
De ce dut il bien estre liez;
Car jamais ne fust repairiez
Se il ne se fust avisés
Des chevilles dont vous oès;
Car par les chevilles aloit
Les chevaus quel part c'on vouloit.
Vers la poitrine retasta,

Recalling that Crompars had turned a peg

he feels about,

finds one on the right, which turns the horse to the right,

discovers more pegs,

and learns to turn the horse in any direction,

or make him softly
come down.

2690 A une cheville assena
Qui en tel fourme faite estoit
Que, si tost que on la tournoit,
Li chevaus, tout en arrestant,
Aloit vers la terre avalant,
Si belement et si soué[1]
Com pluie en avril chiet sor blé.
    Tant fist que il sot la maniere

He gets him under
perfect control.

D'aler et avant et arriere
Et bas et haut quant il vouloit.

Cléomadès is borne by the wonderful horse to a country that is now called Tuscany. Carmans is the king of that country and his wife is named Clarmonde. Their only child is the beautiful Clarmondine. Cléomadès sees a castle with many beautiful towers surrounded by woods and rivers, vineyards and spacious meadows. It was the merry month of May. Cléomadès descends upon a high tower.

There he leaves his
horse, descends by
a stairway,

    Iluec a laissié son cheval.
Par les degrez s'en vint aval.
Moult noble lieu par tout trouva.
Tant ala de çà et de là

and finds a beauti-
ful room

Qu'il est venus en une sale
Qui n'estoit ne laide ne sale,
Mais moult bele et nouviau jonchié.

and a table set

Une table y avoit drecié
D'yvoire à pierres de cristal.
2830 Tout si fait furent li hestal.[2]
Très blanche nape ot desus mise
Ouvrée de diverse guise.

with plenty of food
and good wines.

Sor l'un cor de la table avoit
A mengier kan k'il convenoit,
Et sor l'autre coron à destre
Ot vin si bon que vins pot estre,
En pos d'or et hanas autés.[3]
Viande et vin i ot assés.

After eating and drinking, Cléomadès passes into a rich room in which three damsels are sleeping, the beautiful Clarmondine and two maidens. He kisses Clarmondine, who wakes up. She

---

[1] Softly.   [2] Seats.   [3] In pots of gold and in beakers likewise.

mistakes him for her suitor Bléopatris, and Cléomadès confirms her in her error. But Clarmondine's father is soon informed and has Cléomadès seized and condemned to death in spite of the intercession of Clarmondine, who has fallen in love with the unknown visitor. Cléomadès asks as a favor that he should be killed while sitting on his wonderful horse.

Tant parla au roi et tant dist, — *He spoke so long and so well*
Et si sagement esploita,
3950 Que li rois congié li donna — *that the king gave him leave to mount the horse.*
De monter seur son chevalet.
Et lors s'assemblerent vallet — *Servants came with weapons and sticks.*
Et plousours gens de maintes pars
A espiex, à lances, à dars,
A espées et à bastons;
Grosses pierres en leur girons
Prendoient aucun pour ruer.
Cléomadès ala monter
Seur son cheval si tost qu'il pot
3960 Quant dou roy le congié en ot.
    Liez fu quand il se sent montez, — *As soon as Cléomadès is on his horse*
Car bien sot qu'il fu eschapez.
Lors n'atendi pas longuement,
Ains mist la main apertement
Au front dou cheval, et tourna — *he starts off.*
La cheville, et lors s'en ala
Li chevaus à tout lui errant,
Si très tost parmi l'air fendant,
K'à merveilles s'en esbahirent — *All are amazed and angry.*
3970 Cil qui de là partir le virent.
Moult se tinrent pour deceü
Quant ainsi eschapez lor fu.
Li uns vers l'aultre regardoit.
Chascuns si esbahis estoit
Que il ne savoient que dire;
Corroucié furent et plain d'ire.

After the return of Cléomadès to Seville, the nuptials of his two older sisters are celebrated. Not long after he hastens back to Clarmondine on his magic horse and, having made himself known to her as a son of the King of Spain, he returns with her to Seville. While he goes to his father's castle to prepare a fitting reception for his lady, Clarmondine with the ebony horse waits for him in a garden near the city. There Crompars, who has been lurking in the neighborhood, finds her and through a stratagem persuades her to go off with him on the wonderful steed. While the two, fatigued by their travels, are resting in a meadow Crompars falls asleep and Clarmondine is carried away by Meniadus, king of Salerno. Cléomadès after many adventures finds her there and again by means of the magic horse succeeds in bringing her back to Seville to become his bride.

III. ANALOGUES TO THE CANACEE AND FALCON EPISODES[1]

The Kādambarī, by Bāna, is a Hindu example of a fairly large group of oriental stories concerned with the infidelity of birds. As in the *Squire's Tale* a·female bird complains to a princess who understands her language:

(From *The Kādambarī of Bāna*, trans. C. M. Ridding ["Royal Asiatic Society: New Series," No. 11 [London, 1896], pp. 150–51.)

Then there came up with hasty steps a maina, a very flower. . . . . Close behind her came a parrot. . . . . Angrily the maina began: "Princess Kādambarī, why dost thou not restrain this wretched, ill-mannered, conceited bird from following me? If thou overlookest my being oppressed by him, I will certainly destroy myself. I swear it truly by the lotus feet." At these words Kādambarī smiled; but Mahāç-vetā, not knowing the story, asked Madalekhā what she was saying, and she told the following tale: "This maina, Kalīndī, is a friend of Princess Kādambarī, and was given by her solemnly in marriage to Parishāsa, the parrot. And today, ever since she saw him reciting something at early dawn to Kādambārī's betel-bearer, Tamālikā, alone, she has been filled with jealousy, and in frowardness of wrath will not go near him, or speak, or touch, or look at him; and though we have all tried to soothe her, she will not be soothed."

---

[1] The editor wishes to acknowledge his indebtedness to Professor Haldeen Braddy for the preparation of this section. On the oriental origin of the episode see Haldeen Braddy, *MLR*, XXXI (1936), 11–19; on the possibility of allusions to contemporaries see pp. 180–82 of M. Galway, "Chaucer's Sovereign Lady," *MLR*, XXXIII (1938), 145–99.

Other analogues suggest that Chaucer may have planned to have the falcon's experience influence Canacee in causing her to hate men. The following is taken from the *Arabian Nights:*

(From *The Book of the Thousand Nights and a Night*, trans. Sir Richard F. Burton [Medina ed., n.d.], III, 31–36.)

Taj al Muluk falls in love with Princess Dunyā after hearing her beauty described but then learns from her nurse that the princess despises men. His conversation with the nurse follows:

Asked the Prince, "Tell me what caused her to hate men"; and the old woman answered, "It arose from what she saw in a dream." "And what was this dream?" " 'Twas this: one night, as she lay asleep, she saw a fowler spread his net upon the ground and scatter wheat-grain round it. Then he sat down hard by, and not a bird in the neighbourhood but flocked to his toils. Amongst the rest she beheld a pair of pigeons, male and female; and, whilst she was watching the net, behold, the male bird's foot caught in the meshes and he began to struggle; whereupon all the other birds took fright and flew away. But presently his mate came back and hovered over him, then alighted on the toils unobserved by the fowler, and fell to pecking with her beak and pulling at the mesh in which the male bird's foot was tangled, till she released the toes and they flew away together. Then the fowler came up, mended his net and seated himself afar off. After an hour or so the birds flew back and the female pigeon was caught in the net; whereupon all the other birds took fright and scurried away; and the male pigeon fled with the rest and did not return to his mate, but the fowler came up and took the female pigeon and cut her throat.[1] The Princess awoke, troubled by her dream, and said:—'All males are like this pigeon, worthless creatures: and men in general lack grace and goodness to women.' "

Having disguised himself as a merchant, Tāj al-Mulūk sends the princess costly gifts, but these avail him naught. He finally strikes upon a plan whereby Princess Dunyā and her attendants are to be led into a garden where the scene is differently created in pictures on the walls of a pavilion. His Wazir attends to the task, assisted by a painter:

[1] It is interesting to note that in *John Lane's Continuation of the Squire's Tale,* p. 230, the magic glass of Canacee shows the tercelet the image of her falcon as dead (Part XII, vss. 443–53).

Moreover he sent for gold and lapis lazuli and said to the painter, "Figure me on the wall, at the upper end of this hall, a man-fowler with his nets spread and birds falling into them and a female pigeon entangled in the meshes by her bill." And when the painter had finished his picture on one side, the Wazir said, "Figure me on the other side a similar figure and represent the she-pigeon alone in the snare and the fowler seizing her and setting the knife to her neck; and draw on the third side wall, a great raptor clutching the male pigeon, her mate, and digging talons into him."

When Princess Dunyā later enters the garden and sees the paintings, she exclaims:

"Exalted be Allah! This is the very counterfeit presentment of what I saw in my dream." She continued to gaze at the figures of the birds and the fowler with his net, admiring the work, and presently she said, "O my nurse, I have been wont to blame and hate men, but look now at the fowler how he hath slaughtered the she-bird and set free her mate; who was minded to return to her and aid her to escape when the bird of prey met him and tore him to pieces."[1]

[1] The story of Ardashīr and Hayāt al-Nufūs, which also appears in the *Arabian Nights*, is a variant of the story of Taj al-Mulūk and Princess Dunyā. The differences between these two redactions of an almost identical plot are few in number and of minor importance.

THE FRANKLIN'S TALE

By GERMAINE DEMPSTER AND J. S. P. TATLOCK

IT IS highly probable that Chaucer used as main source the story of Menedon in Boccaccio's *Filocolo* (I), combined it with elements found in the *Historia regum Britanniae* of Geoffrey of Monmouth (II), and gave his tale a Breton background in imitation of the lays (III). His use of St. Jerome's *Adversus Jovinianum* (IV) in this tale is confined to Dorigen's *exempla*.

I. *IL FILOCOLO*

The fourth narrative in the *questioni d'amore* episode in Boccaccio's *Filocolo* is closer to the *Franklin's Tale* than is the almost identical story in *Decameron*, X, 5. Its claims as Chaucer's main source have been presented very convincingly.[1]

(Reprinted from *Il Filocolo*, ed. by Salvatore Battaglia ["Scrittori d' Italia," No. 167, Bari, 1938].)

In a shady spot in a garden a company of young men and women spend the hot hours discussing problems of love. They

[1] See Pio Rajna, pp. 40–43 of "L'Episodio delle questioni d'amore nel *Filocolo* del Boccaccio," *Romania*, XXXI (1902), and, more important, "Le Origini della novella narrata dal *Frankeleyn* nei *Canterbury Tales* del Chaucer," *Romania*, XXXII (1903), 204–67; J. S. P. Tatlock, *The Scene of the "Franklin's Tale" Visited* ("Chaucer Society," 1914), esp. pp. 55–75; J. L. Lowes, "The *Franklin's Tale*, the *Teseide*, and the *Filocolo*," *MP*, XV (1918), 689–728. The theory is accepted by L. Foulet, "Le Prologue du *Franklin's Tale* et les lais bretons," *ZRPh*, XXX (1906), 698–711, and A. Aman, *Die Filiation der "Frankeleynes Tale" in Chaucers "Canterbury Tales"* (Munich diss., Erlangen, 1912), pp. 128–29. Chaucer's use of the *Filocolo* is granted as a possibility by Karl Young, *Origin and Development of the Story of Troilus and Criseyde* ("Chaucer Society," 1908), p. 181n. For features common to the *Fkl. T.* and the *questione* see Rajna, *Romania*, XXXII, 235–42; Tatlock, p. 56 and n. 2; Lowes, pp. 720–22. On their differences see H. Cummings, *The Indebtedness of Chaucer's Works to the Italian Works of Boccaccio* (Cincinnati, 1916), pp. 196–97, and Lowes, pp. 723–25. For comparison of *Dec.*, X, 5 and the *questione* as possible sources see Rajna, *Romania*, XXXI, 42 and n., and XXXII, 234–44, 257. On other indications of Chaucer's acquaintance with the *Filocolo* see Young, pp. 139–81, and his "Chaucer's Use of Boccaccio's *Filocolo*," *MP*, IV (1906), 169–77; Lowes, pp. 705–13; against it, Cummings, pp. 1–12. On related oriental tales see *Originals and Analogues*, pp. 291–325; Rajna, XXXI, 43–45, and XXXII, 258–59; Tatlock, pp. 75–77; A. C. Lee, *The Decameron: Its Sources and Analogues* (London, 1909), pp. 322–28; for full bibliography and numerous summaries see Aman.

377

have elected a queen, Fiammetta, who gives each *questione* its final answer. The fourth question is proposed by Menedon (pp. 311–20).

QUESTIONE IIII

A noble cavalier loves deeply and marries a noble lady.

Nella terra lá dove io nacqui, mi ricorda essere un ricchissimo e nobile cavaliere, il quale di perfettissimo amore amando una donna nobile della terra, per isposa la prese. Della quale donna, essendo bellissima, un altro cavaliere chiamato Tarolfo s'innamorò e di tanto amore l'amava, che oltre a lei non vedeva niuna cosa, né piú disiava, e in molte maniere, forse con sovente passare davanti alle sue case, o giostrando, o armeggiando, o con altri atti, s'ingegnava d'avere l'amore di lei: e spesso mandandole messaggieri, forse promettendole grandissimi doni, per sapere il suo intendimento. Le quali cose la donna tutte celatamente sostenea, senza dare segno o risposta buona al cavaliere, fra sé dicendo: "Poi che questi s'avvedrá che da me né buona risposta né buono atto puote avere, forse elli si rimarrá d'amarmi e di darmi questi stimoli." Ma giá per tutto questo Tarolfo di ciò non si rimaneva, seguendo d'Ovidio gli ammaestramenti, il quale dice: "L'uomo non dee lasciare per durezza della donna di non perserverare, però che per continuanza la molle acqua fora la dura pietra." Ma la donna, dubitando non queste cose venissero a orecchie del marito, ed egli pensasse poi che con volontá di lei questo avvenisse, propose di dirgliele; ma poi mossa da miglior consiglio disse: "Io potrei, s'io il dicessi, commettere tra loro cosa che io mai non viverei lieta: per altro modo si vuole levar via;" e imaginò una sottile malizia. Ella mandò cosí dicendo a Tarolfo: che se egli tanto l'amava quanto mostrava, ella voleva da lui un dono, il quale come l'avesse ricevuto, giurava per i suoi iddii, e per quella leanza che in gentile donna dee essere, che ella farebbe ogni suo piacere; e se quello ch'ella dimandava, donare non le volesse, ponessesi in core di non stimolarla piú avanti, per quanto egli non volesse che essa questo manifestasse al marito. E il dono ch'ella dimandò fu questo. Ella disse che volea del mese di gennaio, in quella terra, un bel giardino e grande, d'erbe e di fiori e d'alberi e di frutti copioso, come se del mese di maggio fosse, tra sé dicendo: "Questa è cosa impossibile, e io mi leverò costui da dosso in questa maniera." Tarolfo, udendo questo, ancora che impossibile gli paresse e che egli conoscesse bene perché la donna questo gli dimandava, rispose che giá mai non riposerebbe né in presenza di lei tornerebbe, infino a tanto che l'addimandato dono le donerebbe. E partitosi della terra con quella compagnia che a lui piacque di prendere, tutto il ponente cercò per avere consiglio di potere pervenire al suo disio;

Tarolfo, another cavalier, discreetly courts her, but in vain.

The lady gives no sign, in hope that he will give over his design.

Lest his persistency might come to the ears of her husband, and be thought due to her own abetting, and end in such a falling-out between the men that she could never again be happy, she bethinks her of a shrewd device to be rid of him; she sends word that she will do his pleasure if he will provide her in January with a garden blooming and fruitful as in May. Otherwise he is to cease troubling her.

"I will neither rest nor return till I can give it."

ma non trovandolo, cercò le piú calde regioni, e pervenne in Tesaglia, In Thessaly
dove per sí fatta bisogna fu mandato da discreto uomo. E quivi
dimorato piú giorni, non avendo ancora trovato quello che cercando
andava, avvenne che essendosi egli quasi del suo avviso disperato,
levatosi una mattina avanti che il sole s'apparecchiasse d'entrare
nell'aurora, incominciò tutto soletto ad andare per lo misero piano
che giá fu tutto del romano sangue bagnato. Ed essendo per grande
spazio andato, egli si vide davanti a' piè d'un monte un uomo, non he comes upon a wretched old fellow, Tebano, collecting herbs and roots,
giovane né di troppa lunga etá, barbuto, e i suoi vestimenti giudica-
vano lui dovere essere povero, picciolo di persona e sparuto molto, il
quale andava cogliendo erbe e cavando con un picciolo coltello diverse
radici, delle quali un lembo della sua gonnella aveva pieno. Il quale
quando Tarolfo vide, si maravigliò e dubitò molto non altro fosse;
ma poi che la stimativa certamente gli rendé lui essere uomo, egli
s'appressò a lui e salutollo, dimandandolo appresso chi fosse e donde, and asks what he is about.
e quel che per quel luogo a cosí fatta ora andava faccendo. A cui il
vecchierello rispose: "Io sono di Tebe, e Tebano è il mio nome, e per
questo piano vo cogliendo queste erbe, acciò che de' liquori d'esse "I am gathering herbs for physic. But who are you, so solitary?"
faccendo alcune cose necessarie e utili a diverse infermitá, io abbia
donde vivere, e a questa ora necessitá e non diletto mi ci costrigne
di venire; ma tu chi se', che nell' aspetto mi sembri nobile, e quinci
sí soletto vai?" A cui Tarolfo rispose: "Io sono dell'ultimo ponente, "I am from the farthest West; I am walking alone to grieve in peace over my hopeless under-taking."
assai ricco cavaliere, e da' pensieri d'una mia impresa vinto e stimo-
lato, non potendola fornire, di qua, per meglio potermi senza impedi-
mento dolermi, mi vo cosí soletto andando." A cui Tebano disse:
"Non sai tu la qualitá del luogo come ella è? E perché inanzi d'altra "Don't you know this place is not canny?"
parte non pigliavi la via? Tu potresti di leggieri qui dai furiosi spiriti
essere vituperato?" Rispose Tarolfo: "In ogni parte puote Iddio "I am in the hands of God."
ugualmente, cosí qui come altrove; egli ha la mia vita e 'l mio onore
in mano; faccia di me secondo che a lui piace: veramente a me sarebbe
la morte un ricchissimo tesoro." Disse allora Tebano: "Qual è la "What is your undertaking?"
tua impresa, per la quale, non potendola fornire, sí dolente dimori?"
A cui Tarolfo rispose: "È tale che impossibile mi pare omai a fornire,
poi che qui non ho trovato consiglio." Disse Tebano: "Osasi dire?"
Rispose Tarolfo: "Sí, ma che utile? forse niuno!" Disse Tebano:
"Ma che danno?" Allora Tarolfo disse: "Io cerco di potere avere "In the coldest month I must have a garden as in May."
consiglio come del piú freddo mese si potesse avere un giardino pieno
di fiori e di frutti e d'erbe, sí bello come del mese di maggio fosse, né
trovo chi a ciò aiuto o consiglio mi doni che vero sia." Tebano stette
un pezzo tutto sospeso senza rispondere, e poi disse: "Tu e molti
altri il sapere e le virtú degli uomini giudicate secondo i vestimenti. "You should not judge me by my garb.
Se la mia roba fosse stata qual è la tua, tu non avresti tanto penato a

dirmi la tua bisogna, o se forse appresso de' ricchi prencipi m'avessi trovato, come tu hai a cogliere erbe; ma molte volte sotto vilissimi drappi grandissimo tesoro di scienza si nasconde: e però a chi proffera consiglio o aiuto niuno celi la sua bisogna, se manifesta non gli può

What would you give him who would provide the garden?"

pregiudicare. Ma che doneresti a chi quello che tu vai cercando ti recasse ad effeto?" Tarolfo rimirava costui nel viso dicendo queste parole, e in sé dubitava non questi si facesse beffe di lui, parendogli incredibile che, se costui non fosse stato Dio, egli avesse potuto avere virtú. Non per tanto egli rispose cosí: "Io signoreggio ne' miei paesi piú

"Half my castles and treasures."

castella, e con esse molti tesori, i quali tutti per mezzo partirei con chi tal piacere mi facesse." "Certo" disse Tebano, "se questo facessi, a me non bisognerebbe d'andare piú cogliendo l'erbe." "Fermamente" disse Tarolfo: "se tu se' quelli che in ciò mi prometti di dar vero effetto, e dallomi, mai non ti bisognerá piú affannare per divenire ricco; ma come e quando mi potrai tu questo fornire?" Disse Tebano: "Il

"When you will; and as to how, you need not trouble yourself, I'll do it."

quando fia a tua posta, del come non ti travagliare. Io me ne verrò teco fidandomi nella tua parola della promessa che mi fai, e quando lá dove ti piacerá saremo, comanderai quello che vorrai, e io fornirò tutto senza fallo." Fu di questo accidente tanto contento in se me-

Tarolfo is well-nigh as joyful as if he had his lady in his arms. "Let us be off."

desimo Tarolfo, che poco piú letizia avrebbe avuta se nelle sue braccia la sua donna allora tenuta avesse, e disse: "Amico, a me si fa tardi che quel che m'imprometti si fornisca, però senza indugio partiamo,

Tebano throws away his herbs, takes his books and other gear of his art, and the two arrive a little before January.

e andiamo lá dove questo si dee fornire." Tebano, gittate via l'erbe, e presi i suoi libri e altre cose al suo mestiere necessarie, con Tarolfo si mise al cammino, e in brieve tempo pervennero alla disiderata città, assai vicini al mese del quale era stato dimandato il giardino. Quivi tacitamente e occulti infine al termine disiderato si riposarono; ma entrato giá il mese, Tarolfo comandò che 'l giardino s'apprestasse,

After waiting a bit, on a night of full moon Tebano issues alone from the city, naked and disheveled.

acciò che donare lo potesse alla sua donna. Come Tebano ebbe il comandamento, egli aspettò la notte, e, venuta, vide i corni della luna tornati in compiuta ritonditá, e videla sopra l'usate terre tutta risplendere. Allora egli uscí della città, lasciati i vestimenti, scalzo, e co' capelli sparti sopra li nudi omeri, tutto solo.

Tebano invokes magical powers that have earlier helped him, flies in a dragon chariot to distant countries, gathers herbs, stones, and the like, returns to the spot chosen for the garden, boils together the ingredients he has gathered and stirs them with a dry olive twig. This turns green and soon bears fruit.

Tebano sprinkles the boiling liquor over the chosen spot,

Come Tebano vide questo, egli prese i boglienti liquori, e sopra l'eletto terreno, nel quale di tanti legni aveva fatto bastoni quanti arbori e di quante maniere voleva quivi, quelli cominciò a spandere e ad inaffiare per tutto: la quale cosa la terra non sentí prima, che ella cominció tutta a fiorire, producendo nuove e belle erbette, e i secchi legni verdi piantoni e fruttiferi divennero tutti. La qual cosa fatta, Tebano rientrò nella terra tornando a Tarolfo. Il quale, quasi pauroso d'essere stato da lui beffato per la lunga dimoranza, trovò tutto pensoso, a cui egli disse: "Tarolfo, fatto è quello che hai dimandato, ed è al piacere tuo." Assai questo piacque a Tarolfo, e dovendo essere il seguente giorno nella città una grandissima solennitá, egli se n'andò davanti alla sua donna, la quale giá era gran tempo che veduta non l'aveva, e cosí le disse: "Madonna, dopo lunga fatica io ho fornito quello che voi comandaste: quando vi piacerá di vederlo o di prenderlo, egli è al vostro piacere." *which straightway blooms and bears fruit.* "Your demand is fulfilled." Next day at a festivity in the city Tarolfo encounters the lady. "*Madonna*, what you commanded is at your pleasure."

La donna, vedendo costui, si maravigliò molto, e piú udendo ciò che egli diceva; e non credendolo, gli rispose: "Assai mi piace; faretelomi vedere domani." Venuto il seguente giorno, Tarolfo andò alla donna, e disse: "Madonna, piacciavi di passare nel giardino, il quale voi mi dimandaste nel freddo mese." Mossesi adunque la donna da molti accompagnata, e, pervenuti al giardino, v'entrarono dentro per una bella porta, e in quello non freddo sí come di fuori, ma un aere temperato e dolce si sentiva. Andò la donna per tutto rimirando e cogliendo erbe e fiori, de' quali molto il vide copioso: e tanto piú ancora avea operato la virtú degli sparti liquori, che i frutti, i quali l'agosto suole produrre, quivi nel salvatico tempo tutti i loro alberi facevano belli: de' quali piú persone, andate con la donna, mangiarono. Questo parve alla donna bellissima cosa e mirabile, né mai un sí bello ne le pareva avere veduto. E poi che essa in molte maniere conobbe quello essere vero giardino, e 'l cavaliere avere adempiuto ciò ch'ella aveva dimandato, ella si voltò a Tarolfo e disse: "Senza fallo, cavaliere, guadagnato avete l'amore mio, e io sono presta d'attenervi ciò ch'io vi promisi; ma veramente vorrei una grazia da voi, che vi piacesse tanto indugiare a richiedermi del vostro disio, che 'l signore mio andasse a caccia, o in altra parte fuori della cittá, acciò che piú saviamente e senza dubitanza alcuna possiate prendere vostro diletto." Piacque a Tarolfo, e, lasciandole il giardino, quasi contento da lei si partí. Questo giardino fu a tutti i paesani manifesto, avvegna che niuno sapesse, se non dopo molto tempo, come venuto si fosse. Ma la gentil donna, che ricevuto l'avea, dolente di quello si partí, tornando alla sua camera piena di noiosa malinconia. E pensando in qual maniera tornar potesse adietro ciò che promesso avea, e non trovando lecita scusa, piú in dolore cresceva. La qual cosa vedendo, il marito si cominciò molto a maravigliare e a dimandarla che cosa ella avesse: la donna diceva che niente aveva, vergognandosi di scoprire al marito With many others she enters the garden, sweet and balmy after the cold outside; she picks flowers and others eat the fruits. "Assuredly, cavalier, you have earned my love, and I am ready to keep my promise. But pray wait till my husband is from home." She enters her chamber full of grief. Her husband asks what is wrong. "Nothing."

la fatta promissione per lo addimandato dono, dubitando non il marito malvagia la tenesse. Ultimamente non potendosi ella a' continui stimoli del marito, che pur la cagione della sua malinconia disiderava di sapere, tenersi, dal principio insino alla fine gli narrò perché dolente dimorava. La qual cosa udendo il cavaliere lungamente pensò, e conoscendo nel pensiero la puritá della donna, cosí le disse: "Va, e copertamente osserva il tuo giuramento, e a Tarolfo ciò che tu promettesti liberamente attieni: egli l' ha ragionevolmente e con grande affanno guadagnato." Cominciò la donna a piangere e a dire: "Facciano gl'iddii da me lontano cotal fallo; in niuna maniera farò questo: aventi m'ucciderei ch'io facessi cosa che disonore o dispiacere vi fosse." A cui il cavaliere disse: "Donna, giá per questo non voglio che tu te n'uccida, né ancora che una sola malinconia tu te ne dia: niuno dispiacere m'è, va e fa quello che impromettesti, ch'io non t'avrò meno cara; ma questo fornito, un'altra volta ti guarda da sí fatte impromesse, non tanto ti paia il dimandato dono impossibile ad avere." Vedendo la donna la volontá del marito, ornatasi e fattasi bella, e presa compagnia, andò all'ostiere di Tarolfo, e di vergogna dipinta gli si presentò dinanzi. Tarolfo come la vide, levatosi da lato a Tebano con cui sedeva, pieno di maraviglia e di letizia le si fece incontro, e lei onorevolmente ricevette, dimandando la cagione della sua venuta. A cui la donna rispose: "Per essere a tutti i tuoi voleri sono venuta; fa di me quel che ti piace." Allora disse Tarolfo: "Senza fine mi fate maravigliare, pensando all'ora e alla compagnia con cui venuta siete: senza novitá stata tra voi e vostro marito non puote essere, ditelomi, io ve ne priego." Narrò allora la donna interamente a Tarolfo come la cosa era tutta per ordine. La qual cosa udendo, Tarolfo piú che prima si cominciò a maravigliare e a pensar forte, e a conoscere cominciò la gran liberalitá del marito di lei che mandata l'avea a lui, e tra sé cominciò a dire che degno di grandissima ripresione sarebbe chi a cosí liberale uomo pensasse villania; e parlando alla donna cosí disse: "Gentil donna, lealmente come valorosa donna avete il vostro dovere servato, per la qual cosa i' ho per ricevuto ciò che di voi disiderava; e però quando piacerá a voi ve ne potrete tornare al vostro marito, e di tanta grazia da mia parte ringraziarlo, e iscusarglimi della follia che per adietro ho usata, accertandolo che per inanzi piú per me mai tali cose non fiano trattate." Ringraziato la donna molto Tarolfo di tanta cortesia, lieta si partí tornando al suo marito, a cui tutto per ordine narrò quello che avvenuto l'era. Ma Tebano ritornato a Tarolfo dimandò come avvenuto egli fosse; Tarolfo glielo contò; a cui Tebano disse: "Dunque per questo avrò io perduto ciò che da te mi fu promesso?" Rispose Tarolfo: "No,

More questioning; she tells him all.

After long thought, perceiving her innocence, "Go," he says, "secretly keep your promise; he has earned it." Tears and protests; "I would rather kill myself."

"Do not, nor even grieve; it is no displeasure to me, nor shall I hold you less dear; but hereafter make no such promises, even though the gift seem impossible."

All adorned, and with attendants, she presents herself bashfully to Tarolfo; who full of joy and wonder receives her with honor and asks why she has come.

"To do your pleasure." "You cannot have come thus without some rare scene with your husband."

Hearing the truth, Tarolfo thinks deeply; he who should think of a churlishness to a man so generous would be most blameworthy.

"Noble lady, you have loyally done your duty. Return to your husband, thank him from me, beg him to forgive my folly. I shall never consider such a thing again."

She thanks him and returns happy to her husband.

Learning of this affair, Tebano asks if he is to lose what Tarolfo has promised him.

anzi, qualora ti piace, va e le mie castella e i miei tesori prendi per "No; take the half of my castles and treasures when you will."
metá, come io ti promisi, però che da te interamente servito mi tengo."
Al quale Tebano rispose: "Unque agl'iddii non piaccia che lá dove il "The gods forbid that I should be less noble than the generous husband, or than you who have been no churl. Keep your possessions."
cavaliere ti fu della sua donna liberale, e tu a lui non fosti villano, io
sia meno cortese. Oltre a tutte le cose del mondo mi piace l'averti
servito, e voglio che ciò che in guiderdone del servigio prendere doveva, tuo si rimanga sí come mai fu;" né di quello di Tarolfo volle
alcuna cosa prendere. Dubitasi ora quale di costoro fosse maggiore Which of the men was most generous?
liberalitá, o quella del cavaliere che concedette alla donna l'andare a
Tarolfo, o quella di Tarolfo, il quale quella donna cui egli avea sempre
disiata, e per cui egli avea tanto fatto per venire a quel punto a che
venuto era, quando la donna venne a lui, rimandò la sopradetta libera
al suo marito; o quella di Tebano, il quale, abbandonate le sue con-
trade, oramai vecchio, e venuto quivi per guadagnare i promessi doni,
e affannatosi per recare a fine ciò che promesso avea, avendoli guada-
gnati, ogni cosa rimise, rimanendosi povero come prima.

Arguing that honor is more precious than wealth or a lover's
pleasure, Fiammetta places the husband's generosity above
that of Tarolfo and Tebano.

II. *HISTORIA REGUM BRITANNIAE*

The similarities between the *Franklin's Tale* and the *Historia
regum Britanniae* are the name of Arviragus as loving husband of Genuissa or Dorigen and the use of magic or skill in a
feat involving rocks and performed at the request of Aurelius.
Those similarities, first taken as pointing to common lost
Celtic antecedents,[1] are now explained as Chaucer's direct borrowings from Geoffrey of Monmouth.[2]

(Text taken, with minor alterations, from Acton Griscom's edition of the
Historia regum Britanniae [London and New York, 1929].)

The Roman Claudius has made peace with the Briton
Arviragus and promised him his daughter.

iv. 15. Emensa hyeme deinde redierunt legati cum filia eamque patri Messengers bring her to her father. She is named Genuissa, and is of
tradiderunt. Erat autem nomen puellæ Genuissa, eratque ei tanta pul-

[1] See pp. 409–18 of W. H. Schofield, "Chaucer's *Franklin's Tale*," *PMLA*,
XVI (1901), 405–49.

[2] F. Lot's review of Schofield, *Moyen-Age*, VI (2d ser., 1902), 108–12; Rajna,
Romania, XXXII, 212–23; Tatlock, pp. 65–68; G. Dempster, *Dramatic Irony in
Chaucer* (Stanford University, 1932), pp. 65–66.

marvelous beauty. Her husband Arviragus is so fired with fervent love that he prefers her to the whole world.

chritudo ut aspicientes in ammirationem duceret. Et, ut maritali lege copulata fuit, tanto fervore amoris succendit regem [Arviragum] ita ut ipsam solam cunctis rebus preferret.

To devise a notable monument for the Britons buried at Stonehenge, the archbishop of Caerleon counsels King Aurelius to send for the wizard Merlinus.

"If any can do this, it is Merlin; none is of more brilliant intellect in soothsaying and in contriving feats."

viii. 10. "Si uspiam est qui preceptum aggredi valuerit, Merlinus, vates Vortegirni, aggredietur. Quippe non estimo alterum esse in regno tuo cui sit clarius ingenium, sive in futuris dicendis sive in operationibus machinandis. Jube eum venire atque ingenio suo uti, ut opus quod affectas constet." Cum itaque de eo multa interrogasset Aurelius, misit diversos nuntios per diversas nationes patriæ, ut inventum illum adducerent.

After a search far and wide Merlin is found and brought to King Aurelius, who asks for divinations.[1] Merlin refuses, "Should I offer them lightly, the spirit who inspires me would forsake me."

"If you desire a perpetual memorial, send for the Giants' Dance in Ireland, a structure of vast rocks. If placed as they are there, they will stand forever."

Denique, cum omnibus repulsam intulisset, noluit eum rex infestare de futuris, sed de operatione premeditata allocutus est. Cui Merlinus: "Si perpetuo opere sepulturam virorum decorare volueris, mitte pro Chorea Gigantum, quæ est in Killarao, monte Hyberniæ. Est etenim ibi structura lapidum, quam nemo hujus ætatis construeret, nisi ingenium arte subnecteret. Grandes sunt lapides, nec est aliquis cujus virtuti cedant. Qui si eo modo, quo ibidem positi sunt, circa plateam locabuntur, stabunt in eternum."

Aurelius' brother Uther Pendragon and fifteen thousand of their men rout the Irish and, with Merlin, reach the Giant's Dance.

"Bestir yourselves, men; see which is better, understanding or force."

viii.12. Circumstantibus itaque cunctis, accessit Merlinus et ait: "Utimini viribus vestris, juvenes, ut in deponendo lapides istos sciatis utrum ingenium virtuti an virtus ingenio cedat." Ad imperium igitur ejus indulserunt unanimiter et multimodis machinationibus aggressi

Their ropes, cords, ladders are of no avail.

sunt Choream deponere. Alii funes, alii restes, alii scalas paraverunt, ut quod affectabant perficerent, nec ullatenus perficere valuerunt.

---

[1] As analogue to the magical performance in the house of the Orleans clerk see *Roman de Merlin*, ed. H. O. Sommer (London, 1894), pp. 224–25; further references in Schofield, p. 419 and n.

Deficientibus itaque cunctis, solutus est Merlinus in risum, suasque *Merlin burst into laughter. By his* machinationes confecit. Denique, cum quaeque necessaria apposuis- *contrivances with incredible ease the* set, levis quam credi potest lapides deposuit; depositos autem fecit *stones are lowered, brought to the* deferri ad naves et interponi; et sic cum gaudio in Britanniam reverti *ships, and carried to Britain and to* coeperunt, et prosperantibus ventis applicant, sepultarasque virorum *the place of the memorial.* cum lapidibus adeunt.

III. THE LAYS

None of the extant lays contains a similar story or could be the source of the *Franklin's Tale*, but many resemblances have been noted, on which the theory was built that Chaucer followed a lay lost to us.[1] Most scholars now believe in Chaucer's imitation of the lay type rather than of one lost lay.

Doon

(P. 61 of Gaston Paris, "Lais inédits," *Romania*, Vol. VIII [1879].)

> Doon, cest lai sévent plusor:
> N'i a gueres bon harpeor
> Ne sache les notes harper;
> Mes je vos voil dire et conter
> L'aventure dont li Breton
> Apelérent cest lai Doon.

Le Freine

(From *The Middle English Lai Le Freine*, ed. Margaret Wattie ["Smith College Studies in Modern Languages" (Northampton, 1928)], p. 1.)[2]

> We redeþ oft & findeþ [ywri]te,   *Lays recited with the harp are of*
> & þis clerkes wele it wite,   *many kinds of aventures; many of*
> Layes þat ben in harping   *faerie, but most of love.*
> Ben yfounde of ferli þing.
> Sum beþe of wer & sum of wo,
> & sum of ioie & mirþe also,

---

[1] See W. H. Schofield; conclusions accepted by Cummings, pp. 181–87, and by Young (who admits that Chaucer may have used the *Filocolo* too), *Origin and Development of the Story of Troilus and Criseyde*, p. 181n. For comparison of the lays with the *Fkl. T.* see Schofield, pp. 425–32; Rajna, *Romania*, XXXII, 224–34; without discussion of source, pp. 208–16 of W. M. Hart, "The *Franklin's Tale*," *Haverford Essays* (Haverford, 1909); Cummings, pp. 185–86. On Chaucer's reference to a Breton source see Rajna, *Romania*, XXXII, 261–67; Tatlock, pp. 58–60; Lowes, 725–28. On early opinions on the *Fkl. T.* source see Rajna, *Romania*, XXXII, 205, nn. 5 and 6; Tatlock, p. 55, n. 2.

[2] Also by Varnhagen, *Anglia*, III (1880), 415–23.

& sum of trecherie & of gile,
Of old auentours þat fel while;
& sum of bourdes & ribaudy,
& mani þer beþ of fairy.
Of al þinge[s] þat men seþ,
Mest o loue for soþe þai beþ.

They were made in Britain.

In Breteyne bi hold time
þis layes were wrouȝt, so seiþ þis rime.
When kinges miȝt our[1] yhere
Of ani meruailes þat þer were,
þai token an harp in gle & game,
& maked a lay & ȝaf it name.[2]

Milun

(Reprinted, like *Equitan* and *Les Dous Amanz*, from *Die Lais der Marie de France*, hrsg. Karl Warnke [Halle, 1925].)

The son of Milun, brought up by an aunt, hears from her of his parents, and especially of his father's knightly fame.

304	Liez fu de ceo qu'il ot oï.
305	A sei meïsmes pense e dit:
	"Mult se deit huem preisier petit,
	Quant il issi fu engendrez
	E sis pere est si alosez,
	S'il ne se met en greignur pris
310	Fors de la terre e del païs." ...
317	A Suhthamptune vait passer;
	Cum il ainz pot, se mist en mer.
	A Barbefluet est arivez;[3]
320	Dreit en Bretaigne en est alez.
	La despendi e turneia;
	As riches humes s'acuinta.
	Unques ne vint en nul estur
	Que l'en nel tenist al meillur.
325	Les povres chevaliers amot;
	Ceo que des riches guaaignot
	Lur donout e sis reteneit,

He too would win high renown in foreign lands.

He crosses from Southampton to Barfleur and proceeds thence to Brittany.

He comes out best in every tourney

[1] Anywhere.

[2] On the relation of this to *Fkl. T.*, see Foulet. Compare opening of *Equitan* quoted on p. 387.

[3] In another lay, *Eliduc*, a knight from "Bretaigne la Menur" crosses over to Great Britain (*Die Lais*, pp. 186–224).

E mult largement despendeit.
Unques sun voel ne surjurna.

330 De tutes les terres de la
Porta le pris e la valur;
Mult fu curteis, mult sot d'onur ...

and wins a great name for courtesy and honor.

341 Milun oï celui loër
E les biens de lui recunter ...

Milun hears of this great knight;

349 D'une chose se purpensa:
Hastivement mer passera,
Si justera al chevalier
Pur lui laidir e empeirier ...

he will cross the sea, joust with him, and lay him low.

373 En Normendie en est passez;
Puis est desqu'en Bretaigne alez.

375 Mult s'aquointa a plusurs genz,
Mult cercha les turneiemenz;
Riches ostels teneit sovent
E si dunot curteisement.
    Tut un yver, ceo m'est a vis,

In Brittany Milun seeks many tournaments and lives as a gracious knight all winter.

380 Conversa Milun el païs.
Plusurs bons chevaliers retint,
De si qu'aprés la paske vint
Qu'il recumencent les turneiz
E les guerres e les desreiz.

After Easter, when tourneys begin, he is the first at the tourney of Mont St. Michel.

385 Al Munt Seint Michiel s'asemblerent;
Norman e Bretun i alerent
E li Flamenc e li Franceis;
Mes n'i ot guaires des Engleis.
Milun i est alez primiers,
390 Ki mult esteit hardiz e fiers.
Le bon chevalier demanda.

After a fight, father and son recognize each other.

Equitan

Mult unt esté noble barun
Cil de Bretaigne, li Bretun.
Jadis suleient par pruësce,
Par curteisie e par noblesce
5   Des aventures que oeient,
Ki a plusurs genz aveneient,
Faire les lais pur remembrance,
Qu'um nes meïst en ubliance ...

The Bretons used to make lays of aventures they heard of.

Equitan is devoted
to pleasure and
love.

Equitan fu mult de grant pris

E mult amez en sun païs.

15 Deduit amout e druërie:

Pur ceo maintint chevalerie.

Cil metent lur vie en nuncure,

Ki d'amer n'unt sen ne mesure;

The test of love is
to forget reason.

Tels est la mesure d'amer

20 Que nuls n'i deit raisun guarder.

King Equitan has come to the castle of his seneschal, whose beautiful wife he is anxious to see.

He finds her so
courteous and dis-
creet and beautiful
that Love's arrow
makes a great
wound in his heart.

55 Mult la trova curteise e sage,

Bele de cors e de visage,

De bel semblant e enveisiee.

Amurs l'a mis en sa maisniee.

Une saiete a vers lui traite,

60 Ki mult grant plaie li a faite:

El quer li a lanciee e mise.

N'i a mestier sens ne cointise:

Pur la dame l'a si suzpris,

Tuz en est murnes e pensis.

He grows pensive
and sleepless.

65 Or l'i estuet del tut entendre,

Ne se purra niënt defendre

La nuit ne dort ne ne repose,

Mes sei meïsme blasme e chose.

"Alas, why did I
come?

"A las," fet il, "quels destinee

70 M'amena en ceste cuntree?

Pur ceste dame qu'ai veüe

M'est une anguisse el quer ferue,

Ki tut le cors me fet trembler.

Jeo quit que mei l'estuet amer.

I shall do ill to love
the wife of him to
whom I owe good
faith, as he to me.

75 E se jo l'aim, jeo ferai mal:

Ceo est la femme al seneschal.

Guarder li dei amur e fei,

Si cum jeo vueil qu'il face a mei.

Se par nul engin le saveit,

80 Bien sai que mult l'en pesereit.

But worse if I go to
pieces!

Mes nepurquant pis iert asez

Que jeo pur li seie afolez.

She ought to have a
lover.

Si bele dame tant mar fust,

S'ele n'amast et dru n'eüst!

85 Que devendreit sa curteisie,

S'ele n'amast de druërie?
Suz ciel n'a hume, s'el l'amast,
Ki durement n'en amendast.
Li seneschals se l'ot cunter,

0   Ne l'en deit mie trop peser;
Suls ne la puet il pas tenir:
Certes, jeo vueil a li partir!"
Quant ceo ot dit, si suspira,
E puis se jut e si pensa.

95   Aprés parla e dist: "De quei
Sui en estrif et en esfrei?
Uncor ne sai ne n'ai seü
S'ele fereit de mei sun dru;
Mes jeo savrai hastivement ... .

117   Sun curage li descovri,
Saveir li fet qu'il muert pur li;
Del tut li puet faire confort

120   E bien li puet doner la mort.
"Sire," la dame li a dit,
"De ceo m'estuet aveir respit.
A ceste primiere feiee
N'en sui jeo mie cunseilliee... .

129   S'aviëz fait vostre talent,
Jeo sai de veir, n'en dut niënt,
Tost m'avriëz entrelaissiee;
J'en sereie mult empeiriee ... .

137   Pur ceo que estes reis puissanz
E mis sire est de vus tenanz,
Quideriëz a mun espeir

140   Le dangier de l'amur aveir.
Amurs n'est pruz, se n'est egals. ...
S'alcuns aime plus haltement
Qu'a sa richesce nen apent,
Cil se dute de tute rien.

150   Li riches huem requide bien
Que nuls ne li toille s'amie
Qu'il vuelt amer par seignurie."
Equitan li respunt aprés:
"Dame, merci! Ne dites mes!

155   Cil ne sunt mie fin curteis,
Ainz est bargaigne de burgeis,
Ki pur aveir ne pur grant fiu

The seneschal oughtn't to care much! He can't have her all; I'll have her."

He lies down and broods.

"Why worry? I don't know if she'll love me. But I'll find out."

He tells her his plight.

"Sir, I must think it over.

If you'd had your will of me, you'd desert me.

You are a king, my lord is your vassal.

Love is not good if it is not equal.

The powerful man thinks to hold his *amie* by might."

"Spare me, lady! This is not the way of the court, but a burgess' bargaining.

Metent lur peine en malvais liu.

Suz ciel n'a dame, s'ele est sage,

There isn't a lady
under heaven wise
and noble, not
cheap and fickle,
whom even the
prince of a castle
should not love, had
she only her coat.

160   Curteise e franche de curage,

Pur quei d'amer se tienge chiere

Qu'el ne seit mie noveliere,

S'el n'eüst fors sul sun mantel,

Qu'uns riches princes de chastel

165   Ne se deüst pur li pener

E leialment e bien amer. ...

Dear lady, I give
myself to you; do
not think me a king,
but your vassal and
ami.

Ma chiere dame, a vus m'otrei!

Ne me tenez mie pur rei,

175   Mes pur vostre hume e vostre ami!

Seürement vus jur e di

Que jeo ferai vostre plaisir.

Let me not die for
your love! You are
lady, and I a serv-
ant, you proud, I
suppliant."

Ne me laissiez pur vus murir!

Vus seiez dame e jeo servanz,

180   Vus orguilluse e jeo preianz."

He cries her mercy
till she promises
him love.

181   Tant a li reis parlé a li

E tant li a crié merci

Que de s'amur l'aseüra.

The rest of the narrative is more like a fabliau than a lay.
The two lovers die in consequence of their attempt to kill the
husband by means of an overheated bath.

Les Dous Amanz

Jadis avint en Normendie

There happened in
Normandy an
aventure of which
the Bretons made
the lay of the two
lovers.

Une aventure mult oïe

De dous enfanz ki s'entramerent,

Par amur ambedui finerent.

5   Un lai en firent li Bretun:

Des Dous Amanz reçut le nun.

In Neustria, which
we call Normandy,
is a marvelously
great hill, on top of
which the two chil-
dren lie buried.

Veritez est qu'en Neüstrie,

Que nus apelum Normendie,

A un halt munt merveilles grant:

10   La sus gisent li dui enfant.

The king of Pistre has a beautiful daughter whose company
is his only joy. In order to keep her, he rejects all her suitors.

Annoyed by peo-
ple's disapproval
he bethinks him of
a way to be rid of
the suitors.

33   Plusur a mal li aturnerent;

Li suen meïsme l'en blasmerent.

35   Quant il oï qu'um en parla,

Mult fu dolenz, mult l'en pesa.

Cumença sei a purpenser
Cument s'en purra delivrer
Que nuls sa fille ne quesist.

40   E luinz e pres manda e dist:

Ki sa fille voldreit aveir,
Une chose seüst de veir:
Sorti esteit e destiné,
Desur le munt fors la cité

45   Entre ses braz la portereit,
Si que ne s'i reposereit.[1]
Quant la nuvele en est seüe
E par la cuntree espandue,
Asez plusur s'i asaierent,

50   Ki nule rien n'i espleitierent.
Tels i ot ki tant s'esforçouent
Que enmi le munt la portoënt,
Ne poeient avant aler:
Iloec l'estut laissier ester.

55   Lung tens remest cele a doner,
Que nuls ne la volt demander.

57   El païs ot un damisel,

Fiz a un cunte, gent e bel.
De bien faire pur aveir pris

60   Sur tuz altres s'est entremis.
En la curt le rei conversot,
Asez sovent i surjurnot;
La fille le rei aama,
E meinte feiz l'araisuna

65   Qu'ele s'amur li otriast
E par druërie l'amast.
Pur ceo que pruz fu e curteis

E que mult le preisot li reis,
Li otria sa druërie,

70   E cil humblement l'en mercie.

He begs her to leave without her father's consent, but she has
a better plan; in the course of the ascent a powerful potion will
keep up his strength.

"En Salerne ai une parente,
Riche femme est, mult a grant rente.

[1] This motif of a seemingly impossible task set to free a lady from her suitors
appears also in the lay of *Doon;* the task is fulfilled by the help of magic. See
Romania, VIII (1879), 61–64 (text); notes on other analogues, pp. 59–61.

105   Plus de trente anz i a esté;
        L'art de phisike a tant usé
        Que mult est saive de mescines.

She knows herbs and roots and will have a plan for you.

        Tant cunuist herbes e racines,
        Se vus a li volez aler
110   E mes letres od vus porter
        E mustrer li vostre aventure,
        Ele en prendra cunseil e cure.

She will give you a sirup to freshen your strength.

        Tels letuaires vus durra
        E tels beivres vus baillera,
115   Que tut vus recunforterunt
        E bone vertu vus durrunt.

When you return, ask to marry me."

        Quant en cest païs revendrez,
        A mun pere me requerrez."

Back from Salerno with the potion the young man agrees to carry her up the hill.

The girl fasts to help her ami.

173   La dameisele s'aturna;
        Mult se destreinst, mult jeüna
175   A sun mangier pur alegier,
        Qu'a sun ami voleit aidier.

On the day the young man was there first (not forgetting his drink).

        Al jur quant tuit furent venu,
        Li damisels primiers i fu;
        Sun beivre n'i ublia mie.

In the meadow by the Seine the king brings his daughter, clad only in her shift.

180   Devers Seigne en la praerie
        En la grant gent tute asemblee
        Li reis a sa fille menee.
        N'ot drap vestu fors la chemise
        Entre ses braz l'aveit cil prise.

The lover takes her in his arms and gives her the phial to carry.

185   La fiolete od tut sun beivre
        (Bien set qu'el nel volt pas deceivre)
        En sa mein a porter li baille;

I fear it will help him little; he has no moderation.

        Mes jo criem que poi ne li vaille,
        Kar n'ot en lui point de mesure.

He goes a great pace to the halfway point, in his joy forgetting the drink, till she feels him flagging.

190   Od li s'en vait grant aleüre;
        Le munt munta de si qu'en mi.
        Pur la joie qu'il ot de li,
        De sun beivre ne li membra;
        Ele senti qu'il alassa.

"Ami, pray drink!"

195   "Amis," fet ele, "kar bevez!
        Jeo sai bien que vus alassez.
        Si recuvrez vostre vertu!"
        Li damisels a respundu:

"Bele, jo sent tut fort mun quer.

200 Ne m'arestereie a nul fuer
Si lungement que jeo beüsse,
Pur quei treis pas aler peüsse.
Ceste genz nus escriëreient,
De lur noise m'esturdireient;

205 Tost me purreient desturber.
Jo ne vueil pas ci arester."
Quant les dous parz fu muntez sus,
Pur un petit qu'il ne chiet jus.
Sovent li prie la meschine:

210 "Amis, bevez vostre mescine!"
Ja ne la volt oïr ne creire.
A grant anguisse od tut li eire.
Sur le munt vint, tant se greva,
Iluec cheï, puis ne leva:

215 Li quers del ventre s'en parti.
La pucele vit sun ami,
Quida qu'il fust en pasmeisuns.
Lez lui se met en genuilluns,
Sun beivre li voleit doner;

220 Mes il ne pout a li pärler.
Issi murut cum jeo vus di.
Ele le pleint a mult halt cri.
Puis a geté e espandu
Le vessel u li beivre fu.

225 Li munz en fu bien arusez;
Mult en a esté amendez
Tuz li païs e la cuntree:
Meinte bone herbe i unt trovee,
Ki del beivre aveient racine.

"My heart is holding out; while I stop I might have taken three steps.

These people would deafen me with their noise; I shall go on."

When he has mounted two-thirds, he almost falls.

Often she begs him, "Ami, drink your medicine!"

He will not listen.

On top he falls, and rises no more; his heart has left him.

The girl thinks him in a faint; she kneels to offer him the drink.

Thus he died as I tell you. She utters a bitter cry and throws away the phial of liquor.

It besprinkles the countryside, and many an herb there found has its root from that marvelous brew.

Grief kills the young woman; the lovers are buried together on the top of the hill.

Sir Tristrem AND The Earl of Toulouse

The "trouthe" motif is a frequent one in the lays.[1] In *Sir Tristrem* King Mark must keep the rash promise made to a minstrel.

(From *Die nordische und die englische Version der Tristan-Sage*, hrsg. v. Eugen Kölbing, Teil II [Heilbronn, 1882], stanzas clxvii and clxviii, p. 51.)

[1] See Schofield, pp. 437–43.

"Harp for me and I will give what you ask."

1827   Mark seyd: "Lat me se,
         Harpi hou þou can,
         And what þou askest me,
1830   ȝiue y schal þe þan!"
         "Bleþely!" seyd he;
         A miri lay he bigan.

After the lay, "Now I have won Ysonde; I shall have your queen or you are false."

         "Sir king of ȝiftes fre,
         Her wiþ Ysonde y wan
1835   Bidene:
         Y proue þe for fals man,
         Or y schal haue þi quen!"

Mark takes counsel;

         Mark to conseyl ȝede
         And asked rede of þo to:

"I must lose my honor, or else Ysonde."

1840   "Lesen y mot mi manhed
         Or ȝeld Ysonde me fro!"
         Mark was ful of drede,

He lets her go.

         Ysonde lete he go.

In *The Earl of Toulouse* an enemy of the emperor loves the empress. One of her followers has promised him to bring him safely to her.

(From *Middle English Metrical Romances*, ed. W. H. French and C. B. Hale [New York 1930], pp. 383–419.)

"I have promised him he shall see his fill of you.

273   "Forsothe y haue hym hyght
         That he schall see yow at hys fylle,
275   Ryght at hys owne wylle;
         Therto my trowthe y plyght.

Lady, he is our enemy; let us kill him; he has done us ill turns."

         Lady, he ys to vs a foo;
         Therfore y rede þat we hym sloo;
         He hath done vs grete grylle."

"You lose your soul if you do; keep your word.

280   The lady seyde, "So mut y goo,
         Thy soule ys loste yf thou do so;
         Thy trowthe þou schalt fulfylle. . . . .

When they ring the mass-bell, bring him to my chapel. No treachery! Keep your word!

289   To-morne when þey rynge þe masbelle,
         Brynge hym into my chapelle,
         And þynke þou on no false sleythe;
         There schall he see me at hys wylle,
         Thy couenaunt to fulfylle;
         Y rede the holde thy trowthe!

If you beguile him, your soul is in peril."

295   Certys, yf thou hym begyle,
         Thy soule ys in grete paryle,
         Syn thou haste made hym othe; . . . ."

IV. *ADVERSUS JOVINIANUM*

To show that chastity was highly esteemed even before Christianity, St. Jerome tells of pagan virgins and widows who preferred death to dishonor or disloyalty. About half of his *exempla* are used in Dorigen's complaint, where their order clearly shows that Chaucer wrote with the Latin text on his desk.[1]

(From J.-P. Migne, *Patrologia Latina*, Vol. XXIII; *Adversus Jovinianum* i. 41–46, cols. 283–88.)

Fkl. T.,   *i. 41:* .... Triginta Atheniensium tyranni cum Phidonem
F 1368   in convivio necassent, filias ejus virgines ad se venire jusserunt, et scortorum more nudari; ac super pavimenta, patris sanguine cruentata, impudicis gestibus ludere: quæ paulisper dissimulato dolore, cum temulentos convivas cernerent, quasi ad requisita naturæ egredientes, invicem se complexæ præcipitaverunt in

Phidon's daughters, forced to dance naked, threw themselves into a cistern to preserve their maidenhood.

F 1426   puteum, ut virginitatem morte servarent. Demotionis Areopagitarum principis virgo filia, audito sponsi Leosthenis interitu, qui bellum Lamiacum concitarat, se interfecit: asserens quanquam intacta esset corpore, tamen si alterum accipere cogeretur,

Demotion's virgin daughter, learning of the death of her betrothed, killed herself; declaring that, if she were forced to take another, he would be like a second husband, since she felt already married to a first.

F 1379   quasi secundum acciperet, cum priori mente nupsisset. Spartiatæ et Messenii diu inter se habuere amicitias, in tantum ut ob quædam sacra etiam virgines ad se mutuo mitterent. Quodam igitur tempore, cum quinquaginta virgines Lacedæmoniorum Messenii violare tentassent, de tanto numero ad stuprum nulla consensit, sed omnes libentissime pro pudicitia occubuerunt. Quamobrem grave bellum et longissimum concitatum est, et post multum temporis Mamertia subversa est.

The Spartans and Messenians were accustomed to send their girls to each other to take part in certain religious rites. One time when the Messenians would violate fifty Spartan virgins, rather than consent they all died. Hence a great war between the cities.

F 1387   Aristoclides Orchomeni tyrannus adamavit virginem Stymphalidem, quæ cum, patre occiso, ad templum Dianæ confugisset, et simulacrum ejus teneret, nec vi posset avelli, in eodem loco confossa est. Ob cujus necem, tanto omnis Arcadia dolore commota est, ut bellum publice sumeret, et necem vir-

The virgin Stymphalis, wooed by the tyrant Aristoclides, fled to the temple of Diana, and held desperately to the image till she was stabbed. All Arcadia was convulsed with grief; made war and avenged her.

F 1428   ginis ulcisceretur. .... Quo ore laudandæ sunt Scedasi filiæ in Leuctris Bœotiæ, quas traditum est, absente patre, duos juvenes prætereuntes jure hospitii suscepisse. Qui multum indulgentes vino vim per noctem intulere virginibus. Quæ amissæ pudicitæ nolentes supervivere, mutuis conciderunt vul-

How can I sufficiently praise the daughters of Scedasus! In their father's absence they received two young travelers as guests, who after heavily drinking forced them. Unwilling to survive their chastity, the girls killed each other.

[1] See G. Dempster, "Chaucer at Work on the Complaint in the *Franklin's Tale*," *MLN*, LII (1937), 16–23, and "A Further Note on Dorigen's *Exempla*," *MLN*, LIV (1939), 137–38.

F 1409 neribus. . . . . Quis valeat silentio præterire septem Milesias
virgines, quæ, Gallorum impetu cuncta vastante, ne quid in-
decens ab hostibus sustinerent, turpitudinem morte fugerunt,
exemplum sui cunctis virginibus relinquentes, honestis mentibus
F 1431 magis pudicitiam curæ esse quam vitam? Nicanor, victis
Thebis atque subversis, unius virginis captivæ amore superatus
est. Cujus conjugium expetens, et voluntarios amplexus,
quod scilicet captiva optare debuerat, sensit pudicis mentibus
plus virginitatem esse quam regnum, et interfectam propria
F 1434 manu flens et lugens amator tenuit. Narrant scriptores Græci
et aliam Thebanam virginem, quam hostis Macedo corruperat,
dissimulasse paulisper dolorem, et violatorem virginitatis suæ
jugulasse postea dormientem: seque interfecisse gladio, ut nec
vivere voluerit post perditam castitatem, nec ante mori quam
sui ultrix exsisteret.

i. 43: . . . . Veniam ad maritatas, quæ mortuis vel occisis
viris supervivere noluerunt, ne cogerentur secundos nosse
concubitus, et quæ mire unicos amaverunt maritos. . . . .
F 1399 Nam Hasdrubalis uxor, capta et incensa urbe, cum se cerneret
a Romanis capiendam esse, apprehensis ab utroque latere
parvulis filiis, in subjectum domus suæ devolavit incendium.
F 1437 *i. 44:* Quid loquar Nicerati conjugem, quæ, impatiens injuriæ
viri, mortem sibi ipsi conscivit, ne triginta tyrannorum, quos
Lysander victis Athenis imposuerat, libidinem sustineret?
F 1451 Artemisia quoque uxor Mausoli insignis pudicitiæ fuisse per-
hibetur. Quæ cum esset regina Cariæ, et nobilium poetarum
atque historicorum laudibus prædicetur, in hoc vel maxime
effertur quod defunctum maritum sic semper amavit ut vivum,
et miræ magnitudinis exstruxit sepulcrum, in tantum ut usque
hodie omnia sepulcra pretiosa ex nomine ejus Mausolæa nun-
F 1453 cupentur. Teuta Illyricorum regina, ut longo tempore viris
fortissimis imperaret, et Romanos sæpe frangeret, miraculo
F 1439 utique meruit castitatis. . . . . Alcibiades ille Socraticus, victis
Atheniensibus, fugit ad Pharnabazum. Qui, accepto pretio
a Lysandro principe Lacedæmoniorum jussit eum interfici.
Cumque suffocato caput esset ablatum, et missum Lysandro
in testimonium cædis expletæ, reliqua pars corporis jacebat
insepulta. Sola igitur concubina, contra crudelissimi hostis imperium, inter extraneos, et imminente discrimine, funeri justa
persolvit, mori parata pro mortuo, quem vivum dilexerat. . . . .
F 1414 *i. 45:* . . . . Xenophon in Cyri majoris scribit infantia,
occiso Abradote viro, quem Panthea uxor miro amore di-

Who could pass over the seven virgins of Miletus, who, during ravages in Gauls, escaped dishonor by death, showing all virgins that to the honorable mind chastity is worth more than life?

At the sack of Thebes, Nicanor loved and would marry a captive virgin. To be sure, she ought to have been willing; but he learned that to the chaste a crown is worth less than virginity, when she killed herself, and in tears he held in his arms her corpse.

Another Theban virgin, violated by a Macedonian invader, dissembled her grief, and while he slept cut his throat, and killed herself. She would not outlive her chastity or die without vengeance.

Let us come to matrons, who would not survive their husbands, nor be forced to a second love affair. ·

Hasdrubal's wife was about to be taken by the Romans at the burning of the city. Embracing her little children she leapt down with them into her blazing house. Why should I speak of Niceratus' wife, who after her husband's murder killed herself to escape the lust of the thirty tyrants?

Artemisa, wife of Mausolus, is distinguished for chastity. Though queen, and lauded in poetry and history, she is most honored for loyal love of her dead husband and for the magnificent tomb she built for him. Hence the word *mausoleum.*

Queen Teuta earned a long and glorious reign by her marvelous chastity.

Alcibiades' head was cut off through treachery and his body lay unburied. His mistress at the risk of death gave it a fair burial.

When Abradatas was killed, his loving wife lay down by his mangled body, stabbed

lexerat, collocasse se juxta corpus lacerum, et confosso pectore,
F 1456 sanguinem suum mariti infudisse vulneribus. . . . . Rhodogune
filia Darii, post mortem viri, nutricem quæ illi secundas nuptias
F 1442 persuadebat, occidit.   Alcestin fabulæ ferunt pro Admeto
F 1443 sponte defunctam; et Penelopes pudicitia Homeri carmen
F 1445 est. Laodamia quoque poetarum ore cantatur, occiso apud
Trojam Protesilao, noluisse supervivere.

　　i. 46: Ad Romanas feminas transeam; et primam ponam
F 1405 Lucretiam, quæ violatæ pudicitiæ nolens supervivere, maculam
F 1455 corporis cruore delevit. Duillius qui primus Romæ navali
certamine triumphavit, Biliam virginem duxit uxorem, tantæ
puditiciæ, ut illo quoque sæculo pro exemplo fuerit, quo im-
pudicitia monstrum erat, non vitium. Is jam senex et trementi
corpore in quodam jurgio audivit exprobrari sibi os fœtidum,
et tristis se domum contulit. Cumque uxori questus esset quare
nunquam se monuisset, ut huic vitio mederetur: Fecissem, inquit illa, nisi putassem omnibus viris sic os olere. Laudanda in
utroque pudica et nobilis femina, et si ignoravit vitium viri, et
si patienter tulit, et quod maritus infelicitatem corporis sui,
F 1448 non uxoris fastidio, sed maledicto sensit inimici. . . . . Brutus
Porciam virginem duxit uxorem; Marciam Cato non virginem;
sed Marcia inter Hortensium Catonemque discurrit, et sine
Catone vivere Marcia potuit; Porcia sine Bruto non potuit.
F 1456 . . . . Valeria Messalarum soror, amisso Servio viro, nulli
volebat nubere. Quæ interrogata cur faceret, ait sibi semper
maritum Servium vivere.

her bosom, and shed her blood into his wounds. Rodogune, after the death of her husband, killed her nurse for urging a second marriage. Alcestis died in place of her husband, and Homer's poetry is of Penelope's chastity. The poets sing of Laodamia that, when Protesilaus had been killed at Troy, she would not survive.

Let us pass to Roman women: and first I put Lucretia, who was unwilling to survive her violation and wiped out her shame with her blood. Duillius married the virgin Bilia, an example from an age when looseness was a monstrosity, not a peccadillo. In his tottering old age, flouted for his bad breath, he asked her why she had never told him. "I thought all men stank so." She is laudable whether she did not notice or merely endured it; and also because he first learned of his failing not through his wife's distaste but through an enemy's jeer.

Brutus married Porcia as a virgin, Cato married Marcia not as a virgin; Marcia was passed about between Cato and Hortensius, and was quite able to live without Cato; but not Porcia without Brutus. Valeria would not remarry after her husband's death; asked why, "My husband is still alive to me."

THE PHYSICIAN'S TALE

By EDGAR F. SHANNON

IN THE *Physician's Tale* Chaucer tells the story of Appius and Virginia. The original source of this tragic tale, so well known in the Middle Ages, was Livy's *History*. To Livy go back Jean de Meun, who cites him by name in *Le Roman de la rose;* John Gower, who tells the tale in the *Confessio amantis;* and Boccaccio, who includes it in *De mulieribus claris.* Pierre Berçuire made a translation of Livy, in which occurs the story of Virginia, into Old French about 1356. All these accounts, as well as Livy's *History*, were theoretically accessible to Chaucer, and a consideration of each of them is involved in the problem of the source of the *Physician's Tale.*

Gower[1] followed Livy very closely, and his treatment and Chaucer's are entirely independent of each other.[2] Scholars, moreover, agree that the *Physician's Tale* was written before the publication of the *Confessio amantis.*[3]

Boccaccio[4] epitomizes Livy's account and fails to give many details used by Chaucer. For instance, Boccaccio does not mention the wife of Virginius; he refers to Virginia's age only as "tenella virgo"; he disregards almost entirely the influence of the friends and advocates of Virginius and Virginia; he does not refer to Virginia as an only child, or even as an only daughter; and he says nothing of the simulation by Appius of the role of an impartial judge. On the other hand, he contributes nothing that is not found in the version of the story in *Le Roman de la rose* or in Livy.

The translation of Livy made by Berçuire was popular in

---

[1] *Confessio amantis*, VII, 5131–5306.

[2] O. Rumbaur, *Die Geschichte von Appius und Virginia in der englischen Litteratur* (Breslau, 1890), pp. 10–17; F. N. Robinson, *Chaucer's Complete Works* (Cambridge, 1933), p. 832; G. C. Macaulay, *Complete Works of John Gower* (Oxford, 1901), II, 535 (note to l. 5131).

[3] J. S. P. Tatlock, *The Development and Chronology of Chaucer's Works* ("Chaucer Society" [London, 1907]), pp. 150–56.

[4] *De mulieribus claris*, chap. 56.

France, Italy, and Spain,[1] and manuscripts were numerous. Though the story of Virginia is not rendered quite literally, it is presented very much as in Livy. It furnishes no details that are not in the original and omits the significant one that Virginia was an only daughter:

Huic si vis adferetur, ego praesentium Quiritium pro sponsa, Verginius militum pro *unica filia,* omnes deorum hominumque implorabimus fidem [Livy, chap. xlv].

Et se te veult faire force *a ceste pucele* ie qui suis son espoux et Virginius en tant que son pere req̄ron la loiaute des romaines et des chevaliers et des dieux aussy [Berçuire, sheet cxix].

The translation offers no evidence in word or phrase that Chaucer made any use of it.[2]

That Chaucer made use of *Le Roman de la rose* is generally accepted,[3] but the French poem does not account for some of the particulars, even though we leave out of consideration such passages as are admittedly original with Chaucer.[4] The brief account of Appius and Virginia in *Le Roman de la rose* (ll. 5589–5658)[5] is quoted below.

[1] L. Petit de Julleville, *Histoire de la langue et de la littérature française* (Paris, 1896), II, 260–62.

[2] As no edition of Berçuire's translation is available in America, it was necessary to have a photostat made from a copy in the Bibliothèque nationale, Paris. The edition used was that of 1486–87, sheets cxviii–cxx and cxxiiii, which is more legible than a later edition of 1514–15, and in which the abbreviations are more easily understood. For the convenience of anyone who may wish to consult Berçuire's translation, this photostat has been placed in the Library of Congress among the Rotograph series sponsored by the Modern Language Association of America.

[3] Thomas Tyrwhitt, *The Canterbury Tales* (London, 1775–78), IV, 305, note to l. 12074; Rumbaur, pp. 6–17; T. R. Lounsbury, *Studies in Chaucer* (New York, 1892), II, 281–84; E. Koeppel, *Anglia,* XIV (1892), 259–60; W. W. Skeat, *Oxford Chaucer* (1900), III, 435 ff., and V, 260 ff.; A. W. Pollard, *Chaucer* (London, 1903), p. 120; E. P. Hammond, *Chaucer: A Bibliographical Manual* (New York, 1908), p. 294; Emile Legouis, *Geoffrey Chaucer,* trans. L. Lailavoix (London, 1913), p. 159; D. S. Fansler, *Chaucer and the Roman de la rose* (New York, 1914), pp. 31–35; R. K. Root, *The Poetry of Chaucer* (rev. ed.; Boston, 1922), pp. 220–22; John Koch, "Chaucer's Belesenheit in den römischen Klassikern," *ES,* LVII (1923), 56–59; Robinson, pp. 832–33.

[4] The passages obviously added by Chaucer are ll. 35–120 and 207–53 (see Robinson, pp. 832–33).

[5] *Le Roman de la rose,* publié par Ernest Langlois ("Société des Anciens Textes Français" [Paris, 1920]), II, 263–66.

Appius made his
retainer undertake
a false complaint
against Virginia, as
says Titus Livius.

5589   Ne fist bien Appius a pendre
   Qui fist a son sergent emprendre
   Par faus tesmoinz fausse querele
5592   Contre Virgine la pucele
   Qui fu fille Virginius
   Si con dit Titus Livius
   Qui bien set le cas raconter.
5596   Pour ce qu'il ne poait donter
   La pucele, qui n'avait cure
   Ne de lui ne de sa luxure,
   Li ribauz dist en audience:

The rascal said, "Sir
Judge, give sentence
for me, for I will
prove her to be my
slave.

5600   "Sire juiges, donez sentence
   Pour mei, car la pucele est meie;
   Pour ma serve la prouveraie
   Contre touz ceus qui sont en vie,
5604   Car, ou qu'ele ait esté nourrie,
   De mon ostel me fu emblee

She was stolen and
carried away to Vir-
ginius.

   Des lors, par po, qu'ele fu nee,
   E bailliee a Virginius:
5608   Si vous requier, sire Appius,
   Que vous me delivrez ma serve,
   Car il est dreiz qu'ele me serve,
   Non pas celui qui l'a nourrie;

If he denies it, I will
prove it by good
witnesses."

5012   E se Virginius le nie,
   Tout ce sui je prez de prouver,
   Car bons tesmoinz en puis trouver."
   Ainsinc palait li maus traistres,
5616   Qui dou faus juige estait menistres,
   E con li plaiz ainsinc alast,
   Ainz que Virginius palast,
   Qui touz estait prez de respondre,

Before Virginius
could respond,
Appius caused the
maiden to be deliv-
ered up to slavery.

5620   Pour ses aversaires confondre,
   Juija par hastive sentence
   Appius que, senz atendance,
   Fust la pucele au serf rendue.
5624   E quant la chose a entendue
   Li beaus preudon devant nomez,
   Bons chevaliers, bien renomez,
   C'est a saveir Virginius,

Virginius, unable to
protect his daugh-
ter against Appius,
cut off her head and
presented it to the
judge in open con-
sistory.

5628   Qui bien veit que vers Appius
   Ne peut pas sa fille defendre,
   Ainz li couvient par force rendre
   E son cors livrer a hontage,

5632 Si change honte pour domage
      Par merveilleus apensement,
      Se Titus Livius ne ment;
      Car il, par amour, senz haïne,
5636 A sa bele fille Virgine
      Tantost a la teste copee
      E puis au juige presentee,
      Devant touz, en plein consistoire;
5640 E li juiges, selonc l'estoire,
      Le comanda tantost a prendre,   Appius commanded
      Pour lui mener ocierre ou pendre.   him to be killed, but
      Mais ne l'ocist ne ne pendi,   the people defended
                                             him.
5644 Car li peuples le defendi,
      Qui fu touz de pitié meüz
      Si tost con li faiz fu seüz.
      Puis fu pour cete mesprison
5648 Appius mis en la prison,   Appius, put in pris-
      E s'ocist la hastivement   on, killed himself
      Ainz le jour de son juigement;   before the day of
                                             his judgment.
      E Claudius li chalengierres   Virginius persuaded
5652 Juigiez iert a mort come lierres   the people to con-
      Se ne l'en cüst respitié   demn Claudius, the
      Virginius par sa pitié,   complainant, to
                                             exile instead of
      Qui tant vost le peuple preier   death.
5656 Qu'en essil le fist enveier;
      E tuit cil condanné mururent   The witnesses in the
      Qui tesmoing de sa cause furent.   case were con-
                                             demned to death.

As Jean de Meun cites Livy as his source, Chaucer might be expected to turn to the Latin version.[1] The question, therefore, is whether there is convincing proof in the *Physician's Tale* that Chaucer used Livy as well as *Le Roman de la rose*.

The story of Appius and Virginia with its attendant circumstances is given by Livy, Book iii, chapters xliv–lviii. Chapters

[1] On the survival of Livy through the Middle Ages see J. E. Sandys, *A History of Classical Scholarship* (2d ed.; Cambridge, 1906), II, 659–61. The proof of use of Livy in Chaucer's poetry rests chiefly upon the *Physician's Tale*. In the story of Lucretia in *Legend of Good Women* there are some rather striking verbal parallels with Livy, but the evidence is not unmistakable (see E. F. Shannon, *Chaucer and the Roman Poets* [Cambridge, 1929], pp. 220–26). It is rather significant that because of similarity in treatment some scholars have suggested that the *Physician's Tale* was originally written to stand with the Lucretia among the *Legends* (see Robinson, p. 832; Root, p. 219; B. ten Brink, *History of English Literature* (New York, 1893), II, 120–21).

xliv–xlviii, presenting the chief events leading up to the death of Virginia at the hands of her father, are appended in full. Chaucer appears to select details and develop suggestions from Livy rather than to follow his entire account. Some of the italicizations made below indicate suggestions rather than verbal translations.

(Reprinted with minor changes from Titus Livius' *Ab urbe condita*, ed. J. Weissenborn and M. Mueller [Leipzig, 1932], I, 183–88.)

xliv. Sequitur aliud in urbe nefas ab libidine ortum, haud minus foedo eventu quam quod per stuprum caedemque Lucretiae urbe regnoque Tarquinios expulerat, ut non finis solum idem *decemviris*[1] qui regibus sed causa etiam eadem imperii amittendi esset. Ap. Claudium virginis plebeiae stuprandae libido cepit. Pater virginis, L. Verginius, honestum ordinem in Algido ducebat, vir exempli recti domi militiaeque. Perinde *uxor*[2] *instituta fuerat liberique instituebantur.* Desponderat filiam L. Icilio tribunicio, viro acri et pro causa plebis expertae virtutis. Hanc *virginem adultam*[3] *forma excellentem*[4] Appius amore amens pretio ac spe perlicere adortus, postquam omnia pudore saepta animadvertit, ad crudelem superbamque vim animum convertit. M. Claudio clienti negotium dedit ut virginem in servitutem adsereret neque cederet secundum libertatem postulantibus vindicias, *quod pater puellae abesset*[5] locum iniuriae esse ratus. *Virgini venienti in forum*[6]—ibi namque in tabernaculis litterarum ludi erant—minister decemviri libidinis manum iniecit, serva sua natam servamque

[Margin note: Appius Claudius, one of the decemvirs, was seized with the desire to debauch a certain maiden of the plebs. Virginius, father of the maiden, was of most exemplary life. He had betrothed his daughter to Icilius, a champion of the people. Appius Claudius, unable to seduce her, commissioned Marcus Claudius to claim her as his slave during her father's absence.

In the Forum the decemvir's agent seized her. A crowd gathered,]

[1] Cf. Chaucer's "That governour was of that regioun" (C 122).

[2] Cf. "by his wyf" (C 5). Chaucer also refers to Virginia's mother:

"This mayde upon a day wente in the toun
   Toward a temple, with hire moder dere" (C 118–19).

"By his wyf" and "with her moder dere" were doubtless inspired by the notice Livy gives to the wife of Virginius in the bringing-up of their children. No reference to her appears in the other accounts except Gower's.

[3] *Virginem adultam* Chaucer renders more explicitly by "This mayde of age twelve yeer was and tweye" (C 30). Twelve years was the legal marriageable age for girls in Chaucer's time.

[4] Cf.

"Fair was this mayde in excellent beautee" (C 7),

"and if that excellent was hire beautee" (C 39),

where Chaucer renders Livy's phrase exactly. In *Le Roman de la rose* she is called *sa bele fille.*

[5] See p. 403, n. 4.

[6] Livy's allusion to Virginia's entering the Forum, where many a temple was, probably suggested to Chaucer the idea that the maiden and her mother "wente—toward a temple" (C 119).

appellans, sequique se iubebat: cunctantem vi abstracturum. Pavida
puella stupente ad clamorem nutricis fidem Quiritium implorantis fit
concursus. *Vergini patris sponsique Icili populare nomen celebrabatur.*   and supported the
Notos gratia eorum, turbam indignitas rei virgini conciliat.[1] Iam a vi   girl.
tuta erat, cum adsertor nihil opus esse multitudine concitata ait;
se iure grassari, non vi. Vocat puellam in ius. Auctoribus qui aderant   The claimant sum-
ut sequeretur ad tribunal Appi perventum est. Notam iudici fabulam   moned the girl to
                                                                       the court of Appius
petitor, quippe apud ipsum auctorem argumenti, peragit: puellam   and there said that
                                                                       she was born in his
domi suae natam furtoque inde in domum Vergini translatam sup-   house and had been
                                                                       carried thence to
positam ei esse; id se indicio compertum adferre probaturumque vel   the home of Vir-
ipso Verginio iudice, ad quem maior pars iniuriae eius pertineat;   ginius.
interim dominum sequi ancillam aequum esse. *Advocati puellae,*[2]   The friends of the
                                                                       maiden demanded
cum *Verginium rei publicae causa dixissent abesse, biduo adfuturum si*   that the case be
                                                                       postponed until the
nuntiatum ei sit, iniquum esse absentem de liberis dimicare,[3] postulant   arrival of the father.
ut rem integram in patris adventum differat, lege ab ipso lata vindicias
det secundum libertatem, neu patiatur *virginem adultam* famae prius
quam libertatis periculum adire.

xlv. Appius decreto praefatur, quam libertati faverit eam ipsam
legem declarare quam *Vergini amici* postulationi suae praetendant;
ceterum ita in ea firmum libertati fore praesidium si nec causis nec per-   Appius said the law
                                                                              must not vary with
sonis variet; in aliis enim qui adserantur in libertatem quia quivis   causes and persons
lege agere possit, id iuris esse: in ea quae in patris manu sit neminem
esse alium cui dominus possessione cedat. *Placere itaque patrem arces-*   and so ordered that
                                                                          the father be sum-
siri, interea iuris sui iacturam adsertorem non facere quin ducat puellam   moned and that
                                                                              meanwhile the
sistendamque in adventum eius qui pater dicatur promittat.[4]   claimant should
                                                                    keep the girl.

[1] Cf. Chaucer's "strong of freendes" of Virginius (C 4), and also,

> "But hastily, er he his tale tolde,
> And wolde have preeved it as sholde a knyght,
> And eek by witnessyng of many a wight,
> That al was fals that sayde his adversarie" (C 192–95).

The strength of the friends of Virginius and of Virginia and their influence in the
daughter's behalf are a conspicuous feature of Livy's story. See also *Vergini amici*
(chap. xlv).

[2] Cf. "For she was strong of freendes" (C 135); see also Livy's *advocati puellae*
(chap. xlvi); *cum ingenti advocatione in forum deducit,* and *cum repelleretur adsertor
virginis a globo mulierum circumstantiumque advocatorum* (chap. xlvii).

[3] Cf. "Thou shalt have al right, and no wrong heere" (C 174).

[4] Cf.

> "The juge answerde, 'Of this, in his absence,
> I may not yeve diffynytyf sentence.
> Lat do hym calle, and I wol gladly heere' " (C 171–73).

Livy represents Appius as thinking the time suitable for the accomplishment of his
plot because the father was absent, *quod pater puellae abesset* (chap. xliv), and
emphasizes the absence of Virginius. See also *Verginio absenti* (chap. xlvi). In
Le Roman de la rose there is no mention of the absence of the father, of his being
summoned by the judge, and of the postponement of the trial.

Adversus iniuriam decreti cum multi magis fremerent quam quisquam unus recusare auderet, P. Numitorius, puellae avus, et sponsus
Icilius interveniunt; dataque inter turbam via, cum multitudo Icili
maxime interventu resisti posse Appio crederet, lictor decresse ait
vociferantemque Icilium submovet. Placidum quoque ingenium tam

atrox iniuria accendisset. "Ferro hinc tibi ,submovendus sum,
Appi," inquit, "ut tacitum feras quod celari vis. Virginem ego hanc
sum ducturus nuptamque pudicam habiturus. Proinde omnes collegarum quoque lictores convoca; expediri virgas et secures iube;
non manebit extra domum patris sponsa Icili. Non, si tribunicium
auxilium et provocationem plebi Romanae, duas arces libertatis
tuendae, ademistis, ideo in liberos quoque nostros coniugesque regnum
vestrae libidini datum est. Saevite in tergum et in cervices nostras:
pudicitia saltem in tuto sit. Huic si vis adferetur, ego praesentium
Quiritium pro sponsa, Verginius militum *pro unica filia*,[1] omnes
deorum hominumque implorabimus fidem, neque tu istud unquam
decretum sine caede nostra referes. Postulo, Appi, etiam atque etiam
consideres quo progrediare. Verginius viderit de filia ubi venerit
quid agat; hoc tantum sciat, sibi si huius vindiciis cesserit condicionem
filiae quaerendam esse. Me vindicantem sponsam in libertatem vita
citius deseret quam fides."

xlvi. Concitata multitudo erat certamenque instare videbatur.
Lictores Icilium circumsteterant; nec ultra minas tamen processum

est, cum Appius non Verginiam defendi ab Icilio, sed inquietum hominem et tribunatum etiam nunc spirantem locum seditionis quaerere
diceret. Non praebiturum se illi eo die materiam; sed ut iam sciret
non id petulantiae suae sed *Verginio absenti* et patrio nomini et libertati datum, ius eo die se non dicturum neque decretum interpositurum:

a M. Claudio petiturum, ut decederet iure suo vindicarique puellam in
posterum diem pateretur; quod nisi pater postero die adfuisset, de-
nuntiare se Icilio similibusque Icili, neque legi suae latorem neque
decemviro constantiam defore. Nec se utique collegarum lictores
convocaturum ad coercendos seditionis auctores: contentum se suis
lictoribus fore.

Cum dilatum tempus iniuriae esset secessissentque *advocati puellae*,
placuit omnium primum fratrem Icili filiumque Numitori, impigros
iuvenes, pergere inde recta ad portam, et quantum adcelerari posset Verginium acciri e castris: in eo verti puellae salutem, si postero die vindex iniuriae ad tempus praesto esset. Iussi pergunt

---

[1] Cf. "No children hadde he mo in al his lyf" (C 6). Livy refers to the training
of the *children* of Virginius, *liberique instituebantur* (chap. xliv). Chaucer intensi-
fies the tragedy by making the only daughter the only child the devoted father
had ever had.

citatisque equis nuntium ad patrem perferunt. Cum instaret adsertor puellae ut vindicaret sponsoresque daret, atque id ipsum agi
diceret Icilius, sedulo tempus terens dum praeciperent iter nuntii missi
in castra, manus tollere undique multitudo et se quisque paratum ad
spondendum Icilio ostendere. Atque ille lacrimabundus "Gratum
est" inquit, "crastina die vestra opera utar: sponsorum nunc satis
est." Ita vindicatur Verginia spondentibus propinquis. Appius paulisper moratus ne eius rei causa sedisse videretur, postquam omissis
rebus aliis prae cura unius nemo adibat, domum se recepit collegisque
in castra scribit, ne Verginio commeatum dent atque etiam in custodia
habeant. Improbum consilium serum, ut debuit, fuit, et iam commeatu sumpto profectus Verginius prima vigilia erat, cum postero
die mane de retinendo eo nequiquam litterae redduntur.

The claimant de-
manded bail of
Icilius, which many
of the people
offered, and Vir-
ginia was set free.

xlvii. At in urbe prima luce cum civitas in foro exspectatione erecta
staret, Verginius sordidatus filiam secum obsoleta veste comitantibus
aliquot matronis *cum ingenti advocatione in forum deducit.*[1] Circumire
ibi et prensare homines coepit et non orare solum precariam opem,
sed pro debita petere: Se pro liberis eorum ac coniugibus cottidie in
acie stare, nec alium virum esse cuius strenue ac fortiter facta in bello
plura memorari possent; quid prodesse si, incolumi urbe, quae capta
ultima timeantur liberis suis sint patienda? Haec prope contionabun-
dus circumibat homines. Similia his ab Icilio iactabantur. Comitatus
muliebris plus tacito fletu quam ulla vox movebat. Adversus quae
omnia obstinato animo Appius—tanta vis amentiae verius quam
amoris mentem turbaverat—in tribunal escendit, et ultro querente
pauca petitore quod ius sibi pridie per ambitionem dictum non esset,
priusquam aut ille postulatum perageret aut Verginio respondendi
daretur locus, Appius interfatur. Quem decreto sermonem praetender-
it, forsan aliquem verum auctores antiqui tradiderint: quia nusquam
ullum in tanta foeditate decreti veri similem invenio, id quod constat
nudum videtur proponendum, decresse vindicias secundum servitutem. Primo stupor omnes admiratione rei tam atrocis defixit; silentium inde aliquamdiu tenuit. Dein cum M. Claudius circumstantibus
matronis iret ad prehendendam virginem, lamentabilisque eum mulierum comploratio excepisset, Verginius intentans in Appium manus,
"Icilio," inquit, "Appi, non tibi filiam despondi, et ad nuptias non ad
stuprum educavi. Placet pecudum ferarumque ritu promisce in
concubitus ruere? Passurine haec isti sint, nescio: non spero esse
passuros, illos, qui arma habent." *Cum repelleretur adsertor virginis
a globo mulierum circumstantiumque advocatorum,* silentium factum
per praeconem.

The next day Vir-
ginius appeared in
the Forum with his
daughter and a
large crowd of wom-
en supporters, ask-
ing aid of the peo-
ple.

Before the claimant
could finish his de-
mand or Virginius
was allowed to re-
ply, Appius inter-
rupted

and made his decree
in favor of the
claims of slavery.

As Marcus Claudi-
us made his way
through the lament-
ing women, Virgini-
us cried out against
Appius.

The claimant of the
maiden was forced
back by the crowd
of women and sup-
porters.

xlviii. Decemvir alienatus ad libidinem animo negat ex hesterno

[1] See p. 403, n. 2.

tantum convicio Icili violentiaque Vergini, cuius testem populum Romanum habeat, sed certis quoque indiciis compertum se habere nocte tota coetus in urbe factos esse ad movendam seditionem. Itaque se haud inscium eius dimicationis cum armatis descendisse, non ut quemquam quietum violaret, sed ut turbantes civitatis otium pro maiestate imperii coerceret. "Proinde quiesse erit melius. I," inquit, "lictor, submove turbam et da viam domino ad prehendendum mancipium." Cum haec intonuisset plenus irae, multitudo ipsa se sua sponte dimovit desertaque praeda iniuriae puella stabat. Tum Verginius ubi nihil usquam auxilii vidit, "Quaeso," inquit, "Appi, primum ignosce patrio dolori, si quo inclementius in te sum invectus; deinde sinas hic coram virgine nutricem percontari quid hoc rei sit, ut si falso pater dictus sum aequiore hinc animo discedam." Data venia seducit filiam ac nutricem prope Cloacinae ad tabernas quibus nunc novis est nomen atque ibi ab lanio cultro arrepto. "Hoc te uno quo possum," ait, "modo, filia, in libertatem vindico." Pectus deinde puellae transfigit respectansque ad tribunal: "Te," inquit, "Appi, tuumque caput sanguine hoc consecro." Clamore ad tam atrox facinus orto excitus Appius comprehendi Verginium iubet. Ille ferro quacumque ibat viam facere, donec multitudine etiam prosequentium tuente ad portam perrexit. Icilius Numitoriusque exsangue corpus sublatum ostentant populo; scelus Appi, puellae infelicem formam, necessitatem patris deplorant. Sequentes clamitant matronae: eamne liberorum procreandorum condicionem, ea pudicitiae praemia esse?—cetera quae in tali re muliebris dolor, quo est maestior imbecillo animo, eo miserabilia magis querentibus subicit. Virorum et maxime Icili vox tota tribuniciae potestatis ac provocationis ad populum ereptae publicarumque indignationum erat.

The decemvir charged Virginius and Icilius with stirring up sedition,

and ordered the lictors to disperse the crowd that the master might take his slave.

Virginius seeing no help anywhere asked permission to talk with the nurse and Virginia and led them to the shrine of Cloacina.

There, seizing a butcher's knife, he exclaimed, "Thus, my daughter, in the only way I can, do I assert your freedom." Then he stabbed her to the heart.

In chapters xlix–lv Livy deals with the uprising of the people in Rome against the tyranny of the decemvirs. In chapters lvi–lviii he gives an account of how Appius Claudius, now deposed from the decemvirate, along with his colleagues was brought to trial: how he was remanded to jail and a day appointed for the continuance of his trial: and how, not waiting for the appointed day to come, he killed himself. At the end of chapter lviii Livy describes the punishment of Marcus Claudius, the claimant of Virginia:

Et M Claudius, adsertor Verginiae, die dicta damnatus, ipso remittente Verginio ultimam poenam dimissus Tibur exsulatum abiit.

In this latter part of the story Chaucer takes nothing specifically from Livy but rather seems to be using Le Roman de la *rose.* Yet there is a certain similarity in his general outline to Livy's.

It is, however, the presence in Chaucer's narrative of details found only in Livy that warrants the conclusion that, while he adopted the skeleton of the story in *Le Roman de la rose,* he supplemented it with material from the Latin original.

An interesting analogue to Chaucer's recital of the maidenly virtues of Virginia is found in the *De virginibus* of St. Ambrose of Milan.[1] Some of the characteristics of Virginia and of the Virgin are so similar as to justify quotations from the *De virginibus.*[2]

Quid nobilius Dei matre? quid splendidius ea, quam Splendor elegit? quid castius ea quae corpus sine corporis contagione generavit? Nam de caeteris ejus virtutibus quid loquar? Virgo erat non solum corpore, sed etiam mente, quae nullo doli ambitu sincerum adulteraret affectum: corde humilis, verbis gravis, animi prudens, loquendi parcior, legendi studiosior: non in incerto divitiarum, sed in prece pauperum spem reponens: intenta operi, verecunda sermone, arbitrum mentis solita non hominem, sed Deum quaerere: nullum laedere, bene velle omnibus, assurgere majoribus natu, aequalibus non invidere, fugere jactantiam, rationem sequi, amare virtutem [ii. ii. 7].

> *What is greater, more glorious, more chaste than the Mother of God? She was a virgin in mind as well as in body, humble in heart, sparing of words, in discourse grave and modest, adorned with all virtues.*

Prodire domo nescia, nisi cum ad Ecclesiam conveniret, et hoc ipsum cum parentibus, aut propinquis. Domestico operosa secreto, forensi stipata comitatu; nullo meliore tamen sui custode quam se ipsa: quae incessu affatuque venerabilis, non tam vestigium pedis tolleret, quam gradum virtutis attolleret [ii. ii. 9].[3]

> *Apart from divine service, to which she went with her parents, she stayed at home, laborious and ever progressing in virtue.*

Sed interdum etiam cum fides tuta sit, juventus suspecta est. Modico itaque vino utere, ne infirmitatem corporis augeas, non ut voluptatem excites; incendunt enim pariter duo, vinum et adolescentia. Infrenent etiam teneram aetatem jejunia, et parcimonia cibi retinaculis quibusdam indomitas cohibeat cupiditates [iii. ii. 5].

> *Youth is not to be trusted. Wine kindles passion and should be used sparingly. A meager diet is advisable.*

[1] Migne, *Patrologia Latina,* Vol. XVI, cols. 193–232.

[2] Attention was first called to Ambrose in connection with the *Physician's Tale* by Professor F. W. Tupper in *MLN,* XXX (1915), 5–7. The passages quoted here include the most striking cited by Mr. Tupper. Ambrose's injunction to parents to teach religion to their daughters is not similar to Chaucer's admonitions to governesses and parents.

[3] This possibly may have suggested the change from the companionship of the nurse mentioned by Livy to the mother (see p. 402, n. 2):

> "This mayde up-on a day wente in the toun
> Toward a temple, with hire moder dere,
> As is of yonge maydens the manere."

Virgins even more
than wives should
keep a modest
silence.
Interroganti non respondere, infantia: respondere, fabula est.
Deesse igitur sermonem virgini, quam superesse malim. Nam si
mulieres etiam de rebus divinis in Ecclesia jubentur tacere, domi
viros suos interrogare: de virginibus quid cautum putamus, in quibus
pudor ornat aetatem, taciturnitas commendat pudorem? [iii. iii. 9].

Unrestrained feasts,
nuptial concerts,
and too much danc-
ing imperil mod-
esty.
Debet igitur bene consciae mentis esse laetitia, non inconditis
comessationibus, non nuptialibus excitata symphoniis; ibi enim intuta
verecundia, illecebra suspecta est, ubi comes deliciarum est extrema
saltatio. Ab hac virgines Dei procul esse desidero [iii. v. 25].

Ambrose refers briefly to St. Pelagia as an example of a virgin
preferring suicide to the loss of her chastity and gives her
speech, which only very slightly resembles the attitude of Virginia toward her sacrifice at the hands of her father.

The similarities between the passages noted tempt the inference that Chaucer may have been reading the Bishop's treatise
when he began to write the story which he later used as the
Physician's Tale.[1] If so, he preserved its classical atmosphere
by references to Pallas, Bacchus, and Venus even while portraying the modest virgin.

[1] In Chaucer's writings the name of Ambrose appears twice, but neither of these
indicates a direct use of his works (see Tupper, *MLN*, XXX [1915], 7, n. 12;
Robinson, pp. 865, 873–74).

THE PARDONER'S PROLOGUE

By GERMAINE DEMPSTER

I. THE PARDONER AND FAUX-SEMBLANT

THERE is no doubt that the character of the Pardoner and the episodes in which he appears are largely the creation of Chaucer.[1] Much of the *Prologue*, however, is paralleled in, and may have been partly inspired by, the speeches of Faux-Semblant in the *Roman de la rose*, where the same device of the public confession is used with great success, and where the sins laid bare—hypocrisy and self-interest—are exactly those of the Pardoner.[2]

(From *Le Roman de la rose*, publié par Ernest Langlois, III [Paris, 1921], 185–223, 311, 322.)

11065	... en quelque leu que je viegne
	Ne coment que je m'i contiegne,
	Nule rien fors barat n'i chaz; ... — *Profit is my one object.*
11181	... Protheüs, qui se soulait
	Muer en tout quanqu'il voulait,
	Ne sot onc tant barat ne guile — *Better than Proteus*
11184	Con je faz, car onques en vile
	N'entrai ou fusse queneüz,
	Tant i fusse oïz ne veüz.
	Trop sai bien mes abiz changier,
11188	Prendre l'un e l'autre estrangier;
	Or sui chevaliers, or sui moines, — *I can change my appearance*
	Or sui prelaz, or sui chanoines, ... — *and play any role.*

[1] See M. P. Hamilton, "The Credentials of Chaucer's Pardoner," *JEGP*, Vol. XL, January, 1941.

[2] That Chaucer must have been very familiar with this brilliant passage, besides being almost inevitable, is suggested by other probable echoes, mainly in the portraits of the Friar in the *General Prologue* and of the friar of the *Summoner's Tale*. On these and the Pardoner see D. S. Fansler, *Chaucer and the Roman de la rose* (New York, 1914), pp. 162–66; for other possible reminiscences see index, p. 266 (Fansler's references are to the edition of Michel, where the confession of Faux-Semblant occupies ll. 11859–12946). The passage may also be partly responsible for Chaucer's frequent use of the public confession on the Canterbury road (Pardoner, Wife of Bath, Canon's Yeoman) and in some tales (Placebo in *Mch. T.*, the friar in *Sum. T.*). On confessions in medieval literature see, in *Harvard Summaries of Theses, 1930* (Cambridge, Mass., 1931), pp. 210–11, a brief outline of an unpublished dissertation by G. M. Rutter.

11211 Or sui none, or sui abaesse,
       Or sui novice, or sui professe,

I go investigating
all religious orders

       E vois par toutes regions
       Cerchant toutes religions;

but care little about
religion.

       Mais de religion, senz faille,

11216 J'en lais le grain e preing la paille; ...

I deceive people.

       (Je faz cheoir dedenz mes pieges
       Le monde par mes privilieges;

I have power to
confess and absolve

       Je puis confessier et assoudre,
       Ce ne me peut nus prelaz toudre,

anybody, anywhere.

       Toutes genz, ou que je les truisse.
       Ne sai nul prelat qui ce puisse)[1]

Caring little for
work,

11520 De labourer n'ai je que faire:
       Trop a grant peine en labourer.

I prefer to pray

       J'aim meauz devant les genz ourer

and practice
deception.

       E afubler ma renardie

11524 Dou mantel de papelardie ...

11565 En aquerre est toute m'entente,

My earnings are
better than my
income.

       Meauz vaut mes pourchaz que ma rente.[2]

I go everywhere,

       S'en me devait tuer ou batre,

11568 Si me vueil je par tout embatre;

confessing

       (Par tout vois les ames curer,
       Nus ne peut mais sanz moi durer

and preaching

       Et preeschier et conseillier,

(never working),

       Senz jamais des mains traveillier.

as authorized by
the pope's bull.

       De l'apostole en ai la bule,
       Qui ne me tient pas pour entule).[3]

I confess the
powerful ones,

11569 Si ne querraie ja cessier
       Ou d'empereeurs confessier,
       Ou reis, ou dus, ou bers, ou contes ...

not the poor;

11575 Je n'ai cure de povres genz:
       Leur estaz n'est ne beaus ne genz ...

11587   E pour le sauvement des ames,

investigate each
one's property,

       J'enquier des seigneurs e des dames,
       E de trestoutes leur maisnies

---

[1] These six lines, taken from the notes of Langlois (pp. 311–15), open a long passage which, with slight variations, occurs in numerous manuscripts after Langlois' l. 11222; it deals with Faux-Semblant as confessor and successful rival of the parish priests. The C fragment of the *Romaunt of the Rose* translates this long passage (ll. 6361–6472), as well as the short one (Langlois, p. 322, *Romaunt*, ll. 6843–48) found in some manuscripts between l. 11568 and l. 11569 and quoted in part below.

[2] Cf. A 256, and see *MLN*, XXIII (1908), 142–44, 200.

[3] On these six lines see above, n. 1.

Les proprietez e les vies ...

11669   E pour aveir des genz loenges,   *flatter the influential*
Des riches omes, par losenges,
Empetrons que letres nous doignent   *for recommendations.*
11672   Qui la bonté de nous tesmoignent,
Si que l'en creie par le monde
Que vertu toute en noùs abonde.
E toujourz povres nous feignons,   *We feign poverty*
11676   Mais, coment que nous nous plaignons,
Nous somes, ce vous faz saveir,
Cil qui tout ont senz riens aveir ...
11709   E di que je sui hors dou monde,   *and unworldliness.*
Mais je m'i plonge e m'i afonde,
E m'i aaise e baigne e noe
Meauz que nus poissons de sa noe ...[1]
11969   Mais a vous n'ose je mentir;
Mais se je peüsse sentir   *If I could,*
Que vous ne l'aperceüssiez,
11972   La mençonge ou poing eüssiez;   *I would deceive you too.*
Certainement je vous boulasse,
Ja pour pechié ne le laissasse; ...

II. THE PARDONER'S "GAUDE," C 377–90

This is the Pardoner's trick of declaring that great sinners, especially adulterous women, must not make offerings to his relics. We shall quote the three earliest analogues known.

A. DER STRICKER'S *Pfaffe Amîs*[2]

Der Stricker wrote in the first half of the thirteenth century. *Pfaffe Amîs* relates the successful frauds of an impoverished English priest traveling to make money. Only the introductory episode before the priest sets out on his journey and the story that concerns us are localized in England.

(From *Erzählungen und Schwänke*, hrsg. v. Hans Lambel [Leipzig, 1883], pp. 34–39.)

Pfaffe Amîs has a precious relic, the head of St. Brandan.

376   "Ez hât gesprochen wider mich,   *"It has requested me to build a monastery,*
Ich sül'm ein münster machen
Mit alsô reinen sachen,   *using only clean gifts,*

[1] Better than any fish with its fin.

[2] The relation to C 377–90 was first noted by W. B. Sedgwick, "Chaucer's Pardoner's Prologue," *MLR*, XIX (1924), 336–37.

Daz got von himel wol gezeme;

380   Unt deich[1] des ophers nine neme,

Daz gebíutet ez mir an den lîp,[2]

Daz mir gebe dehéin[3] wîp

Diu zuo ir élîchem man

Ie deheinen man gewan.

385   Die sô getâne[4] mán hân,

Den gebíut'ich, daz si stille stân;

Wande[5] gæben si mir iht,

Ze wâre, des ennæme ich niht.

Daz lâz' ich iuch wol schouwen."

390   Do begúndén die vrouwen,

Als er begunde singen,

Mit opher zúo dríngen.

Die dâ tougen[6] heten man

Die erbáltén dar an,[7]

395   Unt wurden di aller êrsten dar;

Der opher nam er allez gar.

Als si dô gesâhen,

Dêr begunde enphâhen

Swaz im ze némenné geschach,[8]

400   Unt niemens óphér versprach,

Dô drungen die vrouwen alle

Dar nâch wol mit schalle.

Diu dâ gestanden wære,

Diu het ein bœsez mære

405   Iesâ[9] gemáchét dar an:

Man zige si tougenlîcher man.

Des kunden si sich wol verstân,

Unt begúndén alle zúo gán.

Díu niht phénnínges hâte

410   Diu entlêhent' in vil drâte,[10]

Oder óphérte ein vingerlîn

Guldîn oder silberîn.

Marginal notes:
- refusing those of adulteresses
- as you will see me do."
- Women press with gifts,
- unchaste ones first.
- Seeing him reject nothing,
- all women flock
- to avoid disrepute.
- Some borrow money
- or offer rings.

None can afford to stay out (ll. 413–21, 426–30). There never was such a collection (422–25); some unchaste women made three offerings (431–36).

[1] Dass ich.   [3] Any.   [5] For, because.

[2] Upon my life, emphatically.   [4] Of such kind.   [6] Secret, hidden.

[7] Upon this they gathered courage.

[8] Ll. 397–99: "When they saw that he began to take what he was to accept."

[9] At once. "She would thereby have caused at once a wicked gossip."

[10] She borrowed it (the penny) very hastily.

Dô sprach der phaffe Âmís
440 "Got hât in gótlícher wîs
  Sîn zeichen hiute hie getân,
  Daz wir sus mange vrouwen hân
  Die sich ál sô wol bewárt hánt
  Daz si válscher minne âne stânt,[1]
445 Unt tougenlícher manne.
  Nu gebíut'ich bî dem banne,[2]
  Diu hiute hie gewesen sî
  Daz man si valsches wizze vrî.
  Daz sint si sicherlîche . . . .
457 Die sint sô reine unt sô guot
  Daz si sích vor valsche hânt behuot."
  Sus wart der phaffe rîche,
  Unt gelóbet vil grózlíche
  Von vrouwen unt von wîben.

"God has testified
that so many are
free from sinful
love .

I charge you to
believe this.

All are virtuous."

The priest gets
profit
and much praise
from women.

B. Sercambi's Novella LI, *De ypocriti et fraudatores*[3]

Sercambi's *Novelle* were completed some time after December, 1385. On this date, and on the chance that Chaucer knew something, if not of the *Novelle*, at least of an earlier version, the lost *Novelliero*, see R. A. Pratt and K. Young, pages 22–23, in the present work.

(From MS Trivulziano 193.)[4]

One pretending to be *frate* Chalandrino of the abbey of Vallombrosa stops at Borgo a Mozzano to make a collection on market day.

⟨fol. 82ʳ⟩ Doppo il predicare disse che si facesse bene alla badia di Valombrosa. Ma ben dicea, se fusse alcuno huomo che avesse ucciso alcuno suo compare, non faccia limozina.[5] Et simile, se neuna donna avesse morto o compare o commare, non faccia limosina però che l'abate non l'aciterà. Ditto questa parola, ognuno fe' offerta in quantità. . . . .

He asks for gifts for
his abbey, but mur-
derers cannot offer.

All give generously.

---

[1] That they are without sinful love.   [2] On pain of excommunication.

[3] The analogy to C 377–99 was first pointed out by C. P. Wagner in his paper, "Analogues to the Pardoner's Gaude," presented to the Chaucer section of the M.L.A. in Cincinnati, January 1, 1936, and by B. J. Whiting, "More on Chaucer's *Pardoner's Prologue* (VI [C], 377–390)," *MLN*, LI (1936), 322–27.

[4] For the manuscript and the editorial principles of the present text, kindly prepared by Robert A. Pratt, see pp. 33–35. This *novella* has been printed by Renier, *Novelle inedite di Giovanni Sercambi* (Turin, 1889), pp. 128–31; see above, p. 48.

[5] Here the words *però che l'abate* were written and crossed out (MS).

The *frate* gives Narda, the wife of his host, abundant proof of his licentiousness and insincerity. She assures him that she would rather be burnt than give him another offering. He wages a dinner that he will make her do it.

At collection time he declares, ⟨fol. 83ʳ⟩ Venendo alla lemozina, disse che li omini stessero disepe-rati dalle donne, e così fu. E messo uno tappeto in terra, disse, "A chi vuol far limozina alla badia di Valenbrosa, si dia quello che altra volta si disse. E più dico che qualuncha donna avesse fatto fallo al suo marito, che non dia limozina però che 'l santo abate non l'aceptre'." Le donne, come sentinno tal parola, chi non avea denari si levava la benda di capo e in sul tappeto la gittava. Narda, che vede a furia le femine dare offerta, dice fra se medesima, "Se io offerischo¹ ⟨fol. 83ᵛ⟩ perdo la cena." E diliberato pure l'offerere, si misse mano alla borsa e trassene uno denaro e quasi fu la deretana e offerse. . . . .

"No gift from adulteresses."

All rush with offerings. Narda prefers to lose the dinner.

C. AN *exemplum*

This is known in a fifteenth-century collection only, but earlier collections of *exempla* may have contained this or similar versions.

(From Edward H. Weatherly ["A Note on Chaucer's *Pardoner's Prologue*," *MLN*, L (1935), 310–11], who printed it from Harleian MS 3938, fols. 124*b*–25).

Before collection someone at Ferrara declared: "Our house refuses gifts from adulteresses or otherwise sinful women."

All bring offerings, some borrowing money for them.

Quidem querens quaestam Ferraria post predicationem suam dixit dominabus cum deberent offerre, dixit: Si est aliqua domina quae fecerit fallum de marito, uel de persona sua, non ueniat ad offerendum, quoniam mansio, uel domus nostra, non uult talem pecuniam, uel oblationem, et tunc omnes inerunt ad offerendum, et quae non habebat pecuniam accipiebat mutuo ut non suspicaretur de fallo.

Later versions, some closely related to Sercambi's, others de-rived from Pfaffe Amîs,² give no additional information on Chaucer's possible source or sources.

¹ offerischo: non offerischo (*MS*)—*emend. R.*

² See *Heinrich Bebels Facetien*, I, 63 and 64, ed. G. Bebermeyer ("Stut. Lit. Ver.," Vol. CCLXXVI [Leipzig, 1931]), pp. 27–28; *Ulenspiegel* (story No. 31, pp. 43–45, in J. M. Lappenberg's ed. [Leipzig, 1854]); Hans Sachs, *Sämtliche Fabeln und Schwänke*, II (ed. E. Goetze [Halle, 1894]), 485–88, and IV (ed. E. Goetze and C. Drescher [Halle, 1903]), 66–67; *Wendunmuth von Hans Wilhelm Kirchhof*, ed. H. Oesterley ("Stut. Lit. Ver.," Vol. XCV [Tübingen, 1869]), p. 539; *Les Comptes du monde adventvrevx*, ed. F. Frank (Paris, 1878), I, 60; Henri Estienne *Apologie pour Hérodote*, ed. P. Ristelhuber (Paris, 1879), II, 409–10. About trans-lations of some of those versions see B. J. Whiting, from whose article the above references are taken.

THE PARDONER'S TALE

By FREDERICK TUPPER

NONE of the analogues that has come down to us can claim to be the one direct source of the *Pardoner's Tale*, but those analogues are very numerous and give us considerable data on the source (or sources) used by Chaucer.

The story is particularly widespread in the Orient,[1] but, as none of the oriental versions has in common with Chaucer any feature that is not also present in several Western versions older than Chaucer or at least not dependent on him,[2] and as several striking features found both in Chaucer and in at least one Western version are lacking in all oriental forms of the story,[3] it is clear that the oriental versions could add nothing to the data on Chaucer's source supplied by the occidental versions. The oriental versions shall, accordingly, be left out of consideration.

In the West the story is found mainly in collections of *novelle* and *exempla*, the material of which can safely be accepted as antedating Chaucer. His acquaintance with one or more versions belonging to either or both of those genres seems highly

---

[1] The many citations of Victor Chauvin's *Bibliographie des ouvrages arabes publiés dans l'Europe chrétienne de 1810 à 1885* (Liège, Leipzig, 1904), VIII, 10, and of A. D'Ancona, *Studi di critica e storia letteraria* (Bologna, 1912), II, 136–38, amply sustain belief in oriental origin of the story. Clouston in *Originals and Analogues*, pp. 418–36, has given English renderings of Buddhist, Persian, Arabian, Cashmere, and Tibetan versions. The oriental analogues differ widely from one another. The treasure may be the camel-load of a wealthy merchant or may have a supernatural origin (a shower of precious objects; a mound of earth turned into gold). The companions who stay and poison one another to secure the treasure are usually two, three, or four. The poisoned food is rice, bread, or elephant flesh. In many cases a warning is given and a moral lesson is drawn by a sage, Gautama in a Buddhist version, Jesus in several Arabic and Persian versions.

[2] E.g., the statement that avarice is the root of all destruction or evils. It is found in the Buddhist version (*Originals and Analogues*, p. 421), but also in Morlini and Hans Sachs, neither of whom is at all likely to owe it to Chaucer.

[3] E.g., the quest-of-death motif, the casting of dice or drawing of lots, the mention of rats when the poison is bought, the pledge of secrecy, etc.

probable.[1] In Section I we shall quote most of the *novelle* and *exempla* versions known to us. Section II will give large portions of two plays. In spite of their late date (fifteenth and sixteenth centuries), both are of interest as suggesting that some details present in the *Pardoner's Tale* and not found in our *novelle* or *exempla* were probably not invented by Chaucer. Finally, as parallels and possible sources of some subsidiary material in the *Pardoner's Tale*, a few short passages from different works will be quoted in Section III.

I. *NOVELLE* AND *EXEMPLA*

Our closest analogues to the *Pardoner's Tale* are the *novella* reprinted here under the title *The Hermit, Death, and the Robbers* and the *exemplum De tribus sociis*.

A. *Novelle*

1. CHRIST AND HIS DISCIPLES

This is *novella* No. 83 in the collection edited in 1525 by Gualteruzzi as *Le ciento novelle antike*, the first printed form of what is more generally known as the *Novellino*. The material for this Gualteruzzi collection has been shown to go back in its origin to the thirteenth century.[2]

(Reprinted from *Originals and Analogues of Some of Chaucer's Canterbury Tales* ["Chaucer Society Publications" (1872–78)], p. 131.)

Christ walks thro' a wild country with his disciples.

Come Cristo, andando un giorno co disciepoli suoi per un foresto luogo, uidero molto grande tesoro.

They see some gold piastres, and say to him,

Andando un giorno Cristo co disciepoli suoi per un foresto luogo, nel quale i disciepoli ke ueniano dietro uidero luciere, da una parte, piastre doro fine. Onde essi chiamando Cristo, marauigliandossi

---

[1] For opinions on the relation of our *novelle* and *exempla* versions to Chaucer's source see H. S. Canby, "Some Comments on the Sources of Chaucer's *Pardoner's Tale*," *MP*, II (1905), 477–87, esp. pp. 482–86; G. Dempster, *Dramatic Irony in Chaucer* (Stanford, 1932), pp. 74–77; and Carleton Brown's ed. of the *Pardoner's Tale* (Oxford, 1935), Introd., esp. pp. xxii–xxviii.

[2] A. D'Ancona, *Del Novellino e delle sue Fonti* ("Studi di critica e storia letteraria," Vol. II [Bologna, 1912]), pp. 5 and 136–38. A clear summary of the conclusions of modern scholarship on the origin of the *Novellino* and the stages of its development will be found, with bibliographical references, on pp. vii–xvi of Letterio di Francia's Introduction to his edition of *Le cento novelle antiche o libro di novelle e di bel parlar gentile, detto anche Novellino* (Torino, 1930).

perke non era ristato, ad esso si dissero. "Singniore! prendiamo quello
oro kecci consolera di molte bisongnie." E Cristo si uolse erripreselli,
e disse. "Voi uolete quelle cose ke toglioni al rengnio nostro la maggior parte dellanime. E ke cio sia uero, alla tornata nudirete lassempro," e passaro oltre. Poco stante, due cari compangni lo trou-
aro, onde furo molto lieti, et in concordia andaro alla piu presso uilla
per menare uno mulo, ellaltro rimase a guardia. Ma udite opere ree
kenne seguiro poscia de pensieri rei kel nemico die loro. Quelli torno
col mulo, e disse al compangnio, "io o mangiato alla uilla, ettu dei
auere fame; mangia questi duo pani cosi belli e poi carikeremo."
Quel li rispose, "io non a gran talento di mangiare ora, e pero carichi-
amo prima." Allora presero a caricare. E quando ebbero presso ke
caricato quelli kando per lo mulo, si kino per legar la soma, ellaltro li
corse di dietro a tradimento con uno appuntato coltello, et uccisello.
Poscia prese luno di que pani, e diello al mulo. Ellaltro mangio elli.
Il pane era attoscato: cadde morto elli el mulo inanzi ke mouessero
di quel luogo, elloro rimase libero come di prima. Il nostro Singnior
passo indi con suoi disciepoli nel detto giorno, e mostro loro lassempro
ke detto auea.

Side notes: "Let us take these for our wants." He refuses: "You want that which robs us of souls. As we come back, you'll see." Soon, two companions find the gold. One goes to fetch a mule for it; the other guards it. The first comes back with the mule, and asks his mate to eat two nice loaves that he's brought. His mate refuses, but stabs him as he's stooping. Then he gives the mule one poisoned loaf, eats another himself, and both fall dead. Christ, returning, shows his disciples the dead bodies, as he had foretold.

2. The Hermit, Death, and the Robbers

This *novella* was first printed as No. 82 in Borghini's 1572
Libro di novelle e di bel parlar gentile, a collection largely based
on the Gualteruzzi *Ciento novelle antike*. The manuscript from
which Borghini took this and several other *novelle*,[1] the Codex
Panciatichiano-Palatino 138, dates from the early sixteenth
century,[2] but there is no reason to doubt that its material goes
back to roughly the same time as that of the Gualteruzzi collection.

(From *Originals and Analogues*, pp. 132–33.)

Qui conta d'vno romito che andando per un luogo foresto trouo
molto grande tesoro.

Side note: The Hermit Who Saw a Great Treasure.

Andando vn giorno vn Romito per vn luogo foresto: si trouò vna
grandissima grotta, laquale era molto celata, et ritirandosi verso là
per riposarsi, pero che era assai affaticato; come e'giunse alla grotta

Side note: A hermit lying down in a cave

---

[1] See Letterio di Francia, pp. ix–x. Borghini makes only insignificant changes.
The "sancto romito" of the manuscript becomes "romito," and the moral sentiment, the saving of souls, is converted into a merely prudent warning.

[2] G. Biagi, *Le Novelle antiche dei Codici Panciatichiano-Palatino 138 e Laurenziano-Gaddiano 193* (Firenze, 1880), p. xcvii. Our story is No. 149 in the P-P Codex,
which also contains, as No. 120, the version printed by Gualteruzzi.

sees there much gold.
At once he runs away,

si la vide in certo luogo molto tralucere, impercio che vi hauea molto Oro: e si tosto come il conobbe, incontanente si partio, & comincio a correre per lo diserto, quanto e' ne potea andare. Correndo cosi

and meets three robbers.

questo Romito s'intoppo in tre grandi scherani, liquali stauano in quella foresta per rubare chi unque vi passaua. Ne gia mai si erano

They see no one chasing the hermit,

accorti, che questo oro vi fosse. Hor vedendo costoro, che nascosti si stauano, fuggir cosi questo huomo, non hauendo persona dietro

and ask him what he's running away from.

che'l cacciasse, alquanto hebbero temenza, ma pur se li pararono dinanzi per sapere perche fuggiua, che di cio molto si marauigliauano.

"Death, which is chasing me."

Ed elli rispose & disse: "Fratelli miei, io fuggo la morte, che mi vien dietro cacciando mi." Que' non vedendo ne huomo, ne bestia, che il

"Where is he? Show him to us."
"Come with me, and I will."

cacciasse, dissero: "Mostraci chi ti caccia: & menaci cola oue ella è." Allhora il Romito disse loro: "venite meco, & mostrerrollaui," pregandoli tutta via che non andassero ad essa, impercio che elli per se la fuggia. Ed eglino volendola trouare, per vedere come fosse fatta, nol domandauano di altro. Il Romito vedendo che non potea piu, &

The hermit takes them to the cave, and shows them Death, the gold. They rejoice,

hauendo paura di loro, gli condusse alla grotta, onde egli s'era partito, e disse loro, "Qui è la morte, che mi cacciaua," & mostro loro l'oro che u'era, ed eglino il conobbero incontanènte, & molto si cominciarono a rallegrare, & a fare insieme grande sollazzo. Allhora accommiata-

and say the hermit's a fool.

rono questo buono huomo: & egli sen'ando per i fatti suoi: & quelli cominciarono a dire tra loro, come elli era semplice persona. Rimasero

Then the three robbers consult as to what they shall do.

questi scherani tutti e tre insieme, a guardare questo hauere, e incominciarono a ragionare quello che voleano fare. L'uno rispuose & disse: "A me pare, da che Dio ci ha data cosi alta ventura, che noi non ci partiamo di qui, insino a tanto che noi non ne portiamo tutto

The second proposes that one shall go to the town, buy bread and wine, and all things needful.

questo hauere." Et l'altro disse: "non facciamo cosi. l'vno di noi ne tolga alquanto, & vada alla cittade & vendalo, & rechi del pane & del vino, et di quello che ci bisogna, e di cio s'ingegni il meglio che puote: faccia egli, pur com' elli ci fornisca." A questo s'accordarono tutti e tre insieme. Il Demonio ch'è ingegnoso, e reo d'ordinare di fare

But the crafty Devil puts into the heart of the robber who goes to the town the idea that he shall feed himself,

quanto male e puote, mise in cuore a costui che andaua alla citta per lo fornimento, "da ch'io sarò nella cittade" (dicea fra se medesimo) "io voglio mangiare & bere quanto mi bisogna, & poi fornirmi di certe cose delle quali io ho mestiere hora al presente: & poi auuelenero quello che io

and poison his mates, and have all the treasure.

porto a miei compagni: si che, da ch'elli saranno morti amendue, si sarò io poi Signore di tutto quello hauere, & secondo che mi pare egli è tanto, che io saro poi il piu ricco huomo di tutto questo paese da parte d'hauere": et come li venne in pensiero, cosi fece. Prese viuanda per se quanta gli bisogno, & poi tutta l'altra auuelenoe, et cosi la porto a

While he is gone

que suoi compagni. Intanto ch'ando alla cittad secondo che detto hauemo: se elli pensoe & ordinoe male per uccidere li suoi compagni accio che ogni cosa li rimanesse: quelli pensaro di lui non meglio ch'elli di loro, et dissero tra loro. "Si tosto come questo nostro compagno tornera col pane et col vino, et con l'altre cose che ci bisognano, si l'uccideremo, & poi mangeremo quanto uorremo, e sara poi tra noi due tutto questo grande hauere. Et come meno parti ne saremo, tanto n'haueremo maggior parte ciascuno di noi." Hor viene quelli, che era ito alla cittade a comperare le cose che bisognaua loro. Tornato a suoi compagni incontanente che'l videro, gli furono addosso con le lancie et con le coltella, & l'uccisero. Da che l'hebbero morto, mangiarono di quello che egli hauea recato: & si tosto come furono satolli, amendue caddero morti; & cosi morirono tutti e tre: che l'vno vccise l'altro si come vdito hauete, & non hebbe l'hauere: & cosi paga Domenedio li traditori, che egli andarono caendo la morte, & in questo modo la trouarono, et si come ellino n'erano degni. Et il saggio sauiamenta la fuggio, e l'oro rimase libero come di prima.

[margin: the other robbers plot to murder him as soon as he comes back / and then share the treasure. / Their mate returns from the city, / and they murder him at once. / Then they eat the food he has brought and both fall dead. / Thus does our Lord requite traitors. / The robbers found death. / The wise man fled and the gold was left free.]

3. The Treasure in the Tiber

This is No. 42 in the *Novellae* of Morlinus, a collection of stories first printed at Naples in 1520.

(From *Originals and Analogues*, p. 134. W. A. Clouston copied his text from the 1799 Paris reprint of the Naples edition, and corrected it by a later Paris edition [Bibliothèque Elzévirienne, 1855].)

De illis qui, in Tiberi reperto thesauro, ad inuicem conspirantes, ueneno & ferro periere.

Magus magico susurro in Tiberi delitere thesaurum / quadam in cauea spirituum reuelacione cognouit: quo reperto, cum magnum siclorum cumulum aspiceret, communi uoto pars sotiorum proximum oppidum seu castellum, epulas aliasque res comparaturi, accedunt: ceteri uero copiosum interea ignem instruunt, thesaurumque custodiunt. Dumque in castellum conuenissent, radice malorum cupiditate affecti, ut consotios thesauri parte priuarent, diro ueneno illos interimere statuerunt: cum dicto, in caupona epulantes, ebrii ac uino sepulti / aliquatenus moram fecere. In Tiberi expectantes atque esurientes, consotios de mora incusabant: Iouemque adiurauerunt, repedantes ex oppido atque castello & uita & thesauri parte priuare. Sicque ad inuicem conspirantes, non multo post adueniunt ex pago illi, uinarios utres, pullos, pisces aliaque tuc[etos]i saporis pulmentaria atque prelectum hircum ferentes. Quibus o[b]uiam dederunt ieiuni, illosque omnes morti [im]paratos incautosque insecauere atque crudeli strage perdiderunt. Pone sumptis cibariis [diro] ueneno tabefactis, insigni jocunditate / grauiter cuncta ministrare incipiunt: alter

[margin: The Wizard learnt from the spirits that a treasure lay hid in the Tiber. / On its being found, part of the company go to a town near by to fetch food and liquor. / Moved by avarice, the root of evils, these conspired to buy poison to kill their fellows. / The others, meanwhile, conspired to kill them; / which on their return they do.]

uerrit / alter sternit / pars coquit / atque tuceta concinnat. Pone omnibus scitule appositis, ac mensa largiter instructa edere ceperunt, omniaque ingurgitauerunt. Commodum / ex eis mensa erectis erant quod, morte preuenti, cum sotiis uitam fato reddentes, sub elemento mortui & sepulti remansere.

Nouella indicat: nec esse de malo cogitandum: nam quod quis seminat, metit.

B. *Exempla*[1]

1. *De tribus sociis qui thesaurum invenerunt— exemplum de auaricia*

The manuscript in which this is found was written at Prague in 1406.[2]

(From Joseph Klapper, *Exempla aus Handschriften des Mittelalters, Sammlung mittellateinischer Texte* [Heidelberg, 1911], No. 98.)

Quidam heremita volens in nemore ortum edificare ex casu fodiendo invenit thezaurum statimque clamauit ter magna voce: Mors, mors, mors! Pretereuntes vero tres socij mercatores venerunt dicentes: Vbi est mors, quam clamasti? Ille vero monstrauit eis thezaurum et statim eum abinde repulerunt. Qui recedens venit ad cellam suam. Isti vero cogitantes, quid essent facturi, ordinauerunt, ut vnus ex illis in ciuitatem iret et expensas aportaret. Eo uero abeunte cogittauerunt, ut eum, cum in foueam descenderet, interficerent. Ipse uero vadens eciam cogitauit de perdicione istorum duorum, venenumque comparans omnia cibaria intoxicauit veniensque ad illos dixit: Volumusne prius comedere uel thezaurum excipere? Qui responderunt: Prius thezaurum excipiemus. Feceruntque illum ad foueam descendere, ut eum occiderent. Descendente vero eo ipsum occiderunt et ipsi postmodum comedentes ambo mortui sunt et sic thezaurum intactum reliquerunt. Quo cum heremita (dum) venisset et eos mortuos vidisset, ait: Vere non est aliud thezaurus nisi periculum et mors.

2. *De duobus sociis, qui thesaurum invenerunt*

This is found in a manuscript coming from the Augustine canons of Sagan (Silesia) and written in the middle of the fifteenth century.[3]

(From J. Klapper's *Exempla*, No. 97.)

---

[1] Attention was first drawn to the two *exempla* in Klapper's collection and to the three in British Museum manuscripts by Professor T. F. Crane, "New Analogues of Old Tales," *MP*, X (1913), 310.

[2] MS I F 551 in the Königliche und Universitätsbibliothek at Breslau (see J. Klapper's *Exempla*, p. 79).

[3] Now MS I F 514 in the Königliche und Universitätsbibliothek at Breslau (see Klapper, p. 79).

Per hanc viam ambulauerunt hij duo, de quibus legitur: Duo socij auari ambulauerunt et quoddam pondus auri in via invenerunt. Quod tollere cupientes et pre grauedine non valentes extra viam cum difficultate mouerunt. Simul igitur condixerunt, vt vnus ad civitatem iret pro asino et alius ad auri custodiam remaneret. Vadens igitur vnus cogitauit, qualiter totum aurum posset habere et socium suum interficere. Similiter et qui remanserat eadem cogitabat. Ille igitur qui ad ciuitatem ierat, fecit fieri duos panes et miscuit venenum, ut panem manducans socius moreretur. Veniens igitur cum asino et pane nitebatur aurum asino imponere dicens socio, quod pranderet, ut vires reciperet. Cui socius dixit, quod prius vellet eum iuuare, et statim percuciens eum gladio iugulauit. Quo mortuo, cum esset famelicus, accepit vnum panem, comedit et reliquum asino dedit. Qui ambo manducantes in terram mortui ceciderunt. Hec ad litteram fortassis gesta sunt in hac via spinosa, sed moraliter adhuc semper contingunt.

Two companions find a heap of gold in the road. Unable to carry away the gold, they decide that one go to town for an ass and the other remain on guard. The former plans to kill his comrade and have all the gold. The other has the same intent. The first mixes poison with the bread that he brings, and urges his fellow to eat. The second slays him with his sword. He then eats the bread and gives some of it to the ass. Both fall dead.

3–5. *Exempla* FROM MANUSCRIPTS IN THE BRITISH MUSEUM

Three hitherto unpublished closely related versions are found in three manuscripts now in the British Museum,[1] all three written in Italy and ranging in date from 1400 to the sixteenth century.[2]

(No. 3, from British Museum, Add. MS 11872 [*ca.* 1400], No. 12.)

Cum quidam philosophus ambularet per quoddam nemus cum discipulis suis, invenerunt maximam quantitatem auri et quaesierunt discipuli ab eo quid hoc est. Respondit: "Filii, mala res est; nolite tangere, nam propter illud fiunt homicidia, furta, perjuria." Et his dictis abierunt. Duo autem ex ipsis temptati dixerunt ad invicem: "Unus eat ad emendum panem et alius ad educendum mulum." Ille vero qui panem emerat cogitavit qualiter socium interficeret ut totum aurum haberet. Et acceptis duobus panibus unum toxicaxit ut daret socio. Similiter alter cogitavit qualiter socium occideret et cum venissent ad nemus, dixit ille qui panem portaverat, "Comedamus." Alius dixit: "Expecta me et comede et ego incidam baculum ad educendum mulum." Et ivit et, secto baculo, latenter interfecit socium, et cogitans habere aurum totum cepit comedere panem toxicatum et sic mortuus est et ipse.

Disciples of a philosopher find in a grove a heap of gold, and ask him what it is. He warns against the gold as a source of many evils. Two followers decide to buy bread and get a mule. The buyer of bread poisons this, that he may have the gold after his fellow's death. The other has like intent. When the first urges his fellow to eat, that one cuts a stick and slays him. Then eating the poisoned bread, he too dies.

(No. 4, from British Museum Add. MS 27336 [early fifteenth century], No. 184.)

[1] Herbert's *Catalogue of Romances*, III, 693, 660, 711.

[2] Herbert, III, 692, 647, 709.

The disciples of Jesus walking with him find a sack full of gold and silver.

Jesus forbids them to touch this root of all evils.

Two of the disciples yield to the desire of wealth.

One will buy food

and the other get a mule to carry the gold and silver.

Each considers the death of the other. The one places poison in a loaf.

The other bids his companion wait while he cuts a stick for the mule, meaning to slay him therewith. Returning he kills his fellow

and rejoices in the possession of all the gold. Then partaking of the poisoned loaf, he falls dead.

Legitur in legenda beati Bartolomei quod cum dominus noster, Jesus Christus, ambularet cum discipulis suis per quoddam nemus et vastam solitudinem invenerunt unum saccum auro at argento plenum. Eo invento dixerunt discipuli ad Jesum: "Quid est hoc, Magister?" Qui respondit: "Filioli mei, nolite hoc tangere, quia res pessima est, nam propter hoc saepe fiunt homicidia, perjuria, furta, alia quoque infinita mala et peccata et propter hoc multe anime descendunt ad abissum infernum." Dixerunt discipuli tamen: "Dicas, quid est hoc et quod nomen habet." Dixit ei dominus: "Aurum est et aurum vocatur. Cavere tamen debetis ne illud tangatis." Hoc dicto abire ceperunt. Duo autem ex discipulis temptati ad invicem dicunt: "Eamus et accipiamus aurum; et possidemus illud et sic semper divites et pleni erimus." Qui cum dixerunt ad invicem ut unus eorum iret ad emendum cibaria necessaria et alius ad aquirendum unum mullum qui asportaret auri et argenti saccum quod et factum est. Uterque iam sagita diaboli per invidiam ultra avaritiam percussus cogitavit qualiter alium posset interficere. Ille qui panem emerat in uno pane posuit toxicum ut socium cecideret comedendo panem. Alius vero dixit socio postquam ambo ad saccum pervenerunt: "Expecta me hic donec vadam. Incidam unum baculum ad redeundum mullum"—cogitans et intendans alium suo baculo interficere. Qui, facto baculo, reversus ad socium, invenit eum panem non toxicatum comedentem qui abrecto baculo latentem occidit eum, dicens intra se: "Modo solus totum aurum possidebo." Et accurens ad panem ut comederet, occurrit ei panis in quo toxicum erat, quo gustato et statim cecidit mortuus. Unum sic paruit quod Dominus verum dixit quum dixit: "Filioli mei, nolite hoc tangere quae res pessima est," etc.

Then follows a long exposition upon the accursed love of gold and silver, concluding with a citation from Ecclesiasticus, "Nihil scelestius quam amare pecunias."

(No. 5, from British Museum MS Harley 3938 [sixteenth century], No. 26.)

Christ walking with his disciples tells them that a sack full of money which they have found is death. Two disciples decide to take the gold, one going to buy bread and the other to get an ass to carry the treasure. Each begins to plot the other's death. The first poisons one of the loaves.

Legitur in vita beati Bartolomei quod cum Christus per desertum cum suis discipulis ambularet saccum plenum pecunia invenerunt et cum ab eo quererent quid hoc edit, respondit quod erat mors quia aurum erat quod est causa mortis. Et duo discipuli uterque ordinaverunt aurem accipere. Et dixit unus alteri: "Ego ibo ad emendum panem et duces tu asinum unum ad portandum aurum." Et unus de morte alterius statim cogitare cepit. Unus emit duos panes et unum toxicavit, ut daret socio et occideret. Alter cogitavit mactare socium

in deserto et cum fuissent in loco, dixit unus: "Sta hic et comede et
ego ibo ad accipiendum baculum pro asino," et ille panem bonum
comedit et malum socio remanebat vel reservabat. Et cum ille
venisset et socium mactasset, secure cepit comedere, qui ex veneno
mortuus. Post(ea) Christus hoc sciens ad locum venit et ambos
mortuos reperit. Ex quo apparet quod illud aurum mors fuit; Ecclesiasticus, 6, Qui amat divitias, fructum non capiet ex eis.

II. THE PLAYS

A. *Rappresentazione di Sant' Antonio*

This play was probably written in the fifteenth century. For
detailed comparison with the *Pardoner's Tale* see H. S. Canby,
MP, II (1905), 480–82 and 484–86.[1]

(From *Sacre rappresentazioni dei secoli xiv, xv, e xvi*, ed. A. D.Ancona [Firenze,
1872], II, 54–63.)

The Spirit of Avarice places a mound of gold in the way of
St. Anthony, who warns him that all such temptations are use-
less. Three malefactors meet in the desert; they decide to join
their forces; the spoils will be divided.

Antonio è sanato e va pel diserto: e riscontra e dice loro:

> Fuggite, frate' miei, fuggite forte,
> Tornate a drieto pel vostro migliore,
> Non andate in costà che v' è la morte,
> La qual v' ucciderà con gran dolore.
> Non vi varrà le membra e l'arme accorte,
> Nè vostre gagliardie nè gran valore;
> E se il consiglio mio non seguirete,
> Andando più costà presto morrete.

*Antony, meeting
the malefactors,
counsels them to
turn back for fear
of death.*

Risponde il TAGLIAGAMBE *e dice:*

> Costui debbe esser fuor del sentimento
> E per la fame della cella uscito;
> Questi romiti fanno molto stento,
> Han poco da mangiare e mal vestito;
> Badar con lui è un parlare a vento;
> Però pigliam prestamente partito,
> E andiam questa morte a ritrovare,
> Chè sarà gente ch' e' vorrà campare.

*Tagliagambe bids
the others pay little
heed to the hermit*

*and press on to find
this death.*

---

[1] As the interest both of the Italian and of the German play lies in details paralleled in Chaucer, references to strikingly analogous passages in the *Pardoner's Tale*
will be appended to the marginal summaries of the two plays.

When they discover the mound of gold, Tagliagambe voices their joy in finding this death which is really life;

Vanno più là, e truovano il monte dell' oro, e il TAGLIAGAMBE *dice:*

Guardate, frate' miei, quanta pazia
Regna in quel pazerel, vecchio eremita,
Dicendo che era qua la morte ria!
E' chiama morte quello che è vita.
Se noi non venavam per questa via,
Nostra ventura era per noi fallita.
Questo fia meglio che un prigion da taglia,
E non arem a fare altra battaglia.

he suggests that one go to Damascus for rich food and wine.

Compagni, i' ho pensato, se vi pare,
Che un di voi vada insino a Damasco,
E rechi qualche cosa da mangiare,
E facci anco d' aver qualche buon fiasco.
E ingegnisi chi va, presto tornare,
Perch' io di fame e di sete mi casco;
Rechi confetti, pane, carne e vino,
Se ben dovessi spendere un fiorino.

Let him to whom the lot falls (cf. C 793-94) carry with him a piece of gold.

Facciamo alle buschette chi debba ire,
E chi va porti seco un pezo d' oro:
A qualche banco lo potrà finire,
E facciasi moneta dar da loro.

Risponde CARAPELLO *e dice:*

Carapello eagerly assents to the plan.

Questo mi piace, e debbasi seguire;
E' non si vuol or mai far più dimoro.
Fa', Scaramuccia, e ordina le sorte,
E chi ha la minor, calcagni forte.

Risponde il TAGLIAGAMBE *e dice:*

Scaramuccia, to whom the lot falls, is told what to buy.

Va' presto, Scaramuccia, e non ti scordi
Di trovare il Cibaca o qualche cuoco,
E compera un cappon, pippioni e tordi,
To' duo fiaschi di vin, chè un sare' poco.
Se gniun ti chiama, tien gli orecchi sordi
Ma guarda a non fermarti a qualche giuoco;
Reca un par di bilance da pesare,
Chè poi quest' oro si vuole sterzare.

Scaramuccia muses along the way upon the folly of letting slip a great chance, which may never return. Each one for himself! If he can get the whole treasure, why hesitate?

He will get poison from a chemist,

A me bisogna uno spezial trovare
Che mi venda veleno del più forte;
Un di que' fiaschi potrò avvelenare,

Chè non c'è via più breve a dar lor morte.

deal death to his fellows,

E' m'han creduto e' felloni ingannare
Per far che sie toccato a me la sorte;
Ma sopra lor ritornerà l'inganno,
E l'òr fie tutto mio sanz' altro affanno.

and gain all.

He betakes himself to a bank and haggles with the cashier over the exchange, promising him larger business in future.

Dipoi va allo speziale e dice:

He then goes to a chemist,

 Maestro mio, vo' siate il ben trovato;
I' vengo a voi per aiuto e consiglio.

Risponde lo SPEZIALE:

 Ben sia venuto; i' sono apparecchiato
Di far per te come di proprio figlio.

Risponde SCARAMUCCIA:

and asks poison to kill the rats in his house (C 854).

 Da poco in qua e' m' è in casa arrivato
Gran quantità di topi e gniun ne piglio,
Per modo tal che son tanti e sì vecchi
Che gli hanno ancora a rodermi gli orecchi.
 Di che convien, maestro, che mi diate
Un poco di velen col qual gli spenga;
A vostro modo vò' che vi paghiate;
Pur che sia buon, se viene assai, sí venga.

Risponde lo SPEZIALE *e dice:*

The chemist, warning him against scandal,

 I' tel darò perfetto in veritate,
Ma guarda poi che scandol non ne venga.

provides a box of arsenic

Levati su e fa presto, Domenico,
Recami qua il bossol dell' arsenico.

for two groats.

 Tien qui quel ch' io ti do, dammi duo grossi,
E sotti dir ch' i' t' ho servito bene,
E per men pregio dartelo non puossi
Ma di ragion molto piú se ne viene:

Those who take it will die in great pain.

E, se lo pigliano, e' saran percossi
Di spasimo, e morranno con gran pene.

Risponde SCARAMUCCIA:

 Io non ispesi mai, al parer mio,
Me' mie danari, e fatevi con Dio.

Poi va all' oste e dice:

Then Scaramuccia goes to a public-house to select two flasks of wine, white and red.

 Oste, i' vorrei duo fiaschi d' un buon vino
Bianco e vermiglio che ogniun dolce sia.

*Risponde l'*Oste:

    I' n' ho di Chianti, e vin da san Lorino,
    Trebbian dolci, vernaccia e malvagia.

Risponde lo Scaramuccia:

    Tône duo fiaschi e te' questo fiorino,
    E serba il resto alla tornata mia;
    Intanto infino al cuoco i' voglio andare,
    Per veder se gli ha nulla da mangiare.

He goes to a cook and buys food.

Il Tagliagambe *dice a Carapello:*

In the meantime Tagliagambe and Carapello bind each other to secrecy (C 819, 823).

    Fratel, i' ti vò' dire il pensier mio:
    Con questo, che mi giuri fedelmente.
    Se non ti piace, metterlo in oblio,
    E a persona non ne dir nïente.

Risponde Carapello *e dice:*

    Di' prima tu, e poi ti dirò io
    Un pensier che m'andava per la mente,
    E dimmi arditamente i pensier tuoi,
    Chè quel che noi direm sarà tra noi.

Risponde il Tagliagambe *e dice:*

Tagliagambe then suggests that the gold be divided into two parts rather than three.

    I' ho pensato che questo tesoro
    Che la ventura ci ha fatto trovare,
    Che sol di te e me fusse quest' oro
    Per non l'aver con altri a dimezare.
    La invidia, a dirti il ver, mi dà martoro;
    Però rispondi quel che te ne pare.
    Che altri n'abbi aver, non mi par giuoco,
    E a farne tre parti, e sare' poco.

Carapello agrees.

Risponde Carapello:

    Per certo si, fratel, tu hai ragione.
    Non ti tenendo più celato il vero,
    Io sentia drento una gran passïone
    Ch' era a questo medesimo pensiero;
    E sammi mal che quel ghiotto poltrone,
    Che non val la sua vita un pane intero,
    La ventura abbia avuta per amica,
    E che si goda la nostra fatica.

When their fellow returns, as soon as he sits down (C 826) they will kill him.

    A quel che si vuol far, pigliam partito
    Che, quando e' torna e postosi a sedere,
    Che in un baleno e' sia da noi assalito.
    El pensier nostro lui non può sapere;

In pochi colpi noi l' arem finito;
Ma non si vuol dir nulla al suo venire:
La vita a cento noi abbiam già tolta:
Un più, un men, che monta questa volta?

What matters one more or less?

Scaramuccia torna, e il TAGLIAGAMBE *dice:*
  Che ha' tu venduto quel pezo dell' oro?
  E in queste cose poi quanto spendesti?

Scaramuccia returns and Tagliagambe quarrels with him straightway.

Risponde SCARAMUCCIA:
  Che ne vuo' tu saper, pezo di toro?
  A punto a punto testè lo sapesti.

Risponde il TAGLIAGAMBE:
  Dò, ladroncel, tu non arai il tesoro
  Che con noi insieme divider credesti.
  Poltron gaglioffo, grida se tu sai,
  Che stu non voli, alla barba l'arai.

He shall not have the treasure,

but shall get what he does not want.

Poi che l'hanno morto, il TAGLIAGAMBE *dice a Carapello:*
  Or ti dich'io, fratel mio diletto,
  Che noi potrem mangiare e bere in pace.
  E non abbiam d'avere alcun sospetto,
  Po' che questo gaglioffo morto giace.
  Comincia a tôrre un pezo di confetto,
  Assaggia in prima il vino se ti piace,
  Che noi potremo poi ben giudicare
  S' egli è buono e perfetto: che ti pare?

After slaying him,

they prepare to enjoy the wine and sweetmeats.

CARAPELLO *assaggia el vino e dice:*
  Egli è vantaggiato; assaggia un poco;
  Costui era pur ghiotto e intendente.

The wine delights them,

Il TAGLIAGAMBE *l'assaggia e dice:*
  Questo è un vin che par proprio di fuoco,
  Tanto è gagliardo, sottile e possente.
  Veggiamo or come ci ha trattati il cuoco,
  E trassiniam qualche cosa col dente.
  Di bene in meglio ci siamo abbattuti,
  Sì che con le mascella ogniun s' aiuti.

and the food, too, is excellent.

Quando hanno mangiato, il TAGLIAGAMBE *dice:*
  Or che ci siam cavati ben la sete,
  E il corpo pien, che di nulla si teme,
  E che ci tien l' orezo questo abete,
  Vuolsi che ragioniam di sodo insieme
  Che modo abbiamo a vivere in quïete,
  Fuggendo ogni pensier che l' alma preme.

Hunger and thirst satisfied, they indulge in happy thoughts of the future.

Risponde CARAPELLO *e dice:*

Tu hai ragion, ma io ho poca pratica:
Di' prima tu, che sai ben di gramatica.

Risponde il TAGLIAGAMBE:

They bethink them
how they may be
not only rich but
wise and shun the
turn of the wheel.

Carapel mio, da poi che la ventura
Ci ha fatto diventar tutt' e due ricchi,
Si vuol che noi siam savi, e abbiam cura
Che molto ben la ruota si conficchi
E ribadisca il chiodo, onde paura
Non abbïam che già mai si sconficchi.

Risponde CARAPELLO *e dice:*

El tuo è sanza fallo buon ricordo;
Facciam quel che ti par, ch' i' me n'accordo.

Risponde il TAGLIAGAMBE:

The venom begins
to work: Taglia-
gambe feels great
pains and suspects
the truth.

I' sento, fratel mio, drento un gran caldo
E parmi esser di fuoco tutto pieno,
E sopra al cuore un duol s' è posto saldo
Che tutto quanto mi fa venir meno.
I' ho paura che questo ribaldo
Non abbi in questo vin messo veleno.
Oimè oimè, questo poltrone
Come ranocchi ci ha giunti al boccone.

Risponde CARAPELLO *e dice:*

Carapello also feels
a great heat

and can hardly keep
his eyes open.

I' mi sentia, fratel, drento un gran caldo,
Ma credetti che venissi dal bere,
Chè questi vin che son conci, lo fanno,
Che gli occhi aperti io non posso tenere.
I' non credo che ci abbi fatto inganno,
Chè ancor non gli avàn fatto dispiacere.
Se sarà ver, noi ce n' avedrem tosto:

The finding of the
gold may be a great
loss.

D' aver trovato l' òr ci sarà costo.

Risponde il TAGLIAGAMBE:

A dog is devouring
the vitals.

Che diavol ho io drento alle budella?
E' pare un can che m' abbi divorato.

What gain was the
finding of the gold?

Poco bastommi la buona novella;
Che mi giova tanto oro aver trovato?

Risponde CARAPELLO:

The body hammers,
and seems to be
bursting.

Lascia dir me, che 'l corpo mi martella,
E vedi già ch' i' son tutto gonfiato:
Questo è stato per certo altro che l' oppio!
O diavol, po' che in questo modo scoppio.

Risponde il TAGLIAGAMBE:

Fratel, se tu volessi ir pel Bisticci

I' ti darò tutta la parte mia:

E, se non v'è ,va' pel barbier de' Ricci

Che ha la ricetta a ogni malattia.

Tagliagambe bids
his comrade hasten
for a barber who has
a prescription for
every malady.

Risponde CARAPELLO *e dice:*

Tu vuoi ch' i' vada, e già sento capricci

Della morte crudele acerba e ria,

Che tutte le ricette d' Ipocrasso

Non arien forza farmi andare un passo.

Carapello feels the
tremors of death; he
cannot walk.

The Spirit of Avarice rejoices in the result of his labors. He has led into his master's power not one but three. Satan praises him. An angel speaks the epilogue: You mortals should turn your desires from the treasures of this world to everlasting life.

Guardate, o buona gente, quanti mali

Vengon da questa maladetta lupa,

La qual è nata ne' regni infernali

E la sua fama sanza fin è cupa.

Questo è velen ch' a noi[1] ciechi mortali

La vita toglie e la salute occupa.

Uomini vani, or guardate costoro:

Che utile ha lor fatto il trovar l' oro!

Guardate Anton, che nella giovinezza

Lasciò la robba e la povertà prese, ...

Many evils come
from Avarice,
the accursed wolf,
hell-born,

which takes away
life and safety from
blind mortals.

B. *Der Dot im Stock*

Hans Sachs treated the theme of the three robbers and the treasure first in a *Meisterlied*, then in a play. The *Meisterlied*[2] need not be reprinted here; it is short and could not give us on the sources used by Hans Sachs any information not conveyed by the play. This was written between 1554 and 1556. For a comparison with the *Pardoner's Tale* see W. M. Hart, "The *Pardoner's Tale* and *Der Dot im Stock*," *MP*, IX (1911), 17–22.

(Reprinted from Edmund Goetze, *Sämtliche Fastnachtspiele von Hans Sachs* ["Neudrucke Deutscher Litteraturwerke," Nos. 60–61 (Halle, 1886)], VI, 95–106. We have used the umlaut for the superscript *e*.)

[1] Probably for *voi*.

[2] *Dichtungen von Hans Sachs*, ed. K. Goedeke as Vols. IV–VI (Leipzig, 1883) of "Deutsche Dichter des Sechszehnten Jahrhunderts," hrsg. K. Goedeke und Julius Tittmann. *Der Dot im Stock* is No. 106 in Part I of Sachs's poems (pp. 225–26 of Vol. IV).

Der engel get ein und spricht:

Hear a dreadful example of four people brought to death through avarice.

1 Ir cristen, hört und schweiget stil
   Und merckt ein erschröcklich peyspiel
   Vom aim waltprueder und darpey
   Von verwegener mörder drey,
5 Wie die all vier in ainer süm
   Prachten einander selber üm
   Ob eim schacz aus geiczigem müet,
   Welcher doch kainem kam zw güet,
   Welch pey spil uns die alten eben
10 Haben zw ainem spiegel geben,
   Was üebels noch zu aller zeit
   Sich durch den schnöden geicz pegeit
   Allerley art! . . . .

A hermit, who has long served God with fasting and prayer, sits down to rest in a wood, and listens to the birds' songs of praise.

He discovers in the stump (C 763, 769) a concealed treasure

   Da secz ich mich, ich merck gar wol:
40 Dieser stock ist inwendig hol.
   Ich wil aufsten und schawen nein,
   Was darin mag verporgen sein.

and recognizes that death lurks therein.

   Da ligt ein schacz; pehüet mich got!
   Warhaft steckt darinen der dot,
45 Wan Salomon sagt, das reichtümb
   Seim herren oft zu schaden kümb.
   Doch iderman reichtumb erwelt
   Und im so pegierlich nach stelt
   Paide mit recht und mit unrecht.
He flees from this wealth as a thing of evil.
50 Drümb wil ich in nit haben schlecht,
   Auch nit lenger darpey verziehen,
   Sünder als vor dem dod in fliehen. . . . .

Reflecting, however, on gold's great aid to the poor, he returns, yet finally decides to shun the hoard, and hastens to his cell. Three murderers—Dismas, Barrabas, Jesmas—enter, without booty and in danger of captivity and death. More than death Jesmas fears the judgment of God and the tortures of hell,[1] but his companions make light of such beliefs. If some rich merchant came they would murder him.

[1] Cf. the differentiation of the characters in Chaucer, C 716, 751, 776, 804, 835, 837, 844-45.

DISMAS, *der 1 mörder, dewt und spricht:*

Schawt, schawt! dort lawft ein alter mon
Im holcz forchtsam und sicht oft umb.
Ich glaub, er hab ein grose süm
Gelcz im rock vernet mit im tragen.

130   Kümpt mit! so wöll wir in erschlagen,
In plündern, darnach schicken spat
Umb prot und wein hinein int stat.
Den wöll wir schlemen und liegn im lüeder.

Dismas, seeing a timid old man approaching,

suggests that they rob him and send to the city for bread and wine.

JESMAS *sicht hinaüs, spricht:*

Ach, es ist ein alter waldpruder.

135   O, er tregt weder gelt noch guet,
Er lebet in höchster armuet.
Was wolt wir den den armen zeyen?

Jesmas objects that he is a poor old hermit.

BARRABAS *spricht:*

Schweig sdewffels nam! wilt uns den kheyen?
Wilt gaistlich und parmherzig sein?

140   So kumb in ein kloster hinein
Und uns im wald zw frieden las!
Kümbt! last vürlawffen im die stras?

Barrabas rebukes him for his mercy.

Der waltpruder kümpt, sie lawffen in an. DISMAS *spricht:*

Alter, wan her? peschaide mich!
Warümb schawst so oft hintersich?

145   Sag an! eyllet dir imant nach?

Dismas asks the old man why he looks behind him.

Der waltpruder dewt auf den stock und spricht:

In genem stock den dot ich sach.
Vor dem so flewch ich also vast.
Derhalb mein weg mich lawffen last
Und hüet euch auch vor diesem stock!

The hermit saw death in the stump, and bids them beware.

DISMAS *zeucht von leder und spricht:*

150   Dw muest mir halten ainen pock.
Ich merck: dw dreibst aus uns den spot.
Ich wil dir warmachen den dot.

Dismas draws his sword and threatens him with death.

Der waltpruder felt auf seine knie, hebt paid hent auf und spricht:

Las mich mit fried, pistw ein crist!
Dw waist: dotschlagn verpoten ist.

155   Wer menschen pluet vergiesen thüet,
Dem wirt vergossen auch sein plüet.

The old man begs for mercy,

and recalls to Dismas the fate of murderers. (Cf. C 739–47)

Er schlecht in nider; der waltpruder spricht liegent:

Got wirt mich an eüch allen rechen
Und ewer junge tag abrechen.

Dismas strikes down the old man, who invokes vengeance.

Barrabas, *der 2 mörder, spricht:*

Barrabas suggests
that they throw in-
to a ditch the old
man, who has
warned them
against the stump.

Kümbt! lat den alten kueten pueben
160 Im holcz dort werffen in ain grueben,
Der uns warnt vor des stocks ungnad,
Hat uns darmit drot auf das rad!
Nun, das ist der achzehent mon,
Den wir im wald haben abthon.

Sie dragen in ab.

Sie kumen wider, Dismas *spricht:*

Dismas proposes
that they go to the
stump and look on
death.

165 Kumbt! wöllen zu dem stock uns nehen
Und den dot auch darin pesehen.
Der dot hat den alten erpissen.

Jesmas, *der 3 mörder:*

Jesmas foresees
their death in re-
turn for this mur-
der.

Mich painigt haimlich mein gewissen
Umb dieses frumen mannes sterben.
170 Fuercht, wir müesen all drob verderben.

Sie kumen all 3 zumb stock, sehen hinein. Dismas *spricht:*

They come to the
stump, and find not
death but the
thousand guilders

Pocz marter, schawt! hie ligt kain dot,
Sunder pey dawsent guelden rot.

which the old man
(C 770–71) scorned.

Die hat der alt pertling[1] geschent
Und sie den pitern dot genent.
175 Got geb dem nolhart[2] noch die trües![3]
Der dot wirt uns dreyen gar sües,
Das wir darfon drincken und essen.
Der hünger het uns gar pesessen.

Dismas suggests
that one of them go
to the city for bread
and wine,

Lat uns pald lössen, welcher spat
180 Unter uns nein lauff in die stat
Und pringe uns prot unde wein,
Darpey wir müegen frolich sein,

and that on his re-
turn they divide the
treasure.

Das man darnach den schacz austail!
Der uns dreyen kumbt wol zu hail!

They throw dice
(C 793–804).

Sie knocken all drey nider, werffen mit zway wüerffeln. Barrabas *spricht:*

The lot falls to Jes-
mas and they bid
him go

185 Dich, Jesmas, hat das los getroffen;
Nem den guelden und kümb geloffen!
Pring uns drümb[4] wein und prot wie for,

and avoid arrest,

Nembs zw aller nechst peim stator,[5]

---

[1] The bearded man.

[2] Lay brother.

[3] A curse; *trues,* for *drues,* pestilence.

[4] *Drumb, darum:* for that money.

[5] Take it closest to the city gate.

Auf das dw nit werst ausgespecht,
190   Das dich ergrewffen die statknecht!
Sünst köm wir all mit dir in not,
Und wer im stock gewest der dot.

which would spell
ruin to them all.

JESMAS *nembt den guelden und die flaschen und spricht:*
Ich ge hin und sag uberlawt
Vor forcht grueselt mir gleich die hawt.

Jesmas departs, full
of fears,

195   Fuercht stet, mir kümb auf meinen rüeck
Ein unfürsehens ungelüeck
Auf dem weg oder in der stat,
Wie uns der alt erwünschet hat.

on account of the
old man's curse.

Jesmas get ab mit der flaschen. DISMAS *spricht:*
Barrabas, was dünckt dich des gseln?

Dismas fears be-
trayal by Jesmas

200   Er düt sich gar hündz füetisch[1] steln
Und gancz verzagt zw unsern daten.[2]
Füercht, er werd uns ain mal veraten
Und uns paid pringen in unglüeck.
Nün, zu fuerkümen solche stüeck,

205   So wais ich ainen gueten rat.

and suggests that
they strike him
down upon his re-
turn.

Pald er darnach kùmbt aus der stat
Und thüet uns prot und wein zu tragen,
So woll wir in düeckisch erschlagen.
So dürff wir uns nit mer pesorgen,

210   Das er von uns heut oder morgen
Secze ainen flüechtigen fües.

BARRABAS, *der 2 mörder:*
Deim rat ich auch zw fallen mües,
Mein Dismas, und ist mir auch eben.
Sein dot düt noch ein nücz uns geben,

Barrabas eagerly
assents

215   Das wir diesen schacz uns zw hail
Nür düerffen dailen in zwen dail,
So wirt unser aim pey fünfhundert.
So man aber drey dail ausundert,
Würt aim dreyhundert drey undreissig.

as this will increase
their share of the
treasure.

DISMAS, *der 1 mörder:*
220   Dw rechnest die fach aus gar fleissig.
Nün wöl wir in den thün von prot,
So glob on, in zu schlagen dot.

Dismas suggests
that they strike him
down when he
brings the bread.

[1] *Hundsföttisch:* he behaves himself quite nastily.

[2] "And very hesitantly with respect to our deeds."

Sie geloben einander an. BARRABAS *spricht:*

Ja, das hab dir die trewe mein! . . . .

They go to see if the old man had any money.

Jesmas returns.

JESMAS *kümbt mit wein und prot, schawt hin und her und spricht:*

Wo sint mein zwen geselen hin?
Ich glaub vürwar, es schwindel in
Aus der stat vor der zukünft mein,[1]

He has heavily
poisoned the bread
and wine,

Wan ich hab in das prot und wein
245 Mit ainem herben gift vergift,

to put an end to the
murders of his com-
panions.

Weil sie vil mortz haben gestift
Und hetten auch solicher massen
Ir lebtag nit darfon gelassen.
Des füercht ich mich der sunden minder,
250 Ob ich gleich dise zway mört kinder
Mit herbem gift geschwind und resch
Von diesem ertpoden auslesch,
Das vor in sicher sey weib und mon.
Alsden das gelt allain ich hon.

He will leave the
country,

255 Darmit ich raümen wil das lant
In ein gegent mir unbekant.

repent him of his
sins,

Da wil ich püesen und werden frümb,
Ob mich got zu genad aufnümb
Durch Cristi, seines sünes, sterben,

and thus save his
soul from hell-fire.

260 Das ich nit ewig muest verderben
Hie mit dem leib, dort mit der sel
In des helischen fewers quel.

The other two run
in; Dismas draws
his sword,

Die zwen kumen gelawffen. DISMAS *zewcht von leder, spricht:*

Wie pist so lang aus, dw poswicht?
Ich glaub, dw hast uns vor gericht

accuses Jesmas of
betraying them,

265 Haimlichen in der stat veraten.
Wir wöllen lonen deinen daten.

and threatens him
with death.

Wer dich, dw poswicht! dw must sterben,
E wan wir mit dem rad verderben.

JESMAS *spricht:*

Jesmas denies the
charge,

Ich pin unschuldig in den dingen.
270 Ir mörder, wolt ir mich umpringen?

but is struck down.

Sie schlagen in nider.

[1] Two obscure lines; perhaps "In truth I believe that they may well have been
made dizzy (with apprehension) before my arrival from the city, for I have. . . . ."

BARRABAS *spricht:*

Kümb! las den veretrischen pueben

Zumb alten werffen in die grueben

Und in mit danreis[1] decken zw!

So hab wir vor im rast und rw.

Sie tragen in naus.

Sie kumen wider. DISMAS *spricht:*

275 Nün secz dich! las uns drinckn und essen

Une unsers unmüecz gar vergessen!

Se hin, ich pring dir diesen drünck.

(Er drinckt.)

Wen wir habn gessn und druncken gnünck,

Den wollen wir dailen den schacz

280 Im stock, dem dot zw drücz und dracz.

Den schacz hab wir mit gueten eren.

Darfan hab wir gar lang zu zeren.

BARRABAS *drinckt auch, spricht:*

Ich rat, das wirs gelt dailen pald

Und uns mit heben aus dem wald,

285 Zern weit von hinen in ainr stat

Köstlich nach allem lüest und rat

Mit doppel spil und schönen frawen.

DISMAS, *der erst mörder, grewft und reipt sein pruest und spricht:*

O gsel, wie üebel thüet mir grawen

Une thüet mich gleich ein frost an stosen!

BARRABAS *rüempfft sich auch und spricht:*

290 Und mir auch; hab dir die franczosen!

Wie wirt mir so eng umb das hercz!

Mein ganczer leib pidmet vor schmercz.

Mich dünckt, es grewff mir nach dem leben.

DISMAS, *der erst mörder, spricht:*

Ich glaub, der schalck hab uns vergeben

295 Paide in prot und auch in wein,

Auf das im pleib der schacz allein.

Ich wil auf sten, gen hin und her.

Er stet auff, get lancksam, spricht:

Wie sint mein schenckel mir so schwer!

Kan nit mer auf den füesen sten!

300 Mir wil geleich die sel ausgen.

Er felt nider sam dot.

[1] *Tannenreiser.*

Marginal notes:

Barrabas suggests that they throw the body into the ditch with the hermit.

They return from this errand, pledge each other,

and agree to divide the treasure after their repast,

and to enjoy life.

Barrabas suggests that they find their pleasure in a far-off city

with games of chance and lovely women.

Dismas rubs his breast; he feels a frosty chill;

Barrabas is racked with pain

and fears death.

Dismas suspects that Jesmas has poisoned them.

He stands up and tries to walk,

but falls as dead.

BARRABAS, *der ander mörder, felt auch und spricht krencklich:*

Barrabas also falls,
and now knows the
truth of the her-
mit's saying that
there was death in
the stump.

Der alt schalck in dem graben rock
Hat noch war gsagt, das in dem stock
Der grewlich dot verporgen sey,
Seit darfon er und wir all drey
305 Absterben hie von dieser erd.

He must die full of
evil and bereft of
hope.

Erst ist mein gwissen hart peschwert,
Das ich doch vor pey all mein tagen
Veracht, hab in den wint geschlagen,
Wie gros üebel ich hab gethon.
310 Zw got ich nün kain hoffnung hon,
Far verzweifelt in nobis haus.[1]
Da schlecht das feür zum giebel aus,
Vol ungemachs und ewigs laids.
O we meins elenden abschaids!

He lies as dead.

Er ligt gestreckt sam dot.

The angel comes in

Der engel kümbt und peschlewst:

and warns Chris-
tians to avoid ava-
rice,

315 Ir lieben cristen all gemein,
Last euch dis spil ein warnung sein,
Das ir aus lieb des zeitling güet
Nit solch gros sünt und unrecht thüet!
Wan geicz ist ein wurczl aller süent,

the root of all evils
(C 334, 426, 904–5).

320 Wie den sant Paülus uns verküent,
Weil auch kurcz ist das menschlich leben.
Darfon wir müesen antwort geben
Dem richter am strengen gericht,
Auf das aus solchem üebel nicht
325 Uns ewige pein auf erwachs.
Vor dem uns got phüet, wünscht Hans Sachs.

III. SUBSIDIARY MATERIAL

That the old man in the *Pardoner's Tale* should seek death is
a feature not paralleled in any known analogue of the tale. It
may, with several other features of the mysterious figure, have
been suggested by the story of the Wandering Jew.[2] Some

---

[1] in nobis haus: a rather common expression meaning hell; probably, as Professor Archer Taylor suggests, a popular etymology for *in abyssus*.

[2] This was first suggested in Ten Brink's *History of English Literature*, II
(New York, 1893), 171. For a full discussion of the analogies see N. S. Bushnell,
"The Wandering Jew and the *Pardoner's Tale*," *SP*, XXVIII (1931), 450–60; for a
briefer treatment see Carleton Brown, pp. xxix–xxxi.

other details were almost certainly taken from the first elegy of Maximian.[1]

(From *Maximiani Elegiae ad Fidem Codicis Etonensis*, ed. M. Petschenig [Berlin, 1890], pp. 1–9.)

1 Aemula quid cessas finem properare senectus? cur et in hoc fesso corpore tarda uenis? Solve precor miseram tali de carcere vitam: mors est iam requies, uiuere poena mihi.	Old age lasts too long. I long for death.

. . . .

223 hinc est quod baculo, incumbens ruitura senectus assiduo pigram verbere pulsat humum.	I knock with my staff upon the ground,
225 et numerosa movens certo vestigia plausu talia rugato creditur ore loqui:	as if asking mother earth to have pity
'suscipe me, genetrix, nati miserere laborum: membra peto gremio fessa fouere tuo.'	and receive me.

Parallels to the tavern background of the *Pardoner's Tale* have been noted in *exempla* and moral treatises. The *exempla* are found in the *Liber de apibus* of Thomas of Cantimpré, a Belgian thirteenth-century Dominican.

(From the quotations in K. Petersen's monograph *On the Sources of the "Nonne Prestes Tale"* [1898], pp. 98–99.)[2]

In marchia Flandrie atque Brabantie villa populosissima est sita in qua dedicatio celebrata multos ad spectaculum traxerat et ad lusum. Inter quos quidam tibicen erat qui corizantes juvenes et puellas saltationibus et gesticulationibus suis ad carmina obscena et turpia concitabat [Distinctio Quinta, Exemplum 128]. *In a city of Flanders a religious ceremony is an occasion for dances and obscene songs.*

In Brabantiae partibus urbe lovanio civem vidimus generosum et bonum qui nocte sancta Parasceves ad matutinus surgens transibat ante cellarium in quo perditissimi adolescentes ad ludum tessarum sedentes blasphemiis et juramentis ad invicem contendebant. [Distinctio Quinta, Exemplum 103.] *In Louvain, on Good Friday, young men were playing dice and swearing.*

In his moral treatise entitled *Ayenbite of Inwit*, i.e., *Remorse of Conscience* (ed. Richard Morris ["E.E.T.S.: Original Series,"

---

[1] Professor G. L. Kittredge pointed to this source in *American Journal of Philology*, IX (1888), 84–85. For analogies in *Of Thre Messagers of Death* see M. P. Hamilton, "Death and Old Age in *The Pardoner's Tale*," *SP*, XXXVI (1939), 571–76.

[2] On the relation of those *exempla* to Chaucer's tale see, besides K. Petersen, Carleton Brown, pp. xvi–xviii.

Vol. XXIII (1866)]), a work completed in 1340, Dan Michel discusses "þe zennes þet byeþ ydo in þe taverne."[1]

The tavern is the devil's chapel where he performs his miracles.

þe tauerne ys þe scole of þe dyeule huere his deciples studieþ and his oჳene chapele þer huer ine deþ his seruese and þer huer he makeþ his miracles zuiche as behoueþ to þe dyeule. . . . . Ac þe dyeuel deþ al ayenward ine þe tauerne. Vor huanne þe glotoun geþ in þe tauerne ha geþ opriჳt; huanne he comþ a-yen, he ne heþ uot þet him moჳe sostyeni ne bere [pp. 56–57].

The same ideas are expressed in the anonymous fifteenth-century *Jacob's Well* (ed. Dr. Arthur Brandeis ["E.E.T.S.," Vol. CXV (1900)]).

The tavern is the well of gluttony and the devil's chapel

At þe tauerne often þe glotonye begynneth; for þe tauerne is welle of glotonye, for it may be clepyd þe develys scholehous and þe develys chapel, for þere his dycyples stodyen and syngyn bothe day and nyჳt, and þere þe deuyl doth meraclys to his seruauntys . . . . [p. 147].

The stories of Stilbon and Demetrius (C 603–20) are probably derived from John of Salisbury's *Polycraticus*, I, 5.

(From *Ioannis Sarisberiensis Policraticus*, ed. Clemens Webb [Oxford, 1909], I, 37–38.)

The Sparton Chilon at Corinth found the elders playing dice. He left, refusing to disgrace Sparta by an alliance with gamblers.

Chilon Lacedemonius iungendae societatis causa missus Corinthum duces et seniores populi ludentes inuenit in alea. Infecto itaque negotio reuersus est, dicens se nolle gloriam Sparthanorum, quorum uirtus constructo Bissantio clarescebat, hac maculare infamia ut dicerentur cum aleatoribus contraxisse societatem. Regi quoque Demetrio in obprobrium puerilis leuitatis tali aurei a rege Parthorum dati sunt.

[1] This, the following, and several other analogues to the passage on the taverns were quoted in my article "The Pardoner's Tavern," *JEGP*, XIII (1914), 553–65.

THE SHIPMAN'S TALE

By JOHN WEBSTER SPARGO

IN THE absence of an authentic source, the likeliest thing that can be said is that, if we had one, it would probably be an Old French fabliau very similar to the *Shipman's Tale*, of which the atmosphere is all French. The closest analogue, *Decameron* VIII, 1, is reprinted here simply because it is that, not because it is Chaucer's source. The reasons why this seems true to me are set forth in my monograph (pp. 11–15)[1] and need not detain us here. To me, Sercambi's Novella XIX has precisely the relationship to *Decameron* VIII, 1, that one would expect if the conventional view is accepted that Sercambi's entire collection is an imitation of Boccaccio's. The whole matter is so intricate, and positive evidence either way is so slight, that proof is out of the question; but it may be remarked that more than one scholar can be caught wandering in a vicious circle—that Chaucer knew Boccaccio's *Decameron* because the *Shipman's Tale* resembles *Decameron* VIII, 1, and that Chaucer based his *Shipman's Tale* on *Decameron* VIII, 1, because he knew the *Decameron*. Until such vicious circlers can produce one single piece of reasonably trustworthy evidence in support of either of these main assertions, one is entitled to question both. The same may be said of Sercambi's collection in connection with Chaucer, but Novella XIX is reprinted here so that the reader may do his own comparing.[2]

For the sake of conciseness, I reproduce my outline of the type of story named by Johannes Bolte *Das zurückgewonnene Minnelohn*, "The Lover's Gift Regained," mainly as it appears in the note on pages 54 ff. of my monograph, giving a reference to an important collection in which a variant appears, and addenda.

---

[1] *Chaucer's Shipman's Tale; the Lover's Gift Regained* ("Folklore Fellows' Communications," No. 91 [Helsinki, 1930]), referred to hereafter as "FFC 91."

[2] See Robert A. Pratt, "Chaucer's *Shipman's Tale* and Sercambi," *MLN*, LV (1940), 142–45.

THE LOVER'S GIFT REGAINED

A. The Broken or Removed Article

The lover breaks or removes an article of household equipment and convinces the husband that for this reason the wife has confiscated or held in pledge the gift which he had really given to her.

B. Horse and Wagon as Gift

The lover regains his gift of a horse and wagon by convincing the husband that his wife has confiscated them because he had brought a load of firewood of uneven quality.

C. Borrowing from the Husband and Returning to the Wife

The lover borrows money from the husband with which to purchase the favor of the wife, later telling the husband that the money was returned to the wife during the absence of the husband.

D. Accidental Discovery of Identity

Ignorant of the identity of the husband, the lover tells him of his experiences with his wife. The husband persuades the lover to take him to the scene, where he compels his wife to return to the lover all but a small part of the money, the hire of a prostitute.

E. Piece of Cloth as Gift

The lover regains by a ruse and by thievery the borrowed piece of cloth which he has presented to his mistress.

F. Jewelry as Gift

The lover presents to the wife a valuable piece of jewelry, which he regains by pretending to the husband that he had left it as a pledge.

G. *Anser venalis;* Goose (or Animal) as Gift

The lover regains his gift by a ruse.[1]

[1] In general, see John Webster Spargo, FFC 91.

A. Çukasaptati, Nos. 34, 38 (*Das indische Papageienbuch*, ed. Richard Schmidt [München, 1913]); *Decameron* VIII, 2; FFC 91, pp. 29–34. Add Wesselski's notes in *Archiv orientální*, II (1930), 504 f.

B. L. Erk and F. M. Böhme, *Deutscher Liederhort* (Leipzig, 1893–94), I, 445; FFC 91, pp. 34–37. Add Wesselski, as above, pp. 503 f.; R. Batka in *Die Musik*, XVI (1905), 196 f.; Hoffmann von Fallersleben in Mone's *Anzeiger für Kunde der teutschen Vorzeit*, Vol. II (1833), cols. 33 f.; "The Proud Pedlar" (*Roxburgh Ballads*, III, 656) in *Merry Songs and Ballads prior to the Year 1800*, ed. J. S. Farmer (privately printed, 1897), I, 247 ff.; D. Bax, "Uit de geschiedenis van het Volkslied: Een Boerman hadde een dommen Sin," *Nederlandsch Tijdschrift voor Volkskunde*, XL (1935–36), 10–25.

C. *Decameron* VIII, 1; Chaucer's *Shipman's Tale;* FFC 91, *passim.* Add these imitations of *Decameron* VIII, 1, or VIII, 2: George Whetstone, *An Heptameron of Civill Discourses* (London, 1583), First Day; M.C.-D.F. [=Fumichon?], *Les Hochets d'un sexagénaire* (2 vols.; Paris, 1819), reprinted as *Les Hochets d'un sexagénaire, ou souvenirs d'anecdotes galantes* (2 vols.; Paris: A. Bauche, 1821), Vol. II: *Le Curé de Varlongne.*

D. Karl Euling, *Studien über Heinrich Kaufringer* (Breslau, 1900), pp. 65–69. ["Germanistische Abhandlungen," Vol. XVIII]; FFC 91, pp. 37–39. Add Ragueneau de la Chainaye, *La Chronique indiscrète* (not seen; cited by Fernand Mitton, *Les Femmes et l'adultère de l'antiquité à nos jous* [Paris, 1911], p. 178); *The Deceyte of*

DECAMERON VIII, 1

(*Il Decamerone di Messer Giovanni Boccaccio, riscontrato.... da Pietro Fanfani.* 12ª *impressione....* [Firenze: Felice Le Monnier (1926)], II, 191–93.)

[The introductory paragraph, which is not concerned with the plot of this story, is omitted.]

Fu adunque già in Melano un Tedesco al soldo, il cui nome fu Gulfardo, pro' della persona, et assai leale a coloro ne' cui servigj si mettea, il che rade volte suole de' Tedeschi avvenire: e per ciò che egli era nelle prestanze de' denari che fatte gli erano lealissimo renditore, assai mercatanti avrebbe trovati che per piccolo utile ogni quantità di denari gli avrebber prestata. Pose costui, in Melan dimorando, l'amor suo in una donna assai bella, chiamata madonna Ambruogia, moglie d'un ricco mercatante, che aveva nome Guasparruol Cagastraccio, il quale era assai suo conoscente et amico: et amandola assai discretamente, senza avvedersene il marito nè altri, le mandò un giorno a parlare, pregandola che le dovesse piacere d'esergli del suo amor cortese, e che egli era dalla sua parte presto a dover far ciò che ella gli comandasse. La donna, dopo molte novelle, venne a questa conclusione, che ella era presta di far ciò che Gulfardo volesse, dove due cose ne dovesser seguire: l'una, che questo non dovesse mai per lui esser manifestato ad alcuna persona: l'altra, che, con ciò fosse cosa che ella avesse per alcuna sua cosa bisogno di fiorini du-

[marginal notes:]
In Milan a German soldier named Gulfardo

falls in love with Madonna Ambruogia, wife of Guasparruol Cagastraccio, a rich merchant.

He woos her.

She demands two hundred florins.

Women [London? 1560?]—see *Short Title Catalogue*, Nos. 6451 f.—ed. F. Brie in *Archiv für das Studium der neueren Sprachen und Litteraturen*, CLVI (1929), 44–47.

　　E. *Novelle di Giraldo Giraldi*, ed. D. G. Cioni (Amsterdam, 1796), pp. 6 ff. (Professor Walter L. Bullock refers me here to Giovanni da Prato's *Paradiso degli Alberti*, in *Scelta di curiosità di letteratura italiana*, Nos. 86–88). FFC 91, pp. 48 f. Add *Recueil des plaisants et facétieuses nouvelles de plusieurs auteurs, reveues & corrigees de nouveau. Avec plusieurs autres nouvelles non par cy devant imprimées* (Anvers: Gerard Seelman, 1555), pp. 103 ff., Nouvelle XVI: "D'un Escolier qui donna sa robbe à une ieune apothicaresse d'Orleans, pour iouyr de son amytié, & comment il eut sa robbe"; *Facecieux devis et plaisans contes par le Sʳ de Moulinet, Comédien* ([Paris], 1612), reprinted in *Collection de facéties, raretés et curiosités littéraires ... publiée par les soins de trois bibliophiles* (Paris: Techener, 1829; an alternative title is *Les Joyeusetez faceties et folastres imaginations de Caresme Prenant, Gauthier Garguille ...*), p. 30: "Comme un gentilhomme r'eut dix escus qu'une servante d'hostellerie avoit exigé de luy pour coucher avec elle"; Le Seigneur de La Motte Roulant, *Les facetieux deviz des cent et six nouvelles nouvelles* (Paris: I. Longis et I. Réal, 1550), Nouvelle XVI: "D'un ieune escollier qui donna sa robbe à une apoticaresse d'Orleans, pour avoir son amitié." Add Wesselski, as above, p. 504.

　　F. Heinrich Bebel's *Facetiæ*, trans. A. Wesselski (München and Leipzig,

gento d'oro, voleva che egli, che ricco uomo era, gliele donasse, et
appresso sempre sarebbe al suo servigio. Gulfardo, udendo la'ngordigia
di costei, sdegnato per la viltà di lei, la quale egli credeva che fosse
una valente donna, quasi in odio trasmutò il fervente amore, e pensò
di doverla beffare, e mandolle dicendo che molto volentieri e quello
et ogn'altra cosa, che egli potesse, che le piacesse; e per ciò mandasse-
gli pure a dire quando ella volesse che egli andasse a lei, chè egli
gliele porterebbe, nè che mai di questa cosa alcun sentirebbe, se
non un suo compagno di cui egli si fidava molto, e che sempre in sua
compagnía andava in ciò che faceva. La donna, anzi cattiva femina,
udendo questo, fu contenta, e mandògli dicendo che Guasparruolo
suo marito doveva ivi a poche dì per sue bisogne andare infino a
Genova, et allora ella gliele farebbe assapere, e manderebbe per lui.
Gulfardo, quando tempo gli parve, se n'andò a Guasparruolo e sì gli
disse: Io son per fare un mio fatto, per lo quale mi bisognano fiorini
dugento d'oro, li quali io voglio che tu mi presti con quello utile che
tu mi suogli prestare degli altri. Guasparruolo disse che volentieri, e
di presente gli annoverò i denari. Ivi a pochi giorni Guasparruolo
andò a Genova, come la donna aveva detto: per la qual cosa la donna
mandò a Gulfardo che a lei dovesse venire e recare li dugento fiorin
d'oro. Gulfardo, preso il compagno suo, se n'andò a casa della donna,
e trovatala che l'aspettava, la prima cosa che fece, le mise in mano
questi dugento fiorin d'oro, veggente il suo compagno, e sì le disse:

1907), Vol. I, Book iii, No. 49, with notes in II, 116; J. Frey's *Gartengesellschaft*,
ed. Johannes Bolte (Tübingen, 1896), pp. 90–92; FFC 91, pp. 42–44.

G. *Pogii Fiorentini facetiarum libellus unicus* (London, 1798), I, 76–78, II, 65–
67; FFC 91, pp. 39–42. Add F. H. von der Hagen, *Gesammtabenteuer* (Stuttgart
and Tübingen, 1850), Vol. II, No. XXI, pp. 1–18, "Das Häselein," and cf. No.
XXII, pp. 19–35, "Der Sperber"; *Roxburgh Ballads*, ed. J. Woodfall Ebsworth
(Hertford, 1896 [Ballad Society]), Vol. VIII, Part II, pp. 551 f., "The Fair Maid
of the West; who mortgaged her maidenhead for a high-crown'd hat" (*ca.* 1668
and 1772); and A. Wesselski, as above, p. 504, who cites among others Sacchetti's
Novella No. 231.

Add also these, which do not fall into any one of the subtypes: *Recueil des
plaisantes et facétieuses nouvelles* ... (Anvers, 1555), pp. 119 ff., Nouvelle XXII:
"De la subtilité d'un gentil homme de Bourgongne, qui avoit baille dix escus a
une chambriere d'hostellerie, pour coucher avecques elle: & comment apres son
faict, il les recouvra ..."; Dennis Dominique Cardonne, *A Miscellany of Eastern
Learning. Translated* .... (London, 1771), II, 85–91: "The Singular Stratagem
of a Woman"; *A Hundred Mery Tales* (*ca.* 1525?), ed. W. C. Hazlitt ("Shakespeare
Jest-Books," Vol. I [London, 1864]), No. LXXIV, pp. 102 f.: "Of the husbande
that cryed ble under the bed" (fragment); *The Iests of George Peele*, ed. W. C.
Hazlitt ("Shakespeare Jest-Books," Vol. II [London, 1864]), pp. 291–93: "How
George gulled a Punke, otherwise called a Croshabell."

Madonna, tenete queste denari, e daretegli a vostro marito quando ^{with request to give it to her husband.} serà tornato. La donna gli prese, e non s'avvide perchè Gulfardo ^{She thinks that he only wants to deceive his companion,} dicesse così; ma si credétte che egli il facesse, acciò che'l compagno suo non s'accorgesse che egli a lei per via di prezzo gli desse. Per che ella disse: Io il farò volentieri, ma io voglio veder quanti sono: e versatigli ^{counts the florins,} sopra una tavola e trovatigli esser dugento, seco forte contenta, gli ripose e tornò a Gulfardo, e lui nella sua camera menato, non sola- ^{and grants him her favors.} mente quella notte, ma molte altre, avanti che'l marito tornasse da Genova, della sua persona gli sodisfece. Tornato Guasparruolo da ^{As soon as Guasparruolo returns,} Genova, di presente Gulfardo, avendo appostato che insieme colla ^{Gulfardo goes to the house of the couple} moglie era, se n'andò a lui, et in presenza di lei disse: Guasparruolo, ^{and tells Guasparruolo that in his} i denari, cioè li dugento fiorin d'oro che l'altrier mi prestati, non m'eb- ^{absence he has returned the 200 florins to his wife.} ber luogo, per ciò che io non pote' fornir la bisogna per la quale gli presi; e per ciò io gli recai qui di presente alla donna tua, e sì gliele diedi; e per ciò dannerai la mia ragione. Guasparruolo, vòlto alla moglie, la domandò se avuti gli avea. Ella, che quivi vedeva il testi- ^{As the witness is there, she cannot} monio, nol seppe negare, ma disse: Maisì che io gli ebbi, nè me n'era ^{deny that she received the money;} ancora ricordata di dirloti. Disse allora Guasparruolo: Gulfardo, io son contento: andatevi pur con Dio, che io acconcerò bene la vostra ragione. Gulfardo partitosi, e la donna rimasa scornata, diede al ^{she hands it to her husband.} marito il disonesto prezzo della sua cattività: e così il sagace amante senza costo godè della sua avara donna.

SERCAMBI'S *NOVELLA DE AVARITIA ET LUZURIA*

(From the manuscript [Trivulziano, No. 193] of the *Novelle* of Giovanni Sercambi.)[1]

⟨fol. 53^v⟩ Charissime[2] donne e vo' homini desiderosi di udire alcuna volta l'inganni che si fanno alle donne che per denari vituperano e loro mariti e parenti, dicho che[3] in nella cipta di Perugia, là u' ^{At Perugia lived a banker named} stanotte siamo dimorati, fu um banchieri e merchadante nomato ^{Pierosso} Pierosso, homo servente di denari e maximamente a soldati forestieri, da' quali avea molto guadangno.[4] Avendo il ditto Pierosso una ^{with his young wife,} mogle jovana di xxiiij anni, bella e balda, nomata madonna Soffia; e ^{Sofia, a tricky one prone to deceive her husband for cash.} molte volte avendo fatto fallo al suo marito, più tosto per denari che per amore ad altri portasse, per la qual cosa in alcuno luogo stretto

---

[1] For the manuscript and the editorial principles of the present text, transcribed and prepared by Robert A. Pratt, see above, pp. 33–36. This *novella* has been printed by Renier, *Novelle inedite di Giovanni Sercambi* (Turin, 1889), pp. 81–84; see above, p. 45.

[2] Oharissime *MS.*   [3] di che che *MS, with the second* che *crossed out.*

[4] At this point the manuscript has a marginal note: "di Peirosso e madonna Suffia in Perugia."

Hearing of this, a German soldier named Bernardo sent a go-between to solicit her favors.

fu di lei parlato. E infra l'altre volte che di lei si dicesse si fu um gorno presso a uno carnelevale dove era uno messer Bernardo, tedescho, capo di xxv bacinetti e soldato in Perugia; lo qual messer Bernardo, essendo jovano e cognoscendo madonna Soffia di Pierosso, s'innamorò di lei, pensando se costei con altri à fatto fallo, agevolmente doverne avere diletto. E datosi a sentire e vedere in che modo potrà il suo pensieri mettere in efetto, per una messetta mandò, dicendo il suo volere. La messetta, ch'era già stata altre volte per sì fatte cose a madonna Soffia, li narrò la intensione di messer Bernardo. Madonna Soffia, sentendo quello che la massetta li avea ditto, non avendo di

She replied that the rate was 200 florins, and the time next Sunday, when her husband would be at Ancona on business.

lei vergogna, disse, "Se messer Bernardo mi vuol dare fiorini cc, io sono contenta; e in caso che stia contento, vo' che li dichi che domenicha che serà la domenicha di carnelevale, doppo desnare, che 'l mio marito sarà ito ad Ancona per mercantia, vengna a me e portimi fiorini cc; e io serò contenta che stia mecho lo dì e lla notte seguente; e poi lo lunedì mattina si parta." La messetta, udendo quello mona la puttana, o vuoi dire Soffia, avea ditto, si partiò e messer Bernardo

Bernardo thought she overvalued herself and planned a trick at her expense.

andò e tutta l'anbasciata li disse. Messer Bernardo disse, "Troppo de avere hodorifera la sua giuntana, che sare vasto fusse moscato volerne tanti fiorini." E fra sè pensò um bel modo, e disse alla mes-

He sent word that he would bring a servant along, just to keep the gossips' tongues quiet;

setta, "Va e die a madonna Soffia che io sono contento d'aregarli fiorini cc e star lo dì e lla notte secho; ma perchè altri non si pensi di noi male, dille che io merrò meco uno famiglo, e sensa a lui dire niente, lo mandrò a ffare alcuna imbasciata; e per questo modo persona non si potrà esser acorta che io a liei sia venuto." La me ⟨fol. 54ʳ⟩ sseta disse, "Bene avete ordinato." E tornò alla donna e tutto li disse. La donna, contenta, disse che bene avea fatto, e messosi mano a borsa le diè uno fiorino. E messer Bernardo mandò a dire che tutto era in

then, he borrowed 200 florins from Pierosso,

punto e che lui s'aparechi il gorno ad andare. Messer Bernardo, avendo ordita la tela e bizognandola tessere, pensò chiedere in presto a Pierosso,[1] marito di madonna Soffia, fiorini cc; e andato a lui disse, "O Pierosso, io ò ale mani una mercantia al mio animo desiderosa, la quale m'è promessa per fiorini cc; e sensa quella al presente stare non posso a questo soldo; e però io ti pregho mi debbi servire di fiorini cc; e come arò le miei prime paghe, te li rendrò con quello merito vorrii." Disse Pierosso, "Volentieri"; e aperta una cassa, li presto fiorini cc, dicendo, "A me conviene andare ad Ancona per certe

receiving permission to return them to Sofia during Pierosso's absence.

merchantie. Come avete le paghe, serbatemi li denari." Messer Bernardo disse, "Se quello che m'è promesso inanti non facesse, volete che alla donna vostra questi fiorini renda?" Pierosso disse,

---

[1] Here were written and then crossed out the following words which appear later in the *novella* (MS): "presente madonna Soffia, voi ṣapete che mi prestaste."

"Sì, presti questi denari." E Pierosso messosi in punto per andare ad Ancona, e partisi di Perugia l'altro dì. Messer Bernardo sta allegro. Madonna Soffia aspetta doppia piumata, e per fiorini cc, apresso la sua guntana rienpiuta, sta molto contenta del partimento di Pierosso. Venuto la domenicha di carnolovare, madonna Soffia, invitata dalla vicinansa ali orti, non volea[1] andare, ella rispondendo, "Pierosso mio è ito ad Ancona e non so come si stia; io non voglo oggi uscire di casa, ma lo dì di carnolovare, se altro non sento, verrò." Le vicine, acconciosi, se ne vanno ali orti a ghodere. Madonna Soffia sta aspettare. Messer Bernardo, preso un suo stretto famiglo, avendolo di tutto il suo pensieri informato, secho[2] lo menò a casa di madonna Soffia, e saglie in sala dove madonna Soffia aspettava. Messer Bernardo fingendosi disse, "Il vostro marito mi presto fiorini cc, li quali, non avendoli spesi, ve lli rendo; che, quando Pierosso è ttornato, le li date"; e misseli in sulla taula. Lo famiglo, informato, disse, "Messer, sapete che a casa dovete esser aspettato, e non essendovi,[3] nimo non sapea niente di voi." Or disse messer Bernardo, "Ben ài ditto; e va, e di' a chi viene che io verrò tanto che questi denari abia anomerati." Lo fante subito si partio. Messer Bernardo disse come ci venne fatto che il fante si ricordoe di quello avea a fare. Madonna Soffia disse, "Per certo ongni cosa ci vien fatto. Prima il mio marito esser fuori, apresso noi[4] adutti li fiorini cc, e 'n contrada non esser persona che veduto ci[5] abbia. E però noi possiamo stare in buono agio oggi ⟨fol. 54ᵛ⟩ e stanotte." Messer Bernardo disse, "Voi dite il vero." E inomerati li denari, messer Bernardo prese madonna Soffia, e bacandola disse che le piacesse contentarlo di quello che più volte à diziato.... La mattina coronata di vittoria si partio. E madonna Soffia, allegra che la sua guintana avea portato l'onore sopra tutte le guintane di Perugia, e ralegrandosi de' fiorini auti, e molte volte innomeratoli; e passato alquanti gorni della quaresima, Pierosso tornò d'Ancona. Messer Bernardo, ciò sentendo, subito prese il suo secreto famiglo e a casa di Pierosso se n'andò e fatto richidere Pierosso. Sente che messer Bernardo lo richiede, disse che venisse su. Messer Bernardo, che avea il suo famiglo fatto comprare alquante anguille grosse e alcune tinche de⟨l⟩ lagho di Perugia, e montato in sala, subito Pierosso dicendoli, presente madonna Soffia,

Marginal notes:

Come Sunday, with Pierosso gone, Sofia stays at home, expecting Bernardo,

who comes with a manservant

in whose presence he says: "Your husband lent me 200 florins, which I now return to you."

The servant departed,

and Sofia having earned the 200 florins,

Bernardo went his way.

When Pierosso had returned,

Bernardo called on him,

---

¹ volea *MS;* se volea andare, ella rispondea *emend. R.*

² sendo *MS;* seco *emend. R.*

³ non rispon essendovi entro in casa *MS, with* rispon *and* entro in casa *crossed out.*

⁴ voi *emend R.*   ⁵ v' *emend. R.*

and said in the wife's presence that the money had been returned to her.

"Voi sapete che mi prestaste fiorini cc, quando vi partiste, per alcuno mio[1] bizongno, e io, quello non potendo spendere, li adussi a madonna Soffia, vostra donna, come mi diceste, presente questo mio famiglio; e perchè a me fu sommo servigo, posto che io quelli non spendesse, vo' che voi con madonna Soffia abiate queste anguille e queste tinche e che lle ghodate per mio amore, non per rispetto del servigio, ma per domestichessa." Pierosso, che ode che alla mogle à renduto li fiorini cc, non avendoli nulla ditto, le disse, "O tu non me n'ài ditto nulla." Lo famiglio astuto disse Pierosso, "In mia presensia messer

When the man-servant confirmed this, Sofia had to admit it.

Bernardo lel' diè." La donna subito comprese la malisia di messer Bernardo e disse, "Io pensava dirtelo a più agio, ma poi che messer Bernardo dice che a me li rendeo elli dice vero; ben credea che fussero stati d'altra mercantia che di presto, e arei voluto che alla ragone della mercantia tu li avessi messi." Pierosso disse, "Io lel' prestai il gorno che di qui mi partì." Messer Bernardo: "Voi dite vero, e per certo il servigo fue a me grande, e però sempre mi vi tengo obligato." La donna come baldansosa disse, "Oimè, non vi tenete obligato, già sapete che io sono una volta mogle di Pierosso, e così dovete essere obligato a me come a lui." Messer Bernardo, che di lei avea avuto quello volea, cognoscendola cattiva, disse, "Madonna, in nelle nostre con ⟨fol. 55ʳ⟩ trade li mariti portano le brachi e a lloro si de reverensia, et io vo' oservare la leggie del mio paese, però che a Pierosso de' denari prestati li som senpre obligato e non a voi." Pierosso, che ode sì bel parlare, dice alla donna, "Messer Bernardo à ditto quello che si conviene";[2] e preso l'anguille e lle tinche, messer Bernardo si partio e

Thus tricked she resolved not to be caught again.

Pierosso colla mogle rimane. Madonna Soffia, vedendosi così esser beffata, pensò di non cadere in tal fallo mai con persona che per quel modo riabia quello che dato l'avesse; e così oservò poi.

[1] After *alcuno*, at the end of a line, *m* was written and crossed out (MS).

[2] contiene *emend. R.*

THE PRIORESS'S TALE

By CARLETON BROWN

INTRODUCTION

THE following is a complete list of the known texts of the miracle which forms the theme of the *Prioress's Tale*, classified according to the three main groups into which they arrange themselves. The versions of each group are listed, so far as possible, in chronological order, although this order is based in most cases merely upon the date of the extant manuscript, which must, of course, be distinguished from the date of composition.

GROUP A

1. Bibl. Publ. de Vendôme MS 185, ed. H. Isnard, *Bulletin de la Soc. archéol. scientifique et littéraire du Vendomois*, XXVI (1887), 194–96; reprinted in my *Study of the Miracle of Our Lady Told by Chaucer's Prioress* ("Chaucer Society Publications: Second Series," No. 45 [London, 1910]), pp. 1–2.
2. Bibliothèque nationale MS Lat. 18134, fol. 142ᵛ; printed in my *Study*, pp. 3–4.
3. Gautier de Coincy, *Les Miracles de la Sainte Vierge*, ed. M. l'Abbé Poquet (Paris, 1857), cols. 555–72; printed from MS Harley 4401 in *Originals and Analogues*, pp. 251 ff.
4. Cæsarius of Heisterbach, *Libri VIII Miraculorum*, ed. A. Meister, *Römische Quartalschrift*, XIII Supplementheft (Rom, 1901), pp. 189–91; reprinted in my *Study*, pp. 5–6.
5. John of Garland, *Miracula Beate Virginis*, Royal MS 8. C.IV, fol. 21, col. 1; printed in my *Study*, p. 7.[1]
6. Thomas Cantimpré, *Bonum universale de Apibus*, Lib. ii. cap. xxix. § 13, ed. G. Colvener (Douay, 1605), p. 289; reprinted in my *Study*, p. 8.
7. S. Petrus Celestinus Papa V, *De miraculis Beatæ Mariæ Virginis*, ed. M. de la Bigne, *Max. Bibl. veterum Patrum et Antiq. Script. ecclesiast.* (Lugduni, 1677), XXV, 813–17; reprinted in my *Study*, p. 9. This text is based on No. 1.
8. B. M. Egerton MS 1117, fol. 176ᵛ; printed in my *Study*, pp. 9–10.
9. Mariu Jartegnir, Pergaments Codex, 11, Royal Library Stockholm, ed.

---

[1] Five manuscripts of the *Canterbury Tales* (Hengwrt, Christ Ch., Camb. Dd.4.24, Hatton Donat 1, and Laud 600) insert the text of John of Garland as a gloss on the *Prioress's Tale* (see Manly and Rickert, *Text of the Canterbury Tales* [Chicago, 1940], III, 518).

C. R. Unger, *Mariu Saga* (Christiania, 1871), p. 779; reprinted in my *Study*, pp. 10–11.

10. Thomas Bromyard, *Summa predicantium*, sub voce "Maria," iij, text reprinted by Woodburn O. Ross, *MLN*, L (1935), 307.

11. Sidney Sussex College MS 95, Lib. II, cap. 83, printed in my *Study*, pp. 12–16.

12. Pelbart of Themeswar, *Stellarium corone Beate Virginis*, Lib. XII, pars ultima, cap. 1, ed. Hagenaw (1501); reprinted in my *Study*, pp. 17–18.

13. Hague Kon. Bibl. MS X, 64 (new no. 70, II, 42), fol. 48c; printed in my *Study*, p. 19.

Group A presents what is apparently the earlier form of the legend, which must have been in existence well before the year 1200. The story as it stands in Group A may be outlined as follows.

1. The boy sings the *responsorium* "Gaude Maria"[1] as he passes daily along a street in which Jews dwell, and thereby provokes their resentment.

2. He is slain (either by a single Jew or by a group of them in conspiracy), and his body is buried under the earth in the Jew's house (A 2, 3, 5, 7, 13), in his garden (A 11), in a trench beside his door (A 1), in a stable under the manure (A 4, 8), in a cemetery (A 6), or "sub modio absconsus" (A 12).

3. The boy's mother, in her search for him, passing by the Jew's door, hears the voice of her child and, with the assistance of friends and a crowd of citizens, forces an entrance.

---

[1] Two versions of Group A (5 and 10) refer to the song vaguely as a "Cantilena de beata virgine." The only version which names another song instead of "Gaude Maria" is that by Caesarius (A 4), who first states that the boy sang "Salve regina" *or* the sequence "Ave praeclara," then a little later that he sang "Salve regina" and "Ave Maria," and still later, "Salve regina" *with* the "Ave praeclara." Finally, Caesarius in the latter part of the tale returns to "Salve regina" and "Ave Maria." These vacillations necessarily impair the authority of his narrative in this respect. Besides this overwhelming agreement among the versions of both Groups A and B, it will be noted that the text of the "Gaude Maria," with the line "Erubescat Iudaeus infelix," etc., was specially suited to irritate Jewish auditors:

> "Gaude, Maria virgo, cunctas hereses sola interemisti;
> Quæ Gabrielis archangeli dictis credidisti.
> Dum Virgo Deum et hominem genuisti,
> Et post partum Virgo inviolata permansisti.

Versus: Gabrielem archangelum scimus divinitus te esse affatum;
> Uterum tuum de Spiritu Sancto credimus imprægnatum;
> Erubescat Judæus infelix, qui dicit Christum Joseph semine
> esse natum."

4. The boy is dug up from the earth alive and unharmed.

5. In consequence of this miracle, the Jew (or Jews), according to most versions, is converted. According to others, however, conviction and punishment follow.

GROUP B

1. B.M. Add. MS 32248, fol. 5ᵛ; printed in my *Study*, pp. 20–21.
2. B.M. Add. MS 16589, fol. 87ᵛ, col. 1; printed in my *Study*, p. 22.
3. B.M. Add. MS 18929, fol. 79ᵛ, col. 1; printed in my *Study*, p. 23.
4. Breslau Königliche und Universitäts Bibl. MS I. F.115, ed. Joseph Klapper, *Erzählungen des Mittelalters* ("Wort und Brauch," Heft 12, [Breslau 1914]), p. 301. Agrees verbally with No. 3.
5. Johannes Herolt, *De miraculis Beate Virginis* (an appendix to his *Promptuarium exemplorum*), No. LXVI, reprinted from ed. of 1492 in *PMLA*, XXI (1906), 492.
6. B.M. Add. MS 33956, fol. 73, col. 2; printed in my *Study*, pp. 24–25.
7. *Legender om Jomfru Maria og Hendes Jertegn, Pergaments Cod. 11, Royal Library, Stockholm*, ed. C. R. Unger, *Mariu Saga* (Christiania, 1871), p. 203; printed in my *Study*, pp. 25–28.
8. B.M. Add. MS 27336, fol. 78ᵛ (cf. J. A. Herbert, *Cat. of Romances in Brit. Mus.*, III, 673). This is a collection of religious tales in Latin prose, written in northern Italy in the early fifteenth century—evidently compiled by a Franciscan; printed by Woodburn O. Ross, *MLN*, LII (1936), 24.
9. Jean Mielot, *Miracles de Nostre Dame*, ed. George F. Warner (Roxburghe Club, 1885), pp. 14–15; reprinted in my *Study*, pp. 29–31.
10. Ægidius Aurifaber, *Speculum exemplorum* (Coloniæ, 1485), Dist. octava, cap. lix; reprinted in my *Study*, pp. 31–33.

Group B changes the form of the story in Group A, as outlined above, by introducing several important modifications:

1. The boy is made a chorister and sings his song in the regular services of the church.

2. The boy's mother drops out of the story.

3. The guilty Jew (or Jews) after the murder hears the boy singing as before (either from the spot where he is buried or from his place in the choir, to which the Blessed Virgin has restored him).

4. The Jew (or Jews) thereupon confess the crime before the Christians have learned of it and in most versions are converted and baptized.

Inasmuch as such a series of important changes cannot be coincidental, it is clear that in Group B we have a deliberate adaptation of the earlier story.

GROUP C

 1. Corpus Christi College, Oxford, MS 32, fol. 92
 2. Friar William Herebart, Phillipps MS 8336, fol. 205ᵛ
 3. B.M. Add. MS 11579, fol. 5ᵛ
 4. B.M. Roy. MS 12.E.I, fol. 170
 5. Vernon version (Bodleian MS 3938)
 6. Chaucer's *Prioress's Tale*
 7. Sidney Sussex College MS 95, Lib. II, cap. 84
 8. Sidney Sussex College MS 95, Lib. II, cap. 87
 9. Alphonsus a Spina, *Fortalicium fidei* (Basil, *ca.* 1475)
10. Trinity College, Cambridge, MS O.9.38, fol. 37

The versions of Group C, though uninfluenced by the modifications of the story introduced in Group B, show striking agreement in certain divergences from the narrative of Group A. The following points may be noted as the special characteristics of Group C.

1. The song which the boy sings through Jewry is the antiphon "Alma redemptoris mater" according to seven versions (C 1, 2, 5, 6, 8, 9, 10), and in only one (C 7) the *responsorium* "Gaude Maria," as in nearly all the texts of Group A and Group B. The antiphon "Ave regina," mentioned in C 3, and the "Sancta Maria," in C 4, may be dismissed as mere variants.

2. The body of the murdered boy is thrown into a "jakes" ("cloaca"). This is explicitly stated in every version of this group except C 3 (which is silent on this point).

3. The miracle does not end, as in Group A, with the recovery of the boy's body, but an elaborate funeral scene follows, during which the corpse continues to sing, for in Group C, unlike the others, the story ends tragically. C 4 and 10, which differ in this respect from the other C versions, will be considered later in discussing the development of the versions within the C group.

There are a few cases in which it is not easy to decide how a given text should be classified. Some of the briefer versions lack the details needed to establish their definite relationship. For example, C 3 breaks off with the singing during the funeral service, though a careful comparison with the text of C 7 makes it clear, I think, that in C 3 also the child's restoration was not permanent. Again, some versions show a confusion of elements from different groups. A specially notable example of this is the text in Bromyard's *Summa prædicantium* (A 10) to which Mr. Woodburn Ross has recently called attention.[1] In this the victim is neither a young scholar nor a choirboy but apparently a mature clerk, for he did not make his home in the town where he is slain ("Clericus in villa quadam moram traxisse"). Under these circumstances we should not expect his mother to appear on the scene. The body was thrown into a jakes, and in this betrays unmistakably a borrowing from the Group C tradition. At the same time the author wholly discards the tragic ending and moralizes instead upon the Virgin's protecting care. Accordingly, this story seems to belong in Group A rather than in Group C. Bromyard's *exemplum*, in a word, presents a distorted form of the legend, comparable in this respect to the story of the monk who offended a Jewish apothecary by singing the "Gaude Maria" and was slain by him, but afterward was restored to life by the Virgin.[2] Such sporadic variants, though they testify to the influence of our legend, did not themselves exert any influence upon its development.

THE EARLIEST VERSION OF GROUP C

At the time my former *Study* was published the earliest known versions of Group C were two very brief Latin texts in manuscripts of the early fourteenth century. On the basis of the evidence then available I inferred that the parent-version of this group belonged "to the later decades of the thirteenth century" (p. 86). Recently, however, Dr. Albert C. Friend has discovered an earlier version belonging to Group C in a series of *Anecdota de rebus diversis*, incorporated as Art. 19 of MS 32 in the Library of Corpus Christi College, Oxford.[3] The importance of this newly discovered version makes it necessary to examine in some detail the evidence as to the date of its composition. Dr. Craster, Bodley's librarian, who kindly examined the manuscript at my request, gives it as his opinion that the handwriting of Art. 19 is of the mid-thirteenth century. The

---

[1] *MLN*, L (1935), 307.

[2] I printed the text of this miracle of the monk in my *Study*, p. 51, but did not consider it necessary to list it as an analogue to the *Prioress's Tale*.

[3] "Chaucer's Prioress' Tale: An Early Analogue," *PMLA*, LI (1936), 621-25.

date of the extant manuscript, however, does not necessarily determine the time at which this series of anecdotes was compiled. In regard to this the most trustworthy data are those which the text itself supplies through its references to persons and incidents.

Five of the anecdotes in Art. 19 (Nos. xx, xxi, xxii, xxxv, and xlii), the compiler states, he had by word of mouth ("ex relatu") from persons whose names he records. For Nos. xx and xxi the authority cited is "Magister Ricardus de Buleia," a person whom I am unable to identify. But No. xx is the story of an impoverished Oxford scholar and chaplain, with whom, apparently, Master Richard was personally acquainted, "tempore, scilicet, quo beatus Thomas Cant. futurus martir exulabat in partibus transmarinis" (i.e., November, 1164, to December, 1170). And "Magister Henricus Caluus," named as the authority for No. xxxv, tells us of a certain Ralph, Master of Arts at Oxford, "tempore quo ego ibi scolas frequentavi." This Master Ralph was "nepos" of Master Stephen Langton who *afterward* became Archbishop of Canterbury. The other two anecdotes afford more definite chronological data. Number xxii is headed "Ex Relatu Dom. Egidii Hereford' episcopi" and can therefore be dated before 1216, the year in which Bishop Giles died. And No. xlii, "Ex Relatu Will[i] de Verd' archid' Glouc'," must have been communicated *subsequent* to 1200, the year in which William de Verdun was appointed archdeacon. We are assured, then, that the author of this treatise was engaged in collecting his materials between 1200 and 1216.[1]

These limits are quite consistent with the general chronology of the anecdotes, for while incidents are related of St. Anselm, King Henry I, Theobold Count of Blois (*d.* 1151), and others earlier than the author's own time, it is noteworthy that no mention occurs of persons or events of later date. The mention in No. xxix of "Dni. Stephani Cant' arch' " gives us as the latest positively established date 1207, the year of Stephen Langton's consecration. The account of the generosity of the

---

[1] Mr. Friend (p. 622, n. 5) would date the collection "after the death of Philip Augustus (1223) who is mentioned on Fol. 97*b*," but in this anecdote related of "Philippus rex francie" there is nothing to indicate that he was no longer living.

Abbot of Oseney who in time of famine issued orders to distribute to the poor "quicquid erat panis in domo" (No. xli) probably relates to the famine of 1189, of which we have the following record in the annals of this abbey: "Facta est fames pervalida per Angliam, ita ut multi fame morerentur."[1] The conversation recorded in No. xxxiv between Thomas Carbonel, Abbot of Gloucester, and Alanus, Abbot of Tewksbury, must have taken place before 1202, when the latter died. And No. xxxiii names as the Abbot of Evesham Roger Norrensis, who was deposed from this office in 1213. For two of the anecdotes in this collection (Nos. xxv and xxvi) the authority cited is Walter Map, whose De nugis curialium, according to Dr. James, "may be placed in the years 1181 to 1192 or 1193."[2]

It is not possible to localize this collection of stories with certainty, though there are significant indications pointing to Gloucestershire. Three of the anecdotes (Nos. xxxi, xxxiii, and xlii) are located at Gloucester; one remembers also that Walter Map was parson of Westbury on Severn, in Gloucestershire, and that Hereford (cf. No. xxii) was in an adjoining county. These Gloucestershire allusions in the manuscript are further confirmed by our information concerning the history of the manuscript itself. For, as Mr. Friend has noted, this book was given to Corpus Christi College in 1619 by Henry Parry, whose library included many manuscripts from Llanthony Priory, which was situated in a suburb of Gloucester.[3]

Though the anecdotes for the most part are concerned with persons or occurrences in England, the story of the boy slain by the Jews is located at Carcassonne in the country of the Albigenses. There was a large community of Jews in Carcassonne at the beginning of the thirteenth century,[4] but it is singular that a knowledge of local affairs there should have found its way so directly to England, unless it was through the interest excited by the suppression of the Albigenses. In sup-

[1] Annales monastici ("Rolls Series," Vol. IV [London, 1864–69]), 41.

[2] De nug. cur., ed. M. R. James, Anecdota Oxoniensia, XIV (1914), xxvii.

[3] In this connection one may note also that C 10—the latest of the C versions—was written at Glastonbury, in Somerset, the county adjoining Gloucestershire on the south.

[4] See Thomas Bouges, Histoire ecclésiastique et civile de la ville de Carcassonne (Paris 1741), pp. 191 and 596 ff.

port of this explanation one notes that No. xxi relates an incident concerning "Symon de monte forti," i.e., the elder Simon de Montfort, Vicomte de Carcassonne (*d.* 1218), by whom the Albigenses were crushed.[1] It is altogether likely, therefore, that the text of our *Miracle* preserved in the Corpus Christi manuscript was composed in the very early years of the thirteenth century, perhaps about 1215.

THE RELATION OF GROUP C TO GROUP A

The establishment of such an early date for C 1 obliges us to re-examine the nature of the relationship which was assumed between Group C and Group A. Early versions belonging to Group A to which fairly definite dates can be assigned are the miracle collections of Gautier de Coincy (A 3) and Caesarius of Heisterbach (A 4), which were made, respectively, between 1214 and 1233 and between 1225 and 1237. But, as we now see, both these collections are actually antedated by C 1. In view of this fact, are we still justified in regarding Group A as the parent-group?

Both Caesarius and Gautier, as scholars have long recognized, gathered their material from earlier originals. Without repeating here the detailed comparison of the versions of Group A made in my former *Study* (pp. 62–74), I may set down some of the conclusions which were there reached. The texts of A 1 and A 2, though preserved in manuscripts slightly later than Gautier, are not dependent on him but may be regarded as somewhat condensed versions of the Latin original on which Gautier's narrative was based, which for convenience we may term "Ur-Gautier." Similarly A 6 and A 8, which in important details show special agreements with Caesarius, do not derive from him but from a common source which we may designate as "Ur-Caesarius." But on comparison even Ur-Gautier and Ur-Caesarius are seen to present variant forms of the tradition. Accordingly, the archetype of Group A must be referred to a period considerably earlier than any of the extant manuscripts—certainly well before 1200. From the point of view of chronol·gy, then, there is nothing impossible or

---

[1] Simon assumed the title of count in 1209, but in this manuscript, one notes, his name appears without the title—another evidence of early date.

even improbable in regarding Group C as having developed from the form of the legend represented in Group A.

And from the point of view of narrative development, this relationship between the two groups becomes practically certain. For in the case of miracles as with other narratives the natural development is from the simple to the more complex; and Group A, it is clear, gives the simpler type of story. When the child has been recovered by the searchers who hear his voice (or his song), no further marvels follow. In Group C, on the other hand, the body is borne with ceremony to the church where the funeral rites are celebrated, during which, to the amazement of everyone, the corpse continues the song in praise of the Virgin. As an expansion of the legend this is perfectly intelligible; but, if this funeral scene with the child's song on the bier had been a part of the original legend, it is remarkable that in both the A and B groups it should have dropped out completely.

THE TRAGIC ENDING IN GROUP C

In my former *Study* (pp. 87–95) I emphasized the striking resemblances between the form of the narrative which we find in Group C and the widespread story of Hugh of Lincoln, who was said to have been crucified by the Jews in 1255; and to the influence of this story I attributed the introduction of the tragic ending in Group C. This explanation, however, is now manifestly impossible since we have a version of Group C which antedates the Hugh of Lincoln affair by nearly half a century.

But though the martyrdom of little Hugh is eliminated, the tragic ending in Group C may well be a reflection of earlier stories of Jewish atrocities which were circulating in England. The first of these (and perhaps the model for the others) was that of St. William of Norwich, who is said to have been crucified in 1144. A long Latin history of this affair and the ensuing miracles, composed by Thomas of Monmouth, and preserved in a manuscript written somewhat before 1200, has been published in recent years.[1] Dr. James in his Introduction, after referring

---

[1] A. Jessopp and M. R. James, *Life and Miracles of St. William of Norwich by Thomas of Monmouth, from Cambridge Univ. MS 3037* (Cambridge, 1896).

to an instance of child murder by Jews in the fifth century reported by the church historian Socrates (but in no sense a case of ritual murder) continues: "The story of the child of Inmester comes to us from the fifth century. Between that date and the date of William of Norwich there seems to be a complete blank. There are no child-martyrs, and there is no trace of a belief in ritual murder. After the Norwich story we encounter a rapid succession of child martyrdoms, and the belief in ritual murder appears fully developed" (p. lxiv). The evidences for the martyrdom of William of Norwich need not be examined here. They are no more substantial or convincing than are the numerous miracles which followed. But there is no doubt of their effect in inflaming the imagination of twelfth-century England. Among the other similar atrocities listed by Dr. James, which were reported before the end of the century, it is sufficient to mention the torture and murder of the child Harald at Gloucester in 1168, of which we have a detailed account in the history and cartulary of St. Peter's Abbey.[1]

The legend of the boy slain by the Jews for singing songs in praise of the Virgin is, of course, to be distinguished from these tales of ritual murder. Yet in both types of story a Christian child is represented as suffering martyrdom at the hands of the Jews. And it seems altogether probable that it was through the influence of these stories of ritual murder that the funeral scene was added in Group C of our legend.

Thus in the *Life and Miracles of St. William of Norwich*[2] we read that the child's body "allatus est itaque . . . . cum maximo cleri plebisque tripudio, atque a uenerabili monachorum conuentu processionaliter susceptus, sedisque episcopalis ecclesia introductus, ante sancte crucis altare cum feretro reponitur" (pp. 50–51). Compare this with the statement, in C 7, for example, "Quod quidem corpus cum ingenti gaudio honorifice ad ecclesiam beate virginis allatum coram maius altare cum feretro deponitur." According to Group C, the Jews threw the slain child into a "jakes," and this was also the disposition made of the victim's body in the Anglo-French *Hugues de Lincoln*

---

[1] *Hist. et cartular. Monast. S. Petri Gloucest.*, ed. W. H. Hart ("Rolls Series" [London, 1863]), I, 20–21.

[2] Edited by A. Jessopp and M. R. James (Cambridge, 1896).

(as I pointed out in my *Study*, p. 92). Too much significance, however, should not be attached to this point of agreement. According to the story of William of Norwich (*Life*, pp. 23–24), the Jews proposed in that case also to throw the corpse into a jakes, but the plan was rejected by the wiser heads as unsafe. As I see it now, the occurrence of the "jakes" in Hugues de Lincoln and Group C of our legend is purely a narrative coincidence. Medieval customs being what they were, this detail might make its appearance in stories which had no direct connection.[1]

THE MARVELS ADDED IN LATER VERSIONS OF GROUP C

An examination of the later versions of Group C affords illustration of the general tendency to extend the marvels by adding further incidents. These additions, for the most part, were not connected with the discovery of the crime but with the subsequent funeral service. According to the majority of the C versions, the corpse continued to sing without intermission after the discovery of the body. Thus C 1 (and 8): "Nec cessauit uox illa admirabilis donec corpus sepeliretur," and C 2: "qui tamen a cantu non cessauit," and C 9: "nec aliquando cessabat de die nec de nocte a predicto cantu . . . . nec vnquam cessabat a cantu illo dulcissimo licet mortuus foret."

To be sure, the difficulty of singing after one's throat had been cut seems to have occurred even to the author of the very early Corpus version (C 1), for he offers the ingenious suggestion that it was either the boy himself who sang or an angel whom the Lord had deputed for the purpose. This alternative, however, was felt to be unsatisfactory, and another solution of the difficulty was adopted by some later narrators. According to C 5, 6, 9, and 10, the Virgin placed in the young martyr's mouth an object of some sort—a lily inscribed in letters of gold, "Alma redemptoris mater" in C 5, a "greyn" laid upon the tongue in the *Prioress's Tale* (C 6), a gem ("lapidem preci-

---

[1] Walter Map records another instance of it which occurred while he was attending the schools in Paris. A wealthy Jew seized an unfortunate clerk while a religious procession was passing, "et clericum inde raptum in sentinam domus suae proiecit, quia filium suum lapide leserat" (*De nugis cur.*, ed. M. R. James, p. 226).

osum") in C 9, and a white pebble ("lapillum") in C 10—and
the song continued until this object was removed. It is clear
that the appearance of this magical object in these texts represents an elaboration of the earlier C tradition. But which of
the several objects mentioned in these four texts was most
probably the one originally placed in the boy's mouth? The
lily of the Vernon poem may at once be dismissed, not only
because as an aid to singing it would be a device of doubtful
value but because this was an incident transferred bodily from
the *Miracle*, "De clerico de cuius defuncti ore lilium pullulauit."[1]
Our choice lies then between Chaucer's "greyn" and the precious stone or pebble of C 9 and 10. In deciding this point a
clue is afforded by the conflicting statements as to the manner
of the boy's death.

Among the A versions all except one state that his throat
was cut; and this statement is repeated in the majority of the
C versions. But in A 4 and in C 9 and 10 we read instead that
his tongue was cut out; and it is in just these two versions that
we have the inserted stone "qui locum lingue suppleret"
(C 9). Obviously, therefore, the gem tongue was not based on
earlier tradition but was introduced into these two C texts as
a corollary to the cutting-out of the tongue. Even in relating
miracles some scope must be given for rationalization. On the
other hand, the grain laid upon the tongue, as Professor
Skeat has pointed out,[2] finds at least a distant prototype in
the story of Adam and Seth. It is possible therefore that the
original form of this incident of the magical object is preserved
in the *Prioress's Tale*, even though it is unsupported by any
other version.

An interesting variation, now, from the continuous song of
the corpse, as recorded in the versions which we have been considering, appears in a special group of four versions (C 3, 4, 5,
and 7). The singing in the jakes evidently was regarded as
having fulfilled its function after leading to the discovery of
the body. As in the other C versions, the body was borne in

---

[1] *Miracles de la B.V.M. d'apres un M.S. du XIIIe siècle de la Bibl. de Vendôme*,
ed. H. Isnard (Orleans, 1888), pp. 152–55. The Old French metrical version in
Vie des anciens Pères will be found in B.M. Add. MS 32678, fol. 67 (see J. A.
Herbert, *Cat. Romances in Brit. Mus.*, III, 342 [No. 17]).

[2] *Oxford Chaucer* (1894), V, 491.

state to the church or abbey. The funeral service, however, was postponed until the following day, and apparently during the interim the corpse lay quiet on the bier. But this narrator, who shows special interest in liturgical details, introduced new incidents into the account of the funeral service. The clergy were uncertain whether they should sing the usual requiem mass for the dead or the Office of the Virgin, "Salve sancta parens." But when the officiating priest at length began with "Requiem eternam," the corpse rose from the bier and began the "Salve sancta parens." Thereupon the priest paused in astonishment and the boy's voice likewise ceased. This miraculous interruption of the funeral rites, which was thrice repeated, is clearly a later addition to the legend for the purpose of emphasizing the young martyr's particular devotion to the Virgin. As the Vernon poem puts it:

> Þe Cors aros in heore presens
> Bi-gon þen Salue sancta parens
> Men mihte wel witen þe soþe þer-bi
> Þe child hedde i-seruet vr swete ladi [141–44]

This tendency in the later versions of Group C to amplify the funeral scene by adding new marvels finds its culmination in C 10, the latest version of this group. According to this version, the funeral is followed most unexpectedly by the resuscitation of the victim. The sermon being concluded, the officiating prelate called upon clergy and laity to pour out their prayers and tears for the restoration of the young singer's life.

Orant suppliciter & supplicant confidenter, nec est eis opposita nubes diffidencie ne transiret oracio quia ascendit vsque ad consistorium trinitatis. ffides enim eorum celos penetrauit celeriter & eorum felix confidencia tam fiducialiter quam feliciter impetrauit.

These prayers speedily produced effect:

Subito guttur pueri precisus reseratur, pellis prius dissuta integre restauratur, lingua redditur diuina canenti preconia, cor cum pulmone aut prius ablatum restituitur aut concessum diuinitus de nouo procreatur. Anima ad vas suum & sui vehiculum reuocatur & homo fiat integer carni mortue iterum se maritat spiritus immortalis.

Even with this restoration of the boy to life, however, the "magical object" was not forgotten. The stone was found in the boy's mouth, and, as soon as it was removed, the song ceased. Also the stone itself was preserved in the church as a perpetual memorial and testimony to the miracle.

Clearly this restoration in C 10 is not to be confused with the happy ending of Group A but is merely the final step in the series of marvels in the later development of the Group C tradition. Like the resuscitation of Athelstane in *Ivanhoe*, it may have been added to meet the protests of those who could not reconcile themselves to the tragic ending. And artistically judged, the addition is no less questionable than the scene in Scott's novel, although the narrator did not fail to make effective homiletic use of it.

C 4 also concludes, apparently, with the revival of the boy: "& qualiter post Agnus dei reuixit." But from the very brief outline in this text it is difficult to decide whether this is the real ending of the story or whether we have a truncated narrative. One may compare the concluding sentence of C 3: "surrexit mortuus & incepit magna uoce Salve sancta parens &c." In this case the "et cetera" seems to imply that there were further incidents to follow. Moreover, the use of "mortuus" would suggest that the boy was not really restored to life. Again, it is to be noted that C 4, in which the corpse sings "Salve sancta parens," belongs to what I have styled the special "liturgical group," whereas C 10, in which there can be no question of the boy's restoration, belongs to the "magical object group." It is clear from this that between these two versions there was no direct relationship, so that if the "reuixit" in C 4 means that the boy was permanently restored, we should be obliged to regard the occurrence of the restoration scene in this version as an independent development.

THE IMMEDIATE SOURCE FOR THE
PRIORESS'S TALE

Not only does the *Prioress's Tale* belong definitely to Group C but it betrays no influence from any version of the legend outside this group. It remains, however, to define as closely as we can its relationship to the other versions within this group.

In seeking for Chaucer's immediate source, we may at once set aside the three skeleton versions C 2, 3, and 4, since these are too brief to have served as the basis for his detailed narrative. The Vernon miracle (C 5) may also be dismissed from further consideration, first, because the author of the Vernon miracle gives an altered form of the story of which there is no trace in the *Prioress's Tale*, and, second, because it is very doubtful whether the Vernon manuscript was written early enough for Chaucer to have known it. The Sidney Sussex manuscript, which gives us C 7 and 8, was not written until 1409, and C 9 and 10 are even later, so that it is impossible to regard any of these as the actual text used by Chaucer.

Of all the C versions known to us, therefore, the only one which could possibly be considered the direct source for the *Prioress's Tale* is C 1. Moreover, C 1 not only supplies the main features of Chaucer's narrative but agrees closely in a number of the details. Let us note the most significant of these points of agreement.

1. Chaucer tells us of the clergeon singing his anthem through Jewry:

> Twyes a day it passed thurgh his throte,
> To scoleward and homward whan he wente.
> . . . .
>
> As I haue seyd, thurgh-out the Iewerye
> This litel child, as he cam to and fro,
> Ful merily than wolde he singe and crye
> O Alma redemptoris euer-mo.
> . . . .
>
> He can nat stinte of singing by the weye.

Compare C 1: "In eundo autem & redeundo semper in omnium audiencia cantabat hanc antiphon Alma redemptoris mater, &c. . . . . Ratio vero et dispositio ita se habebat itineris ut a domuncula matris sue ad domum divitis per uicum ubi iudei manebant transire necesse erat. . . . . Puer cotidie a solito cantu non cessabat."

2. Chaucer gives dramatic expression to the resentment of the Jews at the song:

> Is this to yow a thing that is honest,
> That swich a boy shal walken as him lest
> In your despyt, and singe of swich sentence
> Which is agayn your lawes reuerence?

Compare C 1: "Garcio iste qui frequenter transit per nos in obprobrium nostrum & derisum generis nostri tociens replicat canticum illud."

3. Chaucer tells us that the Jews took counsel together to slay the child. (In most versions the murder is conceived and executed by a single Jew.)

> From thennes forth the Iewes han conspyred
> This innocent out of this world to chace;
> An homicyde there-to han they hired.

Compare C 1: "Cogitabant ergo impii quomodo puerum interficerent. Initoque consilio constituerunt duos qui puerum pertranseuntem raperent."

4. Chaucer stresses the anxiety of the boy's mother:

> This povre widwe awaiteth al that night
> After hir litel child, but he cam noght;
> For which, as sone as it was dayes light,
> With face pale of drede and bisy thoght
> She hath at scole and elleswher him soght.

Compare C 1: "Cum autem ad horam constitutam puer non rediret ad matrem, cepit esse sollicita pro filio. . . . . Sustinuit vsque mane. Puero uero non reuertente sequenti die, mater impaciens more baculo innixa cepit ire. Dolor & tristicia filii reparabant ei vires."

5. At length, Chaucer says, the mother got news of the boy:

> Til finally she gan so fer aspye
> That he last seyn was in the Iewerye

Compare C 1: "Ibat igitur filium querens, dictumque est ei quia heri hora illa intrauit in domum illius iudei."

6. Chaucer describes her appeal to the Jews:

> She frayneth and she preyeth pitously
> To euery Iew that dwelte in thilke place,
> To telle hir if hir child wente oght for-by.
> They seyde "nay."

Compare C 1: "Veniens igitur ad ostium. Pulsauit clamans, Reddite mihi filium meum. . . . . Hii uero qui intrinsecus erant . . . . affirmabant se omnino de filio quem querebat nihil scire."

These parallels in C 1 make it certain that Chaucer had before him a detailed narrative instead of a mere outline of the miracle

and also that he was following his source attentively. At the
same time, I do not believe that C 1 was his immediate source.
This will appear when we note a series of agreements between
the *Prioress's Tale* and C 9 and 10, in incidents which are
lacking in C 1.

1. In C 1 the boy did not *speak* at all after his murder. His
corpse continued to sing mechanically, and the song did not
cease until the body was buried. Chaucer, on the other hand,
devotes three stanzas (vs. 197–217) to the boy's own story of
how Our Lady appeared to him and placed the grain upon his
tongue, bidding him sing until it was removed. With this
compare C 9:

> Dixitque omni populo leta et hylari facie qualiter sibi acciderat, sicut
> dictum est, et quomodo virgo beata ad eum venerat et posuerat dictum lapi-
> dem in ore eius vt non cessaret [licet] mortuus ab eius laude. . . . Post hec
> autem vocauit ad se episcopum et dedit sibi pacem similiter & matri, &
> sancta expedicione ob omni populo certificauit eos quod ascendit ad celos in
> societate virginis gloriose.

2. C 1 makes no reference to the school which the boy attended. Both C 9 and 10 give detailed statements concerning
the school and its discipline.

3. C 1 is silent as to the devotion which prompted the boy's
diligence in learning the anthem. Chaucer, however, does not
omit this:

> "And is this song maked in reuerence
> Of Cristes moder?" seyde this innocent:
> "Now certes I wol do my diligence
> To conne it al er Cristemasse is went.
>
> . . . .
>
> I wol it conne our lady to honoure."

Compare C 10: "Amplius ipsum credo ob memoriam & amorem
matris virginis Antiphonam decantare memoratam quam ob
cantus dulcedinem tociens id fecisse."

4. Chaucer declares that it was the "serpent Sathanas that
hath in Iewes hert his waspes nest" who stirred them up to
slay the boy. This is not stated in C 1 but is found in both C 9
and C 10: "consilium habuit cum suis complicibus *quorum corda
dyabolus possidebat*" (C 9) and "Quia fuit sathan inter eos. . . . .
Et ecce sathanas misit in cor eius vt puerum traderet & interficeret innocentem" (C 10).

5. Though, according to the versions of Group C generally, the child's body is thrown into a jakes, Chaucer's phrase curiously resembles that in C 10:

> I say that in a wardrobe[1] they him threwe
> Wher as the Iewes purgen her entraile.

Compare C 10: "corpus extinctum in locum proicitur extreme vilitatis ubi natura se purgat per secessum."

6. Chaucer's statement that the mother was providentially guided to the spot where her child was slain presents a striking parallel to C 9.

> but Iesu, of his grace
> Yaf in hir thought, inwith a litel space,
> That in that place after hir sone she cryde
> Wher he was casten in a pit bisyde.

C 9: "Et disponente deo in fine iiij dierum predictorum mulier illa transiuit per vicum illum in quo filius suus fuerat occisus et in latrinam proiectus."

However, since the existing texts C 9 and 10 are later than the *Prioress's Tale*, we must either dismiss the resemblance in these details as the result of narrative coincidence or (more reasonably it seems to me) assume the existence of an intermediate version not at present known which served as the direct source of these later Latin versions and of Chaucer's narrative.

CHAUCER'S MODIFICATIONS OF THE STORY

Though we have not succeeded in identifying the immediate source of the *Prioress's Tale*, our comparison of the versions of Group C has helped us to define within narrow limits the form of the legend which Chaucer had before him, and thus to draw some valid conclusions as to his methods in shaping the story.

In the first place, it is to be observed that the *Prioress's Tale* shows no special points of agreement with any versions outside the "magical object" group. If Chaucer had worked on the basis of several versions of the story, the chances are that the *Prioress's Tale* in particular details would reveal the impress of versions not falling within this special subgroup. Accordingly,

---

[1] On the medieval use of this term see John W. Draper, *ES*, LX, 238 ff.

we seem justified in concluding that Chaucer did not assemble a variety of texts but based his narrative upon a single source.

More important still are certain narrative features which are peculiar to the *Prioress's Tale,* and which therefore may be assumed to represent Chaucer's own additions to the story.

First of all is his express statement that the "litel clergeon" was "seven yeer of age." In C 9 we are told, "puer etatis annorum X"; moreover, he had already begun the study of grammar (i.e., Latin) and song. In C 10 the boy's age is not stated, but he had finished his elementary studies and had passed on to the study of song. C 1 states merely "puer uero clericus erat" without making any reference to the school which he attended. In stating that the clergeon was seven years old, Chaucer, it would seem, deliberately altered his source in order to heighten the pathos of the story. Seven was the age at which boys ordinarily began school attendance; and, as the clergeon resolved to learn the anthem "er Cristemasse is went," it is clear that the Michaelmas term had not ended and that the clergeon was still in his first term at school.

However, this change in the boy's age involved certain other important modifications of the narrative. A seven-year-old schoolboy, as Chaucer knew very well, would be studying his "prymer" instead of the "antiphoner," as stated in C 9 and 10. And it is to be observed that the clergeon overheard the older scholars singing the "Alma redemptoris mater," but that he himself was supposed to be learning his primer. In Chaucer's narrative, unlike all the others, the child learned the anthem out of school hours and not as a part of his school discipline. In order to bring this about, Chaucer introduced into the scene the figure of "his felaw, which that elder was than he," who became a most important addition to the story.

> His felaw taught him hom-ward prively
> From day to day til he couthe it by rote.

This "felaw" not only served a necessary function in teaching the anthem to the "litel clergeon" but also made it possible to introduce dialogue between the two scholars expounding the meaning of the anthem.

A suggestion for this interpretative dialogue Chaucer may have found in his source. For in both C 9 and C 10 the Jews make inquiry as to the meaning of the song which the boy sings along their street. And in C 10 their question was answered by a Jewish lad who had some slight knowledge of Latin. Chaucer perceived the usefulness of this dialogue in bringing out for the reader the substance of the anthem, but he saw that its effectiveness would be increased by transferring it from Jewry to the school, and thus keeping the action centered about the hero.

Accordingly, he makes the question concerning the anthem come from the clergeon himself and assigns the role of interpreter to the "felaw" who (like the Jewish lad in C 10) had just enough Latin to give a general notion of the meaning of the anthem:

> Nought wiste he what this Latyn was to say,
> For he so yong and tender was of age;
> But on a day his felaw gan he pray
> To expounden him the song in his langage,
> Or telle him what this song was in usage;
> This prayde he him to construe and declare,
> Ful often times upon his knees bare.

We could ill afford to spare this stanza from the narrative of the Prioress. Yet consider that this situation would have been quite impossible had the clergeon been a lad far enough along to be studying grammar and song himself. We see, then, that Chaucer, after first changing the age of his hero, found in this change an opportunity to introduce a most effective situation.

The Prioress's Tale thus illustrates, as clearly perhaps as any of the products of Chaucer's pen, the method of his narrative art. Though Chaucer followed closely the incidents in his source, his imagination by these changes subtly transformed the older miracle into a story of real human action and feeling. The labor involved in investigating his sources is amply rewarded by the pleasure which comes from watching him at his work.

TEXTS OF GROUP C

C 1

Corpus Christi College Oxford MS 32, Art. 19

This manuscript consists of a number of originally separate treatises bound together. Art. 19, which originally was a separate document, had already suffered the loss of leaves both at the beginning and at the end when it was bound up in its present position. H. O. Coxe (*Catalogus Codicum MSS qui in Collegiis Aulisque Oxon. hodie adservantur* [Oxon., 1852], Pars II) assigns MS 32 to the thirteenth century, and gives the following account of this section:

19. Anecdota de rebus diversis, praecipue in Anglia euenientibus: fragmentum, scilicet, libri majoris, hodie enim reliqua sunt modo capita xvii-xlix inclusive.

This text was first recognized as an analogue of the *Prioress's Tale* by Dr. Albert C. Friend, who printed it in *PMLA*, LI (1936), 624–25. It is here reprinted from an independent collation of the manuscript.

⟨fol. 92⟩ Fuit in transmarinis homo diues, burgensis an miles fuerit nescio, in terra Albigeorum in uilla que dicitur Carcassum, habens uetulam quandam pauperem qui quamdiu gressibus pedum libere uti potuit ad mensam ipsius uenire et refici consueuit. Postquam uero ex nimia corporis & etatis inbecillitate ad mensam diuitis accedere per se non potuit, per proprium filium suum paruulum fecit sibi constitutam annonam de domo eiusdem diuitis deferri.

Puer uero clericus erat habens uocem claram. In eundo autem & redeundo semper in omnium audiencia cantabat hanc antiphonam: Alma redemptoris mater &c. & cum finisset eam, reincipiebat. Ratio uero et dispositio ita se habebat itineris ut a domuncula matris sue ad domum diuitis per uicum ubi iudei manebant transire necesse esset. Qui dum singulis diebus per iudeos transiret antiphonam cantando, litigabant iudei ad inuicem dicentes, "Garcio iste qui frequenter transit per nos in obprobrium nostrum & derisum generis nostri tociens replicat canticum illud," & blasplemabant reuerendum illud & suaue nomen illius qui sal[u]tem edidit mundo.

Crescebat impietas iudeorum. Puer uero malignarum cogitationum ignarus cotidie a solito cantu non cessabat. Cogitabant ergo impii quomodo puerum interficerent. Initoque consilio constituerunt duos qui puerum pertranseuntem raperent. Raptus itaque ductus est in interius cubiculum, congregatisque circa eum iudeis nimia crudelitate ceperunt grassari in eum. Nam uentrem innocentis pueri scindentes in modum crucis, interiora eius extraxerunt & ea simul cum corpore in cloacam proiecerunt.

Cum hec ita fierent, in tam crudeli facto gracia dei non defuit, nam cum intrinsecus puer traheretur, cum secaretur, cum proiceretur, a cantu tamen non destitit, uel ipse uel angelus cui a domino iussum est. Sed inter omnia que circa eum impie impii operati sunt eadem uox, idem cantus audiebatur a christianis ⟨fol. 92ᵛ⟩ qui per locum illum transibant, licet nullus eorum aduerteret quod hoc modo puer tractaretur. Iudei uero uocem penitus non audiebant.

Cum autem ad horam constitutam puer non rediret ad matrem, cepit esse sollicita pro filio. Tamen estimans forte quod aliquorsum ab eo mitteretur a quo annonam cotidianam suscipiebat, sustinuit usque mane. Puero uero non reuertente sequenti die, mater impaciens more baculo innixa cepit ire. Dolor autem & tristicia filii reparabant ei uires quas etas consumpserat. Ibat igitur filium querens, dictumque est ei quia heri hora illa intrauit in domum illius iudei. Ueniens igitur ad ostium, pulsauit clamans, "Reddite mihi filium meum quem intrinsecus audio cantantem." Statim enim ex quo accessit ad partem illam audiuit notam sibi filii sui uocem. Hii uero qui intrinsecus erant, putantes se posse latere, delirare eam dicebant, & turpiter eam repellentes, affirmabant se omnino de filio quem querebat nihil scire.

Illa uero angustiata maiorem uille adiit. Ille missis ministris[1] iussit inquiri quid hoc esset. Qui intrantes domum statim uocem audierunt pueri, sed & multi christianorum concurrentes audierunt uocem, requirentesque inuenerunt locum, corpus extraxerunt. Miroque modo omnes christiani qui aderant audierunt melodiam et cantum, soli uero iudei nichil inde audierunt.

Cum magno igitur honore et tripudio tam cleri quam populi ad ecclesiam corpus innocentis est delatum & uenerabiliter sepultum. Nec cessauit uox illa admirabilis donec corpus sepeliretur ad laudem et gloriam gloriose uirginis Marie.

C 2

PHILLIPPS MS 8336

The last quire of this manuscript contains a series of seventeen hymns and antiphons, with the name "Herebert" in the margin opposite the beginning of each, and with an accompanying statement: "Istos hympnos & Antiphonas .... transtulit in Anglicum .... & in manu sua scripsit frater Willelmus Herebert." Herebert was a Franciscan who died, Bale states, in 1333 and was buried in the convent of his order at Hereford. The text of the "Alma redemptoris mater" and the outline of the miracle have been printed in my *Religious Lyrics of the XIVth Century* (Oxford, 1924), pp. 22 and 249.

---

[1] *MS* ministris missis, *marked for transposition.*

ALMA REDEMPTORIS MATER (FOL. 205ᵛ)

Holy moder, þat bere cryst
Buggere of monkunde,
þou art ȝat of heuene blisse
þat prest wey ȝyfst and bunde.
þou sterre of se rer op þe uolk
þat rysing haueht in munde.
In þe þou bere þyn holy uader,
þat mayden were after and raþer,
Whar-of so wondreth kunde.
Of gabrieles mouþe/þou uonge þylke 'Aue';
Lesne ous of sunne nouþe,/so woe bisecheth þe. AMEN.

Hic nota de filio vidue qui semper eundo ad scolas et redeundo de scolis consueuit istam antiphonam decantare; propter quod a iudeis per quos transitum fecit "puer marie" dicebatur; quem ipsi tandem occiderunt et in cloacam proiecerunt, qui tamen a cantu non cessauit, &c.

C 3

BRITISH MUSEUM MS ADDITIONAL 11579

A small quarto vellum manuscript of the early fourteenth century. For a general account of the contents see J. A. Herbert, *Catalogue of Romances in the British Museum*, III, 38: "The whole MS. is a theological miscellany, chiefly in Latin, but with a few passages in French and English; containing abridgments of sermons, notes on various subjects, etc., interspersed with a number of religious tales." In fols. 1–25 are included some thirty tales of a few lines each, together with moral or doctrinal teaching. For a notice of our story see Herbert, p. 528.

⟨fol. 5ᵛ⟩ Erat quidam puer christianus manens in ciuitate vna vbi multi Iudei erant. Qui semper Antiphonam. scilicet Aue regina cantabat coram iudeis & domibus eorum. Quare iudei multum inuidebant ei & tandem per fraudem & munuscula trahebant eum in domibus eorum in vltimo t[h]alamo et amputauerunt capud eius. post hec uero veniens mater pueri querens filium suum semper audiendo uocem filij cantantem Aue regina set non potuit inuenire eum. Deinde uero iuit ad magistros ciuitatis narrando eis quomodo iudei tenuerunt filium suum in carcere. et petijt vt uenirent secum & liberarent filium suum.

Qui venientes omnes uocem audierunt & intrantes & querentes inuenerunt puerum mortuum. & detulerunt eum ad ecclesiam ad sepeliendum. & cum deberent cantare missam pro eo ignorabant

vtrum deberent cantare missam pro mortuis. scilicet Requiem
eternam uel de sancta Maria. scilicet Salue. Et dum hec cogitabant,
surrexit mortuus & incepit magna uoce Salue sancta parens &c.

C 4
ROYAL MS 12.E.1, ART. 19

A small quarto vellum manuscript, early fourteenth century, in various
hands, containing religious tales intermingled with lives of saints and short
theological pieces. For an account of the contents see Herbert, III, 537 ff.

⟨fol. 170⟩ Item quidam puer cotidie reuertens de scolis cotidie per
ostium cuiusdam iudei solebat cantare Sancta maria &c de beata
uirgine. quem iudeus apprehendens proiecit in cloacham apud thole-
tum & qualiter incepit Salue sancta parens. quando sacerdos inceperat
requiem & qualiter post Agnus dei reuixit.

C 5
VERNON MS (BODLEIAN MS 3938)

This text has been printed in *Originals and Analogues of the Canterbury
Tales* ("Chaucer Society Publications"), pp. 281–85, and in *Minor Poems of
the Vernon MS* ("E.E.T.S.: Original Series," No. 98 [1892]), pp. 141–45. Here
reprinted from an independent collation of the manuscript.

HOU þE IEWES, IN DESPIT OF VRE LADY,
þREWE A CHYLD IN A GONGE[1]

fol. 124   Wose loueþ wel vre ladi,
col. 1   Heo wol quiten his wille wel whi,
       Oþur in his lyf or at his ende:
4   þe ladi is so freo and hende.
      Hit fel sum-tyme in Parys,
      As witnesseþ in holy writ Storys.
       In þe Cite bi-fel þis cas:
8   A pore child was of porchas,
      þat wiþ þe beggeri þat he con wynne
      He fond sumdel what of his kinne,
      His ffader, his Moder, and eke him-self;
12   He begged in Cite bi eueri half.
       þe child non oþur Craftus couþe
      But winne his lyflode wiþ his Mouþe.
      þe Childes vois was swete and cler,
16   Men lusted his song wiþ riht good cher;
      Wiþ his song þat was ful swete

---

[1] Title of this piece as given in the Table of Contents.

He gat Mete from strete to strete.
Men herked his song ful likyngly:
20 Hit was an Antimne of vre lady,
He song þat Antimne eueri-wher,
I-Called Alma Redemptoris Mater,
þat is forþrihtly to mene:
24 "Godus Moder, Mylde and Clene,
Heuene ȝate and Sterre of se,
Saue þi peple from synne and we."
þat song was holden deynteous,
28 þe child song hit from hous to hous.
ffor he song hit so lykynglye,
þe Iewes hedde alle to hym Envye.
Til hit fel on A seters-day
32 þe Childes wey þorw þe Iewerie lay:
þe Iewes hedden þat song in hayn,
þerfore þei schope þe child be slayn.
So lykingly þe Child song þer,
36 So lustily song he neuer er.
    On of þe Iewes Malicious
Tilled þe child in to his hous;
His Malice þere he gan to kuyþe:
40 He Cutte þe childes þrote alswiþe.
    þe child ne spared nout for þat wrong,
But neuer-þe-latere song forþ his song;
Whon he hedde endet, he eft bi-gon,
44 His syngyng couþe stoppe no mon.
    þer-of þe Ieuh was sore anuyet.
Leste his Malice mihte ben aspyet,
þe Ieuh bi-þouhte him of a gynne:
48 In to a gonge-put fer wiþ-Inne
þe child adoun þer-Inne he þrong.
þe child song euere þe same song;
So lustily þe child con crie,
52 þat song he neuer er so hyȝe:
Men mihte him here fer and neer,
þe Childes vois was so heiȝ and cleer.
þe Childes moder was wont to a-byde
56 Euery day til þe Non-tyde,
þen was he wont to bringe heom mete,
Such as he mihte wiþ his song gete.
col. 2 Bote þat day was þe tyme a-past.

60　þerfore his Moder was sore a-gast;
　　Wiþ syk and serwe in eueri strete
　　Heo souhte wher heo mihte wiþ him mete.
　　Bote whon heo com in to þe Iewery,
64　Heo herde his vois so clere of cry.
　　Aftur þat vois his Modur dreuh:
　　Wher he was Inne, þerbi heo kneuh.
　　　þen of hire child heo asked a siht.
68　þe Iew wiþ-nayted him a-non riht,
　　And seide þer nas non such child þrinne.
　　þe childes Moder ȝit nolde not blinne,
　　But euer þe Moder criede in on.
72　þe Ieuh seide euere þer nas such non.
　　þen seide þe womman: "þou seist wrong,
　　He is her-Inne, I knowe his song."
　　þe Ieuh bi-gon to stare and swere
76　And seide þer com non such child þere.
　　But neuer-þe-latere men mihte here
　　þe child song euere so loude and clere,
　　And euer þe lengor, herre and herre,
80　Men mihte him here boþe fer and nerre.
　　　þe Modur coude non oþur won:
　　To Meir and Baylyfs heo is gon,
　　Heo pleyneþ þe Ieuh haþ don hire wrong
84　To stelen hire sone so for his song;
　　Heo preyeþ to don hire lawe and riht,
　　Hire sone don come bi-fore heore siht;
　　Heo preyeþ þe Meir par Charite
88　Of him to haue freo lyuere.
　　　þenne heo telleþ þe Meir a-Mong
　　Hou heo lyueþ bi hire sone song.
　　　þe Meir þen haþ of hire pite,
92　And sumneþ þe folk of þat Cite.
　　He telleþ hem of þat wommons sawe,
　　And seiþ he mot don hire þe lawe,
　　And hoteþ hem wiþ hym to wende,
96　To Bringe þis wommons cause to ende.
　　　Whon þei cum þider, for al heore noyse
　　Anon þei herde þe childes voyse,
　　Riht as an Angeles vois hit were,
100　þei herde him neuer synge so clere.
　　　þer þe Meir makeþ entre,

And of þe child he askeþ lyuere.
 þe Ieuh may nouȝt þe Meir refuse,
104 Ne of þe child hym wel excuse,
But nede he moste knouleche his wrong,
A-teynt bi þe childes songe.
 þe Meir let serchen hym, so longe,
108 Til he was founden in þe gonge,
fful depe I-drouned in fulþe of fen.
þe Meir het drawe þe child vp þen,
Wiþ ffen and ffulþe riht foule bi-whoruen,
112 And eke þe childes þrote I-coruen.
Anon-riht, er þei passede forþere,
þe Ieuh was Iugget for þat Morþere.
And er þe peple passede in-sonder,
116 þe Bisschop was comen to seo þat wonder.
 In presence of Bisschop and alle I-fere
þe child song euere I-liche clere.
 þe Bisschop serchede wiþ his hond:
120 Wiþ-inne þe childes þrote he fond
A lilie flour, so briht and cler,
So feir a lylie nas neuere seȝen er,
Wiþ guldene lettres eueriwher:
124 Alma Redemptoris Mater.
 Anon þat lilie out was taken,
þe childes song bi-gon to slaken,
þat swete song was herd no more;
128 But as a ded cors þe child lay þore.
 þe Bisschop wiþ gret solempnete
Bad bere þe cors þorw al þe Cite:
And hym-self wiþ processioun
132 Com wiþ þe Cors þorw al þe toun,
Wiþ prestes and clerkes þat couþen syngen,
And alle þe Belles he het hem ryngen,
Wiþ torches Brennynge and cloþus riche,
136 Wiþ worschipe þei ladden þat holi liche.
In to þe Munstre whon þei kem,
Bi-gonne þe Masse of Requiem,
col. 3 As for þe dede Men is wont.
140 But þus sone þei weren i-stunt:
þe Cors a-Ros in heore presens,
Bi-gon þen Salue sancta parens.
 Men mihte wel witen þe soþe þer-bi:

144 þe child hedde i-seruet vr swete ladi,
þat worschipede him so on erþe her
And brouhte his soule to blisse al cler.
þerfore i rede þat eueri mon
148 Serue þat ladi wel as he con,
And loue hire in his beste wyse:
Heo wol wel quite him his seruise.
Now, Marie, for þi Muchele miht
152 Help vs to heuene þat is so briht!

C 6

Chaucer's *Prioress's Tale*

Registered here in order to bring Chaucer's text into its proper place in the list of versions.

C 7

Sidney Sussex College Cambridge MS
Δ.5.10, Lib. II, Cap. 84

The most extensive known collection of miracles of the Virgin. It is divided into five books, each containing about a hundred miracles. A complete list is given by Dr. M. R. James in his *Catalogue of the MSS of Sidney Sussex College*. The date of the compilation is given in the rubric to the Prologue: "Incipit prologus prime partis tractatus miraculorum beate et perpetue virginis Marie genetricis dei per quemdam monachum *de Thorne* diuersis ex libris collecti et in hanc formam ad laudem eiusdem virginis redacti. Anno domini Millesimo cccc^{mo}. ix." As the words "de Thorne" are written over an erasure, it is impossible to be certain in what monastery this collection of miracles was composed.

DE PUERO CANTANTE RESPONSORIUM GAUDE MARIA A IUDEIS
OCCISO PRO QUO SALUE SANCTA PARENS CELITUS
DECANTARI AUDITUR

Alter quidam scolaris adhuc puerulus in cantu satis edoctus vocem habens dulcem & canorem singulis fere diebus cum de scolis ad vesperum reuerteretur domum Responsorium de beata virgine, scilicet Gaude Maria virgo, in honorem sancte Marie dei genitricis excelsa voce cantare consueuit, itaque omnes beniuolos per quos transiuit vox pueri cantantis exhillarauit. Sed perfidi iudei qui in illis partibus habitabant laudes gloriose virginis supprimere conantes inuidia stimulante puerum illum quadam die ad vesperum per hostium eorum transeuntem apprehenderunt & subito interfecerunt, ac in opprobrium beate virginis corpus eius in cloacam proicientes occuluerunt.

Puer vero more solito domum non regressus inter cognatos & notos
a parentibus & conscolaribus biduo quesitus est nec inuentus. Tercia
autem die ad vesperum audita est ab eis vox cantantis idem responsorium quod puer viuens cantare consueuerat, et videbatur idem puer
more suo decantans. Et hec vox de domo iudeorum vbi puer sus-
pendebatur non destitit resonare donec christiani per iudeorum ostium
preclusum irruentes ad corpus deuenirent. Quod quidem corpus cum
ingenti gaudio honorifice ad ecclesiam beate virginis allatum coram
maius altare cum feretro deponitur.

In crastino vero scolaribus omnibus eiusdem vrbis ad ecclesiam cum
populo conuenientibus vt misse pro eo celebrande reuerenter interes-
sent & pro eius anima deuocius orarent, ac munera sua deo offerrent,
incepit cantor officium Requiem eternam sicud mos est pro defunctis
canere. Et ecce subito vox clara resonans audita est de loculo veluti
ab ipso puero dulci modulamine officium inchoans de beata virgine,
Salua sancta parens. Mox cantor stupefactus subticuit & vox puerilis
prius audita similiter siluit. Quod attendens cantor Requiem eternam
iterum personuit, sed in auribus omnium vox illa dulcissona vocem
cantoris comprimens solenniter reincepit: Salue sancta parens.
Et hoc factum est tercio. Vehementer igitur admirantes clerici in-
spirante deo & persuadente populo totum officium de beata virgine
cum missa prosecuti sunt. ffinita missa corpus terre tradiderunt
glorificantes & laudantes deum eiusque genitricem Mariam cui cum
filio sit honor in secula seculorum. Amen.

C 8

Sidney Sussex College Cambridge MS
Δ.5.10, Lib. II, Cap. 87

This text is based upon the version of C 1, with only a few verbal changes.
It is important as showing that the text of C 1 continued in circulation as late
as 1409.

DE PUERO A IUDEIS INTERFECTO QUI ANTIPHONAM ALMA
REDEMPTORIS CANTARE NON CESSAUIT DONEC
FUNERIS OFFICIUM CONPLERETUR

In terra Albegeorum erat quidam diues potens & nobilis qui quandam vetulam quamdiu ire poterat de mensa sua reficere consueuerat.
Postquam autem per se pre debilitate venire nequiuerat, per filium
eius quem habebat paruulum fecit sibi diues de domo sua annonam
sufficientem deferri. Puer vero clericus erat & sicud illi etati conuenit
vox clara ab eius gutture resonabat. In eundo autem & redeundo
antiphonam Alma redemptoris mater in omnium audiencia decantare

consueuerat. Et cum finisset eam iterum incipiebat, sicque quando ibat vel quando redibat ista sacra melodia de ore pueri non cessabat. Disposicio vero itineris ita se habebat vt a matris sue domuncula ad domum diuitis per vicum iudeorum transire deberet. Qui cum diebus singulis sic beatam virginem clare voce laudans per iudeos incederet grandi murmure stomachati accensi adinuicem loquebantur dicentes: "Puer iste qui frequenter transit per nos cotidie replicat illud canticum in generis nostri derisum & obprobrium." Et ceperunt nomen Marie virginis blasphemare.

Crescebat de die in diem iudeorum impietas & vt puerum inter- ficerent attencius cogitabant. Et dicebant: "Quid faciemus?" Initoque consilio statuerunt duos qui puerum raperent transeuntem. Quod & fecerunt. Raptus itaque ductus est in interius cubiculum & congre- gatis circa eum iudeis nimia crudelitate debacantes, ventrem inno- centis sciderunt per medium & interiora eius extrahentes simul cum corpore in cloacam proiecerunt.

Cumque hec fierent diuina gracia non defuit. Nam cum intrinsecus puer traheretur, secaretur, & in cloacam turpiter proiceretur, a cantu non destitit vel ipse vel forte angelus eius sicud a domino fuerit ordina- tum. Sed semper eadem vox idem cantus a christianis qui per locum illum transibant audiebatur, licet nullus eorum aduerteret quod puer hoc modo ab ipsis perfidis iudeis tractaretur. Sed licet christiani sicud dictum est vocem cantantis euidenter sunt experti, iudei tamen vocem & cantum sunt penitus inexperti.

Cum autem puer ad horam constitutam ex more non rediret, cepit pro filio mater sollicitari. Sustinuit tamen vsque mane. In crastino vero baculo innixa cepit circumire filium suum querens. Vires enim quas etas consumpserat, dolor & tristicia filij reparabant. Cum autem attencius circum circa quereret, dictum est ei quia in domum talis iudei puer illa hora intrauit. Veniens itaque mater ad ostium vbi filium eius audierat intrasse, pulsauit dicens: "Reddite mihi filium meum quem intrinsecus audio more solito decantantem." Ex quo enim ad partem illam accessit, filij sui vocem notam intellexit. Sed iudei qui intrinsecus erant eam delirare dicebant, nil se scire de suo filio asseren- tes turpiter ab ostio repellebant.

Recedens ipsa nunciauit hoc diuiti. A quo missi ministri domum iudei intrantes statim vocem pueri audierunt. Sed & multi christian- orum similiter concurrentes ad istud spectaculum conuenerunt & diligenter requirentes locum inuenerunt, sicque corpus pueri de cloacha merentes extraxerunt. Miro quidem modo omnes christiani melodiam & cantum audierunt, sed sola iudeorum obcecata perfidia non audiuit.

Cum magno igitur honore & gaudio corpus innocentis ad ecclesiam defertur, & ibidem venerabiliter sepelitur. Nec cessauit vox ista admirabilis donec clerus & populus obsequium funeris explerent, & in laude matris christi ad propria remearent.

Et vt hec antiphona nescientibus manifestetur presentibus illam interserere congruum videtur: Alma redemptoris mater que peruia celi porta manens et stella maris succurre cadenti surgere qui curat populo tu que genuisti natura mirante tuum sanctum genitorem virgo prius ac posterius Gabrielis ab ore sumens illud aue peccatorum miserere.

C 9

ALPHONSUS A SPINA, *Fortalicium fidei contra Iudeos, Saracenos, aliosque Christiane fidei inimicos* (1458–60)

Reprinted from the Basel edition, *ca.* 1475. The British Museum possesses what seems to be a slightly earlier edition (Strassburg, 1471?). This work, published anonymously, was first assigned to Alphonsus by Garibay, *Los XL libros d'el compendio historial de las chronicas* (Antwerp, 1571), Lib. XVI, cap. 46. Alphonsus a Spina was a convert from Judaism; at the time he wrote the *Fortalicium* he was Doctor of Theology in the Franciscan College at Salamanca. In 1491 he was sent to Greece as bishop of Thermopylae (see Wadding, *Annales minorum*, XII [1735], 144 and 446; XIV [1735], 523 and the Supplement by Sbaralea [Rome, 1806], p. 27).

The text of our legend, with the omission of the concluding paragraph, was printed in *Originals and Analogues* from the edition of 1500.

DE EXPULSIONE IUDEORUM DE REGNO ANGLORUM

Tercia iudeorum expulsio fuit a regno anglie cuius expulsionis causa duplex assignatur quarum primam legi in quibusdam miraculis sub ordine qui sequitur. In li[n]conia ciuitate regis anglie, Accidit quoddam miraculum quod deus voluit ostendere precibus beate virginis. Vnde mulier quedam vidua et paupercula filium quendam nomine Alfonsum habebat, quem tradidit ad docendum primas litteras et postquam sciuit legere tradidit imbuendum rudimentis gra[m]maticalibus et in musica; qui licet in gra[m]maticalibus processerit, in musicis tamen gratissimus erat. Et quia predicta mulier paupercula erat recommendauit illum cuidam religioso sui generis, vt de victu saltem ipsi prouideret: et ita factum est, quia cottidie post lectiones suas recipiebat suam refectionem cum predicto religioso. Erat autem predictus puer etatis annorum x., cuius erat consuetudo ordinata vt primo cottidie iret ad ecclesiam deinde ad scolas et hora refectionis, vt dictum est, ad domum religiosi. Nocte vero ad matris domicilium se conuertebat.

Cum autem sepe in ecclesia illam preclaram antiphonam Alma
redemptoris audiret cantare, tantam deuocionem concepit in virgine
beata et sic menti impressit predictam antiphonam quod quicunque
iret de die et de nocte per vicos et plateas more puerorum supradictam
antiphonam alta voce dulcissime cantabat. transitus autem eius
erat, cum iret ad domum matris vel rediret ab eadem, per vicum quendam iudeorum; qui audientes frequenter predictam virginis cantacionem ab ore iuuenis quidem [*sic?*] illorum habuit querere a quodam
docto christiano, quis esset sensus illius cantacionis cum eius cantus
tam dulcis esset. Et vt cognouit quod illa erat antiphona quedam que
ad laudem et honorem virginis beate marie matris redemptoris ihesu
christi veri messie decantabatur a fidelibus in ecclesia, concepit dolorem et peperit iniquitatem: quod consilium habuit cum suis complicibus quorum corda dyabolus possidebat, quomodo predictum
infantem morti traderent & occiderent. hora ergo oportuna obseruata
cum paruulus predictus alta voce cantando predictam antiphonam
transiret per eorum vicum, subito sicut a rugientibus leonibus rapitur
& reclusus in domo quadam de modo mortis eius tractauerunt. Et
diffinitum est inter eos quod eius lingua cum qua beatam virginem
laudabat extraheretur per oppositam capitis partem; secundo quod
extraheretur etiam eius cor cum quo cogitabat predictam cantacionem; et vltimo quod corpus eius proiceretur in loco profundissi-
mo et immundissimo fetoribusque pleno qui locus erat eorum continua latrina, vt nullatenus signum eius inueniri posset: et factum
est sic. Set virgo beata, que mater est misericordie & pietatis nec
obliuioni tradit seruicium quodcunque sibi factum, statim sic ille
deuotissimus suus cantor in predicto loco fetito fuit proiectus,
Affuit presens eidem et posuit in eius ore lapidem quendam preciosum, qui locum lingue suppleret, et statim cepit cantare sicut prius
predictam antiphonam ymmo melius et alcius quam primo: nec
aliquando cessabat de die nec de nocte a predicto cantu, & tali modo
stetit in predicto loco paruulus ille iiij. diebus.

Cum vero mater eius videret quod sicut consueuerat ad domum
eius non veniret, celeri gressu ad domum supradicti religiosi peruenit
ac deinde ad scolas, nec poterat inuenire. Discurrebat vndique per
ciuitatem anxia mulier si posset alicubi inuenire filium suum, et
disponente deo in fine iiij. dierum predictorum mulier illa transiuit
per vicum illum in quo filius suus fuerat occisus et in latrinam proiectus; et ecce vox filij sui cantantis dulcissime cantacionem illam
virginis, quam sepissime ab eo audierat, insonuit in auribus eius.
Quo audito clamoribus magnis predicta mulier clamare cepit, et
congregate sunt multe gentes & cum eis iudex ciuitatis, intrauerunt-

que domum illam in qua vox illa audiebatur, et finaliter inuentus est iuuenis in loco predicto et extractus; nec vnquam cessabat a cantu illo dulcissimo licet mortuus foret.

Indutusque alijs vestimentis per dominos qui ibidem venerant, notificatum est episcopo ciuitatis, qui illico veniens ad spectaculum precepit quod poneretur honorifice in quodam lecto; et sic deductus est cum solenni processione & magno honore ad ecclesiam cathedralem predicte ciuitatis: semper tamen continuabat canticum suum. conuenientibus ergo in vnum ad predictam ecclesiam dictus episcopus celebrauit et fecit solempnem sermonem precepitque omnibus audientibus, quod deuotas funderent orationes vt precibus beate virginis deus dignaretur reuelare hoc secretum. Finito vero sermone placuit altissimo et sue beatissime matri quod fuit detecta impijssimorum iudeorum prodicio et crudelitas, quia eadem hora surrexit paruulus ille et stetit pedes in lecto in quo iacebat et extraxit ab ore suo vnum preciosissimum lapidem. Dixitque omni populo leta et hylari facie qualiter sibi acciderat, sicut dictum est, et quomodo virgo beata ad eum venerat et posuerat dictum lapidem in ore eius vt non cessaret [licet]¹ mortuus ab eius laude, et vt ostenderetur gloria filij sui in salutem credencium et perdicionem odiencium et incredulorum.

Post hec autem vocauit ad se episcopum et dedit sibi pacem similiter & matri, & sancta expedicione ab omni populo certificauit eos, quod ascendit ad celos in societate virginis gloriose, et tradidit predictum lapidem preciosum episcopo, vt poneret cum alijs reliquijs in altari. Quo facto, signaculo sancte crucis se insigniuit et coaptans se lecto animam tradidit saluatori. qui honorifice sepultus fuit quodam in sepulcro marmoreo, quod multo tempore preciosos lapides, vt fertur, emanauit quousque quedam pestifera heresis ibidem orta fuit.

Rex vero predicti regni, cum cognouit tam nephandum et horridum iudeorum crimen & propter multa alia que inuenit veridica inquisicione que predicti iudei operabantur in contumeliam et iniuriam ihesu christi saluatoris nostri et sue beatissime matris, ex deliberato et maturo consilio assignata die precepit, quod occiderentur omnes iudei quotquot possent inueniri in predicto regno suo. Et illi qui melius deliberauerunt fuerunt totaliter expoliati ab omnibus bonis et signati ac expulsi a toto regno anglie. Et ab illo tempore nunquam amplius ibi habitauit, nec habitat, nec ausus est apparere aliquis iudeus, quia statim occideretur si cognosceretur.

¹ Between *cessaret* and *mortuus* is a blank space as if a word of five or six letters had fallen out or been removed for correction.

C 10
Trinity College Cambridge MS O.9.38

This is a commonplace book written at the end of the fifteenth and beginning of the sixteenth centuries. For a full list of its contents see Dr. M. R. James, *Catalogue of the MSS of Trinity College* (1900–1904), No. 1450. Dr. James remarks that this manuscript is "evidently the note-book of a Glastonbury monk."

DE CANTU ALMA REDEMPTORIS MATER

⟨fol. 37⟩ Cum mater gracie sui memorum immemor nequaquam existat iugiter ipsius est memoria memoranda, laus ipsi tribuenda propensius & profusius sunt ipsius magnalia predicanda, licet bonorum operum non egeat tocius archa bonitatis tamen vtile et salubre est ipsius bonitatem laudibus cumulare. Prouide sequens capitulum commendandum duximus attramento vt ad noticiam perueniat posterorum et qui audierint ad memoriam virginis sanccius et interius accendantur.

Puer quidam in urbe toletana natus & nutritus matris sue diligencia mediante scolarum subditus discipline, iota & apices non preteriens nectere, didicit elementa et literas literis figura figuris fideliter maritare. Cognito coniugio literarum feliciter ad musicam pertransiuit vt tam vocis quam verbis eidem pateret intellectus diebus singulis soluit debitum leccionis secundum quod eidem prescripsit auctoritas magistralis. Diete debito persoluto hora prandij succedente domum cuiusdam canonici matricis ecclesie puer pauperculus adire consueuit. Cuius suffragio releuabat famem & ventris molestissimi exactoris exaccionem deludebat. Cupiebat saturari de micis diuitis & dabatur ei cotidie ad mensuram de micis que cadebant de mensa dominorum et de fragmentis que superfuerunt hijs qui manducauerant. Puer quod ei dabatur non in pera pastorali set in sacculo pectorali prouide recollegit quod minus fuit & peius in vsus conuertens proprios, maius et melius sue reseruans genetrici. O cordium cognitor & inspector tu nosti quod esset in homine.

Assignabatur puero quadam die pro dieta illa dilectabilis et suauis Antiphona in laudem matris virginis confecta cuius est caput & principium *Alma redemptoris mater*. Puer contumelias & terrores magistri cupiens precanere Antiphonam memoratam assidue ruminabat, tum quia sciendum est difficilis, tum quia delectabilis ad canendum. Amplius ipsum credo ob memoriam & amorem matris virginis Antiphonam decantasse memoratam, quam ob cantus dulcedinem tociens id fecisse; minus enim prodest corda cythare quam cor cytharedi supplicantis ex affectu. Plus amor cordis quam cordis

clamor, plus votum quam vox, iudicem interpellat hominum corda
iudicantem quia cum didicit orare fideliter nouit feliciter perorare.[1]
Quare? quia nunquam sonat vox amene nisi vocis & voti animus sit
precentor.

Cum hora prandij a scolis ⟨fol. 37ᵛ⟩ quadam die puerum absoluisset
& labore quietem subrogasset, puer, vt vitula effraim[2] trituram doc-
tam diligere quod ab vsu didicit hoc exercuit cum effectu, domum adit
canonici de cuius misericordia suam miseriam depellebat. Contigit
ipsum forte ingredi plateas Judaismi, vbi gens dure ceruicis & domus
exasperans habitabat, que Marie virginis fecunditati contradicens dei
filium incarnatum in virginis vtero diffitetur.[3] ffilij synagoge quam
plurimi in domo quadam fuerant congregati & ibi colligacio iniquitatis
& deprimens peccati fasciculus ex ipsorum multitudine amplius fuerat
roboratus. Ad hanc domum puer venit dictam decantans Antiphonam
Alma redemptoris mater, transire cupiens, set illesus non transiuit.
Affuit inter eos quidam adolescens de pueris hebreorum in lingua
latina parumper eruditus quia latinum intelligens ydeoma. Audiunt
cantilenam & mirantur & quia fuit sathan inter eos ecce vnus ex
illis inquirit ab hebreo qui literas nouit latinorum, quid puer con-
cineret christianus. Respondit hebreus puerum Antiphonam in
laudem matris virginis confectam decantare vt ipsius melliflua suaui-
tas ad marie memoriam animis accenderet auditores. Audito virginis
nomine iudeus exclamauit et ecce sathanas misit in cor eius vt puerum
traderet & interficeret innocentem.

Rogat ergo collegam fraudulenter vt puerum introducat et si prece
non possit saltem precio faciat quod deposcit. Innocens vocatur &
introducitur, trahitur ymmo magis traditur. Nam tenetur & facta est
exultacio eorum sicut eius qui deuorat pauperem in abscondito. Sine
mora se preparant occisioni vt condempnent innocentem. Agnum
lupi rapiunt. Apponit vnus cultrum gutturi, lingua crudeliter reseca-
tur,[4] reseratur venter & cor extrahitur cum pulmone. Duplex se
credunt offerre sacrificium, gutture resecato[5] quo vox laudis est
egressa, extracto corde quod virginis memoriam non desijt medi-
tari: arbitrantur obsequium se prestare deo set ymmo ymmolabant
demonijs et non deo. Liuor post fata solet quiescere, set extincto

---

[1] Cf. the following lines which, according to Dr. James's *Catalogue*, are scribbled
in a fifteenth-century hand on the last page of Trinity Coll., Camb., MS 1055:
"Non vox sed votum [*MS* vocum], non musica cordula sed cor,
    Non clamor sed amor cantat in aure dei."

[2] Cf. Hos. 10:11.   [4] rececatur *MS.*

[3] difficetur *MS.*   [5] rececato *MS.*

puero liuor non quieuit, quia corpus extinctum in locum proicitur extreme vilitatis vbi natura se purgat per secessum.

Affuit continuo Alma redemptoris mater quia affuit ipsius misericordia graciosa vt extincto videbatur lapillum album set saxo simillimum ori ipsius apponens & imponens: ⟨fol. 38⟩ lapillo imposito cor & guttur mortui reserant, redit vox cum organo & decantat puer mortuus *Alma redemptoris mater*.

Interim angit mora pueri mentem sue genitricis. Erat enim vnicus filius matris sue. Miratur quod moram faciat longiorem & de mora diuturna subito timet & stupescit. Non enim de facili obliuiscitur mater infantem vteri sui propter gaudium quia natus est homo in mundum. Effecta ergo fere sui impaciens opus manuum pretermittit, plateas ingreditur & vicos circuit ciuitatis circumspicit vndique venientes oculo subtili obuios intuetur. Set nusquam filij sui faciem deprehendit: vltro graditur & vltra progreditur & ingreditur iudaismum, vix se sustinens pre dolore quia dormitauit anima eius pre tedio cum ipsum quem dilexerat viuentem mortuum estimabat. ffit iam vicina domui qua facinus exercuit progenies viperarum audit mater anxia filium suum decantantem *Alma redemptoris mater*. Audiebat quidem vocem set neminem videbat. Idcirco stabat stupefacta set tamen velut ouis solo balatu agnum, sic & ipsa filium proprium proprietate vocis et organi recognoscit, laborabat mater sustinens puerum periendo. Idcirco laborat clamans ori proprio non parcendo non potuit ori suo custodiam; set licet clamando rauce facte fuissent fauces sue tamen clamat indesinenter ad hostia hostium cruentorum: "Reddite filium meum! Reddite filium meum!" Verbi geminacio dolorem animi detegebat. Extra domum filium suum repetit a iudeis, set cum non satisfaceret crudelitas perfidorum in offenso pede adit domum canonici pretaxati, eidem ex ordine referens vniuersa. Accedit canonicus plangens puerum & deplorans. Ab interfectoribus repetit interfectum, set eorum perfidia ipsius voto nullatenus satisfecit. Audit tamen & ipse vocem cognitam innocentis decantantis suauiter *Alma redemptoris mater*.

Currunt ergo pariter ad Archiepiscopum vrbis tolletane eidem rei seriem indicantes.[1] Qui cum innumera manu armatorum currens ad spectaculum, locum perfidie conscium est ingressus, hostia confringit obstancia & seuerius precipit peremptori vt innocentis perempti eximie cicius ostendantur. Credidit enim extinctum quem tanta malicia secrecius occultabat. Vniuersi in puerum necem consencerunt, set pueri precipuus interfector formidans Archiepiscopi maiestatem tocius nequicie veritatem confitetur quomodo cunque ⟨fol. 38ᵛ⟩ ob

---

[1] The scribe wrote *indicantis* and then corrected it by writing *e* above the line.

inuidiam conceptam contra Redemptoris matrem puerum innoxium suffocauit, eo quod in matris virginis memoriam tam suauem concinnit cantilenam. Confessus ymmo magis conuictus ex scelere Archipresulis iudicio se subiecit, misericordiam amplius expetens quam censuram, Archipresul ad manum trahitur. Erant enim ibi tenebre & caligo vbi puer mortuus iacuit in profundo. Tandem voce duce & ductrice ad locum ipsum peruenitur vbi miraculose sine intermissione concinebat puer mortuus *Alma redemptoris mater*. Cum enim vox extincti antiphone finem explicasset idem canticum tota die incepit iterato.

Extrahitur ergo puer tanquam alter Joseph de cisterna, & tam festiue quam festine ad ecclesiam deportatur, nec recedit ab eius ore preconium virginale quia assidue concinit *Alma redemptoris mater*. Conuocato populo, clero cum deuocione maxima assistente, incipit Archipresul in honore beate virginis diuina celebrare. Venit hora qua silencium assistentibus imperatur cum aperitur vox predicantis bonum annunciantis salutem per euangelium. Silet puer ori suo apponens ostium circumstancie ne vox ipsius verba euangelica minus intelligi faciat vel audiri. Auditur euangelium a circumstantibus tam fideliter quam deuote.[1] Ipsoque perlecto salubriter mirabiliter reincepit puer cantilenam *Alma redemptoris mater*. O quanta in clero deuota votorum deuocio! quanto in populo que stabat in gradu suo lacrimarum effusio cum extinctus repecijt quod nuper omisit! Iterans vocis organo quod prius silencio pretermisit. Cum reuerencia tractatur hostia salutaris in altari recolitur memoria dominice passionis organo innocencie marie preconium concinente. Expletis redempcionis nostre misterijs Archipresul se ad populum conuertens sermonem texit in laudem pudicicie virginalis nec christi preconium reticet vel occultat dum marie matris eius memoriam venerabiliter representat. In fine sermonis clerum et populum cum lacrimis exhortatur vt cum deuocionis aromate cum pie oracionis thure vnanimiter natum de virgine deprecentur quatinus meritis matris suo & prece virginis preciose dignetur puerum reddere rediuiuum & eidem mortuo, vite spiraculum inspirare. Plebs & clerus effundunt in se animas suas effundunt sicut aquam cor suum in conspectu domini ⟨fol. 39⟩ fundentes pluuiam voluntariam ac ymbrem serotinum lacrimarum quia lacrime sue in maxillis suis. Orant suppliciter & supplicant confidenter, nec est eis opposita nubes diffidencie ne transiret oracio quia ascendit vsque ad consistorium trinitatis. ffides enim eorum celos penetrauit celeriter & eorum felix confidencia tam fiducialiter quam feliciter impetrauit.

[1] de deuote *MS;* clearly a scribal repetition.

Oracione facta publica seu priuata, matre virgine vt arbitror respiciente in faciem christi filij sui & ipsum vt credo familiariter deprecante, subito guttur pueri precisus reseratur,[1] pellis prius dissuta integre restauratur, lingua redditur diuina canenti preconia, cor cum pulmone aut prius ablatum restituitur aut concessum diuinitus de nouo procreatur. Anima ad vas suum & sui vehiculum reuocatur & homo fiat integer carni mortue iterum se maritat spiritus immortalis. Reuixit qui mortuus fuerat & recedit, puer quasi de graui sompno excitato; set tamen marie preconium non[2] pretermittit set organo mellifluo concinit *Alma redemptoris mater.* O vere alma redemptoris mater que sic succurrit egenti surgere defuncto puero, nam que[3] genitorem natura mirante suum genuit, vitalem spiritum natura mirante mortuo sic infudit sue precis remedio mediante.

Exultat turba fidelium visa miraculi nouitate & de visione resol[u]-untur in lacrimas vniuersi putantes tamen fantasma esse. Intuentur faciem rediuiui, lapillum per mariam impositum in ore reperiunt, inuentum extrahunt & rediuiuus continuo antiphonam pretermittit *Alma redemptoris mater.* Amisit organum qui prius silencium non admisit. Lapis ille in signum repositus est in ecclesia cathedrali in monumentum rei & miraculi testimonium perpetuo reseruandus.

Inquirit ergo pontifex a puero tocius[4] rei seriem & tenorem, & ipse pro voto pontifici satisfaciens, rei processum excessum iudeorum sui martirium & virginis marie suffragium veraciter enarrauit. Totumque dei genetrici ascribebat quicquid circa ipsum actum est per matrem gracie, que de sue habundancia misericordie ipsius miserie sic subuenit. Inter alia suo digito demonstrauit occisorem, et vere resuscitatus a mortuis pro suo peremptore ne mortis reus morti traderetur instanter et humiliter supplicauit. Surgens tandem puer grates vberimas sue reddidit saluatrici, totusque factus incolumis vixit diucius in vrbe tolletana.

Judeus plus venia desperans quam vindicta viso miraculo se reum mortis confitetur set tamen perfundi se postulat lauacro salutari. Pontifex ⟨fol. 39ᵛ⟩ salutem anime eius siciens[5] non criminis vlcionem iudeum baptizatum consignat ecclesie & caractare fidei nostre insignito remittit penam pariter & offensam. Qui postmodum effectus est Marie pijssimus venerator qui prius fuerat sui nominis impijssimus

---

[1] resaratur *MS.*

[2] This word has been written in above the line by the same hand.

[3] naq naq3 *MS.*

[4] The scribe first wrote *tociens* and afterward dotted it for deletion, writing *tocius* above the line.

[5] sciciens *MS.*

persecutor. Gentilis eciam quidam ad hoc venit spectaculum set dum huiusmodi fieret spectator miraculi fidei se subdidit christiane. Vt sic in fide christi lapidis angularis ex circumcisione[1] et prepucio duo parietes[2] iungerentur. Ipse quoque fidus de perfidio, diues opum et habundans diuicijs in honorem matris virginis ecclesiam fabricauit, vbi virginis memoria memoriter celebratur. Sic[3] alma redemptoris mater vtrique subuenit cum effectu, que sui memores deo commendet meritis & iuuet beneficijs. AMEN.

ffinis

[1] circumsicione *MS.*

[2] The scribe wrote first *parites* and then added the *e* above the line.

[3] Sic sic *MS.*

SIR THOPAS

By LAURA HIBBARD LOOMIS

INTRODUCTION

CHAUCER'S *Sir Thopas* has no one source, no one analogue, in any ordinary sense of these words. Irrepressibly
comic and creative, it touches lightly as *a boterflye* on a
variety of romances and other poems. Though obviously a
mock romance, a "Don Quixote in little,"[1] with "its manifest
banter" directed against what Tyrwhitt[2] described as "the
palpable gross fictions, and still more, perhaps, ... the mean-
ness of the language and versification of the common rimers
of Chaucer's own day," it is in no wise a parody on any one
school of romances,[3] if the twelve-line, tail-rhyme romances are,
indeed, to be so designated; it follows no previous pattern of
burlesque or parody, either social or literary.[4] Genius is airily

[1] *Hurd's Letters on Chivalry and Romance*, ed. Edith J. Morley (London, 1911),
pp. 147, 172 ff.; cf. also Caroline Spurgeon, *Five Hundred Years of Chaucer Criticism* (Cambridge, 1925), I, 422; IV, 73. The *Letters* were printed in 1762, 1765, etc.
On the Percy-Warton comments on *Thopas* as a burlesque see Leah Dennis,
"Percy's Essay 'On the Ancient Metrical Romances,'" *PMLA*, XLIX (1934),
90, n. 40.

[2] Thomas Tyrwhitt, *The Canterbury Tales of Chaucer* (London, 1775–78), from
1843 ed., p. lxvi.

[3] A. Trounce ("The English Tail-Rhyme Romances," *Medium Ævum*, I [1932],
89–92) opposed the idea that this "school" of romances was the particular object
of Chaucer's satire.

[4] Medieval French burlesques on the *chansons de geste* or the romances of
chivalry, though analogous in parodistic spirit to *Thopas*, differ from it entirely
in style and substance. Cf. the *Dit d'aventures* (ed. Trebutien [Paris, 1835]), a
tale of preposterous adventures and escapes; the mock-heroic account of Flemish
burghers attacking the Château of Neuville (inedited, MS Suppl. fr. n. 184,
f. 213 ff.; *Hist. Litt.*, XXIII, 498); the gross *Audigier* (Méon and Barbazan,
Fabliaux et contes [Paris, 1808], IV, 217 ff.). For these and other French parodies
see *Hist. Litt.*, XXIII, 501 ff., XXIV, 507; C. Lenient, *La Satire en France* [Paris,
1893], pp. 125–30; H. Schneegans, *Geschichte der grotesken Satire* [Strassburg,
1894], pp. 88, 93; S. M. Tucker, *Verse Satire in England before the Renaissance*
(New York, 1908), p. 25.
For the theory that *Thopas* satirized the Flemings see Lilian Winstanley in her
edition of the *Prioress's Tale* and the *Tale of Sir Thopas* (Cambridge, 1922),

at play in *Thopas*, and the original combinations of old motifs, the unexpected grace of such lines as those describing
the Fairy Queen, are not to be documented. They illustrate
Chaucer's unimpeded originality in the very midst of closest
imitation.

The English poems that excited Chaucer's mirth are in part
indicated by the seven names which he himself cites in *Thopas*.
With the exception of Pleyndamour,[1] for whom no story is now
known, and of Ypotys, the "wise child" of the didactic poem
that bears his name, all the others are titular heroes of extant
"romances of prys." It cannot be shown with certainty that
Chaucer used much more than the titles of *Ypotis* and *Horn
Childe*,[2] or much more than the opening stanzas of *Beves of
Hamtoun* and *Perceval of Gales*.[3] *Guy of Warwick* and, to a less
extent, *Libeaus Desconus*,[4] were, of the romances named, unquestionably, his chief "sources," as from these he culled much

---

pp. lxv ff.; J. M. Manly, "Sir Thopas, a Satire," in *Essays and Studies by Members
of the English Association*, XIII (Oxford, 1928), 52–73, and his edition of the
Canterbury Tales (New York, 1928), pp. 628 ff. The theory is strongly disputed
by W. W. Lawrence, "Satire in Sir Thopas," *PMLA*, L (1935), 81–91.

As an English burlesque *Thopas* belongs with the thirteenth-century *Land of
Cockaygne* (cf. No. 90 in our illustrative extracts) and the fifteenth-century poems,
The Hunting of the Hare (Weber, *Met. Romances*, III, 279 ff.), and the *Tournament
of Tottenham* (French and Hale, *ME Met. Romances*, pp. 989 ff.). In later times
Thopas was in part imitated by Drayton, *Idea* (Eighth Ecl., 1593), and by William
Dunbar, *Of Sir Thomas Norray* (cf. Snyder, *MLN*, XXV [1910], 78 ff.).

[1] Skeat (*Chaucer*, V, 199) noted the name in Malory's *Morte Darthur*, IX, 7,
where Playn de Amours is used for one of three brothers encountered by La Cote
Mal Taillé, a hero whose adventures at this point parallel those of *Libeaus Des-
conus*. Malory presumably drew this part of the story from some expanded
French prose *Tristan*, but no manuscript has yet been found which records the
name Playn de Amours. Cf. Vinaver, *Roman de Tristan dans l'œuvre de Thomas
Malory* (Paris, 1925), p. 170, n. 173. Malory's use of the name militates against the
possibility that Chaucer himself invented it on the model of similar names:
Triamour in *Guy of Warwick*, st. 51(10) and in *Launfal*, vs. 255; Lady Doceamour in
Beves, vs. 161; the Dame d'Amour in *Libeaus*, vs. 1490, the Lady Lufamour in
Perceval, vs. 1565, to say nothing of the titular heroes, Eglamour and Triamour.
On the name of Plenus Amoris for fifteenth-century scribes see F. N. Robinson,
Chaucer, p. 846. On Spenser's *Blandamour* see Magoun, *MP*, XXV, 129; on
Percy's, see Dennis, *MP*, XXIX (1931–32), 232.

[2] For *Ypotis* see No. 17 of the illustrative extracts; for *Horn Childe* see No. 9.

[3] See *Beves*, No. 4 of the illustrative extracts; *Perceval*, No. 14.

[4] See illustrative extracts, *Guy*, A, Nos. 8, 19, 25, 32, 46, 53, 57, 71, 83; and
Libeaus, Nos. 12, 22, 35, 54, 58.

of the phraseology and several of the narrative motifs used in
Thopas. From unnamed romances, from *Launfal, Thomas of
Erceldoune*, and *Eglamour*,[1] he took brief but recognizable
elements. From other romances, *Alisaunder, Amis and Amiloun, Degaré, Degrevant, Gamelyn, Ipomedon, Isumbras, Octavian,
Orfeo, Reinbrun, Richard Cœur de Lion, Seven Sages, Torrent of
Portyngale*, as our illustrative extracts show, he may have taken
hints and phrases, but the brevity of *Thopas* and the conventionality of the romances alike make assurance, in most of
these cases, impossible.

A generous estimate of the evidence afforded by *Thopas*
suggests that Chaucer may have read, or glanced at, fifteen to
twenty of the one hundred and thirteen Middle English romances that are still extant. His amused and eclectic choice was,
no doubt, in large part determined by the manuscript collections in which he found them, for in his day, as also in the
fifteenth century, native vernacular productions were commonly found only in large miscellanies. Two fifteenth-century
collections[2] of this sort still contain the theological *Ypotis* and
the highly romantic *Libeaus*, poems which Chaucer, likewise,
incongruously conjoined in his listing of "romances of prys."
Of these collections, the one in Cotton Caligula A II[3] also included the extraordinary *Trentals* of St. Gregory, and a life of
St. Jerome,[4] two fourteenth-century poems which may account,
since Gregory was called a pope and Jerome was, to the contemporary mind, a cardinal,[5] for the diverting "romances of

[1] See illustrative extracts, *Launfal*, Nos. 49 and 96; *Thomas of Erceldoune*,
No. 51; *Eglamour*, Nos. 7, 56, 64, 70, 79.

[2] Bodleian, Ashmole 61; British Museum, Cotton Caligula A II. Miss Dorothy
Everett (*RES*, VI [1930], 446 ff.) noted that in these two collections *Libeaus,
Ypotis*, and *Isumbras* appeared together, were copied by the same hand, and that
it was probable Chaucer had seen them, similarly associated together, in some
earlier manuscript.

[3] The first part of this manuscript, fols. 3–139, originally Vespasian D 8, including the romances, was copied between 1446 and 1460. Cf. E. Rickert, *Emare*
("E.E.T.S.: Extra Series," Vol. XCIX [1906–8]), pp. ix–x.

[4] For these texts see J. E. Wells, *Manual of Writings in Middle English* (New
Haven, 1916), pp. 172, 311; also Carleton Brown, *Register of Middle English Religious and Didactic Verse* (Oxford, 1920), II, 24, No. 58; II, 271, No. 1836.

[5] In medieval art Jerome was represented with a cardinal's hat from the end of
the thirteenth century (cf. K. Kuenstle, *Ikonographie der Heiligen* [Freiburg-in-

popes and cardinales" in *Thopas*. The same manuscript contains, besides *Libeaus* and *Ypotis*, the unique text of *Launfal*, also *Eglamour*, *Octavian*, and *Isumbras*. The presumption that Chaucer had access to some fourteenth-century prototype of this fifteenth-century manuscript is strong.

Strong too is the presumption that before writing *Thopas* Chaucer had in hand the famous Auchinleck manuscript,[1] written between 1327 and 1340 and in large part by scribes of London,[2] where it may well have remained until Chaucer's day. Despite its many losses, it still contains the only known version of *Horn Childe*, to which Chaucer makes the only known allusion; it alone gives *Horn Childe* in conjunction with *Guy of Warwick* and *Beves of Hamtoun* and so proves that Chaucer's naming of the three together was not a matter of chance. It gives the opening section of *Beves of Hamtoun* (vss. 1–474) in that six-line, tail-rhyme stanza which is the basic form of *Thopas*;[3] the first four lines of *Beves* in this manuscript are closer than in any other now extant to Chaucer's longest instance of verbal borrowing in *Thopas*.[4] The same manuscript contains the unique text of *Sir Tristrem*, which

---

Breisgau, 1926], p. 299). Two illuminations in a splendid Bible executed in England in the latter part of the fourteenth century, probably for Richard II, show Jerome with the cardinal's hat (cf. Brit. Mus., Roy. I E IX, fols. 230, 234 [reproduced by Eric Millar, *English Illuminations of the XIVth Century* (Paris, 1928), Pls. 74, 77]).

[1] The manuscript is now in Edinburgh in the National Library, Adv. MS 19.2.1. On Chaucer's probable use of this manuscript see L. H. Loomis, "Chaucer and the Auchinleck MS: 'Thopas' and 'Guy of Warwick,'" *Studies in Honor of Carleton Brown* (New York, 1940), pp. 111–28.

[2] On this almost unanimously accepted date for the Auchinleck MS see J. M. Booker, *A Middle English Bibliography* (Heidelberg, 1912), p. 54. The A scribe wrote 35 of the 44 extant items in the manuscript (cf. Carr, "A ME Scribe's Methods," *Univ. of Wis., Studies in Lang. and Lit.*, II [1918], 153). This A scribe was established as of London origin by Karl Brunner, *The Seven Sages of Rome* ("E.E.T.S.," Vol. CXCI [1933]), pp. xxv–vii. The London origin of the Y scribe, who copied two poems, was established by Zettl, *Anonymous Short Metrical Chronicle* ("E.E.T.S.," Vol. CXCVI [1935]), pp. xvi ff. The work of the different scribes was first determined by Kölbing, "Vier Romanzen-Handschriften," *ES*, VII (1884), 177–201, whose description of the Auchinleck MS is still the best in print.

[3] Manly, "Stanza Forms in Sir Thopas," *MP*, VIII (1910), 135 ff.

[4] See illustrative extracts, *Beves*, No. 4.

with the exception of *Sir Gawain and the Green Knight*, is the only known Middle English romance to contain stanzas with a one-stress line such as Chaucer used in five stanzas of *Thopas*. Among its seventeen romances are *Alisaunder*, though but a fragment is now left, *Amis*, *Degaré*, *Orfeo*, *Reinbrun*, *Roland and Vernagu*, the *Seven Sages*, a fragment of the "roiale" romance of *King Richard*, and a romantic life of Pope Gregory. Above all, it contains the only known stanzaic version of *Guy of Warwick*, the romance which, in this unique version and in the couplet version preceding it, offers the largest number of verbal parallels to *Thopas* of any known text.[1] It is certain that Chaucer used conjointly these two versions of *Guy*.

The Auchinleck manuscript in its entirety and perhaps some fourteenth-century prototype of Cotton Caligula A II may, then, have been in large part the true begetters of *Thopas*,[2] which has all the air of a sudden tour de force written under the influence of some special stimulus. The use Chaucer made elsewhere of the English popular romances[3] is, by comparison with

---

[1] Miss Caroline Strong ("Sir Thopas and Sir Guy," *MLN*, XXIII [1908], 103 ff.) pointed out over forty verbal correspondences between *Guy* and the parody. Even more convincing are the similar combinations of identical elements (i.e., of the same rhymes, phrases, and concepts) occurring in small groups throughout the two texts. See especially in the illustrative extracts, *Guy*, A, No. 8, p. 500, nn. 2–4, and p. 501, nn. 1–2; No. 25, p. 509, n. 3; No. 32, pp. 512–13; No. 46, p. 517, nn. 1 and 3; No. 53, p. 528, n. 1; No. 57, p. 534, n. 1.

It is of interest to observe that the two rude comments of the Host when he interrupts Chaucer's parody seem both to have come from *Guy*, A:

Now swich a rym the devel I biteche!	*Thopas*
þe deuel biteche ich ȝou ichon.	*Guy*, A, 5834
Thy drasty rymyng is nat worth a toord	*Thopas*
þou nart nouȝt worþ a tord!	*Guy*, A, 3704

Chaucer's own implied satirical criticism of this romance is of special significance in view of the long-continued popularity of *Guy* (see R. S. Crane, "The Vogue of Guy of Warwick," *PMLA*, XXX [1915], 125 ff.).

[2] Trounce, p. 90, in arguing that Chaucer was not parodying "decadent romance," pointed out that the poet's criticisms "would apply with perhaps more force to the early examples of the Auchinleck MS than to those that came later in the century."

[3] Cf. Eleanor Hammond, *Chaucer: A Bibliographical Manual* (New York, 1908), p. 76: "Were it not for the full knowledge of the English metrical romances displayed in the Rime of Sir Thopas, we might have assumed that Chaucer had done no reading in that field, and had picked up his allusions .... from the literary commonplace of his time." Cf. also Howard Patch, "Chaucer and the Romances," *Essays for Barrett Wendell* (Cambridge, 1926), p. 99. The opposite

his use of foreign sources, slight; in *Thopas* his merry wit seems to have been touched off by fresh and concentrated contact with some such bulky and heterogeneous collection as each of these manuscripts presents. Though in general the English romances are short rather than long, running usually from about one thousand to three thousand lines, the Auchinleck manuscript in particular contains some notable examples of prolixity. In it *Guy* runs to over 10,000 lines; *Beves* to 4,620; *Arthur and Merlin* to 9,938; *Alisaunder*, and *Richard Cœur de Lion*, of which only fragments now remain, originally to over 8,000 and 6,000 lines, respectively. In *Guy* and other long-winded and inconsequent stories, "the rambling narrative, the want of plan and method and meaning,"[1] are especially noticeable. Nearly all the romances indulge in extreme exaggerations, especially of the hero's prowess;[2] they make excessive use of insignificant detail;[3] they show the same bourgeois absurdities in setting forth knight-errantry.[4] Above all, they use the same worn devices of minstrel style, the same stereotyped diction, with reiterated commonplace rhymes and phrases.[5]

---

point of view is expressed by R. M. Smith, "Two Chaucer Notes," *MLN*, LI (1936), 314: "Chaucer's familiarity with the romances is to be seen in many of his tales besides *Sir Thopas*." The best list of verbal parallels between Chaucer and the romances is still that of Kittredge in *Harvard Studies in Phil. and Lit.*, I (1892), 56 ff.

It may be noted, as evidence of some exceptional vocabulary influence on *Thopas*, that the poem contains at least twenty-three words which Chaucer uses nowhere else: *aketoun*, *auntrous*, *comyn*, cordewain, *crest*, *dapple-grey*, *destrer*, gyngebreed, hepe (meaning hip), *jambeaux*, lake (meaning linen cloth), launcegay, *leere* (meaning flesh), *mazelyn*, *quyrboilly*, *payndeymayn*, *rewel-boon*, *symphonye*, *spelle* (meaning story), *staf-slynge*, *syklatoun*, trie, wonger. All the italicized words appear in the romances.

[1] W. P. Ker, *English Literature: Medieval* (London, 1912), p. 130.

[2] See Sec. VI, "The Hero in Combat"; Sec. VIII, "The Hero's Praise."

[3] See Sec. III, "The Hero's Pastimes."

[4] See Sec. II, "The Hero's Appearance," and also Sec. III. Cf. Lawrence, *PMLA*, L (1935), 87: "The English romances .... were intended primarily for the simpler middle-class folk. Courtly elegancies are often neglected. .... Chaucer deliberately made his carpet knight plebeian."

[5] For good collections of these conventional phrases see the editions cited in the "Bibliographical Note," especially those for *Amis*, *Athelston*, *Beves*, *Horn*, *Ipomedon*, *Libeaus*, *Octavian*, *Orfeo*, *Perceval*.

Specialized studies of *Thopas* in relation to the romances are: C. J. Bennewitz, *Chaucer's Sir Thopas* (Halle, 1879); E. Kölbing, "Zu Chaucer's Sir Thopas," *ES*, XI (1888), 495–511; W. E. Mead, *The Squyr of Lowe Degre* (Boston, 1904),

The manner, even more than the matter, the phraseology that was the same, whatever the subject or form—pious legend, romance, or lyric[1]—it was this, as he observed it in large collections of contemporary English verse, that aroused Chaucer's derisive wit to parody.

But though Chaucer thus parodied the defects of popular English minstrelsy, especially as they were revealed in the romances, he was not, necessarily, parodying romance as a thing in itself,[2] nor was every line, even in the brief compass of *Thopas*, of equally satiric purpose. Such charming tales "of faery" as *Orfeo* in the Auchinleck manuscript or *Launfal* or *Thomas of Erceldoune*, now preserved only in fifteenth-century manuscripts, but surely once known to him, were far from common in theme and in themselves were neither "mechanical nor absurd." Giants and fays are not associated in Middle English romance, unless the evil enchantress of *Libeaus* is to be so regarded,[3] and, though they are in *Thopas*, Chaucer's purpose in introducing the Fairy Queen need not have been wholly satiric. To make his "carpet knight" still more absurd by having him love an unknown supernatural being was one thing, but the charm of tales "of faery" was palpably upon Chaucer when he sang—as for a medieval Titania—of the Fairy Queen herself, "with harpe and pipe and symphonye," and borrowed from such narratives delightful details, however humorously he used them.

Moreover, slight as are the indications, it is also clear that romances, though the chief source and real occasion of *Thopas*, were not the sole texts in Chaucer's mind. A biblical reminiscence of David and Goliath, possibly through the medium of some Middle English version, influenced his telling of Thopas' encounter with the giant[4] and his "staf-slynge." The bird and

---

pp. lii–lxv, on "The Relation to Chaucer's Sir Thopas"; Miss Strong, "Sir Thopas and Sir Guy," *MLN*, XXIII (1908), 73 ff., 102 ff. For *Guy of Warwick* cf. L. H. Loomis, *Studies . . . . Carleton Brown*, pp. 111 ff. Cf. F. P. Magoun, "The Source of Chaucer's Rime of Sir Thopas," *PMLA*, XLII (1927), 833–44 (on *Libeaus*).

[1] Cf., in the illustrative extracts, Nos. 1 and 88, for examples of legend and lyric.

[2] Cf. Bishop Hurd (*Letters*, p. 175): "He did not mean . . . . to condemn the kind of writing itself: as, I think, we must conclude from the serious air, and very different conduct of the Squire's Tale."

[3] See below, *Libeaus*, No. 58, p. 536, n. 2.   [4] See below, *Cursor mundi*, No. 55.

spice and hero lists, as is shown below,[1] suggest poems that were not romances. Echoes from his own poems are heard, for Chaucer could imitate himself as humorously as he imitated others.[2] And though he was as true a lover of knighthood as of romance, he could, and perhaps did, borrow the basic suggestion for naming his absurd "gem of knighthood," his Flanders-born knight of Poperynghe, from a long French poem which elsewhere he seems to have taken seriously enough.[3] It was by Watriquet de Couvin, a well-known poet of Hainault, who thus, a bit too ornately, praised his sometime noble lord and patron, the Constable of France:[4]

> C'est la jemme et la topase[5]
> Des haus hommes, tous les passoit
> D'honneur faire.

---

[1] See below, Sec. X, "Catalogue Lists."

[2] Mead (pp. lii–lxv) notes that the *it is no nay* of *Thopas* occurs twice in the *Clerk's Tale* (E 817, 1139); that *joye it was to here* occurs in *Prol. to LGW* (vs. 139) with the same rhyme, *clere : here*; that *She sang ful loude and clere* is closely paralleled in the *Merchant's Tale* (E 1845). For bird lists see below, Sec. X, "Catalogue Lists."

Numerous other instances might be cited. Cf. *Hous of Fame* (III, 1198), *Of alle maner of mynstralles,/And gestiours, that tellen tales*, with *Thopas, my mynstrales,/And gestours for to tellen tales;* or the *Pardoner's Tale* (vs. 341), *telle I forth my tales;/ Bulles of popes and cardynales*, with *Thopas, for to tellen tales,/ . . . . Of popes and of cardinales*. The Pardoner also refers to *moyste ale* (vs. 315), and to *saffron* (vs. 345), which are paralleled in *Thopas, ale, moyste or stale*, and *lyk saffroun*. Cf. No. 43.

[3] W. H. Schofield (*Chivalry in English Literature* [Cambridge, 1912], pp. 31, 278) suggested that Chaucer's praise of the noble Knight of the Canterbury Pilgrimage was influenced by that given to the hero of the French poem by Watriquet de Couvin.

[4] *Dits de Watriquet de Couvin*, ed. Scheler (1868), p. 44: *Dit du Connestable de France* (Gauchier de Chatillon, d. 1329). Schofield, p. 278, cited this in connection with *Thopas*.

[5] On the medieval worth and symbolic significance of the topaz see *English Medieval Lapidaries*, ed. Joan Evans and M. S. Serjeantson ("E.E.T.S.," Vol. CXC [1933]), p. 19: "He that bereth þis stone [the topaz] shall the more love to leede his body in chastity"; p. 107: "In the tresor of kynges no þing is mor cler nor mor preciose þen þis preciose ston is." Cf. also Manly, *Canterbury Tales*, p. 630; Ross, *MLN*, XLV (1930), 172. In stressing the peerlessness and chastity of his comic hero, Chaucer may have had these ideas about the topaz in mind. It is also possible, if he knew that *Topyas* was a feminine name in *Richard*, vs. 204, that this suggested effeminacy as a further attribute (cf. R. M. Smith, *MLN*, LI [1936], 314). On Thopas' effeminate traits see below, Sec. II, "The Hero's Appearance." On the hero's chastity see also No. 46, *Guy*, A, sts. 5 and 10.

ILLUSTRATIVE EXTRACTS

As *Thopas* falls, for the purposes of burlesque, into more or less obvious topical sections, the following extracts from Middle English poems are similarly arranged and are designed to illustrate the following topics:

I. Minstrel Comments, Nos. 1–17
II. The Hero's Appearance, Nos. 18–23
III. The Hero's Pastimes, Nos. 24–25
IV. The Hero in Love and Beloved, Nos. 46–51
V. The Hero in Arms, Nos. 52–54
VI. The Hero in Combat, Nos. 55–60
VII. The Hero's Vow, Nos. 61–68
VIII. The Hero's Praise, Nos. 69–76
IX. The Hero "Auntrous," Nos. 77–87
X. Catalogue Lists, Nos. 88–101

The extracts are limited, for the most part, to passages which have not only similarity of theme but also some identity with *Thopas* of word, phrase, or rhyme. Words of this character are italicized in order that the verbal commonplaces which Chaucer was parodying may be distinguished at a glance; also that the occurrence of these identical elements in small but significant groups may be realized. In certain instances they clearly indicate Chaucer's specific source. In each section the extracts are, for convenience of reference, alphabetically arranged according to the title of each poem. References, in the summaries heading each section, are to the extracts immediately following. All citations, unless otherwise indicated in the notes, are from poems dated before 1400 by J. E. Wells, in his *Manual of Writings in Middle English* (New Haven, 1916), and later *Supplements*. The extracts are numbered consecutively and under each title in the "Bibliographical Note" is a complete list of the numbers under which extracts from that text appear. Unless otherwise indicated in the notes, the extracts are from the manuscripts and editions given in the "Bibliographical Note." In general, older editions have been cited, in preference to those of more recent date, as the former contain large collections of parallel passages.

BIBLIOGRAPHICAL NOTE

Alexius, in *Life of St. Alexius*, ed. Furnivall ("E.E.T.S.," Vol. LXIX [1878]), p. 20. MS Oxf., Trin. 57 (late fourteenth century). No. 1.

Alisaunder, Kyng Alisaunder, in *Metrical Romances*, ed. Weber (Edinburgh, 1810), I, 1 ff. MS Lincoln's Inn, L 150 (late fourteenth century or early fifteenth). Nos. 2, 89.

Amis, Amis and Amiloun, ed. Kölbing (Heilbronn, 1884). Auchinleck MS (1327–40). Nos. 3, 29, 38, 69.

Annot and Johon, in *English Lyrics of the XIIIth Century*, ed. Carleton Brown (Oxford, 1932), p. 136. No. 88.

Athelston, ed. Zupitza, in *Englische Studien*, XIII (1889), 331 ff. Unique MS Cbg., Caius Coll. 175 (fifteenth century). Nos. 18, 61.

Avowis of Alexander, in *The Buik of Alexander,* ed. R. L. Ritchie (4 vols.; Edinburgh, 1921–29), III, 248–351. Unique print (*ca.* 1580). No. 62.

Beves, Beves of Hamtoun, ed. Kölbing ("E.E.T.S.: Extra Series," Vols. XLVI, XLVIII, LXV [1885–86, 1894]). Auchinleck MS (1327–40). Nos. 4, 30, 52.

Canterbury Tales, in *Chaucer's Complete Works,* ed. F. N. Robinson (Boston, 1933). Nos. 43, 93. For *Sir Thopas* see *passim.*

Confessio amantis, Book I, in *Complete Works of John Gower,* ed. G. C. Macaulay (Oxford, 1901), Vol. II. No. 82.

Cursor mundi, ed. Morris ("E.E.T.S.," Vols. LVII, LIX, LXII, LXVI, LXVIII–IX, CI [1874–93]). Göttingen Univ. Libr. Theol. 107 (fourteenth century). Nos. 55, 95.

Degaré, in *Middle English Metrical Romances,* ed. French and Hale (New York, 1930), pp. 287 ff. Auchinleck MS (1327–40). Nos. 5, 31, 77.

Degrevant, ed. Luick (Leipzig, 1917). Thornton MS (fifteenth century), Nos. 6, 24, 63, 78.

Eglamour, ed. Schleich in *Palœstra,* Vol. LIII (Berlin, 1906). Thornton MS (fifteenth century). Nos. 7, 56, 64, 70, 79.

Gamelyn, in *Chaucer's Complete Works,* ed. Skeat (Oxford, 1894), IV, 645 ff. MS Harl. 7334 (fifteenth century). No. 44.

Gawain and the Green Knight, ed. Tolkien and Gordon (Oxford, 1925). Unique MS, Cotton Nero A X 4 (late fourteenth century or early fifteenth). No. 80.

Generides, ed. Wright ("E.E.T.S.," Vols. LV, LXX [1873–78]). MS Cbg., Trinity Coll., Gale O 5.2 (fifteenth century). No. 81.

Guy, Guy of Warwick, A, ed. Zupitza ("E.E.T.S.: Extra Series," Vols. XLII, XLIX, LIX [1883–91]). Couplet and unique stanzaic version in the Auchinleck MS (1327–40). Nos. 8, 19, 25, 32, 46, 53, 57, 71, 83.

Horn, in *King Horn,* ed. Hall (Oxford, 1901). MS Cbg. Univ. Libr. Gg. IV, 27.2 (*ca.* 1250–60). No. 20.

Horn Childe, in *King Horn,* ed. Hall (Oxford, 1901). Unique MS, Auchinleck (1327–40). No. 9.

Ipomadon, A (stanzaic version), in *Ipomedon,* ed. Kölbing (Breslau, 1889), pp. 3 ff. Unique MS, Manchester, Chetham 8009 (fifteenth century). Nos. 21, 40, 48, 72, 84.

Ipomydon, B, *Lyfe of Ipomydon* (couplet version), in *Ipomedon,* ed. Kölbing (Breslau, 1889), pp. 257 ff. Unique MS, Harl. 2252 (late fifteenth century). Nos. 10, 26, 33, 39, 47.

Isumbras, Sir Ysumbras, ed. Schleich in *Palœstra,* Vol. XV (Berlin, 1901). Thornton MS (fifteenth century). Nos. 11, 34.

Land of Cockaygne, in *Altenglische Sprachproben,* ed. Mätzner (Berlin, 1867–1900), I, 150. Unique Kildare MS, Harl. 913 (early fourteenth century). No. 90.

Launfal, in *Middle English Metrical Romances,* ed. French and Hale (New York, 1930), pp. 345 ff. Unique MS, Cotton Caligula A II (fifteenth century). Nos. 49, 96.

Libeaus, Libeaus Desconus, ed. Kaluza (Leipzig, 1890). Critical Text. Nos. 12, 22, 35, 54, 58.

Octavian, A (southern version, six-line stanzas), ed. Sarrazin (Heilbronn, 1885), pp. 2 ff. Unique MS, Cotton Caligula A II. Nos. 45, 74, 91.

Octavian, B (northern version, twelve-line stanzas), ed. Sarrazin (Heilbronn, 1885), pp. 64 ff. Thornton MS (fifteenth century). No. 13.

Orfeo, ed. Oscar Zielke (Breslau, 1880). Auchinleck MS (1327–40). No. 27.

Perceval of Gales, ed. Campion and Holthausen (Heidelberg and New York, 1913). Unique copy, Thornton MS (fifteenth century). Nos. 14, 28, 41, 59, 66.

Reinbrun, in *Guy of Warwick* (see above), pp. 631 ff. Unique Auchinleck MS (1327–40). Nos. 36, 75.

Richard, King Richard Cœur de Lion, ed. Karl Brunner (Vienna, 1913). Cbg. Gonville and Caius Coll. 175/96 (fifteenth century). Nos. 86, 92, 97.

Seven Sages, ed. Campbell (Boston, 1907). Cotton Galba E IX (early fifteenth century). Nos. 15, 50, 67.

Speculum vitae, ed. Ullmann, in *Englische Studien*, VII (1884), 469. Cbg. Univ. Libr. Ll. I.8 (late fourteenth century). No. 98.

Squire of Low Degree, ed. Mead (Boston, 1904). (Copeland's ed., *ca.* 1555–60). Nos. 87, 94, 99.

Thomas of Erceldoune, ed. Murray ("E.E.T.S.," Vol. LXI [1875]). Thornton MS (fifteenth century). No. 51.

Torrent of Portyngale, ed. Adam ("E.E.T.S.: Extra Series," Vol. LI [1887]). Unique MS, Manchester, Chetham Library, 8009 (fifteenth century). Nos. 16, 37, 42, 60, 76.

Troy Book (Laud), ed. Wülfing ("E.E.T.S.," Vol. CXXI [1902]). Unique MS, Bodl., Laud Misc. 595 (early fifteenth century). No. 100.

Tryamoure, ed. Halliwell ("Percy Society," Vol. XVI [1846]). MS Cbg. Univ. Libr. Ff.II.38 (fifteenth century). No. 68.

Ypotis, in *Altenglische Legenden*, ed. Horstmann (Heilbronn, 1881), pp. 511 ff. Cotton Cal. A II. No. 17.

I. MINSTREL COMMENTS

Nos. 1–17

English minstrels usually began their narratives, whether of religious or secular character, with a complimentary term of address; they then introduced their hero's name and parentage; they reiterated, especially in transitions, the *so bifel* formula or the *I wol telle* promise to speak, *for sothe*, of exciting things; they constantly used, for the sake of easy rhymes, meaningless expletives; they begged their hearers to listen and keep still.[1] These stereotyped patterns are closely imitated in

---

[1] For illustrations of these conventional elements see Ruth Crosby, "Oral Delivery in the Middle Ages," *Speculum*, XI (1936), 88–110. For *Listeneth, lordynges* or *Herkeneþ* see *Athelston*, ed. Zupitza, vs. 7.; *Libeaus*, ed. Kaluza, vs. 461n.; *King Horn*, ed. Hall, vs. 1n.; Brown, *Register of ME Religious Verse*, II,

Thopas. The first two stanzas are woven from phrases found chiefly in the unique stanzaic version of *Guy of Warwick.*[1] Indeed, the excessive use throughout this romance of stock minstrel expressions seems especially to have inspired Chaucer's derisive imitation. His "murier than the nightyngale" transition, after Thopas' encounter with the giant, is from *Beves of Hamtoun.*[2] His division of *Thopas* into *fits* was probably suggested by the three iterations concerning fits in *Eglamour.*[3] The rude appeal for silence, the *holde youre mouth* of *Thopas*, is most nearly paralleled by that in *Gamelyn.*[4]

1. ST. ALEXIUS

Lesteneþ alle, and herkeneþ me,
Ȝonge and olde, bonde & fre,
   And *ich ȝou telle* sone,
How a ȝong man, *gent* and fre
By-gan þis worldis wele to fle
   Y-born he was in Rome.

2. ALISAUNDER

29   Now pais *holdith*, and leteth cheste,
And ye schole here a noble jeste,
Of Alisaundre, theo riche kyng . . . .
39   *Yef ye wolen* sitte stille,
Ful feole *Y wol yow telle.*

1239   Listenith now, sire and dame,
Now bygynnith a neowe game.

3. AMIS AND AMILOUN

1   For goddes loue in trinyte,[5]
Al þat ben hend, *herkeniþ* to me,
I pray ȝow, *par amoure:*
What whilom fel *beȝond þe see*
Of two barons of grete bounte.

---

176. For *For sothe I telle* see *Amis*, ed. Kölbing, p. xliv; for *so it befel, ibid.*, p. lvii; also *Perceval*, ed. Campion and Holthausen, vss. 233n., 2141n.; *Libeaus*, ed. Kaluza, vs. 31n. For these and other formulas of transition see Schmirgel in *Beves*, ed. Kölbing, p. xlix; *King Horn*, ed. Hall, vss. 29n., 805n.

[1] See *Guy*, A, No. 8, sts. 1–2, and notes.   [2] See *Beves of Hamtoun*, No. 4.

[3] See *Eglamour*, No. 7; *Degrevant*, No. 6; *Thomas of Erceldoune*, No. 51.

[4] See *Gamelyn*, No. 44.

[5] As the first lines of *Amis* in the Auchinleck MS are now lost, vss. 1–5 are quoted from Egerton MS 2862.

1885 *So* it *bifel* þat selue *day,*
    Wiþ tong *as y ȝou tel may,*[1]
    It was midwinter tide.

4. BEVES OF HAMTOUN[2]

1 *Lordinges,* herkneþ *to me tale!*
    Is *merier þan þe niȝtingale,*
    þat y schel singe;
    Of a kniȝt *ich wile ȝow roune,*
    Beues a hiȝte of Hamtoune,
    Wiþ outen lesing.

7 *Ich wile* ȝow *tellen* al to gadre
    Of þat kniȝt and of is fadre,
    Sir Gii:
    Of Hamtoun he was sire
    And of al þat ilche schire,
    To wardi.

5. DEGARÉ

7 In Litel Bretaygne was a kyng
    Of gret poer in alle þing . . . .
11 þer nas no man, *verraiment,*
    þat miȝte in werre ne in *tornament,*
    Ne in iustes for noþing,
    Him out of his sadel bring.

6. DEGREVANT

9 *I wille* ȝow *telle* of a knyghte:

12 He was hardy and wyghte,
    And *doghty* in dede.[3]

---

[1] *Thopas:* And *so bifel* upon a *day,*
    For sothe, *as I yow telle may.*

[2] *Thopas:* Yet listeth, *lordes, to my tale*
    Murier than the nightingale,
    For now *I wol yow roune.*

Cf. Kölbing, *Beves,* p. 219; *ES,* XI (1888), 504. He observed that the better manuscripts in *Sir Thopas* omit *For now.* He maintained, however, that Chaucer did not use the Auchinleck MS for this imitation of *Beves,* but followed a lost manuscript of the type now represented by the fifteenth-century manuscript, Cbg., Univ. Libr. Ff. 2, 38. C has *lystniþ* and omits *is* before *merier.* But Chaucer begins *Thopas* with *listeth* and may have deliberately repeated it here. The agreement of *Thopas* with the rhyming phrase, *to my tale,* of the Auchinleck *Beves* seems decisive evidence. The C MS begins: *Lordinges, lystniþ grete and smale.*

[3] *Thopas: a doghty swayn; a perilous man of dede.* For the stock phrase, *doghty in dede,* see Kölbing, *Amis,* p. xlix; Campion and Holthausen, *Perceval,* vs. 18n.

19 He was knawene for kene,
       þis comely knyghte;
    In Haythynnes and in Spayne,
    In Ffrance and in Bretayne,
    With Perceuelle and Gawayne,
       ffor hardy and wyghte.

    Here endyth þe furst *fit*.[1]
    Howe say ye? *will ye any more of hit?*

7. EGLAMOUR

1   Jesu, þat es hevens kyng,
       Gyff us alle his blyssyng
       And beyld us in his boure . . . .
7   *I will ȝow telle* of a knyghte,
       Þat was bothe hardy and wyght . . . .
11 Þe gre he wynnes with jornaye clere
       And ever in felde *þe floure.*

13 In Artasse[2] *was* getyn and *borne,*
    And his eldirs hym byforne.
       Herkyn! I *will ȝow* saye, ...

---

[1] In MS Cbg., Univ. Libr., Ff. 1, 6, these two lines are inserted after vs. 368;
cf. *Degrevant;* ed. Luick, p. 27, vs. 368n.

  Thopas: Loo, lordes myne, heere is a fit!
       If ye wol any moore of it,
       To telle it wol I fonde.

It seems probable that Chaucer did not adapt these lines from *Degrevant,* but that
some scribe, already familiar with *Thopas,* inserted them in the one manuscript of
Degrevant which contains them. They are written in a different hand from the
rest of the poem. The manuscript itself contains numerous Chaucerian texts, as
Miss Hammond (*Chaucer, Manual,* pp. 344 ff.) has indicated, but not the *Canterbury Tales.*

[2] Cf. also the later passage in *Eglamour,* vss. 905–6:
       Lord, *in* Artas *borne* I *wes;*
       Syr Pryncesamour my *fadir* es,
          es *lorde of þat cuntre.*
with *Thopas:*   *Yborn* he *was in* fer contree,
       In Flaunders, al biyonde the see, ...
       His fader was a man ful fre,
       And *lord* he was *of that contree.*

This unromantic localization of Thopas' birthplace in Flanders may well have been
suggested by the Artois of *Eglamour.* But, as the specific combination of rhymes
and phrases in this second stanza of *Thopas* shows, it was not *Eglamour* but *Guy,*
A, st. 2, that chiefly influenced Chaucer's parody. See below, p. 500, n. 4, and p. 501,
nn. 1–2. Cf. also *Guy,* A, st. 71(5): *þer he was lord of þat cuntre.*

19   Sir Pryncesamour þe erle hight,
Sir Eglamour men callys þe knyght:
Was curtase ever and aye.

Make we mery, so haue we blysse[1]
For þys ys þe fyrst fytte jwys
That we haue vndurtane.

GAMELYN
(See No. 44)

8. GUY OF WARWICK, A

2449   *Lordinges, listeneþ* to me now!

3997   *Listeneþ* now & sitteþ stille.

4790   *More* ȝe schul here *ȝif ȝe wille.*

4793   Of Gyes felawes *y wille ȝou telle*
So y finde in mi *spelle.*

4819   Now wende we oȝain *to* our *spelle,*[2]
þat ȝe me herd er þan *telle.*

7292   *For soþe y ȝou telle may*[3]

1(1–12)   God graunt hem heuen blis to mede
þat herken to mi romaunce rede
    Al of a gentil *kniȝt:*[4]
þe best bodi he was at nede
þat euer miȝt *bistriden stede,* . . . .

(7)   Ouer al þis warld þe priis he wan
As man most of miȝt . . . .

(11)   *His name was* hoten *sir* Gij
Of Warwike, wise & wiȝt.

---

[1] In two fifteenth-century manuscripts these three lines appear after vs. 342 (cf. *Eglamour*, ed. Schleich, p. 23n). They were repeated in almost the same form for the second and third fits (Schleich, pp. 42, 59, 96).

[2] *Thopas:* And herkneth *to* my *spelle;* . . . .
Anon I wol yow *telle.*

[3] *Thopas:* And so bifel upon a day,
For sothe, as I yow telle may.

[4] The first stanza of *Thopas*, like this first stanza of *Guy*, A, combines the exceptional phrase *Al of a knyght* with the stock phrase *His name was* (cf. Nos. 10–15). The first stanza of *Thopas* also combines the exceptional rhyme, *entent* (not *entente*):

     Listeth, *lordes*, in *good entent*,
     And I wol telle *verrayment*,

with the *I* appeal to *lordes*, just as does *Guy*, A, st. 238 (6–9):

     lordinges alle,
     Mine men ȝe ben, *verrament*,
     Ich biseche ȝou wiþ *gode entent*.

2(1–12) Wiȝt he was, *for soþe* to say,
And holden for priis in eueri play
As kniȝt of gret bounde.
Out of þis lond he went his way
þurch mani diuers *cuntray*,
þat was *biȝond þe see*.[1]
Seþþen he com into Inglond,
& Aþelston þe king he fond,
þat was boþe hende & *fre*.
For his loue, ich vnder-stond,
He slouȝ a dragoun in Norþhumberlond,
Ful *fer in* þe norþ *cuntre*.[2]

3(1–5) He & Herhaud, *for soþe* to say,
To Wallingforþ toke þe way
þat was his faders toun.
þan was his fader, *soþe* to say,
Ded & birid in þe clay.

5(1) *On a day* sir Gij gan fond,
8(1) *On a day* þerl gan fond
11(1) *On a day*, wiþouten lesing,
44(1–2) *Now herken*, & ȝe may here
In gest, *ȝif ȝe wil* listen & lere.

9. HORN CHILDE[3]

1 Mi leue frende dere,
Herken & ȝe may here,
& ȝe wil vnder stonde; . . . .
7 *Y wil ȝou telle* of kinges tvo,
Hende haþeolf was on of þo,
þat weld al inglelond.

[1] See above, p. 499, n. 2. The second stanza of *Thopas*, like the second stanza of *Guy*, A, not only uses the same phrases, *in fer (fer in) contree biȝonde the see*, the same four rhyme words, *contree, see, free, contree*, in the same order, but combines these elements with mention of a hero (born or adventured) afar, and of another person (*fader . . . . ful fre, king . . . . hende and fre*).

[2] The precise *Thopas* phrase, *in fer contree*, is repeatedly used in *Guy*, A, vss. 1635, 6117, st. 170(7), *icham of fer contree*.

[3] In the unique copy of this romance in the Auchinleck MS, the title *Horn Childe & maiden Rimnild* (f. 317.c) is written in red and was once followed by a small miniature, now cut out. Trounce's suggestion (*Medium Ævum*, I [1932], 93, n. 1), that Chaucer was referring to the older and finer *King Horn*, seems improbable. The poet took nothing recognizable, save the name, from either romance. He did, however, associate together in *Thopas* the three "romances of prys," *Horn Childe*, *Guy of Warwick*, and *Beves of Hamtoun*. These are found together only in the Auchinleck MS.

10. IPOMYDON, B

1   Mekely, *lordyngis* gentyll and fre,
    Lystene a while and herken to me:
    I shall you telle of a kynge,
4   *A dowghty* man, with owte lesynge; . . . .
11 Of Poyle-lond *lord was he,*
    Gold and syluer he had plente, ...
15 *Hys name was* kynge Ermones.

11. ISUMBRAS

1   Hende in haule, and ȝe *will here*
    Of eldirs, þat byfor vs were,

7   *I will ȝow telle* of a knyghte,
    þat was bothe hardy and wyghte
      And doghty *man* of *dede.*
    His name was called *sir* Ysumbras:
    Swilke a knyghte, als he was,
      Now lyffes nane in lede.

12. LIBEAUS DESCONUS

4   —harkeneþ of a conquerour,
    Wis of witte and wiȝt werrour
      And douȝty *man* in *dede.*
    His name was called Gingelein.

13. OCTAVIAN, B

1   Mekylle and littille, olde and ȝynge,
    Herkyns alle *to my* talkynge—
      Of whayme i wille ȝow kythe.

13 Somtyme byfelle ane auenture:
    In Rome þer was ane emperoure, ...

17 And leuede in joye and grete honoure,
      And *doghety* was *of dede.*
    In *tornament* nor in fyghte
    In þe werlde þer ne was a better knyghte,
      No *worthier* vndir *wede.*
    Octouyane *was his name* thrugheowte.

14. PERCEVAL OF GALES

1   Lef, lythes to me
    Two wordes or thre
    Off one, þat was faire and fre
      And felle in his fighte!

His righte name was *Percyvell*.
He was fosterde in the felle,
He *dranke water of þe welle*,[1]
     And ȝitt was he wyghte.
His fadir was a noble man:
Fro þe tyme, þat he began,
Miche wir(s)chippe he wan,
     When he was made knyghte.

18   He was *doughty of dede*,
     A styffe body on a stede
     Wapynes to wolde.

2141 *So it byfelle appon a day*,
     Now þe *sothe als* I sall say,
     My lorde went hym to play.

15. SEVEN SAGES

1   Lordynges þat here likes to dwell,
    Leues ȝowre speche and heres þis *spell*.
    I sal ȝow tel, if I haue tome,
    Of þe seuen Sages of Rome.
    Whilom lifed a nobil man;
    His name was Dyoclician.

16. TORRENT

10 *I Schall yow tell*, ore I hense pase,
    Off a knyght, þat *Dowghtty* wase,
        In Rome ase clarkys ffynde.

337 *Lorddes*,[2] and ye wol lythe . . . .
1089 *Lordys*, and ye liston wold . . . .

17. YPOTIS[3]

1   He þat wyll of wysdome lere,
    Herkeneth now, & ȝe may here
    Of a tale of holy wryte . . . .
5   How hyt *befell* yn grete Rome.

---

[1] *Thopas:* Hymself *drank water of the well*,
        As dide the knyght sire *Percyvell*.

[2] Here and elsewhere *Torrent* uses the term *lordes* rather than the conventional *lordinges*. Cf. *Thopas: Listeth, lordes*.

[3] This poem was a kind of catechism between the Wise Child, Ypotis (Epictetus), and the Emperor Hadrian. Fourteen Middle English manuscripts survive, the earliest dating from about 1330. Cf. Carleton Brown, *Register of ME Religious and Didactic Verse*, II, 35, No. 140.

II. THE HERO'S APPEARANCE

Nos. 18–23

The popular romances itemized the beauty of women, stressed the strength and prowess of men, and generalized about the excessive richness of clothes worn by men and women alike.[1] Chaucer borrowed for Thopas the proverbial color phrases, *rede as rose, whit as flour,* commonly used for women and children.[2] He enhanced the suggestion of effeminacy by mention of Thopas' nose, his *white leere,* and *sydes smale.*[3] From a dwarf in *Libeaus* Chaucer transferred to Thopas beard, girdle, and shoes; from two elders in the *Seven Sages* he may have taken his hero's *saffroun hair* and *white leere.* The costly foreign stuffs, of India, of Tars, the *sendall,* and the *syklatoun,* worn by notables in romance, he jocosely turned into the variety and cheapness of Thopas' clothes.[4] The allusions in connection with his hero's appearance have been thought to suggest the tradesman.[5]

[1] The most complete list of references to personal attributes in the English romances is given by W. C. Curry, *The ME Ideal of Personal Beauty* (Baltimore, 1916).

[2] For lists of these phrases see Zupitza, *Athelston,* vs. 70n.; Kaluza, *Libeaus,* vs. 489n.; ed. Hall, *Horn,* vs. 15n.; Curry, pp. 82–94. Punning on the word *flour* probably led Chaucer to his own variant, *whit as payndemayn,* a word found in the romances only in *Thopas* and in *Degrevant,* vs. 1291, *þay profird hym payndemayne;* also, vs. 1409, *Paynedemayn . . . . Scho fett.*

[3] Cf. Robinson, *Chaucer,* p. 844 (vs. 836); Camden, "The Physiognomy of Thopas," *RES,* XI (1935), 326 ff. For references to women's noses see Kölbing, *ES,* XI (1888), 498; Curry, p. 63. Cf. No. 51, vs. 68, for *lire white.*

[4] Cf. *Thopas, Of cordewane.* Kölbing (*ES,* XI [1888], 499) noted that the French *Ipomadon,* vs. 1625, has *solleres de cordewan;* but found no other parallel except from sources later than *Thopas. Of Brugges* parodies the *of India* and *of Tars* of the romances. *Syklatoun* is a comparatively rare word found in the romances only in *Guy,* A, vs. 2835 (cf. No. 19) and in *Richard,* vs. 5268, both poems in the Auchinleck MS, and in *Florence of Rome* (ed. Vietor), vs. 177, a story not apparently known to Chaucer.

[5] Cf. Manly, *Canterbury Tales,* p. 630: "The comparison of his face with fine bread, his complexion with a dye for cloth, his beard with a coloring for pies and meats and confectionery; the shoes of cordewain leather, the brown Bruges hose— all suggest the tradesman, as does the silk robe that cost 'many a jane' (ha'penny)."

18. ATHELSTON

65   He gat vpon þe Countas
     Twoo knaue-chyldren dere. . . . .

69   In þe world *was non* here *pere:*
     Also *whyt, so lylye-fflour,*
     Red, as rose, off here colour,
         As bry3t, as blosme on brere.

19. GUY OF WARWICK, A[1]

65   [Hir skynne *was white* of brighte coloure; . . . .
68   Browes bente and *nose* well sittyng]

706 þerl dubbed sir Gij þe fre,
     & wiþ him tventi god gomis, ...
709 Of cloth of Tars & riche cendel
     Was her dobbeing euerich a dei;
     þe panis al of fow & griis,
     þe mantels weren of michel priis.

     [Rich fabrics are offered to Guy.]

2835 Gode cloþes *of sikelatoun* & Alisaundrinis
     Peloure of Matre, & purper & biis,
     To 3our wille as 3e may se.

5688 Oysel sche hete wiþ þe *rode* so rede.
6107 His here, þat was 3alu and bri3t

20. HORN

9   He hadde a sone þat het horn,
     Fairer ne miste non beo born. . . .
13   Fairer nis non þane he was,
     He was bri3t so þe glas,
     He was *whit* so þe flur,
     Rose *red* was his colur.

21. IPOMADON, A

361 He was large of lyme & lythe, ...
367 His dobelett was of red welvet,
     Off bryght golde botuns ibete.

---

[1] Vss. 65–68 are quoted from MS Cbg., Caius 107 (in *Guy*, A, ed. Zupitza), as the parallel lines in the Auchinleck MS are now lost. It will be seen that, like *Thopas*, the Auchinleck *Guy* contained references to white skin, red *rode*, a good *nose*, yellow hair, *sikelatoun*, and to the cost of clothes. But see below, p. 507, n. 1.

370　　　His mantell was of skarlett fyne,
　　　　Furryd with good armyne,
　　　　Ther myght no better been,
　　　　The bordoure all of red sendell;
　　　　That araye became hym wele,
　　　　To wete, wyth outen wene.
　　　　A noble countenavnce he hade, ...
379　　　Also bryght his coloure shone,
　　　　All hym lovyd, that lokyd hym one,
　　　　Bothe lord and lady shene.

2456　　Lyghttly was he clade to ryde,
　　　　In a mantell panyd wyth pryde,
　　　　And semys sette grette plente, ...
2461　　*Hose* he had of clothe of Ynde,
　　　　Suche shull no man now fynde,
　　　　To seke all crystyante.
　　　　Spurrys of gold he had vpon,
　　　　Was neuer kyng better weryd none,
　　　　Ne no mon in no degre.

LAUNFAL

(See No. 49, vss. 232–96; 934–45)

22. LIBEAUS DESCONUS

121　　þat maide was cleped Elene,
　　　　Gentill, briȝt and schene, ...
127　　Sche was cloþed in tars,
　　　　Roume and no þing scars,
　　　　　Pelured wiþ blaunner.
　　　　Her sadell was overgeld
　　　　And wiþ diamaundis fulfeld;
　　　　　Melk whit was her *destrere.*

133　　þe dwerȝ was cloþed in inde,
　　　　Before and ek behinde
　　　　　Stout he was and pert. . . . .
138　　　His surcote was overt.
　　　　His berd was ȝelow as wax,[1]

---

[1] *Thopas:* His heer, *his berd was* lyk saffroun
　　　That *to his girdel* raughte adoun;
　　　His *shoon* of cordewane.

This combined mention of *berd, girdel, shoon,* is anticipated only in *Libeaus,* vss.
139–42, which must be the source of these details in *Thopas.* In *Degaré,* vs. 783–

To his gerdell heng his fax;
  I dar well say in certe.
His schon wiþ gold wer diȝt
And coped as a kniȝt;
  þat semed no poverte.

937 *As rose* her *rode* was *red;*
  þe her schon on hir heed,
    As gold wire schineþ briȝt.
Her browes as selke þrede,
  Y-bent in lengþe and brede;
    Hir *nose* was streiȝt and riȝt,
Her iȝen gray as glas;
  Melk *whit was* her *face*[1]
    So seide, þat siȝ þat siȝt.

23. SEVEN SAGES

51 The iij mayster was a lyght man[2]
With louesum *lere* as *whytte* as swanne,
Hys here was crypse and noo thyng rous,
His name was callyd Lentyllous.

97 An other master come anon,
The ffayrest of them euerychon,
Jesse *was his name* jhoote,
Withowt weme flrom hede to fote.
His here was yelow as the *safferon,*[3]
He loked lustely as a ffawcon.

90, only the dwarf's *beard* and *sschon* are mentioned; in *Reinbrun*, st. 34(10–12) only Heraud's *berde* and *gerder*. All three romances have the *wax:fax* couplet.

[1] *Thopas: Whit was* his *face* as payndemayn,
    His lippes *rede as rose;*
  His *rode* is lyk scarlet in grayn, ...
    He hadde a semely *nose.*
Since *Libeaus*, vss. 937 ff., likewise combines in one stanza mention of a *whit face,* a good *nose, red as rose,* and *rode,* it may be regarded as even more particularly the source of these lines in *Thopas* than the more scattered references in *Guy,* A. See above, p. 505, n. 1.

[2] Vss. 51–54 are from a fifteenth-century manuscript (Egerton 1995) printed in Brunner's edition of the *Seven Sages of Rome* ("E.E.T.S.," Vol. CXCI [1933]).

[3] Vss. 97–101 are from the sixteenth-century manuscript (Oxford, Balliol, 354) printed in Brunner's edition. It should be noted that in the Auchinleck MS the first 122 lines of the *Seven Sages* are now lost. It may, therefore, have contained a suggestion for Thopas' *saffroun hair,* as it still does for another idea that seems to have been incorporated into *Thopas.* See below, p. 546, n. 2.

III. THE HERO'S PASTIMES: HUNTING,
RIDING, SLEEPING, WRESTLING
Nos. 24–45

The hero's accomplishments and pastimes, listed in all seriousness, as in the couplet version of *Ipomydon*, B,[1] usually lack in the romances either pertinence or realism. Chaucer imitated the stereotyped phrases for hunting and riding, and though these occur in many texts, *Guy* seems to have been a special stimulus, since in no other romance is the hero so perpetually leaping on or bestriding or pricking his steed, nor is hunting more often or more conventionally referred to.[2] Thopas' exhausted sleep in the wood is amusingly reminiscent of the forest naps taken by more strenuous heroes, Amis, Ipomadon, or, especially, Torrent or Perceval, since the horses of the last two, shared, like Thopas', their master's rest.[3] From *Perceval* or from *Guy* Chaucer may have taken a hint for Thopas' absurd hunting with a *launcegay*,[4] but it is as likely that no single romance or detail so much inspired the poet to give his hero an equipment so unsuitable for the hunt,[5] or such unknightly prowess in the sports of archery and wrestling,[6] or a taste in food for such plebeian and childish sweets as licorice and gingerbread, as did his own lively apprehension of the general ignorance of courtly ways that the popular romances often displayed. To satirize them, he introduced incongruously homely and humble things, making his knightly hero in nothing more ridiculous than in his bourgeois tastes and pastimes.

[1] *Ipomydon*, B, No. 26.

[2] See *Guy*, A, Nos. 25, 32.

[3] See *Perceval*, No. 41; *Torrent*, No. 42.

[4] See *Perceval*, No. 28. Cf. *Guy*, A, No. 53, vs. 3874.

[5] Thopas had not only the *launcegay* and *long swerd* but also a *grey goshauk*. In *Horn Childe*, vs. 338, a *gentil goshawk* is sent by a lady to her love. In the *Squire of Low Degree*, vs. 775, a lady is promised she shall ride *With goshauke and with gentyll fawcon*. Manly (*Canterbury Tales*, p. 631) quoted Dame Berners, *Boke of Hawkyng* (fol. d 3): "A Goshawke . . . . is for a yeman." In connection with Thopas the goshawk may suggest, then, either the effeminate or the bourgeois character of the knight.

[6] See Nos. 43–45.

1. THE HERO HUNTS

24. DEGREVANT

33   He was faire and *free*,

41   Oþer gamenes he louede mare:
     Grewhundes for *buk* and bare,
     For herte, hynde, *and for hare.*[1]
       By dayes and by nyghte.

49   He walde be vp or daye
     To hunt and to ryvaye,

58   Bothe with horne and with hunde,
     To brynge þe dere to þe grounde,
       Was his maste glewe.

25. GUY OF WARWICK, A[2]

169   Gij a forster fader hadde,
     þat him lerd & him radde
     Of wodes & *riuer* & oþer game: . . . .
175   Michel *he coupe* of hauk & hounde,
     Of estriche faucouns of gret mounde.

2795 þemperour worþschiped Gij þe *fre:* . . . .
2797 To pleyn hem þai went bi riuer
     þat of wilde foule ful were;
     To her wille an hunting hij gos,
     To chace þe hert & þe ros.

6340 In þe cite were mani & mo.
     In þat on half orn þe *riuer*,
     In þat oþer half forest wiþ *wilde dere.*[3]

6717 On hunting went þerl Tirri. . . . .
6719 þai comen into *a fair forest*,
     þer þai fond a bore, *a wilde best.*

---

[1] *Thopas:* Ye, bothe *bukke and hare.*

[2] In addition to the instances here given, other allusions to hunting occur frequently in *Guy*, A. Cf. vss. 1210, 2453, 2510, 3155, 4905, and sts. 4 and 11.

[3] *Thopas:*   *He koude* hunte at *wilde deer,*
          And ride an haukyng for *river* . . . .
          He priketh thurgh *a fair forest,*
          Therinne is many *a wilde best.*

Robinson (*Chaucer*, p. 843, note to vss. 712, 737) observes that Chaucer's rhyme, *deer* : *river* (not *ryvere*) is unusual; also that the meaning *for waterfowl* would here best suit *for river*. *Guy*, A, vss. 170–75, likewise combines this special meaning for *river* (vs. 171) with *he coupe*, and later uses the same rhymes, *wilde dere* : *riuer*, and *fair forest* : *wilde best*. For *he priketh* see below, No. 32, st. 181.

26. IPOMYDON, B[1]

52   Ipomydon resseyueth he now;
    Tholomew, a clerke he toke,
    That taught the child vppon þe boke
    Bothe to synge and to rede,
    And after he taught hym other dede, ...
    Bothe of howndis & haukis game;

62   Aftir he taught hym all & same
    In se, in feld and eke in *ryuere*,
    In wodde to chase the *wilde dere*
    And in the feld to ryde a stede,
    That all men had joy of his dede. . . . .

77   He ys a myghty man for the nonys
    And wele ishape with grete bonys.
    In all that contre was there none,[2]
    To hym myght cast þe tre ne stone.

27. ORFEO

281   þe king *o Fairi* wiþ his rout
    Com to hunt him al about . . . .
302   Sexti leuedis on hors ride, ...
305   And ich a faucoun *on hond* bere
    And *riden on haukin* bi o rivere.

28. PERCEVAL OF GALES

209   Thus he welke in þe lande
    With hys darte *in his hande;* . . . .
213   He wolde schote with his spere
    Bestes and oþer gere
    As many, als he myghte bere;
      He was a gude knave.
    Smalle birdes wolde he slo,
    Hertys, hyndez also.[3]

---

[1] This long passage on the hero's accomplishments has the same rhyme, *ryuere* : *dere*, and the same line, 79 (see n. 2 below), that also appear in *Thopas*. For other romances dealing with the hero's accomplishments see *Alisaunder*, vss. 659–81, where he is taught to dress, to play at ball, *to skyrme and ride*, the seven arts, to joust and fight, and *In grene wode of huntyng,/And of reveryng, and of haukyng; Sir Tristrem*, vss. 287–97: *Of ich maner of glewe; /Old lawes and newe;/More he coupe of veneri.* Hall (*Horn*, vs. 226n.) also cites *Alexis*, vss. 987–89: *And lernen chiualrie,/Of huntyng, & of Ryuere,/Of chesse pleieyng & of tablere.*

[2] Cf. *Thopas:* For *in that contree was ther noon.*

[3] This stanza in which the ignorant young Perceval hunts birds and beasts with a spear offers the only English parallel to Thopas' hunting with a *launcegay*. In

2. THE HERO RIDES[1]

29. AMIS AND AMILOUN

973   Amorwe sir Amis made him ȝare . . . .
976   For no þing nold he spare,
    He priked þe stede, þat him bare,
    Boþe niȝt & day.
    So long he *priked* wiþ-outen abod,
    þe stede, þat he on rode,
    In a fer cuntray
    Was ouercomen & fel doun ded.

1189   Now, hende, *herkneþ*, & y schal say,
    How þat sir Amiloun went his way;
    For no þing wold he spare.
        He priked his stede niȝt & day,
    As a gentil kniȝt, stout & gay.

30. BEVES OF HAMTOUN

1827   A restede him þer a lite tide,
    His gode stede he gan be-stride[2]
    And rod ouer *dale and doun*,
    Til he com to a gret toun.

1942   A gode stede ȝhe let forþ drawe
    And sadeled hit & wel adiȝt,
    And Beues, þat hendi kniȝt,
    Into þe sadel a lippte,
    þat no stirop he ne drippte.

31. DEGARÉ

419   Sire Degarré was wel blithe, ...
421   And lep vpon hiis palefrai,
    And doht him forȝ in his wai.

495   *His gode stede he* gan *bistride.*

---

the burlesque *Audigier* (*Fabliaux*, ed. Barbazan and Meon, IV, 218, vs. 30), the hero's father throws a lance at a spider: *Parmi une iregnie bouta sa lance.* See below, *Guy*, A, No. 53, vss. 3874 and 4131.

[1] Chaucer's parody of the constant references to riding in the romances is marked. In *Thopas* there are six references to the hero's *steed*, one to his *dextrer*, one to its *ambil*, three to *riding*, one to *bestriding*, one, *he worth upon*, eight to *pricking.* See below, *Guy*, No. 32. The word *destrer* occurs in *Guy*, vs. 2354, and in *Libeaus*, vs. 614. For collections of phrases connected with riding see Schmirgel in *Beves* (ed. Kölbing), p. liv; Zupitza, *Athelston*, vs. 381n.; Kaluza, *Libeaus*, vss. 265n., 278n.

[2] See below, p. 512, n. 2.

723 Forȝ he rod in his wai
Mani a pas and mani iurnai;
So longe he passede into west
þat he com into þeld fforest
þer he was biȝeten som while.
728 þerinne he rideȝ mani a mile;
Mani a dai he ride gan; . . . .
731 Ac mani *wilde bestes* he seghȝ,
And foules singen on heghȝ.

32. GUY OF WARWICK, A

Ambling:[1]
1329 Now comeþ Gij soft rideing
Opon a mulet ambling.

4615 Y sett hir on a mule amblinde.

7119 Gij lepe on a mule ambling.

Bestriding:
6411 *His gode stede he bi-strod*[2]
And of-toke hem wiþ-outen abod.

1(4–5) þe best bodi he was at nede
þat euer miȝt *bistriden stede.*

Leaping:[3]
1601 þan he lepe opon his stede.

3864 On hors he lepe wiþ-outen stirop.

97(2) On hors þai lopen fot hot.

259(1) Sir Gij lepe on his stede fot hot.

Pricking:[4]
181(10) & *priked* riȝt *as he were wode.*[5]

---

[1] *Thopas:* His steede . . . ./It gooth an *ambil.*

[2] *Thopas: His goode steede* al *he bistrood.* Numerous instances of this conventional line in the romances are given by Schmirgel in *Beves* (ed. Kölbing), p. liv; also by Kaluza, *Libeaus,* vs. 814n.

[3] Cf. also *Guy,* A, vss. 1611, 2540, 3022, 5757, 6778, and st. 59(10), etc. Chaucer parodied all this leaping, probably the *fot hot* leaps in special, by the leisurely mounting of Thopas: *Into his saddle he clamb.*

[4] Miss Strong (*MLN,* XXIII, 103) remarked: "Over forty times in *Guy* a knight comes *pricking.* It is not by accident that Chaucer repeats the word eight times in eighty-four lines" (cf. *Guy,* A, vss. 899, 949, 958, 973, 995, 1385, 1479, 1521, 1837, etc.). Kölbing (*ES,* Vol. XI [1888]) cited *pricking as þay were wode* from *Ferumbras,* vss. 3021, 3979, 5405, but there is no certain evidence that Chaucer knew this romance (cf. *Thopas: And pryked as he were wood*).

[5] For collections of the phrase *as he (they) were wode* see Kaluza, *Libeaus,* vs. 1215n.; Kölbing, *Tristrem,* vs. 2357n.; Kölbing, *Ipomadon,* A, vs. 8181n.; Zupitza, *Athelston,* vs. 250n.

97(4–6)   þai *priked* þe stedes þat þai on sete . . . .
           & ferd *as þai wer wod.*

Riding and Going; Worth upon:[1]

2827   Þritti mile men may *riden and gon*
           Ne schal men finde man *non.*

4723   *Opon* a mule sche *warþ* anon.

6986   Nim þi stede, & *worþ* þeron.

33. IPOMYDON, B

1488   Ipomydon sterte vp that tyde,
       Anone he *worthyd vppon his stede,*
       They rode to gedyr with good spede.

34. ISUMBRAS

457   When he was horsede on a stede,
      He sprange forthe, *als sparke* one glede,
      With grymly growndyn gare.

35. LIBEAUS DESCONUS

667   Libeaus was redy boun
      And lep out of þe arsoun,
         As sperk doþ *out* of glede.

814   *His stede he gan bestride.*

36. REINBRUN

76(7–12)   Amorwe Reinbroun aros erly,
      And armede him ful hastely,
         For to winne pris.
      A gode stede he bestrod,
      & forþ a went wiþ-oute abod
      To þe forest, ywis.

37. TORRENT

627   On he dyd hys harnes a-geyne
      And *worthe on hys sted,* serteyne,
         And thetherward he sowght.

855   Tho wold he no lenger a-byde,
      He toke ys wey for to Ryde
         On a sted of gret valew. . . . .

864   Thus he *worthe on a stede.*
      In hys wey Cryst hyme sped.

---

[1] Chaucer twice repeats the phrase *ride and go* in *Thopas* and uses the same rhyme, *noon:goon.* See below, p. 546, n. 2. Cf. *Thopas:* He *worth upon* his steede gray.

3. THE HERO SLEEPS IN THE FOREST

38. AMIS AND AMILOUN

992 In to a wilde forest he cam
     Bi tven þe day & þe niȝt.
     So strong slepe ȝede him on,
     To win al þis warldes won,
     No ferþer he no miȝt.

996 þe kniȝt, þat was so hende & fre,
     Wel fair he layd him vnder a tre
     & fel in slepe þat tide.

39. IPOMYDON, B

1457 Ipomydon come by a foreste,
     A while he thoght there to rest,
     He *was* forwakyd & all *werye;*
     To hys men he said on hye:
     "Slepe I muste, with oute fayle
     For I am wery for travayle!"

40. IPOMADON, A

5370 Ipomadon was wonder-sare;
     As he gan *thorow* the *foreste* fare,
     He lyght under a tre,
     There flovris were spryngand, swete of smell;
     Forwery on slepe he fell
     On his cosyns knee.

41. PERCEVAL OF GALES

1205 Now fonde he no sekirnes,
     Bot under þe walle, þer he wes,
     A faire place he hym chese,
        And down there he lighte.
     He laide hym doun in þat tyde,[1]
     His stede stode hym be-syde;
     The fole was fayne for to byde,
        Was wery for þe fyght.

42. TORRENT

1550 Down light this gentill knyght,
     To rest hym a litull wight,

[1] *Thopas:* Sir Thopas eek so *wery was* ....
     That *doun he leyde him in that* plas.

And vnbrydelid *his stede*
And let *hym bayte* on the ground,[1]
And aventid hym in that stound,
There of he had gret nede.

4. THE HERO WRESTLES

43. CANTERBURY TALES, PROLOGUE

545 The Millere was a stout carl for the nones;
547 That proved wel, for over al ther he cam,
At *wrastlynge* he wolde have alwey the *ram*.[2]

44. GAMELYN

169 Litheth, and lesteneth and *holdeth your* tonge,[3]
And ye schul heere talking of Gamelyn the yonge.
There was ther bisyden cryed a *wrastling*,
And therfor ther was set up *a ram* and a ring;
And Gamelyn was in good wil to wende therto,
For to preven his might what he cowthe do.

[He overthrows a mighty wrestler.]

279 Tho that wardeynes were of that wrasteling
Com and broughte Gamelyn the ram and the ring,
And seyden, "*have*, Gamelyn, the ring and *the ram*,
For the beste wrasteler that ever here cam."

45. OCTAVIAN, A

895 At *wrestelyng* and at ston castynge
He wan the prys, without lesynge;
Ther nas nother old ne yynge
So mochell of strength.

---

[1] *Thopas: And by hym baiteth* his dextrer.

[2] *Thopas:* Of *wrastlyng* was ther noon his peer,
Ther any *ram* shal stonde.

For Chaucer's other possible imitations of himself in *Thopas*, see above, Introduction, p. 493, n. 2. Wrestling was a plebeian sport usually practiced only by such heroes in romance as the neglected Gamelyn, or the butcher-bred Octavian. Kölbing (*ES*, XI, 500, vs. 29n.) also cited *Alis.*, vs. 197: *There was champions skyrmyng,/and of other wrastlyng.*

[3] *Thopas:* Now *holde your* mouth, par charitee.

IV.　THE HERO IN LOVE AND BELOVED

Nos. 46–51

For *Thopas* Chaucer seems to have recalled, chiefly from *Guy of Warwick*, the hero's irresistible charm for lovelorn, sleepless ladies, his complaint of being bound by love, and, in a *priue* place in the forest, his love-longing, under the influence of birds' songs. Likewise, the rejection by Felice and Guy of the greatest lords and ladies in the world may well have inspired Thopas' conviction that no woman is worthy to be his *make*, though it is Guy's love, Felice, who uses this specific word. Guy's forswearing of all but one of earth's greatest ladies may also have first suggested an unearthly love for Thopas. Two stories of fairy love were evidently known to Chaucer, *Launfal*, from which he took the identical phrasing and rhyme of the fairy's command that the hero forsake all women for her only, and *Thomas of Erceldoune*, from which Chaucer borrowed for his hero the fairy's *dappill graye* horse, her saddle *of roelle bone*, her bright bridle. The shining fairy ladies of these two stories are closely related to Thopas' elf-queen, but Chaucer may have derived the idea of associating the lady with a giant from *Guy*, A, where a giant has a *leman*, or from *Libeaus Desconus*.[1] Both *Launfal* and *Thomas of Erceldoune* have a setting and situation akin to those in *Thopas;* in both there is a longing hero; in *Launfal* he rests in *a fair forest;* in *Thomas* he hears *throstyll cokke* and *papeioye* singing in the wood; in both the fairy ladies are beings who lie, in fact, not dream, as in *Thopas*, with their mortal loves; in *Launfal* the fairy must be sought *privily*, if not in the *pryve woon of Fairye* of *Thopas;* in *Thomas* music is associated with her, as with the fairy queen of Thopas. Thopas' love for one unknown is a familiar concept illustrated in *Guy* and *Ipomadon*. His dream of the unknown is paralleled in the *Seven Sages*.

46. GUY OF WARWICK, A

237　　þat day Gij dede his miȝt
　　　　To serue þritti *maidens briȝt;*

---

[1] The giant Amoraunt swears to give Guy's head to his own *leman* (*Guy*, A, st. 126[8]). See also *Libeaus*, No. 58, vss. 1489–94.

Al an-amourd on him þai were,[1]
& loued Gij for his feir chere.
Þer of no ȝaf he riȝt nouȝt,
Al anoþer it was his þouȝt:
On Felice þat was so briȝt,
Gij hir loued wiþ al his miȝt. . . . .
279 & grete wonder he haþ *y-wis*[2]
Þat him so hard bifallen *is;*

[Guy resolves to tell his love. Felice rejects him and boasts of those who have loved her unseen.]

397 "Erls, doukes of þe best
In þis world, & þe richest,
Me haue desired apliȝt,
Þat neuer of me hadde siȝt."

[Guy laments his sufferings.]

437 "Loue me doþ to grounde falle,
Þat y ne may stond stef wiþ alle.

477 Allas, Felice, þat ich stounde,
Þi *loue* me haþ so *ybounde!* . . . .[3]
486 Allas! to grounde icham ybrouȝt! . . . .
488 Y brenne so spark on glede."

499 Þerl for him sori *was*
Þer liked non *in that plas.*[4]

[1] *Thopas:* Ful many a *mayde, briȝt in bour,*
They moorne for hym *paramour.*
Cf., in this same extract from *Guy*, A, sts. 5 and 6; also st. 10(7), *He haþ ben desired of mani woman;* and the use, in the same context, of the same rhyming phrases, *briȝt in bour: par amoure,* of st. 11.

[2] This *ywis: is* rhyme is used to absurd excess in *Guy*, A (cf. vss. 251, 296, 551, 985, 991, 1301, 1345, 1689, 1849, 2301, 2371, etc.; also sts. 72[9], 101[7], 117[10], etc.). On *ywis* as a rhyme in the romances see Kaluza, *Libeaus,* vs. 29n. See below, p. 518, n. 3, for the rhyme in *Thopas.*

[3] *Thopas:* O seinte *Marie*, benedicite!
What eyleth this *love* at me
To *bynde* me so soore? . . . .
An elf-queene shal my *lemman* be.
Cf., in this same extract from *Guy*, A, sts. 24 and 26. The conjunction in them of references to *Marie*, to *leman*, to love's binding, establish them as a source for the *Thopas* stanza.

[4] The *plas: was* rhyme is very common in *Guy*, A (cf. vss. 223, 7293, sts. 181[4], 190[4], etc.). See Robinson, *Chaucer*, p. 843, vs. 712n., on this irregular *plas* (not *place*) rhyme in *Thopas.* Cf. above, p. 514, n. 1.

[Again rejected, Guy goes abroad. He performs prodigies of valor
and refuses in marriage several great ladies, including a princess. On
the way home love-longing overcomes him.]

4502   þe weder was hot in somers tide.
         In May it was also ich wene,
         When floures sprede & *springeþ* grene,
         Into a forest sir Gij is go
         Neye a cite, nouȝt fer þer-fro. . . . .

4518   In *priue* stede[1] stode Gij þere;
         So michel *he herd* þo foules *sing*,
         þat him þouȝt he was in gret *longing*.[2]

         [He renews his wooing of Felice.]

5(1–12) On a day sir Gij gan fond,
         & feir Felice he tok bi hond, ...
         "Ichaue," he seyd, "þurch godes sond
         Won þe priis in mani lond
             Of kniȝtes strong & stiþe,
         & me is boden gret anour,
         Kinges douhter & emperour
             To haue to mi wiue.
         Ac, swete Felice," he seyd þan,
         "Y no schal neuer spouse wiman
             Whiles þou art oliue."

6(1–12) þan answerd þat swete wiȝt, ...
         "Icham desired day & niȝt
         Of erl, baroun, & mani a kniȝt,
             For noþing wil þai blinne. . . . .

         & bot ich haue þe to *make*,[3]
         Oþer lord nil y non take,
             For al þis warld to winne."

[Felice confesses her love for Guy to her father, the Earl of Warwick.]

[1] *Thopas:* . . . . he foond, in a *pryve* woon.

[2] *Thopas:* Sir Thopas fil in love-*longynge*,
              Al whan *he herde* the thrustel *synge*.

[3] *Thopas:* An elf-queene wol I love, ywis,
              For in this world no womman is
              Worthy to be my *make*.

The insistence in *Guy*, A, sts. 6–7, on the rejection of the greatest mortals, the
avowal, "Y no schal neuer spouse *wiman*," coupled with the word *make*, suggest at
least one source for Thopas' rejection of mortal ladies.

10(1–12) þan seyd þerl wiþ wordes fre, ...
     "Ich hadde wele leuer þan al mi fe
      Wiþ þan he wald spousy þe,
       þat *douhti man of dede.*
     He haþ ben desired of *mani* woman,
     & he haþ *forsaken* hem euerilcan,
      þat *worþly* were *in wede.*
     Ac naþeless ichil to him fare,
     For to witen of his answare,
      þat *douhti man of dede.*"

11(1–12) On a day, wiþouten lesing,
     þerl him *rode on* dere hunting,
      & sir Gij þe conquerour.
     Als þai riden on her talking
     þai speken togider of mani þing,
      Of leuedis *briȝt in bour.*
     þerl seyd to sir Gij hende and fre,
     "Tel me þe soþe, *par charite,*[1]
      Y pray þe *par amoure:*
     Hastow ment euer in þi liue
     Spouse ani wiman to wiue
      þat falleþ to þine anour?"

12(1–6) Sir Gij answered & seyd þan, ...
     "Bi nouȝt þat y tel can
     Y nil neuer spouse wiman
      Saue on is fre & hende."

[Guy confesses his love for Felice, and her father joyfully promises a bridal party.]

14(4–6) "Now for fourteniȝt it schal be
     þe bridal hold wiþ *gamen & gle*
      At Warwike in þat tyde."

15(6–8) Miche semly folk was gadred þare
     Of erls, barouns lasse & mare,
      & leuedis *briȝt in bour.*

16(10–12) þer was mirþe & melody,
     And al maner menstracie
      As ȝe may forþeward here.

---

[1] *Par charitee* is one of the many expletives which occur time without number in *Guy*, A. For their use in this and other romances see Campion and Holthausen, *Perceval*, vss. 958n., 2285n.; Kölbing, *Amis*, p. xlvii. For the rhyming phrases of this stanza, *briȝt in bour: par amoure,* see above, p. 517, n. 1.

17(1–6)   þer was trumpes & tabour,
           Fiþel, croude, & harpour,[1]
             Her craftes for to kiþe,
           Organisters & gode stiuours,
           Minstrels of mouþe, & mani dysour,
             To glade þo bernes bliþe.

24(1–6)   "*Leman*," seyd Gij oȝain, ...
           "þi *loue* me haþ so *y-bounde*. . . . ."

26(11–12) "God graunt þe, lef, þat haluendel,
             And *Marie*, his moder swete."

47. IPOMYDON, B

95   Ipomydon þat day servyd in halle
       All spake of hym, bothe grete and smalle,
       Ladies & maydens byheld hym on:
       So godely a man they had sene none;
       His feyre chere in halle theym smert,
       That many a lady smote throw the hert.

48. IPOMADON, A

[The hero falls in love with an unknown lady.][2]

176   The worde spronge in the hall
       Of Calabrye the fere;

184   Ipomadon servyd in the hall
       And herde the knyghttes wordes all
       Of that damysell;
       So grette good of her he spake,
       Hym thoughte, hys hertte asvnder brake
       Wyth syghynge and vnsele.

[Ladies are sleepless for his sake.]

698   The lady was full woo;
       She thynkys to haue Ipomadon, ...

---

[1] *Thopas:* With harpe and pipe and symphonie.
Cf. *Guy*, vs. 184 (Sloane MS 1044, ed. Zupitza, *Sitzungsberichte d. Ph.-Hist. Kl. d. Akad. d. Wissenschaften* [Wien, 1873], LXXIV, 628): Feþele, beme, and *cymphanie*.

[2] Instances of Love by Hearsay or Love for the Unseen, a widely popular motif after the troubadour legend of Jaufre Rudel had achieved popularity, may be noted in English in *Alisaunder*, vs. 6662, *King of Tars*, vs. 19, in the *Sowdone of Babylone*, vs. 1887, in Chaucer's *Man of Law's Tale*, vs. 186, etc.

701   Thus turnythe she tow & fro.
"Att the laste *of love drewry*
Dystrwes defawte *of chevallrye:*[1]
Alas, why ys it so?"

908   No thynge sche slepyd all the nyght,
But ofte tymes turnyd and sadely syghte.

7182   . . . . *love* full *sore* hyr *bounden* hase.[2]

[Ipomadon falls into love-longing.]

2444   In to *a foreste feyre* and grene,
Ther foulys song al bedene
On bowes, bothe lesse & mare,
The frithe was full of swete flouris:
Who lyst to love *paramowres*,
Grette lykyng had byn thare.
Ipomadon forgettys nouȝte,
To haue his *leman* in his thoughte,
That made hym sigh full sare.

49. LAUNFAL[3]
[The Hero's Fairy Love.]

217   Pouerly þe knyȝt to hors gan sprynge;
For to dryve away lokynge,
    He rood toward þe west.
Þe weþer was hot þe vndern-tyde;
He lyȝte adoun and gan abyde
    Vnder *a fayr forest;*

223   And for hete of þe wedere,
Hys mantell he felde togydere,
    And sette him doun to reste.

229   As he sat yn sorow and sore,
He sawe come out of holtes hore
    Gentyll maydenes two.
Har kerteles were of Inde-sandel,

[1] *Thopas:* Of bataille and *of chivalry,*
    And of ladyes *love-drury.*

[2] See above, No. 46, vss. 478 and 24(1–6).

[3] The *Lai de Lanval* by Marie de France was turned, in the fourteenth century, into two Middle English versions, one in couplets (Kittredge, *Amer. Jour. Phil.*, X [1889], 7 ff.); the other, the tail-rhyme version by Thomas Chestre. This is printed by French and Hale, *ME Met. Rom.*, in six-line stanzas; in twelve-line stanzas by Kaluza, *ES*, XVIII (1893), 165 ff. The latter has *longinge* for *lokynge*, vs. 218.

235   Hare manteles were of grene felwet,
      Ybordured with gold, ryȝt well ysette.

241   Hare *faces were whyt* as snow on downe;
      Har *rode* was *red*, here eyn were browne;

259   Launfal hem grauntede curteyslyche,
      And wente with hem myldelyche;
      þey wheryn *whyt as floure.*

277   He fond yn þe pauyloun
      þe Kinges douȝter of Olyroun,
      Dame Tryamoure þat hyȝte;
      Here fadyr was kyng *of fayrye,*

283   In þe pauyloun he fond a bed *of prys* . . . .

286   þerinne lay þat lady *gent,*
      þat aftere Sir Launfal hedde ysent,
      þat lefsom lemede *bryȝt.*

292   Sche was as *whyt as lylye* yn May,
      Or snow þat sneweþ yn wynterys day;

295   þe *rede rose*, whan sche ys newe,
      Aȝens here *rode* nes nauȝt of hewe;

301   Sche seyde, "Launfal, *my lemman* swete, ...

303   Swetyng paramour:
      þer nys no man yn Cristente
      þat y love so moche as þe,
          Kyng neyþer emperoure!"

      Launfal beheld þat swete wyȝth . . . .

310   And sat adoun her by*syde,*
      And seyde, "Swetyng, *what so betyde,*[1]
      I am to þyn honoure."

313   She seyde: "Sir knyȝt, gentyl and hende, ...

315   Be nauȝt aschamed of me.
      Yf þou wylt truly to *me take*
      And *alle wemen* for me *forsake,*[2]
          Ryche I wyll make þe."

[1] *Thopas:* A charbocle by his *syde;* . . . .
      Bityde *what so bityde.*

[2] Despite the frequency of the rhyme *take:forsake* as noted by Schmirgel in
Beves, ed. Kölbing, p. lii, by Kaluza, *Libeaus*, v. 214n., and Hall, *Horn*, v. 65n.,
the similar fairy context and phrasing occur together only in *Launfal* and *Thopas.*
Various details suggest Chaucer's use of Chestre's version, not that in couplets.
The latter omits *wemen* from this key couplet. Cf. Thopas: *Alle othere wommen
I forsake,/And to an elf-queene I me take.*

341   þe cloþ was spred, þe bord was sette;
        þey wente to hare sopere.

343   Mete and drynk, þey hadde *afyn,*
        Pyement, claré, and Reynysch *wyn,*[1] . . . .
347   þey wente to bedde and þat anoon,
        Launfal and sche yn fere.

352   Hy seyde to him: "Syr gantyl Knyȝt,
        And þou wylt speke with me any wyȝt,
        To a derne stede þou gon.

    Well *priuyly* I woll come to þe."[2]

934   þe lady was bryȝt as blosme on brere,
        With eyen gray, with louelych chere:
        Her *leyre* lyȝt schoone.

937   As rose on rys her *rode* was red; . . . .
942   þat lofsom lemede lyȝt.

    þe lady was clad yn purpere palle,
    With gentyll body and myddyll *small*
        þat semely was of syȝt.

LIBEAUS DESCONUS

(See No. 58, vss. 1489 ff.)

50. SEVEN SAGES, INCLUSA

[The Dream of the Unknown.]

3235   "Lord," said þe maister, "þis es no ly.
        In þe kingdom of Hungery
        Wond a nobil knyght whylom,
        A rightwis man and whise of dome.
        He dremyd þus opon a nyght,
        þat he lufed a lady bryght,[3]
        Bot he nist in what contre
        þat þe lady myght funden be.
        Him thoght he knew hir wele bi kinde,
        And wele he hopid he sold hir finde.
        þat same time dremyd þat ladi bright

[1] *Thopas:* They fette hym first the swete *wyn.* . . . .
    Of gyngebreed that was ful *fyn.*

[2] *Thopas:* That he foond, in a *pryve* woon,
    The contree *of Fairye.*

[3] *Thopas:* Me dremed al this nyght, pardee,
    An elf-queene shal *my lemman* be.

And thoght þat sho sold luf a knight;
Bot sho wist noght of what land,
Ne in whate stede he was dweland,
Ne his name knew sho nathing."

51. THOMAS OF ERCELDOUNE[1]

[The Hero's Fairy Love.]

Fytte the Firste

25   Als j me wente þis Endres daye,
Ffull faste in mynd makand my mone,
In a mery mornynge of Maye,
By huntle bankkes my-selfe allone,
I herde þe jay, & þe *throstyll cokke*,
The Mawys menyde hir of hir songe,
þe *wodewale* beryde als a belle,
That alle þe wode a-bowte me ronge.
Allonne *in longynge* thus als j laye,
Vndyre-nethe a semely tree,
35   (Saw I wher a lady gay
Came ridand ouer a louely le.)[2]
41   Hir palfraye was a *dappill graye*. . . . .[3]
46   Swylke one ne saghe j neuer none;
Als dose þe *sonne* on someres daye,
þat faire lady hir selfe scho *schone*.[4]

---

[1] References to the famous poet and prophet, Thomas of Erceldoune, occur in early fourteenth-century texts, in the Auchinleck *Sir Tristrem*, in Mannyng's *Chronicle* (to 1338), l. 94, etc. The earliest extant account of his adventure with a fairy lady appears in *Thomas of Erceldoune*, in the Thornton MS (ca. 1430–40), a poem which is closely related to the eighteenth-century ballad, *Thomas Rymer* (Child, *Ballads*, I, 319, No. 37; H. M. Flasdieck, *Tom der Reimer* [Breslau, 1934]). The latest assured historical allusion in *Thomas of Erceldoune*, vss. 469–84, is to the Battle of Otterburn, 1388, though the date, 1401, dubiously proposed by Murray, in his edition of the romance (pp. xxiv f.), has, unfortunately, been often cited since (cf. Burnham, "Thomas of Erceldoune," *PMLA*, XXIII [1908], 379; Wells, *Manual*, p. 225). Murray himself noted that the unrevised prophecy of victory (vss. 350–53), not the actual Scottish defeat, of Halidon Hill, 1333, and the questioning (vss. 345–46), whether Bruce or Baliol should rule, a question needless after 1400, when the Baliols became extinct, suggest that parts of the original version were much earlier than 1401. The story is told, now in the first, now in the third, person.

[2] Vss. 35–36 supplied from MS Cbg., Univ. Lib. Ff. 5.48 (*Th. of E.*, ed. Murray).

[3] *Thopas: His* steede *was* al *dappull gray*.

[4] *Thopas:* Of oon that *shoon* ful brighte.

Hir *selle* it *was of roelle bone*,[1]
Ffull semely was þat syghte to see! . . . .
62   Hir cropoure was of Orpharë:
And als clere golde hir *brydill* it *schone.* . . . .[2]
68   Hir *lire* was *white* as any swan. . . . .[3]

81   Thomas rathely vpe he rase,
85   He knelyde downe appone his knee,
Vndir-nethe þat grenwode *spraye;*
And sayd, "lufly ladye! rewe one mee,
Qwene of heuene als þou wele maye!"
Than spake þat lady Milde of thoghte,
"Thomas! late swylke wordes bee;
Qwene of heuene ne am j noghte, ...

95   I ryde aftyre this *wylde*[4] fee,
My raches rynnys at my devyse."
"If þou be parelde moste of prysee,
And here rydis thus in thy folye,
Of lufe, lady, als þou erte wysse,
Þou gyffe me leue to lye the bye!" . . . .
121   Downe þane lyghte þat ladye bryghte,
Vndir-nethe þat grenewode *spraye;*
And, als the storye tellis full ryghte,
Seuene sythis by hir he *laye.*[5]

177   Scho lede hym in-till a faire herbere,
Whare frwte was g(ro)wan(d gret plentee;)
Pere and appill, bothe ryppe þay were,
The date, and als the damasee;
Þe fygge, and als so þe wyneberye;
The nyghtgales byggande on þair neste;
Þe *papeioyes* faste abowte gane flye;
And *throstylls* sange, wolde hafe no reste.

[1] *Thopas:* His *sadel was of rewel boon.*
[2] *Thopas:* His *brydel as* the sonne *shoon.*
[3] *Thopas:* He dide next his *white leere.*   [4] *Thopas:* Of Fairye/So *wilde.*
[5] *Thopas:* The sparhauk and the *papejay,*
      The *thrustelcok* made eek his *lay,*
      The wodedowve upon the *spray.*

Despite the complete difference of meaning, it is worth noting that *Thomas of Erceldoune* has the same rhyme and a shortly antecedent reference (vss. 29 and 31) to *throstyll cokke* and *wodewale.*

255   Than ladyes come, bothe *faire & gent,*
      With curtassye to hir knelande.
      Harpe & fethill bothe þay fande,
      Getterne, and als so þe sawtrye;
      Lutte and rybybe bothe gangande,
      And all manere of mynstralsye. . . . .
268   Reuelle amanges þame was full ryfe.
      Knyghtis dawnesede by three and three,
      There was revelle, *gamene,* and playe. . . . .
273   Thomas duellide in that solace
      More þane j ȝowe saye *parde.*

V. THE HERO IN ARMS
Nos. 52–54

The arming of the hero in English romance became, early, a
thoroughly conventionalized bit of description which almost
inevitably listed at least helm, shield, horse, and spear.[1] The
specific details concerning Thopas' arming point clearly to *Guy*
and *Libeaus* as chief sources, for *Guy* mentions, in uniquely
combined additions to the hero's usual equipment, a *hawberk*
from Jerusalem, a *charbocle* for decoration, a *flour* upon the
helm; *Libeaus,* in MS Cott. Cal. A II, refers to a *sherte,* a *whyte
gypell,* if not *whit cote-armour,* a *sheeld of gold* with boars'
heads, a spear head *scharp ygrounde.* Thopas' *jambeaux of quyrboilly,*[2]
his too elegant ivory sword-sheath, his too soft *latoun* helm,
find no precise parallels in the romances, but represent, rather,
Chaucer's ironic perception of the burlesque value, in this context, of unusual words and the suggestion of unsuitable materials.

[1] Manly (*Essays and Studies,* XIII [1928], 70) urges that the arming of Thopas
is "absurd from beginning to end," especially in the wearing of an aketoun, and in
putting on over it habergeon and hawberk. I. Linn, "The Arming of Sir Thopas,"
MLN, LI (1936), 302 ff., points out that the romances afford parallels to these irreg-
ularities; also that the triple armings in the fifteenth-century version of *Otuel,* alike
mention the hero's aketoun, hawberk, shield, helmet, steed, sword, and spurs. See
also Herben, *Speculum,* XII (1937), 479 ff. In the Auchinleck versions of *Beves*
(No. 52) and *Guy* (No. 53), the traditional pattern for the hero's arming was already set. As neither romance mentions the hero's spurs, the omission of this
detail in *Thopas* cannot be considered a special absurdity.

[2] For *jambeaux* see *Ferumbras,* ed. Herrtage ("E.E.T.S.: Extra Series," Vol.
XXXIV [1879]), vs. 5615: *Be ys iambeaus forþ he swarf/& ys oþer spore þanne he
carf.* For *quyrboilly* see Barbour's *Bruce,* XII, 22 (ed. Mackenzie [London, 1909]):
On his basnet hye he bar ane hat off qwyrbolle. For *gambisoun,* though not *jambeaux*
see *Guy,* A, No. 53, sts. 93(7), 250(5).

52. BEVES OF HAMTOUN

969 King Ermin þo anon riȝte
Dobbede Beues vn-to kniȝte
And ȝaf him a scheld gode & sur
975 Wiþ þre eglen of asur. . . . .
979 Beues *dede* on *is actoun*,[1]
Hit was worþ mani a toun;[2]
An *hauberk* him brouȝte þat mai,
So seiden alle þat hit isai:
Hit *was* wel *iwrouȝt* & faire,
Non egge tol miȝte it nouȝt paire.
After þat ȝhe ȝaf him a stede,
þat swiþe gode was at nede.

53. GUY OF WARWICK, A

[Guy is armed to fight the Saracens.]
3849 He oxed his armes hastiliche,
And men es him brouȝt sikerliche.
Hosen[3] of iren he haþ on drawe, ...
3853 In a *strong hauberk* he gan him schrede,
Who so it wered, þe ded no þurt him drede.
An *helme* he haþ on him don:
Better no wered neuer kniȝt non;
The sercle of gold þer-on was wrouȝt,
For halfe a cite no worþ it bouȝt: . . . .
3861 Seþþe he gert him wiþ a brond
þat was y-made in eluene lond.
His scheld about his nek he tok,
On hond he nam a spere kerueinde,
Out of þe cite he was rideinde. . . . .
3873 Wel y-armed on his stede,
A launce he bar gode at nede . . . .
4129 Gij anon asked his stede þo
His spere, & his swerd also:
In his hond a gode *swerd* he bar;[4]

[Guy is armed to fight with Amoraunt, a Saracen giant.]

[1] See below, p. 529, n. 2.

[2] Cf. *Guy*, A, No. 53, vs. 3858. From the insistence in such lines on great cost or value sprang, probably, the ironic phrase in *Thopas: coste many a jane.*

[3] Cf. also No. 53, st. 250(5). Contrast the *hosen of mayle* which a good knight should have with Thopas' *Of Brugges were his hosen broun.*

[4] *Thopas:* And *in his hand* a *launcegay,*
   A long *swerd* by his side.

91(1–6)   Gij was ful wele in armes diȝt
          Wiþ *helme*, & *plate*, & brini briȝt,
          þe best þat euer ware.
          þe *hauberk* he hadde was reuis,[1]
          þat was king Clarels, y-wis,
          In Ierusalem when he was þare.

92(1–12) Sir Gij þai toke it in þat *plas*. . . . .
          As briȝt as ani siluer it *was:*
          þe halle *schon* þerof *as sonne* of glas,
          For soþe wiþouten fayle.
          His *helme* was of so michel miȝt,
          Was neuer man ouer comen in fiȝt
          þat hadde it on his ventayle.

93(1–9)   A gode *swerd* he hadde, wiþ-outen faile,
          þat was Ectors in Troye batayle,
          In gest as so men fint. . . . .
          Hose & gambisoun so gode kniȝt schold,
          A targe listed wiþ gold
          About his swere he hint.

[Guy is armed to fight with Colbrand, a Danish giant.]

249(4–12) & Gij was armed swiþe wel
           In a gode *hauberk* of stiel
           Wrouȝt of þe best lawe.
           An *helme* he hadde of michel miȝt

---

[1] *Thopas:* And over that a fyn *hawberk*,
        Was al ywroght of *Iewes* werk.
        Ful strong it was of *plate*.

On the great rarity of medieval references to Jews' work in armor see Ficke, *Phil. Quart.*, VII (1928), 82; L. H. Loomis, *Phil. Quart.*, XIV (1935), 371. It is probable, in view of all of Chaucer's other borrowings from the Auchinleck *Guy*, that his *Iewes* was inspired by the ghost word *reuis*, mis-written for *ieuis*, just as in the very next line *Clarels* was written for *Charles* (Charlemagne). (In Zupitza's ed. of *Guy*, A, p. 52, the word was unfortunately printed *renis*, with a marginal query, *eluis*?) With the immediate reference to Ierusalem that follows *reuis*, it would have been easy for Chaucer to recognize and correct the error and so have achieved his own, *Iewes*. The rhyme that he uses is also found in *Guy*, A, st. 256(1–2):

Of mailes was nouȝt his hauberk:
It was al oî anoþer werk.

It should be observed that the various armings of Guy, in the extracts here given, combine to explain in *Thopas* the following details: the lance (? launcegay), the sword, the Jewish hauberk, the reference to plate mail, the decorative *charbocle*, the *jambeux* (? *gambisoun*), the helmet's *flour*—to say nothing of other less distinctive features. For details drawn from *Libeaus* see No. 54.

With a ce(r)cle of gold, þat schon briȝt,
 Wiþ precious stones on rawe.
In þe frunt stode a *char-bukel* ston:
As briȝt *as ani sonne* it *schon*
 Þat glemes vnder schawe.

250(1–9) *On* þat *helme* stode a *flour:*
 Wrouȝt it was of diuers colour; . . . .
Gloues, & gambisoun, & *hosen* of mayle
 As gode kniȝt haue scholde.
Girt he was wiþ a gode brond
Wele kerueand, biforn his hond
 A targe listed wiþ gold.

251(4–9) Sir Gij opon þat stede wond
Wiþ a gode glaiue *in hond,*
 And *priked* him forþ his way,
&, when he com to þe *plas*
Þer þe batayl loked *was,*
 Gij liȝt wiþ-outen delay.

54. LIBEAUS DESCONUS[1]

217 To army thir knyghtes wer fayn,
The ferste was syr Gaweyn,
 That other syr Percevale,
The thyrthe syr Eweyn,
The ferthde was syr Agrafrayn;
 So seyth the Frenzsch tale.
They caste on hym *a scherte*[2] of selk,
A gypell *as whyte*[3] as melk,
 In that semely sale;
And syght an *hawberk* bryght,
That rychely was adyght,
 Wyth mayles thykke and smale.

---

[1] From MS C, Cott. Calig. A II, in *Ancient Eng. Met. Romances*, ed. Ritson, II (1802), 10 ff. Cf. Kaluza, *Libeaus*, vss. 241–64, 1228–30, 1657–65; 1693–95.

[2] *Thopas:* He did next his white leere, ...
A breech and eek *a sherte;*
And next his sherte an *aketoun*
And over that an haubergeoun
For *percynge* of his herte.

And over that his cote-armour
As whit as is a lilye flour.

[3] Libeaus is later hailed, vs. 1280 (Kaluza, *Libeaus*, vs. 1370), as *þou felaw in whit.* Probably it was from him that Thopas inherited lily-whiteness as a color in which *to debate.* But see also *Launfal*, vs. 742: *His armour þat was whyt as flour; Ipomydon*, B, vs. 830: *Jason . . . . in white harneise dight.*

229 Gaweyn hys owene syre
   Heng abowte hys swyre
    A *scheld* with a gryffoun,
   And Launcelet hym broght a *sper*,
   In werre with hym well to were,
    And also a fell fachoun.
   And syr Oweyn hym broght a stede, ...
238 And an *helm* of ryche atyre,
   That *was* stele, *and noon* yre,
    Percevale sette on hys croun.

1174 Hys foemen were well boun,
   To *perce* hys *acketoun*,
    Gypell, mayl, and plate.

1567 Hys *scheld was of gold* fyn,[1]
   The bores heddes therinne,
    As blak as brond ybrent; . . . .
1573 And of the same paynture
   Was lyngell and trappure
    Iwroght well *fayre and gent;*
   Hys schaft was strong wythall.

1603 Tho he tok a schaft rounde,
   Wyth cornall *scharp ygrounde*,[2]
    And ryde be ryght resoun.

VI. THE HERO IN COMBAT
Nos. 55–60

Thopas' encounter with Olifaunt,[3] like the account of the hero's arming, draws chiefly from *Guy of Warwick* and from *Libeaus*. Alike, *Guy* and *Libeaus* have the horse-killing by the giant, a feat only threatened by Olifaunt; alike, they mention

---

[1] *Thopas: His sheeld was* al *of gold* so reed,
  And *therinne* a *bores heed,*
  A charbocle by his syde.

Kaluza, *Libeaus*, p. xiv, noted Ritson's error in reading *The* for *þre* in vs. 1568. For Thopas' *Charbocle*, see above, *Guy*, A, No. 53, st. 249(10).

[2] *Thopas: His spere was of fyn ciprees*, ...
  The heed ful *sharpe ygrounde.*

[3] Into the one word *Olifaunt* Chaucer condensed the usual prolix descriptions in the romances. No known justification exists for Bishop Hurd's statement (*Letters* [3d ed.], III, 318 that "the Tale of Giant Olyphant and Chylde Topaz is not a fiction of [Chaucer's] own, but a story of antique fame."

Termagaunt, though *Libeaus* alone has the *Termagaunt: geaunt* rhyme of *Thopas;* both *Guy* and *Libeaus* refer to a lady in connection with the giant and to the *grace of God.* The combination of these elements in each romance distinguishes them from others containing the giant combat.[1] *Guy* seems to have suggested the postponed combat and provided the *hill and dale,* the *dale and down,*[2] over which Thopas rode, but Thopas' reason for delay, his declared lack of armor, recalls *Libeaus.*[3] The emphasis in both poems on the littleness of the hero, in contrast to the giant, Guy being called a child, and Libeaus *ʒing and lite,* was, perhaps, the link that suggested the famous combat of David and Goliath, which, evidently, Chaucer had also in mind. In medieval versions of the story, such as that in the *Cursor mundi* composed between 1300 and 1325, David's youth is stressed, and he is called *Childe David.* Chaucer burlesqued both title and incident by transferring to the giant the one-and-only slingshot of fiction, and by having him chase the Child who should have slain him.[4] David's doffing of Saul's armor, his scorn of weapons, may have contributed something to the amusing contrast in *Thopas,* where the hero, already armed, defers battle until he has more armor, and later acquires, piece by piece, a whole panoply. The multiplicity of giants in *Torrent,* the detail of the hero's throwing stones at one of them, may have enhanced Chaucer's perception of the general absurdity of

---

[1] Giant combats occur in the following ME romances: *Beves,* vss. 1881 and 2533; *Degaré,* in some manuscripts; *Eglamour,* No. 56; *Guy,* A, No. 57; *Launfal,* vs. 505; *Libeaus,* No. 58; *King Horn,* vs. 801; *Octavian,* vs. 1075; *Perceval,* No. 59; *Roland and Vernagu* ("E.E.T.S.: Extra Series," Vol. XXXIX), vs. 545; *Tristrem,* (ed. Kölbing), vs. 2722; *Torrent,* No. 60; *Ywain and Gawain* (ed. Schleich), vs. 2430. *Guy* popularized the subject for English romance.

[2] Cf. *Guy,* A, No. 57, st. 64 for the postponed combat. For the *dale* phrases cf. *Guy,* A, st. 29(9); *Barfot bi doun and dale;* st. 42(4), *Heʒede ouer alle bi doun and dale;* also vs. 4038, *Ouer þe dounes & þe dales.* The word *down(s),* but rarely used in the romances, occurs frequently in *Guy,* A, 3033, 3036, 3421, and 3876. Cf. *Thopas: By dale and eek by downe!* For other elements common to the combat episode in *Guy,* A, and *Thopas* see below, p. 536, n. 1.

[3] This detail does not occur in the giant combat, but earlier. Libeaus speaks rudely to Sir Otes de Lile, who is hunting, *y-cloped in inde.* The latter cries out (vss. 1123–25): *Wer ich y-armed nou,/Redy, as art þou, /We wolde fiʒte in same.* Cf. *Thopas:*

> Tomorwe wol I meete with thee,
> Whan I have myn armoure.

[4] Cf. L. H. Loomis, "Thopas and David and Goliath," *MLN,* LI (1936), 311 ff.

the giant theme. But the comic climax of his treatment of Thopas' escape *thurgh Goddes grace* . . . . *and his fair berynge*, was probably inspired by the escape of Eglamour, *thorowe Goddis helpe and his knyfe*.

55. CURSOR MUNDI (DAVID AND GOLIATH)

7443   þai broght wid þaim Goli, þat etin, ...
7447   Be-tuix his eyen, thre fote brad,[1]
      Ful laith it was his visage made.
      Of bodi grett, in graynys lang,
      Vnsterli semid he to be strang;
      Sex elne and mare he was on hiht,
      He was all armid forto fight.
      Of his mete was mesur nan,
      He wild ete seuen schep his an.
      þan said he, "quar es nu saul king? . . . ."

7483   þis herd dauid, and forth gan stand, ...
7485   "I trou treuly in godes miht,
      þat i sal vndertake þe fight,
      Agayn Goly þat es sua grim,
      Wid *goddes grace* sle sal i him;" . . . .
      [Saul commands.]
7519   "Gas and fettis me nou in hi,
      Min aun armur to *child* daui."
      Helm and habiryun on him þai did,
      And gird him wid a suord emid;
      Quen dauid was armyd sua,
      Forth a fote miht he noght ga. . . . .
7531   He tok fiue stanis þar war round,
      And putt þaim in his scrip þat stound,
      And said, "dos away þis ger,
      For certis i can na armis ber. . . . ."

7553   Quen golias on dauid be-helde,
      Ful littel talle of him he teld. . . . .
7575   þan said golias, "þu art bot dede."
      Dauid said, "þat take i godd to rede."
      Said goli, "wil þu fight wid me?
      I rede bi-time þat þu heþen fle."
    "Fle þat wenis haue þe werre,
      For ar i fle i sal come nerre."

---

[1] Cf. *Thopas: a geaunt with hevedes three.*

Wid þis a ston he laid in slinge,[1]
Sua stalworthli he lett it suinge,
þat in his front þe ston he fest,
þat both his eyen vte þai brest. . . . .

7593   Dauid went ham wid gret honour,
All thankid godd þair creatour.

56. EGLAMOUR

229   The knyght sayd: *"So mote I the,*
At my journaye wolde I bee."
He buskede and mad him ȝare.
"Bot a lyttill here by weste
A geant hase *a fayre forest . . . .*
235   With *syprese* trees growand lang."

[Eglamour goes to the forest, kills a stag, and encounters the giant.]

301   When he come ware þe geant was,
"Gude sir," he sayd, "þou latt me passe,
If þat it be thi will!"
"Nay, traytour, þou arte tane:
My chefe herte hase þou slane:
þat sall þe lyk *full* ill."[2]
307   To þe knyght þe geaunt gun gaa,
An iryn clube he gan hym taa: . . . .
313   He sayd: "Traytour, whate does þou here
In my foreste to stele my dere?
Here *sall þou habyde!"*
316   Sir Eglamour his swerde owt droghe.

[After fighting all day, Eglamour kills the giant.]

331   Thorowe Goddis helpe and his knyfe[3]
Thus hase þe geant loste his lyfe.

[1] Cf. *Thopas: stones caste / Out of a fel staf-slynge.* David and his giant-killing slingshot are unique. The first instance of *staff-slinge* in English (*NED*) is in the Auchinleck *Richard,* vs. 5226.

[2] *Thopas: That thou shalt* with this launcegay
    Abyen it *ful* sowre.

[3] *Thopas:* And al it was *thurgh Goddes* gras,
    And thurgh *his* fair berynge.

Manly, *Canterbury Tales,* p. 632, cites *Eglamour* (Cbg., Univ. Libr., Ff II, 38, ed. Halliwell, *Thornton Rom.,* pp. 569 f.): *Of the helpe of God was alle his tryste / And of hys swerde so bryght.* Robinson, *Chaucer,* p. 844, vs. 830n. remarked that the satire here turns on a commonplace sentiment of saga and romance, "Fortuna fortes adjuvat." Orally, he recalls *Havelok,* vs. 2677, where Ubbe would have had his head cut off, *Yif God ne were, and Hue Rauen.*

57. GUY OF WARWICK, A

[Guy fights with Amoraunt, a Saracen giant.]

62(1-9) þan dede he com forþ a Sarrazine, ...
He is so michel & vnrede,
Of his siȝt a man may drede,
Wiþ tong *as y þe telle.*

63(1-6) For he is so michel of bodi y-piȝt,
Oȝains him tvelue men haue no miȝt,
Ben þai neuer so strong;
For he is four fot, sikerly,
More þan ani man stont him bi:
So wonderliche he is long.

[King Triamour is overawed at sight of the giant.]

64(7-12) When he seye Amoraunt so grim
(þer durst no man fiȝt wiþ him,
So grille he was on grounde),
þan asked he respite til a *day,*
To finde anoþer *ȝif he may*[1]
Oȝaines him durst founde.

[Guy undertakes to fight Amoraunt.]

97(4-6) þai *priked* þe stedes þat þai on sete,
& smiten togider wiþ dentes grete,
& ferd *as þai wer wode.*

100(1-2) Sir Amoraunt was agreued in hert,
& smot to Gij a dint ful smert.

101(1-9) þe sadel bowe he clef atvo,
þe stedes nek he dede also,[2]
Wiþ his grimli brond.

[1] *Thopas:* The child seyde, "Also moote I thee,
Tomorwe wol I meete with thee, ...
Thy mawe
Shal I percen, *if I may,* . . . .
Er it be fully pryme of *day,*
For heere thow shalt be slawe."

For another unheroic postponement of a combat, though not with a giant, see above, p. 531, n. 3. *Guy,* A, has many instances of the use of the polite but absurd phrase, *ȝif I (he) may:* vs. 1275, *wald been awreke,* . . . . *ȝif he may;* vs. 3090, *ȝif he may, to deþ he wille him do;* st. 110(8), *to defenden him, ȝif y mouȝt,* etc. For instances in other romances see Campion and Holthausen, *Perceval,* vs. 1982n. For *moote I thee,* see, in this extract from *Guy,* A, st. 110(2).

[2] The giants in romance usually slay the hero's horse. Cf. *Beves,* vs. 1888; *Eglamour,* vs. 581; *Guy,* A, No. 57, 260(10); *Libeaus,* No. 58, vss. 1405-7; *Torrent,* st. 57.

110(1–3)   "Tel me," he *seyd*," wennes þou be;
            For þou art strong, *so mot y the*,
               & of michel miȝt."

117(1–12)   Amoraunt was ful egre of mode,
            & smot to Gij as *he wer wode* . . . .
            Of his scholder þe swerd glod doun,
            þat boþe *plates & hauberioun*
               He carf atvo, y pliȝt,
               Al to þe naked hide, *y-wis*,
               & nouȝt of flesche atamed *is*
               þurch *grace of god* almiȝt.

118(10–12) & when Gij seye þat fair grace,
            þat noþing wounded he was
               Iesu he þanked on heye.

121(1–2)   "Hold þi pes," seyd Amor*aunt*,
            "For, *bi* mi lord sir *Teruagaunt*,[1]

126(5–9)   þi liif þou schalt astite forgon,
            þi bodi schal atvinne,
            & þine heued, *bi Teruagaunt*,
            Mi leman schal haue to presaunt,
               þat comly is of kinne."

[After a terrific combat lasting a whole day, Guy kills the giant.]

[Guy fights with Colbrond, a Danish giant.]

251(4–9)   Sir Gij opon þat stede wond
            Wiþ a gode glaiue in hond,
               & *priked* him forþ his way,
            &, when he com to þe *plas*
            þer þe batayl loked *was*,
               Gij liȝt wiþ-outen delay.

255(2–6)   Colbrond stirt vp in þat stounde:
               To fiȝt he was ful felle.
            He was so michel & so vnrede,
            þat no hors miȝt him lede,
               In gest *as y ȝou telle*.

256(1–12)   Of mailes was nouȝt his *hauberk:*
               It was al of anoþer *werk*, ...

---

[1] See below, p. 538, n. 1. The oath *by Termagaunt* is a commonplace. Cf. Magoun, *PMLA*, XLII (1927), 37, n. 9. The name *Termagaunt* is mentioned five times in *Guy*, A, usually in an oath.

He was so michel & so strong,
& þer-to so wonderliche long:
   In þe world *was non his pere.*

259(1–3)   Sir Gij lepe on his stede fot hot, ...
& wiþ a spere, þat wele bot,
   To him he gan to ride.

260(4–12)   & Colbrond wiþ michel hete
On Gyes helme he wald haue smite, ...
þat sadel & hors atvo he smot,
In to þe erþe wele half a fot,
   & Gij fel doun to grounde.

263(1–3)   & Gij hent his swerd an hond,
& heteliche smot to Colbrond.
   As a *child* he stode him vnder.[1]

269(5–10)   & Gij in þe nek a strok him ȝaf
As he (gan) stoupe for þe brond, ...
þurch *grace of godes* sond
Ded he feld þe glotoun þare.

278(1–5)   Sir Gij went in his way forþ riȝt,
Oft he þonked god almiȝt
þat þe geaunt was slawe.
To Warwike he went, to þat cite
þer *he was lord of þat cuntre.*

58. LIBEAUS DESCONUS[2]

[Libeaus fights with the giant of the Ile d'Or.]

1303   Hit fell in þe monþ of June, ...
1306   þe someris day is long,

[1] See above, p. 534, n. 1; also *Thopas: faire escapeth child Thopas.* Chaucer uses the appelation "Child" only in the giant-combat episode; he uses it as a knightly term, yet gives it a comic suggestiveness. In *Guy*, A, the littleness of the hero is referred to not only in st. 263(3), but also in st. 95(1), *þis litel kniȝt þat stont me by.* Cf. *Childe Dauy* in the *Cursor Mundi*, No. 55.

It should be noted that in the two giant-combat stories of *Guy*, A, and in that of *Thopas*, the following elements are alike combined: the postponement of the fight linked with the phrase *if I (he) may* (*Guy*, A, st. 64), the killing of the hero's horse (actual or threatened), the rhyming of the giant's name (*Amoraunt*, *Guy*, A, st. 121; *Olifaunt*) with *Termagaunt*, the *child* references, the use of such identical phrases as *so moote I thee* and *grace of God* (*Guy*, A, st. 117[12]), and several almost identical lines (*Guy*, A, 97[6], 256[12], 278[5]).

[2] Magoun, "The Source of Chaucer's Sir Thopas," *PMLA*, XLII (1927), 833–44, urges that the whole Ile d'Or episode of *Libeaus* comes nearer to explaining the plot of *Thopas* than does any other romance. Both poems have an otherworld

Mery is þe foules song
And notes of þe niȝtingales:
1309   Þat time Libeaus gan ride
Be a river side
And siȝ a fair cite. . . . .
1315   He axed, what hit hiȝt;
þe maide seide anon riȝt:
"Sir, I will telle þe!
Men clepeþ hit Ile d'or;
Her haþ be fiȝtinge mor,
þan owher in any countre.

1321   For a lady *of pris*,
Roddy *as rose* on rise,
þis countre is in doute.
A geaunt, þat hatte Maugis,
Nowher *his per þer nis*,
Her haþ beleide aboute.
He is as blak as pich;
Nowher þer is non swich
Of dedes sterne and stoute."

1334   He is þritty fote of lengþe,
And miche more of strengþe,
þan oþer kniȝtes five:

1345   Quoþ Libeaus: "Maide hende, ...
1348   Ȝif *God* me *grace* sende,
Er þis day come to ende,
Wiþ fiȝt I hope him spille; . . . .
1354   þauȝ I be ȝing and lite,
To him will I smite;
Let god do his wille!"

1357   þey ride forþ all þre
Toward þat faire cite,
Men clepeþ hit Ile d'or.
Maugis þey gonne y-se

---

setting, both involve the same characters, hero, giant, and lady of supernatural attributes, and the same episode, a combat between the giant and the hero. For comment on the theory, see Miss Everett, *Year's Work in English Studies*, VIII (1927), 107; Rudd, *PQ*, VIII (1929), 303; Patch, *Eng. Stud.*, LXV (1930–31), 353. See also *Launfal*, No. 49, vs. 316, n. 2. It seems difficult to equate the evil enchantress of *Libeaus* with the fairy queen of *Thopas*, even though each lady did have some association with a giant. The giant Amoraunt in *Guy*, A, st. 126(8), speaks of his *leman*.

Upon a bregge of tre,
Beld as wilde bore.

1369   He cride to him in spite:
"Say, þou felaw in whit,
    Tell me, what art þou?
Torne hom aȝain als tit
For þin owe profit,
    Ȝef þou love þy prou!"
Libeaus seide anoon riȝt,
"King Arthour made me kniȝt;
    To him I made avou,
þat I ne schulde never turne bak;
þer fore, þou devell in blak,
    Mak þe redy nou!"

1381   Sir Libeaus and Maugis
On stedes proude *of pris*
    Togeder ride full riȝt.
Boþe lordes and ladis . . . .

1387   . . . . praide god loude and still, ...
1389   Help þat cristen kniȝt,
And þat file *geaunt*,
    þat leved in *Termagaunt*,[1]
þat day to diȝe in fiȝt.

1405   Maugis was queinte and quede
And smitte his stede on þe heed
    And dasched out þe braine.
þe stede fell doune deed;
Libeaus no þing ne sede,
    Bot start him up aȝain.

1477   þe geaunt þis gan se,
þat he schulde slawe be;
    He fliȝ wiþ miȝt and main. . . . . .

[1] *Thopas:* Til that ther cam a greet *geaunt*,
        His name was sire Olifaunt, ...
    A perilous man of dede.
    He seyde, "Child, by *Termagaunt!*
    But if thou prike out of my haunt,
        Anon I sle thy steede."
See *Guy*, A, No. 57, st. 121, for the rhyme of the giant's name, *Amoraunt: bi Terua-*
gaunt. Kölbing (*ES*, XI [1888], 504) compared *Alisaunder*, vs. 6530, *He* (a rhinoce-
ros) *had eres als an olyfant,/ And was wele more þan a geant.*

1484   Libeaus smitte of his heved:
        Þer of he was fain.
        He bar þe heed into þe toun;
        Wiþ a fair processioun
          Þe folk com him again.

1489   A lady, *whit as flour*,
        Þat hiȝte la dame d'amour,
          Afeng him fair and well
        And þonked him wiþ honour,
        Þat he was her socour
          Aȝens þat geaunt fell. . . . .
1498   And profered him wiþ word,
        For to be her lord
          In cite and castell.

1501   Libeaus graunte in haste
        And love to her he caste,
          For sche was *briȝt* and schene.
        Alas! he nadde be *chast;*[1]
        For aftirward, at þe last,
          Sche dede him traie and tene;

1513   For þis fair lady[2]
        Couþe more of sorcery,
          Þen oþer swiche five.
        Sche made him melodie
        Of all maner menstralsy,
          Þat any man miȝte descrive. . . . .
1522   Wiþ fantasme and *fairie*
        Þus sche blered his iȝe,
          Þat evell mot sche þrive.

59. PERCEVAL OF GALES

2005   The geant stode in his holde
        That had those londis in wolde,
        Saw Percevell, þat was bolde,
          One his lande dryfe; . . . .

---

[1] *Thopas:* he was *chaast* and no lechour. The verbal reminiscence in *chaast* suggests that Chaucer had *Libeaus* in mind, rather than, as Kölbing proposed (*ES*, XI, 500), the various places in *Ipomadon*, A (cf. No. 48), where the hero resists lovelorn damsels. Cf. also, *Guy, A*, No. 46, p. 517, n. 1.

[2] *Thopas:* Heere is the queene of Fayerye,
    With harpe and pipe and symphonye,
    Dwellynge in this place.

2009　"How-gate may this fare?
　　　　I se a bolde man ȝare
　　　　　　On my lande ryfe. . . . .

2015　Hym were better hafe been at Rome,
　　　　So ever *mote I thryfe.*"

2045　Than said Percevell the fre:
　　　　"*Thurgh grace of god* so sall I the[1]
　　　　And siche geantez as ȝe,
　　　　　　Sle thaym in the felde."

2049　Siche metyng was seldom sene;
　　　　The *dales* dynned thaym by-twene
　　　　For dynttis, þat þay gaffe by-dene,
　　　　　　When þay so met.

　　　　[Perceval slays the giant.]

60. TORRENT OF PORTYNGALE[2]

[Torrent throws stones in a giant combat.]

1260　The Gyaunt shipped in a while
　　　　And sett hym oute in an yle,
　　　　　　That was grow both grene and gay.
　　　　Sir Torrent com *prekand* on a *stede*,
　　　　Richely armed in his wede;

1287　The Giaunt *said:* "So *must* I *the,*[3]
　　　　Sir, thou art welcom to me,
　　　　　　Thy deth is not to layn!" . . . .

1293　Tho Sir Torent went nere Cate,
　　　　He thought, he wold hym haue slayne.

1295　The theff couth no better wonne,
　　　　In to the see rennyth he sone,
　　　　　　As faste as he myght ffare.
　　　　Sir Torrent gaderid cobled stonys,

---

[1] *Thopas:* For heere thow shalt be *slawe* . . . .
　　　And al it was *thurgh Goddes grace.*

[2] Wells (*Manual,* p. 117) dates *Torrent* between 1400 and 1450; Trounce (*Medium Ævum,* III [1934], 35–36) thinks that "*Torrent* was written in Norfolk proper in the latter half of the 14th century"; also that "it is open to the satire of Chaucer in having a series of incidents, instead of a plot, and the poem may actually have been in Chaucer's mind." In the first two thousand lines Torrent fights five giants and two dragons.

[3] *Thopas:* The child seyde, "Also *moote I thee.*" Cf. *Eglamour,* No. 56, vs. 229; *Guy,* A, No. 57, st. 110(2).

Good and handsom ffor the nonys,
  That good and round ware;
Meny of them to hym he *caste*,
He threw *stonys* on hym so *faste*,[1]
  That he was sad and sare.
To the ground he did hym fell,
Men myght here the fend yell
  Halfe a myle and mare.

VII. THE HERO'S VOW
Nos. 61–68

Thopas' vows to kill the giant, both before and after running
away from him, are a palpable take-off on the braggart oaths
of medieval fiction.[2] That Thopas swears in countrified fashion
on ale and bread may burlesque such fantastic chivalric oaths,
sworn on the body of a bird, as those reported in French and
English versions of the *Avowis of Alexander*[3] and other poems,
but it is as possible that the phrase, *on ale and bread*, sprang
from Chaucer's humorous recollection of the homely fare[4]
which the romancers naïvely ascribed to the nobility, and the
familiar vows of popular phraseology, never to take meat or
drink, or, specifically, never to eat bread.[5]

Though Thopas' two vows against his foe are too brief to
make their antecedents certain, it may be noted that the

---

[1] Cf. also *Torrent:* The Gyaunt yode and gaderid stone
              And sye where the knyght gan gone [1556–57].

[2] *Thopas:* And there he swoor on ale and breed,
              How that the geaunt should be deed,
                Bityde what bityde!

On the medieval custom of making vows see Koschwitz's editions of *Karls des
Grossen Reise nach Jerusalem* (Leipzig, 1901, 1913); also Cross, *MP*, XXV (1927–
28), 349 ff. Cf. *Avowing of Arthur* (ed. French and Hale, *ME. Met. Rom.*, p.
612n.). For oaths and vows in other English romances see Schmirgel in *Beves* (ed.
Kölbing, pp. xlvii, ff.); Kölbing, *Ipomedon*, p. 481; Campion and Holthausen,
Perceval, p. 136 (Schwur); and the various instances given in the extracts here.
French and Hale (pp. 612, 989) note the burlesque boasts in the *Tournament of
Tottenham*, vss. 90 ff.

[3] See below, p. 542, n. 4.

[4] Cf. *King Horn*, vs. 1257, *þer was bred & ale suete,/For riche men þer ete;*
Tristrem, vs. 540 (ed. Kölbing), *þe king ne seyd no more,/Bred þai pard and schare;*
Guy, A, vs. 6852, *Bred & win biforn him þai dede.* Cf. *Richard*, No. 92, vs. 4248.

[5] See Nos. 66–68. Cf. Chaucer's own line, *Certes, I nil never ete breed* (*B of D*,
vs. 92).

familiar rhyme *breed:deed* and the unusual *mawe:slawe*, are
alike paralleled in *Alisaunder*;[1] also that in *Libeaus*, where in
one episode three vows are made, two of them accord with
Thopas' in having a *betide* in one, a *hawberk* in the other.[2]

61. ATHELSTON

169   þanne swoor þe kyng be cros and roode:
"Meete ne drynk schal do me goode,[3]
Tyl þat he *be dede*."

62. AVOWIS OF ALEXANDER[4]

5151   "Lordingis," said auld Cassamus,
"Be all our Goddis and be Marcus,
I rede we to the pacock do
The vsage that coustumit is thair-to.
In this countre the vsage is
That ilk man avow sall his auyse;" . . . .

5207   "This mete for douchty ordaned is
That worthy ar ladeis for to kis.
Heirto suld men avow heyly,
And syne fulfill douchtelly,

---

[1] *Alisaunder:* In litel while was mony y-*slawe*,
    And y-smyte thorough wombe and *mawe* [1259].
    Areches he hutte; now he is *ded*,
    N'ul he no more ete *bred* [2157].

Cf. Schmirgel in *Beves* (ed. Kölbing, p. lxii) on *slawe* as a rhyme word. The rhyme
with *mawe* is rare.

[2] See No. 65, vss. 298, 455.

[3] Zupitza, *Athelston*, vs. 170n., cites *Earl of Toulouse*, vs. 136, *He sware be hym,*
þat dyed on rode, Mete nor drynke schulde do hym gode, Or he vengedd bee; also *Guy*
(Univers.), vs. 3695; *Guy* (Caius), vs. 10030; *Sowdone of Babylone*, vs. 1854 (Haus-
knecht); *Sege of Melayne*, vs. 1189; *Rowlande and Otuell*, vs. 1347. Cf. *Degrevant*,
No. 63; *Perceval*, No. 66. Troilus, IV, vs. 775, swears, *Thanne shal no mete or*
drynke come in me.

[4] The *Avowis of Alexander* makes the second part of the Scottish *Buik of*
Alexander, which is dated 1438 by its epilogue but is assigned by its latest editor,
R. L. Ritchie ([Edinburgh, 1927], I, lxii ff., clviii ff.), to Barbour and the last part
of the fourteenth century. The *Avowis* is based on Jacques de Longuyon's *Voeux*
du Paon, composed about 1310. For instances of solemn chivalric vows sworn on
the body of a bird, a swan, a heron, or a peacock, see Ritchie, I, xxxviii–xl; E. P.
Hammond, *English Verse between Chaucer and Surrey* (Durham, N.C., 1927),
pp. 414–15. Skeat, *Chaucer*, V, 196, on vs. 2062, Miss Hammond, and Robinson,
Chaucer, p. 845, vs. 872n., alike suggest that Thopas' oath *on ale and breed* was a
burlesque of chivalric oaths of this type.

Of armes and of amouris samin;
And I sall first begin the gammin."

[Perdicas makes his vow.]

5287 "That I sall licht in middes the feild
With helme, haubrek, spere and sheild,
Thare sall I duell with thame and fecht
Outher leif or dee quhether God will send."

63. DEGREVANT[1]

1753 þane the ȝorle wax wode,
And swore be bonus and blode:
"Mete ne drynk shall do me gode,
Ar I se þe dye!"

64. EGLAMOUR

564 This fend [i.e., the giant] will felly fyghte.
Sir Eglamour said: "By þe rode,
I sall assaye hym, þofe he be wode,
And sla hym thorow Goddis myghte."

65. LIBEAUS DESCONUS

[The hero vows to attack the mighty William Salebraunche beside
the Chapell Auntrous.]

295 Quoþ Libeaus Desconus:
"Is his fiȝtinge of swich us?
Was he never y-hitte?
For auȝt, þat may *betide*,[2]
To him I will ride
And loke, hou he sit."

[William subsequently tells relatives of his defeat and enforced oath.]

433 "But o þing greviþ me sore,
þat he haþ made me swore
Upon his fauchoun briȝt,
þat I ne schall neuer more,

---

[1] From MS C, Cbg. Univ. Libr. Ff. 1. 6 in *Degrevant*, ed. Luick, p. 113.

[2] Cf. *Orfeo*, vs. 337, *"Parfay," quaþ he, "tide wat bitide"*; *Degaré*, vs. 741, *To
his knaue he seide, "Tide wat tide"*; *Squire of Low Degree*, vs. 275, *This seven yere I
shall you abyde,/Betyde of you what so betyde*; *Beves* M, vs. 351, *Betyde, what so
euer betyde*; vs. 663, *Tyde, what wyll betyde*. For many variant phrases using *betide*
see Zupitza, *Athelston*, vs. 773n.; Campion and Holthausen, *Perceval*, vs. 420n.
See *Launfal*, No. 49, vss. 309–10. Cf. also *Troilus*, V, vs. 750, *bityde what bityde*.

Till I come Arthour before,
Sojourne day ne niȝt."

[The relatives vow to revenge William.]

451 "Wende forþ and do þin oþe,
And þauȝ þe traitour be wroþ,
We schull him asaile:
Er he þis forest passe.
His *hauberk* we will to-rasse,[1]
þauȝ hit be þikke of maile."

66. PERCEVAL OF GALES

381 He sware by grete goddez myȝte: . . . .
383 "Bot if þe kyng make my knyghte,
To-morne I sall hym sloo!"

905 Bot þan spak þe olde knyghte, ...

929 "Hade I bene in the stede,
þer he was done to þe *dede,*
I solde never hafe etyn *brede,*[2]
Are I hade sene hym bren."

67. SEVEN SAGES[3]

505 He swore anon, by saynt Vyncent,
"I schal nevere hete *brede,*
Here the thyfe traytour *be dede.*"

1630 Quod the emperour to the emperesse,
"By hym that made matyns and messe,
I nyll to morwen ete no *brede*
Er the thef traytour *be ded.*"

68. TRYAMOURE[4]

97 Then was the quene wonder wrothe,
And swere mony a grete othe, ...
103 "Y trowe y schalle never ete *bred*
Tylle thou be broght to the *dedd.*"

---

[1] Kaluza (*Libeaus,* vs. 454n.) remarked that Thopas' vow reads (in MS Cbg. Univ. Gg. 4.27, Six Text ed., vs. 2014): *Thyn hauberk schal I percen.* Cf. *Libeaus,* No. 54, vss. 1174–76 (in Kaluza's text, vss. 1228–30).

[2] For other instances in the romances of references to eating bread see above, p. 541, nn. 2 and 4; also, in this section, Nos. 67–68. Cf. Campion and Holthausen, *Perceval,* vs. 929n.

[3] From MS D, Cbg. Univ. Libr., Dd. I. 17 (late fourteenth century), ed. Wright ("Percy Society," Vol. XVI [1846]).

[4] "Composed in the North Midland in 1400–50" (Wells, *Manual,* p. 121).

VIII. THE HERO'S PRAISE
Nos. 69–76

Few passages in the romances better illustrate the lack of originality, the repetitiousness of phrase and theme, which often characterized them, than do the passages devoted to the praise of mighty men; each one was a peerless "flour of chivalrie." Chaucer culled for *Thopas* the most characteristic phrases and made a particularly humorous use of the *none durst* formula which, in *Guy*, was notably overused.

69. AMIS AND AMILOUN

173 Alle þe lond spac of hem þo,
Boþe in tour & toun;
In to what stede þat þai went,
To iustes oþer to *turnament*,
Sir Amis & sir Amiloun,
For *douhti*est þai ware *in* eueri *dede*.

439 Þan was þe boteler, sir Amis,
Ouer al yholden *flour* & priis,
Trewely to telle in tale,
& *douhti*est in eueri *dede*[1]
& *worþli*est in ich a *wede*,[2]
& semliest in sale.

463 It is sir Amis, þe kinges boteler;
In al þis warld nis *his per*,
Noiþer in toun no tour;
He is *douhti*est *in dede*
& *worþli*est *in* eueri *wede*
& chosen for priis & *flour!*

70. EGLAMOUR

126 He hase servede us many a daye
Trewely in his *entent;*
In batelle ne *in tournament.*[3]

71. GUY OF WARWICK, A

45 (In all Englond ne was ther *none*
That durste in wrath ayenste *hym goon.*)

---

[1] See above, *Degrevant*, No. 6, p. 498, n. 3.

[2] *Thopas: So worthy under wede.* For other instances in *Amis* and elsewhere of *worthy in wede* see Kölbing, *Amis*, vs. 30n.

[3] The Thornton MS of *Eglamour* alone has *batelle;* other manuscripts have *justyng.* Cf. *Thopas: In bataille* and *in tourneyment.*

133 þer nas kniȝt in Inglonde
þat wiþ wretþe *durst him* atstonde. . . . .

139 þe(r) nas man in al þis londe
þat *durst him* do schame no schonde.

1675 At ich plas & *turnament*
Gij hadde þe priis *verrament*.
Was þer non in al þat lond,
þat his dent miȝt astond.

1560 þe *flour of* kniȝtes is sleyn þis day.
67(12)　　In warld þai *bere the flour*.[1]

148(7–9) *In* þis warld is man *non*
þat oȝaines him *durst gon*,
Herl, baroun, no kniȝt.[2]

256(12) In þe world *was non his pere*.[3]

72. IPOMADON, A

16 Thereffore in þe world where euer he went,
In justys or *in turnamente*,
Euer more the pryce he wan.

73. LIBEAUS

1615 "Who is ȝoure governoure?"
þey seide: "King Arthour,
Man of moste miȝtes,
Welle of curtesie
And *flour of chivalrie*,
To fille his fon in fiȝtes."

---

[1] *Thopas:* But sir Thopas, he *bereth the flour*
Of roial chivalry!
See *Libeaus*, No. 73; *Octavian*, No. 74; *Torrent.*, No. 76.

[2] *Thopas:* The contree . . . ./ So wilde;
For *in* that contree was ther *noon*,
That to *him durste* ride or *goon*.
Neither wyf ne childe.

In rhyme and rhythm and concept these lines seem to have been inspired by *Guy*, A, st. 148. The substitution of *wyf* ne *childe* was possibly suggested by the *Seven Sages* (ed. Brunner, p. 32), which, like *Thopas*, has the same *wild*:*child* rhyme:
went him forht al barfot
Wiȝ outen leue of wif and *child*
And wente into a forest *wild* [711].
Like *Guy*, A, this copy of the *Seven Sages* is also found in the Auchinleck MS.

[3] See above, p. 515, n. 2; cf. also *Guy*, A, No. 57, st. 256(12); *Reinbrun*, No. 75.

74. OCTAVIAN, A

25 Ottouyan was emperour
  Of all Rome and þe honour;
  Of chyualrye he hadde *þe flour*,
   That any man wyste.
  Here of a nobyll conquerour
   Ye mowyth lyste!

PERCEVAL OF GALES

(See above, No. 14)

75. REINBRUN

107(10–12) "For þow ert of gret power:
  In al þis world *þer nis* þe *per*
  þat man finde miȝte."

113(7–9) For he is man of gret power:
  In al þis world þer *nis is per*,
  Ne of so meche mounde.

76. TORRENT

2494 Of all the Justis, that there ware,
  Torrent *the floure* a way *bare*
2496 And his sonnys, verament.

IX. THE HERO "AUNTROUS"
Nos. 77–87

And for he was a knyght *auntrous*
He nolde slepen in noon hous.

No word in the romances more compactly suggests fantastic knight-errantry than does *auntrous*. In *Degaré, Degrevant, Eglamour, Libeaus,* and *Richard Cœur de Lion,* the heroes are thus designated; in *Ipomadon,* A, the typical career of such a knight is defined. Either *Eglamour* or *Libeaus,* which alike stress the word, may have provided specific inspiration for Thopas as a *knyght auntrous.* Thopas' haste duplicates that of all heroes on quest who, like Guy, never would *abyde.* Thopas' lack of shelter at night, his sleeping in armor, are most nearly paralleled by the similar hardships of Gawain, Generides, or of that later hero, the Squire of Low Degree.

77. DEGARÉ

1006 Iich am an *aunterous kniȝt,*
  For to seche werre and fiȝt.

78. DEGREVANT

421 Scho lokide on þat cheualerouse,
And said: "knyghte *aunterus*, ...
423   My trouthe I þe plyghte."

1385 "Welcome," scho said, "sir *aunterous*,
Me thynke þou art meruelous."

79. EGLAMOUR

466 "My name," he said, "es sir Awntour."

1193 He es *aunterous* in the felde.

1213 He said: "I am *aunterous* in þis stowre
For a lady, whytt als flowre,
   Wyn hir ȝif i may."

80. GAWAIN AND THE GREEN KNIGHT

729 Ner slayn wyth þe slete he sleped in his yrnes
Mo nyȝtez þen innoghe in naked rokkez.

81. GENERIDES

3918 And furth with all the Sowdon had aspyed
Wythynne the logge wher lay Generides,
In his harnes slepyng still opece.

82. CONFESSIO AMANTIS, BOOK I

1523 And thus he wente *forth his weie*[1]
Alone as a knyght *aventurous*.

83. GUY OF WARWICK, A

42(1–3) Þo went Herhaud so trewe in tale . . . .
For noþing he nold abide.[2]

222(8–9) Anon sir Gij him bi-þouȝt
Þat lenger wald he duelle nouȝt.

270(12)   No lenger he nold abide.

84. IPOMADON, A

334   The chyld wolde no lengur to abyde,
But arayde hym ryally to ride . . . .

---

[1] *Thopas: And forth* upon *his way* he glood.

[2] For variant instances of *nolde abyde, ne lenger abyde, noþing abode, wiþ oute bode, wiþ oute dwelling* or *les*, see Campion and Holthausen, *Perceval*, vs. 1018n.; Kölbing, *Ipomadon*, p. cxii, vs. 3276n.; Kölbing, *Amis*, p. xlvi; Zupitza, *Athelston*, vss. 96n., 357n.; Kaluza, *Libeaus*, vss. 56n., 810n.

8670 He is the kyngis sone of Poyle,
　　　 He traveld hathe thorowe many a soyle,
　　　 For your love aventurs sought:
　　　 For your love he made kytte his here,
　　　 For your love he made hym fole euery where,
　　　 For your love grette wonder wrought,
　　　 For your love hathe sufferd payne.

85. LIBEAUS DESCONUS

265　 þe kniȝt to hors gan spring
　　　 And rod to Arthour þe king
　　　　　 And seide: "My lord hende,
　　　 ȝef me þy blessinge!
　　　 Anoon, wiþ oute dwellinge
　　　　　 My will is forþ to wende."

1171　Into þe forest þey rode,
　　　 And Libeaus þer abod
　　　　　 As *aunterous kniȝt* in pride.

1243　Libeaus no lenger abod,
　　　 But aftir him he rod.

1933　þat on rod into þe halle
　　　 And began to calle:
　　　　　 "Sir kniȝt aunterous!"

86. RICHARD CŒUR DE LION

267　Kynge Rycharde gan hym dysguyse. . . . .
271　As a *knyght auentorous.*
　　　 His atyre was orgulous;
　　　 All togyder coleblacke. . . . .
275　*Upon his creste* a rauen stode.
285　He bare a shafte that was grete and stronge,
　　　 It was fourtene fote long.

[Richard vanquishes all opponents. A knight vows his overthrow.]

502　"Tyde me lyff, or tyde me deth,
　　　 I shal mete hym *ȝyff j may!*"
　　　 The *aunterous,* wiþ gret deray,
507　Hys schuldre wiþ hys schafft he brak. . . . .
511　The *aunterous*[1] þo turnyd agayn,
　　　 And houyd stylle for to seyn
　　　 Who durste iouste wiþ hym more.

[1] Richard is referred to as *auntrous* in vss. 473, 477, 495, 504.

87. SQUIRE OF LOW DEGREE[1]

149   Than sayd that lady milde of mode, ...
171   "For, and ye my love should wynne,
        With chyvalry ye must begynne, ...
175   And ryde through many a peryllous place
        As a venterous man to seke your grace,
        Over *hylles and dales,* and hye mountaines,
        In wethers wete, bothe hayle and raynes,
        And yf ye may no harbroughe se,
        Than must ye lodge under a tre,
        Among the beastes wyld and tame, ...
183   And in your armure must ye lye,
        Every nyght than by and by, ...
186   Till seven yere be comen and gone."

X. THE CATALOGUE LISTS[2]
Nos. 88–100

The catalogue list was extravagantly used in medieval poetry.
The *Roman de la rose* in particular had popularized in the
thirteenth century a pattern for tree, bird, flower, and spice
lists that was almost universally imitated—a pattern which
Chaucer himself followed for many years.[3] *Thopas,* a whimsical
mea culpa, parodies the convention with no fewer than seven
lists—of physical attributes,[4] of pastimes,[5] of spices, birds,
food, arms, and heroes of romance. The spice list, comically
substituted for the expected tree list, suggests those in *Alisaunder,* in the lyric *Annot and Johon,* the *Land of Cockaygne,*
the *Romaunt of the Rose;*[6] with the last it shares mention of the

[1] For the date of this romance (*ca.* 1450), see below, p. 551, n. 4.

[2] For convenience of reference, the catalogue lists here cited are divided into
two groups: "I. General" and "II. List of Heroes and Romances."

[3] Cf. Mead, *Squyr of Lowe Degre,* pp. lv–lxiv. He remarks (p. lxiv): "So far as
bird lists are concerned, Chaucer needed only to parody himself." The *sperhauk,*
the *douve,* the *popinjay,* and *throstel,* are all mentioned in the *Parliament of Fowls.*
Cf. also for verbal parallels with *Thopas, Prol. Leg. Good Women,* vs. 139: *somme
songen clere/Layes of love, that joye it was to here; Troilus,* II, 920, *Ful loude sang/
in his briddes wise, a lay/Of love.*

[4] See Sec. II, "The Hero's Appearance."

[5] See Sec. III, "The Hero's Pastimes."

[6] The *Romaunt of the Rose* (No. 93) has five, and *Alisaunder* (No. 89) has six of
the seven condiments named in *Thopas.* For another spice list in romance,
occurring in a list of merchant's wares, cf. *Reinbrun* (in *Guy,* ed. Zupitza, st. 5).
This also mentions a *maslyn.* The lists of birds, trees, spices in the apocryphal
poem, *Susannah* ("E.E.T.S.," Vol. CXVII [1901]), vss. 628 ff., show no correspondences with *Thopas.* Cf. Mead, pp. liii ff.

specific term, *clove-gelofre*, and with the lyric, the same rhyme, *gylofre: cofre*. In the romances the lists ran, commonly, to things not of Nature[1] but of man, to names of places, of heroes, of foods,[2] musical instruments,[3] etc. In no romance, however, were lists of all sorts so absurdly used as in the *Squire of Low Degree*, which, were there any sound reason for believing, as was formerly done,[4] that it antedated *Thopas*, might well be considered in this matter the special object of Chaucer's parody. Apart from other similarities, both poems, in the hero list, mention Guy and Libeaus, and both use the irregular and otherwise unique rhyme, *Gy: chivalry*. Other instances of the hero list are found in the *Cursor mundi, Libeaus, Richard Cœur de Lion*, and the *Speculum vitae*.[5] This last poem, like *Thopas*, mentions *Beves* and *Guy* and story-telling by *menstrales and gestours*, but disapproves of such tales, even as the Host, though on different grounds, testily disapproved of *Thopas*.[6]

I. GENERAL

88. ANNOT AND JOHON[7]

(Flowers)

11 Hire *rode* is *ase rose* þat *red* is on rys,
   Wiþ lilye-*white leres* lossum he is;
   þe primerole he passeþ, þe peruenke *of pris*, ...
15 Coynte ase columbine, such hire cunde ys,
   glad *under gore*[8] in gro[9] in grys;

---

[1] But see *Thomas of Erceldoune*, No. 51, vss. 177–84, for bird and tree lists.

[2] Food lists in romance, in contrast with Thopas' childish diet, usually enumerate hearty meats and potent wines. Cf. *Degrevant*, vss. 1393–1416; alliterative *Morte Arthur*, ed. Brock ("E.E.T.S.," Vol. VIII [1871]), vss. 176–199; *Richard Cœur de Lion*, No. 92; *Squire of Low Degree*, No. 94. Spices and wine only are mentioned in *Horn Childe*, vss. 1257 ff., *Frout & spices sche hem bede,/Wine to drink wite & rede*.

[3] See *Guy*, A, No. 46, st. XVII; and *Alisaunder*, No. 89, and *Octavian*, No. 91. Cf. Mead, p. 93 (vs. 1069n.) for further references.

[4] Mead (pp. lii ff.) gave a history of this opinion from Bishop Percy to Skeat (*Chaucer*, V, 188). He argued, chiefly on the ground of vocabulary, that the date of composition of the romance was about 1450. The earliest extant text is found in a sixteenth-century edition.

[5] Cf. Nos. 95–100.

[6] *Speculum vitae*, No. 98. For the Host's comments see Introduction, p. 490, n. 1.

[7] In relation to *Thopas*, the excessive use, in this short poem, of five lists—of gems, flowers, birds, spices, and heroes—is to be noted. All definitions for the words of this poem are from Carleton Brown, *English Lyrics of the XIIIth Century*.

[8] *Thopas: slepe under my goore*.   [9] In grey fur.

(Birds)

21 he is *papeiai* in pyn þat beteþ me my bale,
    to trewe tortle in a tour y telle þe mi tale;
    he is *þrustle* þryuen in þro þat singeþ in sale,
    þe wilde laueroc ant wolc[1] & þe wodewale, etc.

(Spices)

33 such *licoris* mai leche from lyne to lone,[2]
    such *sucre* mon secheþ þat saneþ men sone, ...
38 ase quibibe & *comyn* cud is in crone,
    Cud *comyn* in court, canel *in cofre,*
    wiþ *gyngyure* & *sedewale* & þe *gylofre.*[3]

89. ALISAUNDER

(Sports and Music)

1040   Now 'gynnith the geste of noblès:
        At theo feste was trumpyng,
        Pipyng, and eke taboryng,
        Sytolyng, and ek harpyng,
        Knyf pleying, and ek syngyng,
        Carolyng, and turneieyng,
        Wrastlyng, and ek skirmyng.

(Spices)

6790   Forth Alisaundre gan wende,
        Til he com to theo trowes ende.
        Notemugge, and the *sedewale,*
        On heom smullith, and the wodewale,
        Theo canel, and the *licoris,*
        And swete savour y-ment, y-wis,
        Theo *gilofre,* quybibe, and mace,
        Gynger, comyn gaven odour grace;
        And, undur sonne, of alle spices
6799   They hadden savour with delices.

GUY OF WARWICK
(See above, No. 46, st. 17)

---

[1] Hawk (Welsh *gwalch*).

[2] From Lyn to Lone, i.e., from Devon to Lancashire.

[3] Kölbing (*Tristram,* vs. 1860n., also *ES,* XI [1888], 501, *Thopas,* vs. 49) suggested Chaucer's possible parody of these lines. The concluding stanza of *Annot and Johon* mentions nine more or less unfamiliar names of heroes and heroines, of whom two were Welsh (cf. Brown, p. 226).

90. LAND OF COCKAYGNE[1]

(Spices, Flowers, Birds)

71 In þe praer[2] is a tre,
Swiþe likful for to se:
þe rote is gingeuir and galingale;
þe siouns[3] beþ al *sedwale;*
Trie maces beþ þe flure;
þe rind, canel[4] of swet odur;
þe frute, *gilofre* of gode smakke;
Of cucubes[5] þer nis no lakke:
þer beþ rosis of rede ble,
And lilie, likful for to se.

95 Ther beþ briddes mani and fale,
þrostil, þruisse, and niʒtingale,
Chalandre and wodwale,
And oþer briddes wiþout tale,
þat stinteþ neuer by har miʒt
Miri to sing dai and niʒt.

91. OCTAVIAN, A

(Music-makers)

55 No man may telle yn tale
þe peple, þat was at that bredale:

67 Ther myʒt men here menstralcye,
Trompys, tabours and cornettys crye,
Roowte, gyterne, lute, and sawtrye,
    Fydelys and othyr mo;
In Parys greet melodye
    They maden þo.

92. RICHARD CŒUR DE LION

(Foods and Drinks)

4246 þey soden fflesch, rost and brede,
And to þe soper faste þay ʒede.

---

[1] The burlesque spirit of this thirteenth-century poem on the Land of Fair Ease, and its brief comic catalogues of spices, flowers, and birds, interestingly anticipate *Thopas.*

[2] Meadow.

[3] Scions, shoots.

[4] Cinnamon.

[5] Cubebs, spice of the pepper family.

Plente þer was of bred and wyn,[1]
Pyment, clarry, good and ffyn;
Off cranes, swannes, and venysoun,
Partryhches, plouers, and heroun,
Off larkes, and small volatyle.

4643   Trumpes blewen, tabours dasshen, ...
4649   Off ryche wyn þer was plente
Pyment and ryche clarre.

93. ROMAUNT OF THE ROSE

(Birds, Trees, Spices)

80   Than is blisful many sithe
The chelaundre and *papyngay*. . . . .
85   Hard is the herte that loveth nought . . .
87   Whan he may on these braunches *here*
The smale briddes syngen *clere*.

657   In many places were nyghtyngales,
Alpes, fynches, and wodewales. . . . .

661   There myghte men see many flokkes
Of turtles and laverokkes.
Chalaundres fele sawe I there. . . . . .

665   And *thrustles*, terins, and mavys,
That songen for to wynne hem prys.

1359   And trees there were, gret foisoun,
That baren notes in her sesoun,
Such as men *notemygges* calle,
That swote of savour ben withalle.
And alemandres gret plente,
Fyges, and many a date-tree
There wexen, if men hadde nede,
Thorough the gardyn in length and brede.
Ther was eke wexyng many a spice,
As *clowe-gelofre*, and *lycorice*,
Gyngevre, and greyn de Parys,
Canell, and *setewule* of prys, ...

1373   And many homly trees ther were
That peches, coynes, and apples beere,
Medlers, plowmes, perys, chesteynes. . . .

1386   And othere trees full many a payre.[2]
What shulde I *tel* you *more of it?*

---

[1] See *Perceval*, No. 66, p. 544, n. 2.

[2] The *Romaunt of the Rose* names, in all, twenty-four trees.

94. THE SQUIRE OF LOW DEGREE

(Birds, Foods, Instruments)[1]

27   And in the garden, as I wene,
      Was an arber fayre and grene,

43   On every braunche sate byrdes thre,
      Syngynge with great melody,
      The lavorocke and the nightyngale,
      The ruddocke (and) the *wood(e)wale*,
      The pee and the *popiniaye*,
      The *thrustele* sange both nyght and daye,
      The marlyn, and the wrenne also,
      The swalowe whippynge to and fro,
      The iaye iangled them amonge,
      The larke began that mery songe,
      The sparowe spredde her *on* her *spraye*.[2]

313 He toke a white yeard in his hande, ...
316 And served the kynge ryght royally,
      With deynty meates that were dere,
      With partryche, pecoke, and plovere,
      With byrdes in bread ybake,
      The tele, the ducke, and the drake.

1067 There was myrth and melody
      With *harpe*, getron, and sautry,
      With rote, ribible, and clokarde,[3]
      With *pypes*, organs, and bumbarde,[4]
      With other mynstrelles them amonge,
      With sytolphe and with sautry songe,
      With fydle, recorde, and dowcemere,
      With trompette and with claryon clere,
      With dulcet pipes of many cordes.

THOMAS OF ERCELDOUNE

(See No. 51, vss. 257–60)

[1] Lists in this romance are used to absurd excess. Among them may be noted the enumeration of thirteen trees, nineteen birds, fourteen meats, seventeen wines, nine pleasures of the world, six musical instruments.

[2] Cf. *Thopas:* The wodedowve *upon the spray.*

[3] Mead, p. 94, suggests for *clokarde* an instrument shaped like a bell tower (clocher).

[4] *Bumbarde*, an instrument of the bassoon family.

II. LISTS OF HEROES AND ROMANCES[1]

95. CURSOR MUNDI

1 Men ȝernis iestis for to here,
   And romance rede on maner sere,
   Of alexander þe conquerour,
   Of Iuli cesar þe emperour
   Of grece & Troye þe strong strijf,
   þere many thosand lesis hir lijf,
   O brut þat berne bolde of hand
   First Conquerour of meri ingland;
   Of king arthour, þat was so riche,
10 Was non in his time funden suiche;
   Of ferlijs þat his knightes fell,
   Of auntris did i. here of tell,
   Of wawain, kay, and other stabil,
   For to were þe runde tabil.
   Hou king charlis and rouland faght—
   Wid sarazins ne wald þai neuer be saght;
   O tristrem, and ysoude þe suete,
   Hu þai wid luffe first gan mete;
   Of king ionet, and ysumbras,
20 Of ydoyne, and of amadas;
   Storijs of diuers thinges,
   Of princes, prelates, and of kinges,[2]

96. LAUNFAL

7 *Douȝty* Artoure som whyle
   Soiournede yn Kardeuyle,
      Wythe ioye and greet solas;

13 Sere *Perseuall* and Sere Gawayn,
   Syr Gyheryes and Syr Agrafrayn
      And Launcelet du Lake;
   Syr Kay and Syr Ewayn,
   þat well couþe fyȝte yn playn,
      Bateles for to take;

---

[1] Cf. Warton, *Hist. Eng. Poet*, I (1824), 126; Halliwell, *The Thornton Romances* (London, 1844), pp. xvi–xx; Allen, "Speculum Vitae," *PMLA*, XXXII (1917), 140. There are long lists of romance heroes and heroines in the *Parlement of Three Ages*, ed. Gollancz (London, 1915), but the only name that corresponds with those in *Thopas* is that of Perceval, vs. 478: *Sir Percevalle de Galeys þat preved had been ofte.*

[2] Cf. *Thopas:* Of romances/Of popes and of cardinales.

Kyng Banboo3t and Kyng Bos—
Of ham þer was a greet los:
   Men sawe nowher here make;—
Syre Galafre and Syr Launfale,
Wherof a noble tale
   Among vs schall awake.

97. RICHARD CŒUR DE LION[1]

8 Ffele romaunses men maken newe,
Off goode kny3tes, stronge and trewe;
Off here dedys men rede romaunce,
Boþe in Engeland and in Ffraunce:
Off Rowelond, and off Olyuer,
And off euery Doseper;
Off Alisaundre, and Charlemayn;
Off kyng Arthour, and off Gawayn,
How þey were knyghtes goode and curteys;
Off Turpyn, and of Oger Daneys;
Off Troye men rede in ryme,
What werre þer was in olde tyme;
Off Ector, and off Achylles,
What folk þey slowe in þat pres.

6723 Now herkenes of my tale soþ,
Þow3 j swere 3ow none oþ!
J wole rede romaunce non
Off Pertenope, ne of Ypomadon,
Off Alisaunder, ne of Charlemayn,
Off Arthour, ne off Sere Gawayn,
Nor off Sere Launcelet-de-Lake,
Off *Beffs*, ne *Gy*, ne Sere Vrrake,
Ne off Ury, ne of Octauyan,
Ne off Hector, the stronge man,
Off Jason, ne off Hercules,
Ne off Eneas, ne off Achylles.
I wene neuere, *par ma fay*,
Þat in þe tyme off here *day*,
Dede ony off hem so *dou3ty dede*
Off strong batayle and gret wy3thede,

---

[1] From Cbg., Caius Coll. MS 175 (fifteenth century). In the *Richard* of the
Auchinleck MS the heroes mentioned (ll. 1–18) are *Rouland, Oliuer, Alisander,
Charlemeyn, Oger, Arthour, Gaweyn.* Cf. *Richard*, ed. Brunner, p. 81; for the second
list, p. 424, vss. 6723 f.

As dede Kyng Rychard, saun fayle,
At Jaffe in þat batayle.

98. SPECULUM VITAE[1]

35 I warne ȝow ferst at þe begynnyng,
I wil make no veyn spekyng
Of dedes of armes ne of amours,
Os don *mynstreles and* oþer *gestours,*[2]
þat make spekyng in many a place
Of Octouian and Isanbrace
And of many oþer gestes,
And namely whan þei come to festes,
Ne of *Beus* of Hamptoun,
þat was a [MS *of*] knyht of gret renoun,
Ne of *sir Gy* of Warewyk,
Al þow it mowe som men like,
I thenke my spekeng schal not be;
For I holde þat nowht bot vanyte. . . . .

53 þere fore gode men þat be now here,
Lysten to me and ȝe may here
Whow ȝe schal reule ȝowre lyf.

99. SQUIRE OF LOW DEGREE

63   And evermore, whan he was wo,
Into that arber wolde he go,

68 And sayd, "Alas, that I was borne!
That I were ryche of gold and fe,
That I might wedde that lady *fre!*

75 Wolde God that I were a kynges sonne,
That ladyes love that I myght wonne!
Or els so bolde in eche fyght,
As Syr *Lybius* that gentell knyght,
Or els so bolde in *chyvalry,*
As Syr Gawayne, or *Syr Guy;*[3]
Or els so doughty of my hande
As was the gyaunte Syr Colbrande."

---

[1] This popular poem, which was cleared of heresy in 1384, is now assigned to William of Nassington (cf. Hope E. Allen, *Writings Ascribed to Richard Rolle* [New York, 1927], p. 372). Brown (*Register of ME Verse*, II, 37) lists 35 manuscripts.

[2] Cf. *Thopas: my mynstrales, And gestours.*

[3] Cf. *Thopas: Of Beves and sir Gy/ . . . . Of roial chivalry!*

100. (LAUD) TROY BOOK[1]

11   Many *speken of men* that *romaunces* rede
       That were sumtyme *doughti in dede,* . . . .

15   Off *Bevis, Gy,* and of Gauwayn,
       Off kyng Richard, & of Owayn,
       Off Tristram, and of Percyuale,
       Off Rouland Ris, and Aglauale,
       Off Archeroun, and of Octouian,
       Off Charles, & of Cassibaldan,
       Off Hauelok, Horne, and of Wade;
       In Romaunces that of hem ben made
       That *gestours* often dos of hem gestes
       At Mangeres and at grete ffestes.
       Here dedis ben in remembraunce
       In many fair Romaunce;
       But of the *worthi*est wyght *in wede*
       That eure *by-strod any stede,*
       Spekes no man, ne in romaunce redes
       Off his batayle ne of his dedis.

[1] The poem and the one manuscript in which it is preserved alike date from the early fifteenth century (cf. Wülfing ["E.E.T.S.," Vol. CXXI (1902)], Preface).

THE TALE OF MELIBEUS

By J. BURKE SEVERS

INTRODUCTION

THE counsels of peace and sweet reasonableness which
constitute the *Tale of Melibeus* were first compiled and
composed by an Italian judge of the thirteenth century,
Albertano of Brescia. Albertano had the pleasant custom of
inditing a Latin tractate and presenting it to each of his sons
as each came of age and entered upon a career. To the eldest,
Vincenzio, in 1238 was dedicated the longest of these guides to
right living, *De amore et dilectione Dei et proximi et aliarum rerum
et de forma vitae.* To Stephano in 1245 was dedicated the shortest, *De arte loquendi et tacendi.* A year later, in 1246, Giovanni,
who was embarking upon a career of surgery, was honored with
the *Liber consolationis et consilii*, a book of consolation and
counsel about half the length of the *De amore et dilectione Dei.*
It is this third tractate—the *Liber consolationis et consilii*—
which is the original of the story of the wise and temperate
Prudence and the proud and headstrong Melibeus.

The *Liber consolationis et consilii* circulated not only in the
original Latin but also in Italian, German, Dutch, and French
translations. At least four different French versions helped
popularize it during the thirteenth and fourteenth centuries.
The oldest of these, dating from the second half of the thirteenth
century and preserved in a manuscript[1] containing similar
translations of Albertano's two other tractates, is a literal rendering of the Latin text. Two other French versions—one in
prose,[2] the other in verse[3]—are of uncertain authorship and
date. The fourth version, which is such a free handling of the
Latin that it must be called an adaptation rather than a translation, was written sometime after 1336 by Renaud de Louens,
a Dominican friar of the convent at Poligny in the Jura. Of all

[1] Bibliothèque nationale, Paris, MS fr. 1142.

[2] Bibliothèque de l'arsenal, Paris, MS 2880.

[3] Bodleian Library, MS 5264 (Marshall 29).

the French redactions, Renaud's was by far the most popular;[1] and, since this was the version which Chaucer converted into the *Tale of Melibeus*, it is profitable to inquire somewhat into the differences between it and its Latin source.

Renaud handled his Latin source boldly and freely, cutting its twenty thousand words to fourteen thousand, to produce a version about two-thirds the length of the original. In order to achieve this abridgment, he completely discarded six of Albertano's fifty-one chapters, omitted almost the whole of eight others, and rejected more than fifty per cent of the material in about half the remaining chapters.[2] Albertano's method of composition allowed Renaud easily to effect large and drastic excisions without seriously impairing the main development of thought. For usually Albertano states an idea succinctly,

---

[1] As against one manuscript for each of the other three French versions, at least twenty-six manuscripts of Renaud's version are extant. See the editor's article in *PMLA*, listed in the bibliography following this introduction.

[2] The nature of the most important of these omissions may be briefly indicated. In the longest, extending for eleven unbroken pages and then, after two very brief breaks, for two pages more, Renaud omits the conclusion of the chapter in praise of women (chap. v, pp. 19–20), all the brief chapters on prudence (vi–ix), the whole of the long chapter on study (x), and virtually the whole of the chapter on counsel (xi). He likewise rejects nearly the whole of the chapters on eschewing covetousness in counsels (xiii), on eschewing the advice of flatterers (xix), on eschewing the advice of those motivated by fear rather than by love (xxi), and on examining counsel (xxvi); the whole chapter on pride (xxxiv); the various types of defense (chap. xxxv, pp. 74–75); the seven species of possibility, with comment on them (chap. xxxvi, pp. 79–81); the similitude between the wounds of Melibeus' daughter and those of Christ, and the distinction of the fivefold will of God (chaps. xxxvii–xxxviii, pp. 84–86); most of the chapter on poverty (xlv); the losses sustained through war and most of the reasons for avoiding war (chaps. xlvi–xlvii, pp. 103–4); most of the chapter on avoiding war through reconciliation (xlviii); the eight cases in which war is permissible (chap. xlix, pp. 108–12); Melibeus' inquiries of his physicians concerning his daughter's convalescence (chap. xlix, p. 119); Melibeus' defense of his desire to punish the transgressors (chap. l, p. 122); and, finally, the submissive action and speech of the offenders when they appear for judgment (chap. li, p. 125).

Most commonly the excisions are less than a page in length. About ten of them run from one to two pages (1.1–1.17, cf. *Mel.* 2156; 5.5–6.2, cf. *Mel.* 2190; 31.14–33.6, cf. *Mel.* 2309; 35.11–37.10, cf. *Mel.* 2320; 37.18–39.4, cf. *Mel.* 2322; 53.12–55.9, cf. *Mel.* 2389; 73.6–74.12, cf. *Mel.* 2526; 79.12–81.15, cf. *Mel.* 2576; 84.23–86.9, cf. *Mel.* 2616; 103.5–104.17, cf. *Mel.* 2842). The two longest are of five and eleven pages, respectively (107.9–112.12, cf. *Mel.* 2883; 19.24–31.1, cf. *Mel.* 2304). (Latin references are to page and line in Sundby's edition, listed in the bibliography following this introduction; references to the *Melibeus* give the line following which the omission occurs.)

then piles up repetitious supporting quotations from various authorities, medieval and classic. Renaud, coming after him, seized upon the chief ideas, then selected at will among the abundance of quotations, sometimes satisfying himself with one or two, sometimes indulging himself more fully, sometimes even rejecting the whole lot. Albertano's elaborate schematism, by rendering the organization of the Latin treatise easily apparent, also aided Renaud in the task of condensation; for not infrequently the French adaptor selected only the skeletonic thought of a section, disregarding the full development of ideas. Yet he reduced the schematism itself by discarding many of Albertano's wooden transitional devices which emphasized it and also, on occasion, by omitting whole sections in which it was offensively present. The result was a briefer, more closely knit, less schematic treatise than Albertano's.

Yet Renaud's alterations did not consist merely in condensation and excision; he also made additions. Occasionally, as he was selecting among the numerous quotations which Albertano offered, he thought of one not present in the *Liber consolationis* and set it down in his own version.[1] Occasionally, too, he expanded or clarified a passage by the addition of a short phrase or sentence.[2] But in the latter half of his adaptation his additions grew more numerous and, in a few instances, very extensive. Throughout his translation of Albertano's chapters on the evils of war (xlvi), on avoiding war (xlvii–xlviii), and on the cases in which war is permissible (xlix), he not only freely discarded large parts of his original but also freely added a score of expansions of his own, ranging in length from one to three or four sentences, which he sandwiched in between the bits retained from Albertano (ll. 935–1139, cf. *Mel.* 2840–3030). Of additions more lengthy than these there are only two. One, running to almost twenty lines in Chaucer's translation, occurs in the speech where Prudence is urging patience upon her irascible spouse; it is substituted by Renaud for a shorter passage in the *Liber consolationis* extolling the same virtue (ll. 748–72, cf. *Mel.* 2681–2700). By far the longest and most important of all the

---

[1] E.g., ll. 140–41, cf. *Mel.* 2237; ll. 266–68, cf. *Mel.* 2307–8; ll. 351–53, cf. *Mel.* 2370; ll. 379–80, cf. *Mel.* 2388; ll. 683–85, cf. *Mel.* 2628, etc.

[2] E.g., ll. 137–39, cf. *Mel.* 2235; ll. 331–34, cf. *Mel.* 2358–59; ll. 650–51, cf. *Mel.* 2603; ll. 703–4, cf. *Mel.* 2641; ll. 721–25, cf. *Mel.* 2657–59, etc.

additions, extending to almost seventy-five lines in Chaucer's translation, consists of a lengthy digression on the acquisition and use of riches (ll. 853–931, cf. *Mel.* 2765–2837) and is composed principally of a dozen scattered passages which Renaud borrowed and pieced together from another of Albertano's tractates, the earlier *De amore et dilectione Dei*.[1] In all, despite the fact that Renaud's adaptation is only two-thirds the length of the Latin original, his additions and expansions account for more than one-sixth of the whole French version.

These extensive differences between the French adaptation and its Latin original render the task of determining Chaucer's source a very easy one indeed. From beginning to end, throughout omissions, additions, and other alterations, the text of Chaucer's translation follows the text of the French adaptation. There is no evidence here, as in the *Clerkes Tale*, of double reliance upon French and Latin; on the contrary, the evidence points to Chaucer's sole reliance upon the French.[2]

[1] Albertano himself suggested the digression by referring the reader of the *Liber consolationis* to the earlier tractate for a fuller discussion: "Secundum quod de hijs plenius notatum invenies in libro de Amore et Dilectione Dei et Proximi et Aliarum Rerum et de Forma Vitae, in titulo: De Acquirendis et Conservandis Opibus, et in sequentibus quatuor titulis" (101.18–102.4). Renaud, following the suggestion, incorporated in his adaptation the passages listed below. (References to the *De amore* are from MS 1 of the John Frederick Lewis Collection of European Manuscripts in the Free Library at Philadelphia, which contains all three of the tractates, plus Albertano's five speeches. The *De amore* occupies fols. 22^{v}1–57^{v}1.) From the opening chapter (no chapter heading), fol. 41^{v}2: ll. 856–62, cf. *Mel.* 2766–70. From "De acquirendis et conservandis opibus," fols. 41^{v}2–42^{r}1: ll. 905–10, cf. *Mel.* 2814–16, 2818–19; fol. 42^{r}2: ll. 911–12, 862–67, cf. *Mel.* 2820–21, 2771–76; fol. 42^{v}1: ll. 908–9, cf. *Mel.* 2817. From "De conscientia boni," fol. 42^{v}1: ll. 912–15, cf. *Mel.* 2822–24; fol. 42^{v}1: ll. 915–17, cf. *Mel.* 2825. From "De bona fama," fol. 42^{v}2: ll. 917–27, cf. *Mel.* 2826–32; fol. 43^{r}2: ll. 869–71, cf. *Mel.* 2777–78. From "De vitandis otio et sompno pigritia atque luxuria," fol. 43^{v}2: ll. 871–77, cf. *Mel.* 2779–83; fol. 43^{v}2: ll. 877–78, cf. *Mel.* 2784. From "De opibus utendis et etiam contempnendis," fol. 44^{v}1: ll. 886–92, cf. *Mel.* 2792–97; fol. 44^{v}2: ll. 900–2, cf. *Mel.* 2809–10; fol. 44^{v}2: ll. 902–5, cf. *Mel.* 2811–13. From "De patientia et impatientia," fols. 54^{r}1–54^{r}2: ll. 810–16, cf. *Mel.* 2729–31.

[2] I call attention in the textual notes (1170–71, 1174–75) to two brief expansions by Chaucer which bear a general similarity in idea to the corresponding passages in the Latin. Lack of similarity in diction and phraseology seems to me to render them nugatory. It may be of some significance, however, that they both occur in the closing paragraphs of the Latin tractate, within thirty lines of each other. At most, this might suggest that Chaucer glanced at the concluding folio of a manuscript of Albertano's Latin tractate and vaguely adopted from it two brief passages.

Had Chaucer had access to the Latin text, he could have recti-
fied certain errors which marred the French manuscript from
which he worked. For his source manuscript was by no means
faultless; it contained not a few scribal blunders, both of com-
mission and of omission. This we may state confidently because
Chaucer's translation is guilty of the same errors and omissions
which we find in some of the French manuscripts. A dozen
passages which Chaucer left out, half of them over ten words in
length, were omitted beyond doubt because he was misled by
identical lacunae in his source manuscript; and a score of faulty
readings may likewise be traced directly to the text from
which he was working.[1] Despite these erroneous readings,
Chaucer's source manuscript was closer to what Renaud de
Louens actually wrote than is *Le Ménagier de Paris*, the only
hitherto available text; for, when *Le Ménagier* is compared with
the manuscripts, it reveals numerous unique readings which
lead one to suspect that its author sometimes gratuitously
altered diction and phraseology, even occasionally suppressing or
adding brief passages. Chaucer's source manuscript, therefore,
though by no means faultless, yielded a text of Renaud's
adaptation in the authentic tradition.

From this source manuscript Chaucer's translation rarely
departs. Sentence for sentence, phrase for phrase, even word
for word, for the most part the *Tale of Melibeus* is a close
translation of Renaud's *Livre de Mellibee et Prudence*. The
extent of Chaucer's deviations the reader may perceive by

---

[1] The omissions are recorded in the textual notes to the present edition. When
the faulty readings are retained in the text proper, the authentic readings are indicated in the notes; otherwise, the faulty readings are recorded along with the
other variants. By faulty reading, of course, I mean one unlike that in the
authentic text of Renaud de Louens. Which of divergent French readings is
authentic has been determined by comparison with the original Latin. When,
therefore, the French manuscripts give divergent readings and Chaucer's translation follows the unauthentic reading, I count the passage in Chaucer as faulty.
Occasionally, it is possible to surmise for some other reason that Chaucer's source
manuscript was corrupt at certain points. For convenience, a list of Chaucer's
faulty readings is appended: "feet," l. 2162; "corage," l. 2257; "grace," l. 2260;
order in ll. 2315–18; "supportacioun," l. 2332; "folwe," l. 2390; "myght to doon,"
l. 2408; "false flatereres," l. 2435; "knowe," ll. 2445–46; "lyeres," l. 2498; "wesele,"
l. 2515; "thynges," l. 2586; "ruyne," l. 2755; "eten," l. 2757; "the myghty men,"
l. 2777; "love," l. 2818; "Seint Jame," l. 2866; "Leeveth," l. 2944; "in exil," l.
3025; "exile," l. 3037; "lord," l. 3050.

consulting the textual notes to the present edition, where they are recorded. Of about twenty-five Chaucerian omissions not accounted for by the French manuscripts, the great majority are short and may have been inadvertently made during the process of translation. Only a half-dozen are more than ten words long. One of these, on the lack of wisdom in youthful kings, was omitted in deference to young Richard; it therefore helps to date the translation after 1377, in the early years of Richard's reign.[1] The others have no special significance, save that it is slightly puzzling why Chaucer chose not to include them.[2] Chaucer's additions are even less important. For the most part, they are caused by a certain redundancy in the translation, a Chaucerian trick (though not confined to Chaucer in this period) of translating a word by a pair of synonyms, and of further explaining an already translated passage with a superfluous "this is to seyn." Disregarding this translator's padding, there are scarcely a dozen brief passages, usually clauses or short sentences, in which Chaucer may be said to have added any ideas to the tale. The most important of these occur at the beginning and at the end. In a short phrase of his initial sentence, Chaucer christens Prudence's daughter, nameless in both Latin and French versions, with the appropriate appellation of "Sophie" (l. 2157). The two lengthiest additions —each a single, fairly long sentence—come near the end of the tale. One occurs at the conclusion of the final speech of the transgressors pleading for mercy (ll. 3015–16), the other at the conclusion of Melibeus' speech granting it (ll. 3074–78); and, since Melibeus' speech draws the tale to its close, this latter addition serves to round out and conclude Chaucer's translation.

In preparing the text of Chaucer's source which is presented

[1] See the textual note to ll. 381–83.

[2] At least one of them is essential to a proper understanding of later references in the tale (ll. 170–73, cf. *Mel.* 2252–53); and its omission, if due really to Chaucer and not to a French or English copyist, would seem to argue that the translator was extremely careless, or performed his translation as an unthinking mechanical exercise. Of course, even though the passages are not omitted in the manuscripts collated for this edition, it is still possible that Chaucer's source manuscript did not contain them; for there are at least twenty additional manuscripts of Renaud's version, some of which might reveal similar omissions.

in the following pages, the editor has selected as base that manuscript which in itself came closest to duplicating the readings of the text from which Chaucer worked when he wrote the *Tale of Melibeus*. This selection was possible only after a thorough, detailed study of the variants in the manuscripts, and after a comparison of them with the readings in Chaucer's tale to determine which French manuscript most frequently corresponded with the English translation. Each departure from the base, however slight, is recorded in the first set of variants, headed "P_3," immediately below the last line of text on each page; and in parentheses have been added the manuscripts from which the emendations have been drawn. Obviously erroneous readings in the base manuscript have been emended, but errors which there is reason to believe were also present in the text which Chaucer used are allowed to stand unaltered. Since every deviation from the base manuscript is scrupulously recorded in the first set of variants, the text and variants together afford an absolutely literal transcription of the base manuscript, excepting only that punctuation and capitalization have been modernized throughout.

In the second set of variants, headed "Var.," have been recorded all manuscript readings which come closer to the content or phraseology of Chaucer's tale than do the corresponding readings in the base. The text, modified by these variants, gives us as close a reproduction of Chaucer's source manuscript as it is possible to achieve. Since Chaucer's *Melibeus* is a straight translation of the *Mellibee*, reflecting in virtually every sentence the wording and phrasing of its source, naturally the number of variants will be larger than for a source less slavishly followed, such, for instance, as the source of the *Clerkes Tale*. In using the text, therefore, it is essential that the variants be consulted at all times, for they are more significant to the student of Chaucer than the corresponding readings in the text proper.

For convenience of reference, the editor has adopted a paragraphing in accordance with that in Professor Robinson's edition of Chaucer's works; and numbers designating the corresponding lines in the *Tale of Melibeus* have been inserted in the margin to the left of the text.

LIST OF MANUSCRIPTS

B Bibliothèque royale, Brussels. MS 9552. Fifteenth (?) century. Fols. 87^r–104^v.

L British Museum, London. MS Royal 19.C.vii. Fifteenth century. Fols. 123^r–148^v.

M Print. *Le Ménagier de Paris*. Edited by Jérôme Pichon. Paris, 1846. Vol. I, pp. 186–235.

P Bibliothèque nationale, Paris. MS fr. 1165. Fifteenth century. Fols. 66^r–85^r.

P$_2$ Bibliothèque nationale, Paris. MS fr. 20042. Fifteenth century (1436). Fols. 1^r–25^v.

P$_3$ Bibliothèque nationale, Paris. MS fr. 578. Fourteenth century. Fols. 56^r–70^v. (This manuscript is the base for the present edition.)

P$_4$ Bibliothèque nationale, Paris. MS fr. 1468. Fifteenth century. Fols. 1^r–35^r.

SELECTED BIBLIOGRAPHY

Cook, A. S. "Chaucer's *Clerk's Tale* and a French Version of His Original," *Romanic Review*, VIII (1917), 219–20.

Gröber, Gustav. *Grundriss der romanischen Philologie*, Vol. II, Part I, pp. 746–47, 1025. Strassburg, 1902.

Koeppel, Emil. "Chaucer und Albertanus Brixiensis," *Archiv für das Studium der neueren Sprachen und Literaturen*, LXXXVI (1891), 29–46.

Landrum, Grace W. "Chaucer's Use of the Vulgate," *Publications of the Modern Language Association*, XXXIX (1924), 75–100.

Mätzner, Eduard. *Altenglische Sprachproben nebst einem Wörterbuche*, Vol. I, Part II, pp. 373–74. Berlin, 1867.

Paris, Paulin. "Jean de Meun," in *Histoire littéraire de la France*, XXVIII, 429. Paris, 1881.

———. *Les Manuscrits françois de la Bibliothèque du roi*, V, 55–65. Paris, 1836–48.

Pichon, J. (ed.). *Le Ménagier de Paris*, I, 186–235. Paris, 1846.

Severs, J. Burke. "The Source of Chaucer's *Melibeus*," *Publications of the Modern Language Association*, L (1935), 92–99.

Sundby, Thor (ed.). *Albertani Brixiensis Liber consolationis et consilii, ex quo hausta est Fabula de Melibeo et Prudentia*. Havniae, 1873.

Tatlock, J. S. P. *The Development and Chronology of Chaucer's Works*, pp. 188–97, 216. "Chaucer Society Publications." London, 1907.

Vayssière, M. A. "Renaut de Louens, poëte franc-comtois du xive siècle," *L'Année dominicaine*, 1873, pp. 141–54.

⟨fol. 56ʳ⟩

CY COMMENCE

LE LIVRE DE MELLIBEE ET PRUDENCE

Aprés ce, ma tres chere dame, que j'ay fait le romment sur *Boece de Consolation* a vostre service et pour vous conforter en Nostre Seigneur, j'ay fait un petit traittié a l'enseingnement et au profit de mon tres cher seigneur, vostre filz, et de tous autres princes et barons qui le vouldront entendre et garder, lequel traittié j'ay fundé et extrait d'une fiction ancienne que j'ay trovee en escript. Et se commence en la maniere qui cy aprés s'ensuit.

Uns jouvenceaulx appellez Mellibee, puissans et riches, ot une
2157 femme appellee Prudence, de laquelle il ot une fille.

Advint un jour qu'il s'ala esbatre et jouer, et laissa en un lieu sa femme et sa fille, et les portes closes. Trois de ses anciens ennemis appuyerent eschielles aus murs de sa maison et par les fenestres en-
2160 trerent dedens et batirent sa femme forment et navrerent sa fille de cinq playes en cinq lieux de son corps, c'est assavoir, es piez, es oreilles, ou neiz, en la bouche, et es mains, et la laisserent presque morte; puis s'en alerent.

Quant Mellibee fut retournez a son hostel et vit cest meschief, si commença forment a plaindre, a plorer, et soy batre en maniere de forsené, et sa robe dessirer.

(**Var.**) 10   un lieu] se maison *B*, son hostel *M*, *P₄*.
13   forment] *om. M*, *P*.
14   playes] plaies mortels *M*.
14–15   oreilles ... mains] mains, es oreilles, ou nes, et en la bouche *P₄*.
17   a son] en son *B*, *P*, *P₂*.
18   et soy batre] *om. P₄*.

---

9   *fille.* Chaucer adds the daughter's name (l. 2157), which appears neither in the Latin original (2.2) nor in the French version.

10   *jouer.* "In the feelds" is Chaucer's addition (l. 2158); it is present in neither the Latin (2.4) nor the French.

12   *appuyerent.* Chaucer's "han it espyed" (l. 2160) may seem to have derived from the Latin *hoc videntes* (2.5); but probably his source manuscript contained a reading like that in P and P₄: *vindrent et appuyerent.* An unnoticed nasal symbol over the *i* might have led Chaucer, or the scribe of his source manuscript to mistake *vindrent* ("came") for *vidrent* ("saw"); or an original *vidrent* in Chaucer's source manuscript may later have been corrupted into the *vindrent* of P and P₄.

14   *piez.* An erroneous reading which Chaucer followed (l. 2162). The true reading is *yeux*, found in B; cf. the Latin original, *oculis* (2.8.)

Lors Prudence sa femme le prist a admonnester qu'il se souffrist;   20
2165 et il tousjours plus fort crioit.

Adonques elle s'appensa de la sentence Ovide, ou *Livre des Remedes d'Amours*, qui dit que celui est fol qui s'efforce d'empescher la mere de plorer en la mort de son enfant jusques a tant qu'elle se soit bien remplie de larmes et saoulee de plorer; lors est il temps de la conforter   25 et d'attremper sa doulour par doulces paroles. Pour ce, Prudence se souffri un pou, et quant elle vit son temps, si lui dist ainsi: "Sire, pour-
2170 quoy vous faites vous sembler fol? Il n'appartient point a sage homme de mener si grant duel. Vostre fille eschappera se Dieu plaist; et se elle estoit ores morte, vous ne vous devez pas destruire pour elle. Car   30 Senecques dit que li sages ne doit prendre grant desconfort de la mort de ses enfans, ains doit souffrir leur mort aussi legierement comme il
2175 attend la sienne propre."

Mellibee respondi: "Cui est cil qui se pourroit tenir de plorer en si grant cause de doulour? Nostre Seigneur Jhesu Crist ⟨fol. 56ᵛ⟩   35 mesmes ploura de la mort du ladre, son amy."

"Certes," dist Prudence, "plour attrempee n'est pas deffendue a celui qui est tristes, mais lui est ottroyee. Car, selon ce que dit Saint Pol l'Appostre en *l'Epistre aux Rommains,* 'On doit mener joye avec ceulz qui joye mainnent, et doit on mener plour et doulour avec ceulz   40 qui l'ont.' Mais ja soit ce que plourer attrempeement soit ottroyez,
2180 toutevoye plourer desmesureement est deffendu. Et pour ce l'on doit garder la mesure que Senecques met: 'Quant tu auras,' dist il, 'perdu ton amy, ton oeil ne soit ne secs ne moistes; car ja soit ce que la lerme viengne a l'ueil, elle n'en doit pas yssir. Car quant tu auras   45 perdu ton ami, efforce toy de un autre recouvrer; car il te vault mieux un autre ami recouvrer que l'ami perdu plorer.' Se tu veulz vivre sagement, oste tristesse de ton cuer. Car, selon ce que dit Jhesu

P₃. 31   Senecques] li sages (Senecques *M, L, B, P, P₂*).

(**Var.**) 21   et il] mais cilz *B.*

22   elle] Prudence *M, L, B, P, P₂, P₄*—*des Remedes*] de Remede *B, P, P₄*, du Remede *L.*

23   s'efforce d'empescher] empesche *B.*

30   pour elle] pour luy *M, B, P, P₂*, pour ce *P₄*—Car] *om. L.*

31   li sages] saiges hons *P₄.*

36   ladre] ladre *corrected to* lazare *in margin P₂.*

38   tristes] triste entre les tristes *L*, triste ou entre les tristes *M, P*, triste en cuer ou entre les tristes *P₄.*

40–41   mener plour ... l'ont] plourer avec ceulx qui pleurent *M, L, B, P, P₂.*

44   secs] trop sec *M, P*—moistes] trop moistes *M, P, P₂, P₄.*

45   Car quant] et quant *M, L, B, P.*

46   autre] autre amy *L, P₄.*

47   veulz] veulx doncques *L, B, P, P₂, P₄.*

Syrac, 'Le cuer lyé et joyeux maintient la personne en la fleur de son
2185 aage, mais l'esperist triste li fait secher les os'; et dit oultre que tristesse   50
occist moult de gens. Et Salemons dit que tout aussi comme la taingne
ou les artuisons nuit a la robe et les vermoissiaulx ou bois, tout aussi
greve tristesse au cuer. Et pour ce nous nous devons porter paciem-
ment en la perte de noz enfans et de noz autres biens temporelz,
ainsi comme Job, lequel quant il ot perdu ses enfans et toute sa sub-   55
stance et ot soustenu moult de tribulations en son corps, il dist:
'Nostre Seigneur le m'a donné; Nostre Seigneur le m'a toulu. Ainsi
2190 comme il l'a voulu faire, il l'a fait. Benoist soit le nom de lui!' "

Mellibee respondi a Prudence sa femme ainsi: "Toutes les choses
que tu dis sont vrayes et profitables, mais mon cuer est si troublé que   60
je ne scey que je doye faire."

Lors Prudence lui dist, "Appelle tous tes loyaulx amis, affins, et
parens, et leur demande conseil de ceste chose, et te gouverne selon
le conseil qu'il te donront. Car Salemon dit, 'Tous tes faiz par conseil
feras; ainsi ne t'en repentiras.' "   65

Adonques Mellibee appella moult de gens, c'est assavoir, cysurgiens,
phisiciens, vieillars et jeunes, et aucuns de ses anciens ennemis
qui estoient reconsiliez par semblance et retournez en sa grace et
2195 amour, et aucuns de ses voisins qui luy portoient reverence plus pour   70
doubtance que pour amour; et avec ce vindrent moult de losengiers
et moult de sages clers et bons advocaz.

Quant ilz furent ensemble, il leur recompta et monstra bien par la
maniere de son parler qu'il estoit moult courrociez et que il avoit
moult grant desir de soy vengier tantost et de faire guerre incontinent;
2200 toutevoye il demanda sur ce leur conseil. Lors un cysurgien, du conseil   75
des autres, se leva et dist:

P₃. 56   en son corps] *om.* (en son corps *M, L, B, P, P₂, P₄*).
69–70   et aucuns de ses voisins ... pour amour] *om.* (et aucuns de ses voisins
qui luy portoient reverence plus pour doubtance que pour amour *P and* [*with
slight variations*] *M, L, B, P₂, P₄*).

(**Var.**) 50   les os] ses os *P₂*—dit oultre] dit ainsi *P, P₄*.
52   les vermoissiaulx] le petit ver *M*.
56   soustenu] receu *M*.
58   l'a voulu] a voulu *L, B, P, P₂, P₄*—lui] nostre seigneur *M, L, B, P, P₂*.
63   parens] tes parens *M, B, P, P₂*.
64   le conseil] leur conseil *P₂, P₄*—Car] *om. L.*
68   et retournez] *om. P₄*.
70–71   losengiers et] lousengiers et de flateurs et aussi *P₄*.
72   Quant] et quant *P₄*—recompta] raconta le cas *L, P, P₄*, raconta le fait
et le cas *P₂*.
76   des autres, se leva] se leva du consentement de tous les autres *P₄*.

"Sire, il appartient a cysurgien que il porte a un chascun proffit et a ⟨fol. 57ʳ⟩ nul dommage, dont il advient aucune foiz que, quant deux hommes par malice se navrent ensemble, un mesme cysurgien garist l'un et l'autre. Et pour ce il n'appartient a nous de norrir   80 guerre ne supporter partie. Mais a ta fille garir, ja soit ce qu'elle soit navree malement, nous mettrons toute nostre cure de jour et de nuit; et a l'aide de Nostre Seigneur nous la te rendrons toute 2205 sainne."

Presque en ceste maniere respondirent les phisiciens et adjousterent   85 que tout aussi comme selon l'art de medecine les maladies se doivent garir par contraire, aussi doit on garir guerre par vengence.

Les voisins jadix ennemis qui en grace estoient retourné, les voisins reconsiliez par semblance, les losengiers firent semblant de plorer et commencerent le fait moult agrever en loant moult Mellibee de puis-   90 sance, d'avoir, et d'amis, en vituperant la puissance de ses adversaires, et dirent que tout oultre il se devoit tantost vengier et incontinent 2210 commencer la guerre.

Adonques un sage advocat, de la voulenté des autres, se leva et dist, "Beaulx seigneurs, la besoingne pourquoy nous sommes yci   95 assemblez est moult haute et pesant pour raison de l'injure et du malefice qui est moult grans, et pour raison des grans maulx qui s'en pevent ensuivre ou temps advenir, et pour raison des richesses et de la puissance des parties, pour lesquelles choses il seroit grant peril 2215 errer en ceste besoingne. Pour ce, des maintenant nous te conseillons,   100 Mellibee, que tu sur toutes choses ayes diligence de garder ta personne en tele maniere qu'il ne te faille ne espies ne gaites pour toy garder. Aprés, tu mettras en ta maison bonnes garnisons et fors pour toy et ta maison deffendre; mais de mouvoir guerre ou de toy venger tantost, nous n'en povons pas bien juger en si pou de temps lequel vault   105 mieux. Si demandons espace d'avoir deliberation, car on dit com- 2220 munément, 'Qui tost juge tost se repent'; et dit on aussi que le juges est tres bons qui tost entend et tart juge. Car ja soit ce que toute

P₃.   90   agrever] agreve (agrever *L, P, P₂, P₄*, a agrever *B*).
92   tantost vengier] *om.* (tantost vengier *M, L, B, P, P₂, P₄*).

(**Var.**)   77   Sire] sire dist il *L, P, P₂*.
83   Nostre Seigneur] dieu *L*.
88   jadix] envieux *M, L, B, P, P₄*.
89   losengiers] lousangiers et flateurs *P₄*.
96   raison de] cause de *M*.
99   grant] moult grans *B*.
100   Pour ce] Pour ce Mellibee *M*.
103   Aprés] et aprés *M, L, P, P₄*.
106   deliberation] deliberation pour nous en advisier *L*.

demeure soit ennuyeuse, toutevoie elle ne fait pas a reprendre en
jugement et en vengence quant elle est souffisant et raisonnable. Et   11(
ce nous monstre par exemple Nostre Seigneur Jhesu Crist quant la
femme qui estoit prinse en avoultire lui fut admenee pour juger que
l'on en devoit faire; car ja soit ce qu'il sceust bien qu'il y devoit
respondre, toutevoye il ne respondi pas tantost, mais va avoir deliberation et escript deux foiz en terre. Pour ces raisons nous demandons   11!
deliberation; laquelle eue, nous te conseillerons, a l'aide de Dieu,
chose qui sera a ton profit."

Lors les jeunes gens et la plus grant partie de tous les autres es-
2225 charnirent cest sage, et firent grant bruit, et dirent que tout aussi
comme l'on ⟨fol. 57ᵛ⟩ doit batre le fer tant comme il est chaut, aussi   12(
l'on doit venger l'injure tant comme elle est fresche, et escrierent a
haute voix, "Guerre! Guerre!"

Adonques se leva un des anciens, et estendit la main, et commanda
que l'on feist scilence, et dist, "Moult de gens crient 'Guerre!' haultement qui ne scevent que guerre se monte. Guerre en son commence-   12!
ment est une chose si large et a si grant entree que un chascun y
puet entrer et la puet trouver legierement, mais a tres grant pene puet
2230 on savoir a quel fin on en puet venir. Car quant la guerre commence, moult de gens ne sont encores nez qui pour cause de la guerre
morront jeunes, ou en vivront en doulour et en misere, et fineront   13(
leur vie en misere et en chetiveté. Et pour ce, avant que l'en mueve
guerre, on doit avoir grant conseil et deliberation." Quant ycellui
ancien cuida confermer son dit par raison, ilz se leverent presque
touz contre lui et intrerompirent son dit souvent et lui dirent qu'il
abregeast ses paroles, car la narration de cellui qui presche a ceulz   13!
qui ne le veulent oïr est ennuyeuse narration, et Jhesu Syrac dit que
musique em plour est ennuyeuse narracion: c'est a dire que autant

P₃. 111 Crist] crit (Crist M, L, B, P, P₂, P₄).
136–37 et Jhesu ... narracion] om. (et Jhesu Syrac dit que musique em plour
est ennuyeuse narracion P, B, and [with slight variations] L).

(Var.) 109   ne fait pas] n'est pas B, P₄, n'est mie L.
110   et en] ne en B, P₂, P₄.
112   admenee] presentee P₄.
114   va] voult M, L, B, P, P₂, P₄.
118–19   escharnirent] se leverent et huerent B, P₄.
119   bruit] noise et grant bruit B.
124   Moult de gens] il y a moult de gens qui P₄, moult de gens sont qui L.
124–25   haultement] guerre B, P, P₂.
126   est une ... entree] a si grant entree et si large B.
131–32   que l'en mueve guerre] qu'elle commence P₂.
132   deliberation] grant deliberation M, L, B, P, P₂, P₄—Quant] Et quant P₄.
133   raison] raisons M, P.

vault parler a cellui a cui il ennuye comme chanter devant celui qui
2235 plore. Quant icellui sage ancien vit qu'il ne pourroit avoir audience,
si s'assist; car Salemon dit, "La ou tu ne pourras avoir audience, ne   140
t'efforce point de parler." Si dist, "Je voy bien maintenant que le
proverbe commun est vray: 'Lors faut le bon conseil quant le grant
besoing est.' " Et ce dit, il s'assist comme tout honteux.

Encor avoir ou conseil Mellibee moult de gens qui lui conseilloient
autre chose en l'oreille et autre chose en appert.   145

Mellibee, quant il ot oÿ tout son conseil, il regarda que la tres
plus grant partie s'accordoit que l'on feist guerre, si s'arresta a leur
2240 sentence et la conferma. Lors Dame Prudence, quant elle vit son
mary qui s'appareilloit de soy venger et de faire guerre, si lui vient
au devant et lui dist moult doulcement, "Sire, je vous pry que vous   150
ne vous hastez et que vous pour tous dons me donnez espace; car
Pierre Alphons dit, 'Qui te fera bien ou mal, ne te haste pas du rendre,
car ainsi plus long temps te attendra ton amy, et plus long temps te
doubtera ton ennemi.' "

Mellibee respondit a Prudence sa femme: "Je ne propose point user   155
de ton conseil pour moult de raisons: premierement, car un chascun
2245 me tendroit pour fol se je par ton conseil et consentement changeoye
ce qui est ordonné par tant de bonnes gens; aprés, car toutes femmes
sont mauvaises, et nesune n'est bonne, selon le dit de Salemon: 'De mil
hommes,' ce dit il, 'en ay trouvé un preudomme, mais ⟨fol. 58ʳ⟩ de   160
toutes les femmes je n'en ay trouvé une bonne.' Aprés, se je me gou-

P₃. 140   si s'assist; car] Et (si s'assist car P, P₄, si s'asist et L.)
144   moult de gens qui lui conseilloient] qui lui conseilloient moult de gens
(moult de gens qui lui conseilloient M, L, B, P₂).
147   si] il (si M, L, B, P, P₂).

(Var.) 138   a cellui] devant cellui M, L, B, P, P₂, P₄.
142   le grant] le plus grant L, B.
145   l'oreille] l'oreille et en secret P₄.
146   Mellibee, quant] Quant Mellibee M, P₄.
148   sentence] conseil P₄.
150   Sire] sire dist elle L, B, P, P₂.
155   user] ouvrer ne user P₂.

147   *s'accordoit.* All other manuscripts (M, L, B, P, P₂, P₄) add *et conseilloit;*
but since Chaucer does not translate the words (l. 2240), we may assume that his
source manuscript, like P₃, omitted them. The Latin (11.8–12) does not
contain their exact equivalent, since the French here is a loose, abbreviated rendering of the original.

154   *ennemi.* Chaucer here adds a sentence (l. 2244) which is present in neither
the French nor the Latin (12.1–3) versions. Cf. *Troilus,* I, 956, and *Parson's Tale,*
1003.

vernoye par ton conseil, il sembleroit que je te donasse sur moy seignorie, laquelle chose ne doit pas estre, car Jhesu Sirac dit, 'Se la femme a la seignorie elle est contraire a son mary'; et Salemon dit, 'A ton fil, a ta femme, a ton frere, a ton amy ne donne puissance sur toy 165 en toute ta vie, car il te vault mieux que tes enfans te requierent ce 2250 que mestier leur sera que toy regarder es mains de tes enfans.' Aprés, se je vouloye user de ton conseil, il convendroit aucune foiz que le conseil fust secret et celé jusques a tant qu'il fust temps du reveller; et ce ne se porroit faire, car il est escript, 'La genglerie des femmes ne 170 puet riens celer fors ce qu'elle ne scet.' Aprés, le philosophe dit, 'En mauvais conseil les femmes vainquent les hommes.' Pour ces raisons je ne doy point user de ton conseil.''

Aprés ce que Dame Prudence ot oÿ debonnairement et en grant patience toutes les choses que son mary voult avant traire, si demanda 175 licence de parler et puis dist: ''Sire, a la premiere raison que vous m'avez avant mise puet on respondre legierement, car je dy qu'il n'est pas folie de changer son conseil quant la chose se change 2255 ou quant elle appert autrement que devant aprés. Et dy encores que se tu avoies promis et juré de faire ton emprinse, et tu la laissoyes de 180 faire par juste cause, l'on ne devroit pas dire que tu feusses mensongier ne parjure, car il est escript, 'Li sages ne ment mie quant il mue son propox en mieux.' Et ja soit ce que ton emprise soit establie et ordonnee par grant multitude de gens, pour ce ne la convient pas adcomplir, car la verité des choses et les profiz sont mieux trouvez par 185 pou de gens sages et parlans par raison que par grant multitude de gens, ou chascun brait et crie a sa voulenté, et tele multitude de gens n'est pas honneste. A la seconde raison, quant vous dittes que toutes

P₃. 171 Aprés] *om.* (Aprés *M, L, B, P, P₂, P₄*).

186 sages et parlans par raison] *om.* (sages et parlans par raison *M, L, B, P, P₂, P₄*).

186–87 multitude de gens] multitude (multitude de gens *M, L, B, P, P₂, P₄*).

(**Var.**) 164–65 A ton fil, a ta femme] a ta femme, a ton filz *P₄*.

168 convendroit] me convendroit *P₂*.

170 faire] estre *L*.

176 puis dist] dist ainsi *P₄*—Sire] sire dist elle *L, B, P, P₂*.

179 elle] la chose *M, L, B, P₂, P₄*—aprés] *om. L, B*.

180 promis et juré] juré et promis *P₄*.

183 propox en] coraige au *P₂*, courage en *M*.

185 les profiz] le prouffit *M, L, B, P, P₂*.

187–88 de gens n'est] n'est *M, L, B, P*.

170–73 *car ... conseil.* In the manuscripts of Chaucer's tale, this passage is lacking (ll. 2252–53). Yet all the French manuscripts and the Latin text (13.2–6) have it.

femmes sont mauvaises et n'en est nulle bonne, sauve vostre reverence,
vous parlez trop generaulment quant vous desprisez ainsi toutes, car   190
2260 il est escript, 'Qui tout desprise a tout desplait.' Et Senecque dit que
cellui qui veult acquerre sapience ne doit nul despriser, mais ce qu'il
scet il le doit enseingnier senz presumption, et ce qu'il ne scet il ne
doit pas avoir honte de demander a mendre de lui. Et que moult de
femmes soient bonnes l'on le puet prouver legierement: premiere-   195
ment, car Nostre Seigneur ne fust onques daingnié descendre en femme se elles fussent toutes mauvaises ainsi comme tu le dis. Aprés,
pour la bonté des femmes, Nostre Seigneur Jhesu Crist, quant il
resuscita de mort a vie, il apparut premier a femme que a homme, car
2265 il apparut premier a Marie Magdelaine ⟨fol. 58ᵛ⟩ que aus appostres.   200
Et quant Salemon dit que de toutes femmes il n'en a trouvé une bonne,
pour ce ne s'ensuist pas que aucune ne soit bonne, car ja soit ce que
il ne l'ait trouvee, moult des autres en ont bien trouvé pluseurs bonnes
et loyaulx; ou, par adventure, quant Salemon dit qu'il n'a point
trouvé de bonne femme, il entend de la bonté souverainne, de laquelle   205
nul n'est bon fors Dieu seulement, selon ce qu'il mesmes le dit en
l'*Euvangille*, car nulle creature n'est tant bonne a cui ne faille aucune
2270 chose senz comparoison a la perfection de son creatour. La tierce chose
est quant tu dis se tu te gouvernoyes par mon conseil il sembleroit
que tu me donasses par dessus toy seignorie. Sauve ta grace, il n'est   210
pas ainsi; car selon ce, nul ne prendroit conseil fors a celui a cui il
vouldroit sur soy puissance, et ce n'est pas voir, car celui qui demande
conseil a puissance et franche voulenté de faire ce que on lui conseille ou
de laisser. Quant a la quarte raison, ou tu dis que la janglerie des
femmes ne puet celer fors ce qu'elle ne scet, ceste parole doit estre   215
entendue d'aucunes tres mauvaises femmes genglerresses ou parler-
2275 resses desquelles on dit: 'Trois choses sont qui gettent l'omme hors de
sa maison: la fumiere, la goutiere, et la mauvaise femme'; et de telle
femme parle Salemon quant il dit, 'Il vauldroit mieux habiter en

P₃.   202   pour ce ... bonne] *om.* (pour ce ne s'ensuist pas que aucune ne soit
bonne P *and* [*with slight variations*] M, L, B, P₂, P₄).

(**Var.**)   189   reverence] grace M, B.
190   vous parlez trop generaulment quant] *om.* P₂.
196   Seigneur] Seigneur Jhesu Crist M, P₄.
199   resuscita] fut ressuscité M.
199–200   a femme ... premier] *om.* M, L, P₂.
203   trouvee] trouvees bonnes L, P₄, trouvé nullez bonnez B.
208   senz comparoison] *om.* B—de son] de dieu son L—chose] raison, L, B, P₄.
214   Quant] et quant P₄.
217   dit: 'Trois choses sont qui] dit que troys choses P₄.
218   maison] maison c'est assavoir M, P₂, P₄.
218–19   telle femme] telles femmes M.

terre deserte que avec femme rioteuse et courrouceuse.' Or scez tu bien   22*
que tu ne m'as pas trouvee telle, ains as souvent esprouvé ma grant
silence et ma grant souffrance et comment j'ay gardees les choses que
l'on doit garder et tenir secretes. Quant a la quinte raison, ou tu dis
qu'en mauvais conseil les femmes vainquent les hommes, ceste raison
2280 n'a point cy son lieu; car tu ne demandes pas conseil de mal faire, et   22*
se tu vouloies ouvrer de mauvais conseil et mal faire, et ta femme t'en
retrait et t'en vainquist, ce ne seroit pas a reprendre, mais a loer; et
ainsi doit on entendre le dit du prophete, 'En mauvais conseil vainquent les femmes les hommes'; car aucune foiz quant les hommes
veulent ouvrer de mauvais conseil, les femmes les en retraient et les   23*
vainquent. Et quant vous blasmez tant les femmes et leur conseil,
je vous monstre par moult de raisons que moult de femmes ont
2285 esté bonnes, et sont, et leur conseil bon et profitable: premierement,
car l'on a acoustumé de dire, 'Conseil de femme, ou il est tres cher,
ou il est tres vil'; car ja soit ce que moult de femmes soient tres mau-   23*
vaises et leur conseil tres vil, toutevoye l'on en trouve assez de bonnes
et qui tres bon conseil et tres cher ont donné. Jacob, par le bon conseil
de Rebeque, sa mere, gaingna ⟨fol. 59ʳ⟩ la beneïçon Ysaac, son pere,
et la seignorie sur tous ses freres. Judith, par son bon conseil, delivra
la cité de Buthulie, ou elle demouroit, des mains Oloferne, qui l'avoit   24*
assigee et la vouloit destruire. Abigal delivra Nabal, son mary, de
David le Roy, qui le vouloit occirre, et l'appaisa par son sens et par
2290 son conseil. Hester, par son bon conseil, esleva moult son pueple ou
royaume de Assuere le Roy. Et ainsi puet on dire de moult d'autres.
Aprés, quant Nostre Seigneur ot creé Adam, le premier homme, il   24*
dist, 'Il n'est pas bon estre l'omme tout seul; faisons lui adjutoire

---

(**Var.**)   222   gardees] gardé et celé *M*.
228   prophete] philosophe *M, L, B*.
228–29   vainquent les femmes] les femmes vainquent *P, P₄*.
231   tant] toutes *P₄*.
232   monstre] monstreray *M, P₄*.
233   leur conseil] leurs conseilz *P₄*.
234   dire, 'Conseil] dire que conseil *L, B*.
235   il est] *om. B*.
236   trouve assez] a assés trouvé *L, B, P₄*.
238   Rebeque] Rebeca *M, P*, Rebecqua *P₂*.
240   Buthulie] bethulie *L, B*.
242   l'appaisa] appaisa le roy *M, P₂*.
243   son conseil] son bon conseil *L, B, P₄*.
244   d'autres] d'aultres femmez *B*.

229–31   *car ... vainquent*. Chaucer omits (l. 2284). All the French manuscripts
contain the passage. The Latin (16.5–17) is even fuller than the French.

semblable a lui.' S'elles donques n'estoient bonnes et leurs conseilz
2295 bons, Nostre Seigneur ne les eust pas appellees a l'omme en adjutoire,
mais en dommage et en nuisement. Aprés, un maistre fait deux vers
es quelz il demande et respont et dit ainsi: 'Quele chose vault mieux 250
que l'or? Jaspe. Quele chose vault plus que jaspe? Sens. Quele chose
vault mieux que sens? Femme. Quelle chose vault mieux que femme?
Riens.' Par ces raisons et par moult d'autres puez tu veoir que moult
de femmes sont bonnes et leur conseil bon et proffitable. Se tu donques
2300 maintenant veulz croire mon conseil, je te rendray ta fille toute sainne 255
et feray tant que tu auras honeur en cest fait.''

Quant Mellibee ot oÿ parler Prudence, si dist: ''Je voy bien que la
parole Salemon est vraye, qui dit, 'Bresches de miel sont paroles bien
ordenees, car elles donnent doulceur a l'ame et senté au corps'; car
par tes paroles tres douces et que j'ay esprouvé ta grant sapience et ta 260
grant loyaulté, je me vueil du tout gouverner par ton conseil.''

''Puis,'' dist Prudence, ''que tu te veulz gouverner par mon conseil,
je te vueil enseingnier comment tu te dois avoir en conseil prendre et
2305 retenir. Premierement, en toutes oeuvres tu dois le conseil de Dieu
demander devant tous autres, et te dois mettre en tel lieu qu'il te 265
daingne conforter et conseiller. Pour ce disoit Thobie a son filz:
'En tout temps beneïz Dieu et lui prie qu'il adresse tes voyes, et tuit
tes conseilz soient en lui tout temps.' Et Saint Jaque dit, 'Se aucun
de vous a mestier de sapience, si la demande a Dieu.' Aprés, tu dois
prendre conseil a toy mesmes et entrer en ta pensee et examiner que 270
2310 mieux te vault. Et lors tu dois oster trois choses de toy qui sont contrarieuses a conseil: c'est assavoir, ire, couvoitise, et hastiveté.

(**Var.**) 248 a l'omme en adjutoire] adjutoires de l'omme L, P, P₄, ayde del
homme B, adjutoires de hommes M.
249 en dommage et en nuisement] domacges et nuisement P₄.
251 Sens. Quele] sens et quelle P₄.
252 Femme. Quelle] femme et quelle P₄.
257 Prudence] Prudence sa femme P₄.
258–59 Bresches ... ordenees] que paroles ordonnees sont bresches de miel P₄.
260 et que] et pour ce aussi que M, et ausi pour ce que P₂, et car P₄.
262 Prudence] dame Prudence P₄.
263 avoir] gouverner P₄.
264 toutes] toutes tes M, L, B, P, P₂, P₄.
266 conforter et conseiller] conseillier et conforter M.

248 *adjutoire.* All other manuscripts (M, L, B, P, P₂, P₄) here add (with
slight variations in reading): *car elles ne fussent pas adjutoire a homme.* Since
Chaucer does not translate the words (l. 2296), we may assume that his source
manuscript, like P₃, omitted them. Since the French translator here recasts and
condenses his original, the words in question are not present in the Latin (18.
1–7).

"Premierement, donques, cellui qui demande conseil a soy mesmes
doit estre senz yre par moult de raisons. La premiere est quar cellui
qui est courreciez cuide tousjours plus povoir faire qu'il ne puet, et   2⁷
pour ce ⟨fol. 59ᵛ⟩ son conseil surmonte tousjours sa force; l'autre, car
cellui qui est courroucié, selon ce que dit Senecques, ne puet parler
2317 fors que choses crimineuses, et par ceste maniere il esmuet les autres
a courrouz et a yre; l'autre, quar celui qui est courcié ne puet bien
2315 juger et par consequant bien conseiller. Aprés, tu dois oster de toy   2⁸
couvoitise; car, selon ce que dit l'appostre, 'Couvoitise est racine de
2320 tous maulx.' Et le couvoiteux ne puet riens juger fors que en la fin
sa couvoitise soit acomplie, qui acomplir ne se puet, car tant com plus a
li couvoiteux, plus desirre. Aprés, tu dois oster de toy hastiveté, car
tu ne dois pas juger pour le meilleur ce que tantost te vendra au devant,   2⁸
ains y doiz penser souvent; car, selon ce que tu as oÿ dessus, l'on dit
2325 communément, 'Qui tost juge tost se repent.' Tu n'es pas toutes
heures en une disposicion, ains trouveras que ce qui aucune foiz te
semblera bon de faire, a l'autre te semblera bon de laisser.

"Quant tu auras prins conseil a toy mesmes et auras jugié a grant   2⁹
deliberation ce que mieux te vault, tien le secret et le garde de reveller a nulle personne se tu ne cuides que en revellant certainnement
2330 tu feras ta condition meilleur et que le reveller te portera proffit.
Car Jhesu Sirac dit, 'A ton ami ne a ton ennemi ne recompte point ton
secret et ta folie, car il te orront et te regarderont et deffendront en   2⁹
ta presence, et par darriere se moqueront de toy.' Et uns autres dit,
'A painnes trouveras tu un tant seulement qui puisse bien celer secret.'
Et Pierre Alphons si dit: 'Tant com ton secret est en ton cuer, tu le
2335 tiens en ta prison; quant tu le reveles, il te tient en la sienne.' Et
pour ce il te vaut mieux taire et ton secret celer que prier cellui a   3(

(**Var.**) 276 l'autre] la seconde P_2.

277–80 selon ... conseiller] ne puet bien jugier, par consequent bien consillier;
la tierche, car cil qui est courouchiez, selon ce que dist Senecques, ne puet parler
fors choses crimineuses, et en telles maniere il esmeut les aultres a courouchier
et a yrer P_2, ne puet bien jugier et par consequent bien conseillier; l'autre si
est car cilz qui est courrouciez, selon ce que dit Seneque, ne puet parler fors
choses crimineuses, et en telle maniere il esmuet les autres a parole et a courroux
et a ire P and [*with slight variations*] L, B, P_4.

280 oster de toy] de ton coeur oster P_2.

295 secret et] secret ne M, B, P, P_4—deffendront] supporteront M, P_2.

297 un tant] une personne P_2.

299 quant] et quant M, B, P_2, P_4—reveles] reveles a autruy M.

275–76 *et pour ... force.* Chaucer omits (l. 2314). All the French manuscripts
contain the passage. It is in the Latin (33.17).

cui tu le revelles qu'il le cele. Car Senecques dit, 'Se tu ne te puez
taire et ton secret celer, comment prieras tu un autre qu'il le cele?'
Se tu cuides que reveller ton secret a un autre face ta condicion meilleur, lors te gouverneras par tel guise: Premierement, tu ne dois faire
semblant a ton conseil quele partie tu veulz tenir ne leur monstrer   305
340 ta voulenté. Car communément tous conseilliers sont losengeours,
et especiaulment ceulz qui sont du conseil des grans seigneurs, car
ilz s'efforcent plus de dire choses plaisans que proffitables. Et pour
ce, riches homs n'aura ja bon conseil se il ne l'a premier de soy mesmes.   310

    "Aprés, tu dois considerer tes amis et tes ennemis. Entre tes amis
tu doiz considerer le plus loyal, le plus sage, le plus ancien, et le plus
345 esprouvé en conseil; et a ceulz tu dois conseil demander. Premierement, donques, tu doiz appeller a ton conseil tes bons et tes loyaulx
amis. Car Salemon dit, 'Aussi comme le cuer ⟨fol. 60ʳ⟩ se delitte en   315
bonne odeur, conseil de bon amy fait a l'ame doulceur.' Et dit aussi,
'A l'amy loyal nulle chose ne se compere, car ne or ne argent ne sont
350 tant dignes comme la bonté du loyal amy.' Et dit encor, 'Amy loyal
est une fort deffense; qui le treuve, il treuve un grant tresor.' Aprés,
tu dois regarder que les loyaulx amis que tu appelles a ton conseil   320
soient sages, car il est escript, 'Requier tousjours le conseil du sage.'
Par ceste mesme raison tu dois appeller les anciens qui assez ont veu
et assez esprouvé. Car il est escript en *Job*, 'Es anciens est la sapience
et en moult de temps est prudence.' Et Tulles dit, 'Les grans besoingnes ne se font pas par force ne par legiereté de corps, mais par   325
bon conseil, et par auctorité de personne, et par science, lesquelles
trois choses n'affoiblissent pas en vieillesse, mais s'efforcent et crois-
355 sent tous les jours.' Aprés, en ton conseil tu dois garder ceste rigle:
car au commencement tu dois appeller pou de gens des plus especiaulx;
car Salemon dit, 'Efforce toy d'avoir pluseurs amis, mais entre mil es- 330
lis en un a ton conseillier.' Quant tu auras eu revelé ton conseil a
pou de gens, si le puez reveller a pluseurs se besoing est. Toutevoye,
les trois condicions que j'ay dictes si doivent estre es conseilliers tous-

(**Var.**)   301   le revelles] l'as revelé *L*, *B*.
302   prieras tu] ose tu prier *M*, *P*₂.
303   secret] conseil *L*, *B*, *P*₄.
304   tel] ceste *P*₄.
305   a ton conseil]   *om. P*₂.
307   et especiaulment] especiaulment *M*, *L*, *B*, *P*, *P*₂, *P*₄.
312   loyal] loial et *M*, loyaulx et *B*, *P*₂—sage] sages et *P*, *P*₂.
313   conseil demander] tout ton conseil demander *B*.
318   bonté] voulenté *M*.
331   a ton] a estre ton *P*₄.

jours gardees, et ne te souffise un conseil tant seulement, mais en
2360 fay pluseurs. Car Salemon dit, 'Sainement est la ou pluseurs conseilz   3:
sont.'

"Aprés ce que je t'ay monstré a cui tu doiz prendre conseil, je te
vueil monstrer lequel conseil tu doiz fuir et eschever. Premierement,
tu dois le conseil des folz eschiver, car Salemon dit, 'A fol ne prens
point de conseil, car il ne te saura conseiller fors ce qu'il aime et   34
qu'il li plaist.' Et si est escript: 'La proprieté du fol est tele car il
croit legierement tous maulx d'autrui et tous biens de lui.' Aprés, tu
doiz fuir le conseil des faintifs losengeurs, lesquelz se efforcent plus
2365 de loer ta personne et a toy plaire que a verité dire; et Tulles dit,
'Entre toutes les pestilences qui sont en amitié, la plus grant est   34
losengerie.' Et pour ce tu dois plus fuir et doubter les doulces paroles
de celui qui te loera que les aigres paroles de celui qui verité te dira.
Car Salemon dit, 'Homme qui dit paroles de losengerie est un lacet
pour prendre les innocens.' Et dit aussi autre part, 'Homme qui parle
a son ami paroles doulces et souees, il lui met devant les piez le laz   3:
pour lui prendre.' Pour ce dit Tulles, 'Garde que tu n'enclines point
tes oreilles a losengeurs, et ne recoip point en ton conseil paroles de
2370 losengerie.' Et Caton dit, 'Advise toy d'eschever paroles doulces et
souees.' Aprés, tu dois fuir le conseil de tes anciens ennemis ⟨fol. 60ᵛ⟩
qui sont reconciliez, car il est escript, 'Nul ne retourne seurement en la   3:
grace de son ennemi.' Et Ysopes dit, 'Ne vous fiez point en ceulz a cui
vous aurez eu guerre et ennemitié anciennement, et ne leur revellez
point voz secrez.' Et la raison conferme Senecques, et dit que il ne puet
estre que la ou a esté le feu longuement qu'il n'y demeure tousjours
2375 aucune vapour. Pour ce dit Salemon, 'En ton ancien ennemi ne te   3(
fie nul temps; et encores se il est reconciliez et se humilie et encline
la teste devant toy, ne le croy, car il le fait plus pour son proffit
que pour amour de toy, a la fin qu'il puisse avoir victoire de toy en

P₃.   350   doulces] doubles (doulces M, P₂, P₄).
353   doulces] doubles (doulces M, P₂, P₄).
363   victoire] vitoire (victoire P, P₂).

(Var.)   334   conseil] conseillier M, L, P₄.
335   la] la chose M—conseilz] conseillers M, P, P₂.
348   Car] om. L.
351   Pour] et pour P₂, P₄—Garde que] om. P₄.
354   Aprés] et aprés B, P₄—fuir] eschever M, P₂, P₄.
358   secrez] consaulx ou secrets M.
359   estre] estre dist il L, P—longuement] long temps B, P₄.
360   Pour]   et pour B, P₄.
361   humilie] humilité est en luy par semblant M, humilité soit en luy par
samblant P₂.
363   victoire de] victoire sur P₂.

soy humiliant et en toy fuyant, laquelle il n'a pas peu avoir en toy
poursuyant.' Et Pierre Alphons dit, 'Ne te compaigne pas a tes anciens   365
ennemis, car ce que tu feras de bien, ilz le pervertiront ou le amenui-
seront.' Aprés, tu dois fuir le conseil de ceulz qui te servent et te portent reverence plus par doubtance que par amour. Car un philosophe
dit, 'Nul n'est bien loyal a cellui que il trop doubte.' Et Tulles dit,
'Nulle puissance d'empire n'est si grant qu'elle puisse durer longue-   370
ment se elle n'a plus l'amour du pueple que la paour.' Aprés, tu doiz
fuir le conseil de ceulz qui sont souvent yvres, car ilz ne scevent riens
celer. Et Salemon dit, 'Nul secret n'est la ou regne yvresse.' Aprés, tu
dois avoir en suspect le conseil de ceulz qui conseillent une chose en
secret et autre dient en appert. Car Cassidoires dit, 'Une maniere   375
de grever son amy est monstrer en appert ce dont l'on veult le contraire.' Aprés, tu dois avoir en suspect le conseil de mauvais homme.
Car il est escript, 'Les conseilz des mauvais hommes sont tousjours
plains de fraude.' Et David dit, 'Bieneureux est l'omme qui n'a suy
le conseil des mauvais.' Aprés, tu dois fuir le conseil des jeunes gens,   380
car le sens des jeunes n'est pas encores meur. Et Salemon dit, 'Doulente la terre qui a enfant a seigneur, de laquelle le prince se des-
jusne matin!'

"Puis que je t'ay monstré a cui tu dois prendre conseil et lequel tu

(marginal line numbers: 2380, 2385)

(**Var.**)   364   laquelle] laquelle victoire M, P_2.
366   pervertiront] pervertiront en mal B, P_4.
366–67   amenuiseront] augmenteront en mal P_2.
368   reverence] reverence car ils le font M, P_2.
370   d'empire] d'empereur P_2, P_4.
373   Et] pour quoy P_2.
374   qui] qui te L, qui toy P_4.
375   dit] dist que c'est B, dit qu'il n'est P_4.
376   monstrer] quant on lui conseille une chose en secret et monstrer L—
est ... l'on] quant il P_4.
377   homme] hommes M, P_4.
378   Les conseilz] le conseil L, B, P, P_2, P_4.
381   le sens ... encores] leur conseil n'est encore pas P.
384   et lequel] et de qui conseil M, P_2.

<hr />

381–83   *Et Salemon ... matin.* Although all the French manuscripts and the
Latin original (53.6–7) have this passage, Chaucer omits it (l. 2389). Cf. J. S. P:
Tatlock, *The Development and Chronology of Chaucer's Works* ("Chaucer Society
Publications" [London, 1907]), p. 192. In M and P_2 the passage is much longer.
between *seigneur* and *de* (382) occurs: *Et le philosophe dit que nous n'eslisons pas
les jeunes en princes, car communément ils n'ont point de prudence; et dit encores
Salemon: dolente est la terre.* This addition is not found in the Latin (53.7).

2390 doiz eschever et fuir, je te vueil monstrer et aprendre comment tu   3
dois conseil examiner. En examinant, donques, ton conseil, selon ce
que Tulles enseingne, tu dois considerer pluseurs choses. Premierement, tu dois considerer que en ce que tu proposes et sur quoy tu
veulz avoir conseil, pure verité soit gardee et dicte. Car l'on ne puet
bien conseiller a celui qui ne dit verité. Aprés, tu dois considerer   3
toutes les choses qui se accordent ad ce que tu proposes faire selon
2395 ton conseil: se raison s'i accorde, se ta puissance s'i accorde, se pluseurs ou meilleurs s'i accordent ⟨fol. 61ʳ⟩ que discordent, ou non.
Aprés, tu dois considerer ce qui s'ensuit au conseil: se c'est hayne ou
amour, paix ou guerre, profit ou dommage; et ainsi de moult d'autres   3
choses. Et en toutes ces choses tu dois tousjours eslire ce qui est a
ton proffit, toutes autres choses refusees et rabatues. Aprés, tu dois
considerer de quelle racine est engendree la matiere de ton conseil et
quel fruit elle puet concevoir et engendrer, et dois encores considerer
2400 toutes causes dont elle est venue. Quant tu auras examiné ton conseil   4
en la maniere devant ditte, et trouvé laquelle partie est meilleur, plus
profitable, et mieux esprouvee de pluseurs sages et anciens, tu dois
considerer se tu la pourras mener a fin. Quar nul ne doit commencer
chose qu'il n'a povoir de faire, et ne doit prendre charge qu'il ne puisse
2405 porter. L'on dit un proverbe: 'Qui trop embrace, pou estraint.' Et   4
Cathon dit: 'Essaye toy de faire ce que tu as povoir de faire, pour
ce que la charge ne te presse tant qu'il couviengne laisser ce que tu
as commencié a faire.' S'il est doubte se tu le pourras mener a fin ou
non, esliz plus tost le souffrir que le commencier. Car Pierre Alphons

P₃.   402   sages] *om.* (sages *M, L, B, P, P₂, P₄*).

(**Var.**)   391   toutes] *om. P₄.*
392   se ta] et si ta *M.*
392–93   pluseurs ou] plusieurs et *M, L, B, P, P₂.*
400   elle est] elles puent estre *P, P₄.*
401   devant] que je t'ay *P₂*—meilleur] la meilleur et *L, B, P₄.*
404   de faire] de la parfaire *M, P₂, P₄,* du parfaire *L,* de parfaire *B.*
405   L'on] car l'on *L, B, P₄.*
407   couviengne] te couviengne *L, B, P, P₂, P₄.*
408   S'il] et s'il *M, P₄.*

385   *fuir.* Chaucer's "folwe" (l. 2390) may have arisen from a confusion
of *suir* with *fuir,* either through misreading or a scribal error. All the French
manuscripts have *fuir.* The clause containing the word does not occur in the
Latin original (53.11).

dit: 'Se tu as paour de dire chose dont il te couviengne repentir, il   410
vault mielx non que si.' C'est a dire, il te vault mielx taire que parler.
Par plus fort raison, doncques, se tu as povoir de faire chose dont il
te couvienge repentir, il te vault mieux souffrir que commencier. Bien
dient ceulz qui deffendent a un chascun chose faire dont il duelt et
doubte se elle est de faire ou non en la fin. Quant tu auras examiné   415
ton conseil par la maniere dessus dicte, et auras trouvé que tu le
pourras mener a fin, adonques le retien et le conferme.

"Or est raison que je te monstre quant et pourquoy l'on doit
changier son conseil senz reprehension. L'on puet changer son conseil et son propox quant la cause cesse ou quant nouvelle cause sur-   420
vient. Car la loy dit, 'Les choses qui de nouvel surviennent ont mestier
de conseil nouvel.' Et Senecques dit, 'Se ton conseil est venu a la
cognoissance de ton ennemi, change ton conseil.' Aprés, l'on puet
changer son conseil quant on trouve aprés que, par erreur ou par
autre cause, mal ou dommage en puet venir; aprés, quant le conseil   425
est deshonneste ou vient de cause deshonneste, car les loys dient que
toutes promesses deshonnestes sont de nulle valeur; aprés, quant il
est impossible ou ne se puet garder bonnement; et en moult d'autres
manieres.

"Aprés, tu doiz ce tenir pour rigle general: que tout conseil est   430
mauvais qui est si fermes que l'on ne le puet changier par condition
qui surviengne."

Mellibee, quant il ot oÿ les enseingnemens Dame Prudence sa femme,
si respondi: "Dame Prudence," dist il, "jusques a l'eure de maintenant, vous m'avez assez enseingnié en general comment je me doy   435

P₃.   410   Se tu as paour de dire chose] paour de faire (Se tu as paour de dire
chose *B*).
      410–13   il vault ... repentir] *om.* (il vault mielx non que si. C'est a dire, il te
vault mielx taire que parler. Par plus fort raison, doncques, se tu as povoir
[paour *B*] de faire chose dont il te couvienge repentir *P, B*).

(**Var.**)   410   paour de dire] povoir de faire *M, P, P₂, P₄*.
      415   en] et a *P₄*.
      416   dessus dicte] que je t'ay dit *P₂*.

      410–13   *il vault ... repentir.* This passage is present only in B and P; M, L, P₂,
P₃, and P₄ all omit it through scribal error in their archetype manuscript. It is present, in longer form, in the Latin (59.24–61.8); Renaud de Louens must therefore
have included it in his translation. Chaucer has it (ll. 2408–10).

      428–29   *et en moult d'autres manieres.* Chaucer omits this passage (l. 2420).
All French manuscripts have it; Renaud uses it to sum up a longer passage in
the Latin (63.2–12).

porter en conseil prendre ⟨fol. 61ᵛ⟩ et retenir. Or vouldroye je moult
que vous descendissiez en especial et me deissiez ce qui vous semble du
2425 conseil que nous avons eu en nostre propre besoingne."

Lors Dame Prudence respondi: "Sire," dist elle, "je te pry que
tu ne repelles point en ton courage se je dy chose qui te desplaise. Car 44⟨
tout ce que je diray, je l'entens dire a ton honneur et a ton proffit, et
ay esperance que tu le porteras en pacience. Et pour ce je te fais
savoir que ton conseil, a parler proprement, ne doit pas estre dit conseil, mais un fol esmouvement senz discretion, ouquel tu as errey en
2430 moult de manieres. 44⟨

"Premierement, tu as errey a assembler ton conseil. Car au commencement tu deusses avoir appellé po de gens, et puis aprés pluseurs
se besoing fust; mais tantost tu as appellé une grant multitude de
gent chargeuse et ennuyeuse. Aprés, tu as errey, car tu deusses
avoir appelley tant seulement tes loyaulx amis sages et anciens; mais 45⟨
avec ceulz tu as appellé gens estranges, jouvenceaulx, folz, losengers,
2435 ennemis reconciliez, et gens qui te portent reverence senz amour.
Aprés, tu as erré quant tu es venu au conseil acompagnié de ire,
couvoitise, et hastiveté, lesquelles trois choses sont contraires au
conseil, et ne les as pas abaissees en toy et en ton conseil, ainsi comme 45⟨
tu deusses. Aprés, tu as erré quant tu demonstres a ton conseil la
voulenté et la grant affeccion de faire guerre que tu avoies incontinent
2439 et de prendre tantost vengence; et pour ce ilz ont plus suy ta voulenté
que ton profit. Aprés, tu as errey, car tu as estey content d'un conseil
tant seulement, et toutesvoies en si grans et si hautes besoingnes es- 46⟨
toient bien neccessaires pluseurs conseilz. Aprés, tu as erré, car tu
n'as pas examiné ton conseil en la maniere dessus ditte. Aprés, tu as

P₃. 439 Sire] Sire Sire *with the first* Sire *underdotted for deletion.*
451 folz] *om.* (folz P, P₂, M).

(**Var.**) 438 propre] presente L, B.
441 diray] dy M.
442 porteras] prendras M.
443 dit] appellé M.
451 folz, losengers] faulx losengiers et B, foulx et faulx losangiers tes P₄.
453 quant] car L, B, P₂. P₄ acompagnié de] car tu avoies avec toy ensemble
M, ensemble avecques toy P, et avoies avec toy P₄.
454 contraires] contrarieuses P.
455 ne les] lesquellez tu n' B- -et en] ne en M, B, P.
456 quant] car M, L, B, P, P₄—demonstres] as demonstré M, L, B, P, P₂.
457 la grant] ta grant L, P₂.
461 conseilz] consilliers P₂.

458 *vengence.* Following this word Chaucer adds a clarifying clause (l. 2440)
found neither in the French manuscripts nor in the Latin original (65.10).

2445 erré, car quant tu as faite la division entre ceulz de ton conseil, tu
n'as pas suy la voulenté de tes loyaulx amis sages et anciens, mais
as regardé tant seulement le plus grant nombre. Et tu scez bien que   465
les folx sont tousjours en plus grant nombre que les sages, et pour ce
le conseil des chapitres et des grans multitudes de gens ou l'en regarde
plus le nombre que la merite des personnes erre souvent, car en tel
2450 conseil les folx l'ont tousjours gaingnié."

Mellibee respondi: "Je confesse bien que j'ay errey, mais tu m'as   470
dit que celui ne fait pas a reprendre qui change son conseil en moult
de cas, pour quoy je suy appareillez de changer a ta voulenté, car
pechié est oeuvre d'omme, mais perseverer en pechié est oeuvre d'ennemy."

2455 Lors dist Prudence: "Examinons tout ton conseil, et veons les-   475
quelz ont parley plus raisonnablement ⟨fol. 62ʳ⟩ et donné meilleur
conseil. Et pour ce que l'examination soit mieux faite, commençons
aux cysurgiens et aus phisiciens, qui premier parlerent. Je," dist
elle, "dy que les cysurgiens et les phisiciens dirent en conseil ce qu'ilz
devoient dire, et parlerent sagement, car a leur office appartient a un   480
chascun proffiter et a nul nuire; et selon leur dit, ilz doivent avoir grant
2460 diligence de la cure de ceulz qu'ilz ont en gouvernement, ainsi comme
il ont dit et respondu sagement. Et pour ce je conseille qu'ilz soient
haultement guerdonné en tele maniere qu'ilz entendent plus lieement
en la cure de ta fille. Car ja soit ce qu'ilz soient tes amis, tu ne dois   485
pas souffrir qu'il te servent pour neant, mais les dois plus largement

P₃.   468   erre] errent (erre *P, M, L*).

(**Var.**)   464   suy] sceu *P*.
470   mais] mais pour ce que *M*.
471   dit] dit dessus *M, L, B, P, P₂*.
473–74   d'ennemy] de deable *M, L, B, P, P₂, P₄*.
475   tout] *om. L*.
481   dit] art *M, L, B, P, P₄*—ilz doivent avoir] avoir *L, B, P*.
482   gouvernement] leur gouvernement *M, P, P₂*.
485   tu] toutesvoies tu *M, L, P, P₂*.

465   *nombre.* In this sentence and in the two preceding sentences Chaucer
translates somewhat more freely than usual, adding occasional phrases (l. 2442–7).
"Ye han cast alle hire wordes in an hochepot" (l. 2447) is an expressive addition
found neither in the French nor in the Latin (65.19–20).

473–74   *d'ennemy.* M and P₂ add: *et pour ce je ne vueil plus en ce perseverer*
[*penser* P₂]. The passage is not present in the Latin (66.12). Chaucer does **not**
have it (l. 2454).

2465 reguerdonner. Mais quant a la proposicion que les phisiciens adjousterent que es maladies un contraire se garist par son contraire, je vouldroye bien savoir comment tu l'entens."

"Certes," dist Mellibee, "je l'entens ainsi: car comme ilz m'ont 49 fait un contraire, que je leur en face un autre. Et pour ce qu'ilz se sont vengez de·moy et m'ont fait injure, je me vengeray d'eulz et leur feray injure, et lors auray curé un contraire par autre contraire."

"Or veez," dist Prudence, "comment un chascun croit legerement ce qu'il vuelt et ce qu'il desirre. Certes," dist elle, "la parole des phisi- 49 ciens ne doit pas estre ainsi entendue. Car mal n'est pas contraire a mal, ne vengence a vengence, ne injure a injure, mais sont semblables. Et pour ce, vengence ne se garit pas par vengence, ne injure par injure, mais accroist tousjours li uns l'autre. Mais la parole doit estre ainsi entendue: car mal et bien sont contraires, paix et guerre, vengence et 50 souffrance, discord et accord; et ainsi de moult d'autres. Mais mal se doit garir par bien, descort par accord, guerre par paix; et ainsi de tous les autres. Et ad ce s'accorde Saint Pol l'Apostre en moult de lieux. 'Ne rendez,' dit il, 'mal pour mal, ne mesdit pour mesdit; mais faites bien a cellui qui mal vous fera, et beneïssez cellui qui vous 50 maudira'; et en moult d'autres lieux il admonneste moult a paix et a accord. Or couvient parler du conseil que donnerent les advocas, les sages, les anciens, qui furent tuit d'un accord et dirent que devant toutes choses tu dois mettre diligence en garder ta personne et en garnir ta maison, et dirent aussi qu'en ceste besoingne l'on doit aler 51 adviseement a grant deliberation. Quant au premier point, qui touche la garde de ta personne, tu dois savoir que cellui qui a guerre doit tousjours humblement et devoltement demander la garde et l'aide de Dieu. Car en cest monde nul ne se puet garder souffisamment senz la garde de Nostre Seigneur. ⟨fol. 62ᵛ⟩ Pour ce dit David le Prophete: 51 'Se Dieu de la cité n'est garde, pour neant veille qui la garde.' Aprés,

P₃.　504　pour mal] pour bien (pour mal *M, L, B, P, P₂, P₄*).
514　se puet] puet (se puet *M, L, P, P₂, P₄*).

(**Var.**)　487　reguerdonner] paier et guerdonner *M, P₂*.
487–88　adjousterent] adjoustent c'est assavoir *P₄*, monstrent *L, B*
488　son] un autre *L, P₄*, autre *M, P₂*, son autre *P*.
493　contraire] *om. M, L, B, P, P₂, P₄*.
494　Prudence] dame Prudence *P₄*.
501　d'autres] d'aultres chozes *B*.
506–7　a paix et a accord] paix et accort *L*.
513　humblement] devant toutes choses humblement *M, P, P₂*, avant toutes autres choses humblement *P₄*.
515　David le Prophete] le Prophete David *P*.

la garde de ta personne, tu la dois commettre a tes loyaulx amis
esprouvez et cogneuz, et a eulx dois demander aide pour toy garder.
Car Cathon dit, 'Se tu as besoing d'aide, demande la a tes amis, car
il n'est nul si bon phisicien comme le loyal amy.' Aprés, tu te dois
garder de toutes gens estranges et mescogneuz et de leur compagnie, et
avoir leur compagnie suspecte. Car Pierre Alphons dit: 'Ne t'acom-
pagne en chemin a nulle personne se tu ne la cognois avant. Et s'il
s'acompaigne a toy senz ta voulenté et enquiert de ta voye, fains que
tu veulz aler plus loing que tu n'as proposé; et se il porte lance, si te
tien a sa destre; s'il porte espee, tien toy a sa senestre.' Aprés, garde
toy sagement de touz ceulz desquelz le conseil je t'ay dit dessus que tu
doiz eschever et fuir. Aprés, garde toy en telle maniere que pour la
presumpcion de ta force tu ne desprises point ton adversaire tant que
tu l'ayes essayé, car sages homs doit tout doubter, especialment ses
ennemis. Et Salemon dit, 'Beneureux est celui qui tousjours se doubte,
car a celui qui pour la durté de son cuer et de soy a trop grant presumpcion, mal lui vendra.' Tu dois donques doubter tous agaiz,
toutes espies. Car, selon ce que dit Senecques, 'Le sage qui doubte
escheve tous maulx.' Et ja soit ce qu'il te soit semblant que tu soies
bien seur et en seur lieu, toutevoye tu dois tousjours avoir diligence

P₃. 517 personne] personnes *with the* s *underdotted for deletion.*
527 desquelz le] lequel (desquieulx le *L*).
528 en telle maniere] *om.* (en telle maniere *M, L, B, P, P₂, P₄*).
531 Et Salemon dit, 'Beneureux] Bien amé (Et Salemon dit Beneureux *M, L,*
B, P, P₂, P₄).

(**Var.**) 521 mescogneuz] menchongniers *P₂, L, B, P₄*.
522 suspecte] en suspect *B*.
524 de ta voye] de ta vie *P*, de ta vie et de ta voie *M*—fains] faing de ta
voie et *P₂*.
526 destre] destre et *B, P*.
527 desquelz le conseil] que *M, P₂, P₄*.
528 doiz] dois leur conseil *M*, dois l'en (?) conseil *P₂*.
530 tu l'ayes essayé] laisses tes gardes *M, P₂*, tu laisses tes gardes *P*.
532 car a] car *B, P₂, P₄*.
534 toutes] et toutes *M, L, B, P₂, P₄*—Senecques] Seneque qui toutes choses
doubte en nulle ne cherra et encores dit il *M, P₂*, Senesque qui toutes les doubte
en nulle ne cherra et encores dit *L and (with minor variations) B, P₄*.
535 tous maulx] maulx *P*.

534–35 *Car ... maulx.* So read P₃ and P; M, L, B, P₂, and P₄ add a passage
after *Senecques* (see *Var.* above). This passage is present also in the Latin (70.15–
16), hence belongs to the text of the French translation. It is reflected in Chaucer
(l. 2511); but Chaucer's order is different and like that in P₃ and P.

de toy garder. Car Senecques dit, 'Qui seur se garde n'a doubte de nul peril.' Aprés, tu te doiz garder non pas tant seulement de ton grant fort ennemi, mais de tout le plus petit. Car Senecques dit, 'Il appartient a homme bien enseingnié qu'il doubte son petit ennemi.'   54
Et Ovide ou *Livre de Remede d'Amours* dit, 'La petite vivre occist le
2515 grant thorel; et le chien, qui n'est pas moult grant, retient bien le sanglier.' Toutesfoiz, tu ne dois pas estre tant doubteux que tu doubtes la ou riens n'a a doubter. Car il est escript, 'Aucunes gens ont enseingnié eulx decevoir, mais ilz ont trop doubté que on ne les   54
deceust.' Aprés, tu te dois garder de venin et de compagnie de moqueurs. Car il est escript, 'Avec le moqueur n'ayes compagnie, mes
2520 la fuy et sa parole comme le venin.'

"Quant au second point, ouquel dirent les sages que tu dois garnir ta maison a grant diligence, je vouldroye bien savoir comment tu en-   55
tens ceste garnison."

"Je," dist Mellibee, "entens ainsi: que je doy garnir ma maison de tours, d'eschaffaulx, d'eschifes, et de autres ediffices, par lesquelz je me puisse garder et deffendre, et pour cause desquelz les ennemis doubtent approucher ma maison."   55

Lors respondi Prudence: "La garnison de tours haultes et de grans

(Var.)   537–38   Car Senecques ... doiz garder] *om. P, P₄*.
541   vivre] mustelle *B, P₄, L*.
544   n'a] n'est *L, B, P₄*.
547   le moqueur] les moqueurs *L, B, P, P₂, P₄*.
548   la fuy et sa parole] fuy leurs paroles *L, P₂*, fuy ces paroles *P*—le venin] venin *B, P₄*.
550–51   entens] l'entens *M, L, B, P, P₂, P₄*.
553   d'eschaffaulx] chasteaulx *M*—d'eschaffaulx ... ediffices] craveaulx, d'es-chieres, de trait, d'elravons (?), de bombardes, et de toutes autres choses *P₄*.
554   deffendre] deffendre ma maison *P₂*—les] mes *L, B, P₄*.
555   doubtent] doubteront *M, P₂*.

537–38   *Car ... garder.* Chaucer's omission of this passage (l. 2512) corresponds with the omission in P and P₄ (see *Var.* above), which was caused by scribal error. The passage is present in the Latin (70. 21–23).

541   *ou Livre de Remede d'Amours.* Chaucer omits (l. 2515); the Latin text (71.3) and all French manuscripts have the passage.

542   *qui n'est pas moult grant.* Chaucer omits (l. 2516); the Latin text (71.5) and all French manuscripts have the passage. After the reference to the bull, Chaucer adds: " 'and the wilde hert.' And the book seith, 'A litel thorn may prikke a kyng ful soore.' " This Chaucerian addition is present neither in any of the French manuscripts nor in the Latin text.

545   *enseingnié eulx decevoir.* The Latin helps to clarify the meaning: *Quidam fallere docuerunt, dum falli timent* (71.19–20). M, L, and P₂ read *leur decevoir.*

525 ediffices appartient aucunes foiz a orgueil. Aprés, l'on ⟨fol. 63ʳ⟩ fait
les tours et les grans ediffices a grant travail et a grans despens; et
quant elles sont faites, elles ne valent riens se elles ne sont deffendues
par sages et par bons amis loyaulx et a grans missions. Et pour ce   560
sachiez que la plus grant garnison et la plus fort que uns riches homs
puisse faire a garder son corps et ses biens, c'est qu'il soit amez de
ses subgez et de ses voisins. Quar Tulles dit, 'Une garnison que l'on ne
530 puet vaincre ne desconfire est l'amour des citiens.'

"Quant au tiers point, ou li sage et li ancien dirent que l'on ne   565
doit point aler en ceste besoingne soudainnement ne hastivement,
mais se doit l'on pourveoir et appareillier a grant diligence et a grant
deliberacion, je croy qu'ilz parlent bien et saigement. Car Tulles dit,
'En toutes besongnes devant c'om les commence, on se doit appareillier
a grant diligence.' En vengence, donques, en guerre, en bataille, et   570
535 en garnison faire, devant ce que on encommence, on doit faire son
appareil en grant deliberacion. Car Tulles dit, 'Long appareillement
de bataille fait brief victoire.' Et Cassidoires dit, 'La garnison est
plus puissant quant elle est de long temps pensee.'

"Or couvient aler au conseil que te donnerent tes voisins qui te   575
540 portent reverence senz amour, tes ennemis reconciliez, les losengers,
ceulz qui te conseilloient d'une chose en secret et disoient autre en
appert, les jeunes gens qui tuit te conseilloient de toy vengier tantost
et faire guerre incontinent. Et certes, ainsi comme je t'ay dit dessus, tu
erras moult en appeller ces gens a ton conseil, lequel conseil est assez   580
reprouvé par les choses dessus dictes. Toutevoie, puis que elles sont
dictes en general, nous descendrons en especial. Or veons, donques,

P₃.   567–70   et a grant … diligence] *om.* (et a grant … diligence L *and* [*with variants*] M, B, P, P₂, P₄).

(**Var.**)   557–58   fait … ediffices] les fait *P₄*.
562   faire] avoir M, L, B, P, P₂, faire et avoir *P₄*.
564   est] c'est M.
568   parlent] parlerent M, B, P, P₂, P₄.
580   ces] telles M, L, B, P₂, P₄.

558   *et les grans ediffices.* This phrase, lacking in the Chaucer manuscripts, has
been supplied by editors of Chaucer from the French source. But cf. P₄ in the
variants above. The phrase is also lacking in the Latin text (73.2), though the
Latin in this passage is much fuller than the French version or Chaucer's translation.

560   *et a grans missions.* Chaucer omits (l. 2526); the Latin text (73.5) and
all French manuscripts have the passage.

581–82   *puis que … general.* Chaucer omits (l. 2545); the Latin text (76.22)
and all French manuscripts have the passage. Possibly Chaucer's source manuscript was faulty or incomprehensible at this point, for in the rest of l. 2545
Chaucer departs from both Latin and French, omitting and condensing.

2545 premierement, selon ce que dit Tulles, la verité de cest conseil. Et
certes de la verité de ceste besoingne ne couvient pas moult enquerre,
quar l'on scet bien cui sont ceulz qui t'ont fait ceste injure, et combien 5?
ilz sont, et comment et quant et quelle injure il ont faite. Examinons,
donques, la seconde condicion que Tulles met, que il appelle 'consente-
2550 ment': c'est a dire, cui sont ceulz, et combien il sont, qui se consentent
a ton conseil et a ta voulenté. Et considerons aussi cui sont ceulz, et
quans, et quelz, qui se consentent a tes adversaires. Quant au premier, 5?
l'on scet bien quelz gens se consentent a ta voulenté, car tous ceulz
que je t'ay nommé dessus qui conseillent que tu faces guerre tantost.
Or veons, donques, que tu es et cui sont ceux que tu tiens tant a
2555 amis. Quant a ta personne, ja soit ce que tu soies riches et puissans,
toutevoye tu es tout seul et n'as nulz enfans masles, fors une fille 5?
tant seulement. Tu n'as freres ne cousins germains ne nulz autres bien
prouchains amis pour paour desquelz tes ennemis cessent de toy pour-
suivre et destruire. Et ta personne destruite, tu scez bien que tes
2560 richesses se mesleront et se diviseront en diverses parties; et quant
⟨fol. 63ᵛ⟩ chascun aura sa piece, il ne te feront force de vengier ta 6?
mort. Mais tes ennemis sont trois et ont moult d'enfans, de freres,
et d'autres bien prouchains amis desquelz, quant tu en auras occis
deux ou trois, encores en demourront assez qui pourront venger leur
mort et te pourront occirre. Et ja soit ce que tes amis soient trop plus
que les amis de tes adversaires, toutevoye il t'appartiennent moult de 6?
2565 loing, et les amis de tes adversaires leur sont prouchains. Et quant

P₃.   598   tu scez bien] *om.* (tu scez bien *M, L, B, P₂, P₄*).

(**Var.**)   590   premier] premier point *B.*
595   enfans masles] enffans *P₂.*
597   amis] parens *M, P₂,* parens ne amis *P₄.*
598   Et ta personne destruite] *om. L, P₂, P₄.*
599   se mesleront] appetiseront *L, B,* se appetisseront *P₄.*
600   piece] partie *M, P₄.*

591-92   *car ... tantost.* The *car* seems to demand a predicate following *tantost*
to complete the sense, and Chaucer has added such a predicate ("ne been nat youre
freendes" [l. 2554]), though neither the French manuscripts nor the Latin text
(77.19) contains Chaucer's addition. P₂ and M omit the *qui.*

593   *que tu es et.* These words Chaucer omits (l. 2555), although they appear
in all the French manuscripts and in the Latin text (77.20).

594   The pointing here adopted (a new sentence beginning at *Quant*) follows
the sense of the Latin (77.22) and the capitalization found in P₃. Chaucer took
quant a ta personne to belong to the preceding sentence (l. 2555); probably his
source manuscript capitalized *ja.*

595   *masles.* Chaucer omits this word (l. 2557) because his source manuscript
also omitted it (cf. *Var.* above). The Latin original reads *filios masculos* (77.25).

ad ce, leur condicion est meilleur que la tienne. Aprés, veons encores
se le conseil que l'on t'a donné de la vengence tantost prendre se consent a raison. Et certes tu scez que non. Car selon droit nul ne doit
faire vengence d'autrui fors le juge qui a la juridicion sur lui, ja soit ce   610
que vengence soit ottroyee ou promisse a aucun quant on la fait
2570 incontinant et attrempeement selon ce que droit le commende. Aprés,
encor sur ce mot 'consentement,' tu dois regarder se ton povoir se
consent a ta voulenté et a ton conseil. Et certes on puet dire que non.
Car, a parler proprement, nous ne povons a riens fors ce que nous   615
povons faire dehuement et selon droit. Et quar selon droit tu ne doiz
2575 prendre vengence de ta propre auctorité, l'on puet dire que ton povoir
ne se consent point a ta voulenté.

"Or couvient examiner le tiers point, que Tulles appelle 'consequent.' Tu dois, donques, savoir que a la vengence que tu veulz faire   620
est consequent et ensuit autre vengence, peril, et guerre, et moult de
2580 maulx et de dommages lesquelz on ne voit pas maintenant.

"Quant au quart point, que Tulles appelle 'engendrement,' tu dois
savoir que ceste injure est engendree de la hayne de tes ennemis; de
la vengence se engendrera autre vengence, hayne, contens, guerre, et   625
degastemens de tes biens.

"Quant aux causes, qui est la darrenier point que Tulles y met, tu
dois savoir que l'injure qui t'a esté faite a deux causes ouvrieres et
2585 efficaces: la loingtaingne et la prouchainne. La lointaingne est Dieu,
qui est cause de toutes causes. La prouchainne sont tes trois ennemis.   630
La cause accidental fu hayne. La cause material sont les cinq playes
de ta fille. La cause formal fut la maniere de faire l'injure: c'est
2590 assavoir car ilz appoyerent eschieles et entrerent par les fenestres. La

(**Var.**)   608–9   se consent] est accordant P_4.
609   scez] scees bien P_4.
610   faire] prendre L, B, P_4.
614   on puet] tu pues M, P_2, P_4.
620   a la] la P_4.
621–22   moult de maulx] d'autres maulx sans nombre M, P_4, moult d'aultres
maulz sans nombre B, d'autre mal sans nombre et sans mesure L.
624–25   de la vengence] et de la vengence P_4.
629   efficaces] efficiens M, B—loingtaingne et la prouchainne. La lointaingne]
cause lontaine et la cause prouchaine. La cause lontaine P_4.
630   causes] choses P, P_4.
633   appoyerent] apporterent L, B, P_4.

628–29   *ouvrieres ... prouchainne.*   Chaucer here introduces Latin terms
(l. 2585) which, with the exception of *efficiens* (=*efficaces,* 629 above), are not
to be found in the Latin text (82.5–6). Moreover, *efficiens* is to be found also in two
of the French manuscripts (see *Var.* above).

cause final fut car ilz vouldrent occirre ta fille, et pour eulz ne demora.
La cause final lointaingne, a quel fin ilz vendront de ceste besoingne,   63⟨
nous ne la povons pas bien savoir, fors que par conjectures et presumpcions. Car nous devons presumer qu'il en vendront a male fin,
par raison du *Decret* qui dit, 'A grant pene sont menees a bonne fin les
choses qui ⟨fol. 64ʳ⟩ sont mal commencees.'

    "Qui me demanderoit pourquoy Dieu a voulu et souffert que l'on   64⟨
2595 t'a fait tel injure, je n'en sauroye pas bien respondre pour certain.
Quar, selon ce que dit l'apposte, 'La science et le jugement Nostre
Seigneur sont si parfont que nulz ne le puet comprendre ne encercher
souffisamment.' Toutevoyes, par aucunes presumpcions je tien et
croy que Dieu, qui est justes et droiturier, a souffert que ce t'est ad-   64⟨
venu par cause juste et raisonnable.

    "Car tu, qui as nom 'Mellibee' (qui vault autant comme cellui
2600 qui boit le miel), as tant voulu boire de miel (c'est a dire, de la douceur
des biens temporelz, des richesses, des delices, et des honneurs de cest
monde) que tu en as esté tout yvre, et as oublié Dieu ton creatour, ne   65⟨
ne lui as porté honneur ne reverence ainsi comme tu deusses. Tu n'as
pas bien retenu en ton memoire la parole de Ovide, qui dit, 'Dessoubz le miel de la doulceur des biens du corps est estendu le venin
2605 qui occist l'ame.' Et Salemon dit, 'Se tu as trouvé le miel, si en boy a
souffisance; car se tu en menjue oultre mesure, il le te couviendra vo-   65⟨
mir.' Pour ce, par adventure Dieu a eu despit de toy, et a tourné sa
face et les oreilles de sa misericorde d'autre part, et a souffert que tu
as esté prins en la maniere que tu as pechié contre lui. Tu as pechié

    P₃. 648 boit le miel), as] le miel a (boit le miel as *B, P, P₂*)—de miel] *om.* (de
miel *B, P, P₂*).
    652 de Ovide] david (de Ovide *L, P, P₂*, d'Ovide *P₄*, Ovide *M, B*).

    (Var.) 635 La cause final lointaingne] Mais la cause final loingtaine *M, L,
B, P₄*, mais la cause lontaigne *P*.
    636–37 presumpcions] par presumpts *M, P, P₄*.
    639 choses] causes *P*.
    641 tel] ceste *P₂*.
    642 le jugement] les jugemens *L, P₄*, li jugement *B*.
    642–43 Nostre Seigneur] de Dieu *P₄*.
    643 si parfont que] parfont *P*—le puet] les puet *L, B, P, P₂, P₄*.
    646 juste et] juste *P*.
    647 qui as] as *P*—autant] autant a dire *L, B, P₄*.
    653 estendu] abscondu *M*, esconduz *P*, repost *L, P₂*, repus *B*.
    654 boy] mengue *M, L, B, P, P₂, P₄*.
    656 a eu despit de toy, et] en despit de toy *M*.
    658 prins] pugnis *L, B, P, P₄*.

    655–56 *vomir.* Chaucer clarifies by adding "and be nedy and povre" (l. 2607),
an expression lacking in both French and Latin (84.6).

2610 contre Nostre Seigneur; car les trois ennemis de l'umain linage, qui
sont le monde, la char, et les dyables, tu les as laissié entrer en ton   660
cuer tout franchement par les fenestres du corps senz toy deffendre
souffisamment contre leurs assaulx et leurs temptations, en tel maniere
qu'il ont navré l'ame de toy de cinq playes, c'est a dire, de tous les
pechiez mortelz, qui entrerent au cuer par les cinq sens du corps. Par
ceste semblance Nostre Seigneur a voulu et souffert que ces trois en-   665
2615 nemis sont entré en ta maison par les fenestres et ont navré ta fille en
la maniere dessus ditte."

"Certes," dist Mellibee, "je voy bien que vous vous efforciez moult
par doulces paroles de moy encliner ad ce que je ne me venge point de
mes ennemis, et m'avez monstré moult sagement les perilz et les maulx   670
qui pourront avenir de ceste vengence. Mais qui voudroit considerer
en toutes vengences touz les perilz et les maulx qui s'en pevent ensuir,
2620 l'on ne feroit jamés vengence; et ce seroit moult grant dommage, car
par vengence les mauvais sont ostez d'entre les bons, et ceulz qui ont
cuer de mal faire se retraient quant ilz voient que l'on punit les mal-   675
faiteurs."

Ad ce respont Dame Prudence: "Certes," dist elle, "je vous ottroye que de venge vient moult de biens, mais faire vengence n'appartient pas a un chascun fors seulement aus juges et a ceulz qui ont
la juridicion sur les malfaiteurs. Et dy plus que aussi comme une per-   680
2625 sonne singuliere ⟨fol. 64ᵛ⟩ pecheroit en faisant vengence, aussi pecheroit le juge en laissant faire vengence. Car Senecques dit, 'Celui nuit
aus bons qui espargne les mauvais.' Et selon ce que dit Cassidoires,
'L'on doubte faire les oultrages quant on scet qu'il desplait aus juges

P₃.   663   tous les] tous (tous les *M, L, B, P, P₂, P₄*).
669   encliner] entamer (encliner *M, L, B, P, P₂, P₄*).

(Var.)   660   les dyables] le deable *M, L, B, P, P₂, P₄*.
661   du] de ton *P₄*.
663   de cinq] en cinq *L, B*—de tous] tous *L*.
665   ces] tes *P₂, P₄*.
677–80   Ad ce ... malfaiteurs] *om. P*.
682   vengence. Car] vengence des delinquens Car *P₄*.

677–80 *Ad ce ... malfaiteurs.* This passage is missing in all the Chaucer
manuscripts; editors of Chaucer have been wont to supply it from the French
source. Since, however, the passage is also missing in P (see *Var.* above) through
scribal error, it seems likely that Chaucer's source manuscript did not contain it,
and that therefore Chaucer did not include it in his translation. It is found in the
Latin (86.24–87.4).

682–83 *Celui ... mauvais.* The French here accurately rephrases the Latin:
Bonis nocet, qui malis parcit (87.9). Chaucer's translation is highly inaccurate
(l. 2627).

et aus souverains.' Et uns autres dit, 'Le juge qui doubte faire les   685
droiz fait les mauvais.' Et Saint Pol l'Appostre dit en l'*Epistre aux*
2630 *Rommains* que le juge ne porte pas le glaive senz cause, mais le porte
pour punir les mauvais et pour deffendre les prodommes. Se tu veulz,
donques, avoir vengence de tes ennemis, tu recourras au juge qui a la
juridicion sur eulx, et il les punira selon droit et encores s'il ont des-   690
servi en leur avoir en telle maniere qu'il demourront pouvre et vivront
a honte."

"He!" dist Mellibee, "ceste vengence ne me plait point. Je regarde
que fortune m'a norri des mon enfance et m'a aidié a passer moult de
2635 fors pas. Je la vueil maintenant essayer, et croy que a l'aide de Dieu   695
elle m'aidera a vengier ma honte."

"Certes," dist Prudence, "se tu veulz ouvrer de mon conseil, tu
n'essaieras point fortune ne ne t'apuyeras a elle. Car, selon le dit de
Senecques, 'Les choses se font folement qui se font en esperance de
fortune.' Car, selon ce qu'il mesmes dit, 'Fortune est une verriere qui   700
de tant comme elle est plus belle et plus clere et resplendissant, de
2640 tant est elle plus tost brisee.' Et pour ce ne te fie point en fortune; car
elle n'est point estable, et la ou tu cuideras estre plus seurs de son aide,
elle te faudra. Et quar fortune t'a norri de ton enfance, je dy que de
tant tu te doiz mains fier en lui et en ton sens. Car Senecque dit que   705
2645 celui que fortune nourrit trop, elle le fait fol. Puis, donques, que tu

P₃. 686 aux] des (aux *L, M, B, P, P₂, P₄*).
691   leur] eulx (leur *M, L, B*).
693   Mellibee] Mallibee (Mellibee *M, L, B, P*).
706   fortune] nature (fortune *M, L, B; P, P₂, P₄*).

(**Var.**)   686   les] les gens *M*.
688   prodommes] bons *P₄*.
689   recourras] retourneras *P₂*.
699   choses] choses qui *P₂*.
701   belle et plus] *om. M, L, B, P, P₂, P₄*.
702   te fie point en fortune] t'y fie point *M, P₂*.
704   Et quar] quant tu dis que *L, B, P₂*, et quant tu diz *P*, et quant diz que
P₄, et pour ce que tu dis que *M*.
705   lui] elle *M, B, P₄*, li *P₂*—ton] son *P₄*.
706   trop] *om. L, P₂*—fol] trop fol *L, P₂*.

690–92 *et encores ... honte.* Chaucer omits this passage (l. 2633); yet all
French manuscripts have it, and its equivalent appears in the Latin (88.18–23).

700 *Fortune est une verriere qui.* Chaucer omits this passage (l. 2640). Although all the French manuscripts have it, no two have it in the same form.
Apparently the passage gave the scribes difficulty, and hence even may have been
incomprehensible in Chaucer's source manuscript. The Latin has the passage
(89.12–13).

demandes vengence, et la vengence qui se fait selon l'ordre de droit et devant le juge ne te plait, et la vengence qui se fait en esperance de fortune est perilleuse et n'est point certainne, tu n'as remede fors que retourner au souverain et vray Juge qui venge toutes les villenies et   710 injures, et il te vengera selon ce qu'il mesmes tesmoingne: 'A moy,'
2650 dit il, 'laisse la vengence, et je la feray.'"

Mellibee respondit: "Se je," dit il, "ne me venge de la villenie que l'on m'a faite, je semondray ceulz qui la m'ont faite et tous autres a moy faire une autre nouvelle villenie. Car il est escript, 'Se tu   715 sueffres senz venger la vieille villenie, tu semons a la nouvelle.' Et ainsi pour mon souffrir l'on me fera tant de villenies de toutes pars que je ne le pourray souffrir ne porter; ains seray au bas du tout en
2655 tout. Car il est escript, 'En moult souffrant, ⟨fol. 65ʳ⟩ t'avendront pou de choses que souffrir ne pourras.'"   720

"Certes," dit Prudence, "je vous ottroye que trop grant souffrance n'est bonne, mais pour ce ne s'ensuit pas que chascune personne a cui l'on fait injure en doye prendre vengence, car ce appartient aus juges tant seulement, qui ne doivent pas souffrir que les villenies et les in-   725 jures ne soient vengees. Et pour ce les deux auttoritez que tu as mises
2660 avant sont entendues tant seulement des juges que, quant ilz souffrent trop faire les injures et les villenies senz punicion, ilz ne semonnent pas tant seulement les nouvelles injures, mais les commandent. Ainsi le dit un sage: 'Le juge,' dit il, 'qui ne corrige le pecheur lui commande a pechier'; et pourroient bien tant souffrir les juges et les souverains de   730 maulx en leur terre que les malfaiteurs les getteroient hors de leur
2665 terre et de leurs lieux, et leur couvendroit perdre en la fin leurs seignories.

"Mais or posons que tu ayes licence de toy vengier. Je dy que tu n'as pas la puissance quant a present; car se veulz faire comparoison de   735

P₃.   707   et la vengence] *om.* (et la vengence *M, L, B, P, P₂*).

(**Var.**)   709–10   que retourner] de recourir *B*, que de recourre *P*, que de toy retourner et avoir recours *P₄*.
      717   ainsi] aussi *P, P₂*—fera] feroit *M, P₂*—villenies] villenie *P₂*.
      720   pou] moult *L, B, P₄*, prou *P*.
      722   s'ensuit] s'ensuit il *M, B, P₂*.
      723   en doye prendre] en prenge *P*.
      724   qui] car ilz *L, B, P₂, P₄*, car *P*.
      726   que, quant] car quant *L, B, P₄*.
      728   les nouvelles injures] faire les nouvelles injures *B, P, P₂*, faire les injures *M, L*, faire lesdits injures *P₄*.

_____
      717   *de toutes pars.* Chaucer omits (l. 2654). All French manuscripts have the passage; the Latin has *undique* (91.20).

ta puissance a la puissance de tes adversaires, tu trouveras en trop de
choses, selon ce que je t'ay monstré dessus, leur condicion meilleur que
la teue. Et pour ce je dy qu'il est bon quant a maintenant de toy
2670 souffrir et avoir patience.

"Aprés, tu scez que l'on dit communément que contendre a plus   740
fort est enragerie; contendre a egal est peril; contendre a mendre est
honte. Et pour ce l'on doit fuir tout contens tant comme l'on puet.
Car Salemon dit qu'il est grant honneur a homme qui se scet getter de
2675 brigue et de contemps. Et se plus fort de toy te grieve, estudie toy
plus en lui appaisier que en toy vengier. Car Senecque dit que celui   745
se met en grant peril qui se courrouce a plus fort de lui. Et Cathon dit,
'Se plus fort de toy te grieve, sueffre toy, car cellui qui t'a une foiz
2680 grevé te pourra une autre foiz aidier.' Or posons que tu ayes licence et
puissance de toy venger; je dy encores que moult de choses sont qui te
doivent retraire et te doivent encliner a toy souffrir et avoir pacience   750
en l'injure que l'on t'a faite et es autres tribulations de cest monde:
premierement, se tu veulx considerer les deffaulx qui sont en toy, pour
lesquelz Dieu a voulu souffrir que ceste tribulacion te soit advenue,
2685 selon ce que je t'ay dit dessus. Car li poetes dit que nous devons porter
en pacience les tribulations qui nous viennent, quant nous pensons   755
que nous les avons bien desservies. Et Saint Gregoire dit que quant un
chascun considere bien le grant nombre des deffaulx et de ses pechiez,
les penes et les tribulations qu'il sueffre ⟨fol. 65ᵛ⟩ lui apperent plus
petites; et de tant comme ses pechiez lui semblent plus pesans, de tant

P₃. 750   te doivent encliner] encliner (te doivent encliner *M, L, B, P, P₂, P₄*)—
pacience] pacience en toy souffrir (pacience *M, L, B, P, P₂, P₄*).
751   et es] es (et es *B, P, P₄*, et aux *M, L, P₂*).
758   il sueffre] ilz sueffrent (il sueffre *M, L, B, P, P₄*, il souffri *P₂*).

(**Var.**)   737   condicion] condicion est *M, P₂*.
740   scez] sces bien *B, P₄*.
741   fort] fort de lui *B*, fort que soy *P₂*, fort de soy *P₄*—enragerie] enragerie et
P₄—egal] egal de soy *P₂*—est peril] c'est peril *M*, est peril et *B, P₄*.
741–42   est honte] c'est honte *M*.
744   brigue] noise *P*.
746   courrouce] contence *P₂*.
748–49   licence et puissance] puissance et licence *P₂, P₄*.
751   que l'on t'a faite] qui t'a esté faicte *M, P₂*.
753   voulu souffrir] souffert *L, B, P₄*.
756   bien desservies] desservies *M, P₂, P₄*.
757   grant] *om. P*—des] de ses *M, P, P₂, P₄*.

751   *et es … monde.* Chaucer omits (l. 2683). All French manuscripts have the
passage. It is lacking in the Latin, for the French adaptation differs considerably
from the Latin at 748–72 (corresponding to Chaucer's ll. 2681–2700).

2690 sa pene lui semble plus legiere. Aprés, moult te doit encliner a pa-   760
cience, la pacience de Nostre Seigneur Jhesu Crist, selon ce que dit
Saint Pierre en ses epistres. 'Jhesu Crist,' dit il, 'a souffert pour nous
et a donné a un chascun exemple de lui ensuivre. Car il ne fist onques
pechié, ne onques de sa bouche ne yssi une villenie. Quant on le maudisoit, il ne maudisoit point; quant on le batoit, il ne menaçoit point.'   765
Aprés, moult te doit encliner a pacience, la grant pacience des sains
qui sont en Paradis, qui ont eu si grant pacience es tribulations qu'ilz
2695 ont souffert senz leur coulpe. Aprés, moult te doit encliner a pacience
ce que les tribulacions de cest monde durent tres petit de temps et sont
tantost passees, et la gloire que l'on acquiert pour avoir pacience est   770
pardurable, selon ce que l'appostre en l'epistre seconde dit a ceulz de
2699 Corinte. Aprés, tien fermement que celui n'est pas bien enseingnié qui
ne scet avoir pacience. Car Salemon dit que la doctrine de l'omme est
cogneue par pacience. Et autre part il mesmes dit que cellui qui est
pacient se gouverne par grant prudence. Et lui mesmes dit, 'L'omme   775
qui est courreceux fait les noises, et le pacient les attrempe.' Aussi dit
2705 il que mieux vault estre bien pacient que bien fort, et plus fait a priser
celui qui puet avoir la seignorie de son cuer que cellui qui par force
prent les grans citez. Et pour ce dit Saint Jaques en son epistre que
pacience est euvre de perfeccion."   780

(**Var.**)   761   la pacience] *om. P₄.*
763   a un chascun exemple] exemple a un chascun *M, L, B, P, P₂, P₄.*
764   villenie] villainne parolle *P₂.*
770   pacience] pacience es tribulations *M, P, P₂.*
771   seconde] *om. L, B.*
771–72   dit ... tien] le scripture raconte et tesmoingne *P₂.*
772   tien] croy *P₄.*
774   qui est] *om. M, L, B, P, P₂, P₄.*
776   attrempe] apaise et attempre *P₂.*
778   force] sa force *B,* sa grant force *P₄.*

---

772   *Corinte.* Chaucer omits the name of the epistle, but adds a direct quotation from it (ll. 2699–2700). The whole reference is lacking in the Latin (93.19–
94.15).

774   *par pacience.* In P₂ and M the following passage occurs after *pacience:
et* [P₂ omits *et*] *nostre Seigneur dit que patience vaint; et encores dit que en nostre
patience* [P₂ reads *encore em pacience*] *nous possiderons* [P₂ reads *procederons*]
nos ames. Chaucer does not have the passage (l. 2702), nor does it occur in the
other French manuscripts, L, B, P, P₃, P₄. Neither is it present in the Latin
(94.18). Its absence from the Latin, however, ought not be interpreted to indicate
that the passage is a spurious, scribal addition, for in the section immediately
preceding the passage under discussion Renaud de Louens has added numerous
sentences not found in his Latin original (see preceding note on 751).

"Certes," dit Mellibee, "je vous ottroye que pacience est une tres grant vertu et de grant parfeccion, mais chascun ne puet pas avoir la parfeccion que vous alez querant. Je ne suy pas du nombre des bien 2710 parfaiz, et pour ce mon cuer ne puet estre en paix jusques a tant qu'il soit vengez. Et ja soit ce que en ceste vengence eust grant peril, je 785 regarde que aussi avoit il grant peril a faire la villenie qui m'a esté faite, et toutesvoies mes adversaires n'ont pas regardé le peril, mais ont hardiement acomplie leur mauvaise voulenté. Et pour ce il me semble que l'on ne me doit pas reprendre se je me met en un po de peril pour moy venger et se je faiz un grant excés. Car l'on dit que 790 excés ne se corrige que par excés; c'est a dire, que oultrage ne se corrige 2715 fors que par oultrage."

"He!" dist Dame Prudence, "vous dictes vostre voulenté, mais certes en cas du monde l'on ne doit faire oultrage par excés pour soy venger ne autrement. Car Cassidoires dit que aussi mal fait celui qui 795 se venge par oultrage comme celui qui fait l'outrage. Et pour ce vous vous devez venger selon l'ordre de droit, non pas par excés ne par oultrage. Car auxi comme vous savez que voz adversaires ⟨fol. 66ʳ⟩ ont pechié encontre vous par leur oultrage, aussi pechiez vous se vous vous voulez venger d'eulz par oultrage et autrement que droit le com- 800 2720 mande. Et pour ce dit Senecques, 'L'on ne doit nul temps venger mauvaitié par mauvaistié.' Et se vous dictes que droit ottroye que l'on

(**Var.**)   781   ottroye] ottroye dame Prudence *M*, *P*, *P₂*.
781–82   une tres grant] une grant *M*, *P*, *P₂*.
785   en ceste vengence eust grant peril] ce soit grans perilz a faire la vengance *B*.
785–86   je regarde ... grant peril] *om. P*.
790–91   Car l'on ... par excés] *om. L*.
794   certes en] en nul *M*—par] ne *M, L, B, P₂, P₄*.
797   non] et non *P₄*.
798–99   auxi comme ... leur oultrage] *om. P*.
800   d'eulz par] de leur *P*.

785–86 *je regarde ... grant peril.* Chaucer omits (l. 2712); hence his source manuscript was probably like P, which also omits this passage (see *Var.* above). Though the passage is not present in the Latin (95.28 ff.), it undoubtedly belongs in the authentic French version. Its omission in P is a scribal blunder due to eyeskip.

790–91 *Car ... par excés.* Chaucer, like L (see *Var.* above), omits this passage. The Latin has it (96.5–7).

795 *ne autrement.* Chaucer omits (l. 2717). All French manuscripts contain the expression. Since the French adaptor is at this point condensing his original, no equivalent exists in the Latin (96.8–16).

798–99 *auxi ... leur oultrage.* Chaucer, like P (see *Var.* above), omits this passage. It is present in the Latin (96.19).

deffende violence par violence et barat par barat, certes c'est verité quant la deffense se fait incontinent senz intervalle et pour soy deffendre, non pas pour soy venger, et se il couvient mettre telle attrempance en deffense que l'on ne puisse reprendre celui qui se deffent d'excés ne d'outrage, car autrement ce seroit contre droit et raison. Or voys tu bien que tu ne fais pas deffense incontinent ne pour toy deffendre, mais pour toy venger; et si n'as pas voulenté de faire ton fait attrempeement. Et pour ce il me semble encores que la pacience est bonne; car Salemon dit que celui qui est impacient y aura dommage."

2725

805

810

"Certes," dist Mellibee, "je vous ottroye que quant un homme est impacient et courrouciez de ce qui ne lui touche et qui ne lui apparti-ent, se dommage lui en vient, il n'est pas merveille. Car la rigle de droit dit que celui est coulpables qui s'entremet de ce qui ne li apparti-ent point. Et Salemon dit es *Proverbes* que celui qui s'entremet de la noise d'autruy est semblables a celui qui prent le chien par les oreilles qu'il ne cognoit: aucune foiz le chien le mort. Aussi est il raison que dommage viengne a cellui qui par impacience et courroux se mesle de la noise d'autrui qui riens ne lui appartient. Mais vous savez bien que ce fait me touche moult de pres. Et pour ce j'en suy courrouciez et impacient, et n'est pas merveille. Et si ne voy pas, sauve vostre grace, que grant dommage me puisse venir de moy venger. Car je suy plus riche et plus puissant que ne sont mes adversaires; et vous savez

2730

2735

815

820

P₃. 816   es *Proverbes*] ou proverbe (es Proverbes *M, P, P₂*).

(**Var.**) 805   non] et non *L, P₄*.
808   ne pour] pour *P₂*.
811   est impacient] n'est pas patient *M, P₂*, n'est patient *P*.
818   qu'il ne ... mort] Car ainsi comme celui qui tient le chien estrange qui ne congnoit si est aucune fois mors du chien *P₂*, Et aussi comme cellui qui tient le chien estange qu'il ne congnoist est aucune fois mors du chien *M*.
821–22   j'en ... impacient, et] se je sui courrouciés et impatiens *B, P*.
824   savez] savez bien *M, P₂*.

816   *es Proverbes*. Chaucer omits (l. 2732). The phrase is present in both Latin (95.13) and French.

818   *qu'il ne ... mort*. P₂ and M expand and alter this passage (see *Var.* above). Chaucer's source manuscript contained the expanded, altered reading. Most of Melibeus' speech in which this passage occurs, and the last sentence of Prudence's preceding speech (810–23), are additions by the French adaptor and therefore have no equivalent in the Latin original at this point (97.7); but Renaud seems to have taken the additions from an earlier passage of the *Liber consolationis* which he had elected to omit from its proper place (cf. *Liber consolationis*, 95.5–15 with *Mel.* 2729–34).

819   *et courroux*. Chaucer omits (l. 2734). It is present in all the French manuscripts, but lacking in the Latin text (95.15).

que par argent et par avoir se gouvernent les choses et le fait de cest   825
2740 monde. Et Salemon dit que toutes choses obeïssent a peccune."

Prudence, quant elle ot oÿ son mary venter de sa richesse et de sa
puissance et despriser la pouvreté de ses adversaires, si dist: "Sire tres
cher, je vous ottroye que vous estes riches et puissans et que les richesses sont bonnes a ceulz qui les ont bien acquises et qui bien en sce-   830
vent user. Car aussi comme le corps ne puet vivre senz l'ame, aussi
ne puet il vivre senz biens temporelz; et par les richesses l'on puet ac-
2745 querre les grans lignages et les grans amis. Et pour ce dit Pemphiles:
'Se la fille d'un bovier est riche, elle puet eslire de mil hommes lequel
qu'elle veult pour mary; car de mil on ne li en refusera pas un.' Et Pam-   835
philes mesmes dit, 'Se tu es amé,—c'est a dire, riches,—tu trouveras
grant nombre de compagnons ⟨fol. 66ᵛ⟩ et d'amis. Et se ta fortune se
2750 change que tu soies pouvres, que tu demourras tout seul!' Et encores
dit Pamphiles que richesses font nobles ceulz qui sont villains de
lignages. Ainsi comme de grans richesses vient moult de biens, aussi   840
de grant povreté vient moult de maulx. Car grant pouvreté contraint
la personne a moult de maulx faire. Et pour ce l'appelle Cassidoires
2755 'mere de crimes.' Et dit aussi Pierre Alphons que l'une des grans adversitez de cest siecle si est quant un homme, franc par nature, est

(**Var.**)   828–29 Sire tres cher] certes tres chier sire *L, B, P*, en ceste maniere
M, P₂.
   830   qui bien] bien *M, P₂*.
   832   par les] par *B*.
   834   fille] fille dist il *P, P₂*.
   835   mary] son mary *M, P₂*.
   836   amé] beneureux *L, M, B, P, P₂*.
   839   richesses font] par richesses sont *M, L, B, P₂*.
   840   Ainsi] et ainsi *M*, et aussi *L, B, P₂*.
   841   grant povreté] povreté *L, B, P*.
   843   dit aussi] pour ce dist *B, P, P₂*—que l'une] une *M, B, P, P₂*.

---

   833 *les grans lignages et.* Chaucer omits (l. 2745). All French manuscripts
(except P₄, which has a lacuna at this point) and the Latin original (98.7–8) have
the expression.

   838 *que tu demourras tout seul!* Chaucer greatly expands this clause (ll. 2749–
50). Cf. *Knight's Tale*, 2779, and *Miller's Tale*, 3204. The whole quotation is
lacking in the Latin (98.12).

   843 *crimes.* Chaucer has "ruyne" (l. 2754). All the French manuscripts
(except P₄, which here has a lengthy lacuna) read *crimes;* the Latin reads *criminum*
(99.5). It seems likely that Chaucer's source manuscript was corrupt in this passage.

contraint par povreté de mengier l'aumosne a son ennemi. Et la   845
raison de ce dit Saint Innocent en un sien livre: 'Doulente et meschant
est la condicion des povres mendians: s'il ne demandent, ilz muerent
de fain; s'ilz demandent, ilz muerent de honte; et toutevoie neccessité
2760 les contraint a demander.' Et pour ce dit Salemon que mieux vault
morir que avoir tele povreté; car, selon ce qu'il dit autre part, 'Mieux   850
vault la mort amere que tele vie.' Par ces raisons que je t'ay dictes,
et par moult d'autres que dire pourroye, je te ottroye que bonnes sont
les richesses a ceulz qui bien les acquierent et qui bien en usent. Et
pour ce je te vueil monstrer comment tu te dois avoir en amassant les
2765 richesses et en usant d'elles.   855

"Premierement, tu les dois acquerre non mie ardamment, mais a
loisir et attrempeement par mesure. Car l'omme qui est trop ardans
d'acquerre richesses se habandonne legierement a tous vices et a touz
autres maulx. Et pour ce dit Salemon, 'Qui trop se haste de soy en-
richir, il ne sera pas innocent,' et aussi autre part, que la richesse has-   860
tivement venue hastivement s'en va, mais celle qui est venue petit et
2770 petit se croist tousjours et se multiplie. Aprés, tu dois acquerir les
richesses par ton sens et par ton labour a ton proffit et senz dommage
d'autrui. Car la loy dit que nulz ne se face riches au dommage d'autruy. Et Tulles dit que doulour, paour, mort, ne autre chose qui puisse   865
2775 advenir a homme n'est tant contre nature comme accroistre sa ri-

P₃.   864–65 Car la loy … d'autruy] om. P₃ (Car la loy … d'autruy M, P, P₂).

(Var.)   845   a] de M, P, P₂.
846   Saint] om. M, L, B, P, P₂—Doulente] doulente dist il L, B, dolente dit P.
847   des povres mendians] du povre mendiant L, B, de povre mendiant P—
il ne demandent, ilz muerent] il ne demande il meurt L, B, P, P₂.
848   ilz demandent, ilz muerent] il demande il meurt L, B, P.
849   les] le L, B, P, P₂.
850   avoir] porter L, B.
857   et attrempeement] attempreement et B.
860   aussi] dit aussi M, L, B, P, P₂—autre part] om. L, B.
863   labour] travail M, L, B, P, P₂.

845   mengier. A scribal error which Chaucer followed (l. 2757). The true
reading is either mendier (M) or demander (L), for the Latin original reads postulare
(99.11).

864–65   dommage d'autruy. Chaucer here adds a sentence (l. 2774) present in
neither French nor Latin originals; but the addition is nothing but a restatement
and clarification of the preceding sentence of his translation.

chesse ou dommage et prejudice d'autrui. Et Cassidoires dit que vouloir acroistre sa richesse de ce petit que le povre mandiant a, surmonte
toute cruauté. Et pour ce que tu les puisse acquerre plus loyaument,
tu ne dois pas estre oiseux ne pareceux de faire ton proffit, mais dois   870
fuir toute oisiveté. Car Salemon dit que oisiveté enseingne faire moult
de maulx, et dit autre part que celui qui traveille et cultive sa terre
2780 mengera du pain, mais celui qui est oiseux cherra en povreté et mourra
de fain. Celui qui est oiseux et pareceux ne treuve nulz temps couve-
nable a faire son proffit. Car selon ce que dit un versifieur, 'Il se excuse   875
en l'iver de ce qu'il fait trop froit, et en l'esté de ce qu'il fait trop
chaut.' Pour ces causes dit Cathon: ⟨fol. 67ʳ⟩ 'Veille,' dit il, 'souvent,
ne t'abandonne a trop dormir, car li trop grans repox norrist les vices.'
Et pour ce dit Saint Innocent: 'Fay tousjours aucunes bonnes euvres
2785 pour ce que l'ennemi te trueuve occuppé.' Car li ennemis ne prent pas   880
legierement en son euvre ceulx qu'il treuve occupez en bonnes euvres.

"En acquerant, donques, les richesses, tu dois fuir oisiveté. Aprés,
des richesses que tu auras acquises par ton sens et par ton travail et
deuement, tu dois user en tele maniere que tu ne soies tenuz pour trop
2790 eschars ne pour trop larges. Car aussi comme fait a blasmer avarice,   885
aussi fait a reprendre fole largesse. Et pour ce dit Cathon: 'Use des

P₃.   869   toute] toute toute (toute *M, P, P₂,* toutes *L, B, P₄*).
876   fait trop froit] fait en trop froit *with* en *underdotted for deletion.*
880   te] ne te (te *L, P, P₄*).
881   son euvre ceulx qu'il treuve occupez] semences qu'il trueuve occupees
(son euvre ceulx qu'il treuve occupez *P,* son euvre celui qui trouve occupés *P₂,*
son euvre celluy qui est occupé *M*).

(**Var.**)   866–67   richesse] prouffit *L, B, P, P₄*.
867   et prejudice] *om. M, L, B, P, P₄*.
874   Celui] Et cellui *L*—ne] et ne *M, L, B, P₂, P₄*.
879   Innocent] Jerosme *L, M, B, P, P₂, P₄*.
883   auras] as *P₂*.
885   trop larges] fol larges *M, L, B, P, P₂, P₄*.
886   reprendre] blasmer et reprendre *M, P₂*—Cathon] Caton *M, P₂*—Use]
Use dist il *B, P, P₂*.

867–69   *Et ... cruauté.* Chaucer omits (l. 2776). The passage is present in all
French manuscripts, except P₂, in which part of it is present (P₂ omits *ou dommage
... sa richesse* [867–68]).

869   *Et pour ... loyaument.* No French manuscript gives a reading like Chaucer's "And though the grete men and the myghty men geten richesses moore lightly than thou" (l. 2777). P reads: *Et pour ce que les puisses acquerre plus loyaument.*
Chaucer's "the grete men and the myghty men" might have come by error from
a manuscript reading *les puisses* (with a nasal symbol over the *e*?); and *loyaument*
might easily have been corrupted into *legierement* to give Chaucer's "lightly."
The Latin original (which here is *De amore et dilectione Dei,* MS 1, fol. 43ʳ2) reads:
Opes igitur bonas et Deo placentes acquiras manibus operando.

richesses que tu auras acquises en tele maniere que l'on ne t'appelle
point aver ne chetif'; car il est escript, 'Grant honte est a l'omme qui a
le cuer pouvre et la bourse riche.' Aussi dit il, 'Use des biens que tu
2795 auras acquis sagement, senz mesuser'; car ceulz qui folement degastent   890
ce qu'il ont, quant ilz n'ont plus riens ilz s'abandonnent legerement a
prendre l'autrui. Je dy, donques, que tu dois fuir avarice en usant des
richesses acquises en tele maniere que l'on ne die pas que tes richesses
2800 soient ensevelies, mais que tu les as en ta puissance. Car un sage reprent l'omme aver, et dit ainsi en deux vers: 'Pourquoy homme qui   895
est cendre et que morir couvient, sevelit son avoir par sa grant avarice,
2805 et pourquoy se joint il tant a son avoir que l'on ne l'en puet dessevrer?'
Car quant il mourra il ne l'emportera pas avec soy. Et pour ce dit
Saint Augustin que l'omme aver est semblables a enfer: quant plus devoure, et plus vuelt devorer. Et aussi comment tu te dois avoir en man-   900
iere que l'on ne te nomme ne aver ne chetif, aussi tu te dois garder que
2810 l'on ne te clame pour un fol large. Pour ce dit Tulles: 'Les biens de ton
hostel ne doivent pas estre tant enclox que pitié et debonnaireté ne les
puissent ouvrir, et ne doivent pas estre tant ouvert qu'ilz soient aban-
donnees a un chascun.' Aprés, en acquerant les richesses et en usant   905
d'elles, tu dois tousjours avoir trois choses en ton cuer: c'est assavoir,
2815 Dieu, conscience, et bonne fame. Tu dois, donques, avoir Dieu en ton
cuer; quar pour nulle richesse tu ne dois faire chose qui desplaise a
Dieu ton creatour. Car selon le dit Salemon, 'Mieux vault petit avoir
et de Dieu la paour, que grant tresor acquerre et perdre son Seigneur.'   910
2820 Et le prophete dit que mieux vault estre preudomme et petit avoir,
que estre mauvais et grans richesses avoir. Et aprés, je dy que tu dois

(**Var.**)   887   auras] as P_2, P_4.
888   il est escript, 'Grant honte est] il est grant honte P, P_2, c'est grant honte
L, P_4, B.
890   auras] as P_2—sagement, senz mesuser] par mesure B, a mesure P, saigement et par mesure P_2—degastent] despendent B.
895   aver] avaricieux P_4.
898   ne l'emportera pas] n'emportera riens B.
899–900   quant plus devoure, et] car tant plus devore et tant L.
912   mauvais] mauvais tenus P.

895–96   *Pourquoy ... avarice*. Chaucer alters the order in this passage and adds
"For deeth is the ende of every man as in this present lyf" (ll. 2802–3). His translation of the immediately following lines (897–98) is also somewhat freer than usual.

910   *paour*. Chaucer's translation reads *love* (l. 2818). Yet *paour* appears in
all the French manuscripts (except P_2, which has *povoir*); and *timore* appears in the
Latin original (which here is *De amore et dilectione Dei*, MS 1, fol. 42^{r}1). Probably
Chaucer's source manuscript contained the erroneous reading *amour*.

acquerre et user des richesses sauve tousjours ta conscience. Car l'appostre dit que la chose dont nous devons avoir plus grant gloire si est
quant nostre ⟨fol. 67ᵛ⟩ conscience nous porte bon tesmoingnage. Et 915
le sage dit, 'Bonne est la conscience quant le pechié n'est en la con-
2825 science.' Aprés, en acquerant les richesses et en usant d'elles, tu dois
avoir grant cure et grant diligence comment ta bonne fame soit tousjours gardee. Quar il est escript, 'Le gaaing doit estre nommé perde
qui sa bonne fame ne garde.' Et Salemon dit, 'Mieux vault la bonne 920
renommee que les grans richesses.' Et pour ce il dit autre part, 'Aies
grant diligence de garder ton bon nom et ta bonne fame, car ce te de-
2830 mourra plus que nul tresor grant et precieux.' Et pour ce il ne doit pas
estre dit gentilz homs qui, toutes autres choses arrieres mises aprés
Dieu et conscience, n'a grant diligence de garder sa bonne fame. Et 925
pour ce dit Cassidoires, 'Il est signe de gentil cuer quant il ayme et
desirre bon nom et bonne fame.' Et pour ce dit Saint Augustin, 'Deux
choses te sont neccessaires: bonne conscience et bonne renomee—
2835 bonne conscience pour toy, bonne fame pour ton voisin.' Et celui qui
tant se fie en sa bonne conscience qu'il neglige sa bonne renommee et 930
ne fait force de lui garder, il est cruel et vilain.

"Or t'ay je monstré comment tu te dois porter en acquerant les
richesses et usant d'elles. Et pour ce que vous fiez tant en voz rich-
esces que pour la fiance que vous y avez vous voulez mouvoir guerre et
faire bataille, je vous conseille que vous ne commencez point guerre, 935
2840 car la grant fiance de voz richesses ne souffit point a guerre maintenir.

(**Var.**) 913 et user] *om. B*—Car] Et *P.*
919–20 Quar ... garde] *om. L.*
921 pour ce] certes *M, L, B, P, P₂.*
924 dit] appellés *B.*
925 conscience] bonne conscience *L.*
927–28 Deux ... neccessaires] il sont a toy necessaires deux choses c'est
assavoir *L.*
928 neccessaires] necessaires c'est assavoir *M, B.*
929 toy] toy et *L, B.*
931 et vilain] vilain *L.*
932 les] *om. L.*
936 car la grant fiance] en la fiance d'icelles *L, B,* en la fiance *P, P₂, P₄*—
de voz] car nulles *L, B, P₄.*

919–20 *Quar ... garde.* Since Chaucer omits this passage (l. 2827), his source
manuscript must have been like L, which also omits it (see *Var.* above). The
omission in the French manuscript was caused by scribal error. The passage is
present in the Latin source (which here is *De amore et dilectione Dei*, MS 1, fol.
42ᵛ2).

Pour ce dit un philosophe, 'L'omme qui guerre vuelt avoir n'aura ja a souffisance d'avoir, car de tant comme l'omme est plus riche, de tant lui couvient il faire plus grans missions se il veult avoir honneur et victoire.' Car Salemon dit, 'Plus as de richesses, plus as de despendeurs.' 940 Aprés, tres cher sire, ja soit ce que par voz richesses vous puissiez avoir moult de gens, touteṿoye pour ce ne vous covient pas commencer guerre la ou vous povez autrement avoir paix a vostre honneur et a 2845 vostre proffit. Car la victoire des batailles de cest monde ne gist pas en grant nombre de gens ne en la vertu des hommes, mais en la main et 945 en la voulenté de Dieu. Et pour ce Judas le Macabee, qui estoit chevalier de Dieu, quant il voult combatre contre son adversaire qui avoit plus grant nombre de gens et plus fort qu'il n'avoit, il reconforta 2850 sa petite compagnie et dit: 'Aussi legierement puet donner Dieu victoire a pou de gens comme a moult; car la victoire des batailles ne vient 950 pas du grant nombre des gens, mais vient du ciel.' Et pour ce, tres cher sire, que nul homme n'est certain s'il est digne que Dieu lui doint victoire, ne plus qu'il est certain s'il est digne de l'amour de Dieu ou non, selon ce que dit Salemon, un chascun doit avoir grant paour ⟨fol. 2855 68ʳ⟩ de guerre commencier, et pour ce que es batailles a moult de 955 perilz, et avient aucune foiz que aussi tost occist on le grant comme le plus petit. Car selon ce qu'il est escript ou second *Livre des Roys*, les faiz des batailles sont aventureux et ne sont pas certains: assez legierement fiert li glaives maintenant l'un, ja tantost l'autre. Et pour ce que peril y a et tout sage homme doit fuir peril, l'on doit fuir guerre 960

(Var.)   937   Pour ce] et pour ce P_4.

937–38   a souffisance d'avoir] souffissance P.

938]   l'omme] il P.

940   Car] Et B, P_4—Plus] qui plus L, B, P_4—as] a M, L, B, P, P_2, P_4— as] a M, L, B, P, P_2, P_4.

942   pour ce] *om.* L, B, P, P_4.

943–44   a vostre proffit] prouffit P_4.

945   nombre] multitude P_4.

946   le Macabee] Machabeus M, B, P_2.

949   dit] dit ainsi L—legierement] legierement dit il L, P, P_2.

950   moult] moult de gens L, P, P_2—des batailles] de la bataille P.

957   plus] *om.* M, L, B, P, P_2, P_4.

958   assez] car assez B, P_4.

960   que peril y a] qu'il y a tres grant peril P_4—et tout ... guerre] tous sages homs doit fuir guerre B, P_4, tout homme sage doit fuir les guerres M.

---

953   *ne plus ... Dieu.* Chaucer omits (l. 2854); the passage is present in the French manuscripts, though P_2 omits the idea preceding Chaucer's omission: *digne que Dieu ... s'il est* (952–53 above). The whole sentence containing the passage is omitted in the Latin original (**104.24**).

2860 tant comme l'on puet bonnement. Car Salemon dit, 'Qui ayme le
peril, il cherra ou peril.' "

Aprés ce que Dame Prudence ot parlé, Mellibee respondit: "Je voy
bien," dist il, "dame, que par voz belles paroles et par les raisons que
vous mettez avant, que la guerre ne vous plait point; mais je n'ay pas   965
encor oÿ vostre conseil comment je me doy porter en ceste besoingne."

"Certes," dist elle, "je vous conseille que vous accordez a voz enne-
2865 mis, et que vous ayez paix avec eulx. Car Senecques dit en ses epistres
que par concorde les petites richesses deviennent grans, et par discorde
les grant richesses vont a declin et se fondent tousjours. Et vous savez   970
que uns des souverains biens de cest monde si est paix. Et pour ce dit
Jhesu Crist a ses appostres: 'Bieneurez sont ceulz qui ayment et pour-
2870 chacent paix, car ilz sont appellez enfans de Dieu.' "

"He!" dist Mellibee, "or voy je bien que vous n'amez pas mon honneur. Vous savez que mes adversaires ont commencié le riot et la   975
brigue par leur oultrage, et veez qu'il ne requierent point la paix et ne
demandent pas la reconciliacion. Voulez donques que je me aille
2875 humilier et crier merci? Certes ce ne seroit pas mon honneur. Car
aussi comme l'on dit que trop grant familiarité engendre mesprise-
ment, aussi fait trop grant humilité."   980

Lors Dame Prudence fist semblant d'estre courroucee, et dist:
"Certes, sire, sauve vostre grace, j'aime vostre honneur et vostre
profit comme le mien propre, et l'ay tousjours aymé; et vous ne autres
ne veistes onques le contraire. Et se je vous avoye dit que vous devez
pourchacer la paix et la reconciliacion, je n'auroye pas tant mespris   985
2880 comme il vous semble. Car un sage dit, 'La discencion commence par
autre, la reconciliacion tousjours par toy.' Et le prophete dit, 'Fuy le
mal et fay le bien; quier paix et la pourchace tant comme tu pourras.'
Toutevoye, je ne vous ay pas dit que vous requerez la paix premier que
voz adversaires, car je vous scey bien de si dur cuer que vous ne feriez   990
2885 a piece tant pour moy. Toutevoye, Salemon dit que mal vendra a la
fin a cellui qui a le cuer trop dur."

(**Var.**)   963   ot] ot ainsi *L*, *B*.
964   dame] dame Prudence *M*, *P*—les] vos *L*.
965   mettez] me mettez *P*, moy mettés *P₄*.
967–68   ennemis] adversaires *M*, *B*, *P*, *P₂*, *P₄*.
968   Senecques] Saint Jaques *P*.
971   souverains biens] grans et souverains biens *B*, *P₄*, grans et des souverains
biens *P*, souverains grans biens *P₂*, grans biens et des souverains *L*, grans biens *M*.
978   humilier et] humilier pardevers eulx et leur *L*, *B*, *P₄*.
987   autre] autre et *M*, *L*, *B*, *P₂*, *P₄*.
991   a piece tant] riens *L*—moy] moy et *M*, *L*, *B*, *P*, *P₂*, *P₄*.

Quant Mellibee oÿ Dame Prudence faire semblant de courroux, si dist, "Dame, je vous prie qu'il ne vous desplaise chose que je die, ⟨fol. 68ᵛ⟩ quar vous savez que je suis courreciez, et n'est pas merveille; 995 et ceulz qui sont courrouciez ne scevent pas bien qu'ilz font ne qu'il 2890 dient. Pour ce dit le philosophe que les troublés ne sont pas bien cler voyant. Mais dittes et conseilliez ce qu'il vous plaira, et je suis appareilliez du faire. Et se vous me reprenez de ma folie, je vous en doy plus priser et amer. Car Salemon dit que celui qui reprent durement 1000 cellui qui foloye, il doit trouver plus grant grace envers lui que cellui 2895 qui le deçoipt par douces paroles."

"Je," dist Dame Prudence, "ne fais semblant d'estre yree ne courroucee fors que pour vostre grant profit. Car Salemon dit, 'Mieux vault cil qui le fol reprent et qui lui monstre semblant d'ire, que lui 1005 loer quant il mesprent et de ses grans folies rire.' Et dit aprés, 'Par la 2900 tritesse du visage corrige le fol son courage.'"

Adonques dist Mellibee, "Dame, je ne sauroye respondre a tant de belles raisons comme vous mettez avant. Dictes briefment vostre voulenté et vostre conseil, et je suy prest de l'acomplir." 1010

Lors Dame Prudence lui descouvri toute sa volenté et lui dist ainsi: "Je conseille que vous, devant toutes choses, faites paix a Dieu et vous 2905 reconciliez a lui. Car selon ce que je vous ay dit autresfoiz, il vous a souffert avenir ceste tribulacion pour voz pechiez. Et se vous faites ce, je vous promet de par lui que il amenera voz adversaires a voz piez 1015 et appareillez de faire toute vostre voulenté. Car Salemon dit, 'Quant les voyes de l'omme plaisent a Dieu, il lui convertist ses ennemis et les 2910 contraint de requerre et de demander la paix.' Aprés, je vous prie qu'il vous plaise que je parle a secret a voz adversaires senz faire sem-

P₃.   997   les troublés] li tromble (les troublés M, L, B, P₂, P₄).
1012   choses] om. (choses M, L, B, P, P₂, P₄).

(Var.)   993   oÿ] ot oÿ P.
994   dist] dist ainsi P₄—chose] de chose L, B, P, P₄.
997   philosophe] prophete L, B, P₄—les troublés ne sont] oeil troublé n'est P.
998   dittes] dittez moi B, P₄.
1000   priser et amer] amer et prisier L, P, P₄.
1001   foloye] fait folie M—envers lui] om. P.
1008   Dame] om. L, B.
1009   mettez] moy mettés P₄.
1012   choses] choses que L, B, P₄.
1015   ce ... lui que] ce que je vous promet de par luy P—il] il vous M, L, B, P, P₂, P₄.
1016   toute] om. L, B, P₄.
1018   Aprés] et aprés P₄.
1019   a secret ... adversaires] a voz adversaires en secret P.

blant que ce viengne de vostre consentement; et lors quant je verray 1020
et sauray leur voulenté, je vous pourray conseiller plus seurement."

2915 "Faites, dame," dist Mellibee, "vostre voulenté, quar je met tout
mon fait en vostre disposicion."

Lors Dame Prudence, quant elle vit la bonne voulenté de son mary,
si ot deliberation en soy mesmes et pensa comment elle pourroit mener 1025
ceste besoingne a bonne fin. Et quant elle vit qu'il fu temps, elle manda les adversaires en lieu secret, et leur proposa sagement les grans
2920 biens qui sont en paix et les grans perilz qui sont en guerre, et leur
enseigna moult doulcement comment ilz se devoient repentir de l'injure qu'ilz avoient faite a Mellibee son seigneur, et a elle, et a sa fille. 1030

Quant ceulz oïrent les doulces paroles de Dame Prudence, ilz furent
si surprins et orent si grant joye que nul ne le pourroit extimer. "He!
Dame Prudence," dirent il, "vous nous avez denoncié en la beneÿson
2925 de doulceur, selon ce que dit David le Prophete; car la reconciliacion
⟨fol. 69ʳ⟩ dont nous ne sommes pas digne et que nous deussions re- 1035
querre a grant devocion et a grant humilité, vous par vostre doulceur la
nous avez presentee. Or veons nous bien que la sentence Salemon est
vraye, qui dit que la douce parole multiplie les amis et fait debonnaire
2930 les ennemis.

"Certes," dirent il, "nous mettons nostre fait en vostre voulenté, et 1040
sommes appareillié en tout et par tout obeïr au dit et commandement
de Monseigneur Mellibee. Et pour ce, tres chere dame et benigne,
nous vous requerons et prions tant humblement comme nous povons
plus, qu'il vous plaise acomplir par fait voz doulces paroles. Toutevoye, tres chiere dame, nous considerons et cognoissons que nous avons 1045
2935 offendu Messire Mellibee oultre mesure et plus que nous ne pourrions
amender. Et pour ce, se nous obligons nous et noz amis a faire sa voulenté et son commandement, par adventure il, comme courrouciez, nous
donra tele painne que nous ne la pourrons porter ne acomplir. Et pour
2940 ce, plaise vous en ce fait avoir tel advisement que nous et noz amis ne 1050
soyons desheritez et perduz par nostre folie."

"Certes," dist Prudence, "il est dure chose et perilleuse que uns

(Var.) 1020–21 verray et] *om. M, L, B, P, P₂, P₄.*
1022 Faites ... Mellibee] Dame dist il faites *P, P₄.*
1026 qu'il fu] son *P₂.*
1033 Prudence] *om. M, P₂—*denoncié en] avancé *P₄.*
1036 vostre] vostre grant *M, L, B, P₂, P₄.*
1040 voulenté] bonne voulenté *M, B, P.*
1042 dame et benigne] et benigne dame *P₄.*
1047 se] *om. M, L, P, P₂, P₄—*sa] toute sa *M, B, P, P₂, P₄.*
1048 par] mais par *M, P₄—*courrouciez] ire contre noz *P₄.*
1050 plaise] **dame plaise** *P₄—*nous et] nous ne *B, P, P₄.*

homs se commette du tout en l'arbitrage et en la puissance de ses ennemis. Car Salemon dit, 'Oyez moy,' dit il, 'tuit pueple et toutes gens et
gouverneurs d'Eglise: a ton fil, a ta femme, a ton frere, a ton cousin, 1055
945 et a ton amy, ne donne puissance sur toy en toute ta vie.' Se il a, donques, deffendu que l'on ne doint point puissance sur soy a son ami,
par plus fort raison il deffent que l'on ne la donne pas a son ennemi.
Toutevoye, je vous donne conseil que vous ne vous deffiez point de
mon seigneur, car je le cognois et scey qu'il est debonnaires, larges, et 1060
950 courtois, et n'est point couvoiteux d'avoir. Il ne desirre en ce monde
fors que honneur tant seulement. Aprés, je scey que en ceste besoingne il ne fera riens senz mon conseil; et je feray, se Dieu plait, que
ceste besoingne venra a bonne fin en telle maniere que vous vous de-
vrez loer de moy."   1065

"Nous," dirent il, "mettons nous et noz biens en tout et par tout en
955 vostre ordonnance et disposicion, et sommes appareillez de venir au
jour que vous nous vouldrez donner, et faire obligations si fors comme
vous plaira que nous acomplirons la voulenté de Messire Mellibee et
la vostre."   1070

Dame Prudence, quant ot oÿe la response d'eulz, si leur commande
aler en leurs lieux secretement, et elle d'autre part retourna vers Melli-
960 bee son seigneur et lui reconta comment elle les avoit trovez repentans
et recognoissans leurs pechiez et appareilliez de souffrir toute pene,
requerans sa pitié et sa misericorde.   1075

P₃.   1056–57   Se il a, donques] S'il deffent dont (Se il a donques P₂, M, L, B,
P₄).
   1067   de venir] *om.* (de venir M, L, B, P, P₂, P₄).
   1068   vous nous] vous (vous nous M, L, B, P, P₄).

(**Var.**)   1054   Oyez] croy P.
   1057   a son ami] a frere ne a ami B, P, P₂, a frere ne ami M, L, P₄.
   1059   donne conseil] conseille M, L, B, P₄.
   1062   scey] sçay bien M.
   1065   moy] moy Lors L, moy Adonc M, moy Et lors P₄.
   1066   dirent il] ilz respondirent dame P₄.
   1070   la vostre] de vous P₄.
   1071   Dame Prudence, quant] Quant Dame Prudence P₄.
   1072–73   Mellibee son seigneur] son seigneur Mellibee M.
   1073   les avoit trovez] avoit trouvé ses adversaires M, avoit retourné ses
adversaires P₂.

   1063–65   *et je ... moy.* Chaucer translates somewhat more freely here than is
his wont, condensing, changing the order, and slightly altering the sense (l. 2954).
It may be of some significance that P, which frequently yields readings like
Chaucer's, has a lacuna in this passage (*ceste ... dirent il:* 1064–66 above). The
whole sentence in which this clause occurs and the two preceding sentences are
lacking in the Latin (115.10).

Lors Mellibee respondi: "Cellui est dignes de pardon qui ne excuse ⟨fol. 69ᵛ⟩ point son pechié, mais le cognoist et s'en repent et demande

2965 indulgence. Car Senecques dit, 'La est remission ou est confession'; car confession est prouchainne a innocence. Et dit autre part, 'Celui est presque ignocent qui a honte de son pechié et le recognoit.' Et pour ce je m'accorde a paix, mais il est bon que nous le facions de la voulenté et consentement de noz amis." 10

Lors Prudence fist une chiere liee et joyant, et dist: "Certes," dist

2970 elle, "vous avez trop bien respondu; car tout aussi comme par le conseil et par l'ayde de voz amis vous avez eu en propox de vous vengier 10 et de faire guerre, aussi senz demander leur conseil vous ne devez accorder ne paix faire. Car la loy dit que nulle chose n'est tant selon nature comme la chose deslier pour ce dont elle a esté liee."

Et lors incontinent Dame Prudence envoya messagiers, et manda querre leurs parens et leurs anciens amis loyaulx et sages, et leur re- 10 compta le fait en la presence de Mellibee tout par ordre par la maniere

2975 qu'il est devisié dessus, et leur demanda quel conseil il donnoient sur ce. Lors les amis Mellibee, toutes les choses dessus dictes deliberees et examinees a grant diligence, donnerent conseil de paix faire et que

2980 l'on les receust a misericorde. 10

Quant Dame Prudence ot le consentement de son seigneur et le conseil de ses amis a son entencion et pour soy, si fut moult liee de cuer. "L'on dit," dist elle, "ou proverbe, 'Du bien que puez faire le

2985 main, ne attend soir ne l'andemain.' Et pour ce je conseille que l'on envoye tantost messagiers sages et advisez a ces gens pour leur dire 11

P₃. 1079   innocence] ygnorance (innocence M, L, B, P, P₂, P₄).

(Var.)   1076   respondi] dist aussi P₄.

1078   remission] la remission L, B, P, P₄—est confession] est la confession L, B.

1084   elle] elle sire P.

1087   tant] tant bonne P₂.

1088   pour] par M, L, B, P, P₂, P₄.

1089   incontinent Dame Prudence] Dame Prudence incontinent P— messagiers] messages P, P₄.

1091   par la maniere] ainsi L.

1095   misericorde] misericorde et a mercy M, B, mercy et a misericorde P₄.

1096   ot] ot oy M, P₂.

1098   "L'on dit," dist elle] et dist On dist B.

1098–99   le main] huy P₂.

1099   ne attend ... l'andemain] n'atendes pas demain P₂, n'atens mie jusques a l'andemain L, n'atens pas jusquez a l'endemain B, n'atens pas a l'endemain P.

1099–1100   l'on envoye] tu envoies M

que, se ilz veulent traittier de paix et d'accord si comme ilz se sont
presentez, que ilz se traient vers nous, et incontinant." Ainsi comme
90 Dame Prudence le conseilla, il fu fait. Quant ces trois malfaiteurs et
repentans de leurs folies oÿrent les messagiers, si furent liez et joyeux,
et respondirent benignement, en rendant graces a Messire Mellibee et 1105
a toute sa compagnie, qu'il estoient prests et appareilliez d'aler vers
eulx senz dilation et d'obeïr en tout et par tout a leur commande-
95 ment.

Et assez tost aprés, ilz se misdrent a la voye d'aler a la court de
Messire Mellibee, ensemble leurs fiances et aucuns de leurs loyaulx 1110
amis. Quant Mellibee les vit en sa presence, si dit: "Il est verité que
00 vous, senz cause et senz raison, avez fait grant injure a moy, a Dame
Prudence ma femme, et a ma fille, en entrant en ma maison en violence
et en faisant tel oultrage comme chascun scet, par laquelle vous avez
mort desservie. Et pour ce je vueil savoir de vous se vous voulez met- 1115
tre du tout la punicion et la vengence de cest oultrage a ma voulenté et
05 de Dame Prudence ma femme."

P₃. 1101   traittier] traittie (traittier *L, M, B, P, P₂, P₄*).
1106   qu'il] et qu'il (qu'il *L, M, B, P, P₂, P₄*).
1114   et en faisant] faisant et (et en faisant: *M, L, B, P₂*).

(**Var.**)   1102   nous, et incontinant] nous incontinent et sans dilation *M*, vous
incontinent et sans dilation *L, B, P₄*.
1103   Quant] Et quant *B, P₄*—trois] *om. P.*
1104   liez] moult liez *L, B, P₄*.
1105   benignement] moult benignement *P.*
1107   leur] son *L, B, P₄*.
1109   d'aler] *om. L.*
1110–11   ensemble ... amis] ensemble avec aucuns de leur loyaux amis faire
leur fiance *P.*
1112   moy] moy et *L, B, P, P₂*.
1112–13   Dame Prudence ma femme] ma femme Prudence *M, B, P₂, P₄*.
1113   fille] fille aussi *B*—en violence] par violence *L, B, P₂, P₄*, a violence *M, P.*

1101–2   *si ... presentez.* Chaucer omits this passage (l. 2987), although it is
present in all the French manuscripts. It is lacking in the Latin (117.11–12).

1102   *et incontinant.* Following *incontinant* all the French manuscripts except
P₃ add the following passage: *et sanz dilacion ensemble leurs pleges loyaulx et con-
venables* (reading of P₄; the other manuscripts exhibit slight variations). Since the
passage is present in the Latin (117.13), it probably is an authentic part of the
French translation. Since Chaucer omits it (l. 2989), his source manuscript must
have been like P₃. The scribe of P₃, however, capitalized *Et* and attached *Et incontinant* to the following sentence. Chaucer rightly took the phrase to go with
what precedes.

1102–3   *Ainsi ... conseilla.* Chaucer omits this (l. 2990). All the French
manuscripts have it, except P₄, which instead reads: *et chascun dist que c'estoit
bien dit et.* The passage is lacking in the Latin (117.14).

Lors l'ainsnel et le plus ⟨fol. 70ʳ⟩ sage des trois respondit pour tous
et dist, "Nous ne sommes pas dignes de venir a la court de tel homme
comme vous estes. Car nous avons tant meffait que voirement nous 11
sommes digne de mort, non pas de vie. Toutevoye, nous nous fyons en
vostre douceur et debonnaireté, dont vous estes renommez par tout
3010 le monde. Et pour ce nous nous offrons a vous, appareilliez d'obeïr a
tous voz commandemens, et vous prions a genoulz et en lermes que
vous ayez de nous pitié et misericorde."   11

3017 Lors Mellibee les releva benignement, et reçupt leur obligation par
leur serement et sur leurs pleges, et leur assigna journee de retourner a
sa court et de eulz offrir a sa presence pour oïr sentence et sa voulenté.
Ces choses ainsi ordonnees, un chascun d'une part et d'autre se departy
3021 d'ensemble.   11

Dame Prudence parla premierement a son seigneur Mellibee et lui
demanda quelle vengence il entendoit prendre de ses adversaires.

"Certes," dist Mellibee, "je les entend a desheriter de tout ce qu'ilz
3025 ont et les envoyer oultre mer senz retour."

"Certes," dist Dame Prudence, "ceste sentence seroit trop felon- 11
nesse et contre raison. Car tu es trop riches et n'as pas besoing de
l'autrui richesse ne de l'autrui argent, et pourroyes estre par raison
notez et reprins de couvoitise, qui est un tres grant vice et racine de

(**Var.**)   1119   et dist] Sire dit il *M, B, P, P₂, P₄,* sires dirent ilz *L*—tel] si noble
ne de tel *M.*
1123   appareilliez] et sommes appareilliés *M.*
1126   leur obligation] leurs obligations *M, L, B.*
1127   leur serement] leurs seremens *L, B, P₂, P₄.*
1130   d'ensemble] d'illec et s'en alerent a leurs maisons *P₄.*
1134   oultre mer] en exil *B, P₄*—senz retour] sans jamais retourner *P₄, P₂.*
1137   richesse ne de l'autrui] *om. L.*

1120   *Car,* etc. From this point to the end of the tale (ll. 3008–78) Chaucer
translates more freely than has been his wont throughout the translation.

1121   *non pas de vie.* Although Chaucer considerably expands the rest of this
sentence, he omits *non pas de vie* (l. 3009). All the French manuscripts have the
passage; it is lacking in the Latin (118.12).

1124   *a genoulz et en lermes.* Here again, although Chaucer expands the sentence in which this phrase occurs, he omits the phrase itself (l. 3013). It is present
in all the French manuscripts and in the Latin (118.17–18).

1125   *misericorde.* Following this sentence occurs one of the very few additions
which Chaucer makes to his source (ll. 3015–16).   The addition is not in the Latin
(118.18), nor, of course, is it in any of the French manuscripts.

1128   *et de … presence.* Though Chaucer expands other parts of the sentence
in which this phrase occurs, he omits the phrase itself (l. 3019). Part of the phrase
(*et de eulz offrir*) is lacking in P; the other French manuscripts and the Latin
(118.26–119.1) have it.

30 tous maulx. Selon ce que dit l'appostre, 'Il te vauldroit mieux tant
perdre du tien que prendre le leur par ceste maniere; mieulx vault 1140
perdre a honneur que gaingnier a honte'; et autre part aussi, 'Le gaing
doit estre appellez perte qui la bonne fame ne garde.' Et dit plus que
l'on ne se doit pas tant seulement garder de faire chose par quoy l'on
perde sa bonne renommee, mais se doit on tous les jours efforcier de
35 faire aucune chose pour acquerre nouvelle fame. Car il est escript, 1145
'La vieille renommee est tost alee quant elle n'est renouvellee.' Aprés,
quant ad ce que tu dis que tu les veulz envoier oultre mer senz jamés
retourner, il me semble que ce seroit mal use de la puissance qu'il t'ont
donnee sur eulx pour faire a toy honneur et reverence. Et le droit dit
que celui est digne de perdre son privilege qui mal use de la puissance 1150
40 qui lui a esté donnee. Et dy plus car supposé que tu leur puisses engendrer tele painne selon droit, laquelle chose je ne te ottroye point,
je dy que tu ne la pourroies pas mener de fait a execucion, ains par
aventure couvendroit retourner a la guerre comme devant. Et pour ce,
se tu veulz que l'on obeïsse a toy, il te couvient sentencier plus cour- 1155
45 toisement. Car il est escript, 'A cellui qui plus courtoisement commande, obeïst on mieulx.' Et pour ce je te prie que en ceste besoingne
te plaise vaincre ton cuer. Car ⟨fol. 70ᵛ⟩ Senecques dit, 'Deux foiz
vaint qui son cuer vaint.' Et Tulles dit, 'Riens ne fait tant a loer en
50 grant seigneur comme quant il est debonnaire et se appaise legiere- 1160
ment.' Et pour ce je te prie qu'il te plaise toy porter en telle maniere en

P₃   1149   sur eulx] *om.* (sur eulx *M, L, B, P, P₂, P₄*).

(**Var.**)   1139   Il te] Et te *L*, et vous *P₄*.
1140   maniere] maniere car il est escript *L, B, P₄*.
1147   oultre mer] en exil *B, P₄*.
1148   mal use] mesure *P₂*.
1150   mal use] mesuse *M, B, P, P₄*.
1151–52   engendrer] enjoindre *M, L, B, P, P₄*.
1152   laquelle chose] que *L, P, P₂, P₄*, ce que *B*.

1139   *Selon*, etc. According to the pointing of P₃, a new sentence begins with
Selon; according to L, however, *selon ... l'appostre* belongs with the preceding sentence. The phrase is not found in the Latin (120.3). Chaucer handles the passage
freely (ll. 3029–31), following neither P₃ nor L.

1147–48   *senz jamés retourner.* Chaucer omits (l. 3037). The passage is present
both in the Latin text (121.20) and in all the French manuscripts.

1149   *pour ... reverence.* Chaucer omits (l. 3039). All the French manuscripts have the passage in one form or another, and it is present in the Latin
(121.21).

1160   *seigneur.* This is the reading of Chaucer's source manuscript (cf. his
translation, "lord," l. 3050). The authentic reading is *homme,* found in all the
other manuscripts (M, L, B, P, P₂, P₄); cf. the Latin original, *viro* (123.11).

ceste vengence que ta bonne renommee soit gardee, et que tu soies loez de pitié et de doulceur, et qu'il ne te couviengne pas repentir de
3055 chose que tu faces. Car Senecques dit, 'Mal vaint qui se repent de sa vittoire.' Pour ces choses je te prie que tu adjoustes a ton jugement misericorde, a celle fin que Dieu ait de toy misericorde en son darrenier jugement. Car Saint Jaques dit en son epistre, 'Jugement senz misericorde sera fait a cellui qui ne fera misericorde.' "

Quant Mellibee ot oÿ toutes les paroles Dame Prudence et ses sages
3060 enseignemens, si fut en grant paix de cuer et loa Dieu, qui lui avoit donné si sage compagnie. Et quant la journee vint que ses adversaires
3065 comparurent en sa presence, il parla a eulz moult doulcement. "Ja soit ce," dist il, "que vous vous soyez portez envers nous moult orguilleusement, et de grant presumpcion vous soit advenu, toutevoie la
3070 grant humilité que je voy en vous me contraint a vous faire grace. Et pour ce nous vous recevons en nostre amitié et en nostre bonne grace, et vous pardonnons toutes injures et tous voz meffaiz encontre nous, a celle fin que Dieu, ou point de la mort, nous vueille pardonner les
3074 nostres." AMEN.

Explicit

(Var.) 1168 fera] aura eu *L*, *P₄*.
1169 toutes] *om. P*—paroles] paroles et raisons de *L*.
1170 loa] loa et regratia *L*.
1172 doulcement] doulcement en ceste maniere *L*.
1173 nous] moy *L*, *B*, *P*, *P₄*.
1176 amitié et en nostre bonne grace] grace et amittié *P₂*.
1177 meffaiz] meffaiz que avez faiz *P₄*.

1170–71 *si fut … compagnie.* Chaucer expands this passage and alters its meaning (ll. 3061–63). His additions are not found at all in the French manuscripts, and bear only a general similarity to the corresponding passage in the Latin (125.6–11).

1174–75 *toutevoie … grace.* Chaucer briefly expands this passage, adding a clause (ll. 3068–70). Cf. the Latin text (126.14–17) for a general similarity of idea.

1179 *nostres.* Chaucer concludes his translation with a long religious sentence (ll. 3075–77), which is found neither in the Latin text (127.7) nor in the French manuscripts. Cf. I John 1:9.

THE MONK'S TALE

By ROBERT K. ROOT

IN FIFTEEN of the fifty-one manuscripts which contain the *Monk's Tale* the tale is labeled, either in an *incipit* or an *explicit* or both, as *De casibus virorum illustrium*. The manuscripts which contain this designation are the following: Cambridge Dd. 4.24, Cambridge Ii.3.26, Cambridge Mm. 2.5, Cardigan, Christ Church, Corpus, Devonshire I, Egerton 2726, Egerton 2864, Ellesmere, Glasgow, Hatton, Lansdowne, Lincoln, Manchester. In addition to these, Huntington contains the title "The Falle of Princis." These sixteen manuscripts do not belong textually to a single group; nine of them, for example, have the so-called "modern instances" at the end of the series of tragedies, seven have the "modern instances" between *Zenobia* and *Nero*. As an example of these manuscript designations one may take the rubrics in Cambridge Dd. 4.24: "Heere endeth the prologe and bigynneth the Monkes tale that is titled De Casibus Virorum Illustrium Chaucer" and "Here endeth the Monkes tale De Casibus Virorum Illustrium."[1]

Whether this designation derives from Chaucer himself, or from some scribal editor, cannot be certainly determined. Its presence in manuscripts textually not of a single type would suggest the former. If, as many scholars have believed, most of the Monk's tragedies had been written before the period of the *Canterbury Tales* as an independent work, Chaucer may have originally given to the series the title *De casibus virorum illustrium*. When later he decided to utilize this material as the *Monk's Tale*, the new title may have been superimposed in his own copy over the earlier title. A scribal editor working with Chaucer's own copy could then easily have derived such a heading as that quoted above from Cambridge Dd.

Whatever its ultimate source, the designation is clearly intended to suggest a similarity between the *Monk's Tale* and the *De casibus virorum illustrium* of Boccaccio, which in nine books

[1] The facts given in this paragraph are derived from Sir William McCormick's *The Manuscripts of Chaucer's Canterbury Tales* (Oxford, 1933).

of Latin prose recounts, with the machinery of a series of visions, and with much moralizing comment, the tragic stories of the great who "from the beginning of the world until our own age" have been cast down from high estate by fickle Fortune. Boccaccio's account of Samson, given below on pages 626–28, may serve as a specimen of its narrative method. For an account of the *De casibus* the student may consult A. Hortis, *Studj sulle opere Latine del Boccaccio* (Trieste, 1879), pages 117–54, 764–69, and the essay by H. Hauvette, "Sur le *De casibus virorum illustrium*," in the miscellany *Entre camarades* (Paris, 1901), pages 279–97. Hauvette thinks that the first version of *De casibus* was finished in 1359 and published in 1363 and that a revised version was finished earlier than October, 1374, when Boccaccio learned of the death of Petrarch. The Paris edition (*ca.* 1508) and manuscripts Harleian 3565 and Cambridge University Library, Ll.II.8, give the earlier text, which is more widely disseminated, particularly in the north of Europe. The Augsburg edition of 1544 gives the revised text. The revisions are chiefly stylistic in character, and it cannot be determined which of the versions was known to Chaucer.

Why Chaucer should have attributed the *De casibus* to "my maister Petrak," as he seems to do in *Monk's Tale*, B 3515 (see below, p. 632), is an unsolved problem of Chaucerian scholarship.

If Boccaccio's *De casibus* suggested to Chaucer the general idea of his series of exemplary tragedies, it contributed very little to the substance of his poem. For not a single one of the Monk's brief biographies is it the primary source. It is the unmistakable source of the last stanza of *Zenobia*, a probable source for the second stanza of *Nero*, and a possible source for the first stanza of *Croesus* and for the *tragedy* of *Pompey* included in *Julius Caesar*. It may have contributed a phrase to *Adam*, and a few lines of moralizing comment to *Samson*. And these are the only ones of the Monk's tragic heroes whose biographies find a place in *De casibus*. Of half a dozen of the Monk's other heroes, *De casibus* makes incidental mention.

There is another analogue which may have suggested to Chaucer the Monk's series of tragedies. In the *Roman de la rose* Reason, having discoursed at length (ll. 5842–6182) to the Lover on the mutability of Fortune, recounts as *exempla* the stories of Nero (ll. 6183–6488) and of Croesus (ll. 6489–6622). And then, after a few sententious lines on Fortune, Reason relates briefly, as recent instances of Fortune's power, the overthrow of Manfred, usurping King of Sicily, and his nephew Conradin at the hands of Charles of Anjou. Here, as in Chaucer, we have tragic heroes of long ago and "modern instances" from the very recent past.[1]

From this *De casibus* section of the *Roman de la rose* Chaucer has drawn the chief substance of two of his tragedies. Jean de Meun's accounts of Nero and of Croesus are the unmistakable primary sources of what the Monk has to say about these two worthies. Since this section of the *Roman de la rose* is an important analogue for the *Monk's Tale* as a whole, the text of the relevant portions, from Langlois' edition ("Société des Anciens Textes Français" [Paris, 1914–22]), is printed below before the sources and analogues of the individual tragedies are considered.

ROMAN DE LA ROSE

The Tragedies of Nero and Croesus

[Reason has been discoursing to the Lover
about the nature of Fortune.]

E pour ce qu'ele est si parverse
Que les bons en la boe verse
E les deseneure e les grieve,
6168   E les mauvais en haut eslieve
E leur done a granz abondances
Dignetez, eneurs e poissances,
Puis, quant li plaist, leur tost ou emble,
6172   N'el ne set qu'el se veaut, ce semble:
Pour ce li ueil bendé li furent
Des anciens, qui la quenurent.
E que Fortune ainsinc le face

The perversity of Fortune. She overthrows the good, and exalts the evil.

---

[1] It is to be noted that fourteen of the authorities for the text of the *Monk's Tale* have the "modern instances" at the end of the series immediately after *Croesus*, and so conform more closely to the model of the *Roman de la rose*. (Harley 7333 has them both at the end and in the middle.)

6176 Que les bons aville e efface
E les mauvais en eneur tiegne,
Car je vueil que bien t'en souviegne,
Ja seit ce que devant dit t'aie
6180 De Socratès, que tant amaie,
E li vaillanz on tant m'amait
Qu'en touz ses faiz me reclamait,

The examples of Seneca and Nero.

Mainz essemples en puis trouver;
6184 E ce peut l'en tantost prouver
E par Seneque e par Neron,
Don la parole tost lairon,
Pour la longueur de la matire,

Nero's crimes.

6188 Car je metraie trop a dire
Les faiz Neron, le cruel ome,
Coment il mist les feus a Rome,
E fist les senateurs ocierre;
6192 Si rot bien cueur plus dur que pierre
Quant il fist ocierre son frere,

Nero dismembers his mother.

Quant il fist desmembrer sa mere,
Pour ce que par lui fust veüz
6196 Li leus ou il fu conceüz;
E puis qu'il la vit desmembree,
Selonc l'estoire remembree,
La beauté des membres juija.
6200 He! Deus! Con ci felon juige a!
N'onc de l'ueil lerme n'en issi,
Car l'estoire le dit issi;
Mais, si come il juijait des membres,
6204 Comanda il que de ses chambres
Li feïst l'en vin aporter,
E but pour son cors deporter.
Mais il l'ot anceis queneüe;
6208 Sa sereur ravait il eüe;
E bailla sei meïsme a ome
Cil desleiaus que je ci nome.

Nero puts to death his master, Seneca.

Seneque mist il a martire,
6212 Son bon maistre, e li fist eslire
De quel mort mourir il vourrait;
Cil vit qu'eschaper ne pourrait,
Tant iere poissanz li maufez:
6216 "Donc seit," dist il, "uns bainz chaufez,
Puis que d'eschaper est neienz,

E me faites saignier laienz
Tant que je muire en l'eve chaude,

Seneca asks that he
may be bled to
death in a hot bath.

6220 E que m'ame joieuse e baude
A Deu qui la fourma se rende,
Qui d'autres tormenz la defende.''
Emprès ce mot, senz arester,

6224 Fist Nerons le baing aprester,
E fist enz le preudome metre,
E puis saignier, ce dit la letre,
Tant qu'il li couvint l'ame rendre,

6228 Tant li fist cil dou sanc espandre;
Ne nule achaison n'i savait
Fors tant que de coustume avait
Nerons que toujourz des s'enfance

Nero unwilling to
show reverence to
his master.

6232 Li soulait porter reverence,
Si con deciples a son maistre:
"Mais ce ne deit," dist il, "pas estre,
Ne n'est pas bel en nule place

6236 Que reverence a ome face
Nus on, puis qu'il est empereres,
Tant seit ses maistres ne ses peres."
E pour ce que trop li grevait

6240 Quant encontre lui se levait,
Quant son maistre voait venir,
N'il ne se poait pas tenir
Qu'il ne li portast reverence

6244 Par la force d'acoustumance,
Fist il destruire le preudome.
Si tint il l'empire de Rome,
Cil desleiaus que je ci di,

6248 E d'orient e de midi,
D'occident, de septentrion
Tint il la juridicion.
E se tu me sez bien entendre,

The gifts of For-
tune do not make
for virtue, but
rather for wicked-
ness.

6252 Par ces paroles peuz aprendre
Que richeces e reverences,
Dignetez, eneurs e poissances,
Ne nules graces de Fortune,

6256 Car je n'en excete nes une,
De si grant force pas ne sont
Qu'eus facent bons ceus qui les ont,
Ne dignes d'aveir les richeces,

6260   Ne les eneurs ne les hauteces.
       Mais s'il ont en aus engrestiez,
       Orgueil, ou queusque mauvaistiez,
       Li grant estat ou il s'encroent
6264   Plus tost les montrent e descloent
       Que se petiz estaz eüssent,
       Par quei si nuire ne peüssent;
       Car, quant de leur poissances usent,
6268   Li fait les volentez encusent,
       Qui demontrance font e signe
       Qu'il ne sont pas ne bon ne digne
       Des richeces, des dignetez,
6272   Des eneurs e des poetez.

It was Fortune that
made the wicked
Nero powerful.

           Or veiz coment Fortune sert
6344   Ça jus en cet mondain desert,
       E coment el fait a despire,
       Qui des mauvais eslut le pire
       E seur touz omes le fist estre
6348   De cet monde seigneur e maistre,
       E fist Seneque ainsinc destruire.
       Fait bien donques sa grace a fuire,
       Quant nus, tant seit de bon eür,
6352   Ne la peut tenir asseür.
       Pour ce vueil que tu la despises,
       E que ses graces riens ne prises.

Therefore, despise
Fortune.

       Laisse plourer enfanz e fames,
       Bestes feibles e variables;
6408   E tu seies forz e estables,
       Quant Fortune verras venir,
       Veauz tu sa roe retenir,
       Qui ne peut estre retenue

But Fortune's wheel
still turns, and Nero
is brought low.

6412   Ne par grant gent ne par menue?
       Cil granz empereres meïsmes,
       Nerons, dont l'essemple meïsmes,
       Qui fu de tout le monde sires,

This great emperor,
lord of all the earth,
comes to a wretched
death, hated by all
his people, and
afraid of being at-
tacked by them.

6416   Tant s'estendait loing ses empires,
       Ne la pot onques arester,
       Tant peüst eneurs conquester;
       Car il, se l'estoire ne ment,
6420   Reçut puis mort mauvaisement,

De tout son peuple anceis haïz,
Don il cremait estre envaïz;
Si manda ses privez amis,
6424 Mais onc li message tramis
Ne trouverent, que qu'il deïssent,
Nus d'aus qui leur uis leur ouvrissent.
Adonc i vint priveement
6428 Nerons mout poereusement,
E hurta de ses propres mains,
N'onc ne l'en firent plus, mais meins,
Car, quant plus chascuns apela,
6432 Chascuns plus s'enclost e cela,
Ne nus ne li vost mot respondre.
Lors le couvint aler repondre,
Si se mist, pour sei herbergier,
6436 O deus siens sers, en un vergier,
Car ja pluseur par tout couraient
Qui pour ocierre le queraient,
E criaient: "Neron! Neron!
6440 Qui le vit? Ou le trouveron?"
Si qu'il neïs bien les oait,
Mais conseil metre n'i poait.
Si s'est si forment esbaïz
6444 Qu'il meïsmes s'est enhaïz;
E quant il se vit en ce point
Qu'il n'ot mais d'esperance point,
Aus sers pria qu'il le tuassent,
6448 Ou qu'a sei tuer li aidassent.
Si s'ocist, mais ainz fist requeste
Que ja nus ne trouvast sa teste,
Pour ce qu'il ne fust queneüz
6452 Se ses cors fust emprès veüz;
E pria que le cors ardissent
Si tost come ardeir le poïssent.
E dit li livres anciens,
6456 Diz *des Doze Cesariens*,
Ou sa mort trouvons en escrit,
Si con Sutonius l'escrit,
Qui la lei crestiene apele
6460 Fausse religion nouvele
E maufaisant, ainsinc la nome,
Veiz ci mot de desleial ome,

He turns to his friends for help, but his messengers cannot find any who will open their door.

With two of his slaves he takes refuge in an orchard. But he can hear his pursuers shouting, "Where shall we find Nero?" and does not know what to do.

He begs the slaves to kill him. Finally he kills himself, begging the slaves to burn his body as soon as possible.

Suetonius describes his death in a book called *The Twelve Caesars.*

Que en Neron fu defenie
6464   Des Cesariens la lignie.
Cist par ses faiz tant pourchaça
Que tout son lignage effaça.

Nepourquant tant fu coustumiers
6468   De bien faire es cinc anz prumiers
Qu'onc si bien ne gouverna terre
Nus princes que l'en seüst querre,
Tant sembla vaillanz e piteus,
6472   Li desleiaus, li despiteus;
E dist en audience a Rome,
Quant il, pour condanner un ome,
Fu requis de la mort escrire,
6476   Ne n'ot pas honte de ce dire,
Qu'il vousist meauz non saveir letre
Que sa main pour escrire i metre.
Si tint, ce veaut li livres dire,
6480   Entour dis e set anz l'empire,
E trente e deus dura sa vie;
Mais ses orgueauz, sa felonie
Si forment l'orent envaï

6484   Que de si haut si bas chaï,
Con tu m'as oï raconter,
Tant l'ot fait Fortune monter,
Qui tant le fist emprès descendre,
6488   Con tu peuz oïr e entendre.
N'onc ne la pot tenir Cresus

Qu'el nou tournast e jus e sus,
Qui refu reis de toute Lide,
6492   Puis li mist l'en au col la bride,
E fu pour ardre au feu livrez,
Quant par pluie fu delivrez,

Qui le grant feu fist tout esteindre,
6496   N'onques nus n'osa la remaindre,
Tuit s'en foïrent pour la pluie:
Cresus se mist tantost en fuie,
Quant il se vit seul en la place,
6500   Senz encombrement e senz chace.
Puis refu sires de sa terre,
E puis resmut nouvele guerre,
Puis refu pris, e puis penduz,

6504 Quant li songes li fu renduz
      Des deus deus qui li aparaient,
      Qui seur l'arbre en haut le servaient:
      Jupiter, ce dist, le lavait,
6508 E Phebus la toaille avait,
      E se penait de l'essuier.
      Mar se vost ou songe apuier,
      Don si grant fiance acuilli
6512 Qu'il come fos s'enorguilli.
      Bien li dist Phanie, sa fille,
      Qui tant estait sage e soutille
      Qu'el savait les songes espondre,
6516 E senz flater li vost respondre:
      "Beaus pere," dist la dameisele,
      "Ci a doulereuse nouvele.
      Vostre orgueauz ne vaut une coque;
6520 Sachiez que Fortune vous moque.
      Par cet songe poez entendre
      Qu'el vous veaut faire au gibet pendre;
      E quant sereiz penduz au vent,
6524 Senz couverture e senz auvent,
      Seur vous plouvra, beaus sires reis,
      E li beaus solauz de ses rais
      Vous essuiera cors e face.
6528 Fortune a cete fin vous chace,
      Qui tost e done les eneurs,
      E fait souvent des granz meneurs,
      E des meneurs refait graigneurs,
6532 E seignourir seur les seigneurs.
      Que vous iraie je flatant?
      Fortune au gibet vous atent,
      E quant au gibet vous tendra,
6536 La hart ou col, el reprendra
      La bele courone doree
      Don vostre teste a couronee;
      S'en iert uns autres couronez,
6540 De cui garde ne vous donez.
        E pour ce que je vous espoigne
      Plus apertement la besoigne,
      Jupiter, qui l'eve vous done,
6544 Cist est li airs qui pleut e tone,
      E Phebus, qui tient la toaille,

King Croesus' dream.

His daughter, Phanie, interprets the dream.

Fortune will bring him to the gibbet.

Jupiter is the air, Phoebus the Sun.

C'est li solauz, senz nule faille;

L'arbre par le gibet vous glose,

6548   Je n'i puis entendre autre chose.

Passer vous couvient cete planche,

Fortune ainsinc le peuple venche

Dou bobant que vous demenez,

6552   Come orguilleus e forsenez.

Si destruit ele maint preudome,

Qu'el ne prise pas une pome

Tricherie ne leiauté,

6556   Ne vil estat, ne reiauté;

Anceis s'en jeue a la pelote,

Come pucele nice e sote,

E giete a grant desordenance

6560   Richece, eneur e reverence;

Dignetez e poissances done,

Ne ne prent garde a quel persone;

Car ses graces, quant les despent,

6564   En despendant si les espant

Qu'el les giete en leu de pouties

Par puteaus e par praeries."

Ainsinc le chastiait Phanie.

Mais fos ne veit en sa folie

Fors que sen e raison ensemble,

6596   Si come en son fol cueur li semble.

Cresus, qui point ne s'umelie,

Touz pleins d'orgueil e de folie,

En touz ses faiz cuide estre sages,

6600   Combien qu'il feïst granz outrages.

"Fille," fait il, "de courteisie

Ne de sen ne m'aprenez mie;

Plus en sai que vous ne savez,

6604   Qui si chastié m'en avez.

E quant par vostre fol respons

M'avez mon songe ainsinc espons,

Servi m'avez de granz mençonges;

6608   Car sachiez que cist nobles songes,

Ou fausse glose voulez metre,

Deit estre entenduz a la letre;

E je meïsmes l'i entens,

6612   Si con nous le verrons en tens.

Thus Fortune destroys many a great man. She is no respecter of persons.

Croesus, in his folly and pride, disregards his daughter's interpretation of the dream.

His dream is to be taken at its face value: the gods are to be his servitors.

Onc ausinc noble vision
N'ot si vil esposicion.
Li deu, sachiez, a mei vendront,
6616 E le servise me rendront
Qu'il m'ont par cet songe tramis,
Tant est chascuns d'aus mes amis,
Car bien l'ai pieç'a deservi."
6620 Veiz con Fortune le servi;
Qu'il ne se pot onques defendre
Qu'el nou feïst au gibet pendre.
N'est ce donc bien chose prouvable
6624 Que sa roe n'est pas tenable,
Quant nus ne la peut retenir,
Tant sache a grant estat venir?
E se tu sez riens de logique,
6628 Qui bien est science autentique,
Puis que li grant seigneur i faillent
Li petit en vain s'i travaillent.
E se les preuves riens ne prises
6632 D'ancienes estoires prises,
Tu les as de ton tens nouveles,
De batailles fresches e beles.

But Fortune brought him to the gibbet. Does this not show that no one can stay her wheel?

But, if examples from long ago do not convince, you may have others from modern times.

[As "modern instances," Jean de Meun tells briefly the stories of Manfred, usurping King of Sicily, and of Conradin, his nephew, overthrown by Charles of Anjou, acting with the sanction of Pope Urban IV. These events of 1264–68 were very recent history when Jean de Meun was writing.]

I AND II. *LUCIFER* AND *ADAM*

For these tragedies, of a single stanza each, no specific source can be assigned. The first tragedy in Boccaccio's *De casibus* (I, 1) is that of Adam and Eve; but there is nothing in this fairly long account which suggests Chaucer's brief epitome, except that Chaucer's location of paradise in "the feeld of Damyssene" may derive from Boccaccio's "ex agro qui postea Damascenus." But this, like the rest of what Chaucer tells us of Lucifer and of Adam, is commonplace which might have been derived from many sources.

III. *SAMSON*

Chaucer cites (B 3236) "*Judicum*" as his authority, and his **primary** source is actually Judges, chapters 13–16. The relevant passages in the Vulgate are 13:1–5; 14:1, 2, 5–7, 15–17, 20; 15:4, 5, 14–20; 16:1–6, 15–30. It is probable that he consulted also the story of Samson in *De casibus* (I, 17), the opening sentence of which may have suggested the beginning of Chaucer's tragedy. There are, however, a number of details in Chaucer's story which Boccaccio's paraphrase of the biblical narrative does not include. Though not the principal source for Chaucer's story of Samson, Boccaccio's version of this "tragedy" is printed as a specimen of the work which may have served as the general model for the *Monk's Tale*. The text given below is based on the Augsburg edition of 1544, corrected by collation with British Museum MS Harleian 3565, Cambridge University Library MS Ll.2.8, and the undated Paris edition of about 1507 (Hortis, No. XI). The corrected text represents, therefore, the earlier, unrevised text of Boccaccio (see above, p. 616).

DE CASIBUS VIRORUM ILLUSTRIUM, LIB. I, CAP. XVII

De Sansone

Samson's birth announced by an angel.

Praenunciante igitur[1] per angelum Deo, ex Manue Israhelita quodam et pulcherrima eius vxore Sanson progenitus est. Qui, cum Nazaraeus esset, comam Dei iussu seruans, et sibi à sicera cauens et vino, in miram[2] iuuentutem atque praeualidam et admirabilem cunctis excreuit. Cuius fortitudinis apparuêre insignia prima,

He kills a lion.

dum ad virginem à se dilectam desponsandam, in Philistinos acres tunc populos, illi ire contingeret, leonem[3] ex abdito in se eleuata fronte venientem impauidus occidit[4] et tacuit. Ingentis animi nobile argumentum, magnalia à se facta imputare Deo et, ni importunitas instet, nunquam in propatulo reserasse.[5] Tandem, illud idem[6] iter dum faceret, in ore[7] oppressae à se belluae mellis fauum[8] reperisset

He proposes a riddle.

et commedisset; et[9] cognatis ex coniuge, appositis soluenti muneribus, problema proposuit inenodabile fere. Cuius occultum cum apperuisset

His wife betrays him.

blanditiis coniugis, aduertit liquidè eius opere ab affinibus solutum esse; ob quod meritum coniugalis amor versus est in odium, et, altera sumpta, illius populi ex affine factus est hostis.

---

[1] *Augs. om.* igitur.

[2] *Augs.* floridam *for* miram.

[3] *Augs.* et Leonem.

[4] *Augs.* expectauit et occidit.

[5] *Harl. and Camb.* reserare.

[6] *Augs.* illuc *for* illud idem.

[7] *Augs.* in ore cranei.

[8] *Augs.* fauum forte.

[9] *Augs. om* et.

Et cum Cereae messes proximam maturitatem ostenderent, nouum et inusitatum genus vltionis commentus, facibus caudis vulpium alligatis, et hostium agris immissis, sata et arbusta exussit omnia, irritassetque facinore Philistaeos. Ab eis Israelitis, in satisfactionem tanti[1] sceleris, vinctus postulatus est. Qui dum ligatus funibus traderetur, eis brachiorum[2] tractu[3] confractis, maxillam asini in conspectu forte iacentem arripuit, qua loco ingentis clauae usus, Philistaeos eum trahentes cecidit atque fudit. Et obtenta victoria sitiens, scaturientem diuino opere fontem ex maxilla videns, potansque,[4] refocillatus est.

He burns the Philistine corn.

He slays the Philistines with the jaw of an ass.

Hoc illi apud suos in cumulum virtutis excessit, iudexque (summi magistratus nomen apud Israhelitas) ille tunc ab eisdem habitus est. Nec defuerunt qui leonem à se occisum Nemaeum dicerent, et Herculem arbitrarentur Sansonem; quod etsi non[5] adfirmem, contradixisse nescio quid resultet.

Samson and Hercules identified.

Is ergo, dum frustatos taliter Philistaeos flocci penderet, in Gazam eorum oppidum tendens, apud meretricem, cuius forsan pellicatu lasciuiens vtebatur, diuertit; noctuque surgens, firmatas ob[6] se capiendum à principibus ciuitatis, seris et ferreis vectibus atque[7] clauibus, portarum fores eas à cardinibus demptas in verticem montis Hebron humeris transportauit, et abiit.

He carries off the gates of Gaza.

Sed quid tanta[8] magna haec erunt, immo permaxima, ad gloriae apicem obtinendum, quam hac in vita felicitatem arbitrantur insipidi.[9] Qui leonem inermis exenterare, qui maxilla hostes conterere, qui reuulsas ex cardinibus valuas in montium vertices portare[10] potuerat, lubricum fortunae ludum sistere non potuit. Nam cum sibi nimium confideret, et meretriculam nomine Dalilam[11] apud hostes degentem adamaret perditè, ab ea corrupta pecunia, post lusiones aliquas, paucis lachrymulis extortum[12] est, in quibus tanti roboris causa permaneret.[13] O bone Deus! à coniuge paulo ante deceptus, à fictis lachrymis verbisque meretriculae victus, iterum se decipiendum tradidit homo ferox. Verum eneruata malitiis mulier,[14] postquam ab

But Fortune is too much for him.

Dalila betrays him.

He should not have been moved by a woman's tears.

---

[1] *Augs. om.* tanti.

[2] brachiorum, *so Harl. and Camb.; Augs. and Paris* brachio.

[3] *Augs.* contracto. [5] *Augs. om.* non. [7] *Augs.* absque.

[4] *Augs.* potans. [6] *Augs.* ad. [8] *Augs.* tam.

[9] *Augs.* arbitramur inscii. *After* insipidi, *Harl. and Camb. add* Sed rerum finis expectandus in omnibus.

[10] *Augs.* apportare. [11] *Harl.* Dalidam. [12] *Augs.* exortum.

[13] *Augs.* ut, in quibus tanti roboris permaneret caussa, certior fieret.

[14] *Augs.* ornata vitiis mulier, uel malitiis.

hostibus instructa dormienti crines, quos ipse a natiuitate sua intactos seruauerat, abstulit, illum etiam fore effeminatum in manibus hostium

He is blinded and forced to work in the mill.

illudendum concessit. Cui euestigio debilitato effodêre oculos et, intrusum carceribus, defatigari iumentorum more ad molas manuarias coegêre. Sic aduersa credulitas, sic amantis pietas, sic mulieris egit inclyta fides; vt quem non poterant homines, non vincula, non

Fortune has turned him to a jest.

ferrum vincere, à mulieribus lachrymulis[1] vinceretur, et, agente fortuna, vbi hostibus suis terrori erat[2] verteretur in ludum.

Grandis quidem,[3] ni fallor, descensus iste, quem vir alias ingentis

He is led to the feast of Dagon.

animi diu tolerasse non potuit. Nam cum illi iam lapsu temporis coma iterum excreuisset,[4] restitutaeque uires deperditae viderentur,[5] congregati Philistaei celebremque[6] diem et publicum sacrum Dagon Deo suo agentes, iam epulis mensisque remotis, iusserant ut eis coram duceretur infelix, ludo diem sollenem hilarem redditurus.[7] Qui à puero ductus, postquam paululum se ludens exercuerat, ridentibus cunctis caecum[8] hominem, Israelitarum iudicem, coram se ludere, quasi fessus, duce puero columnis duabus, quibus omne

He pulls down the temple and perishes with his 3,000 victims.

ferè fani fastigium insidebat, quieturus[9] adhesit. Indignansque secum, ambas tempore sumpto vlnis amplectens clamitansque.[10] "Cum Sansone omnis suus pereat hostis!" miro robore[11] in se traxit, quas[12] in ruinam omne continuo aedificium[13] secutum est, cum Sansone conterens Philistaeorum principes omnes.[14] Quo in casu tria milia virorum oppressa occubuêre.[15] Et sic qui principatum Israelitarum per[16] viginti tenuerat annos,[17] despectus apud hostes, orbusque[18] vitam non ferens, mortem sibi constituit indignam.[19]

Hanc Historiam habes ex ueteri testamento Iudicum 13. et apud Iosephum lib. 5 ca. 13. Antiq. Iud. Philon quoque in libro de biblicis antiquitatibus. Augustinus et alii.

[1] *Augs.* latrunculis, *Par.* lachrymis.

[2] *Augs.* fuit.

[3] *Augs.* equidem.

[4] *Augs.* excreuisset iterum.

[5] *Augs.* viderentur perditè.

[6] *Augs.* celebrem.

[7] *Augs.* reddituros.

[8] *Augs. om.* caecum.

[9] *Augs.* quietus.

[10] *Augs.* clamitans inquit.

[11] *Augs.* Inde miro illas robore.

[12] *Augs.* et *for* quas.

[13] *Augs.* aedificium continuo.

[14] *Augs.* cum Sansone opprimens qui eum ludentes aderant.

[15] *Augs.* mole oppressa graui perière.

[16] *Augs. om.* per.

[17] *Augs.* annis.

[18] *Augs.* orbatusque, *om.* apud hostes.

[19] *Augs.* constituit et hostibus.

IV. *HERCULES*

The story of Hercules was so familiar that many possible sources for Chaucer's account were available. The first two stanzas, which recite the twelve labors of Hercules, quite clearly come from Boethius *De consolatione* iv. m.7. 13–31:

> Herculem duri celebrant labores.
> Ille Centauros domuit superbos,
> 15 Abstulit saeuo spolium leoni
> Fixit et certis uolucres sagittis,
> Poma cernenti rapuit draconi
> Aureo laeuam grauior metallo,
> Cerberum traxit triplici catena.
> 20 Victor immitem posuisse fertur
> Pabulum saeuis dominum quadrigis.
> Hydra combusto periit ueneno,
> Fronte turpatus Achelous amnis
> Ora demersit pudibunda ripis.
> 25 Strauit Antaeum Libycis harenis,
> Cacus Euandri satiauit iras
> Quosque pressurus foret altus orbis
> Saetiger spumis umeros notauit.
> Vltimus caelum labor inreflexo
> 30 Sustulit collo pretiumque rursus
> Vltimi caelum meruit laboris.

For the statement in the third stanza that Hercules set up a pillar at both ends of the world, Chaucer cites the authority of "Trophee." This remains one of the unexplained *cruces* of Chaucerian scholarship (see Professor Robinson's note on the passage for reference to the various attempts at explanation).

Stanzas 4 and 5 contain in brief epitome the story of the death of Hercules, poisoned by the shirt of Nessus, sent to him by his wife, Deianira. All the details given by Chaucer could have been derived from the beginning of the ninth book of Ovid's *Metamorphoses*, of which the relevant passages are printed below. There is, however, no echo of Ovid's phrasing to prove that this version of the story was immediately in his mind. Chaucer certainly knew the *Metamorphoses*. He had, doubtless, also read the lament of Deianira in Ovid's *Heroides* ix. From *Heroides* ix. 67–70, Chaucer may have derived his confusion of Busiris and Diomedes in B 3293–94 (see Shannon,

Chaucer and the Roman Poets [Cambridge, Mass., 1929], pp. 312–17). In Boccaccio's *De claris mulieribus* xxii there is a short account of Deianira. (Boccaccio, like Ovid, absolves Deianira of any evil intentions.) There are only incidental mentions of Hercules in the *De casibus*.

OVID *METAMORPHOSES* BOOK IX

HERCULES AND THE SHIRT OF NESSUS

Hercules mortally wounds the Centaur, Nessus, who gives to Deianira his blood-stained shirt, telling her that it has the power to revive waning love.

125 Haud tamen effugies, quamvis ope fidis equina;
Vulnere, non pedibus te consequar." Ultima dicta
Res probat, et missa fugientia terga sagitta
Traicit. Exstabat ferrum de pectore aduncum
Quod simul evulsum est, sanguis per utrumque foramen
130 Emicuit mixtus Lernaei tabe veneni.
Excipit hunc Nessus: "neque enim moriemur inulti"
Secum ait, et calido velamina tincta cruore
Dat munus raptae velut inritamen amoris.

[Deianira learns that Hercules is in love with Iole]

She sends her husband the poisoned shirt of Nessus, and he puts it on his shoulders.

Incursus animus varios habet. Omnibus illis
Praetulit inbutam Nesseo sanguine vestem
Mittere, quae vires defecto reddat amori,
155 Ignaroque Lichae, quid tradat, nescia, luctus
Ipsa suos tradit blandisque miserrima verbis.
Dona det illa viro, mandat. Capit inscius heros,
Induiturque umeris Lernaeae virus echidnae.
Tura dabat primis et verba precantia flammis,
160 Vinaque marmoreas patera fundebat in aras:
Incaluit vis illa mali, resolutaque flammis
Herculeos abiit late dilapsa per artus.
Dum potuit, solita gemitum virtute repressit.
Victa malis postquam est patientia, reppulit aras,
165 Inplevitque suis nemorosum vocibus Oeten.
Nec mora, letiferam conatur scindere vestem:

The burning poison penetrates his whole body.

Qua trahitur, trahit illa cutem, foedumque relatu,
Aut haeret membris frustra temptata revelli,
Aut laceros artus et grandia detegit ossa.
170 Ipse cruor, gelido ceu quondam lammina candens
Tincta lacu, stridit coquiturque ardente veneno.
Nec modus est, sorbent avidae praecordia flammae,

Caeruleusque fluit toto de corpore sudor,
Ambustique sonant nervi, caecaque medullis
175 Tabe liquefactis tollens ad sidera palmas. . . . .

"Ergo ego foedantem peregrino templa cruore
Busirin domui? Saevoque alimenta parentis
Antaeo eripui? nec me pastoris Hiberi
185 Forma triplex, nec forma triplex tua, Cerbere, movit?
Vosne, manus, validi pressistis cornua tauri?
Vestrum opus Elis habet, vestrum Stymphalides undae,
Partheniumque nemus? Vestra virtute relatus
Thermodontiaco caelatus balteus auro,
190 Pomaque ab insomni concustodita dracone?
Nec mihi centauri potuere resistere, nec mi
Arcadiae vastator aper? Nec profuit hydrae
Crescere per damnum geminasque resumere vires?
Quid, quod Thracis equos humano sanguine pingues
195 Plenaque corporibus laceris praesepia vidi,
Visaque deieci, dominumque ipsosque peremi?
His elisa iacet moles Nemeaea lacertis:
Hac caelum cervice tuli."

Hercules, in his agonizing lament, recounts his mighty labors.

Dixit, perque altum saucius Oeten
205 Haud aliter graditur, quam si venabula taurus
Corpore fixa gerat, factique refugerit auctor.
Saepe illum gemitus edentem, saepe frementem,
Saepe retemptantem totas infringere vestes
Sternentemque trabes irascentemque videres
210 Montibus aut patrio tendentem bracchia caelo.

He goes raging through the mountains.

At tu, Iovis inclita proles,
230 Arboribus caesis, quas ardua gesserat Oete,
Inque pyram structis arcum pharetramque capacem
Regnaque visuras iterum Troiana sagittas
Ferre iubes Poeante satum, quo flamma ministro
Subdita. Dumque avidis comprenditur ignibus agger,
235 Congeriem silvae Nemeaeo vellere summam
Sternis, et inposita clavae cervice recumbis,
Haud alio vultu, quam si conviva iaceres
Inter plena meri redimitus pocula sertis.
Iamque valens et in omne latus diffusa sonabat,
240 Securosque artus contemptoremque petebat
Flamma suum.

Hercules builds a huge funeral pyre and, as the pyre begins to kindle, lays himself down in the flames.

V AND VI. *NEBUCHADNEZZAR* AND *BELSHAZZAR*

Chaucer has drawn his material for these two tragedies from the Book of Daniel, chapters 1–5. The relevant passages in the Vulgate are 1:1–4, 17, 20; 2:1–5, 25–28, 48; 3:1–2; 4:25–31; 5:1–31. There are incidental mentions of Nebuchadnezzar in *De casibus*, II, 15, and of Belshazzar in *De casibus*, II, 19; but there is nothing to suggest that Chaucer consulted Boccaccio for these stories. There are a number of errors in Chaucer's account of Nebuchadnezzar. He did not win Jerusalem *twice* (B 3337); he did not have the children gelded (3342); the golden statue was *six*, not *seven*, cubits broad (3350); Daniel was *not* one of the three children thrown into the fiery furnace (3356). These errors suggest the possibility of a subsidiary source.

VII. *ZENOBIA*

Chaucer's primary source is Boccaccio's *De claris mulieribus*, Caput xcviii, the text of which is printed below. This text is based on the Berne edition of 1539 (Hortis, No. IX) corrected by a collation with Bodleian MS Canon. Misc. 58. The account of Zenobia in *De casibus*, VIII, 6, is a colorless account of her military career without any of those personal, anecdotal touches given in *De claris mulieribus*, which chiefly interested Chaucer. It is apparently to *De casibus* (see above, p. 616) that Chaucer directs us, when he says (B 3509–25) that those who wish to read of Zenobia's battles should

> unto my maister Petrak go,
> That writ ynough of this, I undertake.

He seems to have made no use of the narrative of *De casibus;* but the final stanza of the tragedy is clearly dependent on the moralizing exordium of the *De casibus* passage. I quote this passage (with normalization of spelling, punctuation, and capitalization) from the Huntington Library copy of the *editio princeps* (Hortis, No. X), which is without indication of date or place of publication, but which is attributed in the Huntington Library catalogue to the press of George Husner at Strasbourg (*ca.* 1475):

Mortalium equidem nimium considerata condicio, quam crebris atque dissonis euentibus concussa distrahitur. Haec nuper Persis Syrisque tremenda regibus, nunc paruipenditur a priuatis! Haec nuper imperatoribus ammiranda, nunc venit miseranda plebeis! Haec nuper galeata concionari militibus assueta, nunc velata cogitur muliercularum audire fabellas! Haec nuper Orienti praesidens sceptra gestabat, nunc Romae subiacens colum sicut ceterae baiulat! Quid multa dixerim? Quae se bellicis immixta, quandoque Semiramidem, quandoque Dydonem praedicauerat, nunc Zenobiae nomen, si possit, deleatur exoptat. Ite igitur, humanae condicionis immemores, et scandite celsa, ut aut omnem Fortunae spirantis auram timeatis, aut sopiti, impulso nimio in mortem certissimam corruatis.

DE CLARIS MULIERIBUS, CAP. XCVIII

De Zenobia Palmirenorum Regina

Iuit aduersos montes, per saxa, per hymbres,
    Frigora non curans, nil muliebre morans.
Dura fuit virgo, tandem fit nomine prolis
    Mater, at in reliquis Martia plane manet.

Zenobia Palmirenorum fuit regina, tam eximiae virtutis foemina, priscis testantibus literis, ut caeteris gentilibus inclyta fama[1] praeponenda sit. Haec, ante alia, genere fuit insignis. Nam à Ptolemais Ægyptiorum regibus claram uolunt originem habuisse, parentibus tamen memoriae non concessis. Dicunt autem hanc à pueritia sua, spretis omnino muliebribus officiis, cum iam corpusculum eduxisset in robur, syluas & nemora incoluisse plurimum, & accinctam pharetra, ceruis caprisque cursu atque sagittis fuisse infestam. Inde cum in acriores deuenisset vires, ursos amplecti ausam, pardos leonesque insequi, obuios expectare, capere & occidere, ac in praedam trahere. Et inpauidam,[2] nunc hos, nunc illos saltus & praerupta montium discurrere, lustra perscrutari ferarum, & sub diuo somnos etiam per noctem capere. Hymbres, aestus, & frigora mira tolerantia superare, amores hominum & contubernia spernere adsuetam, & virginitatem summopere colere. Quibus fugata muliebri mollicie, adeo eam[3] in uirile robur duratam aiunt, ut coaetaneos iuuenes luctis, palestricisque ludis omnibus, uiribus superaret. Tandem instante aetate nubili amicorum consilio, Odenato iuueni aequis studiis durato, & longe Palmirenorum nobiliori principi nuptam uolunt. Erat haec speciosa corpore, esto paululum fusca colore, sic enim urente sole regionis illius omnes sunt incolae, praeterea nigris oculis, niueisque dentibus decora. Quae cum cerneret Odenatum, capto à Sapore rege Persarum

Zenobia famed for her virtues.

From her childhood a great huntress.

And a great athlete.

She marries Odenatus.

---

[1] *Ed. om.* fama.   [2] *Ed.* impauida.   [3] *Ed.* adeo & eam.

Valeriano Augusto turpique seruicio damnato, & Galieno filio effoeminate torpescente, ad orientale occupandum imperium intentum, non immemor duriciei pristinae, armis formositatem tegere, & sub uiro militare disposuit. Et cum eo sumpto regio nomine & ornatu, atque cum Herode priuigno, collectis copiis in Saporem, late iam Mesopotamiam occupantem, animose progressa est, & nullis parcens laboribus, nunc ducis, nunc militis officia peragens, non solum acerrimum uirum, & bellorum expertum uirtute armorum superauit, sed creditum eius opere Mesopotamiam in iurisdictionem uenisse, & Saporem, castris eius, cum concubinis, & ingenti praeda captis, usque Ctesiphontem pulsum atque secutum.

Nec multo post Quietum Macriani[1] filium, qui patrio sub nomine orientis imperium intrauerat, ut opprimeretur curauit uigilanti studio. Et cum iam omnem orientem ad Romanos[2] spectantem, una[3] cum uiro pacatum obtinet, & ecce a Maeonio consobrino suo Odenatus,[4] una cum Herode filio occisus est (ut[5] quidam asserunt) ob inuidiam; existimantibus aliis Zenobiam in mortem Herodis praestitisse consensum, eo quod saepius eius damnasset molliciem, & ut filiis Herenniano[6] & Timolao, quos ex Odenato susceperat, successio cederet regni. Et imperante Maeonio aliquandiu quieuit. Verum Maeonio breui à militibus suis trucidato, quasi possessione vacua derelicta, generosi animi mulier, in praedesideratum[7] imperium intrauit continuo, & filiis eius adhuc paruulis, imperiali sagulo humeris[8] perfusa, & regiis ornata, apparuit, filiorumque nomine longe magis quam sexui conueniret, gubernauit imperium, nec segniter, nam in eam, nec Galienus, nec post illum Claudius imperator aliquid attentare ausi sunt. Similiter nec orientales Ægyptii, neque Arabes. Atque[9] Sarraceni uel Armeni populi, quinimò eius timentes potentiam, suos posse seruare terminos fuere contenti. Fuit enim illi tanta bellorum industria, & adeo acris militiae disciplina, vt aeque illam magnipenderent sui exercitus & timerent. Apud quos nunquam contionata est, nisi galeata & in expeditionibus uehiculo carpentario perrarissime vtebatur, equo saepius incedebat, & nonnunquam tribus, vel quatuor milibus passum, cum militibus pedes signa praecedebat. Nec fastidiuit cum ducibus suis quandoque bibisse, cum esset alias sobria; sic cum Persis & Armenis principibus, ut illos vrbanitate & facetia superaret.

Her military campaigns.

Death of her husband, Odenatus.

She reigns in the name of her sons, Herennianus and Timolaus.

No enemy dared to attack her.

Her military prowess.

[1] *Ed.* Matriani.

[2] *Ed.* Rhomanos, *and so throughout.*

[3] *Ed.* uno.

[4] *Ed.* condemnatus.

[5] *Ed.* Et (ut . . . .

[6] *Ed.* Heremiano.

[7] *Ed.* praesideratum.

[8] *Ed.* honoris.

[9] *Ed.* aut.

Fuit tamen adeo pudicitiae severa servatrix, ut nedum ab aliis ab- Her chastity and continence.
stineret omnino,[1] sed etiam Odenato viro suo dum uiueret, se num-
quam exhibere, praeter ad filios procreandos voluisse legimus. Haec
in hac semper habita diligentia, ut post concubitum unum tam diu
abstineret ab altero, donec aduerteret utrum concepisset ex illo,
quod si contigerat, nunquam praeter post partus purgationes à uiro
tangi patiebatur vlterius. Si autem non concepisse perceperat, se
ultro poscenti uiro consentiebat. O laudabile iudicium mulieris!
satis quidem apparet arbitratam, nil ob aliud à natura mortalibus
immissam libidinem, quam ut prolis innouatione continua conse-
ruetur posteritas, & reliquum tanquam superuacaneum vitiosum.
Perrarissimas quidem huiuscemodi moris comperies mulieres.
Haec tamen ne à mente differrent ministeria ad opportuna domestica, praeter eunuchos aetate atque moribus graues, neminem
unquam uel perraro admitti voluit. Vixit praeterea ritu regio, & Her regal state.
magnifico sumptu, usa ea qua reges utuntur pompa. Persicoque more
voluit adorari, & adinstar Romanorum imperatorum conuiuia celebrauit, in eis vasis aureis gemmatisque, quibus olim usam Cleopatram
acceperat; & qua[m]quam seruatrix thesaurorum permaxima esset,
nemo ubi opportunum visum est ea magnificentior aut profusior vsus
est. Etsi plurimum uenacionibus[2] armisque uacasset, non obstitere Her learning. She knew many languages.
haec quin literas Ægyptias nosceret, & sub Longino, philosopho,
praeceptore Graecas etiam disceret. Quarum suffragio, historias
omnes Latinas, Graecas, & Barbaras, summo cum studio vidit, &
memoriae commendauit. Nec haec[3] tantum, quinimò creditum est
illas etiam sub[4] epitomatis breuitate traxisse, & praeter suum idioma
nouit Ægyptium, eoque[5] cum Syriacum sciret vsa[6] est, iussitque filios
Latine loqui. Quid multa? tanti profecto fuit haec, vt Galieno atque
Aureolo & Claudio Augusto sublatis, & Aureliano integrae virtutis
homini, in principatum suffecto, ad ignominiam Romani nominis
expiandam, & ad ingentem gloriam consequendam in se traxerit.
Nam Marcomannico bello peracto, & Romae rebus compositis, The emperor Aurelian attacks her.
Aurelianus cum omni cura Zenobianam[7] expeditionem assumpsit;
& multis egregie aduersus Barbaras nationes eundo confectis, cum
legionibus tandem haud longe Emessam ciuitatem deuenit, quam
penes Zenobia, in nullo perterrita, vna cum Zeba quodam quem belli
susceperat socium, cum exercitu suo consederat,[8] ibi inter Aurelianum
et Zenobiam de summa rerum acriter & diu pugnatum est. Ad vlti-

[1] *Ed.* animo.
[2] *Ed.* uenerationibus.
[3] *Ed.* homo.
[4] *Ed. om.* sub.
[5] *Ed.* eosque.
[6] *Ed.* visa.
[7] *Ed.* Zenobiam.
[8] *Ed.* considerat.

mum cum Romana virtus uideretur superior, Zenobia, cum suis in fugam uersa, Palmira[m] sese recepit, in qua euestigio à victore obsessa est. Quam cum aliquandiu, nullas volens conditiones deditionis audire, mira solertia defendisset, in penuriam opportunarum rerum deducta est. Hinc nequeuntibus Palmirenis Aurelianorum obsistere viribus, interceptis etiam ab eodem Persis Armenisque & Sarracenis auxilio Zenobiae uenientibus, armorum ui ciuitas a Romanis capta est. Ex qua cum Zenobia uecta dromedariis cum filiis in Persas aufugeret, ab Aurelianis militibus secuta & capta, cum filiis Aureliano[1] viva[2] praesentata est. Ex quo non aliter quam si permaximum superasset ducem, & accerrimum reipublicae hostem, Aurelianus gloriatus est, eamque triumpho seruauit, & adduxit cum filiis Romam. Inde ab Aureliano celebratus triumphus spectacula[3] Zenobiae admirandus, in quo inter alia egregia & memoratu dignissima currum duxit, quem sibi ex auro gemmisque praeciosissimum Zenobia fabricari fecerat, sperans se Romam uenturam, non quidem captiuam, sed rerum dominam atque triumphaturam, & Romanum possessuram imperium, quem & ipsa cum filiis praecessit. Verum ipsa cathenis aureis collo manibus pedibusque iniectis, corona & vestimentis regiis, ac margaritis et lapidibus praeciosis onusta, adeo, ut, cum roboris esset inexhausti, pondere fessa persaepe subsisteret. Sanè consum[m]ato triumpho thesauro & uirtute spectabili, aiunt illam priuato in habitu inter Romanas[4] matronas cum filiis senuisse, concessa sibi à Senatu possessione apud Tyburtam, quae Zenobiana[5] diu postmodum ab ea denominata est, haud longe à diui Adriani palatio quod eo in loco est cui Conche ab incolis dicebatur.

Zenobia is defeated and taken prisoner.

Aurelian takes her to Rome, where, decked with gold and jewels, she appears in his triumph.

VIII. *PEDRO OF CASTILE*

For the tragedy of Pedro of Castile, assassinated in 1369, Chaucer probably was dependent on information which came to him by word of mouth. No written source has been discovered.

IX. *PIERRE DE LUSIGNAN*

The single stanza about Pierre de Lusignan, who was assassinated by three of his own knights on January 17, 1369, contains very few details. That he took Alexandria (cf. *Prol.* A 51)

[1] *Ed.* Aurelianae.
[2] *Ed. om.* viva.
[3] *Read* spectaculo?
[4] *Ed.* Rhomanis.
[5] *Ed.* Zenobia.

and harassed the heathen was matter of common knowledge. The account of his death given by Chaucer, which is at variance with historical fact, may have been derived, as Dr. Haldeen Braddy has suggested (*PMLA*, L [1935], 78–80), from Guillaume de Machaut's long biographical poem *La Prise d'Alexandrie*. The following lines are quoted from the edition of M. L. de Mas Latrie (Geneva, 1877).

	Au matinet, à grans eslais,	The barons went to the king's palace at break of day.
	S'en alerent vers le palais,	
	Droit à l'eure que la corneille	
	Les paresseus huche & esveille,	
8635	C'est à dire à l'aube crevant.	
	Devant son lit sont arresté	They draw aside the silk curtain of his bed.
	De mal faire tuit apresté.	
	Li sires d'Absur la courtine,	
	Qui de soie estoit riche & fine,	
8690	Tira, pour le roy mieux veoir,	
	Et pour son cop mieux asseoir.	
	Et si tost com li roys le vit,	
	De son lit en gisant li dist:	
	"Estes vous là, sires d'Absur,	
8695	Faus garson, traître, parjur.	
	Qui vous fait entrer en ma chambre?"	
	Et il respondi sans attendre:	
	"Je ne sui mauvais ne traïtes,	
	Mais tel estes vous, com vous dites;	
8700	Dont vous morrez, sans nul respit,	
	De mes mains." Et en ce despit	
	Lors en son lit sus li coury	The baron strikes two or three blows as he lies in bed.
	Et ij. cos ou iij. le fery.	

X. *BARNABO*

For the tragedy of Barnabo Visconti, killed in 1385, Chaucer was probably dependent on oral information. It is of some interest to note that the story of Barnabo is included by Serdonati in Book i of his continuation (1596) of Boccaccio's *De casibus* (see the Italian translation of *De casibus* by M. Giuseppe Betussi [Florence, 1598], pp. 632–33).

XI. *UGOLINO*

Chaucer tells us (B 3651) that his source is Dante, and his tragedy seems to be derived from *Inferno* xxxiii. 1–90. For a discussion of the differences between Chaucer's version and Dante's see T. Spencer, "The Story of Ugolino in Dante and Chaucer," *Speculum*, IX (1934), 295–301. The text printed below is from the edition of G. A. Scartazzini (Florence, 1899).

DANTE *INFERNO* XXXIII. 1–90

THE STORY OF UGOLINO

In the ninth circle of hell Dante and Virgil come upon Count Ugolino, who is gnawing at the skull of Archbishop Ruggieri. On being questioned, he tells them his story.

La bocca sollevò dal fiero pasto
    Quel peccator, forbendola a' capelli
    Del capo, ch' egli avea di retro guasto.
4 Poi cominciò: "Tu vuoi ch' io rinnovelli
    Disperato dolor che il cor mi preme
    Già pur pensando, pria ch' io ne favelli.
7 Ma se le mie parole esser den semme
    Che frutti infamia al traditor ch' io rodo
    Parlare e lagrimar vedrai insieme.
10 Io non so chi tu sie, né per che modo
    Venuto se' quaggiù; ma Fiorentino
    Mi sembri veramente quand' io t' odo.
13 Tu dèi saper ch' io fui Conte Ugolino,
    E questi l'Arcivescovo Ruggieri;
    Or ti dirò perché i son tal vicino.

Archbishop Ruggieri was responsible for his death.

16 Che per l'effetto de' suo' ma' pensieri,
    Fidandomi di lui, io fossi preso
    E poscia morto dir non è mestieri.
19 Però quel che non puoi avere inteso,
    Ciò è come la morte mia fu cruda,
    Udirai, e saprai s' e' mi ha offeso.
22 Breve pertugio dentro dalla muda
    La qual per me ha il titol della fame,
    E in che conviene ancor ch' altri si chiuda,

After several months of imprisonment in the hunger tower, Ugolino has a foreboding dream.

25 M'avea mostrato per lo suo forame
    Più lune già, quand' io feci il mal sonno
    Che del futuro mi squarciò il velame.
28 Questi pareva a me maestro e donno,
    Cacciando il lupo e i lupicini al monte
    Per che i Pisan' veder Lucca non ponno,

31 Con cagne magre, studiose e conte;
     Gualandi con Sismondi e con Lanfranchi
     S'avea messi dinanzi dalla fronte.

34 In picciol corso mi pareano stanchi
     Lo padre e i figli, e con l'agute scane
     Mi parea lor veder fender li fianchi.

37 Quando fui desto innanzi la dimane,
     Pianger sentii fra il sonno i miei figliuoli
     Ch'eran con meco, e dimandar del pane.

His sons, who are with him, cry out in their sleep, asking for bread.

40 Ben se' crudel, se tu già non ti duoli
     Pensando ciò ch'al mio cor s'annunziava.
     E se non piangi, di che pianger suoli?

43 Già eran desti, e l'ora s'appressava
     Che il cibo ne soleva essere addotto,
     E per suo sogno ciascun dubitava.

46 Ed io sentii chiavar l'uscio di sotto
     All'orribile torre; ond'io guardai
     Nel viso a' miei figliuoi senza far motto.

He hears the locking of the gate.

49 Io non piangeva; sì dentro impietrai;
     Piangevan elli; ed Anselmuccio mio
     Disse: "Tu guardi sì! Padre, che hai?"

52 Però non lagrimai, né rispos'io
     Tutto quel giorno, né la notte appresso,
     Infin che l'altro sol nel mondo uscìo.

They are left all day without food.

55 Come un poco di raggio si fu messo
     Nel doloroso carcere, ed io scorsi
     Per quattro visi lo mio aspetto stesso,

58 Ambo le man' per lo dolor mi morsi
     Ed ei, pensando ch'io il fessi per voglia
     Di manicar, di subito levôrsi,

Ugolino bites his hands in despair. His sons say they would rather that he devoured them.

61 E disser: "Padre, assai ci fia men doglia
     Se tu mangi di noi. Tu ne vestisti
     Queste misere carni; e tu le spoglia."

64 Quetàmi allor per non farli più tristi.
     Lo dì e l'altro stemmo tutti muti.
     Ahi dura terra! perché non t'apristi?

For two days they were silent.

67 Poscia che fummo al quarto dì venuti,
     Gaddo mi si gittò disteso a' piedi,
     Dicendo: "Padre mio, ché non m' ajuti?"

70 Quivi morì. E come tu mi vedi,
     Vidi io cascar li tre ad uno ad uno
     Tra il quinto dì e il sesto; ond'io mi diedi,

On the fourth day Gaddo dies and between the fifth and sixth day the other two also.

After two days
more Ugolino dies
of hunger.

73 Già cieco, a brancolar sovra ciascuno,
      E due dì li chiamai poi che fûr morti.
      Poscia più che il dolor poté il digiuno."

Having told his
story, Ugolino
again gnaws at
Ruggiero's skull.

76 Quand'ebbe detto ciò, con gli occhi torti
      Riprese il teschio misero co' denti
      Che fûro all'osso, come d'un can, forti.

Dante utters an
apostrophe to the
city of Pisa.

79 Ahi Pisa! vitupero delle genti
      Del bel paese là, dove il *Sì* suona;
      Poi che i vicini a te punir son lenti,

82 Movasi la Caprara e la Gorgona,
      E faccian siepe ad Arno in su la foce,
      Sì ch' egli annieghi in te ogni persona.

85 Ché se il Conte Ugolino aveva voce
      D'aver tradita te delle castella,
      Non dovei tu i figliuoi porre a tal croce.

88 Innocenti facea l'età novella,
      Novella Tebe, Uguccione e il Brigata,
      E gli altri duo che il canto suso appella.

XII. *NERO*

Chaucer's primary source is *Roman de la rose* (ll. 6183–6488)
as printed above (pp. 618–22). This accounts adequately for
all of Chaucer's tragedy except the second stanza, with its
account of Nero's extravagant prodigality. This would seem
to have come from Boccaccio's story of Nero (*De casibus*,
VII, 3): "Quibus tam detestandis facinoribus, posita prodi-
galitate, qua aureo rethi, purpureo tracto fune, piscari solitus
erat, et veste nulla bis indui . . . ." (ed. 1544, p. 191). Or Chaucer might have found these details in Suetonius *Nero* xxx. 3:
"Nullam vestem bis induit . . . . piscatus est reti aurato purpura
coccoque funibus nexis." One may compare also Boethius
De consolatione iii. m.4. 1–4:

> Quamuis se Tyrio superbus ostro
>   Comeret et niueis lapillis,
> Inuisus tamen omnibus uigebat
>   Luxuriae Nero saeuientis.

XIII. *HOLOFERNES*

Chaucer's material is derived from the Book of Judith. The
relevant passages in the Vulgate are 2:1–18; 3:13; 4:5–7;
5:29; 12:20; 23:1–12.

XIV. *ANTIOCHUS*

Chaucer is following, for the tragedy of Antiochus Epiphanes, II Maccabees, chapter 9. The relevant verses in the Vulgate are 1–18 and 28.

XV. *ALEXANDER*

At the beginning of the tragedy we are told that

> The storie of Alisaundre is so commune
> That every wight that hath discrecioun
> Hath herd somwhat or al of his fortune.

All that we learn of Alexander in the course of the five stanzas devoted to him consists of commonplaces which might have been derived from any one of many sources. We are told repeatedly that he was a great conqueror; but the detailed information is limited to a very few points. He was fond of wine and women; he conquered Darius; he reigned twelve years; he was the son of Philip of Macedon; he was poisoned by his own people. For the length of his reign Chaucer cites as authority "Machabee." In I Maccabees 1:8 we read: "Et regnauit Alexander annis duodecim, et mortuus est." Chaucer seems also to have had in mind the opening verses of this chapter: "Et factum est, post quam percussit Alexander Philippi Macedo, qui primus regnauit in Graecia. . . . Darium regem Persarum et Medorum: constituit praelia multa, et obtinuit omnium munitiones, et interfecit reges terrae, et pertransiit vsque ad finis terrae" (cf. B 3837–42, 3846–47). Chaucer may conceivably have looked into the *De rebus gestis Alexandri Magni* of Quintus Curtius. In Vincent of Beauvais, *Speculum historiale* (ed. 1473) v. 22–71, the story of Alexander is recounted at great length; but there is nothing to suggest that Vincent was particularly in Chaucer's mind. There is no connected account in Boccaccio's *De casibus*, though incidental mentions of him (including his death by poison) are found in the account of Olympias (IV, 12) and of Darius (IV, 9). It must not be forgotten that Alexander was one of the great heroes of medieval romance.

XVI. *JULIUS CAESAR*

The Monk's account of Julius Caesar, which includes a brief tragedy of Pompey the Great, deals for the most part with generalities for which a precise source cannot be determined. It is only about the tragic ends of "thise grete conqueroures two" that we are given a set of circumstantial details. For the complete stories we are referred (B 3909–10) to Lucan, Suetonius, and Valerius. The *Pharsalia* (*De bello civili*) of Lucan, in ten books of very rhetorical verse, could have provided Chaucer with most of the materials for the first three stanzas of *Julius Caesar;* but I can find no grounds for believing that Lucan was, as Professor Shannon has contended (*Chaucer and the Roman Poets*, pp. 334–39), an immediate source. Lucan's account of the decapitation of Pompey (viii. 592–691) is so overlaid with apostrophe and other rhetorical devices, and is so allusive in character, that it is not easy to winnow out historic statement from rhetorical ornament. Chaucer could, however, have gathered that the perpetrator of the outrage was "oon of his men, a fals traitour" (cf. *Pharsalia* viii. 609–10: "scelus hoc quo nomine dicent, Qui Bruti dixere nefas?").

Professor Lowes has suggested (see note to line 2671 in Robinson's ed. of Chaucer, p. 857) *Li Hystore de Julius Cesar* by Jehan de Tuim, a thirteenth-century prose paraphrase of the *Pharsalia*, as a possible source; but Jehan's account of the treacherous slaying and decapitation of Pompey (ed. Settegast [Halle, 1881], pp. 137–39) offers no close parallels to Chaucer. The traitor Septimius, formerly a follower of Pompey, sends the head to Ptolemy, not to Caesar. One may note, however, that Pompey's tragic end is for Jehan de Tuim an exemplification of the fickleness of Fortune: "Car si tost comme Fortune a mis l'oume en haut, ausi tost le ra ele abatut dou tout. Fortune avoit Pompee montet en grant pris et en grant hounour et en grant dignite, si com vous aves oit, et ore en la fin le ra si dou tout abatut."

Chaucer cites Valerius Maximus as an authority for the stories of Caesar and Pompey, and in *Factorum et dictorum memorabilium* v. i. 10, Chaucer could have read about the decapitation of Pompey and of the tears shed by the victor,

Caesar, when the head was brought to him. The story is one of the "memorable facts" by which Valerius illustrates the theme *De humanitate et clementia*. There is, however, nothing to suggest that Valerius was Chaucer's immediate source for this episode. Valerius does not mention the fact that Pompey's head was cut off by one of his own men. The episode of the decapitation is also given by Boccaccio in his long biography of Pompey in *De casibus*, VI, 9. Boccaccio says that the head was carried through the streets of Alexandria as a spectacle and was then wrapped in a cloth and kept in order to win the favor of the victor (cf. Chaucer's "to wynnen hym favour of Julius"); but he does not mention that the decapitator was a former liege man of Pompey. Chapter 35 of Book vii (ed. 1473) of the *Speculum historiale* is entitled "De fuga et nece Pompei"; but Vincent does not mention the decapitation.

Chaucer's statement that Pompey was Caesar's father-in-law is a reversal of the facts. Pompey was actually Caesar's son-in-law (see Valerius Maximus iii. viii. 7; iv. vi. 4; v. 1. 10; and *Pharsalia* viii. 795). A careless reading of the passage in Lucan might have led to the mistake; but see Robinson's note to line 2680 (B 3870).

For the Monk's reference to Caesar's triumph see Robinson's notes to *Monk's Tale* 2671 (B 3861) and *Man of Law's Tale*, B 400. Caesar was not granted a triumph for his victory in the Civil War, but Suetonius (37–39) describes at length his five-fold triumph for his other victories. His triumphs are described by Jehan de Tuim in the prologue to his paraphrase of Lucan (ed. Settegast, pp. 8–9): "dont s'i faisoit courouner d'un vert chapiel de lorier en senefiance de victore"; and again at the end of the *Hystore de Julius Cesar*, pages 244–45.

For Chaucer's account of the death of Caesar a definite source is found in Suetonius' *Life of Julius Caesar* 82.2:

utque animadvertit undique se strictis pugionibus peti, toga caput obouoluit, simul sinistra manu sinum ad ima crura deduxit, quo honestius caderet etiam inferiore corporis parte uelata. Atque ita tribus et uiginti plagis confossus est uno modo ad primum ictum gemitu sine uoce edito.

This anecdote is recounted also by Valerius Maximus IV. v. 6 as an illustration of *Verecundia*, but Valerius does not tell us that Caesar uttered only a single groan (cf. *Monk's Tale* B 3899).

The passage of Suetonius is quoted with specific attribution to Suetonius by Vincent of Beauvais in his account of Caesar, *Spec. hist.* (ed. 1473) vii. 42. Chapters 2–4, 37–39, and 41 of Book vii are also concerned with Caesar; but there is nothing to suggest that Chaucer had read them. Vincent does not cite Lucan and Valerius Maximus as authorities for the life of Caesar or of Pompey.

If a precise source for the tragedy of Caesar and Pompey is ever discovered, it will presumably be an epitome from which Chaucer could have derived both its substance and its citation of the three authorities.

XVII. *CROESUS*

Chaucer's primary source for the tragedy of Croesus is *Roman de la rose*, lines 6489–6622, as printed above (pp. 622–25). His first stanza, however, is reminiscent of Boethius *De consolatione* ii. pr. 2. 34–36, where Fortune is addressing the author: "Nesciebas Croesum regem Lydorum, Cyro paulo ante formidabilem mox deinde miserandum rogi flammis traditum misso caelitus imbre defensum?" Boccaccio tells the story of Croesus in *De casibus*, III, 20; but Chaucer does not seem to have drawn anything from this account, unless conceivably the escape from the fire: "Hoc satis a fide habeo, Croesum uiuum in maximum ignem fuisse deiectum, a quo antequam laederetur, tantus repente imber cecidit in instanti, ut nec fauilla superesset vnica, et Croesus remaneret illaesus."

THE NUN'S PRIEST'S TALE

By JAMES R. HULBERT

THE classic study of the sources of the *Nun's Priest's Tale* is still Miss Kate Petersen's monograph, *On the Sources of the "Nonne Prestes Tale"* (Boston, 1898). Yet the tendency of scholars of recent years has been not to accept her theory that Chaucer's tale derives from a version nearer to the German analogue than to the French but to hold that the source was a French version close to the *Roman* if not identical with it.[1] To be sure, a careful comparison of the three versions confirms her conclusion that in important respects Chaucer's tale agrees with the German; but it reveals further that both narratives lack consistency and completeness in detail. On the other hand, though the French development of the story is verbose, it does contain all essential details and represents the original exactly. Failure to use the proper names of the French (especially Reynard), however, makes it improbable that Chaucer knew the precise French text that we have. Thus the problem is whether the German and English independently condensed their original and thus by chance reached certain agreements, or whether some of the omissions had been made already in their common source. Since in the German the story is associated with the Reynard cycle but in Chaucer's version even the name Reynard is not used, it seems that in that respect at least the source of the German must have differed from his. But it is logically possible that, though Chaucer's was not identical with that of the German, it was an abbreviated version identical in some respects with the one before the German poet. With the evidence at present available it is probably impossible to solve this problem. That aspect of the problem which concerns Chaucer's failure to preserve any of the names used in the *Roman de Renart* except Chauntecler suggests to Mr. Sisam that Chaucer's immediate source was

[1] Lecompte, in *MP*, XIV (1916), 737–49; Sisam's ed. (Oxford, 1927), p. xxvi, n. 2.

a version—perhaps oral or derived from an oral form—in which the other characters had lost their names.[1]

For other phases of the poem's genesis we are similarly in the dark. The immediate source of the *exempla* given by the Nun's Priest in B 4174 ff. is as uncertain as that of the principal action. Since Chaucer may have encountered the version by Valerius Maximus either in that author's works or in quotations from them made by Robert Holkot or Giraldus Cambrensis or some other medieval compiler, it seems best to print Valerius' versions rather than those of Cicero.[2] Finally, for the mock heroic and sermonistic development of the Priest's tale, no specific source can be cited. Perhaps some passage in Chaucer's original, like the introduction to the story in *Renart*, may have suggested the mock heroic elaboration. Yet, wherever Chaucer got the suggestion, the realization of it is surely his own.

LE ROMAN DE RENART

(Reprinted from Ernest Martin, *Le Roman de Renart* [Strasbourg, 1882], Branch II, ll. 1–468 [Vol. 1, pp. 91–104.].)

You have heard stories of how Paris stole Helen and of Tristan.	Seigneurs, oï avez maint conte Que maint conterre vous raconte, Comment Paris ravi Elaine, Le mal qu'il en ot et la paine: 5 De Tristan qui la chievre fist, Qui assez bellement en dist Et fabliaus et chancon de geste. Romanz de lui et de sa geste Maint autre conte par la terre.
But you have not heard of the war between Renard and Isengrin.	10 Mais onques n'oïstes la guerre, Qui tant fu dure de grant fin, Entre Renart et Ysengrin, Qui moult dura et moult fu dure.
The two barons never liked each other, and there was many a battle between them.	Des deus barons ce est la pure[3] 15 Que ainc ne s'entramerent jour. Mainte mellee et maint estour
Now I shall begin the history of their strife.	Ot entr'eulz deus, ce est la voire. Des or commencerai l'estoire Or oez le conmencement

[1] See Sisam's ed., esp. p. xxiv, and Robinson's *Chaucer* (Boston, 1933).

[2] See Petersen's comparisons, pp. 106 ff.; Sisam, pp. 218 ff.; Robinson, p. 860.

[3] The simple truth.

20 Et de la noise et du content.
    Par quoi et por quel mesestance
    Fu entr'eus deus la desfiance.
        Il avint chose que Renars,
    Qui tant par fu de males ars[1]   Renard came to a
                                                       farm in a wood.
25 Et qui tant sot toz jors de guile,
    S'en vint traiant a une vile.
    La vile seoit en un bos.
    Molt i ot gelines et cos,   There dwelt Con-
                                                       stans des Noes, a
    Anes[2] et malarz, jars et oes.   prosperous farmer
                                                       whose farm abound-
30 Et li sires Constans des Noes,   ed in fowl, salt
    Un vilain qui moult ert garnis,   meat, wheat, and
                                                       fruits.
    Manoit moult pres du plesseïs.[3]
    Plenteïve estoit sa maisons.
    De gelines et de chapons
35 Bien avoit garni son hostel.
    Assez i ot et un et el:
    Char salee, bacons et fliches.[4]
    De ble estoit li vilains riches
    Molt par estoit bien herbergiez,
40 Que moult iert riches ses vergiers.
    Assez i ot bonnes cerises
    Et pluseurs fruis de maintes guises.
    Pommes i ot et autre fruit.
    La vait Renart pour son deduit.
45 Li courtilz estoit bien enclos.   In a yard inclosed
                                                       with thick, sharp
    De piex de chesne agus et gros.   stakes and a haw-
    Hourdes estoit d'aubes espines.   thorn hedge, Con-
                                                       stans kept his hens.
    Laiens avoit mis ses gelines
    Dant Constant pour la forteresce.
50 Et Renart celle part s'adresce,   Thither came Re-
                                                       nard, found a brok-
    Tout coiement le col bessie   en stake and crept
    S'en vint tout droit vers le plessie.   through a hole.
    Moult fu Renart de grant pourchaz.[5]
    Mais la force des espinars
55 Li destourne si son affaire
    Que il n'en puet a bon chief traire,
    Ne pour mucier ne pour saillir:
    N'aus gelines ne veult faillir.
    Acroupiz s'est enmi la voie.

---

[1] Black arts, bad tricks.   [3] Stockade, farm.
[2] Ducks.   [4] Salt meat.   [5] Design, resource.

60   Moult se defripe,[1] moult coloie.[2]
        Il se pourpense que s'il saut,
        Pour quoi il chiece auques de haut,[3]
        Il iert veüz et les gelines
        Se ficheront souz les espines.
65   Si pourroit tost estre seurpris
        Ainz qu'il eüst gaires acquis.
        Moult par estoit en grant esfroi.
        Les gelines veult traire a soi
        Que devant lui voit pasturant.
70   Et Renart vait cheant levant.[4]
        Ou retour de la soif[5] choisist
        Un pel[6] froissie: dedenz se mist.
        La ou li paliz iert desclos,
        Avoit li vilains plante chos:
75   Renart y vint, oultre s'em passe,
        Cheoir se laist en une masse
        Pour ce que la gent ne le voient.
        Mais les gelines en coloient,
        Qui l'ont choisi a sa cheoite.
80   Chascune de fuïr s'esploite.
              Mesire Chantecler li cos
        En une sente les le bos
        Entre deus piex souz la raiere[7]
        S'estoit traiz en une poudriere.
85   Moult fierement leur vient devant
        La plume ou pie, le col tendant.
        Si demande par quel raison
        Elles s'en fuient vers maison.
        Pinte parla qui plus savoit,
90   Celle qui les gros hues ponnoit,
        Qui pres du coc jucoit a destre:
        Si li a raconte son estre
        Et dit "paour avons eüe."
        "Pourquoi? quel chose avez veüe?"
95   "Je ne sai quel beste sauvage
        Qui tost nous puet faire damage,
        Se nous ne vuidons ce pourpris."

[1] He moves to and fro.
[2] Stretches his neck.
[3] Because he would fall from above.
[4] Stumbling.
[5] Palisade.
[6] Stake, picket.
[7] A rail of the fence.

"C'est tout noient, ce vous plevis."
Ce dit li cos: "n'aies peür,
100   Mais estes ci tout asseür."
Dist Pinte "par ma foi jel vi:
Et loiaument le vous affi:
Que je le vi tout a estrouz."[1]
"Et comment le veïstes vous?"
105   "Comment? je vi la soif branler
Et la fuelle du chou trembler
Ou cilz se gist qui est repus."
"Pinte" fait il, "or n'i a plus.
Trives avez, je vous ottroi:

Chantecler assured her that no animal would dare enter the yard, and returned to his sand pile.

110   Que par la foi que je vous doi,
Je ne sai putoiz ne gourpil
Que osast entrer ou courtil.
Ce est gas: retournez arriere."
Cilz se radresce en sa poudriere,
115   Qu'il na paour de nulle riens
Que li face gourpilz ne chiens
De nulle riens n'avoit peür,
Que moult cuidoit estre aseür.
Moult se contint seürement.
120   Ne set gaires q'a l'eil li pent.
Rien ne douta: si fist que fox.
L'un oeil ouvert et l'autre clos,
L'un pie crampi et l'autre droit
S'est apuiez delez un toit.
125   La ou li cos est apoiez
Conme cilz qui iert anuiez
Et de chanter et de veiller,
Si conmenca a someillier.
Ou someillier que il faisoit

There he fell asleep and dreamed that something in the yard came toward him.

130   Et ou dormir qui li plaisoit
Conmenca li cos a songier.
Ne m'en tenes a menconger.
Car il sonja (ce est la voire,
Trover le poez en l'estoire)
135   Que il avoit ne sai quel cose
Dedens la cort, que bien ert close,
Qui li venoit enmi le vis,

[1] Very certainly.

Ensi con il li ert avis,
(Si en avoit molt grant fricon)

140 Et tenoit un ros pelicon

Dont les goles estoient d'os.

Si li metoit par force el dos.

Molt ert Chantecler en grant peine

Del songe qui si le demeine,

145 Endementiers que il somelle.

Et del pelicon se mervelle,

Que la chevece[1] ert en travers:

Et si l'avoit vestu envers.

Estrois estoit en la chevece

150 Si qu'il en a si grant destrece

Qu'a peines s'en est esveilliez.

Mes de ce s'est plus merveilliez

Que blans estoit desos le ventre

Et que par la chevece i entre,

155 Si que la teste est en la faille[2]

Et la coue en la chevecaille.

Por le songe s'est tressailliz,

Que bien cuide estre malbailliz

Por la vision que a veüe,

160 Dont il a grant peor oüe.

Esveillies s'est et esperiz[3]

Li cos et dist "seint esperiz,

Garis hui mon cors de prison

Et met a sauve garison!"

165 Lors s'en torne grant aleüre

Con cil qui point ne s'aseüre

Et vint traiant vers les gelines,

Qui estoient soz les espines.

Tres q'a eles ne se recroit.

170 Pinte apela ou molt se croit,

A une part l'a asenee.

"Pinte, n'i a mester celee.

Molt sui dolanz et esbahiz.

Grant poor ai destre traïz

175 D'oisel ou de beste sauvage.

Qui tost nos puet fere damage."

It wore a red fur coat, the neck of which was of bone, and forced it on Chantecler's back.

With the pain made by the narrow neck, Chantecler awoke.

"Holy Spirit, keep my body from prison," he said.

Hastening to Pinte, he told her his fear of betrayal by some animal.

[1] The neck of the garment.

[2] Head covering.

[3] Conscious, come to his wits.

"Avoi!" fait Pinte "baus dos sire,
Ice ne deves vos pas dire.
Mau fetes qui nos esmaies.
180   Si vos dirai, ca vos traies!
Par trestoz les seinz que l'en prie,
Vos resembles le chen qui crie
Ains que la pierre soit coüe.
Por qu'aves tel poor oüe?
185   Car me dites que vos aves."
"Quoi?" dist li cos "vos ne saves
Que j'ai songie un songe estrange.
Deles cel trou les cele granche,
Et une avision molt male,
190   Por qoi vos me vees si pale.
Tot le songe vos conterai,
Ja riens ne vos en celerai.
Saurees m'en vos conseillier?
Avis me fu el somellier
195   Que ne sai quel beste veneit
Qui un ros pelicon vestoit,
Bien fet sanz cisel et sanz force:[1]
Sil me fesoit vestir a force.
D'os estoit fete l'orleüre,
200   Tote blance, mes molt ert dure:
La chavesce de travers fete,
Estroite, qui molt me dehaite.
Le poil avoit dehors torne.
Le pelicon si atorne
205   Par le chevece le vestoie.
Mais molt petit i arestoie.
Le pelicon vesti ensi:
Mes a reculons m'en issi.
Lors m'en merveillai a cele ore
210   Por la coue qui ert desoure.
Ca sui venus desconseilliez.
Pinte, ne vos en merveilliez,
Se li cuers me fremist et tramble.
Mes dites moi que vos en semble.
215   Molt sui por le songe grevez.
Par cele foi que me devez,
Savez vos que ce senefie?"

"Avoi," said Pinte, "dear sir, you should not frighten us so."

Chantecler recounted his dream.

[1] Shears.

Pinte respont, ou molt se fie,
"Dit m'avez" fait ele "le songe.

220   Mes se dex plest, ce est mencoigne.
Ne porquant si vos voil espondre:
Car bien nos en saurai respondre:
Icele chose que veïstes
El someller que vos feïstes,

Pinte interpreted it
correctly and
warned him against
the fox, which was
now in that bush.

225   Qui le ros pelicon vestoit
Et issi vos desconfortoit
C'est li gorpils, je sai de voir.
Bien le poes apercevoir
Au pelicon qui ros estoit

230   Et qui par force vos vestoit.
Les goles d'os ce sont les denz
A qoi il vos metra dedenz.
La chevece qui n'iert pas droite,
Qui si vos iert male et estroite,

235   Ce est la boce de la beste,
Dont il vos estreindra la teste.
Par iloques i enterois,
Sanz faille vos le vestirois.
Ce que la coue est contremont,

240   Par les seinz de trestot le mont
C'est li gorpils qui vos prendra
Parmi le col, quant il vendra.
Dont sera la coue desore.
Einsi ert, se dex me secore.

245   Ne vos gara argent ne ors.
Li peus qui ert torne defors
C'est voirs, que tot jors porte enverse
Sa pel, quant il mels plot et verse.
Or avez oï sanz faillance

250   De vostre songe la senblance.
Tot soürement le vos di:
Ainz que voiez passe midi,
Vos avandra, ce est la voire.
Mes se vos me volieez croire,

255   Vos retorneriez ariere:
Car il est repos ci derere
En cest boisson, jel sai de voir
Por vos traïr et decevoir."
Quant cil ot oï le respons

260 Del songe, que cele ot espons,
    "Pinte" fait il, "molt par es folc.
    Molt as dit vileine parole,
    Qui diz que je serai sorpris
    Et que la beste est el porpris

265 Qui par fòrce me conquerra.
    Dahez ait qui ja le crera!
    Ne m'as dit rien ou ge me tiegne.
    Ja nel crerai, se biens m'aviegne,
    Que j'aie mal por icest songe."

270 "Sire" fait ele, "dex le dogne!
    Mais s'il n'est si con vos ai dit,
    Je vos otroi senz contredit,
    Je ne soie mes vostre amie."
    "Pinte" fait il, "ce n'i a mie."

275 A fable est li songes tornez.
    A itant s'en est retornez
    En la poudrere a solaller.
    Si reconmance a someller.
    Et quant il fu aseürez,

280 (Molt fu Renars amesurez
    Et voisiez[1] a grant merveille)
    Quant il voit que celui somelle,
    Vers lui aprime sanz demore
    Renars, qui tot le mont acore[2]

285 Et qui tant set de maveis tors.
    Pas avant autre tot sanz cors[3]
    S'en vet Renars le col baissant.
    Se Chantecler le par atent[4]
    Que cil le puisse as denz tenir,

290 Il le fera son jou poïr.[5]
       Quant Renars choisi Chantecler,
    Senpres le volst as denz haper.
    Renars failli, qui fu engres,
    Et Chantecler saut en travers.

295 Renart choisi, bien le conut,
    Desor le fumier s'arestut.
    Quant Renars voit qu'il a failli,
    Forment se tint a malbailli.
    Or se conmence a porpenser,

Marginal notes:

Refusing to believe that there was a beast in the yard, Chantecler returned to the dust heap and fell asleep.

Approaching Chantecler, Renard snapped at him but missed.

Chantecler jumped up.

[1] Canny, foxy.
[2] Kills.
[3] Without hurrying.
[4] Waits long enough.
[5] He will make him repent.

Renard urged
Chantecler not to
flee.

Pleased by Re-
nard's words, Chan-
tecler sang a song.

Renard praised the
singing of Chante-
clin, Chantecler's
father, and said
that when he sang
he closed both his
eyes.

Chantecler suspect-
ed treachery and
sang with one eye
open.

300 Conment il porroit Chantecler
Engignier: car s'il nel manjue,
Dont a il sa voie perdue.
"Chantecler" ce li dist Renart,
"Ne fuir pas, n'aies regart!
305 Molt par sui liez, quant tu es seinz;
Car tu es mes cosins germeins."
Chantecler lors s'asoüra.
Por la joie un sonet chanta.
Ce dist Renars a son cosin,
310 "Membre te mes de Chanteclin,
Ton bon pere qui t'engendra?
Onques nus cos si ne chanta.
D'une grant liue l'ooit on.
Molt bien chantoit en haut un son
315 Et molt par avoit longe aleine
Les deus els clos, la vois ot seine,
D'une leüe ne veoit,
Quant il chantoit et refregnoit."
Dist Chantecler, "Renart cosin,
320 Voles me vos trere a engin?"
"Certes," ce dis Renars, "non voil.
Mes or chantez, so clinnies l'oeil!
D'une char somes et d'un sanc
Meus voudroie estre d'un pie manc
325 Que tu eüses maremenz:
Car tu es trop pres mi parenz."
Dist Chantecler, "pas ne t'en croi.
Un poi te trai ensus de moi
Et je dirai une chancon.
330 N'aura voisin ci environ
Qui bien n'entende mon fauset."
Lores s'en sozrist Renardet:
"Or dont en haut: chantez, cosin!
Je saurai bien, se Chanteclin,
335 Mis oncles, vos fu onc neant."
Lors comenca cil hautement:
Puis jeta Chantecler un bret.
L'un oil ot clos et l'autre overt:
Car molt forment dotoit Renart.
340 Sovent regarde cele part.
Ce dist Renars, "n'as fet neent.

Chanteclins chantoit autrement
A uns lons trez les eilz cligniez:
L'en l'ooit bien par vint plaissiez."

Renard said that Chanteclin sang more loudly.

345   Chantecler quide que voir die.
Lors let aler sa meloudie
Les oilz cligniez par grant aïr.[1]
Lors ne volt plus Renars soffrir.
Par de desoz un roge chol

Then Chantecler shut his eyes.

350   Le prent Renars parmi le col,
Fuiant s'ent va et fait grant joie
De ce qu'il a encontre proie.
Pinte voit que Renars l'enporte,
Dolente est, molt se deconforte.

Renard seized him and fled.

Pinte reproached Chantecler for not following her advice.

355   Si se conmence a dementer,
Quant Chantecler vit enporter,
Et dit, "sire, bien le vos dis
Et vos me gabiez todis
Et si me tenieez por fole.

360   Mes ore est voire la parole,
Dont je vos avoie garni.
Vostre senz vos a escharni.[2]
Fole fui, quant jel vos apris,
Et fox ne crient tant qu'il est pris.

365   Renars vos tient qui vos enporte
Lasse dolente, con sui morte!
Car se je ci pert mon seignor,
A toz jors ai perdu m'onor."
La bone feme del mainil

The woman of the house, coming for the hens, saw Renard and cried "Harou."

370   A overt l'uis de son cortil.
Car vespres ert, per ce voloit
Ses jelines remetre en toit.
Pinte apela, Bise et Rosete.
L'une ne l'autre ne recete.

375   Quant voit que venues ne sont,
Molt se merveille qu'elles font.
Son coc rehuce a grant aleine.
Renart regarde qui l'enmeine.
Lors passe avant por le rescore

380   Et li gorpils conmence a core.
Quant voit que prendre nel porra,
Porpense soi qu'el criera.

---

[1] With great zest.   [2] Deceived, shamed.

"Harou!" escrie a pleine gole.
Li vilein qui sont a la coule,[1]

385   Quant il oent que cele bret,
Trestuit se sont cele part tret.
Si li demandent, que ele a.
En sospirant lor reconta
"Lasse, con m'est mal avenu!"
390   "Coment?" font il. "Car j'ai perdu
Mon coc que li gorpil enporte."

Constans blamed
the woman for not
seizing or hitting
Renard.

Ce dist Costans, "pute vielle orde,
Qu'aves dont fet que nel preïstes?"
"Sire," fait ele, "mar le dites.
395   Par les seinz deu, je nel poi prendre."
"Por quoi?" "Il ne me volt atendre."
"Sel ferissiez?" "Je n'oi de quoi."
"De cest baston." "Par deu ne poi:
Car il s'en vet si grant troton,
400   Nel prendroient deus chen breton."
"Par ou s'en vet?" "Par ci tot droit."

Li vilein corent a esploit.
Tuit s'escrient "or ca, or ca!"
Renars l'oï qui devant va.

Renard ran through
the hole in the
fence.

405   Au pertuis vint, si sailli jus
Qu'a la terre feri li cus.
Le saut qu'il fist ont cil oï.
Tuit sescrient, "or ca, or ci!"
Costans lor dist, "or tost apres!"
410   Li vilein corent a esles.[2]
Costans apele son mastin,
Que tuit apelent Mauvoisin,
"Bardol, Travers, Humbaut, Rebors,
Cores apres Renart le ros!"
415   Au corre qu'il font l'ont veü
Et Renart ont aperceü.
Tuit s'escrient, "vez le gorpil!"
Or est Chanteclers en peril,
S'il ne reseit engin et art.

420   "Conment," fait il, "sire Renart,
Dont n'oez quel honte vos dient,
Cil vilein qui si vos escrient?
Costans vos seut plus que le pas.

---

[1] Who are playing ball.   [2] Running fast.

Car li lanciez un de vos gas
425 A l'issue de cele porte.
Quant il dira, 'Renars l'enporte,'
'Maugrez vostre' ce poes dire,
'Ja nel porres mels desconfire.' "
   N'i a si sage ne foloit.
430 Renars qui tot le mont decoit,
Fu decoüs a cele foiz.
Il s'escria a haute vois.
"Maugre vostre," ce dist Renart,   Renard did so,
"De cestui enpor je ma part."
435 Quant cil senti lache la boce,
Bati les eles, si s'en toche.[1]
Si vint volant sor un pomer.   and Chantecler flew
Renars fu bas sor un fomier,   into an apple tree.
Greinz[2] et maris et trespenses
440 Del coc qui li est escapez.
Chantecler li jeta un ris
"Renart," fait il, "que vos est vis
De cest siegle? que vos en semble?"
Li lecheres fremist et tramle.
445 Si li a dit par felonie:
"La boce," fait il, "soit honie,   Renard said:
Qui s'entremet de noise fere   "Shameful the
                                 mouth which stops
A l'ore qu'ele se doit tere."   to make a noise
"Si soit," fet li cos, "con je voil.   when it should be
                                 still."
450 La male gote li cret l'oil
Qui s'entremet de someller   Chantecler re-
A l'ore que il doit veillier.   joined: "A curse on
Cosins Renart," dist Chantecler,   the eyes that sleep
                                 when they should
"Nus ne se puet en vos fier.   be awake."
455 Dahez ait vostre cosinage!
Il me dut torner a damage.
Renart parjure, ales vos ent!
Se vos estes ci longement,
Vos i lairois vostre gonele."
460 Renars n'a soing de sa favele.
Ne volt plus dire, atant s'en torne.
Ne repose ne ne sejorne,   Disconsolate, Re-
Besongnieus est, le cuer a vein.   nard went his way.
Par une broce[3] lez un plein[4]

---

[1] Took to flight.   [2] Troubled, angry.   [3] Hedge.   [4] Meadow.

465   S'en vait fuiant tot une sente.
      Molt est dolans, molt se demente
      Del coc, qui li est escapes,
      Quant il n'en est bien saoles.

REINHART FUCHS

(From *Heinrichs des Glichezares Reinhart Fuchs*, ed. G. Baesecke [Halle, 1925],
ll. 11–176. Reprinted by permission of Max Niemeyer, publisher.)

      Nu sol ich euch wizzen lan,
      Wavon die rede ist getan.

Near a village re-
sided a well-to-do
farmer, Lanczelin,
and his wife, Ruc-
zela.

      Ein gebure vil riche
      Der saz gemeliche
15 Bei einem dorfe uber ein velt,
      Da hater erbe unde gelt,
      Korn unde hirsez genuc,
      Vil harte eben gienc sin pfluc.
      Der was geheizen Lanczelin,
20 Babe Ruczela daz wip sin.
      Er hatte eine groze clage:

Being troubled by
Reinhart's thefts of
his fowls, Lanczelin
made a stout fence
to protect Scante-
cler and the hens.

      Er muste hûten alle tage
      Siner hûner vor Reinharte.
      Sin hove unde sin garte
25 Waz niht bezunet zu vrumen.[1]
      Davon muster dicke kumen
      Zu schaden, den er ungerne sach.
      Babe Runzela zu im sprach:
      "Alder gouch[2] Lanzelin,
30 Nu han ich der hûner min
      Von Reinharte zehen verlorn,
      Daz muet[3] mich unde ist mir zorn."
      Meister Lanzelin was bescholden[4]
      (Daz ist noch unvergolden),[5]
35 Doch er des niht enliez,
      Ern tete, als in babe Runzela hiez.
      Einen zun machter vil gut,
      Darinne wander[6] han behut
      Scanteclern unde sin wip:

[1] Advantageously, effectively.

[2] Fool.

[3] That bothers me.

[4] Scolded.

[5] Unrequited, not paid back.

[6] He thought.

40   Den riet Reinhart an den lip.[1]
      Eines tages, do die sunne ufgie,
      Reinhart do niht enlie
      Ern gienge zu dem hove mit sinnen:
      Do wolter einer unminnen
45   Scanteclern bereiten.
      Ouch brachtern zu erbeiten.
      Der zun douht in zu dicke unde ze hoch,
      Mit den zenen er dannen zoch
      Einen spachen unde tucte sich do.
50   Als er niman sach, des was er vro.
      Nu wanter sich durch den hag:
      Vil nahen er Schanteclere lag,
      Sin verchvint Reinhart.
      Die henne Pinte sin gewar wart,
55   Scantecler bi der want slief.
      Vor[2] Pinte schre: "Her!" unde rief
      Unde vloch bi eine swellen
      Mit andern iren gellen.
      Scantecler quam gerant
60   Unde hiez si wider zu der want
      Strichen[3] vil schire:
      "Irn durft vor keinem tiere
      Nimmer uwer warten
      In disem bezuntem garten.
65   Doch bitet Got, vil liben wip,
      Daz er mir beschirme minen lip:
      Mir ist getroumet sware,
      Daz sagich euch ze ware,
      Wie ich in einem roten bellitz solde sin,
70   Daz houbetloch was beinein:
      Ich vuhrte, daz sin[4] arbeit.
      Dem heiligen engel sei iz geseit,
      Der erschein mirs zu gute!
      Mir ist swere ze mute."
75   Vrowe Pinte sprach: "Her unde trût,
      Ich sach sich regen in jenem chrût:
      Mich entrigen mine sinne,
      Hi ist ich enweiz was ubeles inne.
      Der riche got beschirme dich!

Reinhart came, pulled out a piece of the fence with his teeth and penetrated within the yard.

He lay down near Scantecler, who was asleep.

Pinte, catching sight of him, shrieked and flew to a perch.

Scantecler came to her and urged her to return to the yard, as the fence protected it from animals.

Yet he had a dream that he was wearing a red fur coat the neck of which was of bone.

Pinte replied that she had seen something move in the cabbages.

[1] R. decided to tackle them.   [3] Stride, hasten.
[2] Frau, Mrs.   [4] To be. "I fear that will be trouble."

80   Mir gat uber erklich,
      Mir grŏwet so, ich vurhte, wir
      Zu noten kumen, daz sagich dir."

Scantecler derided
her and added that
the meaning of
dreams may be
clear after seven
years.

      Scantecler sprach; "Sam mir min lip,
      Mer verzaget ein wip
85   Danne tun viere man:
      Dicke wir vernumen han
      Daz sich erscheinet, daz is war,
      Manic troum uber siben jar."

Pinte advised him
to fly up into a
thorn tree.

      Vor Pinte sprach: "Lazet ewern zorn
90   Unde vliget uf disen dorn,
      Gedenket wol, daz unser kint
      Leider harte cleine sint!
      Verlusest du, herre, dinen lip,
      So muz ich sin ein ruwic wip
95   Und umberaten immer me:
      Mir tut min herze vil wundern we,
      Wen ich so sere vurhte din:
      Nu beschirme dich unser trechtin!"
      Scantecler uf den dorn vlŏch
100   (Reinhart in sit herabe trouch),
      Pinte schire vliende wart,
      Under den dorn lief Reinhart.

He did so.
Reinhart came be-
neath the tree and
started to cajole
him.

      Scantecler im ze hohe saz,
      Reinhart begonde uben baz
105   Sine liste, die er hat:
      Er sprach: "Wer ist, der da uf stat?
      Bistu daz, Sengelin?"

He asked the cock
if he were Sengelin,
Scantecler's father,
and added that Sen-
gelin used to fly to
meet Reinhart's
father and, closing
both his eyes, sing
for joy.

      "Nein ich," sprach Scantecler, "ich enpin,
      Also hiez der vater min."
110   Reinhart sprach: "Daz mac wol sin.
      Nu rewet mich dines vater tot,
      Wen der dem minnisten ere bot,
      Wan trewe undir kunne,
      Daz ist michel wunne.
115   Du gebares zu untare,[1]
      Daz sagich dir zware:
      Din vater was des minen vro,
      Ern gesaz sust hone nie also,
      Gesaech er den vater min,

[1] Unfriendly.

120 Erne vluge zu ime unde hiez in sin
     Willekumen, ouch vermeit er nie,
     Ern swunge sine vitichen ie,
     Iz were spate oder vru,
     Die ougen teter beide zu
125 Unde sang im als ein vrolichez hun."
     Scantecler sprach: "Daz wil ich tun: Scantecler said that his father had taught him to do that.
     Iz larte mich der vater min:
     Du solt groz wilkumen sin!"
     Die vitich begonder swingen   He flew down, closed his eyes, and sang.
130 Unde vrolich nider springen.
     Des was dem toren ze gach,
     Daz gerowe in sere darnach.
     Blinzende er singende wart,
     Bi dem houbete nam in Reinhart,   Reinhart seized him by the head, Pinte shrieked, Reinhart started for the wood.
135 Pinte schrei unde begonde sich missehaben,
     Reinhart tet niht danne draben
     Unde hub sich wundern balde
     Rechte hin gegn dem walde.
     Den schal vernam meister Lanzelin,   Lanczelin heard the noise.
140 Er sprach: "Owe der huner min!"
     Scantecler sprach ze Reinharte: Scantecler urged Reinhart to taunt the farmers.
     "War gahet ir sust harte?
     Wes lazet ir euch disen gebur beschelten?
     Mugt ir iz im niht vergelten?"
145 "Ja ich, sam mir, Reinhart,"   Reinhart did so, and Scantecler twisted his neck from Reinhart's mouth and flew to a tree.
     Sprach er, "ir gat ein uppege vart."
     Scantecler was ungerne da,
     Als er im entweich, da want er sa
     Den hals uz Reinhartes munde.
150 Er vlouc zu der stunde
     Uf einen boum, do er genas.
     Reinhart harte truric was.
     Zuhant Scantecler sprach,   Scantecler told Reinhart that Reinhart couldn't take him again.
     Do er Reinharten under im sach:
155 "Du hast mir gedinet ane danc:
     Der weck douchte mich ze lanc,
     Da du mich her hast getragen.
     Ich wil dir furwar sagen:
     Dune brengest mich dar wider niht,
160 Swaz darumme mir geschiht."

Reinhart replied:
"He is a fool who
avenges himself up-
on his detractors, or
who chatters when
he should be silent."

Reinhart horte wol den spot,

Er sprach: "Er ist tumb, sam mir Got,

Der mit schaden richit,

Daz man im gesprichit,

165　Oder swer[1] danne ist claffens vol,

So er von rechte swigen sol."

Scantecler: "He is
no fool who is al-
ways on his guard."

Do sprach Scantecler: "Er were

Weiz Got niht alwere,[2]

Swer sich behǔtete ze aller zit."

170　Do schiet sich der spot unde ir strit.

Lanczelin came up,
and Reinhart fled.

Meister Lanzelin gienc da hernach,

Reinharten wart dannen gach.

Im was ane maze zorn,

Das er hatte verlorn

175　Sin inbiz, daz er wande han.

Vil harte in hungern began.

EXEMPLA IN VALERIUS MAXIMUS

1. Analogue to B 4174–4252

(Valerius Maximus, *Factorum et dictorum memorabilium, libri novem*, ed. C. Halm [Leipzig, 1865], Lib. i, Cap. vii, ¶ 10.)

Two friends jour-
neying together
came to Megara.
One went to lodg-
ings, the other to an
inn.
The former dreamed
that his friend
prayed him for help
against the treach-
ery of the inn-
keeper.
Aroused, he started
to go to the inn,
but, judging his plan
foolish, went back
to bed.
The friend again ap-
peared and said
that he had been
killed by the inn-
keeper and that his
body in a cart laden
with dung was being
carried to the gate.
The sleeper awoke,
hastened to the gate,
seized the cart, and
caused the innkeep-
er to be executed.

Proximum somnium etsi paulo est longius, propter nimiam tamen euidentiam ne omittatur impetrat. Duo familiares Arcades iter una facientes Megaram uenerunt, quorum alter se ad hospitem contulit, alter in tabernam meritoriam deuertit. is qui in hospitio erat uidit in somnis comitem suum orantem ut sibi coponis insidiis circumuento subueniret: posse enim celeri eius adcursu se inminenti periculo sub-trahi. quo uisu excitatus prociluit tabernamque, in qua is deuers-abatur, petere conatus est. Pestifero deinde fato eius humanissimum propositum tamquam superuacuum damnauit et lectum ac somnum repetiit. tunc idem ei saucius oblatus obsecrauit ut, quoniam uitae suae auxilium ferre neglexisset, neci saltem ultionem non negaret: corpus enim suum a copone trucidatum tum maxime plaustro ferri ad portam stercore coopertum. tam constantibus familiaris precibus conpulsus protinus ad portam cucurrit et plaustrum, quod in quiete demonstratum erat, conprehendit coponemque ad capitale supplicium perduxit.

---

[1] Whoever.　　　　　　　[2] Foolish.

2. ANALOGUE TO B 4254–94

(Valerius Maximus, *Factorum et dictorum memorabilium, libri novem.* Lib. I, Cap. vii, ¶ 3.)

Longe indulgentius dii in poeta Simonide, cuius salutarem inter quietem admonitionem consilii firmitate roborarunt. Is enim cum ad litus nauem appulisset inhumatumque corpus iacens sepulturae mandasset, admonitus ab eo ne proximo die nauigaret, in terra remansit. qui inde soluerant, fluctibus et procellis in conspectu eius obruti sunt: ipse laetatus est quod uitam suam somnio quam naui credere maluisset. memor autem beneficii elegantissimo carmine aeternitati consecrauit, melius illi et diuturnius in animis hominum sepulcrum constituens quam in desertis et ignotis harenis struxerat.

Simonides, admonished by a dead man that he should not sail next day, remained on land.

Those who sailed were submerged in his sight by tempests.

He was happy that he chose to trust his life to a dream rather than to a ship.

THE SECOND NUN'S PROLOGUE AND TALE

By G. H. GEROULD

THE PROLOGUE

NO SOURCE has been discovered for the four stanzas on idleness, with which the prologue begins, nor need one be sought, since the device they embody has been shown to be a convention frequently used in Chaucer's time and later.[1]

The *Invocatio ad Mariam*, which follows (G 36–56), is based primarily on St. Bernard's prayer at the beginning of Canto xxxiii of Dante's *Paradiso:*

O Virgin Mother,	1	"Vergine Madre, figlia del tuo Figlio,
		Umile ed alta più che creatura,
	3	Termine fisso d'eterno consiglio,
who didst so ennoble human nature that the Maker disdained not thy womb,		Tu se' colei, che l'umana natura
		Nobilitasti, sì che il suo Fattore
	6	Non disdegno di farsi sua fattura.
		Nel ventre tuo si raccese l'amore,
		Per lo cui caldo nell'eterna pace
fountain of hope and grace,	9	Così è germinato questo fiore.
		Qui sei a noi meridiana face
		Di caritate, e giuso, intra i mortali,
	12	Sei di speranza fontana vivace.
		Donna, sei tanto grande e tanto vali,
		Che qual vuol grazia ed a te non ricorre,
	15	Sua disianza vuol volar senz' ali.
whose loving kindness anticipates our prayers,		La tua benignità non pur soccorre
		A chi domanda, ma molte fiate
	18	Liberamente al domandar precorre.
in whom is all virtue,		In te misericordia, in te pietate,
		In te magnificenza, in te s'aduna
	21	Quantunque in creatura è di bontate.
grant to this man that he may see the ultimate salvation,		Or questi, che dall'infima lacuna
		Dell'universo infin qui ha vedute

[1] See C. Brown, *MP*, IX (1911), 1–4; F. Tupper, *MLN*, XXX (1915), 10, n. 6; J. S. P. Tatlock, *Anglia*, XXXVII (1913), 106, n. 2.

24   Le vite spiritali ad una ad una,
          Supplica a te, per grazia, di virtute
          Tanto che possa con gli occhi levarsi
27   Più alto verso l'ultima salute.
          Ed io, che mai per mio veder non arsi
          Più ch'io fo per lo suo, tutti i miei preghi
30   Ti porgo, e prego che non sieno scarsi,
          Perchè tu ogni nube gli disleghi   that every cloud of
          Di sua mortalità coi preghi tuoi,   mortality may be
                                                              removed,
33   Sì che il sommo piacer gli si dispieghi.
          Ancor ti prego, Regina che puoi
          Ciò che tu vuoli, che conservi sani,   and his loyal faith
36   Dopo tanto veder, gli affetti suoi.   preserved.
          Vinca tua guardia i movimenti umani;
          Vedi Beatrice con quanti beati
39   Per li miei preghi ti chiudon le mani."[1]

Although it is possible—and even probable—that this passage was the only source consciously in Chaucer's mind, it is clear that other things stored in his memory affected what he wrote. Among these may have been the picture from the *Paradiso*, xxxii, 133–35 (cf. G 69–70).

> Di contro a Pietro vedi sedar Anna,
> Tanto contenta di mirar sua figlia,
> Che non muove occhi per cantare Osanna.

Another may have been a hymn by Venantius Fortunatus, commonly sung at matins (cf. G 45–48).[2]

> Quem terra, pontus, aethera
> colunt, adorant, praedicant,
> trinam regentem machinam,
> claustrum Mariae bajulat.[3]

Still another may have been an anthem in the service at complines (cf. G 62–77).[4]

[1] Chaucer's clear memory of this passage is shown by other echoes of it: ll. 13–18 in *Troilus*, iii, 1261–67, and ll. 16–21 in the *Prologue of the Prioress's Tale*, B 1664–70.

[2] See Tupper, pp. 9–11, and C. Brown, *MLN*, XXX (1915), 231–32.

[3] Mone, *Hymni Latini Medii Aevi* (1853–55), II, 128; Daniel, *Thesaurus hymnologicus* (1855–56), I, 172; Dreves, *Analecta hymnica* (1886–1922), II, 38. First indicated by Brown, *MP*, IX, 6.

[4] See Tupper and Brown, *loc. cit.*

Salve regina, mater misericordiae,
Vita, dulcedo et spes nostra, salve.
Ad te clamamus exules filii Hevae,
Ad te suspiramus gementes et flentes in hac lacrimarum
   valle.
Eia ergo advocata nostra, illos tuos misericordes oculos
   ad nos converte
Et Iesum benedictum fructum ventris tui nobis post
   hoc exilium ostende,
O clemens, o pia, o dulcis virgo Maria.[1]

Single phrases that the poet had heard over and over again in various hymns no doubt came to him in the act of composition and were embodied in his prayer.

Similarly there may be in the *Invocatio* (G 71–74) echoes, directly or indirectly received, of the following passages in the *Commentaria in Somnium Scipionis* by Macrobius:[2]

By one set of virtues (like justice, courage, temperance) a good man guides himself and the state; by a second, in freedom from public duties, he may liberate himself from the contagion of the body and concern himself with divine things;

His uirtutibus uir bonus primum sui atque inde rei publicae rector efficitur, iuste ac prouide gubernans humana, non deserens. secundae, quas purgatorias uocant, hominis sunt, qui diuini capax est, solumque animum eius expediunt, qui decreuit se a corporis contagione purgare et quadam humanorum fuga solis se inserere diuinis. hae sunt otiosorum, qui a rerum publicarum actibus se sequestrant. harum quid singulae uelint, superius expressimus, cum de uirtutibus philosophantium diceremus, quas solas quidem aestimauerunt esse uirtutes.

by a third he may be purged of all worldly stain.

tertiae sunt purgati iam defaecatique animi, et ab omni mundi huius aspergine presse pureque detersi [i. viii. 8–9].

To put the matter briefly,

Et quia totum tractatum, quem ueterum sapientia de inuestigatione huius quaestionis agitauit, in hac latentem uerborum paucitate repperies, ex omnibus aliqua, quibus nos de rei, quam quaerimus, absolutione sufficiet admoneri amore breuitatis excerpsimus. antequam studium philosophiae circa naturae inquisitionem ad tantum

authors of different races have denied that there are other hells than our bodies,

uigoris adolesceret, qui per diuersas gentes auctores constituendis sacris caerimoniarum fuerunt, aliud esse inferos negauerunt quam ipsa corpora, quibus inclusae animae carcerem foedum tenebris

which are the burial-places of our souls.

horridum sordibus et cruore patiuntur. hoc animae sepulcrum, hoc Ditis concaua, hoc inferos uocauerunt et omnia, quae illic esse credidit fabulosa persuasio, in nobismet ipsis et in ipsis humanis corporibus

[1] Daniel, II, 321. First indicated by Holthausen, *Arch. f. das Stud. der neueren Sprachen*, LXXXVII (1891), 265.

[2] Ed. F. Eyssenhardt (1868), pp. 507–18. The analogy was noted by J. L. Lowes, *MP*, XV (1917), 193–202.

adsignare conati sunt: obliuionis fluuium aliud non esse adserentes, quam errorem animae obliuiscentis maiestatem uitae prioris, qua antequam in corpus truderetur, potita est, solamque esse in corpore uitam putantis [i. x. 8–10].

The river of oblivion is forgetting the majesty of our former life, and thinking life to be in the body.

Unde Cicero pariter utrumque significans, corpus esse uinculum, corpus esse sepulcrum, quod carcer est sepultorum ait, qui e corporum uinclis tamquam e carcere euolauerunt [i. xi. 3].

Cicero calls the body a fetter, a grave, a prison.

Secundum hos ergo, quorum sectae amicior est ratio, animae beatae ab omni cuiuscumque contagione corporis liberae caelum possident, quae uero appetentiam corporis et huius, quam in terris uitam uocamus, ab illa specula altissima et perpetua luce despiciens desiderio latenti cogitauerit, pondere ipso terrenae cogitationis paulatim in inferiora delabitur [i. xi. 11).

The souls of the blessed are free from all contagion of the body

and the weight of earthly thought.

There is also to be found a correspondence between certain lines (G 36–49) and a passage in the *Anticlaudianus* by Alanus de Insulis:[1]

Hic superos cives proprio praecellit honore
Virgo, quae proprium pariendi lege pudorem
Non perdens, matris meruit cum virgine nomen.
In qua concordant duo nomina, lite sepulta,
Quae secum pugnare solent, litesque movere,
Nec jam discordant mater virgoque, sed ipsis
Litibus exclusis se pacis ad oscula vertunt.
Hic natura silet, logicae vis exulat omnis,
Rhetoricae perit arbitrium ratioque vacillat.
Haec est quae miro divini muneris usu
Nata patrem, natumque parens concepit, honorem
Virgineum retinens, nec perdens jura parentis,
In cujus ventris thalamo sibi summa paravit
Hospitium deitas, tunicam sibi texuit ipse
Filius artificis summi, nostraeque salutis
Induit ipse togam, nostro vestitus amictu.

The Virgin is exalted by meriting two names, mother and virgin,

that clash by nature and reason.

At once daughter and parent,

in the chamber of her womb the highest divinity made a resting-place, and the Son wove for himself the vestment of our salvation.

THE LEGEND

In considering the source of the legend itself,[2] we must bear in mind Chaucer's own declaration:

I have heer doon my feithful bisynesse
After the legende, in translacioun
Right of thy glorious lif and passioun [G 24–26].

---

[1] Dist. v, cap. ix, ed. T. Wright, *Anglo-Latin Satirical Poets and Epigrammatists of the Twelfth Century* ("Rolls Series," No. 59 [1872]), II, 362.

[2] Including the etymologizing interpretation of the saint's name.

Again, at the end of the prologue,, are his words:

> For bothe have I the wordes and sentence
> Of hym that at the seintes reverence
> The storie wroot, and folwen hire legende [G 81–83],

which with the statement just preceding that:

> I do no diligence
> This ilke storie subtilly to endite [G 79–80],

clearly imply that he was versifying some single text then in his possession. Nothing could be more explicit than this: he was following both "the words and meaning of him who wrote the story, in reverence of the saint." Some one author is indicated. If we add to this the evidence from the rubric found in two manuscripts, *Interpretacio nominis Cecilie quam ponit Frater Jacobus Januensis in Legenda*, and notice how closely the etymologizing preface corresponds to that in *Legenda aurea*, we shall incline to believe that Jacobus de Voragine was the writer meant; and certainly we shall not be content to disregard Chaucer's plain statement as to what he was doing, without definite and convincing proof that he was doing something quite different.

Two forms of the *Passio S. Caeciliae* have been listed by the Bollandists: a longer recension,[1] which has been edited several times in slightly variant texts,[2] and a shorter recension,[3] which also appears in somewhat divergent texts.[4] Besides these

---

[1] *Bibliotheca Hagiographica Latina*, No. 1495.

[2] A. Bosius, *Historia Passionis Beatae Caeciliae* (1600), pp. 1–26; I. Laderchi, *S. Caeciliae Virginis et Martyris Acta*, I (1722), 1–39, II (1723), 181–216; B. Mombritius, *Sanctuarium seu vitae sanctorum* (ca. 1480), I, 188–93 (new ed. 1910, I, 332–41).

[3] *BHL*, No. 1496.

[4] Narbey, *Supplément aux Acta sanctorum* (1899), II, 283–90. See C. F. W. Arnold, *Caesarius von Arlate* (1894), pp. 459–60. A Latin translation of the Greek version of the legend by Simeon Metaphrastes does not concern us, though it has been persistently cited in this connection for the last sixty years, first by Kölbing, *ES*, I (1877), 215–29 (see the note in Robinson's edition, p. 863). Simeon made his translation into Greek from some text of the longer Latin *Passio*. Neither Simeon's Greek text nor the retranslation of it into Latin, which was made in the sixteenth century by Lipomanus (1571) and reissued by Surius (1618), resembles Chaucer's poem in any particular that is not paralleled in the longer recension of the Latin *Passio*. It is unfortunate that the problem of sources should have been confused by reference to the wholly extraneous text of Lipomanus.

two Latin recensions of the legend, the Bollandists enumerate four epitomes that antedate Chaucer: those by Ada, Vincentius Bellovacensis, Petrus de Natalibus, and Jacobus de Voragine.

A survey of this material reveals a close correspondence between what we may call the vulgate or accepted text of *Legenda aurea*[1] and Chaucer through verse 357. Up to this point the differences are as slight as they well could be in a poem of rich tonal beauty compared with a piece of mediocre Latin prose.[2] From verse 358 forward, however, the discrepancies are so marked that by no possibility could the text of Jacobus, as we know it, have served as a basis for what Chaucer wrote. He must have had before him, it is evident, a much longer version of the story. An examination of the text edited by the Milanese scholar and churchman Mombritius,[3] the relevant section of which is hereinafter reprinted, shows it to contain all the matters, except one, which do not appear in *Legenda aurea*—again, as we know it. The text of Mombritius, we must observe, is a representative of the longer recension of the *Passio;* and another representative, that printed by Bosius, supplements Mombritius at the single point, just mentioned, where Chaucer and *Legenda aurea* agree in opposition to him.[4] The latter part of Chaucer's poem thus had as its source some text very similar to that of Mombritius and one which certainly derived from the longer Latin recension.

Three possibilities appear. Either Chaucer followed *Legenda aurea* through the baptism of Tiburce, then turned for the rest of the story to some text of the longer Latin *Passio;* or he had before him a text of *Legenda aurea* much fuller in its later course than the one we know; or else he followed throughout, but with omissions, a text of the *Passio* very similar to the one which Jacobus abbreviated for his compendium.[5] Two things must be remembered about *Legenda aurea*. In the first place, it is

---

[1] Ed. T. Graesse (3d ed.; 1890).

[2] Persistent detractors of the *Second Nun's Tale* ought to be compelled by some Court of Poetry to recite aloud verse 140, for example, until the music of it is revealed to them.

[3] To which attention was called by Holthausen, pp. 266–69.

[4] Vss. 529–32.

[5] Including, of course, the etymologies and the passage from St. Ambrose.

chiefly a compilation, made up of epitomes of earlier legends, rather than an original work. In the second place, it was enormously popular and circulated far and wide all over Europe. No one has yet even attempted to list the extant manuscripts, much less to study their textual history, which, as Graesse pointed out in 1847, would be a formidable task. Modern scholars have been content, quite uncritically, to accept Graesse's edition as representing the pristine state of the work and to brand as deceivers all the medieval writers who have pretended to follow the *Golden Legend* and yet have had the temerity to present texts differing in content from those found in the book as we know it. The case of *St. Caecilia* is not an isolated one. In our complete ignorance of what his copy of *Legenda aurea* may have contained, we must not forget Chaucer's sober statement as to his source.[1]

One other point of interest appears in this connection. Jacobus de Voragine, before he was made archbishop of Genoa toward the end of his life, lived and worked in Lombardy. His collection of legends sometimes has been known, indeed, as *Historia Lombardica*. It may perhaps be significant that Mombritius, pursuing his studies in Milan, should have given us a text of the *Passio S. Caeciliae*, including nearly every detail that Chaucer must have found in his source, though the latter presumably was a briefer version. We are thus justified in conjecturing as a possibility, remembering that it is a possibility merely, that Chaucer had a copy of *Legenda aurea* containing a fuller version of the legend of St. Caecilia than the one appearing in such manuscripts of the work as have been examined.[2] More definite conclusions must await, I think, a full investigation of the textual history of Jacobus' famous work.

In these uncertainties, the best we can do by way of representing the sources of the *Second Nun's Tale* is to print (1) the

---

[1] As does Professor Tatlock, *MLN*, XLV (1930), 298, who also, to my thinking, completely misstates the problem in other particulars. His assumption that either Chaucer or someone before him combined two legends, "constantly and minutely altering Jacobus' vastly admired work," is unsupported by any evidence whatever.

[2] It should be said that the three manuscripts of Jacobus in the Ambrosian Library at Milan have essentially the same text as the English manuscripts of the same period.

text from *Legenda aurea* as found in an English manuscript written before Chaucer's time and (2) the latter part of the *Passio* as edited by Mombritius. The following manuscripts of English origin have nearly identical texts of the *St. Caecilia:* Bodleian Library, MS Bodley 336, from the early fourteenth century, which formerly belonged to Christ Church, Canterbury, and MS Barlow 12, late thirteenth or early fourteenth century; Cambridge University Library, MS Ff.V.31, professedly written in 1299, and MS Gg.II.18, from the fourteenth century; Trinity College, Cambridge, MS R.15.1, from the fourteenth century and formerly at Winchester. I have chosen MS Bodley 336 to represent these, correcting obvious errors with the support of at least two of the other manuscripts.

TEXT OF *LEGENDA AUREA*

(From fourteenth-century MS Bodley 336.)

DE ETHYMOLOGIA NOMINIS

Cecilia quasi celi lilia vel cecis via uel a celo et lya. Uel Cecilia G 85–119[1] quasi cecitate carens. Uel dicitur a celo et leos, quod est populus. Fuit enim celeste lilium per uirginitatis pudorem. Uel dicitur lilium quia habuit candorem mundicie, uirorem consciencie, odorem bone fame. Fuit enim cecis via per exempli informacionem, celum per iugem contemplacionem, lya per assiduam operacionem. Uel dicitur celum quia, sicut dicit Ysidorus,[2] celum philosophi uolubile, rotundum, et ardens esse dixerunt. Sic et ipsa fuit uolubilis per operacionem sollicitam, rotunda per perseueranciam, ardens per caritatem succensam. Fuit enim cecitate carens per sapiencie splendorem. Fuit et celum populi quia in ipsam tanquam in celum spirituale populus ad imitandum intuetur solem, lunam, et stellas, id est sapiencie perspicacitatem, fidei magnanimitatem, et uirtutum uarietatem.

DE SANCTA CECILIA

Cecilia uirgo clarissima ex nobili Romanorum genere exorta, et G 120–40 ab ipsis cunabulis in fide christi nutrita, absconditum semper euangelium Christi gerebat in pectore et non diebus neque noctibus a colloquiis diuinis et oratione cessabat, suamque uirginitatem conseruari

---

[1] On account of the close resemblances between the *Legenda aurea* and much of *SNT*, marginal summaries can here be replaced by references to the corresponding passages in *SNT*. The text of Mombritius will be treated in the same way.

[2] *MS* ysodorus.

a domino exorabat. Cum autem cuidam iuueni, nomine Ualeriano, desponsata fuisset et dies nupciarum instituta esset, illa subtus ad carnem cilicio erat induta et desuper deauratis vestibus tegebatur, et cantantibus organis, illa in corde suo soli domino decantabat dicens: Fiat, domine, cor meum et corpus immaculatum, ut non confundar. Et biduanis ac triduanis ieiuniis orans commendabat se domino, quod timebat. Venit autem nox in qua suscepit una cum sponso suo cubiculi secreta silencia, et ita eum alloquitur: O dulcissime atque amantissime iuuenis, est misterium, quod tibi confitear, si modo tu iuratus asseras cuncta te istud obseruancia custodire. Iurat Valerianus se istud nulla necessitate detegere, nulla racione prodere. Tunc illa ait: Angelum Dei habeo amatorem, qui nimio zelo custodit corpus meum. Hic si uel leuiter senserit quod tu me polluto amore contingas, statim feriet te, et amittes florem tue gratissime iuuentutis. Si autem cognouerit quod me sincero amore diligas, ita quoque diliget te sicut et me, et ostendet tibi gloriam suam. Tunc Valerianus nutu Dei correptus ait: Si uis ut credam tibi, ipsum angelum ostende mihi, et si uere probauero quod angelus sit, faciam quod hortaris; si autem uirum alium diligis, te et ipsum gladio feriam. Cui Cecilia dixit: Si in Deum uerum credideris, et te baptizari promiseris,[1] ipsum uidere ualebis. Vade igitur in tercium miliarum ab urbe, uia que Appia nuncupatur, et pauperibus quos illic inuenies dices: Cecilia me misit ad uos, ut ostendatis mihi sanctum senem Urbanum, quoniam ad ipsum habeo secreta mandata, que perferam. Hunc dum tu uideris, indica ei omnia uerba mea, et postquam ab eo purificatus fueris, rediens ipsum angelum uidebis. Tunc Valerianus perrexit,[2] et secundum signa que acceperat, sanctum Vrbanum episcopum intra sepulcra martirum latitantem inuenit. Cumque ei omnia uerba Cecilie dixisset, ille manus ad celum expandens cum lacrimis ait: Domine Ihesu Christe, seminator casti consilii, suscipe seminum fructus quos in Cecilia seminasti. Domine Ihesu Christe, pastor bone, Cecilia famula tua quasi apis tibi argumentosa deseruit. Nam sponsum, quem quasi leonem ferocem accepit, ad te quasi agnum mansuetissimum destinauit. Et ecce subito apparuit senex quidam niueis uestibus indutus, tenens librum aureis litteris scriptum, quem uidens Ualerianus pre nimio timore quasi mortuus cecidit, et a sene leuatus sic legit: Vnus dominus, una fides, unum baptisma, unus deus et pater omnium, qui est super omnes et per omnia et in omnibus nobis. Cumque hoc legisset, dixit ei senior: Credis ita esse an adhuc dubitas? Tunc exclamauit dicens: Non est aliud quod uerius credi possit sub celo. Statim illo disparente Valerianus a sancto Vrbano baptisma suscepit,

G 141–61

G 162–82

G 183–210

G 211–38

---

[1] *MS* permiseris.   [2] *MS* per exempla.

et rediens, Ceciliam cum angelo loquentem in cubiculo inuenit.
Angelus autem duas coronas ex rosis et liliis in manu habebat, et
vnam Cecilie et alteram Valeriano tradidit dicens: Istas coronas im-
maculato corde et mundo corpore custodite, quia de paradyso Dei
eas attuli, nec unquam marcessent nec odorem amittent, nec ab aliis
nisi quibus castitas placuerit uideri poterunt. Tu autem, Valeriane,
quia utili consilio credidisti, pete quodcumque uolueris. Cui Valerianus: Nichil mihi in hac uita ita dulcius extitit quam unicus fratris
mei affectus; peto igitur ut et ipse mecum ueritatem agnosçat. Cui G 239-59
angelus: Placet domino peticio tua, et ambo cum palma martyrii
ad dominum uenietis. Post hec ingressus[1] Tyburcius frater Valeriani
cum nimium rosarum sensisset odorem, dixit: Miror, hoc tempore,
roseus odor hic et liliorum unde respirat, nam si ipsas rosas uel lilia
in manibus meis tenerem nec sic poterunt odoramenta tante mihi
suauitatis infundere. Confiteor uobis, ita sum refectus ut putem me
subito mutatum. Cui Valerianus: Coronas habemus, quas tui oculi
uidere non preualent, floreo colore et niueo candore uernantes. Et
sicut me interpellante odorem sensisti, sic et, si credideris, uidere
ualebis. Cui Tyburcius: In sompnis hec audio an in ueritate ista G 260-69
tu loqueris, Ualeriane? Cui Ualerianus: In sompnis usque modo
fuimus, sed iam nunc in ueritate manemus. Ad quem Tyburcius:
Vnde hoc nosti? Et Ualerianus: Angelus Dei me docuit, quem
tu uidere poteris si purificatus fueris, et omnibus ydolis abrenunciau-
eris. Huic miraculo de coronis rosarum Ambrosius testatur in pre- G 270-83
facione, sic dicens[2]: Sancta Cecilia sic celesti dono est repleta, ut
martyrii palmam assumeret. Ipsum mundum est cum talamis
exsecrata; testis est Valeriani coniugis et Tyburcii prouocata confessio, quos, domine,[3] angelica manu odoriferis floribus coronasti;
viros uirgo duxit ad gloriam; mundus agnouit quantum ualeat deuocio
castitatis. Hec Ambrosius. Tunc Cecilia euidenter ostendit ei omnia[4] G 284-305
ydola esse insensibilia et muta, ita ut Tyburcius responderet ac
diceret: Qui ita non credit pecus est. Tunc Cecilia osculans pectus
eius dixit: Hodie te fateor meum esse cognatum. Sicut enim amor
Dei fratrem tuum mihi[5] coniugem fecit, ita te mihi cognatum con-
temptus faciet ydolorum. Vade igitur cum fratre tuo ut purificacionem accipias et angelicos uultus[6] uidere ualeas. Dixïtque
Tyburcius fratri suo: Obsecro te, frater, ut mihi dicas ad quem me
ducturus es. Cui Valerianus: ad Urbanum episcopum. Cui Tybur- G 306-32

---

[1] *MS* et egressus.

[2] sic dicens *omitted in MS but supplied by later hand in margin.*

[3] *MS* dominus. [5] *MS* me.

[4] *MS omits* omnia. [6] *MS* angelos.

cius:[1] De illo Urbano dicis qui tociens dampnatus est et adhuc in
latebris commoratur? Hic, si inuentus fuerit, cremabitur, et nos in
illius flammis pariter inuoluemur. Et dum querimus diuinitatem
latentem in celis, incurremus furorem exurentem in terris. Cui
Cecilia: Si hec sola esset uita, iuste hanc solam perdere timeremus.
Est autem alia melior, que nunquam amittitur, quam nobis Dei
filius enarrauit. Omnia enim, que facta sunt, filius ex patre genitus
condidit; vniuersa autem, que condita sunt, ex patre procedens
spiritus animauit. Hic igitur filius Dei in mundum ueniens uerbis

G 333–44   et miraculis aliam uitam esse nobis monstrauit. Cui Tyburcius:
Certe vnum Deum esse asseris, et quomodo nunc tres esse testaris?
Respondit Cecilia: Sicut in una hominis sapientia sunt tria, scilicet
ingenium, memoria, et intellectus, sic et in una diuinitatis essentia
tres persone esse possunt. Tunc cepit ei de aduentu filii Dei et passione predicare, et multas congruitates ipsius passionis ostendere.

Summarized in   [Nam ideo, inquit, filius Dei est peremptus,[2] ut genus humanum dimit-
Chaucer, G 345–48   tatur peccato detentum; benedictus maledicitur, ut homo maledictus benedictionem consequatur; illudi se patitur, ut homo ab
illusione demonum liberetur; spineam coronam accepit in capite,
ut a nobis sententiam auferat capitalem; fel suscepit amarum, ut
saluaret[3] hominis dulcem gustum; expoliatur, ut parentum nos-
trorum nuditatem operiat; in ligno suspenditur, ut ligni preuarica-
cionem tollat. Tunc Tyburcius fratri suo dixit: Miserere mei et

G 349–57 (see   perduc me ad hominem Dei ut purificacionem accipiam.] Ductus
Mombritius)   igitur et purificatus, angelos Dei sepe uidebat, et omnia que postu-

Summarized in   labat protinus habebat.[4] [Valerianus igitur et Tyburcius elemosinis
Chaucer, G 358–63,   insistebant, et sanctorum corpora quos Almachius prefectus occidebat
but see Momb.   sepulture tradebant. Quos Almachius ad se uocans, cur pro suis
sceleribus dampnatos sepeliebant, inquisiuit. Cui Tyburcius: Utinam
eorum serui essemus quos tu dampnatos appelas! Qui contempserunt
quod uidetur esse et non est, et inuenerunt quod non uidetur esse
et est. Cui prefectus: Quid nam illud est? Et Tyburcius: Quod
uidetur esse et non est, est omne quod in hoc mundo est, quod hominem
ad non esse perducit. Quod uero non uidetur esse et est, est uita
iustorum et pena malorum. Cui prefectus: Non puto quod mente
tua loquaris. Tunc iubet astare Valerianum, dicens ei: Quoniam
non est sani capitis frater tuus, tu saltem poteris respondere. Constat plurimum vos errare, qui gaudia respuitis et omnia inimica
gaudiis affectatis. Tunc Valerianus se vidisse ait glaciali tempore

[1] Cui Tyburcius omitted but supplied by later hand in margin.

[2] Other MSS read tentus.

[3] Other MSS read sanaret.   [4] Other MSS read optinebat.

ociosos iocantes et operarios agricolas deridentes, sed estiuo tempore, dum aduenissent gloriosi fructus laborum, gaudentibus illis qui putabantur uani, ceperunt flere qui putabantur urbani. Sic et nos nunc quidem sustinemus ignominiam et laborem. In futuro autem recipiemus gloriam et eternam mercedem. Vos autem qui nunc[1] transitorium habetis gaudium, in futuro autem eternum inuenietis interitum. Cui prefectus: Ergo nos inuictissimi principes eternum habebimus luctum, et uos persone uilissime perpetuum possidebitis gaudium? Cui Valerianus: Homunciones estis et non principes, tempore nostro nati, cicius morituri et Deo rationem plus omnibus reddituri. Dixit autem prefectus: Quid uerborum circuitu immoramur? Offerte diis libamina et illesi abscedite. Sancti responderunt: Nos Deo uero cotidie sacrificium exhibemus. Quibus prefectus: Quod est nomen eius? Cui Valerianus: Nomen eius inuenire non poteris et si pennis uolaueris. Prefectus dixit: Ergo Iubiter nomen dei non est? Cui Valerianus: Nomen est homicide et stupratoris.[2] Ad quem Almachius: Ergo totus mundus errat et tu cum fratre tuo uerum deum nosti? Valerianus respondit: Nos soli non sumus, sed innumerabilis multitudo hanc sanctitatem[3] recepit.] Traduntur igitur sancti in custodiam Maximi. [Quibus ille ait: O iuuentutis flos purpureus, o germanus fraternitatis affectus, quomodo ad mortem quasi ad epulas festinatis? Cui Valerianus: Quod si crediturum promitteret, gloriam animarum eorum post mortem uideret. Et Maximus: Fulminibus igneis consumar si non illum solum Deum confitear, quem adoratis, si contingat quod dicitis. Ipse igitur Maximus et omnis eius familia ac uniuersi carnifices crediderunt et a sancto Urbano, qui illic occulte uenit, baptisma susceperunt.] Igitur dum aurora finem daret, Cecilia exclamauit dicens: Eya milites Christi, abicite opera tenebrarum, et induimini arma lucis. Quarto igitur miliario ab urbe sancti ad statuam Iouis ducuntur, et dum sacrificare nolerunt, pariter decollantur. Tunc Maximus cum iuramento asseruit se in hora passionis eorum angelos uidisse fulgentes, et animas eorum quasi uirgines de thalamo exeuntes, quas in gremio suo usque in celum angeli detulerunt. Almachius uero audiens Maximum christianum effectum, cum plumbatis tamdiu cedi iussit,[4] quousque spiritum excussit.[5] Cuius corpus sancta Cecilia iuxta Valerianum et Tyburcium sepeliuit. Tunc Almachius amborum facultates cepit inquirere, et Ceciliam tanquam Valeriani coniugem coram se fecit astare, iussitque ut ydolis immolaret, aut sententiam mortis acciperet. [Cum autem ad hoc ab apparitoribus urgeretur, et illi uehementer flerent, eo quod

G 367–71

Summarized in Chaucer, G 372–78, but see Momb.

G 379–406 (see Momb.)

G 407–9 (see Momb.)
G 410–13

Summarized in Chaucer, G 414–16

---

[1] *MS omits* nunc.

[2] *MS* strupratoris.

[3] *MS* sanitatem.

[4] *Other MSS* fecit.

[5] *MS* concussit.

puella tam decora et nobilis ultro se morti traderet, dixit ad eos: Hoc, boni iuuenes, non est iuuentutem perdere, sed mutare, dare lutum, et accipere aurum, dare uile habitaculum, et recipere precio- sum, dare breuem angulum et accipere forum perlucidum. Si quis pro nummo solidos daret, nonne uelocius festinaretis? Deus autem quod acceperit simplum reddet centuplum. Creditis hiis que dico?]

G 416–20.

(Not in Chaucer)

Et illi: Credimus Christum uero esse Deum, qui talem possidet famulam. [Vocato igitur Urbano episcopo CCCC et amplius bap-

G 421–41 (see Momb.)

tizati sunt.] Tunc Almachius sanctam Ceciliam ad se uocans ait: Cuius condicionis es? Et illa: Ingenua sum et nobilis. Cui Almachius: Ego te de religione[1] interrogo. Et Cecilia: Interrogacio tua stultum sumit inicium, que duas responsiones una putas inquisicione concludi. Cui Almachius: Vnde tibi tanta presumpcio respondendi? At illa: De consciencia bona et fide non ficta. Cui Almachius: Ignoras cuius potestatis sum? Et illa: Potestas uestra est quasi uter uento reple- tus, quem si acus pupugerit omnis protinus rigor pallescit, et quid-

G 442–86 (see Momb.)

quid in se rigidum habere cernitur incuruatur. Cui Almachius: Ab iniuriis cepisti et in iniuriis perseueras. Cecilia:[2] Iniuria non dicitur nisi quod uerbis fallentibus irrogatur, vnde aut iniuriam doce[3] si falsa locuta sum, aut te ipsum corripe, calumpniam inferentem. Sed nos scientes sanctum Dei nomen omnino negare non possumus. Melius est enim feliciter mori, quam infeliciter uiuere. Cui Almachius: Vt quid cum tanta superbia loqueris? Et illa: Non est superbia sed constancia. Cui Almachius dixit: Infelix, ignoras quia uiuificandi et mortificandi mihi est tradita potestas? Et illa: Contra ueritatem publicam probo te esse mentitum, vitam enim uiuentibus tollere potes, mortuis autem

G 487–511 (see Momb.)

dare uitam non potes. Es minister mortis, non uite. Cui Almachius: Iam depone amenciam tuam et sacrifica diis. Cui Cecilia: Nescio ubi[4] oculos tuos amiseris. Nam quos tu deos dicis, omnes nos saxa esse uidemus. Mitte igitur manum et tangendo disce quod oculis

G 512–25

non uales uidere. Tunc iratus Almachius iussit eam ad domum suam reduci, ibique tota nocte et die iussit in bulliente balneo concremari. Que quasi in loco frigido mansit, nec modicum saltem sudoris persen- sit. Quod cum audisset Almachius, iussit eam in ipso balneo decollari;

G 526–28

quam spiculator tribus ictibus in collo percussit, sed tamen capud

G 529–32 (see Bosius)

eius amputare non potuit, et quia decretum erat ne quartam per- cussionem decollandus acciperet, eam semiuiuam cruentus carnifex

G 533–53

dereliquit. Per triduum autem superuiuens omnia que habebat pau- peribus tradidit, et omnes quos ad fidem conuerterat Urbano episcopo commendauit dicens: Triduanas mihi inducias postulaui, ut hos tue

---

[1] *MS* regione.

[2] *Other MSS insert* respondit.

[3] *MS* date, *other MSS* doce.

[4] *MS* nisi, *other MSS* ubi.

beatitudini commendarem, et hanc domum meam in ecclesiam consecrares. Sanctus autem Urbanus corpus eius inter episcopos sepeliuit,
et domum suam in ecclesiam consecrauit. [Passa est autem circa   Not in Chaucer
annos domini cc xxxvi.[1] tempore Alexandri imperatoris. Alibi tamen
legitur quod passa fuit tempore Marci Aurelii, qui imperauit circa
annos domini cc xx.]

TEXT OF *PASSIO* BY MOMBRITIUS

(From B. Mombritius, *Sanctuarium seu vitae sanctorum* [new ed.; 1910], I,
336–41.)

[Tunc Tyburtius pedibus eius prostratus: ingenti flætu et lachrymis   Not in Chaucer
dixit: Si de ista uita ulterius uel mente tractauero: in illa uita non
inueniar. habeant stulti labentis temporis lucrum. ego qui usque
hodie sine causa uixi: iam non sit sine causa quod uiuo: et his dictis
ad fratrem suum conuersus ait: miserere mei frater carissime: et
rumpe moras: quarum nexus non patior. Dillationes timeo: pondus
ferre non possum. Obsecro te perduc me ad hominem dei: ut me
purificans illius uitæ participem faciat.] Tunc Valerianus perduxit   G 349–57
fratrem suum ad Papam Vrbanum: Cui cum narrasset in uniuersa
quæ fuerunt dicta uel facta: gratias referens deo: suscepit Tyburtium
cum omni gaudio: et baptizans eum secum esse præcepit: quoadus-
que albas deponeret: Quem perfectum doctrina sua per septem dies
Christo militem consecrauit. denique gratiam consecutus est domini:
ut angelos dei uideret quottidie: et omnia quæ poposcisset a domino
protinus consequeretur. Verum quia multum est: ut omnia per
ordinem prosequentes: quæ et quanta per eos dominus mirabilia
fecerit conscribamus: ad gloriosas passiones eorum articulum reuoce-
mus. [Turgidus Almachius urbis præfectus sanctos dei fortiter lani-   Summarized in
abat: et inhumata corpora eorum iubebat derelinqui. Tiburtius uero   Chaucer, G 358–63
et Valerianus ad hoc uocabant quottidie: ut pretiosas martyrum
facerent sepulturas: eleimosynis et pietatibus insistentes. Interea ut
solitum est: bonos odio habent mali: et indicant uniuersa Almachio:
quæ per eos dominus circa egentes ageret: uel quam studiose quos
ille occidi iusserat sepelirent: tenti ab aparitoribus Almachio præ-
sentantur: Quos Almachius his protinus aggressus est uerbis: Cum
uos nobilitatis titulus clarissimos fecerit nasci: cur per nescio quam
superstitionem infelices uos et degeneres exhibetis? Nam facultates
uestras uos audio per nescio quas uiles personas expendendo consumere: ac pro sceleribus suis punitos cum omni gloria tradere sepul-
turæ: ex quo datur intelligi: quod conscii uestri sunt quibus pro

---

[1] This date varies from manuscript to manuscript.

coniuratione honestas traditis sepulturas. Respondens Tyburtius
dixit: Vtinam dignentur nos ut seruos suos computare: quorum tu
estimas nos esse collegas: Qui contempserunt quod uidetur a se;[1] et
non est: et inuenerunt illud quod uidetur non esse: et est. Almachius
præfectus dixit: Quid est: quod uidetur esse: et non est? Tyburtius
dixit: Omnia quæ in isto mundo sunt: quæ inuitant homines ad
mortem perpetuam per læticiam temporalem. Almachius dixit: et
quod non uidetur esse et est? Tyburtius dixit: Vita quæ futura
iustis: et pœna quæ debetur iniustis: ex utroque latere uerum esse
nouimus quod ueniant et infelici dissimulatione quod oculis cordis
nostri scimus uidere oculis corporis nostri subducimus: ut contra
conscientiam: nostram quæ bona sunt malis sermonibus obum-
bremus: et quæ mala sunt bonis sermonibus adornemus. Almachius
dixit: Non puto quod mente tua loquaris. Tyburtius dixit: Non
mente mea loquor: sed eius quem in uisceribus meæ mentis accepi.
Almachius dixit: Nunquid tu ipse scis: quæ loqueris? Tyburtius
respondit: et noui et didici: et credo quod uniuersa quæ a me dicta
sunt: ita ut dicta permanebunt. Almachius dixit: Quare et ego non
aduerto quo ordine ista prosequeris: Tyburtius dixit: Quia ani-
malis homo non percipit quæ sunt spiritus dei. Spiritualis autem
indicat omnia: ipse autem a nemine iudicatur. Tunc ridens præfectus iussit ammoueri Tyburtium: et applicari Valerianum cui et
dixit: Quoniam non est sani capitis frater tuus: tu saltem poteris
sapienter dare responsum. Dicit ei Valerianus: Auditus tuus errorem
parit: quia uiam sermonis nostri non potes intueri. Præfectus dixit:
Nullus sic errat: sicut uos erratis: qui relictis rebus necessariis et
utilibus ineptum sectamini otium: respuentes gaudia: execrantes
læticiam: atque contempnentes omne: quod uitæ blandimento concessum est. Illud tota mentis auiditate suscipitis: quod saluti contrarium inueniri potest et gaudiis inimicum. Valerianus ad hæc respondit: Iocantes et ridentes et uariis diuitiis affluentes uidi glatiali
tempore transire per campos: in quibus campis stabant rustici pasti-
nantes: et cum omni studio sarmenta frangentes: atque spinosa
rosarum sarculo animose et cautissime componentes. Alii quoque
taleas inserebant: alii radicitus noxia quæque truncabant: cunctaque
ruris opera labore nimio excolentes. Tunc illi qui deliciis fruebantur
et epulabantur: cœperunt laborantes irridere: ac dicere: Infelices et
miseri istum superfluum laborem abicite: et nobiscum gaudentes
deliciis uos et uoluptatibus exhibete. Quare sicut insani duro labore
deficientes. uitæ uestræ tempora tristissimis occupationibus fati-
gatis: Et hæc dicentes soluebantur super eos risu: et dabant plausum

---

[1] a se *for* esse.

manibus multis increpationibus insultantes. Hæc illis agentibus:
imbriferis atque algidis mensibus serena tempora successerunt. Et
ecce floribus rosis uernantes campi: nemoribus pampineis ornabantur.
et crispas botrionum sertas exhibebant suo partu sarmenta: et uario
genere taleæ arborum meliflua poma gignebant: in quibus uidemus
usque hodie abundare gratiam: et fructum pariter et decorem. Tunc
gaudentibus illis qui putabantur uani: cœperunt flære omnes qui
uidebantur urbani: et qui in sua fuerant sapientia gloriati. in nimia
pestilentia perierunt: et sera pœnitudine mugitum sui cordis gemi-
tumque reddentes: sibi inuicem loquebantur: Isti sunt quos habuimus
in derisum: laborem ipsorum putabamus obprobrium: uitam eorum
execrabamur ut miseram: personam eorum iudicauimus indignam:
et conuentum eorum sine honore. Isti autem inuenti sunt sapientes:
et nos uani: quando nec ipsi laborauimus: nec ipsis laborantibus
auxilium pro labore præstitimus. Quinimo eis in deliciis positi risimus:
et credidimus dementes: quos nunc fulgentes aspicimus et florentes.
Ad hæc Præfectus ait: Sapienter te quidem uideo prosecutum: sed
non ad interrogationem meam uideris dedisse responsum. Valerianus
dixit: Stultos nos et insipientes esse dixisti: quod facultates nostras
egentibus damus: aduenas suscipimus: uiduis opem ferimus. orphan-
is subuenimus. inhumata corpora tegimus: et honestas dei martyribus
tradimus sepulturas. Insipientes nos esse et insanissimos iudicas:
quod non cum lætantibus lætamur: neque cum uoluptuosis deliciis
resoluimur: aut ignobiles uulgi oculis nos illustres et nobiles osten-
damus. Veniet tempus: in quo fructum huius nostræ tristiciæ col-
ligamus: ut nobis gaudentibus lugeant hi: qui nunc in suis gaudiis
extolluntur. Tempus enim seminandi modo est: qui in ista semi-
nauerint gaudia: in illa uita luctum et gemitum metent. Qui autem
nunc seminauerit lachrymas temporales: in illa uita sunt gaudia
sempiterna messuri. Præfectus dixit: Ergo et nos et inuictissimi
Principes æternum habebimus luctum: Vos uero perpetuum possidebitis gaudium? Valerianus respondit: Quid enim estis uos aut
Principes uestri? homontiones estis tempore nostro nati: tempore
uestro expleto morituri: tantum deo rationem reddituri: quam
uobis tradit summam potestatis. Almachius dixit: Quid uerborum
circuitu in moramur? Offerte diis libamina: et abscedite illæsi:
Responderunt ambo: Nos non diis sed deo quottidie sacrificium exhibemus. Almachius respondit: Quis est deus: cui uestrum uos dicitis
tradere famulatum? Responderunt ambo: et dixerunt: et quis est
deus alius: ut de deo nos interroges? Est enim alius præter unum?
Almachius dixit: ergo Iouis dei nomen non est? Valerianus respondit:
Nomen corruptoris atque stupratoris hominis. Homicidam illum

uestri auctores commemorant: et criminosum litteræ uestræ demon-
strant. hunc tu deum miror qua fronte locutus sis: nisi ab omni
peccato alienus sit: et sit omnibus uirtutibus plenus? Almachius
dixit: Ergo omnis mundus errat: et tu cum fratre tuo uerum deum
nostis? Valerianus respondit: Innumerabilis multitudo christianitatis
sanctitatem suscepit: et magis uos pauci estis: qui sicut astulæ de
naufragio remansistis: ad nihil aliud nisi ut in ignem mitamini.
Tunc iratus Almachius iussit: eum fustibus cædi. Ille autem statim
ut exutus est: cœpit gaudere dicens: Ecce hora quam semper op-
taui: ecce dies omnimodo festiuitate iucundior: Cumque cæderent
eum: uox præconiaria super eum clamabat dicens: Deos et deas
blasphemare noli. Ille autem clamabat populo dicens: Ciues Romani
uidete. ne uos a ueritate ista mea plaga reuocet. Sed state uiriliter:
et deos lapideos quos colit Almachius in calcem conuertite: quia in
æterna tribulatione erunt omnes: qui colunt eos. Tunc Assessor
præfecti Tarquinus lacca dixit præfecto: Inuenisti occasionem:
tolle eos: Nam si moras feceris: et de die protraxeris: omnes facultates
suas errogabunt: et punitis eis tu nihil inuenies.] Tunc iussit carni-

G 364–66

ficibus: ut ab eis ducerentur ad pagum: ubi erat statunculum Iouis:
et jussit: ut si noluissent sacrificare: ambo fratres pariter capitalem

G 367–71

sententiam subirent. Tunc gloriosi martyres tenti a maximo corni-
culario præfecti: ducebantur ad pagum. Qui Maximus cœpit flære

Summarized in
Chaucer, G 372

super eos [dicens: O iuuentutis flos purpureus: o germanus fraternitatis affectus: quem impia definitione uolentes ammittere quasi ad
epulas festinatis. Tunc Tyburtius dixit: Nos nisi pro comperto habe-
remus alteram uitam esse perpetuam: quæ huic uitæ præsenti suc-
cedit: nunquam nos istam ammittere gauderemus. Dicit ei Maximus:
Et quæ potest esse altera uita? Respondit Tyburtius: Sicuti uestitur
uestimentis corpus: ita uestitur anima corpore. Sicut expoliatur uestimentis corpus: ita expoliatur anima corpore. Et corpus quidem quod
terrenum sæmen per libidinem dedit: terreno uentri redditur: ut in
puluerem reductum sicut phœnix futuri luminis aspectu resurgat: Anima uero ad paradisi delicias. si sancta est perferatur: ut in deliciis
affluens. tempus suæ restaurationis expectet. Dicit ei Maximus: Optarem et ego contemnere uitam hanc: si putarem certum apud me habere: quæ loqueris. Dicit ei Valerianus: Quia nihil tibi dicis superesse:
nisi ut probes uera esse: que diximus: in hora qua nos dominus faciat
istam corporis tunicam et a gloriosam nominis sui confessionem deponere: aperiat oculos tuos: et faciat te uidere cum quanta gloria illa
uita suscipitur: si tamen promittas nobis: quod ex animo ad pœniten-
tiam erroris tu uenias. Tunc Maximus denotabat se dicens: Fulminibus igneis consumar: si ex hac hora non illum solum deum confitear:
qui alteram uitam facit huic uitæ succedere. Hoc tantum uos mihi

quod promisistis ostendite.] Dicunt ei ambo fratres: Impetra a car- G 373-78
nificibus: ut domum tuam nos ducant: et hodierni diei inducias ex-
plica: ita ut nos custodiant in domo tua. Illic ad te uenire faciemus
purificatorem: qui te hac nocte purificet. Statim ut purificauerit: faciat te uidere hoc: quod tibi promisimus. Quod cum impetrasset Maximus duxit eos domum suam: ad quorum prædicationem et ipse Maximus cum omni domo sua et ipsi carnifices crediderunt. Tunc Sancta G 379-406
Cæcilia uenit ad eos nocte cum sacerdotibus. et uniuersi ·baptizati
sunt. Igitur cum aurora nocti finem daret: facto mane silentio Cæcilia
dixit: Eia milites Christi abiicite ópera tenebrarum: et induimini arma
lucis. Certamen bonum certauistis: cursum consumastis: fidem
seruastis. Ite ad coronam uitæ: quam dedit nobis deus iustus iudex:
non solum nobis: sed et omnibus: qui diligunt aduentum eius. Locus
igitur qui uocabatur pagus quarto milliario ab urbe situs erat: in quo
per templi ianuam transitus erat: ut omnes qui ingrederentur: si
Ioui tura non ponerentur: punirentur. Venientibus ergo sanctis
offeruntur tura: et recusant. Recusantes ponunt genua: feriuntur
gladio: proiiciunt corpus temporale: et martyrium suscipiunt sempiternum. Tunc Maximus iratus asserabat dicens: uidi angelos dei
fulgentes sicut sol: in qua hora uerberati sunt gladio: et egredientes
animas eorum de corporibus quasi uirgines de thalamo: quas in
gremio suo suscipientes angeli: remigio alarum suarum ferebant ad
cælos. Ista cum lachrymis narrante Maximo: plurimi crediderunt.
et ab idolorum errore conuersi se suo creatori rediderunt. Igitur
cum peruenisset ad Almachium: quod Maximus cornicularius cum
suis factus fuisset christianus: iussit eum tandiu plumbatis tundi:
quandiu redderet spiritum. Quem Sancta Cæcilia iuxta ubi Tyburti- G 407-9
um et Valerianum sepelierat: in nouo sarcophago sepeliuit: [Et Not in Chaucer
iussit: ut in illius sculperetur phœnis ad indicium fidei eius: qui se
resurrectionem inuenturum phœnicis exemplo suscepit.] Factum est G 410-13
autem post hæc: cœpit Almachius quærere facultates amborum:
pro qua inquisitione sanctam Cæciliam quasi Valeriani coniugem
præcepit arctari: Quæ cum uniuersa quæ remanserant pauperibus
ex eorum facultatibus fideliter tradidisset: ipsa quoque ut tura poneret: cœpit compelli. [Tunc apparitoribus qui eam hoc facere com- Summarized in
Chaucer, G 414-16
pellebant dixit: Audite me ciues et fratres: uos ministri estis iudicis
uestri: et uidetur uobis: quod ab eius impietate alieni esse mereamini.
Mihi quidem gloriosum est et ualde optabile omnia pro Christi confessione perferre tormenta: quia cum hac uita nunquam digna sunt
habere amicicias sed de uestra satis doleo iuuentute: quam sine
sollicitudine gerentes facitis quidquid uobis fuerit ab iniusto iudice
imperatum. Tunc illi flætus et uoces dederunt: quod tam elegans
puella et tam sapiens et nobilis etiam optaret occidi: Et rogabant eam

dicentes: ne tale decus ammitteret: nec tantam pulchritudinem uersaret in mortem; quibus flæntibus atque animum reuocare cupientibus: ita respondit: hoc non est iuuentutem perdere; sed mutare. Dare lutum: et accipere aurum. Dare habitaculum uile et paruum: et accipere domum magnam at amplissimam ex lapidibus pretiosis et auro constructam. dare angulum breuem et oppressum: et accipere forum lucidum et margaritis cælestibus coruscantem. dare rem perituram: et accipere quam finem nescit: et mortem ignorat. dare lapidem uilem qui pedibus conculcatur: et accipere lapidem preciosum: qui in diademate regio libranti resplendet aspectu. Hodie si uobis aliquis offerret: ita ut partem summam nummorum gratanter ferret oblatam: nunquid non et uos curreretis ad talem mercaturum: et omnes patentes et notos et affines: et propinquos et caros et amicos faceretis uobiscum concurrere? Quicumque autem uos lachrymis reuocarent: eo quod omnes nummos uestros daretis intrepidi: nunquid non derideretis eos ut ignorantes? Vos autem curreretis exultantes: propterea quod daretis ad commutationem auri preciosi æramentum uile: et nullius summæ iacturam: et tamen pondus ad pondus uos accipere gratularemini. Deus autem non dat pondus ad pondus: sed quod simplum acceperit: centuplum reddet: insuper et uitam æternam. Et his dictis ascendit super lapidem: qui erat iuxta pedes eius: et dicit omnibus: Creditis hæc: quæ dixi:] At illi omnes una uoce dixerunt: Credimus Christum filium dei uerum deum esse: qui te talem possidet famulam. [Dicit eis Cæcilia: Ite ergo: et dicite infelici Almachio me inducias petere: et non urgeat meam passionem. Et huc in domum meam uenire faciam: qui uos omnes faciat uitæ æterna participes. Et ita domino procurante completur. Tunc ueniens papa sanctus Vrbanus baptizauit in domo eius amplius quam quadringentos promiscui sexus: et conditionis et ætatis: quos inter clarissimus uir erat nomine Gordianus. Hic sub umbratione nominis sui domum sanctæ Cæciliæ suo nomini dicauit: ut in occulto ex illa die ex quo ibi baptisma Christi celebratum est: ecclesia fieret: ita ut et papa urbis Vrbanus illic moraretur: licet occulte tamen quottidie redemptionis christi ibi crescerent lucra et infinita fierent diaboli detrimenta.] Sed cum hæc agerentur: Almachius Cæciliam sibi præsentari iubet: Quam interrogans ait: quod tibi nomen est? Respondit: Cæcilia. Almachius dixit: Cuius conditionis es? Cæcilia dixit: Ingenua nobilis clarissima. Almachius respondit: Ego te de religione interrogo. Cæcilia dixit: Interrogatio tua stultum sumit initium: quæ duas responsiones una putat inquisitione concludi. Almachius dixit: Vnde tibi tanta præsumptio respondendi? Cæcilia dixit: De conscientia bona: et fide non ficta. Almachius dixit: Ignoras cuius potestatis sim? Cæcilia respondit: Tu ignoras cuius

G 416–20

Not in Chaucer

G 421–41

potestatis sis. Nam et ego si me interroges de tua potestate: ueris
tibi assertionibus manifestabo. dicit ei Almachius: Dic si quid nosti.
Cæcilia respondit: Omnis potestas hominis sic est: quasi uter uento
repletus: Quem si acus pupugerit: omnis rigor ceruicis eius euanescit.
et quidquid in se rigidum habere cernitur incuruatur. Almachius G 442-57
dixit: Ab iniuriis cœpisti: et in iniuriis perseueras. Cæcilia respondit:
Iniuria non dicitur: nisi cum uerbum fallentibus irrogatur. Vnde
aut iniuriam doce: si falso locuta sum: aut te ipsum corripe calum-
niam inferentem. Almachius dixit: Ignoras quia dominii nostri
inuictissimi principes iusserunt: ut qui se non negauerint esse chris-
tianos puniantur: qui uero negauerint dimittantur? Cæcilia respondit: Sic Imperatores uestri errant: sicut et nobilitas tua: Sententiam enim quam ab eis prolatam esse testaris uos sæuientes et nos
innocentes ostendit. Si enim malum esset hoc nomen: nos negaremus:
uos uero ad confitendum suppliciis urgeretis. Almachius dixit: Pro
pietate sua hoc noluerunt statuere: quomodo uitæ uestræ possit
esse consultum. Cæcilia respondit: Nihil tam impium: nihilque
tam inimicum innocentiæ quam ut reis omnibus tormenta adhibeatis:
ad confitendum qualitatem sceleris. Locum. tempus. conscios socios
omni examinatione perquiritis. Vos uero quos innocentes scitis:
nominis tantum crimen impingitis. Sed nos scientes sanctum nomen:
omnino negare non possumus. Melius est enim feliciter mori: quam
infeliciter uiuere. Nos enim uera dicentes: uos torquemus: qui
mendacium elaboratis audire. Almachius dixit: Elige tibi unum e G 458-86
duobus: Aut sacrifica: aut nega te christianam esse: ut copiam
euadendi suscipias. Tunc surridens beata Cæcilia dixit: O iudicem
necessitate confusum: qui uult ut negem: me esse innocentem: ut
ipse me nocentem faciat. Si uis damnare: cur hortaris negare? Si
uis absoluere: quare uis inquirere? Almachius dixit: Accusatores
præsto sunt: qui te christianam esse testantur. Si negaueris: com-
pendiosum dabis accusantibus finem. Si autem negare nolueris:
dementiæ tuæ reputabis quando sententiæ subiacebis. Cæcilia respondit: Horum mihi accusatio uotiua est: et tua pœna uictoria.
Noli me ut dementem arguere: sed te ipsum increpa: qui christum
me existimas denegare. Almachius dixit: infelix ignoras quoniam
interficiendi et uiuaficandi mihi ab inuictissimis principibus potestas
data est? Vt quid cum tanta superbia loqueris? Cæcilia respondit:
Aliud est esse superbum: aliud est esse constantem. Ego constanter
locuta sum non suberbe: quia superbiam et nos fortiter execramur.
Tu autem si uerum audire non times: iterum docebo te falsissime
nunc locutum. Almachius dixit: Quæ sum falsissime prosecutus?
Cæcilia respondit: hoc quod principes tuos uiuificandi et interficiendi
tibi tradidisse asseris potestatem. Almachius dixit: Ergo mentitus

sum? Cæcilia respondit: Contra ueritatem publicam si iubes probo
te mentitum: Almachius dixit: Doce. Cæcilia respondit: Dixisti
principes tuos uiuificandi: et interficiendi tibi copiam tribuisse: cum
solam mortificandi scias tibi traditam potestatem. uitam enim uiuentibus tollere potes mortuis autem dare non potes. Dic ergo: quia
Imperatores tui mortis te ministrum esse uoluerunt. Nam si quid
plus dixeris: uideberis frustra mentitus. Almachius dixit: Depone
iam audaciam tuam: et sacrifica diis. Cæcilia respondit: Nescio
ubi tu oculos amiseris: Nam quos tu deos dicis: ego et omnes qui
oculos sanos habent saxa uidemus esse: et ærementum: et plumbum.
Almachius dixit: Meas iniurias phylosophando comtempsi: sed
deorum ferre non possum. Cæcilia respondit: ex quo os aperuisti: non
fuit sermo quem non probauerim iniustum stultum et uanum: Sed
nequit deesse: etiam exterioribus oculis te cecatum ostendi. Cum
quod omnes lapides uidemus esse et saxum inutile: hoc tu deum esse
testaris. Do: si iubes: consilium: Mitte manum tuam et tangendo
disce hoc saxum esse: si uidendo non nosti. Nefas est enim: ut
totus populus de te risum habeat. Omnes enim sciunt deum esse in
cælis. Istas autem figuras saxeas per ignem melius in calcem posse
conuerti: quæ modo sui otio pereunt: ut neque tibi pereunti neque
sibi ne in ignem mittantur poterunt subuenire. Tunc iratus uæhem-
enter Almachius iussit eam domum suam reduci: et in sua domo
flammis balnearibus concremari: Cumque fuisset in calore balnei
sui inclusa: subter incendia nimia lignorum pabula ministrarent die
integro et tota nocte quasi in loco frigido illibata perstitit sanitate:
ita ut nec una pars membrorum eius saltem sudoris signo labasset.
Quod cum audisset Almachius: misit qui eam ibidem in ipsis balneis
decollaret. Quam spiculator tertio percussit: et caput eius amputare
non potuit. Sic autem seminecem eam cruentus carnifex dereliquit:[1]
cuius sanguinem omnes bibleis linteaminibus populi qui per eam credi-
derant extergebant. Per triduum autem quo superuixit. non cessauit
omnes mulieres quas enutrierat: et quas educauerat in fide dominica
confirmare: quibus et diuisit uniuersa; quæ habuit: et sancto papæ
Vrbano tradidit commendatas: cui et dixit: Ad hoc mihi triduanas
poposci inducias: ut istas tuæ beatitudini traderem: et hanc domum
meam ecclesiæ nomine consecrares. Tunc sanctus Vrbanus corpus
eius auferens: cum diaconibus nocte sepeliuit eam inter collegas
suos episcopos: ubi sunt omnes confesores et martyres collocati.
Domum autem eius in æternum: sanctæ ecclesiæ nomini tradidit:
in qua domini beneficia exhuberant ad memoriam beatæ Cæciliæ
usque in hodiernum diem.

G 487–511

G 512–25

G 526–28
G 533–53

G 529–32

---

[1] *Bosius inserts:* nam apud veteres lex erat eis imposita, ut si in tribus per-
cussionibus non decollaretur, amplius non audebat.

THE CANON'S YEOMAN'S PRO-LOGUE AND TALE

By JOHN WEBSTER SPARGO

THE background from which Chaucer drew the materials for this prologue and tale, the alchemy of the fourteenth century, happens to be a period in the history of chemistry which is not at all well understood. Some of the more recent studies are signalized in a note, but the suggestions made here must be regarded as purely tentative.[1] From all of these, anyone interested in alchemy will speedily learn that the subject is thus far as the sands of the sea unnumbered. Notably for the fourteenth century, even the main patterns of thought can be but guessed at, for we do not have the texts. Corruptions of Arabic terms combined with garbled manuscripts and mystical interpretations to produce extraordinary confusion, which the editions of the seventeenth century, the best we have as yet, could not set right. Julius F. Ruska, who has devoted much of his brilliant scholarship to the study of alchemical manuscripts in Arabic and medieval Latin, emphasizes the vast amount of fundamental study yet to be carried out before the

---

[1] Lynn Thorndike, *History of Magic and Experimental Science*, Vol. III (New York, 1934); W. J. Wilson, in *Osiris*, Vol. II (1936); John Read, *Prelude to Chemistry* (London, 1936); André de Rassenfosse and G. Guében, *Des alchimistes aux briseurs d'atomes* ("Bibliothèque scientifique belge" [2d ed.; Paris, 1936] cf. especially chap. iv: "L'Alchimie au môyen age," pp. 33–50); J. R. Partington, "Albertus Magnus on Alchemy," in *Ambix, Journal of the Society for the Study of Alchemy and Early Chemistry*, I (London, 1937), 3–20; Gerard Heym, "An Introduction to the Bibliography of Alchemy," *Ambix*, I, 48–60; *Julius Ruska und die Geschichte der Alchemie*, a *Festgabe* offered to Ruska by the Deutsche Gesellschaft für Geschichte der Medizin, Naturwissenschaften und Technik (*Abhandlungen zur Geschichte der Medizin und der Naturwissenschaften*, Vol. XIX [Berlin, 1937]); Wilhelm Ganzenmüller, *Die Alchemie im Mittelalter* ([Paderborn, 1938], a fairly sound popular treatment; see the bibliography, pp. 238–40); S. Harrison Thomson, "The Texts of Michael Scot's *Ars alchemie*," in *Osiris*, V (1938), 523–59. This volume of *Osiris* is also dedicated to Julius Ruska and contains a memoir by Paul Kraus and a list of Ruska's publications. See further W. J. Wilson, "Catalogue of Latin and Vernacular Alchemical Manuscripts in the United States and Canada," *Osiris*, Vol. VI (1939).

alchemy of the period which interests us can be examined in the original sources.[1]

In the absence of the original sources, we can reprint here only the texts which are accessible. The state of these texts is not improved by the facts that the canon of Arnaldus de Villa Nova, for example, is highly suspect, and that it is only now that the identity of the famous "Senior" as a tenth-century Arabian alchemist is beginning to be made known—not to speak of the unsettled state of the canon of this none too well known writer.[2] The status of our subject is illustrated also by the fact that *La Complainte de la Nature*, an alchemical treatise formerly ascribed to Jean de Meun and therefore supposedly a possible source of Chaucer's knowledge of alchemy, turns out

[1] "Wer die Geschichte der Alchemie des Mittelalters nach den Quellen studieren will, steht einer uferlosen Aufgabe gegenüber. . . . . Ganz besonders aber fehlen Untersuchungen über die Quellen und Zusammenhänge der Alchemie des Abendlandes" (*Turba philosophorum*, ed. Julius F. Ruska ["Quellen und Studien zur Geschichte der Naturwissenschaften und der Medizin," I (Berlin, 1926)], p. vii). For a notice of other works by Ruska, all of which are of basic importance, see Rudolf Winderlich's brief article in *Journal of Chemical Education*, XIII (1936), 313–15; and note also Ruska's remark to the effect that the most obscure period in the history of alchemy is that of the thirteenth and fourteenth centuries, in *Annales Guébhard-Séverine*, X (1934), 417. This last is an annual published at Neuchâtel, Switzerland.

[2] On Arnold, see Ruska's edition of the *Turba philosophorum*, p. 339; his edition of the *Tabula smaragdina* (Heidelberg, 1926), p. 190; Paul Diepgen's "Studien zu Arnald von Villanova," in *Archiv für Geschichte der Medizin* as follows: III (1910), 115–30, 188–96, 369–96; V (1911–12), 88–120; VI (1912–13), 380–91; and Thorndike, III (1934), 52–84.

Of "Senior," the identification comes to me through a reference supplied to Professor S. Foster Damon by Dr. George Sarton. It seems that he was Muḥammad ibn Umail, called "al-Ḥakīm," i.e., 'the physician' in the widest sense of medical man, metaphysician, philosopher, and sage. In Latin translation, his work which Chaucer knew was called *Tabula chemica* or *De chemia*. For illuminating expositions of the mangling of "Senior's" Arabic text when translated into Latin, see Ruska in *Isis*, XXIV (1936), 310–42 and his reference to an edition of three texts by this alchemist, together with a Latin rendering of one of these reprinted from Zetzner's *Theatrum chemicum*, Vol. V (Argentorati, 1622), entitled "Senioris Zadith, filii Hamuelis Tabula Chemica," by H. E. Stapleton and M. Hidāyat Ḥussain in *Memoirs of the Asiatic Society of Bengal*, XII (1933), 1–213. At pp. 126 f. of this last is a list of a score of works by this writer, whose full name is given as ʾAbu ʾAbdallah Muḥammad bin Umail al-Ḥakīm aṣ-Ṣādiq at-Tamīmī. Stapleton points out that "Ṣādiq" seems to be the basis of the "Zadith" of the Latin translation. Cf. Philip K. Hitti, *History of the Arabs* (London, 1937), p. 364, and Edmund O. von Lippmann, *Entstehung und Ausbreitung der Alchemie*, II (Berlin, 1931), 149.

to have been written not earlier than the sixteenth century and therefore must be left out of consideration here.[1]

In circumstances thus dubious, it is a relief to turn to a work which gives us welcome clues for the solution of many of the riddlesome problems which abound in alchemical treatises. Until I had read Arthur J. Hopkins' *Alchemy Child of Greek Philosophy* (New York, 1934), I had found such alchemical treatises as I had seen hopelessly confused and self-contradictory. To paraphrase the words of another student of Greek alchemy, a person examining these works with a view to carrying out the processes described in them is in the same kind of dilemma as a builder trying to get practical information from a book on Freemasonry.[2] Mr. Hopkins makes it plain that the difficulty is due in part to failure by medieval writers to understand technical terms which had been transmitted from Greek via Arabic to Latin. Terms used for materials involved in the preparation and use of dyes for textiles were transferred to "dyes" for metals; and in the Occident some did not understand clearly that these "dyes" or "tinctures" for metals operated only externally, as it were merely gilding the surfaces of inferior metals. The colors or dyes or tinctures often run in the cycle black ("earth," i.e., ore), white (silver), yellow or red (gold), purple or violet (the elixir). At a time when competent assayers were not everywhere, many a piece of inferior metal "tinted" with gold passed for the genuine article.[3] Hence the frequent reports of success in transmuting metals to gold. Unless a skilled assayer were at hand to analyze the material, the observer thought that it was solid gold. Such is probably the explanation of the success of Nicolas Flamel, Chaucer's contemporary (about 1330–1417 or 1418), at Paris, who left a most pleasing account of his experiments; such is certainly a part of the experience of a traveling "laborant" or laboratory techni-

---

[1] Lodovico Frati, "Poesie alchimistiche attribuite à Jean de Meun," in *Archivum Romanicum*, III (1919), 321–36, and F. Walker, "Jean de Meun and Alchemy," in *Journal of Chemical Education*, VII (1930), 2863–74. These writers did not know that Brunet (*Manuel du libraire*[5], Vol. III [1862], col. 1679), dated the poem *ca.* 1520.

[2] F. Sherwood Taylor, in *Journal of Hellenic Studies*, L (1930), 138.

[3] On the confusion see the article by Arthur John Hopkins in *Isis*, XXIX (1938), 326–54.

cian—a practical scientist—as it is described in a sixteenth-century treatise attributed to Salomon Trismossin entitled *Splendor Solis;* and such is the reason for the successful trick of the Persian stranger at Damascus who filed gold coins to bits and mixed them up with charcoal and fish glue into pellets which he sold under a fanciful name to a druggist. Then, having let it be known that he understood the secret of transmuting metals, he performed a naturally satisfactory demonstration before the sultan. When the sultan gave him a sum of money with which to procure a further supply of the indispensable drug, the stranger disappeared; and once again a charlatan had performed what looked to bystanders like an authentic transmutation.[1]

With the decree of Pope John XXII before us, we recognize the fact that Chaucer wanted the Canon to be regarded in much the same way that we regard his colleagues in religion, the monk, the friar, and the summoner. On the other hand, the Canon's Yeoman, in contrast with the Canon himself and of course with Chaucer, knows relatively little about the theory behind the laboratory in which he blew and slaved and swept up the pieces. He merely hints at the current color terminology —rather more than do some editors of Chaucer, at that—when he alludes to "watres rubifying," i.e., fluids which transmute to gold, to "citrinacioun," i.e., transmuting to gold, to "watres albificacioun," i.e., fluids which transmute to silver, and to "cementyng," i.e., combining two solids at high temperatures in such a way as to change the properties of one of the substances before melting takes place.[2] The Yeoman knows no

---

[1] Flamel's *Le Livre des figures hiéroglifiques*, ed. Albert Poisson in *Histoire de l'alchimie ... Nicolas Flamel, sa vie, ses fondations, ses œuvres* (Paris, 1893). There is an English translation by "Eirenæus Orandus, *qui est, Vera veris enodans*," entitled *N. Flammel His Exposition of the Hieroglyphicall Figures upon an Arch in St. Innocent Church-yard in Paris* (London, 1624), from which John Read quotes freely at pp. 60 ff. The same writer translates from the German text of *Splendor Solis* at pp. 69 ff. The Persian's trick is summarized from Carra de Vaux by Eric J. Holmyard in *Makers of Chemistry* (Oxford, 1931), pp. 75 f., and is noticed by Hopkins on pp. 198 f.

[2] Other specialized terms cannot be noticed here. Two should be signalized, however: (1) when the Yeoman mentions "enbibing," he means "moistening" or "soaking" (cf. Wilson in *Osiris*, II, 323); (2) "mortifye" in its technical sense means here "to deprive of life, to kill"; but this remains meaningless unless we know that a widespread belief of the time was that mercury (*argentum vivum*) or *quick*silver differed from silver (*argentum*) only in that the mercury was *alive*, i.e., in fluid

more about "this elvysh nyce lore" than the summoner knows about canon law. These servants can repeat like parrots some few of the words which they have heard bandied about, but "grope" them ever so little and they are lost.

The Yeoman's first section gives us some of the terms which the Yeoman recalls by rote, including in the manner of sales talk the usual invective against the art, for this is a clever way in which to break down "sales resistance" in a possible investor. His second section tells us of three tricks by which impostors have succeeded in deceiving gullible persons: (1) "that other" canon slips into the fire beneath the retort a beechen coal in which he has drilled a hole, filled it with silver filings, and then stopped the opening with wax; (2) the molten mixture is stirred by the dupe—the investor—with a hollow rod containing silver; (3) a bar of silver is slipped into the mixture while the victim is not looking. For these extremely simple little tricks we have no specific sources as yet. Finally we have nearly a hundred lines in which the metaphysical import of alchemy is discussed. It is in these last hundred lines that we find mention of "Arnold of the Newe Toun" and of that disciple of Plato who wrote a book called "Senior." Of the latter, mention has already been made; of Arnold's "Rosarie"—a typical alchemical color word, by the way—we must for the time being content ourselves with a bad, even an incomprehensible, text of a work which in itself was purely bookish, never truly experimental. The same may be said of the *Pretiosa margarita novella* by Petrus Bonus Lombardus of Ferrara (Thorndike, III, 147 ff.), and in the main all that can be done here is to illustrate in the most general way some of the types of material which may have come under Chaucer's eye. Many will feel that we can be most sure of the decree of Pope John XXII.

These illustrative materials will be presented arbitrarily under three headings: (I) "Analogues to the Warnings against the Pursuit of Alchemy," (II) "Tricks of Alchemists," and (III) "Sources and Analogues of Passages on the Science of Alchemy."

---

state. Hence, if you could kill mercury by stopping its fluidity or life, you would get ordinary silver (*ibid.*, p. 312, n. 125). See further Edgar Hill Duncan, "The Yeoman's Canon's 'Silver Citrinacioun,' " *MP*, XXXVII (1940), 241–62.

In conclusion, it is pertinent to direct attention to the fact that, although we cannot say that Chaucer was in any sense a genuinely practical scientist—his "exposure" of alchemy (and Petrarch's, too) being due to an ancient convention at least as old as Avicenna (980–1036)—on the other hand, there is no good reason for looking down our noses at Chaucer because of his failure to see through the whole fraud, as some people even today persist in calling it, of alchemy. He did not see through it, because any candid person in those days might well be deceived by the evidence of his own eyes in a laboratory. In the year 1938 the dream of many an alchemist would seem to have come to fruition in the discovery of trialkylphosphineaurus halide, a compound by means of which ten cents' worth of gold may be used to gild a lady's gown. Although the plan of attack was very different from that of the alchemists—and the same thing must be said of the atom-smashing creation of new elements nowadays—it is nonetheless worth pointing out that the alchemists' preoccupation with colors might be justified to a considerable extent by certain inherent qualities which this most malleable and ductile of metals has always possessed. It would be going beyond the evidence to assert that the medieval alchemist used the tests about to be described, but, without chemically pure substances throughout, some of the end products might well be the same. When precipitated from solutions, gold is ruby red in color. At high temperatures, the fumes from heated gold will gild silver which is held in the fumes, say in a sealed retort. Two ordinary tests for the presence of gold involve colors: filter paper soaked in a clear solution of iodine or bromine in water plus the metallic materials to be tested will produce a purple ash if gold is present, and minute quantities in solution may be detected by the addition of a mixture of ferric and stannous chlorides, whereupon a bluish-purple precipitate is thrown down. Were the alchemists mad or perverse or hypocritical, then, in the stress which they laid on precisely these colors? Moreover, as Mr. Wilson points out, "multiplication" of gold is carried on constantly today, as it has been since many a century before Chaucer's time. By adding copper and a little zinc or arsenic to gold, you get 14-carat or 18-carat gold, thus making the noble metal go far-

ther—multiplying its effectiveness. Thus we see that the characteristics of the metal which are scientifically verifiable today
are well calculated to encourage a far better scientist than Chaucer or anybody else in his age could have been to misinterpret
the ambiguous color symbolism inherited from ancient traditions
no longer understood. With unstable and nonstandard reagents,
with gold-bearing mercuric or ferrous or lead ores to start with,
and with tests from assayed pure gold giving analogous results,
might not even a modern chemist be misled?[1]

I

DECREE OF POPE JOHN XXII AGAINST THE CRIME OF ALCHEMY[2]

(From *Corpus juris canonici*, editio Lipsiensis secunda, ed. Friedberg [pârs
secunda; Lipsiae, 1881], col. 1295. "Extravagantes decretales quae a diversis
romanis pontificibus post Sextum emanaverunt ["Extravag. commun."] Lib. V.
tit. vi.")

"DE CRIMINE FALSI"

CAP. UN.

Spondent, quas non exhibent, divitias pauperes alchimistae, pariter
qui se sapientes existimant in foveam incidunt, quam fecerunt. Nam
haud dubie huius artis alchimiae alterutrum se professores ludificant,
quum suae ignorantiae conscii eos, qui supra ipsos aliquid huiusmodi
dixerint, admirantur. Quibus quum veritas quaesita non suppetat,
diem cernunt, facultates exhauriunt, iidemque verbis dissimulant
falsitatem, ut tandem, quod non est in rerum natura esse verum aurum
vel argentum sophistica transmutatione confingant. Eoque interdum eorum temeritas damnata et damnanda progreditur, ut fidis
metallis cudant publicae monetae characteres fidis oculis, et non alias
alchimitum fornacis ignem vulgum ignorantem eludant. Haec itaque
perpetuis volentes exsulare temporibus, hac edictali constitutione
sancimus, ut quicunque huiusmodi aurum vel argentum fecerint,
vel fieri secuto facto mandaverint, vel ad hoc scienter, (dum id fieret,)
facientibus ministraverint, aut scienter vel auro vel argento usi
fuerint vendendo vel dando in solutum: verum tanti ponderis aurum

(marginal notes:)
Alchemists deceive themselves and one another.

After they lose all they have, they try to pass false metals as gold or silver;

they even coin money.

Anyone making or using alchemical gold or silver will be fined the same weight of true gold or silver.

[1] To the late Professor Arthur John Hopkins and to Dr. William Jerome
Wilson the writer is indebted for many helpful suggestions.

[2] On John XXII, pope at Avignon 1316–34, see G. Mollat in *Dictionnaire de
théologie catholique*, VIII, Part I (Paris, 1924), cols. 633 ff. and Noël Valois in
Histoire littéraire de la France, XXXIV (Paris, 1915), 391–630, esp. pp. 419 f.
This decree is quoted from another text and translated by Partington in *Ambix*, I
(1937), 15 f.

vel argentum poenae nomine inferre cogantur in publicum, pauperibus erogandum, quanti alchimitum exsistat, circa quod eos aliquo praedictorum modorum legitime constiterit deliquisse, facientibus nihilominus aurum vel argentum alchimitum, aut ipso (ut praemittitur) scienter utentibus, perpetuae infamiae nota respersis. Quodsi ad praefatam poenam pecuniariam exsolvendam delinquentium ipsorum facultates non sufficiant: poterit discreti moderatio iudicis poenam hanc in aliam, (puta carceris, vel alteram iuxta qualitatem negotii, personarum differentiam aliasque attendendo circumstantias,) commutare. Illos vero qui in tantae ignorantiam infelicitatis proruperint, ut nedum nummos vendant, sed naturalia iuris praecepta contemnant, artis excedant metas, legumque violent interdicta, scienter videlicet adulterinam ex auro et argento alchimito cudendo seu fundendo, cudi seu fundi faciendo monetam, hac animadversione percelli iubemus, ut ipsorum bona deferantur carceri, ipsique perpetuo sint infames. Et si clerici fuerint delinquentes: ipsi ultra praedictas poenas priventur beneficiis habitis, et prorsus reddantur inhabiles ad habenda.[1]

If he cannot pay, the fine will be commuted into some other punishment.

The much worse lawbreakers who make false money will have all their goods confiscated, and will be held criminals.

If clerics, they will also be deprived of benefices for all their lives.

PETRARCH'S DIALOGUE *DE ALCHIMIA*

(From the 1649 Rotterdam edition of *Francisci Petrarchæ De Remediis utriusque Fortunæ*, I, 305–7, Dialogus 111.)

Spes. Spero Alchimiæ prosperos exitus.

Ratio. Mirum unde id speres, quod nec tibi unquam vere accidit, nec cuiquam: &, si accidisse non nullis fama fuerit, ab his ficta, quibus id credi expediret.

Spes. Spero Alchimiæ successum.

Ra. Et quem, quaeso, praeter fumum, cinerem, sudorem, suspiria, verba, dolos, ignominiam? Hi sunt enim Alchimiæ successus, quibus inopem nunquam ad divitias evectum, multos a divitiis ad inopiam redactos sæpe vidimus. Non tamen illud attenditis: tam blandum est sperare, & falli: huc agit vos avaritiæ stimulis impulsa dementia, ut verum opinemini, quod optatis, falsumque, quod cernitis. Notastine aliquos prudentes in reliquis, hac insania laborare? quosdam opulentissimos hac vanitate consumptos? dumque opulentiores fieri student, & fœdo quæstui inhiant, bene parta prodigere, censuque omni in supervacuis effuso, tandem necessariis etiam destituto, alios, civilitate deposita, mœstos semper, atque anxios, dum nec cogitare aliud, quam folles, & forcipes, & carbones, nec aliis, quam suae

I expect alchemy to work.
It never does.

It brings all kinds of troubles, especially poverty.

Cupidity keeps up your blind hopes.

Alchemy ruins some people;

to others it becomes an obsession;

---

[1] Not dated. The companion piece, *De crimine falsi*, printed at col. 1216 of Friedberg's edition, is dated 1322. It specifies penalties for the crime of counterfeiting coins.

hæresis convivere didicerunt, in sylvestres pene homines evasisse: nonnullos denique, amissis primum animi luminibus, in hoc exercitio corporeos insuper oculos amisisse?

it makes some blind both in mind and in body.

Spes. Promissum ab artifice aurum spero.

Ra. Refert cujus artifex, quid promittat. Sunt, quibus promittentibus, nihil credi possit, eoque minus, si promissum jusjurandi religione firmaverint. . . . . Hic, qui tibi aurum suum spondet, cum tuo auro improvisus aufugiet. Novi nihil narro; mos est publicus.

The promises of alchemists are worth nothing.

They take your gold, then disappear.

Yet you keep hoping and exerting yourself in vain. How silly to believe in the promises of beggarly people apparently more concerned about the poverty of others than about their own! If you persist, your home will be a strange sight.

Erunt sufflatores, deceptores, derisores, omnis angulus habebit pulves, & lebetes, & phialas olentium aquarum; herbas praeterea peregrinas; & externos sales, & sulphus, & distillatoria, & caminos. Deque his omnibus tibi in finem curas inutiles, & stultitiam cordis, oris obscœnitatem, & squalorem, & caliginem oculorum, ac sollicitam conflaveris paupertatem: quodque his omnibus pene pejus dixerim, circulatoris nomen, & nocturnis in tenebris, atque infames inter latebras furum vitam.

There will be deceivers and deriders, queer apparatus and ingredients,

and, for you, worry and ailments,

and, worse still, a bad reputation.

(John Gower, *Confessio amantis*, IV, 2559 ff. [*The Complete Works of John Gower*, ed. G. C. Macaulay (Oxford, 1901), II, 370 f.].)

[The "third stone," called Mineral, purifies metals.]

	This Mineral, so as I finde,
2560	Transformeth al the ferste kynde
	And makth hem able to conceive
	Thurgh his vertu, and to receive
	Bothe in substance and in figure
	Of gold and selver the nature.
	For thei tuo ben thextremetes,
	To whiche after the propretes
	Hath every metal his desir,
	With help and confort of the fyr
	Forth with this Ston, as it is seid,
2570	Which to the Sonne and Mone is leid;
	For to the rede and to the whyte
	This Ston hath pouer to profite.
	It makth multiplicacioun
	Of gold, and the fixacioun

A stone called "mineral" transforms baser metals into gold or silver.

It causeth, and of his habit
He doth the werk to be parfit
Of thilke Elixer which men calle
Alconomie, as is befalle
To hem that whilom weren wise.

2580 Bot now it stant al otherwise;
Thei speken faste of thilke Ston,

But the secret of it
is lost,

Bot hou to make it, nou wot non
After the sothe experience.
And natheles gret diligence
Thei setten upon thilke dede,

and the search for it
leads only to pov-
erty.

And spille more than thei spede;
For allewey thei finde a lette,
Which bringeth in poverte and dette
To hem that riche were afore:

2590 The lost [sc. loss?] is had, the lucre is lore,
To gete a pound thei spenden fyve;
I not hou such a craft schal thryve
In the manere as it is used:
It were betre be refused
Than forto worchen upon weene
In thing which stant noght as thei weene.

Yet the science in
itself is sound.

Bot noght forthi, who that it knewe,
The science of himself is trewe
Upon the forme as it was founded,
Wherof the names yit ben grounded
Of hem that ferste it founden oute; . . . .

II

(From Novella XXI of the *Novelle* of Giovanni Sercambi.)

Through a blow-
pipe, Zacchangna
blows from his
mouth more than
an ounce of fine par-
ticles of gold into a
heated crucible.

⟨fol. 40ʳ⟩[1] Zacchangna, avendo in boccha granello d'oro più di oncia j, soffiando con un cannone, in nel cruzuolo lo mettea e la polver n'uscia fuori faccendo fuocho; e soffiando ultimamente quel uncia d'oro che Sachangna avea messo in nel cruzuolo, e così fondeo;

The gold melts, is
cast into a bar, and
taken to Siena to be
sold.

e gittatolo in vergha, disse Sachangna a Pitullo, "Porta quest'oro a Siena e vendelo, e non lo dare per meno di fiorini viii."...

Pitullo sells it for eight florins and returns.

[1] MS Trivulziano No. 193 of the *Novelle* of Giovanni Sercambi. For the manuscript and the editorial principles of the present text see above, pp. 33–36. This *novella*, DE FALSARI, has been printed by D'Ancona, *Scelta*, pp. 155–58; see above, p. 44.

⟨fol. 40ᵛ⟩ E da poi ne fe' di nuovo per lo modo ditto, e[1] Pitullo li portà a Siena, e fiorini nuovi regà in tanto che più che cento fiorini avea già tratto di Siena. Um gorno Pitullo disse fra sè, "Io saprei omai fare questo mestieri, e penso fare patto com Sachangna"; e disseli che saprà fare....

This process is repeated until more than a hundred florins have been brought back from Siena by the intended victim, Pitullo.

Pitullo tries and, of course, fails. For a thousand florins Zacchangna will teach him how to do it.

E prese once vj di quella terra, e messa a fuocho, Zacchangna tenea uno cannone in mano, Pitullo un'altro; e mentre che 'l fuoco si facea, Zachangna dicea, "Soffia[2] così." E mentre che soffiava, misse in nel cruzolo oncia una a buon peso d'oro. Pitullo disse, "Io così farò." Zachangna disse, "Or soffia." Pitullo soffia. Zachangna disse, "Soffia forte." Pitullo soffiava, e questo fe' molte volte, tanto quel oro fu strutto gittato in vergha. Disse Pitullo, "Ormai saprò fare." Sachangna disse, "Stai pressi li fiorini m." Sachangna si parte e vanne a Siena....

Zacchangna gives Pitullo a blow-pipe and shows him how to blow, not telling him of the gold in his mouth.

Pitullo blows along with Zacchangna, and the result is good, as before.

"Now I'll know how to do it." Zacchangna takes his fee and departs.

When Pitullo blows by himself, naturally he gets no farther than the gulled priest in Chaucer's tale.

III

([Petrus Antonius Bonus, *or* Petrus Bonus Ferrariensis], *Pretiosa margarita novella de thesauro, ac pretiosissimo philosophorum lapide* .... [(Venice), 1546.] [This was written about 1330, according to Lynn Thorndike, *History of Magic* ...., III (1934), 147–62.] *Colloquium nuncupatorium, interloquutores Bonus & Lacinius*. [This text is printed in italic throughout in the original.].)

⟨fol. viᵛ⟩ [*Bonus*] .... sed ars ipsa sancta est, & quam non nisi puros ac sanctos homines habere licet. nam ut diui Thomae utra [*sc.* utar?] sententia, Ars ista uel reperit hominem sanctum, aut reddet eius inuentio sanctum. *Laci*[*nius*]. Non sic aiunt moderni nostri, sed dicunt non tantum religiosos omnes: uerum nec uiros probos illa decere. *Bonus.* Et tu quoque horum uulgarium sequeris uocem atque opinionem? *Laci.* Vulgarium? optarem siquidem, sed ut uideo, communis & fere omnium est sententia. *Bonus.* Insanis me hercle, & mihi hæc tuo contentio bilem excitat (nisi de sophistis fiat sermo apud eos) qui quidem non alchimici philosophi censendi sunt, sed fures atque latrones: qua propter uulgus iners atque ignarus alchumistæ nomen,[3] perditis istis simul atque philosophis confundit, qui sicut distat lux a tenebris, verum a falso, Deus ipse a

This is a sacred art known only by pure men.

The modern age does not regard it so.

It enrages me that rogues and robbers should usurp the name of alchemical philosophers.

---

[1] e] *Inserted above the line MS.*   [2] Soffia] Soffra *emend. D'A.*

[3] Omission of this comma would improve the corrupt text.

mammona, bonum a malo, sic isti inter se minime conhærent et ueluti
cacodæmon spiritus angeli nomen adhuc retinens, nihil cum beatis
illis spiritibus,[1] commune possidet in re, nisi forte nomen, sic itidem
isti empyrici sophistæ, falso sibi nomen usurpant, qui quidem suis
latrociniis artem hanc sanctissimam fecere fabulam uulgi. . . . .

⟨fol. viii^v⟩ *Lacinius.* O facinus, quid audio, ut scientia hæc tam
supernaturalis & ars tam rara hodie apud multos illusio & deceptio
uideatur? *Bo[nus].* Nec mirum, quoniam euenit, ut hoc deplorato
seculo omnis generis homines & quidem ignauissimi, audeant artis et
scientiæ huius fœlicissimæ & altissimæ philosophiæ latentes causas
perquirere, arbitrantes lapidem illum beatissimum e chartaceis,
ambagibus ac deceptionibus idiotarum quorundam extorquere at
que furari. ij siquidem sunt fabri, lanarij, lignarij, & id genus
hominum μελαγχολούντων cupientium sine labore ditari. *Laci.* Non
ne illam quærunt similiter & docti, nobiles, principes ac denique
reges? *Bo.* Quid tum? Noui ipse quamplures, sed non ut par est
eos scientiæ huius præstantissimæ, sed tantum auri cupidos uidi,
ita ut iures duros esse silices ex quibus aurum ipsum excauatur, sed
duriorem illorum dices auri famem. & licet eos omnes cunctis in
rebus nasutissimos iudices, hac tamen in re nihil dices habere nasi,
cum eos quandoque uideas stolidissimas chimeras credere ambiguaque
ac falsa, inania atque puerilia, pro ingenti nescio quo semper amplecti
& nunc huic peregrino, nunc uero illi, aures arrigunt, qui ampullosa &
vana pollicitantes, quotidie in arsenicis, sulphuribus, menstruis & his
similibus promptissimi auidissimique inscite atque inepte operantur,
qui tandem hoc fine clauduntur, ut tempus ipsi conterant, aliosque
conterere faciant, & sic pro lapide acquirendo pecuniam dilapidant,
ac demum cum proposito frustratos se esse conspiciant, conantur
quæsitæ longius herbæ,[2] in ualido fugiens argentum sistere succo.
La. O tardas adeo mentes assuetaque falli artificum uarioque;[3]
rerum per inania ductu pectora, quidnam conueniunt ista metallis?
Sed heu quantum a proposito longe uagamur. *Bo.* Minime, nam
omnia quæ dicta sunt ad rem pertinent, ecce iam tua ope in lucem
exeo, non Principum aut Regum dignitate protectus, sed ipsa tantum
uirtute comite, antiquorum ægyptiorum morem partim imitatus,
qui cuncta Mercurio dicabant, tanquam uirtutis ingenijque ipsius
autori ac largitori: partim uero soli tanquam rerum omnium ac
generationis patri. Soli igitur et mercurio dicatum esse uolo ex quorum
fonte cuncta huic operi necessaria profiscuntur. Nec non illis omnibus,
qui uirtutem, & quæcunque recta sunt, colunt; eos autem omnes qui
tantum salis habent, ut quæcunque ipsi non probauerint, negligant

Marginal notes:

It is outrageous that this supernatural science, this rare art, should seem but trickery to many.

No wonder, when the most ignorant folk dare to pursue the secret of the most blessed stone in manuscripts and symbols and deceits; such are smiths, wool-workers, carpenters, and all that black-biled ilk who would get rich quick.

Although the better sort go in for the quest too, they are cursed by greed.

They believe in the most stupid fancies and are deceived by boasts of people who use arsenic, sulphur, and nasty substances unintelligently.

In attempting to discover the stone, they waste money.

They follow the methods of the ancient Egyptians.

---

[1] For punctuation see preceding note.

[2] See p. 695, n. 3.

[3] The semicolon should be omitted.

atque damnent. Inspiciant quæso ipsi opus diligenter, illis opus non autor ipse loquatur. Nam cum autor in sui ipsius commendationem loquitur, male quidem agit, bene uero cum opus ipsum loquitur. Vanus iudicio meo censendus est opifex, qui ab alijs magis quam ab ipso opere laudem expectat atque honorem. Vale.

In my opinion the workman should be deemed no good at all who looks to other people rather than to the work itself for applause and prestige.

(The *Correctorium alchymiae* by Robert or York, "Perscrutator," who flourished *ca.* 1348, is identified by Thorndike [III, 106, 629] as the *Correctorium fatuorum, seu Correctorium Richardi Anglici* listed by Zetzner [1659; VII, 713] and printed by him [II, 385–406] as *Richardi Anglici Libellus utilissimus* περὶ χημείας, *cui titulum fecit, Correctorium.*)

CAPUT II. STUDIUM PHILOSOPHIÆ ESSE NECESSARIUM AD HANC ARTEM

.... Et ideo omnes hujus artis beneficium diligentes, studiis insistere tenentur, & ex libris veritatem exhaurire, & non ex fabulis fictis & operibus mendosis, cum haec ars nullatenus veraciter inveniatur (quamvis hominibus multae sophisticationes appareant) nisi post terminum studii & philosophicorum dictorum cognitionem, seu per scientis fidelem informationem eum docetur. ... [II, 387].

The art of alchemy is learned from books,

after long study of the philosophers or from reliable scholars themselves.

Chaucer had read in some text or other alchemical treatises ascribed to "Senior" and to Arnaldus de Villa Nova (is this Villa Nova perhaps really "Neapolis"? queries Professor Hopkins in a personal letter). These materials he interwove at will. Below some of them are cited in the order in which they appear in the editions from which they are quoted, not in the order in which Chaucer used them.

("Senior," *Tabula chemica*, ed. Lazarus Zetzner, *Theatrum chemicum*, V [1660], 199.)

Et radix hujus aquae sunt ambae aves colligatae, quarum utraque retinet caudum alterius, & radix harum avium est luna plena, & haec est Magnesia & Abarnahas perfectum.

⟨213⟩ Homines vero non intelligunt verba eorum, nec percipiunt quid intenditur, unde falsificant veridicos, & verificant falsidicos opinionibus suis, & sibi debent imponere culpam, non sapientibus. Error enim eorum est ex ignorantia intentionis eorum, quando audiunt diversa verba, sed ignota intellectui eorum, cum sint in intellectu occulto.

All manner of mistakes are made because people do not understand what is meant.

⟨224⟩ Dixit Salomon rex: Recipe lapidem qui dicitur Thitarios, & est lapis rubeus, albus, citrinus, niger, habens multa nomina, & diversos colores.

Dixit etiam naturam unam, & spiritualem, sepultam in arena, & assignavit lapidem coloribus propriis, qui apparent in praepara-

Quoth King Solomon, Take a stone called Thitarios, which is red, white, yellow, and black, has many names and various colors.

tione. Dixit sapiens assigna mihi illum: Dixit, & est corpus magnesiae nobile, quod commendarunt omnes Philosophi. Dixit, Quid est magnesia? Respondit magnesia est aqua composita, congelata, quae repugnant igni. . . . . ⟨227⟩ Et dixit Plato, unumquodque est unum. . . . .[1]

. . . . & hoc est secretum, super quo juraverunt, quod non indicaret in aliquo libro. Nec aliquis eorum declaravit hoc, & attribuerunt illud Deo glorioso, ut inspiraret illud cui vellet, & prohibeatur a quo vellet. Est enim radix sine qua nullum juvabit aes . . . . [sc. ars; Stapleton, as above, p. 183].

⟨234⟩ . . . . sicut dixerunt quidam glossatores, qui recesserunt a veritate, & laboraverunt in capillis, & consumpserent pecuniam suam, & dies in inquisitione vanitatis. Sed opinati sunt, & pervenerunt homines quos vides per falsas opiniones ad vanitatem. Et similiter quicunque dixerunt, quod haec ars est ex ovis, ungulis animalium, urina, sanguine, felle, spermate, & similibus & aliis etiam mineralibus diminutis combustibilibus corruptibilibus & nihil venientibus, falsi sunt, postquam sciverunt, quod sit scientia perfecta magni pretii, & quod est secretum Dei gloriosi, & sublimis, magnum, & multitudo multitudinis, & quae inspirata est a Deo philosophis suis, & electis, & in eum credentibus, & est dignius quam est in mundo, & nihil comparatur ei, & est soror Philosophiae, & habuit esse a Deo per inspirationem. Postquam sciverunt hoc dixerunt, quod esset ex capillis & ovis, arsenicis, & sulphuribus & rebus immundis & sordidis, ita quod quidam ex infirmitate suae rationis fecerunt eam, & ex stercore & urina, & hoc absit a sapientibus Dei gloriosi & sublimis.

(Arnold of Villanova, *De lapide philosophorum*, in Arnold's *Opera* [Lyons, 1532], Cap. ii.)

. . . . ergo lapis iste est ex quatuor elementis compositus.

CAP. III: . . . . quatuor sunt spiritus: sal armonicus: sulphur: arcenicum: argentum vivum: . . . .

CAP. IV: Dixit discipulus quare dicunt philosophi quod mercurius non moritur nisi cum fratre interficiatur: magister dixit primus eorum qui dixit fuit hermes qui dixit quod draco nunquam moritur nisi cum fratre interficiatur: vult dicere quod mercurius nunquam moritur id est congelatur nisi cum fratre suo id est sol et luna.

CAP. V: . . . . nonne oportet quod ego occultem tibi hoc secretum secretorum [with this last might be placed "Senior," as above, p. 195: ". . . . secretum secretorum per me generatur. . . . ."].

Sidenotes:

What is magnesia? —It is made of congealed water, which fire detests.

Some forsake the truth and waste their time and money on foolish things.

Others believe erroneously that with all manner of organic and mineral substances they will get results.

Alchemy is the sister of Philosophy, and as such has its source in God. The nasty materials with which many work have nothing to do with God.

The [Philosopher's] stone is made up of four elements. There are four spirits. Why do the scientists say that mercury does not die unless slain with his brother? Hermes first said that the dragon dies not unless slain with his brother: this means that mercury does not solidify unless with his brother, i.e., the sun and the moon.[2] Should I not conceal from you the great secret?

[1] On Chaucer's use of this passage see Ruska in *Anglia*, LXI (1937), 136 f.

[2] Cf. Lowes, *MLN*, XXVIII (1914), 229.

THE MANCIPLE'S TALE

By JAMES A. WORK

INTRODUCTION

THE material in the *Manciple's Tale* for purposes of analysis may be divided conveniently into two parts: (I) the narrative material, the story of Apollo and the crow, which is the skeleton on which considerable digressive material is hung; and (II) the nonnarrative material, the interpolated castigation of faithless wives, the discourse on plain speech, and the proverbial and sententious remarks on controlling the tongue.

The story of the talking bird who is ill rewarded for his unwise truthfulness is widespread, and numerous oriental and western versions of it are extant.[1] It is clear, however, both from the languages involved and from the stories themselves, that Chaucer did not know and was not influenced by any Indian or Persian versions; therefore, none of these is reprinted here. Of the western European versions, two types are found in the *Seven Sages* and in Ovid's *Metamorphoses*. Since there are a number of similarities in detail between the *Seven Sages* version and Chaucer's, a Middle English text of it has been included here. But since Chaucer's narrative clearly stems from either Ovid or some of his many medieval translators, imitators, and moralizers, the bulk of the following material is Ovidian.[2]

---

[1] See W. A. Clouston, "The Tell-Tale Bird," in *Originals and Analogues of Some of Chaucer's Canterbury Tales* ("Chaucer Society: Second Series," No. 22 [London, 1887]), and Gustav Plessow, *Des Haushälters Erzählung* (Leipzig, 1929), pp. 93 ff.

[2] Limitations of space allow the presentation here of only such texts as bear numerous and consistent resemblances to the *Manciple's Tale* and are most likely to have reached Chaucer. Among the more important of the many other medieval treatments of Ovid's story which attest its widespread popularity and which bear incidental resemblances to the *Manciple's Tale*, are: (1) the second redaction (1342) of the Commentary on Ovid's *Metamorphoses* written by Pierre Berçuire and forming the fifteenth book of his *Reductorium morale;* (2) an anonymous translation and moralization of the *Metamorphoses*, printed in 1484 by Colard Mansion,

In headnotes to the texts printed below I shall call attention
to the chief special resemblances between each of the texts and
Chaucer's story. It may be well to say in advance, however,
that I have found no conclusive evidence that any one of these
texts was Chaucer's source. Each one (save Ovid's) contains
details common to itself and Chaucer and to no other; but none
of these details is so curious that Chaucer could not have
thought of it independently, and there are no general or verbal
parallels that point undeniably to his use of any of these texts.
Certainly any of the Ovidian texts contains all the source
material necessary for Chaucer's mind to transmute into the
Manciple's Tale.

Following the analogues of the narrative material are printed
sources and analogues of a few of the nonnarrative passages
which Chaucer interpolated into his Ovidian tale.

A study of the sources and analogues of the proverbial and
sententious remarks which Chaucer has put into the mouth of
his Manciple is without the scope of this publication. Suffice
it to say that sententious utterances concerning the impossi-
bility of "destreyning" nature, the affinity between words and
deeds, and the wisdom of bridling the tongue are commonplaces
in the proverbial wisdom of many people and times. In almost
all the didactic writings of the Middle Ages, both prose and
verse, were repeated admonitions against (1) speaking too
much, which leads to (2) jangling and backbiting, which in
turn lead to (3) quarrels and lack of peace. Proverbs on these
subjects taken from popular works (especially from the Bible)
occur verbatim in most western European languages. In his
interpolation of proverbial and sententious material into the
Manciple's Tale, and in its popular subject matter, Chaucer is
clearly in the medieval tradition; his sayings are at least metrical paraphrases of common proverbs, and occasionally he fits a
popular proverb into his meter and rhyme verbatim.

---

and reprinted in 1493 by Antoine Vérard under the title *La Bible des poètes;* (3)
the translation and allegory of the *Metamorphoses* made (1375) by Giovanni di
Bonsignore; and (4) the *Metamorphosen* of Albrecht von Halberstadt (thirteenth
century), as transmitted in the redaction (1545) of Georg Wickram.

I. NARRATIVE MATERIAL

PUBLIUS OVIDIUS NASO, *METAMORPHOSES* (A.D. 7)[1]

This text, the "original" of all those printed in this section, presents the basic narrative with fewer moral and sententious comments similar to Chaucer's than do most of the texts which follow. Noteworthy differences between Ovid's story and Chaucer's are found in Chaucer's ignoring all reference to cornix and her story, to corvus' journey to Phebus, to the pregnancy and lament of Coronis, to Phebus' vain attempts to save Coronis, to the cremation of Coronis, and to the birth of Aesculapius.

531   . . . habili Saturnia curru
      ingreditur liquidum pavonibus aethera pictis,
      tam nuper pictis caeso pavonibus Argo,
      quam tu nuper eras, cum candidus ante fuisses,
535   corve loquax, subito nigrantis versus in alas.
      Nam fuit haec quondam niveis argentea pennis
      ales, ut aequaret totas sine labe columbas,
      nec servaturis vigili Capitolia voce
      cederet anseribus nec amanti flumina cygno.
540   Lingua fuit damno: lingua faciente loquaci
      qui color albus erat, nunc est contrarius albo.
        Pulchrior in tota quam Larisaea Coronis
      non fuit Haemonia: placuit tibi, Delphice, certe,
      dum vel casta fuit vel inobservata, sed ales
545   sensit adulterium Phoebeius, utque latentem
      detegeret culpam, non exorabilis index,
      ad dominum tendebat iter. Quem garrula motis
      consequitur pennis, scitetur ut omnia, cornix,
      auditaque viae causa, "Non utile carpis,"
550   inquit, "iter: ne sperne meae praesagia linguae!"

Marginal notes:

- Through the fault of his tongue the raven, once white, was changed to black.
- He discovered the adultery of Coronis and set out to disclose the sin to his master.
- The gossiping crow warned him against this.

For truth-telling I was expelled from Minerva's train. My punishment should warn birds not to invite trouble with their tongues. Minerva once saved me from Neptune; now Nyctimene has taken my place.

596   Talia dicenti, "Tibi," ait, "revocamina," corvus,
      "sint, precor, ista malo: nos vanum spernimus omen";
      nec coeptum dimittit iter dominoque iacentem

Marginal note:

- Spurning the warning, the raven reported the adultery to Phebus.

---

[1] The text is based on that of the "Loeb Classical Library" edition, ed. Frank Justus Miller (London, 1916), Book II, ll. 531–632.

cum iuvene Haemonio vidisse Coronida narrat.

600 Laurea delapsa est audito crimine amantis,

et pariter vultusque deo plectrumque colorque

excidit, utque animus tumida fervebat ab ira,

arma adsueta capit flexumque a cornibus arcum

tendit et illa suo totiens cum pectore iuncta

605 indevitato traiecit pectora telo.

Icta dedit gemitum tractoque a corpore ferro

candida puniceo perfudit membra cruore

et dixit: "Potui poenas tibi, Phoebe, dedisse,

sed peperisse prius; duo nunc moriemur in una."

610 Hactenus, et pariter vitam cum sanguine fudit;

corpus inane animae frigus letale secutum est.

Paenitet heu! sero poenae crudelis amantem,

seque, quod audierit, quod sic exarserit, odit;

odit avem, per quam crimen causamque dolendi

615 scire coactus erat, nec non arcumque manumque

odit cumque manu temeraria tela sagittas.

Conlapsamque fovet seraque ope vincere fata

nititur et medicas exercet inaniter artes.

Quae postquam frustra temptata rogumque parari

620 vidit et arsuros supremis ignibus artus,

tum vero gemitus (neque enim caelestia tingui

ora licet lacrimis) alto de corde petitos

edidit, haud aliter quam cum spectante iuvenca

lactentis vituli dextra libratus ab aure

625 tempora discussit claro cava malleus ictu.

Ut tamen ingratos in pectora fudit odores

et dedit amplexus iniustaque iusta peregit,

non tulit in cineres labi sua Phoebus eosdem

semina, sed natum flammis uteroque parentis

630 eripuit geminique tulit Chironis in antrum.

Sperantemque sibi non falsae praemia linguae

inter aves albas vetuit consistere corvum.

Raging, Phebus transfixed Coronis with an arrow. (marginal note beside line 600)

"First," she said, "I should have borne my child. Now, two die in one." (marginal note beside line 606)

Himself, the informing bird, bow, hand, and arrows, Phebus now hates. (marginal note beside line 612)

Vainly, he tries to save her. (marginal note beside line 617)

He snatched his son from the flames. (marginal note beside line 629)

He forbade the raven to be among white birds. (marginal note beside line 631)

OVIDE MORALISÉ[1]

This text, an elaboration of Ovid, includes, *passim*, many moralistic and sententious comments on the unwisdom of speaking too much and the sin of jangling, which in subject, in

[1] An anonymous translation and moralization (formerly attributed to Philippe de Vitry and to Chrétien Legouais de Sainte-Maure) of the *Metamorphoses*, composed, according to De Boer, between 1316 and 1328. The text is that of *Ovide*

spirit, and occasionally in phraseology are remarkably close to Chaucer. The dishonor to Phebus of Coronis' shame troubles the bird here and in Chaucer; here Phebus "le [the bird] gita puer/De son hostel," in Chaucer, he "out at dore hym slong." Since Chaucer is known to have made use of the *Ovide moralisé* in other of his Ovidian tales, there is a presumption that he may have read this version of the corvus story, whether or not he had it before him while writing the *Manciple's Tale*.

2130	Li corbiaus, qui premierement	The raven, whiter than swan or snow, was blackened by his jangling.
	Avoit eü la couleur blanche	
2132	Plus que cignes—ne noif sor branche,	
	Ne blans coulons ne blance gante	
	N'ot coulour plus blanche et plus gante	
	Que li corbiaux soloit avoir—	
2136	Nercis fu par son non savoir,	
	Si fu muee sa coulour	
	De blanc en noir, par sa folour,	
	Et sa vilz langue jenglerresse,	
2140	Qui fu nuisable et tricheresse,	
	L'ot fet nercir nouvelement.	
	Or vous raconterai comment.	
	—En Thesale ot une pucele,	Phebus loved Coronis, who secretly loved another.
2144	La plus plesant et la plus bele.	
	La colour avoit fresche et fine.	
	Coronis ot non la meschine,	
	Nee en Laurisse la cité,	
2148	Si fu de grant nobilité.	
	Phebus l'ama moult longuement,	
	Mes la bele celeement	
	Amoit un autre damoisiau.	
2152	Phebus ot lors un sien oisiau	Phebus' white raven saw her adultery and went to tell Phebus.
	Que l'en seult apeler corbiau.	
	Lors ne trouvast l'en nul plus biau.	
	La plume avoit bele et deugiee	
2156	Et plus blanche que noif negiee,	
	Puis nerci par sa jenglerie.	

moralisé, poème du commencement du quatorzième siècle, publié d'après tous les manuscrits connus by C. de Boer, Livres I–III (*Verhandelingen der Koninklijke Akademie van Wetenschappen te Amsterdam*, Nieuwe Reeks 15 [Amsterdam, 1915]), Book II, ll. 2130–2548.

Cil aperçut la lecherie
De l'avoultire a la pucele.

2160   A Phebus vait, pour la nouvele
Dire de ce qu'il ot veü.

La cornille l'a conseü,
Si li demande ou il aloit.

2164   Li corbiaus li dist qu'il voloit
A son seigneur tel chose dire,
Et reveler tel avoultire
Dont il a sa dame reprise.

2168   La cornille fu bien aprise,
Qui bien savoit que l'aune en vault,
Si li desloë qu'il n'i ault,
Quar trop puet avoir grant damage

2172   Cil qui porte mauves message:
"Trop isneaux vient cil a la porte
Qui mauvese nouvele aporte:
Ja si tart ne savra venir.

2176   Trop te pourra mesavenir
De descouvrir ceste avoutire.

Tuit voir ne sont pas bon a dire:
Souvent pert l'en a dire voir.

2180   Cil n'est mie de grant savoir
Qui quanqu'il set veult reveler.

Mieux vault son corage celer
Que descouvrir par non savoir

2184   Riens dont l'en doie mal avoir.

Bien sai, quant Phebus le savroit,
Corrous et pesance en avroit,
Si ne quit qu'il li pleüst mie

2188   Oïr mesdire de s'amie.
Se tu li dis, il t'en harra
Et trop mescheoir t'en porra.
Pieç'a l'ai bien aperceü,

2192   Que voir dire m'a trop neü.

Ma loiautez m'a fet damage.
Tuit autre oisel, se il sont sage,
Se doivent por moi chastoier,

2196   Quar qui voit autrui foloier
Et mescheoir de sa folie,
Trop est folz s'il ne s'en chastie.

Bien dois mes proverbes noter.
2200 Se tu me deignes escouter,
Je te dirai con grant damage
J'oi jadis d'un autre message."

Note my proverbs and hear my story."

For my jangling (although it was truthful) Pallas chased me from her house. When I reported that Aglauros had discovered the secret of Ericthonius, my mistress chased me from her service. Formerly she had saved me from Neptune by turning me into a bird, but now Nyctimene has been put in my place.

2339 Li corbiaus laidenge et maudist
2340 La cornille qui ce li dist:
"Dieus te doinst grant male aventure,"
Dist il. "De ton sens n'ai je cure.
Ja pour ton sermon nel lairai.
2344 Je ne croi pas tant en charai
Que je face tel tricherie.
Soufferrai je la puterie
De ma dame et la deshonour
2348 Et la honte de mon seignour?
Ja certes ne le soufferrai,
Ains m'en vois, si li conterai."
Lors vait a Phebus, si li conte
2352 La vilonnie et la grant honte
Que Coronis li avoit faite,
Et comme elle a s'amor enfraite,
S'a nouvel avoutre acointié,
2356 Cui elle a donné s'amistié,
Si l'en a reprise prouvee
Et en present forfait trouvee.
Quant Phebus oit la vilanie
2360 Et la reprouche de s'amie,
Trop fu dolens, trop s'esbahi.
Sa harpe des mains li cheï
Et li arçons que il tenoit.
2364 De nul geu ne li souvenoit.
La coronne li chut dou chief.
Trop fu a duel et a meschief.
Trop ot grant ire en son corage.
2368 En cele ire et en cele rage,
Dont il avoit le cuer espris,

The scornful raven replied, "I will not suffer my master to be dishonored."

He told Phebus the shame Coronis had brought upon him, as he had discovered it.

Grieving, Phebus transfixed Coronis with an arrow.

A son arc et ses fleches pris.
L'arc entoise et la fleche trait.
2372 Ne failli mie a celui trait,
Ains a jusqu'au cuer entamee
La bele qu'il ot tant amee.

This was wrong!

Ce fu damages et pechiez!
2376 Ses cors tendres, blans et deugiez
Taint tous de sanguine coulour.
Cele se pasme de dolour:
2379 Li trouble toute la veüe.

Dying, she said, "I deserved death, but should first have borne your child."

Grief-stricken, Phebus repents too late.

2397 A cest cop chiet la bele morte.
Phebus se deult et desconforte,
Quant voit que l'ame s'en depart:
2400 Il se repent, mes c'est a tart.
Puis qu'ele est morte sans doutance,
Poi profite la repentance.

He hates the bird who brought the evil news, and himself, for listening to it.

Il het son arc et sa saiete
2404 Et la main dont il l'avoit traite;
Il het l'oisel qui de la bele
Li porta la male nouvele,
Et il meïsmes s'en haï,
2408 Dont il onques avoit oï
Ce dont il ot si grant pesance.

He repents having taken undeserved vengeance.

Moult se repent de tel vengance:
Bien li samble qu'el n'avoit mie
2412 Pour tel forfait mort deservie.
La morte prent et si l'embrace.
Baise li la bouche et la face.
Le cors oint, moult piteusement,
2416 De moult precieus oignement,
Qui de par l'art de medecine
Retenist l'ame en la meschine,
2419 Mes riens ne vault, qu'el n'i est mie.

Phebus delivered Aesculapius and cremated Coronis' body.

He evilly requited the raven by turning his whiteness to black.

2449 Li corbiaus atendoit merite
De la nouvele qu'il ot dite,
Et Phebus male la li rent:
2452 Autre qu'il n'aloit esperent:

Noire plume li a donnee,
Et sa blanchour en noir tornee.
　—Ces fables espondrai briement

I will explicate
these stories.

2456　Par histoire, et puis autrement.
Phebus, uns jovenciaux prisiez,
Preux et apers et envoisiez,
Coronis la bele acointa

Phebus, an estima-
ble youth, loved Co-
ronis, who secretly
took another lover.

2460　Par amours, et si l'ençainta
D'un fil, qui puis fu preux et sages,
Si sot contre divers malages
Trouver remede et medecine.

2464　Phebus ama moult la meschine,
Si la maintint honestement,
Mes la bele celeement
D'un autre avoutre s'acointa.

2468　Ce sot et de ce l'acointa
Uns siens sers, fel et folz parliers,
Losengierres et nouveliers,
Si cuida que, pour lui voir dire

One of Phebus'
servants, a flatterer
and a gossip, told
him of the adultery.

2472　Et pour descouvrir l'avoultire
Ou il ot sa dame trouvee
Et en present prise prouvee,
Deüst grant guerredon avoir.

2476　Tantost com Phebus pot savoir
Que s'amie ot vers lui mespris,
Trop fu de jalousie espris,
Trop fu plains d'ire et de pesance.

Phebus at once
killed her.

2480　En cele ire, sans demourance,
D'un mortel glaive la feri,
Si qu'a poi qu'en lui ne peri
La porteüre qu'ele avoit,

2484　Que briement enfanter devoit.
Quant vit que mort l'avoit ferue,
Si que ne pot estre garue
La bele que tant seult amer,

2488　Si la fist fendre et entamer
Phebus, pour l'enfant garantir,
Si l'en trait vif, et, sans mentir,
Le serf qui, par sa genglerie,

He hated so much
the servant whose
jangling had made
him kill his love
that he threw him
out of his house.

2492　Li ot fait ocirre s'amie,
Dont il ot grant pesance au cuer,
Haï tant, qu'il le gita puer

De son hostel, et, sans demour,
2496 Li toli sa grace et s'amour,
N'onc puis n'en vault avoir merci:
C'est li blans corbiaux qui nerci
Par sa jengle, et cis nous enseigne
2500 Que nulz jenglerres ne deviengne,
Quar, pour jenglerie a conter,
Ne puet nulz en grant pris monter.

No one should re-
ward janglers or
believe flatterers.

Nulz ne doit amer jengleour,
2504 Ne soi croire en losengeour.
Qui s'i croit il est deceüs.
Pluiseur s'en sont aperceüs

They do more harm
than thieves.

Que faulz losengiers et jenglerres
2508 Est assez plus mauves que lerres.
C'est assez legier a savoir:
Li lerres n'emble que l'avoir,
Mes ce puet l'en bien recouvrer
2512 Par espargnier ou par ouvrer,
Mes qui sert de losengerie
Emble et tault par sa jenglerie
Aus gens lor bone renomee,
2516 Qui ne puet estre recouvree.

God confound
flatterers!
Many men are de-
famed by lying
janglers.

Dieus confonde losengeours!
Par les mesdisans jengleours
Sont maint et maintes diffamé
2520 Qui dou fet dont il sont blasmé
Ne sont coupable n'entechié.

In janglery is great
sin.

En jenglerie a grant pechié.
Par les faulses losengeries
2524 Et par les males jengleries
Sont maint prodomme mis a mort.
Faulz est qui a jengler s'amort,
Quar trop y a mauves mehaing.

The defamer loses
men's affection, as
did the raven.

2528 Li corbiaux atendoit gaaing
Pour sa jenglerie a avoir:
Bien puet chascuns apercevoir,
En ce qu'il n'i gaaigna mie,
2532 Que nulz ne doit autrui amie
Devant son ami diffamer.
Nulz ne vaudroit oïr blasmer
Devant soi s'amie ou sa fame,
2536 Et s'aucuns est qui la diffame

Devant lui de riens qu'ele face,

Il se tault s'amour et sa grace,

Autresi com fist li corbiaux,

2540   Qui jadis estoit blans et biaux,

Puis nercist a sa deshonnour.

Nulz homs, por plere a son seignor,   *No one ought to say evil of his master's lady.*

Ne doit de sa dame mesdire,

2544   Et s'ele veult faire avoultire,

Il ne s'i doit pas consentir

N'encuser la. Mieux doit mentir,   *Better to lie or to be silent, that one may have peace, than to suffer for telling the truth.*

Ou taire soi, pour pais avoir,

2548   Que mal souffrir pour dire voir.

JOHN GOWER, *CONFESSIO AMANTIS* (ca. 1390)[1]

Gower, like Chaucer, compares the bird with only a swan; ignores all reference to cornix and her story, to corvus' journey to Phebus, to the lament of Coronis, to Phebus' vain attempts to save Coronis, and to the birth of Aesculapius; and introduces the sententious comments of the narrator with the "my son" formula. Gower's raven is blackened in "tokne" of his wicked speech; Chaucer's crow, in "tokenynge" that he has caused the death of Phebus' wife. Gower follows a medieval tradition in making Phebus kill Coronis with a sword and departs from both classical and medieval tradition in making Coronis the owner of the bird. As long as the dates of Chaucer's and Gower's stories remain unfixed, their relationship must remain uncertain and they can be considered merely as analogues.

768   Mi Sone, be thou war ther by,   *My son, hold your tongue; the blabber loses where he would gain.*

And hold thi tunge stille clos:

770   For who that hath his word desclos

Er that he wite what he mene,

He is folofte nyh his tene

And lest ful many time grace,

Wher that he wolde his thonk pourchace.

775   And over this, my Sone diere,   *If you overhear other men's affairs, keep them secret.*

Of othre men, if thou miht hiere

In privete what thei have wroght,

---

[1] The text is that of G. C. Macaulay, *The English Works of John Gower* (London, 1900), Book III, ll. 768–835.

Hold conseil and descoevere it noght,
For Cheste can no conseil hele,
780 Or be it wo or be it wele:
And tak a tale into thi mynde,
The which of olde ensample I finde.
    Phebus, which makth the daies lihte,

A love he hadde, which tho hihte
785 Cornide, whom aboven alle
He pleseth: bot what schal befalle
Of love ther is noman knoweth,
Bot as fortune hire happes throweth.
So it befell upon a chaunce,
790 A yong kniht tok hire aqueintance
And hadde of hire al that he wolde:

Bot a fals bridd, which sche hath holde
And kept in chambre of pure yowthe,
Discoevereth all that evere he cowthe.
795 This briddes name was as tho
Corvus, the which was thanne also
Welmore whyt than eny Swan,
And he, that schrewe, al that he can
Of his ladi to Phebus seide;
800 And he for wraththe his swerd outbreide,
With which Cornide anon he slowh.
Bot after him was wo ynowh,

And tok a full gret repentance,
Wherof in tokne and remembrance
805 Of hem whiche usen wicke speche,
Upon this bridd he tok this wreche,
That ther he was snow whyt tofore,
Evere afterward colblak therfore
He was transformed, as it scheweth,
810 And many a man yit him beschreweth,
And clepen him into this day
A Raven, be whom yit men mai
Take evidence, whan he crieth,
That som mishapp it signefieth.

815 Be war therfore and sei the beste,
If thou wolt be thiself in reste,
Mi goode Sone, as I the rede. . . .

831   Mi Sone, be thou non of tho,   *Be neither jangler*
        To jangle and telle tales so,   *nor tale-teller.*
        And namely that thou ne chyde,
        For Cheste can no conseil hide,
835   For Wraththe seide nevere wel.

GUILLAUME DE MACHAUT, *LE LIVRE DU VOIR DIT* (ca. 1364)[1]

Special points common to Machaut and Chaucer include the joy taken by Phebus in his bird; the presentation of Phebus as a sweet singer; the direct (and vigorous) discourse between Phebus and the bird; the bird's "swearing" he *saw* the lechery; and the reaction of Phebus: he turns the crow (raven) *and all crows* (ravens) black in memory of this one's deed, he declares that probably Coronis was innocent and the bird has lied, and he dooms the bird forever to jangle and cry.

7773   Li Corbiaus jadis plume blanche   *The raven was once*
        Avoit plus que la noif sur branche,   *whiter than a swan;*
7775   Ne que coulon, gante, ne cine,
        Ne que la fleur de l'aube-espine.
        Brief en li n'avoit riens de lait,
        Car il estoit plus blans que lait.
        Phebus l'amoit moult chierement,   *Phebus took greater*
7780   Et y prenoit esbatement   *pleasure in him*
        Plus qu'en son arson n'en sa harpe, *than in bow or harp.*
        Dont il s'esbat souvent & harpe.
        Or vous diray comment ç'avint
        Qua sa blancheur noire devint.
7785   En Thessale ot une pucelle   *Phebus loved Coro-*
        Qui estoit avenant & belle,   *nis,*
        Et de grace la plus loée
        Qui fust en toute la contrée;
        Née en la cité de Laurice
7790   Fu, si n'estoit rude ne nice;
        Ains estoit cointe, aperte & sage,
        Et estraite de haut lignage.
        Coronis ot nom la meschine.
        Phebus l'en amoit d'amour fine,

[1] The text is that of Paulin Paris, *Le Livre du voir dit, publié pour la Société des Bibliophiles Français* (Paris, 1875), ll. 7773–8110.

7795 Si fermement & de tel cuer
Qu'il ne l'oubliast à nul-fuer.

but she loved a youth more than Phebus loved his white bird.

Mais elle amoit un damoisel
Plus que Phebus son blanc oysel.
Brief riens tant n'amoit autre chose:
7800 Bien y parut à la parclose;

The raven saw them joined according to nature,

Car li Corbiaus les vit ensemble,
Joins par nature, ce me semble,
Que chascuns prenoit son desduit,
Si com nature les y duit.
7805 Quant li Courbiaus vit l'avoutire,
Il les commença à maudire,

and swore that he would tell Phebus.

Et si jura grant sairement
Qu'il yroit dire isnellement
A Phebus la grant lecherie
7810 Qu'il a véu en son amie.
De ses ailes l'air accola,
Et sans plus dire s'envola
Pour dire à Phebus la nouvelle
Du damoisel & de la belle,
7815 Comment il les avoit trouvé
Presentement en fait prouvé.

He told the crow,

La Corneille qui l'encontra
Pris son vol en son encontre a,
Moult enquist où voler vouloit
7820 Qui si hastivement voloit?
Li Corbiaus tantost li respont
Et de chief en chief li espont
De Coronis tout l'avoutire,

declaring that he would not conceal this shame from his master.

Et dit qu'à Phebus le va dire,
7825 Car pas ne vuet celer la honte
7826 De son signeur, qu'il ne li conte.

Corneille warned: "Do not risk arousing Phebus' anger against you; Pallas expelled me for tale-telling."

The raven said he would not rest until he had told Phebus about Coronis.

7969   Li Corbiaus dit que non fera,
7970 Et que jamais ne cessera,
Tant qu'à Phebus ait recité
De Coronis la verité.
Il fiert de l'elle & si s'en vole.
N'a pas esté à bonne escole;

He was not wise; trouble often comes from speaking when

7975 Car il avient souvent contraire

De parler, quant on se doit taire.

Si qu'il en ara telle paie

Comme raison aus gengleurs paie,

Au moins à ceus qui ont à faire

7980 A gens qui sont de bon affaire.

 De ses elles l'air accolant,

Sen va li Corbiaus en volant,

Sans voie & sans chemin ferré;

Tant a cerchié, tant a erré

7985 Qu'il est venus droit en Tessale.

Phebus estoit en une sale

D'or, d'argent & de pierrerie

Bien & richement entaillie.

Du son qui de sa harpe issoit

7990 Moult doucement retentissoit

La sale & tous li lieus d'entour;

N'il n'y avoit chambre ne tour

Dont on ne le péust oïr.

Li blans Corbiaus à resjoïr

7995 Se prist moult fort, quant il l'entent:

Grant chiere & grant salaire attent;

Mais il faurra à son entente.

Il ressemble au cisne qui chante

Et resjoïst contre sa mort,

8000 Car cils est trop fols qui s'amort

A dire chose qui desplaise

A son seigneur, quant il est aise.

Et vraiement trop parler nuit.

N'onques, ne de soir ne de nuit,

8005 Ne fu janglerie en saison.

Quant li Corbiaus vit la maison

De Phebus, l'air fent & depart,

Et tost s'en vole celle part.

Phebus le vit, si li commande

8010 Que raison li die & li rende

Dont il vient, car moult longuement

A pris hors son esbatement.

Li Corbiaus en l'eure li conte

L'outrage, le lait & la honte

8015 De Coronis & l'avanture;

Encore lui dist-il: "Biau sire,

Par tous les sairemens qu'on fait,

Side notes:

one should be silent; he will receive thereof a jangler's reward.

He flew until he found Phebus in a golden room,

filling the place with the sweet sounds of his harp.

The raven rejoiced:

but he is a fool who kills himself to say something which displeases his master.

To talk too much is harmful; janglery is never seasonable.

When Phebus asked why he had come,

the raven told him of the shame of Coronis:

"Sire, I swear I saw their misdeed."

Je les vi en present mesfait;
A vous le di j'y fui tenus,
8020   Et pour ce sui-je cy venus."
        Quant Phebus oÿ la nouvelle
Du Corbel, qui dist que la belle
Qu'il aime de fin cuer entier
Le laist pour un autre acointier,
8025   De son chief chéy sa coronne,
Et sa harpe qui souef sonne
De ses mains chéy à ses piez.
S'il fust ferus de .ii. espiez
Parmy le corps, il ne fust mie
8030   Plus dolens qu'il est pour s'amie,
De ce qu'on li a raporté
Que vers li a fait fausseté.
Mais, ce n'est pas necessité
Que quanqu'on dit soit verité;
8035   N'en ce qu'on dit n'a pas le quart
De verité, se Dieus me gart.
Phebus trop forment se tourmente,
Trop se complaint, trop se demente,
Trop a de mal & de dolour;
8040   En sa rage & en sa furour,
D'aventure la belle vit.
Or orrez comme il se chevit:
L'arc prist, la flesche mist en coche,
Et si roidement la descoche
8045   Qu'à Coronis l'a traite ou pis,
Pour ce qu'elle fu acoupis.
Coronis chiet toute estendue,
Li cuers li fault & la véue
Li trouble en chief & de la plaie,
8050   Li sans jusqu'à la terre raie.
En morant dist: "Lasse dolente!
Bien voy que la mort m'est presente;
Et si n'ay pas mort desservi,
S'en vo gré ne vous ay servi.
8055   Amis, mais vous vous hastez trop,
Car .ii. en tuez à .i. cop.
Au moins entendez ma complainte:
Je suis de vous grosse & enseinte,
Et li enfes n'a rien meffait,

8060   Dous amis, que vous m'avez fait."
      Après ce mot, l'ame rendi.
      Quant Phebus la belle entendi
      Et qu'il vit qu'elle est toute morte,
      Trop mortelment se desconforte;
8065   Trop fu courciés, trop fu dolens,
      Il maudist tous oisiaus volans,
      Especialment le Corbel
      Qui dessus tous avoit corps bel.
      Il maudist l'arc & la saiette,
8070   Et la main dont il l'avoit traitte.
      Le corps fist aromatiser
      D'oingnement qu'on doit moult prisier,
      Fait par maniere si soutive
      Qu'elle semble encor toute vive.
8075   Ou temple Venus la déesse
      Fu là mise, à moult grant richesce,
      Mais il la fist ouvrir & fendre
      Avant toute euvre, & l'enfant prendre,
      Qui fu puis de moult grant renon:
8080   Esculapius ot à non,
      Et si sceust plus de surgerie
      Que nul homme qui fust en vie.
      Car il faisoit les mors revivre,
      Si com je le truis en mon livre.
8085   Li Corbiaus attendoit merite
      De la nouvelle qu'il a dite;
      Moult le desire, moult li tarde.
      Phebus le vit & le regarde
      Et dit: "En signe de memoire,
8090   Sera ta blanche plume noire,
      Et tuit li corbel qui l'ont blanche
      L'aront plus noire que n'est anche,
      A tousjours perpetuelment;
      Ne sera jamais autrement,
8095   Pour ta mauvaise janglerie
      Qui m'a tolu ma druerie
      De la plus belle de ce monde.
      Et puet estre qu'elle estoit monde
      De ce fait, & que menti m'as.
8100   Dont dolens suis tristes & mas.

Marginalia:

At this, he cursed all birds, especially the beautiful raven.

He cared for her body

and delivered Aesculapius.

The raven awaited his reward.

Phebus said, "In token of this, your white feathers will be black and all white ravens will be black forever;

never will they be otherwise, because of your evil janglery which has lost me my love.

Probably she was innocent and you have lied to me.

Forever will you
only jangle.

> Jamais ne feras que jangler;
> Maus aigles te puist estrangler!

Get out! You are
banished."

> Va-t'en! de ma court es banis,
> Se plus y viens, tu es honnis."

Thus was the raven
requited.

> 8105 Ainsi fu li Corbiaus paiez:
> Si s'envola tous esmaiez,
> Et devint lerres; c'est la somme.

Since then he only
jangles and cries.

> Et si, le scevent bien maint homme,
> Qu'en tous les leus où il repaire,
> 8110 Il ne fait que jangler & braire.

INTEGUMENTA OVIDII[1]

This brief text is perhaps unique in stressing, with Chaucer, the facts that the bird was dear (sacred) to Phebus because of his vocal ability and that his cry presages "tempests."

Corvus is sacred to
[Phebus] because of
his voice,

⟨fol. 54ʳ⟩ Item de coruo: Coruus Ioui [sic] sacratus dicitur quia quadraginta quatuor vocum interpretaciones habet et ad Phebum

or because he pre-
sages tempests.
Because he detected
Coronis' adultery,
corvus was changed
from white to black

pertinet vocum interpretacio, vel quia futuras presignet tempestates sicut et Phebus. Coruus, quia Phebo Coronidis detexit adulterium, de albo mutatus est in nigrum. Quia dum dominum suum habebat propicium reputabatur candidus, sed niger existimatus est, reversa in contrarium.

THE SEVEN SAGES OF ROME[2]

Chaucer's allusion to the chough in the *Wife of Bath's Prologue* (D 231–34) suggests that he was familiar with this or a closely related version of the tale. Similarities between this version and the *Manciple's Tale* are as follows: the hero kept his bird in a cage in his hall; the bird spoke and could "telle tales" ("telle a tale"); the word "lemman" is applied to the wife's lover; when the hero was absent, "þe wif . . . sente here co-piner fore" ("His wyf anon hath for hir lemman sent"); the hero returned to his caged bird in his hall where he received the

---

[1] An expanded version of the *Integumenta Ovidii* of Johannes Anglicus (? thirteenth century). The text is taken from MS Lansdowne 728: *Expositio vel Commentarius in libros xv Ovidii Metamorphoseon, cum tabulis genealogicis Deorum* (listed in British Museum, *Catalogue of Lansdowne MSS* [London, 1819], II, 165).

[2] This early fourteenth-century text is taken from that edited by Karl Brunner ("E.E.T.S., Original Series" No. 191, [London, 1933]), ll. 2193–2292. For a discussion of other Middle English versions and of their French sources see Brunner, pp. ix ff.

news of his wife's lechery (in the Ovidian versions the bird, never caged, flies to Phebus); the bird greeted his returning master in direct discourse, beginning, "By God"; the bird mentioned the "mochel sschame" ("greet shame") which the wife had done her husband; the merchant beat his wife "ate dore" (Phebus slung the crow "out at dore"); the merchant sent his wife "On alder twenti deuel wai" (Phebus slung the crow "Unto the devel, which I hym bitake"); and there is brief moralizing on rash actions and on man's need of good counsel.

2193	A burgeis was in Rome toun,	A wealthy merchant had a fair wife
	A riche man of gret renoun.	
	Marchaunt he was of gret auoir	
	And had a wif was queint and fair.	
	But sche was fikel vnder hir lok,	who was false to him.
	And hadde a parti of Eue smok.	
	And manie ben ȝit of hire kinne,	
2200	þat ben al bilapped þer inne!	
	þe burgeis hadde a pie in his halle,	In a cage in his hall he kept a pie, who could tell tales.
	þat couþe telle tales alle	
	Apertlich, in freinch langage,	
	And heng in a fair cage	
	And seþ lemmans comen and gon,	The pie saw his mistress' lemans come and go, and told his master,
	And teld hire louerd sone anon.	
	And for þat þe pie hadde isaid,	
	þe wif was ofte iuel ipaid.	
	And þe burgeis louede his pie,	who loved him.
2210	For he wiste he couþe nowt lie.	
	So hit bifil, vpon a dai,	One day when the merchant was away the wife sent for her ,eman.
	þe burgeis fram home tok his wai,	
	And wente aboute his marchaundise,	
	þe wif waited anon hire prise,	
	And sente here copiner fore;	
	And whanne he com to þe halle dore,	
	He no dorste nowt in hie	
	For þe wreiing of þe pie.	
	þe wif him bi þe hond hent,	
2220	And in to chaumbre anon þai went.	
	þe pie bigan to grede anon,	When the pie threatened to tell his master,
	"Ȝa, now mi louerd is out igon,	
	þou comest hider for no gode,	

I schal ȝou wraie bi þe rode!"

the wife kept him awake with a simulated storm.

þe wif þouȝt schent ȝe was,
A wrenche ȝhe þouȝte naþelas,
And clepede a maide to make here bed,
And after, bi hir boþer red,
A laddre þai sette þe halle to,
2230 And vndede a tile or two.
Ouer þe pie þai gan handel
A cler bacyn and a candel.
A pot ful of water cler
þai sschadde vpon þe pies swer.
Wiȝ bacyn beting and kandel liȝt
þai bobbed þe pie bi niȝt
And water on him gan schenche:
þis was on of wommannes wrenche.
þo þe dai dawen gan,
2240 Awai stal þe ȝongeman.
Men vnlek dore and windowe
þe pie him sschok wiȝ mochel howe,
For ssche was fain þat hit was dai
þe copiner was went his wai.

When his master returned, the pie said,

þe gode burgeis was him icome
In to þe halle þe wai he nome.

"By God, a lover was here who has done you much shame.

þe pie saide "Bi god almiȝt
þe copiner was her to niȝt
And haþ idon þe mochel sschame,
2250 Imad an hore of oure dame!

And there was rain and thunder."

And ȝit hit had ben to niȝt
Gret rain and þonder briȝt.
Sehthen ich was brid in mi nest
I ne hadde neuere so iuel rest."

The wife said, "It's outrageous to believe this pie: the night was clear."

þe wif haþ þe tale iherd
And þouȝte wel to ben amered,
And saide "Sire þou hast outrage
To leue a pie in a kage.
To niȝt was þe weder fair and cler
2260 And þe firmament wel fair,
And sche saiþ hit haþ ben þonder.
Sche haþ ilowe mani a wonder
But ich be awreke of here swiþe,
Ne schal i neuer ben womman bliþe."

þe godeman askede his neȝebours

Of þat niȝt and of þe ours

And þai saide þat al þat niȝt

Was þe weder cler and briȝt.

When the neighbors agreed that the night had been clear,

þe burgeis saide þe pie

2270 Ne scholde him nammore lie.

Nammo wordes he þar spak,

But also swiþe his nekke tobrak.

the merchant declared that the pie should never again lie to him, and broke his neck.

And whanne he seȝ his pie ded

For sorewe coude he no Red.

When he saw his pie dead, he was distraught.

He seȝgh hir [wete] and his cage

He þouȝte of gile and of outrage.

He wente him out, þe ladder he segȝ

And vp to þe halle Rof he stegȝ.

He discovered his wife's treachery,

þe pot wiȝ þe water he fond,

2280 þat he brak wiȝ his hand,

And manie oþer trecherie

þat was idon to his pie.

He went him doun wiȝ outen oþ

In his herte grim and wroþ.

And wiȝ a god staf ful sket

His wif ate dore he bet,

And bad hir go þat ilche dai

On alder twenti deuel wai.

beat her at the door, and bade her go the way of twenty devils.

Lo sire, he saide, for a foles red,

2290 þe pie þat saide soht, was ded.

The truthful pie was dead;

Hadde he taken god conseil

2292 His pie hadde ben hol and hail.

had the merchant but taken good counsel, the bird would have been well.

II. NONNARRATIVE MATERIAL

Sources or Analogues of H 163–74

1. BOETHIUS, *DE CONSOLATIONE PHILOSOPHIAE* (ca. 524)[1]

Quae canit altis garrula ramis

Ales, caveae clauditur antro:

Huic licet illita pocula melle,

Largasque dapes dulci studio

Ludens hominum cura ministret,

The caged bird, though delicately fed,

[1] The text is taken from an edition published at Leyden in 1671, Book III m. ii, 17–26.

on escaping, desires the woods.

Si tamen, arto saliens tecto,
Nemorum gratas viderit umbras;
Sparsas pedibus proterit escas,
Silvas tantum maesta requirit,
Silvas dulci voce susurrat.

2.   JEAN DE MEUN, *LE ROMAN DE LA ROSE*[1]

When a bird is taken and caged and fed deliciously,

Li oisillons dou vert boschage,
Quant il est pris e mis en cage,
Nourriz mout ententivement
Laienz delicieusement,
E chante, tant con sera vis,
De cueur gai, ce vous est avis,

it yet desires the woods,

Si desierre il les bois ramez
Qu'il a naturelment amez,
E voudrait seur les arbres estre,
Ja si bien nou savra l'en paistre;

and studies ever to recover its freedom.

Toujourz i pense e s'estudie
A recouvrer sa franche vie.
Sa viande a ses piez demarche,
O l'ardeur qui son cueur li charche,
E va par sa cage traçant,
A grant angoisse pourchaçant
Coment fenestre ou pertuis truisse
Par quei voler au bois s'en puisse.

SOURCE OR ANALOGUE OF H 175–80

JEAN DE MEUN, *LE ROMAN DE LA ROSE*[2]

Take a cat which has never seen rat or mouse and feed it delicately;

Qui prendrait, beaus fiz, un chaton
Qui onques rate ne raton
Veü n'avrait, puis fust nourriz
Senz ja voeir rat ne souriz,
Lonc tens, par ententive cure,
De delicieuse pasture,

when it sees a mouse, nothing can restrain it.

E puis veïst souriz venir,
N'est riens qui le peüst tenir,
Se l'en le laissait eschaper,

---

[1] The text is that of Ernest Langlois, *Le Roman de la rose*, IV ("S.A.T.F." [Paris, 1922]), ll. 13941–58.

[2] The text is that of Langlois, ll. 14039–52.

Qu'il ne l'alast tantost haper;
Trestouz ses mes en laisserait,
Ja si familleus ne serait;
N'est riens qui pais entr'aus feïst,
Pour peine que l'en i meïst.

It will leave all its prepared food for it.

Sources or Analogues of H 183–86

1. JEAN DE MEUN, *LE ROMAN DE LA ROSE*[1]

Le vaillant ome arriere boute
E prent le pire de la route;
La nourrist ses amours e couve
Tout autresinc come la louve,
Cui sa folie tant empire
Qu'el prent adès des lous le pire.

Man takes the worst of the company,

like the wolf, who always takes the worst wolf.

2. GASTON PHEBUS, *LE LIVRE DE CHASSE* (ca. 1387)[2]

The bitch wolf, in heat, leads the males six or eight days without food or rest; then she chooses him who has labored hardest for her, as her mate.

And þerfore men seyen *by ȝonde þe see in somme contres* whan eny woman doþ amys, that she is like to þe wolf bicche for she takeþ hure to the worst and þe foulest and to þe moost wreech; and it is soth that þe biche of þe wolf takeþ hure to þe foulest and to the moost wreche, for he haþ moost trauaylled, most goo and fastest for hure þan oþere han, and he moost poor, moost lene, and most wrecch.

Men say an erring woman is like a bitch wolf,

who takes the most wretched wolf

because he has most exhausted himself for her.

Source or Analogue of H 329–33

JEAN DE MEUN, *LE ROMAN DE LA ROSE*[3]

Langue deit estre refrenee,
Car nous lisons de Tholomee
Une parole mout oneste,
Au comencier de l'*Almageste:*

The tongue should be restrained.

[1] Langlois, ll. 7761–66.

[2] The text is taken, with modernized punctuation, from the translation of Edward, Second Duke of York, in *The Master of Game* (1406–13), ed. William A. and F. Baillie-Grohman (London, 1904), p. 31. The italicized words do not appear in the original French.

[3] Langlois, ll. 7037–57.

He is wise who re-
strains his tongue,
except when he
speaks of God.

No one can praise
God too much.

Cato says

the first virtue is to
restrain the tongue.[1]

Que sages est cil qui met peine
A ce que sa langue refreine,
Fors, senz plus, quant de Deu parole.
La n'a l'en pas trop de parole,
Car nus ne peut Deu trop loer
Ne trop pour seigneur avoer,
Trop craindre ne trop obeïr,
Trop amer ne trop beneïr,
Crier merci ne graces rendre;
A ce ne peut nus trop entendre,
Car toujourz reclamer le deivent
Tuit cil qui biens de lui receivent.
Chatons meïsmes s'i acorde,
S'il est qui son livre recorde:
La peuz en escrit trouver tu
Que la prumeraine vertu
C'est de metre a sa langue frein.

[1] "Virtutem primam esse puto compescere linguam:
Proximus ille deo est qui scit racione tacere" (*Distichs of Cato*, 1.3).

THE PARSON'S TALE[1]

By GERMAINE DEMPSTER

AS HAS been shown by Kate O. Petersen,[2] the sections on Penance proper in the *Parson's Tale* (the first quarter and the last eighth of the tale) are derived from the chapter "De poenitentiis et remissionibus" in the *Summa* of St. Raymund of Pennaforte,[3] while the intervening treatise on the Seven Deadly Sins is derived from the *Summa vitiorum* of Guilielmus Peraldus.[4] But the relation to Pennaforte is very different from that to Peraldus. Pennaforte's treatment of Penance is not much longer than the corresponding sections in

[1] I take pleasure in acknowledging my indebtedness to Professor James M. Cline of the University of California, who, in preparation for this chapter, made a study of various analogues of the *Pa. T.* but was unable to continue and allowed me to use his material. Dr. Cline discovered that the compilation in Fonds français 6276 of the Bibliothèque nationale was dependent both on Pennaforte and on Peraldus; it was he who singled out for especial study that very interesting work.

My very special thanks are due to Professor George L. Hamilton, who generously consented to examine the galley of the present work, and suggested several important additions to my bibliographical and explanatory notes.

[2] *The Sources of the Parson's Tale* (Boston, 1901).

[Mrs. Dempster and I have disagreed concerning the presentation of the introductory material to this section on the *Parson's Tale.* I should have wished to remove what appear to me to be incongruities in statement and to present more directly and explicitly Miss Petersen's own conclusions—W. F. BRYAN.]

[3] On St. Raymund and his works see J. F. von Schulte, *Die Geschichte der Quellen und Literatur des canonischen Rechts von Gratian bis auf die Gegenwart*, II (Stuttgart, 1877), 408–13; Johannes Dietterle, "Die Summae Confessorum," *Zeit. f. Kirchengesch.*, Vols. XXIV–XXVIII (1903–7; on Pennaforte, XXIV, 530–48); Stephan Kuttner, *Repertorium der Kanonistik, 1140–1234* (Vatican City, 1937), pp. 438–52; and A. Teetaert, "Raymond de Penyafort," in *Dictionnaire de théologie catholique* (Paris: A Vacant, E. Mangenot & E. Amann, 1909——). The *Summa* was written soon after the Fourth Lateran Council, 1215, had made annual confession compulsory; von Schulte dates it between 1234 and 1243, Kuttner between 1222 and 1229. On Penance before 1215 see Oscar D. Watkins, *A History of Penance* (London, 1920), and the extensive treatments of "Pénitence," "Satisfaction," etc., in *Dict. de théol. cath.*

[4] This is the second half of the *Summa de vitiis et virtutibus*, written before 1261 (see Petersen, p. 2, n. 3). On the author see the brief notes in *La grande encyclopédie* and *The Catholic Encyclopedia.*

Chaucer—only one and a half times as long;[1] that it is their main source is abundantly indicated by the general lines of the exposition[2] and by verbal parallelism. In contrast to this, Peraldus' treatise on the sins is thirteen times as long as Chaucer's; for much of what Chaucer has there is in Peraldus no parallel either close or remote, and the parallel passages listed by Miss Petersen frequently occur in the two works in such different sequence and surroundings as to make derivation highly doubtful. The *Summa vitiorum* must be considered as the ultimate source of only a small part of the treatise on the sins in the *Parson's Tale.*[3]

That intermediaries lie between the works both of St. Raymund and of Peraldus and the *Parson's Tale* is hardly open to question.[4] It is strongly suggested by important additions to the material derived from the *summae*, by several gaps and other traces of attempts to combine different plans, and it is confirmed by the existence of a vast late thirteenth- and fourteenth-century Latin and vernacular literature of religious manuals[5] similar in content to what we would suspect the source or sources of the *Parson's Tale* to have been, and sharing with it a number of features foreign to the two *summae:* the loose

[1] A wrong impression would be conveyed by the Verona, 1744, edition chosen by Miss Petersen; it is full of late accretions, some as late as 1600 at least.

[2] In spite of long additions or expansions, mainly I 111–26, 161–282, 322–86.

[3] Chaucer's debt to Peraldus varies in the different parts of his treatise on the sins. Most of the versets in his section on pride and nearly all versets in his section on envy (remedies excluded) find parallels (though scattered, and some very remote [see Petersen, pp. 36–49]) in the corresponding tracts of Peraldus; but for lust only one-third, and for avarice much less than one-third of Chaucer's versets find in Peraldus any analogue, close or remote (Petersen, pp. 71–78, 66–70), though Peraldus' chapter on lust is five times as long as Chaucer's, and that on avarice twenty-two times.

[4] See Petersen, pp. 78–81; H. Spies, "Chaucer's religiöse Grundstimmung und die Echtheit der *Parson's Tale,*" *Festschrift für L. Morsbach* (Halle, 1913), p. 647; H. G. Pfander, "Some Medieval Manuals of Religious Instruction in England and Observations on Chaucer's *Parson's Tale,*" *JEGP,* XXXV (1936), 243–58, esp. 254.

[5] For a good introduction to this literature see H. G. Pfander. Dr. Pfander is undoubtedly right in insisting that the *Pa. T.* is a treatise or manual, not a sermon (see esp. pp. 253–54 and n. 30). It is only as part of Chaucer's pilgrimage fiction that we must think of the *Pa. T.* as orally delivered. Chaucer himself calls it a treatise (I 957, 1081), not a sermon.

planning and rambling exposition (Peraldus was very long, rarely rambling), the frequent tone of exhortation and appeal to sentiment as against the detached exposition in the *summae*, the larger space given to practical advice at the expense of patristic and biblical authorities or the discussion of canonical law, the more colorful and picturesque language—in brief, the adaptation of the genre to the needs and tastes of the laity and of the less-educated members of the clergy.

Whether the two treatises that constitute the *Parson's Tale* were first combined by Chaucer or by some predecessor still remains an open question. The fact that grafting surveys of the sins on the discussion of Confession (as had been done by Pennaforte[1] and before him[2]) had become a practice long before Chaucer[3] can hardly be said to favor either of the two possibilities. The unparalleled length of the digression on the sins in the *Parson's Tale*,[4] and perhaps also the absence of a satisfactory logical link at I 386,[5] might be taken to favor the view that Chaucer himself made the junction.[6] But nothing short of the discovery of closer analogues can be expected to clear the question.

[1] See text quoted below, pp. 740–41.

[2] I am grateful to Mr. C. A. Robson, of Christ Church, Oxford, for drawing my attention to this (and other) features of the still unpublished *Penitentiale* of Robertus Flamesburiensis. On its contents see Dietterle, Vol. XXIV, pp. 368–69; S. Baluze, *Miscellaneorum Liber Septimus* (Paris, 1715), pp. 345–46; and *Dict. de théol. cath.* under "Pénitence," col. 903. On its date, probably between 1207 and 1212, see Dietterle, p. 373. That Pennaforte knew and used the work of Robertus Flamesburiensis is taken for granted by most scholars.

[3] See Petersen, p. 35, and the contents of many manuals of religious instruction as given by Pfander.

[4] It is longer than the discussion of Penance proper.

[5] Most penitentials come to a survey of the sins from comments on the questions to be asked by the confessor; the logical connection is made very clear. That the *Pa. T.* announces the subject in I 321 does not make up for the lack of a link at the proper place.

[6] See Emil Koeppel, "Über das Verhältnis von Chaucers Prosawerken zu seinen Dichtungen und die Echtheit der *Parson's Tale*," *Herrig's Archiv*, LXXXVII (1891), 33–54, where it is argued that Chaucer had first written the treatise on the sins and later incorporated it into the discussion of Penance prepared for the Parson of the Canterbury pilgrimage. Professor Manly suggests that the two treatises may not have been combined until after Chaucer's death (*The Text of the Canterbury Tales* [Chicago, 1940], II, 455).

The passages selected for quotation are from four works:

I. "De poenitentiis et remissionibus," the last chapter of the *Summa* of Raymund of Pennaforte. As no abbreviation or imitation of this in Latin or any vernacular has been found whose use by Chaucer or his predecessors could account for the parallels between the *Summa* and the *Parson's Tale*,[1] we must, in spite of the unlikelihood of Chaucer's direct use of it, quote sections from the *Summa* itself:[2]

A, the introductory section on Penance in general;

B, part of the section on Contrition;

C, portions of the section on Confession.

II. Guilielmus Peraldus' *Summa vitiorum:*

A, outline of the tract on sloth,[3]

B and C, two short sections, chosen among those to which Chaucer is indebted, will illustrate differences in treatment (B, part of the section on the kinds of gluttony; and C, part of that on the remedies against lust).

III. The Anglo-Norman *Compileison* in MS R.14.7 of Trinity College, Cambridge.[4] Neither the treatise on the sins nor that

---

[1] A fragment of a Latin penitential preserved in MS Lambeth 182, fols. 173^r–184^v, and noted by Dr. Pfander (p. 257) as being close to *Pa. T.*, is nowhere more so than is Raymund's *Summa* itself, copied almost verbatim for long stretches. It is important, for such work of comparison, to secure a trustworthy *unexpanded* text of the *Summa*.

[2] The length of "De poenitentiis et remissionibus" forbids its inclusion *in extenso* in the present work. For the sections which we omit see the exhaustive lists of parallels in Miss Petersen's book.

[3] Sloth has been chosen as a good average both in its relation to *Pa. T.* and in its length. It covers, in the Basel, 1497, edition, 15 folios; envy and gluttony cover, respectively, 2 and 3; avarice and pride, 37 and 44.

[4] No. 883 in M. R. James, *The Western MSS in the Library of Trinity College, Cambridge* (Cambridge, 1901), II, 289–91. The *Compileison* treats of sin (fols. 1^r–36^r), Penance (36^r–115^v), the Ten Commandments (115^v–121^r), the roads to salvation (121^r–124^v), *La Vie de gent de religion* (124^v–154^v, unfinished), the *Symbolum* (154^v–155^r) the Pater Noster (155^r–156^r), *Coment l'homme doit regarder son estat* (156^r–157^r; here the manuscript breaks off).

As noted by Miss Hope E. Allen (*TLS*, October 24, 1936), *La Vie de gent de religion* found in this compilation is a close analogue of *The Ancren Riwle* (as are also some sections of the treatises on the sins and on Penance). Some features of the compilation of interest in this connection are discussed by Miss Allen in "Wynkyn de Worde and a Second French Compilation from the 'Ancren Riwle' with a Description of the First (Trinity Coll. Camb. MS 883)," *Essays and Studies in Honor of Carleton Brown* (New York, 1940), pp. 182–219. The whole work will

on Penance found in this compilation could be the source, direct or indirect, of the corresponding sections of the *Parson's Tale:* the interest of the work is accordingly that of an analogue. As such it presents one unwelcome feature—its length, doubtless a good deal greater than that of the direct source or sources.[1] But none of the shorter works examined[2] was found to combine as many features shared, certainly or almost certainly, by antecedents of the *Parson's Tale.* To list those features: The *Compileison,* like the *Parson's Tale,* is indebted both to Peraldus' *Summa* and to Pennaforte's "De poenitentiis et remissionibus."[3] Though the two treatises on the sins and on Penance are not combined as are their analogues in Chaucer, but are merely placed side by side, the position of Chaucer's treatise on the sins as a digression from that on Penance is paralleled in the *Compileison* by the occurrence, at the end of the section on Confession, of a three-thousand-word survey of the sins. The sins, both in the longer treatise and in this digression, are taken in the same order as in Chaucer.[4] The *Compileison* offers very good analogues to at least some *Parson's Tale* passages derived neither from Peraldus nor from Pennaforte. It includes a trea-

---

probably be published in "E.E.T.S." Miss Allen also recognized the ninth and last section of the treatise on Penance (fols. 111ᵛ–115ᵛ) as the tract on the Pains of Purgatory often attributed to Grosseteste; this section will be studied by Miss Ruth Dean. Exactly the same compilation exists in a manuscript of the Bibliothèque nationale (Fonds français 6276), from which transcriptions were made by Professor Cline. I am grateful to Miss Dean and Miss Allen for recognizing the work and directing me to the manuscript of Trinity College, whose text, at least in the sections of interest in connection with *Pa. T.*, is distinctly better.

[1] The total length of the treatises on the sins and on Penance is about four times that of *Pa. T.*

[2] Most of the ground is still to be covered: the manuals of religious instructions are legion, and the study of Anglo-Norman literature is only beginning.

[3] The debt to Peraldus is small (a few sections from the *Summa vitiorum,* some also from *Summa virtutum,* as, e.g., the remedies against pride [fols. 7ʳ–9ᵛ]); that to Pennaforte is more extensive, as is the case in *Pa. T.* But the *Compileison* is definitely not in the line of transmission between either Peraldus or Pennaforte and Chaucer.

[4] It is that of St. Gregory and of Pennaforte, except that in their works pride is the source of seven sins, of which the first is *inanis gloria;* it is also the order in *Ancren Riwle,* in *Jacob's Well,* and in some Anglo-Norman penitentials derived from Robertus Flamesburiensis, but otherwise is not very current in thirteenth- or fourteenth- century manuals. In Peraldus the order is: gluttony, lust, avarice, sloth, pride, envy, anger, and—eighth—the sins of the tongue.

tise on the Ten Commandments and one on the Pater Noster,
as did undoubtedly some of the antecedents of the *Parson's
Tale*.¹ The approximate date of the work,² its almost certain
Anglo-Norman origin, and the Anglo-Norman character of the
dialect of the scribes of the two manuscripts in which it is
known³ make it reasonable to suppose that works rather closely
related were within the reach of Chaucer and his predecessors
in the field. Of this compilation we shall quote:

A, part of the introduction on sin in general, and the introduction to the section on pride;

B and C, two sections paralleled in Chaucer's treatise on the
sins, but not in Peraldus (B, species of pride; C, part of
species on envy);

D and E, derivatives of the two Peraldus passages to be
quoted under II B and II C (kinds of gluttony and
remedies against lust);

F, the incentives to Contrition (derived from Pennaforte);

G, part of the digression on the sins.

IV. *Le Livre de vices et de vertus* or *Somme le roy* of Frère
Laurent,⁴ written 1279. As indebtedness of Chaucer to this

¹ Fols. 115ᵛ–121ʳ, 155ʳ–156ʳ; cf. I 956, 1040–44.

² Probably not much older than the two manuscripts in which it is found. Mr. J.
A. Herbert, quoted by Miss Allen in her note in *TLS*, places the Trinity College
manuscript in the late thirteenth or early fourteenth century; Miss Ruth Dean
and Professor S. H. Thomson, who kindly examined my photographs of the Bibl.
nat. manuscript, date it, respectively, *ca.* 1300 and in the third decade of the
fourteenth century.

³ Professors M. K. Pope and W. H. Trethewey, whom I thank for their kind
assistance, agree that, though the scribes have none of the grosser Anglo-Nor-
manisms, there is no doubt about their dialect. As to the writers, no characteristic Anglo-Norman construction has been noted in the sections examined, but the
references to the king of England in *exempla* in the treatise on Penance (fols. 45ᵛ
and 94ʳ) and to the water of all England in the treatise on the sins (fol. 24ᵛ) indicate beyond doubt that the writer of at least some of the portions that interest us
was insular. (One suspects also that at least some of the gathering of material
for the section on Penance is the work of a Franciscan. It was done, we are told
[fol. 111ᵛ], *al honur Deu tut puissant e de ma douce dame Seinte Marie e de Seint
Franceys*.)

⁴ On Frère Laurent see P. Mandonnet, "Laurent d'Orléans, auteur de la *Somme
le Roi*," *Revue des langues romanes*, LVI (1913), 20–23; Ch. V. Langlois, *La Vie en
France au moyen âge d'après des moralistes du temps* (Paris, 1926), pp. xiii–xiv;
F. Serra, "Frère Lorens e Remigio Girolamo," *Atti della Reale Accademia delle
Scienze di Torino*, LXX, Tomo II (1935), 306. In MS 2292 of the Bibliothèque

short work seems now improbable,[1] a brief passage in which we find several parallels to features found in the *Parson's Tale* but not in Peraldus or in our Anglo-Norman compilation, will be of interest as an indication of the intricacy and the number of the streams that seem to converge in the *Parson's Tale*.

I. THE *SUMMA* OF ST. RAYMUND OF PENNAFORTE

(From MS 2517 of the Bibliothèque royale, Brussels. The handwriting indicates the middle of the thirteenth century.[2] Some of the content suggests England or Normandy. The text is very good except for a few obvious slips which we correct mainly from the Rome, 1603, edition, known as the best edition but often inferior to MS 2517; such corrections are not indicated. The spelling, capitalization, and punctuation have been modernized, and most abbreviations have been expanded. Italics are used for subtitles and for references. As it is often impossible to determine the extent of the quotations, no italics or quotation marks will indicate them.)

A. INTRODUCTORY SECTION ON PENANCE IN GENERAL[3]

⟨fol. 94ᵛ⟩ *De poenitentiis et remissionibus.*[4] Post abyssum et laqueos Babylonis, de quibus superius aliqua memoravimus ad cautelam, videlicet, ut cognoscantur et cognita melius evitentur, restat ut ad portum quietis ac serenitatis aeternae solliciti festinemus, inquirentes viam rectam, necessariam et infallibilem, quae quidem est poenitentia; circa quam videndum quid sit ⟨fol. 95ʳ⟩ poenitentia, unde dicatur, de tribus actionibus poenitentiae, de tribus speciebus

Outline of chapter.

---

royale of Brussels he is called *Laurens du Bois, docteur et lisant de l'ordre des prescheurs en la cité de Paris;* MS 2293 adds the title of *maistre en divinité* (J. van den Gheyn, *Cat. des manuscripts de la Bibliothèque royale,* III [Brussels, 1903], 400, 402).

[1] For an exhaustive list of the parallels between the *Somme* and *Pa. T.* see W. Eilers, "Dissertation on the *Parson's Tale* and the *Somme de vices et de vertus* of Frère Lorens," in *Essays on Chaucer,* Part V ("Chaucer Society Publications" [London, 1884]). The discovery of Miss Petersen has deprived most of the parallels of the significance that Eilers attached to them.

[2] I wish to thank Dr. F. Lyna, keeper of the manuscripts of the Bibliothèque royale, for giving me his opinion on this question. J van den Gheyn (Vol. IV, pp. 16–17) is mistaken on the date (fourteenth century) and also in calling the work *Summula.* This word is found as title in a later hand only; the text is that of the unabbreviated *Summa.*

[3] Cf. I 75–127.

[4] This subtitle covers all our quotations from the *Summa.*

ejusdem, quae sunt necessaria ad poenitentiam veram, de clavibus, de remissionibus, de impedimentis poenitentiae, et aliqua alia dubitabilia interponemus circa istam materiam.

Poenitentia est, ut ait Ambrosius, et mala praeterita plangere, et plangenda iterum non committere. Item Augustinus: Poenitentia est quaedam dolentis vindicta puniens in se quod dolet commisisse. Dicitur autem poenitentia, quasi poenae tentio, a poenitendo, quia per illam quis punit illicita quae commisit. Probantur haec *De Poenitentia dist. 3, circa princi.*[1]

Occasione illius verbi positi in auctoritate Ambrosii—et plangenda iterum non committere—dixerunt quidam quod, si aliquis vere poenitet, numquam postea peccabit mortaliter; et si contigerit ipsum peccare postea, probatur per hoc quod prima non fuit vera poenitentia. Item muniunt se aliis auctoritatibus multis. Isidorus: Irrisor est, non poenitens, qui adhuc agit quod poenitet, nec videtur Deum poscere subditus sed subsannare superbus. Item Augustinus: Inanis est poenitentia quam sequens culpa coinquinat. Idem: Nihil prosunt lamenta si replicantur peccata. Ad hoc dicendum quod verba posita in auctoritate praedicta Ambrosii et similibus, non ad diversa tempora, sed ad illud in quo quis poenitet, sunt referenda, scilicet, ut tempore quo plangit commissa mala, non committat voluntate vel opere flenda. Et hoc aperte innuit Gregorius dicens: Poenitentiam agere est et praeterita mala plangere et plangenda non committere. Nam qui sic deplorat ut tamen alia committat, adhuc poenitentiam agere aut ignorat, aut dissimulat. Quid enim prodest si peccata luxuriae quis defleat, et tamen adhuc avaritiae aestibus anhelat? Item Isidorus, post illa verba—irrisor est, etc.—statim subjunxit exponens quod dixerat: Multi enim lacrymas indesinenter fundunt, et peccare non desinunt; quosdam accipere lacrymas ad poenitentiam cerno et affectum poenitentiae non habere. Sufficit ergo ad veritatem poenitentiae ut quis plangat praeterita et proponat in animo plangenda iterum non committere. . . . .[2]

---

[1] Marginal notes by Guilielmus Redonensis complete this and similar references in the 1603 edition (and probably others) and in manuscripts, some of which, according to Dietterle (p. 543), are as old as 1260. As such notes have left no mark on *Pa. T.*, we shall not add them to the bare text as found in our manuscript. The references to *De poenitentia* are confusing; this first one is to *De vera et falsa poenitentia*, formerly attributed to Augustine (*S. Agustini opera omnia*, Vol. VI [Paris, 1837], col. 1632); some seem to be to the *De poenitentia* of St. Ambrose (*Patr. Lat.*, Vol. XVI, cols. 485–546), others to sermons and homilies of St. John Chrysostom (*Patr. Gr.*, Vol. XLIX, cols. 277–348, and Vol. LX, esp. "Homilies on II Corinthians," IV.6, col. 426).

[2] The discussion fills two columns more.

⟨fol. 95ᵛ⟩ *De tribus actionibus poenitentiae.* Actiones autem poenitentiae, ut ait Augustinus, sunt tres. Una est quae novum hominem parturit, et fit ante baptismum. Nisi enim baptizandus poeniteat vitae veteris, vitam novam inchoare non potest; et si baptizetur accipit characterem, sed non gratiam nec remissionem peccatorum, donec recedat fictio de corde suo. Non tamen tenetur iste ad exteriorem poenitentiam agendam quia sufficit ei poenitentia interior. Ab hac poenitentia cum baptizantur soli parvuli sunt immunes eo quod non possunt uti libero arbitrio. Altera vero poenitentia est, sive actio poenitentiae, quam quis facit post baptismum de mortalibus peccatis. Tertia est quae fit de peccatis venialibus et quotidianis; de hac Augustinus: Poenitentia humilium et bonorum fidelium, poena quotidiana. Probantur haec omnia *De Poenitentia, dist. 1: Tres actiones, De consecratione, dist. 4, Tunc valere, Agunt, Ne quod absit, Sine poenitentia.* Dona sunt et vocatio Dei, quia gratia Dei in baptismo non requirit gemitum neque planctum vel opus aliquod, sed solam fidem, et omnia gratis condonat.

Circa secundam autem actionem est, quantum ad praesentem materiam, principaliter insistendum.

De tribus speciebus poenitentiae. Species poenitentiae sunt tres, nam alia est solemnis, alia publica, alia privata. Solemnis est quae fit in capite quadragesimae cum solemnitate, quae est *dist. 50 in capite.* Dicitur etiam solemnis, licet non ita proprie, quando aliquis invitus ad poenitentiam agendam mittitur in monasterium; *dist. 50, Si ille.* Haec debet imponi ab episcopo tantum, vel de mandato ejus a sacerdote, et debet imponi pro crimine publico et vulgarissimo quod totam commoverit urbem. Item non debet imponi clerico nisi deposito, quia qui semel egit eam non debet postea promoveri nec ministrare in ordine suscepto. Item non debet contrahere matrimonium; si tamen contraxerit, tenebit. Probantur ⟨fol. 96ʳ⟩ haec *dist. 50: Confirmandum, Illud, Alienum, 26 q.6c. ultimo.* Et require haec et alia de ista materia supra, de solemne poenitentia et de sacramento iterando vel non § *circa.* Publica est quae supra dicta est solemnis ideo quia publice fit; proprie tamen dicitur illa quae fit in facie Ecclesiae, non cum praedicta solemnitate, sed cum injungitur peregrinatio per mundum cum baculo, cubitali et scapulari, vel veste aliqua ad hoc consueta. Hanc posset imponere quilibet sacerdos parochiano suo, quia non invenio sibi prohibitum, nisi consuetudo esset contraria in aliqua Ecclesia. Item non debet imponi clerico nisi deposito, nec debet imponi nisi pro crimine enormi et manifesto. *De Poenitentia, dist. 6: Sacerdos.* Item solemnis poenitentia non debet iterari, sed alia quaelibet potest et debet iterari quotiens

The functions of Penance are three: before Baptism,

for deadly sins,

for venial sins.

Authorities.

The second function concerns us most.

The species of Penance are three: it is solemn,

public,

homo peccat. *De Poenitentia, dist. 3:* reperiuntur *Septies cadit justus,*

Adhuc instant perfidi. Privata dicitur illa poenitentia quae singulariter fit quotidie et cum quis peccata sua secrete sacerdoti confitetur.

Quae sint necessaria ad veram poenitentiam. Sequitur videre quae sint necessaria in poenitentia vera et perfecta: et quidem tria, videlicet: cordis contritio, oris confessio, operis satisfactio.[1] Johannes Os Aureum: Perfecta poenitentia cogit peccatorem omnia libenter sufferre: in ore enim confessio, in corde contritio, in opere tota humilitas. Haec est fructuosa poenitentia. *De Poenitentia. dist. 1: Perfecta.*

Quia enim tribus modis Deum offendimus, scilicet delectatione cogitationis, impudentia locutionis, et superbia operis, secundum regulam ut contraria contrariis curentur tribus modis oppositis satisfaciamus.

De hiis etiam Jeronimus exponens verba Amos ait: Super tribus sceleribus Damasci, et super quattuor non convertam eum. Juxta tropologiam hoc possumus dicere: Primum peccatum est cogitasse quae mala sunt; secundum, cogitationibus adquievisse perversis; tertium, quod mente decreveris opere complevisse; quartum, post peccatum non agere poenitentiam et suo sibi complacere delicto. *De*

Poenitentia, dist. 1: Super tribus. Et isti sunt tres mortui quos legitur Dominus suscitasse, scilicet filia Archisynagogi, filius viduae, et Lazarus. Puellam suscitavit in domo—ecce peccatum cogitationis; puerum in porta civitatis—ecce peccatum locutionis; Lazarum in sepulcro quatriduanum fetentem—ecce peccatum operationis; vel dic, per puerum peccatum operationis, per Lazarum peccatum consuetudinis. Item, puellam verbo, puerum motu, Lazarum strepitu, clamore et lacrimis suscitavit. Unde versus:

Mens mala mors intus, malus actus mors foris, usus,
Tumba, puella, puer, Lazarus ista notant.
Hanc verbo, hunc motu, lacrimando suscitat illum,

scilicet Christus. Haec ergo poenitentia est illud felix triduum de quo ait Moyses: Deus Hebraeorum vocavit nos ut eamus viam trium dierum in solitudine et sacrificemus Domino Deo nostro ne forte accidat nobis pestis aut gladius—pestis, id est culpa in praesenti;

gladius, scilicet poena in futuro. In hoc triduo quaesivit Virgo Maria filium et invenit. Haec est scala cum tribus gradibus quam vidit Jacob erectam a terra usque in caelum,[2] et Dominum innixum scale

---

[1] Much of this passage is derived from the *Sententiae* of Peter Lombard (Lib. IV, dist. xvi, cap. 1), written about the middle of the twelfth century.

[2] In a homily of Godefroy, abbot of Admont (d. 1165), Jacob's ladder with its three steps or rounds is interpreted to mean Mary and the virtues of love, chastity, and humility (*Patr. Latin.*, Vol. CLXXIV: *Homiliae festivales,* lxxvi, col. 1011).

propter tria: primum, ut gigas nomine substantiae fortiter eam sus-
tineat; secundum, ut manum, si necesse fuerit, ascendenti per eam
porrigat; tertium, ut ascendens, cum laboraverit et fatigatus fuerit,
in ipsum respiciat, jactans totam curam suam in ipsum; non est enim
ita crudelis, ut ait Augustinus, ut ipsum cadere permittat. In prima
dieta sive gradu est dolor, in secunda pudor, in tertia labor. Singulas
dietas per ordinem prosequamur.

B. Of Contrition[1]

De prima dieta, hae contritione. Prima dieta est contritio, circa
quam quattuor sunt consideranda, scilicet quid ipsa sit, et quae sunt
causae inductivae ipsius, qualis debeat esse, et quis sit ejus effectus.

Outline of section on Contrition.

Quid sit contritio. Contritio est dolor pro peccatis assumptus cum
proposito confitendi et satisfaciendi. Hoc praecipitur a Domino per
Prophetam ubi dicitur: Scindite corda vestra, etc. Iste dolor debet
esse triplex, ut ait Bernardus: acer, acrior, acerrimus—acer, quia
offendimus Dominum et creatorem omnium; acrior, quia patrem
nostrum caelestem qui nos pascit multipliciter; acerrimus, quia
Redemptorem nostrum qui nos liberavit proprio sanguine a vinculis
peccatorum, crudelitate daemonum, et acerbitate gehennae.

Contrition is sorrow over one's sins.

Quae inducunt contritione. Causae inductivae contritionis sunt sex:
cogitatio, et ex ea pudor de peccatis commissis, detestatio vilitatis
ipsius peccati, timor de die judicii et poenae gehennae, dolor de amissione patriae caelestis et multiplici offensa ⟨fol. 96ᵛ⟩ creatoris, et
spes triplex: veniae, gratiae, gloriae—veniae, qua peccata remittun-
tur; gratiae, qua bene operabitur; gloriae, qua pro bono opere adhuc
remunerabitur.

Six causes lead to it:

De primo, scilicet de cogitatione, Ezechias: Recogitabo omnes
annos meos in amaritudine animae meae. De secundo, scilicet de
pudore, Job: Res dignas confusione agunt. Nahum iii: Revelabo
pudenda tua in facie tua. Jerem. in Tren. iv:[2] Denigrata est super
carbones facies illorum. De tertio, scilicet de detestatione peccati,
propter cujus vilitatem peccator vilis factus est, Jerem. ii: Quam vilis
facta es nimis iterans vias tuas. Petrus in Canonica: Qui facit peccatum servus est peccati. Augustinus: Appende te ex pretio ne tibi
vilescas. Philosophus: Major sum et ad majora natus quam ut fiam
mancipium corporis mei. Seneca: Si scirem Deos ignoscituros, homines
autem ignoraturos, tamen abhorrerem peccatum. De quarto, scilicet
de timore de die judicii et poena inferni, Jeron.: Quotiens hunc diem
considero toto corde contremisco. Idem: Sive comedo, sive bibo, sive
aliquid aliud facio, semper videtur in aure mea illa tuba horribilis

i. meditation about sin,
ii. shame for sin,

iii. hatred of sin,

iv. fear of Last Judgment and Hell,

---

[1] Cf. I 128–315.   [2] *Threni,* i.e., the lamentations of Jeremiah.

insonuisse, etc. Augustinus: Ascendat homo tribunal mentis suae, etc.
Gregorius: Quid faciet virgula deserti ubi concutietur cedrus paradisi?
Petrus in Canonica, iv: Si justus vix salvabitur, impius et peccator
ubi apparebit? Apoc. xviii: Apprehensa est bestia et cum illa pseudo-
propheta et qui acceperunt characterem bestiae et qui adoraverunt
imaginem ejus; missi sunt hi duo in stagnum ignis, etc. Item Apoc.
xx: Timidis et incredulis et exsecratis et homicidis et fornicatoribus et
veneficis et idolatris et omnibus mendacibus, pars illorum in stagno
ardenti, igne et sulphure, quod est mors secunda. Item Apostol. ad
Roman. vi: Stipendia peccati mors. De quinto, [scilicet de amissione
caelestis gloriae,] Apoc. iii: Tene quod habes ut nemo accipiat
coronam tuam. In eodem, xvi: Beatus qui vigilat et custodit vesti-
menta sua, ne nudus ambulet et videant turpitudinem ejus. Et require supra eodem § circa principium in auctoritate Bernardi. De
sexto, scilicet de spe, ipsemet Dominus: Ecce ego sto ante ostium
et pulso. Si quis audiens vocem meam aperuerit mihi januam,
intrabo ad illum et coenabo cum illo et ille mecum. Qui vicerit sedebit
mecum in throno meo. Item, tam ipse quam praecursor ejus clamant
in suae praedicationis exordio: Poenitentiam agite; et statim sub-
jungunt de praemio dicentes: Appropinquat enim regnum caelorum.
Item: Non veni vocare justos sed peccatores ad poenitentiam. At-
tende etiam, peccatrix anima, quod non solum Dominus sed tota illa
caelestis curia cum ipso domino tam pie, tam dulciter te hortantur ad
poenitentiam, dicentes: Revertere, revertere, Sunamitis, revertere,
revertere, ut intueamur te. Nota: quater dicunt revertere propter
quattuor genera peccatorum. Dicunt ergo, O Sunamitis, id est, O
anima captiva—scilicet, quam diabolus propter delicias hujus mundi
captivam duxit ad inferos—revertere a peccato pravae cogitationis,
revertere a peccato locutionis, revertere a peccato operationis, revertere a peccato perversae consuetudinis. Item, revertere per cordis
contritionem, revertere per oris confessionem, revertere per operis
satisfactionem, revertere per bonae vitae continuationem, quoniam
qui perseveraverit usque in finem, hic salvus erit. Ut intueamur te,
id est, ut sic possimus videre in te imaginem et similitudinem Dei
quod ferventi desidero optamus. Item Dominus per Osee, ii, ad
animam peccatricem: Sponsabo te mihi in fide, sponsabo te mihi in
judicio et justitia et in misericordia et miserationibus, et sponsabo te
mihi in sempiternum.

"Sponsabo" is then discussed morally and anagogically, and
the section closes with general reflections on forgiveness and
Penance. We omit also the next two sections on the qualities
and the effects of Contrition.

[margin: v. sorrow at loss of Heaven,]

[margin: vi. hope of salvation.]

C. Of Confession[1]

⟨fol. 97ᵛ⟩ Secunda dieta est confessio, circa quam sunt 7 consideranda, videlicet quid ipsa sit; an necessario sit facienda, et cui; quae sint necessaria ad veram confessionem; utrum, et de quibus, et qualiter sint interrogationes faciendae; et de poena sacerdotis revelantis confessionem.

Outline of section on Confession.

Quid sit confessio. Confessio est legitima coram sacerdote peccatorum declaratio. Et dicitur confessio quasi simul, vel ex toto, vel undique fassio; nam ille confitetur qui totum fatetur. Tenetur poenitens peccata sua necessario confiteri, et breviter haec tria—contritio, confessio et satisfactio—sunt in praecepto. Contritio praecipitur in Joele—scindite corda vestra; confessio in Tren.—effunde sicut aquam cor tuum; item Psal.—effundite coram illo cora vestra; et Jacobus—confitemini alterutrum peccata vestra; satisfactio in Joan.—facite dignos fructus poenitentiae. Item omnia haec praecipiuntur a Domino cum dicit: Poenitentiam agite, etc. Ergo videtur quod non est salus sine confessione; quod verum est ubi quis habere potest cui confiteatur; alias secus. Require infra eod. §, *Sed numquid in articulo.*

Confession is full declaration of sins to a priest;
it is compulsory;

Cui confitendum est. Debet quilibet regulariter confiteri sacerdoti, nam sacerdotibus dedit Dominus potestatem ligandi atque solvendi cum dixit: Quorum remiseritis peccata, etc.

it must be made to a priest.

The conditions are discussed in which confession may be heard by regulars, or laymen, or must be heard by the bishop. The question whether venial sins also should be confessed is answered in the affirmative.

⟨fol. 98ᵛ⟩ *Quae sunt necessaria ad veram confessionem.* Ad hoc dicas quod quattuor, videlicet quod sit amara, festina, frequens, integra.

The conditions for true Confession are four:

De primo, scilicet de amaritudine, Jerem.: Statue tibi speculam, pone tibi amaritudines, dirige cor tuum in viam rectam. Signa hujus amaritudinis sunt verecundia, humilitas, lacrimae, fortitudo vincens pudorem, et pronitas oboedientiae. De primo signo, scilicet de verecundia, Augustinus: Laborat mens patiendo erubescentiam; et quoniam verecundia est magna poena, qui erubescit pro Christo fit dignus misericordia; *De Poenitentia, dist. 1: Quem poenitet.* De secundo, scilicet de humilitate, Apostolus: Humiliamini sub potenti manu Dei. Unde et publicanus non audebat oculos ad caelum levare. De tertio, scilicet de lacrimis: Deduc quasi torrentem lacrimas per diem et noctem, non des requiem tibi neque taceant pupillae oculi tui. Item Johan. Chrysost.: Lacrimae lavant delictum quod pudor

i. It must be bitter.
The signs are
1. shame,
2. humility,
3. tears,

---

[1] Cf. I 316–21 and 957–1027; I 322–86 have no close parallel in Pennaforte.

est ore confiteri, id est, cum pudore et verecundia est confitendum.
4. courage, Item Psalm.: Fluminis impetus laetificat civitatem Dei. De quarto,
scilicet de fortitudine, exemplum Mariae Magdalenae quae adeo fortis
fuit in confitendo propter amaram interius compunctionem quod, nullo
5. obedience. pudore obstante, publice fuit confessa turpitudinem peccatorum. De
quinto, scilicet de pronitate oboedientiae, exemplum Domini, qui factus est pro nobis oboediens usque ad mortem, mortem autem crucis.
Item Aug.: Ponat se poenitens omnino in potestate judicis, in judicio
sacerdotis, nihil sibi reservans sui, ut omnia eo jubente paratus sit
facere pro recipienda vita animae quaecumque faceret pro evitanda
corporis morte, et hoc cum desiderio, quia vitam recuperat infinitam
ut Deus. Cum gaudio enim debet facere immortalis futurus quae
faceret pro differenda morte moriturus. *De Poenit. dist. 5: Consideret.*

Quod confessio debet esse festina. Debet esse festina confessio.
ii. It must be
prompt Salom.: Ne tardes converti ad Deum et ne differas de die in diem;
subito enim veniet ira illius, et in tempore vindictae disperdet te.
for five reasons. Debet ergo festinare propter quinque: Primum, propter incertitudi-
nem horae mortis; Luc: Veniet Dominus servi illius in die qua non
sperat et hora qua nescit, et dividet eum, partemque ejus cum in-
fidelibus ponet. Item diviti promittenti sibi longam vitam dictum
est: Stulte, hac nocte repetent animam tuam a te; quae autem con-
gregasti cujus erunt? Secundum est quod morans in peccato semper
accumulat peccatum peccato et per consequens poenam poenae.
Apoc.: Qui in sordibus est sordescat adhuc. Apostolus: An ignoras
quoniam benignitas Dei ad poenitentiam te adducit? Secundum
duritiam autem tuam et cor impoenitens, thesaurizas tibi iram in die
quando reddet unicuique juxta opera sua. Item Osee: Maledictum
et homicidium et mendacium et furtum inundaverunt, et sanguis
sanguinem tetigit. Item Gregorius: Peccatum quod non per poenitentiam diluitur mox pondere suo ad aliud trahit. Tertium est quod
quanto majorem moram fecerit in peccato tanto magis elongabitur
a Domino, et per consequens tanto difficilior erit conversio. Unde
illuc:

> Qui non est hodie cras minus aptus erit.
> Principiis obsta, sero medicina paratur
> Cum mala per longas invaluere moras.

Et Psal.: Domine, qui elongant se a te peribunt. ⟨fol. 99ʳ⟩ Quartum,
quia in extrema aegritudine potest vix aliquis poenitere vere sed etiam
cogitare. Jeron.: Cum aegritudine opprimeris vix aliud potes cogitare quam quod sentis, et illuc rapitur intentio mentis ubi est vis
doloris. Multa enim, ut ait Augustinus, occurrunt tunc impedimenta,
nam morbus urget, poena terret, filii, quos illicite dilexit, uxor et mun-

dus eum ad se vocant. Tene ergo certum et dimitte incertum, id est, age poenitentiam dum sanus es, non differas usque ad infirmitatem. *De Poen. dist. 7: Qui egerit; Nullus exspectet.* Quintum, quia, nisi in vita praesenti exaudierit Dominus clamantem, clamabit ipse postea ad Dominum et non exaudietur. Clamavit enim dives in inferno sepultus et non est exauditus etiam in gutta aquae. Item clamabant virgines fatuae, "Domine, Domine, aperi nobis," et respondit Dominus, "Amen dico vobis, nescio vos." Item de talibus Dominus per Jerem.: Ego inducam super eos mala de quibus exire non poterunt, et clamabunt ad me et non exaudiam eos. Festina ergo, et noli procrastinare dicens, "sine modo, sine modo," quia, ut ait Augustinus, illud "modo" non habet modum.

Quod confessio debet esse integra. Item debet confessio esse integra, scilicet ut peccata omnia dicat, non dividendo ea inter diversos sacerdotes, sed uni; Dominus enim summae bonitatis opus imperfectionis non novit; aut totum hominem sanat aut nihil. Augustinus: Caveas ne, verecundia ductus, dividas confessionem. Ad idem Jerem. in Tren.: Effunde sicut aquam cor tuum ante conspectum Domini Dei tui. Item Psalmus: Effundite coram illo corda vestra. *[iii. It must be complete,]*

Ad hoc autem, quod integra sit confessio, ista novem exiguntur, scilicet quod sit voluntaria, fidelis, propria, accusatoria, vera, nuda, discreta, pura, morosa. *[which involves nine conditions: it must]*

Voluntaria debet esse, ut non sit sicut confessio Achor, sed sicut confessio dextri latronis in cruce. Licet enim dolere debeat propter peccata quae commisit, debet tamen gaudere propter vitam quam recuperat; unde simul contingit dolorem et gaudium esse in eodem sujecto. Psalm.: Secundum multitudinem dolorum meorum in corde meo consolationes tuae laetificaverunt animam meam. *[1. be voluntary,]*

Fidelis, ut tam ipse confitens quam sacerdos cui confitetur sint in fide catholica, ut fiat confessio secundum doctrinam Ecclesiae, non secundum doctrinam haereticorum. Item, quod fiat sub spe veniae; aliter non valeret. *De Poenitentia, dist. 1: Quem poenitet, et dist. 6: Qui vult.* *[2. be consistent with church rules,]*

Propria, ut seipsum tantum accuset, et non alium. Psalm.: Meditatus sum nocte cum corde. Item: Deus, vitam meam nuntiavi tibi. Aliter, si crimen alterius diceret, non esset erroris illius corrector, sed proditor vel detractor. Fallit hoc ubi circumstantia facti talis est quod aliter non posset confiteri peccatum, ut si cognovit matrem suam vel filiam vel simile; et tunc non est dicendus proditor, quia non dicit ut alium prodat vel gravet, sed ut se liberet, quod aliter facere non posset. *[3. be personal,]*

4. be accusatory,

Accusatoria, ut sic dicat commisisse se peccatum ex propria malitia, se fortiter accusando, non praetendens excusationes in peccatis sicut primi parentes. Salom. in Parab. xviii: Justus prior accusator est sui; venit amicus ejus et investigabit ipsum. Nisi modo se accuset coram isto amico, id est, coram Deo vel sacerdote Dei vicario, in futuro habebit accusatores Deum et propriam conscientiam, diabolum, peccata, et etiam totum mundum, quia pugnabit orbis terrarum contra peccata regum. Si vero modo se accusat Deus excusabit eum. Augustinus super Psalmum: Veritas de terra orta est, etc. Veritas de terra orta, id est, confessio de homine, ut accuset se. Et sic justitia de caelo prospexit, quasi Deus dicat: Parcamus huic quia non parcit sibi; ignoscamus quia non ignoscit. De caelo enim prospicit, id est, a Deo data est justificatio poenitenti.

5. be honest,

Vera, id est, non tacens verum nec admiscens falsum etiam humilitatis causa. Augustinus: Cum causa humilitatis mentiris, si non eras peccator antequam mentireris, mentiendo efficeris quod devitaveras. Item: Non est veritas nisi ita te dixeris peccatorem ut etiam esse cognoscas; veritas autem ipsa est ut quod est dicas. Nam quomodo est humilitas ubi regnat falsitas? Sed contradicit Joh. Eg. in Canonica I: Si dixerimus quod peccatum non habemus, ipsi nos seducimus, et veritas in nobis non est. Item Gregorius: Bonarum mentium est ibi culpas suas agnoscere ubi culpa non est. Sed dic quod debet se dicere peccatorem in genere, quia nemo sine crimine vivit; in specie vero non dicat se perpetrasse peccatum nisi sciat vel credat ita esse. Objicitur etiam de generali confessione in qua sacerdotes et alii confitentur interdum specialiter se commisisse omnia peccata. Sed dic quod taliter confitens loquitur in persona Ecclesiae, vel quia, sicut ait Augustinus, in uno peccato multa peccata possunt notari. Quod autem dicit: In omnibus vitiis in quibus miser homo, etc., ibi comprehendit genera singulorum et non singula generum, quasi diceret: Peccavi cogitatione, locutione, et opere, et omissione.

6. be viva voce,

Nuda, quia non debet confiteri ⟨fol 99ᵛ⟩ per nuntium vel per epistolam, sed viva voce et ore proprio, et praesentialiter, ut qui per se peccavit per seipsum erubescat. Praecepit enim Dominus mundatis ut ostenderent se sacerdotibus; et Augustinus, *De Poen., dist. 1: Quem poenitet.* . . . .

(The sinner must call each sin by its name, tell all circumstances, etc.)

7. treat the sins one by one,

Discreta similiter debet esse confessio, scilicet ut distincte ac separatim confiteatur singula peccata, non confuse, juxta illud: Lavabo per singulas noctes lectum meum, etc., id est, per singula peccata conscientiam meam. Item ut eligat peritum judicem; Aug.: Sacerdotem quaere qui te sciat ligare et solvere. Sed quid, si sacerdos suus imperitus et indiscretus non vult dare ei licentiam eundi ad alium discretum? Numquid poterit ire auctoritate propria? Non; videtur arg. ext. eod. . . . . et *De Poen., dist 6: Placuit.* Tutius ergo est ei agere per superiorem. *Ext. De jure patron.; Nullus laicus.* Require de his alia supra eo, § *Debet quilibet.*

Pura, quoad intentionem, ut non ad vanam gloriam vel hypocrisim vel timore servili, sed timore filiali et sine omni fictione fiat. *De Poen., dist. 1: Quem poenitet, et § Item taciturnitas.* 8. be done in good faith,

Item morosa, ut non dicantur peccata in transcursu ut campsores vel computatores qui computant nummos, sed cum mora et deliberatione, ut ex hoc accendatur devotio et major habeatur contritio et verecundia. 9. and seriously.

Confiteatur ergo poenitens integre juxta formam praedictam explicans omnia. Jerem. ii: Scito quid feceris, cursor levis explicans vias tuas. Alioquin si noluerint hic lavare animas suas per integram confessionem, fiet eis prout dicit Amos iv: Levabunt vos in contis, et reliquias vestras in ollis ferventibus, et projiciemini in Armon.

(About fifteen lines are devoted to the explanation of this passage.)

⟨fol. 100ʳ⟩ *Quod confessio debet esse frequens.* Item debet confessio esse frequens, quod dupliciter est intelligendum: uno modo, ut si frequenter ceciderit per peccatum etiam mortale frequenter resurgat per poenitentiam—require supra eodem *Species, 5: Item solemnis;* alio modo, ut etiam eadem peccata frequenter confiteatur. Non tamen tenetur quis, nisi in casibus quos require infra eodem §, *Sed numquid peccata.* Augustinus: Quanto pluribus confitebitur quis sub spe veniae turpitudinem criminis, tanto facilius consequetur gratiam remissionis; *De Poen., dist. 1, Quem poenitet.* Item Ysa xxii: Sume citharam, circui civitatem, meretrix oblivione tradita; bene cane, frequenta canticum, ut memoria tui sit. Item nota penalem constitutionem emanasse contra negligentes confiteri peccata, scilicet quod saltem semel in anno tenetur quilibet, postquam ad annos discretionis pervenerit, confiteri omnia peccata sua et reverenter suscipere ad minus in Pascha Eucharistiae sacramentum, nisi forte de consilio proprii sacerdotis ob aliquam rationabilem causam ad tempus ab ejus perceptione duxerit abstinendum; alioquin, et vivens ab ingressu ecclesiae arceatur, et moriens Christiana careat sepultura. Unde hoc salutare statutum debet frequenter in ecclesiis publicari, ne quisquam ex ignoran- iv. It must be frequent,

at least once a year.

Physicians must
urge the sick to see
a priest first.
tiae caecitate velamen excusationis assumat. Item nota quod statutum
est et praeceptum [a Papa Innocentio][1] medicis corporum ut infirmos,
ad quos vocati fuerint, ante omnia moneant et inducant ut medicos
advocent animarum, ut, postquam fuerit de salute animarum pro-
visum, ad corporale medicinae remedium salubrius procedatur. Si
quis a tem medicorum, postquam per praelatos locorum fuerit haec
constitutio promulgata, transgressor exstiterit, tamdiu ab ingressu
ecclesiae arceatur donec pro transgressione hujusmodi satisfecerit
competenter. Prohibetur autem sub interminatione anathematis ne
quis medicorum pro corporali salute aliquid aegro suadeat quod in
periculum animae convertatur. Hae constitutiones sunt extra eo.
Omnis utriusque, et *Cum infirmitas.*

A discussion follows "utrum sint faciendae interrogationes in
confessione a sacerdote, et de quibus et qualiter," which leads
to a brief survey of the Seven Deadly Sins:

The Seven Capital
Sins
⟨fol. 101ʳ⟩ Sunt autem ista septem crimina capitalia, quae continentur in hoc versu:

Luxus, gustus, avet, tristis, furit, invidet, ambit.

Ut autem scias propagationem istorum criminum nota doctrinam
are derived from
pride.
quam tradit Gregorius super Job: Radix totius mali est superbia,
etc. Et infra: De hoc quippe beluo, de radice scilicet superbia, septem
principalia vitia oriuntur: inanis gloria, invidia, ira, tristitia, avaritia,
ventris ingluvies, et luxuria. Et quia hiis septem vitiis nos doluit cap-
tos Redemptor noster, idcirco ad spiritualis proelii luctamen gratia
Each has its
progeny:
the progeny of
vain-glory,
septiformis spiritus venit plenus. Sed habent haec singula contra nos
exercitum suum.[2] Nam de inani gloria oriuntur haec septem vitia,
scilicet inoboedentia, jactantia, hypocrisis, contentio, pertinacia, dis-
of envy,
cordia, novitatum praesumptio. De invidia nascuntur haec quinque:
odium, susurratio, detractio, exultatio in adversis, afflictio in prosperis
of ire,
proximi. De ira pullulant ista sex: rixae, tumor mentis, contumeliae,
of dejection,
clamor, indignatio, blasphemiae. De tristitia similiter procedunt sex:
malitia, rancor, pusillanimitas, desperatio, torpor erga praecepta,
of avarice,
vagatio mentis circa illicita. De avaritia nascuntur sex: proditio,
fraus, fallacia, perjurium, inquietudo, et contra misericordiam cordis

[1] These words, missing in our manuscript, are found in most others and in the
Rome, 1603, edition.

[2] This sentence and the rest of the paragraph are taken almost verbatim from
Gregory's *Moralium libri* xxxi. 45 (*Patr. Lat.,* Vol. LXXVI [1878], col. 621). It is
interesting to note that this passage is used and referred to in the corresponding
(but longer) digression on the sins in the treatise on Penance in our Anglo-Norman
compilation; see below, p. 756.

obduratio. De ventris ingluvie propagantur quinque: inepta laetitia, *of gluttony,*
scurrilitas, immunditia, multiloquium, hebetudo sensuum circa in-
telligentiam. De luxuria generantur octo: caecitas mentis, incon- *of lust.*
sideratio, inconstantia, praecipitatio, amor sui, odium Dei, affectus
praesentis saeculi, horror vel desperatio futuri saeculi.

Item interroget sacerdos si aliquando temptetur, et qua tempta-
tione, qualiter resistat, etc. . . . .

A brief discussion of these and related questions closes the
section on Confession.

The relation between the *Summa* and the *Parson's Tale*
remains the same in the section on Satisfaction (for an exhaustive list of the parallels see Petersen, pp. 27–34).

II. THE *SUMMA VITIORUM* OF GUILIELMUS PERALDUS

(From the Basel, 1497, edition. Punctuation, capitalization, and spelling are
modernized, and some abbreviations are expanded.)

A. OUTLINE OF TRACT V, "DE ACCIDIA"[1]

Part I. De his quae valere possunt ad detestationem accidiae (fols. 58^r–
61^r).

Cap. i. De ordine dicendorum in isto tractatu, et de diversis exemplis quae
valere possunt ad detestationem accidiae. **ii.** De verbis Sacrae Scripturae
quae laborem suadent et otium vel pigritiam dissuadent. **iii.** Quantum peccatum accidiae Deo displiceat. Quod peccatum accidiae multum placeat
diabolo. Quantum accidia noceat proprio subjecto, et quod ipsa repleat
hominem malis poenae. Quomodo accidia repleat hominem malis culpae.
Quomodo accidia auferat homini bona gloriae, gratiae, et naturae. De octo
quae valere possunt ad temporis conservationem: (1) verba Scripturae, (2)
exempla creaturarum, (3) natura temporis, (4) preciositas temporis, (5) . . . .
si consideramus nos debitores esse totius temporis nostri, (6) . . . . quod
oportebit districtam rationem de eo reddere coram Deo, (7) . . . . quod
tempus . . . . est nostra possessio, (8) . . . . quod temporis amissio quaedam
mors est. **iv.** De aliis sex quae valere possunt ad detestationem accidiae:
(1) quod ipsa inquinat pulchriorem partem Ecclesiae, scilicet viros con-
templativos, (2) quod ille qui hoc vitio a diabolo capitur ignominiosius capitur
ceteris peccatoribus, (3) quod homo accidiosus valde ignominiose detinetur
captus, (4) quod vitium istud . . . . homines infestat . . . . qui sunt in servitio
Dei, (5) quod accidia est valde gravis infirmitas (three reasons), (6) quod
accidiosus iniquus est in Deum, ... in proximum, ... in seipsum.

---

[1] Fols. 58^r–73^v; on the length of this and the other tracts see p. 726, n. 3.

Part II. De diversis generibus peccatorum quae ad hoc vitium pertinent (fols. 61ʳ–72ʳ).

Cap. i. De tepiditate et malis quae in homine tepiditas facit. **ii.** De mollitie. **iii.** De somnolentia. **iv.** De otiositate, et quod stultus sit otiosus. De xii stultitiis hominis otiosi: (1) quod ipse diabolo locum facit, (2) quod otiosus in tali statu se ponit quod brutis animalibus inferior est, etc. (We omit ten of the twelve points.) Quod reprehensibiles sint otiosi tempore gratiae. Quod tria sint attendenda circa occupationem. **v.** De vitio dilationis, et de primo de dilatione conversionis. De duobus quae impediunt ne Deus intret ad cor peccatoris, et de repromissione ejus qui differt converti. De octo quae movere deberent ad accelerationem conversionis: (1) mortis incertitudo, (2) octo bona quae sequuntur ex acceleratione [conversionis], (3) periculum malae consuetudinis, (4) quod conversio dilata difficilior est (twelve reasons), (5) quod ille qui differt converti iniquus est in Deum (six reasons), ... in angelum (three reasons), ... in seipsum, ... in proximum (three reasons), in inferiores creaturas, (6) quod difficile est aliquem vere converti, (7) quod status peccatoris est valde periculosus, (8) magna stultitia quae ostenditur esse in dilatione conversionis. Octo casus sunt in quibus fatua solet reputari dilatio [conversionis]. De dilatione confessionis et de fatuitate eorum qui differunt confiteri (eight points). **vi..** De vitio tarditatis, et de sex quae hoc vitium dissuadent. **vii.** De vitio negligentiae. De sex quae faciunt ad detestationem negligentiae. De remediis contra negligentiam (three remedies). De tribus quae impediunt diligentiam studii. **viii..** De vitio inconsummationis sed imperseverantiae. **ix.** De vitio remissionis. **x.** De vitio quod potest vocari dissolutionis. **xi.** De vitio incuriae. **xii.** De vitio ignaviae. **xiii.** De vitio indevotionis. **xiv.** De vitio tristitiae in divino servitio. **xv.** De taedio vitae. **xvi.** De desesperatione, et unde praevenire consuevit. **xvii.** De accidia claustralium, et xii malis quae ex ea proveniunt.

Pars III. De octo remediis contra accidiam (fol. 72ʳ, about 2 cols.). (1) diversas occupationes, (2) consideratio poenae futurae, (3) consideratio aeterni praemii, (4) societas bonorum, (5) exemplum illius qui piger non fuit, (6) consideratio periculorum in quibus sumus in praesenti, (7) amor Dei, (8) gratia Dei.

Pars IV. De indiscreto fervore qui accidiae videtur esse contrarius (fols. 72ʳ–73ᵛ).

Cap. i. De fervore indiscreto et de his qui exiguntur ad hoc ut aliquis Deo discrete serviat. **ii.** De multiplici malo quod ex indiscreto fervore provenit. **iii.** De duodecim stultitiis indiscreti fervoris. **iv.** De malis quae faciunt delicata cibaria. **v.** De condescensione patrum spiritualium circa fratres.

B. The Types of Gluttony[1]

Gregory distinguishes five kinds of gluttony: eating

⟨fol. 8ʳ⟩ Aliter distinguuntur quinque species hujus vitii a Gregorio; super istud Gen. xxv, ubi dixit Esau Jacob: "Da mihi de coctione

---

[1] Cf. I 828–30. In the rest of Chaucer's treatment of the species of gluttony, resemblances to Peraldus seem accidental (see Petersen, pp. 70–71).

hac rufa." Prima est cum quis horam comedendi praevenit ut legitur *i. too soon, as Jonathan,* de Ionatha, I Reg. xiv. Talis timere potest illam maledictionem quae habetur Eccs. x: Vae tibi terra cujus rex puer est et cujus principes mane comedunt. Terra intelligitur hic homo—terra enim est et in terram ibit; rex est liberum arbitrium quod animam habet regere; principes intelliguntur quinque sensus. Sicut illi qui verum deum colunt ab honore et obsequio divino diem incohare volunt, sic illi quorum deus venter est primo quaerunt regnum dei sui. Regnum dei eorum est esca et potus. Secunda species est quando aliquis nimis *ii. food too delicate, as the Jews in the desert,* delicata vult habere, ut legitur Nume. xi de filiis Israel qui in eremo carnes desiderabant; et in Luc. legitur de divite epulone quod epulabatur quotidie splendide. Seneca: Palatum tuum fames excitet, non sapores. Triplici ratione ostenditur quare homo non debeat quaerere delicata.

(The three reasons are stated and supported with quotations from the Bible and from St. Bernard.)

Tertia species est quando quis nimis sumit, ut legitur de Sodomitis, *iii. too much, as the people of Sodom,* Ezech. xvi. Hiero.: Pluvia illa optima est quae sensim descendit; subitus autem et nimius et praeceps imber arva subvertit. Similiter nimius cibus nocet. Quarta species est studiositas quae pertinet ad sollici- *iv. food prepared with undue care, as the sons of Eli,* tudinem et curiositatem laute praeparandi, ut legitur de filiis Heli, I Regnum ii. De studioso dicit Isidorus: Tota die epulas ruminat qui ad explendam gulam vespere delitias praeparat. Talis est quasi animal ruminans. Scilicet in hoc differt a ruminantibus animalibus quod bruta animalia ruminantia ruminant post sumptionem cibi sed talis ruminat ante. Quinta species est cum quis nimis avide vel *v. greedily, as Esau.* ardenter sumit cibum, ut legitur de Esau, Gen. xxv. Unde Ecci. xxxvii: Noli avidus esse in omni epulatione neque te effundas super omnem escam. Et Augustinus: Melius est piscibus vesci more domini quam lenticula more jumentorum. Signum foedae aviditatis est in sumendo cibum tremor manuum cyphum et bolum tenentium, effusio vultus exterioris super cibaria cum torvis oculis quam comitatur effusio vultus interioris super escam, quae est quando sic animus ad cibum ardore trahitur ut aliud cogitare non sinatur. Signum etiam hujus foedae aviditatis est inordinatio scindendi panem, masticandi cibum, et sumendi. Bern.: Etiam ad sanitatem corporis, quanto cibus honestius et ordinatius ingeritur, tanto facilius et salubrius digeritur. Contra aviditatem istam consilium est interponere psalmum vel aliam orationem. Hae species continentur in hoc versu:

Praepropere, laute, nimis, ardenter, studiose.

To these five kinds of *gula* as given in Gregory, Peraldus adds four others: having meals too frequently, food too varied, new dishes, food too costly.

C. Some Remedies against Lust[1]

⟨fol. 15ᵛ⟩ *De triplici remedio contra peccatum luxuriae.* Dictum est de his quae dant occasionem luxuriae; consequenter dicendum est de remediis contra hoc peccatum. Cum autem luxuria sit ignis, sicut patet ex praedictis, necessario erit triplex remedium contra eam, sicut contra ignem nimium triplex solet adhiberi remedium, scilicet, aut per aquae effusionem, aut lignorum subtractionem, aut elongationem. Verbi gratia, si olla quae juxta ignem est adeo ebulliat ut effundatur quod in ea continetur, aliquod horum trium fieri consuevit: vel aqua frigida ollae infunditur, vel de lignis subtrahitur, vel olla ab igne elongatur. Sic etiam faciendum est contra ignem luxuriae. Si quis videret se temptari a peccato illo consilium unum est ut ad aquam recurrat, vel ad aquam frigidam quam projiciat super se, ad litteram, vel ad aquam lacrimarum, vel ad aquam, id est tribulationem quamcumque, vel recipiat disciplinam bonam, vel pungat se fortiter, vel trahat sibi pilos barbae vel capitis, vel, si non vult adhibere tribulationis praesentiam, saltem adhibeat ejus memoriam ut cogitet de poenis quae debentur peccato luxuriae. Ad istud remedium pertinet quod legitur Prover. xx: Dolor[2] vulneris absterget mala. Ecci. xi: Malitia unius horae oblivionem facit luxuriae maximae. Ad idem pertinet quod legitur in vitis patrum de quodam sene qui, cum temptaretur graviter de quadam muliere quam receperat in hospitio suo, ipse accendit lucernam et combussit omnes digitos suos. Sicut autem ille merito combureretur super cujus vestem ignis caderet, qui prae pigritia illum a se non excuteret, nec esset compatiendum ei, et sicut merito domum suam amitteret qui, videns domum suam comburi, aquam non quaereret, sic merito ignis luxuriae eos consumit qui ad aquam tribulationis non currunt cum vident ignem consumere non vestes suas vel domum sed seipsos. In qua pigritia satis ostendunt quod magis vilipendunt seipsos quam aliqua suorum. Seneca: Nihil est homini seipso vilius. Si homo tunc intraret in aquam frigidam usque ad pectus, ex quo non immineret ei ex hoc periculum, non esset hoc malum.

Sidenotes:

Since lust is like fire, the same three remedies can be applied:

i. water, either literally,

or in the sense of tribulation through discipline, etc.,

[1] Cf. I 951–55. In the rest of Chaucer's chapter on the remedies against lust, the debt to Peraldus (a very small one) is to "De temperantia" in the *Summa virtutum* (Petersen, p. 76). For the remedies against the other six sins Chaucer does not seem to owe anything to either the *Summa virtutum* or the *Summa vitiorum*.

[2] Vulgate *livor*.

Secundum consilium est ut homo subtrahat sibi de cibo et potu. *ii. abstention from exciting foods or drinks,* Secundum enim ligna silvae exardescit ignis, ut legitur Ecci. xxviii. Pamphilus: Detrahe ligna foco, protinus ignis abest. Et praecipue de illis generibus ciborum et potuum quae inflammant ad luxuriam, ut sunt fortia vina et acuti sapores. Ista enim sunt non qualiacumque ligna ad nutrimentum luxuriae, sed sunt quasi faculae ardentes ad eam incendendam. Unde, sicut deridendus esset ille qui faculis ardentibus domum suam accenderet si diceret quod combustio ejus sibi displiceret, sic deridendi sunt qui dicunt se velle continere cum talibus cibis et potibus domos suas incendant.

Tertium remedium est ut homo elonget se ab igne luxuriae. Hoc *iii. avoidance of object of temptation.* remedium docet nos Apostolus, I ad Cor. vi, dicens: Fugite fornicationem. Super quod verbum dicit Ambrosius: Cum aliis nempe vitiis potest expectari conflictus; hanc fugite ne approximetis, quia non potest aliter melius vinci. Ad idem monemur exemplo Joseph, de quo legitur Gen. xxxix quod, cum domina sua diceret ei "Dormi mecum," ipse, relicto in manu ejus pallio, fugit et egressus est foras.

Other remedies discussed in a later chapter (fol. 18ᵛ) are prayer, an honest occupation, wisdom, almsgiving, and meditation on the state of the flesh after death.

III. AN ANGLO-NORMAN *COMPILEISON*[1]

(From a microfilm of MS R.14.7 of Trinity College, Cambridge, on which see above, pp. 726–28. Except for the correction of a few obvious mistakes, the spelling, in the Latin quotations as well as in the French text, has been reproduced in all its variations; abbreviations have been resolved but not indicated;[2] accents, apostrophes, and cedillas have been added; the word division has been normalized; the punctuation and the use of capitals and italics are mine. In a few cases where MS 6276 of the Bibliothèque nationale offered a better reading than our *TC* manuscript, that reading has been adopted.)

A. Introduction on the Seven Sins and on Pride[3]

⟨fol. 1ʳ⟩ ... *Pur quei les set pechez sunt apellez pechez capitaus.* Il *Why the Seven Sins are called "capital."* sunt apellez pecchez capitals pur ceo ke de ceus set ausi com de set testes neesunt tuz autres pechez. Kar checun de ceus set ad mout de

[1] For much valued help in the preparation of this text I wish to express my gratitude to Mr. C. A. Robson of Christ Church, Oxford, and Professor W. H. Trethewey of the University of Toronto.

[2] We trust that the dialectal color will not be affected by this, as forms fully written out (often in two or more different ways) were always found near the abbreviated forms.

[3] Cf. I 386–90.

membres e mout de branches, c'est a saver mout des especes, des
queus les plosours sunt morteus ... .

⟨fol. 4ʳ⟩ Li primer donc de ces set deuant diz pecchez si est orgoil,
li secunde est enuie, li tierz est ire, li quarte est accidie, li quint est
auarice, li sime est gule, li seme est luxure. Ceo est li ost au deable de
enfern dunt il guerreie humeine lignee; e plusours de ceo ueint il par
acun de ceus set pecchez hu par acun de lur especes, e les enprisone
issi primes en sa prison par pecché, e enapres les enserre en la prison
pardurable de enfern par peine, si Deu par sa grace en ceste uie ne
les repele par uerraie repentance. E pur ceo de ceus set pecchez se
deit checun crestien garder e defendre a soun poer, si com il ueut se
memes sauuer de la prison de enfern e de la peine pardurable deliuerer.
E si il se sent cupable de nul de ceus deuant diz set pecchez, il se deit
tanttost umblement de ceo en sun quer repentir, e a Deu merci souent
crier, e apertement de ceo sei a prestre confesser, e par uerraie satis-
faccion a Deu sei acorder, ki tut le pardurra, sanz ren duter. E bien
sachez ke a peine est nul homme ki ne eit acune espece de ceus set
pecchez, kar il i ad mout des especes si com vus isci oier porrez si
vus bon escut e bon entendement i metet quant vus les especes de
checun pecché par sei lire orrez. Mes pur ceo ke orgoil, solom Seinte
Escripture, est racine e comencement de tuz maus, pur ceo adeprimes
commencerom de li un especial sermon; e enapres, par le deuant dit
ordre, des autres sis morteus pecchez dirrom, par la grace de Deu,
solonc ceo ke nus en Seint Escripture troué les avom. E nostre duz
Seignur Ihesu Crist nus doint ceo fere al honur de lui e a sauacion des
almes.

*Isci commence un especial sermon[1] de orgoil; si ad sis chapitles si
cum est tuché ci en le prologo de orgoil. Li primer chapitle si ad treis
perografs.*

Initium omnis peccati est superbia. Ceste auctorité est escrite en le
liuere de Ecclesiastikus, e dit ke orgoil est commencement de checun
pecché; de ki nus, par la grace de Deu, dirrom adeprimes quei orgoil
fet, e quei il est, ke homme le puisse conustre; e comment orgoil est
mortel pecché; e de quatre maners de orgoil solom Sein Gregorie, ki
sunt mout a hair; puis tocherom les especes ki uenent de orgoil e lur
efect en homme, les queus homme deit eschieure solum sun poer;
enapres tocherom nus coment orgoil fet homme peccher de quor, de
bouche e de fest; e apres ceo dirrom nus un amonicioun a hommes e a
femmes ki se acesment trop queintement pur enginier e pur deceiuere
les genz; puis dirrom pur quei homme deit mout hair orgoil e echieure

[1] The word *sermon* is often used loosely for sections of such treatises or manuals
(see above, p. 724, n. 5).

Side notes:

They are pride, envy, ire, sloth, avarice, gluttony, and lust.

They lead to Hell,

unless the sinner repents, confesses, and does Satisfaction.

Pride, as root of all sins, will be treated first.

Contents of section on pride.

e fuir; e audrein[1] tocherom nus les medicines e les remedies encontre
orgoil.

B. THE SPECIES OF PRIDE[2]

⟨fol. 4ᵛ⟩ *Isci sunt nomez les especes de orgoil.* De orgoil vent veine
glorie, ipocrisie, auauntance, inobedience, noun reuerence, noun
uergoigne, estrif, despit, presumpcioun hu surquiderie, arrogance, insolence, iangle, curiosité, elacioun, contumace, non suffrance, duresce.

Isci sunt mis descripcions des especes de orgoil. Ore escutez, ore
entendez des filies de orgoil les propretez, les queles si vus ben entendez par tut echieure les porrez. E primes orrez de veine glorie.
Trop est sot ki ceo uoille. Veine glorie fet homme fere ben pur los e
pur pris du secle auer, ceo ke dut fere pur Deu e pur la uie pardurable
auer. Ipocrisie fet homme parrer bon quant il est mauueis, si come
feindre sei plus seint ke il ne est e plus ualer ke il ne fest. Auantance
fet homme priser ses fes demeine,[3] e auanter sei de ceo ke il ad si come
de la grace Deu hu de autre ben hu de pecché ke il a fet, hu de ceo ke
il ne ad pas ausi com de lui uenist. Non reuerence est desprisement en
corage de soen souerein hu de son prelast, e ceo fet homme lesser de
porter reuerence a ceus ke il deust honurer par dreit e pur meuz ualiant
tenir; c'est a dire... .[4] Inobedience est en ouere, e ceo fet homme enrefre[5] encontre ceus a ki il dust ⟨fol. 5ʳ⟩ obeir, ceo est encountre
souereins e ses prelaz, kar ne suffit mie sulement de obeir par ouere a
sun souerein hu a sun prelast si l'em ne face de bon quer e debonere-
ment en sun corage, e si ne eime e prise en sun quer si il est prelast hu
ordiné hu sun souerein, ia tiel ne seit nent[6] pur sa persone, mes pur la

The species of pride:

vainglory,

hypocrisy,

boasting,

irreverence,

disobedience,

---

[1] *Audrein, au derrein,* at the end. The plan for every one of the sins is almost
identical.

[2] Cf. I 390–406. Mr. C. A. Robson generously informed me that he had found in
the penitential of Robertus Flamesburiensis the sources of Chaucer's species of
pride and of his remarks on backbiting (clearly the sources also of the two passages
in our *Compileison*), and that Robert's section on the species of pride was used also
in the Anglo-Norman treatise *Les Set morteus pecches* (Vesp. D. iii), where the
passage, as Mr. Robson notes, comes closer to Chaucer than does Robertus. It
does not, however, come as close as our *Compileison* (or Bodl. 90, whose text here,
quoted in parts by M. Liddell [Academy, XLIX (1896), 448], seems identical
with ours). The passage on backbiting quoted hereafter has not been found in
any other Anglo-Norman work examined by Mr. Robson or myself.

[3] Adj.: "his own deeds."

[4] This and the other brief passages omitted in this section are merely repetitions
of what precedes.

[5] *Enrefre, enrevre, enrievre,* malicious, stubborn (see Meyer-Lübke, *Rom. Etym.
Wört.*, 4453).

[6] *nent, neent, nient,* in no wise.

amur de celui ki[1] liu tient en terre par hautesce de ordre e par digneté de office hu par (de)acune maners de prelacie. Non uergoigne fest homme effronté e hounte perdre e affaitement de tut oblier. Estrif fest homme estut e contrarius e fel e purueirs. Despit fet homme despire les autres pur bien ke il quide en se meimes, c'est a dire … . Les maus ke homme veit en autres deit il despire e ne mie les hommes. Presumpcion—ceo est surquiderie—fet homme estre surquiders e par ceo li fet enprendre chose utre sun poer e uiure sanz consail, pur ceo ke lui est auis ke nul ne le sace consailler meuz de sei meimes. E ceo fet homme quider estre plus sages hu meliour hu meuz valiant ke il ne seit. Arrogance est utrage ke fet homme utraius, e le fet uoler estre plus honuré ke a lui ne apent, e si il ne est, de ce lui fet auer dedeing, e lui fet autre mester enprendre ki ne affert pas a lui. Insolence fet homme despire les autres, e ses paroles e ses fez hu sun aler hu sun abit en acune manere especifier. Iangle fet homme mout parler e iangler, e, pur ceo ke lui semble ke nul nel contreualie en resoun ne en ualue ne en sauer, il uout auer tut soul totes les paroles del ostel. Curiosité fet homme estre curious e pensif e entremettant des mout des choses pur sei esleuer e pur sun poer e pur sa ualur mustrer, c'est a dire … . Elacioun fet homme enfler e hautein e orgoillous de quoer ke il ne uout suffrir de auer souerein ne per. Contumace fet homme estre rebel e contumax encontre le auctorité de ses souereins hu de ses prelaz par despit. Non suffrance fet homme ke il ne ueut rien suffrir ne restreindre les mauueis mouemenz de sun queor, c'est tant a dire … . Contempt ou despit fet homme negligent e dedeignous de quoer, ke il ne ueut fere ceo ke il deit fere par droit. Duresce fet homme auer le quoer dur e endurci ke il ne ueut fere ceo ke il deust par resoun e par dreiture fere. Plusurs autres maneres d'especes ki isci ne sunt pas nomez ne escrites i a ki descendent de orgoil e de ses branches, mes ces sunt celes ki plus sunt vsez e les plus couenables.

shamelessness, dissention, contempt,

presumption,

arrogance,

insolence,

loquacity,

ostentation,

elation, contumacy,

lack of self-mastery,

neglect of duties, obduracy.

Other species are less important.

C. Backbiting as a Species of Envy[2]

Detraction in its various forms.

⟨fol 9ᵛ⟩ Detraccion fet homme mesdire de autre par dereres, e la hu il ne peut de tut le bien esteindre, amenuser le ueut au plus ke il peut. E si come Seint Anselme dit, detraccion est a checune feiez quant homme dit, de autre acune chose par tele entente dont il puet

---

[1] Gen.; *celui ki = celui dont.* The structure is not clear; the sense is that sovereigns and priests, even if they have no merit of their own, should be loved and honored for the love of Him whose place they hold in this world.

[2] Cf. I 493–97. In the rest of the passage on the species of envy, analogies to *Pa. T.* are few and remote. (The species listed, for the other sins as well as for envy, correspond to the species in the short *Set morteus pecches* in Vesp. D. iii, a transcription of which I owe to the kindness of Mr. Robson.)

estre meins amé ou prisé. Deprauacion est quant un homme dit de un autre issi, "mult ure uolunters e iune e fet amones," e un autre ⟨fol. 10ʳ⟩ respont e dit, "veire, pur el le fet ke pur Deu,"[1] e le depraue issi, ceo est, il torne a mal autri bienfet. Conpression est si un dit de acun issi, "celi est prodom," e li autre respont, "oil, mes ne mie autresi prodhome cum vus le tenez." E issi li un amenuse le bien del autre par compression en sa response, e li autre li amenuse par deprauacion.

D. The Five Manners of Gluttony[2]

⟨fol. 19ᵛ⟩ *De cinc maners de gule.* Ceste gule si ad cinc maners. La primere manere de gule si est quant homme mangue trop par tens sanz cause renable, si come fit Ionathas li fiz Saul; kar Saul soen pere, ki fu rei des Gieus, adonc auoit defendu ke nul homme ne mangast un iour deske au uespre. E Ionathas manga un pou de miel deuant le uespre, dont son pere, quant il aparçust, li eust occis, ne eust esté li pople ki fu tant encontre si come counte le Liuere de Reis: "*Maledictus*," inquit, "*uir qui comederit panem usque ad uesperam.*" *Et infra ait Ionathas:* "*Gustans gustavi paululum mellis et ecce morior.*" *Sequitur:* "*Liberauit populus Ionathan ut non moreretur.*"

The five manners of gluttony are: i. eating too soon, as Jonathan,

La secunde manere de gule est quant homme mangue plus precious uiandis e plus costuses ke mester ne seit solonc soun estat, si com firent les fiz de Israel en desert. Kar li pople de Israel, si come conte l'Escripture, desirra trop a manger char en desert; e nekedent si en urent il a grant plenté a manger de manne—ceo fu une uiande ke Deu lour enuea du ciel, en la quele fu sauor de checun delitable uiande. "*Vulgus*," inquit, "*promiscuum flagrauit desiderio carnium, sedens et flens cum filiis Israel, et ait: Quis dabit nobis ad vescendas carnes? Recordamur piscium quos commedebamus in Egypto.*" *Et post:* "*Anima nostra arida est; nihil aliud respiciunt oculi nostri nisi manna.*"

ii. food too delicate, as the Jews in the desert,

La tierce manere de gule est quant homme mangue trop en quantité —ceo est utre mesure—si come firent les hommes de Sodome, de ki dit Ezechiel li prophete: "*Haec fuit*," inquit, "*iniquitas Sodomae, superbia, saturitas panis et habundantia et otium, et manum egeno et pauperi non porrigebant.*"

iii. too much, as the people of Sodom,

---

[1] This is clearer in Robertus Flamesburiensis: Cum dico, "iste multum orat, multum ieiunat, multas facit elemosinas," et tu respondes, "frater, hec non facit pro Deo sed quia ad istam et illam aspirat dignitatem," depravacio est (from the transcriptions made by Mr. Robson from manuscripts in the Bibl. nat.).

[2] Cf. I 828–30, and Peraldus as quoted above, II, B, pp. 742–43. A second section on the kinds of gluttony (*les especes de gule*, fols. 20ʳ–20ᵛ) bears no close relation to anything in *Pa.T.*

iv. greedily, as
Esau,

La quarte manere de gule est quant homme mangue trop egrement e trop ardaument, e quant il par sa gule deuoure sa uiande sanz bien mascher la, si come fit Esau de la uiande ke Iacob soen frere auoit fet de lentille, pur le grant desir de quele uiande il uendi a Iacob sa einesce, kar il dit issi en Genesi: *"En,"* inquit, *"morior; et quid proderunt mihi primogenita?"* Et sequitur: *"Iurauit Iacob Esau, et uendidit ei primogenita."*

v. giving too much
thought to it, as the
sons of Eli.

La quinte manere de gule est quant li penser de homme e la con-treuoure est pleine de estudie entour delitables uiandes ou beiuers pur assez fere a sa gule, si com firent Ofni e Phinees, les fiz Hely le prestre, des queus nus lisom en le primer Liure des Reis issi: *"Porro filii Heli filii Belial nescientes Dominum neque officium sacerdotum, quorum puer rapiebat carnes crudas de olla sacrificantium antequam adolebant adhipem Domino."*

E. Some Remedies against Lust[1]

There are other
remedies against
lust. It is like fire

⟨fol. 29ʳ⟩ Plusours autre medecines[2] e remedies sunt encountre luxure, si com vus orrez isci apres. Luxure est come feu de enfern, si come dit Seint Iob: "Luxure est," fet il, "feu deuorant deke a perdicioun." Kar ki ke luxure enprent[3] ele le deuoure com feu fet le sarment e l'ameine a perdicion hastiuement e esrace en ueie toz ses biens de cors e de alme ensement. *"Ignis,"* inquit, *"est usque ad per-*

and should be
fought in the same
four ways:

dicionem deuorans et cuncta eradicans genimina." Par ceo apert ke en-countre luxure, ki est ausi come feu, sunt quatre remedies, car en quatre maners sout hom tenir la liquor boillant en uessel au feu: par mettre eaue freide en uessel, ou par retrere la bouche,[4] ou par enloigner le pot du feu, ou par bien mouer le pot ou le uessel boliant.

i. by using water

(or thinking of
Christ's Passion),

En itele manere cil ou cele ki est tempté par luxure, ki est ausi comme feu ardaunt, beiue eaue freide pur sei refreider, ou pense de cel sanc e de cele eaue ki raa hors du costé nostre douz Seignur Ihesu Crist en la Croiz pur lui lauer de ses pechez, e il serra tost refreidé par la grace Deu, pur uerité le vus di. La quele medecine aparust bien en un hom-me de religioun, li quel esteit forment tempté de luxure. ...[5]

ii. by abstaining
from exciting foods
or drinks,

⟨fol. 29ᵛ⟩ La secunde medecine si est ceste ki ensuit: par retrere la bouche sauue l'em la liquor e le pot boilliant par feu, e tot ausi li

---

[1] Cf. I 951–55 and Peraldus as quoted above, II, C, pp. 744–45.

[2] The remedies advocated (fols. 27ᵛ–29ʳ) are prayer, meditation on Christ's Passion, and discipline, with especial emphasis on the wisdom of resisting tempta-tion as soon as it starts.

[3] Kindles.   [4] The log.

[5] We omit about twenty lines on repeated temptations ending in salvation through prayer in front of a crucifix.

homme ki uout sauuer sa alme il deit sustrere a soen cors les mangers e
les beiuers ki lui eschaufent e ki lui enticent a luxure, si come sauses
chaudes e forz uins e teles autres fortes choses. Kar issi dit Eclesiasti-
kus: "Solonc les chaudes uiandes e les chaudes boiures est li cors de
homme eschauffé e tempté par luxure." Kar "solonc la bouche de
bois art li feu; *secundum ligna siluae exardet ignis.*" Si com donc li
home serreit digne de estre escharni ki de hastes ardantes arsist sa
meson si il deit[1] ke le arson li despleut, en tele manere sunt il a es-
charnir ki dient ke il uolent estre chastes e checun iour enbracent lour
cors de chaudes uiandes e de chauz boiueres.

La tierce medecine encountre luxure est ke cil ki est de ceo tempté iii. by avoiding the object of tempta-tion,
ke il s'eloigne du feu de luxure—ceo est de la persone dont il est tempté
—si com Seint Poel nus commaunda e dit: "Fuiez," fet il, "lecherie."
"Fugite," inquit, *"fornicationem."* Sur cel moz dit Seint Ambrose: "O
les autres uices puet homme," fet il, "attendre la bataille, mes luxure
fuiez e si n'en aprochez pas a lui, kar ele ne puet pas meuz estre uencue
ke par fuite." *"Cum aliis,"* inquit, *"viciis potest expectari conflictus;*
hanc fugite, ne aproximetis, quia non potest melius vinci."

La quarte medecine[2] est ke l'em deit bien mouer le pot ki uoudra iv. by tiring the body.
sauuer la liquor. En tele manere homme ki est tempté de luxure il
deit bien trauailier soen cors par ueiller e par urer e par discipliner e
par autres labours honestes, e par ceo en abatera il la temptacion;
autrement porra il tost chair en luxure si come dit li sage homme. Si
homme demande pur quei Egistus seit fet lecheorz la cause est preste:
il fu odif e ne trauailla point soen cors ausi com il deit. Si il eust soen
cors trauaillé, de sa luxure fust il sauué. *Queritur Egistus quare sit*
factus adulter; in promptu causa est: desidiosus erat.

Un autre medecine encountre luxure est de penser de la peine ke li Another remedy is to think of the pun-ishment in Hell.
lecheor auera enterienement pur sa lecherie en enfer, de la quele peine
parout Seint Gregorie, e dit issi: "Curt est," fet il, "li delit de lecherie,
mes la peine du lecheor serra sanz fin."

A few more lines on this subject close the section on the
remedies against lust.

F. The Incentives to Contrition[3]

⟨fol. 44ʳ⟩ *Isci comence li secund chapitle de contricion de quer, en*
lequel sunt mustrez les sis choses principaus ki ameinent uerraie con- Six main causes lead to Contrition:
tricion en le quer du peccheour. Si ad set perogras.

---

[1] *deit* for *deist.*   [2] This fourth one is not in Peraldus.

[3] Cf. I 134–291, and Pennaforte as quoted above, I, B, pp. 733–34.

(the sinner should indeed feel bitter sorrow).

Luctum unigeniti fac tibi planctum amarum. Home ki ueut auer contricion e dolour pur ses pecchez il deit regarder totes les choses ki lui poruochent a dolir pur ses pecchez, comme fet la femme ki ne ad fors un soul fiz e celui ueit giser deuant lui morz. Mout deut ele e mout amere pleinte fet pur ceo ke ele ad perdu soen fiz ke ele tant ama e ki tant sa mere solaça. Mes mout plus deit li peccheour doloir e amere pleinte fere ki ad perdu nostre douz Seignur par soen pecché, ki solaz e confort lui fu en totes choses en totes ses bosoignes. E pur ce parout Nostre Sire al alme peccherese en le auctorité au comencement du chapitle deuant toché e dit issi: "Plorez," fet il, "e amere pleinte fetes pur vos pecchez com fet la femme ki ne ad for un fiz e le ueit mort deuant lui."

Queles choses ameinent homme a contricion. Apres ceo donc ke vus auez oi quei seit contricion, isci entendez queles choses ameinent contricion en quer de homme. E vus deuez sauoir ke sis choses ameinent

Those causes enumerated;

contricion en le quer del homme, ceo est a sauoir: pensee de ses pecchez e par la pensee amertume e dolour du pecché, honte des pecchez ke ad fet, haine de la uilté du pecché, pour du grant iour de iugement e de la peine de enfern, dolour de la perte de la ioie du ciel e de la grant ire dont il ad Deu corucé, e trebble esperance—ceo est a sauoir: esperance de pardon par ont ses pecchez lui serrunt touz pardonez, esperance de la grace de Deu par ont il fra les bones oueres apres e leira les mauueis, e(a)esperance de glorie dont il serra reguerdoné pur ses biensfez. *Sex enim sunt causae inductivae contritionis.*[1]

treated separately: i. The sinner's meditation about his sins

Coment li peccheour deit penser de ses pecchez. De la pensee des pecchez, dont amertume de quer ensuit, lisoms nus en Ysaie le prophet ke Ezechie li rei dist: "Ieo penserai al honur de vus, Sire Deu, touz mes anz"—ceo est a dire touz mes pecchez ke ieo ai fet puis ke ieo sauoie pecchier—"en amertume de ma alme"—ceo est en dolour de moun quer. *Hinc est illud Ysaie: "Recogitabo," inquit, "tibi omnes annos meos in amaritudine animae meae."* Mout deit bien li peccheour repenser ses pecchez ou grant dolour, ke il par sa contricion en puisse

in preparation for the Day of Judgment.

de Deu auer pardon, kar autrement demené mout dour serra quant il au iour de iuisse acountes rendra, e ne mie seulement de ses oueres, mes de checune odiue parole ke il ad parlé folement, e de checune mauueise pensee ensement, e de checune eure de tens ke il ad despendu malement, si come Seinte Escripture temoigne apertement: *"Omnes nos," inquit Apostolus, "manifestari oportet ante tribunal Christi, ut referat unusquisque propria corporis, prout gessit, sive bonum, sive malum." Et in Euangelio legitur: "De omni verbo otioso reddent homines*

---

[1] The source passage in St. Raymund's *Summa* is quoted *in extenso,* substantially as on pp. 733–34.

rationem in die iudicii, et non solum de verbis otiosis sed etiam de mini-
mis cogitationibus." Et sicut dicit beatus Anselmus: "In illa die exige-
tur a te omne tempus uiuendi tibi inpensum qualiter fuerit a te expen-
sum."

De hontage de pecché. Del hontage ke li peccheour deit auer pur ses
pecchez parout Seint Iob en soun liuere ou il dit issi: "Les peccheours," fet il, "sunt dignes de grant hontage." E ke ceo est ueirs
vus poez clerement ueer en cest exsample: Si un homme eust une mout
bele face e clere, e il feist une chose par ont il perdesist tantost cele
beauté e receust une leide face e plus neire ke carbon, ne deust il de cel
fet auer grant huntage e grant ⟨fol. 44ᵛ⟩ contricion? Mes la alme ki
est sanz pecché mortel trop bele face ad deuant Deu, dont Deu se
delite de esgarder le, si come il memes dit quant il a sa spuse parout
issi; il dit: "Mustre," fet il, "ta face, car est mout bele." *"Ostende,"*
inquit, "mihi faciem tuam; facies tua decora." Mes si tost com ele eit
mortument pecchié receit ele une face plus leide e plus neire ke carbon,
si com dit Ieremie li prophete: "La face," fet il, "del alme du peccheour est enneircie plus ke carbon." *"Denigrata," inquit, "facies*
eorum super carbones."

De la haine de pecché. De la hayne de pecché, pur la uilté de ki li
peccheour est fet trop uil deuant Deu, dit derechief Ieremie li prophete
parlant al alme peccheresse, e dit issi: "A," fet il "com vus estes fet
trop uilles pur les pecchez ke vus auez fet." *"Quamuis facta vilis," in-*
quit, "es nimis iterans vias tuas." E ke ele seit fet mout uile vus poet
bien veer par cest essample: Si la emperice de le emperur de tot cest
mond, ki eust en sei totes les beautez e totes les bontes ke onkes homme auoit, eust fet auouterie oue le plus mauueis e ou le plus leid ribaud
ki fust en terre, e ke il fust mortel enemi al emperur, e en ki nule bonté
ne nule ualour ne fuist, ne se deueroist ele par droit tenir sei mout uile
quant ele de ceo enpensast? Oil, certes. Mes checun alme de crestiene[1]
est la espuse de Ihesu Crist e la emperice del emperur de tretot le
mond e du ciel e de la terre e de quanke en eus soit, si come dit Seint
Augustin. La quele, si tost come ele fet morteu pecché, deuient ele
auoutre au diable de enfern, ki est trop leid ribaud par pecché e
sanz totes bontez par sa malice. *"Omnis," inquit, "anima christiana*
aut est Christi sponsa aut dyaboli adultera." Mout deit donc homme
auer grant dolour e grant pité quant il est cheuz en si grant uilté par
pecché. Dont, si homme bien regardast la grant uilté ke il encurt par
pecché, il elirroit plus tost assez de morir ke de peccher morteument.
Mout hai ceste uilté li sage Seneke quant il dit issi: "Si ieo susse,"

[1] Probably intended as a noun; the final *e* is of no significance, especially before
a vowel. BN 6276 has *alme cristiene.*

(marginal notes:)

ii. His shame of sin,

by which he is
indeed degraded.

iii. His hatred
of sin that made
him most vile

as shown by a
comparison.

fet il, "ke Deu le pecchié me pardorroit e ke nul homme moun pecché ne saueroit, nekedent si aueroie ieo hydour de pecchier." *"Si scirem," inquit, "deos ignoscituros, homines autem ignoraturos, tamen abhorrerem peccatum."*

iv. (a) His fear of the Last Judgment.

De la pour del iour de iuisse. De la grant pour del ior de iuise parla Seint Ierome issi e dit: "Checune foit," fet il, "quant ieo enterienement enpens du grant iour de iugement, si comence ieo a trembler de la pour ke ieo en ai de tot moun cors subitement." *"Quotiens," inquit, "diem illum considero, toto corpore contremisco."* Quant si prodomme

St. Jerome shivered at the thought,

donc come fu Seint Ierome de tot soen cors trembla quant il enterienement du iour de iuise enpensa, mout deit plus trembler li peccheour a checune fez ke il enpense de ceu grant iour quant touz li mauueis pur lour pecchiez serrunt liuerez en enfernal peine, ou il arderont en cors

and Job wished that he might, that day, hide in Hell.

e en alme a[1] remanant en feu ardant e en suffre puant. Pur la doute de ceu iour trouoms nus en Seinte Escripture ke li plus prodomme ki fuist donc en terre desirra de estre en enfern iceu iour tant come Nostre Seignur fera le iugement, mes ke il put enapres reuenir a Nostre Seignur en la ioie. Cist prodomme fu Seint Iob, ki dit cestes paroles en soen liuere: "A, ki me donast," fet il, "ke ieo fuisse en enfern desouz vostre proteccion, Sire Deu, muscé, deske si tant ke vostre grant ire au iour de iuise soit passé, e me donessez tens quant ieo serrais repellé." *"Deus," inquit, "mihi tribuat ut in inferno protegas me et abscondas me donec pertranseat furor tuus et constituas mihi tempus in*

The wrath of God on the Day of Judgment.

quo recorderis mei." E ceo ne fu pas merueille ke il lui parla issi, kar la Deu ire serra si grant a iceu iour encontre peccheours ke il ses fiz demeine, ke il rechata par soen precious sanc, gettera trez enz en le feu de enfern, si il troue en eus mortel pecché, quant il dirra a eus ceste doleruse parole: "Departiez de moi, vus, maleruz, pur vos pecchiez enz en le feu pardurable ki est apparaliez au diable e as ses angeles." *"Discedite," inquit, "a me, maledicti, in ignem eternum qui paratus est dyabolo et angelis eius."* Alas, chettifs peccheours, ke from nus a iceu iour, quant si prodomme requiert Nostre Seignur de estre mucé en enfern deske la ire de lui a iceu ⟨fol. 45ʳ⟩ iour seit passé? Ieo vus

The only safeguard is in repentance and amendment,

dirrai, si Deu plet, sanz fauseté bone medicine e seine, kar sachez bien certeinement si nus seom ore en ceste uie isci uerrai repentanz e ueraiement confes de toz nos mauueitez e les lessoms du tot pur le

which will lead us to Heaven.

amur e pur la pour de Deu, sanz nule doute nus serroms la a dextre de lui au iour de iugement, cele beneite parole e douce oianz: "Uenez, les benez fiz de moun pere, e receuez le regne du ciel ki vus est apparaillez du comencement del mond." Le regne, dit il, pur ceo ke il serront pur

---

[1] a = *en.*

uoirs tretuz reis coronez quanke serrunt en la glorie du ciel translatez e sauuez. *"Venite," inquit, "benedicti Patris mei; possidete regnum paratum uobis a constitutione mundi."* Lessom nus donc ore isci nos uileinies e nos pecches, e nus serroms la adonc sanz fin fes fiz Deu beneiz apellez, e ou nostre pere Deu tut puissant enz en la ioie pardurable coronez. E ceo nus otreie le douz rei de magestez. Amen.

De la peine de enfern.[1] De la peine de enfern, ke li peccheour deit mout doter, dit Seint Davi li prophe[te] par le Seint Espirit issi: "Ausi come les ouuaille," fet il, "sunt esparkees e encloses enz en la faude ou dedenz lour curt, en tele manere serront les peccheours enclos en enfern, e la mort les pestera," c'est a dire, si come les ouuailles encloses en la faude ou en lour toit enparkees n'en issunt iames si lour pastour ne les deferme, ausi les peccheours ki une feit entrent en enfern, en cele doleruse habitacion, n'en ystrent iames fors pur auoir bien ne rançon. *"Sicut oves," inquit, "in inferno positi sunt; mors depascet eos."* Kar en enfern ne est nule rançon, si come dit Seinte Escripture e le temoigne: *"quia in inferno nulla est remdemptio."* Nekedent au iour de iuise li peccheours s'en istrent, mes tantost arere reboutez serront, ausi com fet li limaçon ki entre e yst hors de sa meson. Kar au iour de iuise, quant li cors e le alme par la Deu assise ensemble serront assemblez, en la peine pulente de enfern serront tost rebotez, ou sanz nule fin peinez serront pur lour pecchez. E la chose ke li peccheours ore isci plus heent—c'est la mort—illokes serra adonc de eus coueité come deliciouses uiandes. ... Kar iames fin ne auerunt si come li seinz hommes le dient e temoignent. *"Quia desiderabunt," inquit, "mori et fugiet mors ab eis."*

Qeu boiure li mauueis en enfern beiuerunt, si dit la Seinte Diuine Escripture en tele manere: "En le boiure des peccheours illoc serra feu ardant mellé oue suffre puant." E, ke cestes deus choses soent bien enchaufees, il i serra ausi com un uent de tempeste mellez, ki lour boiure eschaufera e le feu oue le suffre mellera. *"Ignis," inquit, "sulphur et spiritus procellarum, pars calicis eorum."* En liu de uin boiuereunt illukes les peccheours le fiel des dragons e le uenim des serpenz. *"Quia scerpentum et fel draconum uinum eorum et uenenum aspidum insanabile."* Kar si grant seif illukes aueront li dampnez ke il suscheront le uenim hors de la teste des serpens si come lisons en Iob: *"Caput," inquit, "aspidum suggent."* Certes a mal eure cil onkes nasquit, e mar peccha ensement, e mar en issit uerraiement, ki la en tele dolour demorra pardurablement.

---

[1] Pennaforte treats this subject very briefly (see above, pp. 733–34); to this long development, paralleled in many penitentials, cf. I 168–230.

Marginal notes:

(b) His fear of Hell.

The sinners shall be inclosed like sheep

beyond hope of redemption,

craving for death in vain.

Their drink shall be fire and sulphur,

the poison of dragons and the venom of asps.

Meditation on such punishment should bring you to Contrition.

Cestes deuant dites e....es[1] peines ke li peccheour en enfern auera, de quer lisez, e bien a ceo uostre entente metez, ou lire par deuant vus le facet, e souent les rehercetz e relisez enterienement, de ceo en uostre quer enpensez e en uostre memorie ferm les enfichez, e par uerraie contricion a Deu vus acordez, ke vus sanz fin enz cele peine dampnez ne seez. Dont Deu vus en defend par sa grant pitez. Amen.

v. Sorrow at the loss of Heaven.

Of the next section, *De la dolour de la perte de la ioie du ciel* (nearly two columns), we quote only a comparison suggestive of English origin:

⟨fol. 45ᵛ⟩ ... E ke li peccheour deit mout dolir pur ceo ke il ad perdu le regne du ciel, vus bien apertement le poez ueer par cest essample. Mout aueroit li fiz li rei de Engletere grant materie de dolir e trop grant doil demener si il seust ke il eust perdu le regne temporel de Engletere par acun pecché ke il eust fet encountre soen pere. Mes mout deit plus de assez doloir checun crestien, kar il ne a mie perdu soulement le regne temporel mes le regne du ciel si tost com il fet mortel pecché. ...

We omit the sixth and last of the causes that lead to Contrition, viz., hope. Of the three points announced in the outline—hope of forgiveness, of grace, and of glory—only the first is treated (cf. I 283–91).

G. Survey of the Sins in the Section on Confession

The confessant must examine himself as to the Ten Commandments and the Seven Deadly Sins

⟨fol. 70ʳ⟩ *Isci comence li quart chapitle de la secunde partie de la tierce partie de confession, ki nus mustre coment li uerrai regehissant se deit confesser de dis comandemenz[2] e de set morteus pecchez e lour especes solonc le enseignement de Seint Gregorie.[3] Si ad set perografs.*

Laua a malitia cor tuum. Home ki se ueut par confession lauer il deit soen quer de malice purger solonc ceste auctorité en Ieremie le prophete, par ki Nostre Seignur nus amoneste de lauer nostre quer de pecché. Vus deuez donc sauoir ke il couient le uerrai regehissant confesser sei de dis comaundemenz de la lei si il en eit nul enfreint. De ceo querez en la compeleison de dis comandemenz. E il se deit

---

[1] Word illegible, not the expected *escrites*.

[2] Cf. I 956. In this section of the *Compileison* the subject of the Ten Commandments will be dismissed with mere reference to the separate treatise on the Commandments, fols. 115ᵛ–121ʳ.

[3] The allusion is to the passage of *Moralium libri* which Pennaforte incorporated into his work at the corresponding place, i.e., at the end of the section on Confession (see p. 740). The Anglo-Norman compiler quotes a little of it, with reference.

confesser de set morteus pecchez, si il eit pecché par nul de ceus, les
queus sunt orgoil, enuie, ire, accidie, auarice, gule, e luxurie, de queus, from which all
others are derived.
si come dit Seint Gregorie, est deriué la uniuersité de tuz uices.

The sins are treated twice in the above order.[1] The first survey enumerates the *especes* or derivatives of the sins. We shall
quote the section on *gule:*

⟨fol. 70r⟩ *Des especes de gule.* De gule uient peresce, sompnolence, The derivatives of
gule;
yueresce, uouchement,[2] uomite, non acceptable leesce, ribaudie,
ueine parole, non nettesce, legierté, non estable de pensee e de cors,
lecherie, rebuchement de sen.[3] Gule tout le us de menbres, enpire le
engin e la ueue. Les cinc maneres de gule sunt cestes:[4] trop tost man- its five manners.
ger—ceo est deuant eure, deliciousement, trop artaument, estudiouse-
ment.[5] De ces nons querez en la compileison de set pecchez morteus
en la chapitle des especes de gule. *De gula nascitur torpor, somp-
nolencia. ...* Species gulae notantur in hiis versibus:

> Praepropere, laute, nimis, ardenter, studiose,
> Mel Ionathe, carnes heremi, panes Sodomite,
> Lens Esau, Phinees arguit olla gulam.

The second survey tells of the ways and circumstances in
which the sins are committed. We shall quote the introduction
to this survey and the section on *gule:*

⟨fol. 71r⟩ E ke ieo soie mieuz entendu des simples genz e meins
sotils, ieo mettrai ci apres la enqueste des set morteus pecchez, ceo I shall add a review
of the Seven Deadly
est a dire coment li confessour doit enquere du regehissant de checun Sins for the use of
confessors
pecché mortel par sei si mester soit, e coment checun simple homme e and confessants.
meins entendant puisse ci auoir mirour de confession en le quel i se
puisse esmirer e esgarder, e par ceo aparceuer si il soit en nul de ces
set morteus pecchez. *Isci comence le quint chapitle de la secunde
partie. ...*

[1] On this order see above, p. 727 and n. 4.

[2] BN 6276: *bouchement. Bouchement* is found only in the sense of appeal in justice;
vouchier, vouģier is known in the sense of to be nauseated, to vomit (Godefroy).
The list of *especes* of each sin in French is followed by its Latin equivalent; the
corresponding word there is *nausea.*

[3] In the Latin, *hebetudo.*

[4] Apart from this passage on the five manners of gluttony and what comes
below on the same subject, nothing in the whole digression on the sins is clearly
related to either Peraldus or Chaucer. For their analogues to the passage see
above, pp. 742–43 and I 828–30.

[5] One of the five—eating too much—is omitted here in both manuscripts.

Of the ways in
which the sin of
gule is committed.

La enqueste de gule. De gule deit la enqueste estre fete issi: Auez trop mangé ou beu deske uoucheison[1] ou a yueresce ou a uomite, e si vus deuant la uomite de nuuel esteiet acomunié.[2] Si vus auez esté yuere, ueez coment: ou deske a perturbacion de sen seulement, ou deske a defaute de langue ou de ueue ou de aler, ou deske ou. Si vus par yveresce auez estriué oue nul homme, ou a nul homme maudit ou feru, ou lecherie encoru ou autre pecché en tant ke l'emdemein esteiez malade. Ou dormistis quant vus deuiez aler a muster e as autres oures de iustice e de misericorde. Auez esté pareceus, e si a ceo auez esté acustummers. Si vus auez mangé ou beu aucune foiz de chose emblee, pur quele chose sentence de excomunicacion fu donnee par auenture. Ou auez mangé ou beu de aucune chose a tort purchacee. Si vus auez mangé ou beu a scient ou[3] escomuniez. Si vus auez prouoché vus meime a apetit de plus manger par sauses ou par deliciouses uiandes. Si vus auez mangé ou beu deuant tens en iour de iune pur glotonie plus ke pur mester. Auez treiné auant uostre soer au manger trop longement pur[4] la iune. Estes vus cheu en les cinc circumstances de gule: ou en maniant trop tost deuant tens, si com fist Ionathas, le fiz Saul le rei, e pur ceo fu il iugé a mort; ou deliciousement, si come les Geus firent, ki prierent char en desert e ne furent mie paiez de manne dunt Deu les past quarante anz en desert; ou trop, si come la gent de Sodome firent, des ques li pecché fu abundance de pain; ou ardaument, si com Esau fist, ki la uille lentille trop ardaument coueita; ou par grant estudie, si come firent les fiz Hely le prestre, ki trop grant apparaillement firunt entour lour uiandes.

A survey of the sins against the Sacrament closes the section on Confession.

---

[1] Apparently the equivalent of *uouchement* (see p. 757, n. 2).

[2] The sin referred to is that of overeating immediately after receiving Holy Communion, and thus allowing one's self to vomit the sacred host.

[3] ou, with: "Have you knowingly eaten or drunk with an excommunicated person?"

[4] pur, because: "Did you, because it was fasting time, sit very long at a meal?" i.e., have you tried to make up for having only one meal a day by sitting an exceptionally long time at it?

IV. *LA SOMME LE ROY, OU LIVRE DES VICES ET DES VERTUS*

This work is very brief; the following quotations cover over one-third of the chapter on lust.

(From Rotograph 306 of MLA Rotograph Collection; the manuscript is Royal 19.c.11 of the British Museum.)[1]

⟨fol. 17ʳ⟩ *Li viᵉ chief.* Li sizemes chiez de la beste si est luxure, qui est mout outrageuse et desordenee au delit des vains ou au delit charnel. De tel pechié faire enorte li dyables en v manieres[2] se comme dit Saint Grigoire: premierement de fol regart, apres en folement parler, apres en fols atouchemens, apres en fols e fels baisiers, apres vient l'en au fait. Ensi soutiuement fait entrer li dyables de l'un en l'autre. *(The sixth of the Seven Sins is lust. There are five steps to it.)*

Cils pechiez se deuise premierement en ii manieres, car il y a luxure de cuer et luxure de cors. *(It includes lust of the heart)*

Luxure de cuer. La luxure du cuer si a iiii degrez.

Those are the thought of the sin, pleasure in this thought, consent of heart and reason, and the wish to commit the sin. Women are warned against the sinful wearing of clothes that lead men to *luxure de cuer*.

De la luxure du cors. Luxure de cors se deuise en luxure d'yex, d'oreilles, de bouche, de mains, de tous les sens du cors, et especiaument de l'ueure vilaine. A ce pechié appartiennent toutes les choses par quoi la char se(s) muet a desirer tele oeure, comme ⟨fol. 17ᵛ⟩ sont les outrages de boiure e de menger, les souez lis, robes delicieuses, et toutes manieres d'aises de cors outre necessité. *(and lust of the body.)*

Le pechié de l'ueure de luxure se deuise en mout de manieres selonc l'estat des personnes qui les font, et va en montant de mal en mal. Li premiers est de home ou de fame qui n'ont nuls liens ne de veu de mariage ne de ordre ne de religion ne autre. Li secons est en fame commune. Cils pechiez est plus griez car il est plus vils et pour ce que tels fames sont a la foiz mariees ou de religion, ou ne refusent *(The guilt varies with the status of the sinners: people free from vows, prostitutes,)*

---

[1] The French *Somme* (written 1279) is not published; *Dan Michel's Ayenbite of Inwyt* (ed. Richard Morris, "E.E.T.S." [London, 1866]) and *Des Coninx Summe* (ed. D. C. Tinbergen [Leiden, 1900]) are largely translations of it.

[2] Cf. I 852–64. Nothing corresponds to this in Peraldus or in our Anglo-Norman *Compileison*. The devil's hand is in Peraldus, but the five fingers there correspond to fornication, violation, adultery, incest, and the sins against nature (fols. 10ᵛ–11ʳ).

widows and
widowers,
maidens,
adulteresses;
nului, ne frere ne cousin ne fil ne pere. Li tiers est d'ome deslié a fame veue ou la reuerse. Li quars est aus puceles. Li quins est es fames mariees; c'est pechié d'auoutire, qui est moult grief car il y a trespassement de foy que l'un doit porter a l'autre; apres il y a sacrilege quant l'en brise sacrement de mariage dont il vient desheritemens, deshonneur et faus mariage. Cils pechiez se double aucune foiz quant il est de home marié et de fame qui a son mari.

sin between hus-
band and wife,
Li siziemes est quant li homs a sa propre fame fait chose deffendue et desordenee contre nature de home et de ordre de mariage. Et de sa propre espee se puet i home occirre, et aussi puet il auec sa propre fame pechier mortelment.[1] Pour ce feri Diex Onan le neueu Jacob; et li dyables auoit non Hamodeus estrangla les vii maris la sainte damoisiele Saira, qui puis fu fame au jone Thobie. Car tous les sacremens de Sainte Eglise l'en doit traitier netement et tenir

between relatives
by baptism.
les et auoir en grant reuerence. Li septismes est de homme a sa commere ou a sa fillueille ou du fillueil aus enfans son parrin ou sa marrine.[2] Car tels personnes ne se pueent assambler sanz pechiez mortel ne par mariage.

Or the sin may be between relatives by blood or by marriage, or one sinner or both may be bound by religious vows.

[1] Cf. I 859 (also, *Mcht. T.*, E 1839–40) and I 904–6. Peraldus and the Anglo-Norman compilation only touch upon this question; neither has the comparison with the knife.

[2] Cf. I 909; there is nothing similar in Peraldus; the Anglo-Norman compilation has only a brief allusion to *parenté espirituele* (fol. 23ᵛ). In various portions some other manuscripts of the *Somme* offer better parallels to *Pa.T.* than does the British Museum manuscript of which we are using a rotograph. E.g., the points of superiority of the Pater Noster over other prayers are found in MS 24780 of the Bibliothèque nationale and in others very much as in Chaucer, I 1040–42; cf. Rotograph 306, fol. 38ʳ. (The clear distinction between the three points—[a] dignity of origin, [b] brevity, and [c] adequacy—shows how the passage in *Pa. T.* should be punctuated.)

INDEX

[The Table of Contents and the Index are planned as complements in order to make the material in *Sources and Analogues* readily accessible. It is hoped that the Contents will give a serviceable guide to the material in each section. The Index is designed to point to the authors, titles, genres, and significant subjects and motifs in the entire work. The spelling of names and titles is, of course, that used by the contributors of the individual sections. The titles of modern studies and the names of the scholars who have made these studies are not included in the Index.—W. F. BRYAN.]